In Praise of *Computer Architecture: A Quantitative Approach* Fifth Edition

"The 5th edition of *Computer Architecture: A Quantitative Approach* continues the legacy, providing students of computer architecture with the most up-to-date information on current computing platforms, and architectural insights to help them design future systems. A highlight of the new edition is the significantly revised chapter on data-level parallelism, which demystifies GPU architectures with clear explanations using traditional computer architecture terminology."

—Krste Asanović, University of California, Berkeley

"*Computer Architecture: A Quantitative Approach* is a classic that, like fine wine, just keeps getting better. I bought my first copy as I finished up my under-graduate degree and it remains one of my most frequently referenced texts today. When the fourth edition came out, there was so much new material that I needed to get it to stay current in the field. And, as I review the fifth edition, I realize that Hennessy and Patterson have done it again. The entire text is heavily updated and Chapter 6 alone makes this new edition required reading for those wanting to really understand cloud and warehouse scale-computing. Only Hennessy and Patterson have access to the insiders at Google, Amazon, Microsoft, and other cloud computing and internet-scale application providers and there is no better coverage of this important area anywhere in the industry."

—James Hamilton, Amazon Web Services

"Hennessy and Patterson wrote the first edition of this book when graduate stu-dents built computers with 50,000 transistors. Today, warehouse-size computers contain that many servers, each consisting of dozens of independent processors and billions of transistors. The evolution of computer architecture has been rapid and relentless, but *Computer Architecture: A Quantitative Approach* has kept pace, with each edition accurately explaining and analyzing the important emerg-ing ideas that make this field so exciting."

—James Larus, Microsoft Research

"This new edition adds a superb new chapter on data-level parallelism in vector, SIMD, and GPU architectures. It explains key architecture concepts inside mass-market GPUs, maps them to traditional terms, and compares them with vector and SIMD architectures. It's timely and relevant with the widespread shift to GPU parallel computing. *Computer Architecture: A Quantitative Approach* fur-thers its string of firsts in presenting comprehensive architecture coverage of sig-nificant new developments!"

—John Nickolls, NVIDIA

"The new edition of this now classic textbook highlights the ascendance of explicit parallelism (data, thread, request) by devoting a whole chapter to each type. The chapter on data parallelism is particularly illuminating: the comparison and contrast between Vector SIMD, instruction level SIMD, and GPU cuts through the jargon associated with each architecture and exposes the similarities and differences between these architectures."

—Kunle Olukotun, Stanford University

"The fifth edition of *Computer Architecture: A Quantitative Approach* explores the various parallel concepts and their respective tradeoffs. As with the previous editions, this new edition covers the latest technology trends. Two highlighted are the explosive growth of Personal Mobile Devices (PMD) and Warehouse Scale Computing (WSC)—where the focus has shifted towards a more sophisticated balance of performance and energy efficiency as compared with raw performance. These trends are fueling our demand for ever more processing capability which in turn is moving us further down the parallel path."

—Andrew N. Sloss, Consultant Engineer, ARM
Author of *ARM System Developer's Guide*

Computer Architecture

A Quantitative Approach

Fifth Edition

John L. Hennessy is the tenth president of Stanford University, where he has been a member of the faculty since 1977 in the departments of electrical engineering and computer science. Hennessy is a Fellow of the IEEE and ACM; a member of the National Academy of Engineering, the National Academy of Science, and the American Philosophical Society; and a Fellow of the American Academy of Arts and Sciences. Among his many awards are the 2001 Eckert-Mauchly Award for his contributions to RISC technology, the 2001 Seymour Cray Computer Engineering Award, and the 2000 John von Neumann Award, which he shared with David Patterson. He has also received seven honorary doctorates.

In 1981, he started the MIPS project at Stanford with a handful of graduate students. After completing the project in 1984, he took a leave from the university to cofound MIPS Computer Systems (now MIPS Technologies), which developed one of the first commercial RISC microprocessors. As of 2006, over 2 billion MIPS microprocessors have been shipped in devices ranging from video games and palmtop computers to laser printers and network switches. Hennessy subsequently led the DASH (Director Architecture for Shared Memory) project, which prototyped the first scalable cache coherent multiprocessor; many of the key ideas have been adopted in modern multiprocessors. In addition to his technical activities and university responsibilities, he has continued to work with numerous start-ups both as an early-stage advisor and an investor.

David A. Patterson has been teaching computer architecture at the University of California, Berkeley, since joining the faculty in 1977, where he holds the Pardee Chair of Computer Science. His teaching has been honored by the Distinguished Teaching Award from the University of California, the Karlstrom Award from ACM, and the Mulligan Education Medal and Undergraduate Teaching Award from IEEE. Patterson received the IEEE Technical Achievement Award and the ACM Eckert-Mauchly Award for contributions to RISC, and he shared the IEEE Johnson Information Storage Award for contributions to RAID. He also shared the IEEE John von Neumann Medal and the C & C Prize with John Hennessy. Like his co-author, Patterson is a Fellow of the American Academy of Arts and Sciences, the Computer History Museum, ACM, and IEEE, and he was elected to the National Academy of Engineering, the National Academy of Sciences, and the Silicon Valley Engineering Hall of Fame. He served on the Information Technology Advisory Committee to the U.S. President, as chair of the CS division in the Berkeley EECS department, as chair of the Computing Research Association, and as President of ACM. This record led to Distinguished Service Awards from ACM and CRA.

At Berkeley, Patterson led the design and implementation of RISC I, likely the first VLSI reduced instruction set computer, and the foundation of the commercial SPARC architecture. He was a leader of the Redundant Arrays of Inexpensive Disks (RAID) project, which led to dependable storage systems from many companies. He was also involved in the Network of Workstations (NOW) project, which led to cluster technology used by Internet companies and later to cloud computing. These projects earned three dissertation awards from ACM. His current research projects are Algorithm-Machine-People Laboratory and the Parallel Computing Laboratory, where he is director. The goal of the AMP Lab is develop scalable machine learning algorithms, warehouse-scale-computer-friendly programming models, and crowd-sourcing tools to gain valueable insights quickly from big data in the cloud. The goal of the Par Lab is to develop technologies to deliver scalable, portable, efficient, and productive software for parallel personal mobile devices.

Computer Architecture
A Quantitative Approach

Fifth Edition

John L. Hennessy
Stanford University

David A. Patterson
University of California, Berkeley

With Contributions by

Krste Asanović
University of California, Berkeley

Jason D. Bakos
University of South Carolina

Robert P. Colwell
R&E Colwell & Assoc. Inc.

Thomas M. Conte
North Carolina State University

José Duato
Universitat Politècnica de València and Simula

Diana Franklin
University of California, Santa Barbara

David Goldberg
The Scripps Research Institute

Norman P. Jouppi
HP Labs

Sheng Li
HP Labs

Naveen Muralimanohar
HP Labs

Gregory D. Peterson
University of Tennessee

Timothy M. Pinkston
University of Southern California

Parthasarathy Ranganathan
HP Labs

David A. Wood
University of Wisconsin–Madison

Amr Zaky
University of Santa Clara

ELSEVIER

Amsterdam • Boston • Heidelberg • London
New York • Oxford • Paris • San Diego
San Francisco • Singapore • Sydney • Tokyo

Acquiring Editor: Todd Green
Development Editor: Nate McFadden
Project Manager: Paul Gottehrer
Designer: Joanne Blank

Morgan Kaufmann is an imprint of Elsevier
225 Wyman Street, Waltham, MA 02451, USA

Library of Congress Cataloging-in-Publication Data
Application submitted

British Library Cataloguing-in-Publication Data
A catalogue record for this book is available from the British Library.

ISBN: 978-0-12-383872-8

For information on all MK publications
visit our website at *www.mkp.com*

Printed in the United States of America
11 12 13 14 15   10 9 8 7 6 5 4 3 2 1

Typeset by: diacriTech, Chennai, India

To Andrea, Linda, and our four sons

Foreword

by Luiz André Barroso, Google Inc.

The first edition of Hennessy and Patterson's *Computer Architecture: A Quantitative Approach* was released during my first year in graduate school. I belong, therefore, to that first wave of professionals who learned about our discipline using this book as a compass. Perspective being a fundamental ingredient to a useful Foreword, I find myself at a disadvantage given how much of my own views have been colored by the previous four editions of this book. Another obstacle to clear perspective is that the student-grade reverence for these two superstars of Computer Science has not yet left me, despite (or perhaps because of) having had the chance to get to know them in the years since. These disadvantages are mitigated by my having practiced this trade continuously since this book's first edition, which has given me a chance to enjoy its evolution and enduring relevance.

The last edition arrived just two years after the rampant industrial race for higher CPU clock frequency had come to its official end, with Intel cancelling its 4 GHz single-core developments and embracing multicore CPUs. Two years was plenty of time for John and Dave to present this story not as a random product line update, but as a defining computing technology inflection point of the last decade. That fourth edition had a reduced emphasis on instruction-level parallelism (ILP) in favor of added material on thread-level parallelism, something the current edition takes even further by devoting two chapters to thread- and data-level parallelism while limiting ILP discussion to a single chapter. Readers who are being introduced to new graphics processing engines will benefit especially from the new Chapter 4 which focuses on data parallelism, explaining the different but slowly converging solutions offered by multimedia extensions in general-purpose processors and increasingly programmable graphics processing units. Of notable practical relevance: If you have ever struggled with CUDA terminology check out Figure 4.24 (teaser: "Shared Memory" is really local, while "Global Memory" is closer to what you'd consider shared memory).

Even though we are still in the middle of that multicore technology shift, this edition embraces what appears to be the next major one: cloud computing. In this case, the ubiquity of Internet connectivity and the evolution of compelling Web services are bringing to the spotlight very small devices (smart phones, tablets) and very large ones (warehouse-scale computing systems). The ARM Cortex A8, a popular CPU for smart phones, appears in Chapter 3's "Putting It All Together" section, and a whole new Chapter 6 is devoted to request- and data-level parallelism in the context of warehouse-scale computing systems. In this new chapter, John and Dave present these new massive clusters as a distinctively new class of computers—an open invitation for computer architects to help shape this emerging field. Readers will appreciate how this area has evolved in the last decade by comparing the Google cluster architecture described in the third edition with the more modern incarnation presented in this version's Chapter 6.

Return customers of this book will appreciate once again the work of two outstanding computer scientists who over their careers have perfected the art of combining an academic's principled treatment of ideas with a deep understanding of leading-edge industrial products and technologies. The authors' success in industrial interactions won't be a surprise to those who have witnessed how Dave conducts his biannual project retreats, forums meticulously crafted to extract the most out of academic–industrial collaborations. Those who recall John's entrepreneurial success with MIPS or bump into him in a Google hallway (as I occasionally do) won't be surprised by it either.

Perhaps most importantly, return and new readers alike will get their money's worth. What has made this book an enduring classic is that each edition is not an update but an extensive revision that presents the most current information and unparalleled insight into this fascinating and quickly changing field. For me, after over twenty years in this profession, it is also another opportunity to experience that student-grade admiration for two remarkable teachers.

Contents

Chapter 6 **Warehouse-Scale Computers to Exploit Request-Level and Data-Level Parallelism**

Appendix A **Instruction Set Principles**

Appendix B **Review of Memory Hierarchy**

Appendix C Pipelining: Basic and Intermediate Concepts

Online Appendices

Preface

Why We Wrote This Book

Through five editions of this book, our goal has been to describe the basic principles underlying what will be tomorrow's technological developments. Our excitement about the opportunities in computer architecture has not abated, and we echo what we said about the field in the first edition: "It is not a dreary science of paper machines that will never work. No! It's a discipline of keen intellectual interest, requiring the balance of marketplace forces to cost-performance-power, leading to glorious failures and some notable successes."

Our primary objective in writing our first book was to change the way people learn and think about computer architecture. We feel this goal is still valid and important. The field is changing daily and must be studied with real examples and measurements on real computers, rather than simply as a collection of definitions and designs that will never need to be realized. We offer an enthusiastic welcome to anyone who came along with us in the past, as well as to those who are joining us now. Either way, we can promise the same quantitative approach to, and analysis of, real systems.

As with earlier versions, we have strived to produce a new edition that will continue to be as relevant for professional engineers and architects as it is for those involved in advanced computer architecture and design courses. Like the first edition, this edition has a sharp focus on new platforms—personal mobile devices and warehouse-scale computers—and new architectures—multicore and GPUs. As much as its predecessors, this edition aims to demystify computer architecture through an emphasis on cost-performance-energy trade-offs and good engineering design. We believe that the field has continued to mature and move toward the rigorous quantitative foundation of long-established scientific and engineering disciplines.

This Edition

We said the fourth edition of *Computer Architecture: A Quantitative Approach* may have been the most significant since the first edition due to the switch to multicore chips. The feedback we received this time was that the book had lost the sharp focus of the first edition, covering everthing equally but without emphasis and context. We're pretty sure that won't be said about the fifth edition.

We believe most of the excitement is at the extremes in size of computing, with personal mobile devices (PMDs) such as cell phones and tablets as the clients and warehouse-scale computers offering cloud computing as the server. (Observant readers may seen the hint for cloud computing on the cover.) We are struck by the common theme of these two extremes in cost, performance, and energy efficiency despite their difference in size. As a result, the running context through each chapter is computing for PMDs and for warehouse scale computers, and Chapter 6 is a brand-new chapter on the latter topic.

The other theme is parallelism in all its forms. We first idetify the two types of application-level parallelism in Chapter 1: *data-level parallelism (DLP)*, which arises because there are many data items that can be operated on at the same time, and *task-level parallelism (TLP)*, which arises because tasks of work are created that can operate independently and largely in parallel. We then explain the four architectural styles that exploit DLP and TLP: *instruction-level parallelism (ILP)* in Chapter 3; *vector architectures* and *graphic processor units (GPUs)* in Chapter 4, which is a brand-new chapter for this edition; *thread-level parallelism* in Chapter 5; and *request-level parallelism* (RLP) via warehouse-scale computers in Chapter 6, which is also a brand-new chapter for this edition. We moved memory hierarchy earlier in the book to Chapter 2, and we moved the storage systems chapter to Appendix D. We are particularly proud about Chapter 4, which contains the most detailed and clearest explanation of GPUs yet, and Chapter 6, which is the first publication of the most recent details of a Google Warehouse-scale computer.

As before, the first three appendices in the book give basics on the MIPS instruction set, memory hierachy, and pipelining for readers who have not read a book like *Computer Organization and Design*. To keep costs down but still supply supplemental material that are of interest to some readers, available online at http://booksite.mkp.com/9780123838728/ are nine more appendices. There are more pages in these appendices than there are in this book!

This edition continues the tradition of using real-world examples to demonstrate the ideas, and the "Putting It All Together" sections are brand new. The "Putting It All Together" sections of this edition include the pipeline organizations and memory hierarchies of the ARM Cortex A8 processor, the Intel core i7 processor, the NVIDIA GTX-280 and GTX-480 GPUs, and one of the Google warehouse-scale computers.

Topic Selection and Organization

As before, we have taken a conservative approach to topic selection, for there are many more interesting ideas in the field than can reasonably be covered in a treatment of basic principles. We have steered away from a comprehensive survey of every architecture a reader might encounter. Instead, our presentation focuses on core concepts likely to be found in any new machine. The key criterion remains that of selecting ideas that have been examined and utilized successfully enough to permit their discussion in quantitative terms.

Our intent has always been to focus on material that is not available in equivalent form from other sources, so we continue to emphasize advanced content wherever possible. Indeed, there are several systems here whose descriptions cannot be found in the literature. (Readers interested strictly in a more basic introduction to computer architecture should read *Computer Organization and Design: The Hardware/Software Interface.*)

An Overview of the Content

Chapter 1 has been beefed up in this edition. It includes formulas for energy, static power, dynamic power, integrated circuit costs, reliability, and availability. (These formulas are also found on the front inside cover.) Our hope is that these topics can be used through the rest of the book. In addition to the classic quantitative principles of computer design and performance measurement, the PIAT section has been upgraded to use the new SPECPower benchmark.

Our view is that the instruction set architecture is playing less of a role today than in 1990, so we moved this material to Appendix A. It still uses the MIPS64 architecture. (For quick review, a summary of the MIPS ISA can be found on the back inside cover.) For fans of ISAs, Appendix K covers 10 RISC architectures, the 80x86, the DEC VAX, and the IBM 360/370.

We then move onto memory hierarchy in Chapter 2, since it is easy to apply the cost-performance-energy principles to this material and memory is a critical resource for the rest of the chapters. As in the past edition, Appendix B contains an introductory review of cache principles, which is available in case you need it. Chapter 2 discusses 10 advanced optimizations of caches. The chapter includes virtual machines, which offers advantages in protection, software management, and hardware management and play an important role in cloud computing. In addition to covering SRAM and DRAM technologies, the chapter includes new material on Flash memory. The PIAT examples are the ARM Cortex A8, which is used in PMDs, and the Intel Core i7, which is used in servers.

Chapter 3 covers the exploitation of instruction-level parallelism in high-performance processors, including superscalar execution, branch prediction, speculation, dynamic scheduling, and multithreading. As mentioned earlier, Appendix C is a review of pipelining in case you need it. Chapter 3 also surveys the limits of ILP. Like Chapter 2, the PIAT examples are again the ARM Cortex A8 and the Intel Core i7. While the third edition contained a great deal on Itanium and VLIW, this material is now in Appendix H, indicating our view that this architecture did not live up to the earlier claims.

The increasing importance of multimedia applications such as games and video processing has also increased the importance of achitectures that can exploit data-level parallelism. In particular, there is a rising interest in computing using graphical processing units (GPUs), yet few architects understand how GPUs really work. We decided to write a new chapter in large part to unveil this new style of computer architecture. Chapter 4 starts with an introduction to vector architectures, which acts as a foundation on which to build explanations of multimedia SIMD instruction set extensions and GPUs. (Appendix G goes into even more depth on vector architectures.) The section on GPUs was the most difficult to write in this book, in that it took many iterations to get an accurate description that was also easy to understand. A significant challenge was the terminology. We decided to go with our own terms and then provide a translation between our terms and the official NVIDIA terms. (A copy of that table can be found in the back inside cover pages.) This chapter introduces the Roofline performance model and then uses it to compare the Intel Core i7 and the NVIDIA GTX 280 and GTX 480 GPUs. The chapter also describes the Tegra 2 GPU for PMDs.

Chapter 5 describes multicore processors. It explores symmetric and distributed-memory architectures, examining both organizational principles and performance. Topics in synchronization and memory consistency models are next. The example is the Intel Core i7. Readers interested in interconnection networks on a chip should read Appendix F, and those interested in larger scale multiprocessors and scientific applications should read Appendix I.

As mentioned earlier, Chapter 6 describes the newest topic in computer architecture, warehouse-scale computers (WSCs). Based on help from engineers at Amazon Web Services and Google, this chapter integrates details on design, cost, and performance of WSCs that few architects are aware of. It starts with the popular MapReduce programming model before describing the architecture and physical implemention of WSCs, including cost. The costs allow us to explain the emergence of cloud computing, whereby it can be cheaper to compute using WSCs in the cloud than in your local datacenter. The PIAT example is a description of a Google WSC that includes information published for the first time in this book.

This brings us to Appendices A through L. Appendix A covers principles of ISAs, including MIPS64, and Appendix K describes 64-bit versions of Alpha, MIPS, PowerPC, and SPARC and their multimedia extensions. It also includes some classic architectures (80x86, VAX, and IBM 360/370) and popular embedded instruction sets (ARM, Thumb, SuperH, MIPS16, and Mitsubishi M32R). Appendix H is related, in that it covers architectures and compilers for VLIW ISAs.

As mentioned earlier, Appendices B and C are tutorials on basic caching and pipelining concepts. Readers relatively new to caching should read Appendix B before Chapter 2 and those new to pipelining should read Appendix C before Chapter 3.

Appendix D, "Storage Systems," has an expanded discussion of reliability and availability, a tutorial on RAID with a description of RAID 6 schemes, and rarely found failure statistics of real systems. It continues to provide an introduction to queuing theory and I/O performance benchmarks. We evaluate the cost, performance, and reliability of a real cluster: the Internet Archive. The "Putting It All Together" example is the NetApp FAS6000 filer.

Appendix E, by Thomas M. Conte, consolidates the embedded material in one place.

Appendix F, on interconnection networks, has been revised by Timothy M. Pinkston and José Duato. Appendix G, written originally by Krste Asanović, includes a description of vector processors. We think these two appendices are some of the best material we know of on each topic.

Appendix H describes VLIW and EPIC, the architecture of Itanium.

Appendix I describes parallel processing applications and coherence protocols for larger-scale, shared-memory multiprocessing. Appendix J, by David Goldberg, describes computer arithmetic.

Appendix L collects the "Historical Perspective and References" from each chapter into a single appendix. It attempts to give proper credit for the ideas in each chapter and a sense of the history surrounding the inventions. We like to think of this as presenting the human drama of computer design. It also supplies references that the student of architecture may want to pursue. If you have time, we recommend reading some of the classic papers in the field that are mentioned in these sections. It is both enjoyable and educational to hear the ideas directly from the creators. "Historical Perspective" was one of the most popular sections of prior editions.

Navigating the Text

There is no single best order in which to approach these chapters and appendices, except that all readers should start with Chapter 1. If you don't want to read everything, here are some suggested sequences:

- *Memory Hierarchy:* Appendix B, Chapter 2, and Appendix D.
- *Instruction-Level Parallelism:* Appendix C, Chapter 3, and Appendix H
- *Data-Level Parallelism:* Chapters 4 and 6, Appendix G
- *Thread-Level Parallelism:* Chapter 5, Appendices F and I
- *Request-Level Parallelism:* Chapter 6
- *ISA:* Appendices A and K

Appendix E can be read at any time, but it might work best if read after the ISA and cache sequences. Appendix J can be read whenever arithmetic moves you. You should read the corresponding portion of Appendix L after you complete each chapter.

Chapter Structure

The material we have selected has been stretched upon a consistent framework that is followed in each chapter. We start by explaining the ideas of a chapter. These ideas are followed by a "Crosscutting Issues" section, a feature that shows how the ideas covered in one chapter interact with those given in other chapters. This is followed by a "Putting It All Together" section that ties these ideas together by showing how they are used in a real machine.

Next in the sequence is "Fallacies and Pitfalls," which lets readers learn from the mistakes of others. We show examples of common misunderstandings and architectural traps that are difficult to avoid even when you know they are lying in wait for you. The "Fallacies and Pitfalls" sections is one of the most popular sections of the book. Each chapter ends with a "Concluding Remarks" section.

Case Studies with Exercises

Each chapter ends with case studies and accompanying exercises. Authored by experts in industry and academia, the case studies explore key chapter concepts and verify understanding through increasingly challenging exercises. Instructors should find the case studies sufficiently detailed and robust to allow them to create their own additional exercises.

Brackets for each exercise (<chapter.section>) indicate the text sections of primary relevance to completing the exercise. We hope this helps readers to avoid exercises for which they haven't read the corresponding section, in addition to providing the source for review. Exercises are rated, to give the reader a sense of the amount of time required to complete an exercise:

[10] Less than 5 minutes (to read and understand)

[15] 5–15 minutes for a full answer

[20] 15–20 minutes for a full answer

[25] 1 hour for a full written answer

[30] Short programming project: less than 1 full day of programming

[40] Significant programming project: 2 weeks of elapsed time

[Discussion] Topic for discussion with others

Solutions to the case studies and exercises are available for instructors who register at *textbooks.elsevier.com*.

Supplemental Materials

A variety of resources are available online at http://booksite.mkp.com/9780123838728/, including the following:

- Reference appendices—some guest authored by subject experts—covering a range of advanced topics
- Historical Perspectives material that explores the development of the key ideas presented in each of the chapters in the text
- Instructor slides in PowerPoint
- Figures from the book in PDF, EPS, and PPT formats
- Links to related material on the Web
- List of errata

New materials and links to other resources available on the Web will be added on a regular basis.

Helping Improve This Book

Finally, it is possible to make money while reading this book. (Talk about cost-performance!) If you read the Acknowledgments that follow, you will see that we went to great lengths to correct mistakes. Since a book goes through many printings, we have the opportunity to make even more corrections. If you uncover any remaining resilient bugs, please contact the publisher by electronic mail (*ca5bugs@mkp.com*).

We welcome general comments to the text and invite you to send them to a separate email address at *ca5comments@mkp.com*.

Concluding Remarks

Once again this book is a true co-authorship, with each of us writing half the chapters and an equal share of the appendices. We can't imagine how long it would have taken without someone else doing half the work, offering inspiration when the task seemed hopeless, providing the key insight to explain a difficult concept, supplying reviews over the weekend of chapters, and commiserating when the weight of our other obligations made it hard to pick up the pen. (These obligations have escalated exponentially with the number of editions, as the biographies attest.) Thus, once again we share equally the blame for what you are about to read.

John Hennessy ■ *David Patterson*

Acknowledgments

Although this is only the fifth edition of this book, we have actually created ten different versions of the text: three versions of the first edition (alpha, beta, and final) and two versions of the second, third, and fourth editions (beta and final). Along the way, we have received help from hundreds of reviewers and users. Each of these people has helped make this book better. Thus, we have chosen to list all of the people who have made contributions to some version of this book.

Contributors to the Fifth Edition

Like prior editions, this is a community effort that involves scores of volunteers. Without their help, this edition would not be nearly as polished.

Reviewers

Jason D. Bakos, University of South Carolina; Diana Franklin, The University of California, Santa Barbara; Norman P. Jouppi, HP Labs; Gregory Peterson, University of Tennessee; Parthasarathy Ranganathan, HP Labs; Mark Smotherman, Clemson University; Gurindar Sohi, University of Wisconsin–Madison; Mateo Valero, Universidad Politécnica de Cataluña; Sotirios G. Ziavras, New Jersey Institute of Technology

Members of the University of California–Berkeley Par Lab and RAD Lab who gave frequent reviews of Chapter 1, 4, and 6 and shaped the explanation of GPUs and WSCs: Krste Asanović, Michael Armbrust, Scott Beamer, Sarah Bird, Bryan Catanzaro, Jike Chong, Henry Cook, Derrick Coetzee, Randy Katz, Yunsup Lee, Leo Meyervich, Mark Murphy, Zhangxi Tan, Vasily Volkov, and Andrew Waterman

Advisory Panel

Luiz André Barroso, Google Inc.; Robert P. Colwell, R&E Colwell & Assoc. Inc.; Krisztian Flautner, VP of R&D at ARM Ltd.; Mary Jane Irwin, Penn State;

David Kirk, NVIDIA; Grant Martin, Chief Scientist, Tensilica; Gurindar Sohi, University of Wisconsin–Madison; Mateo Valero, Universidad Politécnica de Cataluña

Appendices

Krste Asanović, University of California, Berkeley (Appendix G); Thomas M. Conte, North Carolina State University (Appendix E); José Duato, Universitat Politècnica de València and Simula (Appendix F); David Goldberg, Xerox PARC (Appendix J); Timothy M. Pinkston, University of Southern California (Appendix F)

José Flich of the Universidad Politécnica de Valencia provided significant contributions to the updating of Appendix F.

Case Studies with Exercises

Jason D. Bakos, University of South Carolina (Chapters 3 and 4); Diana Franklin, University of California, Santa Barbara (Chapter 1 and Appendix C); Norman P. Jouppi, HP Labs (Chapter 2); Naveen Muralimanohar, HP Labs (Chapter 2); Gregory Peterson, University of Tennessee (Appendix A); Parthasarathy Ranganathan, HP Labs (Chapter 6); Amr Zaky, University of Santa Clara (Chapter 5 and Appendix B)

Jichuan Chang, Kevin Lim, and Justin Meza assisted in the development and testing of the case studies and exercises for Chapter 6.

Additional Material

John Nickolls, Steve Keckler, and Michael Toksvig of NVIDIA (Chapter 4 NVIDIA GPUs); Victor Lee, Intel (Chapter 4 comparison of Core i7 and GPU); John Shalf, LBNL (Chapter 4 recent vector architectures); Sam Williams, LBNL (Roofline model for computers in Chapter 4); Steve Blackburn of Australian National University and Kathryn McKinley of University of Texas at Austin (Intel performance and power measurements in Chapter 5); Luiz Barroso, Urs Hölzle, Jimmy Clidaris, Bob Felderman, and Chris Johnson of Google (the Google WSC in Chapter 6); James Hamilton of Amazon Web Services (power distribution and cost model in Chapter 6)

Jason D. Bakos of the University of South Carolina developed the new lecture slides for this edition.

Finally, a special thanks once again to Mark Smotherman of Clemson University, who gave a final technical reading of our manuscript. Mark found numerous bugs and ambiguities, and the book is much cleaner as a result.

This book could not have been published without a publisher, of course. We wish to thank all the Morgan Kaufmann/Elsevier staff for their efforts and support. For this fifth edition, we particularly want to thank our editors Nate McFadden and Todd Green, who coordinated surveys, the advisory panel, development of the case studies and exercises, focus groups, manuscript reviews, and the updating of the appendices.

We must also thank our university staff, Margaret Rowland and Roxana Infante, for countless express mailings, as well as for holding down the fort at Stanford and Berkeley while we worked on the book.

Our final thanks go to our wives for their suffering through increasingly early mornings of reading, thinking, and writing.

Contributors to Previous Editions

Reviewers

George Adams, Purdue University; Sarita Adve, University of Illinois at Urbana–Champaign; Jim Archibald, Brigham Young University; Krste Asanović, Massachusetts Institute of Technology; Jean-Loup Baer, University of Washington; Paul Barr, Northeastern University; Rajendra V. Boppana, University of Texas, San Antonio; Mark Brehob, University of Michigan; Doug Burger, University of Texas, Austin; John Burger, SGI; Michael Butler; Thomas Casavant; Rohit Chandra; Peter Chen, University of Michigan; the classes at SUNY Stony Brook, Carnegie Mellon, Stanford, Clemson, and Wisconsin; Tim Coe, Vitesse Semiconductor; Robert P. Colwell; David Cummings; Bill Dally; David Douglas; José Duato, Universitat Politècnica de València and Simula; Anthony Duben, Southeast Missouri State University; Susan Eggers, University of Washington; Joel Emer; Barry Fagin, Dartmouth; Joel Ferguson, University of California, Santa Cruz; Carl Feynman; David Filo; Josh Fisher, Hewlett-Packard Laboratories; Rob Fowler, DIKU; Mark Franklin, Washington University (St. Louis); Kourosh Gharachorloo; Nikolas Gloy, Harvard University; David Goldberg, Xerox Palo Alto Research Center; Antonio González, Intel and Universitat Politècnica de Catalunya; James Goodman, University of Wisconsin–Madison; Sudhanva Gurumurthi, University of Virginia; David Harris, Harvey Mudd College; John Heinlein; Mark Heinrich, Stanford; Daniel Helman, University of California, Santa Cruz; Mark D. Hill, University of Wisconsin–Madison; Martin Hopkins, IBM; Jerry Huck, Hewlett-Packard Laboratories; Wen-mei Hwu, University of Illinois at Urbana–Champaign; Mary Jane Irwin, Pennsylvania State University; Truman Joe; Norm Jouppi; David Kaeli, Northeastern University; Roger Kieckhafer, University of Nebraska; Lev G. Kirischian, Ryerson University; Earl Killian; Allan Knies, Purdue University; Don Knuth; Jeff Kuskin, Stanford; James R. Larus, Microsoft Research; Corinna Lee, University of Toronto; Hank Levy; Kai Li, Princeton University; Lori Liebrock, University of Alaska, Fairbanks; Mikko Lipasti, University of Wisconsin–Madison; Gyula A. Mago, University of North Carolina, Chapel Hill; Bryan Martin; Norman Matloff; David Meyer; William Michalson, Worcester Polytechnic Institute; James Mooney; Trevor Mudge, University of Michigan; Ramadass Nagarajan, University of Texas at Austin; David Nagle, Carnegie Mellon University; Todd Narter; Victor Nelson; Vojin Oklobdzija, University of California, Berkeley; Kunle Olukotun, Stanford University; Bob Owens, Pennsylvania State University; Greg Papadapoulous, Sun

Microsystems; Joseph Pfeiffer; Keshav Pingali, Cornell University; Timothy M. Pinkston, University of Southern California; Bruno Preiss, University of Waterloo; Steven Przybylski; Jim Quinlan; Andras Radics; Kishore Ramachandran, Georgia Institute of Technology; Joseph Rameh, University of Texas, Austin; Anthony Reeves, Cornell University; Richard Reid, Michigan State University; Steve Reinhardt, University of Michigan; David Rennels, University of California, Los Angeles; Arnold L. Rosenberg, University of Massachusetts, Amherst; Kaushik Roy, Purdue University; Emilio Salgueiro, Unysis; Karthikeyan Sankaralingam, University of Texas at Austin; Peter Schnorf; Margo Seltzer; Behrooz Shirazi, Southern Methodist University; Daniel Siewiorek, Carnegie Mellon University; J. P. Singh, Princeton; Ashok Singhal; Jim Smith, University of Wisconsin–Madison; Mike Smith, Harvard University; Mark Smotherman, Clemson University; Gurindar Sohi, University of Wisconsin–Madison; Arun Somani, University of Washington; Gene Tagliarin, Clemson University; Shyamkumar Thoziyoor, University of Notre Dame; Evan Tick, University of Oregon; Akhilesh Tyagi, University of North Carolina, Chapel Hill; Dan Upton, University of Virginia; Mateo Valero, Universidad Politécnica de Cataluña, Barcelona; Anujan Varma, University of California, Santa Cruz; Thorsten von Eicken, Cornell University; Hank Walker, Texas A&M; Roy Want, Xerox Palo Alto Research Center; David Weaver, Sun Microsystems; Shlomo Weiss, Tel Aviv University; David Wells; Mike Westall, Clemson University; Maurice Wilkes; Eric Williams; Thomas Willis, Purdue University; Malcolm Wing; Larry Wittie, SUNY Stony Brook; Ellen Witte Zegura, Georgia Institute of Technology; Sotirios G. Ziavras, New Jersey Institute of Technology

Appendices

The vector appendix was revised by Krste Asanović of the Massachusetts Institute of Technology. The floating-point appendix was written originally by David Goldberg of Xerox PARC.

Exercises

George Adams, Purdue University; Todd M. Bezenek, University of Wisconsin–Madison (in remembrance of his grandmother Ethel Eshom); Susan Eggers; Anoop Gupta; David Hayes; Mark Hill; Allan Knies; Ethan L. Miller, University of California, Santa Cruz; Parthasarathy Ranganathan, Compaq Western Research Laboratory; Brandon Schwartz, University of Wisconsin–Madison; Michael Scott; Dan Siewiorek; Mike Smith; Mark Smotherman; Evan Tick; Thomas Willis

Case Studies with Exercises

Andrea C. Arpaci-Dusseau, University of Wisconsin–Madison; Remzi H. Arpaci-Dusseau, University of Wisconsin–Madison; Robert P. Colwell, R&E Colwell & Assoc., Inc.; Diana Franklin, California Polytechnic State University, San Luis Obispo; Wen-mei W. Hwu, University of Illinois at Urbana–Champaign; Norman P. Jouppi, HP Labs; John W. Sias, University of Illinois at Urbana–Champaign; David A. Wood, University of Wisconsin–Madison

Special Thanks

Duane Adams, Defense Advanced Research Projects Agency; Tom Adams; Sarita Adve, University of Illinois at Urbana–Champaign; Anant Agarwal; Dave Albonesi, University of Rochester; Mitch Alsup; Howard Alt; Dave Anderson; Peter Ashenden; David Bailey; Bill Bandy, Defense Advanced Research Projects Agency; Luiz Barroso, Compaq's Western Research Lab; Andy Bechtolsheim; C. Gordon Bell; Fred Berkowitz; John Best, IBM; Dileep Bhandarkar; Jeff Bier, BDTI; Mark Birman; David Black; David Boggs; Jim Brady; Forrest Brewer; Aaron Brown, University of California, Berkeley; E. Bugnion, Compaq's Western Research Lab; Alper Buyuk-tosunoglu, University of Rochester; Mark Callaghan; Jason F. Cantin; Paul Carrick; Chen-Chung Chang; Lei Chen, University of Rochester; Pete Chen; Nhan Chu; Doug Clark, Princeton University; Bob Cmelik; John Crawford; Zarka Cvetanovic; Mike Dahlin, University of Texas, Austin; Merrick Darley; the staff of the DEC Western Research Laboratory; John DeRosa; Lloyd Dickman; J. Ding; Susan Eggers, University of Washington; Wael El-Essawy, University of Rochester; Patty Enriquez, Mills; Milos Ercegovac; Robert Garner; K. Gharachorloo, Compaq's Western Research Lab; Garth Gibson; Ronald Greenberg; Ben Hao; John Henning, Compaq; Mark Hill, University of Wisconsin–Madison; Danny Hillis; David Hodges; Urs Hölzle, Google; David Hough; Ed Hudson; Chris Hughes, University of Illinois at Urbana–Champaign; Mark Johnson; Lewis Jordan; Norm Jouppi; William Kahan; Randy Katz; Ed Kelly; Richard Kessler; Les Kohn; John Kowaleski, Compaq Computer Corp; Dan Lambright; Gary Lauterbach, Sun Microsystems; Corinna Lee; Ruby Lee; Don Lewine; Chao-Huang Lin; Paul Losleben, Defense Advanced Research Projects Agency; Yung-Hsiang Lu; Bob Lucas, Defense Advanced Research Projects Agency; Ken Lutz; Alan Mainwaring, Intel Berkeley Research Labs; Al Marston; Rich Martin, Rutgers; John Mashey; Luke McDowell; Sebastian Mirolo, Trimedia Corporation; Ravi Murthy; Biswadeep Nag; Lisa Noordergraaf, Sun Microsystems; Bob Parker, Defense Advanced Research Projects Agency; Vern Paxson, Center for Internet Research; Lawrence Prince; Steven Przybylski; Mark Pullen, Defense Advanced Research Projects Agency; Chris Rowen; Margaret Rowland; Greg Semeraro, University of Rochester; Bill Shannon; Behrooz Shirazi; Robert Shomler; Jim Slager; Mark Smotherman, Clemson University; the SMT research group at the University of Washington; Steve Squires, Defense Advanced Research Projects Agency; Ajay Sreekanth; Darren Staples; Charles Stapper; Jorge Stolfi; Peter Stoll; the students at Stanford and Berkeley who endured our first attempts at creating this book; Bob Supnik; Steve Swanson; Paul Taysom; Shreekant Thakkar; Alexander Thomasian, New Jersey Institute of Technology; John Toole, Defense Advanced Research Projects Agency; Kees A. Vissers, Trimedia Corporation; Willa Walker; David Weaver; Ric Wheeler, EMC; Maurice Wilkes; Richard Zimmerman.

John Hennessy ■ *David Patterson*

Fundamentals of Quantitative Design and Analysis

I think it's fair to say that personal computers have become the most empowering tool we've ever created. They're tools of communication, they're tools of creativity, and they can be shaped by their user.

Bill Gates, February 24, 2004

1.1 Introduction

Computer technology has made incredible progress in the roughly 65 years since the first general-purpose electronic computer was created. Today, less than $500 will purchase a mobile computer that has more performance, more main memory, and more disk storage than a computer bought in 1985 for $1 million. This rapid improvement has come both from advances in the technology used to build computers and from innovations in computer design.

Although technological improvements have been fairly steady, progress arising from better computer architectures has been much less consistent. During the first 25 years of electronic computers, both forces made a major contribution, delivering performance improvement of about 25% per year. The late 1970s saw the emergence of the microprocessor. The ability of the microprocessor to ride the improvements in integrated circuit technology led to a higher rate of performance improvement—roughly 35% growth per year.

This growth rate, combined with the cost advantages of a mass-produced microprocessor, led to an increasing fraction of the computer business being based on microprocessors. In addition, two significant changes in the computer marketplace made it easier than ever before to succeed commercially with a new architecture. First, the virtual elimination of assembly language programming reduced the need for object-code compatibility. Second, the creation of standardized, vendor-independent operating systems, such as UNIX and its clone, Linux, lowered the cost and risk of bringing out a new architecture.

These changes made it possible to develop successfully a new set of architectures with simpler instructions, called RISC (Reduced Instruction Set Computer) architectures, in the early 1980s. The RISC-based machines focused the attention of designers on two critical performance techniques, the exploitation of *instruction-level parallelism* (initially through pipelining and later through multiple instruction issue) and the use of caches (initially in simple forms and later using more sophisticated organizations and optimizations).

The RISC-based computers raised the performance bar, forcing prior architectures to keep up or disappear. The Digital Equipment Vax could not, and so it was replaced by a RISC architecture. Intel rose to the challenge, primarily by translating 80x86 instructions into RISC-like instructions internally, allowing it to adopt many of the innovations first pioneered in the RISC designs. As transistor counts soared in the late 1990s, the hardware overhead of translating the more complex x86 architecture became negligible. In low-end applications, such as cell phones, the cost in power and silicon area of the x86-translation overhead helped lead to a RISC architecture, ARM, becoming dominant.

Figure 1.1 shows that the combination of architectural and organizational enhancements led to 17 years of sustained growth in performance at an annual rate of over 50%—a rate that is unprecedented in the computer industry.

The effect of this dramatic growth rate in the 20th century has been fourfold. First, it has significantly enhanced the capability available to computer users. For many applications, the highest-performance microprocessors of today outperform the supercomputer of less than 10 years ago.

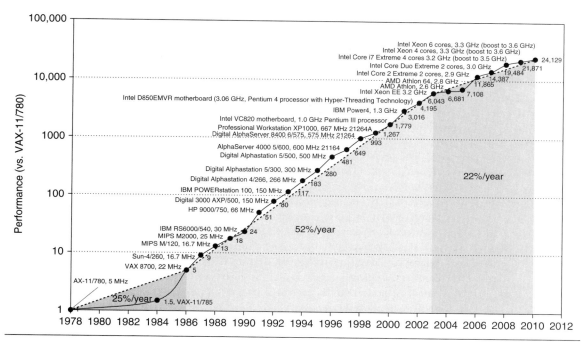

Figure 1.1 Growth in processor performance since the late 1970s. This chart plots performance relative to the VAX 11/780 as measured by the SPEC benchmarks (see Section 1.8). Prior to the mid-1980s, processor performance growth was largely technology driven and averaged about 25% per year. The increase in growth to about 52% since then is attributable to more advanced architectural and organizational ideas. By 2003, this growth led to a difference in performance of about a factor of 25 versus if we had continued at the 25% rate. Performance for floating-point-oriented calculations has increased even faster. Since 2003, the limits of power and available instruction-level parallelism have slowed uniprocessor performance, to no more than 22% per year, or about 5 times slower than had we continued at 52% per year. (The fastest SPEC performance since 2007 has had automatic parallelization turned on with increasing number of cores per chip each year, so uniprocessor speed is harder to gauge. These results are limited to single-socket systems to reduce the impact of automatic parallelization.) Figure 1.11 on page 24 shows the improvement in clock rates for these same three eras. Since SPEC has changed over the years, performance of newer machines is estimated by a scaling factor that relates the performance for two different versions of SPEC (e.g., SPEC89, SPEC92, SPEC95, SPEC2000, and SPEC2006).

Second, this dramatic improvement in cost-performance leads to new classes of computers. Personal computers and workstations emerged in the 1980s with the availability of the microprocessor. The last decade saw the rise of smart cell phones and tablet computers, which many people are using as their primary computing platforms instead of PCs. These mobile client devices are increasingly using the Internet to access warehouses containing tens of thousands of servers, which are being designed as if they were a single gigantic computer.

Third, continuing improvement of semiconductor manufacturing as predicted by Moore's law has led to the dominance of microprocessor-based computers across the entire range of computer design. Minicomputers, which were traditionally made from off-the-shelf logic or from gate arrays, were replaced by servers made using microprocessors. Even mainframe computers and high-performance supercomputers are all collections of microprocessors.

The hardware innovations above led to a renaissance in computer design, which emphasized both architectural innovation and efficient use of technology improvements. This rate of growth has compounded so that by 2003, high-performance microprocessors were 7.5 times faster than what would have been obtained by relying solely on technology, including improved circuit design; that is, 52% per year versus 35% per year.

This hardware renaissance led to the fourth impact, which is on software development. This 25,000-fold performance improvement since 1978 (see Figure 1.1) allowed programmers today to trade performance for productivity. In place of performance-oriented languages like C and C++, much more programming today is done in managed programming languages like Java and C#. Moreover, scripting languages like Python and Ruby, which are even more productive, are gaining in popularity along with programming frameworks like Ruby on Rails. To maintain productivity and try to close the performance gap, interpreters with just-in-time compilers and trace-based compiling are replacing the traditional compiler and linker of the past. Software deployment is changing as well, with Software as a Service (SaaS) used over the Internet replacing shrink-wrapped software that must be installed and run on a local computer.

The nature of applications also changes. Speech, sound, images, and video are becoming increasingly important, along with predictable response time that is so critical to the user experience. An inspiring example is Google Goggles. This application lets you hold up your cell phone to point its camera at an object, and the image is sent wirelessly over the Internet to a warehouse-scale computer that recognizes the object and tells you interesting information about it. It might translate text on the object to another language; read the bar code on a book cover to tell you if a book is available online and its price; or, if you pan the phone camera, tell you what businesses are nearby along with their websites, phone numbers, and directions.

Alas, Figure 1.1 also shows that this 17-year hardware renaissance is over. Since 2003, single-processor performance improvement has dropped to less than 22% per year due to the twin hurdles of maximum power dissipation of air-cooled chips and the lack of more instruction-level parallelism to exploit efficiently. Indeed, in 2004 Intel canceled its high-performance uniprocessor projects and joined others in declaring that the road to higher performance would be via multiple processors per chip rather than via faster uniprocessors.

This milestone signals a historic switch from relying solely on instruction-level parallelism (ILP), the primary focus of the first three editions of this book, to *data-level parallelism* (DLP) and *thread-level parallelism* (TLP), which were featured in the fourth edition and expanded in this edition. This edition also adds warehouse-scale computers and *request-level parallelism* (RLP). Whereas the compiler and hardware conspire to exploit ILP implicitly without the programmer's attention, DLP, TLP, and RLP are explicitly parallel, requiring the restructuring of the application so that it can exploit explicit parallelism. In some instances, this is easy; in many, it is a major new burden for programmers.

This text is about the architectural ideas and accompanying compiler improvements that made the incredible growth rate possible in the last century, the reasons for the dramatic change, and the challenges and initial promising approaches to architectural ideas, compilers, and interpreters for the 21st century. At the core is a quantitative approach to computer design and analysis that uses empirical observations of programs, experimentation, and simulation as its tools. It is this style and approach to computer design that is reflected in this text. The purpose of this chapter is to lay the quantitative foundation on which the following chapters and appendices are based.

This book was written not only to explain this design style but also to stimulate you to contribute to this progress. We believe this approach will work for explicitly parallel computers of the future just as it worked for the implicitly parallel computers of the past.

1.2   Classes of Computers

These changes have set the stage for a dramatic change in how we view computing, computing applications, and the computer markets in this new century. Not since the creation of the personal computer have we seen such dramatic changes in the way computers appear and in how they are used. These changes in computer use have led to five different computing markets, each characterized by different applications, requirements, and computing technologies. Figure 1.2 summarizes these mainstream classes of computing environments and their important characteristics.

Feature	Personal mobile device (PMD)	Desktop	Server	Clusters/warehouse-scale computer	Embedded
Price of system	$100–$1000	$300–$2500	$5000–$10,000,000	$100,000–$200,000,000	$10–$100,000
Price of microprocessor	$10–$100	$50–$500	$200–$2000	$50–$250	$0.01–$100
Critical system design issues	Cost, energy, media performance, responsiveness	Price-performance, energy, graphics performance	Throughput, availability, scalability, energy	Price-performance, throughput, energy proportionality	Price, energy, application-specific performance

Figure 1.2 A summary of the five mainstream computing classes and their system characteristics. Sales in 2010 included about 1.8 billion PMDs (90% cell phones), 350 million desktop PCs, and 20 million servers. The total number of embedded processors sold was nearly 19 billion. In total, 6.1 billion ARM-technology based chips were shipped in 2010. Note the wide range in system price for servers and embedded systems, which go from USB keys to network routers. For servers, this range arises from the need for very large-scale multiprocessor systems for high-end transaction processing.

Personal Mobile Device (PMD)

Personal mobile device (*PMD*) is the term we apply to a collection of wireless devices with multimedia user interfaces such as cell phones, tablet computers, and so on. Cost is a prime concern given the consumer price for the whole product is a few hundred dollars. Although the emphasis on energy efficiency is frequently driven by the use of batteries, the need to use less expensive packaging—plastic versus ceramic—and the absence of a fan for cooling also limit total power consumption. We examine the issue of energy and power in more detail in Section 1.5. Applications on PMDs are often Web-based and media-oriented, like the Google Goggles example above. Energy and size requirements lead to use of Flash memory for storage (Chapter 2) instead of magnetic disks.

Responsiveness and predictability are key characteristics for media applications. A *real-time performance* requirement means a segment of the application has an absolute maximum execution time. For example, in playing a video on a PMD, the time to process each video frame is limited, since the processor must accept and process the next frame shortly. In some applications, a more nuanced requirement exists: the average time for a particular task is constrained as well as the number of instances when some maximum time is exceeded. Such approaches—sometimes called *soft real-time*—arise when it is possible to occasionally miss the time constraint on an event, as long as not too many are missed. Real-time performance tends to be highly application dependent.

Other key characteristics in many PMD applications are the need to minimize memory and the need to use energy efficiently. Energy efficiency is driven by both battery power and heat dissipation. The memory can be a substantial portion of the system cost, and it is important to optimize memory size in such cases. The importance of memory size translates to an emphasis on code size, since data size is dictated by the application.

Desktop Computing

The first, and probably still the largest market in dollar terms, is desktop computing. Desktop computing spans from low-end netbooks that sell for under $300 to high-end, heavily configured workstations that may sell for $2500. Since 2008, more than half of the desktop computers made each year have been battery operated laptop computers.

Throughout this range in price and capability, the desktop market tends to be driven to optimize *price-performance*. This combination of performance (measured primarily in terms of compute performance and graphics performance) and price of a system is what matters most to customers in this market, and hence to computer designers. As a result, the newest, highest-performance microprocessors and cost-reduced microprocessors often appear first in desktop systems (see Section 1.6 for a discussion of the issues affecting the cost of computers).

Desktop computing also tends to be reasonably well characterized in terms of applications and benchmarking, though the increasing use of Web-centric, interactive applications poses new challenges in performance evaluation.

Servers

As the shift to desktop computing occurred in the 1980s, the role of servers grew to provide larger-scale and more reliable file and computing services. Such servers have become the backbone of large-scale enterprise computing, replacing the traditional mainframe.

For servers, different characteristics are important. First, availability is critical. (We discuss availability in Section 1.7.) Consider the servers running ATM machines for banks or airline reservation systems. Failure of such server systems is far more catastrophic than failure of a single desktop, since these servers must operate seven days a week, 24 hours a day. Figure 1.3 estimates revenue costs of downtime for server applications.

A second key feature of server systems is scalability. Server systems often grow in response to an increasing demand for the services they support or an increase in functional requirements. Thus, the ability to scale up the computing capacity, the memory, the storage, and the I/O bandwidth of a server is crucial.

Finally, servers are designed for efficient throughput. That is, the overall performance of the server—in terms of transactions per minute or Web pages served per second—is what is crucial. Responsiveness to an individual request remains important, but overall efficiency and cost-effectiveness, as determined by how many requests can be handled in a unit time, are the key metrics for most servers. We return to the issue of assessing performance for different types of computing environments in Section 1.8.

Application	Cost of downtime per hour	Annual losses with downtime of		
		1% (87.6 hrs/yr)	0.5% (43.8 hrs/yr)	0.1% (8.8 hrs/yr)
Brokerage operations	$6,450,000	$565,000,000	$283,000,000	$56,500,000
Credit card authorization	$2,600,000	$228,000,000	$114,000,000	$22,800,000
Package shipping services	$150,000	$13,000,000	$6,600,000	$1,300,000
Home shopping channel	$113,000	$9,900,000	$4,900,000	$1,000,000
Catalog sales center	$90,000	$7,900,000	$3,900,000	$800,000
Airline reservation center	$89,000	$7,900,000	$3,900,000	$800,000
Cellular service activation	$41,000	$3,600,000	$1,800,000	$400,000
Online network fees	$25,000	$2,200,000	$1,100,000	$200,000
ATM service fees	$14,000	$1,200,000	$600,000	$100,000

Figure 1.3 Costs rounded to nearest $100,000 of an unavailable system are shown by analyzing the cost of downtime (in terms of immediately lost revenue), assuming three different levels of availability and that downtime is distributed uniformly. These data are from Kembel [2000] and were collected and analyzed by Contingency Planning Research.

Clusters/Warehouse-Scale Computers

The growth of Software as a Service (SaaS) for applications like search, social networking, video sharing, multiplayer games, online shopping, and so on has led to the growth of a class of computers called *clusters*. Clusters are collections of desktop computers or servers connected by local area networks to act as a single larger computer. Each node runs its own operating system, and nodes communicate using a networking protocol. The largest of the clusters are called *warehouse-scale computers* (WSCs), in that they are designed so that tens of thousands of servers can act as one. Chapter 6 describes this class of the extremely large computers.

Price-performance and power are critical to WSCs since they are so large. As Chapter 6 explains, 80% of the cost of a $90M warehouse is associated with power and cooling of the computers inside. The computers themselves and networking gear cost another $70M and they must be replaced every few years. When you are buying that much computing, you need to buy wisely, as a 10% improvement in price-performance means a savings of $7M (10% of $70M).

WSCs are related to servers, in that availability is critical. For example, Amazon.com had $13 billion in sales in the fourth quarter of 2010. As there are about 2200 hours in a quarter, the average revenue per hour was almost $6M. During a peak hour for Christmas shopping, the potential loss would be many times higher. As Chapter 6 explains, the difference from servers is that WSCs use redundant inexpensive components as the building blocks, relying on a software layer to catch and isolate the many failures that will happen with computing at this scale. Note that scalability for a WSC is handled by the local area network connecting the computers and not by integrated computer hardware, as in the case of servers.

Supercomputers are related to WSCs in that they are equally expensive, costing hundreds of millions of dollars, but supercomputers differ by emphasizing floating-point performance and by running large, communication-intensive batch programs that can run for weeks at a time. This tight coupling leads to use of much faster internal networks. In contrast, WSCs emphasize interactive applications, large-scale storage, dependability, and high Internet bandwidth.

Embedded Computers

Embedded computers are found in everyday machines; microwaves, washing machines, most printers, most networking switches, and all cars contain simple embedded microprocessors.

The processors in a PMD are often considered embedded computers, but we are keeping them as a separate category because PMDs are platforms that can run externally developed software and they share many of the characteristics of desktop computers. Other embedded devices are more limited in hardware and software sophistication. We use the ability to run third-party software as the dividing line between non-embedded and embedded computers.

Embedded computers have the widest spread of processing power and cost. They include 8-bit and 16-bit processors that may cost less than a dime, 32-bit microprocessors that execute 100 million instructions per second and cost under $5, and high-end processors for network switches that cost $100 and can execute billions of instructions per second. Although the range of computing power in the embedded computing market is very large, price is a key factor in the design of computers for this space. Performance requirements do exist, of course, but the primary goal is often meeting the performance need at a minimum price, rather than achieving higher performance at a higher price.

Most of this book applies to the design, use, and performance of embedded processors, whether they are off-the-shelf microprocessors or microprocessor cores that will be assembled with other special-purpose hardware. Indeed, the third edition of this book included examples from embedded computing to illustrate the ideas in every chapter.

Alas, most readers found these examples unsatisfactory, as the data that drive the quantitative design and evaluation of other classes of computers have not yet been extended well to embedded computing (see the challenges with EEMBC, for example, in Section 1.8). Hence, we are left for now with qualitative descriptions, which do not fit well with the rest of the book. As a result, in this and the prior edition we consolidated the embedded material into Appendix E. We believe a separate appendix improves the flow of ideas in the text while allowing readers to see how the differing requirements affect embedded computing.

Classes of Parallelism and Parallel Architectures

Parallelism at multiple levels is now the driving force of computer design across all four classes of computers, with energy and cost being the primary constraints. There are basically two kinds of parallelism in applications:

1. *Data-Level Parallelism (DLP)* arises because there are many data items that can be operated on at the same time.

2. *Task-Level Parallelism (TLP)* arises because tasks of work are created that can operate independently and largely in parallel.

Computer hardware in turn can exploit these two kinds of application parallelism in four major ways:

1. *Instruction-Level Parallelism* exploits data-level parallelism at modest levels with compiler help using ideas like pipelining and at medium levels using ideas like speculative execution.

2. *Vector Architectures* and *Graphic Processor Units (GPUs)* exploit data-level parallelism by applying a single instruction to a collection of data in parallel.

3. *Thread-Level Parallelism* exploits either data-level parallelism or task-level parallelism in a tightly coupled hardware model that allows for interaction among parallel threads.

4. *Request-Level Parallelism* exploits parallelism among largely decoupled tasks specified by the programmer or the operating system.

These four ways for hardware to support the data-level parallelism and task-level parallelism go back 50 years. When Michael Flynn [1966] studied the parallel computing efforts in the 1960s, he found a simple classification whose abbreviations we still use today. He looked at the parallelism in the instruction and data streams called for by the instructions at the most constrained component of the multiprocessor, and placed all computers into one of four categories:

1. *Single instruction stream, single data stream* (SISD)—This category is the uniprocessor. The programmer thinks of it as the standard sequential computer, but it can exploit instruction-level parallelism. Chapter 3 covers SISD architectures that use ILP techniques such as superscalar and speculative execution.

2. *Single instruction stream, multiple data streams* (SIMD)—The same instruction is executed by multiple processors using different data streams. SIMD computers exploit *data-level parallelism* by applying the same operations to multiple items of data in parallel. Each processor has its own data memory (hence the MD of SIMD), but there is a single instruction memory and control processor, which fetches and dispatches instructions. Chapter 4 covers DLP and three different architectures that exploit it: vector architectures, multimedia extensions to standard instruction sets, and GPUs.

3. *Multiple instruction streams, single data stream* (MISD)—No commercial multiprocessor of this type has been built to date, but it rounds out this simple classification.

4. *Multiple instruction streams, multiple data streams* (MIMD)—Each processor fetches its own instructions and operates on its own data, and it targets task-level parallelism. In general, MIMD is more flexible than SIMD and thus more generally applicable, but it is inherently more expensive than SIMD. For example, MIMD computers can also exploit data-level parallelism, although the overhead is likely to be higher than would be seen in an SIMD computer. This overhead means that grain size must be sufficiently large to exploit the parallelism efficiently. Chapter 5 covers tightly coupled MIMD architectures, which exploit *thread-level parallelism* since multiple cooperating threads operate in parallel. Chapter 6 covers loosely coupled MIMD architectures—specifically, *clusters* and *warehouse-scale computers*—that exploit *request-level parallelism*, where many independent tasks can proceed in parallel naturally with little need for communication or synchronization.

This taxonomy is a coarse model, as many parallel processors are hybrids of the SISD, SIMD, and MIMD classes. Nonetheless, it is useful to put a framework on the design space for the computers we will see in this book.

1.3   **Defining Computer Architecture**

The task the computer designer faces is a complex one: Determine what attributes are important for a new computer, then design a computer to maximize performance and energy efficiency while staying within cost, power, and availability constraints. This task has many aspects, including instruction set design, functional organization, logic design, and implementation. The implementation may encompass integrated circuit design, packaging, power, and cooling. Optimizing the design requires familiarity with a very wide range of technologies, from compilers and operating systems to logic design and packaging.

Several years ago, the term *computer architecture* often referred only to instruction set design. Other aspects of computer design were called *implementation,* often insinuating that implementation is uninteresting or less challenging.

We believe this view is incorrect. The architect's or designer's job is much more than instruction set design, and the technical hurdles in the other aspects of the project are likely more challenging than those encountered in instruction set design. We'll quickly review instruction set architecture before describing the larger challenges for the computer architect.

Instruction Set Architecture: The Myopic View of Computer Architecture

We use the term *instruction set architecture* (ISA) to refer to the actual programmer-visible instruction set in this book. The ISA serves as the boundary between the software and hardware. This quick review of ISA will use examples from 80x86, ARM, and MIPS to illustrate the seven dimensions of an ISA. Appendices A and K give more details on the three ISAs.

1. *Class of ISA*—Nearly all ISAs today are classified as general-purpose register architectures, where the operands are either registers or memory locations. The 80x86 has 16 general-purpose registers and 16 that can hold floating-point data, while MIPS has 32 general-purpose and 32 floating-point registers (see Figure 1.4). The two popular versions of this class are *register-memory* ISAs, such as the 80x86, which can access memory as part of many instructions, and *load-store* ISAs, such as ARM and MIPS, which can access memory only with load or store instructions. All recent ISAs are load-store.

2. *Memory addressing*—Virtually all desktop and server computers, including the 80x86, ARM, and MIPS, use byte addressing to access memory operands. Some architectures, like ARM and MIPS, require that objects must be *aligned.* An access to an object of size s bytes at byte address A is aligned if $A \bmod s = 0$. (See Figure A.5 on page A-8.) The 80x86 does not require alignment, but accesses are generally faster if operands are aligned.

3. *Addressing modes*—In addition to specifying registers and constant operands, addressing modes specify the address of a memory object. MIPS addressing

Name	Number	Use	Preserved across a call?
$zero	0	The constant value 0	N.A.
$at	1	Assembler temporary	No
$v0–$v1	2–3	Values for function results and expression evaluation	No
$a0–$a3	4–7	Arguments	No
$t0–$t7	8–15	Temporaries	No
$s0–$s7	16–23	Saved temporaries	Yes
$t8–$t9	24–25	Temporaries	No
$k0–$k1	26–27	Reserved for OS kernel	No
$gp	28	Global pointer	Yes
$sp	29	Stack pointer	Yes
$fp	30	Frame pointer	Yes
$ra	31	Return address	Yes

Figure 1.4 MIPS registers and usage conventions. In addition to the 32 general-purpose registers (R0–R31), MIPS has 32 floating-point registers (F0–F31) that can hold either a 32-bit single-precision number or a 64-bit double-precision number.

modes are Register, Immediate (for constants), and Displacement, where a constant offset is added to a register to form the memory address. The 80x86 supports those three plus three variations of displacement: no register (absolute), two registers (based indexed with displacement), and two registers where one register is multiplied by the size of the operand in bytes (based with scaled index and displacement). It has more like the last three, minus the displacement field, plus register indirect, indexed, and based with scaled index. ARM has the three MIPS addressing modes plus PC-relative addressing, the sum of two registers, and the sum of two registers where one register is multiplied by the size of the operand in bytes. It also has autoincrement and autodecrement addressing, where the calculated address replaces the contents of one of the registers used in forming the address.

4. *Types and sizes of operands*—Like most ISAs, 80x86, ARM, and MIPS support operand sizes of 8-bit (ASCII character), 16-bit (Unicode character or half word), 32-bit (integer or word), 64-bit (double word or long integer), and IEEE 754 floating point in 32-bit (single precision) and 64-bit (double precision). The 80x86 also supports 80-bit floating point (extended double precision).

5. *Operations*—The general categories of operations are data transfer, arithmetic logical, control (discussed next), and floating point. MIPS is a simple and easy-to-pipeline instruction set architecture, and it is representative of the RISC architectures being used in 2011. Figure 1.5 summarizes the MIPS ISA. The 80x86 has a much richer and larger set of operations (see Appendix K).

Instruction type/opcode	Instruction meaning
Data transfers	*Move data between registers and memory, or between the integer and FP or special registers; only memory address mode is 16-bit displacement + contents of a GPR*
LB, LBU, SB	Load byte, load byte unsigned, store byte (to/from integer registers)
LH, LHU, SH	Load half word, load half word unsigned, store half word (to/from integer registers)
LW, LWU, SW	Load word, load word unsigned, store word (to/from integer registers)
LD, SD	Load double word, store double word (to/from integer registers)
L.S, L.D, S.S, S.D	Load SP float, load DP float, store SP float, store DP float
MFC0, MTC0	Copy from/to GPR to/from a special register
MOV.S, MOV.D	Copy one SP or DP FP register to another FP register
MFC1, MTC1	Copy 32 bits to/from FP registers from/to integer registers
Arithmetic/logical	*Operations on integer or logical data in GPRs; signed arithmetic trap on overflow*
DADD, DADDI, DADDU, DADDIU	Add, add immediate (all immediates are 16 bits); signed and unsigned
DSUB, DSUBU	Subtract, signed and unsigned
DMUL, DMULU, DDIV, DDIVU, MADD	Multiply and divide, signed and unsigned; multiply-add; all operations take and yield 64-bit values
AND, ANDI	And, and immediate
OR, ORI, XOR, XORI	Or, or immediate, exclusive or, exclusive or immediate
LUI	Load upper immediate; loads bits 32 to 47 of register with immediate, then sign-extends
DSLL, DSRL, DSRA, DSLLV, DSRLV, DSRAV	Shifts: both immediate (DS__) and variable form (DS__V); shifts are shift left logical, right logical, right arithmetic
SLT, SLTI, SLTU, SLTIU	Set less than, set less than immediate, signed and unsigned
Control	*Conditional branches and jumps; PC-relative or through register*
BEQZ, BNEZ	Branch GPRs equal/not equal to zero; 16-bit offset from PC + 4
BEQ, BNE	Branch GPR equal/not equal; 16-bit offset from PC + 4
BC1T, BC1F	Test comparison bit in the FP status register and branch; 16-bit offset from PC + 4
MOVN, MOVZ	Copy GPR to another GPR if third GPR is negative, zero
J, JR	Jumps: 26-bit offset from PC + 4 (J) or target in register (JR)
JAL, JALR	Jump and link: save PC + 4 in R31, target is PC-relative (JAL) or a register (JALR)
TRAP	Transfer to operating system at a vectored address
ERET	Return to user code from an exception; restore user mode
Floating point	*FP operations on DP and SP formats*
ADD.D, ADD.S, ADD.PS	Add DP, SP numbers, and pairs of SP numbers
SUB.D, SUB.S, SUB.PS	Subtract DP, SP numbers, and pairs of SP numbers
MUL.D, MUL.S, MUL.PS	Multiply DP, SP floating point, and pairs of SP numbers
MADD.D, MADD.S, MADD.PS	Multiply-add DP, SP numbers, and pairs of SP numbers
DIV.D, DIV.S, DIV.PS	Divide DP, SP floating point, and pairs of SP numbers
CVT._._	Convert instructions: CVT.x.y converts from type x to type y, where x and y are L (64-bit integer), W (32-bit integer), D (DP), or S (SP). Both operands are FPRs.
C.__.D, C.__.S	DP and SP compares: "__" = LT,GT,LE,GE,EQ,NE; sets bit in FP status register

Figure 1.5 Subset of the instructions in MIPS64. SP = single precision; DP = double precision. Appendix A gives much more detail on MIPS64. For data, the most significant bit number is 0; least is 63.

6. *Control flow instructions*—Virtually all ISAs, including these three, support conditional branches, unconditional jumps, procedure calls, and returns. All three use PC-relative addressing, where the branch address is specified by an address field that is added to the PC. There are some small differences. MIPS conditional branches (BE, BNE, etc.) test the contents of registers, while the 80x86 and ARM branches test condition code bits set as side effects of arithmetic/logic operations. The ARM and MIPS procedure call places the return address in a register, while the 80x86 call (CALLF) places the return address on a stack in memory.

7. *Encoding an ISA*—There are two basic choices on encoding: *fixed length* and *variable length*. All ARM and MIPS instructions are 32 bits long, which simplifies instruction decoding. Figure 1.6 shows the MIPS instruction formats. The 80x86 encoding is variable length, ranging from 1 to 18 bytes. Variable-length instructions can take less space than fixed-length instructions, so a program compiled for the 80x86 is usually smaller than the same program compiled for MIPS. Note that choices mentioned above will affect how the instructions are encoded into a binary representation. For example, the number of registers and the number of addressing modes both have a significant impact on the size of instructions, as the register field and addressing mode field can appear many times in a single instruction. (Note that ARM and MIPS later offered extensions to offer 16-bit length instructions so as to reduce program size, called Thumb or Thumb-2 and MIPS16, respectively.)

Basic instruction formats

R	opcode	rs	rt	rd	shamt	funct
	31 26	25 21	20 16	15 11	10 6	5 0

I	opcode	rs	rt	immediate
	31 26	25 21	20 16	15

J	opcode	address
	31 26	25

Floating-point instruction formats

FR	opcode	fmt	ft	fs	fd	funct
	31 26	25 21	20 16	15 11	10 6	5 0

FI	opcode	fmt	ft	immediate
	31 26	25 21	20 16	15

Figure 1.6 MIPS64 instruction set architecture formats. All instructions are 32 bits long. The R format is for integer register-to-register operations, such as DADDU, DSUBU, and so on. The I format is for data transfers, branches, and immediate instructions, such as LD, SD, BEQZ, and DADDIs. The J format is for jumps, the FR format for floating-point operations, and the FI format for floating-point branches.

The other challenges facing the computer architect beyond ISA design are particularly acute at the present, when the differences among instruction sets are small and when there are distinct application areas. Therefore, starting with the last edition, the bulk of instruction set material beyond this quick review is found in the appendices (see Appendices A and K).

We use a subset of MIPS64 as the example ISA in this book because it is both the dominant ISA for networking and it is an elegant example of the RISC architectures mentioned earlier, of which ARM (Advanced RISC Machine) is the most popular example. ARM processors were in 6.1 billion chips shipped in 2010, or roughly 20 times as many chips that shipped with 80x86 processors.

Genuine Computer Architecture: Designing the Organization and Hardware to Meet Goals and Functional Requirements

The implementation of a computer has two components: organization and hardware. The term *organization* includes the high-level aspects of a computer's design, such as the memory system, the memory interconnect, and the design of the internal processor or CPU (central processing unit—where arithmetic, logic, branching, and data transfer are implemented). The term *microarchitecture* is also used instead of organization. For example, two processors with the same instruction set architectures but different organizations are the AMD Opteron and the Intel Core i7. Both processors implement the x86 instruction set, but they have very different pipeline and cache organizations.

The switch to multiple processors per microprocessor led to the term *core* to also be used for processor. Instead of saying multiprocessor microprocessor, the term *multicore* has caught on. Given that virtually all chips have multiple processors, the term central processing unit, or CPU, is fading in popularity.

Hardware refers to the specifics of a computer, including the detailed logic design and the packaging technology of the computer. Often a line of computers contains computers with identical instruction set architectures and nearly identical organizations, but they differ in the detailed hardware implementation. For example, the Intel Core i7 (see Chapter 3) and the Intel Xeon 7560 (see Chapter 5) are nearly identical but offer different clock rates and different memory systems, making the Xeon 7560 more effective for server computers.

In this book, the word *architecture* covers all three aspects of computer design—instruction set architecture, organization or microarchitecture, and hardware.

Computer architects must design a computer to meet functional requirements as well as price, power, performance, and availability goals. Figure 1.7 summarizes requirements to consider in designing a new computer. Often, architects also must determine what the functional requirements are, which can be a major task. The requirements may be specific features inspired by the market. Application software often drives the choice of certain functional requirements by determining how the computer will be used. If a large body of software exists for a certain instruction set architecture, the architect may decide that a new computer

Functional requirements	Typical features required or supported
Application area	*Target of computer*
Personal mobile device	Real-time performance for a range of tasks, including interactive performance for graphics, video, and audio; energy efficiency (Ch. 2, 3, 4, 5; App. A)
General-purpose desktop	Balanced performance for a range of tasks, including interactive performance for graphics, video, and audio (Ch. 2, 3, 4, 5; App. A)
Servers	Support for databases and transaction processing; enhancements for reliability and availability; support for scalability (Ch. 2, 5; App. A, D, F)
Clusters/warehouse-scale computers	Throughput performance for many independent tasks; error correction for memory; energy proportionality (Ch 2, 6; App. F)
Embedded computing	Often requires special support for graphics or video (or other application-specific extension); power limitations and power control may be required; real-time constraints (Ch. 2, 3, 5; App. A, E)
Level of software compatibility	*Determines amount of existing software for computer*
At programming language	Most flexible for designer; need new compiler (Ch. 3, 5; App. A)
Object code or binary compatible	Instruction set architecture is completely defined—little flexibility—but no investment needed in software or porting programs (App. A)
Operating system requirements	*Necessary features to support chosen OS (Ch. 2; App. B)*
Size of address space	Very important feature (Ch. 2); may limit applications
Memory management	Required for modern OS; may be paged or segmented (Ch. 2)
Protection	Different OS and application needs: page vs. segment; virtual machines (Ch. 2)
Standards	*Certain standards may be required by marketplace*
Floating point	Format and arithmetic: IEEE 754 standard (App. J), special arithmetic for graphics or signal processing
I/O interfaces	For I/O devices: Serial ATA, Serial Attached SCSI, PCI Express (App. D, F)
Operating systems	UNIX, Windows, Linux, CISCO IOS
Networks	Support required for different networks: Ethernet, Infiniband (App. F)
Programming languages	Languages (ANSI C, C++, Java, Fortran) affect instruction set (App. A)

Figure 1.7 Summary of some of the most important functional requirements an architect faces. The left-hand column describes the class of requirement, while the right-hand column gives specific examples. The right-hand column also contains references to chapters and appendices that deal with the specific issues.

should implement an existing instruction set. The presence of a large market for a particular class of applications might encourage the designers to incorporate requirements that would make the computer competitive in that market. Later chapters examine many of these requirements and features in depth.

Architects must also be aware of important trends in both the technology and the use of computers, as such trends affect not only the future cost but also the longevity of an architecture.

Trends in Technology

If an instruction set architecture is to be successful, it must be designed to survive rapid changes in computer technology. After all, a successful new instruction set architecture may last decades—for example, the core of the IBM mainframe has been in use for nearly 50 years. An architect must plan for technology changes that can increase the lifetime of a successful computer.

To plan for the evolution of a computer, the designer must be aware of rapid changes in implementation technology. Five implementation technologies, which change at a dramatic pace, are critical to modern implementations:

■   *Integrated circuit logic technology*—Transistor density increases by about 35% per year, quadrupling somewhat over four years. Increases in die size are less predictable and slower, ranging from 10% to 20% per year. The combined effect is a growth rate in transistor count on a chip of about 40% to 55% per year, or doubling every 18 to 24 months. This trend is popularly known as Moore's law. Device speed scales more slowly, as we discuss below.

■   *Semiconductor DRAM* (dynamic random-access memory)—Now that most DRAM chips are primarily shipped in DIMM modules, it is harder to track chip capacity, as DRAM manufacturers typically offer several capacity products at the same time to match DIMM capacity. Capacity per DRAM chip has increased by about 25% to 40% per year recently, doubling roughly every two to three years. This technology is the foundation of main memory, and we discuss it in Chapter 2. Note that the rate of improvement has continued to slow over the editions of this book, as Figure 1.8 shows. There is even concern as whether the growth rate will stop in the middle of this decade due to the increasing difficulty of efficiently manufacturing even smaller DRAM cells [Kim 2005]. Chapter 2 mentions several other technologies that may replace DRAM if it hits a capacity wall.

CA:AQA Edition	Year	DRAM growth rate	Characterization of impact on DRAM capacity
1	1990	60%/year	Quadrupling every 3 years
2	1996	60%/year	Quadrupling every 3 years
3	2003	40%–60%/year	Quadrupling every 3 to 4 years
4	2007	40%/year	Doubling every 2 years
5	2011	25%–40%/year	Doubling every 2 to 3 years

Figure 1.8 Change in rate of improvement in DRAM capacity over time. The first two editions even called this rate the DRAM Growth Rule of Thumb, since it had been so dependable since 1977 with the 16-kilobit DRAM through 1996 with the 64-megabit DRAM. Today, some question whether DRAM capacity can improve at all in 5 to 7 years, due to difficulties in manufacturing an increasingly three-dimensional DRAM cell [Kim 2005].

- *Semiconductor Flash* (electrically erasable programmable read-only memory)—This nonvolatile semiconductor memory is the standard storage device in PMDs, and its rapidly increasing popularity has fueled its rapid growth rate in capacity. Capacity per Flash chip has increased by about 50% to 60% per year recently, doubling roughly every two years. In 2011, Flash memory is 15 to 20 times cheaper per bit than DRAM. Chapter 2 describes Flash memory.

- *Magnetic disk technology*—Prior to 1990, density increased by about 30% per year, doubling in three years. It rose to 60% per year thereafter, and increased to 100% per year in 1996. Since 2004, it has dropped back to about 40% per year, or doubled every three years. Disks are 15 to 25 times cheaper per bit than Flash. Given the slowed growth rate of DRAM, disks are now 300 to 500 times cheaper per bit than DRAM. This technology is central to server and warehouse scale storage, and we discuss the trends in detail in Appendix D.

- *Network technology*—Network performance depends both on the performance of switches and on the performance of the transmission system. We discuss the trends in networking in Appendix F.

These rapidly changing technologies shape the design of a computer that, with speed and technology enhancements, may have a lifetime of three to five years. Key technologies such as DRAM, Flash, and disk change sufficiently that the designer must plan for these changes. Indeed, designers often design for the next technology, knowing that when a product begins shipping in volume that the next technology may be the most cost-effective or may have performance advantages. Traditionally, cost has decreased at about the rate at which density increases.

Although technology improves continuously, the impact of these improvements can be in discrete leaps, as a threshold that allows a new capability is reached. For example, when MOS technology reached a point in the early 1980s where between 25,000 and 50,000 transistors could fit on a single chip, it became possible to build a single-chip, 32-bit microprocessor. By the late 1980s, first-level caches could go on a chip. By eliminating chip crossings within the processor and between the processor and the cache, a dramatic improvement in cost-performance and energy-performance was possible. This design was simply infeasible until the technology reached a certain point. With multicore microprocessors and increasing numbers of cores each generation, even server computers are increasingly headed toward a single chip for all processors. Such technology thresholds are not rare and have a significant impact on a wide variety of design decisions.

Performance Trends: Bandwidth over Latency

As we shall see in Section 1.8, *bandwidth* or *throughput* is the total amount of work done in a given time, such as megabytes per second for a disk transfer. In contrast, *latency* or *response time* is the time between the start and the completion of an event, such as milliseconds for a disk access. Figure 1.9 plots the relative

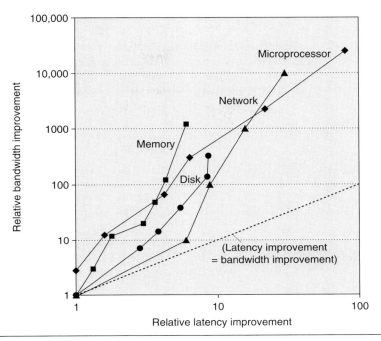

Figure 1.9 Log–log plot of bandwidth and latency milestones from Figure 1.10 relative to the first milestone. Note that latency improved 6X to 80X while bandwidth improved about 300X to 25,000X. Updated from Patterson [2004].

improvement in bandwidth and latency for technology milestones for microprocessors, memory, networks, and disks. Figure 1.10 describes the examples and milestones in more detail.

Performance is the primary differentiator for microprocessors and networks, so they have seen the greatest gains: 10,000–25,000X in bandwidth and 30–80X in latency. Capacity is generally more important than performance for memory and disks, so capacity has improved most, yet bandwidth advances of 300–1200X are still much greater than gains in latency of 6–8X.

Clearly, bandwidth has outpaced latency across these technologies and will likely continue to do so. A simple rule of thumb is that bandwidth grows by at least the square of the improvement in latency. Computer designers should plan accordingly.

Scaling of Transistor Performance and Wires

Integrated circuit processes are characterized by the *feature size*, which is the minimum size of a transistor or a wire in either the x or y dimension. Feature sizes have decreased from 10 microns in 1971 to 0.032 microns in 2011; in fact, we have switched units, so production in 2011 is referred to as "32 nanometers," and 22 nanometer chips are under way. Since the transistor count per square

Microprocessor	16-bit address/ bus, microcoded	32-bit address/ bus, microcoded	5-stage pipeline, on-chip I & D caches, FPU	2-way superscalar, 64-bit bus	Out-of-order 3-way superscalar	Out-of-order superpipelined, on-chip L2 cache	Multicore OOO 4-way on chip L3 cache, Turbo
Product	Intel 80286	Intel 80386	Intel 80486	Intel Pentium	Intel Pentium Pro	Intel Pentium 4	Intel Core i7
Year	1982	1985	1989	1993	1997	2001	2010
Die size (mm^2)	47	43	81	90	308	217	240
Transistors	134,000	275,000	1,200,000	3,100,000	5,500,000	42,000,000	1,170,000,000
Processors/chip	1	1	1	1	1	1	4
Pins	68	132	168	273	387	423	1366
Latency (clocks)	6	5	5	5	10	22	14
Bus width (bits)	16	32	32	64	64	64	196
Clock rate (MHz)	12.5	16	25	66	200	1500	3333
Bandwidth (MIPS)	2	6	25	132	600	4500	50,000
Latency (ns)	320	313	200	76	50	15	4

Memory module	DRAM	Page mode DRAM	Fast page mode DRAM	Fast page mode DRAM	Synchronous DRAM	Double data rate SDRAM	DDR3 SDRAM
Module width (bits)	16	16	32	64	64	64	64
Year	1980	1983	1986	1993	1997	2000	2010
Mbits/DRAM chip	0.06	0.25	1	16	64	256	2048
Die size (mm^2)	35	45	70	130	170	204	50
Pins/DRAM chip	16	16	18	20	54	66	134
Bandwidth (MBytes/s)	13	40	160	267	640	1600	16,000
Latency (ns)	225	170	125	75	62	52	37

Local area network	Ethernet	Fast Ethernet	Gigabit Ethernet	10 Gigabit Ethernet	100 Gigabit Ethernet		
IEEE standard	802.3	803.3u	802.3ab	802.3ac	802.3ba		
Year	1978	1995	1999	2003	2010		
Bandwidth (Mbits/sec)	10	100	1000	10,000	100,000		
Latency (μsec)	3000	500	340	190	100		

Hard disk	3600 RPM	5400 RPM	7200 RPM	10,000 RPM	15,000 RPM	15,000 RPM	
Product	CDC WrenI 94145-36	Seagate ST41600	Seagate ST15150	Seagate ST39102	Seagate ST373453	Seagate ST3600057	
Year	1983	1990	1994	1998	2003	2010	
Capacity (GB)	0.03	1.4	4.3	9.1	73.4	600	
Disk form factor	5.25 inch	5.25 inch	3.5 inch	3.5 inch	3.5 inch	3.5 inch	
Media diameter	5.25 inch	5.25 inch	3.5 inch	3.0 inch	2.5 inch	2.5 inch	
Interface	ST-412	SCSI	SCSI	SCSI	SCSI	SAS	
Bandwidth (MBytes/s)	0.6	4	9	24	86	204	
Latency (ms)	48.3	17.1	12.7	8.8	5.7	3.6	

Figure 1.10 **Performance milestones over 25 to 40 years for microprocessors, memory, networks, and disks.** The microprocessor milestones are several generations of IA-32 processors, going from a 16-bit bus, microcoded 80286 to a 64-bit bus, multicore, out-of-order execution, superpipelined Core i7. Memory module milestones go from 16-bit-wide, plain DRAM to 64-bit-wide double data rate version 3 synchronous DRAM. Ethernet advanced from 10 Mbits/sec to 100 Gbits/sec. Disk milestones are based on rotation speed, improving from 3600 RPM to 15,000 RPM. Each case is best-case bandwidth, and latency is the time for a simple operation assuming no contention. Updated from Patterson [2004].

millimeter of silicon is determined by the surface area of a transistor, the density of transistors increases quadratically with a linear decrease in feature size.

The increase in transistor performance, however, is more complex. As feature sizes shrink, devices shrink quadratically in the horizontal dimension and also shrink in the vertical dimension. The shrink in the vertical dimension requires a reduction in operating voltage to maintain correct operation and reliability of the transistors. This combination of scaling factors leads to a complex interrelationship between transistor performance and process feature size. To a first approximation, transistor performance improves linearly with decreasing feature size.

The fact that transistor count improves quadratically with a linear improvement in transistor performance is both the challenge and the opportunity for which computer architects were created! In the early days of microprocessors, the higher rate of improvement in density was used to move quickly from 4-bit, to 8-bit, to 16-bit, to 32-bit, to 64-bit microprocessors. More recently, density improvements have supported the introduction of multiple processors per chip, wider SIMD units, and many of the innovations in speculative execution and caches found in Chapters 2, 3, 4, and 5.

Although transistors generally improve in performance with decreased feature size, wires in an integrated circuit do not. In particular, the signal delay for a wire increases in proportion to the product of its resistance and capacitance. Of course, as feature size shrinks, wires get shorter, but the resistance and capacitance per unit length get worse. This relationship is complex, since both resistance and capacitance depend on detailed aspects of the process, the geometry of a wire, the loading on a wire, and even the adjacency to other structures. There are occasional process enhancements, such as the introduction of copper, which provide one-time improvements in wire delay.

In general, however, wire delay scales poorly compared to transistor performance, creating additional challenges for the designer. In the past few years, in addition to the power dissipation limit, wire delay has become a major design limitation for large integrated circuits and is often more critical than transistor switching delay. Larger and larger fractions of the clock cycle have been consumed by the propagation delay of signals on wires, but power now plays an even greater role than wire delay.

1.5   Trends in Power and Energy in Integrated Circuits

Today, power is the biggest challenge facing the computer designer for nearly every class of computer. First, power must be brought in and distributed around the chip, and modern microprocessors use hundreds of pins and multiple interconnect layers just for power and ground. Second, power is dissipated as heat and must be removed.

Power and Energy: A Systems Perspective

How should a system architect or a user think about performance, power, and energy? From the viewpoint of a system designer, there are three primary concerns.

First, what is the maximum power a processor ever requires? Meeting this demand can be important to ensuring correct operation. For example, if a processor attempts to draw more power than a power supply system can provide (by drawing more current than the system can supply), the result is typically a voltage drop, which can cause the device to malfunction. Modern processors can vary widely in power consumption with high peak currents; hence, they provide voltage indexing methods that allow the processor to slow down and regulate voltage within a wider margin. Obviously, doing so decreases performance.

Second, what is the sustained power consumption? This metric is widely called the *thermal design power* (TDP), since it determines the cooling requirement. TDP is neither peak power, which is often 1.5 times higher, nor is it the actual average power that will be consumed during a given computation, which is likely to be lower still. A typical power supply for a system is usually sized to exceed the TDP, and a cooling system is usually designed to match or exceed TDP. Failure to provide adequate cooling will allow the junction temperature in the processor to exceed its maximum value, resulting in device failure and possibly permanent damage. Modern processors provide two features to assist in managing heat, since the maximum power (and hence heat and temperature rise) can exceed the long-term average specified by the TDP. First, as the thermal temperature approaches the junction temperature limit, circuitry reduces the clock rate, thereby reducing power. Should this technique not be successful, a second thermal overload trip is activated to power down the chip.

The third factor that designers and users need to consider is energy and energy efficiency. Recall that power is simply energy per unit time: 1 watt = 1 joule per second. Which metric is the right one for comparing processors: energy or power? In general, energy is always a better metric because it is tied to a specific task and the time required for that task. In particular, the energy to execute a workload is equal to the average power times the execution time for the workload.

Thus, if we want to know which of two processors is more efficient for a given task, we should compare energy consumption (not power) for executing the task. For example, processor A may have a 20% higher average power consumption than processor B, but if A executes the task in only 70% of the time needed by B, its energy consumption will be $1.2 \times 0.7 = 0.84$, which is clearly better.

One might argue that in a large server or cloud, it is sufficient to consider average power, since the workload is often assumed to be infinite, but this is misleading. If our cloud were populated with processor Bs rather than As, then the cloud would do less work for the same amount of energy expended. Using energy to compare the alternatives avoids this pitfall. Whenever we have a fixed workload, whether for a warehouse-size cloud or a smartphone, comparing energy will be the right way to compare processor alternatives, as the electricity bill for the cloud and the battery lifetime for the smartphone are both determined by the energy consumed.

When is power consumption a useful measure? The primary legitimate use is as a constraint: for example, a chip might be limited to 100 watts. It can be used as a metric if the workload is fixed, but then it's just a variation of the true metric of energy per task.

Energy and Power within a Microprocessor

For CMOS chips, the traditional primary energy consumption has been in switching transistors, also called *dynamic energy*. The energy required per transistor is proportional to the product of the capacitive load driven by the transistor and the square of the voltage:

$$\text{Energy}_{\text{dynamic}} \propto \text{Capacitive load} \times \text{Voltage}^2$$

This equation is the energy of pulse of the logic transition of $0 \rightarrow 1 \rightarrow 0$ or $1 \rightarrow 0 \rightarrow 1$. The energy of a single transition ($0 \rightarrow 1$ or $1 \rightarrow 0$) is then:

$$\text{Energy}_{\text{dynamic}} \propto 1/2 \times \text{Capacitive load} \times \text{Voltage}^2$$

The power required per transistor is just the product of the energy of a transition multiplied by the frequency of transitions:

$$\text{Power}_{\text{dynamic}} \propto 1/2 \times \text{Capacitive load} \times \text{Voltage}^2 \times \text{Frequency switched}$$

For a fixed task, slowing clock rate reduces power, but not energy.

Clearly, dynamic power and energy are greatly reduced by lowering the voltage, so voltages have dropped from 5V to just under 1V in 20 years. The capacitive load is a function of the number of transistors connected to an output and the technology, which determines the capacitance of the wires and the transistors.

Example   Some microprocessors today are designed to have adjustable voltage, so a 15% reduction in voltage may result in a 15% reduction in frequency. What would be the impact on dynamic energy and on dynamic power?

Answer   Since the capacitance is unchanged, the answer for energy is the ratio of the voltages since the capacitance is unchanged:

$$\frac{\text{Energy}_{\text{new}}}{\text{Energy}_{\text{old}}} = \frac{(\text{Voltage} \times 0.85)^2}{\text{Voltage}^2} = 0.85^2 = 0.72$$

thereby reducing energy to about 72% of the original. For power, we add the ratio of the frequencies

$$\frac{\text{Power}_{\text{new}}}{\text{Power}_{\text{old}}} = 0.72 \times \frac{(\text{Frequency switched} \times 0.85)}{\text{Frequency switched}} = 0.61$$

shrinking power to about 61% of the original.

As we move from one process to the next, the increase in the number of transistors switching and the frequency with which they switch dominate the decrease in load capacitance and voltage, leading to an overall growth in power consumption and energy. The first microprocessors consumed less than a watt and the first 32-bit microprocessors (like the Intel 80386) used about 2 watts, while a 3.3 GHz Intel Core i7 consumes 130 watts. Given that this heat must be dissipated from a chip that is about 1.5 cm on a side, we have reached the limit of what can be cooled by air.

Given the equation above, you would expect clock frequency growth to slow down if we can't reduce voltage or increase power per chip. Figure 1.11 shows that this has indeed been the case since 2003, even for the microprocessors in Figure 1.1 that were the highest performers each year. Note that this period of flat clock rates corresponds to the period of slow performance improvement range in Figure 1.1.

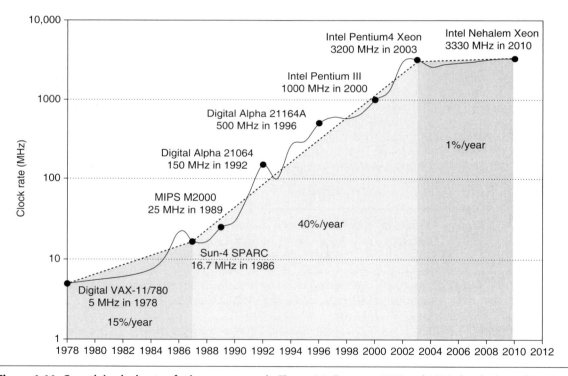

Figure 1.11 Growth in clock rate of microprocessors in Figure 1.1. Between 1978 and 1986, the clock rate improved less than 15% per year while performance improved by 25% per year. During the "renaissance period" of 52% performance improvement per year between 1986 and 2003, clock rates shot up almost 40% per year. Since then, the clock rate has been nearly flat, growing at less than 1% per year, while single processor performance improved at less than 22% per year.

Distributing the power, removing the heat, and preventing hot spots have become increasingly difficult challenges. Power is now the major constraint to using transistors; in the past, it was raw silicon area. Hence, modern microprocessors offer many techniques to try to improve energy efficiency despite flat clock rates and constant supply voltages:

1. *Do nothing well.* Most microprocessors today turn off the clock of inactive modules to save energy and dynamic power. For example, if no floating-point instructions are executing, the clock of the floating-point unit is disabled. If some cores are idle, their clocks are stopped.

2. *Dynamic Voltage-Frequency Scaling (DVFS).* The second technique comes directly from the formulas above. Personal mobile devices, laptops, and even servers have periods of low activity where there is no need to operate at the highest clock frequency and voltages. Modern microprocessors typically offer a few clock frequencies and voltages in which to operate that use lower power and energy. Figure 1.12 plots the potential power savings via DVFS for a server as the workload shrinks for three different clock rates: 2.4 GHz, 1.8 GHz, and 1 GHz. The overall server power savings is about 10% to 15% for each of the two steps.

3. *Design for typical case.* Given that PMDs and laptops are often idle, memory and storage offer low power modes to save energy. For example, DRAMs have a series of increasingly lower power modes to extend battery life in PMDs and laptops, and there have been proposals for disks that have a mode that spins at lower rates when idle to save power. Alas, you cannot access DRAMs or disks in these modes, so you must return to fully active mode to read or write, no matter how low the access rate. As mentioned

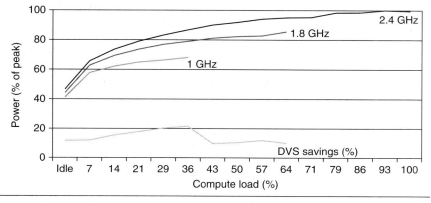

Figure 1.12 Energy savings for a server using an AMD Opteron microprocessor, 8 GB of DRAM, and one ATA disk. At 1.8 GHz, the server can only handle up to two-thirds of the workload without causing service level violations, and, at 1.0 GHz, it can only safely handle one-third of the workload. (Figure 5.11 in Barroso and Hölzle [2009].)

above, microprocessors for PCs have been designed instead for a more typical case of heavy use at high operating temperatures, relying on on-chip temperature sensors to detect when activity should be reduced automatically to avoid overheating. This "emergency slowdown" allows manufacturers to design for a more typical case and then rely on this safety mechanism if someone really does run programs that consume much more power than is typical.

4. *Overclocking.* Intel started offering *Turbo mode* in 2008, where the chip decides that it is safe to run at a higher clock rate for a short time possibly on just a few cores until temperature starts to rise. For example, the 3.3 GHz Core i7 can run in short bursts for 3.6 GHz. Indeed, the highest-performing microprocessors each year since 2008 in Figure 1.1 have all offered temporary overclocking of about 10% over the nominal clock rate. For single threaded code, these microprocessors can turn off all cores but one and run it at an even higher clock rate. Note that while the operating system can turn off Turbo mode there is no notification once it is enabled, so the programmers may be surprised to see their programs vary in performance due to room temperature!

Although dynamic power is traditionally thought of as the primary source of power dissipation in CMOS, static power is becoming an important issue because leakage current flows even when a transistor is off:

$$\text{Power}_{static} \propto \text{Current}_{static} \times \text{Voltage}$$

That is, static power is proportional to number of devices.

Thus, increasing the number of transistors increases power even if they are idle, and leakage current increases in processors with smaller transistor sizes. As a result, very low power systems are even turning off the power supply (*power gating*) to inactive modules to control loss due to leakage. In 2011, the goal for leakage is 25% of the total power consumption, with leakage in high-performance designs sometimes far exceeding that goal. Leakage can be as high as 50% for such chips, in part because of the large SRAM caches that need power to maintain the storage values. (The S in SRAM is for static.) The only hope to stop leakage is to turn off power to subsets of the chips.

Finally, because the processor is just a portion of the whole energy cost of a system, it can make sense to use a faster, less energy-efficient processor to allow the rest of the system to go into a sleep mode. This strategy is known as *race-to-halt.*

The importance of power and energy has increased the scrutiny on the efficiency of an innovation, so the primary evaluation now is tasks per joule or performance per watt as opposed to performance per mm^2 of silicon. This new metric affects approaches to parallelism, as we shall see in Chapters 4 and 5.

1.6   Trends in Cost

Although costs tend to be less important in some computer designs—specifically supercomputers—cost-sensitive designs are of growing significance. Indeed, in the past 30 years, the use of technology improvements to lower cost, as well as increase performance, has been a major theme in the computer industry.

Textbooks often ignore the cost half of cost-performance because costs change, thereby dating books, and because the issues are subtle and differ across industry segments. Yet, an understanding of cost and its factors is essential for computer architects to make intelligent decisions about whether or not a new feature should be included in designs where cost is an issue. (Imagine architects designing skyscrapers without any information on costs of steel beams and concrete!)

This section discusses the major factors that influence the cost of a computer and how these factors are changing over time.

The Impact of Time, Volume, and Commoditization

The cost of a manufactured computer component decreases over time even without major improvements in the basic implementation technology. The underlying principle that drives costs down is the *learning curve*—manufacturing costs decrease over time. The learning curve itself is best measured by change in *yield*—the percentage of manufactured devices that survives the testing procedure. Whether it is a chip, a board, or a system, designs that have twice the yield will have half the cost.

Understanding how the learning curve improves yield is critical to projecting costs over a product's life. One example is that the price per megabyte of DRAM has dropped over the long term. Since DRAMs tend to be priced in close relationship to cost—with the exception of periods when there is a shortage or an oversupply—price and cost of DRAM track closely.

Microprocessor prices also drop over time, but, because they are less standardized than DRAMs, the relationship between price and cost is more complex. In a period of significant competition, price tends to track cost closely, although microprocessor vendors probably rarely sell at a loss.

Volume is a second key factor in determining cost. Increasing volumes affect cost in several ways. First, they decrease the time needed to get down the learning curve, which is partly proportional to the number of systems (or chips) manufactured. Second, volume decreases cost, since it increases purchasing and manufacturing efficiency. As a rule of thumb, some designers have estimated that cost decreases about 10% for each doubling of volume. Moreover, volume decreases the amount of development cost that must be amortized by each computer, thus allowing cost and selling price to be closer.

Commodities are products that are sold by multiple vendors in large volumes and are essentially identical. Virtually all the products sold on the shelves of grocery stores are commodities, as are standard DRAMs, Flash memory, disks, monitors, and keyboards. In the past 25 years, much of the personal computer industry has become a commodity business focused on building desktop and laptop computers running Microsoft Windows.

Because many vendors ship virtually identical products, the market is highly competitive. Of course, this competition decreases the gap between cost and selling price, but it also decreases cost. Reductions occur because a commodity market has both volume and a clear product definition, which allows multiple suppliers to compete in building components for the commodity product. As a result, the overall product cost is lower because of the competition among the suppliers of the components and the volume efficiencies the suppliers can achieve. This rivalry has led to the low end of the computer business being able to achieve better price-performance than other sectors and yielded greater growth at the low end, although with very limited profits (as is typical in any commodity business).

Cost of an Integrated Circuit

Why would a computer architecture book have a section on integrated circuit costs? In an increasingly competitive computer marketplace where standard parts—disks, Flash memory, DRAMs, and so on—are becoming a significant portion of any system's cost, integrated circuit costs are becoming a greater portion of the cost that varies between computers, especially in the high-volume, cost-sensitive portion of the market. Indeed, with personal mobile devices' increasing reliance of whole *systems on a chip* (SOC), the cost of the integrated circuits is much of the cost of the PMD. Thus, computer designers must understand the costs of chips to understand the costs of current computers.

Although the costs of integrated circuits have dropped exponentially, the basic process of silicon manufacture is unchanged: A *wafer* is still tested and chopped into *dies* that are packaged (see Figures 1.13, 1.14, and 1.15). Thus, the cost of a packaged integrated circuit is

$$\text{Cost of integrated circuit} = \frac{\text{Cost of die} + \text{Cost of testing die} + \text{Cost of packaging and final test}}{\text{Final test yield}}$$

In this section, we focus on the cost of dies, summarizing the key issues in testing and packaging at the end.

Learning how to predict the number of good chips per wafer requires first learning how many dies fit on a wafer and then learning how to predict the percentage of those that will work. From there it is simple to predict cost:

$$\text{Cost of die} = \frac{\text{Cost of wafer}}{\text{Dies per wafer} \times \text{Die yield}}$$

The most interesting feature of this first term of the chip cost equation is its sensitivity to die size, shown below.

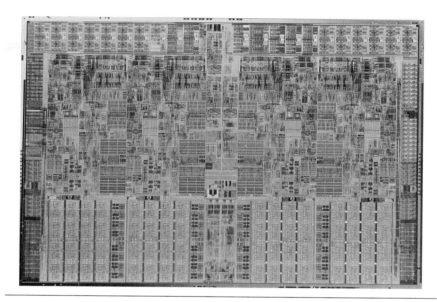

Figure 1.13 Photograph of an Intel Core i7 microprocessor die, which is evaluated in Chapters 2 through 5. The dimensions are 18.9 mm by 13.6 mm (257 mm²) in a 45 nm process. (Courtesy Intel.)

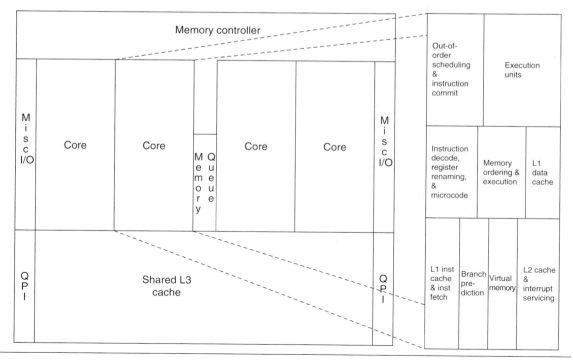

Figure 1.14 Floorplan of Core i7 die in Figure 1.13 on left with close-up of floorplan of second core on right.

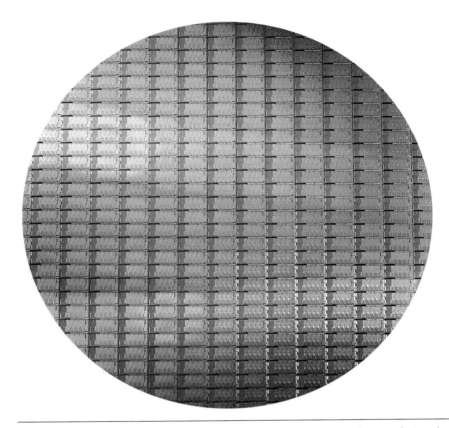

Figure 1.15 This 300 mm wafer contains 280 full Sandy Bridge dies, each 20.7 by 10.5 mm in a 32 nm process. (Sandy Bridge is Intel's successor to Nehalem used in the Core i7.) At 216 mm², the formula for dies per wafer estimates 282. (Courtesy Intel.)

The number of dies per wafer is approximately the area of the wafer divided by the area of the die. It can be more accurately estimated by

$$\text{Dies per wafer} = \frac{\pi \times (\text{Wafer diameter}/2)^2}{\text{Die area}} - \frac{\pi \times \text{Wafer diameter}}{\sqrt{2} \times \text{Die area}}$$

The first term is the ratio of wafer area (πr^2) to die area. The second compensates for the "square peg in a round hole" problem—rectangular dies near the periphery of round wafers. Dividing the circumference (πd) by the diagonal of a square die is approximately the number of dies along the edge.

Example   Find the number of dies per 300 mm (30 cm) wafer for a die that is 1.5 cm on a side and for a die that is 1.0 cm on a side.

Answer   When die area is 2.25 cm^2:

$$\text{Dies per wafer} = \frac{\pi \times (30/2)^2}{2.25} - \frac{\pi \times 30}{\sqrt{2 \times 2.25}} = \frac{706.9}{2.25} - \frac{94.2}{2.12} = 270$$

Since the area of the larger die is 2.25 times bigger, there are roughly 2.25 as many smaller dies per wafer:

$$\text{Dies per wafer} = \frac{\pi \times (30/2)^2}{1.00} - \frac{\pi \times 30}{\sqrt{2 \times 1.00}} = \frac{706.9}{1.00} - \frac{94.2}{1.41} = 640$$

However, this formula only gives the maximum number of dies per wafer. The critical question is: What is the fraction of good dies on a wafer, or the *die yield*? A simple model of integrated circuit yield, which assumes that defects are randomly distributed over the wafer and that yield is inversely proportional to the complexity of the fabrication process, leads to the following:

$$\text{Die yield} = \text{Wafer yield} \times 1/(1 + \text{Defects per unit area} \times \text{Die area})^N$$

This Bose–Einstein formula is an empirical model developed by looking at the yield of many manufacturing lines [Sydow 2006]. *Wafer yield* accounts for wafers that are completely bad and so need not be tested. For simplicity, we'll just assume the wafer yield is 100%. Defects per unit area is a measure of the random manufacturing defects that occur. In 2010, the value was typically 0.1 to 0.3 defects per square inch, or 0.016 to 0.057 defects per square centimeter, for a 40 nm process, as it depends on the maturity of the process (recall the learning curve, mentioned earlier). Finally, N is a parameter called the process-complexity factor, a measure of manufacturing difficulty. For 40 nm processes in 2010, N ranged from 11.5 to 15.5.

Example   Find the die yield for dies that are 1.5 cm on a side and 1.0 cm on a side, assuming a defect density of 0.031 per cm^2 and N is 13.5.

Answer   The total die areas are 2.25 cm^2 and 1.00 cm^2. For the larger die, the yield is

$$\text{Die yield} = 1/(1 + 0.031 \times 2.25)^{13.5} = 0.40$$

For the smaller die, the yield is

$$\text{Die yield} = 1/(1 + 0.031 \times 1.00)^{13.5} = 0.66$$

That is, less than half of all the large dies are good but two-thirds of the small dies are good.

The bottom line is the number of good dies per wafer, which comes from multiplying dies per wafer by die yield to incorporate the effects of defects. The examples above predict about 109 good 2.25 cm^2 dies from the 300 mm wafer and 424 good 1.00 cm^2 dies. Many microprocessors fall between these two sizes. Low-end embedded 32-bit processors are sometimes as small as 0.10 cm^2, and processors used for embedded control (in printers, microwaves, and so on) are often less than 0.04 cm^2.

Given the tremendous price pressures on commodity products such as DRAM and SRAM, designers have included redundancy as a way to raise yield. For a number of years, DRAMs have regularly included some redundant memory cells, so that a certain number of flaws can be accommodated. Designers have used similar techniques in both standard SRAMs and in large SRAM arrays used for caches within microprocessors. Obviously, the presence of redundant entries can be used to boost the yield significantly.

Processing of a 300 mm (12-inch) diameter wafer in a leading-edge technology cost between $5000 and $6000 in 2010. Assuming a processed wafer cost of $5500, the cost of the 1.00 cm^2 die would be around $13, but the cost per die of the 2.25 cm^2 die would be about $51, or almost four times the cost for a die that is a little over twice as large.

What should a computer designer remember about chip costs? The manufacturing process dictates the wafer cost, wafer yield, and defects per unit area, so the sole control of the designer is die area. In practice, because the number of defects per unit area is small, the number of good dies per wafer, and hence the cost per die, grows roughly as the square of the die area. The computer designer affects die size, and hence cost, both by what functions are included on or excluded from the die and by the number of I/O pins.

Before we have a part that is ready for use in a computer, the die must be tested (to separate the good dies from the bad), packaged, and tested again after packaging. These steps all add significant costs.

The above analysis has focused on the variable costs of producing a functional die, which is appropriate for high-volume integrated circuits. There is, however, one very important part of the fixed costs that can significantly affect the cost of an integrated circuit for low volumes (less than 1 million parts), namely, the cost of a mask set. Each step in the integrated circuit process requires a separate mask. Thus, for modern high-density fabrication processes with four to six metal layers, mask costs exceed $1M. Obviously, this large fixed cost affects the cost of prototyping and debugging runs and, for small-volume production, can be a significant part of the production cost. Since mask costs are likely to continue to increase, designers may incorporate reconfigurable logic to enhance the flexibility of a part or choose to use gate arrays (which have fewer custom mask levels) and thus reduce the cost implications of masks.

Cost versus Price

With the commoditization of computers, the margin between the cost to manufacture a product and the price the product sells for has been shrinking. Those margins pay for a company's research and development (R&D), marketing, sales, manufacturing equipment maintenance, building rental, cost of financing, pretax profits, and taxes. Many engineers are surprised to find that most companies spend only 4% (in the commodity PC business) to 12% (in the high-end server business) of their income on R&D, which includes all engineering.

Cost of Manufacturing versus Cost of Operation

For the first four editions of this book, cost meant the cost to build a computer and price meant price to purchase a computer. With the advent of warehouse-scale computers, which contain tens of thousands of servers, the cost to operate the computers is significant in addition to the cost of purchase.

As Chapter 6 shows, the amortized purchase price of servers and networks is just over 60% of the monthly cost to operate a warehouse-scale computer, assuming a short lifetime of the IT equipment of 3 to 4 years. About 30% of the monthly operational costs are for power use and the amortized infrastructure to distribute power and to cool the IT equipment, despite this infrastructure being amortized over 10 years. Thus, to lower operational costs in a warehouse-scale computer, computer architects need to use energy efficiently.

1.7   Dependability

Historically, integrated circuits were one of the most reliable components of a computer. Although their pins may be vulnerable, and faults may occur over communication channels, the error rate inside the chip was very low. That conventional wisdom is changing as we head to feature sizes of 32 nm and smaller, as both transient faults and permanent faults will become more commonplace, so architects must design systems to cope with these challenges. This section gives a quick overview of the issues in dependability, leaving the official definition of the terms and approaches to Section D.3 in Appendix D.

Computers are designed and constructed at different layers of abstraction. We can descend recursively down through a computer seeing components enlarge themselves to full subsystems until we run into individual transistors. Although some faults are widespread, like the loss of power, many can be limited to a single component in a module. Thus, utter failure of a module at one level may be considered merely a component error in a higher-level module. This distinction is helpful in trying to find ways to build dependable computers.

One difficult question is deciding when a system is operating properly. This philosophical point became concrete with the popularity of Internet services. Infrastructure providers started offering *service level agreements* (SLAs) or *service level objectives* (SLOs) to guarantee that their networking or power service would be dependable. For example, they would pay the customer a penalty if they did not meet an agreement more than some hours per month. Thus, an SLA could be used to decide whether the system was up or down.

Systems alternate between two states of service with respect to an SLA:

1. *Service accomplishment*, where the service is delivered as specified
2. *Service interruption*, where the delivered service is different from the SLA

Transitions between these two states are caused by *failures* (from state 1 to state 2) or *restorations* (2 to 1). Quantifying these transitions leads to the two main measures of dependability:

■ *Module reliability* is a measure of the continuous service accomplishment (or, equivalently, of the time to failure) from a reference initial instant. Hence, the *mean time to failure* (MTTF) is a reliability measure. The reciprocal of MTTF is a rate of failures, generally reported as failures per billion hours of operation, or *FIT* (for *failures in time*). Thus, an MTTF of 1,000,000 hours equals $10^9/10^6$ or 1000 FIT. Service interruption is measured as *mean time to repair* (MTTR). *Mean time between failures* (MTBF) is simply the sum of MTTF + MTTR. Although MTBF is widely used, MTTF is often the more appropriate term. If a collection of modules has exponentially distributed lifetimes—meaning that the age of a module is not important in probability of failure—the overall failure rate of the collection is the sum of the failure rates of the modules.

■ *Module availability* is a measure of the service accomplishment with respect to the alternation between the two states of accomplishment and interruption. For nonredundant systems with repair, module availability is

$$\text{Module availability} = \frac{\text{MTTF}}{(\text{MTTF} + \text{MTTR})}$$

Note that reliability and availability are now quantifiable metrics, rather than synonyms for dependability. From these definitions, we can estimate reliability of a system quantitatively if we make some assumptions about the reliability of components and that failures are independent.

Example   Assume a disk subsystem with the following components and MTTF:

■ 10 disks, each rated at 1,000,000-hour MTTF
■ 1 ATA controller, 500,000-hour MTTF
■ 1 power supply, 200,000-hour MTTF
■ 1 fan, 200,000-hour MTTF
■ 1 ATA cable, 1,000,000-hour MTTF

Using the simplifying assumptions that the lifetimes are exponentially distributed and that failures are independent, compute the MTTF of the system as a whole.

Answer   The sum of the failure rates is

$$\text{Failure rate}_{system} = 10 \times \frac{1}{1,000,000} + \frac{1}{500,000} + \frac{1}{200,000} + \frac{1}{200,000} + \frac{1}{1,000,000}$$

$$= \frac{10 + 2 + 5 + 5 + 1}{1,000,000 \text{ hours}} = \frac{23}{1,000,000} = \frac{23,000}{1,000,000,000 \text{ hours}}$$

or 23,000 FIT. The MTTF for the system is just the inverse of the failure rate:

$$\text{MTTF}_{system} = \frac{1}{\text{Failure rate}_{system}} = \frac{1,000,000,000 \text{ hours}}{23,000} = 43,500 \text{ hours}$$

or just under 5 years.

The primary way to cope with failure is redundancy, either in time (repeat the operation to see if it still is erroneous) or in resources (have other components to take over from the one that failed). Once the component is replaced and the system fully repaired, the dependability of the system is assumed to be as good as new. Let's quantify the benefits of redundancy with an example.

Example   Disk subsystems often have redundant power supplies to improve dependability. Using the components and MTTFs from above, calculate the reliability of redundant power supplies. Assume one power supply is sufficient to run the disk subsystem and that we are adding one redundant power supply.

Answer   We need a formula to show what to expect when we can tolerate a failure and still provide service. To simplify the calculations, we assume that the lifetimes of the components are exponentially distributed and that there is no dependency between the component failures. MTTF for our redundant power supplies is the mean time until one power supply fails divided by the chance that the other will fail before the first one is replaced. Thus, if the chance of a second failure before repair is small, then the MTTF of the pair is large.

Since we have two power supplies and independent failures, the mean time until one disk fails is $\text{MTTF}_{power\ supply}/2$. A good approximation of the probability of a second failure is MTTR over the mean time until the other power supply fails. Hence, a reasonable approximation for a redundant pair of power supplies is

$$\text{MTTF}_{power\ supply\ pair} = \frac{\text{MTTF}_{power\ supply}/2}{\dfrac{\text{MTTR}_{power\ supply}}{\text{MTTF}_{power\ supply}}} = \frac{\text{MTTF}^2_{power\ supply}/2}{\text{MTTR}_{power\ supply}} = \frac{\text{MTTF}^2_{power\ supply}}{2 \times \text{MTTR}_{power\ supply}}$$

Using the MTTF numbers above, if we assume it takes on average 24 hours for a human operator to notice that a power supply has failed and replace it, the reliability of the fault tolerant pair of power supplies is

$$\text{MTTF}_{power\ supply\ pair} = \frac{\text{MTTF}^2_{power\ supply}}{2 \times \text{MTTR}_{power\ supply}} = \frac{200,000^2}{2 \times 24} \cong 830,000,000$$

making the pair about 4150 times more reliable than a single power supply.

Having quantified the cost, power, and dependability of computer technology, we are ready to quantify performance.

Measuring, Reporting, and Summarizing Performance

When we say one computer is faster than another is, what do we mean? The user of a desktop computer may say a computer is faster when a program runs in less time, while an Amazon.com administrator may say a computer is faster when it completes more transactions per hour. The computer user is interested in reducing *response time*—the time between the start and the completion of an event—also referred to as *execution time*. The operator of a warehouse-scale computer may be interested in increasing *throughput*—the total amount of work done in a given time.

In comparing design alternatives, we often want to relate the performance of two different computers, say, X and Y. The phrase "X is faster than Y" is used here to mean that the response time or execution time is lower on X than on Y for the given task. In particular, "X is n times faster than Y" will mean:

$$\frac{\text{Execution time}_Y}{\text{Execution time}_X} = n$$

Since execution time is the reciprocal of performance, the following relationship holds:

$$n = \frac{\text{Execution time}_Y}{\text{Execution time}_X} = \frac{\dfrac{1}{\text{Performance}_Y}}{\dfrac{1}{\text{Performance}_X}} = \frac{\text{Performance}_X}{\text{Performance}_Y}$$

The phrase "the throughput of X is 1.3 times higher than Y" signifies here that the number of tasks completed per unit time on computer X is 1.3 times the number completed on Y.

Unfortunately, time is not always the metric quoted in comparing the performance of computers. Our position is that the only consistent and reliable measure of performance is the execution time of real programs, and that all proposed alternatives to time as the metric or to real programs as the items measured have eventually led to misleading claims or even mistakes in computer design.

Even execution time can be defined in different ways depending on what we count. The most straightforward definition of time is called *wall-clock time*, *response time*, or *elapsed time*, which is the latency to complete a task, including disk accesses, memory accesses, input/output activities, operating system overhead—everything. With multiprogramming, the processor works on another program while waiting for I/O and may not necessarily minimize the elapsed time of one program. Hence, we need a term to consider this activity. *CPU time* recognizes this distinction and means the time the processor is computing, *not* including the time waiting for I/O or running other programs. (Clearly, the response time seen by the user is the elapsed time of the program, not the CPU time.)

Computer users who routinely run the same programs would be the perfect candidates to evaluate a new computer. To evaluate a new system the users would simply compare the execution time of their *workloads*—the mixture of programs and operating system commands that users run on a computer. Few are in this happy situation, however. Most must rely on other methods to evaluate computers, and often other evaluators, hoping that these methods will predict performance for their usage of the new computer.

Benchmarks

The best choice of benchmarks to measure performance is real applications, such as Google Goggles from Section 1.1. Attempts at running programs that are much simpler than a real application have led to performance pitfalls. Examples include:

■ *Kernels*, which are small, key pieces of real applications

■ *Toy programs*, which are 100-line programs from beginning programming assignments, such as quicksort

■ *Synthetic benchmarks*, which are fake programs invented to try to match the profile and behavior of real applications, such as Dhrystone

All three are discredited today, usually because the compiler writer and architect can conspire to make the computer appear faster on these stand-in programs than on real applications. Depressingly for your authors—who dropped the fallacy about using synthetic programs to characterize performance in the fourth edition of this book since we thought computer architects agreed it was disreputable—the synthetic program Dhrystone is still the most widely quoted benchmark for embedded processors!

Another issue is the conditions under which the benchmarks are run. One way to improve the performance of a benchmark has been with benchmark-specific flags; these flags often caused transformations that would be illegal on many programs or would slow down performance on others. To restrict this process and increase the significance of the results, benchmark developers often require the vendor to use one compiler and one set of flags for all the programs in the same language (C++ or C). In addition to the question of compiler flags, another question is whether source code modifications are allowed. There are three different approaches to addressing this question:

1. No source code modifications are allowed.

2. Source code modifications are allowed but are essentially impossible. For example, database benchmarks rely on standard database programs that are tens of millions of lines of code. The database companies are highly unlikely to make changes to enhance the performance for one particular computer.

3. Source modifications are allowed, as long as the modified version produces the same output.

The key issue that benchmark designers face in deciding to allow modification of the source is whether such modifications will reflect real practice and provide useful insight to users, or whether such modifications simply reduce the accuracy of the benchmarks as predictors of real performance.

To overcome the danger of placing too many eggs in one basket, collections of benchmark applications, called *benchmark suites*, are a popular measure of performance of processors with a variety of applications. Of course, such suites are only as good as the constituent individual benchmarks. Nonetheless, a key advantage of such suites is that the weakness of any one benchmark is lessened by the presence of the other benchmarks. The goal of a benchmark suite is that it will characterize the relative performance of two computers, particularly for programs not in the suite that customers are likely to run.

A cautionary example is the Electronic Design News Embedded Microprocessor Benchmark Consortium (or EEMBC, pronounced "embassy") benchmarks. It is a set of 41 kernels used to predict performance of different embedded applications: automotive/industrial, consumer, networking, office automation, and telecommunications. EEMBC reports unmodified performance and "full fury" performance, where almost anything goes. Because these benchmarks use kernels, and because of the reporting options, EEMBC does not have the reputation of being a good predictor of relative performance of different embedded computers in the field. This lack of success is why Dhrystone, which EEMBC was trying to replace, is still used.

One of the most successful attempts to create standardized benchmark application suites has been the SPEC (Standard Performance Evaluation Corporation), which had its roots in efforts in the late 1980s to deliver better benchmarks for workstations. Just as the computer industry has evolved over time, so has the need for different benchmark suites, and there are now SPEC benchmarks to cover many application classes. All the SPEC benchmark suites and their reported results are found at *www.spec.org*.

Although we focus our discussion on the SPEC benchmarks in many of the following sections, many benchmarks have also been developed for PCs running the Windows operating system.

Desktop Benchmarks

Desktop benchmarks divide into two broad classes: processor-intensive benchmarks and graphics-intensive benchmarks, although many graphics benchmarks include intensive processor activity. SPEC originally created a benchmark set focusing on processor performance (initially called SPEC89), which has evolved into its fifth generation: SPEC CPU2006, which follows SPEC2000, SPEC95 SPEC92, and SPEC89. SPEC CPU2006 consists of a set of 12 integer benchmarks (CINT2006) and 17 floating-point benchmarks (CFP2006). Figure 1.16 describes the current SPEC benchmarks and their ancestry.

SPEC benchmarks are real programs modified to be portable and to minimize the effect of I/O on performance. The integer benchmarks vary from part of a C

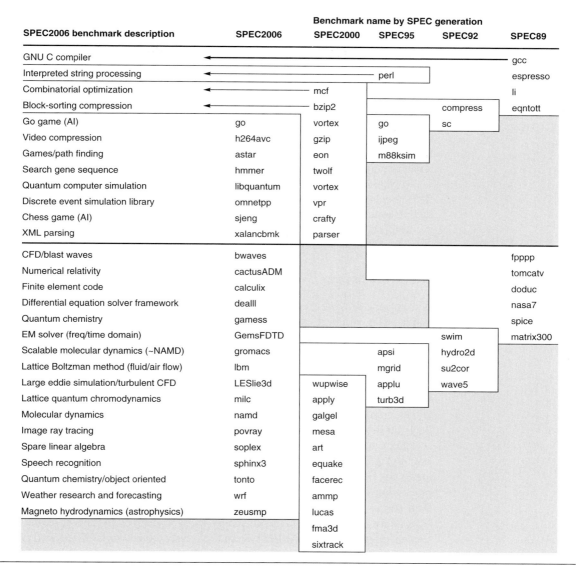

SPEC2006 benchmark description	Benchmark name by SPEC generation				
	SPEC2006	SPEC2000	SPEC95	SPEC92	SPEC89
GNU C compiler					gcc
Interpreted string processing			perl		espresso
Combinatorial optimization		mcf			li
Block-sorting compression		bzip2		compress	eqntott
Go game (AI)	go	vortex	go	sc	
Video compression	h264avc	gzip	ijpeg		
Games/path finding	astar	eon	m88ksim		
Search gene sequence	hmmer	twolf			
Quantum computer simulation	libquantum	vortex			
Discrete event simulation library	omnetpp	vpr			
Chess game (AI)	sjeng	crafty			
XML parsing	xalancbmk	parser			
CFD/blast waves	bwaves				fpppp
Numerical relativity	cactusADM				tomcatv
Finite element code	calculix				doduc
Differential equation solver framework	dealll				nasa7
Quantum chemistry	gamess				spice
EM solver (freq/time domain)	GemsFDTD			swim	matrix300
Scalable molecular dynamics (~NAMD)	gromacs		apsi	hydro2d	
Lattice Boltzman method (fluid/air flow)	lbm		mgrid	su2cor	
Large eddie simulation/turbulent CFD	LESlie3d	wupwise	applu	wave5	
Lattice quantum chromodynamics	milc	apply	turb3d		
Molecular dynamics	namd	galgel			
Image ray tracing	povray	mesa			
Spare linear algebra	soplex	art			
Speech recognition	sphinx3	equake			
Quantum chemistry/object oriented	tonto	facerec			
Weather research and forecasting	wrf	ammp			
Magneto hydrodynamics (astrophysics)	zeusmp	lucas			
		fma3d			
		sixtrack			

Figure 1.16   SPEC2006 programs and the evolution of the SPEC benchmarks over time, with integer programs above the line and floating-point programs below the line. Of the 12 SPEC2006 integer programs, 9 are written in C, and the rest in C++. For the floating-point programs, the split is 6 in Fortran, 4 in C++, 3 in C, and 4 in mixed C and Fortran. The figure shows all 70 of the programs in the 1989, 1992, 1995, 2000, and 2006 releases. The benchmark descriptions on the left are for SPEC2006 only and do not apply to earlier versions. Programs in the same row from different generations of SPEC are generally not related; for example, fpppp is not a CFD code like bwaves. Gcc is the senior citizen of the group. Only 3 integer programs and 3 floating-point programs survived three or more generations. Note that all the floating-point programs are new for SPEC2006. Although a few are carried over from generation to generation, the version of the program changes and either the input or the size of the benchmark is often changed to increase its running time and to avoid perturbation in measurement or domination of the execution time by some factor other than CPU time.

compiler to a chess program to a quantum computer simulation. The floating-point benchmarks include structured grid codes for finite element modeling, particle method codes for molecular dynamics, and sparse linear algebra codes for fluid dynamics. The SPEC CPU suite is useful for processor benchmarking for both desktop systems and single-processor servers. We will see data on many of these programs throughout this text. However, note that these programs share little with programming languages and environments and the Google Goggles application that Section 1.1 describes. Seven use C++, eight use C, and nine use Fortran! They are even statically linked, and the applications themselves are dull. It's not clear that SPECINT2006 and SPECFP2006 capture what is exciting about computing in the 21st century.

In Section 1.11, we describe pitfalls that have occurred in developing the SPEC benchmark suite, as well as the challenges in maintaining a useful and predictive benchmark suite.

SPEC CPU2006 is aimed at processor performance, but SPEC offers many other benchmarks.

Server Benchmarks

Just as servers have multiple functions, so are there multiple types of benchmarks. The simplest benchmark is perhaps a processor throughput-oriented benchmark. SPEC CPU2000 uses the SPEC CPU benchmarks to construct a simple throughput benchmark where the processing rate of a multiprocessor can be measured by running multiple copies (usually as many as there are processors) of each SPEC CPU benchmark and converting the CPU time into a rate. This leads to a measurement called the SPECrate, and it is a measure of request-level parallelism from Section 1.2. To measure thread-level parallelism, SPEC offers what they call high-performance computing benchmarks around OpenMP and MPI.

Other than SPECrate, most server applications and benchmarks have significant I/O activity arising from either disk or network traffic, including benchmarks for file server systems, for Web servers, and for database and transaction-processing systems. SPEC offers both a file server benchmark (SPECSFS) and a Web server benchmark (SPECWeb). SPECSFS is a benchmark for measuring NFS (Network File System) performance using a script of file server requests; it tests the performance of the I/O system (both disk and network I/O) as well as the processor. SPECSFS is a throughput-oriented benchmark but with important response time requirements. (Appendix D discusses some file and I/O system benchmarks in detail.) SPECWeb is a Web server benchmark that simulates multiple clients requesting both static and dynamic pages from a server, as well as clients posting data to the server. SPECjbb measures server performance for Web applications written in Java. The most recent SPEC benchmark is SPECvirt_Sc2010, which evaluates end-to-end performance of virtualized datacenter servers, including hardware, the virtual machine layer, and the virtualized guest operating system. Another recent SPEC benchmark measures power, which we examine in Section 1.10.

Transaction-processing (TP) benchmarks measure the ability of a system to handle transactions that consist of database accesses and updates. Airline reservation systems and bank ATM systems are typical simple examples of TP; more sophisticated TP systems involve complex databases and decision-making. In the mid-1980s, a group of concerned engineers formed the vendor-independent Transaction Processing Council (TPC) to try to create realistic and fair benchmarks for TP. The TPC benchmarks are described at *www.tpc.org*.

The first TPC benchmark, TPC-A, was published in 1985 and has since been replaced and enhanced by several different benchmarks. TPC-C, initially created in 1992, simulates a complex query environment. TPC-H models ad hoc decision support—the queries are unrelated and knowledge of past queries cannot be used to optimize future queries. TPC-E is a new On-Line Transaction Processing (OLTP) workload that simulates a brokerage firm's customer accounts. The most recent effort is TPC Energy, which adds energy metrics to all the existing TPC benchmarks.

All the TPC benchmarks measure performance in transactions per second. In addition, they include a response time requirement, so that throughput performance is measured only when the response time limit is met. To model real-world systems, higher transaction rates are also associated with larger systems, in terms of both users and the database to which the transactions are applied. Finally, the system cost for a benchmark system must also be included, allowing accurate comparisons of cost-performance. TPC modified its pricing policy so that there is a single specification for all the TPC benchmarks and to allow verification of the prices that TPC publishes.

Reporting Performance Results

The guiding principle of reporting performance measurements should be *reproducibility*—list everything another experimenter would need to duplicate the results. A SPEC benchmark report requires an extensive description of the computer and the compiler flags, as well as the publication of both the baseline and optimized results. In addition to hardware, software, and baseline tuning parameter descriptions, a SPEC report contains the actual performance times, shown both in tabular form and as a graph. A TPC benchmark report is even more complete, since it must include results of a benchmarking audit and cost information. These reports are excellent sources for finding the real costs of computing systems, since manufacturers compete on high performance and cost-performance.

Summarizing Performance Results

In practical computer design, you must evaluate myriad design choices for their relative quantitative benefits across a suite of benchmarks believed to be relevant. Likewise, consumers trying to choose a computer will rely on performance measurements from benchmarks, which hopefully are similar to the user's applications. In both cases, it is useful to have measurements for a suite of benchmarks so that the performance of important applications is similar to that of one or more benchmarks in the suite and that variability in performance can be understood. In the ideal case, the suite resembles a statistically valid sample of the application space, but such a sample requires more benchmarks than are typically found in most suites and requires a randomized sampling, which essentially no benchmark suite uses.

Once we have chosen to measure performance with a benchmark suite, we would like to be able to summarize the performance results of the suite in a single number. A straightforward approach to computing a summary result would be to compare the arithmetic means of the execution times of the programs in the suite. Alas, some SPEC programs take four times longer than others do, so those programs would be much more important if the arithmetic mean were the single number used to summarize performance. An alternative would be to add a weighting factor to each benchmark and use the weighted arithmetic mean as the single number to summarize performance. The problem would then be how to pick weights; since SPEC is a consortium of competing companies, each company might have their own favorite set of weights, which would make it hard to reach consensus. One approach is to use weights that make all programs execute an equal time on some reference computer, but this biases the results to the performance characteristics of the reference computer.

Rather than pick weights, we could normalize execution times to a reference computer by dividing the time on the reference computer by the time on the computer being rated, yielding a ratio proportional to performance. SPEC uses this approach, calling the ratio the SPECRatio. It has a particularly useful property that it matches the way we compare computer performance throughout this text—namely, comparing performance ratios. For example, suppose that the SPECRatio of computer A on a benchmark was 1.25 times higher than computer B; then we would know:

$$1.25 = \frac{\text{SPECRatio}_A}{\text{SPECRatio}_B} = \frac{\dfrac{\text{Execution time}_{\text{reference}}}{\text{Execution time}_A}}{\dfrac{\text{Execution time}_{\text{reference}}}{\text{Execution time}_B}} = \frac{\text{Execution time}_B}{\text{Execution time}_A} = \frac{\text{Performance}_A}{\text{Performance}_B}$$

Notice that the execution times on the reference computer drop out and the choice of the reference computer is irrelevant when the comparisons are made as a ratio, which is the approach we consistently use. Figure 1.17 gives an example.

Because a SPECRatio is a ratio rather than an absolute execution time, the mean must be computed using the *geometric* mean. (Since SPECRatios have no units, comparing SPECRatios arithmetically is meaningless.) The formula is

$$\text{Geometric mean} = \sqrt[n]{\prod_{i=1}^{n} sample_i}$$

Benchmarks	Ultra 5 time (sec)	Opteron time (sec)	SPECRatio	Itanium 2 time (sec)	SPECRatio	Opteron/Itanium times (sec)	Itanium/Opteron SPECRatios
wupwise	1600	51.5	31.06	56.1	28.53	0.92	0.92
swim	3100	125.0	24.73	70.7	43.85	1.77	1.77
mgrid	1800	98.0	18.37	65.8	27.36	1.49	1.49
applu	2100	94.0	22.34	50.9	41.25	1.85	1.85
mesa	1400	64.6	21.69	108.0	12.99	0.60	0.60
galgel	2900	86.4	33.57	40.0	72.47	2.16	2.16
art	2600	92.4	28.13	21.0	123.67	4.40	4.40
equake	1300	72.6	17.92	36.3	35.78	2.00	2.00
facerec	1900	73.6	25.80	86.9	21.86	0.85	0.85
ammp	2200	136.0	16.14	132.0	16.63	1.03	1.03
lucas	2000	88.8	22.52	107.0	18.76	0.83	0.83
fma3d	2100	120.0	17.48	131.0	16.09	0.92	0.92
sixtrack	1100	123.0	8.95	68.8	15.99	1.79	1.79
apsi	2600	150.0	17.36	231.0	11.27	0.65	0.65
Geometric mean			20.86		27.12	1.30	1.30

Figure 1.17 SPECfp2000 execution times (in seconds) for the Sun Ultra 5—the reference computer of SPEC2000—and execution times and SPECRatios for the AMD Opteron and Intel Itanium 2. (SPEC2000 multiplies the ratio of execution times by 100 to remove the decimal point from the result, so 20.86 is reported as 2086.) The final two columns show the ratios of execution times and SPECRatios. This figure demonstrates the irrelevance of the reference computer in relative performance. The ratio of the execution times is identical to the ratio of the SPECRatios, and the ratio of the geometric means (27.12/20.86 = 1.30) is identical to the geometric mean of the ratios (1.30).

In the case of SPEC, $sample_i$ is the SPECRatio for program i. Using the geometric mean ensures two important properties:

1. The geometric mean of the ratios is the same as the ratio of the geometric means.

2. The ratio of the geometric means is equal to the geometric mean of the performance ratios, which implies that the choice of the reference computer is irrelevant.

Hence, the motivations to use the geometric mean are substantial, especially when we use performance ratios to make comparisons.

Example   Show that the ratio of the geometric means is equal to the geometric mean of the performance ratios, and that the reference computer of SPECRatio matters not.

Answer   Assume two computers A and B and a set of SPECRatios for each.

$$\frac{\text{Geometric mean}_A}{\text{Geometric mean}_B} = \frac{\sqrt[n]{\prod_{i=1}^{n} \text{SPECRatio A}_i}}{\sqrt[n]{\prod_{i=1}^{n} \text{SPECRatio B}_i}} = \sqrt[n]{\prod_{i=1}^{n} \frac{\text{SPECRatio A}_i}{\text{SPECRatio B}_i}}$$

$$= \sqrt[n]{\prod_{i=1}^{n} \frac{\dfrac{\text{Execution time}_{\text{reference}_i}}{\text{Execution time}_{A_i}}}{\dfrac{\text{Execution time}_{\text{reference}_i}}{\text{Execution time}_{B_i}}}} = \sqrt[n]{\prod_{i=1}^{n} \frac{\text{Execution time}_{B_i}}{\text{Execution time}_{A_i}}} = \sqrt[n]{\prod_{i=1}^{n} \frac{\text{Performance}_{A_i}}{\text{Performance}_{B_i}}}$$

That is, the ratio of the geometric means of the SPECRatios of A and B is the geometric mean of the performance ratios of A to B of all the benchmarks in the suite. Figure 1.17 demonstrates this validity using examples from SPEC.

1.9   Quantitative Principles of Computer Design

Now that we have seen how to define, measure, and summarize performance, cost, dependability, energy, and power, we can explore guidelines and principles that are useful in the design and analysis of computers. This section introduces important observations about design, as well as two equations to evaluate alternatives.

Take Advantage of Parallelism

Taking advantage of parallelism is one of the most important methods for improving performance. Every chapter in this book has an example of how performance is enhanced through the exploitation of parallelism. We give three brief examples here, which are expounded on in later chapters.

Our first example is the use of parallelism at the system level. To improve the throughput performance on a typical server benchmark, such as SPECWeb or TPC-C, multiple processors and multiple disks can be used. The workload of handling requests can then be spread among the processors and disks, resulting in improved throughput. Being able to expand memory and the number of processors and disks is called *scalability*, and it is a valuable asset for servers. Spreading of data across many disks for parallel reads and writes enables data-level parallelism. SPECWeb also relies on request-level parallelism to use many processors while TPC-C uses thread-level parallelism for faster processing of database queries.

At the level of an individual processor, taking advantage of parallelism among instructions is critical to achieving high performance. One of the simplest ways to do this is through pipelining. (It is explained in more detail in Appendix C and is a major focus of Chapter 3.) The basic idea behind pipelining is to overlap instruction execution to reduce the total time to complete an instruction sequence. A key insight that allows pipelining to work is that not every instruction depends on its immediate predecessor, so executing the instructions completely or partially in parallel may be possible. Pipelining is the best-known example of instruction-level parallelism.

Parallelism can also be exploited at the level of detailed digital design. For example, set-associative caches use multiple banks of memory that are typically searched in parallel to find a desired item. Modern ALUs (arithmetic-logical units) use carry-lookahead, which uses parallelism to speed the process of computing sums from linear to logarithmic in the number of bits per operand. These are more examples of data-level parallelism.

Principle of Locality

Important fundamental observations have come from properties of programs. The most important program property that we regularly exploit is the *principle of locality*: Programs tend to reuse data and instructions they have used recently. A widely held rule of thumb is that a program spends 90% of its execution time in only 10% of the code. An implication of locality is that we can predict with reasonable accuracy what instructions and data a program will use in the near future based on its accesses in the recent past. The principle of locality also applies to data accesses, though not as strongly as to code accesses.

Two different types of locality have been observed. *Temporal locality* states that recently accessed items are likely to be accessed in the near future. *Spatial locality* says that items whose addresses are near one another tend to be referenced close together in time. We will see these principles applied in Chapter 2.

Focus on the Common Case

Perhaps the most important and pervasive principle of computer design is to focus on the common case: In making a design trade-off, favor the frequent case over the infrequent case. This principle applies when determining how to spend resources, since the impact of the improvement is higher if the occurrence is frequent.

Focusing on the common case works for power as well as for resource allocation and performance. The instruction fetch and decode unit of a processor may be used much more frequently than a multiplier, so optimize it first. It works on dependability as well. If a database server has 50 disks for every processor, storage dependability will dominate system dependability.

In addition, the frequent case is often simpler and can be done faster than the infrequent case. For example, when adding two numbers in the processor, we can expect overflow to be a rare circumstance and can therefore improve performance by optimizing the more common case of no overflow. This emphasis may slow down the case when overflow occurs, but if that is rare then overall performance will be improved by optimizing for the normal case.

We will see many cases of this principle throughout this text. In applying this simple principle, we have to decide what the frequent case is and how much performance can be improved by making that case faster. A fundamental law, called *Amdahl's law,* can be used to quantify this principle.

Amdahl's Law

The performance gain that can be obtained by improving some portion of a computer can be calculated using Amdahl's law. Amdahl's law states that the performance improvement to be gained from using some faster mode of execution is limited by the fraction of the time the faster mode can be used.

Amdahl's law defines the *speedup* that can be gained by using a particular feature. What is speedup? Suppose that we can make an enhancement to a computer that will improve performance when it is used. Speedup is the ratio:

$$\text{Speedup} = \frac{\text{Performance for entire task using the enhancement when possible}}{\text{Performance for entire task without using the enhancement}}$$

Alternatively,

$$\text{Speedup} = \frac{\text{Execution time for entire task without using the enhancement}}{\text{Execution time for entire task using the enhancement when possible}}$$

Speedup tells us how much faster a task will run using the computer with the enhancement as opposed to the original computer.

Amdahl's law gives us a quick way to find the speedup from some enhancement, which depends on two factors:

1. *The fraction of the computation time in the original computer that can be converted to take advantage of the enhancement*—For example, if 20 seconds of the execution time of a program that takes 60 seconds in total can use an enhancement, the fraction is 20/60. This value, which we will call $\text{Fraction}_{\text{enhanced}}$, is always less than or equal to 1.

2. *The improvement gained by the enhanced execution mode, that is, how much faster the task would run if the enhanced mode were used for the entire program*—This value is the time of the original mode over the time of the enhanced mode. If the enhanced mode takes, say, 2 seconds for a portion of the program, while it is 5 seconds in the original mode, the improvement is 5/2. We will call this value, which is always greater than 1, $\text{Speedup}_{\text{enhanced}}$.

The execution time using the original computer with the enhanced mode will be the time spent using the unenhanced portion of the computer plus the time spent using the enhancement:

$$\text{Execution time}_{\text{new}} = \text{Execution time}_{\text{old}} \times \left((1 - \text{Fraction}_{\text{enhanced}}) + \frac{\text{Fraction}_{\text{enhanced}}}{\text{Speedup}_{\text{enhanced}}} \right)$$

The overall speedup is the ratio of the execution times:

$$\text{Speedup}_{\text{overall}} = \frac{\text{Execution time}_{\text{old}}}{\text{Execution time}_{\text{new}}} = \frac{1}{(1 - \text{Fraction}_{\text{enhanced}}) + \dfrac{\text{Fraction}_{\text{enhanced}}}{\text{Speedup}_{\text{enhanced}}}}$$

Example Suppose that we want to enhance the processor used for Web serving. The new processor is 10 times faster on computation in the Web serving application than the original processor. Assuming that the original processor is busy with computation 40% of the time and is waiting for I/O 60% of the time, what is the overall speedup gained by incorporating the enhancement?

Answer $\text{Fraction}_{\text{enhanced}} = 0.4$; $\text{Speedup}_{\text{enhanced}} = 10$; $\text{Speedup}_{\text{overall}} = \dfrac{1}{0.6 + \dfrac{0.4}{10}} = \dfrac{1}{0.64} \approx 1.56$

Amdahl's law expresses the law of diminishing returns: The incremental improvement in speedup gained by an improvement of just a portion of the computation diminishes as improvements are added. An important corollary of Amdahl's law is that if an enhancement is only usable for a fraction of a task then we can't speed up the task by more than the reciprocal of 1 minus that fraction.

A common mistake in applying Amdahl's law is to confuse "fraction of time converted *to use an enhancement*" and "fraction of time *after enhancement is in use*." If, instead of measuring the time that we *could use* the enhancement in a computation, we measure the time *after* the enhancement is in use, the results will be incorrect!

Amdahl's law can serve as a guide to how much an enhancement will improve performance and how to distribute resources to improve cost-performance. The goal, clearly, is to spend resources proportional to where time is spent. Amdahl's law is particularly useful for comparing the overall system performance of two alternatives, but it can also be applied to compare two processor design alternatives, as the following example shows.

Example A common transformation required in graphics processors is square root. Implementations of floating-point (FP) square root vary significantly in performance, especially among processors designed for graphics. Suppose FP square root (FPSQR) is responsible for 20% of the execution time of a critical graphics benchmark. One proposal is to enhance the FPSQR hardware and speed up this operation by a factor of 10. The other alternative is just to try to make all FP instructions in the graphics processor run faster by a factor of 1.6; FP instructions are responsible for half of the execution time for the application. The design team believes that they can make all FP instructions run 1.6 times faster with the same effort as required for the fast square root. Compare these two design alternatives.

Answer   We can compare these two alternatives by comparing the speedups:

$$\text{Speedup}_{\text{FPSQR}} = \frac{1}{(1-0.2) + \frac{0.2}{10}} = \frac{1}{0.82} = 1.22$$

$$\text{Speedup}_{\text{FP}} = \frac{1}{(1-0.5) + \frac{0.5}{1.6}} = \frac{1}{0.8125} = 1.23$$

Improving the performance of the FP operations overall is slightly better because of the higher frequency.

Amdahl's law is applicable beyond performance. Let's redo the reliability example from page 35 after improving the reliability of the power supply via redundancy from 200,000-hour to 830,000,000-hour MTTF, or 4150X better.

Example   The calculation of the failure rates of the disk subsystem was

$$\text{Failure rate}_{\text{system}} = 10 \times \frac{1}{1{,}000{,}000} + \frac{1}{500{,}000} + \frac{1}{200{,}000} + \frac{1}{200{,}000} + \frac{1}{1{,}000{,}000}$$

$$= \frac{10 + 2 + 5 + 5 + 1}{1{,}000{,}000 \text{ hours}} = \frac{23}{1{,}000{,}000 \text{ hours}}$$

Therefore, the fraction of the failure rate that could be improved is 5 per million hours out of 23 for the whole system, or 0.22.

Answer   The reliability improvement would be

$$\text{Improvement}_{\text{power supply pair}} = \frac{1}{(1-0.22) + \frac{0.22}{4150}} = \frac{1}{0.78} = 1.28$$

Despite an impressive 4150X improvement in reliability of one module, from the system's perspective, the change has a measurable but small benefit.

In the examples above, we needed the fraction consumed by the new and improved version; often it is difficult to measure these times directly. In the next section, we will see another way of doing such comparisons based on the use of an equation that decomposes the CPU execution time into three separate components. If we know how an alternative affects these three components, we can determine its overall performance. Furthermore, it is often possible to build simulators that measure these components before the hardware is actually designed.

The Processor Performance Equation

Essentially all computers are constructed using a clock running at a constant rate. These discrete time events are called *ticks*, *clock ticks*, *clock periods*, *clocks*, *cycles*, or *clock cycles*. Computer designers refer to the time of a clock period by its duration (e.g., 1 ns) or by its rate (e.g., 1 GHz). CPU time for a program can then be expressed two ways:

$$\text{CPU time} = \text{CPU clock cycles for a program} \times \text{Clock cycle time}$$

or

$$\text{CPU time} = \frac{\text{CPU clock cycles for a program}}{\text{Clock rate}}$$

In addition to the number of clock cycles needed to execute a program, we can also count the number of instructions executed—the *instruction path length* or *instruction count* (IC). If we know the number of clock cycles and the instruction count, we can calculate the average number of *clock cycles per instruction* (CPI). Because it is easier to work with, and because we will deal with simple processors in this chapter, we use CPI. Designers sometimes also use *instructions per clock* (IPC), which is the inverse of CPI.

CPI is computed as

$$\text{CPI} = \frac{\text{CPU clock cycles for a program}}{\text{Instruction count}}$$

This processor figure of merit provides insight into different styles of instruction sets and implementations, and we will use it extensively in the next four chapters.

By transposing the instruction count in the above formula, clock cycles can be defined as IC × CPI. This allows us to use CPI in the execution time formula:

$$\text{CPU time} = \text{Instruction count} \times \text{Cycles per instruction} \times \text{Clock cycle time}$$

Expanding the first formula into the units of measurement shows how the pieces fit together:

$$\frac{\text{Instructions}}{\text{Program}} \times \frac{\text{Clock cycles}}{\text{Instruction}} \times \frac{\text{Seconds}}{\text{Clock cycle}} = \frac{\text{Seconds}}{\text{Program}} = \text{CPU time}$$

As this formula demonstrates, processor performance is dependent upon three characteristics: clock cycle (or rate), clock cycles per instruction, and instruction count. Furthermore, CPU time is *equally* dependent on these three characteristics; for example, a 10% improvement in any one of them leads to a 10% improvement in CPU time.

Unfortunately, it is difficult to change one parameter in complete isolation from others because the basic technologies involved in changing each characteristic are interdependent:

■ *Clock cycle time*—Hardware technology and organization

■ *CPI*—Organization and instruction set architecture

■ *Instruction count*—Instruction set architecture and compiler technology

Luckily, many potential performance improvement techniques primarily improve one component of processor performance with small or predictable impacts on the other two.

Sometimes it is useful in designing the processor to calculate the number of total processor clock cycles as

$$\text{CPU clock cycles} = \sum_{i=1}^{n} IC_i \times CPI_i$$

where IC_i represents the number of times instruction i is executed in a program and CPI_i represents the average number of clocks per instruction for instruction i. This form can be used to express CPU time as

$$\text{CPU time} = \left(\sum_{i=1}^{n} IC_i \times CPI_i \right) \times \text{Clock cycle time}$$

and overall CPI as

$$CPI = \frac{\displaystyle\sum_{i=1}^{n} IC_i \times CPI_i}{\text{Instruction count}} = \sum_{i=1}^{n} \frac{IC_i}{\text{Instruction count}} \times CPI_i$$

The latter form of the CPI calculation uses each individual CPI_i and the fraction of occurrences of that instruction in a program (i.e., $IC_i \div$ Instruction count). CPI_i should be measured and not just calculated from a table in the back of a reference manual since it must include pipeline effects, cache misses, and any other memory system inefficiencies.

Consider our performance example on page 47, here modified to use measurements of the frequency of the instructions and of the instruction CPI values, which, in practice, are obtained by simulation or by hardware instrumentation.

Example   Suppose we have made the following measurements:

Frequency of FP operations = 25%

Average CPI of FP operations = 4.0

Average CPI of other instructions = 1.33

Frequency of FPSQR = 2%

CPI of FPSQR = 20

Assume that the two design alternatives are to decrease the CPI of FPSQR to 2 or to decrease the average CPI of all FP operations to 2.5. Compare these two design alternatives using the processor performance equation.

Answer   First, observe that only the CPI changes; the clock rate and instruction count remain identical. We start by finding the original CPI with neither enhancement:

$$CPI_{original} = \sum_{i=1}^{n} CPI_i \times \left(\frac{IC_i}{Instruction\ count}\right)$$

$$= (4 \times 25\%) + (1.33 \times 75\%) = 2.0$$

We can compute the CPI for the enhanced FPSQR by subtracting the cycles saved from the original CPI:

$$CPI_{with\ new\ FPSQR} = CPI_{original} - 2\% \times (CPI_{old\ FPSQR} - CPI_{of\ new\ FPSQR\ only})$$

$$= 2.0 - 2\% \times (20 - 2) = 1.64$$

We can compute the CPI for the enhancement of all FP instructions the same way or by summing the FP and non-FP CPIs. Using the latter gives us:

$$CPI_{new\ FP} = (75\% \times 1.33) + (25\% \times 2.5) = 1.625$$

Since the CPI of the overall FP enhancement is slightly lower, its performance will be marginally better. Specifically, the speedup for the overall FP enhancement is

$$Speedup_{new\ FP} = \frac{CPU\ time_{original}}{CPU\ time_{new\ FP}} = \frac{IC \times Clock\ cycle \times CPI_{original}}{IC \times Clock\ cycle \times CPI_{new\ FP}}$$

$$= \frac{CPI_{original}}{CPI_{new\ FP}} = \frac{2.00}{1.625} = 1.23$$

Happily, we obtained this same speedup using Amdahl's law on page 46.

It is often possible to measure the constituent parts of the processor performance equation. This is a key advantage of using the processor performance equation versus Amdahl's law in the previous example. In particular, it may be difficult to measure things such as the fraction of execution time for which a set of instructions is responsible. In practice, this would probably be computed by summing the product of the instruction count and the CPI for each of the instructions in the set. Since the starting point is often individual instruction count and CPI measurements, the processor performance equation is incredibly useful.

To use the processor performance equation as a design tool, we need to be able to measure the various factors. For an existing processor, it is easy to obtain the execution time by measurement, and we know the default clock speed. The challenge lies in discovering the instruction count or the CPI. Most new processors include counters for both instructions executed and for clock cycles. By periodically monitoring these counters, it is also possible to attach execution time and instruction count to segments of the code, which can be helpful to programmers trying to understand and tune the performance of an application. Often, a designer or programmer will want to understand performance at a more fine-grained level than what is available from the hardware counters. For example, they may want to know why the CPI is what it is. In such cases, simulation techniques used are like those for processors that are being designed.

Techniques that help with energy efficiency, such as dynamic voltage frequency scaling and overclocking (see Section 1.5), make this equation harder to use, since the clock speed may vary while we measure the program. A simple approach is to turn off those features to make the results reproducible. Fortunately, as performance and energy efficiency are often highly correlated—taking less time to run a program generally saves energy—it's probably safe to consider performance without worrying about the impact of DVFS or overclocking on the results.

1.10 Putting It All Together: Performance, Price, and Power

In the "Putting It All Together" sections that appear near the end of every chapter, we provide real examples that use the principles in that chapter. In this section, we look at measures of performance and power-performance in small servers using the SPECpower benchmark.

Figure 1.18 shows the three multiprocessor servers we are evaluating along with their price. To keep the price comparison fair, all are Dell PowerEdge servers. The first is the PowerEdge R710, which is based on the Intel Xeon X5670 microprocessor with a clock rate of 2.93 GHz. Unlike the Intel Core i7 in Chapters 2 through 5, which has 4 cores and an 8 MB L3 cache, this Intel chip has 6 cores and a 12 MB L3 cache, although the cores themselves are identical. We selected a two-socket system with 12 GB of ECC-protected 1333 MHz DDR3 DRAM. The next server is the PowerEdge R815, which is based on the AMD Opteron 6174 microprocessor. A chip has 6 cores and a 6 MB L3 cache, and it runs at 2.20 GHz, but AMD puts two of these chips into a single socket. Thus, a socket has 12 cores and two 6 MB L3 caches. Our second server has two sockets with 24 cores and 16 GB of ECC-protected 1333 MHz DDR3 DRAM, and our third server (also a PowerEdge R815) has four sockets with 48 cores and 32 GB of DRAM. All are running the IBM J9 JVM and the Microsoft Windows 2008 Server Enterprise x64 Edition operating system.

Note that due to the forces of benchmarking (see Section 1.11), these are unusually configured servers. The systems in Figure 1.18 have little memory relative to the amount of computation, and just a tiny 50 GB solid-state disk. It is inexpensive to add cores if you don't need to add commensurate increases in memory and storage!

Rather than run statically linked C programs of SPEC CPU, SPECpower uses a more modern software stack written in Java. It is based on SPECjbb, and it represents the server side of business applications, with performance measured as the number transactions per second, called *ssj_ops* for *server side Java operations per second*. It exercises not only the processor of the server, as does SPEC

	System 1		System 2		System 3	
Component		**Cost (% Cost)**		**Cost (% Cost)**		**Cost (% Cost)**
Base server	PowerEdge R710	$653 (7%)	PowerEdge R815	$1437 (15%)	PowerEdge R815	$1437 (11%)
Power supply	570 W		1100 W		1100 W	
Processor	Xeon X5670	$3738 (40%)	Opteron 6174	$2679 (29%)	Opteron 6174	$5358 (42%)
Clock rate	2.93 GHz		2.20 GHz		2.20 GHz	
Total cores	12		24		48	
Sockets	2		2		4	
Cores/socket	6		12		12	
DRAM	12 GB	$484 (5%)	16 GB	$693 (7%)	32 GB	$1386 (11%)
Ethernet Inter.	Dual 1-Gbit	$199 (2%)	Dual 1-Gbit	$199 (2%)	Dual 1-Gbit	$199 (2%)
Disk	50 GB SSD	$1279 (14%)	50 GB SSD	$1279 (14%)	50 GB SSD	$1279 (10%)
Windows OS		$2999 (32%)		$2999 (33%)		$2999 (24%)
Total		$9352 (100%)		$9286 (100%)		$12,658 (100%)
Max ssj_ops	910,978		926,676		1,840,450	
Max ssj_ops/$	97		100		145	

Figure 1.18 **Three Dell PowerEdge servers being measured and their prices as of August 2010.** We calculated the cost of the processors by subtracting the cost of a second processor. Similarly, we calculated the overall cost of memory by seeing what the cost of extra memory was. Hence, the base cost of the server is adjusted by removing the estimated cost of the default processor and memory. Chapter 5 describes how these multi-socket systems are connected together.

CPU, but also the caches, memory system, and even the multiprocessor interconnection system. In addition, it exercises the Java Virtual Machine (JVM), including the JIT runtime compiler and garbage collector, as well as portions of the underlying operating system.

As the last two rows of Figure 1.18 show, the performance and price-performance winner is the PowerEdge R815 with four sockets and 48 cores. It hits 1.8M ssj_ops, and the ssj_ops per dollar is highest at 145. Amazingly, the computer with the largest number of cores is the most cost effective. In second place is the two-socket R815 with 24 cores, and the R710 with 12 cores is in last place.

While most benchmarks (and most computer architects) care only about performance of systems at peak load, computers rarely run at peak load. Indeed, Figure 6.2 in Chapter 6 shows the results of measuring the utilization of tens of thousands of servers over 6 months at Google, and less than 1% operate at an average utilization of 100%. The majority have an average utilization of between 10% and 50%. Thus, the SPECpower benchmark captures power as the target workload varies from its peak in 10% intervals all the way to 0%, which is called Active Idle.

Figure 1.19 plots the ssj_ops (SSJ operations/second) per watt and the average power as the target load varies from 100% to 0%. The Intel R710 always has the lowest power and the best ssj_ops per watt across each target workload level.

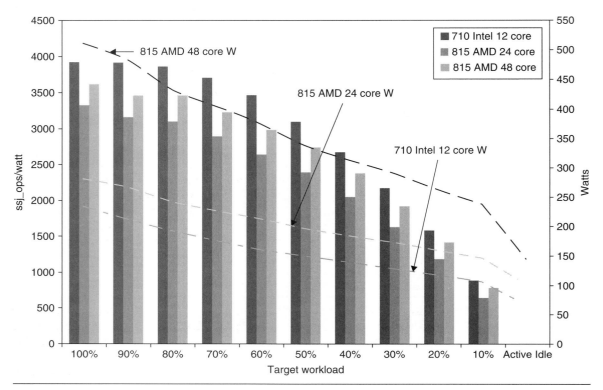

Figure 1.19 Power-performance of the three servers in Figure 1.18. Ssj_ops/watt values are on the left axis, with the three columns associated with it, and watts are on the right axis, with the three lines associated with it. The horizontal axis shows the target workload, as it varies from 100% to Active Idle. The Intel-based R715 has the best ssj_ops/watt at each workload level, and it also consumes the lowest power at each level.

One reason is the much larger power supply for the R815, at 1100 watts versus 570 in the R715. As Chapter 6 shows, power supply efficiency is very important in the overall power efficiency of a computer. Since watts = joules/second, this metric is proportional to SSJ operations per joule:

$$\frac{\text{ssj\_operations/sec}}{\text{Watt}} = \frac{\text{ssj\_operations/sec}}{\text{Joule/sec}} = \frac{\text{ssj\_operations}}{\text{Joule}}$$

To calculate a single number to use to compare the power efficiency of systems, SPECpower uses:

$$\text{Overall ssj\_ops/watt} = \frac{\sum \text{ssj\_ops}}{\sum \text{power}}$$

The overall ssj_ops/watt of the three servers is 3034 for the Intel R710, 2357 for the AMD dual-socket R815, and 2696 for the AMD quad-socket R815. Hence, the Intel R710 has the best power-performance. Dividing by the price of the servers, the ssj_ops/watt/$1000 is 324 for the Intel R710, 254 for the dual-socket AMD R815, and 213 for the quad-socket MD R815. Thus, adding power reverses the results of the price-performance competition, and the price-power-performance trophy goes to Intel R710; the 48-core R815 comes in last place.

1.11   Fallacies and Pitfalls

The purpose of this section, which will be found in every chapter, is to explain some commonly held misbeliefs or misconceptions that you should avoid. We call such misbeliefs *fallacies*. When discussing a fallacy, we try to give a counterexample. We also discuss *pitfalls*—easily made mistakes. Often pitfalls are generalizations of principles that are true in a limited context. The purpose of these sections is to help you avoid making these errors in computers that you design.

Fallacy   *Multiprocessors are a silver bullet.*

The switch to multiple processors per chip around 2005 did not come from some breakthrough that dramatically simplified parallel programming or made it easy to build multicore computers. The change occurred because there was no other option due to the ILP walls and power walls. Multiple processors per chip do not guarantee lower power; it's certainly possible to design a multicore chip that uses more power. The potential is just that it's possible to continue to improve performance by replacing a high-clock-rate, inefficient core with several lower-clock-rate, efficient cores. As technology improves to shrink transistors, this can shrink both capacitance and the supply voltage a bit so that we can get a modest increase in the number of cores per generation. For example, for the last few years Intel has been adding two cores per generation.

As we shall see in Chapters 4 and 5, performance is now a programmer's burden. The La-Z-Boy programmer era of relying on hardware designers to make their programs go faster without lifting a finger is officially over. If programmers want their programs to go faster with each generation, they must make their programs more parallel.

The popular version of Moore's law—increasing performance with each generation of technology—is now up to programmers.

Pitfall   *Falling prey to Amdahl's heartbreaking law.*

Virtually every practicing computer architect knows Amdahl's law. Despite this, we almost all occasionally expend tremendous effort optimizing some feature before we measure its usage. Only when the overall speedup is disappointing do we recall that we should have measured first before we spent so much effort enhancing it!

Pitfall   *A single point of failure.*

The calculations of reliability improvement using Amdahl's law on page 48 show that dependability is no stronger than the weakest link in a chain. No matter how much more dependable we make the power supplies, as we did in our example, the single fan will limit the reliability of the disk subsystem. This Amdahl's law observation led to a rule of thumb for fault-tolerant systems to make sure that every component was redundant so that no single component failure could bring down the whole system. Chapter 6 shows how a software layer avoids single points of failure inside warehouse-scale computers.

Fallacy   *Hardware enhancements that increase performance improve energy efficiency or are at worst energy neutral.*

Esmaeilzadeh et al. [2011] measured SPEC2006 on just one core of a 2.67 GHz Intel Core i7 using Turbo mode (Section 1.5). Performance increased by a factor of 1.07 when the clock rate increased to 2.94 GHz (or a factor of 1.10), but the i7 used a factor of 1.37 more joules and a factor of 1.47 more watt-hours!

Fallacy   *Benchmarks remain valid indefinitely.*

Several factors influence the usefulness of a benchmark as a predictor of real performance, and some change over time. A big factor influencing the usefulness of a benchmark is its ability to resist "benchmark engineering" or "benchmarketing." Once a benchmark becomes standardized and popular, there is tremendous pressure to improve performance by targeted optimizations or by aggressive interpretation of the rules for running the benchmark. Small kernels or programs that spend their time in a small amount of code are particularly vulnerable.

For example, despite the best intentions, the initial SPEC89 benchmark suite included a small kernel, called matrix300, which consisted of eight different 300×300 matrix multiplications. In this kernel, 99% of the execution time was in a single line (see SPEC [1989]). When an IBM compiler optimized this inner loop (using an idea called *blocking*, discussed in Chapters 2 and 4), performance improved by a factor of 9 over a prior version of the compiler! This benchmark tested compiler tuning and was not, of course, a good indication of overall performance, nor of the typical value of this particular optimization.

Over a long period, these changes may make even a well-chosen benchmark obsolete; Gcc is the lone survivor from SPEC89. Figure 1.16 on page 39 lists the status of all 70 benchmarks from the various SPEC releases. Amazingly, almost 70% of all programs from SPEC2000 or earlier were dropped from the next release.

Fallacy   *The rated mean time to failure of disks is 1,200,000 hours or almost 140 years, so disks practically never fail.*

The current marketing practices of disk manufacturers can mislead users. How is such an MTTF calculated? Early in the process, manufacturers will put thousands of disks in a room, run them for a few months, and count the number that fail. They compute MTTF as the total number of hours that the disks worked cumulatively divided by the number that failed.

One problem is that this number far exceeds the lifetime of a disk, which is commonly assumed to be 5 years or 43,800 hours. For this large MTTF to make some sense, disk manufacturers argue that the model corresponds to a user who buys a disk and then keeps replacing the disk every 5 years—the planned lifetime of the disk. The claim is that if many customers (and their great-grandchildren) did this for the next century, on average they would replace a disk 27 times before a failure, or about 140 years.

A more useful measure would be percentage of disks that fail. Assume 1000 disks with a 1,000,000-hour MTTF and that the disks are used 24 hours a day. If you replaced failed disks with a new one having the same reliability characteristics, the number that would fail in a year (8760 hours) is

$$\text{Failed disks} = \frac{\text{Number of disks} \times \text{Time period}}{\text{MTTF}} = \frac{1000 \text{ disks} \times 8760 \text{ hours/drive}}{1,000,000 \text{ hours/failure}} = 9$$

Stated alternatively, 0.9% would fail per year, or 4.4% over a 5-year lifetime.

Moreover, those high numbers are quoted assuming limited ranges of temperature and vibration; if they are exceeded, then all bets are off. A survey of disk drives in real environments [Gray and van Ingen 2005] found that 3% to 7% of drives failed per year, for an MTTF of about 125,000 to 300,000 hours. An even larger study found annual disk failure rates of 2% to 10% [Pinheiro, Weber, and Barroso 2007]. Hence, the real-world MTTF is about 2 to 10 times worse than the manufacturer's MTTF.

Fallacy   *Peak performance tracks observed performance.*

The only universally true definition of peak performance is "the performance level a computer is guaranteed not to exceed." Figure 1.20 shows the percentage of peak performance for four programs on four multiprocessors. It varies from 5% to 58%. Since the gap is so large and can vary significantly by benchmark, peak performance is not generally useful in predicting observed performance.

Pitfall   *Fault detection can lower availability.*

This apparently ironic pitfall is because computer hardware has a fair amount of state that may not always be critical to proper operation. For example, it is not fatal if an error occurs in a branch predictor, as only performance may suffer.

In processors that try to aggressively exploit instruction-level parallelism, not all the operations are needed for correct execution of the program. Mukherjee et al. [2003] found that less than 30% of the operations were potentially on the critical path for the SPEC2000 benchmarks running on an Itanium 2.

The same observation is true about programs. If a register is "dead" in a program—that is, the program will write it before it is read again—then errors do

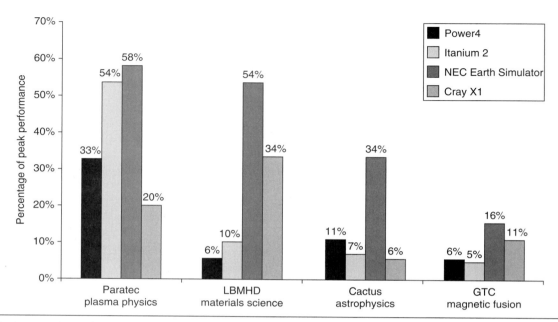

Figure 1.20 **Percentage of peak performance for four programs on four multiprocessors scaled to 64 processors.** The Earth Simulator and X1 are vector processors (see Chapter 4 and Appendix G). Not only did they deliver a higher fraction of peak performance, but they also had the highest peak performance and the lowest clock rates. Except for the Paratec program, the Power 4 and Itanium 2 systems delivered between 5% and 10% of their peak. From Oliker et al. [2004].

not matter. If you were to crash the program upon detection of a transient fault in a dead register, it would lower availability unnecessarily.

Sun Microsystems lived this pitfall in 2000 with an L2 cache that included parity, but not error correction, in its Sun E3000 to Sun E10000 systems. The SRAMs they used to build the caches had intermittent faults, which parity detected. If the data in the cache were not modified, the processor simply reread the data from the cache. Since the designers did not protect the cache with ECC (error-correcting code), the operating system had no choice but to report an error to dirty data and crash the program. Field engineers found no problems on inspection in more than 90% of the cases.

To reduce the frequency of such errors, Sun modified the Solaris operating system to "scrub" the cache by having a process that proactively writes dirty data to memory. Since the processor chips did not have enough pins to add ECC, the only hardware option for dirty data was to duplicate the external cache, using the copy without the parity error to correct the error.

The pitfall is in detecting faults without providing a mechanism to correct them. These engineers are unlikely to design another computer without ECC on external caches.

1.12 Concluding Remarks

This chapter has introduced a number of concepts and provided a quantitative framework that we will expand upon throughout the book. Starting with this edition, energy efficiency is the new companion to performance.

In Chapter 2, we start with the all-important area of memory system design. We will examine a wide range of techniques that conspire to make memory look infinitely large while still being as fast as possible. (Appendix B provides introductory material on caches for readers without much experience and background in them.) As in later chapters, we will see that hardware–software cooperation has become a key to high-performance memory systems, just as it has to high-performance pipelines. This chapter also covers virtual machines, an increasingly important technique for protection.

In Chapter 3, we look at instruction-level parallelism (ILP), of which pipelining is the simplest and most common form. Exploiting ILP is one of the most important techniques for building high-speed uniprocessors. Chapter 3 begins with an extensive discussion of basic concepts that will prepare you for the wide range of ideas examined in both chapters. Chapter 3 uses examples that span about 40 years, drawing from one of the first supercomputers (IBM 360/91) to the fastest processors in the market in 2011. It emphasizes what is called the *dynamic* or *run time approach* to exploiting ILP. It also talks about the limits to ILP ideas and introduces multithreading, which is further developed in both Chapters 4 and 5. Appendix C provides introductory material on pipelining for readers without much experience and background in pipelining. (We expect it to be a review for many readers, including those of our introductory text, *Computer Organization and Design: The Hardware/Software Interface*.)

Chapter 4 is new to this edition, and it explains three ways to exploit data-level parallelism. The classic and oldest approach is vector architecture, and we start there to lay down the principles of SIMD design. (Appendix G goes into greater depth on vector architectures.) We next explain the SIMD instruction set extensions found in most desktop microprocessors today. The third piece is an in-depth explanation of how modern graphics processing units (GPUs) work. Most GPU descriptions are written from the programmer's perspective, which usually hides how the computer really works. This section explains GPUs from an insider's perspective, including a mapping between GPU jargon and more traditional architecture terms.

Chapter 5 focuses on the issue of achieving higher performance using multiple processors, or multiprocessors. Instead of using parallelism to overlap individual instructions, multiprocessing uses parallelism to allow multiple instruction streams to be executed simultaneously on different processors. Our focus is on the dominant form of multiprocessors, shared-memory multiprocessors, though we introduce other types as well and discuss the broad issues that arise in any multiprocessor. Here again, we explore a variety of techniques, focusing on the important ideas first introduced in the 1980s and 1990s.

Chapter 6 is also new to this edition. We introduce clusters and then go into depth on warehouse-scale computers (WSCs), which computer architects help design. The designers of WSCs are the professional descendents of the pioneers of supercomputers such as Seymour Cray in that they are designing extreme computers. They contain tens of thousands of servers, and the equipment and building that holds them cost nearly $200 M. The concerns of price-performance and energy efficiency of the earlier chapters applies to WSCs, as does the quantitative approach to making decisions.

This book comes with an abundance of material online (see Preface for more details), both to reduce cost and to introduce readers to a variety of advanced topics. Figure 1.21 shows them all. Appendices A, B, and C, which appear in the book, will be review for many readers.

In Appendix D, we move away from a processor-centric view and discuss issues in storage systems. We apply a similar quantitative approach, but one based on observations of system behavior and using an end-to-end approach to performance analysis. It addresses the important issue of how to efficiently store and retrieve data using primarily lower-cost magnetic storage technologies. Our focus is on examining the performance of disk storage systems for typical I/O-intensive workloads, like the OLTP benchmarks we saw in this chapter. We extensively explore advanced topics in RAID-based systems, which use redundant disks to achieve both high performance and high availability. Finally, the chapter introduces queuing theory, which gives a basis for trading off utilization and latency.

Appendix E applies an embedded computing perspective to the ideas of each of the chapters and early appendices.

Appendix F explores the topic of system interconnect broadly, including wide area and system area networks that allow computers to communicate.

Appendix	Title
A	Instruction Set Principles
B	Review of Memory Hierarchies
C	Pipelining: Basic and Intermediate Concepts
D	Storage Systems
E	Embedded Systems
F	Interconnection Networks
G	Vector Processors in More Depth
H	Hardware and Software for VLIW and EPIC
I	Large-Scale Multiprocessors and Scientific Applications
J	Computer Arithmetic
K	Survey of Instruction Set Architectures
L	Historical Perspectives and References

Figure 1.21 List of appendices.

Appendix H reviews VLIW hardware and software, which, in contrast, are less popular than when EPIC appeared on the scene just before the last edition.

Appendix I describes large-scale multiprocessors for use in high-performance computing.

Appendix J is the only appendix that remains from the first edition, and it covers computer arithmetic.

Appendix K provides a survey of instruction architectures, including the 80x86, the IBM 360, the VAX, and many RISC architectures, including ARM, MIPS, Power, and SPARC.

We describe Appendix L below.

1.13   Historical Perspectives and References

Appendix L (available online) includes historical perspectives on the key ideas presented in each of the chapters in this text. These historical perspective sections allow us to trace the development of an idea through a series of machines or describe significant projects. If you're interested in examining the initial development of an idea or machine or interested in further reading, references are provided at the end of each history. For this chapter, see Section L.2, The Early Development of Computers, for a discussion on the early development of digital computers and performance measurement methodologies.

As you read the historical material, you'll soon come to realize that one of the important benefits of the youth of computing, compared to many other engineering fields, is that many of the pioneers are still alive—we can learn the history by simply asking them!

Case Studies and Exercises by Diana Franklin

Case Study 1: Chip Fabrication Cost

Concepts illustrated by this case study

- Fabrication Cost
- Fabrication Yield
- Defect Tolerance through Redundancy

There are many factors involved in the price of a computer chip. New, smaller technology gives a boost in performance and a drop in required chip area. In the smaller technology, one can either keep the small area or place more hardware on the chip in order to get more functionality. In this case study, we explore how different design decisions involving fabrication technology, area, and redundancy affect the cost of chips.

Chip	Die size (mm^2)	Estimated defect rate (per cm^2)	Manufacturing size (nm)	Transistors (millions)
IBM Power5	389	.30	130	276
Sun Niagara	380	.75	90	279
AMD Opteron	199	.75	90	233

Figure 1.22 Manufacturing cost factors for several modern processors.

1.1　[10/10] <1.6> Figure 1.22 gives the relevant chip statistics that influence the cost of several current chips. In the next few exercises, you will be exploring the effect of different possible design decisions for the IBM Power5.

　　a.　[10] <1.6> What is the yield for the IBM Power5?

　　b.　[10] <1.6> Why does the IBM Power5 have a lower defect rate than the Niagara and Opteron?

1.2　[20/20/20/20] <1.6> It costs $1 billion to build a new fabrication facility. You will be selling a range of chips from that factory, and you need to decide how much capacity to dedicate to each chip. Your Woods chip will be 150 mm^2 and will make a profit of $20 per defect-free chip. Your Markon chip will be 250 mm^2 and will make a profit of $25 per defect-free chip. Your fabrication facility will be identical to that for the Power5. Each wafer has a 300 mm diameter.

　　a.　[20] <1.6> How much profit do you make on each wafer of Woods chip?

　　b.　[20] <1.6> How much profit do you make on each wafer of Markon chip?

　　c.　[20] <1.6> Which chip should you produce in this facility?

　　d.　[20] <1.6> What is the profit on each new Power5 chip? If your demand is 50,000 Woods chips per month and 25,000 Markon chips per month, and your facility can fabricate 150 wafers a month, how many wafers should you make of each chip?

1.3　[20/20] <1.6> Your colleague at AMD suggests that, since the yield is so poor, you might make chips more cheaply if you placed an extra core on the die and only threw out chips on which both processors had failed. We will solve this exercise by viewing the yield as a probability of no defects occurring in a certain area given the defect rate. Calculate probabilities based on each Opteron core separately (this may not be entirely accurate, since the yield equation is based on empirical evidence rather than a mathematical calculation relating the probabilities of finding errors in different portions of the chip).

　　a.　[20] <1.6> What is the probability that a defect will occur on no more than one of the two processor cores?

　　b.　[20] <1.6> If the old chip cost $20 dollars per chip, what will the cost be of the new chip, taking into account the new area and yield?

Case Study 2: Power Consumption in Computer Systems

Concepts illustrated by this case study

- Amdahl's Law
- Redundancy
- MTTF
- Power Consumption

Power consumption in modern systems is dependent on a variety of factors, including the chip clock frequency, efficiency, disk drive speed, disk drive utilization, and DRAM. The following exercises explore the impact on power that different design decisions and use scenarios have.

1.4 [20/10/20] <1.5> Figure 1.23 presents the power consumption of several computer system components. In this exercise, we will explore how the hard drive affects power consumption for the system.

    a. [20] <1.5> Assuming the maximum load for each component, and a power supply efficiency of 80%, what wattage must the server's power supply deliver to a system with an Intel Pentium 4 chip, 2 GB 240-pin Kingston DRAM, and one 7200 rpm hard drive?

    b. [10] <1.5> How much power will the 7200 rpm disk drive consume if it is idle roughly 60% of the time?

    c. [20] <1.5> Given that the time to read data off a 7200 rpm disk drive will be roughly 75% of a 5400 rpm disk, at what idle time of the 7200 rpm disk will the power consumption be equal, on average, for the two disks?

1.5 [10/10/20] <1.5> One critical factor in powering a server farm is cooling. If heat is not removed from the computer efficiently, the fans will blow hot air back onto the computer, not cold air. We will look at how different design decisions affect the necessary cooling, and thus the price, of a system. Use Figure 1.23 for your power calculations.

Component type	Product	Performance	Power
Processor	Sun Niagara 8-core	1.2 GHz	72–79 W peak
	Intel Pentium 4	2 GHz	48.9–66 W
DRAM	Kingston X64C3AD2 1 GB	184-pin	3.7 W
	Kingston D2N3 1 GB	240-pin	2.3 W
Hard drive	DiamondMax 16	5400 rpm	7.0 W read/seek, 2.9 W idle
	DiamondMax 9	7200 rpm	7.9 W read/seek, 4.0 W idle

Figure 1.23 Power consumption of several computer components.

a. [10] <1.5> A cooling door for a rack costs $4000 and dissipates 14 KW (into the room; additional cost is required to get it out of the room). How many servers with an Intel Pentium 4 processor, 1 GB 240-pin DRAM, and a single 7200 rpm hard drive can you cool with one cooling door?

b. [10] <1.5> You are considering providing fault tolerance for your hard drive. RAID 1 doubles the number of disks (see Chapter 6). Now how many systems can you place on a single rack with a single cooler?

c. [20] <1.5> Typical server farms can dissipate a maximum of 200 W per square foot. Given that a server rack requires 11 square feet (including front and back clearance), how many servers from part (a) can be placed on a single rack, and how many cooling doors are required?

1.6 [Discussion] <1.8> Figure 1.24 gives a comparison of power and performance for several benchmarks comparing two servers: Sun Fire T2000 (which uses Niagara) and IBM x346 (using Intel Xeon processors). This information was reported on a Sun Web site. There are two pieces of information reported: power and speed on two benchmarks. For the results shown, the Sun Fire T2000 is clearly superior. What other factors might be important and thus cause someone to choose the IBM x346 if it were superior in those areas?

1.7 [20/20/20/20] <1.6, 1.9> Your company's internal studies show that a single-core system is sufficient for the demand on your processing power; however, you are exploring whether you could save power by using two cores.

a. [20] <1.9> Assume your application is 80% parallelizable. By how much could you decrease the frequency and get the same performance?

b. [20] <1.6> Assume that the voltage may be decreased linearly with the frequency. Using the equation in Section 1.5, how much dynamic power would the dual-core system require as compared to the single-core system?

c. [20] <1.6, 1.9> Now assume the voltage may not decrease below 25% of the original voltage. This voltage is referred to as the *voltage floor*, and any voltage lower than that will lose the state. What percent of parallelization gives you a voltage at the voltage floor?

d. [20] <1.6, 1.9> Using the equation in Section 1.5, how much dynamic power would the dual-core system require as compared to the single-core system when taking into account the voltage floor?

	Sun Fire T2000	IBM x346
Power (watts)	298	438
SPECjbb (operations/sec)	63,378	39,985
Power (watts)	330	438
SPECWeb (composite)	14,001	4348

Figure 1.24 Sun power/performance comparison as selectively reported by Sun.

Exercises

1.8 [10/15/15/10/10] <1.4, 1.5> One challenge for architects is that the design created today will require several years of implementation, verification, and testing before appearing on the market. This means that the architect must project what the technology will be like several years in advance. Sometimes, this is difficult to do.

a. [10] <1.4> According to the trend in device scaling observed by Moore's law, the number of transistors on a chip in 2015 should be how many times the number in 2005?

b. [15] <1.5> The increase in clock rates once mirrored this trend. Had clock rates continued to climb at the same rate as in the 1990s, approximately how fast would clock rates be in 2015?

c. [15] <1.5> At the current rate of increase, what are the clock rates now projected to be in 2015?

d. [10] <1.4> What has limited the rate of growth of the clock rate, and what are architects doing with the extra transistors now to increase performance?

e. [10] <1.4> The rate of growth for DRAM capacity has also slowed down. For 20 years, DRAM capacity improved by 60% each year. That rate dropped to 40% each year and now improvement is 25 to 40% per year. If this trend continues, what will be the approximate rate of growth for DRAM capacity by 2020?

1.9 [10/10] <1.5> You are designing a system for a real-time application in which specific deadlines must be met. Finishing the computation faster gains nothing. You find that your system can execute the necessary code, in the worst case, twice as fast as necessary.

a. [10] <1.5> How much energy do you save if you execute at the current speed and turn off the system when the computation is complete?

b. [10] <1.5> How much energy do you save if you set the voltage and frequency to be half as much?

1.10 [10/10/20/20] <1.5> Server farms such as Google and Yahoo! provide enough compute capacity for the highest request rate of the day. Imagine that most of the time these servers operate at only 60% capacity. Assume further that the power does not scale linearly with the load; that is, when the servers are operating at 60% capacity, they consume 90% of maximum power. The servers could be turned off, but they would take too long to restart in response to more load. A new system has been proposed that allows for a quick restart but requires 20% of the maximum power while in this "barely alive" state.

a. [10] <1.5> How much power savings would be achieved by turning off 60% of the servers?

b. [10] <1.5> How much power savings would be achieved by placing 60% of the servers in the "barely alive" state?

    c. [20] <1.5> How much power savings would be achieved by reducing the voltage by 20% and frequency by 40%?

    d. [20] <1.5> How much power savings would be achieved by placing 30% of the servers in the "barely alive" state and 30% off?

1.11   [10/10/20] <1.7> Availability is the most important consideration for designing servers, followed closely by scalability and throughput.

    a. [10] <1.7> We have a single processor with a failures in time (FIT) of 100. What is the mean time to failure (MTTF) for this system?

    b. [10] <1.7> If it takes 1 day to get the system running again, what is the availability of the system?

    c. [20] <1.7> Imagine that the government, to cut costs, is going to build a supercomputer out of inexpensive computers rather than expensive, reliable computers. What is the MTTF for a system with 1000 processors? Assume that if one fails, they all fail.

1.12   [20/20/20] <1.1, 1.2, 1.7> In a server farm such as that used by Amazon or eBay, a single failure does not cause the entire system to crash. Instead, it will reduce the number of requests that can be satisfied at any one time.

    a. [20] <1.7> If a company has 10,000 computers, each with a MTTF of 35 days, and it experiences catastrophic failure only if 1/3 of the computers fail, what is the MTTF for the system?

    b. [20] <1.1, 1.7> If it costs an extra $1000, per computer, to double the MTTF, would this be a good business decision? Show your work.

    c. [20] <1.2> Figure 1.3 shows, on average, the cost of downtimes, assuming that the cost is equal at all times of the year. For retailers, however, the Christmas season is the most profitable (and therefore the most costly time to lose sales). If a catalog sales center has twice as much traffic in the fourth quarter as every other quarter, what is the average cost of downtime per hour during the fourth quarter and the rest of the year?

1.13   [10/20/20] <1.9> Your company is trying to choose between purchasing the Opteron or Itanium 2. You have analyzed your company's applications, and 60% of the time it will be running applications similar to wupwise, 20% of the time applications similar to ammp, and 20% of the time applications similar to apsi.

    a. [10] If you were choosing just based on overall SPEC performance, which would you choose and why?

    b. [20] What is the weighted average of execution time ratios for this mix of applications for the Opteron and Itanium 2?

    c. [20] What is the speedup of the Opteron over the Itanium 2?

1.14   [20/10/10/10/15] <1.9> In this exercise, assume that we are considering enhancing a machine by adding vector hardware to it. When a computation is run in vector mode on the vector hardware, it is 10 times faster than the normal mode of execution. We call the percentage of time that could be spent using vector mode the *percentage of vectorization.* Vectors are discussed in Chapter 4, but you don't need to know anything about how they work to answer this question!

a. [20] <1.9> Draw a graph that plots the speedup as a percentage of the computation performed in vector mode. Label the *y*-axis "Net speedup" and label the *x*-axis "Percent vectorization."

b. [10] <1.9> What percentage of vectorization is needed to achieve a speedup of 2?

c. [10] <1.9> What percentage of the computation run time is spent in vector mode if a speedup of 2 is achieved?

d. [10] <1.9> What percentage of vectorization is needed to achieve one-half the maximum speedup attainable from using vector mode?

e. [15] <1.9> Suppose you have measured the percentage of vectorization of the program to be 70%. The hardware design group estimates it can speed up the vector hardware even more with significant additional investment. You wonder whether the compiler crew could increase the percentage of vectorization, instead. What percentage of vectorization would the compiler team need to achieve in order to equal an addition 2× speedup in the vector unit (beyond the initial 10×)?

1.15 [15/10] <1.9> Assume that we make an enhancement to a computer that improves some mode of execution by a factor of 10. Enhanced mode is used 50% of the time, measured as a percentage of the execution time *when the enhanced mode is in use.* Recall that Amdahl's law depends on the fraction of the original, *unenhanced* execution time that could make use of enhanced mode. Thus, we cannot directly use this 50% measurement to compute speedup with Amdahl's law.

a. [15] <1.9> What is the speedup we have obtained from fast mode?

b. [10] <1.9> What percentage of the original execution time has been converted to fast mode?

1.16 [20/20/15] <1.9> When making changes to optimize part of a processor, it is often the case that speeding up one type of instruction comes at the cost of slowing down something else. For example, if we put in a complicated fast floating-point unit, that takes space, and something might have to be moved farther away from the middle to accommodate it, adding an extra cycle in delay to reach that unit. The basic Amdahl's law equation does not take into account this trade-off.

a. [20] <1.9> If the new fast floating-point unit speeds up floating-point operations by, on average, 2×, and floating-point operations take 20% of the original program's execution time, what is the overall speedup (ignoring the penalty to any other instructions)?

b. [20] <1.9> Now assume that speeding up the floating-point unit slowed down data cache accesses, resulting in a 1.5× slowdown (or 2/3 speedup). Data cache accesses consume 10% of the execution time. What is the overall speedup now?

c. [15] <1.9> After implementing the new floating-point operations, what percentage of execution time is spent on floating-point operations? What percentage is spent on data cache accesses?

1.17 [10/10/20/20] <1.10> Your company has just bought a new Intel Core i5 dual-core processor, and you have been tasked with optimizing your software for this processor. You will run two applications on this dual core, but the resource requirements are not equal. The first application requires 80% of the resources, and the other only 20% of the resources. Assume that when you parallelize a portion of the program, the speedup for that portion is 2.

a. [10] <1.10> Given that 40% of the first application is parallelizable, how much speedup would you achieve with that application if run in isolation?

b. [10] <1.10> Given that 99% of the second application is parallelizable, how much speedup would this application observe if run in isolation?

c. [20] <1.10> Given that 40% of the first application is parallelizable, how much *overall system speedup* would you observe if you parallelized it?

d. [20] <1.10> Given that 99% of the second application is parallelizable, how much overall system speedup would you observe if you parallelized it?

1.18 [10/20/20/20/25] <1.10> When parallelizing an application, the ideal speedup is speeding up by the number of processors. This is limited by two things: percentage of the application that can be parallelized and the cost of communication. Amdahl's law takes into account the former but not the latter.

a. [10] <1.10> What is the speedup with N processors if 80% of the application is parallelizable, ignoring the cost of communication?

b. [20] <1.10> What is the speedup with 8 processors if, for every processor added, the communication overhead is 0.5% of the original execution time.

c. [20] <1.10> What is the speedup with 8 processors if, for every time the number of processors is doubled, the communication overhead is increased by 0.5% of the original execution time?

d. [20] <1.10> What is the speedup with N processors if, for every time the number of processors is doubled, the communication overhead is increased by 0.5% of the original execution time?

e. [25] <1.10> Write the general equation that solves this question: What is the number of processors with the highest speedup in an application in which $P\%$ of the original execution time is parallelizable, and, for every time the number of processors is doubled, the communication is increased by 0.5% of the original execution time?

2

Memory Hierarchy
Design

Ideally one would desire an indefinitely large memory capacity such that any particular … word would be immediately available. … We are … forced to recognize the possibility of constructing a hierarchy of memories, each of which has greater capacity than the preceding but which is less quickly accessible.

A. W. Burks, H. H. Goldstine,
and J. von Neumann
Preliminary Discussion of the
Logical Design of an Electronic
Computing Instrument (1946)

Introduction

Computer pioneers correctly predicted that programmers would want unlimited amounts of fast memory. An economical solution to that desire is a *memory hierarchy*, which takes advantage of locality and trade-offs in the cost-performance of memory technologies. The *principle of locality*, presented in the first chapter, says that most programs do not access all code or data uniformly. Locality occurs in time (*temporal locality*) and in space (*spatial locality*). This principle, plus the guideline that for a given implementation technology and power budget smaller hardware can be made faster, led to hierarchies based on memories of different speeds and sizes. Figure 2.1 shows a multilevel memory hierarchy, including typical sizes and speeds of access.

Since fast memory is expensive, a memory hierarchy is organized into several levels—each smaller, faster, and more expensive per byte than the next lower level, which is farther from the processor. The goal is to provide a memory system with cost per byte almost as low as the cheapest level of memory and speed almost as fast as the fastest level. In most cases (but not all), the data contained in a lower level are a superset of the next higher level. This property, called the *inclusion property*, is always required for the lowest level of the hierarchy, which consists of main memory in the case of caches and disk memory in the case of virtual memory.

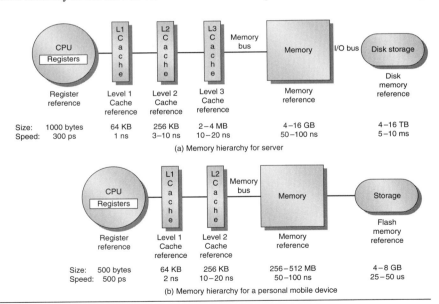

Figure 2.1 The levels in a typical memory hierarchy in a server computer shown on top (a) and in a personal mobile device (PMD) on the bottom (b). As we move farther away from the processor, the memory in the level below becomes slower and larger. Note that the time units change by a factor of 10^9—from picoseconds to milliseconds—and that the size units change by a factor of 10^{12}—from bytes to terabytes. The PMD has a slower clock rate and smaller caches and main memory. A key difference is that servers and desktops use disk storage as the lowest level in the hierarchy while PMDs use Flash, which is built from EEPROM technology.

The importance of the memory hierarchy has increased with advances in performance of processors. Figure 2.2 plots single processor performance projections against the historical performance improvement in time to access main memory. The processor line shows the increase in memory requests per second on average (i.e., the inverse of the latency between memory references), while the memory line shows the increase in DRAM accesses per second (i.e., the inverse of the DRAM access latency). The situation in a uniprocessor is actually somewhat worse, since the peak memory access rate is faster than the average rate, which is what is plotted.

More recently, high-end processors have moved to multiple cores, further increasing the bandwidth requirements versus single cores. In fact, the aggregate peak bandwidth essentially grows as the numbers of cores grows. A modern high-end processor such as the Intel Core i7 can generate two data memory references per core each clock cycle; with four cores and a 3.2 GHz clock rate, the i7 can generate a peak of 25.6 billion 64-bit data memory references per second, in addition to a peak instruction demand of about 12.8 billion 128-bit instruction references; this is a total peak bandwidth of 409.6 GB/sec! This incredible bandwidth is achieved by multiporting and pipelining the caches; by the use of multiple levels of caches, using separate first- and sometimes second-level caches per core; and by using a separate instruction and data cache at the first level. In contrast, the peak bandwidth to DRAM main memory is only 6% of this (25 GB/sec).

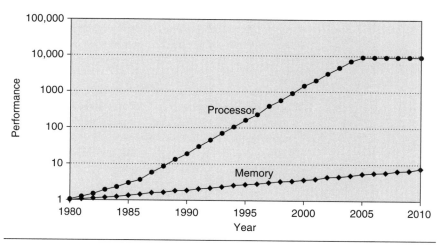

Figure 2.2 Starting with 1980 performance as a baseline, the gap in performance, measured as the difference in the time between processor memory requests (for a single processor or core) and the latency of a DRAM access, is plotted over time. Note that the vertical axis must be on a logarithmic scale to record the size of the processor–DRAM performance gap. The memory baseline is 64 KB DRAM in 1980, with a 1.07 per year performance improvement in latency (see Figure 2.13 on page 99). The processor line assumes a 1.25 improvement per year until 1986, a 1.52 improvement until 2000, a 1.20 improvement between 2000 and 2005, and no change in processor performance (on a per-core basis) between 2005 and 2010; see Figure 1.1 in Chapter 1.

Traditionally, designers of memory hierarchies focused on optimizing average memory access time, which is determined by the cache access time, miss rate, and miss penalty. More recently, however, power has become a major consideration. In high-end microprocessors, there may be 10 MB or more of on-chip cache, and a large second- or third-level cache will consume significant power both as leakage when not operating (called *static power*) and as active power, as when performing a read or write (called *dynamic power*), as described in Section 2.3. The problem is even more acute in processors in PMDs where the CPU is less aggressive and the power budget may be 20 to 50 times smaller. In such cases, the caches can account for 25% to 50% of the total power consumption. Thus, more designs must consider both performance and power trade-offs, and we will examine both in this chapter.

Basics of Memory Hierarchies: A Quick Review

The increasing size and thus importance of this gap led to the migration of the basics of memory hierarchy into undergraduate courses in computer architecture, and even to courses in operating systems and compilers. Thus, we'll start with a quick review of caches and their operation. The bulk of the chapter, however, describes more advanced innovations that attack the processor–memory performance gap.

When a word is not found in the cache, the word must be fetched from a lower level in the hierarchy (which may be another cache or the main memory) and placed in the cache before continuing. Multiple words, called a *block* (or *line*), are moved for efficiency reasons, and because they are likely to be needed soon due to spatial locality. Each cache block includes a *tag* to indicate which memory address it corresponds to.

A key design decision is where blocks (or lines) can be placed in a cache. The most popular scheme is *set associative*, where a *set* is a group of blocks in the cache. A block is first mapped onto a set, and then the block can be placed anywhere within that set. Finding a block consists of first mapping the block address to the set and then searching the set—usually in parallel—to find the block. The set is chosen by the address of the data:

$$(Block\ address)\ \text{MOD}\ (Number\ of\ sets\ in\ cache)$$

If there are *n* blocks in a set, the cache placement is called *n-way set associative*. The end points of set associativity have their own names. A *direct-mapped* cache has just one block per set (so a block is always placed in the same location), and a *fully associative* cache has just one set (so a block can be placed anywhere).

Caching data that is only read is easy, since the copy in the cache and memory will be identical. Caching writes is more difficult; for example, how can the copy in the cache and memory be kept consistent? There are two main strategies. A *write-through* cache updates the item in the cache *and* writes through to update main memory. A *write-back* cache only updates the copy in the cache. When the block is about to be replaced, it is copied back to memory. Both write strategies can use a *write buffer* to allow the cache to proceed as soon as the data are placed in the buffer rather than wait the full latency to write the data into memory.

One measure of the benefits of different cache organizations is miss rate. *Miss rate* is simply the fraction of cache accesses that result in a miss—that is, the number of accesses that miss divided by the number of accesses.

To gain insights into the causes of high miss rates, which can inspire better cache designs, the three Cs model sorts all misses into three simple categories:

■ *Compulsory*—The very first access to a block *cannot* be in the cache, so the block must be brought into the cache. Compulsory misses are those that occur even if you had an infinite sized cache.

■ *Capacity*—If the cache cannot contain all the blocks needed during execution of a program, capacity misses (in addition to compulsory misses) will occur because of blocks being discarded and later retrieved.

■ *Conflict*—If the block placement strategy is not fully associative, conflict misses (in addition to compulsory and capacity misses) will occur because a block may be discarded and later retrieved if multiple blocks map to its set and accesses to the different blocks are intermingled.

Figures B.8 and B.9 on pages B-24 and B-25 show the relative frequency of cache misses broken down by the three Cs. As we will see in Chapters 3 and 5, multithreading and multiple cores add complications for caches, both increasing the potential for capacity misses as well as adding a fourth C, for *coherency* misses due to cache flushes to keep multiple caches coherent in a multiprocessor; we will consider these issues in Chapter 5.

Alas, miss rate can be a misleading measure for several reasons. Hence, some designers prefer measuring *misses per instruction* rather than misses per memory reference (miss rate). These two are related:

$$\frac{\text{Misses}}{\text{Instruction}} = \frac{\text{Miss rate} \times \text{Memory accesses}}{\text{Instruction count}} = \text{Miss rate} \times \frac{\text{Memory accesses}}{\text{Instruction}}$$

(It is often reported as misses per 1000 instructions to use integers instead of fractions.)

The problem with both measures is that they don't factor in the cost of a miss. A better measure is the *average memory access time*:

$$\text{Average memory access time} = \text{Hit time} + \text{Miss rate} \times \text{Miss penalty}$$

where *hit time* is the time to hit in the cache and *miss penalty* is the time to replace the block from memory (that is, the cost of a miss). Average memory access time is still an indirect measure of performance; although it is a better measure than miss rate, it is not a substitute for execution time. In Chapter 3 we will see that speculative processors may execute other instructions during a miss, thereby reducing the effective miss penalty. The use of multithreading (introduced in Chapter 3) also allows a processor to tolerate missses without being forced to idle. As we will examine shortly, to take advantage of such latency tolerating techniques we need caches that can service requests while handling an outstanding miss.

If this material is new to you, or if this quick review moves too quickly, see Appendix B. It covers the same introductory material in more depth and includes examples of caches from real computers and quantitative evaluations of their effectiveness.

Section B.3 in Appendix B presents six basic cache optimizations, which we quickly review here. The appendix also gives quantitative examples of the benefits of these optimizations. We also comment briefly on the power implications of these trade-offs.

1. *Larger block size to reduce miss rate*—The simplest way to reduce the miss rate is to take advantage of spatial locality and increase the block size. Larger blocks reduce compulsory misses, but they also increase the miss penalty. Because larger blocks lower the number of tags, they can slightly reduce static power. Larger block sizes can also increase capacity or conflict misses, especially in smaller caches. Choosing the right block size is a complex trade-off that depends on the size of cache and the miss penalty.

2. *Bigger caches to reduce miss rate*—The obvious way to reduce capacity misses is to increase cache capacity. Drawbacks include potentially longer hit time of the larger cache memory and higher cost and power. Larger caches increase both static and dynamic power.

3. *Higher associativity to reduce miss rate*—Obviously, increasing associativity reduces conflict misses. Greater associativity can come at the cost of increased hit time. As we will see shortly, associativity also increases power consumption.

4. *Multilevel caches to reduce miss penalty*—A difficult decision is whether to make the cache hit time fast, to keep pace with the high clock rate of processors, or to make the cache large to reduce the gap between the processor accesses and main memory accesses. Adding another level of cache between the original cache and memory simplifies the decision (see Figure 2.3). The first-level cache can be small enough to match a fast clock cycle time, yet the second-level (or third-level) cache can be large enough to capture many accesses that would go to main memory. The focus on misses in second-level caches leads to larger blocks, bigger capacity, and higher associativity. Multilevel caches are more power efficient than a single aggregate cache. If L1 and L2 refer, respectively, to first- and second-level caches, we can redefine the average memory access time:

$$\text{Hit time}_{L1} + \text{Miss rate}_{L1} \times (\text{Hit time}_{L2} + \text{Miss rate}_{L2} \times \text{Miss penalty}_{L2})$$

5. *Giving priority to read misses over writes to reduce miss penalty*—A write buffer is a good place to implement this optimization. Write buffers create hazards because they hold the updated value of a location needed on a read

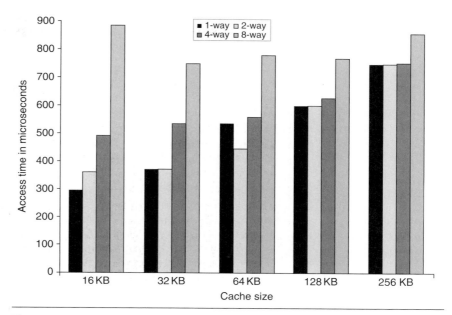

Figure 2.3 **Access times generally increase as cache size and associativity are increased.** These data come from the CACTI model 6.5 by Tarjan, Thoziyoor, and Jouppi [2005]. The data assume a 40 nm feature size (which is between the technology used in Intel's fastest and second fastest versions of the i7 and the same as the technology used in the fastest ARM embedded processors), a single bank, and 64-byte blocks. The assumptions about cache layout and the complex trade-offs between interconnect delays (that depend on the size of a cache block being accessed) and the cost of tag checks and multiplexing lead to results that are occasionally surprising, such as the lower access time for a 64 KB with two-way set associativity versus direct mapping. Similarly, the results with eight-way set associativity generate unusual behavior as cache size is increased. Since such observations are highly dependent on technology and detailed design assumptions, tools such as CACTI serve to reduce the search space rather than precision analysis of the trade-offs.

miss—that is, a read-after-write hazard through memory. One solution is to check the contents of the write buffer on a read miss. If there are no conflicts, and if the memory system is available, sending the read before the writes reduces the miss penalty. Most processors give reads priority over writes. This choice has little effect on power consumption.

6. *Avoiding address translation during indexing of the cache to reduce hit time*—Caches must cope with the translation of a virtual address from the processor to a physical address to access memory. (Virtual memory is covered in Sections 2.4 and B.4.) A common optimization is to use the page offset—the part that is identical in both virtual and physical addresses—to index the cache, as described in Appendix B, page B-38. This virtual index/ physical tag method introduces some system complications and/or

limitations on the size and structure of the L1 cache, but the advantages of removing the translation lookaside buffer (TLB) access from the critical path outweigh the disadvantages.

Note that each of the six optimizations above has a potential disadvantage that can lead to increased, rather than decreased, average memory access time.

The rest of this chapter assumes familiarity with the material above and the details in Appendix B. In the Putting It All Together section, we examine the memory hierarchy for a microprocessor designed for a high-end server, the Intel Core i7, as well as one designed for use in a PMD, the Arm Cortex-A8, which is the basis for the processor used in the Apple iPad and several high-end smartphones. Within each of these classes, there is a significant diversity in approach due to the intended use of the computer. While the high-end processor used in the server has more cores and bigger caches than the Intel processors designed for desktop uses, the processors have similar architectures. The differences are driven by performance and the nature of the workload; desktop computers are primarily running one application at a time on top of an operating system for a single user, whereas server computers may have hundreds of users running potentially dozens of applications simultaneously. Because of these workload differences, desktop computers are generally concerned more with average latency from the memory hierarchy, whereas server computers are also concerned about memory bandwidth. Even within the class of desktop computers there is wide diversity from lower end netbooks with scaled-down processors more similar to those found in high-end PMDs, to high-end desktops whose processors contain multiple cores and whose organization resembles that of a low-end server.

In contrast, PMDs not only serve one user but generally also have smaller operating systems, usually less multitasking (running of several applications simultaneously), and simpler applications. PMDs also typically use Flash memory rather than disks, and most consider both performance and energy consumption, which determines battery life.

2.2 Ten Advanced Optimizations of Cache Performance

The average memory access time formula above gives us three metrics for cache optimizations: hit time, miss rate, and miss penalty. Given the recent trends, we add cache bandwidth and power consumption to this list. We can classify the ten advanced cache optimizations we examine into five categories based on these metrics:

1. *Reducing the hit time*—Small and simple first-level caches and way-prediction. Both techniques also generally decrease power consumption.

2. *Increasing cache bandwidth*—Pipelined caches, multibanked caches, and nonblocking caches. These techniques have varying impacts on power consumption.

3. *Reducing the miss penalty*—Critical word first and merging write buffers. These optimizations have little impact on power.

4. *Reducing the miss rate*—Compiler optimizations. Obviously any improvement at compile time improves power consumption.

5. *Reducing the miss penalty or miss rate via parallelism*—Hardware prefetching and compiler prefetching. These optimizations generally increase power consumption, primarily due to prefetched data that are unused.

In general, the hardware complexity increases as we go through these optimizations. In addition, several of the optimizations require sophisticated compiler technology. We will conclude with a summary of the implementation complexity and the performance benefits of the ten techniques presented in Figure 2.11 on page 96. Since some of these are straightforward, we cover them briefly; others require more description.

First Optimization: Small and Simple First-Level Caches to Reduce Hit Time and Power

The pressure of both a fast clock cycle and power limitations encourages limited size for first-level caches. Similarly, use of lower levels of associativity can reduce both hit time and power, although such trade-offs are more complex than those involving size.

The critical timing path in a cache hit is the three-step process of addressing the tag memory using the index portion of the address, comparing the read tag value to the address, and setting the multiplexor to choose the correct data item if the cache is set associative. Direct-mapped caches can overlap the tag check with the transmission of the data, effectively reducing hit time. Furthermore, lower levels of associativity will usually reduce power because fewer cache lines must be accessed.

Although the total amount of on-chip cache has increased dramatically with new generations of microprocessors, due to the clock rate impact arising from a larger L1 cache, the size of the L1 caches has recently increased either slightly or not at all. In many recent processors, designers have opted for more associativity rather than larger caches. An additional consideration in choosing the associativity is the possibility of eliminating address aliases; we discuss this shortly.

One approach to determining the impact on hit time and power consumption in advance of building a chip is to use CAD tools. CACTI is a program to estimate the access time and energy consumption of alternative cache structures on CMOS microprocessors within 10% of more detailed CAD tools. For a given minimum feature size, CACTI estimates the hit time of caches as cache size varies, associativity, number of read/write ports, and more complex parameters. Figure 2.3 shows the estimated impact on hit time as cache size and associativity are varied. Depending on cache size, for these parameters the model suggests that the hit time for direct mapped is slightly faster than two-way set associative and that two-way set associative is 1.2 times faster than four-way and four-way is 1.4 times faster than eight-way. Of course, these estimates depend on technology as well as the size of the cache.

Example   Using the data in Figure B.8 in Appendix B and Figure 2.3, determine whether a 32 KB four-way set associative L1 cache has a faster memory access time than a 32 KB two-way set associative L1 cache. Assume the miss penalty to L2 is 15 times the access time for the faster L1 cache. Ignore misses beyond L2. Which has the faster average memory access time?

Answer   Let the access time for the two-way set associative cache be 1. Then, for the two-way cache:

$$\text{Average memory access time}_{2\text{-way}} = \text{Hit time} + \text{Miss rate} \times \text{Miss penalty}$$
$$= 1 + 0.038 \times 15 = 1.38$$

For the four-way cache, the access time is 1.4 times longer. The elapsed time of the miss penalty is $15/1.4 = 10.1$. Assume 10 for simplicity:

$$\text{Average memory access time}_{4\text{-way}} = \text{Hit time}_{2\text{-way}} \times 1.4 + \text{Miss rate} \times \text{Miss penalty}$$
$$= 1.4 + 0.037 \times 10 = 1.77$$

Clearly, the higher associativity looks like a bad trade-off; however, since cache access in modern processors is often pipelined, the exact impact on the clock cycle time is difficult to assess.

Energy consumption is also a consideration in choosing both the cache size and associativity, as Figure 2.4 shows. The energy cost of higher associativity ranges from more than a factor of 2 to negligible in caches of 128 KB or 256 KB when going from direct mapped to two-way set associative.

In recent designs, there are three other factors that have led to the use of higher associativity in first-level caches. First, many processors take at least two clock cycles to access the cache and thus the impact of a longer hit time may not be critical. Second, to keep the TLB out of the critical path (a delay that would be larger than that associated with increased associativity), almost all L1 caches should be virtually indexed. This limits the size of the cache to the page size times the associativity, because then only the bits within the page are used for the index. There are other solutions to the problem of indexing the cache before address translation is completed, but increasing the associativity, which also has other benefits, is the most attractive. Third, with the introduction of multithreading (see Chapter 3), conflict misses can increase, making higher associativity more attractive.

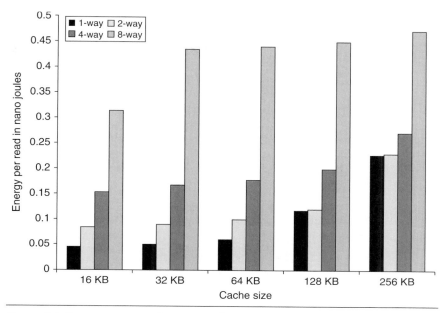

Figure 2.4 Energy consumption per read increases as cache size and associativity are increased. As in the previous figure, CACTI is used for the modeling with the same technology parameters. The large penalty for eight-way set associative caches is due to the cost of reading out eight tags and the corresponding data in parallel.

Second Optimization: Way Prediction to Reduce Hit Time

Another approach reduces conflict misses and yet maintains the hit speed of direct-mapped cache. In *way prediction*, extra bits are kept in the cache to predict the way, or block within the set of the *next* cache access. This prediction means the multiplexor is set early to select the desired block, and only a single tag comparison is performed that clock cycle in parallel with reading the cache data. A miss results in checking the other blocks for matches in the next clock cycle.

Added to each block of a cache are block predictor bits. The bits select which of the blocks to try on the *next* cache access. If the predictor is correct, the cache access latency is the fast hit time. If not, it tries the other block, changes the way predictor, and has a latency of one extra clock cycle. Simulations suggest that set prediction accuracy is in excess of 90% for a two-way set associative cache and 80% for a four-way set associative cache, with better accuracy on I-caches than D-caches. Way prediction yields lower average memory access time for a two-way set associative cache if it is at least 10% faster, which is quite likely. Way prediction was first used in the MIPS R10000 in the mid-1990s. It is popular in processors that use two-way set associativity and is used in the ARM Cortex-A8 with four-way set associative caches. For very fast processors, it may be challenging to implement the one cycle stall that is critical to keeping the way prediction penalty small.

An extended form of way prediction can also be used to reduce power consumption by using the way prediction bits to decide which cache block to actually access (the way prediction bits are essentially extra address bits); this approach, which might be called *way selection*, saves power when the way prediction is correct but adds significant time on a way misprediction, since the access, not just the tag match and selection, must be repeated. Such an optimization is likely to make sense only in low-power processors. Inoue, Ishihara, and Murakami [1999] estimated that using the way selection approach with a four-way set associative cache increases the average access time for the I-cache by 1.04 and for the D-cache by 1.13 on the SPEC95 benchmarks, but it yields an average cache power consumption relative to a normal four-way set associative cache that is 0.28 for the I-cache and 0.35 for the D-cache. One significant drawback for way selection is that it makes it difficult to pipeline the cache access.

Example   Assume that there are half as many D-cache accesses as I-cache accesses, and that the I-cache and D-cache are responsible for 25% and 15% of the processor's power consumption in a normal four-way set associative implementation. Determine if way selection improves performance per watt based on the estimates from the study above.

Answer   For the I-cache, the savings in power is $25 \times 0.28 = 0.07$ of the total power, while for the D-cache it is $15 \times 0.35 = 0.05$ for a total savings of 0.12. The way prediction version requires 0.88 of the power requirement of the standard 4-way cache. The increase in cache access time is the increase in I-cache average access time plus one-half the increase in D-cache access time, or $1.04 + 0.5 \times 0.13 = 1.11$ times longer. This result means that way selection has 0.90 of the performance of a standard four-way cache. Thus, way selection improves performance per joule very slightly by a ratio of $0.90/0.88 = 1.02$. This optimization is best used where power rather than performance is the key objective.

Third Optimization: Pipelined Cache Access to Increase Cache Bandwidth

This optimization is simply to pipeline cache access so that the effective latency of a first-level cache hit can be multiple clock cycles, giving fast clock cycle time and high bandwidth but slow hits. For example, the pipeline for the instruction cache access for Intel Pentium processors in the mid-1990s took 1 clock cycle, for the Pentium Pro through Pentium III in the mid-1990s through 2000 it took 2 clocks, and for the Pentium 4, which became available in 2000, and the current Intel Core i7 it takes 4 clocks. This change increases the number of pipeline stages, leading to a greater penalty on mispredicted branches and more clock cycles between issuing the load and using the data (see Chapter 3), but it does make it easier to incorporate high degrees of associativity.

Fourth Optimization: Nonblocking Caches to Increase Cache Bandwidth

For pipelined computers that allow out-of-order execution (discussed in Chapter 3), the processor need not stall on a data cache miss. For example, the processor could continue fetching instructions from the instruction cache while waiting for the data cache to return the missing data. A *nonblocking cache* or *lockup-free cache* escalates the potential benefits of such a scheme by allowing the data cache to continue to supply cache hits during a miss. This "hit under miss" optimization reduces the effective miss penalty by being helpful during a miss instead of ignoring the requests of the processor. A subtle and complex option is that the cache may further lower the effective miss penalty if it can overlap multiple misses: a "hit under multiple miss" or "miss under miss" optimization. The second option is beneficial only if the memory system can service multiple misses; most high-performance processors (such as the Intel Core i7) usually support both, while lower end processors, such as the ARM A8, provide only limited nonblocking support in L2.

To examine the effectiveness of nonblocking caches in reducing the cache miss penalty, Farkas and Jouppi [1994] did a study assuming 8 KB caches with a 14-cycle miss penalty; they observed a reduction in the effective miss penalty of 20% for the SPECINT92 benchmarks and 30% for the SPECFP92 benchmarks when allowing one hit under miss.

Li, Chen, Brockman, and Jouppi [2011] recently updated this study to use a multilevel cache, more modern assumptions about miss penalties, and the larger and more demanding SPEC2006 benchmarks. The study was done assuming a model based on a single core of an Intel i7 (see Section 2.6) running the SPEC2006 benchmarks. Figure 2.5 shows the reduction in data cache access latency when allowing 1, 2, and 64 hits under a miss; the caption describes further details of the memory system. The larger caches and the addition of an L3 cache since the earlier study have reduced the benefits with the SPECINT2006 benchmarks showing an average reduction in cache latency of about 9% and the SPECFP2006 benchmarks about 12.5%.

Example   Which is more important for floating-point programs: two-way set associativity or hit under one miss for the primary data caches? What about integer programs? Assume the following average miss rates for 32 KB data caches: 5.2% for floating-point programs with a direct-mapped cache, 4.9% for these programs with a two-way set associative cache, 3.5% for integer programs with a direct-mapped cache, and 3.2% for integer programs with a two-way set associative cache. Assume the miss penalty to L2 is 10 cycles, and the L2 misses and penalties are the same.

Answer   For floating-point programs, the average memory stall times are

$$\text{Miss rate}_{DM} \times \text{Miss penalty} = 5.2\% \times 10 = 0.52$$

$$\text{Miss rate}_{2\text{-way}} \times \text{Miss penalty} = 4.9\% \times 10 = 0.49$$

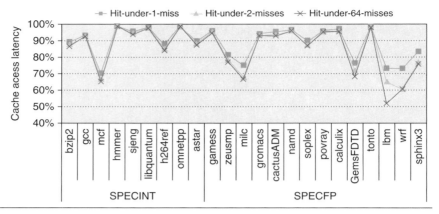

Figure 2.5 The effectiveness of a nonblocking cache is evaluated by allowing 1, 2, or 64 hits under a cache miss with 9 SPECINT (on the left) and 9 SPECFP (on the right) benchmarks. The data memory system modeled after the Intel i7 consists of a 32KB L1 cache with a four cycle access latency. The L2 cache (shared with instructions) is 256 KB with a 10 clock cycle access latency. The L3 is 2 MB and a 36-cycle access latency. All the caches are eight-way set associative and have a 64-byte block size. Allowing one hit under miss reduces the miss penalty by 9% for the integer benchmarks and 12.5% for the floating point. Allowing a second hit improves these results to 10% and 16%, and allowing 64 results in little additional improvement.

The cache access latency (including stalls) for two-way associativity is 0.49/0.52 or 94% of direct-mapped cache. The caption of Figure 2.5 says hit under one miss reduces the average data cache access latency for floating point programs to 87.5% of a blocking cache. Hence, for floating-point programs, the direct mapped data cache supporting one hit under one miss gives better performance than a two-way set-associative cache that blocks on a miss.

For integer programs, the calculation is

$$\text{Miss rate}_{DM} \times \text{Miss penalty} = 3.5\% \times 10 = 0.35$$

$$\text{Miss rate}_{2\text{-way}} \times \text{Miss penalty} = 3.2\% \times 10 = 0.32$$

The data cache access latency of a two-way set associative cache is thus 0.32/0.35 or 91% of direct-mapped cache, while the reduction in access latency when allowing a hit under one miss is 9%, making the two choices about equal.

The real difficulty with performance evaluation of nonblocking caches is that a cache miss does not necessarily stall the processor. In this case, it is difficult to judge the impact of any single miss and hence to calculate the average memory access time. The effective miss penalty is not the sum of the misses but the non-overlapped time that the processor is stalled. The benefit of nonblocking caches is complex, as it depends upon the miss penalty when there are multiple misses, the memory reference pattern, and how many instructions the processor can execute with a miss outstanding.

In general, out-of-order processors are capable of hiding much of the miss penalty of an L1 data cache miss that hits in the L2 cache but are not capable of hiding a significant fraction of a lower level cache miss. Deciding how many outstanding misses to support depends on a variety of factors:

- The temporal and spatial locality in the miss stream, which determines whether a miss can initiate a new access to a lower level cache or to memory

- The bandwidth of the responding memory or cache

- To allow more outstanding misses at the lowest level of the cache (where the miss time is the longest) requires supporting at least that many misses at a higher level, since the miss must initiate at the highest level cache

- The latency of the memory system

The following simplified example shows the key idea.

Example   Assume a main memory access time of 36 ns and a memory system capable of a sustained transfer rate of 16 GB/sec. If the block size is 64 bytes, what is the maximum number of outstanding misses we need to support assuming that we can maintain the peak bandwidth given the request stream and that accesses never conflict. If the probability of a reference colliding with one of the previous four is 50%, and we assume that the access has to wait until the earlier access completes, estimate the number of maximum outstanding references. For simplicity, ignore the time between misses.

Answer   In the first case, assuming that we can maintain the peak bandwidth, the memory system can support $(16 \times 10)^9/64 = 250$ million references per second. Since each reference takes 36 ns, we can support $250 \times 10^6 \times 36 \times 10^{-9} = 9$ references. If the probability of a collision is greater than 0, then we need more outstanding references, since we cannot start work on those references; the memory system needs more independent references not fewer! To approximate this, we can simply assume that half the memory references need not be issued to the memory. This means that we must support twice as many outstanding references, or 18.

In Li, Chen, Brockman, and Jouppi's study they found that the reduction in CPI for the integer programs was about 7% for one hit under miss and about 12.7% for 64. For the floating point programs, the reductions were 12.7% for one hit under miss and 17.8% for 64. These reductions track fairly closely the reductions in the data cache access latency shown in Figure 2.5.

Fifth Optimization: Multibanked Caches to Increase Cache Bandwidth

Rather than treat the cache as a single monolithic block, we can divide it into independent banks that can support simultaneous accesses. Banks were originally

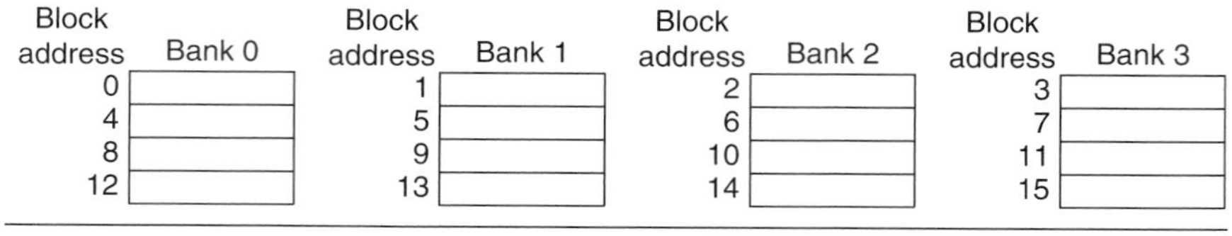

Figure 2.6 Four-way interleaved cache banks using block addressing. Assuming 64 bytes per blocks, each of these addresses would be multiplied by 64 to get byte addressing.

used to improve performance of main memory and are now used inside modern DRAM chips as well as with caches. The Arm Cortex-A8 supports one to four banks in its L2 cache; the Intel Core i7 has four banks in L1 (to support up to 2 memory accesses per clock), and the L2 has eight banks.

Clearly, banking works best when the accesses naturally spread themselves across the banks, so the mapping of addresses to banks affects the behavior of the memory system. A simple mapping that works well is to spread the addresses of the block sequentially across the banks, called *sequential interleaving*. For example, if there are four banks, bank 0 has all blocks whose address modulo 4 is 0, bank 1 has all blocks whose address modulo 4 is 1, and so on. Figure 2.6 shows this interleaving. Multiple banks also are a way to reduce power consumption both in caches and DRAM.

Sixth Optimization: Critical Word First and Early Restart to Reduce Miss Penalty

This technique is based on the observation that the processor normally needs just one word of the block at a time. This strategy is impatience: Don't wait for the full block to be loaded before sending the requested word and restarting the processor. Here are two specific strategies:

■ *Critical word first*—Request the missed word first from memory and send it to the processor as soon as it arrives; let the processor continue execution while filling the rest of the words in the block.

■ *Early restart*—Fetch the words in normal order, but as soon as the requested word of the block arrives send it to the processor and let the processor continue execution.

Generally, these techniques only benefit designs with large cache blocks, since the benefit is low unless blocks are large. Note that caches normally continue to satisfy accesses to other blocks while the rest of the block is being filled.

Alas, given spatial locality, there is a good chance that the next reference is to the rest of the block. Just as with nonblocking caches, the miss penalty is not simple to calculate. When there is a second request in critical word first, the effective miss penalty is the nonoverlapped time from the reference until the second piece arrives. The benefits of critical word first and early restart depend on the size of the block and the likelihood of another access to the portion of the block that has not yet been fetched.

Seventh Optimization: Merging Write Buffer to Reduce Miss Penalty

Write-through caches rely on write buffers, as all stores must be sent to the next lower level of the hierarchy. Even write-back caches use a simple buffer when a block is replaced. If the write buffer is empty, the data and the full address are written in the buffer, and the write is finished from the processor's perspective; the processor continues working while the write buffer prepares to write the word to memory. If the buffer contains other modified blocks, the addresses can be checked to see if the address of the new data matches the address of a valid write buffer entry. If so, the new data are combined with that entry. *Write merging* is the name of this optimization. The Intel Core i7, among many others, uses write merging.

If the buffer is full and there is no address match, the cache (and processor) must wait until the buffer has an empty entry. This optimization uses the memory more efficiently since multiword writes are usually faster than writes performed one word at a time. Skadron and Clark [1997] found that even a merging four-entry write buffer generated stalls that led to a 5% to 10% performance loss.

The optimization also reduces stalls due to the write buffer being full. Figure 2.7 shows a write buffer with and without write merging. Assume we had four entries in the write buffer, and each entry could hold four 64-bit words. Without this optimization, four stores to sequential addresses would fill the buffer at one word per entry, even though these four words when merged exactly fit within a single entry of the write buffer.

Note that input/output device registers are often mapped into the physical address space. These I/O addresses *cannot* allow write merging because separate I/O registers may not act like an array of words in memory. For example, they may require one address and data word per I/O register rather than use multiword writes using a single address. These side effects are typically implemented by marking the pages as requiring nonmerging write through by the caches.

Eighth Optimization: Compiler Optimizations to Reduce Miss Rate

Thus far, our techniques have required changing the hardware. This next technique reduces miss rates without any hardware changes.

This magical reduction comes from optimized software—the hardware designer's favorite solution! The increasing performance gap between processors and main memory has inspired compiler writers to scrutinize the memory hierarchy to see if compile time optimizations can improve performance. Once again, research

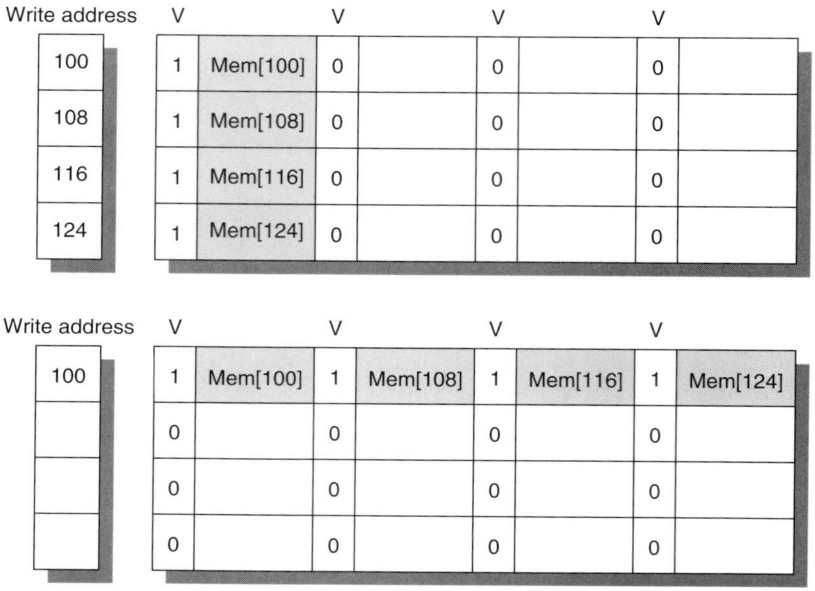

Figure 2.7 To illustrate write merging, the write buffer on top does not use it while the write buffer on the bottom does. The four writes are merged into a single buffer entry with write merging; without it, the buffer is full even though three-fourths of each entry is wasted. The buffer has four entries, and each entry holds four 64-bit words. The address for each entry is on the left, with a valid bit (V) indicating whether the next sequential 8 bytes in this entry are occupied. (Without write merging, the words to the right in the upper part of the figure would only be used for instructions that wrote multiple words at the same time.)

is split between improvements in instruction misses and improvements in data misses. The optimizations presented below are found in many modern compilers.

Loop Interchange

Some programs have nested loops that access data in memory in nonsequential order. Simply exchanging the nesting of the loops can make the code access the data in the order in which they are stored. Assuming the arrays do not fit in the cache, this technique reduces misses by improving spatial locality; reordering maximizes use of data in a cache block before they are discarded. For example, if x is a two-dimensional array of size [5000,100] allocated so that x[i,j] and x[i,j+1] are adjacent (an order called row major, since the array is laid out by rows), then the two pieces of code below show how the accesses can be optimized:

```
/* Before */
for (j = 0; j < 100; j = j+1)
        for (i = 0; i < 5000; i = i+1)
                x[i][j] = 2 * x[i][j];
```

```
/* After */
for (i = 0; i < 5000; i = i+1)
      for (j = 0; j < 100; j = j+1)
            x[i][j] = 2 * x[i][j];
```

The original code would skip through memory in strides of 100 words, while the revised version accesses all the words in one cache block before going to the next block. This optimization improves cache performance without affecting the number of instructions executed.

Blocking

This optimization improves temporal locality to reduce misses. We are again dealing with multiple arrays, with some arrays accessed by rows and some by columns. Storing the arrays row by row (*row major order*) or column by column (*column major order*) does not solve the problem because both rows and columns are used in every loop iteration. Such orthogonal accesses mean that transformations such as loop interchange still leave plenty of room for improvement.

Instead of operating on entire rows or columns of an array, blocked algorithms operate on submatrices or *blocks*. The goal is to maximize accesses to the data loaded into the cache before the data are replaced. The code example below, which performs matrix multiplication, helps motivate the optimization:

```
/* Before */
for (i = 0; i < N; i = i+1)
      for (j = 0; j < N; j = j+1)
            {r = 0;
             for (k = 0; k < N; k = k + 1)
                   r = r + y[i][k]*z[k][j];
             x[i][j] = r;
            };
```

The two inner loops read all N-by-N elements of z, read the same N elements in a row of y repeatedly, and write one row of N elements of x. Figure 2.8 gives a snapshot of the accesses to the three arrays. A dark shade indicates a recent access, a light shade indicates an older access, and white means not yet accessed.

The number of capacity misses clearly depends on N and the size of the cache. If it can hold all three N-by-N matrices, then all is well, provided there are no cache conflicts. If the cache can hold one N-by-N matrix and one row of N, then at least the ith row of y and the array z may stay in the cache. Less than that and misses may occur for both x and z. In the worst case, there would be $2N^3 + N^2$ memory words accessed for N^3 operations.

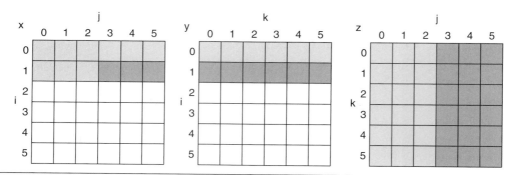

Figure 2.8 A snapshot of the three arrays x, y, and z when *N* = 6 and i = 1. The age of accesses to the array elements is indicated by shade: white means not yet touched, light means older accesses, and dark means newer accesses. Compared to Figure 2.9, elements of y and z are read repeatedly to calculate new elements of x. The variables i, j, and k are shown along the rows or columns used to access the arrays.

To ensure that the elements being accessed can fit in the cache, the original code is changed to compute on a submatrix of size B by B. Two inner loops now compute in steps of size B rather than the full length of x and z. B is called the *blocking factor.* (Assume x is initialized to zero.)

```
/* After */
for (jj = 0; jj < N; jj = jj+B)
for (kk = 0; kk < N; kk = kk+B)
for (i = 0; i < N; i = i+1)
        for (j = jj; j < min(jj+B,N); j = j+1)
            {r = 0;
            for (k = kk; k < min(kk+B,N); k = k + 1)
                    r = r + y[i][k]*z[k][j];
            x[i][j] = x[i][j] + r;
            };
```

Figure 2.9 illustrates the accesses to the three arrays using blocking. Looking only at capacity misses, the total number of memory words accessed is $2N^3/B + N^2$. This total is an improvement by about a factor of B. Hence, blocking exploits a combination of spatial and temporal locality, since y benefits from spatial locality and z benefits from temporal locality.

Although we have aimed at reducing cache misses, blocking can also be used to help register allocation. By taking a small blocking size such that the block can be held in registers, we can minimize the number of loads and stores in the program.

As we shall see in Section 4.8 of Chapter 4, cache blocking is absolutely necessary to get good performance from cache-based processors running applications using matrices as the primary data structure.

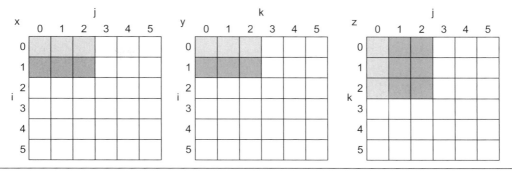

Figure 2.9 **The age of accesses to the arrays x, y, and z when** $B = 3$. Note that, in contrast to Figure 2.8, a smaller number of elements is accessed.

Ninth Optimization: Hardware Prefetching of Instructions and Data to Reduce Miss Penalty or Miss Rate

Nonblocking caches effectively reduce the miss penalty by overlapping execution with memory access. Another approach is to prefetch items before the processor requests them. Both instructions and data can be prefetched, either directly into the caches or into an external buffer that can be more quickly accessed than main memory.

Instruction prefetch is frequently done in hardware outside of the cache. Typically, the processor fetches two blocks on a miss: the requested block and the next consecutive block. The requested block is placed in the instruction cache when it returns, and the prefetched block is placed into the instruction stream buffer. If the requested block is present in the instruction stream buffer, the original cache request is canceled, the block is read from the stream buffer, and the next prefetch request is issued.

A similar approach can be applied to data accesses [Jouppi 1990]. Palacharla and Kessler [1994] looked at a set of scientific programs and considered multiple stream buffers that could handle either instructions or data. They found that eight stream buffers could capture 50% to 70% of all misses from a processor with two 64 KB four-way set associative caches, one for instructions and the other for data.

The Intel Core i7 supports hardware prefetching into both L1 and L2 with the most common case of prefetching being accessing the next line. Some earlier Intel processors used more aggressive hardware prefetching, but that resulted in reduced performance for some applications, causing some sophisticated users to turn off the capability.

Figure 2.10 shows the overall performance improvement for a subset of SPEC2000 programs when hardware prefetching is turned on. Note that this figure includes only 2 of 12 integer programs, while it includes the majority of the SPEC floating-point programs.

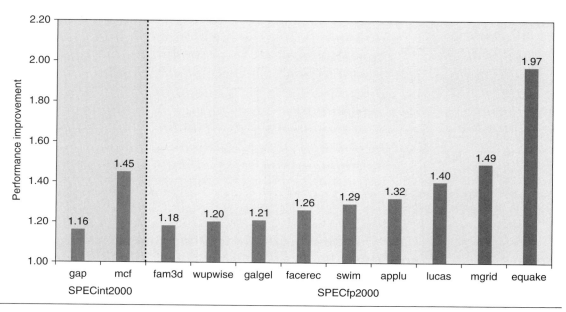

Figure 2.10 Speedup due to hardware prefetching on Intel Pentium 4 with hardware prefetching turned on for 2 of 12 SPECint2000 benchmarks and 9 of 14 SPECfp2000 benchmarks. Only the programs that benefit the most from prefetching are shown; prefetching speeds up the missing 15 SPEC benchmarks by less than 15% [Singhal 2004].

Prefetching relies on utilizing memory bandwidth that otherwise would be unused, but if it interferes with demand misses it can actually lower performance. Help from compilers can reduce useless prefetching. When prefetching works well its impact on power is negligible. When prefetched data are not used or useful data are displaced, prefetching will have a very negative impact on power.

Tenth Optimization: Compiler-Controlled Prefetching to Reduce Miss Penalty or Miss Rate

An alternative to hardware prefetching is for the compiler to insert prefetch instructions to request data before the processor needs it. There are two flavors of prefetch:

■ *Register prefetch* will load the value into a register.

■ *Cache prefetch* loads data only into the cache and not the register.

Either of these can be *faulting* or *nonfaulting*; that is, the address does or does not cause an exception for virtual address faults and protection violations. Using this terminology, a normal load instruction could be considered a "faulting register prefetch instruction." Nonfaulting prefetches simply turn into no-ops if they would normally result in an exception, which is what we want.

The most effective prefetch is "semantically invisible" to a program: It doesn't change the contents of registers and memory, *and* it cannot cause virtual memory faults. Most processors today offer nonfaulting cache prefetches. This section assumes nonfaulting cache prefetch, also called *nonbinding* prefetch.

Prefetching makes sense only if the processor can proceed while prefetching the data; that is, the caches do not stall but continue to supply instructions and data while waiting for the prefetched data to return. As you would expect, the data cache for such computers is normally nonblocking.

Like hardware-controlled prefetching, the goal is to overlap execution with the prefetching of data. Loops are the important targets, as they lend themselves to prefetch optimizations. If the miss penalty is small, the compiler just unrolls the loop once or twice, and it schedules the prefetches with the execution. If the miss penalty is large, it uses software pipelining (see Appendix H) or unrolls many times to prefetch data for a future iteration.

Issuing prefetch instructions incurs an instruction overhead, however, so compilers must take care to ensure that such overheads do not exceed the benefits. By concentrating on references that are likely to be cache misses, programs can avoid unnecessary prefetches while improving average memory access time significantly.

Example   For the code below, determine which accesses are likely to cause data cache misses. Next, insert prefetch instructions to reduce misses. Finally, calculate the number of prefetch instructions executed and the misses avoided by prefetching. Let's assume we have an 8 KB direct-mapped data cache with 16-byte blocks, and it is a write-back cache that does write allocate. The elements of a and b are 8 bytes long since they are double-precision floating-point arrays. There are 3 rows and 100 columns for a and 101 rows and 3 columns for b. Let's also assume they are not in the cache at the start of the program.

```
for (i = 0; i < 3; i = i+1)
    for (j = 0; j < 100; j = j+1)
        a[i][j] = b[j][0] * b[j+1][0];
```

Answer   The compiler will first determine which accesses are likely to cause cache misses; otherwise, we will waste time on issuing prefetch instructions for data that would be hits. Elements of a are written in the order that they are stored in memory, so a will benefit from spatial locality: The even values of j will miss and the odd values will hit. Since a has 3 rows and 100 columns, its accesses will lead to $3 \times (100/2)$, or 150 misses.

The array b does not benefit from spatial locality since the accesses are not in the order it is stored. The array b does benefit twice from temporal locality: The same elements are accessed for each iteration of i, and each iteration of j uses the same value of b as the last iteration. Ignoring potential conflict misses, the misses due to b will be for b[j+1][0] accesses when i = 0, and also the first access to b[j][0] when j = 0. Since j goes from 0 to 99 when i = 0, accesses to b lead to 100 + 1, or 101 misses.

Thus, this loop will miss the data cache approximately 150 times for a plus 101 times for b, or 251 misses.

To simplify our optimization, we will not worry about prefetching the first accesses of the loop. These may already be in the cache, or we will pay the miss penalty of the first few elements of a or b. Nor will we worry about suppressing the prefetches at the end of the loop that try to prefetch beyond the end of a (a[i][100] ... a[i][106]) and the end of b (b[101][0] ... b[107][0]). If these were faulting prefetches, we could not take this luxury. Let's assume that the miss penalty is so large we need to start prefetching at least, say, seven iterations in advance. (Stated alternatively, we assume prefetching has no benefit until the eighth iteration.) We underline the changes to the code above needed to add prefetching.

```
for (j = 0; j < 100; j = j+1) {
      prefetch(b[j+7][0]);
      /* b(j,0) for 7 iterations later */
      prefetch(a[0][j+7]);
      /* a(0,j) for 7 iterations later */
      a[0][j] = b[j][0] * b[j+1][0];};
  for (i = 1; i < 3; i = i+1)
      for (j = 0; j < 100; j = j+1) {
            prefetch(a[i][j+7]);
            /* a(i,j) for +7 iterations */
            a[i][j] = b[j][0] * b[j+1][0];}
```

This revised code prefetches a[i][7] through a[i][99] and b[7][0] through b[100][0], reducing the number of nonprefetched misses to

- 7 misses for elements b[0][0], b[1][0], ..., b[6][0] in the first loop
- 4 misses ($\lceil 7/2 \rceil$) for elements a[0][0], a[0][1], ..., a[0][6] in the first loop (spatial locality reduces misses to 1 per 16-byte cache block)
- 4 misses ($\lceil 7/2 \rceil$) for elements a[1][0], a[1][1], ..., a[1][6] in the second loop
- 4 misses ($\lceil 7/2 \rceil$) for elements a[2][0], a[2][1], ..., a[2][6] in the second loop

or a total of 19 nonprefetched misses. The cost of avoiding 232 cache misses is executing 400 prefetch instructions, likely a good trade-off.

Example   Calculate the time saved in the example above. Ignore instruction cache misses and assume there are no conflict or capacity misses in the data cache. Assume that prefetches can overlap with each other and with cache misses, thereby transferring at the maximum memory bandwidth. Here are the key loop times ignoring cache misses: The original loop takes 7 clock cycles per iteration, the first prefetch loop takes 9 clock cycles per iteration, and the second prefetch loop takes 8 clock cycles per iteration (including the overhead of the outer for loop). A miss takes 100 clock cycles.

Answer   The original doubly nested loop executes the multiply 3×100 or 300 times. Since the loop takes 7 clock cycles per iteration, the total is 300×7 or 2100 clock cycles plus cache misses. Cache misses add 251×100 or 25,100 clock cycles, giving a total of 27,200 clock cycles. The first prefetch loop iterates 100 times; at 9 clock cycles per iteration the total is 900 clock cycles plus cache misses. Now add 11×100 or 1100 clock cycles for cache misses, giving a total of 2000. The second loop executes 2×100 or 200 times, and at 8 clock cycles per iteration it takes 1600 clock cycles plus 8×100 or 800 clock cycles for cache misses. This gives a total of 2400 clock cycles. From the prior example, we know that this code executes 400 prefetch instructions during the $2000 + 2400$ or 4400 clock cycles to execute these two loops. If we assume that the prefetches are completely overlapped with the rest of the execution, then the prefetch code is 27,200/4400, or 6.2 times faster.

Although array optimizations are easy to understand, modern programs are more likely to use pointers. Luk and Mowry [1999] have demonstrated that compiler-based prefetching can sometimes be extended to pointers as well. Of 10 programs with recursive data structures, prefetching all pointers when a node is visited improved performance by 4% to 31% in half of the programs. On the other hand, the remaining programs were still within 2% of their original performance. The issue is both whether prefetches are to data already in the cache and whether they occur early enough for the data to arrive by the time it is needed.

Many processors support instructions for cache prefetch, and high-end processors (such as the Intel Core i7) often also do some type of automated prefetch in hardware.

Cache Optimization Summary

The techniques to improve hit time, bandwidth, miss penalty, and miss rate generally affect the other components of the average memory access equation as well as the complexity of the memory hierarchy. Figure 2.11 summarizes these techniques and estimates the impact on complexity, with + meaning that the technique improves the factor, – meaning it hurts that factor, and blank meaning it has no impact. Generally, no technique helps more than one category.

Technique	Hit time	Band-width	Miss penalty	Miss rate	Power consumption	Hardware cost/ complexity	Comment
Small and simple caches	+			−	+	0	Trivial; widely used
Way-predicting caches	+				+	1	Used in Pentium 4
Pipelined cache access	−	+				1	Widely used
Nonblocking caches		+	+			3	Widely used
Banked caches		+			+	1	Used in L2 of both i7 and Cortex-A8
Critical word first and early restart			+			2	Widely used
Merging write buffer			+			1	Widely used with write through
Compiler techniques to reduce cache misses				+		0	Software is a challenge, but many compilers handle common linear algebra calculations
Hardware prefetching of instructions and data			+	+	−	2 instr., 3 data	Most provide prefetch instructions; modern high-end processors also automatically prefetch in hardware.
Compiler-controlled prefetching			+	+		3	Needs nonblocking cache; possible instruction overhead; in many CPUs

Figure 2.11 Summary of 10 advanced cache optimizations showing impact on cache performance, power consumption, and complexity. Although generally a technique helps only one factor, prefetching can reduce misses if done sufficiently early; if not, it can reduce miss penalty. + means that the technique improves the factor, − means it hurts that factor, and blank means it has no impact. The complexity measure is subjective, with 0 being the easiest and 3 being a challenge.

2.3 Memory Technology and Optimizations

… the one single development that put computers on their feet was the invention of a reliable form of memory, namely, the core memory. … Its cost was reasonable, it was reliable and, because it was reliable, it could in due course be made large. [p. 209]

Maurice Wilkes
Memoirs of a Computer Pioneer (1985)

Main memory is the next level down in the hierarchy. Main memory satisfies the demands of caches and serves as the I/O interface, as it is the destination of input as well as the source for output. Performance measures of main memory emphasize both latency and bandwidth. Traditionally, main memory latency (which affects the cache miss penalty) is the primary concern of the cache, while main memory bandwidth is the primary concern of multiprocessors and I/O.

Although caches benefit from low-latency memory, it is generally easier to improve memory bandwidth with new organizations than it is to reduce latency. The popularity of multilevel caches and their larger block sizes make main memory bandwidth important to caches as well. In fact, cache designers increase block size to take advantage of the high memory bandwidth.

The previous sections describe what can be done with cache organization to reduce this processor–DRAM performance gap, but simply making caches larger or adding more levels of caches cannot eliminate the gap. Innovations in main memory are needed as well.

In the past, the innovation was how to organize the many DRAM chips that made up the main memory, such as multiple memory banks. Higher bandwidth is available using memory banks, by making memory and its bus wider, or by doing both. Ironically, as capacity per memory chip increases, there are fewer chips in the same-sized memory system, reducing possibilities for wider memory systems with the same capacity.

To allow memory systems to keep up with the bandwidth demands of modern processors, memory innovations started happening inside the DRAM chips themselves. This section describes the technology inside the memory chips and those innovative, internal organizations. Before describing the technologies and options, let's go over the performance metrics.

With the introduction of burst transfer memories, now widely used in both Flash and DRAM, memory latency is quoted using two measures—access time and cycle time. *Access time* is the time between when a read is requested and when the desired word arrives, and *cycle time* is the minimum time between unrelated requests to memory.

Virtually all computers since 1975 have used DRAMs for main memory and SRAMs for cache, with one to three levels integrated onto the processor chip with the CPU. In PMDs, the memory technology often balances power and speed, with higher end systems using fast, high-bandwidth memory technology.

SRAM Technology

The first letter of SRAM stands for *static*. The dynamic nature of the circuits in DRAM requires data to be written back after being read—hence the difference between the access time and the cycle time as well as the need to refresh. SRAMs don't need to refresh, so the access time is very close to the cycle time. SRAMs typically use six transistors per bit to prevent the information from being disturbed when read. SRAM needs only minimal power to retain the charge in standby mode.

In earlier times, most desktop and server systems used SRAM chips for their primary, secondary, or tertiary caches; today, all three levels of caches are integrated onto the processor chip. Currently, the largest on-chip, third-level caches are 12 MB, while the memory system for such a processor is likely to have 4 to

16 GB of DRAM. The access times for large, third-level, on-chip caches are typically two to four times that of a second-level cache, which is still three to five times faster than accessing DRAM memory.

DRAM Technology

As early DRAMs grew in capacity, the cost of a package with all the necessary address lines was an issue. The solution was to multiplex the address lines, thereby cutting the number of address pins in half. Figure 2.12 shows the basic DRAM organization. One-half of the address is sent first during the *row access strobe* (RAS). The other half of the address, sent during the *column access strobe* (CAS), follows it. These names come from the internal chip organization, since the memory is organized as a rectangular matrix addressed by rows and columns.

An additional requirement of DRAM derives from the property signified by its first letter, *D*, for *dynamic*. To pack more bits per chip, DRAMs use only a single transistor to store a bit. Reading that bit destroys the information, so it must be restored. This is one reason why the DRAM cycle time was traditionally longer than the access time; more recently, DRAMs have introduced multiple banks, which allow the rewrite portion of the cycle to be hidden. In addition, to prevent loss of information when a bit is not read or written, the bit must be "refreshed" periodically. Fortunately, all the bits in a row can be refreshed simultaneously just by reading that row. Hence, every DRAM in the memory system must access every row within a certain time window, such as 8 ms. Memory controllers include hardware to refresh the DRAMs periodically.

This requirement means that the memory system is occasionally unavailable because it is sending a signal telling every chip to refresh. The time for a refresh is typically a full memory access (RAS and CAS) for each row of the DRAM. Since the memory matrix in a DRAM is conceptually square, the number of steps

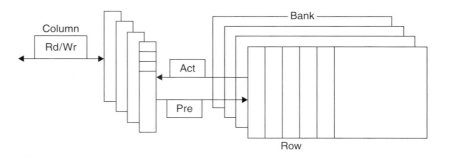

Figure 2.12 Internal organization of a DRAM. Modern DRAMs are organized in banks, typically four for DDR3. Each bank consists of a series of rows. Sending a PRE (precharge) command opens or closes a bank. A row address is sent with an Act (activate), which causes the row to transfer to a buffer. When the row is in the buffer, it can be transferred by successive column addresses at whatever the width of the DRAM is (typically 4, 8, or 16 bits in DDR3) or by specifying a block transfer and the starting address. Each command, as well as block transfers, are synchronized with a clock.

in a refresh is usually the square root of the DRAM capacity. DRAM designers try to keep time spent refreshing to less than 5% of the total time.

So far we have presented main memory as if it operated like a Swiss train, consistently delivering the goods exactly according to schedule. Refresh belies that analogy, since some accesses take much longer than others do. Thus, refresh is another reason for variability of memory latency and hence cache miss penalty.

Amdahl suggested as a rule of thumb that memory capacity should grow linearly with processor speed to keep a balanced system, so that a 1000 MIPS processor should have 1000 MB of memory. Processor designers rely on DRAMs to supply that demand. In the past, they expected a fourfold improvement in capacity every three years, or 55% per year. Unfortunately, the performance of DRAMs is growing at a much slower rate. Figure 2.13 shows a performance improvement in row access time, which is related to latency, of about 5% per year. The CAS or data transfer time, which is related to bandwidth, is growing at more than twice that rate.

Although we have been talking about individual chips, DRAMs are commonly sold on small boards called *dual inline memory modules* (DIMMs). DIMMs typically contain 4 to 16 DRAMs, and they are normally organized to be 8 bytes wide (+ ECC) for desktop and server systems.

Production year	Chip size	DRAM type	Row access strobe (RAS)		Column access strobe (CAS)/ data transfer time (ns)	Cycle time (ns)
			Slowest DRAM (ns)	Fastest DRAM (ns)		
1980	64K bit	DRAM	180	150	75	250
1983	256K bit	DRAM	150	120	50	220
1986	1M bit	DRAM	120	100	25	190
1989	4M bit	DRAM	100	80	20	165
1992	16M bit	DRAM	80	60	15	120
1996	64M bit	SDRAM	70	50	12	110
1998	128M bit	SDRAM	70	50	10	100
2000	256M bit	DDR1	65	45	7	90
2002	512M bit	DDR1	60	40	5	80
2004	1G bit	DDR2	55	35	5	70
2006	2G bit	DDR2	50	30	2.5	60
2010	4G bit	DDR3	36	28	1	37
2012	8G bit	DDR3	30	24	0.5	31

Figure 2.13 Times of fast and slow DRAMs vary with each generation. (Cycle time is defined on page 97.) Performance improvement of row access time is about 5% per year. The improvement by a factor of 2 in column access in 1986 accompanied the switch from NMOS DRAMs to CMOS DRAMs. The introduction of various burst transfer modes in the mid-1990s and SDRAMs in the late 1990s has significantly complicated the calculation of access time for blocks of data; we discuss this later in this section when we talk about SDRAM access time and power. The DDR4 designs are due for introduction in mid- to late 2012. We discuss these various forms of DRAMs in the next few pages.

In addition to the DIMM packaging and the new interfaces to improve the data transfer time, discussed in the following subsections, the biggest change to DRAMs has been a slowing down in capacity growth. DRAMs obeyed Moore's law for 20 years, bringing out a new chip with four times the capacity every three years. Due to the manufacturing challenges of a single-bit DRAM, new chips only double capacity every two years since 1998. In 2006, the pace slowed further, with the four years from 2006 to 2010 seeing only a doubling of capacity.

Improving Memory Performance Inside a DRAM Chip

As Moore's law continues to supply more transistors and as the processor–memory gap increases pressure on memory performance, the ideas of the previous section have made their way inside the DRAM chip. Generally, innovation has led to greater bandwidth, sometimes at the cost of greater latency. This subsection presents techniques that take advantage of the nature of DRAMs.

As mentioned earlier, a DRAM access is divided into row access and column access. DRAMs must buffer a row of bits inside the DRAM for the column access, and this row is usually the square root of the DRAM size—for example, 2 Kb for a 4 Mb DRAM. As DRAMs grew, additional structure and several opportunities for increasing bandwith were added.

First, DRAMs added timing signals that allow repeated accesses to the row buffer without another row access time. Such a buffer comes naturally, as each array will buffer 1024 to 4096 bits for each access. Initially, separate column addresses had to be sent for each transfer with a delay after each new set of column addresses.

Originally, DRAMs had an asynchronous interface to the memory controller, so every transfer involved overhead to synchronize with the controller. The second major change was to add a clock signal to the DRAM interface, so that the repeated transfers would not bear that overhead. *Synchronous DRAM* (SDRAM) is the name of this optimization. SDRAMs typically also have a programmable register to hold the number of bytes requested, and hence can send many bytes over several cycles per request. Typically, 8 or more 16-bit transfers can occur without sending any new addresses by placing the DRAM in burst mode; this mode, which supports critical word first transfers, is the only way that the peak bandwidths shown in Figure 2.14 can be achieved.

Third, to overcome the problem of getting a wide stream of bits from the memory without having to make the memory system too large as memory system density increased, DRAMS were made wider. Initially, they offered a four-bit transfer mode; in 2010, DDR2 and DDR3 DRAMS had up to 16-bit buses.

The fourth major DRAM innovation to increase bandwidth is to transfer data on both the rising edge and falling edge of the DRAM clock signal, thereby doubling the peak data rate. This optimization is called *double data rate* (DDR).

To provide some of the advantages of interleaving, as well to help with power management, SDRAMs also introduced *banks*, breaking a single SDRAM into 2 to 8 blocks (in current DDR3 DRAMs) that can operate independently. (We have already seen banks used in internal caches, and they were often used in large

Standard	Clock rate (MHz)	M transfers per second	DRAM name	MB/sec /DIMM	DIMM name
DDR	133	266	DDR266	2128	PC2100
DDR	150	300	DDR300	2400	PC2400
DDR	200	400	DDR400	3200	PC3200
DDR2	266	533	DDR2-533	4264	PC4300
DDR2	333	667	DDR2-667	5336	PC5300
DDR2	400	800	DDR2-800	6400	PC6400
DDR3	533	1066	DDR3-1066	8528	PC8500
DDR3	666	1333	DDR3-1333	10,664	PC10700
DDR3	800	1600	DDR3-1600	12,800	PC12800
DDR4	1066–1600	2133–3200	DDR4-3200	17,056–25,600	PC25600

Figure 2.14 Clock rates, bandwidth, and names of DDR DRAMS and DIMMs in 2010. Note the numerical relationship between the columns. The third column is twice the second, and the fourth uses the number from the third column in the name of the DRAM chip. The fifth column is eight times the third column, and a rounded version of this number is used in the name of the DIMM. Although not shown in this figure, DDRs also specify latency in clock cycles as four numbers, which are specified by the DDR standard. For example, DDR3-2000 CL 9 has latencies of 9-9-9-28. What does this mean? With a 1 ns clock (clock cycle is one-half the transfer rate), this indicates 9 ns for row to columns address (RAS time), 9 ns for column access to data (CAS time), and a minimum read time of 28 ns. Closing the row takes 9 ns for precharge but happens only when the reads from that row are finished. In burst mode, transfers occur on every clock on both edges, when the first RAS and CAS times have elapsed. Furthermore, the precharge is not needed until the entire row is read. DDR4 will be produced in 2012 and is expected to reach clock rates of 1600 MHz in 2014, when DDR5 is expected to take over. The exercises explore these details further.

main memories.) Creating multiple banks inside a DRAM effectively adds another segment to the address, which now consists of bank number, row address, and column address. When an address is sent that designates a new bank, that bank must be opened, incurring an additional delay. The management of banks and row buffers is completely handled by modern memory control interfaces, so that when subsequent access specifies the same row for an open bank, the access can happen quickly, sending only the column address.

When DDR SDRAMs are packaged as DIMMs, they are confusingly labeled by the peak *DIMM* bandwidth. Hence, the DIMM name PC2100 comes from 133 MHz × 2 × 8 bytes, or 2100 MB/sec. Sustaining the confusion, the chips themselves are labeled with *the number of bits per second* rather than their clock rate, so a 133 MHz DDR chip is called a DDR266. Figure 2.14 shows the relationships among clock rate, transfers per second per chip, chip name, DIMM bandwidth, and DIMM name.

DDR is now a sequence of standards. DDR2 lowers power by dropping the voltage from 2.5 volts to 1.8 volts and offers higher clock rates: 266 MHz, 333 MHz, and 400 MHz. DDR3 drops voltage to 1.5 volts and has a maximum clock speed of 800 MHz. DDR4, scheduled for production in 2014, drops the voltage to 1 to 1.2 volts and has a maximum expected clock rate of 1600 MHz. DDR5 will follow in about 2014 or 2015. (As we discuss in the next section, GDDR5 is a graphics RAM and is based on DDR3 DRAMs.)

Graphics Data RAMs

GDRAMs or GSDRAMs (Graphics or Graphics Synchronous DRAMs) are a special class of DRAMs based on SDRAM designs but tailored for handling the higher bandwidth demands of graphics processing units. GDDR5 is based on DDR3 with earlier GDDRs based on DDR2. Since Graphics Processor Units (GPUs; see Chapter 4) require more bandwidth per DRAM chip than CPUs, GDDRs have several important differences:

1. GDDRs have wider interfaces: 32-bits versus 4, 8, or 16 in current designs.

2. GDDRs have a higher maximum clock rate on the data pins. To allow a higher transfer rate without incurring signaling problems, GDRAMS normally connect directly to the GPU and are attached by soldering them to the board, unlike DRAMs, which are normally arranged in an expandable array of DIMMs.

Altogether, these characteristics let GDDRs run at two to five times the bandwidth per DRAM versus DDR3 DRAMs, a significant advantage in supporting GPUs. Because of the lower locality of memory requests in a GPU, burst mode generally is less useful for a GPU, but keeping open multiple memory banks and managing their use improves effective bandwidth.

Reducing Power Consumption in SDRAMs

Power consumption in dynamic memory chips consists of both dynamic power used in a read or write and static or standby power; both depend on the operating voltage. In the most advanced DDR3 SDRAMs the operating voltage has been dropped to 1.35 to 1.5 volts, significantly reducing power versus DDR2 SDRAMs. The addition of banks also reduced power, since only the row in a single bank is read and precharged.

In addition to these changes, all recent SDRAMs support a power down mode, which is entered by telling the DRAM to ignore the clock. Power down mode disables the SDRAM, except for internal automatic refresh (without which entering power down mode for longer than the refresh time will cause the contents of memory to be lost). Figure 2.15 shows the power consumption for three situations in a 2 Gb DDR3 SDRAM. The exact delay required to return from low power mode depends on the SDRAM, but a typical timing from autorefresh low power mode is 200 clock cycles; additional time may be required for resetting the mode register before the first command.

Flash Memory

Flash memory is a type of EEPROM (Electronically Erasable Programmable Read-Only Memory), which is normally read-only but can be erased. The other key property of Flash memory is that it holds it contents without any power.

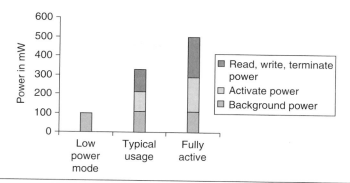

Figure 2.15 Power consumption for a DDR3 SDRAM operating under three conditions: low power (shutdown) mode, typical system mode (DRAM is active 30% of the time for reads and 15% for writes), and fully active mode, where the DRAM is continuously reading or writing when not in precharge. Reads and writes assume bursts of 8 transfers. These data are based on a Micron 1.5V 2Gb DDR3-1066.

Flash is used as the backup storage in PMDs in the same manner that a disk functions in a laptop or server. In addition, because most PMDs have a limited amount of DRAM, Flash may also act as a level of the memory hierarchy, to a much larger extent than it might have to do so in the desktop or server with a main memory that might be 10 to 100 times larger.

Flash uses a very different architecture and has different properties than standard DRAM. The most important differences are

1. Flash memory must be erased (hence the name Flash for the "flash" erase process) before it is overwritten, and it is erased in blocks (in high-density Flash, called NAND Flash, which is what is used in most computer applications) rather than individual bytes or words. This means when data must be written to Flash, an entire block must be assembled, either as new data or by merging the data to be written and the rest of the block's contents.

2. Flash memory is static (i.e., it keeps its contents even when power is not applied) and draws significantly less power when not reading or writing (from less than half in standby mode to zero when completely inactive).

3. Flash memory has a limited number of write cycles for any block, typically at least 100,000. By ensuring uniform distribution of written blocks throughout the memory, a system can maximize the lifetime of a Flash memory system.

4. High-density Flash is cheaper than SDRAM but more expensive than disks: roughly $2/GB for Flash, $20 to $40/GB for SDRAM, and $0.09/GB for magnetic disks.

5. Flash is much slower than SDRAM but much faster than disk. For example, a transfer of 256 bytes from a typical high-density Flash memory takes about 6.5 μs (using burst mode transfer similar to but slower than that used in SDRAM). A comparable transfer from a DDR SDRAM takes about one-quarter as long, and for a disk about 1000 times longer. For writes, the

difference is considerably larger, with the SDRAM being at least 10 and as much as 100 times faster than Flash depending on the circumstances.

The rapid improvements in high-density Flash in the past decade have made the technology a viable part of memory hierarchies in mobile devices and as solid-state replacements for disks. As the rate of increase in DRAM density continues to drop, Flash could play an increased role in future memory systems, acting as both a replacement for hard disks and as an intermediate storage between DRAM and disk.

Enhancing Dependability in Memory Systems

Large caches and main memories significantly increase the possibility of errors occurring both during the fabrication process and dynamically, primarily from cosmic rays striking a memory cell. These dynamic errors, which are changes to a cell's contents, not a change in the circuitry, are called *soft errors*. All DRAMs, Flash memory, and many SRAMs are manufactured with spare rows, so that a small number of manufacturing defects can be accommodated by programming the replacement of a defective row by a spare row. In addition to fabrication errors that must be fixed at configuration time, *hard errors*, which are permanent changes in the operation of one of more memory cells, can occur in operation.

Dynamic errors can be detected by parity bits and detected and fixed by the use of Error Correcting Codes (ECCs). Because instruction caches are read-only, parity suffices. In larger data caches and in main memory, ECC is used to allow errors to be both detected and corrected. Parity requires only one bit of overhead to detect a single error in a sequence of bits. Because a multibit error would be undetected with parity, the number of bits protected by a parity bit must be limited. One parity bit per 8 data bits is a typical ratio. ECC can detect two errors and correct a single error with a cost of 8 bits of overhead per 64 data bits.

In very large systems, the possibility of multiple errors as well as complete failure of a single memory chip becomes significant. Chipkill was introduced by IBM to solve this problem, and many very large systems, such as IBM and SUN servers and the Google Clusters, use this technology. (Intel calls their version SDDC.) Similar in nature to the RAID approach used for disks, Chipkill distributes the data and ECC information, so that the complete failure of a single memory chip can be handled by supporting the reconstruction of the missing data from the remaining memory chips. Using an analysis by IBM and assuming a 10,000 processor server with 4 GB per processor yields the following rates of unrecoverable errors in three years of operation:

- Parity only—about 90,000, or one unrecoverable (or undetected) failure every 17 minutes

- ECC only—about 3500, or about one undetected or unrecoverable failure every 7.5 hours

- Chipkill—6, or about one undetected or unrecoverable failure every 2 months

Another way to look at this is to find the maximum number of servers (each with 4 GB) that can be protected while achieving the same error rate as demonstrated for Chipkill. For parity, even a server with only one processor will have an unrecoverable error rate higher than a 10,000-server Chipkill protected system. For ECC, a 17-server system would have about the same failure rate as a 10,000-server Chipkill system. Hence, Chipkill is a requirement for the 50,000 to 100,00 servers in warehouse-scale computers (see Section 6.8 of Chapter 6).

2.4 Protection: Virtual Memory and Virtual Machines

A virtual machine is taken to be an efficient, isolated duplicate *of the real machine. We explain these notions through the idea of a* virtual machine monitor *(VMM). . . . a VMM has three essential characteristics. First, the VMM provides an environment for programs which is essentially identical with the original machine; second, programs run in this environment show at worst only minor decreases in speed; and last, the VMM is in complete control of system resources.*

Gerald Popek and Robert Goldberg
"Formal requirements for virtualizable third generation architectures,"
Communications of the ACM (July 1974)

Security and privacy are two of the most vexing challenges for information technology in 2011. Electronic burglaries, often involving lists of credit card numbers, are announced regularly, and it's widely believed that many more go unreported. Hence, both researchers and practitioners are looking for new ways to make computing systems more secure. Although protecting information is not limited to hardware, in our view real security and privacy will likely involve innovation in computer architecture as well as in systems software.

This section starts with a review of the architecture support for protecting processes from each other via virtual memory. It then describes the added protection provided from virtual machines, the architecture requirements of virtual machines, and the performance of a virtual machine. As we will see in Chapter 6, virtual machines are a foundational technology for cloud computing.

Protection via Virtual Memory

Page-based virtual memory, including a translation lookaside buffer that caches page table entries, is the primary mechanism that protects processes from each other. Sections B.4 and B.5 in Appendix B review virtual memory, including a detailed description of protection via segmentation and paging in the 80x86. This subsection acts as a quick review; refer to those sections if it's too quick.

Multiprogramming, where several programs running concurrently would share a computer, led to demands for protection and sharing among programs and to the concept of a *process*. Metaphorically, a process is a program's breathing air and living space—that is, a running program plus any state needed to continue running it. At any instant, it must be possible to switch from one process to another. This exchange is called a *process switch* or *context switch*.

The operating system and architecture join forces to allow processes to share the hardware yet not interfere with each other. To do this, the architecture must limit what a process can access when running a user process yet allow an operating system process to access more. At a minimum, the architecture must do the following:

1. Provide at least two modes, indicating whether the running process is a user process or an operating system process. This latter process is sometimes called a *kernel* process or a *supervisor* process.

2. Provide a portion of the processor state that a user process can use but not write. This state includes a user/supervisor mode bit, an exception enable/disable bit, and memory protection information. Users are prevented from writing this state because the operating system cannot control user processes if users can give themselves supervisor privileges, disable exceptions, or change memory protection.

3. Provide mechanisms whereby the processor can go from user mode to supervisor mode and vice versa. The first direction is typically accomplished by a *system call*, implemented as a special instruction that transfers control to a dedicated location in supervisor code space. The PC is saved from the point of the system call, and the processor is placed in supervisor mode. The return to user mode is like a subroutine return that restores the previous user/supervisor mode.

4. Provide mechanisms to limit memory accesses to protect the memory state of a process without having to swap the process to disk on a context switch.

Appendix A describes several memory protection schemes, but by far the most popular is adding protection restrictions to each page of virtual memory. Fixed-sized pages, typically 4 KB or 8 KB long, are mapped from the virtual address space into physical address space via a page table. The protection restrictions are included in each page table entry. The protection restrictions might determine whether a user process can read this page, whether a user process can write to this page, and whether code can be executed from this page. In addition, a process can neither read nor write a page if it is not in the page table. Since only the OS can update the page table, the paging mechanism provides total access protection.

Paged virtual memory means that every memory access logically takes at least twice as long, with one memory access to obtain the physical address and a second access to get the data. This cost would be far too dear. The solution is to rely on the principle of locality; if the accesses have locality, then the *address translations* for the accesses must also have locality. By keeping these address translations in a special cache, a memory access rarely requires a second access to translate the address. This special address translation cache is referred to as a *translation lookaside buffer* (TLB).

A TLB entry is like a cache entry where the tag holds portions of the virtual address and the data portion holds a physical page address, protection field, valid bit, and usually a use bit and a dirty bit. The operating system changes these bits by changing the value in the page table and then invalidating the corresponding TLB entry. When the entry is reloaded from the page table, the TLB gets an accurate copy of the bits.

Assuming the computer faithfully obeys the restrictions on pages and maps virtual addresses to physical addresses, it would seem that we are done. Newspaper headlines suggest otherwise.

The reason we're not done is that we depend on the accuracy of the operating system as well as the hardware. Today's operating systems consist of tens of millions of lines of code. Since bugs are measured in number per thousand lines of code, there are thousands of bugs in production operating systems. Flaws in the OS have led to vulnerabilities that are routinely exploited.

This problem and the possibility that not enforcing protection could be much more costly than in the past have led some to look for a protection model with a much smaller code base than the full OS, such as Virtual Machines.

Protection via Virtual Machines

An idea related to virtual memory that is almost as old are Virtual Machines (VMs). They were first developed in the late 1960s, and they have remained an important part of mainframe computing over the years. Although largely ignored in the domain of single-user computers in the 1980s and 1990s, they have recently gained popularity due to

- The increasing importance of isolation and security in modern systems
- The failures in security and reliability of standard operating systems
- The sharing of a single computer among many unrelated users, such as in a datacenter or cloud
- The dramatic increases in the raw speed of processors, which make the overhead of VMs more acceptable

The broadest definition of VMs includes basically all emulation methods that provide a standard software interface, such as the Java VM. We are interested in VMs that provide a complete system-level environment at the binary instruction set architecture (ISA) level. Most often, the VM supports the same ISA as the underlying hardware; however, it is also possible to support a different ISA, and such approaches are often employed when migrating between ISAs, so as to allow software from the departing ISA to be used until it can be ported to the new ISA. Our focus here will be in VMs where the ISA presented by the VM and the underlying hardware match. Such VMs are called (Operating) *System Virtual Machines*. IBM VM/370, VMware ESX Server, and Xen are examples. They present the illusion that the users of a VM have an entire computer to themselves, including a copy of the operating system. A single computer runs multiple VMs and can support a number of different operating systems (OSes). On a conventional platform, a single OS "owns" all the hardware resources, but with a VM multiple OSes all share the hardware resources.

The software that supports VMs is called a *virtual machine monitor* (VMM) or *hypervisor*; the VMM is the heart of virtual machine technology. The underlying hardware platform is called the *host*, and its resources are shared among the *guest* VMs. The VMM determines how to map virtual resources to physical resources: A physical resource may be time-shared, partitioned, or even emulated in software. The VMM is much smaller than a traditional OS; the isolation portion of a VMM is perhaps only 10,000 lines of code.

In general, the cost of processor virtualization depends on the workload. User-level processor-bound programs, such as SPEC CPU2006, have zero virtualization overhead because the OS is rarely invoked so everything runs at native speeds. Conversely, I/O-intensive workloads generally are also OS-intensive and execute many system calls (which doing I/O requires) and privileged instructions that can result in high virtualization overhead. The overhead is determined by the number of instructions that must be emulated by the VMM and how slowly they are emulated. Hence, when the guest VMs run the same ISA as the host, as we assume here, the goal of the architecture and the VMM is to run almost all instructions directly on the native hardware. On the other hand, if the I/O-intensive workload is also *I/O-bound*, the cost of processor virtualization can be completely hidden by low processor utilization since it is often waiting for I/O.

Although our interest here is in VMs for improving protection, VMs provide two other benefits that are commercially significant:

1. *Managing software*—VMs provide an abstraction that can run the complete software stack, even including old operating systems such as DOS. A typical deployment might be some VMs running legacy OSes, many running the current stable OS release, and a few testing the next OS release.

2. *Managing hardware*—One reason for multiple servers is to have each application running with its own compatible version of the operating system on separate computers, as this separation can improve dependability. VMs allow these separate software stacks to run independently yet share hardware, thereby consolidating the number of servers. Another example is that some VMMs support migration of a running VM to a different computer, either to balance load or to evacuate from failing hardware.

These two reasons are why cloud-based servers, such as Amazon's, rely on virtual machines.

Requirements of a Virtual Machine Monitor

What must a VM monitor do? It presents a software interface to guest software, it must isolate the state of guests from each other, and it must protect itself from guest software (including guest OSes). The qualitative requirements are

- Guest software should behave on a VM exactly as if it were running on the native hardware, except for performance-related behavior or limitations of fixed resources shared by multiple VMs.

- Guest software should not be able to change allocation of real system resources directly.

To "virtualize" the processor, the VMM must control just about everything—access to privileged state, address translation, I/O, exceptions and interrupts—even though the guest VM and OS currently running are temporarily using them.

For example, in the case of a timer interrupt, the VMM would suspend the currently running guest VM, save its state, handle the interrupt, determine which guest VM to run next, and then load its state. Guest VMs that rely on a timer interrupt are provided with a virtual timer and an emulated timer interrupt by the VMM.

To be in charge, the VMM must be at a higher privilege level than the guest VM, which generally runs in user mode; this also ensures that the execution of any privileged instruction will be handled by the VMM. The basic requirements of system virtual machines are almost identical to those for paged virtual memory listed above:

- At least two processor modes, system and user.

- A privileged subset of instructions that is available only in system mode, resulting in a trap if executed in user mode. All system resources must be controllable only via these instructions.

(Lack of) Instruction Set Architecture Support for Virtual Machines

If VMs are planned for during the design of the ISA, it's relatively easy to both reduce the number of instructions that must be executed by a VMM and how long it takes to emulate them. An architecture that allows the VM to execute directly on the hardware earns the title *virtualizable*, and the IBM 370 architecture proudly bears that label.

Alas, since VMs have been considered for desktop and PC-based server applications only fairly recently, most instruction sets were created without virtualization in mind. These culprits include 80x86 and most RISC architectures.

Because the VMM must ensure that the guest system only interacts with virtual resources, a conventional guest OS runs as a user mode program on top of the VMM. Then, if a guest OS attempts to access or modify information related to hardware resources via a privileged instruction—for example, reading or writing the page table pointer—it will trap to the VMM. The VMM can then effect the appropriate changes to corresponding real resources.

Hence, if any instruction that tries to read or write such sensitive information traps when executed in user mode, the VMM can intercept it and support a virtual version of the sensitive information as the guest OS expects.

In the absence of such support, other measures must be taken. A VMM must take special precautions to locate all problematic instructions and ensure that they behave correctly when executed by a guest OS, thereby increasing the complexity of the VMM and reducing the performance of running the VM.

Sections 2.5 and 2.7 give concrete examples of problematic instructions in the 80x86 architecture.

Impact of Virtual Machines on Virtual Memory and I/O

Another challenge is virtualization of virtual memory, as each guest OS in every VM manages its own set of page tables. To make this work, the VMM separates the notions of *real* and *physical memory* (which are often treated synonymously) and makes real memory a separate, intermediate level between virtual memory and physical memory. (Some use the terms *virtual memory, physical memory*, and *machine memory* to name the same three levels.) The guest OS maps virtual memory to real memory via its page tables, and the VMM page tables map the guests' real memory to physical memory. The virtual memory architecture is specified either via page tables, as in IBM VM/370 and the 80x86, or via the TLB structure, as in many RISC architectures.

Rather than pay an extra level of indirection on every memory access, the VMM maintains a *shadow page table* that maps directly from the guest virtual address space to the physical address space of the hardware. By detecting all modifications to the guest's page table, the VMM can ensure the shadow page table entries being used by the hardware for translations correspond to those of the guest OS environment, with the exception of the correct physical pages substituted for the real pages in the guest tables. Hence, the VMM must trap any attempt by the guest OS to change its page table or to access the page table pointer. This is commonly done by write protecting the guest page tables and trapping any access to the page table pointer by a guest OS. As noted above, the latter happens naturally if accessing the page table pointer is a privileged operation.

The IBM 370 architecture solved the page table problem in the 1970s with an additional level of indirection that is managed by the VMM. The guest OS keeps its page tables as before, so the shadow pages are unnecessary. AMD has proposed a similar scheme for their Pacifica revision to the 80x86.

To virtualize the TLB in many RISC computers, the VMM manages the real TLB and has a copy of the contents of the TLB of each guest VM. To pull this off, any instructions that access the TLB must trap. TLBs with Process ID tags can support a mix of entries from different VMs and the VMM, thereby avoiding flushing of the TLB on a VM switch. Meanwhile, in the background, the VMM supports a mapping between the VMs' virtual Process IDs and the real Process IDs.

The final portion of the architecture to virtualize is I/O. This is by far the most difficult part of system virtualization because of the increasing number of I/O devices attached to the computer *and* the increasing diversity of I/O device types. Another difficulty is the sharing of a real device among multiple VMs, and yet another comes from supporting the myriad of device drivers that are required, especially if different guest OSes are supported on the same VM system. The VM illusion can be maintained by giving each VM generic versions of each type of I/O device driver, and then leaving it to the VMM to handle real I/O.

The method for mapping a virtual to physical I/O device depends on the type of device. For example, physical disks are normally partitioned by the VMM to create virtual disks for guest VMs, and the VMM maintains the mapping of virtual tracks and sectors to the physical ones. Network interfaces are often shared between VMs in very short time slices, and the job of the VMM is to keep track of messages for the virtual network addresses to ensure that guest VMs receive only messages intended for them.

An Example VMM: The Xen Virtual Machine

Early in the development of VMs, a number of inefficiencies became apparent. For example, a guest OS manages its virtual to real page mapping, but this mapping is ignored by the VMM, which performs the actual mapping to physical pages. In other words, a significant amount of wasted effort is expended just to keep the guest OS happy. To reduce such inefficiencies, VMM developers decided that it may be worthwhile to allow the guest OS to be aware that it is running on a VM. For example, a guest OS could assume a real memory as large as its virtual memory so that no memory management is required by the guest OS.

Allowing small modifications to the guest OS to simplify virtualization is referred to as *paravirtualization*, and the open source Xen VMM is a good example. The Xen VMM, which is used in Amazon's Web services data centers, provides a guest OS with a virtual machine abstraction that is similar to the physical hardware, but it drops many of the troublesome pieces. For example, to avoid flushing the TLB, Xen maps itself into the upper 64 MB of the address space of each VM. It allows the guest OS to allocate pages, just checking to be sure it does not violate protection restrictions. To protect the guest OS from the user programs in the VM, Xen takes advantage of the four protection levels available in the 80x86. The Xen VMM runs at the highest privilege level (0), the guest OS runs at the next level (1), and the applications run at the lowest privilege level (3). Most OSes for the 80x86 keep everything at privilege levels 0 or 3.

For subsetting to work properly, Xen modifies the guest OS to not use problematic portions of the architecture. For example, the port of Linux to Xen changes about 3000 lines, or about 1% of the 80x86-specific code. These changes, however, do not affect the application-binary interfaces of the guest OS.

To simplify the I/O challenge of VMs, Xen assigned privileged virtual machines to each hardware I/O device. These special VMs are called *driver domains*. (Xen calls its VMs "domains.") Driver domains run the physical device drivers, although interrupts are still handled by the VMM before being sent to the appropriate driver domain. Regular VMs, called *guest domains*, run simple virtual device drivers that must communicate with the physical device drivers in the driver domains over a channel to access the physical I/O hardware. Data are sent between guest and driver domains by page remapping.

Crosscutting Issues: The Design of Memory Hierarchies

This section describes three topics discussed in other chapters that are fundamental to memory hierarchies.

Protection and Instruction Set Architecture

Protection is a joint effort of architecture and operating systems, but architects had to modify some awkward details of existing instruction set architectures when virtual memory became popular. For example, to support virtual memory in the IBM 370, architects had to change the successful IBM 360 instruction set architecture that had been announced just 6 years before. Similar adjustments are being made today to accommodate virtual machines.

For example, the 80x86 instruction POPF loads the flag registers from the top of the stack in memory. One of the flags is the Interrupt Enable (IE) flag. Until recent changes to support virtualization, running the POPF instruction in user mode, rather than trapping it, simply changed all the flags except IE. In system mode, it does change the IE flag. Since a guest OS runs in user mode inside a VM, this was a problem, as it would expect to see a changed IE. Extensions of the 80x86 architecture to support virtualization eliminated this problem.

Historically, IBM mainframe hardware and VMM took three steps to improve performance of virtual machines:

1. Reduce the cost of processor virtualization.

2. Reduce interrupt overhead cost due to the virtualization.

3. Reduce interrupt cost by steering interrupts to the proper VM without invoking VMM.

IBM is still the gold standard of virtual machine technology. For example, an IBM mainframe ran thousands of Linux VMs in 2000, while Xen ran 25 VMs in 2004 [Clark et al. 2004]. Recent versions of Intel and AMD chipsets have added special instructions to support devices in a VM, to mask interrupts at lower levels from each VM, and to steer interrupts to the appropriate VM.

Coherency of Cached Data

Data can be found in memory and in the cache. As long as the processor is the sole component changing or reading the data and the cache stands between the processor and memory, there is little danger in the processor seeing the old or *stale* copy. As we will see, multiple processors and I/O devices raise the opportunity for copies to be inconsistent and to read the wrong copy.

The frequency of the cache coherency problem is different for multiprocessors than I/O. Multiple data copies are a rare event for I/O—one to be avoided whenever possible—but a program running on multiple processors will *want* to have copies of the same data in several caches. Performance of a multiprocessor program depends on the performance of the system when sharing data.

The *I/O cache coherency* question is this: Where does the I/O occur in the computer—between the I/O device and the cache or between the I/O device and main memory? If input puts data into the cache and output reads data from the cache, both I/O and the processor see the same data. The difficulty in this approach is that it interferes with the processor and can cause the processor to stall for I/O. Input may also interfere with the cache by displacing some information with new data that are unlikely to be accessed soon.

The goal for the I/O system in a computer with a cache is to prevent the stale data problem while interfering as little as possible. Many systems, therefore, prefer that I/O occur directly to main memory, with main memory acting as an I/O buffer. If a write-through cache were used, then memory would have an up-to-date copy of the information, and there would be no stale data issue for output. (This benefit is a reason processors used write through.) Alas, write through is usually found today only in first-level data caches backed by an L2 cache that uses write back.

Input requires some extra work. The software solution is to guarantee that no blocks of the input buffer are in the cache. A page containing the buffer can be marked as noncachable, and the operating system can always input to such a page. Alternatively, the operating system can flush the buffer addresses from the cache before the input occurs. A hardware solution is to check the I/O addresses on input to see if they are in the cache. If there is a match of I/O addresses in the cache, the cache entries are invalidated to avoid stale data. All of these approaches can also be used for output with write-back caches.

Processor cache coherency is a critical subject in the age of multicore processors, and we will examine it in detail in Chapter 5.

| 2.6 | **Putting It All Together: Memory Hierachies in the ARM Cortex-A8 and Intel Core i7** |

This section reveals the ARM Cortex-A8 (hereafter called the Cortex-A8) and Intel Core i7 (hereafter called i7) memory hierarchies and shows the performance of their components on a set of single threaded benchmarks. We examine the Cortex-A8 first because it has a simpler memory system; we go into more detail for the i7, tracing out a memory reference in detail. This section presumes that readers are familiar with the organization of a two-level cache hierarchy using virtually indexed caches. The basics of such a memory system are explained in detail in Appendix B, and readers who are uncertain of the organization of such a system are strongly advised to review the Opteron example in Appendix B. Once they understand the organization of the Opteron, the brief explanation of the Cortex-A8 system, which is similar, will be easy to follow.

The ARM Cortex-A8

The Cortex-A8 is a configurable core that supports the ARMv7 instruction set architecture. It is delivered as an IP (Intellectual Property) core. IP cores are the dominant form of technology delivery in the embedded, PMD, and related markets; billions of ARM and MIPS processors have been created from these IP cores. Note that IP cores are different than the cores in the Intel i7 or AMD Athlon multicores. An IP core (which may itself be a multicore) is designed to be incorporated with other logic (hence it is the core of a chip), including application-specific processors (such as an encoder or decoder for video), I/O interfaces, and memory interfaces, and then fabricated to yield a processor optimized for a particular application. For example, the Cortex-A8 IP core is used in the Apple iPad and smartphones by several manufacturers including Motorola and Samsung. Although the processor core is almost identical, the resultant chips have many differences.

Generally, IP cores come in two flavors. Hard cores are optimized for a particular semiconductor vendor and are black boxes with external (but still on-chip) interfaces. Hard cores typically allow parametrization only of logic outside the core, such as L2 cache sizes, and the IP core cannot be modified. Soft cores are usually delivered in a form that uses a standard library of logic elements. A soft core can be compiled for different semiconductor vendors and can also be modified, although extensive modifications are very difficult due to the complexity of modern-day IP cores. In general, hard cores provide higher performance and smaller die area, while soft cores allow retargeting to other vendors and can be more easily modified.

The Cortex-A8 can issue two instructions per clock at clock rates up to 1GHz. It can support a two-level cache hierarchy with the first level being a pair of caches (for I & D), each 16 KB or 32 KB organized as four-way set associative and using way prediction and random replacement. The goal is to have single-cycle access latency for the caches, allowing the Cortex-A8 to maintain a load-to-use delay of one cycle, simpler instruction fetch, and a lower penalty for fetching the correct instruction when a branch miss causes the wrong instruction to be prefetched. The optional second-level cache when present is eight-way set associative and can be configured with 128 KB up to 1 MB; it is organized into one to four banks to allow several transfers from memory to occur concurrently. An external bus of 64 to 128 bits handles memory requests. The first-level cache is virtually indexed and physically tagged, and the second-level cache is physically indexed and tagged; both levels use a 64-byte block size. For the D-cache of 32 KB and a page size of 4 KB, each physical page could map to two different cache addresses; such aliases are avoided by hardware detection on a miss as in Section B.3 of Appendix B.

Memory management is handled by a pair of TLBs (I and D), each of which are fully associative with 32 entries and a variable page size (4 KB, 16 KB, 64 KB, 1 MB, and 16 MB); replacement in the TLB is done by a round robin algorithm. TLB misses are handled in hardware, which walks a page table structure in memory. Figure 2.16 shows how the 32-bit virtual address is used to index the TLB and the caches, assuming 32 KB primary caches and a 512 KB secondary cache with 16 KB page size.

Performance of the Cortex-A8 Memory Hierarchy

The memory hierarchy of the Cortex-A8 was simulated with 32 KB primary caches and a 1 MB eight-way set associative L2 cache using the integer Minnespec benchmarks (see **KleinOsowski and Lilja [2002]**). Minnespec is a set of benchmarks consisting of the SPEC2000 benchmarks but with different inputs that reduce the running times by several orders of magnitude. Although the use of smaller inputs does not change the instruction mix, it does affect the

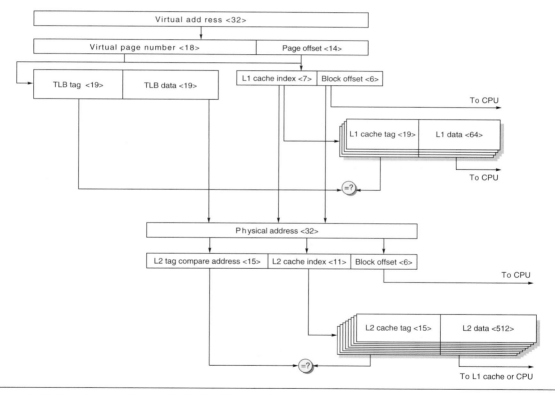

Figure 2.16 **The virtual address, physical address, indexes, tags, and data blocks for the ARM Cortex-A8 data caches and data TLB.** Since the instruction and data hierarchies are symmetric, we show only one. The TLB (instruction or data) is fully associative with 32 entries. The L1 cache is four-way set associative with 64-byte blocks and 32 KB capacity. The L2 cache is eight-way set associative with 64-byte blocks and 1 MB capacity. This figure doesn't show the valid bits and protection bits for the caches and TLB, nor the use of the way prediction bits that would dictate the predicted bank of the L1 cache.

cache behavior. For example, on mcf, the most memory-intensive SPEC2000 integer benchmark, Minnespec has a miss rate for a 32 KB cache that is only 65% of the miss rate for the full SPEC version. For a 1 MB cache the difference is a factor of 6! On many other benchmarks the ratios are similar to those on mcf, but the absolute miss rates are much smaller. For this reason, one cannot compare the Minniespec benchmarks against the SPEC2000 benchmarks. Instead, the data are useful for looking at the relative impact of L1 and L2 misses and on overall CPI, as we do in the next chapter.

The instruction cache miss rates for these benchmarks (and also for the full SPEC2000 versions on which Minniespec is based) are very small even for just the L1: close to zero for most and under 1% for all of them. This low rate probably results from the computationally intensive nature of the SPEC programs and the four-way set associative cache that eliminates most conflict misses. Figure 2.17 shows the data cache results, which have significant L1 and L2 miss rates. The L1 miss penalty for a 1 GHz Cortex-A8 is 11 clock cycles, while the

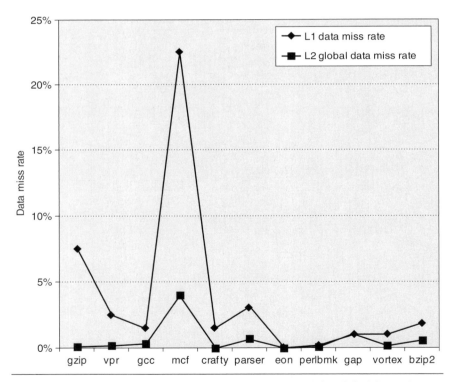

Figure 2.17 The data miss rate for ARM with a 32 KB L1 and the global data miss rate for a 1 MB L2 using the integer Minnespec benchmarks are significantly affected by the applications. Applications with larger memory footprints tend to have higher miss rates in both L1 and L2. Note that the L2 rate is the global miss rate, that is counting all references, including those that hit in L1. Mcf is known as a cache buster.

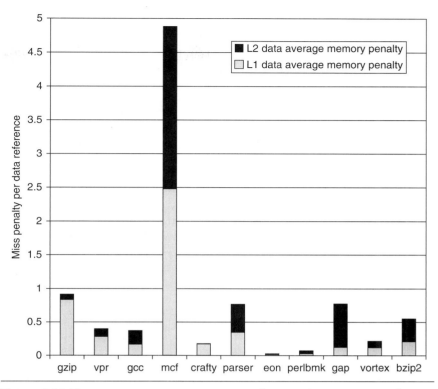

Figure 2.18 The average memory access penalty per data memory reference coming from L1 and L2 is shown for the ARM processor when running Minniespec. Although the miss rates for L1 are significantly higher, the L2 miss penalty, which is more than five times higher, means that the L2 misses can contribute significantly.

L2 miss penalty is 60 clock cycles, using DDR SDRAMs for the main memory. Using these miss penalties, Figure 2.18 shows the average penalty per data access. In the next chapter, we will examine the impact of the cache misses on overall CPI.

The Intel Core i7

The i7 supports the x86-64 instruction set architecture, a 64-bit extension of the 80x86 architecture. The i7 is an out-of-order execution processor that includes four cores. In this chapter, we focus on the memory system design and performance from the viewpoint of a single core. The system performance of multiprocessor designs, including the i7 multicore, is examined in detail in Chapter 5.

Each core in an i7 can execute up to four 80x86 instructions per clock cycle, using a multiple issue, dynamically scheduled, 16-stage pipeline, which we describe in detail in Chapter 3. The i7 can also support up to two simultaneous threads per processor, using a technique called simultaneous multithreading, described in Chapter 4. In 2010, the fastest i7 had a clock rate of 3.3 GHz, which yields a peak instruction execution rate of 13.2 billion instructions per second, or over 50 billion instructions per second for the four-core design.

The i7 can support up to three memory channels, each consisting of a separate set of DIMMs, and each of which can transfer in parallel. Using DDR3-1066 (DIMM PC8500), the i7 has a peak memory bandwith of just over 25 GB/sec.

i7 uses 48-bit virtual addresses and 36-bit physical addresses, yielding a maximum physical memory of 36 GB. Memory management is handled with a two-level TLB (see Appendix B, Section B.4), summarized in Figure 2.19.

Figure 2.20 summarizes the i7's three-level cache hierarchy. The first-level caches are virtually indexed and physically tagged (see Appendix B, Section B.3), while the L2 and L3 caches are physically indexed. Figure 2.21 is labeled with the

Characteristic	Instruction TLB	Data DLB	Second-level TLB
Size	128	64	512
Associativity	4-way	4-way	4-way
Replacement	Pseudo-LRU	Pseudo-LRU	Pseudo-LRU
Access latency	1 cycle	1 cycle	6 cycles
Miss	7 cycles	7 cycles	Hundreds of cycles to access page table

Figure 2.19 Characteristics of the i7's TLB structure, which has separate first-level instruction and data TLBs, both backed by a joint second-level TLB. The first-level TLBs support the standard 4 KB page size, as well as having a limited number of entries of large 2 to 4 MB pages; only 4 KB pages are supported in the second-level TLB.

Characteristic	L1	L2	L3
Size	32 KB I/32 KB D	256 KB	2 MB per core
Associativity	4-way I/8-way D	8-way	16-way
Access latency	4 cycles, pipelined	10 cycles	35 cycles
Replacement scheme	Pseudo-LRU	Pseudo-LRU	Pseudo-LRU but with an ordered selection algorihtm

Figure 2.20 Characteristics of the three-level cache hierarchy in the i7. All three caches use write-back and a block size of 64 bytes. The L1 and L2 caches are separate for each core, while the L3 cache is shared among the cores on a chip and is a total of 2 MB per core. All three caches are nonblocking and allow multiple outstanding writes. A merging write buffer is used for the L1 cache, which holds data in the event that the line is not present in L1 when it is written. (That is, an L1 write miss does not cause the line to be allocated.) L3 is inclusive of L1 and L2; we explore this property in further detail when we explain multiprocessor caches. Replacement is by a variant on pseudo-LRU; in the case of L3 the block replaced is always the lowest numbered way whose access bit is turned off. This is not quite random but is easy to compute.

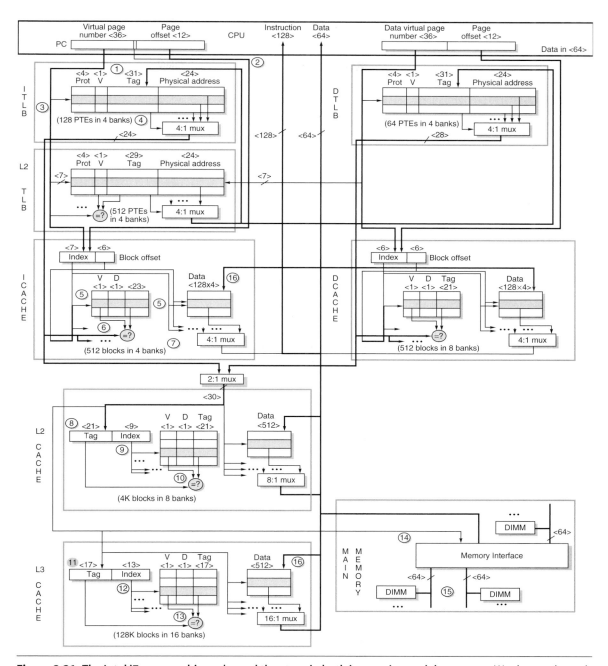

Figure 2.21 The Intel i7 memory hierarchy and the steps in both instruction and data access. We show only reads for data. Writes are similar, in that they begin with a read (since caches are write back). Misses are handled by simply placing the data in a write buffer, since the L1 cache is not write allocated.

steps of an access to the memory hierarchy. First, the PC is sent to the instruction cache. The instruction cache index is

$$2^{\text{Index}} = \frac{\text{Cache size}}{\text{Block size} \times \text{Set associativity}} = \frac{32\text{K}}{64 \times 4} = 128 = 2^7$$

or 7 bits. The page frame of the instruction's address (36 = 48 − 12 bits) is sent to the instruction TLB (step 1). At the same time the 7-bit index (plus an additional 2 bits from the block offset to select the appropriate 16 bytes, the instruction fetch amount) from the virtual address is sent to the instruction cache (step 2). Notice that for the four-way associative instruction cache, 13 bits are needed for the cache address: 7 bits to index the cache plus 6 bits of block offset for the 64-byte block, but the page size is 4 KB = 2^{12}, which means that 1 bit of the cache index must come from the virtual address. This use of 1 bit of virtual address means that the corresponding block could actually be in two different places in the cache, since the corresponding physical address could have either a 0 or 1 in this location. For instructions this does not pose a problem, since even if an instruction appeared in the cache in two different locations, the two versions must be the same. If such duplication, or aliasing, of data is allowed, the cache must be checked when the page map is changed, which is an infrequent event. Note that a very simple use of page coloring (see Appendix B, Section B.3) can eliminate the possibility of these aliases. If even-address virtual pages are mapped to even-address physical pages (and the same for odd pages), then these aliases can never occur because the low-order bit in the virtual and physical page number will be identical.

The instruction TLB is accessed to find a match between the address and a valid Page Table Entry (PTE) (steps 3 and 4). In addition to translating the address, the TLB checks to see if the PTE demands that this access result in an exception due to an access violation.

An instruction TLB miss first goes to the L2 TLB, which contains 512 PTEs of 4 KB page sizes and is four-way set associative. It takes two clock cycles to load the L1 TLB from the L2 TLB. If the L2 TLB misses, a hardware algorithm is used to walk the page table and update the TLB entry. In the worst case, the page is not in memory, and the operating system gets the page from disk. Since millions of instructions could execute during a page fault, the operating system will swap in another process if one is waiting to run. Otherwise, if there is no TLB exception, the instruction cache access continues.

The index field of the address is sent to all four banks of the instruction cache (step 5). The instruction cache tag is 36 − 7 bits (index) − 6 bits (block offset), or 23 bits. The four tags and valid bits are compared to the physical page frame from the instruction TLB (step 6). As the i7 expects 16 bytes each instruction fetch, an additional 2 bits are used from the 6-bit block offset to select the appropriate 16 bytes. Hence, 7 + 2 or 9 bits are used to send 16 bytes of instructions to the processor. The L1 cache is pipelined, and the latency of a hit is 4 clock cycles (step 7). A miss goes to the second-level cache.

As mentioned earlier, the instruction cache is virtually addressed and physically tagged. Because the second-level caches are physically addressed, the physical page address from the TLB is composed with the page offset to make an address to access the L2 cache. The L2 index is

$$2^{\text{Index}} = \frac{\text{Cache size}}{\text{Block size} \times \text{Set associativity}} = \frac{256\text{K}}{64 \times 8} = 512 = 2^9$$

so the 30-bit block address (36-bit physical address − 6-bit block offset) is divided into a 21-bit tag and a 9-bit index (step 8). Once again, the index and tag are sent to all eight banks of the unified L2 cache (step 9), which are compared in parallel. If one matches and is valid (step 10), it returns the block in sequential order after the initial 10-cycle latency at a rate of 8 bytes per clock cycle.

If the L2 cache misses, the L3 cache is accessed. For a four-core i7, which has an 8 MB L3, the index size is

$$2^{\text{Index}} = \frac{\text{Cache size}}{\text{Block size} \times \text{Set associativity}} = \frac{8M}{64 \times 16} = 8192 = 2^{13}$$

The 13-bit index (step 11) is sent to all 16 banks of the L3 (step 12). The L3 tag, which is $36 − (13 + 6) = 17$ bits, is compared against the physical address from the TLB (step 13). If a hit occurs, the block is returned after an initial latency at a rate of 16 bytes per clock and placed into both L1 and L3. If L3 misses, a memory access is initiated.

If the instruction is not found in the L3 cache, the on-chip memory controller must get the block from main memory. The i7 has three 64-bit memory channels that can act as one 192-bit channel, since there is only one memory controller and the same address is sent on both channels (step 14). Wide transfers happen when both channels have identical DIMMs. Each channel supports up to four DDR DIMMs (step 15). When the data return they are placed into L3 and L1 (step 16) because L3 is inclusive.

The total latency of the instruction miss that is serviced by main memory is approximately 35 processor cycles to determine that an L3 miss has occurred, plus the DRAM latency for the critical instructions. For a single-bank DDR1600 SDRAM and 3.3 GHz CPU, the DRAM latency is about 35 ns or 100 clock cycles to the first 16 bytes, leading to a total miss penalty of 135 clock cycles. The memory controller fills the remainder of the 64-byte cache block at a rate of 16 bytes per memory clock cycle, which takes another 15 ns or 45 clock cycles.

Since the second-level cache is a write-back cache, any miss can lead to an old block being written back to memory. The i7 has a 10-entry merging write buffer that writes back dirty cache lines when the next level in the cache is unused for a read. The write buffer is snooped by any miss to see if the cache line exists in the buffer; if so, the miss is filled from the buffer. A similar buffer is used between the L1 and L2 caches.

If this initial instruction is a load, the data address is sent to the data cache and data TLBs, acting very much like an instruction cache access with one key difference. The first-level data cache is eight-way set associative, meaning that the index is 6 bits (versus 7 for the instruction cache) and the address used to access the cache is the same as the page offset. Hence aliases in the data cache are not a worry.

Suppose the instruction is a store instead of a load. When the store issues, it does a data cache lookup just like a load. A miss causes the block to be placed in a write buffer, since the L1 cache does not allocate the block on a write miss. On a hit, the store does not update the L1 (or L2) cache until later, after it is known to be nonspeculative. During this time the store resides in a load-store queue, part of the out-of-order control mechanism of the processor.

The I7 also supports prefetching for L1 and L2 from the next level in the hierarchy. In most cases, the prefetched line is simply the next block in the cache. By prefetching only for L1 and L2, high-cost unnecessary fetches to memory are avoided.

Performance of the i7 Memory System

We evaluate the performance of the i7 cache structure using 19 of the SPECCPU2006 benchmarks (12 integer and 7 floating point), which were described in Chapter 1. The data in this section were collected by Professor Lu Peng and Ph.D. student Ying Zhang, both of Louisiana State University.

We begin with the L1 cache. The 32 KB, four-way set associative instruction cache leads to a very low instruction miss rate, especially because the instruction prefetch in the i7 is quite effective. Of course, how we evaluate the miss rate is a bit tricky, since the i7 does not generate individual requests for single instruction units, but instead prefetches 16 bytes of instruction data (between four and five instructions typically). If, for simplicity, we examine the instruction cache miss rate as if single instruction references were handled, then the L1 instruction cache miss rate varies from 0.1% to 1.8%, averaging just over 0.4%. This rate is in keeping with other studies of instruction cache behavior for the SPECCPU2006 benchmarks, which showed low instruction cache miss rates.

The L1 data cache is more interesting and even trickier to evaluate for three reasons:

1. Because the L1 data cache is not write allocated, writes can hit but never really miss, in the sense that a write that does not hit simply places its data in the write buffer and does not record as a miss.

2. Because speculation may sometimes be wrong (see Chapter 3 for an extensive discussion), there are references to the L1 data cache that do not correspond to loads or stores that eventually complete execution. How should such misses be treated?

3. Finally, the L1 data cache does automatic prefetching. Should prefetches that miss be counted, and, if so, how?

To address these issues, while keeping the amount of data reasonable, Figure 2.22 shows the L1 data cache misses in two ways: relative to the number of loads that actually complete (often called graduation or retirement) and relative to all the L1 data cache accesses from any source. As we can see, the miss rate when measured against only completed loads is 1.6 times higher (an average of 9.5% versus 5.9%). Figure 2.23 shows the same data in table form.

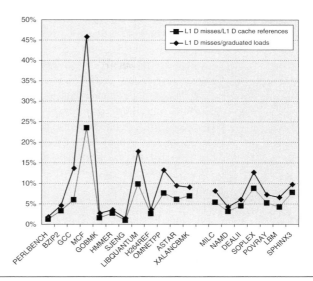

Figure 2.22 **The L1 data cache miss rate for 17 SPECCPU2006 benchmarks is shown in two ways: relative to the actual loads that complete execution successfully and relative to all the references to L1, which also includes prefetches, speculative loads that do not complete, and writes, which count as references, but do not generate misses.** These data, like the rest in this section, were collected by Professor Lu Peng and Ph.D. student Ying Zhang, both of Louisiana State University, based on earlier studies of the Intel Core Duo and other processors (see Peng et al. [2008]).

Benchmark	L1 data misses/ graduated loads	L1 data misses/ L1 data cache references
PERLBENCH	2%	1%
BZIP2	5%	3%
GCC	14%	6%
MCF	46%	24%
GOBMK	3%	2%
HMMER	4%	3%
SJENG	2%	1%
LIBQUANTUM	18%	10%
H264REF	4%	3%
OMNETPP	13%	8%
ASTAR	9%	6%
XALANCBMK	9%	7%
MILC	8%	5%
NAMD	4%	3%
DEALII	6%	5%
SOPLEX	13%	9%
POVRAY	7%	5%
LBM	7%	4%
SPHINX3	10%	8%

Figure 2.23 **The primary data cache misses are shown versus all loads that complete and all references (which includes speculative and prefetch requests).**

With L1 data cache miss rates running 5% to 10%, and sometimes higher, the importance of the L2 and L3 caches should be obvious. Figure 2.24 shows the miss rates of the L2 and L3 caches versus the number of L1 references (and Figure 2.25 shows the data in tabular form). Since the cost for a miss to memory is over 100 cycles and the average data miss rate in L2 is 4%, L3 is obviously critical. Without L3 and assuming about half the instructions are loads or stores, L2 cache misses could add two cycles per instruction to the CPI! In comparison, the average L3 data miss rate of 1% is still significant but four times lower than the L2 miss rate and six times less than the L1 miss rate. In the next chapter, we will examine the relationship between the i7 CPI and cache misses, as well as other pipeline effects.

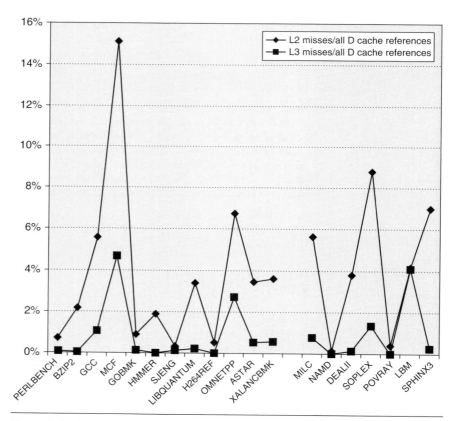

Figure 2.24 The L2 and L3 data cache miss rates for 17 SPECCPU2006 benchmarks are shown relative to all the references to L1, which also includes prefetches, speculative loads that do not complete, and program–generated loads and stores. These data, like the rest in this section, were collected by Professor Lu Peng and Ph.D. student Ying Zhang, both of Louisiana State University.

	L2 misses/all data cache references	L3 misses/all data cache references
PERLBENCH	1%	0%
BZIP2	2%	0%
GCC	6%	1%
MCF	15%	5%
GOBMK	1%	0%
HMMER	2%	0%
SJENG	0%	0%
LIBQUANTUM	3%	0%
H264REF	1%	0%
OMNETPP	7%	3%
ASTAR	3%	1%
XALANCBMK	4%	1%
MILC	6%	1%
NAMD	0%	0%
DEALII	4%	0%
SOPLEX	9%	1%
POVRAY	0%	0%
LBM	4%	4%
SPHINX3	7%	0%

Figure 2.25 The L2 and L3 miss rates shown in table form versus the number of data requests.

2.7   Fallacies and Pitfalls

As the most naturally quantitative of the computer architecture disciplines, memory hierarchy would seem to be less vulnerable to fallacies and pitfalls. Yet we were limited here not by lack of warnings, but by lack of space!

Fallacy   *Predicting cache performance of one program from another.*

Figure 2.26 shows the instruction miss rates and data miss rates for three programs from the SPEC2000 benchmark suite as cache size varies. Depending on the program, the data misses per thousand instructions for a 4096 KB cache are 9, 2, or 90, and the instruction misses per thousand instructions for a 4 KB cache are 55, 19, or 0.0004. Commercial programs such as databases will have significant miss rates even in large second-level caches, which is generally not the case for the SPEC programs. Clearly, generalizing cache performance from one program to another is unwise. As Figure 2.24 reminds us, there is a great deal of variation,

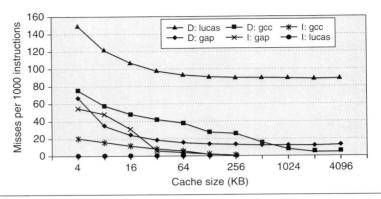

Figure 2.26 Instruction and data misses per 1000 instructions as cache size varies from 4 KB to 4096 KB. Instruction misses for gcc are 30,000 to 40,000 times larger than lucas, and, conversely, data misses for lucas are 2 to 60 times larger than gcc. The programs gap, gcc, and lucas are from the SPEC2000 benchmark suite.

and even predictions about the relative miss rates of integer and floating-point-intensive programs can be wrong as mcf and sphnix3 remind us!

Pitfall *Simulating enough instructions to get accurate performance measures of the memory hierarchy.*

There are really three pitfalls here. One is trying to predict performance of a large cache using a small trace. Another is that a program's locality behavior is not constant over the run of the entire program. The third is that a program's locality behavior may vary depending on the input.

Figure 2.27 shows the cumulative average instruction misses per thousand instructions for five inputs to a single SPEC2000 program. For these inputs, the average memory rate for the first 1.9 billion instructions is very different from the average miss rate for the rest of the execution.

Pitfall *Not delivering high memory bandwidth in a cache-based system.*

Caches help with average cache memory latency but may not deliver high memory bandwidth to an application that must go to main memory. The architect must design a high bandwidth memory behind the cache for such applications. We will revisit this pitfall in Chapters 4 and 5.

Pitfall *Implementing a virtual machine monitor on an instruction set architecture that wasn't designed to be virtualizable.*

Many architects in the 1970s and 1980s weren't careful to make sure that all instructions reading or writing information related to hardware resource information were privileged. This *laissez faire* attitude causes problems for VMMs

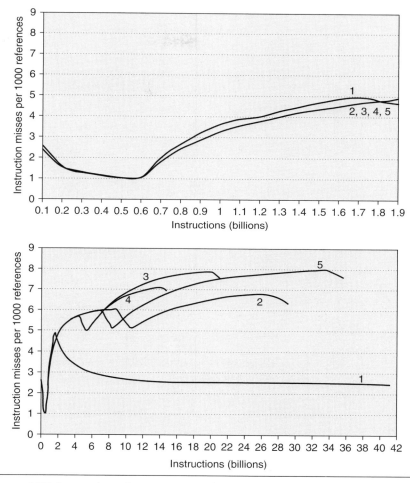

Figure 2.27 Instruction misses per 1000 references for five inputs to the perl benchmark from SPEC2000. There is little variation in misses and little difference between the five inputs for the first 1.9 billion instructions. Running to completion shows how misses vary over the life of the program and how they depend on the input. The top graph shows the running average misses for the first 1.9 billion instructions, which starts at about 2.5 and ends at about 4.7 misses per 1000 references for all five inputs. The bottom graph shows the running average misses to run to completion, which takes 16 to 41 billion instructions depending on the input. After the first 1.9 billion instructions, the misses per 1000 references vary from 2.4 to 7.9 depending on the input. The simulations were for the Alpha processor using separate L1 caches for instructions and data, each two-way 64 KB with LRU, and a unified 1 MB direct-mapped L2 cache.

for all of these architectures, including the 80x86, which we use here as an example.

Figure 2.28 describes the 18 instructions that cause problems for virtualization [Robin and Irvine 2000]. The two broad classes are instructions that

- Read control registers in user mode that reveal that the guest operating system is running in a virtual machine (such as POPF mentioned earlier)

- Check protection as required by the segmented architecture but assume that the operating system is running at the highest privilege level.

Virtual memory is also challenging. Because the 80x86 TLBs do not support process ID tags, as do most RISC architectures, it is more expensive for the VMM and guest OSes to share the TLB; each address space change typically requires a TLB flush.

Problem category	Problem 80x86 instructions
Access sensitive registers without trapping when running in user mode	Store global descriptor table register (SGDT) Store local descriptor table register (SLDT) Store interrupt descriptor table register (SIDT) Store machine status word (SMSW) Push flags (PUSHF, PUSHFD) Pop flags (POPF, POPFD)
When accessing virtual memory mechanisms in user mode, instructions fail the 80x86 protection checks	Load access rights from segment descriptor (LAR) Load segment limit from segment descriptor (LSL) Verify if segment descriptor is readable (VERR) Verify if segment descriptor is writable (VERW) Pop to segment register (POP CS, POP SS, …) Push segment register (PUSH CS, PUSH SS, …) Far call to different privilege level (CALL) Far return to different privilege level (RET) Far jump to different privilege level (JMP) Software interrupt (INT) Store segment selector register (STR) Move to/from segment registers (MOVE)

Figure 2.28 Summary of 18 80x86 instructions that cause problems for virtualization [Robin and Irvine 2000]. The first five instructions of the top group allow a program in user mode to read a control register, such as a descriptor table register, without causing a trap. The pop flags instruction modifies a control register with sensitive information but fails silently when in user mode. The protection checking of the segmented architecture of the 80x86 is the downfall of the bottom group, as each of these instructions checks the privilege level implicitly as part of instruction execution when reading a control register. The checking assumes that the OS must be at the highest privilege level, which is not the case for guest VMs. Only the MOVE to segment register tries to modify control state, and protection checking foils it as well.

Virtualizing I/O is also a challenge for the 80x86, in part because it both supports memory-mapped I/O and has separate I/O instructions, but more importantly because there are a very large number and variety of types of devices and device drivers of PCs for the VMM to handle. Third-party vendors supply their own drivers, and they may not properly virtualize. One solution for conventional VM implementations is to load real device drivers directly into the VMM.

To simplify implementations of VMMs on the 80x86, both AMD and Intel have proposed extensions to the architecture. Intel's VT-x provides a new execution mode for running VMs, a architected definition of the VM state, instructions to swap VMs rapidly, and a large set of parameters to select the circumstances where a VMM must be invoked. Altogether, VT-x adds 11 new instructions for the 80x86. AMD's Secure Virtual Machine (SVM) provides similar functionality.

After turning on the mode that enables VT-x support (via the new VMXON instruction), VT-x offers four privilege levels for the guest OS that are lower in priority than the original four (and fix issues like the problem with the POPF instruction mentioned earlier). VT-x captures all the states of a Virtual Machine in the Virtual Machine Control State (VMCS), and then provides atomic instructions to save and restore a VMCS. In addition to critical state, the VMCS includes configuration information to determine when to invoke the VMM and then specifically what caused the VMM to be invoked. To reduce the number of times the VMM must be invoked, this mode adds shadow versions of some sensitive registers and adds masks that check to see whether critical bits of a sensitive register will be changed before trapping. To reduce the cost of virtualizing virtual memory, AMD's SVM adds an additional level of indirection, called *nested page tables*. It makes shadow page tables unnecessary.

2.8   Concluding Remarks: Looking Ahead

Over the past thirty years there have been several predictions of the eminent [sic] cessation of the rate of improvement in computer performance. Every such prediction was wrong. They were wrong because they hinged on unstated assumptions that were overturned by subsequent events. So, for example, the failure to foresee the move from discrete components to integrated circuits led to a prediction that the speed of light would limit computer speeds to several orders of magnitude slower than they are now. Our prediction of the memory wall is probably wrong too but it suggests that we have to start thinking "out of the box."

Wm. A. Wulf and Sally A. McKee
Hitting the Memory Wall: Implications of the Obvious
Department of Computer Science, University of Virginia (December 1994)
This paper introduced the term *memory wall.*

The possibility of using a memory hierarchy dates back to the earliest days of general-purpose digital computers in the late 1940s and early 1950s. Virtual memory was introduced in research computers in the early 1960s and into IBM mainframes in the 1970s. Caches appeared around the same time. The basic concepts have been expanded and enhanced over time to help close the access time gap between main memory and processors, but the basic concepts remain.

One trend that could cause a significant change in the design of memory hierarchies is a continued slowdown in both density and access time of DRAMs. In the last decade, both these trends have been observed. While some increases in DRAM bandwidth have been achieved, decreases in access time have come much more slowly, partly because to limit power consumption voltage levels have been going down. One concept being explored to increase bandwidth is to have multiple overlapped accesses per bank. This provides an alternative to increasing the number of banks while allowing higher bandwidth. Manufacturing challenges to the conventional DRAM design that uses a capacitor in each cell, typically placed in a deep trench, have also led to slowdowns in the rate of increase in density. As this book was going to press, one manufacturer announced a new DRAM that does not require the capacitor, perhaps providing the opportunity for continued enhancement of DRAM technology.

Independently of improvements in DRAM, Flash memory is likely to play a larger role because of potential advantages in power and density. Of course, in PMDs, Flash has already replaced disk drives and offers advantages such as "instant on" that many desktop computers do not provide. Flash's potential advantage over DRAMs—the absence of a per-bit transistor to control writing—is also its Achilles heel. Flash must use bulk erase-rewrite cycles that are considerably slower. As a result, several PMDs, such as the Apple iPad, use a relatively small SDRAM main memory combined with Flash, which acts as both the file system and the page storage system to handle virtual memory.

In addition, several completely new approaches to memory are being explored. These include MRAMs, which use magnetic storage of data, and phase change RAMs (known as PCRAM, PCME, and PRAM), which use a glass that can be changed between amorphous and crystalline states. Both types of memories are nonvolatile and offer potentially higher densities than DRAMs. These are not new ideas; magnetoresistive memory technologies and phase change memories have been around for decades. Either technology may become an alternative to current Flash; replacing DRAM is a much tougher task. Although the improvements in DRAMs have slowed down, the possibility of a capacitor-free cell and other potential improvements make it hard to bet against DRAMs at least for the next decade.

For some years, a variety of predictions have been made about the coming memory wall (see quote and paper cited above), which would lead to fundamental decreases in processor performance. However, the extension of caches to multiple levels, more sophisticated refill and prefetch schemes, greater compiler and programmer awareness of the importance of locality, and the use of parallelism to hide what latency remains have helped keep the memory wall at bay. The introduction of out-of-order pipelines with multiple outstanding misses allowed available instruction-level parallelism to hide the memory latency remaining in a cache-based system. The introduction of multithreading and more thread-level parallelism took this a step further by providing more parallelism and hence more latency-hiding opportunities. It is likely that the use of instruction- and thread-level parallelism will be the primary tool to combat whatever memory delays are encountered in modern multilevel cache systems.

One idea that periodically arises is the use of programmer-controlled scratch-pad or other high-speed memories, which we will see are used in GPUs. Such ideas have never made the mainstream for several reasons: First, they break the memory model by introducing address spaces with different behavior. Second, unlike compiler-based or programmer-based cache optimizations (such as prefetching), memory transformations with scratchpads must completely handle the remapping from main memory address space to the scratchpad address space. This makes such transformations more difficult and limited in applicability. In GPUs (see Chapter 4), where local scratchpad memories are heavily used, the burden for managing them currently falls on the programmer.

Although one should be cautious about predicting the future of computing technology, history has shown that caching is a powerful and highly extensible idea that is likely to allow us to continue to build faster computers and ensure that the memory hierarchy can deliver the instructions and data needed to keep such systems working well.

2.9   Historical Perspective and References

In Section L.3 (available online) we examine the history of caches, virtual memory, and virtual machines. IBM plays a prominent role in the history of all three. References for further reading are included.

Case Studies and Exercises by Norman P. Jouppi, Naveen Muralimanohar, and Sheng Li

Case Study 1: Optimizing Cache Performance via Advanced Techniques

Concepts illustrated by this case study

- Non-blocking Caches
- Compiler Optimizations for Caches
- Software and Hardware Prefetching
- Calculating Impact of Cache Performance on More Complex Processors

The transpose of a matrix interchanges its rows and columns; this is illustrated below:

$$\begin{bmatrix} A11 & A12 & A13 & A14 \\ A21 & A22 & A23 & A24 \\ A31 & A32 & A33 & A34 \\ A41 & A42 & A43 & A44 \end{bmatrix} \Rightarrow \begin{bmatrix} A11 & A21 & A31 & A41 \\ A12 & A22 & A32 & A42 \\ A13 & A23 & A33 & A43 \\ A14 & A24 & A34 & A44 \end{bmatrix}$$

Here is a simple C loop to show the transpose:

```
for (i = 0; i < 3; i++) {
for (j = 0; j < 3; j++) {
output[j][i] = input[i][j];
}
}
```

Assume that both the input and output matrices are stored in the row major order (*row major order* means that the row index changes fastest). Assume that you are executing a 256 × 256 double-precision transpose on a processor with a 16 KB fully associative (don't worry about cache conflicts) least recently used (LRU) replacement L1 data cache with 64 byte blocks. Assume that the L1 cache misses or prefetches require 16 cycles and always hit in the L2 cache, and that the L2 cache can process a request every two processor cycles. Assume that each iteration of the inner loop above requires four cycles if the data are present in the L1 cache. Assume that the cache has a write-allocate fetch-on-write policy for write misses. Unrealistically, assume that writing back dirty cache blocks requires 0 cycles.

2.1 [10/15/15/12/20] <2.2> For the simple implementation given above, this execution order would be nonideal for the input matrix; however, applying a loop interchange optimization would create a nonideal order for the output matrix. Because loop interchange is not sufficient to improve its performance, it must be blocked instead.

a. [10] <2.2> What should be the minimum size of the cache to take advantage of blocked execution?

b. [15] <2.2> How do the relative number of misses in the blocked and unblocked versions compare in the minimum sized cache above?

c. [15] <2.2> Write code to perform a transpose with a block size parameter *B* which uses *B* × *B* blocks.

d. [12] <2.2> What is the minimum associativity required of the L1 cache for consistent performance independent of both arrays' position in memory?

e. [20] <2.2> Try out blocked and nonblocked 256 × 256 matrix transpositions on a computer. How closely do the results match your expectations based on what you know about the computer's memory system? Explain any discrepancies if possible.

2.2 [10] <2.2> Assume you are designing a hardware prefetcher for the *unblocked* matrix transposition code above. The simplest type of hardware prefetcher only prefetches sequential cache blocks after a miss. More complicated "non-unit stride" hardware prefetchers can analyze a miss reference stream and detect and prefetch non-unit strides. In contrast, software prefetching can determine non-unit strides as easily as it can determine unit strides. Assume prefetches write directly into the cache and that there is no "pollution" (overwriting data that must be used before the data that are prefetched). For best performance given a non-unit stride prefetcher, in the steady state of the inner loop how many prefetches must be outstanding at a given time?

2.3 [15/20] <2.2> With software prefetching it is important to be careful to have the prefetches occur in time for use but also to minimize the number of outstanding prefetches to live within the capabilities of the microarchitecture and minimize cache pollution. This is complicated by the fact that different processors have different capabilities and limitations.

a. [15] <2.2> Create a blocked version of the matrix transpose with software prefetching.

b. [20] <2.2> Estimate and compare the performance of the blocked and unblocked transpose codes both with and without software prefetching.

Case Study 2: Putting It All Together: Highly Parallel Memory Systems

Concept illustrated by this case study

■ Crosscutting Issues: The Design of Memory Hierarchies

The program in Figure 2.29 can be used to evaluate the behavior of a memory system. The key is having accurate timing and then having the program stride through memory to invoke different levels of the hierarchy. Figure 2.29 shows the code in C. The first part is a procedure that uses a standard utility to get an accurate measure of the user CPU time; this procedure may have to be changed to work on some systems. The second part is a nested loop to read and write memory at different strides and cache sizes. To get accurate cache timing, this code is repeated many times. The third part times the nested loop overhead only so that it can be subtracted from overall measured times to see how long the accesses were. The results are output in .csv file format to facilitate importing into spreadsheets. You may need to change CACHE_MAX depending on the question you are answering and the size of memory on the system you are measuring. Running the program in single-user mode or at least without other active applications will give more consistent results. The code in Figure 2.29 was derived from a program written by Andrea Dusseau at the University of California–Berkeley

```c
#include "stdafx.h"
#include <stdio.h>
#include <time.h>
#define ARRAY_MIN (1024) /* 1/4 smallest cache */
#define ARRAY_MAX (4096*4096) /* 1/4 largest cache */
int x[ARRAY_MAX]; /* array going to stride through */

double get_seconds() { /* routine to read time in seconds */
    __time64_t ltime;
    _time64( &ltime );
    return (double) ltime;
}
int label(int i) {/* generate text labels */
    if (i<1e3) printf("%1dB,",i);
    else if (i<1e6) printf("%1dK,",i/1024);
    else if (i<1e9) printf("%1dM,",i/1048576);
    else printf("%1dG,",i/1073741824);
    return 0;
}
int _tmain(int argc, _TCHAR* argv[]) {
int register nextstep, i, index, stride;
int csize;
double steps, tsteps;
double loadtime, lastsec, sec0, sec1, sec; /* timing variables */

/* Initialize output */
printf(" ,");
for (stride=1; stride <= ARRAY_MAX/2; stride=stride*2)
    label(stride*sizeof(int));
printf("\n");

/* Main loop for each configuration */
for (csize=ARRAY_MIN; csize <= ARRAY_MAX; csize=csize*2) {
    label(csize*sizeof(int)); /* print cache size this loop */
    for (stride=1; stride <= csize/2; stride=stride*2) {

        /* Lay out path of memory references in array */
        for (index=0; index < csize; index=index+stride)
            x[index] = index + stride; /* pointer to next */
        x[index-stride] = 0; /* loop back to beginning */

        /* Wait for timer to roll over */
        lastsec = get_seconds();
        sec0 = get_seconds(); while (sec0 == lastsec);

        /* Walk through path in array for twenty seconds */
        /* This gives 5% accuracy with second resolution */
        steps = 0.0; /* number of steps taken */
        nextstep = 0; /* start at beginning of path */
        sec0 = get_seconds(); /* start timer */
        { /* repeat until collect 20 seconds */
            (i=stride;i!=0;i=i-1) { /* keep samples same */
                nextstep = 0;
                do nextstep = x[nextstep]; /* dependency */
                while (nextstep != 0);
            }
            steps = steps + 1.0; /* count loop iterations */
            sec1 = get_seconds(); /* end timer */
        } while ((sec1 - sec0) < 20.0); /* collect 20 seconds */
        sec = sec1 - sec0;

        /* Repeat empty loop to loop subtract overhead */
        tsteps = 0.0; /* used to match no. while iterations */
        sec0 = get_seconds(); /* start timer */
        { /* repeat until same no. iterations as above */
            (i=stride;i!=0;i=i-1) { /* keep samples same */
                index = 0;
                do index = index + stride;
                while (index < csize);
            }
            tsteps = tsteps + 1.0;
            sec1 = get_seconds(); /* - overhead */
        } while (tsteps<steps); /* until = no. iterations */
        sec = sec - (sec1 - sec0);
        loadtime = (sec*1e9)/(steps*csize);
        /* write out results in .csv format for Excel */
        printf("%4.1f,", (loadtime<0.1) ? 0.1 : loadtime);
    }; /* end of inner for loop */
    printf("\n");
}; /* end of outer for loop */
return 0;
}
```

Figure 2.29 C program for evaluating memory system.

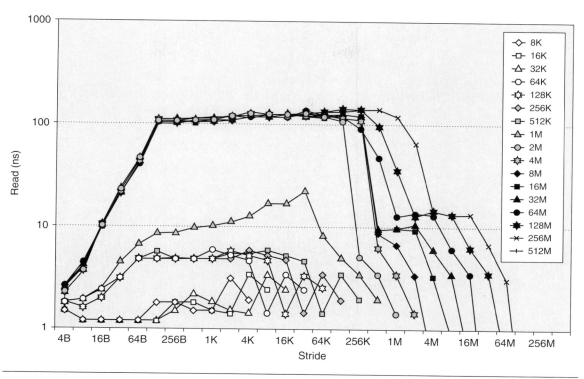

Figure 2.30 Sample results from program in Figure 2.29.

and was based on a detailed description found in Saavedra-Barrera [1992]. It has been modified to fix a number of issues with more modern machines and to run under Microsoft Visual C++. It can be downloaded from *www.hpl.hp.com/research/cacti/aca_ch2_cs2.c*.

The program above assumes that program addresses track physical addresses, which is true on the few machines that use virtually addressed caches, such as the Alpha 21264. In general, virtual addresses tend to follow physical addresses shortly after rebooting, so you may need to reboot the machine in order to get smooth lines in your results. To answer the questions below, assume that the sizes of all components of the memory hierarchy are powers of 2. Assume that the size of the page is much larger than the size of a block in a second-level cache (if there is one), and the size of a second-level cache block is greater than or equal to the size of a block in a first-level cache. An example of the output of the program is plotted in Figure 2.30; the key lists the size of the array that is exercised.

2.4   [12/12/12/10/12] <2.6> Using the sample program results in Figure 2.30:

a.   [12] <2.6> What are the overall size and block size of the second-level cache?

b.   [12] <2.6> What is the miss penalty of the second-level cache?

c. [12] <2.6> What is the associativity of the second-level cache?

d. [10] <2.6> What is the size of the main memory?

e. [12] <2.6> What is the paging time if the page size is 4 KB?

2.5 [12/15/15/20] <2.6> If necessary, modify the code in Figure 2.29 to measure the following system characteristics. Plot the experimental results with elapsed time on the *y*-axis and the memory stride on the *x*-axis. Use logarithmic scales for both axes, and draw a line for each cache size.

a. [12] <2.6> What is the system page size?

b. [15] <2.6> How many entries are there in the *translation lookaside buffer (TLB)*?

c. [15] <2.6> What is the miss penalty for the TLB?

d. [20] <2.6> What is the associativity of the TLB?

2.6 [20/20] <2.6> In multiprocessor memory systems, lower levels of the memory hierarchy may not be able to be saturated by a single processor but should be able to be saturated by multiple processors working together. Modify the code in Figure 2.29, and run multiple copies at the same time. Can you determine:

a. [20] <2.6> How many actual processors are in your computer system and how many system processors are just additional multithreaded contexts?

b. [20] <2.6> How many memory controllers does your system have?

2.7 [20] <2.6> Can you think of a way to test some of the characteristics of an instruction cache using a program? *Hint:* The compiler may generate a large number of non obvious instructions from a piece of code. Try to use simple arithmetic instructions of known length in your instruction set architecture (ISA).

Exercises

2.8 [12/12/15] <2.2> The following questions investigate the impact of small and simple caches using CACTI and assume a 65 nm (0.065 µm) technology. (CACTI is available in an online form at *http://quid.hpl.hp.com:9081/cacti/*.)

a. [12] <2.2> Compare the access times of 64 KB caches with 64 byte blocks and a single bank. What are the relative access times of two-way and four-way set associative caches in comparison to a direct mapped organization?

b. [12] <2.2> Compare the access times of four-way set associative caches with 64 byte blocks and a single bank. What are the relative access times of 32 KB and 64 KB caches in comparison to a 16 KB cache?

c. [15] <2.2> For a 64 KB cache, find the cache associativity between 1 and 8 with the lowest average memory access time given that misses per instruction for a certain workload suite is 0.00664 for direct mapped, 0.00366 for two-way set associative, 0.000987 for four-way set associative, and 0.000266 for eight-way set associative cache. Overall, there are 0.3 data references per instruction. Assume cache misses take 10 ns in all models. To calculate the hit time in cycles, assume the cycle time output using CACTI, which corresponds to the maximum frequency a cache can operate without any bubbles in the pipeline.

2.9   [12/15/15/10] <2.2> You are investigating the possible benefits of a way-predicting L1 cache. Assume that a 64 KB four-way set associative single-banked L1 data cache is the cycle time limiter in a system. As an alternative cache organization you are considering a way-predicted cache modeled as a 64 KB direct-mapped cache with 80% prediction accuracy. Unless stated otherwise, assume that a mispredicted way access that hits in the cache takes one more cycle. Assume the miss rates and the miss penalties in question 2.8 part (c).

a.   [12] <2.2> What is the average memory access time of the current cache (in cycles) versus the way-predicted cache?

b.   [15] <2.2> If all other components could operate with the faster way-predicted cache cycle time (including the main memory), what would be the impact on performance from using the way-predicted cache?

c.   [15] <2.2> Way-predicted caches have usually been used only for instruction caches that feed an instruction queue or buffer. Imagine that you want to try out way prediction on a data cache. Assume that you have 80% prediction accuracy and that subsequent operations (e.g., data cache access of other instructions, dependent operations) are issued assuming a correct way prediction. Thus, a way misprediction necessitates a pipe flush and replay trap, which requires 15 cycles. Is the change in average memory access time per load instruction with data cache way prediction positive or negative, and how much is it?

d.   [10] <2.2> As an alternative to way prediction, many large associative L2 caches serialize tag and data access, so that only the required dataset array needs to be activated. This saves power but increases the access time. Use CACTI's detailed Web interface for a 0.065 µm process 1 MB four-way set associative cache with 64 byte blocks, 144 bits read out, 1 bank, only 1 read/write port, 30 bit tags, and ITRS-HP technology with global wires. What is the ratio of the access times for serializing tag and data access in comparison to parallel access?

2.10   [10/12] <2.2> You have been asked to investigate the relative performance of a banked versus pipelined L1 data cache for a new microprocessor. Assume a 64 KB two-way set associative cache with 64 byte blocks. The pipelined cache would consist of three pipestages, similar in capacity to the Alpha 21264 data cache. A banked implementation would consist of two 32 KB two-way set associative banks. Use CACTI and assume a 65 nm (0.065 µm) technology to answer the following questions. The cycle time output in the Web version shows at what frequency a cache can operate without any bubbles in the pipeline.

a.   [10] <2.2> What is the cycle time of the cache in comparison to its access time, and how many pipestages will the cache take up (to two decimal places)?

b. [12] <2.2> Compare the area and total dynamic read energy per access of the pipelined design versus the banked design. State which takes up less area and which requires more power, and explain why that might be.

2.11 [12/15] <2.2> Consider the usage of critical word first and early restart on L2 cache misses. Assume a 1 MB L2 cache with 64 byte blocks and a refill path that is 16 bytes wide. Assume that the L2 can be written with 16 bytes every 4 processor cycles, the time to receive the first 16 byte block from the memory controller is 120 cycles, each additional 16 byte block from main memory requires 16 cycles, and data can be bypassed directly into the read port of the L2 cache. Ignore any cycles to transfer the miss request to the L2 cache and the requested data to the L1 cache.

a. [12] <2.2> How many cycles would it take to service an L2 cache miss with and without critical word first and early restart?

b. [15] <2.2> Do you think critical word first and early restart would be more important for L1 caches or L2 caches, and what factors would contribute to their relative importance?

2.12 [12/12] <2.2> You are designing a write buffer between a write-through L1 cache and a write-back L2 cache. The L2 cache write data bus is 16 B wide and can perform a write to an independent cache address every 4 processor cycles.

a. [12] <2.2> How many bytes wide should each write buffer entry be?

b. [15] <2.2> What speedup could be expected in the steady state by using a merging write buffer instead of a nonmerging buffer when zeroing memory by the execution of 64-bit stores if all other instructions could be issued in parallel with the stores and the blocks are present in the L2 cache?

c. [15] <2.2> What would the effect of possible L1 misses be on the number of required write buffer entries for systems with blocking and nonblocking caches?

2.13 [10/10/10] <2.3> Consider a desktop system with a processor connected to a 2 GB DRAM with *error-correcting code (ECC)*. Assume that there is only one memory channel of width 72 bits to 64 bits for data and 8 bits for ECC.

a. [10] <2.3> How many DRAM chips are on the DIMM if 1 GB DRAM chips are used, and how many data I/Os must each DRAM have if only one DRAM connects to each DIMM data pin?

b. [10] <2.3> What burst length is required to support 32 B L2 cache blocks?

c. [10] <2.3> Calculate the peak bandwidth for DDR2-667 and DDR2-533 DIMMs for reads from an active page excluding the ECC overhead.

2.14 [10/10] <2.3> A sample DDR2 SDRAM timing diagram is shown in Figure 2.31. tRCD is the time required to activate a row in a bank, and column address strobe (CAS) latency (CL) is the number of cycles required to read out a column in a row Assume that the RAM is on a standard DDR2 DIMM with ECC, having 72 data lines. Also assume burst lengths of 8 which read out 8 bits, or a total of 64 B from

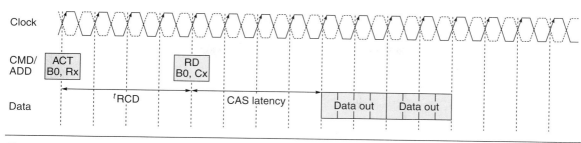

Figure 2.31 DDR2 SDRAM timing diagram.

the DIMM. Assume `tRCD = CAS (or CL) * clock_frequency`, and `clock_frequency = transfers_per_second/2`. The on-chip latency on a cache miss through levels 1 and 2 and back, not including the DRAM access, is 20 ns.

a. [10] <2.3> How much time is required from presentation of the activate command until the last requested bit of data from the DRAM transitions from valid to invalid for the DDR2-667 1 GB CL = 5 DIMM? Assume that for every request we automatically prefetch another adjacent cacheline in the same page.

b. [10] <2.3> What is the relative latency when using the DDR2-667 DIMM of a read requiring a bank activate versus one to an already open page, including the time required to process the miss inside the processor?

2.15 [15] <2.3> Assume that a DDR2-667 2 GB DIMM with CL = 5 is available for $130 and a DDR2-533 2 GB DIMM with CL = 4 is available for $100. Assume that two DIMMs are used in a system, and the rest of the system costs $800. Consider the performance of the system using the DDR2-667 and DDR2-533 DIMMs on a workload with 3.33 L2 misses per 1K instructions, and assume that 80% of all DRAM reads require an activate. What is the cost-performance of the entire system when using the different DIMMs, assuming only one L2 miss is outstanding at a time and an in-order core with a CPI of 1.5 not including L2 cache miss memory access time?

2.16 [12] <2.3> You are provisioning a server with eight-core 3 GHz CMP, which can execute a workload with an overall CPI of 2.0 (assuming that L2 cache miss refills are not delayed). The L2 cache line size is 32 bytes. Assuming the system uses DDR2-667 DIMMs, how many independent memory channels should be provided so the system is not limited by memory bandwidth if the bandwidth required is sometimes twice the average? The workloads incur, on an average, 6.67 L2 misses per 1K instructions.

2.17 [12/12] <2.3> A large amount (more than a third) of DRAM power can be due to page activation (see *http://download.micron.com/pdf/technotes/ddr2/TN4704.pdf* and *www.micron.com/systemcalc*). Assume you are building a system with 2 GB of memory using either 8-bank 2 GB x8 DDR2 DRAMs or 8-bank 1 GB x8 DRAMs, both with the same speed grade. Both use a page size of 1 KB, and the last level cacheline size is 64 bytes. Assume that DRAMs that are not active are in precharged standby and dissipate negligible power. Assume that the time to transition from standby to active is not significant.

a. [12] <2.3> Which type of DRAM would be expected to provide the higher system performance? Explain why.

b. [12] <2.3> How does a 2 GB DIMM made of 1 GB x8 DDR2 DRAMs compare against a DIMM with similar capacity made of 1 Gb x4 DDR2 DRAMs in terms of power?

2.18 [20/15/12] <2.3> To access data from a typical DRAM, we first have to activate the appropriate row. Assume that this brings an entire page of size 8 KB to the row buffer. Then we select a particular column from the row buffer. If subsequent accesses to DRAM are to the same page, then we can skip the activation step; otherwise, we have to close the current page and precharge the bitlines for the next activation. Another popular DRAM policy is to proactively close a page and precharge bitlines as soon as an access is over. Assume that every read or write to DRAM is of size 64 bytes and DDR bus latency (Data out in Figure 2.30) for sending 512 bits is Tddr.

a. [20] <2.3> Assuming DDR2-667, if it takes five cycles to precharge, five cycles to activate, and four cycles to read a column, for what value of the row buffer hit rate (r) will you choose one policy over another to get the best access time? Assume that every access to DRAM is separated by enough time to finish a random new access.

b. [15] <2.3> If 10% of the total accesses to DRAM happen back to back or contiguously without any time gap, how will your decision change?

c. [12] <2.3> Calculate the difference in average DRAM energy per access between the two policies using the row buffer hit rate calculated above. Assume that precharging requires 2 nJ and activation requires 4 nJ and that 100 pJ/bit are required to read or write from the row buffer.

2.19 [15] <2.3> Whenever a computer is idle, we can either put it in stand by (where DRAM is still active) or we can let it hibernate. Assume that, to hibernate, we have to copy just the contents of DRAM to a nonvolatile medium such as Flash. If reading or writing a cacheline of size 64 bytes to Flash requires 2.56 μJ and DRAM requires 0.5 nJ, and if idle power consumption for DRAM is 1.6 W (for 8 GB), how long should a system be idle to benefit from hibernating? Assume a main memory of size 8 GB.

2.20 [10/10/10/10/10] <2.4> Virtual Machines (VMs) have the potential for adding many beneficial capabilities to computer systems, such as improved total cost of ownership (TCO) or availability. Could VMs be used to provide the following capabilities? If so, how could they facilitate this?

a. [10] <2.4> Test applications in production environments using development machines?

b. [10] <2.4> Quick redeployment of applications in case of disaster or failure?

   c. [10] <2.4> Higher performance in I/O-intensive applications?

   d. [10] <2.4> Fault isolation between different applications, resulting in higher availability for services?

   e. [10] <2.4> Performing software maintenance on systems while applications are running without significant interruption?

2.21   [10/10/12/12] <2.4> Virtual machines can lose performance from a number of events, such as the execution of privileged instructions, TLB misses, traps, and I/O. These events are usually handled in system code. Thus, one way of estimating the slowdown when running under a VM is the percentage of application execution time in system versus user mode. For example, an application spending 10% of its execution in system mode might slow down by 60% when running on a VM. Figure 2.32 lists the early performance of various system calls under native execution, pure virtualization, and paravirtualization for LMbench using Xen on an Itanium system with times measured in microseconds (courtesy of Matthew Chapman of the University of New South Wales).

   a. [10] <2.4> What types of programs would be expected to have smaller slowdowns when running under VMs?

   b. [10] <2.4> If slowdowns were linear as a function of system time, given the slowdown above, how much slower would a program spending 20% of its execution in system time be expected to run?

   c. [12] <2.4> What is the median slowdown of the system calls in the table above under pure virtualization and paravirtualization?

   d. [12] <2.4> Which functions in the table above have the largest slowdowns? What do you think the cause of this could be?

Benchmark	Native	Pure	Para
Null call	0.04	0.96	0.50
Null I/O	0.27	6.32	2.91
Stat	1.10	10.69	4.14
Open/close	1.99	20.43	7.71
Install sighandler	0.33	7.34	2.89
Handle signal	1.69	19.26	2.36
Fork	56.00	513.00	164.00
Exec	316.00	2084.00	578.00
Fork + exec sh	1451.00	7790.00	2360.00

Figure 2.32 Early performance of various system calls under native execution, pure virtualization, and paravirtualization.

2.22   [12] <2.4> Popek and Goldberg's definition of a virtual machine said that it would be indistinguishable from a real machine except for its performance. In this question, we will use that definition to find out if we have access to native execution on a processor or are running on a virtual machine. The Intel VT-x technology effectively provides a second set of privilege levels for the use of the virtual machine. What would a virtual machine running on top of another virtual machine have to do, assuming VT-x technology?

2.23   [20/25] <2.4> With the adoption of virtualization support on the x86 architecture, virtual machines are actively evolving and becoming mainstream. Compare and contrast the Intel VT-x and AMD's AMD-V virtualization technologies. (Information on AMD-V can be found at *http://sites.amd.com/us/business/it-solutions/ virtualization/Pages/resources.aspx.*)

   a. [20] <2.4> Which one could provide higher performance for memory-intensive applications with large memory footprints?

   b. [25] <2.4> Information on AMD's IOMMU support for virtualized I/O can be found in *http://developer.amd.com/documentation/articles/pages/892006101.aspx.* What do Virtualization Technology and an input/output memory management unit (IOMMU) do to improve virtualized I/O performance?

2.24   [30] <2.2, 2.3> Since instruction-level parallelism can also be effectively exploited on in-order superscalar processors and *very long instruction word (VLIW)* processors with speculation, one important reason for building an out-of-order (OOO) superscalar processor is the ability to tolerate unpredictable memory latency caused by cache misses. Hence, you can think about hardware supporting OOO issue as being part of the memory system! Look at the floorplan of the Alpha 21264 in Figure 2.33 to find the relative area of the integer and floating-point issue queues and mappers versus the caches. The queues schedule instructions for issue, and the mappers rename register specifiers. Hence, these are necessary additions to support OOO issue. The 21264 only has L1 data and instruction caches on chip, and they are both 64 KB two-way set associative. Use an OOO superscalar simulator such as SimpleScalar (*www.cs.wisc.edu/~mscalar/ simplescalar.html*) on memory-intensive benchmarks to find out how much performance is lost if the area of the issue queues and mappers is used for additional L1 data cache area in an in-order superscalar processor, instead of OOO issue in a model of the 21264. Make sure the other aspects of the machine are as similar as possible to make the comparison fair. Ignore any increase in access or cycle time from larger caches and effects of the larger data cache on the floorplan of the chip. (Note that this comparison will not be totally fair, as the code will not have been scheduled for the in-order processor by the compiler.)

2.25   [20/20/20] <2.6> The Intel performance analyzer VTune can be used to make many measurements of cache behavior. A free evaluation version of VTune on both Windows and Linux can be downloaded from *http://software.intel.com/en-us/articles/intel-vtune-amplifier-xe/.* The program (`aca_ch2_cs2.c`) used in Case Study 2 has been modified so that it can work with VTune out of the box on Microsoft Visual C++. The program can be downloaded from *www.hpl.hp.com/*

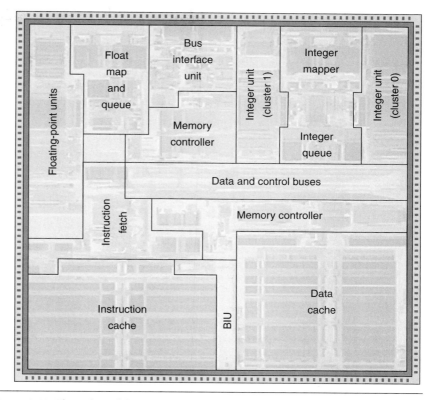

Figure 2.33 Floorplan of the Alpha 21264 [Kessler 1999].

research/cacti/aca_ch2_cs2_vtune.c. Special VTune functions have been inserted to exclude initialization and loop overhead during the performance analysis process. Detailed VTune setup directions are given in the README section in the program. The program keeps looping for 20 seconds for every configuration. In the following experiment you can find the effects of data size on cache and overall processor performance. Run the program in VTune on an Intel processor with the input dataset sizes of 8 KB, 128 KB, 4 MB, and 32 MB, and keep a stride of 64 bytes (stride one cache line on Intel i7 processors). Collect statistics on overall performance and L1 data cache, L2, and L3 cache performance.

a.   [20] <2.6> List the number of misses per 1K instruction of L1 data cache, L2, and L3 for each dataset size and your processor model and speed. Based on the results, what can you say about the L1 data cache, L2, and L3 cache sizes on your processor? Explain your observations.

b.   [20] <2.6> List the *instructions per clock* (IPC) for each dataset size and your processor model and speed. Based on the results, what can you say about the L1, L2, and L3 miss penalties on your processor? Explain your observations.

c. [20] <2.6> Run the program in VTune with input dataset size of 8 KB and 128 KB on an Intel OOO processor. List the number of L1 data cache and L2 cache misses per 1K instructions and the CPI for both configurations. What can you say about the effectiveness of memory latency hiding techniques in high-performance OOO processors? *Hint:* You need to find the L1 data cache miss latency for your processor. For recent Intel i7 processors, it is approximately 11 cycles.

3

Instruction-Level Parallelism and Its Exploitation

"Who's first?"

"America."

"Who's second?"

"Sir, there is no second."

Dialog between two observers of the sailing race later named "The America's Cup" and run every few years—the inspiration for John Cocke's naming of the IBM research processor as "America." This processor was the precursor to the RS/6000 series and the first superscalar microprocessor.

Instruction-Level Parallelism: Concepts and Challenges

All processors since about 1985 use pipelining to overlap the execution of instructions and improve performance. This potential overlap among instructions is called *instruction-level parallelism* (ILP), since the instructions can be evaluated in parallel. In this chapter and Appendix H, we look at a wide range of techniques for extending the basic pipelining concepts by increasing the amount of parallelism exploited among instructions.

This chapter is at a considerably more advanced level than the material on basic pipelining in Appendix C. If you are not thoroughly familiar with the ideas in Appendix C, you should review that appendix before venturing into this chapter.

We start this chapter by looking at the limitation imposed by data and control hazards and then turn to the topic of increasing the ability of the compiler and the processor to exploit parallelism. These sections introduce a large number of concepts, which we build on throughout this chapter and the next. While some of the more basic material in this chapter could be understood without all of the ideas in the first two sections, this basic material is important to later sections of this chapter.

There are two largely separable approaches to exploiting ILP: (1) an approach that relies on hardware to help discover and exploit the parallelism dynamically, and (2) an approach that relies on software technology to find parallelism statically at compile time. Processors using the dynamic, hardware-based approach, including the Intel Core series, dominate in the desktop and server markets. In the personal mobile device market, where energy efficiency is often the key objective, designers exploit lower levels of instruction-level parallelism. Thus, in 2011, most processors for the PMD market use static approaches, as we will see in the ARM Cortex-A8; however, future processors (e.g., the new ARM Cortex-A9) are using dynamic approaches. Aggressive compiler-based approaches have been attempted numerous times beginning in the 1980s and most recently in the Intel Itanium series. Despite enormous efforts, such approaches have not been successful outside of the narrow range of scientific applications.

In the past few years, many of the techniques developed for one approach have been exploited within a design relying primarily on the other. This chapter introduces the basic concepts and both approaches. A discussion of the limitations on ILP approaches is included in this chapter, and it was such limitations that directly led to the movement to multicore. Understanding the limitations remains important in balancing the use of ILP and thread-level parallelism.

In this section, we discuss features of both programs and processors that limit the amount of parallelism that can be exploited among instructions, as well as the critical mapping between program structure and hardware structure, which is key to understanding whether a program property will actually limit performance and under what circumstances.

The value of the CPI (cycles per instruction) for a pipelined processor is the sum of the base CPI and all contributions from stalls:

Pipeline CPI = Ideal pipeline CPI + Structural stalls + Data hazard stalls + Control stalls

Technique	Reduces	Section
Forwarding and bypassing	Potential data hazard stalls	C.2
Delayed branches and simple branch scheduling	Control hazard stalls	C.2
Basic compiler pipeline scheduling	Data hazard stalls	C.2, 3.2
Basic dynamic scheduling (scoreboarding)	Data hazard stalls from true dependences	C.7
Loop unrolling	Control hazard stalls	3.2
Branch prediction	Control stalls	3.3
Dynamic scheduling with renaming	Stalls from data hazards, output dependences, and antidependences	3.4
Hardware speculation	Data hazard and control hazard stalls	3.6
Dynamic memory disambiguation	Data hazard stalls with memory	3.6
Issuing multiple instructions per cycle	Ideal CPI	3.7, 3.8
Compiler dependence analysis, software pipelining, trace scheduling	Ideal CPI, data hazard stalls	H.2, H.3
Hardware support for compiler speculation	Ideal CPI, data hazard stalls, branch hazard stalls	H.4, H.5

Figure 3.1 The major techniques examined in Appendix C, Chapter 3, and Appendix H are shown together with the component of the CPI equation that the technique affects.

The *ideal pipeline CPI* is a measure of the maximum performance attainable by the implementation. By reducing each of the terms of the right-hand side, we decrease the overall pipeline CPI or, alternatively, increase the IPC (instructions per clock). The equation above allows us to characterize various techniques by what component of the overall CPI a technique reduces. Figure 3.1 shows the techniques we examine in this chapter and in Appendix H, as well as the topics covered in the introductory material in Appendix C. In this chapter, we will see that the techniques we introduce to decrease the ideal pipeline CPI can increase the importance of dealing with hazards.

What Is Instruction-Level Parallelism?

All the techniques in this chapter exploit parallelism among instructions. The amount of parallelism available within a *basic block*—a straight-line code sequence with no branches in except to the entry and no branches out except at the exit—is quite small. For typical MIPS programs, the average dynamic branch frequency is often between 15% and 25%, meaning that between three and six instructions execute between a pair of branches. Since these instructions are likely to depend upon one another, the amount of overlap we can exploit within a basic block is likely to be less than the average basic block size. To obtain substantial performance enhancements, we must exploit ILP across multiple basic blocks.

The simplest and most common way to increase the ILP is to exploit parallelism among iterations of a loop. This type of parallelism is often called *loop-level parallelism*. Here is a simple example of a loop that adds two 1000-element arrays and is completely parallel:

```
for (i=0; i<=999; i=i+1)
    x[i] = x[i] + y[i];
```

Every iteration of the loop can overlap with any other iteration, although within each loop iteration there is little or no opportunity for overlap.

We will examine a number of techniques for converting such loop-level parallelism into instruction-level parallelism. Basically, such techniques work by unrolling the loop either statically by the compiler (as in the next section) or dynamically by the hardware (as in Sections 3.5 and 3.6).

An important alternative method for exploiting loop-level parallelism is the use of SIMD in both vector processors and Graphics Processing Units (GPUs), both of which are covered in Chapter 4. A SIMD instruction exploits data-level parallelism by operating on a small to moderate number of data items in parallel (typically two to eight). A vector instruction exploits data-level parallelism by operating on many data items in parallel using both parallel execution units and a deep pipeline. For example, the above code sequence, which in simple form requires seven instructions per iteration (two loads, an add, a store, two address updates, and a branch) for a total of 7000 instructions, might execute in one-quarter as many instructions in some SIMD architecture where four data items are processed per instruction. On some vector processors, this sequence might take only four instructions: two instructions to load the vectors x and y from memory, one instruction to add the two vectors, and an instruction to store back the result vector. Of course, these instructions would be pipelined and have relatively long latencies, but these latencies may be overlapped.

Data Dependences and Hazards

Determining how one instruction depends on another is critical to determining how much parallelism exists in a program and how that parallelism can be exploited. In particular, to exploit instruction-level parallelism we must determine which instructions can be executed in parallel. If two instructions are *parallel*, they can execute simultaneously in a pipeline of arbitrary depth without causing any stalls, assuming the pipeline has sufficient resources (and hence no structural hazards exist). If two instructions are dependent, they are not parallel and must be executed in order, although they may often be partially overlapped. The key in both cases is to determine whether an instruction is dependent on another instruction.

Data Dependences

There are three different types of dependences: *data dependences* (also called true data dependences), *name dependences*, and *control dependences*. An instruction *j* is *data dependent* on instruction *i* if either of the following holds:

- Instruction *i* produces a result that may be used by instruction *j*.
- Instruction *j* is data dependent on instruction *k*, and instruction *k* is data dependent on instruction *i*.

The second condition simply states that one instruction is dependent on another if there exists a chain of dependences of the first type between the two instructions. This dependence chain can be as long as the entire program. Note that a dependence within a single instruction (such as ADDD R1,R1,R1) is not considered a dependence.

For example, consider the following MIPS code sequence that increments a vector of values in memory (starting at 0(R1) and with the last element at 8(R2)) by a scalar in register F2. (For simplicity, throughout this chapter, our examples ignore the effects of delayed branches.)

```
Loop:    L.D     F0,0(R1)        ;F0=array element
         ADD.D   F4,F0,F2        ;add scalar in F2
         S.D     F4,0(R1)        ;store result
         DADDUI  R1,R1,#-8       ;decrement pointer 8 bytes
         BNE     R1,R2,LOOP      ;branch R1!=R2
```

The data dependences in this code sequence involve both floating-point data:

```
Loop:    L.D     F0,0(R1)        ;F0=array element
         ADD.D   F4,F0,F2        ;add scalar in F2
         S.D     F4,0(R1)        ;store result
```

and integer data:

```
         DADDIU  R1,R1,#-8       ;decrement pointer
                                 ;8 bytes (per DW)
         BNE     R1,R2,Loop      ;branch R1!=R2
```

In both of the above dependent sequences, as shown by the arrows, each instruction depends on the previous one. The arrows here and in following examples show the order that must be preserved for correct execution. The arrow points from an instruction that must precede the instruction that the arrowhead points to.

If two instructions are data dependent, they must execute in order and cannot execute simultaneously or be completely overlapped. The dependence implies that there would be a chain of one or more data hazards between the two instructions. (See Appendix C for a brief description of data hazards, which we will define precisely in a few pages.) Executing the instructions simultaneously will cause a processor with pipeline interlocks (and a pipeline depth longer than the distance between the instructions in cycles) to detect a hazard and stall, thereby reducing or eliminating the overlap. In a processor without interlocks that relies on compiler scheduling, the compiler cannot schedule dependent instructions in such a way that they completely overlap, since the program will not execute correctly. The presence of a data dependence in an instruction sequence reflects a data dependence in the source code from which the instruction sequence was generated. The effect of the original data dependence must be preserved.

Dependences are a property of *programs*. Whether a given dependence results in an actual hazard being detected and whether that hazard actually causes a stall are properties of the *pipeline organization*. This difference is critical to understanding how instruction-level parallelism can be exploited.

A data dependence conveys three things: (1) the possibility of a hazard, (2) the order in which results must be calculated, and (3) an upper bound on how much parallelism can possibly be exploited. Such limits are explored in Section 3.10 and in Appendix H in more detail.

Since a data dependence can limit the amount of instruction-level parallelism we can exploit, a major focus of this chapter is overcoming these limitations. A dependence can be overcome in two different ways: (1) maintaining the dependence but avoiding a hazard, and (2) eliminating a dependence by transforming the code. Scheduling the code is the primary method used to avoid a hazard without altering a dependence, and such scheduling can be done both by the compiler and by the hardware.

A data value may flow between instructions either through registers or through memory locations. When the data flow occurs in a register, detecting the dependence is straightforward since the register names are fixed in the instructions, although it gets more complicated when branches intervene and correctness concerns force a compiler or hardware to be conservative.

Dependences that flow through memory locations are more difficult to detect, since two addresses may refer to the same location but look different: For example, 100(R4) and 20(R6) may be identical memory addresses. In addition, the effective address of a load or store may change from one execution of the instruction to another (so that 20(R4) and 20(R4) may be different), further complicating the detection of a dependence.

In this chapter, we examine hardware for detecting data dependences that involve memory locations, but we will see that these techniques also have limitations. The compiler techniques for detecting such dependences are critical in uncovering loop-level parallelism.

Name Dependences

The second type of dependence is a *name dependence*. A name dependence occurs when two instructions use the same register or memory location, called a *name*, but there is no flow of data between the instructions associated with that name. There are two types of name dependences between an instruction *i* that *precedes* instruction *j* in program order:

1. An *antidependence* between instruction *i* and instruction *j* occurs when instruction *j* writes a register or memory location that instruction *i* reads. The original ordering must be preserved to ensure that *i* reads the correct value. In the example on page 151, there is an antidependence between S.D and DADDIU on register R1.

2. An *output dependence* occurs when instruction *i* and instruction *j* write the same register or memory location. The ordering between the instructions

must be preserved to ensure that the value finally written corresponds to instruction *j*.

Both antidependences and output dependences are name dependences, as opposed to true data dependences, since there is no value being transmitted between the instructions. Because a name dependence is not a true dependence, instructions involved in a name dependence can execute simultaneously or be reordered, if the name (register number or memory location) used in the instructions is changed so the instructions do not conflict.

This renaming can be more easily done for register operands, where it is called *register renaming*. Register renaming can be done either statically by a compiler or dynamically by the hardware. Before describing dependences arising from branches, let's examine the relationship between dependences and pipeline data hazards.

Data Hazards

A hazard exists whenever there is a name or data dependence between instructions, and they are close enough that the overlap during execution would change the order of access to the operand involved in the dependence. Because of the dependence, we must preserve what is called *program order*—that is, the order that the instructions would execute in if executed sequentially one at a time as determined by the original source program. The goal of both our software and hardware techniques is to exploit parallelism by preserving program order *only where it affects the outcome of the program.* Detecting and avoiding hazards ensures that necessary program order is preserved.

Data hazards, which are informally described in Appendix C, may be classified as one of three types, depending on the order of read and write accesses in the instructions. By convention, the hazards are named by the ordering in the program that must be preserved by the pipeline. Consider two instructions *i* and *j*, with *i* preceding *j* in program order. The possible data hazards are

- RAW *(read after write)*—*j* tries to read a source before *i* writes it, so *j* incorrectly gets the *old* value. This hazard is the most common type and corresponds to a true data dependence. Program order must be preserved to ensure that *j* receives the value from *i*.

- WAW *(write after write)*—*j* tries to write an operand before it is written by *i*. The writes end up being performed in the wrong order, leaving the value written by *i* rather than the value written by *j* in the destination. This hazard corresponds to an output dependence. WAW hazards are present only in pipelines that write in more than one pipe stage or allow an instruction to proceed even when a previous instruction is stalled.

- WAR *(write after read)*—*j* tries to write a destination before it is read by *i*, so *i* incorrectly gets the *new* value. This hazard arises from an antidependence (or name dependence). WAR hazards cannot occur in most static issue pipelines— even deeper pipelines or floating-point pipelines—because all reads are early (in ID in the pipeline in Appendix C) and all writes are late (in WB in the pipeline in Appendix C). A WAR hazard occurs either when there are some instructions that write results early in the instruction pipeline *and* other instructions that read a source late in the pipeline, or when instructions are reordered, as we will see in this chapter.

Note that the RAR *(read after read)* case is not a hazard.

Control Dependences

The last type of dependence is a *control dependence.* A control dependence determines the ordering of an instruction, *i,* with respect to a branch instruction so that instruction *i* is executed in correct program order and only when it should be. Every instruction, except for those in the first basic block of the program, is control dependent on some set of branches, and, in general, these control dependences must be preserved to preserve program order. One of the simplest examples of a control dependence is the dependence of the statements in the "then" part of an if statement on the branch. For example, in the code segment

```
if p1 {
      S1;
};
if p2 {
      S2;
}
```

S1 is control dependent on p1, and S2 is control dependent on p2 but not on p1. In general, two constraints are imposed by control dependences:

1. An instruction that is control dependent on a branch cannot be moved *before* the branch so that its execution *is no longer controlled* by the branch. For example, we cannot take an instruction from the then portion of an if statement and move it before the if statement.

2. An instruction that is not control dependent on a branch cannot be moved *after* the branch so that its execution *is controlled* by the branch. For example, we cannot take a statement before the if statement and move it into the then portion.

When processors preserve strict program order, they ensure that control dependences are also preserved. We may be willing to execute instructions that should not have been executed, however, thereby violating the control dependences, *if* we can do so without affecting the correctness of the program. Thus, control dependence is not the critical property that must be preserved. Instead, the two properties critical to program correctness—and normally preserved by maintaining both data and control dependences—are the *exception behavior* and the *data flow.*

Preserving the exception behavior means that any changes in the ordering of instruction execution must not change how exceptions are raised in the program.

Often this is relaxed to mean that the reordering of instruction execution must not cause any new exceptions in the program. A simple example shows how maintaining the control and data dependences can prevent such situations. Consider this code sequence:

```
        DADDU   R2,R3,R4
        BEQZ    R2,L1
        LW      R1,0(R2)
L1:
```

In this case, it is easy to see that if we do not maintain the data dependence involving R2, we can change the result of the program. Less obvious is the fact that if we ignore the control dependence and move the load instruction before the branch, the load instruction may cause a memory protection exception. Notice that *no data dependence* prevents us from interchanging the BEQZ and the LW; it is only the control dependence. To allow us to reorder these instructions (and still preserve the data dependence), we would like to just ignore the exception when the branch is taken. In Section 3.6, we will look at a hardware technique, *speculation*, which allows us to overcome this exception problem. Appendix H looks at software techniques for supporting speculation.

The second property preserved by maintenance of data dependences and control dependences is the data flow. The *data flow* is the actual flow of data values among instructions that produce results and those that consume them. Branches make the data flow dynamic, since they allow the source of data for a given instruction to come from many points. Put another way, it is insufficient to just maintain data dependences because an instruction may be data dependent on more than one predecessor. Program order is what determines which predecessor will actually deliver a data value to an instruction. Program order is ensured by maintaining the control dependences.

For example, consider the following code fragment:

```
        DADDU   R1,R2,R3
        BEQZ    R4,L
        DSUBU   R1,R5,R6
L:      ...

        OR      R7,R1,R8
```

In this example, the value of R1 used by the OR instruction depends on whether the branch is taken or not. Data dependence alone is not sufficient to preserve correctness. The OR instruction is data dependent on both the DADDU and DSUBU instructions, but preserving that order alone is insufficient for correct execution.

Instead, when the instructions execute, the data flow must be preserved: If the branch is not taken, then the value of R1 computed by the DSUBU should be used by the OR, and, if the branch is taken, the value of R1 computed by the DADDU should be used by the OR. By preserving the control dependence of the OR on the branch, we prevent an illegal change to the data flow. For similar reasons, the DSUBU instruction cannot be moved above the branch. Speculation, which helps with the exception problem, will also allow us to lessen the impact of the control dependence while still maintaining the data flow, as we will see in Section 3.6.

Sometimes we can determine that violating the control dependence cannot affect either the exception behavior or the data flow. Consider the following code sequence:

```
        DADDU    R1,R2,R3
        BEQZ     R12,skip
        DSUBU    R4,R5,R6
        DADDU    R5,R4,R9
skip:   OR       R7,R8,R9
```

Suppose we knew that the register destination of the DSUBU instruction (R4) was unused after the instruction labeled skip. (The property of whether a value will be used by an upcoming instruction is called *liveness.*) If R4 were unused, then changing the value of R4 just before the branch would not affect the data flow since R4 would be *dead* (rather than live) in the code region after skip. Thus, if R4 were dead and the existing DSUBU instruction could not generate an exception (other than those from which the processor resumes the same process), we could move the DSUBU instruction before the branch, since the data flow cannot be affected by this change.

If the branch is taken, the DSUBU instruction will execute and will be useless, but it will not affect the program results. This type of code scheduling is also a form of speculation, often called software speculation, since the compiler is betting on the branch outcome; in this case, the bet is that the branch is usually not taken. More ambitious compiler speculation mechanisms are discussed in Appendix H. Normally, it will be clear when we say speculation or speculative whether the mechanism is a hardware or software mechanism; when it is not clear, it is best to say "hardware speculation" or "software speculation."

Control dependence is preserved by implementing control hazard detection that causes control stalls. Control stalls can be eliminated or reduced by a variety of hardware and software techniques, which we examine in Section 3.3.

3.2 Basic Compiler Techniques for Exposing ILP

This section examines the use of simple compiler technology to enhance a processor's ability to exploit ILP. These techniques are crucial for processors that use static issue or static scheduling. Armed with this compiler technology, we will shortly examine the design and performance of processors using static issuing. Appendix H will investigate more sophisticated compiler and associated hardware schemes designed to enable a processor to exploit more instruction-level parallelism.

Basic Pipeline Scheduling and Loop Unrolling

To keep a pipeline full, parallelism among instructions must be exploited by finding sequences of unrelated instructions that can be overlapped in the pipeline. To avoid a pipeline stall, the execution of a dependent instruction must be separated from the source instruction by a distance in clock cycles equal to the pipeline latency of that source instruction. A compiler's ability to perform this scheduling depends both on the amount of ILP available in the program and on the latencies of the functional units in the pipeline. Figure 3.2 shows the FP unit latencies we assume in this chapter, unless different latencies are explicitly stated. We assume the standard five-stage integer pipeline, so that branches have a delay of one clock cycle. We assume that the functional units are fully pipelined or replicated (as many times as the pipeline depth), so that an operation of any type can be issued on every clock cycle and there are no structural hazards.

In this subsection, we look at how the compiler can increase the amount of available ILP by transforming loops. This example serves both to illustrate an important technique as well as to motivate the more powerful program transformations described in Appendix H. We will rely on the following code segment, which adds a scalar to a vector:

```
for (i=999; i>=0; i=i-1)
    x[i] = x[i] + s;
```

We can see that this loop is parallel by noticing that the body of each iteration is independent. We formalize this notion in Appendix H and describe how we can test whether loop iterations are independent at compile time. First, let's look at the performance of this loop, showing how we can use the parallelism to improve its performance for a MIPS pipeline with the latencies shown above.

The first step is to translate the above segment to MIPS assembly language. In the following code segment, R1 is initially the address of the element in the array with the highest address, and F2 contains the scalar value s. Register R2 is precomputed, so that 8(R2) is the address of the last element to operate on.

Instruction producing result	Instruction using result	Latency in clock cycles
FP ALU op	Another FP ALU op	3
FP ALU op	Store double	2
Load double	FP ALU op	1
Load double	Store double	0

Figure 3.2 Latencies of FP operations used in this chapter. The last column is the number of intervening clock cycles needed to avoid a stall. These numbers are similar to the average latencies we would see on an FP unit. The latency of a floating-point load to a store is 0, since the result of the load can be bypassed without stalling the store. We will continue to assume an integer load latency of 1 and an integer ALU operation latency of 0.

The straightforward MIPS code, not scheduled for the pipeline, looks like this:

```
Loop:   L.D       F0,0(R1)      ;F0=array element
        ADD.D     F4,F0,F2      ;add scalar in F2
        S.D       F4,0(R1)      ;store result
        DADDUI    R1,R1,#-8     ;decrement pointer
                                ;8 bytes (per DW)
        BNE       R1,R2,Loop    ;branch R1!=R2
```

Let's start by seeing how well this loop will run when it is scheduled on a simple pipeline for MIPS with the latencies from Figure 3.2.

Example   Show how the loop would look on MIPS, both scheduled and unscheduled, including any stalls or idle clock cycles. Schedule for delays from floating-point operations, but remember that we are ignoring delayed branches.

Answer   Without any scheduling, the loop will execute as follows, taking nine cycles:

Clock cycle issued

```
Loop:   L.D       F0,0(R1)        1
        stall                     2
        ADD.D     F4,F0,F2        3
        stall                     4
        stall                     5
        S.D       F4,0(R1)        6
        DADDUI    R1,R1,#-8       7
        stall                     8
        BNE       R1,R2,Loop      9
```

We can schedule the loop to obtain only two stalls and reduce the time to seven cycles:

```
Loop:   L.D       F0,0(R1)
        DADDUI    R1,R1,#-8
        ADD.D     F4,F0,F2
        stall
        stall
        S.D       F4,8(R1)
        BNE       R1,R2,Loop
```

The stalls after ADD.D are for use by the S.D.

In the previous example, we complete one loop iteration and store back one array element every seven clock cycles, but the actual work of operating on the array element takes just three (the load, add, and store) of those seven clock cycles. The remaining four clock cycles consist of loop overhead—the DADDUI and BNE—and two stalls. To eliminate these four clock cycles we need to get more operations relative to the number of overhead instructions.

A simple scheme for increasing the number of instructions relative to the branch and overhead instructions is *loop unrolling*. Unrolling simply replicates the loop body multiple times, adjusting the loop termination code.

Loop unrolling can also be used to improve scheduling. Because it eliminates the branch, it allows instructions from different iterations to be scheduled together. In this case, we can eliminate the data use stalls by creating additional independent instructions within the loop body. If we simply replicated the instructions when we unrolled the loop, the resulting use of the same registers could prevent us from effectively scheduling the loop. Thus, we will want to use different registers for each iteration, increasing the required number of registers.

Example   Show our loop unrolled so that there are four copies of the loop body, assuming R1 − R2 (that is, the size of the array) is initially a multiple of 32, which means that the number of loop iterations is a multiple of 4. Eliminate any obviously redundant computations and do not reuse any of the registers.

Answer   Here is the result after merging the DADDUI instructions and dropping the unnecessary BNE operations that are duplicated during unrolling. Note that R2 must now be set so that 32(R2) is the starting address of the last four elements.

```
Loop:   L.D       F0,0(R1)
        ADD.D     F4,F0,F2
        S.D       F4,0(R1)        ;drop DADDUI & BNE
        L.D       F6,-8(R1)
        ADD.D     F8,F6,F2
        S.D       F8,-8(R1)       ;drop DADDUI & BNE
        L.D       F10,-16(R1)
        ADD.D     F12,F10,F2
        S.D       F12,-16(R1)     ;drop DADDUI & BNE
        L.D       F14,-24(R1)
        ADD.D     F16,F14,F2
        S.D       F16,-24(R1)
        DADDUI    R1,R1,#-32
        BNE       R1,R2,Loop
```

We have eliminated three branches and three decrements of R1. The addresses on the loads and stores have been compensated to allow the DADDUI instructions on R1 to be merged. This optimization may seem trivial, but it is not; it requires symbolic substitution and simplification. Symbolic substitution and simplification will rearrange expressions so as to allow constants to be collapsed, allowing an expression such as $((i + 1) + 1)$ to be rewritten as $(i + (1 + 1))$ and then simplified to $(i + 2)$. We will see more general forms of these optimizations that eliminate dependent computations in Appendix H.

Without scheduling, every operation in the unrolled loop is followed by a dependent operation and thus will cause a stall. This loop will run in 27 clock cycles—each LD has 1 stall, each ADDD 2, the DADDUI 1, plus 14 instruction issue cycles—or 6.75 clock cycles for each of the four elements, but it can be scheduled to improve performance significantly. Loop unrolling is normally done early in the compilation process, so that redundant computations can be exposed and eliminated by the optimizer.

In real programs we do not usually know the upper bound on the loop. Suppose it is *n*, and we would like to unroll the loop to make *k* copies of the body. Instead of a single unrolled loop, we generate a pair of consecutive loops. The first executes (*n* mod *k*) times and has a body that is the original loop. The second is the unrolled body surrounded by an outer loop that iterates (*n/k*) times. (As we shall see in Chapter 4, this technique is similar to a technique called *strip mining*, used in compilers for vector processors.) For large values of *n*, most of the execution time will be spent in the unrolled loop body.

In the previous example, unrolling improves the performance of this loop by eliminating overhead instructions, although it increases code size substantially. How will the unrolled loop perform when it is scheduled for the pipeline described earlier?

Example   Show the unrolled loop in the previous example after it has been scheduled for the pipeline with the latencies from Figure 3.2.

Answer
```
Loop:   L.D      F0,0(R1)
        L.D      F6,-8(R1)
        L.D      F10,-16(R1)
        L.D      F14,-24(R1)
        ADD.D    F4,F0,F2
        ADD.D    F8,F6,F2
        ADD.D    F12,F10,F2
        ADD.D    F16,F14,F2
        S.D      F4,0(R1)
        S.D      F8,-8(R1)
        DADDUI   R1,R1,#-32
        S.D      F12,16(R1)
        S.D      F16,8(R1)
        BNE      R1,R2,Loop
```

The execution time of the unrolled loop has dropped to a total of 14 clock cycles, or 3.5 clock cycles per element, compared with 9 cycles per element before any unrolling or scheduling and 7 cycles when scheduled but not unrolled.

The gain from scheduling on the unrolled loop is even larger than on the original loop. This increase arises because unrolling the loop exposes more computation that can be scheduled to minimize the stalls; the code above has no stalls. Scheduling the loop in this fashion necessitates realizing that the loads and stores are independent and can be interchanged.

Summary of the Loop Unrolling and Scheduling

Throughout this chapter and Appendix H, we will look at a variety of hardware and software techniques that allow us to take advantage of instruction-level parallelism to fully utilize the potential of the functional units in a processor. The key to most of these techniques is to know when and how the ordering among instructions may be changed. In our example we made many such changes, which to us, as human beings, were obviously allowable. In practice, this process must be performed in a methodical fashion either by a compiler or by hardware. To obtain the final unrolled code we had to make the following decisions and transformations:

- Determine that unrolling the loop would be useful by finding that the loop iterations were independent, except for the loop maintenance code.

- Use different registers to avoid unnecessary constraints that would be forced by using the same registers for different computations (e.g., name dependences).

- Eliminate the extra test and branch instructions and adjust the loop termination and iteration code.

- Determine that the loads and stores in the unrolled loop can be interchanged by observing that the loads and stores from different iterations are independent. This transformation requires analyzing the memory addresses and finding that they do not refer to the same address.

- Schedule the code, preserving any dependences needed to yield the same result as the original code.

The key requirement underlying all of these transformations is an understanding of how one instruction depends on another and how the instructions can be changed or reordered given the dependences.

Three different effects limit the gains from loop unrolling: (1) a decrease in the amount of overhead amortized with each unroll, (2) code size limitations, and (3) compiler limitations. Let's consider the question of loop overhead first. When we unrolled the loop four times, it generated sufficient parallelism among the instructions that the loop could be scheduled with no stall cycles. In fact, in 14 clock cycles, only 2 cycles were loop overhead: the DADDUI, which maintains the index value, and the BNE, which terminates the loop. If the loop is unrolled eight times, the overhead is reduced from 1/2 cycle per original iteration to 1/4.

A second limit to unrolling is the growth in code size that results. For larger loops, the code size growth may be a concern particularly if it causes an increase in the instruction cache miss rate.

Another factor often more important than code size is the potential shortfall in registers that is created by aggressive unrolling and scheduling. This secondary effect that results from instruction scheduling in large code segments is called *register pressure*. It arises because scheduling code to increase ILP causes the number of live values to increase. After aggressive instruction scheduling, it may not be possible to allocate all the live values to registers. The transformed code, while theoretically faster, may lose some or all of its advantage because it generates a shortage of registers. Without unrolling, aggressive scheduling is sufficiently limited by branches so that register pressure is rarely a problem. The combination of unrolling and aggressive scheduling can, however, cause this problem. The problem becomes especially challenging in multiple-issue processors that require the exposure of more independent instruction sequences whose execution can be overlapped. In general, the use of sophisticated high-level transformations, whose potential improvements are difficult to measure before detailed code generation, has led to significant increases in the complexity of modern compilers.

Loop unrolling is a simple but useful method for increasing the size of straight-line code fragments that can be scheduled effectively. This transformation is useful in a variety of processors, from simple pipelines like those we have examined so far to the multiple-issue superscalars and VLIWs explored later in this chapter.

3.3 Reducing Branch Costs with Advanced Branch Prediction

Because of the need to enforce control dependences through branch hazards and stalls, branches will hurt pipeline performance. Loop unrolling is one way to reduce the number of branch hazards; we can also reduce the performance losses of branches by predicting how they will behave. In Appendix C, we examine simple branch predictors that rely either on compile-time information or on the observed dynamic behavior of a branch in isolation. As the number of instructions in flight has increased, the importance of more accurate branch prediction has grown. In this section, we examine techniques for improving dynamic prediction accuracy.

Correlating Branch Predictors

The 2-bit predictor schemes use only the recent behavior of a single branch to predict the future behavior of that branch. It may be possible to improve the prediction accuracy if we also look at the recent behavior of *other* branches rather than just the branch we are trying to predict. Consider a small code fragment from the eqntott benchmark, a member of early SPEC benchmark suites that displayed particularly bad branch prediction behavior:

```
if (aa==2)
        aa=0;
if (bb==2)
        bb=0;
if (aa!=bb) {
```

Here is the MIPS code that we would typically generate for this code fragment assuming that aa and bb are assigned to registers R1 and R2:

```
            DADDIU    R3,R1,#-2
            BNEZ      R3,L1           ;branch b1    (aa!=2)
            DADD      R1,R0,R0        ;aa=0
    L1:     DADDIU    R3,R2,#-2
            BNEZ      R3,L2           ;branch b2    (bb!=2)
            DADD      R2,R0,R0        ;bb=0
    L2:     DSUBU     R3,R1,R2        ;R3=aa-bb
            BEQZ      R3,L3           ;branch b3    (aa==bb)
```

Let's label these branches b1, b2, and b3. The key observation is that the behavior of branch b3 is correlated with the behavior of branches b1 and b2. Clearly, if branches b1 and b2 are both not taken (i.e., if the conditions both evaluate to true and aa and bb are both assigned 0), then b3 will be taken, since aa and bb are clearly equal. A predictor that uses only the behavior of a single branch to predict the outcome of that branch can never capture this behavior.

Branch predictors that use the behavior of other branches to make a prediction are called *correlating predictors* or *two-level predictors*. Existing correlating predictors add information about the behavior of the most recent branches to decide how to predict a given branch. For example, a (1,2) predictor uses the behavior of the last branch to choose from among a pair of 2-bit branch predictors in predicting a particular branch. In the general case, an (m,n) predictor uses the behavior of the last m branches to choose from 2^m branch predictors, each of which is an n-bit predictor for a single branch. The attraction of this type of correlating branch predictor is that it can yield higher prediction rates than the 2-bit scheme and requires only a trivial amount of additional hardware.

The simplicity of the hardware comes from a simple observation: The global history of the most recent m branches can be recorded in an m-bit shift register, where each bit records whether the branch was taken or not taken. The branch-prediction buffer can then be indexed using a concatenation of the low-order bits from the branch address with the m-bit global history. For example, in a (2,2) buffer with 64 total entries, the 4 low-order address bits of the branch (word address) and the 2 global bits representing the behavior of the two most recently executed branches form a 6-bit index that can be used to index the 64 counters.

How much better do the correlating branch predictors work when compared with the standard 2-bit scheme? To compare them fairly, we must compare predictors that use the same number of state bits. The number of bits in an (m,n) predictor is

$$2^m \times n \times \text{Number of prediction entries selected by the branch address}$$

A 2-bit predictor with no global history is simply a (0,2) predictor.

Example   How many bits are in the (0,2) branch predictor with 4K entries? How many entries are in a (2,2) predictor with the same number of bits?

Answer   The predictor with 4K entries has

$$2^0 \times 2 \times 4K = 8K \text{ bits}$$

How many branch-selected entries are in a (2,2) predictor that has a total of 8K bits in the prediction buffer? We know that

$$2^2 \times 2 \times \text{Number of prediction entries selected by the branch} = 8K$$

Hence, the number of prediction entries selected by the branch = 1K.

Figure 3.3 compares the misprediction rates of the earlier (0,2) predictor with 4K entries and a (2,2) predictor with 1K entries. As you can see, this correlating predictor not only outperforms a simple 2-bit predictor with the same total number of state bits, but it also often outperforms a 2-bit predictor with an unlimited number of entries.

Tournament Predictors: Adaptively Combining Local and Global Predictors

The primary motivation for correlating branch predictors came from the observation that the standard 2-bit predictor using only local information failed on some important branches and that, by adding global information, the performance could be improved. *Tournament predictors* take this insight to the next level, by using multiple predictors, usually one based on global information and one based on local information, and combining them with a selector. Tournament predictors can achieve both better accuracy at medium sizes (8K–32K bits) and also make use of very large numbers of prediction bits effectively. Existing tournament predictors use a 2-bit saturating counter per branch to choose among two different predictors based on which predictor (local, global, or even some mix) was most effective in recent predictions. As in a simple 2-bit predictor, the saturating counter requires two mispredictions before changing the identity of the preferred predictor.

The advantage of a tournament predictor is its ability to select the right predictor for a particular branch, which is particularly crucial for the integer benchmarks. A typical tournament predictor will select the global predictor almost 40% of the time for the SPEC integer benchmarks and less than 15% of the time for the SPEC FP benchmarks. In addition to the Alpha processors that pioneered tournament predictors, recent AMD processors, including both the Opteron and Phenom, have used tournament-style predictors.

Figure 3.4 looks at the performance of three different predictors (a local 2-bit predictor, a correlating predictor, and a tournament predictor) for different

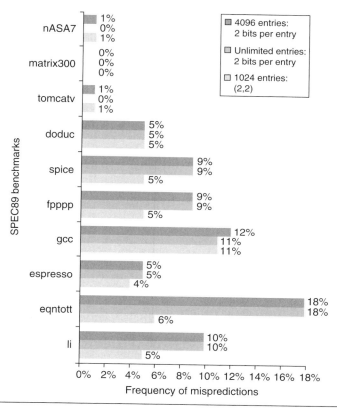

Figure 3.3 Comparison of 2-bit predictors. A noncorrelating predictor for 4096 bits is first, followed by a noncorrelating 2-bit predictor with unlimited entries and a 2-bit predictor with 2 bits of global history and a total of 1024 entries. Although these data are for an older version of SPEC, data for more recent SPEC benchmarks would show similar differences in accuracy.

numbers of bits using SPEC89 as the benchmark. As we saw earlier, the prediction capability of the local predictor does not improve beyond a certain size. The correlating predictor shows a significant improvement, and the tournament predictor generates slightly better performance. For more recent versions of the SPEC, the results would be similar, but the asymptotic behavior would not be reached until slightly larger predictor sizes.

The local predictor consists of a two-level predictor. The top level is a local history table consisting of 1024 10-bit entries; each 10-bit entry corresponds to the most recent 10 branch outcomes for the entry. That is, if the branch was taken 10 or more times in a row, the entry in the local history table will be all 1s. If the branch is alternately taken and untaken, the history entry consists of alternating 0s and 1s. This 10-bit history allows patterns of up to 10 branches to be discovered and predicted. The selected entry from the local history table is used to

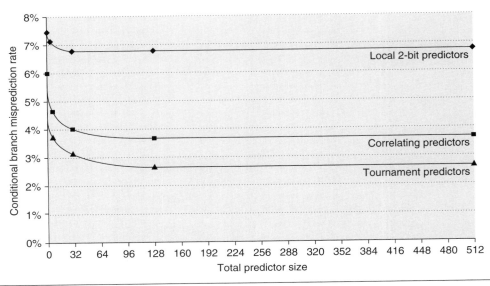

Figure 3.4 The misprediction rate for three different predictors on SPEC89 as the total number of bits is increased. The predictors are a local 2-bit predictor, a correlating predictor that is optimally structured in its use of global and local information at each point in the graph, and a tournament predictor. Although these data are for an older version of SPEC, data for more recent SPEC benchmarks would show similar behavior, perhaps converging to the asymptotic limit at slightly larger predictor sizes.

index a table of 1K entries consisting of 3-bit saturating counters, which provide the local prediction. This combination, which uses a total of 29K bits, leads to high accuracy in branch prediction.

The Intel Core i7 Branch Predictor

Intel has released only limited amounts of information about the Core i7's branch predictor, which is based on earlier predictors used in the Core Duo chip. The i7 uses a two-level predictor that has a smaller first-level predictor, designed to meet the cycle constraints of predicting a branch every clock cycle, and a larger second-level predictor as a backup. Each predictor combines three different predictors: (1) the simple two-bit predictor, which was introduced in Appendix C (and used in the tournament predictor discussed above); (2) a global history predictor, like those we just saw; and (3) a loop exit predictor. The loop exit predictor uses a counter to predict the exact number of taken branches (which is the number of loop iterations) for a branch that is detected as a loop branch. For each branch, the best prediction is chosen from among the three predictors by tracking the accuracy of each prediction, like a tournament predictor. In addition to this multilevel main predictor, a separate unit predicts target addresses for indirect branches, and a stack to predict return addresses is also used.

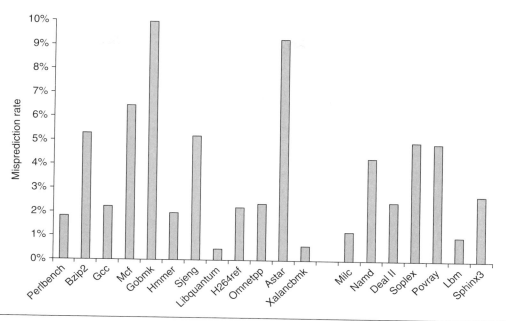

Figure 3.5 **The misprediction rate for 19 of the SPECCPU2006 benchmarks versus the number of successfully retired branches is slightly higher on average for the integer benchmarks than for the FP (4% versus 3%).** More importantly, it is much higher for a few benchmarks.

As in other cases, speculation causes some challenges in evaluating the predictor, since a mispredicted branch may easily lead to another branch being fetched and mispredicted. To keep things simple, we look at the number of mispredictions as a percentage of the number of successfully completed branches (those that were not the result of misspeculation). Figure 3.5 shows these data for 19 of the SPECCPU 2006 benchmarks. These benchmarks are considerably larger than SPEC89 or SPEC2000, with the result being that the misprediction rates are slightly higher than those in Figure 3.4 even with a more elaborate combination of predictors. Because branch misprediction leads to ineffective speculation, it contributes to the wasted work, as we will see later in this chapter.

3.4 Overcoming Data Hazards with Dynamic Scheduling

A simple statically scheduled pipeline fetches an instruction and issues it, unless there is a data dependence between an instruction already in the pipeline and the fetched instruction that cannot be hidden with bypassing or forwarding. (Forwarding logic reduces the effective pipeline latency so that the certain dependences do not result in hazards.) If there is a data dependence that cannot be hidden, then the hazard detection hardware stalls the pipeline starting with the instruction that uses the result. No new instructions are fetched or issued until the dependence is cleared.

In this section, we explore *dynamic scheduling*, in which the hardware rearranges the instruction execution to reduce the stalls while maintaining data flow and exception behavior. Dynamic scheduling offers several advantages. First, it allows code that was compiled with one pipeline in mind to run efficiently on a different pipeline, eliminating the need to have multiple binaries and recompile for a different microarchitecture. In today's computing environment, where much of the software is from third parties and distributed in binary form, this advantage is significant. Second, it enables handling some cases when dependences are unknown at compile time; for example, they may involve a memory reference or a data-dependent branch, or they may result from a modern programming environment that uses dynamic linking or dispatching. Third, and perhaps most importantly, it allows the processor to tolerate unpredictable delays, such as cache misses, by executing other code while waiting for the miss to resolve. In Section 3.6, we explore hardware speculation, a technique with additional performance advantages, which builds on dynamic scheduling. As we will see, the advantages of dynamic scheduling are gained at a cost of significant increase in hardware complexity.

Although a dynamically scheduled processor cannot change the data flow, it tries to avoid stalling when dependences are present. In contrast, static pipeline scheduling by the compiler (covered in Section 3.2) tries to minimize stalls by separating dependent instructions so that they will not lead to hazards. Of course, compiler pipeline scheduling can also be used on code destined to run on a processor with a dynamically scheduled pipeline.

Dynamic Scheduling: The Idea

A major limitation of simple pipelining techniques is that they use in-order instruction issue and execution: Instructions are issued in program order, and if an instruction is stalled in the pipeline no later instructions can proceed. Thus, if there is a dependence between two closely spaced instructions in the pipeline, this will lead to a hazard and a stall will result. If there are multiple functional units, these units could lie idle. If instruction *j* depends on a long-running instruction *i*, currently in execution in the pipeline, then all instructions after *j* must be stalled until *i* is finished and *j* can execute. For example, consider this code:

```
DIV.D    F0,F2,F4
ADD.D    F10,F0,F8
SUB.D    F12,F8,F14
```

The SUB.D instruction cannot execute because the dependence of ADD.D on DIV.D causes the pipeline to stall; yet, SUB.D is not data dependent on anything in the pipeline. This hazard creates a performance limitation that can be eliminated by not requiring instructions to execute in program order.

In the classic five-stage pipeline, both structural and data hazards could be checked during instruction decode (ID): When an instruction could execute without hazards, it was issued from ID knowing that all data hazards had been resolved.

To allow us to begin executing the SUB.D in the above example, we must separate the issue process into two parts: checking for any structural hazards and waiting for the absence of a data hazard. Thus, we still use in-order instruction issue (i.e., instructions issued in program order), but we want an instruction to begin execution as soon as its data operands are available. Such a pipeline does *out-of-order execution*, which implies *out-of-order completion*.

Out-of-order execution introduces the possibility of WAR and WAW hazards, which do not exist in the five-stage integer pipeline and its logical extension to an in-order floating-point pipeline. Consider the following MIPS floating-point code sequence:

```
DIV.D     F0,F2,F4
ADD.D     F6,F0,F8
SUB.D     F8,F10,F14
MUL.D     F6,F10,F8
```

There is an antidependence between the ADD.D and the SUB.D, and if the pipeline executes the SUB.D before the ADD.D (which is waiting for the DIV.D), it will violate the antidependence, yielding a WAR hazard. Likewise, to avoid violating output dependences, such as the write of F6 by MUL.D, WAW hazards must be handled. As we will see, both these hazards are avoided by the use of register renaming.

Out-of-order completion also creates major complications in handling exceptions. Dynamic scheduling with out-of-order completion must preserve exception behavior in the sense that *exactly* those exceptions that would arise if the program were executed in strict program order *actually* do arise. Dynamically scheduled processors preserve exception behavior by delaying the notification of an associated exception until the processor knows that the instruction should be the next one completed.

Although exception behavior must be preserved, dynamically scheduled processors could generate *imprecise* exceptions. An exception is *imprecise* if the processor state when an exception is raised does not look exactly as if the instructions were executed sequentially in strict program order. Imprecise exceptions can occur because of two possibilities:

1. The pipeline may have *already completed* instructions that are *later* in program order than the instruction causing the exception.

2. The pipeline may have *not yet completed* some instructions that are *earlier* in program order than the instruction causing the exception.

Imprecise exceptions make it difficult to restart execution after an exception. Rather than address these problems in this section, we will discuss a solution that provides precise exceptions in the context of a processor with speculation in Section 3.6. For floating-point exceptions, other solutions have been used, as discussed in Appendix J.

To allow out-of-order execution, we essentially split the ID pipe stage of our simple five-stage pipeline into two stages:

1. *Issue*—Decode instructions, check for structural hazards.

2. *Read operands*—Wait until no data hazards, then read operands.

An instruction fetch stage precedes the issue stage and may fetch either into an instruction register or into a queue of pending instructions; instructions are then issued from the register or queue. The execution stage follows the read operands stage, just as in the five-stage pipeline. Execution may take multiple cycles, depending on the operation.

We distinguish when an instruction *begins execution* and when it *completes execution*; between the two times, the instruction is *in execution*. Our pipeline allows multiple instructions to be in execution at the same time; without this capability, a major advantage of dynamic scheduling is lost. Having multiple instructions in execution at once requires multiple functional units, pipelined functional units, or both. Since these two capabilities—pipelined functional units and multiple functional units—are essentially equivalent for the purposes of pipeline control, we will assume the processor has multiple functional units.

In a dynamically scheduled pipeline, all instructions pass through the issue stage in order (in-order issue); however, they can be stalled or bypass each other in the second stage (read operands) and thus enter execution out of order. *Scoreboarding* is a technique for allowing instructions to execute out of order when there are sufficient resources and no data dependences; it is named after the CDC 6600 scoreboard, which developed this capability. Here, we focus on a more sophisticated technique, called *Tomasulo's algorithm.* The primary difference is that Tomasulo's algorithm handles antidependences and output dependences by effectively renaming the registers dynamically. Additionally, Tomasulo's algorithm can be extended to handle *speculation*, a technique to reduce the effect of control dependences by predicting the outcome of a branch, executing instructions at the predicted destination address, and taking corrective actions when the prediction was wrong. While the use of scoreboarding is probably sufficient to support a simple two-issue superscalar like the ARM A8, a more aggressive processor, like the four-issue Intel i7, benefits from the use of out-of-order execution.

Dynamic Scheduling Using Tomasulo's Approach

The IBM 360/91 floating-point unit used a sophisticated scheme to allow out-of-order execution. This scheme, invented by Robert Tomasulo, tracks when operands for instructions are available to minimize RAW hazards and introduces register renaming in hardware to minimize WAW and WAR hazards. There are many variations on this scheme in modern processors, although the key concepts of tracking instruction dependences to allow execution as soon as operands are available and renaming registers to avoid WAR and WAW hazards are common characteristics.

IBM's goal was to achieve high floating-point performance from an instruction set and from compilers designed for the entire 360 computer family, rather than from specialized compilers for the high-end processors. The 360 architecture had only four double-precision floating-point registers, which limits the effectiveness of compiler scheduling; this fact was another motivation for the Tomasulo approach. In addition, the IBM 360/91 had long memory accesses and long floating-point delays, which Tomasulo's algorithm was designed to overcome. At the end of the section, we will see that Tomasulo's algorithm can also support the overlapped execution of multiple iterations of a loop.

We explain the algorithm, which focuses on the floating-point unit and load-store unit, in the context of the MIPS instruction set. The primary difference between MIPS and the 360 is the presence of register-memory instructions in the latter architecture. Because Tomasulo's algorithm uses a load functional unit, no significant changes are needed to add register-memory addressing modes. The IBM 360/91 also had pipelined functional units, rather than multiple functional units, but we describe the algorithm as if there were multiple functional units. It is a simple conceptual extension to also pipeline those functional units.

As we will see, RAW hazards are avoided by executing an instruction only when its operands are available, which is exactly what the simpler scoreboarding approach provides. WAR and WAW hazards, which arise from name dependences, are eliminated by register renaming. *Register renaming* eliminates these hazards by renaming all destination registers, including those with a pending read or write for an earlier instruction, so that the out-of-order write does not affect any instructions that depend on an earlier value of an operand.

To better understand how register renaming eliminates WAR and WAW hazards, consider the following example code sequence that includes potential WAR and WAW hazards:

```
DIV.D    F0,F2,F4
ADD.D    F6,F0,F8
S.D      F6,0(R1)
SUB.D    F8,F10,F14
MUL.D    F6,F10,F8
```

There are two antidependences: between the ADD.D and the SUB.D and between the S.D and the MUL.D. There is also an output dependence between the ADD.D and the MUL.D, leading to three possible hazards: WAR hazards on the use of F8 by ADD.D and the use of F6 by the SUB.D, as well as a WAW hazard since the ADD.D may finish later than the MUL.D. There are also three true data dependences: between the DIV.D and the ADD.D, between the SUB.D and the MUL.D, and between the ADD.D and the S.D.

These three name dependences can all be eliminated by register renaming. For simplicity, assume the existence of two temporary registers, S and T. Using S and T, the sequence can be rewritten without any dependences as:

```
DIV.D    F0,F2,F4
ADD.D    S,F0,F8
S.D      S,0(R1)
SUB.D    T,F10,F14
MUL.D    F6,F10,T
```

In addition, any subsequent uses of F8 must be replaced by the register T. In this code segment, the renaming process can be done statically by the compiler. Finding any uses of F8 that are later in the code requires either sophisticated compiler analysis or hardware support, since there may be intervening branches between the above code segment and a later use of F8. As we will see, Tomasulo's algorithm can handle renaming across branches.

In Tomasulo's scheme, register renaming is provided by *reservation stations*, which buffer the operands of instructions waiting to issue. The basic idea is that a reservation station fetches and buffers an operand as soon as it is available, eliminating the need to get the operand from a register. In addition, pending instructions designate the reservation station that will provide their input. Finally, when successive writes to a register overlap in execution, only the last one is actually used to update the register. As instructions are issued, the register specifiers for pending operands are renamed to the names of the reservation station, which provides register renaming.

Since there can be more reservation stations than real registers, the technique can even eliminate hazards arising from name dependences that could not be eliminated by a compiler. As we explore the components of Tomasulo's scheme, we will return to the topic of register renaming and see exactly how the renaming occurs and how it eliminates WAR and WAW hazards.

The use of reservation stations, rather than a centralized register file, leads to two other important properties. First, hazard detection and execution control are distributed: The information held in the reservation stations at each functional unit determines when an instruction can begin execution at that unit. Second, results are passed directly to functional units from the reservation stations where they are buffered, rather than going through the registers. This bypassing is done with a common result bus that allows all units waiting for an operand to be loaded simultaneously (on the 360/91 this is called the *common data bus*, or CDB). In pipelines with multiple execution units and issuing multiple instructions per clock, more than one result bus will be needed.

Figure 3.6 shows the basic structure of a Tomasulo-based processor, including both the floating-point unit and the load/store unit; none of the execution control tables is shown. Each reservation station holds an instruction that has been issued and is awaiting execution at a functional unit and either the operand values for that instruction, if they have already been computed, or else the names of the reservation stations that will provide the operand values.

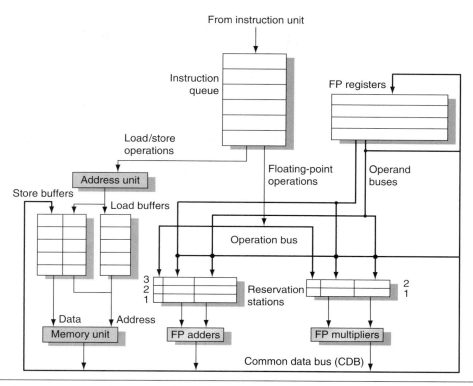

Figure 3.6 The basic structure of a MIPS floating-point unit using Tomasulo's algorithm. Instructions are sent from the instruction unit into the instruction queue from which they are issued in first-in, first-out (FIFO) order. The reservation stations include the operation and the actual operands, as well as information used for detecting and resolving hazards. Load buffers have three functions: (1) hold the components of the effective address until it is computed, (2) track outstanding loads that are waiting on the memory, and (3) hold the results of completed loads that are waiting for the CDB. Similarly, store buffers have three functions: (1) hold the components of the effective address until it is computed, (2) hold the destination memory addresses of outstanding stores that are waiting for the data value to store, and (3) hold the address and value to store until the memory unit is available. All results from either the FP units or the load unit are put on the CDB, which goes to the FP register file as well as to the reservation stations and store buffers. The FP adders implement addition and subtraction, and the FP multipliers do multiplication and division.

The load buffers and store buffers hold data or addresses coming from and going to memory and behave almost exactly like reservation stations, so we distinguish them only when necessary. The floating-point registers are connected by a pair of buses to the functional units and by a single bus to the store buffers. All results from the functional units and from memory are sent on the common data bus, which goes everywhere except to the load buffer. All reservation stations have tag fields, employed by the pipeline control.

Before we describe the details of the reservation stations and the algorithm, let's look at the steps an instruction goes through. There are only three steps, although each one can now take an arbitrary number of clock cycles:

1. *Issue*—Get the next instruction from the head of the instruction queue, which is maintained in FIFO order to ensure the maintenance of correct data flow. If there is a matching reservation station that is empty, issue the instruction to the station with the operand values, if they are currently in the registers. If there is not an empty reservation station, then there is a structural hazard and the instruction stalls until a station or buffer is freed. If the operands are not in the registers, keep track of the functional units that will produce the operands. This step renames registers, eliminating WAR and WAW hazards. (This stage is sometimes called *dispatch* in a dynamically scheduled processor.)

2. *Execute*—If one or more of the operands is not yet available, monitor the common data bus while waiting for it to be computed. When an operand becomes available, it is placed into any reservation station awaiting it. When all the operands are available, the operation can be executed at the corresponding functional unit. By delaying instruction execution until the operands are available, RAW hazards are avoided. (Some dynamically scheduled processors call this step "issue," but we use the name "execute," which was used in the first dynamically scheduled processor, the CDC 6600.)

   Notice that several instructions could become ready in the same clock cycle for the same functional unit. Although independent functional units could begin execution in the same clock cycle for different instructions, if more than one instruction is ready for a single functional unit, the unit will have to choose among them. For the floating-point reservation stations, this choice may be made arbitrarily; loads and stores, however, present an additional complication.

   Loads and stores require a two-step execution process. The first step computes the effective address when the base register is available, and the effective address is then placed in the load or store buffer. Loads in the load buffer execute as soon as the memory unit is available. Stores in the store buffer wait for the value to be stored before being sent to the memory unit. Loads and stores are maintained in program order through the effective address calculation, which will help to prevent hazards through memory, as we will see shortly.

   To preserve exception behavior, no instruction is allowed to initiate execution until all branches that precede the instruction in program order have completed. This restriction guarantees that an instruction that causes an exception during execution really would have been executed. In a processor using branch prediction (as all dynamically scheduled processors do), this means that the processor must know that the branch prediction was correct before allowing an instruction after the branch to begin execution. If the processor records the occurrence of the exception, but does not actually raise it, an instruction can start execution but not stall until it enters write result.

   As we will see, speculation provides a more flexible and more complete method to handle exceptions, so we will delay making this enhancement and show how speculation handles this problem later.

3. *Write result*—When the result is available, write it on the CDB and from there into the registers and into any reservation stations (including store buffers) waiting for this result. Stores are buffered in the store buffer until both the value to be stored and the store address are available, then the result is written as soon as the memory unit is free.

The data structures that detect and eliminate hazards are attached to the reservation stations, to the register file, and to the load and store buffers with slightly different information attached to different objects. These tags are essentially names for an extended set of virtual registers used for renaming. In our example, the tag field is a 4-bit quantity that denotes one of the five reservation stations or one of the five load buffers. As we will see, this produces the equivalent of 10 registers that can be designated as result registers (as opposed to the four double-precision registers that the 360 architecture contains). In a processor with more real registers, we would want renaming to provide an even larger set of virtual registers. The tag field describes which reservation station contains the instruction that will produce a result needed as a source operand.

Once an instruction has issued and is waiting for a source operand, it refers to the operand by the reservation station number where the instruction that will write the register has been assigned. Unused values, such as zero, indicate that the operand is already available in the registers. Because there are more reservation stations than actual register numbers, WAW and WAR hazards are eliminated by renaming results using reservation station numbers. Although in Tomasulo's scheme the reservation stations are used as the extended virtual registers, other approaches could use a register set with additional registers or a structure like the reorder buffer, which we will see in Section 3.6.

In Tomasulo's scheme, as well as the subsequent methods we look at for supporting speculation, results are broadcast on a bus (the CDB), which is monitored by the reservation stations. The combination of the common result bus and the retrieval of results from the bus by the reservation stations implements the forwarding and bypassing mechanisms used in a statically scheduled pipeline. In doing so, however, a dynamically scheduled scheme introduces one cycle of latency between source and result, since the matching of a result and its use cannot be done until the Write Result stage. Thus, in a dynamically scheduled pipeline, the effective latency between a producing instruction and a consuming instruction is at least one cycle longer than the latency of the functional unit producing the result.

It is important to remember that the tags in the Tomasulo scheme refer to the buffer or unit that will produce a result; the register names are discarded when an instruction issues to a reservation station. (This is a key difference between Tomasulo's scheme and scoreboarding: In scoreboarding, operands stay in the registers and are only read after the producing instruction completes and the consuming instruction is ready to execute.)

Each reservation station has seven fields:

- Op—The operation to perform on source operands S1 and S2.

- Qj, Qk—The reservation stations that will produce the corresponding source operand; a value of zero indicates that the source operand is already available in Vj or Vk, or is unnecessary.

- Vj, Vk—The value of the source operands. Note that only one of the V fields or the Q field is valid for each operand. For loads, the Vk field is used to hold the offset field.

- A—Used to hold information for the memory address calculation for a load or store. Initially, the immediate field of the instruction is stored here; after the address calculation, the effective address is stored here.

- Busy—Indicates that this reservation station and its accompanying functional unit are occupied.

The register file has a field, Qi:

- Qi—The number of the reservation station that contains the operation whose result should be stored into this register. If the value of Qi is blank (or 0), no currently active instruction is computing a result destined for this register, meaning that the value is simply the register contents.

The load and store buffers each have a field, A, which holds the result of the effective address once the first step of execution has been completed.

In the next section, we will first consider some examples that show how these mechanisms work and then examine the detailed algorithm.

3.5 Dynamic Scheduling: Examples and the Algorithm

Before we examine Tomasulo's algorithm in detail, let's consider a few examples that will help illustrate how the algorithm works.

Example Show what the information tables look like for the following code sequence when only the first load has completed and written its result:

1.	L.D	F6,32(R2)
2.	L.D	F2,44(R3)
3.	MUL.D	F0,F2,F4
4.	SUB.D	F8,F2,F6
5.	DIV.D	F10,F0,F6
6.	ADD.D	F6,F8,F2

Answer Figure 3.7 shows the result in three tables. The numbers appended to the names Add, Mult, and Load stand for the tag for that reservation station—Add1 is the tag for the result from the first add unit. In addition, we have included an

Instruction		Instruction status		
Instruction		Issue	Execute	Write result
L.D	F6,32(R2)	√	√	√
L.D	F2,44(R3)	√	√	
MUL.D	F0,F2,F4	√		
SUB.D	F8,F2,F6	√		
DIV.D	F10,F0,F6	√		
ADD.D	F6,F8,F2	√		

Reservation stations								
Name	Busy	Op	Vj	Vk		Qj	Qk	A
Load1	No							
Load2	Yes	Load						44 + Regs[R3]
Add1	Yes	SUB		Mem[32 + Regs[R2]]		Load2		
Add2	Yes	ADD				Add1	Load2	
Add3	No							
Mult1	Yes	MUL		Regs[F4]		Load2		
Mult2	Yes	DIV		Mem[32 + Regs[R2]]		Mult1		

Register status									
Field	F0	F2	F4	F6	F8	F10	F12	...	F30
Qi	Mult1	Load2		Add2	Add1	Mult2			

Figure 3.7 **Reservation stations and register tags shown when all of the instructions have issued, but only the first load instruction has completed and written its result to the CDB.** The second load has completed effective address calculation but is waiting on the memory unit. We use the array Regs[] to refer to the register file and the array Mem[] to refer to the memory. Remember that an operand is specified by either a Q field or a V field at any time. Notice that the ADD.D instruction, which has a WAR hazard at the WB stage, has issued and could complete before the DIV.D initiates.

instruction status table. This table is included only to help you understand the algorithm; it is *not* actually a part of the hardware. Instead, the reservation station keeps the state of each operation that has issued.

Tomasulo's scheme offers two major advantages over earlier and simpler schemes: (1) the distribution of the hazard detection logic, and (2) the elimination of stalls for WAW and WAR hazards.

The first advantage arises from the distributed reservation stations and the use of the CDB. If multiple instructions are waiting on a single result, and each instruction already has its other operand, then the instructions can be released simultaneously by the broadcast of the result on the CDB. If a centralized register file were used, the units would have to read their results from the registers when register buses are available.

The second advantage, the elimination of WAW and WAR hazards, is accomplished by renaming registers using the reservation stations and by the process of storing operands into the reservation station as soon as they are available.

For example, the code sequence in Figure 3.7 issues both the DIV.D and the ADD.D, even though there is a WAR hazard involving F6. The hazard is eliminated in one of two ways. First, if the instruction providing the value for the DIV.D has completed, then Vk will store the result, allowing DIV.D to execute independent of the ADD.D (this is the case shown). On the other hand, if the L.D had not completed, then Qk would point to the Load1 reservation station, and the DIV.D instruction would be independent of the ADD.D. Thus, in either case, the ADD.D can issue and begin executing. Any uses of the result of the DIV.D would point to the reservation station, allowing the ADD.D to complete and store its value into the registers without affecting the DIV.D.

We'll see an example of the elimination of a WAW hazard shortly. But let's first look at how our earlier example continues execution. In this example, and the ones that follow in this chapter, assume the following latencies: load is 1 clock cycle, add is 2 clock cycles, multiply is 6 clock cycles, and divide is 12 clock cycles.

Example Using the same code segment as in the previous example (page 176), show what the status tables look like when the MUL.D is ready to write its result.

Answer The result is shown in the three tables in Figure 3.8. Notice that ADD.D has completed since the operands of DIV.D were copied, thereby overcoming the WAR hazard. Notice that even if the load of F6 was delayed, the add into F6 could be executed without triggering a WAW hazard.

Tomasulo's Algorithm: The Details

Figure 3.9 specifies the checks and steps that each instruction must go through. As mentioned earlier, loads and stores go through a functional unit for effective address computation before proceeding to independent load or store buffers. Loads take a second execution step to access memory and then go to write result to send the value from memory to the register file and/or any waiting reservation stations. Stores complete their execution in the write result stage, which writes the result to memory. Notice that all writes occur in write result, whether the destination is a register or memory. This restriction simplifies Tomasulo's algorithm and is critical to its extension with speculation in Section 3.6.

Instruction		Instruction status		
		Issue	Execute	Write result
L.D	F6,32(R2)	√	√	√
L.D	F2,44(R3)	√	√	√
MUL.D	F0,F2,F4	√	√	
SUB.D	F8,F2,F6	√	√	√
DIV.D	F10,F0,F6	√		
ADD.D	F6,F8,F2	√	√	√

			Reservation stations				
Name	Busy	Op	Vj	Vk	Qj	Qk	A
Load1	No						
Load2	No						
Add1	No						
Add2	No						
Add3	No						
Mult1	Yes	MUL	Mem[44 + Regs[R3]]	Regs[F4]			
Mult2	Yes	DIV		Mem[32 + Regs[R2]]	Mult1		

				Register status				
Field	F0	F2	F4	F6	F8	F10	F12	...	F30
Qi	Mult1					Mult2			

Figure 3.8 Multiply and divide are the only instructions not finished.

Tomasulo's Algorithm: A Loop-Based Example

To understand the full power of eliminating WAW and WAR hazards through dynamic renaming of registers, we must look at a loop. Consider the following simple sequence for multiplying the elements of an array by a scalar in F2:

```
Loop:    L.D      F0,0(R1)
         MUL.D    F4,F0,F2
         S.D      F4,0(R1)
         DADDIU   R1,R1,-8
         BNE      R1,R2,Loop;  branches if R1¦R2
```

If we predict that branches are taken, using reservation stations will allow multiple executions of this loop to proceed at once. This advantage is gained without changing the code—in effect, the loop is unrolled dynamically by the hardware using the reservation stations obtained by renaming to act as additional registers.

Instruction state	Wait until	Action or bookkeeping

Issue
FP operation
	Station r empty	`if (RegisterStat[rs].Qi¦0)`
		`    {RS[r].Qj ← RegisterStat[rs].Qi}`
		`else {RS[r].Vj ← Regs[rs]; RS[r].Qj ← 0};`
		`if (RegisterStat[rt].Qi¦0)`
		`    {RS[r].Qk ← RegisterStat[rt].Qi`
		`else {RS[r].Vk ← Regs[rt]; RS[r].Qk ← 0};`
		`RS[r].Busy ← yes; RegisterStat[rd].Q ← r;`

Load or store	Buffer r empty	`if (RegisterStat[rs].Qi¦0)`
		`    {RS[r].Qj ← RegisterStat[rs].Qi}`
		`else {RS[r].Vj ← Regs[rs]; RS[r].Qj ← 0};`
		`RS[r].A ← imm; RS[r].Busy ← yes;`

Load only		`RegisterStat[rt].Qi ← r;`

Store only		`if (RegisterStat[rt].Qi¦0)`
		`    {RS[r].Qk ← RegisterStat[rs].Qi}`
		`else {RS[r].Vk ← Regs[rt]; RS[r].Qk ← 0};`

Execute FP operation	`(RS[r].Qj = 0)` and `(RS[r].Qk = 0)`	Compute result: operands are in Vj and Vk
Load/store step 1	`RS[r].Qj = 0 & r is head of` load-store queue	`RS[r].A ← RS[r].Vj + RS[r].A;`
Load step 2	Load step 1 complete	Read from `Mem[RS[r].A]`

Write result
FP operation
or load
	Execution complete at r &
	CDB available
		`∀x(if (RegisterStat[x].Qi=r) {Regs[x] ← result;`
		`    RegisterStat[x].Qi ← 0});`
		`∀x(if (RS[x].Qj=r) {RS[x].Vj ← result;RS[x].Qj ←`
		`    0});`
		`∀x(if (RS[x].Qk=r) {RS[x].Vk ← result;RS[x].Qk ←`
		`    0});`
		`RS[r].Busy ← no;`

Store	Execution complete at r & `RS[r].Qk = 0`	`Mem[RS[r].A] ← RS[r].Vk;` `RS[r].Busy ← no;`

Figure 3.9 Steps in the algorithm and what is required for each step. For the issuing instruction, rd is the destination, rs and rt are the source register numbers, imm is the sign-extended immediate field, and r is the reservation station or buffer that the instruction is assigned to. RS is the reservation station data structure. The value returned by an FP unit or by the load unit is called result. RegisterStat is the register status data structure (not the register file, which is Regs[]). When an instruction is issued, the destination register has its Qi field set to the number of the buffer or reservation station to which the instruction is issued. If the operands are available in the registers, they are stored in the V fields. Otherwise, the Q fields are set to indicate the reservation station that will produce the values needed as source operands. The instruction waits at the reservation station until both its operands are available, indicated by zero in the Q fields. The Q fields are set to zero either when this instruction is issued or when an instruction on which this instruction depends completes and does its write back. When an instruction has finished execution and the CDB is available, it can do its write back. All the buffers, registers, and reservation stations whose values of Qj or Qk are the same as the completing reservation station update their values from the CDB and mark the Q fields to indicate that values have been received. Thus, the CDB can broadcast its result to many destinations in a single clock cycle, and if the waiting instructions have their operands they can all begin execution on the next clock cycle. Loads go through two steps in execute, and stores perform slightly differently during write result, where they may have to wait for the value to store. Remember that, to preserve exception behavior, instructions should not be allowed to execute if a branch that is earlier in program order has not yet completed. Because any concept of program order is not maintained after the issue stage, this restriction is usually implemented by preventing any instruction from leaving the issue step, if there is a pending branch already in the pipeline. In Section 3.6, we will see how speculation support removes this restriction.

Let's assume we have issued all the instructions in two successive iterations of the loop, but none of the floating-point load/stores or operations has completed. Figure 3.10 shows reservation stations, register status tables, and load and store buffers at this point. (The integer ALU operation is ignored, and it is assumed the branch was predicted as taken.) Once the system reaches this state, two copies of the loop could be sustained with a CPI close to 1.0, provided the multiplies could complete in four clock cycles. With a latency of six cycles, additional iterations will need to be processed before the steady state can be reached. This requires more reservation stations to hold instructions that are in execution.

		Instruction status		
Instruction	From iteration	Issue	Execute	Write result
L.D F0,0(R1)	1	√	√	
MUL.D F4,F0,F2	1	√		
S.D F4,0(R1)	1	√		
L.D F0,0(R1)	2	√	√	
MUL.D F4,F0,F2	2	√		
S.D F4,0(R1)	2	√		

			Reservation stations				
Name	Busy	Op	Vj	Vk	Qj	Qk	A
Load1	Yes	Load					Regs[R1] + 0
Load2	Yes	Load					Regs[R1] − 8
Add1	No						
Add2	No						
Add3	No						
Mult1	Yes	MUL		Regs[F2]	Load1		
Mult2	Yes	MUL		Regs[F2]	Load2		
Store1	Yes	Store	Regs[R1]			Mult1	
Store2	Yes	Store	Regs[R1] − 8			Mult2	

				Register status				
Field	F0	F2	F4	F6	F8	F10	F12	...	F30
Qi	Load2		Mult2						

Figure 3.10   Two active iterations of the loop with no instruction yet completed. Entries in the multiplier reservation stations indicate that the outstanding loads are the sources. The store reservation stations indicate that the multiply destination is the source of the value to store.

As we will see later in this chapter, when extended with multiple instruction issue, Tomasulo's approach can sustain more than one instruction per clock.

A load and a store can safely be done out of order, provided they access different addresses. If a load and a store access the same address, then either

- The load is before the store in program order and interchanging them results in a WAR hazard, or

- The store is before the load in program order and interchanging them results in a RAW hazard.

Similarly, interchanging two stores to the same address results in a WAW hazard.

Hence, to determine if a load can be executed at a given time, the processor can check whether any uncompleted store that precedes the load in program order shares the same data memory address as the load. Similarly, a store must wait until there are no unexecuted loads or stores that are earlier in program order and share the same data memory address. We consider a method to eliminate this restriction in Section 3.9.

To detect such hazards, the processor must have computed the data memory address associated with any earlier memory operation. A simple, but not necessarily optimal, way to guarantee that the processor has all such addresses is to perform the effective address calculations in program order. (We really only need to keep the relative order between stores and other memory references; that is, loads can be reordered freely.)

Let's consider the situation of a load first. If we perform effective address calculation in program order, then when a load has completed effective address calculation, we can check whether there is an address conflict by examining the A field of all active store buffers. If the load address matches the address of any active entries in the store buffer, that load instruction is not sent to the load buffer until the conflicting store completes. (Some implementations bypass the value directly to the load from a pending store, reducing the delay for this RAW hazard.)

Stores operate similarly, except that the processor must check for conflicts in both the load buffers and the store buffers, since conflicting stores cannot be reordered with respect to either a load or a store.

A dynamically scheduled pipeline can yield very high performance, provided branches are predicted accurately—an issue we addressed in the last section. The major drawback of this approach is the complexity of the Tomasulo scheme, which requires a large amount of hardware. In particular, each reservation station must contain an associative buffer, which must run at high speed, as well as complex control logic. The performance can also be limited by the single CDB. Although additional CDBs can be added, each CDB must interact with each reservation station, and the associative tag-matching hardware would have to be duplicated at each station for each CDB.

In Tomasulo's scheme, two different techniques are combined: the renaming of the architectural registers to a larger set of registers and the buffering of source operands from the register file. Source operand buffering resolves WAR hazards that arise when the operand is available in the registers. As we will see later, it is also possible to eliminate WAR hazards by the renaming of a register together with the buffering of a result until no outstanding references to the earlier version of the register remain. This approach will be used when we discuss hardware speculation.

Tomasulo's scheme was unused for many years after the 360/91, but was widely adopted in multiple-issue processors starting in the 1990s for several reasons:

1. Although Tomasulo's algorithm was designed before caches, the presence of caches, with the inherently unpredictable delays, has become one of the major motivations for dynamic scheduling. Out-of-order execution allows the processors to continue executing instructions while awaiting the completion of a cache miss, thus hiding all or part of the cache miss penalty.

2. As processors became more aggressive in their issue capability and designers are concerned with the performance of difficult-to-schedule code (such as most nonnumeric code), techniques such as register renaming, dynamic scheduling, and speculation became more important.

3. It can achieve high performance without requiring the compiler to target code to a specific pipeline structure, a valuable property in the era of shrink-wrapped mass market software.

3.6   Hardware-Based Speculation

As we try to exploit more instruction-level parallelism, maintaining control dependences becomes an increasing burden. Branch prediction reduces the direct stalls attributable to branches, but for a processor executing multiple instructions per clock, just predicting branches accurately may not be sufficient to generate the desired amount of instruction-level parallelism. A wide issue processor may need to execute a branch every clock cycle to maintain maximum performance. Hence, exploiting more parallelism requires that we overcome the limitation of control dependence.

Overcoming control dependence is done by speculating on the outcome of branches and executing the program as if our guesses were correct. This mechanism represents a subtle, but important, extension over branch prediction with dynamic scheduling. In particular, with speculation, we fetch, issue, and *execute* instructions, as if our branch predictions were always correct; dynamic scheduling only fetches and issues such instructions. Of course, we need mechanisms to handle the situation where the speculation is incorrect. Appendix H discusses a variety of mechanisms for supporting speculation by the compiler. In this section, we explore *hardware speculation,* which extends the ideas of dynamic scheduling.

Hardware-based speculation combines three key ideas: (1) dynamic branch prediction to choose which instructions to execute, (2) speculation to allow the execution of instructions before the control dependences are resolved (with the ability to undo the effects of an incorrectly speculated sequence), and (3) dynamic scheduling to deal with the scheduling of different combinations of basic blocks. (In comparison, dynamic scheduling without speculation only partially overlaps basic blocks because it requires that a branch be resolved before actually executing any instructions in the successor basic block.)

Hardware-based speculation follows the predicted flow of data values to choose when to execute instructions. This method of executing programs is essentially a *data flow execution*: Operations execute as soon as their operands are available.

To extend Tomasulo's algorithm to support speculation, we must separate the bypassing of results among instructions, which is needed to execute an instruction speculatively, from the actual completion of an instruction. By making this separation, we can allow an instruction to execute and to bypass its results to other instructions, without allowing the instruction to perform any updates that cannot be undone, until we know that the instruction is no longer speculative.

Using the bypassed value is like performing a speculative register read, since we do not know whether the instruction providing the source register value is providing the correct result until the instruction is no longer speculative. When an instruction is no longer speculative, we allow it to update the register file or memory; we call this additional step in the instruction execution sequence *instruction commit*.

The key idea behind implementing speculation is to allow instructions to execute out of order but to force them to commit *in order* and to prevent any irrevocable action (such as updating state or taking an exception) until an instruction commits. Hence, when we add speculation, we need to separate the process of completing execution from instruction commit, since instructions may finish execution considerably before they are ready to commit. Adding this commit phase to the instruction execution sequence requires an additional set of hardware buffers that hold the results of instructions that have finished execution but have not committed. This hardware buffer, which we call the *reorder buffer*, is also used to pass results among instructions that may be speculated.

The reorder buffer (ROB) provides additional registers in the same way as the reservation stations in Tomasulo's algorithm extend the register set. The ROB holds the result of an instruction between the time the operation associated with the instruction completes and the time the instruction commits. Hence, the ROB is a source of operands for instructions, just as the reservation stations provide operands in Tomasulo's algorithm. The key difference is that in Tomasulo's algorithm, once an instruction writes its result, any subsequently issued instructions will find the result in the register file. With speculation, the register file is not updated until the instruction commits (and we know definitively that the instruction should execute); thus, the ROB supplies operands in the interval between completion of instruction execution and instruction commit. The ROB is similar to the store buffer in Tomasulo's algorithm, and we integrate the function of the store buffer into the ROB for simplicity.

Each entry in the ROB contains four fields: the instruction type, the destination field, the value field, and the ready field. The instruction type field indicates whether the instruction is a branch (and has no destination result), a store (which has a memory address destination), or a register operation (ALU operation or load, which has register destinations). The destination field supplies the register number (for loads and ALU operations) or the memory address (for stores) where the instruction result should be written. The value field is used to hold the value of the instruction result until the instruction commits. We will see an example of ROB entries shortly. Finally, the ready field indicates that the instruction has completed execution, and the value is ready.

Figure 3.11 shows the hardware structure of the processor including the ROB. The ROB subsumes the store buffers. Stores still execute in two steps, but the second step is performed by instruction commit. Although the renaming

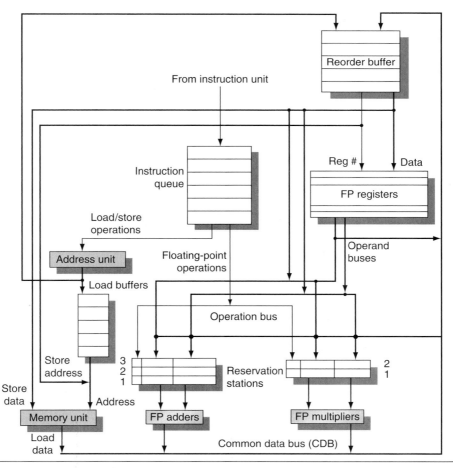

Figure 3.11 **The basic structure of a FP unit using Tomasulo's algorithm and extended to handle speculation.** Comparing this to Figure 3.6 on page 173, which implemented Tomasulo's algorithm, the major change is the addition of the ROB and the elimination of the store buffer, whose function is integrated into the ROB. This mechanism can be extended to multiple issue by making the CDB wider to allow for multiple completions per clock.

function of the reservation stations is replaced by the ROB, we still need a place to buffer operations (and operands) between the time they issue and the time they begin execution. This function is still provided by the reservation stations. Since every instruction has a position in the ROB until it commits, we tag a result using the ROB entry number rather than using the reservation station number. This tagging requires that the ROB assigned for an instruction must be tracked in the reservation station. Later in this section, we will explore an alternative implementation that uses extra registers for renaming and a queue that replaces the ROB to decide when instructions can commit.

Here are the four steps involved in instruction execution:

1. *Issue*—Get an instruction from the instruction queue. Issue the instruction if there is an empty reservation station and an empty slot in the ROB; send the operands to the reservation station if they are available in either the registers or the ROB. Update the control entries to indicate the buffers are in use. The number of the ROB entry allocated for the result is also sent to the reservation station, so that the number can be used to tag the result when it is placed on the CDB. If either all reservations are full or the ROB is full, then instruction issue is stalled until both have available entries.

2. *Execute*—If one or more of the operands is not yet available, monitor the CDB while waiting for the register to be computed. This step checks for RAW hazards. When both operands are available at a reservation station, execute the operation. Instructions may take multiple clock cycles in this stage, and loads still require two steps in this stage. Stores need only have the base register available at this step, since execution for a store at this point is only effective address calculation.

3. *Write result*—When the result is available, write it on the CDB (with the ROB tag sent when the instruction issued) and from the CDB into the ROB, as well as to any reservation stations waiting for this result. Mark the reservation station as available. Special actions are required for store instructions. If the value to be stored is available, it is written into the Value field of the ROB entry for the store. If the value to be stored is not available yet, the CDB must be monitored until that value is broadcast, at which time the Value field of the ROB entry of the store is updated. For simplicity we assume that this occurs during the write results stage of a store; we discuss relaxing this requirement later.

4. *Commit*—This is the final stage of completing an instruction, after which only its result remains. (Some processors call this commit phase "completion" or "graduation.") There are three different sequences of actions at commit depending on whether the committing instruction is a branch with an incorrect prediction, a store, or any other instruction (normal commit). The normal commit case occurs when an instruction reaches the head of the ROB and its result is present in the buffer; at this point, the processor updates the register with the result and removes the instruction from the ROB. Committing a store is similar except that memory is updated rather than a result register. When a branch with incorrect prediction reaches the head of the ROB, it indicates that the speculation

was wrong. The ROB is flushed and execution is restarted at the correct successor of the branch. If the branch was correctly predicted, the branch is finished.

Once an instruction commits, its entry in the ROB is reclaimed and the register or memory destination is updated, eliminating the need for the ROB entry. If the ROB fills, we simply stop issuing instructions until an entry is made free. Now, let's examine how this scheme would work with the same example we used for Tomasulo's algorithm.

Example   Assume the same latencies for the floating-point functional units as in earlier examples: add is 2 clock cycles, multiply is 6 clock cycles, and divide is 12 clock cycles. Using the code segment below, the same one we used to generate Figure 3.8, show what the status tables look like when the MUL.D is ready to go to commit.

```
L.D     F6,32(R2)
L.D     F2,44(R3)
MUL.D   F0,F2,F4
SUB.D   F8,F2,F6
DIV.D   F10,F0,F6
ADD.D   F6,F8,F2
```

Answer   Figure 3.12 shows the result in the three tables. Notice that although the SUB.D instruction has completed execution, it does not commit until the MUL.D commits. The reservation stations and register status field contain the same basic information that they did for Tomasulo's algorithm (see page 176 for a description of those fields). The differences are that reservation station numbers are replaced with ROB entry numbers in the Qj and Qk fields, as well as in the register status fields, and we have added the Dest field to the reservation stations. The Dest field designates the ROB entry that is the destination for the result produced by this reservation station entry.

The above example illustrates the key important difference between a processor with speculation and a processor with dynamic scheduling. Compare the content of Figure 3.12 with that of Figure 3.8 on page 179, which shows the same code sequence in operation on a processor with Tomasulo's algorithm. The key difference is that, in the example above, no instruction after the earliest uncompleted instruction (MUL.D above) is allowed to complete. In contrast, in Figure 3.8 the SUB.D and ADD.D instructions have also completed.

One implication of this difference is that the processor with the ROB can dynamically execute code while maintaining a precise interrupt model. For example, if the MUL.D instruction caused an interrupt, we could simply wait until it reached the head of the ROB and take the interrupt, flushing any other pending instructions from the ROB. Because instruction commit happens in order, this yields a precise exception.

By contrast, in the example using Tomasulo's algorithm, the SUB.D and ADD.D instructions could both complete before the MUL.D raised the exception.

Reorder buffer

Entry	Busy	Instruction		State	Destination	Value
1	No	L.D	F6,32(R2)	Commit	F6	Mem[32 + Regs[R2]]
2	No	L.D	F2,44(R3)	Commit	F2	Mem[44 + Regs[R3]]
3	Yes	MUL.D	F0,F2,F4	Write result	F0	#2 × Regs[F4]
4	Yes	SUB.D	F8,F2,F6	Write result	F8	#2 − #1
5	Yes	DIV.D	F10,F0,F6	Execute	F10	
6	Yes	ADD.D	F6,F8,F2	Write result	F6	#4 + #2

Reservation stations

Name	Busy	Op	Vj	Vk	Qj	Qk	Dest	A
Load1	No							
Load2	No							
Add1	No							
Add2	No							
Add3	No							
Mult1	No	MUL.D	Mem[44 + Regs[R3]]	Regs[F4]			#3	
Mult2	Yes	DIV.D		Mem[32 + Regs[R2]]	#3		#5	

FP register status

Field	F0	F1	F2	F3	F4	F5	F6	F7	F8	F10
Reorder #	3						6		4	5
Busy	Yes	No	No	No	No	No	Yes	...	Yes	Yes

Figure 3.12 At the time the MUL.D is ready to commit, only the two L.D instructions have committed, although several others have completed execution. The MUL.D is at the head of the ROB, and the two L.D instructions are there only to ease understanding. The SUB.D and ADD.D instructions will not commit until the MUL.D instruction commits, although the results of the instructions are available and can be used as sources for other instructions. The DIV.D is in execution, but has not completed solely due to its longer latency than MUL.D. The Value column indicates the value being held; the format #X is used to refer to a value field of ROB entry X. Reorder buffers 1 and 2 are actually completed but are shown for informational purposes. We do not show the entries for the load/store queue, but these entries are kept in order.

The result is that the registers F8 and F6 (destinations of the SUB.D and ADD.D instructions) could be overwritten, and the interrupt would be imprecise.

Some users and architects have decided that imprecise floating-point exceptions are acceptable in high-performance processors, since the program will likely terminate; see Appendix J for further discussion of this topic. Other types of exceptions, such as page faults, are much more difficult to accommodate if they are imprecise, since the program must transparently resume execution after handling such an exception.

The use of a ROB with in-order instruction commit provides precise exceptions, in addition to supporting speculative execution, as the next example shows.

Example   Consider the code example used earlier for Tomasulo's algorithm and shown in Figure 3.10 in execution:

```
Loop:   L.D      F0,0(R1)
        MUL.D    F4,F0,F2
        S.D      F4,0(R1)
        DADDIU   R1,R1,#-8
        BNE      R1,R2,Loop      ;branches if R1¦R2
```

Assume that we have issued all the instructions in the loop twice. Let's also assume that the L.D and MUL.D from the first iteration have committed and all other instructions have completed execution. Normally, the store would wait in the ROB for both the effective address operand (R1 in this example) and the value (F4 in this example). Since we are only considering the floating-point pipeline, assume the effective address for the store is computed by the time the instruction is issued.

Answer   Figure 3.13 shows the result in two tables.

		Reorder buffer			
Entry	Busy	Instruction	State	Destination	Value
1	No	L.D F0,0(R1)	Commit	F0	Mem[0 + Regs[R1]]
2	No	MUL.D F4,F0,F2	Commit	F4	#1 × Regs[F2]
3	Yes	S.D F4,0(R1)	Write result	0 + Regs[R1]	#2
4	Yes	DADDIU R1,R1,#-8	Write result	R1	Regs[R1] − 8
5	Yes	BNE R1,R2,Loop	Write result		
6	Yes	L.D F0,0(R1)	Write result	F0	Mem[#4]
7	Yes	MUL.D F4,F0,F2	Write result	F4	#6 × Regs[F2]
8	Yes	S.D F4,0(R1)	Write result	0 + #4	#7
9	Yes	DADDIU R1,R1,#-8	Write result	R1	#4 − 8
10	Yes	BNE R1,R2,Loop	Write result		

			FP register status					
Field	F0	F1	F2	F3	F4	F5	F6	F7	F8
Reorder #	6				7				
Busy	Yes	No	No	No	Yes	No	No	...	No

Figure 3.13 Only the L.D and MUL.D instructions have committed, although all the others have completed execution. Hence, no reservation stations are busy and none is shown. The remaining instructions will be committed as quickly as possible. The first two reorder buffers are empty, but are shown for completeness.

Because neither the register values nor any memory values are actually written until an instruction commits, the processor can easily undo its speculative actions when a branch is found to be mispredicted. Suppose that the branch BNE is not taken the first time in Figure 3.13. The instructions prior to the branch will simply commit when each reaches the head of the ROB; when the branch reaches the head of that buffer, the buffer is simply cleared and the processor begins fetching instructions from the other path.

In practice, processors that speculate try to recover as early as possible after a branch is mispredicted. This recovery can be done by clearing the ROB for all entries that appear after the mispredicted branch, allowing those that are before the branch in the ROB to continue, and restarting the fetch at the correct branch successor. In speculative processors, performance is more sensitive to the branch prediction, since the impact of a misprediction will be higher. Thus, all the aspects of handling branches—prediction accuracy, latency of misprediction detection, and misprediction recovery time—increase in importance.

Exceptions are handled by not recognizing the exception until it is ready to commit. If a speculated instruction raises an exception, the exception is recorded in the ROB. If a branch misprediction arises and the instruction should not have been executed, the exception is flushed along with the instruction when the ROB is cleared. If the instruction reaches the head of the ROB, then we know it is no longer speculative and the exception should really be taken. We can also try to handle exceptions as soon as they arise and all earlier branches are resolved, but this is more challenging in the case of exceptions than for branch mispredict and, because it occurs less frequently, not as critical.

Figure 3.14 shows the steps of execution for an instruction, as well as the conditions that must be satisfied to proceed to the step and the actions taken. We show the case where mispredicted branches are not resolved until commit. Although speculation seems like a simple addition to dynamic scheduling, a comparison of Figure 3.14 with the comparable figure for Tomasulo's algorithm in Figure 3.9 shows that speculation adds significant complications to the control. In addition, remember that branch mispredictions are somewhat more complex as well.

There is an important difference in how stores are handled in a speculative processor versus in Tomasulo's algorithm. In Tomasulo's algorithm, a store can update memory when it reaches write result (which ensures that the effective address has been calculated) and the data value to store is available. In a speculative processor, a store updates memory only when it reaches the head of the ROB. This difference ensures that memory is not updated until an instruction is no longer speculative.

Figure 3.14 has one significant simplification for stores, which is unneeded in practice. Figure 3.14 requires stores to wait in the write result stage for the register source operand whose value is to be stored; the value is then moved from the Vk field of the store's reservation station to the Value field of the store's ROB entry. In reality, however, the value to be stored need not arrive

Status	Wait until	Action or bookkeeping

Issue
all
instructions
	Reservation station (r) and ROB (b) both available	`if (RegisterStat[rs].Busy)/*in-flight instr. writes rs*/`
		`    {h ← RegisterStat[rs].Reorder;`
		`    if (ROB[h].Ready)/* Instr completed already */`
		`        {RS[r].Vj ← ROB[h].Value; RS[r].Qj ← 0;}`
		`    else {RS[r].Qj ← h;} /* wait for instruction */`
		`} else {RS[r].Vj ← Regs[rs]; RS[r].Qj ← 0;};`
		`RS[r].Busy ← yes; RS[r].Dest ← b;`
		`ROB[b].Instruction ← opcode; ROB[b].Dest ← rd;ROB[b].Ready ← no;`

FP operations and stores		`if (RegisterStat[rt].Busy) /*in-flight instr writes rt*/`
		`    {h ← RegisterStat[rt].Reorder;`
		`    if (ROB[h].Ready)/* Instr completed already */`
		`        {RS[r].Vk ← ROB[h].Value; RS[r].Qk ← 0;}`
		`    else {RS[r].Qk ← h;} /* wait for instruction */`
		`} else {RS[r].Vk ← Regs[rt]; RS[r].Qk ← 0;};`

FP operations		`RegisterStat[rd].Reorder ← b; RegisterStat[rd].Busy ← yes;` `ROB[b].Dest ← rd;`
Loads		`RS[r].A ← imm; RegisterStat[rt].Reorder ← b;` `RegisterStat[rt].Busy ← yes; ROB[b].Dest ← rt;`
Stores		`RS[r].A ← imm;`
Execute FP op	`(RS[r].Qj == 0) and (RS[r].Qk == 0)`	Compute results—operands are in Vj and Vk
Load step 1	`(RS[r].Qj == 0)` and there are no stores earlier in the queue	`RS[r].A ← RS[r].Vj + RS[r].A;`
Load step 2	Load step 1 done and all stores earlier in ROB have different address	Read from `Mem[RS[r].A]`
Store	`(RS[r].Qj == 0)` and store at queue head	`ROB[h].Address ← RS[r].Vj + RS[r].A;`

Write result all but store	Execution done at r and CDB available	`b ← RS[r].Dest; RS[r].Busy ← no;`
		`∀x(if (RS[x].Qj==b) {RS[x].Vj ← result; RS[x].Qj ← 0});`
		`∀x(if (RS[x].Qk==b) {RS[x].Vk ← result; RS[x].Qk ← 0});`
		`ROB[b].Value ← result; ROB[b].Ready ← yes;`

Store	Execution done at r and `(RS[r].Qk == 0)`	`ROB[h].Value ← RS[r].Vk;`

Commit	Instruction is at the head of the ROB (entry h) and `ROB[h].ready == yes`	`d ← ROB[h].Dest; /* register dest, if exists */`
		`if (ROB[h].Instruction==Branch)`
		`    {if (branch is mispredicted)`
		`        {clear ROB[h], RegisterStat; fetch branch dest;};}`
		`else if (ROB[h].Instruction==Store)`
		`        {Mem[ROB[h].Destination] ← ROB[h].Value;}`
		`else /* put the result in the register destination */`
		`    {Regs[d] ← ROB[h].Value;};`
		`ROB[h].Busy ← no; /* free up ROB entry */`
		`/* free up dest register if no one else writing it */`
		`if (RegisterStat[d].Reorder==h) {RegisterStat[d].Busy ← no;};`

Figure 3.14 Steps in the algorithm and what is required for each step. For the issuing instruction, rd is the destination, rs and rt are the sources, r is the reservation station allocated, b is the assigned ROB entry, and h is the head entry of the ROB. RS is the reservation station data structure. The value returned by a reservation station is called the result. RegisterStat is the register data structure, Regs represents the actual registers, and ROB is the reorder buffer data structure.

until *just before* the store commits and can be placed directly into the store's ROB entry by the sourcing instruction. This is accomplished by having the hardware track when the source value to be stored is available in the store's ROB entry and searching the ROB on every instruction completion to look for dependent stores.

This addition is not complicated, but adding it has two effects: We would need to add a field to the ROB, and Figure 3.14, which is already in a small font, would be even longer! Although Figure 3.14 makes this simplification, in our examples, we will allow the store to pass through the write result stage and simply wait for the value to be ready when it commits.

Like Tomasulo's algorithm, we must avoid hazards through memory. WAW and WAR hazards through memory are eliminated with speculation because the actual updating of memory occurs in order, when a store is at the head of the ROB, and, hence, no earlier loads or stores can still be pending. RAW hazards through memory are maintained by two restrictions:

1. Not allowing a load to initiate the second step of its execution if any active ROB entry occupied by a store has a Destination field that matches the value of the A field of the load.

2. Maintaining the program order for the computation of an effective address of a load with respect to all earlier stores.

Together, these two restrictions ensure that any load that accesses a memory location written to by an earlier store cannot perform the memory access until the store has written the data. Some speculative processors will actually bypass the value from the store to the load directly, when such a RAW hazard occurs. Another approach is to predict potential collisions using a form of value prediction; we consider this in Section 3.9.

Although this explanation of speculative execution has focused on floating point, the techniques easily extend to the integer registers and functional units. Indeed, speculation may be more useful in integer programs, since such programs tend to have code where the branch behavior is less predictable. Additionally, these techniques can be extended to work in a multiple-issue processor by allowing multiple instructions to issue and commit every clock. In fact, speculation is probably most interesting in such processors, since less ambitious techniques can probably exploit sufficient ILP within basic blocks when assisted by a compiler.

3.7   Exploiting ILP Using Multiple Issue and Static Scheduling

The techniques of the preceding sections can be used to eliminate data, control stalls, and achieve an ideal CPI of one. To improve performance further we would like to decrease the CPI to less than one, but the CPI cannot be reduced below one if we issue only one instruction every clock cycle.

The goal of the *multiple-issue processors*, discussed in the next few sections, is to allow multiple instructions to issue in a clock cycle. Multiple-issue processors come in three major flavors:

1. Statically scheduled superscalar processors
2. VLIW (very long instruction word) processors
3. Dynamically scheduled superscalar processors

The two types of superscalar processors issue varying numbers of instructions per clock and use in-order execution if they are statically scheduled or out-of-order execution if they are dynamically scheduled.

VLIW processors, in contrast, issue a fixed number of instructions formatted either as one large instruction or as a fixed instruction packet with the parallelism among instructions explicitly indicated by the instruction. VLIW processors are inherently statically scheduled by the compiler. When Intel and HP created the IA-64 architecture, described in Appendix H, they also introduced the name EPIC—explicitly parallel instruction computer—for this architectural style.

Although statically scheduled superscalars issue a varying rather than a fixed number of instructions per clock, they are actually closer in concept to VLIWs, since both approaches rely on the compiler to schedule code for the processor. Because of the diminishing advantages of a statically scheduled superscalar as the issue width grows, statically scheduled superscalars are used primarily for narrow issue widths, normally just two instructions. Beyond that width, most designers choose to implement either a VLIW or a dynamically scheduled superscalar. Because of the similarities in hardware and required compiler technology, we focus on VLIWs in this section. The insights of this section are easily extrapolated to a statically scheduled superscalar.

Figure 3.15 summarizes the basic approaches to multiple issue and their distinguishing characteristics and shows processors that use each approach.

The Basic VLIW Approach

VLIWs use multiple, independent functional units. Rather than attempting to issue multiple, independent instructions to the units, a VLIW packages the multiple operations into one very long instruction, or requires that the instructions in the issue packet satisfy the same constraints. Since there is no fundamental difference in the two approaches, we will just assume that multiple operations are placed in one instruction, as in the original VLIW approach.

Since the advantage of a VLIW increases as the maximum issue rate grows, we focus on a wider issue processor. Indeed, for simple two-issue processors, the overhead of a superscalar is probably minimal. Many designers would probably argue that a four-issue processor has manageable overhead, but as we will see later in this chapter, the growth in overhead is a major factor limiting wider issue processors.

Common name	Issue structure	Hazard detection	Scheduling	Distinguishing characteristic	Examples
Superscalar (static)	Dynamic	Hardware	Static	In-order execution	Mostly in the embedded space: MIPS and ARM, including the ARM Cortex-A8
Superscalar (dynamic)	Dynamic	Hardware	Dynamic	Some out-of-order execution, but no speculation	None at the present
Superscalar (speculative)	Dynamic	Hardware	Dynamic with speculation	Out-of-order execution with speculation	Intel Core i3, i5, i7; AMD Phenom; IBM Power 7
VLIW/LIW	Static	Primarily software	Static	All hazards determined and indicated by compiler (often implicitly)	Most examples are in signal processing, such as the TI C6x
EPIC	Primarily static	Primarily software	Mostly static	All hazards determined and indicated explicitly by the compiler	Itanium

Figure 3.15 The five primary approaches in use for multiple-issue processors and the primary characteristics that distinguish them. This chapter has focused on the hardware-intensive techniques, which are all some form of superscalar. Appendix H focuses on compiler-based approaches. The EPIC approach, as embodied in the IA-64 architecture, extends many of the concepts of the early VLIW approaches, providing a blend of static and dynamic approaches.

Let's consider a VLIW processor with instructions that contain five operations, including one integer operation (which could also be a branch), two floating-point operations, and two memory references. The instruction would have a set of fields for each functional unit—perhaps 16 to 24 bits per unit, yielding an instruction length of between 80 and 120 bits. By comparison, the Intel Itanium 1 and 2 contain six operations per instruction packet (i.e., they allow concurrent issue of two three-instruction bundles, as Appendix H describes).

To keep the functional units busy, there must be enough parallelism in a code sequence to fill the available operation slots. This parallelism is uncovered by unrolling loops and scheduling the code within the single larger loop body. If the unrolling generates straight-line code, then *local scheduling* techniques, which operate on a single basic block, can be used. If finding and exploiting the parallelism require scheduling code across branches, a substantially more complex *global scheduling* algorithm must be used. Global scheduling algorithms are not only more complex in structure, but they also must deal with significantly more complicated trade-offs in optimization, since moving code across branches is expensive.

In Appendix H, we will discuss *trace scheduling*, one of these global scheduling techniques developed specifically for VLIWs; we will also explore special hardware support that allows some conditional branches to be eliminated, extending the usefulness of local scheduling and enhancing the performance of global scheduling.

For now, we will rely on loop unrolling to generate long, straight-line code sequences, so that we can use local scheduling to build up VLIW instructions and focus on how well these processors operate.

Example   Suppose we have a VLIW that could issue two memory references, two FP operations, and one integer operation or branch in every clock cycle. Show an unrolled version of the loop x[i] = x[i] + s (see page 158 for the MIPS code) for such a processor. Unroll as many times as necessary to eliminate any stalls. Ignore delayed branches.

Answer   Figure 3.16 shows the code. The loop has been unrolled to make seven copies of the body, which eliminates all stalls (i.e., completely empty issue cycles), and runs in 9 cycles. This code yields a running rate of seven results in 9 cycles, or 1.29 cycles per result, nearly twice as fast as the two-issue superscalar of Section 3.2 that used unrolled and scheduled code.

For the original VLIW model, there were both technical and logistical problems that make the approach less efficient. The technical problems are the increase in code size and the limitations of lockstep operation. Two different elements combine to increase code size substantially for a VLIW. First, generating enough operations in a straight-line code fragment requires ambitiously unrolling loops (as in earlier examples), thereby increasing code size. Second, whenever instructions are not full, the unused functional units translate to wasted bits in the instruction encoding. In Appendix H, we examine software scheduling

Memory reference 1	Memory reference 2	FP operation 1	FP operation 2	Integer operation/branch
L.D F0,0(R1)	L.D F6,-8(R1)			
L.D F10,-16(R1)	L.D F14,-24(R1)			
L.D F18,-32(R1)	L.D F22,-40(R1)	ADD.D F4,F0,F2	ADD.D F8,F6,F2	
L.D F26,-48(R1)		ADD.D F12,F10,F2	ADD.D F16,F14,F2	
		ADD.D F20,F18,F2	ADD.D F24,F22,F2	
S.D F4,0(R1)	S.D F8,-8(R1)	ADD.D F28,F26,F2		
S.D F12,-16(R1)	S.D F16,-24(R1)			DADDUI R1,R1,#-56
S.D F20,24(R1)	S.D F24,16(R1)			
S.D F28,8(R1)				BNE R1,R2,Loop

Figure 3.16 VLIW instructions that occupy the inner loop and replace the unrolled sequence. This code takes 9 cycles assuming no branch delay; normally the branch delay would also need to be scheduled. The issue rate is 23 operations in 9 clock cycles, or 2.5 operations per cycle. The efficiency, the percentage of available slots that contained an operation, is about 60%. To achieve this issue rate requires a larger number of registers than MIPS would normally use in this loop. The VLIW code sequence above requires at least eight FP registers, while the same code sequence for the base MIPS processor can use as few as two FP registers or as many as five when unrolled and scheduled.

approaches, such as software pipelining, that can achieve the benefits of unrolling without as much code expansion.

To combat this code size increase, clever encodings are sometimes used. For example, there may be only one large immediate field for use by any functional unit. Another technique is to compress the instructions in main memory and expand them when they are read into the cache or are decoded. In Appendix H, we show other techniques, as well as document the significant code expansion seen on IA-64.

Early VLIWs operated in lockstep; there was no hazard-detection hardware at all. This structure dictated that a stall in any functional unit pipeline must cause the entire processor to stall, since all the functional units must be kept synchronized. Although a compiler may be able to schedule the deterministic functional units to prevent stalls, predicting which data accesses will encounter a cache stall and scheduling them are very difficult. Hence, caches needed to be blocking and to cause *all* the functional units to stall. As the issue rate and number of memory references becomes large, this synchronization restriction becomes unacceptable. In more recent processors, the functional units operate more independently, and the compiler is used to avoid hazards at issue time, while hardware checks allow for unsynchronized execution once instructions are issued.

Binary code compatibility has also been a major logistical problem for VLIWs. In a strict VLIW approach, the code sequence makes use of both the instruction set definition and the detailed pipeline structure, including both functional units and their latencies. Thus, different numbers of functional units and unit latencies require different versions of the code. This requirement makes migrating between successive implementations, or between implementations with different issue widths, more difficult than it is for a superscalar design. Of course, obtaining improved performance from a new superscalar design may require recompilation. Nonetheless, the ability to run old binary files is a practical advantage for the superscalar approach.

The EPIC approach, of which the IA-64 architecture is the primary example, provides solutions to many of the problems encountered in early VLIW designs, including extensions for more aggressive software speculation and methods to overcome the limitation of hardware dependence while preserving binary compatibility.

The major challenge for all multiple-issue processors is to try to exploit large amounts of ILP. When the parallelism comes from unrolling simple loops in FP programs, the original loop probably could have been run efficiently on a vector processor (described in the next chapter). It is not clear that a multiple-issue processor is preferred over a vector processor for such applications; the costs are similar, and the vector processor is typically the same speed or faster. The potential advantages of a multiple-issue processor versus a vector processor are their ability to extract some parallelism from less structured code and their ability to easily cache all forms of data. For these reasons multiple-issue approaches have become the primary method for taking advantage of instruction-level parallelism, and vectors have become primarily an extension to these processors.

Exploiting ILP Using Dynamic Scheduling, Multiple Issue, and Speculation

So far, we have seen how the individual mechanisms of dynamic scheduling, multiple issue, and speculation work. In this section, we put all three together, which yields a microarchitecture quite similar to those in modern microprocessors. For simplicity, we consider only an issue rate of two instructions per clock, but the concepts are no different from modern processors that issue three or more instructions per clock.

Let's assume we want to extend Tomasulo's algorithm to support multiple-issue superscalar pipeline with separate integer, load/store, and floating-point units (both FP multiply and FP add), each of which can initiate an operation on every clock. We do not want to issue instructions to the reservation stations out of order, since this could lead to a violation of the program semantics. To gain the full advantage of dynamic scheduling we will allow the pipeline to issue any combination of two instructions in a clock, using the scheduling hardware to actually assign operations to the integer and floating-point unit. Because the interaction of the integer and floating-point instructions is crucial, we also extend Tomasulo's scheme to deal with both the integer and floating-point functional units and registers, as well as incorporating speculative execution. As Figure 3.17 shows, the basic organization is similar to that of a processor with speculation with one issue per clock, except that the issue and completion logic must be enhanced to allow multiple instructions to be processed per clock.

Issuing multiple instructions per clock in a dynamically scheduled processor (with or without speculation) is very complex for the simple reason that the multiple instructions may depend on one another. Because of this the tables must be updated for the instructions in parallel; otherwise, the tables will be incorrect or the dependence may be lost.

Two different approaches have been used to issue multiple instructions per clock in a dynamically scheduled processor, and both rely on the observation that the key is assigning a reservation station and updating the pipeline control tables. One approach is to run this step in half a clock cycle, so that two instructions can be processed in one clock cycle; this approach cannot be easily extended to handle four instructions per clock, unfortunately.

A second alternative is to build the logic necessary to handle two or more instructions at once, including any possible dependences between the instructions. Modern superscalar processors that issue four or more instructions per clock may include both approaches: They both pipeline and widen the issue logic. A key observation is that we cannot simply pipeline away the problem. By making instruction issues take multiple clocks because new instructions are issuing every clock cycle, we must be able to assign the reservation station and to update the pipeline tables, so that a dependent instruction issuing on the next clock can use the updated information.

This issue step is one of the most fundamental bottlenecks in dynamically scheduled superscalars. To illustrate the complexity of this process, Figure 3.18

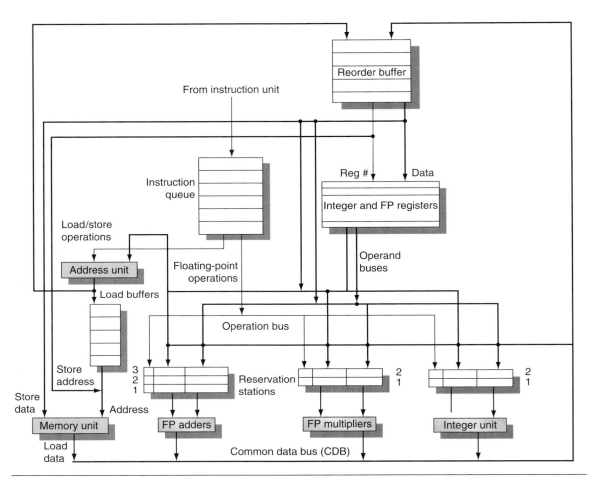

Figure 3.17 The basic organization of a multiple issue processor with speculation. In this case, the organization could allow a FP multiply, FP add, integer, and load/store to all issues simultaneously (assuming one issue per clock per functional unit). Note that several datapaths must be widened to support multiple issues: the CDB, the operand buses, and, critically, the instruction issue logic, which is not shown in this figure. The last is a difficult problem, as we discuss in the text.

shows the issue logic for one case: issuing a load followed by a dependent FP operation. The logic is based on that in Figure 3.14 on page 191, but represents only one case. In a modern superscalar, every possible combination of dependent instructions that is allowed to issue in the same clock cycle must be considered. Since the number of possibilities climbs as the square of the number of instructions that can be issued in a clock, the issue step is a likely bottleneck for attempts to go beyond four instructions per clock.

We can generalize the detail of Figure 3.18 to describe the basic strategy for updating the issue logic and the reservation tables in a dynamically scheduled superscalar with up to n issues per clock as follows:

Action or bookkeeping	Comments

`if (RegisterStat[rs1].Busy)/*in-flight instr. writes rs*/`
`{h ← RegisterStat[rs1].Reorder;`
`if (ROB[h].Ready)/* Instr completed already */`
`{RS[r1].Vj ← ROB[h].Value; RS[r1].Qj ← 0;}`
`else {RS[r1].Qj ← h;} /* wait for instruction */`
`} else {RS[r1].Vj ← Regs[rs]; RS[r1].Qj ← 0;};`
`RS[r1].Busy ← yes; RS[r1].Dest ← b1;`
`ROB[b1].Instruction ← Load; ROB[b1].Dest ← rd1;`
`ROB[b1].Ready ← no;`
`RS[r].A ← imm1; RegisterStat[rt1].Reorder ← b1;`
`RegisterStat[rt1].Busy ← yes; ROB[b1].Dest ← rt1;`
	Updating the reservation tables for the load instruction, which has a single source operand. Because this is the first instruction in this issue bundle, it looks no different than what would normally happen for a load.

`RS[r2].Qj ← b1;} /* wait for load instruction */`	Since we know that the first operand of the FP operation is from the load, this step simply updates the reservation station to point to the load. Notice that the dependence must be analyzed on the fly and the ROB entries must be allocated during this issue step so that the reservation tables can be correctly updated.

`if (RegisterStat[rt2].Busy) /*in-flight instr writes rt*/`
`{h ← RegisterStat[rt2].Reorder;`
`if (ROB[h].Ready)/* Instr completed already */`
`{RS[r2].Vk ← ROB[h].Value; RS[r2].Qk ← 0;}`
`else {RS[r2].Qk ← h;} /* wait for instruction */`
`} else {RS[r2].Vk ← Regs[rt2]; RS[r2].Qk ← 0;};`
`RegisterStat[rd2].Reorder ← b2;`
`RegisterStat[rd2].Busy ← yes;`
`ROB[b2].Dest ← rd2;`
	Since we assumed that the second operand of the FP instruction was from a prior issue bundle, this step looks like it would in the single-issue case. Of course, if this instruction was dependent on something in the same issue bundle the tables would need to be updated using the assigned reservation buffer.

`RS[r2].Busy ← yes; RS[r2].Dest ← b2;`
`ROB[b2].Instruction ← FP operation; ROB[b2].Dest ← rd2;`
`ROB[b2].Ready ← no;`
	This section simply updates the tables for the FP operation, and is independent of the load. Of course, if further instructions in this issue bundle depended on the FP operation (as could happen with a four-issue superscalar), the updates to the reservation tables for those instructions would be effected by this instruction.

Figure 3.18 The issue steps for a pair of dependent instructions (called 1 and 2) where instruction 1 is FP load and instruction 2 is an FP operation whose first operand is the result of the load instruction; r1 and r2 are the assigned reservation stations for the instructions; and b1 and b2 are the assigned reorder buffer entries. For the issuing instructions, rd1 and rd2 are the destinations; rs1, rs2, and rt2 are the sources (the load only has one source); r1 and r2 are the reservation stations allocated; and b1 and b2 are the assigned ROB entries. RS is the reservation station data structure. RegisterStat is the register data structure, Regs represents the actual registers, and ROB is the reorder buffer data structure. Notice that we need to have assigned reorder buffer entries for this logic to operate properly and recall that all these updates happen in a single clock cycle in parallel, not sequentially!

1. Assign a reservation station and a reorder buffer for *every* instruction that *might* be issued in the next issue bundle. This assignment can be done before the instruction types are known, by simply preallocating the reorder buffer entries sequentially to the instructions in the packet using *n* available reorder buffer entries and by ensuring that enough reservation stations are available to issue the whole bundle, independent of what it contains. By limiting the number of instructions of a given class (say, one FP, one integer, one load,

one store), the necessary reservation stations can be preallocated. Should sufficient reservation stations not be available (such as when the next few instructions in the program are all of one instruction type), the bundle is broken, and only a subset of the instructions, in the original program order, is issued. The remainder of the instructions in the bundle can be placed in the next bundle for potential issue.

2. Analyze all the dependences among the instructions in the issue bundle.

3. If an instruction in the bundle depends on an earlier instruction in the bundle, use the assigned reorder buffer number to update the reservation table for the dependent instruction. Otherwise, use the existing reservation table and reorder buffer information to update the reservation table entries for the issuing instruction.

Of course, what makes the above very complicated is that it is all done in parallel in a single clock cycle!

At the back-end of the pipeline, we must be able to complete and commit multiple instructions per clock. These steps are somewhat easier than the issue problems since multiple instructions that can actually commit in the same clock cycle must have already dealt with and resolved any dependences. As we will see, designers have figured out how to handle this complexity: The Intel i7, which we examine in Section 3.13, uses essentially the scheme we have described for speculative multiple issue, including a large number of reservation stations, a reorder buffer, and a load and store buffer that is also used to handle nonblocking cache misses.

From a performance viewpoint, we can show how the concepts fit together with an example.

Example   Consider the execution of the following loop, which increments each element of an integer array, on a two-issue processor, once without speculation and once with speculation:

```
Loop:    LD       R2,0(R1)      ;R2=array element
         DADDIU   R2,R2,#1      ;increment R2
         SD       R2,0(R1)      ;store result
         DADDIU   R1,R1,#8      ;increment pointer
         BNE      R2,R3,LOOP    ;branch if not last element
```

Assume that there are separate integer functional units for effective address calculation, for ALU operations, and for branch condition evaluation. Create a table for the first three iterations of this loop for both processors. Assume that up to two instructions of any type can commit per clock.

Answer   Figures 3.19 and 3.20 show the performance for a two-issue dynamically scheduled processor, without and with speculation. In this case, where a branch can be a critical performance limiter, speculation helps significantly. The third branch in

Iteration number	Instructions		Issues at clock cycle number	Executes at clock cycle number	Memory access at clock cycle number	Write CDB at clock cycle number	Comment
1	LD	R2,0(R1)	1	2	3	4	First issue
1	DADDIU	R2,R2,#1	1	5		6	Wait for LW
1	SD	R2,0(R1)	2	3	7		Wait for DADDIU
1	DADDIU	R1,R1,#8	2	3		4	Execute directly
1	BNE	R2,R3,LOOP	3	7			Wait for DADDIU
2	LD	R2,0(R1)	4	8	9	10	Wait for BNE
2	DADDIU	R2,R2,#1	4	11		12	Wait for LW
2	SD	R2,0(R1)	5	9	13		Wait for DADDIU
2	DADDIU	R1,R1,#8	5	8		9	Wait for BNE
2	BNE	R2,R3,LOOP	6	13			Wait for DADDIU
3	LD	R2,0(R1)	7	14	15	16	Wait for BNE
3	DADDIU	R2,R2,#1	7	17		18	Wait for LW
3	SD	R2,0(R1)	8	15	19		Wait for DADDIU
3	DADDIU	R1,R1,#8	8	14		15	Wait for BNE
3	BNE	R2,R3,LOOP	9	19			Wait for DADDIU

Figure 3.19 The time of issue, execution, and writing result for a dual-issue version of our pipeline *without* speculation. Note that the LD following the BNE cannot start execution earlier because it must wait until the branch outcome is determined. This type of program, with data-dependent branches that cannot be resolved earlier, shows the strength of speculation. Separate functional units for address calculation, ALU operations, and branch-condition evaluation allow multiple instructions to execute in the same cycle. Figure 3.20 shows this example with speculation.

the speculative processor executes in clock cycle 13, while it executes in clock cycle 19 on the nonspeculative pipeline. Because the completion rate on the nonspeculative pipeline is falling behind the issue rate rapidly, the nonspeculative pipeline will stall when a few more iterations are issued. The performance of the nonspeculative processor could be improved by allowing load instructions to complete effective address calculation before a branch is decided, but unless speculative memory accesses are allowed, this improvement will gain only 1 clock per iteration.

This example clearly shows how speculation can be advantageous when there are data-dependent branches, which otherwise would limit performance. This advantage depends, however, on accurate branch prediction. Incorrect speculation does not improve performance; in fact, it typically harms performance and, as we shall see, dramatically lowers energy efficiency.

Iteration number	Instructions		Issues at clock number	Executes at clock number	Read access at clock number	Write CDB at clock number	Commits at clock number	Comment
1	LD	R2,0(R1)	1	2	3	4	5	First issue
1	DADDIU	R2,R2,#1	1	5		6	7	Wait for LW
1	SD	R2,0(R1)	2	3			7	Wait for DADDIU
1	DADDIU	R1,R1,#8	2	3		4	8	Commit in order
1	BNE	R2,R3,LOOP	3	7			8	Wait for DADDIU
2	LD	R2,0(R1)	4	5	6	7	9	No execute delay
2	DADDIU	R2,R2,#1	4	8		9	10	Wait for LW
2	SD	R2,0(R1)	5	6			10	Wait for DADDIU
2	DADDIU	R1,R1,#8	5	6		7	11	Commit in order
2	BNE	R2,R3,LOOP	6	10			11	Wait for DADDIU
3	LD	R2,0(R1)	7	8	9	10	12	Earliest possible
3	DADDIU	R2,R2,#1	7	11		12	13	Wait for LW
3	SD	R2,0(R1)	8	9			13	Wait for DADDIU
3	DADDIU	R1,R1,#8	8	9		10	14	Executes earlier
3	BNE	R2,R3,LOOP	9	13			14	Wait for DADDIU

Figure 3.20 The time of issue, execution, and writing result for a dual-issue version of our pipeline *with* speculation. Note that the LD following the BNE can start execution early because it is speculative.

3.9

Advanced Techniques for Instruction Delivery and Speculation

In a high-performance pipeline, especially one with multiple issues, predicting branches well is not enough; we actually have to be able to deliver a high-bandwidth instruction stream. In recent multiple-issue processors, this has meant delivering 4 to 8 instructions every clock cycle. We look at methods for increasing instruction delivery bandwidth first. We then turn to a set of key issues in implementing advanced speculation techniques, including the use of register renaming versus reorder buffers, the aggressiveness of speculation, and a technique called *value prediction*, which attempts to predict the result of a computation and which could further enhance ILP.

Increasing Instruction Fetch Bandwidth

A multiple-issue processor will require that the average number of instructions fetched every clock cycle be at least as large as the average throughput. Of course, fetching these instructions requires wide enough paths to the instruction cache, but the most difficult aspect is handling branches. In this section, we look

at two methods for dealing with branches and then discuss how modern processors integrate the instruction prediction and prefetch functions.

Branch-Target Buffers

To reduce the branch penalty for our simple five-stage pipeline, as well as for
deeper pipelines, we must know whether the as-yet-undecoded instruction is a
branch and, if so, what the next program counter (PC) should be. If the
instruction is a branch and we know what the next PC should be, we can have a
branch penalty of zero. A branch-prediction cache that stores the predicted
address for the next instruction after a branch is called a *branch-target buffer* or
branch-target cache. Figure 3.21 shows a branch-target buffer.

Because a branch-target buffer predicts the next instruction address and will
send it out *before* decoding the instruction, we *must* know whether the fetched
instruction is predicted as a taken branch. If the PC of the fetched instruction
matches an address in the prediction buffer, then the corresponding predicted PC
is used as the next PC. The hardware for this branch-target buffer is essentially
identical to the hardware for a cache.

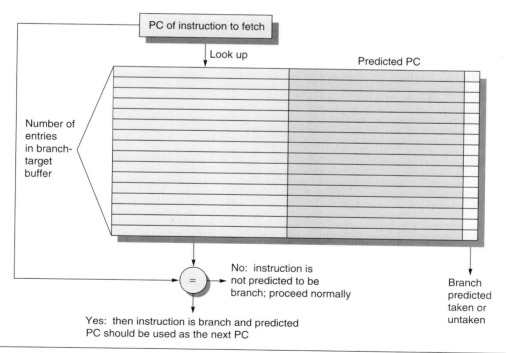

Figure 3.21 A branch-target buffer. The PC of the instruction being fetched is matched against a set of instruction
addresses stored in the first column; these represent the addresses of known branches. If the PC matches one of
these entries, then the instruction being fetched is a taken branch, and the second field, predicted PC, contains the
prediction for the next PC after the branch. Fetching begins immediately at that address. The third field, which is
optional, may be used for extra prediction state bits.

If a matching entry is found in the branch-target buffer, fetching begins immediately at the predicted PC. Note that unlike a branch-prediction buffer, the predictive entry must be matched to this instruction because the predicted PC will be sent out before it is known whether this instruction is even a branch. If the processor did not check whether the entry matched this PC, then the wrong PC would be sent out for instructions that were not branches, resulting in worse performance. We only need to store the predicted-taken branches in the branch-target buffer, since an untaken branch should simply fetch the next sequential instruction, as if it were not a branch.

Figure 3.22 shows the steps when using a branch-target buffer for a simple five-stage pipeline. From this figure we can see that there will be no branch delay

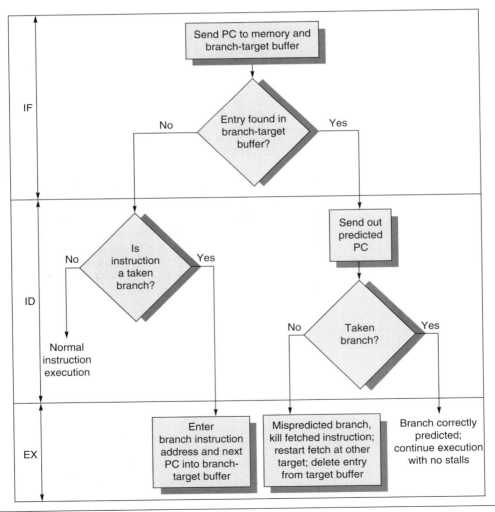

Figure 3.22 The steps involved in handling an instruction with a branch-target buffer.

Instruction in buffer	Prediction	Actual branch	Penalty cycles
Yes	Taken	Taken	0
Yes	Taken	Not taken	2
No		Taken	2
No		Not taken	0

Figure 3.23 Penalties for all possible combinations of whether the branch is in the buffer and what it actually does, assuming we store only taken branches in the buffer. There is no branch penalty if everything is correctly predicted and the branch is found in the target buffer. If the branch is not correctly predicted, the penalty is equal to one clock cycle to update the buffer with the correct information (during which an instruction cannot be fetched) and one clock cycle, if needed, to restart fetching the next correct instruction for the branch. If the branch is not found and taken, a two-cycle penalty is encountered, during which time the buffer is updated.

if a branch-prediction entry is found in the buffer and the prediction is correct. Otherwise, there will be a penalty of at least two clock cycles. Dealing with the mispredictions and misses is a significant challenge, since we typically will have to halt instruction fetch while we rewrite the buffer entry. Thus, we would like to make this process fast to minimize the penalty.

To evaluate how well a branch-target buffer works, we first must determine the penalties in all possible cases. Figure 3.23 contains this information for a simple five-stage pipeline.

Example Determine the total branch penalty for a branch-target buffer assuming the penalty cycles for individual mispredictions from Figure 3.23. Make the following assumptions about the prediction accuracy and hit rate:

■ Prediction accuracy is 90% (for instructions in the buffer).

■ Hit rate in the buffer is 90% (for branches predicted taken).

Answer We compute the penalty by looking at the probability of two events: the branch is predicted taken but ends up being not taken, and the branch is taken but is not found in the buffer. Both carry a penalty of two cycles.

Probability (branch in buffer, but actually not taken) = Percent buffer hit rate × Percent incorrect predictions
= 90% × 10% = 0.09
Probability (branch not in buffer, but actually taken) = 10%
Branch penalty = $(0.09 + 0.10) \times 2$
Branch penalty = 0.38

This penalty compares with a branch penalty for delayed branches, which we evaluate in Appendix C, of about 0.5 clock cycles per branch. Remember, though, that the improvement from dynamic branch prediction will grow as the pipeline length and, hence, the branch delay grows; in addition, better predictors will yield a larger performance advantage. Modern high-performance processors have branch misprediction delays on the order of 15 clock cycles; clearly, accurate prediction is critical!

One variation on the branch-target buffer is to store one or more *target instructions* instead of, or in addition to, the predicted *target address*. This variation has two potential advantages. First, it allows the branch-target buffer access to take longer than the time between successive instruction fetches, possibly allowing a larger branch-target buffer. Second, buffering the actual target instructions allows us to perform an optimization called *branch folding*. Branch folding can be used to obtain 0-cycle unconditional branches and sometimes 0-cycle conditional branches.

Consider a branch-target buffer that buffers instructions from the predicted path and is being accessed with the address of an unconditional branch. The only function of the unconditional branch is to change the PC. Thus, when the branch-target buffer signals a hit and indicates that the branch is unconditional, the pipeline can simply substitute the instruction from the branch-target buffer in place of the instruction that is returned from the cache (which is the unconditional branch). If the processor is issuing multiple instructions per cycle, then the buffer will need to supply multiple instructions to obtain the maximum benefit. In some cases, it may be possible to eliminate the cost of a conditional branch.

Return Address Predictors

As we try to increase the opportunity and accuracy of speculation we face the challenge of predicting indirect jumps, that is, jumps whose destination address varies at runtime. Although high-level language programs will generate such jumps for indirect procedure calls, select or case statements, and FORTRAN-computed gotos, the vast majority of the indirect jumps come from procedure returns. For example, for the SPEC95 benchmarks, procedure returns account for more than 15% of the branches and the vast majority of the indirect jumps on average. For object-oriented languages such as C++ and Java, procedure returns are even more frequent. Thus, focusing on procedure returns seems appropriate.

Though procedure returns can be predicted with a branch-target buffer, the accuracy of such a prediction technique can be low if the procedure is called from multiple sites and the calls from one site are not clustered in time. For example, in SPEC CPU95, an aggressive branch predictor achieves an accuracy of less than 60% for such return branches. To overcome this problem, some designs use a small buffer of return addresses operating as a stack. This structure caches the most recent return addresses: pushing a return address on the stack at a call and popping one off at a return. If the cache is sufficiently large (i.e., as large as the maximum call depth), it will predict the returns perfectly. Figure 3.24 shows the performance of such a return buffer with 0 to 16 elements for a number of the SPEC CPU95 benchmarks. We will use a similar return predictor when we examine the studies of

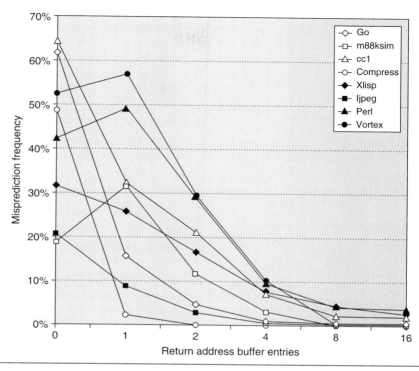

Figure 3.24 Prediction accuracy for a return address buffer operated as a stack on a number of SPEC CPU95 benchmarks. The accuracy is the fraction of return addresses predicted correctly. A buffer of 0 entries implies that the standard branch prediction is used. Since call depths are typically not large, with some exceptions, a modest buffer works well. These data come from Skadron et al. [1999] and use a fix-up mechanism to prevent corruption of the cached return addresses.

ILP in Section 3.10. Both the Intel Core processors and the AMD Phenom processors have return address predictors.

Integrated Instruction Fetch Units

To meet the demands of multiple-issue processors, many recent designers have chosen to implement an integrated instruction fetch unit as a separate autonomous unit that feeds instructions to the rest of the pipeline. Essentially, this amounts to recognizing that characterizing instruction fetch as a simple single pipe stage given the complexities of multiple issue is no longer valid.

Instead, recent designs have used an integrated instruction fetch unit that integrates several functions:

1. *Integrated branch prediction*—The branch predictor becomes part of the instruction fetch unit and is constantly predicting branches, so as to drive the fetch pipeline.

2. *Instruction prefetch*—To deliver multiple instructions per clock, the instruction fetch unit will likely need to fetch ahead. The unit autonomously manages the prefetching of instructions (see Chapter 2 for a discussion of techniques for doing this), integrating it with branch prediction.

3. *Instruction memory access and buffering*—When fetching multiple instructions per cycle a variety of complexities are encountered, including the difficulty that fetching multiple instructions may require accessing multiple cache lines. The instruction fetch unit encapsulates this complexity, using prefetch to try to hide the cost of crossing cache blocks. The instruction fetch unit also provides buffering, essentially acting as an on-demand unit to provide instructions to the issue stage as needed and in the quantity needed.

Virtually all high-end processors now use a separate instruction fetch unit connected to the rest of the pipeline by a buffer containing pending instructions.

Speculation: Implementation Issues and Extensions

In this section we explore four issues that involve the design trade-offs in speculation, starting with the use of register renaming, the approach that is often used instead of a reorder buffer. We then discuss one important possible extension to speculation on control flow: an idea called *value prediction*.

Speculation Support: Register Renaming versus Reorder Buffers

One alternative to the use of a reorder buffer (ROB) is the explicit use of a larger physical set of registers combined with register renaming. This approach builds on the concept of renaming used in Tomasulo's algorithm and extends it. In Tomasulo's algorithm, the values of the *architecturally visible registers* (R0, ..., R31 and F0, ..., F31) are contained, at any point in execution, in some combination of the register set and the reservation stations. With the addition of speculation, register values may also temporarily reside in the ROB. In either case, if the processor does not issue new instructions for a period of time, all existing instructions will commit, and the register values will appear in the register file, which directly corresponds to the architecturally visible registers.

In the register-renaming approach, an extended set of physical registers is used to hold both the architecturally visible registers as well as temporary values. Thus, the extended registers replace most of the function of the ROB and the reservation stations; only a queue to ensure that instructions complete in order is needed. During instruction issue, a renaming process maps the names of architectural registers to physical register numbers in the extended register set, allocating a new unused register for the destination. WAW and WAR hazards are avoided by renaming of the destination register, and speculation recovery is handled because a physical register holding an instruction destination does not become the architectural register until the instruction commits. The renaming map is a simple data structure that supplies the physical register number of the register that currently corresponds to the specified architectural register, a function performed by the register status table in Tomasulo's algorithm. When an instruction commits, the renaming table is permanently updated to indicate that a physical register corresponds to the actual architectural register, thus effectively finalizing the update to the processor state. Although an ROB is not necessary with register renaming, the hardware must still track instructions in a queue-like structure and update the renaming table in strict order.

An advantage of the renaming approach versus the ROB approach is that instruction commit is slightly simplified, since it requires only two simple actions: (1) record that the mapping between an architectural register number and physical register number is no longer speculative, and (2) free up any physical registers being used to hold the "older" value of the architectural register. In a design with reservation stations, a station is freed up when the instruction using it completes execution, and a ROB entry is freed up when the corresponding instruction commits.

With register renaming, deallocating registers is more complex, since before we free up a physical register, we must know that it no longer corresponds to an architectural register and that no further uses of the physical register are outstanding. A physical register corresponds to an architectural register until the architectural register is rewritten, causing the renaming table to point elsewhere. That is, if no renaming entry points to a particular physical register, then it no longer corresponds to an architectural register. There may, however, still be uses of the physical register outstanding. The processor can determine whether this is the case by examining the source register specifiers of all instructions in the functional unit queues. If a given physical register does not appear as a source and it is not designated as an architectural register, it may be reclaimed and reallocated.

Alternatively, the processor can simply wait until another instruction that writes the same architectural register commits. At that point, there can be no further uses of the older value outstanding. Although this method may tie up a physical register slightly longer than necessary, it is easy to implement and is used in most recent superscalars.

One question you may be asking is how do we ever know which registers are the architectural registers if they are constantly changing? Most of the time when the program is executing, it does not matter. There are clearly cases, however, where another process, such as the operating system, must be able to know exactly where the contents of a certain architectural register reside. To understand how this capability is provided, assume the processor does not issue instructions for some period of time. Eventually all instructions in the pipeline will commit, and the mapping between the architecturally visible registers and physical registers will become stable. At that point, a subset of the physical registers contains the architecturally visible registers, and the value of any physical register not associated with an architectural register is unneeded. It is then easy to move the architectural registers to a fixed subset of physical registers so that the values can be communicated to another process.

Both register renaming and reorder buffers continue to be used in high-end processors, which now feature the ability to have as many as 40 or 50 instructions (including loads and stores waiting on the cache) in flight. Whether renaming or a reorder buffer is used, the key complexity bottleneck for a dynamically schedule superscalar remains issuing bundles of instructions with dependences within the bundle. In particular, dependent instructions in an issue bundle must be issued with the assigned virtual registers of the instructions on which they depend. A strategy for instruction issue with register renaming similar to that used for multiple issue with reorder buffers (see page 198) can be deployed, as follows:

1. The issue logic pre-reserves enough physical registers for the entire issue bundle (say, four registers for a four-instruction bundle with at most one register result per instruction).

2. The issue logic determines what dependences exist within the bundle. If a dependence does not exist within the bundle, the register renaming structure is used to determine the physical register that holds, or will hold, the result on which instruction depends. When no dependence exists within the bundle the result is from an earlier issue bundle, and the register renaming table will have the correct register number.

3. If an instruction depends on an instruction that is earlier in the bundle, then the pre-reserved physical register in which the result will be placed is used to update the information for the issuing instruction.

Note that just as in the reorder buffer case, the issue logic must both determine dependences within the bundle and update the renaming tables in a single clock, and, as before, the complexity of doing this for a larger number of instructions per clock becomes a chief limitation in the issue width.

How Much to Speculate

One of the significant advantages of speculation is its ability to uncover events that would otherwise stall the pipeline early, such as cache misses. This potential advantage, however, comes with a significant potential disadvantage. Speculation is not free. It takes time and energy, and the recovery of incorrect speculation further reduces performance. In addition, to support the higher instruction execution rate needed to benefit from speculation, the processor must have additional resources, which take silicon area and power. Finally, if speculation causes an exceptional event to occur, such as a cache or translation lookaside buffer (TLB) miss, the potential for significant performance loss increases, if that event would not have occurred without speculation.

To maintain most of the advantage, while minimizing the disadvantages, most pipelines with speculation will allow only low-cost exceptional events (such as a first-level cache miss) to be handled in speculative mode. If an expensive exceptional event occurs, such as a second-level cache miss or a TLB miss, the processor will wait until the instruction causing the event is no longer speculative before handling the event. Although this may slightly degrade the performance of some programs, it avoids significant performance losses in others, especially those that suffer from a high frequency of such events coupled with less-than-excellent branch prediction.

In the 1990s, the potential downsides of speculation were less obvious. As processors have evolved, the real costs of speculation have become more apparent, and the limitations of wider issue and speculation have been obvious. We return to this issue shortly.

Speculating through Multiple Branches

In the examples we have considered in this chapter, it has been possible to resolve a branch before having to speculate on another. Three different situations can benefit from speculating on multiple branches simultaneously: (1) a very high branch frequency, (2) significant clustering of branches, and (3) long delays in functional units. In the first two cases, achieving high performance may mean that multiple branches are speculated, and it may even mean handling more than one branch per clock. Database programs, and other less structured integer computations, often exhibit these properties, making speculation on multiple branches important. Likewise, long delays in functional units can raise the importance of speculating on multiple branches as a way to avoid stalls from the longer pipeline delays.

Speculating on multiple branches slightly complicates the process of speculation recovery but is straightforward otherwise. As of 2011, no processor has yet combined full speculation with resolving multiple branches per cycle, and it is unlikely that the costs of doing so would be justified in terms of performance versus complexity and power.

Speculation and the Challenge of Energy Efficiency

What is the impact of speculation on energy efficiency? At first glance, one might argue that using speculation always decreases energy efficiency, since whenever speculation is wrong it consumes excess energy in two ways:

1. The instructions that were speculated and whose results were not needed generated excess work for the processor, wasting energy.

2. Undoing the speculation and restoring the state of the processor to continue execution at the appropriate address consumes additional energy that would not be needed without speculation.

Certainly, speculation will raise the power consumption and, if we could control speculation, it would be possible to measure the cost (or at least the dynamic power cost). But, if speculation lowers the execution time by more than it increases the average power consumption, then the total energy consumed may be less.

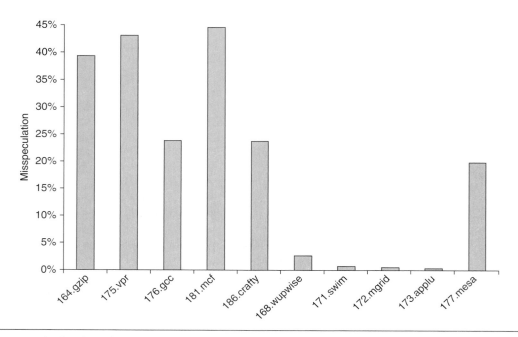

Figure 3.25 The fraction of instructions that are executed as a result of misspeculation is typically much higher for integer programs (the first five) versus FP programs (the last five).

Thus, to understand the impact of speculation on energy efficiency, we need to look at how often speculation is leading to unnecessary work. If a significant number of unneeded instructions is executed, it is unlikely that speculation will improve running time by a comparable amount! Figure 3.25 shows the fraction of instructions that are executed from misspeculation. As we can see, this fraction is small in scientific code and significant (about 30% on average) in integer code. Thus, it is unlikely that speculation is energy efficient for integer applications. Designers could avoid speculation, try to reduce the misspeculation, or think about new approaches, such as only speculating on branches that are known to be highly predictable.

Value Prediction

One technique for increasing the amount of ILP available in a program is value prediction. *Value prediction* attempts to predict the value that will be produced by an instruction. Obviously, since most instructions produce a different value every time they are executed (or at least a different value from a set of values), value prediction can have only limited success. There are, however, certain instructions for which it is easier to predict the resulting value—for example, loads that load from a constant pool or that load a value that changes infrequently. In addition, when an instruction produces a value chosen from a small set of potential values, it may be possible to predict the resulting value by correlating it with other program behavior.

Value prediction is useful if it significantly increases the amount of available ILP. This possibility is most likely when a value is used as the source of a chain of dependent computations, such as a load. Because value prediction is used to enhance speculations and incorrect speculation has detrimental performance impact, the accuracy of the prediction is critical.

Although many researchers have focused on value prediction in the past ten years, the results have never been sufficiently attractive to justify their incorporation in real processors. Instead, a simpler and older idea, related to value prediction, has been used: address aliasing prediction. *Address aliasing prediction* is a simple technique that predicts whether two stores or a load and a store refer to the same memory address. If two such references do not refer to the same address, then they may be safely interchanged. Otherwise, we must wait until the memory addresses accessed by the instructions are known. Because we need not actually predict the address values, only whether such values conflict, the prediction is both more stable and simpler. This limited form of address value speculation has been used in several processors already and may become universal in the future.

3.10   Studies of the Limitations of ILP

Exploiting ILP to increase performance began with the first pipelined processors in the 1960s. In the 1980s and 1990s, these techniques were key to achieving rapid performance improvements. The question of how much ILP exists was critical to our long-term ability to enhance performance at a rate that exceeds the increase in speed of the base integrated circuit technology. On a shorter scale, the critical question of what is needed to exploit more ILP is crucial to both computer designers and compiler writers. The data in this section also provide us with a way to examine the value of ideas that we have introduced in this chapter, including memory disambiguation, register renaming, and speculation.

In this section we review a portion of one of the studies done of these questions (based on Wall's 1993 study). All of these studies of available parallelism operate by making a set of assumptions and seeing how much parallelism is available under those assumptions. The data we examine here are from a study that makes the fewest assumptions; in fact, the ultimate hardware model is probably unrealizable. Nonetheless, all such studies assume a certain level of compiler technology, and some of these assumptions could affect the results, despite the use of incredibly ambitious hardware.

As we will see, for hardware models that have reasonable cost, it is unlikely that the costs of very aggressive speculation can be justified: the inefficiencies in power and use of silicon are simply too high. While many in the research community and the major processor manufacturers were betting in favor of much greater exploitable ILP and were initially reluctant to accept this possibility, by 2005 they were forced to change their minds.

The Hardware Model

To see what the limits of ILP might be, we first need to define an ideal processor. An ideal processor is one where all constraints on ILP are removed. The only limits on ILP in such a processor are those imposed by the actual data flows through either registers or memory.

The assumptions made for an ideal or perfect processor are as follows:

1. *Infinite register renaming*—There are an infinite number of virtual registers available, and hence all WAW and WAR hazards are avoided and an unbounded number of instructions can begin execution simultaneously.

2. *Perfect branch prediction*—Branch prediction is perfect. All conditional branches are predicted exactly.

3. *Perfect jump prediction*—All jumps (including jump register used for return and computed jumps) are perfectly predicted. When combined with perfect branch prediction, this is equivalent to having a processor with perfect speculation and an unbounded buffer of instructions available for execution.

4. *Perfect memory address alias analysis*—All memory addresses are known exactly, and a load can be moved before a store provided that the addresses are not identical. Note that this implements perfect address alias analysis.

5. *Perfect caches*—All memory accesses take one clock cycle. In practice, superscalar processors will typically consume large amounts of ILP hiding cache misses, making these results highly optimistic.

Assumptions 2 and 3 eliminate *all* control dependences. Likewise, assumptions 1 and 4 eliminate *all but the true* data dependences. Together, these four assumptions mean that *any* instruction in the program's execution can be scheduled on the cycle immediately following the execution of the predecessor on which it depends. It is even possible, under these assumptions, for the *last* dynamically executed instruction in the program to be scheduled on the very first cycle! Thus, this set of assumptions subsumes both control and address speculation and implements them as if they were perfect.

Initially, we examine a processor that can issue an unlimited number of instructions at once, looking arbitrarily far ahead in the computation. For all the processor models we examine, there are no restrictions on what types of instructions can execute in a cycle. For the unlimited-issue case, this means there may be an unlimited number of loads or stores issuing in one clock cycle. In addition, all functional unit latencies are assumed to be one cycle, so that any sequence of dependent instructions can issue on successive cycles. Latencies longer than one cycle would decrease the number of issues per cycle, although not the number of instructions under execution at any point. (The instructions in execution at any point are often referred to as *in flight*.)

Of course, this ideal processor is probably unrealizable. For example, the IBM Power7 (see Wendell et. al. [2010]) is the most advanced superscalar processor announced to date. The Power7 issues up to six instructions per clock and initiates execution on up to 8 of 12 execution units (only two of which are load/store units), supports a large set of renaming registers (allowing hundreds of instructions to be in flight), uses a large aggressive branch predictor, and employs dynamic memory disambiguation. The Power7 continued the move toward using more thread-level parallelism by increasing the width of simultaneous multithreading (SMT) support (to four threads per core) and the number of cores per chip to eight. After looking at the parallelism available for the perfect processor, we will examine what might be achievable in any processor likely to be designed in the near future.

To measure the available parallelism, a set of programs was compiled and optimized with the standard MIPS optimizing compilers. The programs were instrumented and executed to produce a trace of the instruction and data references. Every instruction in the trace is then scheduled as early as possible, limited only by the data dependences. Since a trace is used, perfect branch prediction and perfect alias analysis are easy to do. With these mechanisms, instructions may be scheduled much earlier than they would otherwise, moving across large numbers of instructions on which they are not data dependent, including branches, since branches are perfectly predicted.

Figure 3.26 shows the average amount of parallelism available for six of the SPEC92 benchmarks. Throughout this section the parallelism is measured by the average instruction issue rate. Remember that all instructions have a one-cycle latency; a longer latency would reduce the average number of instructions per clock. Three of these benchmarks (fpppp, doduc, and tomcatv) are floating-point intensive, and the other three are integer programs. Two of the floating-point benchmarks (fpppp and tomcatv) have extensive parallelism, which could be exploited by a vector computer or by a multiprocessor (the structure in fpppp is quite messy, however, since some hand transformations have been done on the code). The doduc program has extensive parallelism, but the parallelism does not occur in simple parallel loops as it does in fpppp and tomcatv. The program li is a LISP interpreter that has many short dependences.

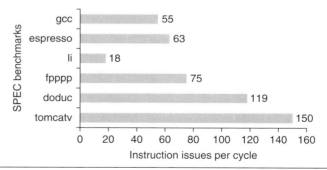

Figure 3.26 **ILP available in a perfect processor for six of the SPEC92 benchmarks.** The first three programs are integer programs, and the last three are floating-point programs. The floating-point programs are loop intensive and have large amounts of loop-level parallelism.

Limitations on ILP for Realizable Processors

In this section we look at the performance of processors with ambitious levels of hardware support equal to or better than what is available in 2011 or, given the events and lessons of the last decade, likely to be available in the near future. In particular, we assume the following fixed attributes:

1. Up to 64 instruction issues per clock with *no* issue restrictions, or more than 10 times the total issue width of the widest processor in 2011. As we discuss later, the practical implications of very wide issue widths on clock rate, logic complexity, and power may be the most important limitations on exploiting ILP.

2. A tournament predictor with 1K entries and a 16-entry return predictor. This predictor is comparable to the best predictors in 2011; the predictor is not a primary bottleneck.

3. Perfect disambiguation of memory references done dynamically—this is ambitious but perhaps attainable for small window sizes (and hence small issue rates and load/store buffers) or through address aliasing prediction.

4. Register renaming with 64 additional integer and 64 additional FP registers, which is slightly less than the most aggressive processor in 2011. The Intel Core i7 has 128 entries in its reorder buffer, although they are not split between integer and FP, while the IBM Power7 has almost 200. Note that we assume a pipeline latency of one cycle, which significantly reduces the need for reorder buffer entries. Both the Power7 and the i7 have latencies of 10 cycles or greater.

Figure 3.27 shows the result for this configuration as we vary the window size. This configuration is more complex and expensive than any existing implementations, especially in terms of the number of instruction issues, which is more than 10 times larger than the largest number of issues available on any processor in 2011. Nonetheless, it gives a useful bound on what future implementations might yield. The data in these figures are likely to be very optimistic for another reason. There are no issue restrictions among the 64 instructions: They may all be memory references. No one would even contemplate this capability in a processor in the near future. Unfortunately, it is quite difficult to bound the performance of a processor with reasonable issue restrictions; not only is the space of possibilities quite large, but the existence of issue restrictions requires that the parallelism be evaluated with an accurate instruction scheduler, making the cost of studying processors with large numbers of issues very expensive.

In addition, remember that in interpreting these results cache misses and non-unit latencies have not been taken into account, and both these effects will have significant impact!

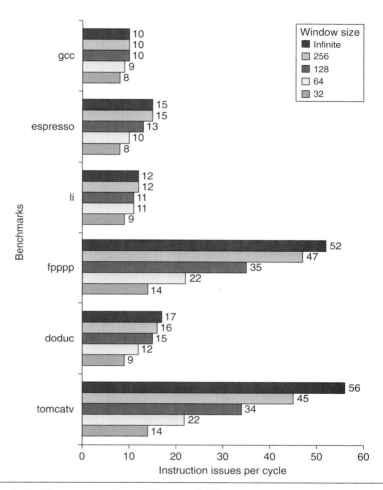

Figure 3.27 The amount of parallelism available versus the window size for a variety of integer and floating-point programs with up to 64 arbitrary instruction issues per clock. Although there are fewer renaming registers than the window size, the fact that all operations have one-cycle latency and the number of renaming registers equals the issue width allows the processor to exploit parallelism within the entire window. In a real implementation, the window size and the number of renaming registers must be balanced to prevent one of these factors from overly constraining the issue rate.

The most startling observation from Figure 3.27 is that, with the realistic processor constraints listed above, the effect of the window size for the integer programs is not as severe as for FP programs. This result points to the key difference between these two types of programs. The availability of loop-level parallelism in two of the FP programs means that the amount of ILP that can be exploited is higher, but for integer programs other factors—such as branch prediction, register renaming, and less parallelism, to start with—are all important limitations. This observation is critical because of the increased emphasis on integer performance since the explosion of the World Wide Web and cloud computing starting in the mid-1990s. Indeed, most of the market growth in the last decade—transaction processing, Web servers, and the like—depended on integer performance, rather than floating point. As we will see in the next section, for a realistic processor in 2011, the actual performance levels are much lower than those shown in Figure 3.27.

Given the difficulty of increasing the instruction rates with realistic hardware designs, designers face a challenge in deciding how best to use the limited resources available on an integrated circuit. One of the most interesting trade-offs is between simpler processors with larger caches and higher clock rates versus more emphasis on instruction-level parallelism with a slower clock and smaller caches. The following example illustrates the challenges, and in the next chapter we will see an alternative approach to exploiting fine-grained parallelism in the form of GPUs.

Example   Consider the following three hypothetical, but not atypical, processors, which we run with the SPEC gcc benchmark:

1. A simple MIPS two-issue static pipe running at a clock rate of 4 GHz and achieving a pipeline CPI of 0.8. This processor has a cache system that yields 0.005 misses per instruction.

2. A deeply pipelined version of a two-issue MIPS processor with slightly smaller caches and a 5 GHz clock rate. The pipeline CPI of the processor is 1.0, and the smaller caches yield 0.0055 misses per instruction on average.

3. A speculative superscalar with a 64-entry window. It achieves one-half of the ideal issue rate measured for this window size. (Use the data in Figure 3.27.) This processor has the smallest caches, which lead to 0.01 misses per instruction, but it hides 25% of the miss penalty on every miss by dynamic scheduling. This processor has a 2.5 GHz clock.

Assume that the main memory time (which sets the miss penalty) is 50 ns. Determine the relative performance of these three processors.

Answer   First, we use the miss penalty and miss rate information to compute the contribution to CPI from cache misses for each configuration. We do this with the following formula:

$$\text{Cache CPI} = \text{Misses per instruction} \times \text{Miss penalty}$$

We need to compute the miss penalties for each system:

$$\text{Miss penalty} = \frac{\text{Memory access time}}{\text{Clock cycle}}$$

The clock cycle times for the processors are 250 ps, 200 ps, and 400 ps, respectively. Hence, the miss penalties are

$$\text{Miss penalty}_1 = \frac{50 \text{ ns}}{250 \text{ ps}} = 200 \text{ cycles}$$

$$\text{Miss penalty}_2 = \frac{50 \text{ ns}}{200 \text{ ps}} = 250 \text{ cycles}$$

$$\text{Miss penalty}_3 = \frac{0.75 \times 50 \text{ ns}}{400 \text{ ps}} = 94 \text{ cycles}$$

Applying this for each cache:

$$\text{Cache CPI}_1 = 0.005 \times 200 = 1.0$$
$$\text{Cache CPI}_2 = 0.0055 \times 250 = 1.4$$
$$\text{Cache CPI}_3 = 0.01 \times 94 = 0.94$$

We know the pipeline CPI contribution for everything but processor 3; its pipeline CPI is given by:

$$\text{Pipeline CPI}_3 = \frac{1}{\text{Issue rate}} = \frac{1}{9 \times 0.5} = \frac{1}{4.5} = 0.22$$

Now we can find the CPI for each processor by adding the pipeline and cache CPI contributions:

$$\text{CPI}_1 = 0.8 + 1.0 = 1.8$$
$$\text{CPI}_2 = 1.0 + 1.4 = 2.4$$
$$\text{CPI}_3 = 0.22 + 0.94 = 1.16$$

Since this is the same architecture, we can compare instruction execution rates in millions of instructions per second (MIPS) to determine relative performance:

$$\text{Instruction execution rate} = \frac{\text{CR}}{\text{CPI}}$$

$$\text{Instruction execution rate}_1 = \frac{4000 \text{ MHz}}{1.8} = 2222 \text{ MIPS}$$

$$\text{Instruction execution rate}_2 = \frac{5000 \text{ MHz}}{2.4} = 2083 \text{ MIPS}$$

$$\text{Instruction execution rate}_3 = \frac{2500 \text{ MHz}}{1.16} = 2155 \text{ MIPS}$$

In this example, the simple two-issue static superscalar looks best. In practice, performance depends on both the CPI and clock rate assumptions.

Beyond the Limits of This Study

Like any limit study, the study we have examined in this section has its own limitations. We divide these into two classes: limitations that arise even for the perfect speculative processor, and limitations that arise for one or more realistic models. Of course, all the limitations in the first class apply to the second. The most important limitations that apply even to the perfect model are

1. *WAW and WAR hazards through memory*—The study eliminated WAW and WAR hazards through register renaming, but not in memory usage. Although at first glance it might appear that such circumstances are rare (especially WAW hazards), they arise due to the allocation of stack frames. A called procedure reuses the memory locations of a previous procedure on the stack, and this can lead to WAW and WAR hazards that are unnecessarily limiting. Austin and Sohi [1992] examined this issue.

2. *Unnecessary dependences*—With infinite numbers of registers, all but true register data dependences are removed. There are, however, dependences arising from either recurrences or code generation conventions that introduce unnecessary true data dependences. One example of these is the dependence on the control variable in a simple for loop. Since the control variable is incremented on every loop iteration, the loop contains at least one dependence. As we show in Appendix H, loop unrolling and aggressive algebraic optimization can remove such dependent computation. Wall's study includes a limited amount of such optimizations, but applying them more aggressively could lead to increased amounts of ILP. In addition, certain code generation conventions introduce unneeded dependences, in particular the use of return address registers and a register for the stack pointer (which is incremented and decremented in the call/return sequence). Wall removes the effect of the return address register, but the use of a stack pointer in the linkage convention can cause "unnecessary" dependences. Postiff et al. [1999] explored the advantages of removing this constraint.

3. *Overcoming the data flow limit*—If value prediction worked with high accuracy, it could overcome the data flow limit. As of yet, none of the more than 100 papers on the subject has achieved a significant enhancement in ILP when using a realistic prediction scheme. Obviously, perfect data value prediction would lead to effectively infinite parallelism, since every value of every instruction could be predicted *a priori*.

For a less-than-perfect processor, several ideas have been proposed that could expose more ILP. One example is to speculate along multiple paths. This idea was discussed by Lam and Wilson [1992] and explored in the study covered in this section. By speculating on multiple paths, the cost of incorrect recovery is reduced and more parallelism can be uncovered. It only makes sense to evaluate this scheme for a limited number of branches because the hardware resources required grow exponentially. Wall [1993] provided data for speculating in both directions on up to eight branches. Given the costs of pursuing both paths, knowing that one will be thrown away (and the growing amount of useless computation as such a process is followed through multiple branches), every commercial design has instead devoted additional hardware to better speculation on the correct path.

It is critical to understand that none of the limits in this section is fundamental in the sense that overcoming them requires a change in the laws of physics! Instead, they are practical limitations that imply the existence of some formidable barriers to exploiting additional ILP. These limitations—whether they be window size, alias detection, or branch prediction—represent challenges for designers and researchers to overcome.

Attempts to break through these limits in the first five years of this century met with frustration. Some techniques produced small improvements, but often at significant increases in complexity, increases in the clock cycle, and disproportionate increases in power. In summary, designers discovered that trying to extract more ILP was simply too inefficient. We will return to this discussion in our concluding remarks.

3.11 Cross-Cutting Issues: ILP Approaches and the Memory System

Hardware versus Software Speculation

The hardware-intensive approaches to speculation in this chapter and the software approaches of Appendix H provide alternative approaches to exploiting ILP. Some of the trade-offs, and the limitations, for these approaches are listed below:

- To speculate extensively, we must be able to disambiguate memory references. This capability is difficult to do at compile time for integer programs that contain pointers. In a hardware-based scheme, dynamic runtime disambiguation of memory addresses is done using the techniques we saw earlier for Tomasulo's algorithm. This disambiguation allows us to move loads past stores at runtime. Support for speculative memory references can help overcome the conservatism of the compiler, but unless such approaches are used carefully, the overhead of the recovery mechanisms may swamp the advantages.

- Hardware-based speculation works better when control flow is unpredictable and when hardware-based branch prediction is superior to software-based branch prediction done at compile time. These properties hold for many integer programs. For example, a good static predictor has a misprediction rate of about 16% for four major integer SPEC92 programs, and a hardware predictor has a misprediction rate of under 10%. Because speculated instructions may slow down the computation when the prediction is incorrect, this difference is significant. One result of this difference is that even statically scheduled processors normally include dynamic branch predictors.

- Hardware-based speculation maintains a completely precise exception model even for speculated instructions. Recent software-based approaches have added special support to allow this as well.

- Hardware-based speculation does not require compensation or bookkeeping code, which is needed by ambitious software speculation mechanisms.

- Compiler-based approaches may benefit from the ability to see further in the code sequence, resulting in better code scheduling than a purely hardware-driven approach.

- Hardware-based speculation with dynamic scheduling does not require different code sequences to achieve good performance for different implementations of an architecture. Although this advantage is the hardest to quantify, it may be the most important in the long run. Interestingly, this was one of the motivations for the IBM 360/91. On the other hand, more recent explicitly parallel architectures, such as IA-64, have added flexibility that reduces the hardware dependence inherent in a code sequence.

The major disadvantage of supporting speculation in hardware is the complexity and additional hardware resources required. This hardware cost must be evaluated against both the complexity of a compiler for a software-based approach and the amount and usefulness of the simplifications in a processor that relies on such a compiler.

Some designers have tried to combine the dynamic and compiler-based approaches to achieve the best of each. Such a combination can generate interesting and obscure interactions. For example, if conditional moves are combined with register renaming, a subtle side effect appears. A conditional move that is annulled must still copy a value to the destination register, since it was renamed earlier in the instruction pipeline. These subtle interactions complicate the design and verification process and can also reduce performance.

The Intel Itanium processor was the most ambitious computer ever designed based on the software support for ILP and speculation. It did not deliver on the hopes of the designers, especially for general-purpose, nonscientific code. As designers' ambitions for exploiting ILP were reduced in light of the difficulties discussed in Section 3.10, most architectures settled on hardware-based mechanisms with issue rates of three to four instructions per clock.

Speculative Execution and the Memory System

Inherent in processors that support speculative execution or conditional instructions is the possibility of generating invalid addresses that would not occur without speculative execution. Not only would this be incorrect behavior if protection exceptions were taken, but the benefits of speculative execution would be swamped by false exception overhead. Hence, the memory system must identify speculatively executed instructions and conditionally executed instructions and suppress the corresponding exception.

By similar reasoning, we cannot allow such instructions to cause the cache to stall on a miss because again unnecessary stalls could overwhelm the benefits of speculation. Hence, these processors must be matched with nonblocking caches.

In reality, the penalty of an L2 miss is so large that compilers normally only speculate on L1 misses. Figure 2.5 on page 84 shows that for some well-behaved scientific programs the compiler can sustain multiple outstanding L2 misses to cut the L2 miss penalty effectively. Once again, for this to work the memory system behind the cache must match the goals of the compiler in number of simultaneous memory accesses.

3.12

3.12 Multithreading: Exploiting Thread-Level Parallelism to Improve Uniprocessor Throughput

The topic we cover in this section, multithreading, is truly a cross-cutting topic, since it has relevance to pipelining and superscalars, to graphics processing units (Chapter 4), and to multiprocessors (Chapter 5). We introduce the topic here and explore the use of multithreading to increase uniprocessor throughput by using multiple threads to hide pipeline and memory latencies. In the next chapter, we will see how multithreading provides the same advantages in GPUs, and finally, Chapter 5 will explore the combination of multithreading and multiprocessing. These topics are closely interwoven, since multithreading is a primary technique for exposing more parallelism to the hardware. In a strict sense, multithreading uses thread-level parallelism, and thus is properly the subject of Chapter 5, but its role in both improving pipeline utilization and in GPUs motivates us to introduce the concept here.

Although increasing performance by using ILP has the great advantage that it is reasonably transparent to the programmer, as we have seen ILP can be quite limited or difficult to exploit in some applications. In particular, with reasonable instruction issue rates, cache misses that go to memory or off-chip caches are unlikely to be hidden by available ILP. Of course, when the processor is stalled waiting on a cache miss, the utilization of the functional units drops dramatically.

Since attempts to cover long memory stalls with more ILP have limited effectiveness, it is natural to ask whether other forms of parallelism in an application could be used to hide memory delays. For example, an online transaction-processing system has natural parallelism among the multiple queries and updates that are presented by requests. Of course, many scientific applications contain natural parallelism since they often model the three-dimensional, parallel structure of nature, and that structure can be exploited by using separate threads. Even desktop applications that use modern Windows-based operating systems often have multiple active applications running, providing a source of parallelism.

Multithreading allows multiple threads to share the functional units of a single processor in an overlapping fashion. In contrast, a more general method to exploit *thread-level parallelism* (TLP) is with a multiprocessor that has multiple independent threads operating at once and in parallel. Multithreading, however, does not duplicate the entire processor as a multiprocessor does. Instead, multithreading shares most of the processor core among a set of threads, duplicating only private state, such as the registers and program counter. As we will see in

Chapter 5, many recent processors incorporate both multiple processor cores on a single chip and provide multithreading within each core.

Duplicating the per-thread state of a processor core means creating a separate register file, a separate PC, and a separate page table for each thread. The memory itself can be shared through the virtual memory mechanisms, which already support multiprogramming. In addition, the hardware must support the ability to change to a different thread relatively quickly; in particular, a thread switch should be much more efficient than a process switch, which typically requires hundreds to thousands of processor cycles. Of course, for multithreading hardware to achieve performance improvements, a program must contain multiple threads (we sometimes say that the application is multithreaded) that could execute in concurrent fashion. These threads are identified either by a compiler (typically from a language with parallelism constructs) or by the programmer.

There are three main hardware approaches to multithreading. *Fine-grained multithreading* switches between threads on each clock, causing the execution of instructions from multiple threads to be interleaved. This interleaving is often done in a round-robin fashion, skipping any threads that are stalled at that time. One key advantage of fine-grained multithreading is that it can hide the throughput losses that arise from both short and long stalls, since instructions from other threads can be executed when one thread stalls, even if the stall is only for a few cycles. The primary disadvantage of fine-grained multithreading is that it slows down the execution of an individual thread, since a thread that is ready to execute without stalls will be delayed by instructions from other threads. It trades an uncrease in multithreaded throughput for a loss in the performance (as measured by latency) of a single thread. The Sun Niagara processor, which we examine shortly, uses simple fine-grained multithreading, as do the Nvidia GPUs, which we look at in the next chapter.

Coarse-grained multithreading was invented as an alternative to fine-grained multithreading. Coarse-grained multithreading switches threads only on costly stalls, such as level two or three cache misses. This change relieves the need to have thread-switching be essentially free and is much less likely to slow down the execution of any one thread, since instructions from other threads will only be issued when a thread encounters a costly stall.

Coarse-grained multithreading suffers, however, from a major drawback: It is limited in its ability to overcome throughput losses, especially from shorter stalls. This limitation arises from the pipeline start-up costs of coarse-grained multithreading. Because a CPU with coarse-grained multithreading issues instructions from a single thread, when a stall occurs the pipeline will see a bubble before the new thread begins executing. Because of this start-up overhead, coarse-grained multithreading is much more useful for reducing the penalty of very high-cost stalls, where pipeline refill is negligible compared to the stall time. Several research projects have explored coarse grained multithreading, but no major current processors use this technique.

The most common implementation of multithreading is called *Simultaneous multithreading* (SMT). Simultaneous multithreading is a variation on fine-grained multithreading that arises naturally when fine-grained multithreading is implemented on top of a multiple-issue, dynamically scheduled processor. As with other forms of multithreading, SMT uses thread-level parallelism to hide long-latency events in a processor, thereby increasing the usage of the functional units. The key insight in SMT is that register renaming and dynamic scheduling allow multiple instructions from independent threads to be executed without regard to the dependences among them; the resolution of the dependences can be handled by the dynamic scheduling capability.

Figure 3.28 conceptually illustrates the differences in a processor's ability to exploit the resources of a superscalar for the following processor configurations:

- A superscalar with no multithreading support
- A superscalar with coarse-grained multithreading
- A superscalar with fine-grained multithreading
- A superscalar with simultaneous multithreading

In the superscalar without multithreading support, the use of issue slots is limited by a lack of ILP, including ILP to hide memory latency. Because of the length of L2 and L3 cache misses, much of the processor can be left idle.

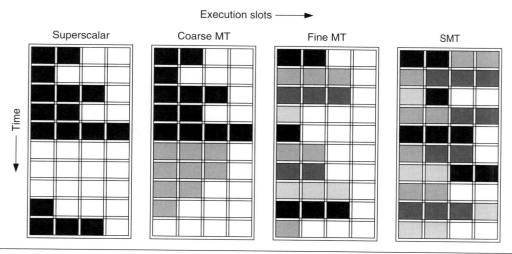

Figure 3.28 How four different approaches use the functional unit execution slots of a superscalar processor. The horizontal dimension represents the instruction execution capability in each clock cycle. The vertical dimension represents a sequence of clock cycles. An empty (white) box indicates that the corresponding execution slot is unused in that clock cycle. The shades of gray and black correspond to four different threads in the multithreading processors. Black is also used to indicate the occupied issue slots in the case of the superscalar without multithreading support. The Sun T1 and T2 (aka Niagara) processors are fine-grained multithreaded processors, while the Intel Core i7 and IBM Power7 processors use SMT. The T2 has eight threads, the Power7 has four, and the Intel i7 has two. In all existing SMTs, instructions issue from only one thread at a time. The difference in SMT is that the subsequent decision to execute an instruction is decoupled and could execute the operations coming from several different instructions in the same clock cycle.

In the coarse-grained multithreaded superscalar, the long stalls are partially hidden by switching to another thread that uses the resources of the processor. This switching reduces the number of completely idle clock cycles. In a coarse-grained multithreaded processor, however, thread switching only occurs when there is a stall. Because the new thread has a start-up period, there are likely to be some fully idle cycles remaining.

In the fine-grained case, the interleaving of threads can eliminate fully empty slots. In addition, because the issuing thread is changed on every clock cycle, longer latency operations can be hidden. Because instruction issue and execution are connected, a thread can only issue as many instructions as are ready. With a narrow issue width this is not a problem (a cycle is either occupied or not), which is why fine-grained multithreading works perfectly for a single issue processor, and SMT would make no sense. Indeed, in the Sun T2, there are two issues per clock, but they are from different threads. This eliminates the need to implement the complex dynamic scheduling approach and relies instead on hiding latency with more threads.

If one implements fine-grained threading on top of a multiple-issue dynamically schedule processor, the result is SMT. In all existing SMT implementations, all issues come from one thread, although instructions from different threads can initiate execution in the same cycle, using the dynamic scheduling hardware to determine what instructions are ready. Although Figure 3.28 greatly simplifies the real operation of these processors, it does illustrate the potential performance advantages of multithreading in general and SMT in wider issue, dynamically scheduled processors.

Simultaneous multithreading uses the insight that a dynamically scheduled processor already has many of the hardware mechanisms needed to support the mechanism, including a large virtual register set. Multithreading can be built on top of an out-of-order processor by adding a per-thread renaming table, keeping separate PCs, and providing the capability for instructions from multiple threads to commit.

Effectiveness of Fine-Grained Multithreading on the Sun T1

In this section, we use the Sun T1 processor to examine the ability of multithreading to hide latency. The T1 is a fine-grained multithreaded multicore microprocessor introduced by Sun in 2005. What makes T1 especially interesting is that it is almost totally focused on exploiting thread-level parallelism (TLP) rather than instruction-level parallelism (ILP). The T1 abandoned the intense focus on ILP (just shortly after the most aggressive ILP processors ever were introduced), returned to a simple pipeline strategy, and focused on exploiting TLP, using both multiple cores and multithreading to produce throughput.

Each T1 processor contains eight processor cores, each supporting four threads. Each processor core consists of a simple six-stage, single-issue pipeline (a standard five-stage RISC pipeline like that of Appendix C, with one stage added for thread switching). T1 uses fine-grained multithreading (but not SMT), switching to a new thread on each clock cycle, and threads that are idle because they are waiting due to

Characteristic	Sun T1
Multiprocessor and multithreading support	Eight cores per chip; four threads per core. Fine-grained thread scheduling. One shared floating-point unit for eight cores. Supports only on-chip multiprocessing.
Pipeline structure	Simple, in-order, six-deep pipeline with three-cycle delays for loads and branches.
L1 caches	16 KB instructions; 8 KB data. 64-byte block size. Miss to L2 is 23 cycles, assuming no contention.
L2 caches	Four separate L2 caches, each 750 KB and associated with a memory bank. 64-byte block size. Miss to main memory is 110 clock cycles assuming no contention.
Initial implementation	90 nm process; maximum clock rate of 1.2 GHz; power 79 W; 300 M transistors; 379 mm^2 die.

Figure 3.29 A summary of the T1 processor.

a pipeline delay or cache miss are bypassed in the scheduling. The processor is idle only when all four threads are idle or stalled. Both loads and branches incur a three-cycle delay that can only be hidden by other threads. A single set of floating-point functional units is shared by all eight cores, as floating-point performance was not a focus for T1. Figure 3.29 summarizes the T1 processor.

T1 Multithreading Unicore Performance

The T1 makes TLP its focus, both through the multithreading on an individual core and through the use of many simple cores on a single die. In this section, we will look at the effectiveness of the T1 in increasing the performance of a single core through fine-grained multithreading. In Chapter 5, we will return to examine the effectiveness of combining multithreading with multiple cores.

To examine the performance of the T1, we use three server-oriented benchmarks: TPC-C, SPECJBB (the SPEC Java Business Benchmark), and SPECWeb99. Since multiple threads increase the memory demands from a single processor, they could overload the memory system, leading to reductions in the potential gain from multithreading. Figure 3.30 shows the relative increase in the miss rate and the observed miss latency when executing with one thread per core versus executing four threads per core for TPC-C. Both the miss rates and the miss latencies increase, due to increased contention in the memory system. The relatively small increase in miss latency indicates that the memory system still has unused capacity.

By looking at the behavior of an average thread, we can understand the interaction among the threads and their ability to keep a core busy. Figure 3.31 shows the percentage of cycles for which a thread is executing, ready but not executing, and not ready. Remember that not ready does not imply that the core with that thread is stalled; it is only when all four threads are not ready that the core will stall.

Threads can be not ready due to cache misses, pipeline delays (arising from long latency instructions such as branches, loads, floating point, or integer multiply/divide), and a variety of smaller effects. Figure 3.32 shows the relative

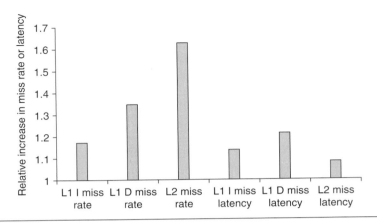

Figure 3.30 **The relative change in the miss rates and miss latencies when executing with one thread per core versus four threads per core on the TPC-C benchmark.** The latencies are the actual time to return the requested data after a miss. In the four-thread case, the execution of other threads could potentially hide much of this latency.

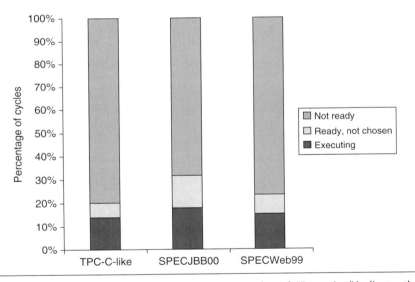

Figure 3.31 **Breakdown of the status on an average thread.** "Executing" indicates the thread issues an instruction in that cycle. "Ready but not chosen" means it could issue but another thread has been chosen, and "not ready" indicates that the thread is awaiting the completion of an event (a pipeline delay or cache miss, for example).

frequency of these various causes. Cache effects are responsible for the thread not being ready from 50% to 75% of the time, with L1 instruction misses, L1 data misses, and L2 misses contributing roughly equally. Potential delays from the pipeline (called "pipeline delay") are most severe in SPECJBB and may arise from its higher branch frequency.

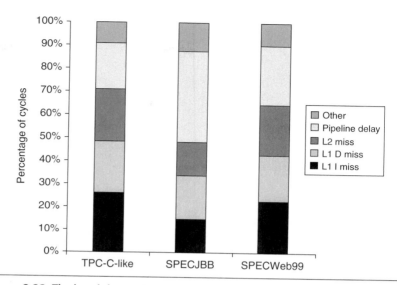

Figure 3.32 The breakdown of causes for a thread being not ready. The contribution to the "other" category varies. In TPC-C, store buffer full is the largest contributor; in SPEC-JBB, atomic instructions are the largest contributor; and in SPECWeb99, both factors contribute.

Benchmark	Per-thread CPI	Per-core CPI
TPC-C	7.2	1.80
SPECJBB	5.6	1.40
SPECWeb99	6.6	1.65

Figure 3.33 The per-thread CPI, the per-core CPI, the effective eight-core CPI, and the effective IPC (inverse of CPI) for the eight-core T1 processor.

Figure 3.33 shows the per-thread and per-core CPI. Because T1 is a fine-grained multithreaded processor with four threads per core, with sufficient parallelism the ideal effective CPI per thread would be four, since that would mean that each thread was consuming one cycle out of every four. The ideal CPI per core would be one. In 2005, the IPC for these benchmarks running on aggressive ILP cores would have been similar to that seen on a T1 core. The T1 core, however, was very modest in size compared to the aggressive ILP cores of 2005, which is why the T1 had eight cores compared to the two to four offered on other processors of the same vintage. As a result, in 2005 when it was introduced, the Sun T1 processor had the best performance on integer applications with extensive TLP and demanding memory performance, such as SPECJBB and transaction processing workloads.

Effectiveness of Simultaneous Multithreading on Superscalar Processors

A key question is, How much performance can be gained by implementing SMT? When this question was explored in 2000–2001, researchers assumed that dynamic superscalars would get much wider in the next five years, supporting six to eight issues per clock with speculative dynamic scheduling, many simultaneous loads and stores, large primary caches, and four to eight contexts with simultaneous issue and retirement from multiple contexts. No processor has gotten close to this level.

As a result, simulation research results that showed gains for multiprogrammed workloads of two or more times are unrealistic. In practice, the existing implementations of SMT offer only two to four contexts with fetching and issue from only one, and up to four issues per clock. The result is that the gain from SMT is also more modest.

For example, in the Pentium 4 Extreme, as implemented in HP-Compaq servers, the use of SMT yields a performance improvement of 1.01 when running the SPECintRate benchmark and about 1.07 when running the SPECfpRate benchmark. Tuck and Tullsen [2003] reported that, on the SPLASH parallel benchmarks, they found single-core multithreaded speedups ranging from 1.02 to 1.67, with an average speedup of about 1.22.

With the availability of recent extensive and insightful measurements done by Esmaeilzadeh et al. [2011], we can look at the performance and energy benefits of using SMT in a single i7 core using a set of multithreaded applications. The benchmarks we use consist of a collection of parallel scientific applications and a set of multithreaded Java programs from the DaCapo and SPEC Java suite, as summarized in Figure 3.34. The Intel i7 supports SMT with two threads. Figure 3.35 shows the performance ratio and the energy efficiency ratio of the these benchmarks run on one core of the i7 with SMT turned off and on. (We plot the energy efficiency ratio, which is the inverse of energy consumption, so that, like speedup, a higher ratio is better.)

The harmonic mean of the speedup for the Java benchmarks is 1.28, despite the two benchmarks that see small gains. These two benchmarks, pjbb2005 and tradebeans, while multithreaded, have limited parallelism. They are included because they are typical of a multithreaded benchmark that might be run on an SMT processor with the hope of extracting some performance, which they find in limited amounts. The PARSEC benchmarks obtain somewhat better speedups than the full set of Java benchmarks (harmonic mean of 1.31). If tradebeans and pjbb2005 were omitted, the Java workload would actually have significantly better speedup (1.39) than the PARSEC benchmarks. (See the discussion of the implication of using harmonic mean to summarize the results in the caption of Figure 3.36.)

Energy consumption is determined by the combination of speedup and increase in power consumption. For the Java benchmarks, on average, SMT delivers the same energy efficiency as non-SMT (average of 1.0), but it is brought down by the two poor performing benchmarks; without tradebeans and pjbb2005, the average

blackscholes	Prices a portfolio of options with the Black-Scholes PDE
bodytrack	Tracks a markerless human body
canneal	Minimizes routing cost of a chip with cache-aware simulated annealing
facesim	Simulates motions of a human face for visualization purposes
ferret	Search engine that finds a set of images similar to a query image
fluidanimate	Simulates physics of fluid motion for animation with SPH algorithm
raytrace	Uses physical simulation for visualization
streamcluster	Computes an approximation for the optimal clustering of data points
swaptions	Prices a portfolio of swap options with the Heath–Jarrow–Morton framework
vips	Applies a series of transformations to an image
x264	MPG-4 AVC/H.264 video encoder
eclipse	Integrated development environment
lusearch	Text search tool
sunflow	Photo-realistic rendering system
tomcat	Tomcat servlet container
tradebeans	Tradebeans Daytrader benchmark
xalan	An XSLT processor for transforming XML documents
pjbb2005	Version of SPEC JBB2005 (but fixed in problem size rather than time)

Figure 3.34 The parallel benchmarks used here to examine multithreading, as well as in Chapter 5 to examine multiprocessing with an i7. The top half of the chart consists of PARSEC benchmarks collected by Biena et al. [2008]. The PARSEC benchmarks are meant to be indicative of compute-intensive, parallel applications that would be appropriate for multicore processors. The lower half consists of multithreaded Java benchmarks from the DaCapo collection (see Blackburn et al. [2006]) and pjbb2005 from SPEC. All of these benchmarks contain some parallelism; other Java benchmarks in the DaCapo and SPEC Java workloads use multiple threads but have little or no true parallelism and, hence, are not used here. See Esmaeilzadeh et al. [2011] for additional information on the characteristics of these benchmarks, relative to the measurements here and in Chapter 5.

energy efficiency for the Java benchmarks is 1.06, which is almost as good as the PARSEC benchmarks. In the PARSEC benchmarks, SMT reduces energy by $1 - (1/1.08) = 7\%$. Such energy-reducing performance enhancements are *very difficult* to find. Of course, the static power associated with SMT is paid in both cases, thus the results probably slightly overstate the energy gains.

These results clearly show that SMT in an aggressive speculative processor with extensive support for SMT can improve performance in an energy efficient fashion, which the more aggressive ILP approaches have failed to do. In 2011, the balance between offering multiple simpler cores and fewer more sophisticated cores has shifted in favor of more cores, with each core typically being a three- to four-issue superscalar with SMT supporting two to four threads. Indeed, Esmaeilzadeh et al. [2011] show that the energy improvements from SMT are even larger on the Intel i5 (a processor similar to the i7, but with smaller caches and a lower clock rate) and the Intel Atom (an 80×86 processor designed for the netbook market and described in Section 3.14).

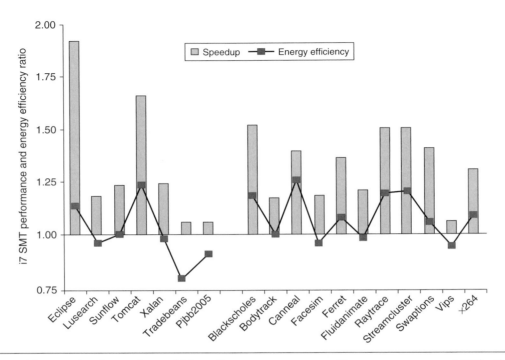

Figure 3.35 **The speedup from using multithreading on one core on an i7 processor averages 1.28 for the Java benchmarks and 1.31 for the PARSEC benchmarks (using an unweighted harmonic mean, which implies a workload where the total time spent executing each benchmark in the single-threaded base set was the same).** The energy efficiency averages 0.99 and 1.07, respectively (using the harmonic mean). Recall that anything above 1.0 for energy efficiency indicates that the feature reduces execution time by more than it increases average power. Two of the Java benchmarks experience little speedup and have significant negative energy efficiency because of this. Turbo Boost is off in all cases. These data were collected and analyzed by Esmaeilzadeh et al. [2011] using the Oracle (Sun) HotSpot build 16.3-b01 Java 1.6.0 Virtual Machine and the gcc v4.4.1 native compiler.

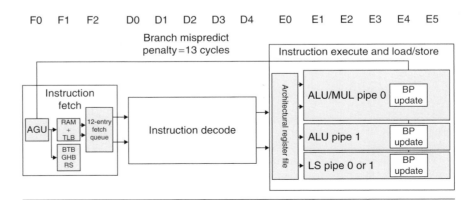

Figure 3.36 **The basic structure of the A8 pipeline is 13 stages.** Three cycles are used for instruction fetch and four for instruction decode, in addition to a five-cycle integer pipeline. This yields a 13-cycle branch misprediction penalty. The instruction fetch unit tries to keep the 12-entry instruction queue filled.

Putting It All Together: The Intel Core i7 and ARM Cortex-A8

In this section we explore the design of two multiple issue processors: the ARM Cortex-A8 core, which is used as the basis for the Apple A9 processor in the iPad, as well as the processor in the Motorola Droid and the iPhones 3GS and 4, and the Intel Core i7, a high-end, dynamically scheduled, speculative processor, intended for high-end desktops and server applications. We begin with the simpler processor.

The ARM Cortex-A8

The A8 is a dual-issue, statically scheduled superscalar with dynamic issue detection, which allows the processor to issue one or two instructions per clock. Figure 3.36 shows the basic pipeline structure of the 13-stage pipeline.

The A8 uses a dynamic branch predictor with a 512-entry two-way set associative branch target buffer and a 4K-entry global history buffer, which is indexed by the branch history and the current PC. In the event that the branch target buffer misses, a prediction is obtained from the global history buffer, which can then be used to compute the branch address. In addition, an eight-entry return stack is kept to track return addresses. An incorrect prediction results in a 13-cycle penalty as the pipeline is flushed.

Figure 3.37 shows the instruction decode pipeline. Up to two instructions per clock can be issued using an in-order issue mechanism. A simple scoreboard structure is used to track when an instruction can issue. A pair of dependent instructions can be processed through the issue logic, but, of course, they will be serialized at the scoreboard, unless they can be issued so that the forwarding paths can resolve the dependence.

Figure 3.38 shows the execution pipeline for the A8 processor. Either instruction 1 or instruction 2 can go to the load/store pipeline. Fully bypassing is supported among the pipelines. The ARM Cortex-A8 pipeline uses a simple two-issue statically scheduled superscalar to allow reasonably high clock rate with lower power. In contrast, the i7 uses a reasonably aggressive, four-issue dynamically scheduled speculative pipeline structure.

Performance of the A8 Pipeline

The A8 has an ideal CPI of 0.5 due to its dual-issue structure. Pipeline stalls can arise from three sources:

1. Functional hazards, which occur because two adjacent instructions selected for issue simultaneously use the same functional pipeline. Since the A8 is statically scheduled, it is the compiler's task to try to avoid such conflicts. When they cannot be avoided, the A8 can issue at most one instruction in that cycle.

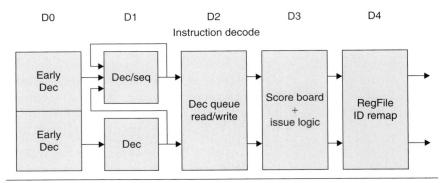

Figure 3.37 The five-stage instruction decode of the A8. In the first stage, a PC produced by the fetch unit (either from the branch target buffer or the PC incrementer) is used to retrieve an 8-byte block from the cache. Up to two instructions are decoded and placed into the decode queue; if neither instruction is a branch, the PC is incremented for the next fetch. Once in the decode queue, the scoreboard logic decides when the instructions can issue. In the issue, the register operands are read; recall that in a simple scoreboard, the operands always come from the registers. The register operands and opcode are sent to the instruction execution portion of the pipeline.

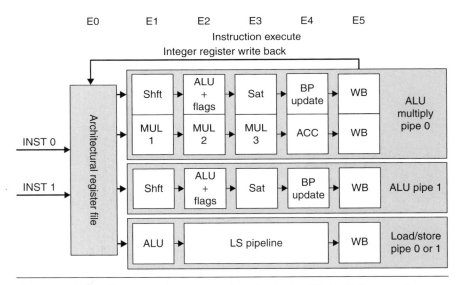

Figure 3.38 The five-stage instruction decode of the A8. Multiply operations are always performed in ALU pipeline 0.

2. Data hazards, which are detected early in the pipeline and may stall either both instructions (if the first cannot issue, the second is always stalled) or the second of a pair. The compiler is responsible for preventing such stalls when possible.

3. Control hazards, which arise only when branches are mispredicted.

In addition to pipeline stalls, L1 and L2 misses both cause stalls.

Figure 3.39 shows an estimate of the factors that contribute to the actual CPI for the Minnespec benchmarks, which we saw in Chapter 2. As we can see, pipeline delays rather than memory stalls are the major contributor to the CPI. This result is partially due to the effect that Minnespec has a smaller cache footprint than full SPEC or other large programs.

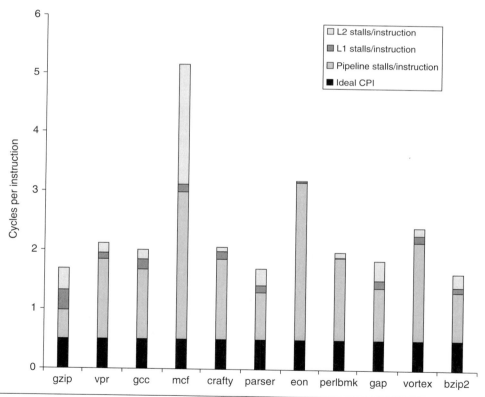

Figure 3.39 The estimated composition of the CPI on the ARM A8 shows that pipeline stalls are the primary addition to the base CPI. eon deserves some special mention, as it does integer-based graphics calculations (ray tracing) and has very few cache misses. It is computationally intensive with heavy use of multiples, and the single multiply pipeline becomes a major bottleneck. This estimate is obtained by using the L1 and L2 miss rates and penalties to compute the L1 and L2 generated stalls per instruction. These are subtracted from the CPI measured by a detailed simulator to obtain the pipeline stalls. Pipeline stalls include all three hazards plus minor effects such as way misprediction.

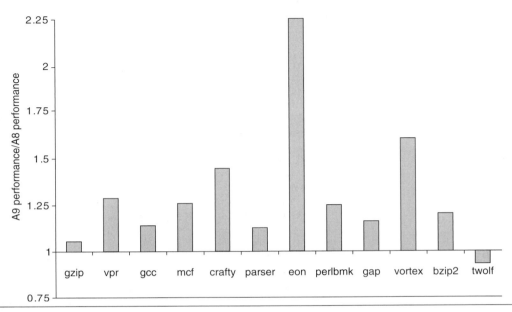

Figure 3.40 The performance ratio for the A9 compared to the A8, both using a 1 GHz clock and the same size caches for L1 and L2, shows that the A9 is about 1.28 times faster. Both runs use a 32 KB primary cache and a 1 MB secondary cache, which is 8-way set associative for the A8 and 16-way for the A9. The block sizes in the caches are 64 bytes for the A8 and 32 bytes for the A9. As mentioned in the caption of Figure 3.39, eon makes intensive use of integer multiply, and the combination of dynamic scheduling and a faster multiply pipeline significantly improves performance on the A9. twolf experiences a small slowdown, likely due to the fact that its cache behavior is worse with the smaller L1 block size of the A9.

The insight that the pipeline stalls created significant performance losses probably played a key role in the decision to make the ARM Cortex-A9 a dynamically scheduled superscalar. The A9, like the A8, issues up to two instructions per clock, but it uses dynamic scheduling and speculation. Up to four pending instructions (two ALUs, one load/store or FP/multimedia, and one branch) can begin execution in a clock cycle. The A9 uses a more powerful branch predictor, instruction cache prefetch, and a nonblocking L1 data cache. Figure 3.40 shows that the A9 outperforms the A8 by a factor of 1.28 on average, assuming the same clock rate and virtually identical cache configurations.

The Intel Core i7

The i7 uses an aggressive out-of-order speculative microarchitecture with reasonably deep pipelines with the goal of achieving high instruction throughput by combining multiple issue and high clock rates. Figure 3.41 shows the overall structure of the i7 pipeline. We will examine the pipeline by starting with

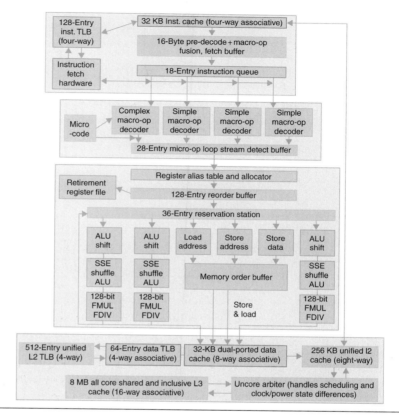

Figure 3.41 The Intel Core i7 pipeline structure shown with the memory system components. The total pipeline depth is 14 stages, with branch mispredictions costing 17 cycles. There are 48 load and 32 store buffers. The six independent functional units can each begin execution of a ready micro-op in the same cycle.

instruction fetch and continuing on to instruction commit, following steps labeled on the figure.

1. Instruction fetch—The processor uses a multilevel branch target buffer to achieve a balance between speed and prediction accuracy. There is also a return address stack to speed up function return. Mispredictions cause a penalty of about 15 cycles. Using the predicted address, the instruction fetch unit fetches 16 bytes from the instruction cache.

2. The 16 bytes are placed in the predecode instruction buffer—In this step, a process called macro-op fusion is executed. *Macro-op fusion* takes instruction combinations such as compare followed by a branch and fuses them into a single operation. The predecode stage also breaks the 16 bytes into individual x86 instructions. This predecode is nontrivial since the length of an x86

instruction can be from 1 to 17 bytes and the predecoder must look through a number of bytes before it knows the instruction length. Individual x86 instructions (including some fused instructions) are placed into the 18-entry instruction queue.

3. Micro-op decode—Individual x86 instructions are translated into micro-ops. Micro-ops are simple MIPS-like instructions that can be executed directly by the pipeline; this approach of translating the x86 instruction set into simple operations that are more easily pipelined was introduced in the Pentium Pro in 1997 and has been used since. Three of the decoders handle x86 instructions that translate directly into one micro-op. For x86 instructions that have more complex semantics, there is a microcode engine that is used to produce the micro-op sequence; it can produce up to four micro-ops every cycle and continues until the necessary micro-op sequence has been generated. The micro-ops are placed according to the order of the x86 instructions in the 28-entry micro-op buffer.

4. The micro-op buffer preforms *loop stream detection* and *microfusion*—If there is a small sequence of instructions (less than 28 instructions or 256 bytes in length) that comprises a loop, the loop stream detector will find the loop and directly issue the micro-ops from the buffer, eliminating the need for the instruction fetch and instruction decode stages to be activated. Microfusion combines instruction pairs such as load/ALU operation and ALU operation/store and issues them to a single reservation station (where they can still issue independently), thus increasing the usage of the buffer. In a study of the Intel Core architecture, which also incorporated microfusion and macrofusion, Bird et al. [2007] discovered that microfusion had little impact on performance, while macrofusion appears to have a modest positive impact on integer performance and little impact on floating-point performance.

5. Perform the basic instruction issue—Looking up the register location in the register tables, renaming the registers, allocating a reorder buffer entry, and fetching any results from the registers or reorder buffer before sending the micro-ops to the reservation stations.

6. The i7 uses a 36-entry centralized reservation station shared by six functional units. Up to six micro-ops may be dispatched to the functional units every clock cycle.

7. Micro-ops are executed by the individual function units and then results are sent back to any waiting reservation station as well as to the register retirement unit, where they will update the register state, once it is known that the instruction is no longer speculative. The entry corresponding to the instruction in the reorder buffer is marked as complete.

8. When one or more instructions at the head of the reorder buffer have been marked as complete, the pending writes in the register retirement unit are executed, and the instructions are removed from the reorder buffer.

Performance of the i7

In earlier sections, we examined the performance of the i7's branch predictor and also the performance of SMT. In this section, we look at single-thread pipeline performance. Because of the presence of aggressive speculation as well as non-blocking caches, it is difficult to attribute the gap between idealized performance and actual performance accurately. As we will see, relatively few stalls occur because instructions cannot issue. For example, only about 3% of the loads are delayed because no reservation station is available. Most losses come either from branch mispredicts or cache misses. The cost of a branch mispredict is 15 cycles, while the cost of an L1 miss is about 10 cycles; L2 misses are slightly more than three times as costly as an L1 miss, and L3 misses cost about 13 times what an L1 miss costs (130–135 cycles)! Although the processor will attempt to find alternative instructions to execute for L3 misses and some L2 misses, it is likely that some of the buffers will fill before the miss completes, causing the processor to stop issuing instructions.

To examine the cost of mispredicts and incorrect speculation, Figure 3.42 shows the fraction of the work (measured by the numbers of micro-ops dispatched into the pipeline) that do not retire (i.e., their results are annulled),

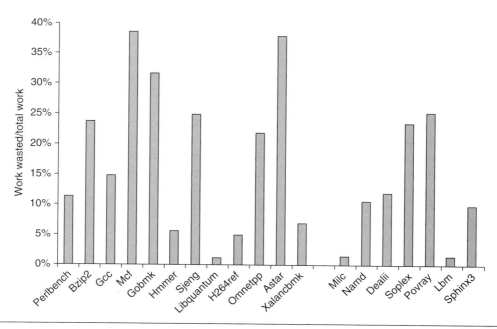

Figure 3.42 The amount of "wasted work" is plotted by taking the ratio of dispatched micro-ops that do not graduate to all dispatched micro-ops. For example, the ratio is 25% for sjeng, meaning that 25% of the dispatched and executed micro-ops are thrown away. The data in this section were collected by Professor Lu Peng and Ph.D. student Ying Zhang, both of Louisiana State University.

relative to all micro-op dispatches. For sjeng, for example, 25% of the work is wasted, since 25% of the dispatched micro-ops are never retired.

Notice that the wasted work in some cases closely matches the branch misprediction rates shown in Figure 3.5 on page 167, but in several instances, such as mcf, the wasted work seems relatively larger than the misprediction rate. In such cases, a likely explanation arises from the memory behavior. With the very high data cache miss rates, mcf will dispatch many instructions during an incorrect speculation as long as sufficient reservation stations are available for the stalled memory references. When the branch misprediction is detected, the micro-ops corresponding to these instructions will be flushed, but there will be congestion around the caches, as speculated memory references try to complete. There is no simple way for the processor to halt such cache requests once they are initiated.

Figure 3.43 shows the overall CPI for the 19 SPECCPU2006 benchmarks. The integer benchmarks have a CPI of 1.06 with very large variance (0.67 standard deviation). MCF and OMNETPP are the major outliers, both having a CPI over 2.0 while most other benchmarks are close to, or less than, 1.0 (gcc, the next highest, is 1.23). This variance derives from differences in the accuracy of branch

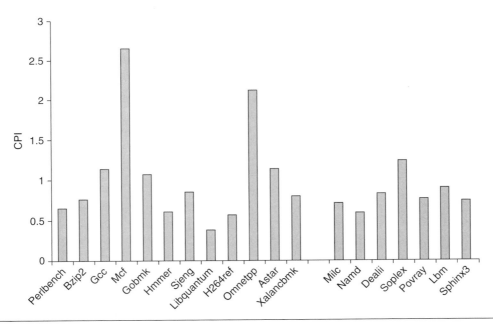

Figure 3.43 The CPI for the 19 SPECCPU2006 benchmarks shows an average CPI for 0.83 for both the FP and integer benchmarks, although the behavior is quite different. In the integer case, the CPI values range from 0.44 to 2.66 with a standard deviation of 0.77, while the variation in the FP case is from 0.62 to 1.38 with a standard deviation of 0.25. The data in this section were collected by Professor Lu Peng and Ph.D. student Ying Zhang, both of Louisiana State University.

prediction and in cache miss rates. For the integer benchmarks, the L2 miss rate is the best predictor of CPI, and the L3 miss rate (which is very small) has almost no effect.

The FP benchmarks achieve higher performance with a lower average CPI (0.89) and a lower standard deviation (0.25). For the FP benchmarks, L1 and L2 are equally important in determining the CPI, while L3 plays a smaller but significant role. While the dynamic scheduling and nonblocking capabilities of the i7 can hide some miss latency, cache memory behavior is still a major contributor. This reinforces the role of multithreading as another way to hide memory latency.

3.14   Fallacies and Pitfalls

Our few fallacies focus on the difficulty of predicting performance and energy efficiency and extrapolating from single measures such as clock rate or CPI. We also show that different architectural approaches can have radically different behaviors for different benchmarks.

Fallacy   *It is easy to predict the performance and energy efficiency of two different versions of the same instruction set architecture, if we hold the technology constant.*

Intel manufactures a processor for the low-end Netbook and PMD space that is quite similar in its microarchitecture of the ARM A8, called the Atom 230. Interestingly, the Atom 230 and the Core i7 920 have both been fabricated in the same 45 nm Intel technology. Figure 3.44 summarizes the Intel Core i7, the ARM Cortex-A8, and Intel Atom 230. These similarities provide a rare opportunity to directly compare two radically different microarchitectures for the same instruction set while holding constant the underlying fabrication technology. Before we do the comparison, we need to say a little more about the Atom 230.

The Atom processors implement the x86 architecture using the standard technique of translating x86 instructions into RISC-like instructions (as every x86 implementation since the mid-1990s has done). Atom uses a slightly more powerful microoperation, which allows an arithmetic operation to be paired with a load or a store. This means that on average for a typical instruction mix only 4% of the instructions require more than one microoperation. The microoperations are then executed in a 16-deep pipeline capable of issuing two instructions per clock, in order, as in the ARM A8. There are dual-integer ALUs, separate pipelines for FP add and other FP operations, and two memory operation pipelines, supporting more general dual execution than the ARM A8 but still limited by the in-order issue capability. The Atom 230 has a 32 KB instruction cache and a 24 KB data cache, both backed by a shared 512 KB L2 on the same die. (The Atom 230 also supports multithreading with two threads, but we will consider only one single threaded comparisons.) Figure 3.46 summarizes the i7, A8, and Atom processors and their key characteristics.

We might expect that these two processors, implemented in the same technology and with the same instruction set, would exhibit predictable behavior, in

Area	Specific characteristic	Intel i7 920 Four cores, each with FP	ARM A8 One core, no FP	Intel Atom 230 One core, with FP
Physical chip properties	Clock rate	2.66 GHz	1 GHz	1.66 GHz
	Thermal design power	130 W	2 W	4 W
	Package	1366-pin BGA	522-pin BGA	437-pin BGA
Memory system	TLB	Two-level All four-way set associative 128 I/64 D 512 L2	One-level fully associative 32 I/32 D	Two-level All four-way set associative 16 I/16 D 64 L2
	Caches	Three-level 32 KB/32 KB 256 KB 2–8 MB	Two-level 16/16 or 32/32 KB 128 KB–1MB	Two-level 32/24 KB 512 KB
	Peak memory BW	17 GB/sec	12 GB/sec	8 GB/sec
Pipeline structure	Peak issue rate	4 ops/clock with fusion	2 ops/clock	2 ops/clock
	Pipeline scheduling	Speculating out of order	In-order dynamic issue	In-order dynamic issue
	Branch prediction	Two-level	Two-level 512-entry BTB 4K global history 8-entry return stack	Two-level

Figure 3.44 An overview of the four-core Intel i7 920, an example of a typical Arm A8 processor chip (with a 256 MB L2, 32K L1s, and no floating point), and the Intel ARM 230 clearly showing the difference in design philosophy between a processor intended for the PMD (in the case of ARM) or netbook space (in the case of Atom) and a processor for use in servers and high-end desktops. Remember, the i7 includes four cores, each of which is several times higher in performance than the one-core A8 or Atom. All these processors are implemented in a comparable 45 nm technology.

terms of relative performance and energy consumption, meaning that power and performance would scale close to linearly. We examine this hypothesis using three sets of benchmarks. The first sets is a group of Java, single-threaded benchmarks that come from the DaCapo benchmarks, and the SPEC JVM98 benchmarks (see Esmaeilzadeh et al. [2011] for a discussion of the benchmarks and measurements). The second and third sets of benchmarks are from SPEC CPU2006 and consist of the integer and FP benchmarks, respectively.

As we can see in Figure 3.45, the i7 significantly outperforms the Atom. All benchmarks are at least four times faster on the i7, two SPECFP benchmarks are over ten times faster, and one SPECINT benchmark runs over eight times faster!

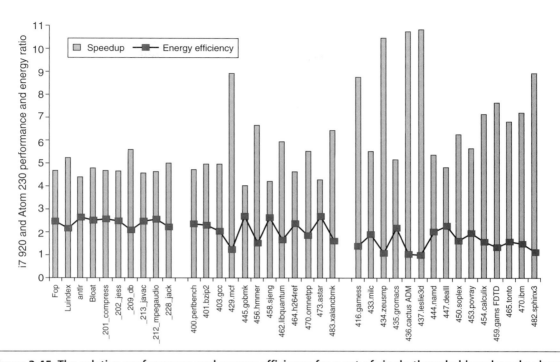

Figure 3.45 The relative performance and energy efficiency for a set of single-threaded benchmarks shows the i7 920 is 4 to over 10 times faster than the Atom 230 but that it is about 2 times *less* power efficient on average! Performance is shown in the columns as i7 relative to Atom, which is execution time (i7)/execution time (Atom). Energy is shown with the line as Energy (Atom)/Energy (i7). The i7 never beats the Atom in energy efficiency, although it is essentially as good on four benchmarks, three of which are floating point. The data shown here were collected by Esmaeilzadeh et al. [2011]. The SPEC benchmarks were compiled with optimization on using the standard Intel compiler, while the Java benchmarks use the Sun (Oracle) Hotspot Java VM. Only one core is active on the i7, and the rest are in deep power saving mode. Turbo Boost is used on the i7, which increases its performance advantage but slightly decreases its relative energy efficiency.

Since the ratio of clock rates of these two processors is 1.6, most of the advantage comes from a much lower CPI for the i7: a factor of 2.8 for the Java benchmarks, a factor of 3.1 for the SPECINT benchmarks, and a factor of 4.3 for the SPECFP benchmarks.

But, the average power consumption for the i7 is just under 43 W, while the average power consumption of the Atom is 4.2 W, or about one-tenth of the power! Combining the performance and power leads to a energy efficiency advantage for the Atom that is typically more than 1.5 times better and often 2 times better! This comparison of two processors using the same underlying technology makes it clear that the performance advantages of an aggressive superscalar with dynamic scheduling and speculation come with a significant disadvantage in energy efficiency.

Fallacy   *Processors with lower CPIs will always be faster.*

Fallacy   *Processors with faster clock rates will always be faster.*

The key is that it is the product of CPI and clock rate that determines performance. A high clock rate obtained by deeply pipelining the CPU must maintain a low CPI to get the full benefit of the faster clock. Similarly, a simple processor with a high clock rate but a low CPI may be slower.

As we saw in the previous fallacy, performance and energy efficiency can diverge significantly among processors designed for different environments even when they have the same ISA. In fact, large differences in performance can show up even within a family of processors from the same company all designed for high-end applications. Figure 3.46 shows the integer and FP performance of two different implementations of the x86 architecture from Intel, as well as a version of the Itanium architecture, also by Intel.

The Pentium 4 was the most aggressively pipelined processor ever built by Intel. It used a pipeline with over 20 stages, had seven functional units, and cached micro-ops rather than x86 instructions. Its relatively inferior performance given the aggressive implementation, was a clear indication that the attempt to exploit more ILP (there could easily be 50 instructions in flight) had failed. The Pentium's power consumption was similar to the i7, although its transistor count was lower, as its primary caches were half as large as the i7, and it included only a 2 MB secondary cache with no tertiary cache.

The Intel Itanium is a VLIW-style architecture, which despite the potential decrease in complexity compared to dynamically scheduled superscalars, never attained competitive clock rates with the mainline x86 processors (although it appears to achieve an overall CPI similar to that of the i7). In examining these results, the reader should be aware that they use different implementation technologies, giving the i7 an advantage in terms of transistor speed and hence clock rate for an equivalently pipelined processor. Nonetheless, the wide variation in performance—more than three times between the Pentium and i7—is astonishing. The next pitfall explains where a significant amount of this advantage comes from.

Processor	Clock rate	SPECCInt2006 base	SPECCFP2006 baseline
Intel Pentium 4 670	3.8 GHz	11.5	12.2
Intel Itanium -2	1.66 GHz	14.5	17.3
Intel i7	3.3 GHz	35.5	38.4

Figure 3.46 Three different Intel processors vary widely. Although the Itanium processor has two cores and the i7 four, only one core is used in the benchmarks.

Pitfall   *Sometimes bigger and dumber is better.*

Much of the attention in the early 2000s went to building aggressive processors to exploit ILP, including the Pentium 4 architecture, which used the deepest pipeline ever seen in a microprocessor, and the Intel Itanium, which had the highest peak issue rate per clock ever seen. What quickly became clear was that the main limitation in exploiting ILP often turned out to be the memory system. Although speculative out-of-order pipelines were fairly good at hiding a significant fraction of the 10- to 15-cycle miss penalties for a first-level miss, they could do very little to hide the penalties for a second-level miss that, when going to main memory, were likely to be 50 to100 clock cycles.

The result was that these designs never came close to achieving the peak instruction throughput despite the large transistor counts and extremely sophisticated and clever techniques. The next section discusses this dilemma and the turning away from more aggressive ILP schemes to multicore, but there was another change that exemplifies this pitfall. Instead of trying to hide even more memory latency with ILP, designers simply used the transistors to build much larger caches. Both the Itanium 2 and the i7 use three-level caches compared to the two-level cache of the Pentium 4, and the third-level caches are 9 MB and 8 MB compared to the 2 MB second-level cache of the Pentium 4. Needless to say, building larger caches is a lot easier than designing the 20+ -stage Pentium 4 pipeline and, from the data in Figure 3.46, seems to be more effective.

3.15   Concluding Remarks: What's Ahead?

As 2000 began, the focus on exploiting instruction-level parallelism was at its peak. Intel was about to introduce Itanium, a high-issue-rate statically scheduled processor that relied on a VLIW-like approach with intensive compiler support. MIPS, Alpha, and IBM processors with dynamically scheduled speculative execution were in their second generation and had gotten wider and faster. The Pentium 4, which used speculative scheduling, had also been announced that year with seven functional units and a pipeline more than 20 stages deep. But there were storm clouds on the horizon.

Research such as that covered in Section 3.10 was showing that pushing ILP much further would be extremely difficult, and, while peak instruction throughput rates had risen from the first speculative processors some 3 to 5 years earlier, sustained instruction execution rates were growing much more slowly.

The next five years were telling. The Itanium turned out to be a good FP processor but only a mediocre integer processor. Intel still produces the line, but there are not many users, the clock rate lags the mainline Intel processors, and Microsoft no longer supports the instruction set. The Intel Pentium 4, while achieving good performance, turned out to be inefficient in terms of performance/watt (i.e., energy use), and the complexity of the processor made it unlikely that further advances would be possible by increasing the issue rate. The end of a 20-year road of achieving new performance levels in microprocessors by exploiting ILP had come. The Pentium 4 was widely acknowledged to have gone beyond the point of diminishing returns, and the aggressive and sophisticated Netburst microarchitecture was abandoned.

By 2005, Intel and all the other major processor manufacturers had revamped their approach to focus on multicore. Higher performance would be achieved through thread-level parallelism rather than instruction-level parallelism, and the responsibility for using the processor efficiently would largely shift from the hardware to the software and the programmer. This change was the most significant change in processor architecture since the early days of pipelining and instruction-level parallelism some 25+ years earlier.

During the same period, designers began to explore the use of more data-level parallelism as another approach to obtaining performance. SIMD extensions enabled desktop and server microprocessors to achieve moderate performance increases for graphics and similar functions. More importantly, graphics processing units (GPUs) pursued aggressive use of SIMD, achieving significant performance advantages for applications with extensive data-level parallelism. For scientific applications, such approaches represent a viable alternative to the more general, but less efficient, thread-level parallelism exploited in multicores. The next chapter explores these developments in the use of data-level parallelism.

Many researchers predicted a major retrenchment in the use of ILP, predicting that two issue superscalar processors and larger numbers of cores would be the future. The advantages, however, of slightly higher issue rates and the ability of speculative dynamic scheduling to deal with unpredictable events, such as level-one cache misses, led to moderate ILP being the primary building block in multicore designs. The addition of SMT and its effectiveness (both for performance and energy efficiency) further cemented the position of the moderate issue, out-of-order, speculative approaches. Indeed, even in the embedded market, the newest processors (e.g., the ARM Cortex-A9) have introduced dynamic scheduling, speculation, and wider issues rates.

It is highly unlikely that future processors will try to increase the width of issue significantly. It is simply too inefficient both from the viewpoint of silicon utilization and power efficiency. Consider the data in Figure 3.47 that show the most recent four processors in the IBM Power series. Over the past decade, there has been a modest improvement in the ILP support in the Power processors, but the dominant portion of the increase in transistor count (a factor of almost 7 from the Power 4 to the Power7) went to increasing the caches and the number of cores per die. Even the expansion in SMT support seems to be more a focus than an increase in the ILP throughput: The ILP structure from Power4 to Power7 went from 5 issues to 6, from 8 functional units to 12 (but not increasing from the original 2 load/store units), while the SMT support went from nonexistent to 4 threads/processor. It seems clear that even for the most advanced ILP processor in 2011 (the Power7), the focus has moved beyond instruction-level parallelism. The next two chapters focus on approaches that exploit data-level and thread-level parallelism.

	Power4	Power5	Power6	Power7
Introduced	2001	2004	2007	2010
Initial clock rate (GHz)	1.3	1.9	4.7	3.6
Transistor count (M)	174	276	790	1200
Issues per clock	5	5	7	6
Functional units	8	8	9	12
Cores/chip	2	2	2	8
SMT threads	0	2	2	4
Total on-chip cache (MB)	1.5	2	4.1	32.3

Figure 3.47 Characteristics of four IBM Power processors. All except the Power6 were dynamically scheduled, which is static, and in-order, and all the processors support two load/store pipelines. The Power6 has the same functional units as the Power5 except for a decimal unit. Power7 uses DRAM for the L3 cache.

3.16   Historical Perspective and References

Section L.5 (available online) features a discussion on the development of pipelining and instruction-level parallelism. We provide numerous references for further reading and exploration of these topics. Section L.5 covers both Chapter 3 and Appendix H.

Case Studies and Exercises by Jason D. Bakos and Robert P. Colwell

Case Study: Exploring the Impact of Microarchitectural Techniques

Concepts illustrated by this case study

- Basic Instruction Scheduling, Reordering, Dispatch
- Multiple Issue and Hazards
- Register Renaming
- Out-of-Order and Speculative Execution
- Where to Spend Out-of-Order Resources

You are tasked with designing a new processor microarchitecture, and you are trying to figure out how best to allocate your hardware resources. Which of the hardware and software techniques you learned in Chapter 3 should you apply? You have a list of latencies for the functional units and for memory, as well as some representative code. Your boss has been somewhat vague about the performance requirements of your new design, but you know from experience that, all else being equal, faster is usually better. Start with the basics. Figure 3.48 provides a sequence of instructions and list of latencies.

3.1 [10] <1.8, 3.1, 3.2> What would be the baseline performance (in cycles, per loop iteration) of the code sequence in Figure 3.48 if no new instruction's execution could be initiated until the previous instruction's execution had completed? Ignore front-end fetch and decode. Assume for now that execution does not stall for lack of the next instruction, but only one instruction/cycle can be issued. Assume the branch is taken, and that there is a one-cycle branch delay slot.

3.2 [10] <1.8, 3.1, 3.2> Think about what latency numbers really mean—they indicate the number of cycles a given function requires to produce its output, nothing more. If the overall pipeline stalls for the latency cycles of each functional unit, then you are at least guaranteed that any pair of back-to-back instructions (a "producer" followed by a "consumer") will execute correctly. But not all instruction pairs have a producer/consumer relationship. Sometimes two adjacent instructions have nothing to do with each other. How many cycles would the loop body in the code sequence in Figure 3.48 require if the pipeline detected true data dependences and only stalled on those, rather than blindly stalling everything just because one functional unit is busy? Show the code with <stall> inserted where necessary to accommodate stated latencies. (*Hint:* An instruction with latency +2 requires two <stall> cycles to be inserted into the code sequence. Think of it this way: A one-cycle instruction has latency 1 + 0, meaning zero extra wait states. So, latency 1 + 1 implies one stall cycle; latency 1 + N has N extra stall cycles.

3.3 [15] <3.6, 3.7> Consider a multiple-issue design. Suppose you have two execution pipelines, each capable of beginning execution of one instruction per cycle, and enough fetch/decode bandwidth in the front end so that it will not stall your

			Latencies beyond single cycle	
Loop:	LD	F2,0(RX)	Memory LD	+4
I0:	DIVD	F8,F2,F0	Memory SD	+1
I1:	MULTD	F2,F6,F2	Integer ADD, SUB	+0
I2:	LD	F4,0(Ry)	Branches	+1
I3:	ADDD	F4,F0,F4	ADDD	+1
I4:	ADDD	F10,F8,F2	MULTD	+5
I5:	ADDI	Rx,Rx,#8	DIVD	+12
I6:	ADDI	Ry,Ry,#8		
I7:	SD	F4,0(Ry)		
I8:	SUB	R20,R4,Rx		
I9:	BNZ	R20,Loop		

Figure 3.48 Code and latencies for Exercises 3.1 through 3.6.

execution. Assume results can be immediately forwarded from one execution unit to another, or to itself. Further assume that the only reason an execution pipeline would stall is to observe a true data dependency. Now how many cycles does the loop require?

3.4 [10] <3.6, 3.7> In the multiple-issue design of Exercise 3.3, you may have recognized some subtle issues. Even though the two pipelines have the exact same instruction repertoire, they are neither identical nor interchangeable, because there is an implicit ordering between them that must reflect the ordering of the instructions in the original program. If instruction $N + 1$ begins execution in Execution Pipe 1 at the same time that instruction N begins in Pipe 0, and $N + 1$ happens to require a shorter execution latency than N, then $N + 1$ will complete before N (even though program ordering would have implied otherwise). Recite at least two reasons why that could be hazardous and will require special considerations in the microarchitecture. Give an example of two instructions from the code in Figure 3.48 that demonstrate this hazard.

3.5 [20] <3.7> Reorder the instructions to improve performance of the code in Figure 3.48. Assume the two-pipe machine in Exercise 3.3 and that the out-of-order completion issues of Exercise 3.4 have been dealt with successfully. Just worry about observing true data dependences and functional unit latencies for now. How many cycles does your reordered code take?

3.6 [10/10/10] <3.1, 3.2> Every cycle that does not initiate a new operation in a pipe is a lost opportunity, in the sense that your hardware is not living up to its potential.

  a. [10] <3.1, 3.2> In your reordered code from Exercise 3.5, what fraction of all cycles, counting both pipes, were wasted (did not initiate a new op)?

  b. [10] <3.1, 3.2> Loop unrolling is one standard compiler technique for finding more parallelism in code, in order to minimize the lost opportunities for performance. Hand-unroll two iterations of the loop in your reordered code from Exercise 3.5.

  c. [10] <3.1, 3.2> What speedup did you obtain? (For this exercise, just color the $N + 1$ iteration's instructions green to distinguish them from the Nth iteration's instructions; if you were actually unrolling the loop, you would have to reassign registers to prevent collisions between the iterations.)

3.7 [15] <2.1> Computers spend most of their time in loops, so multiple loop iterations are great places to speculatively find more work to keep CPU resources busy. Nothing is ever easy, though; the compiler emitted only one copy of that loop's code, so even though multiple iterations are handling distinct data, they will appear to use the same registers. To keep multiple iterations' register usages from colliding, we rename their registers. Figure 3.49 shows example code that we would like our hardware to rename. A compiler could have simply unrolled the loop and used different registers to avoid conflicts, but if we expect our hardware to unroll the loop, it must also do the register renaming. How? Assume your hardware has a pool of temporary registers (call them T registers, and assume that

```
Loop: LD      F4,0(Rx)
I0:   MULTD   F2,F0,F2
I1:   DIVD    F8,F4,F2
I2:   LD      F4,0(Ry)
I3:   ADDD    F6,F0,F4
I4:   SUBD    F8,F8,F6
I5:   SD      F8,0(Ry)
```

Figure 3.49 Sample code for register renaming practice.

```
I0:   LD      T9,0(Rx)
I1:   MULTD   T10,F0,T9
...
```

Figure 3.50 *Hint:* Expected output of register renaming.

there are 64 of them, T0 through T63) that it can substitute for those registers designated by the compiler. This rename hardware is indexed by the src (source) register designation, and the value in the table is the T register of the last destination that targeted that register. (Think of these table values as producers, and the src registers are the consumers; it doesn't much matter where the producer puts its result as long as its consumers can find it.) Consider the code sequence in Figure 3.49. Every time you see a destination register in the code, substitute the next available T, beginning with T9. Then update all the src registers accordingly, so that true data dependences are maintained. Show the resulting code. (*Hint:* See Figure 3.50.)

3.8 [20] <3.4> Exercise 3.7 explored simple register renaming: when the hardware register renamer sees a source register, it substitutes the destination T register of the last instruction to have targeted that source register. When the rename table sees a destination register, it substitutes the next available T for it, but superscalar designs need to handle multiple instructions per clock cycle at every stage in the machine, including the register renaming. A simple scalar processor would therefore look up both src register mappings for each instruction and allocate a new dest mapping per clock cycle. Superscalar processors must be able to do that as well, but they must also ensure that any dest-to-src relationships between the two concurrent instructions are handled correctly. Consider the sample code sequence in Figure 3.51. Assume that we would like to simultaneously rename the first two instructions. Further assume that the next two available T registers to be used are known at the beginning of the clock cycle in which these two instructions are being renamed. Conceptually, what we want is for the first instruction to do its rename table lookups and then update the table per its destination's T register. Then the second instruction would do exactly the same thing, and any

I0:	SUBD	F1,F2,F3
I1:	ADDD	F4,F1,F2
I2:	MULTD	F6,F4,F1
I3:	DIVD	F0,F2,F6

Figure 3.51 Sample code for superscalar register renaming.

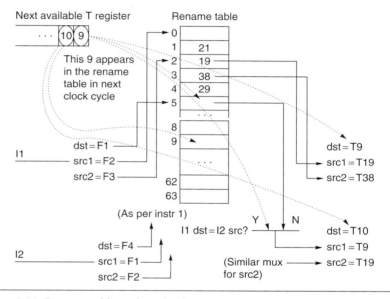

Figure 3.52 Rename table and on-the-fly register substitution logic for superscalar machines. (Note that src is source, and dest is destination.)

interinstruction dependency would thereby be handled correctly. But there's not enough time to write that T register designation into the renaming table and then look it up again for the second instruction, all in the same clock cycle. That register substitution must instead be done live (in parallel with the register rename table update). Figure 3.52 shows a circuit diagram, using multiplexers and comparators, that will accomplish the necessary on-the-fly register renaming. Your task is to show the cycle-by-cycle state of the rename table for every instruction of the code shown in Figure 3.51. Assume the table starts out with every entry equal to its index (T0 = 0; T1 = 1, ...).

3.9 [5] <3.4> If you ever get confused about what a register renamer has to do, go back to the assembly code you're executing, and ask yourself what has to happen for the right result to be obtained. For example, consider a three-way superscalar machine renaming these three instructions concurrently:

```
ADDI R1, R1, R1
ADDI R1, R1, R1
ADDI R1, R1, R1
```

If the value of R1 starts out as 5, what should its value be when this sequence has executed?

3.10 [20] <3.4, 3.9> Very long instruction word (VLIW) designers have a few basic choices to make regarding architectural rules for register use. Suppose a VLIW is designed with self-draining execution pipelines: once an operation is initiated, its results will appear in the destination register at most L cycles later (where L is the latency of the operation). There are never enough registers, so there is a temptation to wring maximum use out of the registers that exist. Consider Figure 3.53. If loads have a $1 + 2$ cycle latency, unroll this loop once, and show how a VLIW capable of two loads and two adds per cycle can use the minimum number of registers, in the absence of any pipeline interruptions or stalls. Give an example of an event that, in the presence of self-draining pipelines, could disrupt this pipelining and yield wrong results.

3.11 [10/10/10] <3.3> Assume a five-stage single-pipeline microarchitecture (fetch, decode, execute, memory, write-back) and the code in Figure 3.54. All ops are one cycle except LW and SW, which are $1 + 2$ cycles, and branches, which are $1 + 1$ cycles. There is no forwarding. Show the phases of each instruction per clock cycle for one iteration of the loop.

   a. [10] <3.3> How many clock cycles per loop iteration are lost to branch overhead?

   b. [10] <3.3> Assume a static branch predictor, capable of recognizing a backwards branch in the Decode stage. Now how many clock cycles are wasted on branch overhead?

   c. [10] <3.3> Assume a dynamic branch predictor. How many cycles are lost on a correct prediction?

```
Loop:  LW        R4,0(R0)  ;  ADDI     R11,R3,#1
       LW        R5,8(R1)  ;  ADDI     R20,R0,#1
       <stall>
       ADDI      R10,R4,#1;
       SW        R7,0(R6)  ;  SW       R9,8(R8)
       ADDI      R2,R2,#8
       SUB       R4,R3,R2
       BNZ       R4,Loop
```

Figure 3.53 Sample VLIW code with two adds, two loads, and two stalls.

```
Loop:   LW      R3,0(R0)
        LW      R1,0(R3)
        ADDI    R1,R1,#1
        SUB     R4,R3,R2
        SW      R1,0(R3)
        BNZ     R4, Loop
```

Figure 3.54 Code loop for Exercise 3.11.

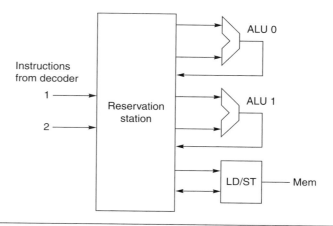

Figure 3.55 An out-of-order microarchitecure.

3.12 [15/20/20/10/20] <3.4, 3.7, 3.14> Let's consider what dynamic scheduling might achieve here. Assume a microarchitecture as shown in Figure 3.55. Assume that the arithmetic-logical units (ALUs) can do all arithmetic ops (MULTD, DIVD, ADDD, ADDI, SUB) and branches, and that the Reservation Station (RS) can dispatch at most one operation to each functional unit per cycle (one op to each ALU plus one memory op to the LD/ST).

   a. [15] <3.4> Suppose all of the instructions from the sequence in Figure 3.48 are present in the RS, with no renaming having been done. Highlight any instructions in the code where register renaming would improve perfor-mance. (*Hint:* Look for read-after-write and write-after-write hazards. Assume the same functional unit latencies as in Figure 3.48.)

   b. [20] <3.4> Suppose the register-renamed version of the code from part (a) is resident in the RS in clock cycle *N*, with latencies as given in Figure 3.48. Show how the RS should dispatch these instructions out of order, clock by clock, to obtain optimal performance on this code. (Assume the same RS restrictions as in part (a). Also assume that results must be written into the RS before they're available for use—no bypassing.) How many clock cycles does the code sequence take?

c. [20] <3.4> Part (b) lets the RS try to optimally schedule these instructions. But in reality, the whole instruction sequence of interest is not usually present in the RS. Instead, various events clear the RS, and as a new code sequence streams in from the decoder, the RS must choose to dispatch what it has. Suppose that the RS is empty. In cycle 0, the first two register-renamed instructions of this sequence appear in the RS. Assume it takes one clock cycle to dispatch any op, and assume functional unit latencies are as they were for Exercise 3.2. Further assume that the front end (decoder/register-renamer) will continue to supply two new instructions per clock cycle. Show the cycle-by-cycle order of dispatch of the RS. How many clock cycles does this code sequence require now?

d. [10] <3.14> If you wanted to improve the results of part (c), which would have helped most: (1) Another ALU? (2) Another LD/ST unit? (3) Full bypassing of ALU results to subsequent operations? or (4) Cutting the longest latency in half? What's the speedup?

e. [20] <3.7> Now let's consider speculation, the act of fetching, decoding, and executing beyond one or more conditional branches. Our motivation to do this is twofold: The dispatch schedule we came up with in part (c) had lots of nops, and we know computers spend most of their time executing loops (which implies the branch back to the top of the loop is pretty predictable). Loops tell us where to find more work to do; our sparse dispatch schedule suggests we have opportunities to do some of that work earlier than before. In part (d) you found the critical path through the loop. Imagine folding a second copy of that path onto the schedule you got in part (b). How many more clock cycles would be required to do two loops' worth of work (assuming all instructions are resident in the RS)? (Assume all functional units are fully pipelined.)

Exercises

3.13 [25] <3.13> In this exercise, you will explore performance trade-offs between three processors that each employ different types of multithreading. Each of these processors is superscalar, uses in-order pipelines, requires a fixed three-cycle stall following all loads and branches, and has identical L1 caches. Instructions from the same thread issued in the same cycle are read in program order and must not contain any data or control dependences.

■ Processor A is a superscalar SMT architecture, capable of issuing up to two instructions per cycle from two threads.

■ Processor B is a fine MT architecture, capable of issuing up to four instructions per cycle from a single thread and switches threads on any pipeline stall.

- Processor C is a coarse MT architecture, capable of issuing up to eight instructions per cycle from a single thread and switches threads on an L1 cache miss.

Our application is a list searcher, which scans a region of memory for a specific value stored in R9 between the address range specified in R16 and R17. It is parallelized by evenly dividing the search space into four equal-sized contiguous blocks and assigning one search thread to each block (yielding four threads). Most of each thread's runtime is spent in the following unrolled loop body:

```
loop:   LD R1,0(R16)
        LD R2,8(R16)
        LD R3,16(R16)
        LD R4,24(R16)
        LD R5,32(R16)
        LD R6,40(R16)
        LD R7,48(R16)
        LD R8,56(R16)
        BEQAL R9,R1,match0
        BEQAL R9,R2,match1
        BEQAL R9,R3,match2
        BEQAL R9,R4,match3
        BEQAL R9,R5,match4
        BEQAL R9,R6,match5
        BEQAL R9,R7,match6
        BEQAL R9,R8,match7
        DADDIU R16,R16,#64
        BLT R16,R17,loop
```

Assume the following:

- A barrier is used to ensure that all threads begin simultaneously.
- The first L1 cache miss occurs after two iterations of the loop.
- None of the BEQAL branches is taken.
- The BLT is always taken.
- All three processors schedule threads in a round-robin fashion.

Determine how many cycles are required for each processor to complete the first two iterations of the loop.

3.14   [25/25/25] <3.2, 3.7> In this exercise, we look at how software techniques can extract instruction-level parallelism (ILP) in a common vector loop. The following loop is the so-called DAXPY loop (double-precision *aX* plus *Y*) and is the central operation in Gaussian elimination. The following code implements the DAXPY operation, $Y = aX + Y$, for a vector length 100. Initially, R1 is set to the base address of array *X* and R2 is set to the base address of *Y*:

```
          DADDIU   R4,R1,#800   ; R1 = upper bound for X
foo:      L.D      F2,0(R1)     ; (F2) = X(i)
          MUL.D    F4,F2,F0     ; (F4) = a*X(i)
          L.D      F6,0(R2)     ; (F6) = Y(i)
          ADD.D    F6,F4,F6     ; (F6) = a*X(i) + Y(i)
          S.D      F6,0(R2)     ; Y(i) = a*X(i) + Y(i)
          DADDIU   R1,R1,#8     ; increment X index
          DADDIU   R2,R2,#8     ; increment Y index
          DSLTU    R3,R1,R4     ; test: continue loop?
          BNEZ     R3,foo       ; loop if needed
```

Assume the functional unit latencies as shown in the table below. Assume a one-cycle delayed branch that resolves in the ID stage. Assume that results are fully bypassed.

Instruction producing result	Instruction using result	Latency in clock cycles
FP multiply	FP ALU op	6
FP add	FP ALU op	4
FP multiply	FP store	5
FP add	FP store	4
Integer operations and all loads	Any	2

a. [25] <3.2> Assume a single-issue pipeline. Show how the loop would look both unscheduled by the compiler and after compiler scheduling for both floating-point operation and branch delays, including any stalls or idle clock cycles. What is the execution time (in cycles) per element of the result vector, *Y*, unscheduled and scheduled? How much faster must the clock be for processor hardware alone to match the performance improvement achieved by the scheduling compiler? (Neglect any possible effects of increased clock speed on memory system performance.)

b. [25] <3.2> Assume a single-issue pipeline. Unroll the loop as many times as necessary to schedule it without any stalls, collapsing the loop overhead instructions. How many times must the loop be unrolled? Show the instruction schedule. What is the execution time per element of the result?

c. [25] <3.7> Assume a VLIW processor with instructions that contain five operations, as shown in Figure 3.16. We will compare two degrees of loop unrolling. First, unroll the loop 6 times to extract ILP and schedule it without any stalls (i.e., completely empty issue cycles), collapsing the loop overhead instructions, and then repeat the process but unroll the loop 10 times. Ignore the branch delay slot. Show the two schedules. What is the execution time per element of the result vector for each schedule? What percent of the operation slots are used in each schedule? How much does the size of the code differ between the two schedules? What is the total register demand for the two schedules?

3.15 [20/20] <3.4, 3.5, 3.7, 3.8> In this exercise, we will look at how variations on Tomasulo's algorithm perform when running the loop from Exercise 3.14. The functional units (FUs) are described in the table below.

FU Type	Cycles in EX	Number of FUs	Number of reservation stations
Integer	1	1	5
FP adder	10	1	3
FP multiplier	15	1	2

Assume the following:

■ Functional units are not pipelined.

■ There is no forwarding between functional units; results are communicated by the common data bus (CDB).

■ The execution stage (EX) does both the effective address calculation and the memory access for loads and stores. Thus, the pipeline is IF/ID/IS/EX/WB.

■ Loads require one clock cycle.

■ The issue (IS) and write-back (WB) result stages each require one clock cycle.

■ There are five load buffer slots and five store buffer slots.

■ Assume that the Branch on Not Equal to Zero (BNEZ) instruction requires one clock cycle.

a. [20] <3.4–3.5> For this problem use the single-issue Tomasulo MIPS pipeline of Figure 3.6 with the pipeline latencies from the table above. Show the number of stall cycles for each instruction and what clock cycle each instruction begins execution (i.e., enters its first EX cycle) for three iterations of the loop. How many cycles does each loop iteration take? Report your answer in the form of a table with the following column headers:

■ Iteration (loop iteration number)

■ Instruction

■ Issues (cycle when instruction issues)

■ Executes (cycle when instruction executes)

- Memory access (cycle when memory is accessed)

- Write CDB (cycle when result is written to the CDB)

- Comment (description of any event on which the instruction is waiting)

Show three iterations of the loop in your table. You may ignore the first instruction.

b. [20] <3.7, 3.8> Repeat part (a) but this time assume a two-issue Tomasulo algorithm and a fully pipelined floating-point unit (FPU).

3.16 [10] <3.4> Tomasulo's algorithm has a disadvantage: Only one result can compute per clock per CDB. Use the hardware configuration and latencies from the previous question and find a code sequence of no more than 10 instructions where Tomasulo's algorithm must stall due to CDB contention. Indicate where this occurs in your sequence.

3.17 [20] <3.3> An (*m,n*) correlating branch predictor uses the behavior of the most recent *m* executed branches to choose from 2^m predictors, each of which is an *n*-bit predictor. A two-level local predictor works in a similar fashion, but only keeps track of the past behavior of each individual branch to predict future behavior.

There is a design trade-off involved with such predictors: Correlating predictors require little memory for history which allows them to maintain 2-bit predictors for a large number of individual branches (reducing the probability of branch instructions reusing the same predictor), while local predictors require substantially more memory to keep history and are thus limited to tracking a relatively small number of branch instructions. For this exercise, consider a (1,2) correlating predictor that can track four branches (requiring 16 bits) versus a (1,2) local predictor that can track two branches using the same amount of memory. For the following branch outcomes, provide each prediction, the table entry used to make the prediction, any updates to the table as a result of the prediction, and the final misprediction rate of each predictor. Assume that all branches up to this point have been taken. Initialize each predictor to the following:

Correlating predictor

Entry	Branch	Last outcome	Prediction
0	0	T	T with one misprediction
1	0	NT	NT
2	1	T	NT
3	1	NT	T
4	2	T	T
5	2	NT	T
6	3	T	NT with one misprediction
7	3	NT	NT

Local predictor

Entry	Branch	Last 2 outcomes (right is most recent)	Prediction
0	0	T,T	T with one misprediction
1	0	T,NT	NT
2	0	NT,T	NT
3	0	NT	T
4	1	T,T	T
5	1	T,NT	T with one misprediction
6	1	NT,T	NT
7	1	NT,NT	NT

Branch PC (word address)	Outcome
454	T
543	NT
777	NT
543	NT
777	NT
454	T
777	NT
454	T
543	T

3.18 [10] <3.9> Suppose we have a deeply pipelined processor, for which we implement a branch-target buffer for the conditional branches only. Assume that the misprediction penalty is always four cycles and the buffer miss penalty is always three cycles. Assume a 90% hit rate, 90% accuracy, and 15% branch frequency. How much faster is the processor with the branch-target buffer versus a processor that has a fixed two-cycle branch penalty? Assume a base clock cycle per instruction (CPI) without branch stalls of one.

3.19 [10/5] <3.9> Consider a branch-target buffer that has penalties of zero, two, and two clock cycles for correct conditional branch prediction, incorrect prediction, and a buffer miss, respectively. Consider a branch-target buffer design that distinguishes conditional and unconditional branches, storing the target address for a conditional branch and the target instruction for an unconditional branch.

    a. [10] <3.9> What is the penalty in clock cycles when an unconditional branch is found in the buffer?

    b. [10] <3.9> Determine the improvement from branch folding for unconditional branches. Assume a 90% hit rate, an unconditional branch frequency of 5%, and a two-cycle penalty for a buffer miss. How much improvement is gained by this enhancement? How high must the hit rate be for this enhancement to provide a performance gain?

4

Data-Level Parallelism in Vector, SIMD, and GPU Architectures

We call these algorithms *data parallel* algorithms because their parallelism comes from simultaneous operations across large sets of data, rather than from multiple threads of control.

W. Daniel Hillis and Guy L. Steele
"Data Parallel Algorithms," *Comm. ACM* (1986)

If you were plowing a field, which would you rather use: two strong oxen or 1024 chickens?

Seymour Cray, Father of the Supercomputer
*(arguing for two powerful vector processors
versus many simple processors)*

4.1 Introduction

A question for the single instruction, multiple data (SIMD) architecture, which Chapter 1 introduced, has always been just how wide a set of applications has significant data-level parallelism (DLP). Fifty years later, the answer is not only the matrix-oriented computations of scientific computing, but also the media-oriented image and sound processing. Moreover, since a single instruction can launch many data operations, SIMD is potentially more energy efficient than multiple instruction multiple data (MIMD), which needs to fetch and execute one instruction per data operation. These two answers make SIMD attractive for Personal Mobile Devices. Finally, perhaps the biggest advantage of SIMD versus MIMD is that the programmer continues to think sequentially yet achieves parallel speedup by having parallel data operations.

This chapter covers three variations of SIMD: vector architectures, multimedia SIMD instruction set extensions, and graphics processing units (GPUs).[1]

The first variation, which predates the other two by more than 30 years, means essentially pipelined execution of many data operations. These *vector architectures* are easier to understand and to compile to than other SIMD variations, but they were considered too expensive for microprocessors until recently. Part of that expense was in transistors and part was in the cost of sufficient DRAM bandwidth, given the widespread reliance on caches to meet memory performance demands on conventional microprocessors.

The second SIMD variation borrows the SIMD name to mean basically simultaneous parallel data operations and is found in most instruction set architectures today that support multimedia applications. For x86 architectures, the SIMD instruction extensions started with the MMX (Multimedia Extensions) in 1996, which were followed by several SSE (Streaming SIMD Extensions) versions in the next decade, and they continue to this day with AVX (Advanced Vector Extensions). To get the highest computation rate from an x86 computer, you often need to use these SIMD instructions, especially for floating-point programs.

The third variation on SIMD comes from the GPU community, offering higher potential performance than is found in traditional multicore computers today. While GPUs share features with vector architectures, they have their own distinguishing characteristics, in part due to the ecosystem in which they evolved. This environment has a system processor and system memory in addition to the GPU and its graphics memory. In fact, to recognize those distinctions, the GPU community refers to this type of architecture as *heterogeneous*.

---

[1] This chapter is based on material in Appendix F, "Vector Processors," by Krste Asanovic, and Appendix G, "Hardware and Software for VLIW and EPIC" from the 4th edition of this book; on material in Appendix A, "Graphics and Computing GPUs," by John Nickolls and David Kirk, from the 4th edition of *Computer Organization and Design*; and to a lesser extent on material in "Embracing and Extending 20th-Century Instruction Set Architectures," by Joe Gebis and David Patterson, *IEEE Computer*, April 2007.

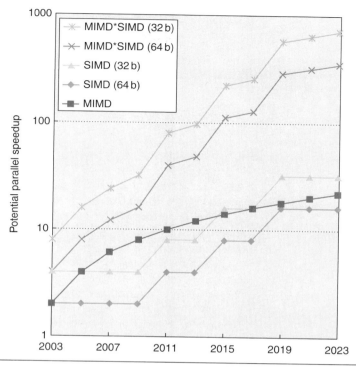

Figure 4.1   Potential speedup via parallelism from MIMD, SIMD, and both MIMD and SIMD over time for x86 computers. This figure assumes that two cores per chip for MIMD will be added every two years and the number of operations for SIMD will double every four years.

For problems with lots of data parallelism, all three SIMD variations share the advantage of being easier for the programmer than classic parallel MIMD programming. To put into perspective the importance of SIMD versus MIMD, Figure 4.1 plots the number of cores for MIMD versus the number of 32-bit and 64-bit operations per clock cycle in SIMD mode for x86 computers over time.

For x86 computers, we expect to see two additional cores per chip every two years and the SIMD width to double every four years. Given these assumptions, over the next decade the potential speedup from SIMD parallelism is twice that of MIMD parallelism. Hence, it's as least as important to understand SIMD parallelism as MIMD parallelism, although the latter has received much more fanfare recently. For applications with both data-level parallelism and thread-level parallelism, the potential speedup in 2020 will be an order of magnitude higher than today.

The goal of this chapter is for architects to understand why vector is more general than multimedia SIMD, as well as the similarities and differences between vector and GPU architectures. Since vector architectures are supersets of the multimedia SIMD instructions, including a better model for compilation, and since GPUs share several similarities with vector architectures, we start with vector architectures to set the foundation for the following two sections. The next section introduces vector architectures, while Appendix G goes much deeper into the subject.

| 4.2 | **Vector Architecture** |

The most efficient way to execute a vectorizable application is a vector processor.

Jim Smith
International Symposium on Computer Architecture (1994)

Vector architectures grab sets of data elements scattered about memory, place them into large, sequential register files, operate on data in those register files, and then disperse the results back into memory. A single instruction operates on vectors of data, which results in dozens of register–register operations on independent data elements.

These large register files act as compiler-controlled buffers, both to hide memory latency and to leverage memory bandwidth. Since vector loads and stores are deeply pipelined, the program pays the long memory latency only once per vector load or store versus once per element, thus amortizing the latency over, say, 64 elements. Indeed, vector programs strive to keep memory busy.

VMIPS

We begin with a vector processor consisting of the primary components that Figure 4.2 shows. This processor, which is loosely based on the Cray-1, is the foundation for discussion throughout this section. We will call this instruction set architecture *VMIPS*; its scalar portion is MIPS, and its vector portion is the logical vector extension of MIPS. The rest of this subsection examines how the basic architecture of VMIPS relates to other processors.

The primary components of the instruction set architecture of VMIPS are the following:

■ *Vector registers*—Each vector register is a fixed-length bank holding a single vector. VMIPS has eight vector registers, and each vector register holds 64 elements, each 64 bits wide. The vector register file needs to provide enough ports to feed all the vector functional units. These ports will allow a high degree of overlap among vector operations to different vector registers. The read and write ports, which total at least 16 read ports and 8 write ports, are connected to the functional unit inputs or outputs by a pair of crossbar switches.

■ *Vector functional units*—Each unit is fully pipelined, and it can start a new operation on every clock cycle. A control unit is needed to detect hazards, both structural hazards for functional units and data hazards on register accesses. Figure 4.2 shows that VMIPS has five functional units. For simplicity, we focus exclusively on the floating-point functional units.

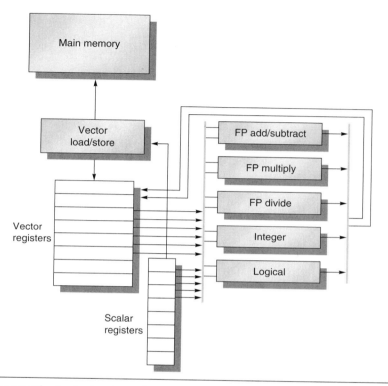

Figure 4.2 The basic structure of a vector architecture, VMIPS. This processor has a scalar architecture just like MIPS. There are also eight 64-element vector registers, and all the functional units are vector functional units. This chapter defines special vector instructions for both arithmetic and memory accesses. The figure shows vector units for logical and integer operations so that VMIPS looks like a standard vector processor that usually includes these units; however, we will not be discussing these units. The vector and scalar registers have a significant number of read and write ports to allow multiple simultaneous vector operations. A set of crossbar switches (thick gray lines) connects these ports to the inputs and outputs of the vector functional units.

- *Vector load/store unit*—The vector memory unit loads or stores a vector to or from memory. The VMIPS vector loads and stores are fully pipelined, so that words can be moved between the vector registers and memory with a bandwidth of one word per clock cycle, after an initial latency. This unit would also normally handle scalar loads and stores.

- *A set of scalar registers*—Scalar registers can also provide data as input to the vector functional units, as well as compute addresses to pass to the vector load/store unit. These are the normal 32 general-purpose registers and 32 floating-point registers of MIPS. One input of the vector functional units latches scalar values as they are read out of the scalar register file.

Instruction	Operands	Function
ADDVV.D ADDVS.D	V1,V2,V3 V1,V2,F0	Add elements of V2 and V3, then put each result in V1. Add F0 to each element of V2, then put each result in V1.
SUBVV.D SUBVS.D SUBSV.D	V1,V2,V3 V1,V2,F0 V1,F0,V2	Subtract elements of V3 from V2, then put each result in V1. Subtract F0 from elements of V2, then put each result in V1. Subtract elements of V2 from F0, then put each result in V1.
MULVV.D MULVS.D	V1,V2,V3 V1,V2,F0	Multiply elements of V2 and V3, then put each result in V1. Multiply each element of V2 by F0, then put each result in V1.
DIVVV.D DIVVS.D DIVSV.D	V1,V2,V3 V1,V2,F0 V1,F0,V2	Divide elements of V2 by V3, then put each result in V1. Divide elements of V2 by F0, then put each result in V1. Divide F0 by elements of V2, then put each result in V1.
LV	V1,R1	Load vector register V1 from memory starting at address R1.
SV	R1,V1	Store vector register V1 into memory starting at address R1.
LVWS	V1,(R1,R2)	Load V1 from address at R1 with stride in R2 (i.e., R1 + i × R2).
SVWS	(R1,R2),V1	Store V1 to address at R1 with stride in R2 (i.e., R1 + i × R2).
LVI	V1,(R1+V2)	Load V1 with vector whose elements are at R1 + V2(i) (i.e., V2 is an index).
SVI	(R1+V2),V1	Store V1 to vector whose elements are at R1 + V2(i) (i.e., V2 is an index).
CVI	V1,R1	Create an index vector by storing the values 0, 1 × R1, 2 × R1, ..., 63 × R1 into V1.
S--VV.D S--VS.D	V1,V2 V1,F0	Compare the elements (EQ, NE, GT, LT, GE, LE) in V1 and V2. If condition is true, put a 1 in the corresponding bit vector; otherwise put 0. Put resulting bit vector in vector-mask register (VM). The instruction S--VS.D performs the same compare but using a scalar value as one operand.
POP	R1,VM	Count the 1s in vector-mask register VM and store count in R1.
CVM		Set the vector-mask register to all 1s.
MTC1 MFC1	VLR,R1 R1,VLR	Move contents of R1 to vector-length register VL. Move the contents of vector-length register VL to R1.
MVTM MVFM	VM,F0 F0,VM	Move contents of F0 to vector-mask register VM. Move contents of vector-mask register VM to F0.

Figure 4.3 The VMIPS vector instructions, showing only the double-precision floating-point operations. In addition to the vector registers, there are two special registers, VLR and VM, discussed below. These special registers are assumed to live in the MIPS coprocessor 1 space along with the FPU registers. The operations with stride and uses of the index creation and indexed load/store operations are explained later.

Figure 4.3 lists the VMIPS vector instructions. In VMIPS, vector operations use the same names as scalar MIPS instructions, but with the letters "VV" appended. Thus, ADDVV.D is an addition of two double-precision vectors. The vector instructions take as their input either a pair of vector registers (ADDVV.D) or a vector register and a scalar register, designated by appending "VS" (ADDVS.D). In the latter case, all operations use the same value in the scalar register as one input: The operation ADDVS.D will add the contents of a scalar register to each element in a vector register. The vector functional unit gets a copy of the scalar value at issue time. Most vector operations have a vector destination register, although a few (such as population count) produce a scalar value, which is stored to a scalar register.

The names LV and SV denote vector load and vector store, and they load or store an entire vector of double-precision data. One operand is the vector register to be loaded or stored; the other operand, which is a MIPS general-purpose register, is the starting address of the vector in memory. As we shall see, in addition to the vector registers, we need two additional special-purpose registers: the vector-length and vector-mask registers. The former is used when the natural vector length is not 64 and the latter is used when loops involve IF statements.

The power wall leads architects to value architectures that can deliver high performance without the energy and design complexity costs of highly out-of-order superscalar processors. Vector instructions are a natural match to this trend, since architects can use them to increase performance of simple in-order scalar processors without greatly increasing energy demands and design complexity. In practice, developers can express many of the programs that ran well on complex out-of-order designs more efficiently as data-level parallelism in the form of vector instructions, as Kozyrakis and Patterson [2002] showed.

With a vector instruction, the system can perform the operations on the vector data elements in many ways, including operating on many elements simultaneously. This flexibility lets vector designs use slow but wide execution units to achieve high performance at low power. Further, the independence of elements within a vector instruction set allows scaling of functional units without performing additional costly dependency checks, as superscalar processors require.

Vectors naturally accommodate varying data sizes. Hence, one view of a vector register size is 64 64-bit data elements, but 128 32-bit elements, 256 16-bit elements, and even 512 8-bit elements are equally valid views. Such hardware multiplicity is why a vector architecture can be useful for multimedia applications as well as scientific applications.

How Vector Processors Work: An Example

We can best understand a vector processor by looking at a vector loop for VMIPS. Let's take a typical vector problem, which we use throughout this section:

$$Y = a \times X + Y$$

X and Y are vectors, initially resident in memory, and a is a scalar. This problem is the so-called *SAXPY* or *DAXPY* loop that forms the inner loop of the Linpack benchmark. (SAXPY stands for single-precision a × X plus Y; DAXPY for double precision a × X plus Y.) Linpack is a collection of linear algebra routines, and the Linpack benchmark consists of routines for performing Gaussian elimination.

For now, let us assume that the number of elements, or length, of a vector register (64) matches the length of the vector operation we are interested in. (This restriction will be lifted shortly.)

Example   Show the code for MIPS and VMIPS for the DAXPY loop. Assume that the starting addresses of X and Y are in Rx and Ry, respectively.

Answer   Here is the MIPS code.

```
            L.D        F0,a            ;load scalar a
            DADDIU     R4,Rx,#512      ;last address to load
    Loop:   L.D        F2,0(Rx)        ;load X[i]
            MUL.D      F2,F2,F0        ;a × X[i]
            L.D        F4,0(Ry)        ;load Y[i]
            ADD.D      F4,F4,F2        ;a × X[i] + Y[i]
            S.D        F4,9(Ry)        ;store into Y[i]
            DADDIU     Rx,Rx,#8        ;increment index to X
            DADDIU     Ry,Ry,#8        ;increment index to Y
            DSUBU      R20,R4,Rx       ;compute bound
            BNEZ       R20,Loop        ;check if done
```

Here is the VMIPS code for DAXPY.

```
            L.D        F0,a            ;load scalar a
            LV         V1,Rx           ;load vector X
            MULVS.D    V2,V1,F0        ;vector-scalar multiply
            LV         V3,Ry           ;load vector Y
            ADDVV.D    V4,V2,V3        ;add
            SV         V4,Ry           ;store the result
```

The most dramatic difference is that the vector processor greatly reduces the dynamic instruction bandwidth, executing only 6 instructions versus almost 600 for MIPS. This reduction occurs because the vector operations work on 64 elements and the overhead instructions that constitute nearly half the loop on MIPS are not present in the VMIPS code. When the compiler produces vector instructions for such a sequence and the resulting code spends much of its time running in vector mode, the code is said to be *vectorized* or *vectorizable*. Loops can be vectorized when they do not have dependences between iterations of a loop, which are called *loop-carried dependences* (see Section 4.5).

Another important difference between MIPS and VMIPS is the frequency of pipeline interlocks. In the straightforward MIPS code, every ADD.D must wait for a MUL.D, and every S.D must wait for the ADD.D. On the vector processor, each vector instruction will only stall for the first element in each vector, and then subsequent elements will flow smoothly down the pipeline. Thus, pipeline stalls are required only once per vector *instruction*, rather than once per vector *element*. Vector architects call forwarding of element-dependent operations *chaining*, in that the dependent operations are "chained" together. In this example, the pipeline stall frequency on MIPS will be about 64× higher than it is on VMIPS. Software pipelining or loop unrolling (Appendix H) can reduce the pipeline stalls on MIPS; however, the large difference in instruction bandwidth cannot be reduced substantially.

Vector Execution Time

The execution time of a sequence of vector operations primarily depends on three factors: (1) the length of the operand vectors, (2) structural hazards among the operations, and (3) the data dependences. Given the vector length and the *initiation rate*, which is the rate at which a vector unit consumes new operands and produces new results, we can compute the time for a single vector instruction. All modern vector computers have vector functional units with multiple parallel pipelines (or *lanes*) that can produce two or more results per clock cycle, but they may also have some functional units that are not fully pipelined. For simplicity, our VMIPS implementation has one lane with an initiation rate of one element per clock cycle for individual operations. Thus, the execution time in clock cycles for a single vector instruction is approximately the vector length.

To simplify the discussion of vector execution and vector performance, we use the notion of a *convoy*, which is the set of vector instructions that could potentially execute together. As we shall soon see, you can estimate performance of a section of code by counting the number of convoys. The instructions in a convoy *must not* contain any structural hazards; if such hazards were present, the instructions would need to be serialized and initiated in different convoys. To keep the analysis simple, we assume that a convoy of instructions must complete execution before any other instructions (scalar or vector) can begin execution.

It might seem that in addition to vector instruction sequences with structural hazards, sequences with read-after-write dependency hazards should also be in separate convoys, but chaining allows them to be in the same convoy.

Chaining allows a vector operation to start as soon as the individual elements of its vector source operand become available: The results from the first functional unit in the chain are "forwarded" to the second functional unit. In practice, we often implement chaining by allowing the processor to read and write a particular vector register at the same time, albeit to different elements. Early implementations of chaining worked just like forwarding in scalar pipelining, but this restricted the timing of the source and destination instructions in the chain. Recent implementations use *flexible chaining*, which allows a vector instruction to chain to essentially any other active vector instruction, assuming that we don't generate a structural hazard. All modern vector architectures support flexible chaining, which we assume in this chapter.

To turn convoys into execution time we need a timing metric to estimate the time for a convoy. It is called a *chime*, which is simply the unit of time taken to execute one convoy. Thus, a vector sequence that consists of m convoys executes in m chimes; for a vector length of n, for VMIPS this is approximately $m \times n$ clock cycles. The chime approximation ignores some processor-specific overheads, many of which are dependent on vector length. Hence, measuring time in chimes is a better approximation for long vectors than for short ones. We will use the chime measurement, rather than clock cycles per result, to indicate explicitly that we are ignoring certain overheads.

If we know the number of convoys in a vector sequence, we know the execution time in chimes. One source of overhead ignored in measuring chimes is any limitation on initiating multiple vector instructions in a single clock cycle. If only one vector instruction can be initiated in a clock cycle (the reality in most vector processors), the chime count will underestimate the actual execution time of a convoy. Because the length of vectors is typically much greater than the number of instructions in the convoy, we will simply assume that the convoy executes in one chime.

Example   Show how the following code sequence lays out in convoys, assuming a single copy of each vector functional unit:

```
LV          V1,Rx       ;load vector X
MULVS.D     V2,V1,F0    ;vector-scalar multiply
LV          V3,Ry       ;load vector Y
ADDVV.D     V4,V2,V3    ;add two vectors
SV          V4,Ry       ;store the sum
```

How many chimes will this vector sequence take? How many cycles per FLOP (floating-point operation) are needed, ignoring vector instruction issue overhead?

Answer   The first convoy starts with the first LV instruction. The MULVS.D is dependent on the first LV, but chaining allows it to be in the same convoy.

The second LV instruction must be in a separate convoy since there is a structural hazard on the load/store unit for the prior LV instruction. The ADDVV.D is dependent on the second LV, but it can again be in the same convoy via chaining. Finally, the SV has a structural hazard on the LV in the second convoy, so it must go in the third convoy. This analysis leads to the following layout of vector instructions into convoys:

1. LV   MULVS.D

2. LV   ADDVV.D

3. SV

The sequence requires three convoys. Since the sequence takes three chimes and there are two floating-point operations per result, the number of cycles per FLOP is 1.5 (ignoring any vector instruction issue overhead). Note that, although we allow the LV and MULVS.D both to execute in the first convoy, most vector machines will take two clock cycles to initiate the instructions.

This example shows that the chime approximation is reasonably accurate for long vectors. For example, for 64-element vectors, the time in chimes is 3, so the sequence would take about 64×3 or 192 clock cycles. The overhead of issuing convoys in two separate clock cycles would be small.

Another source of overhead is far more significant than the issue limitation. The most important source of overhead ignored by the chime model is vector *start-up time*. The start-up time is principally determined by the pipelining latency of the vector functional unit. For VMIPS, we will use the same pipeline depths as the Cray-1, although latencies in more modern processors have tended to increase, especially for vector loads. All functional units are fully pipelined.

The pipeline depths are 6 clock cycles for floating-point add, 7 for floating-point multiply, 20 for floating-point divide, and 12 for vector load.

Given these vector basics, the next several subsections will give optimizations that either improve the performance or increase the types of programs that can run well on vector architectures. In particular, they will answer the questions:

- How can a vector processor execute a single vector faster than one element per clock cycle? Multiple elements per clock cycle improve performance.

- How does a vector processor handle programs where the vector lengths are not the same as the length of the vector register (64 for VMIPS)? Since most application vectors don't match the architecture vector length, we need an efficient solution to this common case.

- What happens when there is an IF statement inside the code to be vectorized? More code can vectorize if we can efficiently handle conditional statements.

- What does a vector processor need from the memory system? Without sufficient memory bandwidth, vector execution can be futile.

- How does a vector processor handle multiple dimensional matrices? This popular data structure must vectorize for vector architectures to do well.

- How does a vector processor handle sparse matrices? This popular data structure must vectorize also.

- How do you program a vector computer? Architectural innovations that are a mismatch to compiler technology may not get widespread use.

The rest of this section introduces each of these optimizations of the vector architecture, and Appendix G goes into greater depth.

Multiple Lanes: Beyond One Element per Clock Cycle

A critical advantage of a vector instruction set is that it allows software to pass a large amount of parallel work to hardware using only a single short instruction. A single vector instruction can include scores of independent operations yet be encoded in the same number of bits as a conventional scalar instruction. The parallel semantics of a vector instruction allow an implementation to execute these elemental operations using a deeply pipelined functional unit, as in the VMIPS implementation we've studied so far; an array of parallel functional units; or a combination of parallel and pipelined functional units. Figure 4.4 illustrates how to improve vector performance by using parallel pipelines to execute a vector add instruction.

The VMIPS instruction set has the property that all vector arithmetic instructions only allow element N of one vector register to take part in operations with element N from other vector registers. This dramatically simplifies the construction of a highly parallel vector unit, which can be structured as multiple parallel *lanes*. As with a traffic highway, we can increase the peak throughput of a vector unit by adding more lanes. Figure 4.5 shows the structure of a four-lane vector

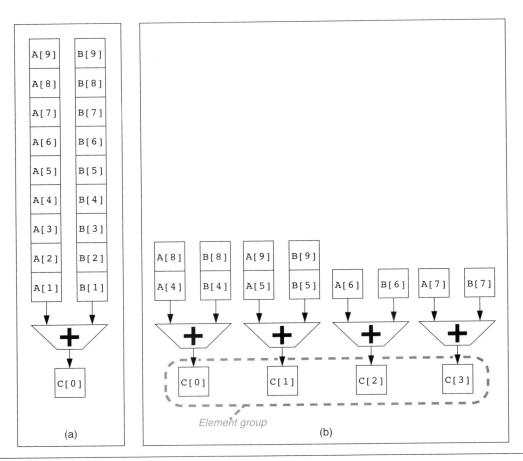

Figure 4.4 Using multiple functional units to improve the performance of a single vector add instruction, C = A + B. The vector processor (a) on the left has a single add pipeline and can complete one addition per cycle. The vector processor (b) on the right has four add pipelines and can complete four additions per cycle. The elements within a single vector add instruction are interleaved across the four pipelines. The set of elements that move through the pipelines together is termed an *element group*. (Reproduced with permission from Asanovic [1998].)

unit. Thus, going to four lanes from one lane reduces the number of clocks for a chime from 64 to 16. For multiple lanes to be advantageous, both the applications and the architecture must support long vectors; otherwise, they will execute so quickly that you'll run out of instruction bandwidth, requiring ILP techniques (see Chapter 3) to supply enough vector instructions.

Each lane contains one portion of the vector register file and one execution pipeline from each vector functional unit. Each vector functional unit executes vector instructions at the rate of one element group per cycle using multiple pipelines, one per lane. The first lane holds the first element (element 0) for all vector registers, and so the first element in any vector instruction will have its source

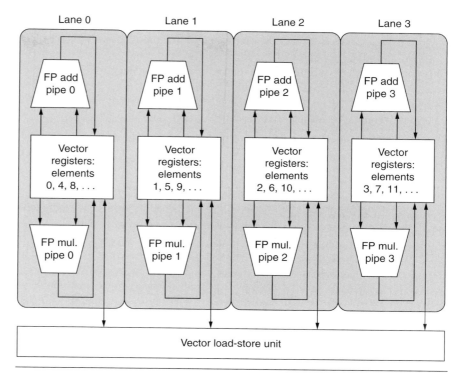

Figure 4.5 Structure of a vector unit containing four lanes. The vector register storage is divided across the lanes, with each lane holding every fourth element of each vector register. The figure shows three vector functional units: an FP add, an FP multiply, and a load-store unit. Each of the vector arithmetic units contains four execution pipelines, one per lane, which act in concert to complete a single vector instruction. Note how each section of the vector register file only needs to provide enough ports for pipelines local to its lane. This figure does not show the path to provide the scalar operand for vector-scalar instructions, but the scalar processor (or control processor) broadcasts a scalar value to all lanes.

and destination operands located in the first lane. This allocation allows the arithmetic pipeline local to the lane to complete the operation without communicating with other lanes. Accessing main memory also requires only intralane wiring. Avoiding interlane communication reduces the wiring cost and register file ports required to build a highly parallel execution unit, and helps explain why vector computers can complete up to 64 operations per clock cycle (2 arithmetic units and 2 load/store units across 16 lanes).

Adding multiple lanes is a popular technique to improve vector performance as it requires little increase in control complexity and does not require changes to existing machine code. It also allows designers to trade off die area, clock rate, voltage, and energy without sacrificing peak performance. If the clock rate of a vector processor is halved, doubling the number of lanes will retain the same potential performance.

Vector-Length Registers: Handling Loops Not Equal to 64

A vector register processor has a natural vector length determined by the number of elements in each vector register. This length, which is 64 for VMIPS, is unlikely to match the real vector length in a program. Moreover, in a real program the length of a particular vector operation is often *unknown* at compile time. In fact, a single piece of code may require different vector lengths. For example, consider this code:

```
for (i=0; i <n;  i=i+1)
    Y[i] = a * X[i] + Y[i];
```

The size of all the vector operations depends on n, which may not even be known until run time! The value of n might also be a parameter to a procedure containing the above loop and therefore subject to change during execution.

The solution to these problems is to create a *vector-length register* (VLR). The VLR controls the length of any vector operation, including a vector load or store. The value in the VLR, however, cannot be greater than the length of the vector registers. This solves our problem as long as the real length is less than or equal to the *maximum vector length* (MVL). The MVL determines the number of data elements in a vector of an architecture. This parameter means the length of vector registers can grow in later computer generations without changing the instruction set; as we shall see in the next section, multimedia SIMD extensions have no equivalent of MVL, so they change the instruction set every time they increase their vector length.

What if the value of n is not known at compile time and thus may be greater than the MVL? To tackle the second problem where the vector is longer than the maximum length, a technique called *strip mining* is used. Strip mining is the generation of code such that each vector operation is done for a size less than or equal to the MVL. We create one loop that handles any number of iterations that is a multiple of the MVL and another loop that handles any remaining iterations and must be less than the MVL. In practice, compilers usually create a single strip-mined loop that is parameterized to handle both portions by changing the length. We show the strip-mined version of the DAXPY loop in C:

```
low = 0;
VL = (n % MVL); /*find odd-size piece using modulo op % */
for (j = 0; j <= (n/MVL);  j=j+1) { /*outer loop*/
    for (i = low; i < (low+VL); i=i+1) /*runs for length VL*/
        Y[i] = a * X[i] + Y[i] ; /*main operation*/
    low = low + VL; /*start of next vector*/
    VL = MVL; /*reset the length to maximum vector length*/
}
```

The term n/MVL represents truncating integer division. The effect of this loop is to block the vector into segments that are then processed by the inner loop. The

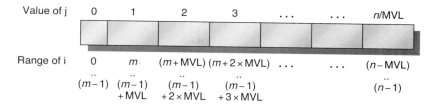

Figure 4.6 A vector of arbitrary length processed with strip mining. All blocks but the first are of length MVL, utilizing the full power of the vector processor. In this figure, we use the variable *m* for the expression (n % MVL). (The C operator % is modulo.)

length of the first segment is (n % MVL), and all subsequent segments are of length MVL. Figure 4.6 shows how to split the long vector into segments.

The inner loop of the preceding code is vectorizable with length VL, which is equal to either (n % MVL) or MVL. The VLR register must be set twice in the code, once at each place where the variable VL in the code is assigned.

Vector Mask Registers: Handling IF Statements in Vector Loops

From Amdahl's law, we know that the speedup on programs with low to moderate levels of vectorization will be very limited. The presence of conditionals (IF statements) inside loops and the use of sparse matrices are two main reasons for lower levels of vectorization. Programs that contain IF statements in loops cannot be run in vector mode using the techniques we have discussed so far because the IF statements introduce control dependences into a loop. Likewise, we cannot implement sparse matrices efficiently using any of the capabilities we have seen so far. We discuss strategies for dealing with conditional execution here, leaving the discussion of sparse matrices for later.

Consider the following loop written in C:

```
for (i = 0; i < 64;  i=i+1)
   if (X[i] != 0)
      X[i] = X[i] - Y[i];
```

This loop cannot normally be vectorized because of the conditional execution of the body; however, if the inner loop could be run for the iterations for which $X[i] \neq 0$, then the subtraction could be vectorized.

The common extension for this capability is *vector-mask control*. Mask registers essentially provide conditional execution of each element operation in a vector instruction. The vector-mask control uses a Boolean vector to control the execution of a vector instruction, just as conditionally executed instructions use a Boolean condition to determine whether to execute a scalar instruction. When the *vector-mask register* is enabled, any vector instructions executed operate only on the vector elements whose corresponding entries in the vector-mask register are one. The entries in the destination vector register that correspond to a zero in the mask register are unaffected by the vector operation. Clearing the vector-mask register sets it to all ones, making subsequent vector instructions operate on all vector elements. We can now use the following code for the previous loop, assuming that the starting addresses of X and Y are in Rx and Ry, respectively:

```
LV        V1,Rx      ;load vector X into V1
LV        V2,Ry      ;load vector Y
L.D       F0,#0      ;load FP zero into F0
SNEVS.D   V1,F0      ;sets VM(i) to 1 if V1(i)!=F0
SUBVV.D   V1,V1,V2   ;subtract under vector mask
SV        V1,Rx      ;store the result in X
```

Compiler writers call the transformation to change an IF statement to a straight-line code sequence using conditional execution *if conversion*.

Using a vector-mask register does have overhead, however. With scalar architectures, conditionally executed instructions still require execution time when the condition is not satisfied. Nonetheless, the elimination of a branch and the associated control dependences can make a conditional instruction faster even if it sometimes does useless work. Similarly, vector instructions executed with a vector mask still take the same execution time, even for the elements where the mask is zero. Likewise, even with a significant number of zeros in the mask, using vector-mask control may still be significantly faster than using scalar mode.

As we shall see in Section 4.4, one difference between vector processors and GPUs is the way they handle conditional statements. Vector processors make the mask registers part of the architectural state and rely on compilers to manipulate mask registers explicitly. In contrast, GPUs get the same effect using hardware to manipulate internal mask registers that are invisible to GPU software. In both cases, the hardware spends the time to execute a vector element whether the mask is zero or one, so the GFLOPS rate drops when masks are used.

Memory Banks: Supplying Bandwidth for Vector Load/Store Units

The behavior of the load/store vector unit is significantly more complicated than that of the arithmetic functional units. The start-up time for a load is the time to get the first word from memory into a register. If the rest of the vector can be supplied without stalling, then the vector initiation rate is equal to the rate at which new words are fetched or stored. Unlike simpler functional units, the initiation rate may not necessarily be one clock cycle because memory bank stalls can reduce effective throughput.

Typically, penalties for start-ups on load/store units are higher than those for arithmetic units—over 100 clock cycles on many processors. For VMIPS we assume a start-up time of 12 clock cycles, the same as the Cray-1. (More recent vector computers use caches to bring down latency of vector loads and stores.)

To maintain an initiation rate of one word fetched or stored per clock, the memory system must be capable of producing or accepting this much data. Spreading accesses across multiple independent memory banks usually delivers the desired rate. As we will soon see, having significant numbers of banks is useful for dealing with vector loads or stores that access rows or columns of data.

Most vector processors use memory banks, which allow multiple independent accesses rather than simple memory interleaving for three reasons:

1. Many vector computers support multiple loads or stores per clock, and the memory bank cycle time is usually several times larger than the processor cycle time. To support simultaneous accesses from multiple loads or stores, the memory system needs multiple banks and to be able to control the addresses to the banks independently.

2. Most vector processors support the ability to load or store data words that are not sequential. In such cases, independent bank addressing, rather than interleaving, is required.

3. Most vector computers support multiple processors sharing the same memory system, so each processor will be generating its own independent stream of addresses.

In combination, these features lead to a large number of independent memory banks, as the following example shows.

Example   The largest configuration of a Cray T90 (Cray T932) has 32 processors, each capable of generating 4 loads and 2 stores per clock cycle. The processor clock cycle is 2.167 ns, while the cycle time of the SRAMs used in the memory system is 15 ns. Calculate the minimum number of memory banks required to allow all processors to run at full memory bandwidth.

Answer   The maximum number of memory references each cycle is 192: 32 processors times 6 references per processor. Each SRAM bank is busy for $15/2.167 = 6.92$ clock cycles, which we round up to 7 processor clock cycles. Therefore, we require a minimum of $192 \times 7 = 1344$ memory banks!

The Cray T932 actually has 1024 memory banks, so the early models could not sustain full bandwidth to all processors simultaneously. A subsequent memory upgrade replaced the 15 ns asynchronous SRAMs with pipelined synchronous SRAMs that more than halved the memory cycle time, thereby providing sufficient bandwidth.

Taking a higher level perspective, vector load/store units play a similar role to prefetch units in scalar processors in that both try to deliver data bandwidth by supplying processors with streams of data.

Stride: Handling Multidimensional Arrays in Vector Architectures

The position in memory of adjacent elements in a vector may not be sequential. Consider this straightforward code for matrix multiply in C:

```
for (i = 0; i < 100;  i=i+1)
    for (j = 0; j < 100;  j=j+1) {
        A[i][j] = 0.0;
        for (k = 0; k < 100; k=k+1)
            A[i][j] = A[i][j] + B[i][k] * D[k][j];
    }
```

We could vectorize the multiplication of each row of B with each column of D and strip-mine the inner loop with k as the index variable.

To do so, we must consider how to address adjacent elements in B and adjacent elements in D. When an array is allocated memory, it is linearized and must be laid out in either row-major (as in C) or column-major (as in Fortran) order. This linearization means that either the elements in the row or the elements in the column are not adjacent in memory. For example, the C code above allocates in row-major order, so the elements of D that are accessed by iterations in the inner loop are separated by the row size times 8 (the number of bytes per entry) for a total of 800 bytes. In Chapter 2, we saw that blocking could improve locality in cache-based systems. For vector processors without caches, we need another technique to fetch elements of a vector that are not adjacent in memory.

This distance separating elements to be gathered into a single register is called the *stride*. In this example, matrix D has a stride of 100 double words (800 bytes), and matrix B would have a stride of 1 double word (8 bytes). For column-major order, which is used by Fortran, the strides would be reversed. Matrix D would have a stride of 1, or 1 double word (8 bytes), separating successive elements, while matrix B would have a stride of 100, or 100 double words (800 bytes). Thus, without reordering the loops, the compiler can't hide the long distances between successive elements for both B and D.

Once a vector is loaded into a vector register, it acts as if it had logically adjacent elements. Thus, a vector processor can handle strides greater than one, called *non-unit strides*, using only vector load and vector store operations with stride capability. This ability to access nonsequential memory locations and to reshape them into a dense structure is one of the major advantages of a vector processor. Caches inherently deal with unit stride data; increasing block size can help reduce miss rates for large scientific datasets with unit stride, but increasing block size can even have a negative effect for data that are accessed with non-unit strides. While blocking techniques can solve some of these problems (see Chapter 2), the ability to access data efficiently that is not contiguous remains an advantage for vector processors on certain problems, as we shall see in Section 4.7.

On VMIPS, where the addressable unit is a byte, the stride for our example would be 800. The value must be computed dynamically, since the size of the matrix may not be known at compile time or—just like vector length—may change for different executions of the same statement. The vector stride, like the vector starting address, can be put in a general-purpose register. Then the VMIPS instruction LVWS (load vector with stride) fetches the vector into a vector register. Likewise, when storing a non-unit stride vector, use the instruction SVWS (store vector with stride).

Supporting strides greater than one complicates the memory system. Once we introduce non-unit strides, it becomes possible to request accesses from the same bank frequently. When multiple accesses contend for a bank, a memory bank conflict occurs, thereby stalling one access. A bank conflict and, hence, a stall will occur if

$$\frac{\text{Number of banks}}{\text{Least common multiple (Stride, Number of banks)}} < \text{Bank busy time}$$

Example   Suppose we have 8 memory banks with a bank busy time of 6 clocks and a total memory latency of 12 cycles. How long will it take to complete a 64-element vector load with a stride of 1? With a stride of 32?

Answer   Since the number of banks is larger than the bank busy time, for a stride of 1 the load will take $12 + 64 = 76$ clock cycles, or 1.2 clock cycles per element. The worst possible stride is a value that is a multiple of the number of memory banks, as in this case with a stride of 32 and 8 memory banks. Every access to memory (after the first one) will collide with the previous access and will have to wait for the 6-clock-cycle bank busy time. The total time will be $12 + 1 + 6 * 63 = 391$ clock cycles, or 6.1 clock cycles per element.

Gather-Scatter: Handling Sparse Matrices in Vector Architectures

As mentioned above, sparse matrices are commonplace so it is important to have techniques to allow programs with sparse matrices to execute in vector mode. In a sparse matrix, the elements of a vector are usually stored in some compacted form and then accessed indirectly. Assuming a simplified sparse structure, we might see code that looks like this:

```
for (i = 0; i < n;   i=i+1)
    A[K[i]] = A[K[i]] + C[M[i]];
```

This code implements a sparse vector sum on the arrays A and C, using index vectors K and M to designate the nonzero elements of A and C. (A and C must have the same number of nonzero elements—n of them—so K and M are the same size.) The primary mechanism for supporting sparse matrices is *gather-scatter operations* using index vectors. The goal of such operations is to support moving between a compressed representation (i.e., zeros are not included) and normal representation (i.e., the zeros are included) of a sparse matrix. A *gather* operation takes an *index vector* and fetches the vector whose elements are at the addresses given by adding a base address to the offsets given in the index vector. The result is a dense vector in a vector register. After these elements are operated on in dense form, the sparse vector can be stored in expanded form by a *scatter* store, using the same index vector. Hardware support for such operations is called *gather-scatter* and it appears on nearly all modern vector processors. The VMIPS instructions are LVI (load vector indexed or gather) and SVI (store vector indexed or scatter). For example, if Ra, Rc, Rk, and Rm contain the starting addresses of the vectors in the previous sequence, we can code the inner loop with vector instructions such as:

```
LV        Vk, Rk          ;load K
LVI       Va, (Ra+Vk)     ;load A[K[]]
LV        Vm, Rm          ;load M
LVI       Vc, (Rc+Vm)     ;load C[M[]]
ADDVV.D   Va, Va, Vc      ;add them
SVI       (Ra+Vk), Va     ;store A[K[]]
```

This technique allows code with sparse matrices to run in vector mode. A simple vectorizing compiler could not automatically vectorize the source code above because the compiler would not know that the elements of K are distinct values, and thus that no dependences exist. Instead, a programmer directive would tell the compiler that it was safe to run the loop in vector mode.

Although indexed loads and stores (gather and scatter) can be pipelined, they typically run much more slowly than non-indexed loads or stores, since the memory banks are not known at the start of the instruction. Each element has an individual address, so they can't be handled in groups, and there can be conflicts at many places throughout the memory system. Thus, each individual access incurs significant latency. However, as Section 4.7 shows, a memory system can deliver better performance by designing for this case and by using more hardware resources versus when architects have a *laissez faire* attitude toward such accesses.

As we shall see in Section 4.4, all loads are gathers and all stores are scatters in GPUs. To avoid running slowly in the frequent case of unit strides, it is up to the GPU programmer to ensure that all the addresses in a gather or scatter are to adjacent locations. In addition, the GPU hardware must recognize the sequence of these addresses during execution to turn the gathers and scatters into the more efficient unit stride accesses to memory.

Programming Vector Architectures

An advantage of vector architectures is that compilers can tell programmers at compile time whether a section of code will vectorize or not, often giving hints as to why it did not vectorize the code. This straightforward execution model allows experts in other domains to learn how to improve performance by revising their code or by giving hints to the compiler when it's OK to assume independence between operations, such as for gather-scatter data transfers. It is this dialog between the compiler and the programmer, with each side giving hints to the other on how to improve performance, that simplifies programming of vector computers.

Today, the main factor that affects the success with which a program runs in vector mode is the structure of the program itself: Do the loops have true data dependences (see Section 4.5), or can they be restructured so as not to have such dependences? This factor is influenced by the algorithms chosen and, to some extent, by how they are coded.

As an indication of the level of vectorization achievable in scientific programs, let's look at the vectorization levels observed for the Perfect Club benchmarks. Figure 4.7 shows the percentage of operations executed in vector mode for two versions of the code running on the Cray Y-MP. The first version is that obtained with just compiler optimization on the original code, while the second version uses extensive hints from a team of Cray Research programmers. Several studies of the performance of applications on vector processors show a wide variation in the level of compiler vectorization.

Benchmark name	Operations executed in vector mode, compiler-optimized	Operations executed in vector mode, with programmer aid	Speedup from hint optimization
BDNA	96.1%	97.2%	1.52
MG3D	95.1%	94.5%	1.00
FLO52	91.5%	88.7%	N/A
ARC3D	91.1%	92.0%	1.01
SPEC77	90.3%	90.4%	1.07
MDG	87.7%	94.2%	1.49
TRFD	69.8%	73.7%	1.67
DYFESM	68.8%	65.6%	N/A
ADM	42.9%	59.6%	3.60
OCEAN	42.8%	91.2%	3.92
TRACK	14.4%	54.6%	2.52
SPICE	11.5%	79.9%	4.06
QCD	4.2%	75.1%	2.15

Figure 4.7 **Level of vectorization among the Perfect Club benchmarks when executed on the Cray Y-MP [Vajapeyam 1991].** The first column shows the vectorization level obtained with the compiler without hints, while the second column shows the results after the codes have been improved with hints from a team of Cray Research programmers.

The hint-rich versions show significant gains in vectorization level for codes the compiler could not vectorize well by itself, with all codes now above 50% vectorization. The median vectorization improved from about 70% to about 90%.

4.3   SIMD Instruction Set Extensions for Multimedia

SIMD Multimedia Extensions started with the simple observation that many media applications operate on narrower data types than the 32-bit processors were optimized for. Many graphics systems used 8 bits to represent each of the three primary colors plus 8 bits for transparency. Depending on the application, audio samples are usually represented with 8 or 16 bits. By partitioning the carry chains within, say, a 256-bit adder, a processor could perform simultaneous operations on short vectors of thirty-two 8-bit operands, sixteen 16-bit operands, eight 32-bit operands, or four 64-bit operands. The additional cost of such partitioned adders was small. Figure 4.8 summarizes typical multimedia SIMD instructions. Like vector instructions, a SIMD instruction specifies the same operation on vectors of data. Unlike vector machines with large register files such as the VMIPS vector register, which can hold as many as sixty-four 64-bit elements in each of 8 vector registers, SIMD instructions tend to specify fewer operands and hence use much smaller register files.

In contrast to vector architectures, which offer an elegant instruction set that is intended to be the target of a vectorizing compiler, SIMD extensions have three major omissions:

■   Multimedia SIMD extensions fix the number of data operands in the opcode, which has led to the addition of hundreds of instructions in the MMX, SSE, and AVX extensions of the x86 architecture. Vector architectures have a vector length register that specifies the number of operands for the current operation. These variable-length vector registers easily accommodate programs that naturally have shorter vectors than the maximum size the architecture supports. Moreover, vector architectures have an implicit maximum vector length in the architecture, which combined with the vector length register avoids the use of many opcodes.

Instruction category	Operands
Unsigned add/subtract	Thirty-two 8-bit, sixteen 16-bit, eight 32-bit, or four 64-bit
Maximum/minimum	Thirty-two 8-bit, sixteen 16-bit, eight 32-bit, or four 64-bit
Average	Thirty-two 8-bit, sixteen 16-bit, eight 32-bit, or four 64-bit
Shift right/left	Thirty-two 8-bit, sixteen 16-bit, eight 32-bit, or four 64-bit
Floating point	Sixteen 16-bit, eight 32-bit, four 64-bit, or two 128-bit

Figure 4.8 Summary of typical SIMD multimedia support for 256-bit-wide operations. Note that the IEEE 754-2008 floating-point standard added half-precision (16-bit) and quad-precision (128-bit) floating-point operations.

- Multimedia SIMD does not offer the more sophisticated addressing modes of vector architectures, namely strided accesses and gather-scatter accesses. These features increase the number of programs that a vector compiler can successfully vectorize (see Section 4.7).

- Multimedia SIMD usually does not offer the mask registers to support conditional execution of elements as in vector architectures.

These omissions make it harder for the compiler to generate SIMD code and increase the difficulty of programming in SIMD assembly language.

For the x86 architecture, the MMX instructions added in 1996 repurposed the 64-bit floating-point registers, so the basic instructions could perform eight 8-bit operations or four 16-bit operations simultaneously. These were joined by parallel MAX and MIN operations, a wide variety of masking and conditional instructions, operations typically found in digital signal processors, and ad hoc instructions that were believed to be useful in important media libraries. Note that MMX reused the floating-point data transfer instructions to access memory.

The Streaming SIMD Extensions (SSE) successor in 1999 added separate registers that were 128 bits wide, so now instructions could simultaneously perform sixteen 8-bit operations, eight 16-bit operations, or four 32-bit operations. It also performed parallel single-precision floating-point arithmetic. Since SSE had separate registers, it needed separate data transfer instructions. Intel soon added double-precision SIMD floating-point data types via SSE2 in 2001, SSE3 in 2004, and SSE4 in 2007. Instructions with four single-precision floating-point operations or two parallel double-precision operations increased the peak floating-point performance of the x86 computers, as long as programmers place the operands side by side. With each generation, they also added ad hoc instructions whose aim is to accelerate specific multimedia functions perceived to be important.

The Advanced Vector Extensions (AVX), added in 2010, doubles the width of the registers again to 256 bits and thereby offers instructions that double the number of operations on all narrower data types. Figure 4.9 shows AVX instructions useful for double-precision floating-point computations. AVX includes preparations to extend the width to 512 bits and 1024 bits in future generations of the architecture.

In general, the goal of these extensions has been to accelerate carefully written libraries rather than for the compiler to generate them (see Appendix H), but recent x86 compilers are trying to generate such code, particularly for floating-point-intensive applications.

Given these weaknesses, why are Multimedia SIMD Extensions so popular? First, they cost little to add to the standard arithmetic unit and they were easy to implement. Second, they require little extra state compared to vector architectures, which is always a concern for context switch times. Third, you need a lot of memory bandwidth to support a vector architecture, which many computers don't have. Fourth, SIMD does not have to deal with problems in

AVX Instruction	Description
VADDPD	Add four packed double-precision operands
VSUBPD	Subtract four packed double-precision operands
VMULPD	Multiply four packed double-precision operands
VDIVPD	Divide four packed double-precision operands
VFMADDPD	Multiply and add four packed double-precision operands
VFMSUBPD	Multiply and subtract four packed double-precision operands
VCMPxx	Compare four packed double-precision operands for EQ, NEQ, LT, LE, GT, GE, …
VMOVAPD	Move aligned four packed double-precision operands
VBROADCASTSD	Broadcast one double-precision operand to four locations in a 256-bit register

Figure 4.9 AVX instructions for x86 architecture useful in double-precision floating-point programs. Packed-double for 256-bit AVX means four 64-bit operands executed in SIMD mode. As the width increases with AVX, it is increasingly important to add data permutation instructions that allow combinations of narrow operands from different parts of the wide registers. AVX includes instructions that shuffle 32-bit, 64-bit, or 128-bit operands within a 256-bit register. For example, BROADCAST replicates a 64-bit operand 4 times in an AVX register. AVX also includes a large variety of fused multiply-add/subtract instructions; we show just two here.

virtual memory when a single instruction that can generate 64 memory accesses can get a page fault in the middle of the vector. SIMD extensions use separate data transfers per SIMD group of operands that are aligned in memory, and so they cannot cross page boundaries. Another advantage of short, fixed-length "vectors" of SIMD is that it is easy to introduce instructions that can help with new media standards, such as instructions that perform permutations or instructions that consume either fewer or more operands than vectors can produce. Finally, there was concern about how well vector architectures can work with caches. More recent vector architectures have addressed all of these problems, but the legacy of past flaws shaped the skeptical attitude toward vectors among architects.

Example   To give an idea of what multimedia instructions look like, assume we added 256-bit SIMD multimedia instructions to MIPS. We concentrate on floating-point in this example. We add the suffix "4D" on instructions that operate on four double-precision operands at once. Like vector architectures, you can think of a SIMD processor as having lanes, four in this case. MIPS SIMD will reuse the floating-point registers as operands for 4D instructions, just as double-precision reused single-precision registers in the original MIPS. This example shows MIPS SIMD code for the DAXPY loop. Assume that the starting addresses of X and Y are in Rx and Ry, respectively. Underline the changes to the MIPS code for SIMD.

Answer   Here is the MIPS code:

```
        L.D      F0,a          ;load scalar a
        MOV      F1, F0        ;copy a into F1 for SIMD MUL
        MOV      F2, F0        ;copy a into F2 for SIMD MUL
        MOV      F3, F0        ;copy a into F3 for SIMD MUL
        DADDIU   R4,Rx,#512    ;last address to load
Loop:   L.4D     F4,0(Rx)      ;load X[i], X[i+1], X[i+2], X[i+3]
        MUL.4D   F4,F4,F0      ;a×X[i],a×X[i+1],a×X[i+2],a×X[i+3]
        L.4D     F8,0(Ry)      ;load Y[i], Y[i+1], Y[i+2], Y[i+3]
        ADD.4D   F8,F8,F4      ;a×X[i]+Y[i], ...., a×X[i+3]+Y[i+3]
        S.4D     F8,0(Rx)      ;store into Y[i], Y[i+1], Y[i+2], Y[i+3]
        DADDIU   Rx,Rx,#32     ;increment index to X
        DADDIU   Ry,Ry,#32     ;increment index to Y
        DSUBU    R20,R4,Rx     ;compute bound
        BNEZ     R20,Loop      ;check if done
```

The changes were replacing every MIPS double-precision instruction with its 4D equivalent, increasing the increment from 8 to 32, and changing the registers from F2 and F4 to F4 and F8 to get enough space in the register file for four sequential double-precision operands. So that each SIMD lane would have its own copy of the scalar a, we copied the value of F0 into registers F1, F2, and F3. (Real SIMD instruction extensions have an instruction to broadcast a value to all other registers in a group.) Thus, the multiply does F4*F0, F5*F1, F6*F2, and F7*F3. While not as dramatic as the 100× reduction of dynamic instruction bandwidth of VMIPS, SIMD MIPS does get a 4× reduction: 149 versus 578 instructions executed for MIPS.

Programming Multimedia SIMD Architectures

Given the ad hoc nature of the SIMD multimedia extensions, the easiest way to use these instructions has been through libraries or by writing in assembly language.

Recent extensions have become more regular, giving the compiler a more reasonable target. By borrowing techniques from vectorizing compilers, compilers are starting to produce SIMD instructions automatically. For example, advanced compilers today can generate SIMD floating-point instructions to deliver much higher performance for scientific codes. However, programmers must be sure to align all the data in memory to the width of the SIMD unit on which the code is run to prevent the compiler from generating scalar instructions for otherwise vectorizable code.

The Roofline Visual Performance Model

One visual, intuitive way to compare potential floating-point performance of variations of SIMD architectures is the Roofline model [Williams et al. 2009].

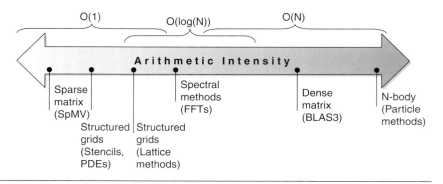

Figure 4.10 Arithmetic intensity, specified as the number of floating-point operations to run the program divided by the number of bytes accessed in main memory [Williams et al. 2009]. Some kernels have an arithmetic intensity that scales with problem size, such as dense matrix, but there are many kernels with arithmetic intensities independent of problem size.

It ties together floating-point performance, memory performance, and arithmetic intensity in a two-dimensional graph. *Arithmetic intensity* is the ratio of floating-point operations per byte of memory accessed. It can be calculated by taking the total number of floating-point operations for a program divided by the total number of data bytes transferred to main memory during program execution. Figure 4.10 shows the relative arithmetic intensity of several example kernels.

Peak floating-point performance can be found using the hardware specifications. Many of the kernels in this case study do not fit in on-chip caches, so peak memory performance is defined by the memory system behind the caches. Note that we need the peak memory bandwidth that is available to the processors, not just at the DRAM pins as in Figure 4.27 on page 325. One way to find the (delivered) peak memory performance is to run the Stream benchmark.

Figure 4.11 shows the Roofline model for the NEC SX-9 vector processor on the left and the Intel Core i7 920 multicore computer on the right. The vertical Y-axis is achievable floating-point performance from 2 to 256 GFLOP/sec. The horizontal X-axis is arithmetic intensity, varying from 1/8th FLOP/DRAM byte accessed to 16 FLOP/ DRAM byte accessed in both graphs. Note that the graph is a log–log scale, and that Rooflines are done just once for a computer.

For a given kernel, we can find a point on the X-axis based on its arithmetic intensity. If we drew a vertical line through that point, the performance of the kernel on that computer must lie somewhere along that line. We can plot a horizontal line showing peak floating-point performance of the computer. Obviously, the actual floating-point performance can be no higher than the horizontal line, since that is a hardware limit.

How could we plot the peak memory performance? Since the X-axis is FLOP/ byte and the Y-axis is FLOP/sec, bytes/sec is just a diagonal line at a 45-degree angle in this figure. Hence, we can plot a third line that gives the maximum floating-point performance that the memory system of that computer can support

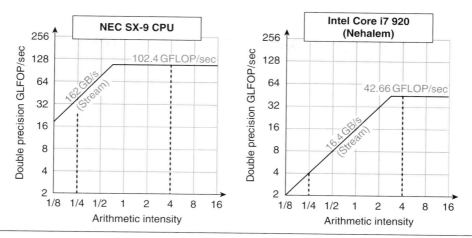

Figure 4.11 Roofline model for one NEC SX-9 vector processor on the left and the Intel Core i7 920 multicore computer with SIMD Extensions on the right [Williams et al. 2009]. This Roofline is for unit-stride memory accesses and double-precision floating-point performance. NEC SX-9 is a vector supercomputer announced in 2008 that costs millions of dollars. It has a peak DP FP performance of 102.4 GFLOP/sec and a peak memory bandwidth of 162 GBytes/sec from the Stream benchmark. The Core i7 920 has a peak DP FP performance of 42.66 GFLOP/sec and a peak memory bandwidth of 16.4 GBytes/sec. The dashed vertical lines at an arithmetic intensity of 4 FLOP/byte show that both processors operate at peak performance. In this case, the SX-9 at 102.4 FLOP/sec is 2.4× faster than the Core i7 at 42.66 GFLOP/sec. At an arithmetic intensity of 0.25 FLOP/byte, the SX-9 is 10× faster at 40.5 GFLOP/sec versus 4.1 GFLOP/sec for the Core i7.

for a given arithmetic intensity. We can express the limits as a formula to plot these lines in the graphs in Figure 4.11:

$$\text{Attainable GFLOPs/sec} = \text{Min}(\text{Peak Memory BW} \times \text{Arithmetic Intensity}, \text{Peak Floating-Point Perf.})$$

The horizontal and diagonal lines give this simple model its name and indicate its value. The "Roofline" sets an upper bound on performance of a kernel depending on its arithmetic intensity. If we think of arithmetic intensity as a pole that hits the roof, either it hits the flat part of the roof, which means performance is computationally limited, or it hits the slanted part of the roof, which means performance is ultimately limited by memory bandwidth. In Figure 4.11, the vertical dashed line on the right (arithmetic intensity of 4) is an example of the former and the vertical dashed line on the left (arithmetic intensity of 1/4) is an example of the latter. Given a Roofline model of a computer, you can apply it repeatedly, since it doesn't vary by kernel.

Note that the "ridge point," where the diagonal and horizontal roofs meet, offers an interesting insight into the computer. If it is far to the right, then only kernels with very high arithmetic intensity can achieve the maximum performance of that computer. If it is far to the left, then almost any kernel can potentially hit the maximum performance. As we shall see, this vector processor has both much higher memory bandwidth and a ridge point far to the left when compared to other SIMD processors.

Figure 4.11 shows that the peak computational performance of the SX-9 is 2.4× faster than Core i7, but the memory performance is 10× faster. For programs with an arithmetic intensity of 0.25, the SX-9 is 10× faster (40.5 versus 4.1 GFLOP/sec). The higher memory bandwidth moves the ridge point from 2.6 in the Core i7 to 0.6 on the SX-9, which means many more programs can reach peak computational performance on the vector processor.

4.4   Graphics Processing Units

For a few hundred dollars, anyone can buy a GPU with hundreds of parallel floating-point units, which makes high-performance computing more accessible. The interest in GPU computing blossomed when this potential was combined with a programming language that made GPUs easier to program. Hence, many programmers of scientific and multimedia applications today are pondering whether to use GPUs or CPUs.

GPUs and CPUs do not go back in computer architecture genealogy to a common ancestor; there is no Missing Link that explains both. As Section 4.10 describes, the primary ancestors of GPUs are graphics accelerators, as doing graphics well is the reason why GPUs exist. While GPUs are moving toward mainstream computing, they can't abandon their responsibility to continue to excel at graphics. Thus, the design of GPUs may make more sense when architects ask, given the hardware invested to do graphics well, how can we supplement it to improve the performance of a wider range of applications?

Note that this section concentrates on using GPUs for computing. To see how GPU computing combines with the traditional role of graphics acceleration, see "Graphics and Computing GPUs," by John Nickolls and David Kirk (Appendix A in the 4th edition of *Computer Organization and Design* by the same authors as this book).

Since the terminology and some hardware features are quite different from vector and SIMD architectures, we believe it will be easier if we start with the simplified programming model for GPUs before we describe the architecture.

Programming the GPU

CUDA is an elegant solution to the problem of representing parallelism in algorithms, not all algorithms, but enough to matter. It seems to resonate in some way with the way we think and code, allowing an easier, more natural expression of parallelism beyond the task level.

Vincent Natol
"Kudos for CUDA," *HPC Wire* (2010)

The challenge for the GPU programmer is not simply getting good performance on the GPU, but also in coordinating the scheduling of computation on the system processor and the GPU and the transfer of data between system memory and GPU memory. Moreover, as we see shall see later in this section, GPUs have virtually every type of parallelism that can be captured by the programming environment: multithreading, MIMD, SIMD, and even instruction-level.

NVIDIA decided to develop a C-like language and programming environment that would improve the productivity of GPU programmers by attacking both the challenges of heterogeneous computing and of multifaceted parallelism. The name of their system is *CUDA*, for Compute Unified Device Architecture. CUDA produces C/C++ for the system processor (*host*) and a C and C++ dialect for the GPU (*device*, hence the D in CUDA). A similar programming language is OpenCL, which several companies are developing to offer a vendor-independent language for multiple platforms.

NVIDIA decided that the unifying theme of all these forms of parallelism is the *CUDA Thread*. Using this lowest level of parallelism as the programming primitive, the compiler and the hardware can gang thousands of CUDA Threads together to utilize the various styles of parallelism within a GPU: multithreading, MIMD, SIMD, and instruction-level parallelism. Hence, NVIDIA classifies the CUDA programming model as Single Instruction, Multiple Thread (*SIMT*). For reasons we shall soon see, these threads are blocked together and executed in groups of 32 threads, called a *Thread Block*. We call the hardware that executes a whole block of threads a *multithreaded SIMD Processor*.

We need just a few details before we can give an example of a CUDA program:

- To distinguish between functions for the GPU (device) and functions for the system processor (host), CUDA uses __device__ or __global__ for the former and __host__ for the latter.

- CUDA variables declared as in the __device__ or __global__ functions are allocated to the GPU Memory (see below), which is accessible by all multithreaded SIMD processors.

- The extended function call syntax for the function *name* that runs on the GPU is

      name<<<dimGrid, dimBlock>>>(... *parameter list* ...)

  where dimGrid and dimBlock specify the dimensions of the code (in blocks) and the dimensions of a block (in threads).

- In addition to the identifier for blocks (blockIdx) and the identifier for threads per block (threadIdx), CUDA provides a keyword for the number of threads per block (blockDim), which comes from the dimBlock parameter in the bullet above.

Before seeing the CUDA code, let's start with conventional C code for the DAXPY loop from Section 4.2:

```
// Invoke DAXPY
daxpy(n, 2.0, x, y);
// DAXPY in C
void daxpy(int n, double a, double *x, double *y)
{
        for (int i = 0; i < n; ++i)
                y[i] = a*x[i] + y[i];
}
```

Below is the CUDA version. We launch n threads, one per vector element, with 256 CUDA Threads per thread block in a multithreaded SIMD Processor. The GPU function starts by calculating the corresponding element index i based on the block ID, the number of threads per block, and the thread ID. As long as this index is within the array (i < n), it performs the multiply and add.

```
// Invoke DAXPY with 256 threads per Thread Block
__host__
int nblocks = (n+ 255) / 256;
    daxpy<<<nblocks, 256>>>(n, 2.0, x, y);
// DAXPY in CUDA
__device__
void daxpy(int n, double a, double *x, double *y)
{
    int i = blockIdx.x*blockDim.x + threadIdx.x;
    if (i < n) y[i] = a*x[i] + y[i];
}
```

Comparing the C and CUDA codes, we see a common pattern to parallelizing data-parallel CUDA code. The C version has a loop where each iteration is independent of the others, allowing the loop to be transformed straightforwardly into a parallel code where each loop iteration becomes an independent thread. (As mentioned above and described in detail in Section 4.5, vectorizing compilers also rely on a lack of dependences between iterations of a loop, which are called *loop carried dependences*.) The programmer determines the parallelism in CUDA explicitly by specifying the grid dimensions and the number of threads per SIMD Processor. By assigning a single thread to each element, there is no need to synchronize among threads when writing results to memory.

The GPU hardware handles parallel execution and thread management; it is not done by applications or by the operating system. To simplify scheduling by the hardware, CUDA requires that thread blocks be able to execute independently and in any order. Different thread blocks cannot communicate directly, although they can *coordinate* using atomic memory operations in Global Memory.

As we shall soon see, many GPU hardware concepts are not obvious in CUDA. That is a good thing from a programmer productivity perspective, but most programmers are using GPUs instead of CPUs to get performance. Performance programmers must keep the GPU hardware in mind when writing in CUDA. For reasons explained shortly, they know that they need to keep groups of 32 threads together in control flow to get the best performance from multithreaded SIMD Processors, and create many more threads per multithreaded SIMD Processor to hide latency to DRAM. They also need to keep the data addresses localized in one or a few blocks of memory to get the expected memory performance.

Like many parallel systems, a compromise between productivity and performance is for CUDA to include intrinsics to give programmers explicit control of the hardware. The struggle between productivity on one hand versus allowing the programmer to be able to express anything that the hardware can do on the other happens often in parallel computing. It will be interesting to see how the language evolves in this classic productivity–performance battle as well as to see if CUDA becomes popular for other GPUs or even other architectural styles.

NVIDIA GPU Computational Structures

The uncommon heritage mentioned above helps explain why GPUs have their own architectural style and their own terminology independent from CPUs. One obstacle to understanding GPUs has been the jargon, with some terms even having misleading names. This obstacle has been surprisingly difficult to overcome, as the many rewrites of this chapter can attest. To try to bridge the twin goals of making the architecture of GPUs understandable *and* learning the many GPU terms with non traditional definitions, our final solution is to use the CUDA terminology for software but initially use more descriptive terms for the hardware, sometimes borrowing terms used by OpenCL. Once we explain the GPU architecture in our terms, we'll map them into the official jargon of NVIDIA GPUs.

From left to right, Figure 4.12 lists the more descriptive term used in this section, the closest term from mainstream computing, the official NVIDIA GPU term in case you are interested, and then a short description of the term. The rest of this section explains the microarchitetural features of GPUs using these descriptive terms from the left of the figure.

We use NVIDIA systems as our example as they are representative of GPU architectures. Specifically, we follow the terminology of the CUDA parallel programming language above and use the Fermi architecture as the example (see Section 4.7).

Like vector architectures, GPUs work well only with data-level parallel problems. Both styles have gather-scatter data transfers and mask registers, and GPU processors have even more registers than do vector processors. Since they do not have a close-by scalar processor, GPUs sometimes implement a feature at runtime in hardware that vector computers implement at compiler time in software. Unlike most vector architectures, GPUs also rely on multithreading within a single multithreaded SIMD processor to hide memory latency (see Chapters 2 and 3). However, efficient code for both vector architectures and GPUs requires programmers to think in groups of SIMD operations.

A *Grid* is the code that runs on a GPU that consists of a set of *Thread Blocks*. Figure 4.12 draws the analogy between a grid and a vectorized loop and between a Thread Block and the body of that loop (after it has been strip-mined, so that it is a full computation loop). To give a concrete example, let's suppose we want to multiply two vectors together, each 8192 elements long. We'll return to this example throughout this section. Figure 4.13 shows the relationship between this example and these first two GPU terms. The GPU code that works on the whole 8192 element multiply is called a *Grid* (or vectorized loop). To break it down into more manageable sizes, a Grid is composed of *Thread Blocks* (or body of a vectorized loop), each with up to 512 elements. Note that a SIMD instruction executes 32 elements at a time. With 8192 elements in the vectors, this example thus has 16 Thread Blocks since $16 = 8192 \div 512$. The Grid and Thread Block

Type	More descriptive name	Closest old term outside of GPUs	Official CUDA/ NVIDIA GPU term	Book definition
Program abstractions	Vectorizable Loop	Vectorizable Loop	Grid	A vectorizable loop, executed on the GPU, made up of one or more Thread Blocks (bodies of vectorized loop) that can execute in parallel.
	Body of Vectorized Loop	Body of a (Strip-Mined) Vectorized Loop	Thread Block	A vectorized loop executed on a multithreaded SIMD Processor, made up of one or more threads of SIMD instructions. They can communicate via Local Memory.
	Sequence of SIMD Lane Operations	One iteration of a Scalar Loop	CUDA Thread	A vertical cut of a thread of SIMD instructions corresponding to one element executed by one SIMD Lane. Result is stored depending on mask and predicate register.
Machine object	A Thread of SIMD Instructions	Thread of Vector Instructions	Warp	A traditional thread, but it contains just SIMD instructions that are executed on a multithreaded SIMD Processor. Results stored depending on a per-element mask.
	SIMD Instruction	Vector Instruction	PTX Instruction	A single SIMD instruction executed across SIMD Lanes.
Processing hardware	Multithreaded SIMD Processor	(Multithreaded) Vector Processor	Streaming Multiprocessor	A multithreaded SIMD Processor executes threads of SIMD instructions, independent of other SIMD Processors.
	Thread Block Scheduler	Scalar Processor	Giga Thread Engine	Assigns multiple Thread Blocks (bodies of vectorized loop) to multithreaded SIMD Processors.
	SIMD Thread Scheduler	Thread scheduler in a Multithreaded CPU	Warp Scheduler	Hardware unit that schedules and issues threads of SIMD instructions when they are ready to execute; includes a scoreboard to track SIMD Thread execution.
	SIMD Lane	Vector Lane	Thread Processor	A SIMD Lane executes the operations in a thread of SIMD instructions on a single element. Results stored depending on mask.
Memory hardware	GPU Memory	Main Memory	Global Memory	DRAM memory accessible by all multithreaded SIMD Processors in a GPU.
	Private Memory	Stack or Thread Local Storage (OS)	Local Memory	Portion of DRAM memory private to each SIMD Lane.
	Local Memory	Local Memory	Shared Memory	Fast local SRAM for one multithreaded SIMD Processor, unavailable to other SIMD Processors.
	SIMD Lane Registers	Vector Lane Registers	Thread Processor Registers	Registers in a single SIMD Lane allocated across a full thread block (body of vectorized loop).

Figure 4.12 Quick guide to GPU terms used in this chapter. We use the first column for hardware terms. Four groups cluster these 11 terms. From top to bottom: Program Abstractions, Machine Objects, Processing Hardware, and Memory Hardware. Figure 4.21 on page 309 associates vector terms with the closest terms here, and Figure 4.24 on page 313 and Figure 4.25 on page 314 reveal the official CUDA/NVIDIA and AMD terms and definitions along with the terms used by OpenCL.

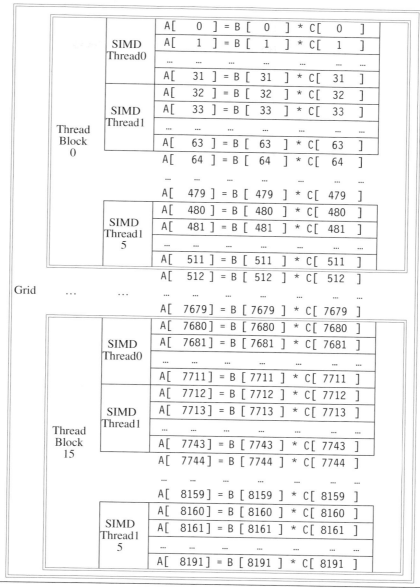

Figure 4.13 The mapping of a Grid (vectorizable loop), Thread Blocks (SIMD basic blocks), and threads of SIMD instructions to a vector–vector multiply, with each vector being 8192 elements long. Each thread of SIMD instructions calculates 32 elements per instruction, and in this example each Thread Block contains 16 threads of SIMD instructions and the Grid contains 16 Thread Blocks. The hardware Thread Block Scheduler assigns Thread Blocks to multithreaded SIMD Processors and the hardware Thread Scheduler picks which thread of SIMD instructions to run each clock cycle within a SIMD Processor. Only SIMD Threads in the same Thread Block can communicate via Local Memory. (The maximum number of SIMD Threads that can execute simultaneously per Thread Block is 16 for Tesla-generation GPUs and 32 for the later Fermi-generation GPUs.)

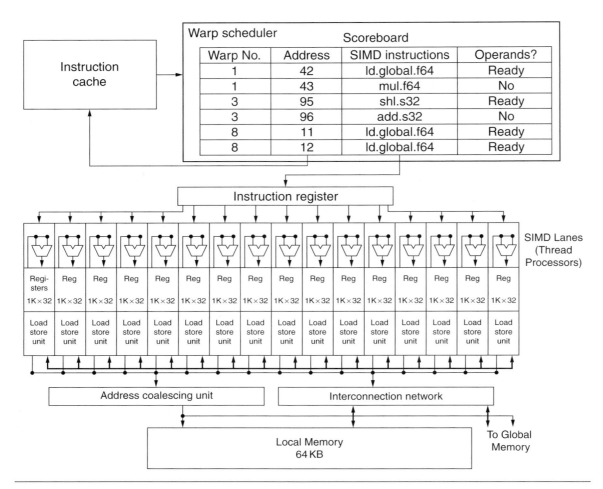

Figure 4.14 Simplified block diagram of a Multithreaded SIMD Processor. It has 16 SIMD lanes. The SIMD Thread Scheduler has, say, 48 independent threads of SIMD instructions that it schedules with a table of 48 PCs.

are programming abstractions implemented in GPU hardware that help programmers organize their CUDA code. (The Thread Block is analogous to a stripminded vector loop with a vector length of 32.)

A Thread Block is assigned to a processor that executes that code, which we call a *multithreaded SIMD Processor*, by the *Thread Block Scheduler*. The Thread Block Scheduler has some similarities to a control processor in a vector architecture. It determines the number of thread blocks needed for the loop and keeps allocating them to different multithreaded SIMD Processors until the loop is completed. In this example, it would send 16 Thread Blocks to multithreaded SIMD Processors to compute all 8192 elements of this loop.

Figure 4.14 shows a simplified block diagram of a multithreaded SIMD Processor. It is similar to a Vector Processor, but it has many parallel functional units

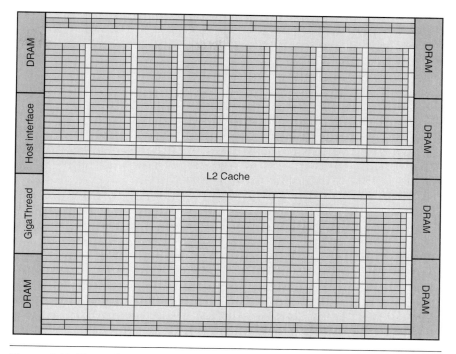

Figure 4.15 Floor plan of the Fermi GTX 480 GPU. This diagram shows 16 multi-threaded SIMD Processors. The Thread Block Scheduler is highlighted on the left. The GTX 480 has 6 GDDR5 ports, each 64 bits wide, supporting up to 6 GB of capacity. The Host Interface is PCI Express 2.0 x 16. Giga Thread is the name of the scheduler that distributes thread blocks to Multiprocessors, each of which has its own SIMD Thread Scheduler.

instead of a few that are deeply pipelined, as does a Vector Processor. In the programming example in Figure 4.13, each multithreaded SIMD Processor is assigned 512 elements of the vectors to work on. SIMD Processors are full processors with separate PCs and are programmed using threads (see Chapter 3).

The GPU hardware then contains a collection of multithreaded SIMD Processors that execute a Grid of Thread Blocks (bodies of vectorized loop); that is, a GPU is a multiprocessor composed of multithreaded SIMD Processors.

The first four implementations of the Fermi architecture have 7, 11, 14, or 15 multithreaded SIMD Processors; future versions may have just 2 or 4. To provide transparent scalability across models of GPUs with differing number of multi-threaded SIMD Processors, the Thread Block Scheduler assigns Thread Blocks (bodies of a vectorized loop) to multithreaded SIMD Processors. Figure 4.15 shows the floor plan of the GTX 480 implementation of the Fermi architecture.

Dropping down one more level of detail, the machine object that the hardware creates, manages, schedules, and executes is a *thread of SIMD instructions*. It is a traditional thread that contains exclusively SIMD instructions. These threads of SIMD instructions have their own PCs and they run on a multithreaded SIMD Processor. The *SIMD Thread Scheduler* includes a scoreboard that lets it know which threads of SIMD instructions are ready to run, and then it sends them off to a dispatch unit to be run on the multithreaded SIMD Processor. It is identical to a hardware thread scheduler in a traditional multithreaded processor (see Chapter 3), just that it is scheduling threads of SIMD instructions. Thus, GPU hardware has two levels of hardware schedulers: (1) the *Thread Block Scheduler* that assigns Thread Blocks (bodies of vectorized loops) to multithreaded SIMD Processors, which ensures that thread blocks are assigned to the processors whose local memories have the corresponding data, and (2) the SIMD Thread Scheduler *within* a SIMD Processor, which schedules when threads of SIMD instructions should run.

The SIMD instructions of these threads are 32 wide, so each thread of SIMD instructions in this example would compute 32 of the elements of the computation. In this example, Thread Blocks would contain $512/32 = 16$ SIMD threads (see Figure 4.13).

Since the thread consists of SIMD instructions, the SIMD Processor must have parallel functional units to perform the operation. We call them *SIMD Lanes*, and they are quite similar to the Vector Lanes in Section 4.2.

The number of lanes per SIMD processor varies across GPU generations. With Fermi, each 32-wide thread of SIMD instructions is mapped to 16 physical SIMD Lanes, so each SIMD instruction in a thread of SIMD instructions takes two clock cycles to complete. Each thread of SIMD instructions is executed in lock step and only scheduled at the beginning. Staying with the analogy of a SIMD Processor as a vector processor, you could say that it has 16 lanes, the vector length would be 32, and the chime is 2 clock cycles. (This wide but shallow nature is why we use the term SIMD Processor instead of vector processor as it is more descriptive.)

Since by definition the threads of SIMD instructions are independent, the SIMD Thread Scheduler can pick whatever thread of SIMD instructions is ready, and need not stick with the next SIMD instruction in the sequence within a thread. The SIMD Thread Scheduler includes a scoreboard (see Chapter 3) to keep track of up to 48 threads of SIMD instructions to see which SIMD instruction is ready to go. This scoreboard is needed because memory access instructions can take an unpredictable number of clock cycles due to memory bank conflicts, for example. Figure 4.16 shows the SIMD Thread Scheduler picking threads of SIMD instructions in a different order over time. The assumption of GPU architects is that GPU applications have so many threads of SIMD instructions that multithreading can both hide the latency to DRAM and increase utilization of multithreaded SIMD Processors. However, to hedge their bets, the recent NVIDIA Fermi GPU includes an L2 cache (see Section 4.7).

Continuing our vector multiply example, each multithreaded SIMD Processor must load 32 elements of two vectors from memory into registers, perform the multiply by reading and writing registers, and store the product back from registers into memory. To hold these memory elements, a SIMD Processor has an impressive 32,768 32-bit registers. Just like a vector processor, these registers are divided logically across the vector lanes or, in this case, SIMD Lanes. Each SIMD Thread is limited to no more than 64 registers, so you might think of a SIMD

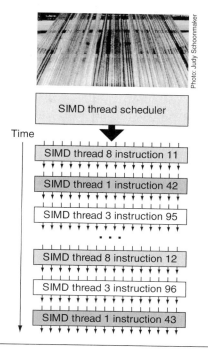

Figure 4.16 Scheduling of threads of SIMD instructions. The scheduler selects a ready thread of SIMD instructions and issues an instruction synchronously to all the SIMD Lanes executing the SIMD thread. Because threads of SIMD instructions are independent, the scheduler may select a different SIMD thread each time.

Thread as having up to 64 vector registers, with each vector register having 32 elements and each element being 32 bits wide. (Since double-precision floating-point operands use two adjacent 32-bit registers, an alternative view is that each SIMD Thread has 32 vector registers of 32 elements, each of which is 64 bits wide.)

Since Fermi has 16 physical SIMD Lanes, each contains 2048 registers. (Rather than trying to design hardware registers with many read ports and write ports per bit, GPUs will use simpler memory structures but divide them into banks to get sufficient bandwidth, just as vector processors do.) Each CUDA Thread gets one element of each of the vector registers. To handle the 32 elements of each thread of SIMD instructions with 16 SIMD Lanes, the CUDA Threads of a Thread block collectively can use up to half of the 2048 registers.

To be able to execute many threads of SIMD instructions, each is dynamically allocated a set of the physical registers on each SIMD Processor when threads of SIMD instructions are created and freed when the SIMD Thread exits.

Note that a CUDA thread is just a vertical cut of a thread of SIMD instructions, corresponding to one element executed by one SIMD Lane. Beware that CUDA Threads are very different from POSIX threads; you can't make arbitrary system calls from a CUDA Thread.

We're now ready to see what GPU instructions look like.

NVIDA GPU Instruction Set Architecture

Unlike most system processors, the instruction set target of the NVIDIA compilers is an abstraction of the hardware instruction set. *PTX* (*Parallel Thread Execution*) provides a stable instruction set for compilers as well as compatibility across generations of GPUs. The hardware instruction set is hidden from the programmer. PTX instructions describe the operations on a single CUDA thread, and usually map one-to-one with hardware instructions, but one PTX can expand to many machine instructions, and vice versa. PTX uses virtual registers, so the compiler figures out how many physical vector registers a SIMD thread needs, and then an optimizer divides the available register storage between the SIMD threads. This optimizer also eliminates dead code, folds instructions together, and calculates places where branches might diverge and places where diverged paths could converge.

While there is some similarity between the x86 microarchitectures and PTX, in that both translate to an internal form (microinstructions for x86), the difference is that this translation happens in hardware at runtime during execution on the x86 versus in software and load time on a GPU.

The format of a PTX instruction is

```
opcode.type d, a, b, c;
```

where d is the destination operand; a, b, and c are source operands; and the operation type is one of the following:

Type	.type Specifier
Untyped bits 8, 16, 32, and 64 bits	.b8, .b16, .b32, .b64
Unsigned integer 8, 16, 32, and 64 bits	.u8, .u16, .u32, .u64
Signed integer 8, 16, 32, and 64 bits	.s8, .s16, .s32, .s64
Floating Point 16, 32, and 64 bits	.f16, .f32, .f64

Source operands are 32-bit or 64-bit registers or a constant value. Destinations are registers, except for store instructions.

Figure 4.17 shows the basic PTX instruction set. All instructions can be predicated by 1-bit predicate registers, which can be set by a set predicate instruction (setp). The control flow instructions are functions call and return, thread exit, branch, and barrier synchronization for threads within a thread block (bar.sync). Placing a predicate in front of a branch instruction gives us conditional branches. The compiler or PTX programmer declares virtual registers as 32-bit or 64-bit typed or untyped values. For example, R0, R1, ... are for 32-bit values and RD0, RD1, ... are for 64-bit registers. Recall that the assignment of virtual registers to physical registers occurs at load time with PTX.

Group	Instruction	Example	Meaning	Comments
Arithmetic	arithmetic .type = .s32, .u32, .f32, .s64, .u64, .f64			
	add.type	add.f32 d, a, b	d = a + b;	
	sub.type	sub.f32 d, a, b	d = a − b;	
	mul.type	mul.f32 d, a, b	d = a * b;	
	mad.type	mad.f32 d, a, b, c	d = a * b + c;	multiply-add
	div.type	div.f32 d, a, b	d = a / b;	multiple microinstructions
	rem.type	rem.u32 d, a, b	d = a % b;	integer remainder
	abs.type	abs.f32 d, a	d = |a|;	
	neg.type	neg.f32 d, a	d = 0 - a;	
	min.type	min.f32 d, a, b	d = (a < b)? a:b;	floating selects non-NaN
	max.type	max.f32 d, a, b	d = (a > b)? a:b;	floating selects non-NaN
	setp.cmp.type	setp.lt.f32 p, a, b	p = (a < b);	compare and set predicate
	numeric .cmp = eq, ne, lt, le, gt, ge; unordered cmp = equ, neu, ltu, leu, gtu, geu, num, nan			
	mov.type	mov.b32 d, a	d = a;	move
	selp.type	selp.f32 d, a, b, p	d = p? a: b;	select with predicate
	cvt.dtype.atype	cvt.f32.s32 d, a	d = convert(a);	convert atype to dtype
Special Function	special .type = .f32 (some .f64)			
	rcp.type	rcp.f32 d, a	d = 1/a;	reciprocal
	sqrt.type	sqrt.f32 d, a	d = sqrt(a);	square root
	rsqrt.type	rsqrt.f32 d, a	d = 1/sqrt(a);	reciprocal square root
	sin.type	sin.f32 d, a	d = sin(a);	sine
	cos.type	cos.f32 d, a	d = cos(a);	cosine
	lg2.type	lg2.f32 d, a	d = log(a)/log(2)	binary logarithm
	ex2.type	ex2.f32 d, a	d = 2 ** a;	binary exponential
Logical	logic.type = .pred,.b32, .b64			
	and.type	and.b32 d, a, b	d = a & b;	
	or.type	or.b32 d, a, b	d = a | b;	
	xor.type	xor.b32 d, a, b	d = a ^ b;	
	not.type	not.b32 d, a, b	d = ~a;	one's complement
	cnot.type	cnot.b32 d, a, b	d = (a==0)? 1:0;	C logical not
	shl.type	shl.b32 d, a, b	d = a << b;	shift left
	shr.type	shr.s32 d, a, b	d = a >> b;	shift right
Memory Access	memory.space = .global, .shared, .local, .const; .type = .b8, .u8, .s8, .b16, .b32, .b64			
	ld.space.type	ld.global.b32 d, [a+off]	d = *(a+off);	load from memory space
	st.space.type	st.shared.b32 [d+off], a	*(d+off) = a;	store to memory space
	tex.nd.dtyp.btype	tex.2d.v4.f32.f32 d, a, b	d = tex2d(a, b);	texture lookup
	atom.spc.op.type	atom.global.add.u32 d,[a], b atom.global.cas.b32 d,[a], b, c	atomic { d = *a; *a = op(*a, b); }	atomic read-modify-write operation
	atom.op = and, or, xor, add, min, max, exch, cas; .spc = .global; .type = .b32			
Control Flow	branch	@p bra target	if (p) goto target;	conditional branch
	call	call (ret), func, (params)	ret = func(params);	call function
	ret	ret	return;	return from function call
	bar.sync	bar.sync d	wait for threads	barrier synchronization
	exit	exit	exit;	terminate thread execution

Figure 4.17 Basic PTX GPU thread instructions.

The following sequence of PTX instructions is for one iteration of our DAXPY loop on page 289:

```
shl.u32 R8, blockIdx, 9    ; Thread Block ID * Block size (512 or 2⁹)
add.u32 R8, R8, threadIdx  ; R8 = i = my CUDA Thread ID
shl.u32 R8, R8, 3          ; byte offset
ld.global.f64 RD0, [X+R8]  ; RD0 = X[i]
ld.global.f64 RD2, [Y+R8]  ; RD2 = Y[i]
mul.f64 RD0, RD0, RD4      ; Product in RD0 = RD0 * RD4 (scalar a)
add.f64 RD0, RD0, RD2      ; Sum in RD0 = RD0 + RD2 (Y[i])
st.global.f64 [Y+R8], RD0  ; Y[i] = sum (X[i]*a + Y[i])
```

As demonstrated above, the CUDA programming model assigns one CUDA Thread to each loop iteration and offers a unique identifier number to each thread block (blockIdx) and one to each CUDA Thread within a block (threadIdx). Thus, it creates 8192 CUDA Threads and uses the unique number to address each element in the array, so there is no incrementing or branching code. The first three PTX instructions calculate that unique element byte offset in R8, which is added to the base of the arrays. The following PTX instructions load two double-precision floating-point operands, multiply and add them, and store the sum. (We'll describe the PTX code corresponding to the CUDA code "if (i < n)" below.)

Note that unlike vector architectures, GPUs don't have separate instructions for sequential data transfers, strided data transfers, and gather-scatter data transfers. All data transfers are gather-scatter! To regain the efficiency of sequential (unit-stride) data transfers, GPUs include special Address Coalescing hardware to recognize when the SIMD Lanes within a thread of SIMD instructions are collectively issuing sequential addresses. That runtime hardware then notifies the Memory Interface Unit to request a block transfer of 32 sequential words. To get this important performance improvement, the GPU programmer must ensure that adjacent CUDA Threads access nearby addresses at the same time that can be coalesced into one or a few memory or cache blocks, which our example does.

Conditional Branching in GPUs

Just like the case with unit-stride data transfers, there are strong similarities between how vector architectures and GPUs handle IF statements, with the former implementing the mechanism largely in software with limited hardware support and the latter making use of even more hardware. As we shall see, in addition to explicit predicate registers, GPU branch hardware uses internal masks, a branch synchronization stack, and instruction markers to manage when a branch diverges into multiple execution paths and when the paths converge.

At the PTX assembler level, control flow of one CUDA thread is described by the PTX instructions branch, call, return, and exit, plus individual per-thread-lane predication of each instruction, specified by the programmer with per-thread-lane 1-bit predicate registers. The PTX assembler analyzes the PTX branch graph and optimizes it to the fastest GPU hardware instruction sequence.

At the GPU hardware instruction level, control flow includes branch, jump, jump indexed, call, call indexed, return, exit, and special instructions that manage the branch synchronization stack. GPU hardware provides each SIMD thread with its own stack; a stack entry contains an identifier token, a target instruction address, and a target thread-active mask. There are GPU special instructions that push stack entries for a SIMD thread and special instructions and instruction markers that pop a stack entry or unwind the stack to a specified entry and branch to the target instruction address with the target thread-active mask. GPU hardware instructions also have individual per-lane predication (enable/disable), specified with a 1-bit predicate register for each lane.

The PTX assembler typically optimizes a simple outer-level IF/THEN/ELSE statement coded with PTX branch instructions to just predicated GPU instructions, without any GPU branch instructions. A more complex control flow typically results in a mixture of predication and GPU branch instructions with special instructions and markers that use the branch synchronization stack to push a stack entry when some lanes branch to the target address, while others fall through. NVIDIA says a branch *diverges* when this happens. This mixture is also used when a SIMD Lane executes a synchronization marker or *converges*, which pops a stack entry and branches to the stack-entry address with the stack-entry thread-active mask.

The PTX assembler identifies loop branches and generates GPU branch instructions that branch to the top of the loop, along with special stack instructions to handle individual lanes breaking out of the loop and converging the SIMD Lanes when all lanes have completed the loop. GPU indexed jump and indexed call instructions push entries on the stack so that when all lanes complete the switch statement or function call the SIMD thread converges.

A GPU set predicate instruction (setp in the figure above) evaluates the conditional part of the IF statement. The PTX branch instruction then depends on that predicate. If the PTX assembler generates predicated instructions with no GPU branch instructions, it uses a per-lane predicate register to enable or disable each SIMD Lane for each instruction. The SIMD instructions in the threads inside the THEN part of the IF statement broadcast operations to all the SIMD Lanes. Those lanes with the predicate set to one perform the operation and store the result, and the other SIMD Lanes don't perform an operation or store a result. For the ELSE statement, the instructions use the complement of the predicate (relative to the THEN statement), so the SIMD Lanes that were idle now perform the operation and store the result while their formerly active siblings don't. At the end of the ELSE statement, the instructions are unpredicated so the original computation can proceed. Thus, for equal length paths, an IF-THEN-ELSE operates at 50% efficiency.

IF statements can be nested, hence the use of a stack, and the PTX assembler typically generates a mix of predicated instructions and GPU branch and special synchronization instructions for complex control flow. Note that deep nesting can mean that most SIMD Lanes are idle during execution of nested conditional statements. Thus, doubly nested IF statements with equal-length paths run at 25% efficiency, triply nested at 12.5% efficiency, and so on. The analogous case would be a vector processor operating where only a few of the mask bits are ones.

Dropping down a level of detail, the PTX assembler sets a "branch synchronization" marker on appropriate conditional branch instructions that pushes the current active mask on a stack inside each SIMD thread. If the conditional branch diverges the (some lanes take the branch, some fall through), it pushes a stack entry and sets the current internal active mask based on the condition. A branch synchronization marker pops the diverged branch entry and flips the mask bits before the ELSE portion. At the end of the IF statement, the PTX assembler adds another branch synchronization marker that pops the prior active mask off the stack into the current active mask.

If all the mask bits are set to one, then the branch instruction at the end of the THEN skips over the instructions in the ELSE part. There is a similar optimization for the THEN part in case all the mask bits are zero, as the conditional branch jumps over the THEN instructions. Parallel IF statements and PTX branches often use branch conditions that are unanimous (all lanes agree to follow the same path), such that the SIMD thread does not diverge into different individual lane control flow. The PTX assembler optimizes such branches to skip over blocks of instructions that are not executed by any lane of a SIMD thread. This optimization is useful in error condition checking, for example, where the test must be made but is rarely taken.

The code for a conditional statement similar to the one in Section 4.2 is

```
if (X[i] != 0)
    X[i] = X[i] – Y[i];
else X[i] = Z[i];
```

This IF statement could compile to the following PTX instructions (assuming that R8 already has the scaled thread ID), with *Push*, *Comp*, *Pop* indicating the branch synchronization markers inserted by the PTX assembler that push the old mask, complement the current mask, and pop to restore the old mask:

```
        ld.global.f64 RD0, [X+R8]      ; RD0 = X[i]
        setp.neq.s32 P1, RD0, #0       ; P1 is predicate register 1
        @!P1, bra ELSE1, *Push         ; Push old mask, set new mask bits
                                       ; if P1 false, go to ELSE1
        ld.global.f64 RD2, [Y+R8]      ; RD2 = Y[i]
        sub.f64 RD0, RD0, RD2          ; Difference in RD0
        st.global.f64 [X+R8], RD0      ; X[i] = RD0
        @P1, bra ENDIF1, *Comp         ; complement mask bits
                                       ; if P1 true, go to ENDIF1
ELSE1:  ld.global.f64 RD0, [Z+R8]      ; RD0 = Z[i]
        st.global.f64 [X+R8], RD0      ; X[i] = RD0
ENDIF1: <next instruction>, *Pop       ; pop to restore old mask
```

Once again, normally all instructions in the IF-THEN-ELSE statement are executed by a SIMD Processor. It's just that only some of the SIMD Lanes are enabled for the THEN instructions and some lanes for the ELSE instructions. As mentioned above, in the surprisingly common case that the individual lanes agree on the predicated branch—such as branching on a parameter value that is the same for all lanes so that all active mask bits are zeros or all are ones—the branch skips the THEN instructions or the ELSE instructions.

This flexibility makes it appear that an element has its own program counter; however, in the slowest case only one SIMD Lane could store its result every two clock cycles, with the rest idle. The analogous slowest case for vector architectures is operating with only one mask bit set to one. This flexibility can lead naive GPU programmers to poor performance, but it can be helpful in the early stages of program development. Keep in mind, however, that the only choice for a SIMD Lane in a clock cycle is to perform the operation specified in the PTX instruction or be idle; two SIMD Lanes cannot simultaneously execute different instructions.

This flexibility also helps explain the name *CUDA Thread* given to each element in a thread of SIMD instructions, since it gives the illusion of acting independently. A naive programmer may think that this thread abstraction means GPUs handle conditional branches more gracefully. Some threads go one way, the rest go another, which seems true as long as you're not in a hurry. Each CUDA Thread is executing the same instruction as every other thread in the thread block or it is idle. This synchronization makes it easier to handle loops with conditional branches since the mask capability can turn off SIMD Lanes and it detects the end of the loop automatically.

The resulting performance sometimes belies that simple abstraction. Writing programs that operate SIMD Lanes in this highly independent MIMD mode is like writing programs that use lots of virtual address space on a computer with a smaller physical memory. Both are correct, but they may run so slowly that the programmer could be displeased with the result.

Vector compilers could do the same tricks with mask registers as GPUs do in hardware, but it would involve scalar instructions to save, complement, and restore mask registers. Conditional execution is a case where GPUs do in runtime hardware what vector architectures do at compile time. One optimization available at runtime for GPUs but not at compile time for vector architectures is to skip the THEN or ELSE parts when mask bits are all zeros or all ones.

Thus, the efficiency with which GPUs execute conditional statements comes down to how frequently the branches would diverge. For example, one calculation of eigenvalues has deep conditional nesting, but measurements of the code show that around 82% of clock cycle issues have between 29 and 32 out of the 32 mask bits set to one, so GPUs execute this code more efficiently than one might expect.

Note that the same mechanism handles the strip-mining of vector loops— when the number of elements doesn't perfectly match the hardware. The example at the beginning of this section shows that an IF statement checks to see if this SIMD Lane element number (stored in R8 in the example above) is less than the limit ($i < n$), and it sets masks appropriately.

NVIDIA GPU Memory Structures

Figure 4.18 shows the memory structures of an NVIDIA GPU. Each SIMD Lane in a multithreaded SIMD Processor is given a private section of off-chip DRAM, which we call the *Private Memory*. It is used for the stack frame, for spilling registers, and for private variables that don't fit in the registers. SIMD Lanes do *not* share Private Memories. Recent GPUs cache this Private Memory in the L1 and L2 caches to aid register spilling and to speed up function calls.

We call the on-chip memory that is local to each multithreaded SIMD Processor *Local Memory*. It is shared by the SIMD Lanes within a multithreaded SIMD Processor, but this memory is not shared between multithreaded SIMD Processors. The multithreaded SIMD Processor dynamically allocates portions of the Local Memory to a thread block when it creates the thread block, and frees the memory when all the threads of the thread block exit. That portion of Local Memory is private to that thread block.

Finally, we call the off-chip DRAM shared by the whole GPU and all thread blocks *GPU Memory*. Our vector multiply example only used GPU Memory.

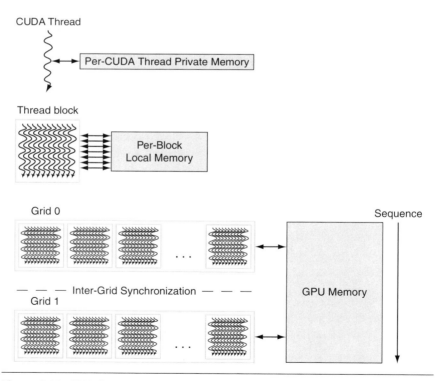

Figure 4.18 GPU Memory structures. GPU Memory is shared by all Grids (vectorized loops), Local Memory is shared by all threads of SIMD instructions within a thread block (body of a vectorized loop), and Private Memory is private to a single CUDA Thread.

The system processor, called the *host*, can read or write GPU Memory. Local Memory is unavailable to the host, as it is private to each multithreaded SIMD processor. Private Memories are unavailable to the host as well.

Rather than rely on large caches to contain the whole working sets of an application, GPUs traditionally use smaller streaming caches and rely on extensive multithreading of threads of SIMD instructions to hide the long latency to DRAM, since their working sets can be hundreds of megabytes. Given the use of multithreading to hide DRAM latency, the chip area used for caches in system processors is spent instead on computing resources and on the large number of registers to hold the state of many threads of SIMD instructions. In contrast, as mentioned above, vector loads and stores amortize the latency across many elements, since they only pay the latency once and then pipeline the rest of the accesses.

While hiding memory latency is the underlying philosophy, note that the latest GPUs and vector processors have added caches. For example, the recent Fermi architecture has added caches, but they are thought of as either bandwidth filters to reduce demands on GPU Memory or as accelerators for the few variables whose latency cannot be hidden by multithreading. Thus, local memory for stack frames, function calls, and register spilling is a good match to caches, since latency matters when calling a function. Caches also save energy, since on-chip cache accesses take much less energy than accesses to multiple, external DRAM chips.

To improve memory bandwidth and reduce overhead, as mentioned above, PTX data transfer instructions coalesce individual parallel thread requests from the same SIMD thread together into a single memory block request when the addresses fall in the same block. These restrictions are placed on the GPU program, somewhat analogous to the guidelines for system processor programs to engage hardware prefetching (see Chapter 2). The GPU memory controller will also hold requests and send ones to the same open page together to improve memory bandwidth (see Section 4.6). Chapter 2 describes DRAM in sufficient detail to understand the potential benefits of grouping related addresses.

Innovations in the Fermi GPU Architecture

The multithreaded SIMD Processor of Fermi is more complicated than the simplified version in Figure 4.14. To increase hardware utilization, each SIMD Processor has two SIMD Thread Schedulers and two instruction dispatch units. The dual SIMD Thread Scheduler selects two threads of SIMD instructions and issues one instruction from each to two sets of 16 SIMD Lanes, 16 load/store units, or 4 special function units. Thus, two threads of SIMD instructions are scheduled every two clock cycles to any of these collections. Since the threads are independent, there is no need to check for data dependences in the instruction stream. This innovation would be analogous to a multithreaded vector processor that can issue vector instructions from two independent threads.

Figure 4.19 shows the Dual Scheduler issuing instructions and Figure 4.20 shows the block diagram of the multithreaded SIMD Processor of a Fermi GPU.

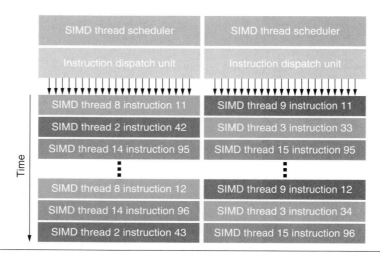

Figure 4.19 Block Diagram of Fermi's Dual SIMD Thread Scheduler. Compare this design to the single SIMD Thread Design in Figure 4.16.

Fermi introduces several innovations to bring GPUs much closer to mainstream system processors than Tesla and previous generations of GPU architectures:

■ *Fast Double-Precision Floating-Point Arithmetic*—Fermi matches the relative double-precision speed of conventional processors of roughly half the speed of single precision versus a tenth the speed of single precision in the prior Tesla generation. That is, there is no order of magnitude temptation to use single precision when the accuracy calls for double precision. The peak double-precision performance grew from 78 GFLOP/sec in the predecessor GPU to 515 GFLOP/sec when using multiply-add instructions.

■ *Caches for GPU Memory*—While the GPU philosophy is to have enough threads to hide DRAM latency, there are variables that are needed across threads, such as local variables mentioned above. Fermi includes both an L1 Data Cache and L1 Instruction Cache for each multithreaded SIMD Processor and a single 768 KB L2 cache shared by all multithreaded SIMD Processors in the GPU. As mentioned above, in addition to reducing bandwidth pressure on GPU Memory, caches can save energy by staying on-chip rather than going off-chip to DRAM. The L1 cache actually cohabits the same SRAM as Local Memory. Fermi has a mode bit that offers the choice of using 64 KB of SRAM as a 16 KB L1 cache with 48 KB of Local Memory or as a 48 KB L1 cache with 16 KB of Local Memory. Note that the GTX 480 has an inverted memory hierarchy: The size of the aggregate register file is 2 MB, the size of all the L1 data caches is between 0.25 and 0.75 MB (depending on whether they are 16 KB or 48 KB), and the size of the L2 cache is 0.75 MB. It will be interesting to see the impact of this inverted ratio on GPU applications.

■ *64-Bit Addressing and a Unified Address Space for All GPU Memories*—This innovation makes it much easier to provide the pointers needed for C and C++.

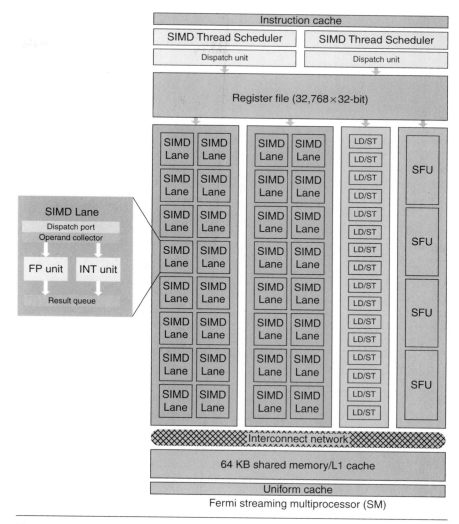

Figure 4.20 Block diagram of the multithreaded SIMD Processor of a Fermi GPU.
Each SIMD Lane has a pipelined floating-point unit, a pipelined integer unit, some logic
for dispatching instructions and operands to these units, and a queue for holding
results. The four Special Function units (SFUs) calculate functions such as square roots,
reciprocals, sines, and cosines.

- *Error Correcting Codes* to detect and correct errors in memory and registers
  (see Chapter 2)—To make long-running applications dependable on thousands of servers, ECC is the norm in the datacenter (see Chapter 6).

- *Faster Context Switching*—Given the large state of a multithreaded SIMD
  Processor, Fermi has hardware support to switch contexts much more
  quickly. Fermi can switch in less than 25 microseconds, about 10× faster than
  its predecessor can.

■ *Faster Atomic Instructions*—First included in the Tesla architecture, Fermi improves performance of Atomic instructions by 5 to 20×, to a few microseconds. A special hardware unit associated with the L2 cache, not inside the multithreaded SIMD Processors, handles atomic instructions.

Similarities and Differences between Vector Architectures and GPUs

As we have seen, there really are many similarities between vector architectures and GPUs. Along with the quirky jargon of GPUs, these similarities have contributed to the confusion in architecture circles about how novel GPUs really are. Now that you've seen what is under the covers of vector computers and GPUs, you can appreciate both the similarities and the differences. Since both architectures are designed to execute data-level parallel programs, but take different paths, this comparison is in depth to try to gain better understanding of what is needed for DLP hardware. Figure 4.21 shows the vector term first and then the closest equivalent in a GPU.

A SIMD Processor is like a vector processor. The multiple SIMD Processors in GPUs act as independent MIMD cores, just as many vector computers have multiple vector processors. This view would consider the NVIDIA GTX 480 as a 15-core machine with hardware support for multithreading, where each core has 16 lanes. The biggest difference is multithreading, which is fundamental to GPUs and missing from most vector processors.

Looking at the registers in the two architectures, the VMIPS register file holds entire vectors—that is, a contiguous block of 64 doubles. In contrast, a single vector in a GPU would be distributed across the registers of all SIMD Lanes. A VMIPS processor has 8 vector registers with 64 elements, or 512 elements total. A GPU thread of SIMD instructions has up to 64 registers with 32 elements each, or 2048 elements. These extra GPU registers support multithreading.

Figure 4.22 is a block diagram of the execution units of a vector processor on the left and a multithreaded SIMD Processor of a GPU on the right. For pedagogic purposes, we assume the vector processor has four lanes and the multithreaded SIMD Processor also has four SIMD Lanes. This figure shows that the four SIMD Lanes act in concert much like a four-lane vector unit, and that a SIMD Processor acts much like a vector processor.

In reality, there are many more lanes in GPUs, so GPU "chimes" are shorter. While a vector processor might have 2 to 8 lanes and a vector length of, say, 32—making a chime 4 to 16 clock cycles—a multithreaded SIMD Processor might have 8 or 16 lanes. A SIMD thread is 32 elements wide, so a GPU chime would just be 2 or 4 clock cycles. This difference is why we use "SIMD Processor" as the more descriptive term because it is closer to a SIMD design than it is to a traditional vector processor design.

The closest GPU term to a vectorized loop is Grid, and a PTX instruction is the closest to a vector instruction since a SIMD Thread broadcasts a PTX instruction to all SIMD Lanes.

Type	Vector term	Closest CUDA/NVIDIA GPU term	Comment
Program abstractions	Vectorized Loop	Grid	Concepts are similar, with the GPU using the less descriptive term.
	Chime	--	Since a vector instruction (PTX Instruction) takes just two cycles on Fermi and four cycles on Tesla to complete, a chime is short in GPUs.
Machine objects	Vector Instruction	PTX Instruction	A PTX instruction of a SIMD thread is broadcast to all SIMD Lanes, so it is similar to a vector instruction.
	Gather/Scatter	Global load/store (ld.global/st.global)	All GPU loads and stores are gather and scatter, in that each SIMD Lane sends a unique address. It's up to the GPU Coalescing Unit to get unit-stride performance when addresses from the SIMD Lanes allow it.
	Mask Registers	Predicate Registers and Internal Mask Registers	Vector mask registers are explicitly part of the architectural state, while GPU mask registers are internal to the hardware. The GPU conditional hardware adds a new feature beyond predicate registers to manage masks dynamically.
Processing and memory hardware	Vector Processor	Multithreaded SIMD Processor	These are similar, but SIMD Processors tend to have many lanes, taking a few clock cycles per lane to complete a vector, while vector architectures have few lanes and take many cycles to complete a vector. They are also multithreaded where vectors usually are not.
	Control Processor	Thread Block Scheduler	The closest is the Thread Block Scheduler that assigns Thread Blocks to a multithreaded SIMD Processor. But GPUs have no scalar-vector operations and no unit-stride or strided data transfer instructions, which Control Processors often provide.
	Scalar Processor	System Processor	Because of the lack of shared memory and the high latency to communicate over a PCI bus (1000s of clock cycles), the system processor in a GPU rarely takes on the same tasks that a scalar processor does in a vector architecture.
	Vector Lane	SIMD Lane	Both are essentially functional units with registers.
	Vector Registers	SIMD Lane Registers	The equivalent of a vector register is the same register in all 32 SIMD Lanes of a multithreaded SIMD Processor running a thread of SIMD instructions. The number of registers per SIMD thread is flexible, but the maximum is 64, so the maximum number of vector registers is 64.
	Main Memory	GPU Memory	Memory for GPU versus System memory in vector case.

Figure 4.21 GPU equivalent to vector terms.

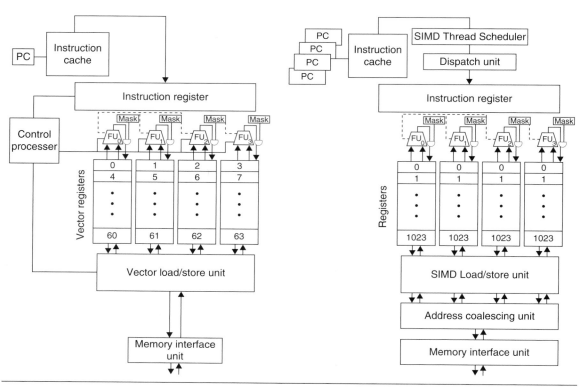

Figure 4.22 A vector processor with four lanes on the left and a multithreaded SIMD Processor of a GPU with four SIMD Lanes on the right. (GPUs typically have 8 to 16 SIMD Lanes.) The control processor supplies scalar operands for scalar-vector operations, increments addressing for unit and non-unit stride accesses to memory, and performs other accounting-type operations. Peak memory performance only occurs in a GPU when the Address Coalescing unit can discover localized addressing. Similarly, peak computational performance occurs when all internal mask bits are set identically. Note that the SIMD Processor has one PC per SIMD thread to help with multithreading.

With respect to memory access instructions in the two architectures, all GPU loads are gather instructions and all GPU stores are scatter instructions. If data addresses of CUDA Threads refer to nearby addresses that fall in the same cache/memory block at the same time, the Address Coalescing Unit of the GPU will ensure high memory bandwidth. The *explicit* unit-stride load and store instructions of vector architectures versus the *implicit* unit stride of GPU programming is why writing efficient GPU code requires that programmers think in terms of SIMD operations, even though the CUDA programming model looks like MIMD. As CUDA Threads can generate their own addresses, strided as well as gather-scatter, addressing vectors are found in both vector architectures and GPUs.

As we mentioned several times, the two architectures take very different approaches to hiding memory latency. Vector architectures amortize it across all the elements of the vector by having a deeply pipelined access so you pay the latency only once per vector load or store. Hence, vector loads and stores are like a block transfer between memory and the vector registers. In contrast, GPUs hide memory latency using multithreading. (Some researchers are investigating adding multithreading to vector architectures to try to capture the best of both worlds.)

With respect to conditional branch instructions, both architectures implement them using mask registers. Both conditional branch paths occupy time and/or space even when they do not store a result. The difference is that the vector compiler manages mask registers explicitly in software while the GPU hardware and assembler manages them implicitly using branch synchronization markers and an internal stack to save, complement, and restore masks.

As mentioned above, the conditional branch mechanism of GPUs gracefully handles the strip-mining problem of vector architectures. When the vector length is unknown at compile time, the program must calculate the modulo of the application vector length and the maximum vector length and store it in the vector length register. The strip-minded loop then resets the vector length register to the maximum vector length for the rest of the loop. This case is simpler with GPUs since they just iterate the loop until all the SIMD Lanes reach the loop bound. On the last iteration, some SIMD Lanes will be masked off and then restored after the loop completes.

The control processor of a vector computer plays an important role in the execution of vector instructions. It broadcasts operations to all the vector lanes and broadcasts a scalar register value for vector-scalar operations. It also does implicit calculations that are explicit in GPUs, such as automatically incrementing memory addresses for unit-stride and non-unit-stride loads and stores. The control processor is missing in the GPU. The closest analogy is the Thread Block Scheduler, which assigns Thread Blocks (bodies of vector loop) to multithreaded SIMD Processors. The runtime hardware mechanisms in a GPU that both generate addresses and then discover if they are adjacent, which is commonplace in many DLP applications, are likely less power efficient than using a control processor.

The scalar processor in a vector computer executes the scalar instructions of a vector program; that is, it performs operations that would be too slow to do in the vector unit. Although the system processor that is associated with a GPU is the closest analogy to a scalar processor in a vector architecture, the separate address spaces plus transferring over a PCle bus means thousands of clock cycles of overhead to use them together. The scalar processor can be slower than a vector processor for floating-point computations in a vector computer, but not by the same ratio as the system processor versus a multithreaded SIMD Processor (given the overhead).

Hence, each "vector unit" in a GPU must do computations that you would expect to do on a scalar processor in a vector computer. That is, rather than calculate on the system processor and communicate the results, it can be faster to disable all but one SIMD Lane using the predicate registers and built-in masks and do the scalar work with one SIMD Lane. The relatively simple scalar processor in a vector computer is likely to be faster and more power efficient than the GPU solution. If system processors and GPUs become more closely tied together in the future, it will be interesting to see if system processors can play the same role as scalar processors do for vector and Multimedia SIMD architectures.

Similarities and Differences between Multimedia SIMD Computers and GPUs

At a high level, multicore computers with Multimedia SIMD instruction extensions do share similarities with GPUs. Figure 4.23 summarizes the similarities and differences.

Both are multiprocessors whose processors use multiple SIMD lanes, although GPUs have more processors and many more lanes. Both use hardware multithreading to improve processor utilization, although GPUs have hardware support for many more threads. Recent innovations in GPUs mean that now both have similar performance ratios between single-precision and double-precision floating-point arithmetic. Both use caches, although GPUs use smaller streaming caches and multicore computers use large multilevel caches that try to contain whole working sets completely. Both use a 64-bit address space, although the physical main memory is much smaller in GPUs. While GPUs support memory protection at the page level, they do not support demand paging.

In addition to the large numerical differences in processors, SIMD lanes, hardware thread support, and cache sizes, there are many architectural differences. The scalar processor and Multimedia SIMD instructions are tightly integrated in traditional computers; they are separated by an I/O bus in GPUs, and they even have separate main memories. The multiple SIMD processors in a GPU use a single address space, but the caches are not coherent as they are in traditional multicore computers. Unlike GPUs, multimedia SIMD instructions do not support gather-scatter memory accesses, which Section 4.7 shows is a significant omission.

Feature	Multicore with SIMD	GPU
SIMD processors	4 to 8	8 to 16
SIMD lanes/processor	2 to 4	8 to 16
Multithreading hardware support for SIMD threads	2 to 4	16 to 32
Typical ratio of single-precision to double-precision performance	2:1	2:1
Largest cache size	8 MB	0.75 MB
Size of memory address	64-bit	64-bit
Size of main memory	8 GB to 256 GB	4 to 6 GB
Memory protection at level of page	Yes	Yes
Demand paging	Yes	No
Integrated scalar processor/SIMD processor	Yes	No
Cache coherent	Yes	No

Figure 4.23 Similarities and differences between multicore with Multimedia SIMD extensions and recent GPUs.

Summary

Now that the veil has been lifted, we can see that GPUs are really just multi-threaded SIMD processors, although they have more processors, more lanes per processor, and more multithreading hardware than do traditional multicore computers. For example, the Fermi GTX 480 has 15 SIMD processors with 16 lanes per processor and hardware support for 32 SIMD threads. Fermi even embraces instruction-level parallelism by issuing instructions from two SIMD threads to two sets of SIMD lanes. They also have less cache memory—Fermi's L2 cache is 0.75 megabyte—and it is not coherent with the distant scalar processor.

Type	More descriptive name used in this book	Official CUDA/ NVIDIA term	Book definition and AMD and OpenCL terms	Official CUDA/NVIDIA definition
Program abstractions	Vectorizable loop	Grid	A vectorizable loop, executed on the GPU, made up of one or more "Thread Blocks" (or bodies of vectorized loop) that can execute in parallel. OpenCL name is "index range." AMD name is "NDRange".	A grid is an array of thread blocks that can execute concurrently, sequentially, or a mixture.
	Body of Vectorized loop	Thread Block	A vectorized loop executed on a multithreaded SIMD Processor, made up of one or more threads of SIMD instructions. These SIMD Threads can communicate via Local Memory. AMD and OpenCL name is "work group".	A thread block is an array of CUDA Threads that execute concurrently together and can cooperate and communicate via Shared Memory and barrier synchronization. A Thread Block has a Thread Block ID within its Grid.
	Sequence of SIMD Lane operations	CUDA Thread	A vertical cut of a thread of SIMD instructions corresponding to one element executed by one SIMD Lane. Result is stored depending on mask. AMD and OpenCL call a CUDA Thread a "work item."	A CUDA Thread is a lightweight thread that executes a sequential program and can cooperate with other CUDA Threads executing in the same Thread Block. A CUDA Thread has a thread ID within its Thread Block.
Machine object	A Thread of SIMD instructions	Warp	A traditional thread, but it contains just SIMD instructions that are executed on a multithreaded SIMD Processor. Results are stored depending on a per-element mask. AMD name is "wavefront."	A warp is a set of parallel CUDA Threads (e.g., 32) that execute the same instruction together in a multithreaded SIMT/SIMD Processor.
	SIMD instruction	PTX instruction	A single SIMD instruction executed across the SIMD Lanes. AMD name is "AMDIL" or "FSAIL" instruction.	A PTX instruction specifies an instruction executed by a CUDA Thread.

Figure 4.24 Conversion from terms used in this chapter to official NVIDIA/CUDA and AMD jargon. OpenCL names are given in the book definition.

Type	More descriptive name used in this book	Official CUDA/ NVIDIA term	Book definition and AMD and OpenCL terms	Official CUDA/NVIDIA definition
Processing hardware	Multithreaded SIMD processor	Streaming multi-processor	Multithreaded SIMD Processor that executes thread of SIMD instructions, independent of other SIMD Processors. Both AMD and OpenCL call it a "compute unit." However, the CUDA Programmer writes program for one lane rather than for a "vector" of multiple SIMD Lanes.	A streaming multiprocessor (SM) is a multithreaded SIMT/ SIMD Processor that executes warps of CUDA Threads. A SIMT program specifies the execution of one CUDA Thread, rather than a vector of multiple SIMD Lanes.
	Thread block scheduler	Giga thread engine	Assigns multiple bodies of vectorized loop to multithreaded SIMD Processors. AMD name is "Ultra-Threaded Dispatch Engine".	Distributes and schedules thread blocks of a grid to streaming multiprocessors as resources become available.
	SIMD Thread scheduler	Warp scheduler	Hardware unit that schedules and issues threads of SIMD instructions when they are ready to execute; includes a scoreboard to track SIMD Thread execution. AMD name is "Work Group Scheduler".	A warp scheduler in a streaming multiprocessor schedules warps for execution when their next instruction is ready to execute.
	SIMD Lane	Thread processor	Hardware SIMD Lane that executes the operations in a thread of SIMD instructions on a single element. Results are stored depending on mask. OpenCL calls it a "processing element." AMD name is also "SIMD Lane".	A thread processor is a datapath and register file portion of a streaming multiprocessor that executes operations for one or more lanes of a warp.
Memory hardware	GPU Memory	Global Memory	DRAM memory accessible by all multithreaded SIMD Processors in a GPU. OpenCL calls it "Global Memory."	Global memory is accessible by all CUDA Threads in any thread block in any grid; implemented as a region of DRAM, and may be cached.
	Private Memory	Local Memory	Portion of DRAM memory private to each SIMD Lane. Both AMD and OpenCL call it "Private Memory."	Private "thread-local" memory for a CUDA Thread; implemented as a cached region of DRAM.
	Local Memory	Shared Memory	Fast local SRAM for one multithreaded SIMD Processor, unavailable to other SIMD Processors. OpenCL calls it "Local Memory." AMD calls it "Group Memory".	Fast SRAM memory shared by the CUDA Threads composing a thread block, and private to that thread block. Used for communication among CUDA Threads in a thread block at barrier synchronization points.
	SIMD Lane registers	Registers	Registers in a single SIMD Lane allocated across body of vectorized loop. AMD also calls them "Registers".	Private registers for a CUDA Thread; implemented as multithreaded register file for certain lanes of several warps for each thread processor.

Figure 4.25 Conversion from terms used in this chapter to official NVIDIA/CUDA and AMD jargon. Note that our descriptive terms "Local Memory" and "Private Memory" use the OpenCL terminology. NVIDIA uses SIMT, single-instruction multiple-thread, rather than SIMD, to describe a streaming multiprocessor. SIMT is preferred over SIMD because the per-thread branching and control flow are unlike any SIMD machine.

The CUDA programming model wraps up all these forms of parallelism around a single abstraction, the CUDA Thread. Thus, the CUDA programmer can think of programming thousands of threads, although they are really executing each block of 32 threads on the many lanes of the many SIMD Processors. The CUDA programmer who wants good performance keeps in mind that these threads are blocked and executed 32 at a time and that addresses need to be to adjacent addresses to get good performance from the memory system.

Although we've used CUDA and the NVIDIA GPU in this section, rest assured that the same ideas are found in the OpenCL programming language and in GPUs from other companies.

Now that you understand better how GPUs work, we reveal the real jargon. Figures 4.24 and 4.25 match the descriptive terms and definitions of this section with the official CUDA/NVIDIA and AMD terms and definitions. We also include the OpenCL terms. We believe the GPU learning curve is steep in part because of using terms such as "Streaming Multiprocessor" for the SIMD Processor, "Thread Processor" for the SIMD Lane, and "Shared Memory" for Local Memory—especially since Local Memory is *not* shared between SIMD Processors! We hope that this two-step approach gets you up that curve quicker, even if it's a bit indirect.

4.5   Detecting and Enhancing Loop-Level Parallelism

Loops in programs are the fountainhead of many of the types of parallelism we discussed above and in Chapter 5. In this section, we discuss compiler technology for discovering the amount of parallelism that we can exploit in a program as well as hardware support for these compiler techniques. We define precisely when a loop is parallel (or vectorizable), how dependence can prevent a loop from being parallel, and techniques for eliminating some types of dependences. Finding and manipulating loop-level parallelism is critical to exploiting both DLP and TLP, as well as the more aggressive static ILP approaches (e.g., VLIW) that we examine in Appendix H.

Loop-level parallelism is normally analyzed at the source level or close to it, while most analysis of ILP is done once instructions have been generated by the compiler. Loop-level analysis involves determining what dependences exist among the operands in a loop across the iterations of that loop. For now, we will consider only data dependences, which arise when an operand is written at some point and read at a later point. Name dependences also exist and may be removed by the renaming techniques discussed in Chapter 3.

The analysis of loop-level parallelism focuses on determining whether data accesses in later iterations are dependent on data values produced in earlier iterations; such dependence is called a *loop-carried dependence*. Most of the examples we considered in Chapters 2 and 3 had no loop-carried dependences and, thus, are loop-level parallel. To see that a loop is parallel, let us first look at the source representation:

```
for (i=999; i>=0; i=i-1)
    x[i] = x[i] + s;
```

In this loop, the two uses of x[i] are dependent, but this dependence is within a single iteration and is not loop carried. There is a loop-carried dependence between successive uses of i in different iterations, but this dependence involves an induction variable that can be easily recognized and eliminated. We saw examples of how to eliminate dependences involving induction variables during loop unrolling in Section 2.2 of Chapter 2, and we will look at additional examples later in this section.

Because finding loop-level parallelism involves recognizing structures such as loops, array references, and induction variable computations, the compiler can do this analysis more easily at or near the source level, as opposed to the machine-code level. Let's look at a more complex example.

Example   Consider a loop like this one:

```
for (i=0; i<100; i=i+1) {
    A[i+1] = A[i] + C[i];    /* S1 */
    B[i+1] = B[i] + A[i+1];  /* S2 */
}
```

Assume that A, B, and C are distinct, nonoverlapping arrays. (In practice, the arrays may sometimes be the same or may overlap. Because the arrays may be passed as parameters to a procedure that includes this loop, determining whether arrays overlap or are identical often requires sophisticated, interprocedural analysis of the program.) What are the data dependences among the statements S1 and S2 in the loop?

Answer   There are two different dependences:

1. S1 uses a value computed by S1 in an earlier iteration, since iteration i computes A[i+1], which is read in iteration i+1. The same is true of S2 for B[i] and B[i+1].

2. S2 uses the value A[i+1] computed by S1 in the same iteration.

These two dependences are different and have different effects. To see how they differ, let's assume that only one of these dependences exists at a time. Because the dependence of statement S1 is on an earlier iteration of S1, this dependence is loop carried. This dependence forces successive iterations of this loop to execute in series.

The second dependence (S2 depending on S1) is within an iteration and is not loop carried. Thus, if this were the only dependence, multiple iterations of the loop could execute in parallel, as long as each pair of statements in an iteration were kept in order. We saw this type of dependence in an example in Section 2.2, where unrolling was able to expose the parallelism. These intra-loop dependences are common; for example, a sequence of vector instructions that uses chaining exhibits exactly this sort of dependence.

It is also possible to have a loop-carried dependence that does not prevent parallelism, as the next example shows.

Example   Consider a loop like this one:

```
for (i=0; i<100; i=i+1) {
      A[i] = A[i] + B[i];    /* S1 */
      B[i+1] = C[i] + D[i]; /* S2 */
}
```

What are the dependences between S1 and S2? Is this loop parallel? If not, show how to make it parallel.

Answer   Statement S1 uses the value assigned in the previous iteration by statement S2, so there is a loop-carried dependence between S2 and S1. Despite this loop-carried dependence, this loop can be made parallel. Unlike the earlier loop, this dependence is not circular; neither statement depends on itself, and although S1 depends on S2, S2 does not depend on S1. A loop is parallel if it can be written without a cycle in the dependences, since the absence of a cycle means that the dependences give a partial ordering on the statements.

Although there are no circular dependences in the above loop, it must be transformed to conform to the partial ordering and expose the parallelism. Two observations are critical to this transformation:

1. There is no dependence from S1 to S2. If there were, then there would be a cycle in the dependences and the loop would not be parallel. Since this other dependence is absent, interchanging the two statements will not affect the execution of S2.

2. On the first iteration of the loop, statement S2 depends on the value of B[0] computed *prior* to initiating the loop.

These two observations allow us to replace the loop above with the following code sequence:

```
A[0] = A[0] + B[0];
for (i=0; i<99; i=i+1) {
      B[i+1] = C[i] + D[i];
      A[i+1] = A[i+1] + B[i+1];
}
B[100] = C[99] + D[99];
```

The dependence between the two statements is no longer loop carried, so that iterations of the loop may be overlapped, provided the statements in each iteration are kept in order.

Our analysis needs to begin by finding all loop-carried dependences. This dependence information is *inexact*, in the sense that it tells us that such dependence *may* exist. Consider the following example:

```
for (i=0;i<100;i=i+1) {
      A[i] = B[i] + C[i]
      D[i] = A[i] * E[i]
}
```

The second reference to A in this example need not be translated to a load instruction, since we know that the value is computed and stored by the previous statement; hence, the second reference to A can simply be a reference to the register into which A was computed. Performing this optimization requires knowing that the two references are *always* to the same memory address and that there is no intervening access to the same location. Normally, data dependence analysis only tells that one reference *may* depend on another; a more complex analysis is required to determine that two references *must be* to the exact same address. In the example above, a simple version of this analysis suffices, since the two references are in the same basic block.

Often loop-carried dependences are in the form of a *recurrence*. A recurrence occurs when a variable is defined based on the value of that variable in an earlier iteration, often the one immediately preceding, as in the following code fragment:

```
for (i=1;i<100;i=i+1) {
      Y[i] = Y[i-1] + Y[i];
}
```

Detecting a recurrence can be important for two reasons: Some architectures (especially vector computers) have special support for executing recurrences, and, in an ILP context, it may still be possible to exploit a fair amount of parallelism.

Finding Dependences

Clearly, finding the dependences in a program is important both to determine which loops might contain parallelism and to eliminate name dependences. The complexity of dependence analysis arises also because of the presence of arrays and pointers in languages such as C or C++, or pass-by-reference parameter passing in Fortran. Since scalar variable references explicitly refer to a name, they can usually be analyzed quite easily with aliasing because of pointers and reference parameters causing some complications and uncertainty in the analysis.

How does the compiler detect dependences in general? Nearly all dependence analysis algorithms work on the assumption that array indices are *affine*. In simplest terms, a one-dimensional array index is affine if it can be written in the form $a \times i + b$, where a and b are constants and i is the loop index variable. The index of a multidimensional array is affine if the index in each dimension is affine. Sparse array accesses, which typically have the form x[y[i]], are one of the major examples of non-affine accesses.

Determining whether there is a dependence between two references to the same array in a loop is thus equivalent to determining whether two affine functions can have the same value for different indices between the bounds of the loop. For example, suppose we have stored to an array element with index value $a \times i + b$ and loaded from the same array with index value $c \times i + d$, where i is the for-loop index variable that runs from m to n. A dependence exists if two conditions hold:

1. There are two iteration indices, j and k, that are both within the limits of the for loop. That is, $m \le j \le n$, $m \le k \le n$.

2. The loop stores into an array element indexed by $a \times j + b$ and later fetches from that *same* array element when it is indexed by $c \times k + d$. That is, $a \times j + b = c \times k + d$.

In general, we cannot determine whether dependence exists at compile time. For example, the values of a, b, c, and d may not be known (they could be values in other arrays), making it impossible to tell if a dependence exists. In other cases, the dependence testing may be very expensive but decidable at compile time; for example, the accesses may depend on the iteration indices of multiple nested loops. Many programs, however, contain primarily simple indices where a, b, c, and d are all constants. For these cases, it is possible to devise reasonable compile time tests for dependence.

As an example, a simple and sufficient test for the absence of a dependence is the *greatest common divisor* (GCD) test. It is based on the observation that if a loop-carried dependence exists, then GCD (c,a) must divide $(d - b)$. (Recall that an integer, x, *divides* another integer, y, if we get an integer quotient when we do the division y/x and there is no remainder.)

Example   Use the GCD test to determine whether dependences exist in the following loop:

```
for (i=0; i<100; i=i+1) {
      X[2*i+3] = X[2*i] * 5.0;
}
```

Answer   Given the values $a = 2$, $b = 3$, $c = 2$, and $d = 0$, then GCD$(a,c) = 2$, and $d - b = -3$. Since 2 does not divide -3, no dependence is possible.

The GCD test is sufficient to guarantee that no dependence exists; however, there are cases where the GCD test succeeds but no dependence exists. This can arise, for example, because the GCD test does not consider the loop bounds.

In general, determining whether a dependence actually exists is NP-complete. In practice, however, many common cases can be analyzed precisely at low cost. Recently, approaches using a hierarchy of exact tests increasing in generality and cost have been shown to be both accurate and efficient. (A test is *exact* if it precisely determines whether a dependence exists. Although the general case is NP-complete, there exist exact tests for restricted situations that are much cheaper.)

In addition to detecting the presence of a dependence, a compiler wants to classify the type of dependence. This classification allows a compiler to recognize name dependences and eliminate them at compile time by renaming and copying.

Example   The following loop has multiple types of dependences. Find all the true dependences, output dependences, and antidependences, and eliminate the output dependences and antidependences by renaming.

```
for (i=0; i<100; i=i+1) {
    Y[i] = X[i] / c; /* S1 */
    X[i] = X[i] + c; /* S2 */
    Z[i] = Y[i] + c; /* S3 */
    Y[i] = c - Y[i]; /* S4 */
}
```

Answer   The following dependences exist among the four statements:

1. There are true dependences from S1 to S3 and from S1 to S4 because of Y[i]. These are not loop carried, so they do not prevent the loop from being considered parallel. These dependences will force S3 and S4 to wait for S1 to complete.

2. There is an antidependence from S1 to S2, based on X[i].

3. There is an antidependence from S3 to S4 for Y[i].

4. There is an output dependence from S1 to S4, based on Y[i].

The following version of the loop eliminates these false (or pseudo) dependences.

```
for (i=0; i<100; i=i+1 {
    T[i] = X[i] / c; /* Y renamed to T to remove output dependence */
    X1[i] = X[i] + c;/* X renamed to X1 to remove antidependence */
    Z[i] = T[i] + c;/* Y renamed to T to remove antidependence */
    Y[i] = c - T[i];
}
```

After the loop, the variable X has been renamed X1. In code that follows the loop, the compiler can simply replace the name X by X1. In this case, renaming does not require an actual copy operation, as it can be done by substituting names or by register allocation. In other cases, however, renaming will require copying.

Dependence analysis is a critical technology for exploiting parallelism, as well as for the transformation-like blocking that Chapter 2 covers. For detecting loop-level parallelism, dependence analysis is the basic tool. Effectively compiling programs for vector computers, SIMD computers, or multiprocessors depends critically on this analysis. The major drawback of dependence analysis is that it applies only under a limited set of circumstances, namely, among references within a single loop nest and using affine index functions. Thus, there are many situations where array-oriented dependence analysis *cannot* tell us what we want to know; for example, analyzing accesses done with pointers, rather than with array indices can be much harder. (This is one reason why Fortran is still preferred over C and C++ for many scientific applications designed for parallel computers.) Similarly, analyzing references across procedure calls is extremely difficult. Thus, while analysis of code written in sequential languages remains important, we also need approaches such as OpenMP and CUDA that write explicitly parallel loops.

Eliminating Dependent Computations

As mentioned above, one of the most important forms of dependent computations is a recurrence. A dot product is a perfect example of a recurrence:

```
for (i=9999; i>=0; i=i-1)
        sum = sum + x[i] * y[i];
```

This loop is not parallel because it has a loop-carried dependence on the variable sum. We can, however, transform it to a set of loops, one of which is completely parallel and the other that can be partly parallel. The first loop will execute the completely parallel portion of this loop. It looks like:

```
for (i=9999; i>=0; i=i-1)
        sum[i] = x[i] * y[i];
```

Notice that sum has been expanded from a scalar into a vector quantity (a transformation called *scalar expansion*) and that this transformation makes this new loop completely parallel. When we are done, however, we need to do the reduce step, which sums up the elements of the vector. It looks like:

```
for (i=9999; i>=0; i=i-1)
        finalsum = finalsum + sum[i];
```

Although this loop is not parallel, it has a very specific structure called a *reduction*. Reductions are common in linear algebra and, as we shall see in Chapter 6, they are also a key part of the primary parallelism primitive MapReduce used in warehouse-scale computers. In general, any function can be used as a reduction operator, and common cases include operators such as max and min.

Reductions are sometimes handled by special hardware in a vector and SIMD architecture that allows the reduce step to be done much faster than it could be done in scalar mode. These work by implementing a technique similar to what can be done in a multiprocessor environment. While the general transformation works with any number of processors, suppose for simplicity we have 10 processors. In the first step of reducing the sum, each processor executes the following (with p as the processor number ranging from 0 to 9):

```
for (i=999; i>=0; i=i-1)
        finalsum[p] = finalsum[p] + sum[i+1000*p];
```

This loop, which sums up 1000 elements on each of the ten processors, is completely parallel. A simple scalar loop can then complete the summation of the last ten sums. Similar approaches are used in vector and SIMD processors.

It is important to observe that the above transformation relies on associativity of addition. Although arithmetic with unlimited range and precision is associative, computer arithmetic is not associative, for either integer arithmetic, because of limited range, or floating-point arithmetic, because of both range and precision. Thus, using these restructuring techniques can sometimes lead to erroneous behavior, although such occurrences are rare. For this reason, most compilers require that optimizations that rely on associativity be explicitly enabled.

4.6 Crosscutting Issues

Energy and DLP: Slow and Wide versus Fast and Narrow

A fundamental energy advantage of data-level parallel architectures comes from the energy equation in Chapter 1. Since we assume ample data-level parallelism, the performance is the same if we halve the clock rate and double the execution resources: twice the number of lanes for a vector computer, wider registers and ALUs for multimedia SIMD, and more SIMD lanes for GPUs. If we can lower the voltage while dropping the clock rate, we can actually reduce energy as well as the power for the computation while maintaining the same peak performance. Hence, DLP processors tend to have lower clock rates than system processors, which rely on high clock rates for performance (see Section 4.7).

Compared to out-of-order processors, DLP processors can have simpler control logic to launch a large number of operations per clock cycle; for example, the control is identical for all lanes in vector processors, and there is no logic to decide on multiple instruction issue or speculative execution logic. Vector architectures can also make it easier to turn off unused portions of the chip. Each vector instruction explicitly describes all the resources it needs for a number of cycles when the instruction issues.

Banked Memory and Graphics Memory

Section 4.2 noted the importance of substantial memory bandwidth for vector architectures to support unit stride, non-unit stride, and gather-scatter accesses.

To achieve their high performance, GPUs also require substantial memory bandwidth. Special DRAM chips designed just for GPUs, called *GDRAM* for *graphics DRAM*, help deliver this bandwidth. GDRAM chips have higher bandwidth often at lower capacity than conventional DRAM chips. To deliver this bandwidth, GDRAM chips are often soldered directly onto the same board as the GPU rather than being placed into DIMM modules that are inserted into slots on a board, as is the case for system memory. DIMM modules allow for much greater capacity and for the system to be upgraded, unlike GDRAM. This limited capacity—about 4 GB in 2011—is in conflict with the goal of running bigger problems, which is a natural use of the increased computational power of GPUs.

To deliver the best possible performance, GPUs try to take into account all the features of GDRAMs. They are typically arranged internally as 4 to 8 banks, with a power of 2 number of rows (typically 16,384) and a power of 2 number of bits per row (typically 8192). Chapter 2 describes the details of DRAM behavior that GPUs try to match.

Given all the potential demands on the GDRAMs from both the computation tasks and the graphics acceleration tasks, the memory system could see a large number of uncorrelated requests. Alas, this diversity hurts memory performance. To cope, the GPU's memory controller maintains separate queues of traffic bound for different GDRAM banks, waiting until there is enough traffic to justify opening a row and transferring all requested data at once. This delay improves bandwidth but stretches latency, and the controller must ensure that no processing units starve while waiting for data, for otherwise neighboring processors could become idle. Section 4.7 shows that gather-scatter techniques and memory-bank-aware access techniques can deliver substantial increases in performance versus conventional cache-based architectures.

Strided Accesses and TLB Misses

One problem with strided accesses is how they interact with the translation lookaside buffer (TLB) for virtual memory in vector architectures or GPUs. (GPUs use TLBs for memory mapping.) Depending on how the TLB is organized and the size of the array being accessed in memory, it is even possible to get one TLB miss for every access to an element in the array!

4.7   Putting It All Together: Mobile versus Server GPUs and Tesla versus Core i7

Given the popularity of graphics applications, GPUs are now found in both mobile clients as well as traditional servers or heavy-duty desktop computers. Figure 4.26 lists the key characteristics of the NVIDIA Tegra 2 for mobile clients, which is used in the LG Optimus 2X and runs Android OS, and the Fermi GPU for servers. GPU server engineers hope to be able to do live animation within five years after a movie is released. GPU mobile engineers in turn want within five more years that a mobile client can do what a server or game console does today. More concretely, the overarching goal is for the graphics quality of a movie such as *Avatar* to be achieved in real time on a server GPU in 2015 and on your mobile GPU in 2020.

The NVIDIA Tegra 2 for mobile devices provides both the system processor and the GPU in a single chip using a single physical memory. The system processor is a dual-core ARM Cortex-A9, with each core using out-of-order execution and dual instruction issue. Each core includes the optional floating-point unit.

The GPU has hardware acceleration for programmable pixel shading, programmable vertex and lighting, and 3D graphics, but it does not include the GPU computing features needed to run CUDA or OpenCL programs.

	NVIDIA Tegra 2	NVIDIA Fermi GTX 480
Market	Mobile client	Desktop, server
System processor	Dual-Core ARM Cortex-A9	Not applicable
System interface	Not applicable	PCI Express 2.0×16
System interface bandwidth	Not applicable	6 GBytes/sec (each direction), 12 GBytes/sec (total)
Clock rate	Up to 1 GHz	1.4 GHz
SIMD multiprocessors	Unavailable	15
SIMD lanes/SIMD multiprocessor	Unavailable	32
Memory interface	32-bit LP-DDR2/DDR2	384-bit GDDR5
Memory bandwidth	2.7 GBytes/sec	177 GBytes/sec
Memory capacity	1 GByte	1.5 GBytes
Transistors	242 M	3030 M
Process	40 nm TSMC process G	40 nm TSMC process G
Die area	57 mm^2	520 mm^2
Power	1.5 watts	167 watts

Figure 4.26 Key features of the GPUs for mobile clients and servers. The Tegra 2 is the reference platform for Android OS and is found in the LG Optimus 2X cell phone.

The die size is 57 mm^2 (7.5×7.5 mm) in a 40 nm TSMC process, and it contains 242 million transistors. It uses 1.5 watts.

The NVIDIA GTX 480 in Figure 4.26 is the first implementation of the Fermi architecture. The clock rate is 1.4 GHz, and it includes 15 SIMD processors. The chip itself has 16, but to improve yield only 15 of the 16 need work for this product. The path to GDDR5 memory is 384 (6×64) bits wide, and it interfaces that clock at 1.84 GHz, offering a peak memory bandwidth of 177 GBytes/sec by transferring on both clock edges of double data rate memory. It connects to the host system processor and memory via a PCI Express 2.0×16 link, which has a peak bidirectional rate of 12 GBytes/sec.

All physical characteristics of the GTX 480 die are impressively large: It contains 3.0 billion transistors, the die size is 520 mm^2 (22.8×22.8 mm) in a 40 nm TSMC process, and the typical power is 167 watts. The whole module is 250 watts, which includes the GPU, GDRAMs, fans, power regulators, and so on.

Comparison of a GPU and a MIMD with Multimedia SIMD

A group of Intel researchers published a paper [Lee et al. 2010] comparing a quad-core Intel i7 (see Chapter 3) with multimedia SIMD extensions to the previous generation GPU, the Tesla GTX 280. Figure 4.27 lists the characteristics

	Core i7-960	GTX 280	GTX 480	Ratio 280/i7	Ratio 480/i7
Number of processing elements (cores or SMs)	4	30	15	7.5	3.8
Clock frequency (GHz)	3.2	1.3	1.4	0.41	0.44
Die size	263	576	520	2.2	2.0
Technology	Intel 45 nm	TSMC 65 nm	TSMC 40 nm	1.6	1.0
Power (chip, not module)	130	130	167	1.0	1.3
Transistors	700 M	1400 M	3030 M	2.0	4.4
Memory bandwidth (GBytes/sec)	32	141	177	4.4	5.5
Single-precision SIMD width	4	8	32	2.0	8.0
Double-precision SIMD width	2	1	16	0.5	8.0
Peak single-precision scalar FLOPS (GFLOP/Sec)	26	117	63	4.6	2.5
Peak single-precision SIMD FLOPS (GFLOP/Sec)	102	311 to 933	515 or 1344	3.0–9.1	6.6–13.1
(SP 1 add or multiply)	N.A.	(311)	(515)	(3.0)	(6.6)
(SP 1 instruction fused multiply-adds)	N.A.	(622)	(1344)	(6.1)	(13.1)
(Rare SP dual issue fused multiply-add and multiply)	N.A.	(933)	N.A.	(9.1)	--
Peak double-precision SIMD FLOPS (GFLOP/sec)	51	78	515	1.5	10.1

Figure 4.27 Intel Core i7-960, NVIDIA GTX 280, and GTX 480 specifications. The rightmost columns show the ratios of GTX 280 and GTX 480 to Core i7. For single-precision SIMD FLOPS on the GTX 280, the higher speed (933) comes from a very rare case of dual issuing of fused multiply-add and multiply. More reasonable is 622 for single fused multiply-adds. Although the case study is between the 280 and i7, we include the 480 to show its relationship to the 280 since it is described in this chapter. Note that these memory bandwidths are higher than in Figure 4.28 because these are DRAM pin bandwidths and those in Figure 4.28 are at the processors as measured by a benchmark program. (From Table 2 in Lee et al. [2010].)

of the two systems. Both products were purchased in Fall 2009. The Core i7 is in Intel's 45-nanometer semiconductor technology while the GPU is in TSMC's 65-nanometer technology. Although it might have been more fair to have a comparison by a neutral party or by both interested parties, the purpose of this section is *not* to determine how much faster one product is than another, but to try to understand the relative value of features of these two contrasting architecture styles.

The rooflines of the Core i7 920 and GTX 280 in Figure 4.28 illustrate the differences in the computers. The 920 has a slower clock rate than the 960 (2.66 GHz versus 3.2 GHz), but the rest of the system is the same. Not only does the GTX 280 have much higher memory bandwidth and double-precision floating-point performance, but also its double-precision ridge point is considerably to the left. As mentioned above, it is much easier to hit peak computational performance the further the ridge point of the roofline is to the left. The double-precision ridge point is 0.6 for the GTX 280 versus 2.6 for the Core i7. For single-precision performance, the ridge point moves far to the right, as it's much harder to hit the roof of single-precision performance because it is so

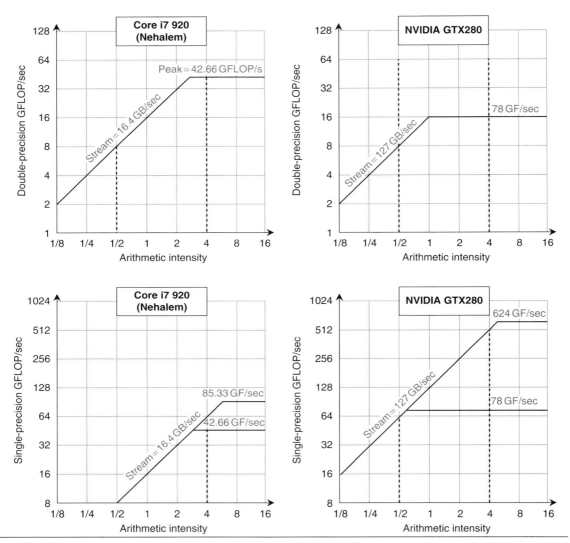

Figure 4.28 Roofline model [Williams et al. 2009]. These rooflines show double-precision floating-point performance in the top row and single-precision performance in the bottom row. (The DP FP performance ceiling is also in the bottom row to give perspective.) The Core i7 920 on the left has a peak DP FP performance of 42.66 GFLOP/sec, a SP FP peak of 85.33 GFLOP/sec, and a peak memory bandwidth of 16.4 GBytes/sec. The NVIDIA GTX 280 has a DP FP peak of 78 GFLOP/sec, SP FP peak of 624 GFLOP/sec, and 127 GBytes/sec of memory bandwidth. The dashed vertical line on the left represents an arithmetic intensity of 0.5 FLOP/byte. It is limited by memory bandwidth to no more than 8 DP GFLOP/sec or 8 SP GFLOP/sec on the Core i7. The dashed vertical line to the right has an arithmetic intensity of 4 FLOP/byte. It is limited only computationally to 42.66 DP GFLOP/sec and 64 SP GFLOP/sec on the Core i7 and 78 DP GFLOP/sec and 512 DP GFLOP/sec on the GTX 280. To hit the highest computation rate on the Core i7 you need to use all 4 cores and SSE instructions with an equal number of multiplies and adds. For the GTX 280, you need to use fused multiply-add instructions on all multithreaded SIMD processors. Guz et al. [2009] have an interesting analytic model for these two architectures.

much higher. Note that the arithmetic intensity of the kernel is based on the bytes that go to main memory, not the bytes that go to cache memory. Thus, caching can change the arithmetic intensity of a kernel on a particular computer, presuming that most references really go to the cache. The Rooflines help explain the relative performance in this case study. Note also that this bandwidth is for unit-stride accesses in both architectures. Real gather-scatter addresses that are not coalesced are slower on the GTX 280 and on the Core i7, as we shall see.

The researchers said that they selected the benchmark programs by analyzing the computational and memory characteristics of four recently proposed benchmark suites and then "formulated the set of *throughput computing kernels* that capture these characteristics." Figure 4.29 describes these 14 kernels, and Figure 4.30 shows the performance results, with larger numbers meaning faster.

Kernel	Application	SIMD	TLP	Characteristics
SGEMM (**SGEMM**)	Linear algebra	Regular	Across 2D tiles	Compute bound after tiling
Monte Carlo (**MC**)	Computational finance	Regular	Across paths	Compute bound
Convolution (**Conv**)	Image analysis	Regular	Across pixels	Compute bound; BW bound for small filters
FFT (**FFT**)	Signal processing	Regular	Across smaller FFTs	Compute bound or BW bound depending on size
SAXPY (**SAXPY**)	Dot product	Regular	Across vector	BW bound for large vectors
LBM (**LBM**)	Time migration	Regular	Across cells	BW bound
Constraint solver (**Solv**)	Rigid body physics	Gather/Scatter	Across constraints	Synchronization bound
SpMV (**SpMV**)	Sparse solver	Gather	Across non-zero	BW bound for typical large matrices
GJK (**GJK**)	Collision detection	Gather/Scatter	Across objects	Compute bound
Sort (**Sort**)	Database	Gather/Scatter	Across elements	Compute bound
Ray casting (**RC**)	Volume rendering	Gather	Across rays	4-8 MB first level working set; over 500 MB last level working set
Search (**Search**)	Database	Gather/Scatter	Across queries	Compute bound for small tree, BW bound at bottom of tree for large tree
Histogram (**Hist**)	Image analysis	Requires conflict detection	Across pixels	Reduction/synchronization bound

Figure 4.29 Throughput computing kernel characteristics (from Table 1 in Lee et al. [2010].) The name in parentheses identifies the benchmark name in this section. The authors suggest that code for both machines had equal optimization effort.

Kernel	Units	Core i7-960	GTX 280	GTX 280/ i7-960
SGEMM	GFLOP/sec	94	364	3.9
MC	Billion paths/sec	0.8	1.4	1.8
Conv	Million pixels/sec	1250	3500	2.8
FFT	GFLOP/sec	71.4	213	3.0
SAXPY	GBytes/sec	16.8	88.8	5.3
LBM	Million lookups/sec	85	426	5.0
Solv	Frames/sec	103	52	0.5
SpMV	GFLOP/sec	4.9	9.1	1.9
GJK	Frames/sec	67	1020	15.2
Sort	Million elements/sec	250	198	0.8
RC	Frames/sec	5	8.1	1.6
Search	Million queries/sec	50	90	1.8
Hist	Million pixels/sec	1517	2583	1.7
Bilat	Million pixels/sec	83	475	5.7

Figure 4.30 Raw and relative performance measured for the two platforms. In this study, SAXPY is just used as a measure of memory bandwidth, so the right unit is GBytes/sec and not GFLOP/sec. (Based on Table 3 in [Lee et al. 2010].)

Given that the raw performance specifications of the GTX 280 vary from 2.5× slower (clock rate) to 7.5× faster (cores per chip) while the performance varies from 2.0× slower (Solv) to 15.2× faster (GJK), the Intel researchers explored the reasons for the differences:

■ *Memory bandwidth.* The GPU has 4.4× the memory bandwidth, which helps explain why LBM and SAXPY run 5.0 and 5.3× faster; their working sets are hundreds of megabytes and hence don't fit into the Core i7 cache. (To access memory intensively, they did not use cache blocking on SAXPY.) Hence, the slope of the rooflines explains their performance. SpMV also has a large working set, but it only runs 1.9× because the double-precision floating point of the GTX 280 is only 1.5× faster than the Core i7. (Recall that the Fermi GTX 480 double-precision is 4× faster than the Tesla GTX 280.)

■ *Compute bandwidth.* Five of the remaining kernels are compute bound: SGEMM, Conv, FFT, MC, and Bilat. The GTX is faster by 3.9, 2.8, 3.0, 1.8, and 5.7, respectively. The first three of these use single-precision floating-point arithmetic, and GTX 280 single precision is 3 to 6× faster. (The 9× faster than the Core i7 as shown in Figure 4.27 occurs only in the very special case when the GTX 280 can issue a fused multiply-add and a multiply per clock cycle.) MC uses double precision, which explains why it's only 1.8× faster since DP performance is only 1.5× faster. Bilat uses transcendental functions, which the GTX 280 supports directly (see Figure 4.17). The

Core i7 spends two-thirds of its time calculating transcendental functions, so the GTX 280 is 5.7× faster. This observation helps point out the value of hardware support for operations that occur in your workload: double-precision floating point and perhaps even transcendentals.

■ *Cache benefits.* Ray casting (RC) is only 1.6× faster on the GTX because cache blocking with the Core i7 caches prevents it from becoming memory bandwidth bound, as it is on GPUs. Cache blocking can help Search, too. If the index trees are small so that they fit in the cache, the Core i7 is twice as fast. Larger index trees make them memory bandwidth bound. Overall, the GTX 280 runs search 1.8× faster. Cache blocking also helps Sort. While most programmers wouldn't run Sort on a SIMD processor, it can be written with a 1-bit Sort primitive called *split*. However, the split algorithm executes many more instructions than a scalar sort does. As a result, the GTX 280 runs only 0.8× as fast as the Core i7. Note that caches also help other kernels on the Core i7, since cache blocking allows SGEMM, FFT, and SpMV to become compute bound. This observation re-emphasizes the importance of cache blocking optimizations in Chapter 2. (It would be interesting to see how caches of the Fermi GTX 480 will affect the six kernels mentioned in this paragraph.)

■ *Gather-Scatter.* The multimedia SIMD extensions are of little help if the data are scattered throughout main memory; optimal performance comes only when data are aligned on 16-byte boundaries. Thus, GJK gets little benefit from SIMD on the Core i7. As mentioned above, GPUs offer gather-scatter addressing that is found in a vector architecture but omitted from SIMD extensions. The address coalescing unit helps as well by combining accesses to the same DRAM line, thereby reducing the number of gathers and scatters. The memory controller also batches accesses to the same DRAM page together. This combination means the GTX 280 runs GJK a startling 15.2× faster than the Core i7, which is larger than any single physical parameter in Figure 4.27. This observation reinforces the importance of gather-scatter to vector and GPU architectures that is missing from SIMD extensions.

■ *Synchronization.* The performance synchronization of is limited by atomic updates, which are responsible for 28% of the total runtime on the Core i7 despite its having a hardware fetch-and-increment instruction. Thus, Hist is only 1.7× faster on the GTX 280. As mentioned above, the atomic updates of the Fermi GTX 480 are 5 to 20× faster than those of the Tesla GTX 280, so once again it would be interesting to run Hist on the newer GPU. Solv solves a batch of independent constraints in a small amount of computation followed by barrier synchronization. The Core i7 benefits from the atomic instructions and a memory consistency model that ensures the right results even if not all previous accesses to memory hierarchy have completed. Without the memory consistency model, the GTX 280 version launches some batches from the system processor, which leads to the GTX 280 running 0.5× as fast as the Core i7. This observation points out how synchronization performance can be important for some data parallel problems.

It is striking how often weaknesses in the Tesla GTX 280 that were uncovered by kernels selected by Intel researchers were already being addressed in the successor architecture to Tesla: Fermi has faster double-precision floating-point performance, atomic operations, and caches. (In a related study, IBM researchers made the same observation [Bordawekar 2010].) It was also interesting that the gather-scatter support of vector architectures that predate the SIMD instructions by decades was so important to the effective usefulness of these SIMD extensions, which some had predicted before the comparison [Gebis and Patterson 2007] The Intel researchers noted that 6 of the 14 kernels would exploit SIMD better with more efficient gather-scatter support on the Core i7. This study certainly establishes the importance of cache blocking as well. It will be interesting to see if future generations of the multicore and GPU hardware, compilers, and libraries respond with features that improve performance on such kernels.

We hope that there will be more such multicore-GPU comparisons. Note that an important feature missing from this comparison was describing the level of effort to get the results for the two systems. Ideally, future comparisons would release the code used on both systems so that others could recreate the same experiments on different hardware platforms and possibly improve on the results.

4.8   Fallacies and Pitfalls

While data-level parallelism is the easiest form of parallelism after ILP from the programmer's perspective, and plausibly the easiest from the architect's perspective, it still has many fallacies and pitfalls.

Fallacy   *GPUs suffer from being coprocessors.*

While the split between main memory and GPU memory has disadvantages, there are advantages to being at a distance from the CPU.

For example, PTX exists in part because of the I/O device nature of GPUs. This level of indirection between the compiler and the hardware gives GPU architects much more flexibility than system processor architects. It's often hard to know in advance whether an architecture innovation will be well supported by compilers and libraries and be important to applications. Sometimes a new mechanism will even prove useful for one or two generations and then fade in importance as the IT world changes. PTX allows GPU architects to try innovations speculatively and drop them in subsequent generations if they disappoint or fade in importance, which encourages experimentation. The justification for inclusion is understandably much higher for system processors—and hence much less experimentation can occur—as distributing binary machine code normally implies that new features must be supported by all future generations of that architecture.

A demonstration of the value of PTX is that the Fermi architecture radically changed the hardware instruction set—from being memory-oriented like x86 to being register-oriented like MIPS *as well as* doubling the address size to 64 bits—without disrupting the NVIDIA software stack.

Pitfall *Concentrating on peak performance in vector architectures and ignoring start-up overhead.*

Early memory-memory vector processors such as the TI ASC and the CDC STAR-100 had long start-up times. For some vector problems, vectors had to be longer than 100 for the vector code to be faster than the scalar code! On the CYBER 205—derived from the STAR-100—the start-up overhead for DAXPY is 158 clock cycles, which substantially increases the break-even point. If the clock rates of the Cray-1 and the CYBER 205 were identical, the Cray-1 would be faster until the vector length is greater than 64. Because the Cray-1 clock was also faster (even though the 205 was newer), the crossover point was a vector length over 100.

Pitfall *Increasing vector performance, without comparable increases in scalar performance.*

This imbalance was a problem on many early vector processors, and a place where Seymour Cray (the architect of the Cray computers) rewrote the rules. Many of the early vector processors had comparatively slow scalar units (as well as large start-up overheads). Even today, a processor with lower vector performance but better scalar performance can outperform a processor with higher peak vector performance. Good scalar performance keeps down overhead costs (strip mining, for example) and reduces the impact of Amdahl's law.

A good example of this comes from comparing a fast scalar processor and a vector processor with lower scalar performance. The Livermore Fortran kernels are a collection of 24 scientific kernels with varying degrees of vectorization. Figure 4.31 shows the performance of two different processors on this benchmark. Despite the vector processor's higher peak performance, its low scalar

Processor	Minimum rate for any loop (MFLOPS)	Maximum rate for any loop (MFLOPS)	Harmonic mean of all 24 loops (MFLOPS)
MIPS M/120-5	0.80	3.89	1.85
Stardent-1500	0.41	10.08	1.72

Figure 4.31 Performance measurements for the Livermore Fortran kernels on two different processors. Both the MIPS M/120-5 and the Stardent-1500 (formerly the Ardent Titan-1) use a 16.7 MHz MIPS R2000 chip for the main CPU. The Stardent-1500 uses its vector unit for scalar FP and has about half the scalar performance (as measured by the minimum rate) of the MIPS M/120-5, which uses the MIPS R2010 FP chip. The vector processor is more than a factor of 2.5× faster for a highly vectorizable loop (maximum rate). However, the lower scalar performance of the Stardent-1500 negates the higher vector performance when total performance is measured by the harmonic mean on all 24 loops.

performance makes it slower than a fast scalar processor as measured by the harmonic mean.

The flip of this danger today is increasing vector performance—say, by increasing the number of lanes—without increasing scalar performance. Such myopia is another path to an unbalanced computer.

The next fallacy is closely related.

Fallacy *You can get good vector performance without providing memory bandwidth.*

As we saw with the DAXPY loop and the Roofline model, memory bandwidth is quite important to all SIMD architectures. DAXPY requires 1.5 memory references per floating-point operation, and this ratio is typical of many scientific codes. Even if the floating-point operations took no time, a Cray-1 could not increase the performance of the vector sequence used, since it is memory limited. The Cray-1 performance on Linpack jumped when the compiler used blocking to change the computation so that values could be kept in the vector registers. This approach lowered the number of memory references per FLOP and improved the performance by nearly a factor of two! Thus, the memory bandwidth on the Cray-1 became sufficient for a loop that formerly required more bandwidth.

Fallacy *On GPUs, just add more threads if you don't have enough memory performance.*

GPUs use many CUDA threads to hide the latency to main memory. If memory accesses are scattered or not correlated among CUDA threads, the memory system will get progressively slower in responding to each individual request. Eventually, even many threads will not cover the latency. For the "more CUDA threads" strategy to work, not only do you need lots of CUDA Threads, but the CUDA threads themselves also must be well behaved in terms of locality of memory accesses.

4.9 Concluding Remarks

Data-level parallelism is increasing in importance for personal mobile devices, given the popularity of applications showing the importance of audio, video, and games on these devices. When combined with an easier to program model than task-level parallelism and potentially better energy efficiency, it's easy to predict a renaissance for data-level parallelism in this next decade. Indeed, we can already see this emphasis in products, as both GPUs and traditional processors have been increasing the number of SIMD lanes at least as fast as they have been adding processors (see Figure 4.1 on page 263).

Hence, we are seeing system processors take on more of the characteristics of GPUs, and vice versa. One of the biggest differences in performance between conventional processors and GPUs has been for gather-scatter addressing. Traditional vector architectures show how to add such addressing to SIMD instructions, and we expect to see more ideas added from the well-proven vector architectures to SIMD extensions over time.

As we said at the opening of Section 4.4, the GPU question is not simply which architecture is best, but, given the hardware investment to do graphics well, how can it be enhanced to support computation that is more general? Although vector architectures have many advantages on paper, it remains to be proven whether vector architectures can be as good a foundation for graphics as GPUs.

GPU SIMD processors and compilers are still of relatively simple design. Techniques that are more aggressive will likely be introduced over time to increase GPU utilization, especially since GPU computing applications are just starting to be developed. By studying these new programs, GPU designers will surely discover and implement new machine optimizations. One question is whether the scalar processor (or control processor), which serves to save hardware and energy in vector processors, will appear within GPUs.

The Fermi architecture has already included many features found in conventional processors to make GPUs more mainstream, but there are still others necessary to close the gap. Here are a few we expect to be addressed in the near future.

- *Virtualizable GPUs.* Virtualization has proved important for servers and is the foundation of cloud computing (see Chapter 6). For GPUs to be included in the cloud, they will need to be just as virtualizable as the processors and memory that they are attached to.

- *Relatively small size of GPU memory.* A commonsense use of faster computation is to solve bigger problems, and bigger problems often have a larger memory footprint. This GPU inconsistency between speed and size can be addressed with more memory capacity. The challenge is to maintain high bandwidth while increasing capacity.

- *Direct I/O to GPU memory.* Real programs do I/O to storage devices as well as to frame buffers, and large programs can require a lot of I/O as well as a sizeable memory. Today's GPU systems must transfer between I/O devices and system memory and then between system memory and GPU memory. This extra hop significantly lowers I/O performance in some programs, making GPUs less attractive. Amdahl's law warns us what happens when you neglect one piece of the task while accelerating others. We expect that future GPUs will make all I/O first-class citizens, just as it does for frame buffer I/O today.

- *Unified physical memories.* An alternative solution to the prior two bullets is to have a single physical memory for the system and GPU, just as some inexpensive GPUs do for PMDs and laptops. The AMD Fusion architecture, announced just as this edition was being finished, is an initial merger between traditional GPUs and traditional CPUs. NVIDIA also announced Project Denver, which combines an ARM scalar processor with NVIDIA GPUs in a single address space. When these systems are shipped, it will be interesting to learn just how tightly integrated they are and the impact of integration on performance and energy of both data parallel and graphics applications.

Having covered the many versions of SIMD, the next chapter dives into the realm of MIMD.

Historical Perspective and References

Section L.6 (available online) features a discussion on the Illiac IV (a representative of the early SIMD architectures) and the Cray-1 (a representative of vector architectures). We also look at multimedia SIMD extensions and the history of GPUs.

Case Study and Exercises by Jason D. Bakos

Case Study: Implementing a Vector Kernel on a Vector Processor and GPU

Concepts illustrated by this case study

■ Programming Vector Processors

■ Programming GPUs

■ Performance Estimation

MrBayes is a popular and well-known computational biology application for inferring the evolutionary histories among a set of input species based on their multiply-aligned DNA sequence data of length n. MrBayes works by performing a heuristic search over the space of all binary tree topologies for which the inputs are the leaves. In order to evaluate a particular tree, the application must compute an $n \times 4$ conditional likelihood table (named clP) for each interior node. The table is a function of the conditional likelihood tables of the node's two descendent nodes (clL and clR, single precision floating point) and their associated $n \times 4 \times 4$ transition probability tables (tiPL and tiPR, single precision floating point). One of this application's kernels is the computation of this conditional likelihood table and is shown below:

```
for (k=0; k<seq_length; k++) {

   clP[h++] = (tiPL[AA]*clL[A] + tiPL[AC]*clL[C] + tiPL[AG]*clL[G] + tiPL[AT]*clL[T])
             *(tiPR[AA]*clR[A] + tiPR[AC]*clR[C] + tiPR[AG]*clR[G] + tiPR[AT]*clR[T]);

   clP[h++] = (tiPL[CA]*clL[A] + tiPL[CC]*clL[C] + tiPL[CG]*clL[G] + tiPL[CT]*clL[T])
             *(tiPR[CA]*clR[A] + tiPR[CC]*clR[C] + tiPR[CG]*clR[G] + tiPR[CT]*clR[T]);

   clP[h++] = (tiPL[GA]*clL[A] + tiPL[GC]*clL[C] + tiPL[GG]*clL[G] + tiPL[GT]*clL[T])
             *(tiPR[GA]*clR[A] + tiPR[GC]*clR[C] + tiPR[GG]*clR[G] + tiPR[GT]*clR[T]);

   clP[h++] = (tiPL[TA]*clL[A] + tiPL[TC]*clL[C] + tiPL[TG]*clL[G] + tiPL[TT]*clL[T])
             *(tiPR[TA]*clR[A] + tiPR[TC]*clR[C] + tiPR[TG]*clR[G] + tiPR[TT]*clR[T]);

   clL += 4;

   clR += 4;

   tiPL += 16;

   tiPR += 16;

}
```

Constants	Values
AA,AC,AG,AT	0,1,2,3
CA,CC,CG,CT	4,5,6,7
GA,GC,GG,GT	8,9,10,11
TA,TC,TG,TT	12,13,14,15
A,C,G,T	0,1,2,3

Figure 4.32 Constants and values for the case study.

4.1 [25] <4.2, 4.3> Assume the constants shown in Figure 4.32. Show the code for MIPS and VMIPS. Assume we cannot use scatter-gather loads or stores. Assume the starting addresses of tiPL, tiPR, clL, clR, and clP are in RtiPL, RtiPR, RclL, RclR, and RclP, respectively. Assume the VMIPS register length is user programmable and can be assigned by setting the special register VL (e.g., li VL 4). To facilitate vector addition reductions, assume that we add the following instructions to VMIPS:

SUMR.S Fd, Vs Vector Summation Reduction Single Precision:

This instruction performs a summation reduction on a vector register Vs, writing to the sum into scalar register Fd.

4.2 [5] <4.2, 4.3> Assuming seq_length == 500, what is the dynamic instruction count for both implementations?

4.3 [25] <4.2, 4.3> Assume that the vector reduction instruction is executed on the vector functional unit, similar to a vector add instruction. Show how the code sequence lays out in convoys assuming a single instance of each vector functional unit. How many chimes will the code require? How many cycles per FLOP are needed, ignoring vector instruction issue overhead?

4.4 [15] <4.2, 4.3> Now assume that we can use scatter-gather loads and stores (LVI and SVI). Assume that tiPL, tiPR, clL, clR, and clP are arranged consecutively in memory. For example, if seq_length==500, the tiPR array would begin 500 * 4 bytes after the tiPL array. How does this affect the way you can write the VMIPS code for this kernel? Assume that you can initialize vector registers with integers using the following technique which would, for example, initialize vector register V1 with values (0,0,2000,2000):

```
LI R2,0
SW R2,vec
SW R2,vec+4
LI R2,2000
SW R2,vec+8
SW R2,vec+12
LV V1,vec
```

Assume the maximum vector length is 64. Is there any way performance can be improved using gather-scatter loads? If so, by how much?

4.5 [25] <4.4> Now assume we want to implement the MrBayes kernel on a GPU using a single thread block. Rewrite the C code of the kernel using CUDA. Assume that pointers to the conditional likelihood and transition probability tables are specified as parameters to the kernel. Invoke one thread for each iteration of the loop. Load any reused values into shared memory before performing operations on it.

4.6 [15] <4.4> With CUDA we can use coarse-grain parallelism at the block level to compute the conditional likelihoods of multiple nodes in parallel. Assume that we want to compute the conditional likelihoods from the bottom of the tree up. Assume that the conditional likelihood and transition probability arrays are organized in memory as described in question 4 and the group of tables for each of the 12 leaf nodes is also stored in consecutive memory locations in the order of node number. Assume that we want to compute the conditional likelihood for nodes 12 to 17, as shown in Figure 4.33. Change the method by which you compute the array indices in your answer from Exercise 4.5 to include the block number.

4.7 [15] <4.4> Convert your code from Exercise 4.6 into PTX code. How many instructions are needed for the kernel?

4.8 [10] <4.4> How well do you expect this code to perform on a GPU? Explain your answer.

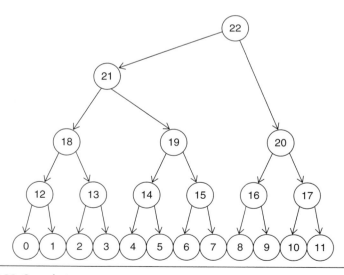

Figure 4.33 Sample tree.

Exercises

4.9   [10/20/20/15/15] <4.2> Consider the following code, which multiplies two vectors that contain single-precision complex values:

```
for (i=0;i<300;i++) {
        c_re[i] = a_re[i] * b_re[i] - a_im[i] * b_im[i];
        c_im[i] = a_re[i] * b_im[i] + a_im[i] * b_re[i];
}
```

Assume that the processor runs at 700 MHz and has a maximum vector length of 64. The load/store unit has a start-up overhead of 15 cycles; the multiply unit, 8 cycles; and the add/subtract unit, 5 cycles.

   a. [10] <4.2> What is the arithmetic intensity of this kernel? Justify your answer.

   b. [20] <4.2> Convert this loop into VMIPS assembly code using strip mining.

   c. [20] <4.2> Assuming chaining and a single memory pipeline, how many chimes are required? How many clock cycles are required per complex result value, including start-up overhead?

   d. [15] <4.2> If the vector sequence is chained, how many clock cycles are required per complex result value, including overhead?

   e. [15] <4.2> Now assume that the processor has three memory pipelines and chaining. If there are no bank conflicts in the loop's accesses, how many clock cycles are required per result?

4.10   [30] <4.4> In this problem, we will compare the performance of a vector processor with a hybrid system that contains a scalar processor and a GPU-based coprocessor. In the hybrid system, the host processor has superior scalar performance to the GPU, so in this case all scalar code is executed on the host processor while all vector code is executed on the GPU. We will refer to the first system as the vector computer and the second system as the hybrid computer. Assume that your target application contains a vector kernel with an arithmetic intensity of 0.5 FLOPs per DRAM byte accessed; however, the application also has a scalar component which that must be performed before and after the kernel in order to prepare the input vectors and output vectors, respectively. For a sample dataset, the scalar portion of the code requires 400 ms of execution time on both the vector processor and the host processor in the hybrid system. The kernel reads input vectors consisting of 200 MB of data and has output data consisting of 100 MB of data. The vector processor has a peak memory bandwidth of 30 GB/sec and the GPU has a peak memory bandwidth of 150 GB/sec. The hybrid system has an additional overhead that requires all input vectors to be transferred between the host memory and GPU local memory before and after the kernel is invoked. The hybrid system has a direct memory access (DMA) bandwidth of 10 GB/sec and an average latency of 10 ms. Assume that both the vector processor and GPU are performance bound by memory bandwidth. Compute the execution time required by both computers for this application.

4.11 [15/25/25] <4.4, 4.5> Section 4.5 discussed the reduction operation that reduces a vector down to a scalar by repeated application of an operation. A reduction is a special type of a loop recurrence. An example is shown below:

```
dot=0.0;
for (i=0;i<64;i++) dot = dot + a[i] * b[i];
```

A vectorizing compiler might apply a transformation called *scalar expansion*, which expands dot into a vector and splits the loop such that the multiply can be performed with a vector operation, leaving the reduction as a separate scalar operation:

```
for (i=0;i<64;i++) dot[i] = a[i] * b[i];
for (i=1;i<64;i++) dot[0] = dot[0] + dot[i];
```

As mentioned in Section 4.5, if we allow the floating-point addition to be associative, there are several techniques available for parallelizing the reduction.

a. [15] <4.4, 4.5> One technique is called recurrence doubling, which adds sequences of progressively shorter vectors (i.e., two 32-element vectors, then two 16-element vectors, and so on). Show how the C code would look for executing the second loop in this way.

b. [25] <4.4, 4.5> In some vector processors, the individual elements within the vector registers are addressable. In this case, the operands to a vector operation may be two different parts of the same vector register. This allows another solution for the reduction called *partial sums*. The idea is to reduce the vector to m sums where m is the total latency through the vector functional unit, including the operand read and write times. Assume that the VMIPS vector registers are addressable (e.g., you can initiate a vector operation with the operand V1(16), indicating that the input operand begins with element 16). Also, assume that the total latency for adds, including the operand read and result write, is eight cycles. Write a VMIPS code sequence that reduces the contents of V1 to eight partial sums.

c. [25] <4.4, 4.5> When performing a reduction on a GPU, one thread is associated with each element in the input vector. The first step is for each thread to write its corresponding value into shared memory. Next, each thread enters a loop that adds each pair of input values. This reduces the number of elements by half after each iteration, meaning that the number of active threads also reduces by half after each iteration. In order to maximize the performance of the reduction, the number of fully populated warps should be maximized throughout the course of the loop. In other words, the active threads should be contiguous. Also, each thread should index the shared array in such a way as to avoid bank conflicts in the shared memory. The following loop violates only the first of these guidelines and also uses the modulo operator which is very expensive for GPUs:

```
unsigned int tid = threadIdx.x;
for(unsigned int s=1; s < blockDim.x; s *= 2) {
if ((tid % (2*s)) == 0) {
sdata[tid] += sdata[tid + s];
}
__syncthreads();
}
```

Rewrite the loop to meet these guidelines and eliminate the use of the modulo operator. Assume that there are 32 threads per warp and a bank conflict occurs whenever two or more threads from the same warp reference an index whose modulo by 32 are equal.

4.12 [10/10/10/10] <4.3> The following kernel performs a portion of the finite-difference time-domain (FDTD) method for computing Maxwell's equations in a three-dimensional space, part of one of the SPEC06fp benchmarks:

```
for (int x=0; x<NX-1; x++) {
for (int y=0; y<NY-1; y++) {
for (int z=0; z<NZ-1; z++) {
int index = x*NY*NZ + y*NZ + z;
if (y>0 && x >0) {
material = IDx[index];
dH1 = (Hz[index] - Hz[index-incrementY])/dy[y];
dH2 = (Hy[index] - Hy[index-incrementZ])/dz[z];
Ex[index] = Ca[material]*Ex[index]+Cb[material]*(dH2-dH1);
}}}}
```

Assume that dH1, dH2, Hy, Hz, dy, dz, Ca, Cb, and Ex are all single-precision floating-point arrays. Assume IDx is an array of unsigned int.

a. [10] <4.3> What is the arithmetic intensity of this kernel?

b. [10] <4.3> Is this kernel amenable to vector or SIMD execution? Why or why not?

c. [10] <4.3> Assume this kernel is to be executed on a processor that has 30 GB/sec of memory bandwidth. Will this kernel be memory bound or compute bound?

d. [10] <4.3> Develop a roofline model for this processor, assuming it has a peak computational throughput of 85 GFLOP/sec.

4.13 [10/15] <4.4> Assume a GPU architecture that contains 10 SIMD processors. Each SIMD instruction has a width of 32 and each SIMD processor contains 8 lanes for single-precision arithmetic and load/store instructions, meaning that each non-diverged SIMD instruction can produce 32 results every 4 cycles. Assume a kernel that has divergent branches that causes on average 80% of threads to be active. Assume that 70% of all SIMD instructions executed are single-precision arithmetic and 20% are load/store. Since not all memory latencies are covered, assume an average SIMD instruction issue rate of 0.85. Assume that the GPU has a clock speed of 1.5 GHz.

a. [10] <4.4> Compute the throughput, in GFLOP/sec, for this kernel on this GPU.

b. [15] <4.4> Assume that you have the following choices:

(1) Increasing the number of single-precision lanes to 16

(2) Increasing the number of SIMD processors to 15 (assume this change doesn't affect any other performance metrics and that the code scales to the additional processors)

(3) Adding a cache that will effectively reduce memory latency by 40%, which will increase instruction issue rate to 0.95

What is speedup in throughput for each of these improvements?

4.14 [10/15/15] <4.5> In this exercise, we will examine several loops and analyze their potential for parallelization.

a. [10] <4.5> Does the following loop have a loop-carried dependency?

```
for (i=0;i<100;i++) {
A[i] = B[2*i+4];
B[4*i+5] = A[i];
}
```

b. [15] <4.5> In the following loop, find all the true dependences, output dependences, and antidependences. Eliminate the output dependences and antidependences by renaming.

```
for (i=0;i<100;i++) {
A[i] = A[i] * B[i]; /* S1 */
B[i] = A[i] + c; /* S2 */
A[i] = C[i] * c; /* S3 */
C[i] = D[i] * A[i]; /* S4 */
```

c. [15] <4.5> Consider the following loop:

```
for (i=0;i < 100;i++) {
A[i] = A[i] + B[i]; /* S1 */
B[i+1] = C[i] + D[i]; /* S2 */
}
```

Are there dependences between S1 and S2? Is this loop parallel? If not, show how to make it parallel.

4.15　[10] <4.4> List and describe at least four factors that influence the performance of GPU kernels. In other words, which runtime behaviors that are caused by the kernel code cause a reduction in resource utilization during kernel execution?

4.16　[10] <4.4> Assume a hypothetical GPU with the following characteristics:

- Clock rate 1.5 GHz

- Contains 16 SIMD processors, each containing 16 single-precision floating-point units

- Has 100 GB/sec off-chip memory bandwidth

Without considering memory bandwidth, what is the peak single-precision floating-point throughput for this GPU in GLFOP/sec, assuming that all memory latencies can be hidden? Is this throughput sustainable given the memory bandwidth limitation?

4.17　[60] <4.4> For this programming exercise, you will write and characterize the behavior of a CUDA kernel that contains a high amount of data-level parallelism but also contains conditional execution behavior. Use the NVIDIA CUDA Toolkit along with GPU-SIM from the University of British Columbia (*http://www.ece.ubc.ca/~aamodt/gpgpu-sim/*) or the CUDA Profiler to write and compile a CUDA kernel that performs 100 iterations of Conway's Game of Life for a 256 × 256 game board and returns the final state of the game board to the host. Assume that the board is initialized by the host. Associate one thread with each cell. Make sure you add a barrier after each game iteration. Use the following game rules:

- Any live cell with fewer than two live neighbors dies.

- Any live cell with two or three live neighbors lives on to the next generation.

- Any live cell with more than three live neighbors dies.

- Any dead cell with exactly three live neighbors becomes a live cell.

After finishing the kernel answer the following questions:

a.　[60] <4.4> Compile your code using the –ptx option and inspect the PTX representation of your kernel. How many PTX instructions make up the PTX implementation of your kernel? Did the conditional sections of your kernel include branch instructions or only predicated non-branch instructions?

b.　[60] <4.4> After executing your code in the simulator, what is the dynamic instruction count? What is the achieved instructions per cycle (IPC) or instruction issue rate? What is the dynamic instruction breakdown in terms of control instructions, arithmetic-logical unit (ALU) instructions, and memory instructions? Are there any shared memory bank conflicts? What is the effective off-chip memory bandwidth?

c.　[60] <4.4> Implement an improved version of your kernel where off-chip memory references are coalesced and observe the differences in runtime performance.

5

Thread-Level Parallelism

The turning away from the conventional organization came in the middle 1960s, when the law of diminishing returns began to take effect in the effort to increase the operational speed of a computer. . . . Electronic circuits are ultimately limited in their speed of operation by the speed of light . . . and many of the circuits were already operating in the nanosecond range.

W. Jack Bouknight et al.
The Illiac IV System (1972)

We are dedicating all of our future product development to multicore designs. We believe this is a key inflection point for the industry.

Intel President Paul Otellini,
describing Intel's future direction at the
Intel Developer Forum in 2005

5.1 Introduction

As the quotations that open this chapter show, the view that advances in uni-processor architecture were nearing an end has been held by some researchers for many years. Clearly, these views were premature; in fact, during the period of 1986–2003, uniprocessor performance growth, driven by the microprocessor, was at its highest rate since the first transistorized computers in the late 1950s and early 1960s.

Nonetheless, the importance of multiprocessors was growing throughout the 1990s as designers sought a way to build servers and supercomputers that achieved higher performance than a single microprocessor, while exploiting the tremendous cost-performance advantages of commodity microprocessors. As we discussed in Chapters 1 and 3, the slowdown in uniprocessor performance arising from diminishing returns in exploiting instruction-level parallelism (ILP) combined with growing concern over power, is leading to a new era in computer architecture—an era where multiprocessors play a major role from the low end to the high end. The second quotation captures this clear inflection point.

This increased importance of multiprocessing reflects several major factors:

- The dramatically lower efficiencies in silicon and energy use that were encountered between 2000 and 2005 as designers attempted to find and exploit more ILP, which turned out to be inefficient, since power and silicon costs grew faster than performance. Other than ILP, the only scalable and general-purpose way we know how to increase performance faster than the basic technology allows (from a switching perspective) is through multiprocessing.

- A growing interest in high-end servers as cloud computing and software-as-a-service become more important.

- A growth in data-intensive applications driven by the availability of massive amounts of data on the Internet.

- The insight that increasing performance on the desktop is less important (outside of graphics, at least), either because current performance is acceptable or because highly compute- and data-intensive applications are being done in the cloud.

- An improved understanding of how to use multiprocessors effectively, especially in server environments where there is significant natural parallelism, arising from large datasets, natural parallelism (which occurs in scientific codes), or parallelism among large numbers of independent requests (request-level parallelism).

- The advantages of leveraging a design investment by replication rather than unique design; all multiprocessor designs provide such leverage.

In this chapter, we focus on exploiting thread-level parallelism (TLP). TLP implies the existence of multiple program counters and hence is exploited primarily through MIMDs. Although MIMDs have been around for decades, the movement of thread-level parallelism to the forefront across the range of computing from embedded applications to high-end severs is relatively recent. Likewise, the extensive use of thread-level parallelism for general-purpose applications, versus scientific applications, is relatively new.

Our focus in this chapter is on *multiprocessors*, which we define as computers consisting of tightly coupled processors whose coordination and usage are typically controlled by a single operating system and that share memory through a shared address space. Such systems exploit thread-level parallelism through two different software models. The first is the execution of a tightly coupled set of threads collaborating on a single task, which is typically called *parallel processing*. The second is the execution of multiple, relatively independent processes that may originate from one or more users, which is a form of *request-level parallelism*, although at a much smaller scale than what we explore in the next chapter. Request-level parallelism may be exploited by a single application running on multiple processors, such as a database responding to queries, or multiple applications running independently, often called *multiprogramming*.

The multiprocessors we examine in this chapter typically range in size from a dual processor to dozens of processors and communicate and coordinate through the sharing of memory. Although sharing through memory implies a shared address space, it does not necessarily mean there is a single physical memory. Such multiprocessors include both single-chip systems with multiple cores, known as *multicore*, and computers consisting of multiple chips, each of which may be a multicore design.

In addition to true multiprocessors, we will return to the topic of multithreading, a technique that supports multiple threads executing in an interleaved fashion on a single multiple issue processor. Many multicore processors also include support for multithreading.

In the next chapter, we consider ultrascale computers built from very large numbers of processors, connected with networking technology and often called *clusters*; these large-scale systems are typically used for cloud computing with a model that assumes either massive numbers of independent requests or highly parallel, intensive compute tasks. When these clusters grow to tens of thousands of servers and beyond, we call them *warehouse-scale computers*.

In addition to the multiprocessors we study here and the warehouse-scaled systems of the next chapter, there are a range of special large-scale multiprocessor systems, sometimes called *multicomputers*, which are less tightly coupled than the multiprocessors examined in this chapter but more tightly coupled than the warehouse-scale systems of the next. The primary use for such multicomputers is in high-end scientific computation. Many other books, such as Culler, Singh, and Gupta [1999], cover such systems in detail. Because of the large and changing nature of the field of multiprocessing (the just-mentioned Culler et al. reference is over 1000 pages and discusses only multiprocessing!), we have chosen to focus our attention on what we believe is the most important and general-purpose portions of the computing space. Appendix I discusses some of the issues that arise in building such computers in the context of large-scale scientific applications.

Thus, our focus will be on multiprocessors with a small to moderate number of processors (2 to 32). Such designs vastly dominate in terms of both units and dollars. We will pay only slight attention to the larger-scale multiprocessor design space (33 or more processors), primarily in Appendix I, which covers more aspects of the design of such processors, as well as the behavior performance for parallel scientific workloads, a primary class of applications for large-scale multiprocessors. In large-scale multiprocessors, the interconnection networks are a critical part of the design; Appendix F focuses on that topic.

Multiprocessor Architecture: Issues and Approach

To take advantage of an MIMD multiprocessor with n processors, we must usually have at least n threads or processes to execute. The independent threads within a single process are typically identified by the programmer or created by the operating system (from multiple independent requests). At the other extreme, a thread may consist of a few tens of iterations of a loop, generated by a parallel compiler exploiting data parallelism in the loop. Although the amount of computation assigned to a thread, called the *grain size*, is important in considering how to exploit thread-level parallelism efficiently, the important qualitative distinction from instruction-level parallelism is that thread-level parallelism is identified at a high level by the software system or programmer and that the threads consist of hundreds to millions of instructions that may be executed in parallel.

Threads can also be used to exploit data-level parallelism, although the overhead is likely to be higher than would be seen with an SIMD processor or with a GPU (see Chapter 4). This overhead means that grain size must be sufficiently large to exploit the parallelism efficiently. For example, although a vector processor or GPU may be able to efficiently parallelize operations on short vectors, the resulting grain size when the parallelism is split among many threads may be so small that the overhead makes the exploitation of the parallelism prohibitively expensive in an MIMD.

Existing shared-memory multiprocessors fall into two classes, depending on the number of processors involved, which in turn dictates a memory organization and interconnect strategy. We refer to the multiprocessors by their memory organization because what constitutes a small or large number of processors is likely to change over time.

The first group, which we call *symmetric (shared-memory) multiprocessors* (SMPs), or *centralized shared-memory multiprocessors*, features small numbers of cores, typically eight or fewer. For multiprocessors with such small processor counts, it is possible for the processors to share a single centralized memory that all processors have equal access to, hence the term *symmetric*. In multicore chips, the memory is effectively shared in a centralized fashion among the cores, and all existing multicores are SMPs. When more than one multicore is connected, there are separate memories for each multicore, so the memory is distributed rather than centralized.

SMP architectures are also sometimes called *uniform memory access* (UMA) multiprocessors, arising from the fact that all processors have a uniform latency from memory, even if the memory is organized into multiple banks. Figure 5.1 shows what these multiprocessors look like. The architecture of SMPs is the topic of Section 5.2, and we explain the approach in the context of a multicore.

The alternative design approach consists of multiprocessors with physically distributed memory, called *distributed shared memory* (DSM). Figure 5.2 shows what these multiprocessors look like. To support larger processor counts, memory must be distributed among the processors rather than centralized; otherwise, the memory system would not be able to support the bandwidth demands of a larger number of processors without incurring excessively long access latency. With the rapid increase in processor performance and the associated increase in a processor's memory bandwidth requirements, the size of a multiprocessor for which distributed memory is preferred continues to shrink. The introduction of multicore processors has meant that even two-chip multiprocessors use distributed memory. The larger number of processors also raises the need for a high-bandwidth interconnect, of which we will see examples in Appendix F. Both

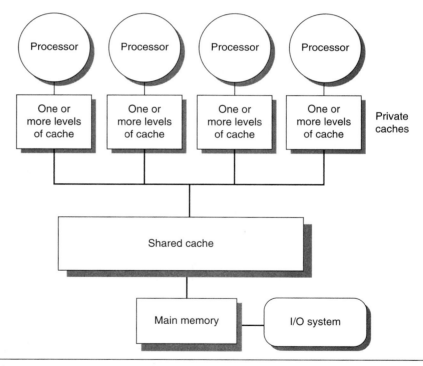

Figure 5.1 Basic structure of a centralized shared-memory multiprocessor based on a multicore chip. Multiple processor–cache subsystems share the same physical memory, typically with one level of shared cache, and one or more levels of private per-core cache. The key architectural property is the uniform access time to all of the memory from all of the processors. In a multichip version the shared cache would be omitted and the bus or interconnection network connecting the processors to memory would run between chips as opposed to within a single chip.

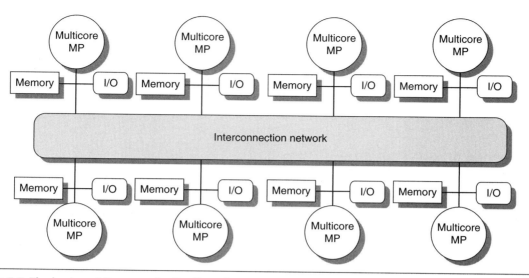

Figure 5.2 The basic architecture of a distributed-memory multiprocessor in 2011 typically consists of a multi-core multiprocessor chip with memory and possibly I/O attached and an interface to an interconnection network that connects all the nodes. Each processor core shares the entire memory, although the access time to the lock memory attached to the core's chip will be much faster than the access time to remote memories.

directed networks (i.e., switches) and indirect networks (typically multidimensional meshes) are used.

Distributing the memory among the nodes both increases the bandwidth and reduces the latency to local memory. A DSM multiprocessor is also called a *NUMA* (nonuniform memory access), since the access time depends on the location of a data word in memory. The key disadvantages for a DSM are that communicating data among processors becomes somewhat more complex, and a DSM requires more effort in the software to take advantage of the increased memory bandwidth afforded by distributed memories. Because all multicore-based multiprocessors with more than one processor chip (or socket) use distributed memory, we will explain the operation of distributed memory multiprocessors from this viewpoint.

In both SMP and DSM architectures, communication among threads occurs through a shared address space, meaning that a memory reference can be made by any processor to any memory location, assuming it has the correct access rights. The term *shared memory* associated with both SMP and DSM refers to the fact that the *address space* is shared.

In contrast, the clusters and warehouse-scale computers of the next chapter look like individual computers connected by a network, and the memory of one processor cannot be accessed by another processor without the assistance of software protocols running on both processors. In such designs, message-passing protocols are used to communicate data among processors.

Challenges of Parallel Processing

The application of multiprocessors ranges from running independent tasks with essentially no communication to running parallel programs where threads must communicate to complete the task. Two important hurdles, both explainable with Amdahl's law, make parallel processing challenging. The degree to which these hurdles are difficult or easy is determined both by the application and by the architecture.

The first hurdle has to do with the limited parallelism available in programs, and the second arises from the relatively high cost of communications. Limitations in available parallelism make it difficult to achieve good speedups in any parallel processor, as our first example shows.

Example   Suppose you want to achieve a speedup of 80 with 100 processors. What fraction of the original computation can be sequential?

Answer   Recall from Chapter 1 that Amdahl's law is

$$\text{Speedup} = \frac{1}{\dfrac{\text{Fraction}_{enhanced}}{\text{Speedup}_{enhanced}} + (1 - \text{Fraction}_{enhanced})}$$

For simplicity in this example, assume that the program operates in only two modes: parallel with all processors fully used, which is the enhanced mode, or serial with only one processor in use. With this simplification, the speedup in enhanced mode is simply the number of processors, while the fraction of enhanced mode is the time spent in parallel mode. Substituting into the previous equation:

$$80 = \frac{1}{\dfrac{\text{Fraction}_{parallel}}{100} + (1 - \text{Fraction}_{parallel})}$$

Simplifying this equation yields:

$$0.8 \times \text{Fraction}_{parallel} + 80 \times (1 - \text{Fraction}_{parallel}) = 1$$
$$80 - 79.2 \times \text{Fraction}_{parallel} = 1$$
$$\text{Fraction}_{parallel} = \frac{80 - 1}{79.2}$$
$$\text{Fraction}_{parallel} = 0.9975$$

Thus, to achieve a speedup of 80 with 100 processors, only 0.25% of the original computation can be sequential. Of course, to achieve linear speedup (speedup of n with n processors), the entire program must usually be parallel with no serial portions. In practice, programs do not just operate in fully parallel or sequential mode, but often use less than the full complement of the processors when running in parallel mode.

The second major challenge in parallel processing involves the large latency of remote access in a parallel processor. In existing shared-memory multiprocessors, communication of data between separate cores may cost 35 to 50 clock cycles and among cores on separate chips anywhere from 100 clock cycles to as much as 500 or more clock cycles (for large-scale multiprocessors), depending on the communication mechanism, the type of interconnection network, and the scale of the multiprocessor. The effect of long communication delays is clearly substantial. Let's consider a simple example.

Example   Suppose we have an application running on a 32-processor multiprocessor, which has a 200 ns time to handle reference to a remote memory. For this application, assume that all the references except those involving communication hit in the local memory hierarchy, which is slightly optimistic. Processors are stalled on a remote request, and the processor clock rate is 3.3 GHz. If the base CPI (assuming that all references hit in the cache) is 0.5, how much faster is the multiprocessor if there is no communication versus if 0.2% of the instructions involve a remote communication reference?

 Answer   It is simpler to first calculate the clock cycles per instruction. The effective CPI for the multiprocessor with 0.2% remote references is

$$\text{CPI} = \text{Base CPI} + \text{Remote request rate} \times \text{Remote request cost}$$
$$= 0.5 + 0.2\% \times \text{Remote request cost}$$

The remote request cost is

$$\frac{\text{Remote access cost}}{\text{Cycle time}} = \frac{200 \text{ ns}}{0.3 \text{ ns}} = 666 \text{ cycles}$$

Hence, we can compute the CPI:

$$\text{CPI} = 0.5 + 1.2 = 1.7$$

The multiprocessor with all local references is $1.7/0.5 = 3.4$ times faster. In practice, the performance analysis is much more complex, since some fraction of the noncommunication references will miss in the local hierarchy and the remote access time does not have a single constant value. For example, the cost of a remote reference could be quite a bit worse, since contention caused by many references trying to use the global interconnect can lead to increased delays.

These problems—insufficient parallelism and long-latency remote communication—are the two biggest performance challenges in using multiprocessors. The problem of inadequate application parallelism must be attacked primarily in software with new algorithms that offer better parallel performance, as well as by software systems that maximize the amount of time spent executing with the full complement of processors. Reducing the impact of long remote latency can be attacked both by the architecture and by the programmer. For example, we can reduce the frequency of remote accesses with either hardware mechanisms, such as caching shared data, or software mechanisms, such as restructuring the data to make more accesses local. We can try to tolerate the latency by using multi-threading (discussed later in this chapter) or by using prefetching (a topic we cover extensively in Chapter 2).

Much of this chapter focuses on techniques for reducing the impact of long remote communication latency. For example, Sections 5.2 through 5.4 discuss how caching can be used to reduce remote access frequency, while maintaining a coherent view of memory. Section 5.5 discusses synchronization, which, because it inherently involves interprocessor communication and also can limit parallelism, is a major potential bottleneck. Section 5.6 covers latency-hiding techniques and memory consistency models for shared memory. In Appendix I, we focus primarily on larger-scale multiprocessors that are used predominantly for scientific work. In that appendix, we examine the nature of such applications and the challenges of achieving speedup with dozens to hundreds of processors.

5.2 Centralized Shared-Memory Architectures

The observation that the use of large, multilevel caches can substantially reduce the memory bandwidth demands of a processor is the key insight that motivates centralized memory multiprocessors. Originally, these processors were all single-core and often took an entire board, and memory was located on a shared bus. With more recent, higher-performance processors, the memory demands have outstripped the capability of reasonable buses, and recent microprocessors directly connect memory to a single chip, which is sometimes called a *backside* or *memory bus* to distinguish it from the bus used to connect to I/O. Accessing a chip's local memory whether for an I/O operation or for an access from another chip requires going through the chip that "owns" that memory. Thus, access to memory is asymmetric: faster to the local memory and slower to the remote memory. In a multicore that memory is shared among all the cores on a single chip, but the asymmetric access to the memory of one multicore from the memory of another remains.

Symmetric shared-memory machines usually support the caching of both shared and private data. *Private data* are used by a single processor, while *shared data* are used by multiple processors, essentially providing communication among the processors through reads and writes of the shared data. When a private item is cached, its location is migrated to the cache, reducing the average access time as well as the memory bandwidth required. Since no other processor uses the data, the program behavior is identical to that in a uniprocessor. When shared data are cached, the shared value may be replicated in multiple caches. In addition to the reduction in access latency and required memory bandwidth, this replication also provides a reduction in contention that may exist for shared data items that are being read by multiple processors simultaneously. Caching of shared data, however, introduces a new problem: cache coherence.

What Is Multiprocessor Cache Coherence?

Unfortunately, caching shared data introduces a new problem because the view of memory held by two different processors is through their individual caches, which, without any additional precautions, could end up seeing two different values. Figure 5.3 illustrates the problem and shows how two different processors can have two different values for the same location. This difficulty is generally referred to as the *cache coherence problem*. Notice that the coherence problem exists because we have both a global state, defined primarily by the main memory, and a local state, defined by the individual caches, which are private to each processor core. Thus, in a multicore where some level of caching may be shared (for example, an L3), while some levels are private (for example, L1 and L2), the coherence problem still exists and must be solved.

Informally, we could say that a memory system is coherent if any read of a data item returns the most recently written value of that data item. This definition, although intuitively appealing, is vague and simplistic; the reality is much more complex. This simple definition contains two different aspects of memory system behavior, both of which are critical to writing correct shared-memory programs. The first aspect, called *coherence*, defines what values can be returned by a read. The second aspect, called *consistency*, determines when a written value will be returned by a read. Let's look at coherence first.

A memory system is coherent if

1. A read by processor P to location X that follows a write by P to X, with no writes of X by another processor occurring between the write and the read by P, always returns the value written by P.

Time	Event	Cache contents for processor A	Cache contents for processor B	Memory contents for location X
0				1
1	Processor A reads X	1		1
2	Processor B reads X	1	1	1
3	Processor A stores 0 into X	0	1	0

Figure 5.3 The cache coherence problem for a single memory location (X), read and written by two processors (A and B). We initially assume that neither cache contains the variable and that X has the value 1. We also assume a write-through cache; a write-back cache adds some additional but similar complications. After the value of X has been written by A, A's cache and the memory both contain the new value, but B's cache does not, and if B reads the value of X it will receive 1!

2. A read by a processor to location X that follows a write by another processor
    to X returns the written value if the read and write are sufficiently separated
    in time and no other writes to X occur between the two accesses.

3. Writes to the same location are *serialized*; that is, two writes to the same loca-
    tion by any two processors are seen in the same order by all processors. For
    example, if the values 1 and then 2 are written to a location, processors can
    never read the value of the location as 2 and then later read it as 1.

The first property simply preserves program order—we expect this property
to be true even in uniprocessors. The second property defines the notion of
what it means to have a coherent view of memory: If a processor could
continuously read an old data value, we would clearly say that memory was
incoherent.

The need for write serialization is more subtle, but equally important. Suppose we did not serialize writes, and processor P1 writes location X followed by
P2 writing location X. Serializing the writes ensures that every processor will see
the write done by P2 at some point. If we did not serialize the writes, it might be
the case that some processors could see the write of P2 first and then see the write
of P1, maintaining the value written by P1 indefinitely. The simplest way to
avoid such difficulties is to ensure that all writes to the same location are seen in
the same order; this property is called *write serialization*.

Although the three properties just described are sufficient to ensure coherence, the question of when a written value will be seen is also important. To see
why, observe that we cannot require that a read of X instantaneously see the
value written for X by some other processor. If, for example, a write of X on one
processor precedes a read of X on another processor by a very small time, it may
be impossible to ensure that the read returns the value of the data written, since
the written data may not even have left the processor at that point. The issue of
exactly *when* a written value must be seen by a reader is defined by a *memory
consistency model*—a topic discussed in Section 5.6.

Coherence and consistency are complementary: Coherence defines the
behavior of reads and writes to the same memory location, while consistency
defines the behavior of reads and writes with respect to accesses to other memory locations. For now, make the following two assumptions. First, a write does
not complete (and allow the next write to occur) until all processors have seen
the effect of that write. Second, the processor does not change the order of any
write with respect to any other memory access. These two conditions mean
that, if a processor writes location A followed by location B, any processor that
sees the new value of B must also see the new value of A. These restrictions
allow the processor to reorder reads, but forces the processor to finish a write in
program order. We will rely on this assumption until we reach Section 5.6,
where we will see exactly the implications of this definition, as well as the
alternatives.

Basic Schemes for Enforcing Coherence

The coherence problem for multiprocessors and I/O, although similar in origin, has different characteristics that affect the appropriate solution. Unlike I/O, where multiple data copies are a rare event—one to be avoided whenever possible—a program running on multiple processors will normally have copies of the same data in several caches. In a coherent multiprocessor, the caches provide both *migration* and *replication* of shared data items.

Coherent caches provide migration, since a data item can be moved to a local cache and used there in a transparent fashion. This migration reduces both the latency to access a shared data item that is allocated remotely and the bandwidth demand on the shared memory.

Coherent caches also provide replication for shared data that are being simultaneously read, since the caches make a copy of the data item in the local cache. Replication reduces both latency of access and contention for a read shared data item. Supporting this migration and replication is critical to performance in accessing shared data. Thus, rather than trying to solve the problem by avoiding it in software, multiprocessors adopt a hardware solution by introducing a protocol to maintain coherent caches.

The protocols to maintain coherence for multiple processors are called *cache coherence protocols*. Key to implementing a cache coherence protocol is tracking the state of any sharing of a data block. There are two classes of protocols in use, each of which uses different techniques to track the sharing status:

- *Directory based*—The sharing status of a particular block of physical memory is kept in one location, called the *directory*. There are two very different types of directory-based cache coherence. In an SMP, we can use one centralized directory, associated with the memory or some other single serialization point, such as the outermost cache in a multicore. In a DSM, it makes no sense to have a single directory, since that would create a single point of contention and make it difficult to scale to many multicore chips given the memory demands of multicores with eight or more cores. Distributed directories are more complex than a single directory, and such designs are the subject of Section 5.4.

- *Snooping*—Rather than keeping the state of sharing in a single directory, every cache that has a copy of the data from a block of physical memory could track the sharing status of the block. In an SMP, the caches are typically all accessible via some broadcast medium (e.g., a bus connects the per-core caches to the shared cache or memory), and all cache controllers monitor or *snoop* on the medium to determine whether or not they have a copy of a block that is requested on a bus or switch access. Snooping can also be used as the coherence protocol for a multichip multiprocessor, and some designs support a snooping protocol on top of a directory protocol within each multicore!

Snooping protocols became popular with multiprocessors using microprocessors (single-core) and caches attached to a single shared memory by a bus.

The bus provided a convenient broadcast medium to implement the snooping protocols. Multicore architectures changed the picture significantly, since all multicores share some level of cache on the chip. Thus, some designs switched to using directory protocols, since the overhead was small. To allow the reader to become familiar with both types of protocols, we focus on a snooping protocol here and discuss a directory protocol when we come to DSM architectures.

Snooping Coherence Protocols

There are two ways to maintain the coherence requirement described in the prior subsection. One method is to ensure that a processor has exclusive access to a data item before it writes that item. This style of protocol is called a *write invalidate protocol* because it invalidates other copies on a write. It is by far the most common protocol. Exclusive access ensures that no other readable or writable copies of an item exist when the write occurs: All other cached copies of the item are invalidated.

Figure 5.4 shows an example of an invalidation protocol with write-back caches in action. To see how this protocol ensures coherence, consider a write followed by a read by another processor: Since the write requires exclusive access, any copy held by the reading processor must be invalidated (hence, the protocol name). Thus, when the read occurs, it misses in the cache and is forced to fetch a new copy of the data. For a write, we require that the writing processor have exclusive access, preventing any other processor from being able to write

Processor activity	Bus activity	Contents of processor A's cache	Contents of processor B's cache	Contents of memory location X
				0
Processor A reads X	Cache miss for X	0		0
Processor B reads X	Cache miss for X	0	0	0
Processor A writes a 1 to X	Invalidation for X	1		0
Processor B reads X	Cache miss for X	1	1	1

Figure 5.4 An example of an invalidation protocol working on a snooping bus for a single cache block (X) with write-back caches. We assume that neither cache initially holds X and that the value of X in memory is 0. The processor and memory contents show the value after the processor and bus activity have both completed. A blank indicates no activity or no copy cached. When the second miss by B occurs, processor A responds with the value canceling the response from memory. In addition, both the contents of B's cache and the memory contents of X are updated. This update of memory, which occurs when a block becomes shared, simplifies the protocol, but it is possible to track the ownership and force the write-back only if the block is replaced. This requires the introduction of an additional state called "owner," which indicates that a block may be shared, but the owning processor is responsible for updating any other processors and memory when it changes the block or replaces it. If a multicore uses a shared cache (e.g., L3), then all memory is seen through the shared cache; L3 acts like the memory in this example, and coherency must be handled for the private L1 and L2 for each core. It is this observation that led some designers to opt for a directory protocol within the multicore. To make this work the L3 cache must be inclusive (see page 397).

simultaneously. If two processors do attempt to write the same data simultaneously, one of them wins the race (we'll see how we decide who wins shortly), causing the other processor's copy to be invalidated. For the other processor to complete its write, it must obtain a new copy of the data, which must now contain the updated value. Therefore, this protocol enforces write serialization.

The alternative to an invalidate protocol is to update all the cached copies of a data item when that item is written. This type of protocol is called a *write update* or *write broadcast* protocol. Because a write update protocol must broadcast all writes to shared cache lines, it consumes considerably more bandwidth. For this reason, recent multiprocessors have opted to implement a write invalidate protocol, and we will focus only on invalidate protocols for the rest of the chapter.

Basic Implementation Techniques

The key to implementing an invalidate protocol in a multicore is the use of the bus, or another broadcast medium, to perform invalidates. In older multiple-chip multiprocessors, the bus used for coherence is the shared-memory access bus. In a multicore, the bus can be the connection between the private caches (L1 and L2 in the Intel Core i7) and the shared outer cache (L3 in the i7). To perform an invalidate, the processor simply acquires bus access and broadcasts the address to be invalidated on the bus. All processors continuously snoop on the bus, watching the addresses. The processors check whether the address on the bus is in their cache. If so, the corresponding data in the cache are invalidated.

When a write to a block that is shared occurs, the writing processor must acquire bus access to broadcast its invalidation. If two processors attempt to write shared blocks at the same time, their attempts to broadcast an invalidate operation will be serialized when they arbitrate for the bus. The first processor to obtain bus access will cause any other copies of the block it is writing to be invalidated. If the processors were attempting to write the same block, the serialization enforced by the bus also serializes their writes. One implication of this scheme is that a write to a shared data item cannot actually complete until it obtains bus access. All coherence schemes require some method of serializing accesses to the same cache block, either by serializing access to the communication medium or another shared structure.

In addition to invalidating outstanding copies of a cache block that is being written into, we also need to locate a data item when a cache miss occurs. In a write-through cache, it is easy to find the recent value of a data item, since all written data are always sent to the memory, from which the most recent value of a data item can always be fetched. (Write buffers can lead to some additional complexities and must effectively be treated as additional cache entries.)

For a write-back cache, the problem of finding the most recent data value is harder, since the most recent value of a data item can be in a private cache rather than in the shared cache or memory. Happily, write-back caches can use the same snooping scheme both for cache misses and for writes: Each processor snoops every address placed on the shared bus. If a processor finds that it has a dirty copy of the requested cache block, it provides that cache block in response to the read request and causes the memory (or L3) access to be aborted. The additional complexity comes from having to retrieve the cache block from another processor's private cache (L1 or L2), which can often take longer than retrieving it from L3. Since write-back caches generate lower requirements for memory bandwidth, they can support larger numbers of faster processors. As a result, all multicore processors use write-back at the outermost levels of the cache, and we will examine the implementation of coherence with write-back caches.

The normal cache tags can be used to implement the process of snooping, and the valid bit for each block makes invalidation easy to implement. Read misses, whether generated by an invalidation or by some other event, are also straightforward since they simply rely on the snooping capability. For writes we would like to know whether any other copies of the block are cached because, if there are no other cached copies, then the write need not be placed on the bus in a write-back cache. Not sending the write reduces both the time to write and the required bandwidth.

To track whether or not a cache block is shared, we can add an extra state bit associated with each cache block, just as we have a valid bit and a dirty bit. By adding a bit indicating whether the block is shared, we can decide whether a write must generate an invalidate. When a write to a block in the shared state occurs, the cache generates an invalidation on the bus and marks the block as *exclusive*. No further invalidations will be sent by that core for that block. The core with the sole copy of a cache block is normally called the *owner* of the cache block.

When an invalidation is sent, the state of the owner's cache block is changed from shared to unshared (or exclusive). If another processor later requests this cache block, the state must be made shared again. Since our snooping cache also sees any misses, it knows when the exclusive cache block has been requested by another processor and the state should be made shared.

Every bus transaction must check the cache-address tags, which could potentially interfere with processor cache accesses. One way to reduce this interference is to duplicate the tags and have snoop accesses directed to the duplicate tags. Another approach is to use a directory at the shared L3 cache; the directory indicates whether a given block is shared and possibly which cores have copies. With the directory information, invalidates can be directed only to those caches with copies of the cache block. This requires that L3 must always have a copy of any data item in L1 or L2, a property called *inclusion*, which we will return to in Section 5.7.

An Example Protocol

A snooping coherence protocol is usually implemented by incorporating a finite-state controller in each core. This controller responds to requests from the processor in the core and from the bus (or other broadcast medium), changing the state of the selected cache block, as well as using the bus to access data or to invalidate it. Logically, you can think of a separate controller being associated with each block; that is, snooping operations or cache requests for different blocks can proceed independently. In actual implementations, a single controller allows multiple operations to distinct blocks to proceed in interleaved fashion (that is, one operation may be initiated before another is completed, even though only one cache access or one bus access is allowed at a time). Also, remember that, although we refer to a bus in the following description, any interconnection network that supports a broadcast to all the coherence controllers and their associated private caches can be used to implement snooping.

The simple protocol we consider has three states: invalid, shared, and modified. The shared state indicates that the block in the private cache is potentially shared, while the modified state indicates that the block has been updated in the private cache; note that the modified state *implies* that the block is exclusive. Figure 5.5 shows the requests generated by a core (in the top half of the table)

Request	Source	State of addressed cache block	Type of cache action	Function and explanation
Read hit	Processor	Shared or modified	Normal hit	Read data in local cache.
Read miss	Processor	Invalid	Normal miss	Place read miss on bus.
Read miss	Processor	Shared	Replacement	Address conflict miss: place read miss on bus.
Read miss	Processor	Modified	Replacement	Address conflict miss: write-back block, then place read miss on bus.
Write hit	Processor	Modified	Normal hit	Write data in local cache.
Write hit	Processor	Shared	Coherence	Place invalidate on bus. These operations are often called upgrade or *ownership* misses, since they do not fetch the data but only change the state.
Write miss	Processor	Invalid	Normal miss	Place write miss on bus.
Write miss	Processor	Shared	Replacement	Address conflict miss: place write miss on bus.
Write miss	Processor	Modified	Replacement	Address conflict miss: write-back block, then place write miss on bus.
Read miss	Bus	Shared	No action	Allow shared cache or memory to service read miss.
Read miss	Bus	Modified	Coherence	Attempt to share data: place cache block on bus and change state to shared.
Invalidate	Bus	Shared	Coherence	Attempt to write shared block; invalidate the block.
Write miss	Bus	Shared	Coherence	Attempt to write shared block; invalidate the cache block.
Write miss	Bus	Modified	Coherence	Attempt to write block that is exclusive elsewhere; write-back the cache block and make its state invalid in the local cache.

Figure 5.5 The cache coherence mechanism receives requests from both the core's processor and the shared bus and responds to these based on the type of request, whether it hits or misses in the local cache, and the state of the local cache block specified in the request. The fourth column describes the type of cache action as normal hit or miss (the same as a uniprocessor cache would see), replacement (a uniprocessor cache replacement miss), or coherence (required to maintain cache coherence); a normal or replacement action may cause a coherence action depending on the state of the block in other caches. For read, misses, write misses, or invalidates snooped from the bus, an action is required *only* if the read or write addresses match a block in the local cache and the block is valid.

as well as those coming from the bus (in the bottom half of the table). This protocol is for a write-back cache but is easily changed to work for a write-through cache by reinterpreting the modified state as an exclusive state and updating the cache on writes in the normal fashion for a write-through cache. The most common extension of this basic protocol is the addition of an exclusive state, which describes a block that is unmodified but held in only one private cache. We describe this and other extensions on page 362.

When an invalidate or a write miss is placed on the bus, any cores whose private caches have copies of the cache block invalidate it. For a write miss in a write-back cache, if the block is exclusive in just one private cache, that cache also writes back the block; otherwise, the data can be read from the shared cache or memory.

Figure 5.6 shows a finite-state transition diagram for a single private cache block using a write invalidation protocol and a write-back cache. For simplicity, the three states of the protocol are duplicated to represent transitions based on processor requests (on the left, which corresponds to the top half of the table in Figure 5.5), as opposed to transitions based on bus requests (on the right, which corresponds to the bottom half of the table in Figure 5.5). Boldface type is used to distinguish the bus actions, as opposed to the conditions on which a state transition depends. The state in each node represents the state of the selected private cache block specified by the processor or bus request.

All of the states in this cache protocol would be needed in a uniprocessor cache, where they would correspond to the invalid, valid (and clean), and dirty states. Most of the state changes indicated by arcs in the left half of Figure 5.6 would be needed in a write-back uniprocessor cache, with the exception being the invalidate on a write hit to a shared block. The state changes represented by the arcs in the right half of Figure 5.6 are needed only for coherence and would not appear at all in a uniprocessor cache controller.

As mentioned earlier, there is only one finite-state machine per cache, with stimuli coming either from the attached processor or from the bus. Figure 5.7 shows how the state transitions in the right half of Figure 5.6 are combined with those in the left half of the figure to form a single state diagram for each cache block.

To understand why this protocol works, observe that any valid cache block is either in the shared state in one or more private caches or in the exclusive state in exactly one cache. Any transition to the exclusive state (which is required for a processor to write to the block) requires an invalidate or write miss to be placed on the bus, causing all local caches to make the block invalid. In addition, if some other local cache had the block in exclusive state, that local cache generates a write-back, which supplies the block containing the desired address. Finally, if a read miss occurs on the bus to a block in the exclusive state, the local cache with the exclusive copy changes its state to shared.

The actions in gray in Figure 5.7, which handle read and write misses on the bus, are essentially the snooping component of the protocol. One other property that is preserved in this protocol, and in most other protocols, is that any memory block in the shared state is always up to date in the outer shared cache (L2 or L3,

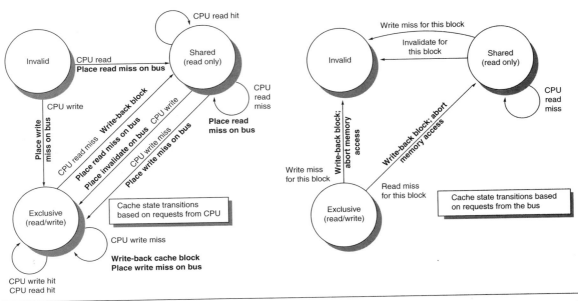

Figure 5.6 A write invalidate, cache coherence protocol for a private write-back cache showing the states and state transitions for each block in the cache. The cache states are shown in circles, with any access permitted by the local processor without a state transition shown in parentheses under the name of the state. The stimulus causing a state change is shown on the transition arcs in regular type, and any bus actions generated as part of the state transition are shown on the transition arc in bold. The stimulus actions apply to a block in the private cache, not to a specific address in the cache. Hence, a read miss to a block in the shared state is a miss for that cache block but for a different address. The left side of the diagram shows state transitions based on actions of the processor associated with this cache; the right side shows transitions based on operations on the bus. A read miss in the exclusive or shared state and a write miss in the exclusive state occur when the address requested by the processor does not match the address in the local cache block. Such a miss is a standard cache replacement miss. An attempt to write a block in the shared state generates an invalidate. Whenever a bus transaction occurs, all private caches that contain the cache block specified in the bus transaction take the action dictated by the right half of the diagram. The protocol assumes that memory (or a shared cache) provides data on a read miss for a block that is clean in all local caches. In actual implementations, these two sets of state diagrams are combined. In practice, there are many subtle variations on invalidate protocols, including the introduction of the exclusive unmodified state, as to whether a processor or memory provides data on a miss. In a multicore chip, the shared cache (usually L3, but sometimes L2) acts as the equivalent of memory, and the bus is the bus between the private caches of each core and the shared cache, which in turn interfaces to the memory.

or memory if there is no shared cache), which simplifies the implementation. In fact, it does not matter whether the level out from the private caches is a shared cache or memory; the key is that all accesses from the cores go through that level.

Although our simple cache protocol is correct, it omits a number of complications that make the implementation much trickier. The most important of these is that the protocol assumes that operations are *atomic*—that is, an operation can be done in such a way that no intervening operation can occur. For example, the protocol described assumes that write misses can be detected, acquire the bus, and

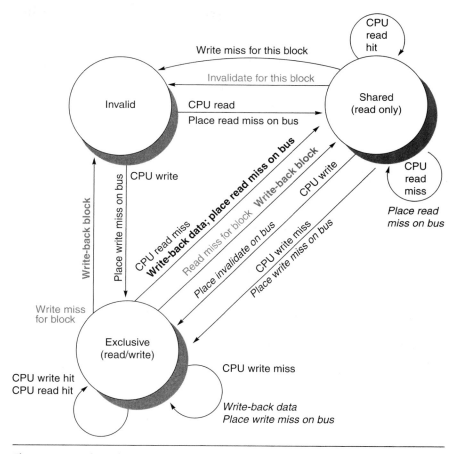

Figure 5.7 Cache coherence state diagram with the state transitions induced by the local processor shown in black and by the bus activities shown in gray. As in Figure 5.6, the activities on a transition are shown in bold.

receive a response as a single atomic action. In reality this is not true. In fact, even a read miss might not be atomic; after detecting a miss in the L2 of a multicore, the core must arbitrate for access to the bus connecting to the shared L3. Nonatomic actions introduce the possibility that the protocol can *deadlock*, meaning that it reaches a state where it cannot continue. We will explore these complications later in this section and when we examine DSM designs.

With multicore processors, the coherence among the processor cores is all implemented on chip, using either a snooping or simple central directory protocol. Many dual-processor chips, including the Intel Xeon and AMD Opteron, supported multichip multiprocessors that could be built by connecting a high-speed interface (called Quickpath or Hypertransport, respectively). These next-level interconnects are not just extensions of the shared bus, but use a different approach for interconnecting multicores.

A multiprocessor built with multiple multicore chips will have a distributed memory architecture and will need an interchip coherency mechanism above and beyond the one within the chip. In most cases, some form of directory scheme is used.

Extensions to the Basic Coherence Protocol

The coherence protocol we have just described is a simple three-state protocol and is often referred to by the first letter of the states, making it a MSI (Modified, Shared, Invalid) protocol. There are many extensions of this basic protocol, which we mentioned in the captions of figures in this section. These extensions are created by adding additional states and transactions, which optimize certain behaviors, possibly resulting in improved performance. Two of the most common extensions are

1. *MESI* adds the state Exclusive to the basic MSI protocol to indicate when a cache block is resident only in a single cache but is clean. If a block is in the E state, it can be written without generating any invalidates, which optimizes the case where a block is read by a single cache before being written by that same cache. Of course, when a read miss to a block in the E state occurs, the block must be changed to the S state to maintain coherence. Because all subsequent accesses are snooped, it is possible to maintain the accuracy of this state. In particular, if another processor issues a read miss, the state is changed from exclusive to shared. The advantage of adding this state is that a subsequent write to a block in the exclusive state by the same core need not acquire bus access or generate an invalidate, since the block is known to be exclusively in this local cache; the processor merely changes the state to modified. This state is easily added by using the bit that encodes the coherent state as an exclusive state and using the dirty bit to indicate that a bock is modified. The popular MESI protocol, which is named for the four states it includes (Modified, Exclusive, Shared, and Invalid), uses this structure. The Intel i7 uses a variant of a MESI protocol, called MESIF, which adds a state (Forward) to designate which sharing processor should respond to a request. It is designed to enhance performance in distributed memory organizations.

2. *MOESI* adds the state Owned to the MESI protocol to indicate that the associated block is owned by that cache and out-of-date in memory. In MSI and MESI protocols, when there is an attempt to share a block in the Modified state, the state is changed to Shared (in both the original and newly sharing cache), and the block must be written back to memory. In a MOESI protocol, the block can be changed from the Modified to Owned state in the original cache without writing it to memory. Other caches, which are newly sharing the block, keep the block in the Shared state; the O state, which only the original cache holds, indicates that the main memory copy is out of date and that the designated cache is the owner. The owner of the block must supply it on a miss, since memory is not up to date and must write the block back to memory if it is replaced. The AMD Opteron uses the MOESI protocol.

The next section examines the performance of these protocols for our parallel and multiprogrammed workloads; the value of these extensions to a basic protocol will be clear when we examine the performance. But, before we do that, let's take a brief look at the limitations on the use of a symmetric memory structure and a snooping coherence scheme.

Limitations in Symmetric Shared-Memory Multiprocessors and Snooping Protocols

As the number of processors in a multiprocessor grows, or as the memory demands of each processor grow, any centralized resource in the system can become a bottleneck. Using the higher bandwidth connection available on-chip and a shared L3 cache, which is faster than memory, designers have managed to support four to eight high-performance cores in a symmetric fashion. Such an approach is unlikely to scale much past eight cores, and it will not work once multiple multicores are combined.

Snooping bandwidth at the caches can also become a problem, since every cache must examine every miss placed on the bus. As we mentioned, duplicating the tags is one solution. Another approach, which has been adopted in some recent multicores, is to place a directory at the level of the outermost cache. The directory explicitly indicates which processor's caches have copies of every item in the outermost cache. This is the approach Intel uses on the i7 and Xeon 7000 series. Note that the use of this directory does not eliminate the bottleneck due to a shared bus and L3 among the processors, but it is much simpler to implement than the distributed directory schemes that we will examine in Section 5.4.

How can a designer increase the memory bandwidth to support either more or faster processors? To increase the communication bandwidth between processors and memory, designers have used multiple buses as well as interconnection networks, such as crossbars or small point-to-point networks. In such designs, the memory system (either main memory or a shared cache) can be configured into multiple physical banks, so as to boost the effective memory bandwidth while retaining uniform access time to memory. Figure 5.8 shows how such a system might look if it where implemented with a single-chip multicore. Although such an approach might be used to allow more than four cores to be interconnected on a single chip, it does not scale well to a multichip multiprocessor that uses multicore building blocks, since the memory is already attached to the individual multicore chips, rather than centralized.

The AMD Opteron represents another intermediate point in the spectrum between a snooping and a directory protocol. Memory is directly connected to each multicore chip, and up to four multicore chips can be connected. The system is a NUMA, since local memory is somewhat faster. The Opteron implements its coherence protocol using the point-to-point links to broadcast up to three other chips. Because the interprocessor links are not shared, the only way a processor can know when an invalid operation has completed is by an explicit acknowledgment. Thus, the coherence protocol uses a broadcast to

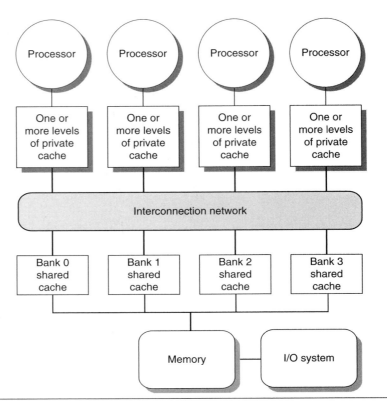

Figure 5.8 A multicore single-chip multiprocessor with uniform memory access through a banked shared cache and using an interconnection network rather than a bus.

find potentially shared copies, like a snooping protocol, but uses the acknowledgments to order operations, like a directory protocol. Because local memory is only somewhat faster than remote memory in the Opteron implementation, some software treats an Opteron multiprocessor as having uniform memory access.

A snooping cache coherence protocol can be used without a centralized bus, but still requires that a broadcast be done to snoop the individual caches on every miss to a potentially shared cache block. This cache coherence traffic creates another limit on the scale and the speed of the processors. Because coherence traffic is unaffected by larger caches, faster processors will inevitably overwhelm the network and the ability of each cache to respond to snoop requests from *all* the other caches. In Section 5.4, we examine directory-based protocols, which eliminate the need for broadcast to all caches on a miss. As processor speeds and the number of cores per processor increase, more designers are likely to opt for such protocols to avoid the broadcast limit of a snooping protocol.

Implementing Snooping Cache Coherence

The devil is in the details.

Classic proverb

When we wrote the first edition of this book in 1990, our final "Putting It All Together" was a 30-processor, single-bus multiprocessor using snoop-based coherence; the bus had a capacity of just over 50 MB/sec, which would not be enough bus bandwidth to support even one core of an Intel i7 in 2011! When we wrote the second edition of this book in 1995, the first cache coherence multiprocessors with more than a single bus had recently appeared, and we added an appendix describing the implementation of snooping in a system with multiple buses. In 2011, most multicore processors that support only a single-chip multiprocessor have opted to use a shared bus structure connecting to either a shared memory or a shared cache. In contrast, *every* multicore multiprocessor system that supports 16 or more cores uses an interconnect other than a single bus, and designers must face the challenge of implementing snooping without the simplification of a bus to serialize events.

As we said earlier, the major complication in actually implementing the snooping coherence protocol we have described is that write and upgrade misses are not atomic in any recent multiprocessor. The steps of detecting a write or upgrade miss, communicating with the other processors and memory, getting the most recent value for a write miss and ensuring that any invalidates are processed, and updating the cache cannot be done as if they took a single cycle.

In a single multicore chip, these steps can be made effectively atomic by arbitrating for the bus to the shared cache or memory first (before changing the cache state) and not releasing the bus until all actions are complete. How can the processor know when all the invalidates are complete? In some multicores, a single line is used to signal when all necessary invalidates have been received and are being processed. Following that signal, the processor that generated the miss can release the bus, knowing that any required actions will be completed before any activity related to the next miss. By holding the bus exclusively during these steps, the processor effectively makes the individual steps atomic.

In a system without a bus, we must find some other method of making the steps in a miss atomic. In particular, we must ensure that two processors that attempt to write the same block at the same time, a situation which is called a *race*, are strictly ordered: One write is processed and precedes before the next is begun. It does not matter which of two writes in a race wins the race, just that there be only a single winner whose coherence actions are completed first. In a snooping system, ensuring that a race has only one winner is accomplished by using broadcast for all misses as well as some basic properties of the interconnection network. These properties, together with the ability to restart the miss handling of the loser in a race, are the keys to implementing snooping cache coherence without a bus. We explain the details in Appendix I.

It is possible to combine snooping and directories, and several designs use snooping within a multicore and directories among multiple chips or, *vice versa*, directories within a multicore and snooping among multiple chips.

<table>
<tr><td>5.3</td><td></td></tr>
</table>

5.3 Performance of Symmetric Shared-Memory Multiprocessors

In a multicore using a snooping coherence protocol, several different phenomena combine to determine performance. In particular, the overall cache performance is a combination of the behavior of uniprocessor cache miss traffic and the traffic caused by communication, which results in invalidations and subsequent cache misses. Changing the processor count, cache size, and block size can affect these two components of the miss rate in different ways, leading to overall system behavior that is a combination of the two effects.

Appendix B breaks the uniprocessor miss rate into the three C's classification (capacity, compulsory, and conflict) and provides insight into both application behavior and potential improvements to the cache design. Similarly, the misses that arise from interprocessor communication, which are often called *coherence misses*, can be broken into two separate sources.

The first source is the so-called *true sharing misses* that arise from the communication of data through the cache coherence mechanism. In an invalidation-based protocol, the first write by a processor to a shared cache block causes an invalidation to establish ownership of that block. Additionally, when another processor attempts to read a modified word in that cache block, a miss occurs and the resultant block is transferred. Both these misses are classified as true sharing misses since they directly arise from the sharing of data among processors.

The second effect, called *false sharing*, arises from the use of an invalidation-based coherence algorithm with a single valid bit per cache block. False sharing occurs when a block is invalidated (and a subsequent reference causes a miss) because some word in the block, other than the one being read, is written into. If the word written into is actually used by the processor that received the invalidate, then the reference was a true sharing reference and would have caused a miss independent of the block size. If, however, the word being written and the word read are different and the invalidation does not cause a new value to be communicated, but only causes an extra cache miss, then it is a false sharing miss. In a false sharing miss, the block is shared, but no word in the cache is actually shared, and the miss would not occur if the block size were a single word. The following example makes the sharing patterns clear.

Example   Assume that words x1 and x2 are in the same cache block, which is in the shared state in the caches of both P1 and P2. Assuming the following sequence of events, identify each miss as a true sharing miss, a false sharing miss, or a hit.

Any miss that would occur if the block size were one word is designated a true sharing miss.

Time	P1	P2
1	Write x1	
2		Read x2
3	Write x1	
4		Write x2
5	Read x2	

Answer   Here are the classifications by time step:

1. This event is a true sharing miss, since x1 was read by P2 and needs to be invalidated from P2.

2. This event is a false sharing miss, since x2 was invalidated by the write of x1 in P1, but that value of x1 is not used in P2.

3. This event is a false sharing miss, since the block containing x1 is marked shared due to the read in P2, but P2 did not read x1. The cache block containing x1 will be in the shared state after the read by P2; a write miss is required to obtain exclusive access to the block. In some protocols this will be handled as an *upgrade request*, which generates a bus invalidate, but does not transfer the cache block.

4. This event is a false sharing miss for the same reason as step 3.

5. This event is a true sharing miss, since the value being read was written by P2.

Although we will see the effects of true and false sharing misses in commercial workloads, the role of coherence misses is more significant for tightly coupled applications that share significant amounts of user data. We examine their effects in detail in Appendix I, when we consider the performance of a parallel scientific workload.

A Commercial Workload

In this section, we examine the memory system behavior of a four-processor shared-memory multiprocessor when running a general-purpose commercial workload. The study we examine was done with a four-processor Alpha system in 1998, but it remains the most comprehensive and insightful study of the performance of a multiprocessor for such workloads. The results were collected either on an AlphaServer 4100 or using a configurable simulator modeled after the AlphaServer 4100. Each processor in the AlphaServer 4100 is an Alpha 21164, which issues up to four instructions per clock and runs at 300 MHz.

Although the clock rate of the Alpha processor in this system is considerably slower than processors in systems designed in 2011, the basic structure of the system, consisting of a four-issue processor and a three-level cache hierarchy, is very similar to the multicore Intel i7 and other processors, as shown in Figure 5.9. In particular, the Alpha caches are somewhat smaller, but the miss times are also lower than on an i7. Thus, the behavior of the Alpha system should provide interesting insights into the behavior of modern multicore designs.

The workload used for this study consists of three applications:

1. An online transaction-processing (OLTP) workload modeled after TPC-B (which has memory behavior similar to its newer cousin TPC-C, described in Chapter 1) and using Oracle 7.3.2 as the underlying database. The workload consists of a set of client processes that generate requests and a set of servers that handle them. The server processes consume 85% of the user time, with the remaining going to the clients. Although the I/O latency is hidden by careful tuning and enough requests to keep the processor busy, the server processes typically block for I/O after about 25,000 instructions.

2. A decision support system (DSS) workload based on TPC-D, the older cousin of the heavily used TPC-E, which also uses Oracle 7.3.2 as the underlying database. The workload includes only 6 of the 17 read queries in TPC-D,

Cache level	Characteristic	Alpha 21164	Intel i7
L1	Size	8 KB I/8 KB D	32 KB I/32 KB D
	Associativity	Direct mapped	4-way I/8-way D
	Block size	32 B	64 B
	Miss penalty	7	10
L2	Size	96 KB	256 KB
	Associativity	3-way	8-way
	Block size	32 B	64 B
	Miss penalty	21	35
L3	Size	2 MB	2 MB per core
	Associativity	Direct mapped	16-way
	Block size	64 B	64 B
	Miss penalty	80	~100

Figure 5.9 The characteristics of the cache hierarchy of the Alpha 21164 used in this study and the Intel i7. Although the sizes are larger and the associativity is higher on the i7, the miss penalties are also higher, so the behavior may differ only slightly. For example, from Appendix B, we can estimate the miss rates of the smaller Alpha L1 cache as 4.9% and 3% for the larger i7 L1 cache, so the average L1 miss penalty per reference is 0.34 for the Alpha and 0.30 for the i7. Both systems have a high penalty (125 cycles or more) for a transfer required from a private cache. The i7 also shares its L3 among all the cores.

Benchmark	% Time user mode	% Time kernel	% Time processor idle
OLTP	71	18	11
DSS (average across all queries)	87	4	9
AltaVista	>98	<1	<1

Figure 5.10   The distribution of execution time in the commercial workloads. The OLTP benchmark has the largest fraction of both OS time and processor idle time (which is I/O wait time). The DSS benchmark shows much less OS time, since it does less I/O, but still more than 9% idle time. The extensive tuning of the AltaVista search engine is clear in these measurements. The data for this workload were collected by Barroso, Gharachorloo, and Bugnion [1998] on a four-processor AlphaServer 4100.

although the 6 queries examined in the benchmark span the range of activities in the entire benchmark. To hide the I/O latency, parallelism is exploited both within queries, where parallelism is detected during a query formulation process, and across queries. Blocking calls are much less frequent than in the OLTP benchmark; the 6 queries average about 1.5 million instructions before blocking.

3. A Web index search (AltaVista) benchmark based on a search of a memory-mapped version of the AltaVista database (200 GB). The inner loop is heavily optimized. Because the search structure is static, little synchronization is needed among the threads. AltaVista was the most popular Web search engine before the arrival of Google.

Figure 5.10 shows the percentages of time spent in user mode, in the kernel, and in the idle loop. The frequency of I/O increases both the kernel time and the idle time (see the OLTP entry, which has the largest I/O-to-computation ratio). AltaVista, which maps the entire search database into memory and has been extensively tuned, shows the least kernel or idle time.

Performance Measurements of the Commercial Workload

We start by looking at the overall processor execution for these benchmarks on the four-processor system; as discussed on page 367, these benchmarks include substantial I/O time, which is ignored in the processor time measurements. We group the six DSS queries as a single benchmark, reporting the average behavior. The effective CPI varies widely for these benchmarks, from a CPI of 1.3 for the AltaVista Web search, to an average CPI of 1.6 for the DSS workload, to 7.0 for the OLTP workload. Figure 5.11 shows how the execution time breaks down into instruction execution, cache and memory system access time, and other stalls (which are primarily pipeline resource stalls but also include translation lookaside buffer (TLB) and branch mispredict stalls). Although the performance of the DSS

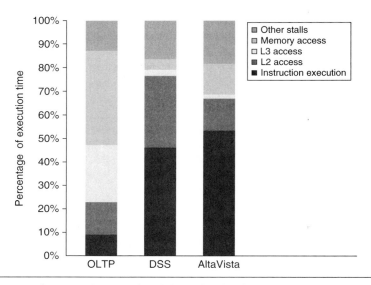

Figure 5.11 The execution time breakdown for the three programs (OLTP, DSS, and AltaVista) in the commercial workload. The DSS numbers are the average across six different queries. The CPI varies widely from a low of 1.3 for AltaVista, to 1.61 for the DSS queries, to 7.0 for OLTP. (Individually, the DSS queries show a CPI range of 1.3 to 1.9.) "Other stalls" includes resource stalls (implemented with replay traps on the 21164), branch mispredict, memory barrier, and TLB misses. For these benchmarks, resource-based pipeline stalls are the dominant factor. These data combine the behavior of user and kernel accesses. Only OLTP has a significant fraction of kernel accesses, and the kernel accesses tend to be better behaved than the user accesses! All the measurements shown in this section were collected by Barroso, Gharachorloo, and Bugnion [1998].

and AltaVista workloads is reasonable, the performance of the OLTP workload is very poor, due to a poor performance of the memory hierarchy.

Since the OLTP workload demands the most from the memory system with large numbers of expensive L3 misses, we focus on examining the impact of L3 cache size, processor count, and block size on the OLTP benchmark. Figure 5.12 shows the effect of increasing the cache size, using two-way set associative caches, which reduces the large number of conflict misses. The execution time is improved as the L3 cache grows due to the reduction in L3 misses. Surprisingly, almost all of the gain occurs in going from 1 to 2 MB, with little additional gain beyond that, despite the fact that cache misses are still a cause of significant performance loss with 2 MB and 4 MB caches. The question is, Why?

To better understand the answer to this question, we need to determine what factors contribute to the L3 miss rate and how they change as the L3 cache grows. Figure 5.13 shows these data, displaying the number of memory access cycles contributed per instruction from five sources. The two largest sources of L3 memory access cycles with a 1 MB L3 are instruction and capacity/conflict

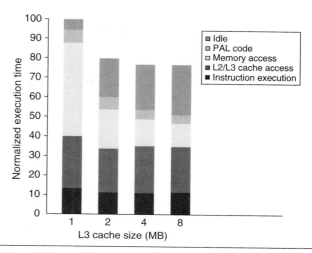

Figure 5.12 The relative performance of the OLTP workload as the size of the L3 cache, which is set as two-way set associative, grows from 1 MB to 8 MB. The idle time also grows as cache size is increased, reducing some of the performance gains. This growth occurs because, with fewer memory system stalls, more server processes are needed to cover the I/O latency. The workload could be retuned to increase the computation/communication balance, holding the idle time in check. The PAL code is a set of sequences of specialized OS-level instructions executed in privileged mode; an example is the TLB miss handler.

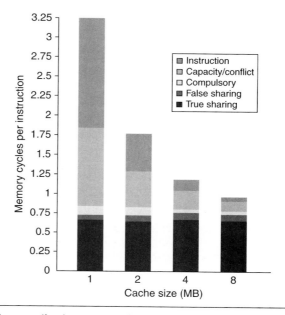

Figure 5.13 The contributing causes of memory access cycle shift as the cache size is increased. The L3 cache is simulated as two-way set associative.

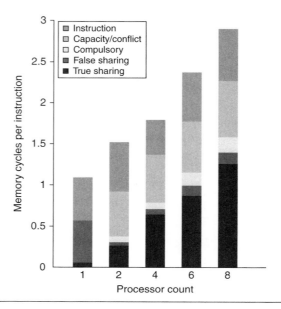

Figure 5.14 The contribution to memory access cycles increases as processor count increases primarily due to increased true sharing. The compulsory misses slightly increase since each processor must now handle more compulsory misses.

misses. With a larger L3, these two sources shrink to be minor contributors. Unfortunately, the compulsory, false sharing, and true sharing misses are unaffected by a larger L3. Thus, at 4 MB and 8 MB, the true sharing misses generate the dominant fraction of the misses; the lack of change in true sharing misses leads to the limited reductions in the overall miss rate when increasing the L3 cache size beyond 2 MB.

Increasing the cache size eliminates most of the uniprocessor misses while leaving the multiprocessor misses untouched. How does increasing the processor count affect different types of misses? Figure 5.14 shows these data assuming a base configuration with a 2 MB, two-way set associative L3 cache. As we might expect, the increase in the true sharing miss rate, which is not compensated for by any decrease in the uniprocessor misses, leads to an overall increase in the memory access cycles per instruction.

The final question we examine is whether increasing the block size—which should decrease the instruction and cold miss rate and, within limits, also reduce the capacity/conflict miss rate and possibly the true sharing miss rate—is helpful for this workload. Figure 5.15 shows the number of misses per 1000 instructions as the block size is increased from 32 to 256 bytes. Increasing the block size from 32 to 256 bytes affects four of the miss rate components:

■ The true sharing miss rate decreases by more than a factor of 2, indicating some locality in the true sharing patterns.

■ The compulsory miss rate significantly decreases, as we would expect.

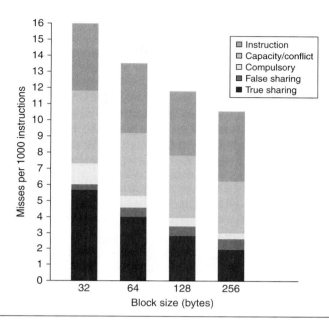

Figure 5.15 The number of misses per 1000 instructions drops steadily as the block size of the L3 cache is increased, making a good case for an L3 block size of at least 128 bytes. The L3 cache is 2 MB, two-way set associative.

- The conflict/capacity misses show a small decrease (a factor of 1.26 compared to a factor of 8 increase in block size), indicating that the spatial locality is not high in the uniprocessor misses that occur with L3 caches larger than 2 MB.

- The false sharing miss rate, although small in absolute terms, nearly doubles.

The lack of a significant effect on the instruction miss rate is startling. If there were an instruction-only cache with this behavior, we would conclude that the spatial locality is very poor. In the case of a mixed L2 cache, other effects such as instruction-data conflicts may also contribute to the high instruction cache miss rate for larger blocks. Other studies have documented the low spatial locality in the instruction stream of large database and OLTP workloads, which have lots of short basic blocks and special-purpose code sequences. Based on these data, the miss penalty for a larger block size L3 to perform as well as the 32-byte block size L3 can be expressed as a multiplier on the 32-byte block size penalty:

Block size	Miss penalty relative to 32-byte block miss penalty
64 bytes	1.19
128 bytes	1.36
256 bytes	1.52

With modern DDR SDRAMs that make block access fast, these numbers seem attainable, especially at the 128 byte block size. Of course, we must also worry about the effects of the increased traffic to memory and possible contention for the memory with other cores. This latter effect may easily negate the gains obtained from improving the performance of a single processor.

A Multiprogramming and OS Workload

Our next study is a multiprogrammed workload consisting of both user activity and OS activity. The workload used is two independent copies of the compile phases of the Andrew benchmark, a benchmark that emulates a software development environment. The compile phase consists of a parallel version of the Unix "make" command executed using eight processors. The workload runs for 5.24 seconds on eight processors, creating 203 processes and performing 787 disk requests on three different file systems. The workload is run with 128 MB of memory, and no paging activity takes place.

The workload has three distinct phases: compiling the benchmarks, which involves substantial compute activity; installing the object files in a library; and removing the object files. The last phase is completely dominated by I/O, and only two processes are active (one for each of the runs). In the middle phase, I/O also plays a major role, and the processor is largely idle. The overall workload is much more system and I/O intensive than the highly tuned commercial workload.

For the workload measurements, we assume the following memory and I/O systems:

■ *Level 1 instruction cache*—32 KB, two-way set associative with a 64-byte block, 1 clock cycle hit time.

■ *Level 1 data cache*—32 KB, two-way set associative with a 32-byte block, 1 clock cycle hit time. We vary the L1 data cache to examine its effect on cache behavior.

■ *Level 2 cache*—1 MB unified, two-way set associative with a 128-byte block, 10 clock cycle hit time.

■ *Main memory*—Single memory on a bus with an access time of 100 clock cycles.

■ *Disk system*—Fixed-access latency of 3 ms (less than normal to reduce idle time).

Figure 5.16 shows how the execution time breaks down for the eight processors using the parameters just listed. Execution time is broken down into four components:

1. *Idle*—Execution in the kernel mode idle loop

2. *User*—Execution in user code

3. *Synchronization*—Execution or waiting for synchronization variables

4. *Kernel*—Execution in the OS that is neither idle nor in synchronization access

	User execution	Kernel execution	Synchronization wait	Processor idle (waiting for I/O)
Instructions executed	27%	3%	1%	69%
Execution time	27%	7%	2%	64%

Figure 5.16 The distribution of execution time in the multiprogrammed parallel "make" workload. The high fraction of idle time is due to disk latency when only one of the eight processors is active. These data and the subsequent measurements for this workload were collected with the SimOS system [Rosenblum et al. 1995]. The actual runs and data collection were done by M. Rosenblum, S. Herrod, and E. Bugnion of Stanford University.

This multiprogramming workload has a significant instruction cache performance loss, at least for the OS. The instruction cache miss rate in the OS for a 64-byte block size, two-way set associative cache varies from 1.7% for a 32 KB cache to 0.2% for a 256 KB cache. User-level instruction cache misses are roughly one-sixth of the OS rate, across the variety of cache sizes. This partially accounts for the fact that, although the user code executes nine times as many instructions as the kernel, those instructions take only about four times as long as the smaller number of instructions executed by the kernel.

Performance of the Multiprogramming and OS Workload

In this subsection, we examine the cache performance of the multiprogrammed workload as the cache size and block size are changed. Because of differences between the behavior of the kernel and that of the user processes, we keep these two components separate. Remember, though, that the user processes execute more than eight times as many instructions, so that the overall miss rate is determined primarily by the miss rate in user code, which, as we will see, is often one-fifth of the kernel miss rate.

Although the user code executes more instructions, the behavior of the operating system can cause more cache misses than the user processes for two reasons beyond larger code size and lack of locality. First, the kernel initializes all pages before allocating them to a user, which significantly increases the compulsory component of the kernel's miss rate. Second, the kernel actually shares data and thus has a nontrivial coherence miss rate. In contrast, user processes cause coherence misses only when the process is scheduled on a different processor, and this component of the miss rate is small.

Figure 5.17 shows the data miss rate versus data cache size and versus block size for the kernel and user components. Increasing the data cache size affects the user miss rate more than it affects the kernel miss rate. Increasing the block size has beneficial effects for both miss rates, since a larger fraction of the misses arise from compulsory and capacity, both of which can be potentially

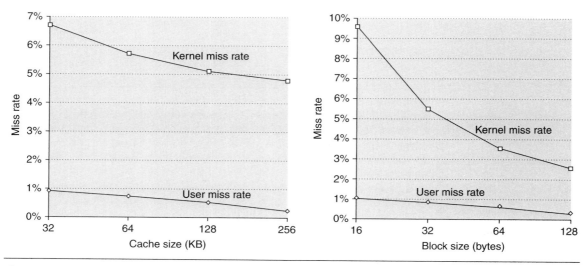

Figure 5.17 **The data miss rates for the user and kernel components behave differently for increases in the L1 data cache size (on the left) versus increases in the L1 data cache block size (on the right).** Increasing the L1 data cache from 32 KB to 256 KB (with a 32-byte block) causes the user miss rate to decrease proportionately more than the kernel miss rate: the user-level miss rate drops by almost a factor of 3, while the kernel-level miss rate drops only by a factor of 1.3. The miss rate for both user and kernel components drops steadily as the L1 block size is increased (while keeping the L1 cache at 32 KB). In contrast to the effects of increasing the cache size, increasing the block size improves the kernel miss rate more significantly (just under a factor of 4 for the kernel references when going from 16-byte to 128-byte blocks versus just under a factor of 3 for the user references).

improved with larger block sizes. Since coherence misses are relatively rarer, the negative effects of increasing block size are small. To understand why the kernel and user processes behave differently, we can look at how the kernel misses behave.

Figure 5.18 shows the variation in the kernel misses versus increases in cache size and in block size. The misses are broken into three classes: compulsory misses, coherence misses (from both true and false sharing), and capacity/conflict misses (which include misses caused by interference between the OS and the user process and between multiple user processes). Figure 5.18 confirms that, for the kernel references, increasing the cache size reduces only the uniprocessor capacity/conflict miss rate. In contrast, increasing the block size causes a reduction in the compulsory miss rate. The absence of large increases in the coherence miss rate as block size is increased means that false sharing effects are probably insignificant, although such misses may be offsetting some of the gains from reducing the true sharing misses.

If we examine the number of bytes needed per data reference, as in Figure 5.19, we see that the kernel has a higher traffic ratio that grows with block size. It is easy to see why this occurs: When going from a 16-byte block to a 128-byte block, the miss rate drops by about 3.7, but the number of bytes

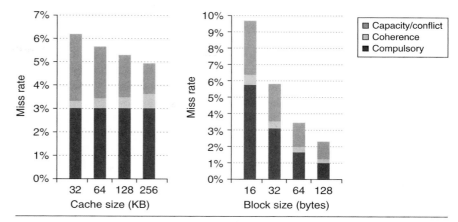

Figure 5.18 The components of the kernel data miss rate change as the L1 data cache size is increased from 32 KB to 256 KB, when the multiprogramming workload is run on eight processors. The compulsory miss rate component stays constant, since it is unaffected by cache size. The capacity component drops by more than a factor of 2, while the coherence component nearly doubles. The increase in coherence misses occurs because the probability of a miss being caused by an invalidation increases with cache size, since fewer entries are bumped due to capacity. As we would expect, the increasing block size of the L1 data cache substantially reduces the compulsory miss rate in the kernel references. It also has a significant impact on the capacity miss rate, decreasing it by a factor of 2.4 over the range of block sizes. The increased block size has a small reduction in coherence traffic, which appears to stabilize at 64 bytes, with no change in the coherence miss rate in going to 128-byte lines. Because there are no significant reductions in the coherence miss rate as the block size increases, the fraction of the miss rate due to coherence grows from about 7% to about 15%.

transferred per miss increases by 8, so the total miss traffic increases by just over a factor of 2. The user program also more than doubles as the block size goes from 16 to 128 bytes, but it starts out at a much lower level.

For the multiprogrammed workload, the OS is a much more demanding user of the memory system. If more OS or OS-like activity is included in the workload, and the behavior is similar to what was measured for this workload, it will become very difficult to build a sufficiently capable memory system. One possible route to improving performance is to make the OS more cache aware, through either better programming environments or through programmer assistance. For example, the OS reuses memory for requests that arise from different system calls. Despite the fact that the reused memory will be completely overwritten, the hardware, not recognizing this, will attempt to preserve coherency and the possibility that some portion of a cache block may be read, even if it is not. This behavior is analogous to the reuse of stack locations on procedure invocations. The IBM Power series has support to allow the compiler to indicate this type of behavior on procedure invocations, and the newest

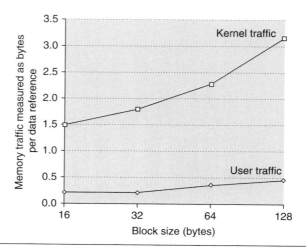

Figure 5.19 The number of bytes needed per data reference grows as block size is increased for both the kernel and user components. It is interesting to compare this chart against the data on scientific programs shown in Appendix I.

AMD processors have similar support. It is harder to detect such behavior by the OS, and doing so may require programmer assistance, but the payoff is potentially even greater.

OS and commercial workloads pose tough challenges for multiprocessor memory systems, and unlike scientific applications, which we examine in Appendix I, they are less amenable to algorithmic or compiler restructuring. As the number of cores increases predicting the behavior of such applications is likely to get more difficult. Emulation or simulation methodologies that allow the simulation of hundreds of cores with large applications (including operating systems) will be crucial to maintaining an analytical and quantitative approach to design.

5.4 Distributed Shared-Memory and Directory-Based Coherence

As we saw in Section 5.2, a snooping protocol requires communication with all caches on every cache miss, including writes of potentially shared data. The absence of any centralized data structure that tracks the state of the caches is both the fundamental advantage of a snooping-based scheme, since it allows it to be inexpensive, as well as its Achilles' heel when it comes to scalability.

For example, consider a multiprocessor composed of four 4-core multicores capable of sustaining one data reference per clock and a 4 GHz clock. From the data in Section I.5 of Appendix I, we can see that the applications may require 4 GB/sec to 170 GB/sec of bus bandwidth. Although the caches in those experiments are small, most of the traffic is coherence traffic, which is unaffected by cache size. Although a modern bus might accommodate 4 GB/sec, 170 GB/sec is far beyond the capability of any bus-based system. In the last few years, the development of multicore processors forced all designers to shift to some form of distributed memory to support the bandwidth demands of the individual processors.

We can increase the memory bandwidth and interconnection bandwidth by distributing the memory, as shown in Figure 5.2 on page 348; this immediately separates local memory traffic from remote memory traffic, reducing the bandwidth demands on the memory system and on the interconnection network. Unless we eliminate the need for the coherence protocol to broadcast on every cache miss, distributing the memory will gain us little.

As we mentioned earlier, the alternative to a snooping-based coherence protocol is a *directory protocol*. A directory keeps the state of every block that may be cached. Information in the directory includes which caches (or collections of caches) have copies of the block, whether it is dirty, and so on. Within a multicore with a shared outermost cache (say, L3), it is easy to implement a directory scheme: Simply keep a bit vector of the size equal to the number of cores for each L3 block. The bit vector indicates which private caches may have copies of a block in L3, and invalidations are only sent to those caches. This works perfectly for a single multicore if L3 is inclusive, and this scheme is the one used in the Intel i7.

The solution of a single directory used in a multicore is not scalable, even though it avoids broadcast. The directory must be distributed, but the distribution must be done in a way that the coherence protocol knows where to find the directory information for any cached block of memory. The obvious solution is to distribute the directory along with the memory, so that different coherence requests can go to different directories, just as different memory requests go to different memories. A distributed directory retains the characteristic that the sharing status of a block is always in a single known location. This property, together with the maintenance of information that says what other nodes may be caching the block, is what allows the coherence protocol to avoid broadcast. Figure 5.20 shows how our distributed-memory multiprocessor looks with the directories added to each node.

The simplest directory implementations associate an entry in the directory with each memory block. In such implementations, the amount of information is proportional to the product of the number of memory blocks (where each block is the same size as the L2 or L3 cache block) times the number of nodes, where a node is a single multicore processor or a small collection of processors that implements coherence internally. This overhead is not a problem for multiprocessors with less than a few hundred processors (each of which might be a multicore) because the directory overhead with a reasonable block size will be tolerable. For larger multiprocessors, we need methods to allow the directory structure to be efficiently scaled, but only supercomputer-sized systems need to worry about this.

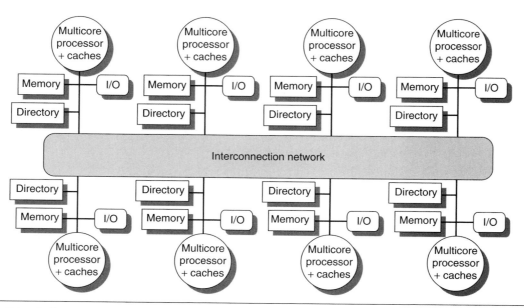

Figure 5.20 **A directory is added to each node to implement cache coherence in a distributed-memory multi-processor.** In this case, a node is shown as a single multicore chip, and the directory information for the associated memory may reside either on or off the multicore. Each directory is responsible for tracking the caches that share the memory addresses of the portion of memory in the node. The coherence mechanism would handle both the maintenance of the directory information and any coherence actions needed within the multicore node.

Directory-Based Cache Coherence Protocols: The Basics

Just as with a snooping protocol, there are two primary operations that a directory protocol must implement: handling a read miss and handling a write to a shared, clean cache block. (Handling a write miss to a block that is currently shared is a simple combination of these two.) To implement these operations, a directory must track the state of each cache block. In a simple protocol, these states could be the following:

- *Shared*—One or more nodes have the block cached, and the value in memory is up to date (as well as in all the caches).

- *Uncached*—No node has a copy of the cache block.

- *Modified*—Exactly one node has a copy of the cache block, and it has written the block, so the memory copy is out of date. The processor is called the *owner* of the block.

In addition to tracking the state of each potentially shared memory block, we must track which nodes have copies of that block, since those copies will need to be invalidated on a write. The simplest way to do this is to keep a bit vector for each memory block. When the block is shared, each bit of the vector indicates whether the corresponding processor chip (which is likely a multicore) has a copy of that block. We can also use the bit vector to keep track of the owner of the block when the block is in the exclusive state. For efficiency reasons, we also track the state of each cache block at the individual caches.

The states and transitions for the state machine at each cache are identical to what we used for the snooping cache, although the actions on a transition are slightly different. The processes of invalidating and locating an exclusive copy of a data item are different, since they both involve communication between the requesting node and the directory and between the directory and one or more remote nodes. In a snooping protocol, these two steps are combined through the use of a broadcast to all the nodes.

Before we see the protocol state diagrams, it is useful to examine a catalog of the message types that may be sent between the processors and the directories for the purpose of handling misses and maintaining coherence. Figure 5.21 shows the types of messages sent among nodes. The *local node* is the node where a request originates. The *home node* is the node where the memory location and the

Message type	Source	Destination	Message contents	Function of this message
Read miss	Local cache	Home directory	P, A	Node P has a read miss at address A; request data and make P a read sharer.
Write miss	Local cache	Home directory	P, A	Node P has a write miss at address A; request data and make P the exclusive owner.
Invalidate	Local cache	Home directory	A	Request to send invalidates to all remote caches that are caching the block at address A.
Invalidate	Home directory	Remote cache	A	Invalidate a shared copy of data at address A.
Fetch	Home directory	Remote cache	A	Fetch the block at address A and send it to its home directory; change the state of A in the remote cache to shared.
Fetch/invalidate	Home directory	Remote cache	A	Fetch the block at address A and send it to its home directory; invalidate the block in the cache.
Data value reply	Home directory	Local cache	D	Return a data value from the home memory.
Data write-back	Remote cache	Home directory	A, D	Write-back a data value for address A.

Figure 5.21 **The possible messages sent among nodes to maintain coherence, along with the source and destination node, the contents (where P = requesting node number, A = requested address, and D = data contents), and the function of the message.** The first three messages are requests sent by the local node to the home. The fourth through sixth messages are messages sent to a remote node by the home when the home needs the data to satisfy a read or write miss request. Data value replies are used to send a value from the home node back to the requesting node. Data value write-backs occur for two reasons: when a block is replaced in a cache and must be written back to its home memory, and also in reply to fetch or fetch/invalidate messages from the home. Writing back the data value whenever the block becomes shared simplifies the number of states in the protocol, since any dirty block must be exclusive and any shared block is always available in the home memory.

directory entry of an address reside. The physical address space is statically distributed, so the node that contains the memory and directory for a given physical address is known. For example, the high-order bits may provide the node number, while the low-order bits provide the offset within the memory on that node. The local node may also be the home node. The directory must be accessed when the home node is the local node, since copies may exist in yet a third node, called a *remote node*.

A remote node is the node that has a copy of a cache block, whether exclusive (in which case it is the only copy) or shared. A remote node may be the same as either the local node or the home node. In such cases, the basic protocol does not change, but interprocessor messages may be replaced with intraprocessor messages.

In this section, we assume a simple model of memory consistency. To minimize the type of messages and the complexity of the protocol, we make an assumption that messages will be received and acted upon in the same order they are sent. This assumption may not be true in practice and can result in additional complications, some of which we address in Section 5.6 when we discuss memory consistency models. In this section, we use this assumption to ensure that invalidates sent by a node are honored before new messages are transmitted, just as we assumed in the discussion of implementing snooping protocols. As we did in the snooping case, we omit some details necessary to implement the coherence protocol. In particular, the serialization of writes and knowing that the invalidates for a write have completed are not as simple as in the broadcast-based snooping mechanism. Instead, explicit acknowledgments are required in response to write misses and invalidate requests. We discuss these issues in more detail in Appendix I.

An Example Directory Protocol

The basic states of a cache block in a directory-based protocol are exactly like those in a snooping protocol, and the states in the directory are also analogous to those we showed earlier. Thus, we can start with simple state diagrams that show the state transitions for an individual cache block and then examine the state diagram for the directory entry corresponding to each block in memory. As in the snooping case, these state transition diagrams do not represent all the details of a coherence protocol; however, the actual controller is highly dependent on a number of details of the multiprocessor (message delivery properties, buffering structures, and so on). In this section, we present the basic protocol state diagrams. The knotty issues involved in implementing these state transition diagrams are examined in Appendix I.

Figure 5.22 shows the protocol actions to which an individual cache responds. We use the same notation as in the last section, with requests coming from outside the node in gray and actions in bold. The state transitions for an individual cache are caused by read misses, write misses, invalidates, and data fetch requests; Figure 5.22 shows these operations. An individual cache also generates read miss, write miss, and invalidate messages that are sent to the home directory. Read and write misses require data value replies, and these events wait for replies before changing state. Knowing when invalidates complete is a separate problem and is handled separately.

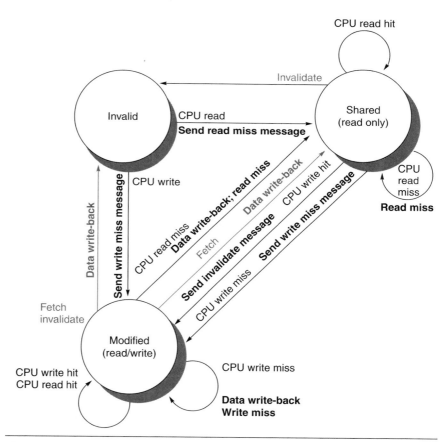

Figure 5.22 State transition diagram for an individual cache block in a directory-based system. Requests by the local processor are shown in black, and those from the home directory are shown in gray. The states are identical to those in the snooping case, and the transactions are very similar, with explicit invalidate and write-back requests replacing the write misses that were formerly broadcast on the bus. As we did for the snooping controller, we assume that an attempt to write a shared cache block is treated as a miss; in practice, such a transaction can be treated as an ownership request or upgrade request and can deliver ownership without requiring that the cache block be fetched.

The operation of the state transition diagram for a cache block in Figure 5.22 is essentially the same as it is for the snooping case: The states are identical, and the stimulus is almost identical. The write miss operation, which was broadcast on the bus (or other network) in the snooping scheme, is replaced by the data fetch and invalidate operations that are selectively sent by the directory controller. Like the snooping protocol, any cache block must be in the exclusive state when it is written, and any shared block must be up to date in memory. In many multicore processors, the outermost level in the processor cache is shared among the cores (as is the L3 in the Intel i7, the AMD Opteron, and the IBM Power7), and hardware at that level maintains coherence among the private caches of each core on the same chip, using either an internal directory or snooping. Thus, the on-chip multicore coherence mechanism can be used to extend coherence among a larger set of processors by simply interfacing to the outermost shared cache. Because this interface is at L3, contention between the processor and coherence requests is less of an issue, and duplicating the tags could be avoided.

In a directory-based protocol, the directory implements the other half of the coherence protocol. A message sent to a directory causes two different types of actions: updating the directory state and sending additional messages to satisfy the request. The states in the directory represent the three standard states for a block; unlike in a snooping scheme, however, the directory state indicates the state of all the cached copies of a memory block, rather than for a single cache block.

The memory block may be uncached by any node, cached in multiple nodes and readable (shared), or cached exclusively and writable in exactly one node. In addition to the state of each block, the directory must track the set of nodes that have a copy of a block; we use a set called *Sharers* to perform this function. In multiprocessors with fewer than 64 nodes (each of which may represent four to eight times as many processors), this set is typically kept as a bit vector. Directory requests need to update the set Sharers and also read the set to perform invalidations.

Figure 5.23 shows the actions taken at the directory in response to messages received. The directory receives three different requests: read miss, write miss, and data write-back. The messages sent in response by the directory are shown in bold, while the updating of the set Sharers is shown in bold italics. Because all the stimulus messages are external, all actions are shown in gray. Our simplified protocol assumes that some actions are atomic, such as requesting a value and sending it to another node; a realistic implementation cannot use this assumption.

To understand these directory operations, let's examine the requests received and actions taken state by state. When a block is in the uncached state, the copy in memory is the current value, so the only possible requests for that block are

■ *Read miss*—The requesting node is sent the requested data from memory, and the requestor is made the only sharing node. The state of the block is made shared.

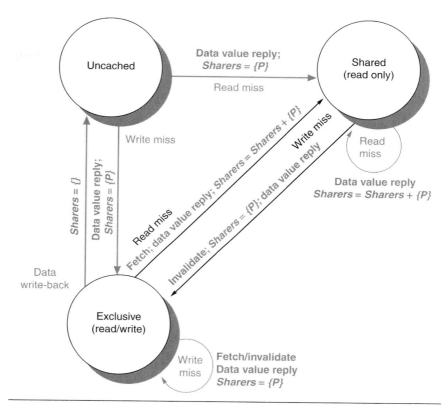

Figure 5.23 The state transition diagram for the directory has the same states and structure as the transition diagram for an individual cache. All actions are in gray because they are all externally caused. Bold indicates the action taken by the directory in response to the request.

- *Write miss*—The requesting node is sent the value and becomes the sharing node. The block is made exclusive to indicate that the only valid copy is cached. Sharers indicates the identity of the owner.

When the block is in the shared state, the memory value is up to date, so the same two requests can occur:

- *Read miss*—The requesting node is sent the requested data from memory, and the requesting node is added to the sharing set.
- *Write miss*—The requesting node is sent the value. All nodes in the set Sharers are sent invalidate messages, and the Sharers set is to contain the identity of the requesting node. The state of the block is made exclusive.

When the block is in the exclusive state, the current value of the block is held in a cache on the node identified by the set Sharers (the owner), so there are three possible directory requests:

▪ *Read miss*—The owner is sent a data fetch message, which causes the state of the block in the owner's cache to transition to shared and causes the owner to send the data to the directory, where it is written to memory and sent back to the requesting processor. The identity of the requesting node is added to the set Sharers, which still contains the identity of the processor that was the owner (since it still has a readable copy).

▪ *Data write-back*—The owner is replacing the block and therefore must write it back. This write-back makes the memory copy up to date (the home directory essentially becomes the owner), the block is now uncached, and the Sharers set is empty.

▪ *Write miss*—The block has a new owner. A message is sent to the old owner, causing the cache to invalidate the block and send the value to the directory, from which it is sent to the requesting node, which becomes the new owner. Sharers is set to the identity of the new owner, and the state of the block remains exclusive.

This state transition diagram in Figure 5.23 is a simplification, just as it was in the snooping cache case. In the case of a directory, as well as a snooping scheme implemented with a network other than a bus, our protocols will need to deal with nonatomic memory transactions. Appendix I explores these issues in depth.

The directory protocols used in real multiprocessors contain additional optimizations. In particular, in this protocol when a read or write miss occurs for a block that is exclusive, the block is first sent to the directory at the home node. From there it is stored into the home memory and also sent to the original requesting node. Many of the protocols in use in commercial multiprocessors forward the data from the owner node to the requesting node directly (as well as performing the write-back to the home). Such optimizations often add complexity by increasing the possibility of deadlock and by increasing the types of messages that must be handled.

Implementing a directory scheme requires solving most of the same challenges we discussed for snooping protocols beginning on page 365. There are, however, new and additional problems, which we describe in Appendix I. In Section 5.8, we briefly describe how modern multicores extend coherence beyond a single chip. The combinations of multichip coherence and multicore coherence include all four possibilities of snooping/snooping (AMD Opteron), snooping/directory, directory/snooping, and directory/directory!

5.5   Synchronization: The Basics

Synchronization mechanisms are typically built with user-level software routines that rely on hardware-supplied synchronization instructions. For smaller multiprocessors or low-contention situations, the key hardware capability is an uninterruptible instruction or instruction sequence capable of atomically retrieving and changing a value. Software synchronization mechanisms are then constructed using this capability. In this section, we focus on the implementation of lock and unlock synchronization operations. Lock and unlock can be used straightforwardly to create mutual exclusion, as well as to implement more complex synchronization mechanisms.

In high-contention situations, synchronization can become a performance bottleneck because contention introduces additional delays and because latency is potentially greater in such a multiprocessor. We discuss how the basic synchronization mechanisms of this section can be extended for large processor counts in Appendix I.

Basic Hardware Primitives

The key ability we require to implement synchronization in a multiprocessor is a set of hardware primitives with the ability to atomically read and modify a memory location. Without such a capability, the cost of building basic synchronization primitives will be too high and will increase as the processor count increases. There are a number of alternative formulations of the basic hardware primitives, all of which provide the ability to atomically read and modify a location, together with some way to tell if the read and write were performed atomically. These hardware primitives are the basic building blocks that are used to build a wide variety of user-level synchronization operations, including things such as locks and barriers. In general, architects do not expect users to employ the basic hardware primitives, but instead expect that the primitives will be used by system programmers to build a synchronization library, a process that is often complex and tricky. Let's start with one such hardware primitive and show how it can be used to build some basic synchronization operations.

One typical operation for building synchronization operations is the *atomic exchange*, which interchanges a value in a register for a value in memory. To see how to use this to build a basic synchronization operation, assume that we want to build a simple lock where the value 0 is used to indicate that the lock is free and 1 is used to indicate that the lock is unavailable. A processor tries to set the lock by doing an exchange of 1, which is in a register, with the memory address corresponding to the lock. The value returned from the exchange instruction is 1 if some other processor had already claimed access and 0 otherwise. In the latter case, the value is also changed to 1, preventing any competing exchange from also retrieving a 0.

For example, consider two processors that each try to do the exchange simultaneously: This race is broken since exactly one of the processors will perform the exchange first, returning 0, and the second processor will return 1 when it does the exchange. The key to using the exchange (or swap) primitive to implement synchronization is that the operation is atomic: The exchange is indivisible, and two simultaneous exchanges will be ordered by the write serialization mechanisms. It is impossible for two processors trying to set the synchronization variable in this manner to both think they have simultaneously set the variable.

There are a number of other atomic primitives that can be used to implement synchronization. They all have the key property that they read and update a memory value in such a manner that we can tell whether or not the two operations executed atomically. One operation, present in many older multiprocessors, is *test-and-set*, which tests a value and sets it if the value passes the test. For example, we could define an operation that tested for 0 and set the value to 1, which can be used in a fashion similar to how we used atomic exchange. Another atomic synchronization primitive is *fetch-and-increment*: It returns the value of a memory location and atomically increments it. By using the value 0 to indicate that the synchronization variable is unclaimed, we can use fetch-and-increment, just as we used exchange. There are other uses of operations like fetch-and-increment, which we will see shortly.

Implementing a single atomic memory operation introduces some challenges, since it requires both a memory read and a write in a single, uninterruptible instruction. This requirement complicates the implementation of coherence, since the hardware cannot allow any other operations between the read and the write, and yet must not deadlock.

An alternative is to have a pair of instructions where the second instruction returns a value from which it can be deduced whether the pair of instructions was executed as if the instructions were atomic. The pair of instructions is effectively atomic if it appears as if all other operations executed by any processor occurred before or after the pair. Thus, when an instruction pair is effectively atomic, no other processor can change the value between the instruction pair.

The pair of instructions includes a special load called a *load linked* or *load locked* and a special store called a *store conditional*. These instructions are used in sequence: If the contents of the memory location specified by the load linked are changed before the store conditional to the same address occurs, then the store conditional fails. If the processor does a context switch between the two instructions, then the store conditional also fails. The store conditional is defined to return 1 if it was successful and a 0 otherwise. Since the load linked returns the initial value and the store conditional returns 1 only if it succeeds, the following sequence implements an atomic exchange on the memory location specified by the contents of R1:

```
try:    MOV R3,R4  ;mov exchange value
        LL  R2,0(R1);load linked
        SC  R3,0(R1);store conditional
        BEQZ R3,try ;branch store fails
        MOV R4,R2   ;put load value in R4
```

At the end of this sequence the contents of R4 and the memory location specified by R1 have been atomically exchanged (ignoring any effect from delayed branches). Anytime a processor intervenes and modifies the value in memory between the LL and SC instructions, the SC returns 0 in R3, causing the code sequence to try again.

An advantage of the load linked/store conditional mechanism is that it can be used to build other synchronization primitives. For example, here is an atomic fetch-and-increment:

```
try:    LL   R2,0(R1) ;load linked
        DADDUIR3,R2,#1 ;increment
        SC   R3,0(R1) ;store conditional
        BEQZ R3,try ;branch store fails
```

These instructions are typically implemented by keeping track of the address specified in the LL instruction in a register, often called the *link register*. If an interrupt occurs, or if the cache block matching the address in the link register is invalidated (for example, by another SC), the link register is cleared. The SC instruction simply checks that its address matches that in the link register. If so, the SC succeeds; otherwise, it fails. Since the store conditional will fail after either another attempted store to the load linked address or any exception, care must be taken in choosing what instructions are inserted between the two instructions. In particular, only register-register instructions can safely be permitted; otherwise, it is possible to create deadlock situations where the processor can never complete the SC. In addition, the number of instructions between the load linked and the store conditional should be small to minimize the probability that either an unrelated event or a competing processor causes the store conditional to fail frequently.

Implementing Locks Using Coherence

Once we have an atomic operation, we can use the coherence mechanisms of a multiprocessor to implement *spin locks*—locks that a processor continuously tries to acquire, spinning around a loop until it succeeds. Spin locks are used when programmers expect the lock to be held for a very short amount of time and when they want the process of locking to be low latency when the lock is available. Because spin locks tie up the processor, waiting in a loop for the lock to become free, they are inappropriate in some circumstances.

The simplest implementation, which we would use if there were no cache coherence, would be to keep the lock variables in memory. A processor could continually try to acquire the lock using an atomic operation, say, atomic exchange from page 387, and test whether the exchange returned the lock as free. To release the lock, the processor simply stores the value 0 to the lock. Here is the code sequence to lock a spin lock whose address is in R1 using an atomic exchange:

```
        DADDUIR2,R0,#1
lockit: EXCHR2,0(R1)    ;atomic exchange
        BNEZR2,lockit   ;already locked?
```

If our multiprocessor supports cache coherence, we can cache the locks using the coherence mechanism to maintain the lock value coherently. Caching locks has two advantages. First, it allows an implementation where the process of "spinning" (trying to test and acquire the lock in a tight loop) could be done on a local cached copy rather than requiring a global memory access on each attempt to acquire the lock. The second advantage comes from the observation that there is often locality in lock accesses; that is, the processor that used the lock last will use it again in the near future. In such cases, the lock value may reside in the cache of that processor, greatly reducing the time to acquire the lock.

Obtaining the first advantage—being able to spin on a local cached copy rather than generating a memory request for each attempt to acquire the lock—requires a change in our simple spin procedure. Each attempt to exchange in the loop directly above requires a write operation. If multiple processors are attempting to get the lock, each will generate the write. Most of these writes will lead to write misses, since each processor is trying to obtain the lock variable in an exclusive state.

Thus, we should modify our spin lock procedure so that it spins by doing reads on a local copy of the lock until it successfully sees that the lock is available. Then it attempts to acquire the lock by doing a swap operation. A processor first reads the lock variable to test its state. A processor keeps reading and testing until the value of the read indicates that the lock is unlocked. The processor then races against all other processes that were similarly "spin waiting" to see who can lock the variable first. All processes use a swap instruction that reads the old value and stores a 1 into the lock variable. The single winner will see the 0, and the losers will see a 1 that was placed there by the winner. (The losers will continue to set the variable to the locked value, but that doesn't matter.) The winning processor executes the code after the lock and, when finished, stores a 0 into the lock variable to release the lock, which starts the race all over again. Here is the code to perform this spin lock (remember that 0 is unlocked and 1 is locked):

```
lockit:   LD R2,0(R1)       ;load of lock
          BNEZ R2,lockit     ;not available-spin
          DADDUI R2,R0,#1    ;load locked value
          EXCH R2,0(R1)      ;swap
          BNEZ R2,lockit     ;branch if lock wasn't 0
```

Let's examine how this "spin lock" scheme uses the cache coherence mechanisms. Figure 5.24 shows the processor and bus or directory operations for multiple processes trying to lock a variable using an atomic swap. Once the processor with the lock stores a 0 into the lock, all other caches are invalidated and must fetch the new value to update their copy of the lock. One such cache gets the copy of the unlocked value (0) first and performs the swap. When the cache miss of other processors is satisfied, they find that the variable is already locked, so they must return to testing and spinning.

Step	P0	P1	P2	Coherence state of lock at end of step	Bus/directory activity
1	Has lock	Begins spin, testing if lock = 0	Begins spin, testing if lock = 0	Shared	Cache misses for P1 and P2 satisfied in either order. Lock state becomes shared.
2	Set lock to 0	(Invalidate received)	(Invalidate received)	Exclusive (P0)	Write invalidate of lock variable from P0.
3		Cache miss	Cache miss	Shared	Bus/directory services P2 cache miss; write-back from P0; state shared.
4		(Waits while bus/directory busy)	Lock = 0 test succeeds	Shared	Cache miss for P2 satisfied
5		Lock = 0	Executes swap, gets cache miss	Shared	Cache miss for P1 satisfied
6		Executes swap, gets cache miss	Completes swap: returns 0 and sets lock = 1	Exclusive (P2)	Bus/directory services P2 cache miss; generates invalidate; lock is exclusive.
7		Swap completes and returns 1, and sets lock = 1	Enter critical section	Exclusive (P1)	Bus/directory services P1 cache miss; sends invalidate and generates write-back from P2.
8		Spins, testing if lock = 0			None

Figure 5.24 Cache coherence steps and bus traffic for three processors, P0, P1, and P2. This figure assumes write invalidate coherence. P0 starts with the lock (step 1), and the value of the lock is 1 (i.e., locked); it is initially exclusive and owned by P0 before step 1 begins. P0 exits and unlocks the lock (step 2). P1 and P2 race to see which reads the unlocked value during the swap (steps 3 to 5). P2 wins and enters the critical section (steps 6 and 7), while P1's attempt fails so it starts spin waiting (steps 7 and 8). In a real system, these events will take many more than 8 clock ticks, since acquiring the bus and replying to misses take much longer. Once step 8 is reached, the process can repeat with P2, eventually getting exclusive access and setting the lock to 0.

This example shows another advantage of the load linked/store conditional primitives: The read and write operations are explicitly separated. The load linked need not cause any bus traffic. This fact allows the following simple code sequence, which has the same characteristics as the optimized version using exchange (R1 has the address of the lock, the LL has replaced the LD, and the SC has replaced the EXCH):

```
lockit:   LLR2,0(R1)        ;load linked
          BNEZR2,lockit     ;not available-spin
          DADDUIR2,R0,#1    ;locked value
          SCR2,0(R1)        ;store
          BEQZR2,lockit     ;branch if store fails
```

The first branch forms the spinning loop; the second branch resolves races when two processors see the lock available simultaneously.

Models of Memory Consistency: An Introduction

Cache coherence ensures that multiple processors see a consistent view of memory. It does not answer the question of *how* consistent the view of memory must be. By "how consistent" we are really asking when must a processor see a value that has been updated by another processor? Since processors communicate through shared variables (used both for data values and for synchronization), the question boils down to this: In what order must a processor observe the data writes of another processor? Since the only way to "observe the writes of another processor" is through reads, the question becomes what properties must be enforced among reads and writes to different locations by different processors?

Although the question of how consistent memory must be seems simple, it is remarkably complicated, as we can see with a simple example. Here are two code segments from processes P1 and P2, shown side by side:

```
P1:     A = 0;          P2:     B = 0;
        .....                   .....
        A = 1;                  B = 1;
L1:     if (B == 0)...   L2:    if (A == 0)...
```

Assume that the processes are running on different processors, and that locations A and B are originally cached by both processors with the initial value of 0. If writes always take immediate effect and are immediately seen by other processors, it will be impossible for *both* if statements (labeled L1 and L2) to evaluate their conditions as true, since reaching the if statement means that either A or B must have been assigned the value 1. But suppose the write invalidate is delayed, and the processor is allowed to continue during this delay. Then, it is possible that both P1 and P2 have not seen the invalidations for B and A (respectively) *before* they attempt to read the values. The question now is should this behavior be allowed, and, if so, under what conditions?

The most straightforward model for memory consistency is called *sequential consistency*. Sequential consistency requires that the result of any execution be the same as if the memory accesses executed by each processor were kept in order and the accesses among different processors were arbitrarily interleaved. Sequential consistency eliminates the possibility of some nonobvious execution in the previous example because the assignments must be completed before the if statements are initiated.

The simplest way to implement sequential consistency is to require a processor to delay the completion of any memory access until all the invalidations caused by that access are completed. Of course, it is equally effective to delay the next memory access until the previous one is completed. Remember that memory consistency involves operations among different variables: The two accesses that must be ordered are actually to different memory locations. In our example, we must delay the read of A or B (A == 0 or B == 0) until the previous write has completed (B = 1 or A = 1). Under sequential consistency, we cannot, for example, simply place the write in a write buffer and continue with the read.

Although sequential consistency presents a simple programming paradigm, it reduces potential performance, especially in a multiprocessor with a large number of processors or long interconnect delays, as we can see in the following example.

Example   Suppose we have a processor where a write miss takes 50 cycles to establish ownership, 10 cycles to issue each invalidate after ownership is established, and 80 cycles for an invalidate to complete and be acknowledged once it is issued. Assuming that four other processors share a cache block, how long does a write miss stall the writing processor if the processor is sequentially consistent? Assume that the invalidates must be explicitly acknowledged before the coherence controller knows they are completed. Suppose we could continue executing after obtaining ownership for the write miss without waiting for the invalidates; how long would the write take?

Answer   When we wait for invalidates, each write takes the sum of the ownership time plus the time to complete the invalidates. Since the invalidates can overlap, we need only worry about the last one, which starts $10 + 10 + 10 + 10 = 40$ cycles after ownership is established. Hence, the total time for the write is $50 + 40 + 80 = 170$ cycles. In comparison, the ownership time is only 50 cycles. With appropriate write buffer implementations, it is even possible to continue before ownership is established.

To provide better performance, researchers and architects have explored two different routes. First, they developed ambitious implementations that preserve sequential consistency but use latency-hiding techniques to reduce the penalty; we discuss these in Section 5.7. Second, they developed less restrictive memory consistency models that allow for faster hardware. Such models can affect how the programmer sees the multiprocessor, so before we discuss these less restrictive models, let's look at what the programmer expects.

The Programmer's View

Although the sequential consistency model has a performance disadvantage, from the viewpoint of the programmer it has the advantage of simplicity. The challenge is to develop a programming model that is simple to explain and yet allows a high-performance implementation.

One such programming model that allows us to have a more efficient implementation is to assume that programs are *synchronized*. A program is synchronized if all accesses to shared data are ordered by synchronization operations. A data reference is ordered by a synchronization operation if, in every possible execution, a write of a variable by one processor and an access (either a read or a write) of that variable by another processor are separated by a pair of synchronization operations, one executed after the write by the writing processor and one executed before the access by the second processor. Cases where variables may be updated without ordering by synchronization are called *data races* because the execution outcome depends on the relative speed of the processors, and, like races in hardware design, the outcome is unpredictable, which leads to another name for synchronized programs: *data-race-free*.

As a simple example, consider a variable being read and updated by two different processors. Each processor surrounds the read and update with a lock and an unlock, both to ensure mutual exclusion for the update and to ensure that the read is consistent. Clearly, every write is now separated from a read by the other processor by a pair of synchronization operations: one unlock (after the write) and one lock (before the read). Of course, if two processors are writing a variable with no intervening reads, then the writes must also be separated by synchronization operations.

It is a broadly accepted observation that most programs are synchronized. This observation is true primarily because if the accesses were unsynchronized, the behavior of the program would likely be unpredictable because the speed of execution would determine which processor won a data race and thus affect the results of the program. Even with sequential consistency, reasoning about such programs is very difficult.

Programmers could attempt to guarantee ordering by constructing their own synchronization mechanisms, but this is extremely tricky, can lead to buggy programs, and may not be supported architecturally, meaning that they may not work in future generations of the multiprocessor. Instead, almost all programmers will choose to use synchronization libraries that are correct and optimized for the multiprocessor and the type of synchronization.

Finally, the use of standard synchronization primitives ensures that even if the architecture implements a more relaxed consistency model than sequential consistency, a synchronized program will behave as if the hardware implemented sequential consistency.

Relaxed Consistency Models: The Basics

The key idea in relaxed consistency models is to allow reads and writes to complete out of order, but to use synchronization operations to enforce ordering, so that a synchronized program behaves as if the processor were sequentially consistent. There are a variety of relaxed models that are classified according to what read and write orderings they relax. We specify the orderings by a set of rules of the form X→Y, meaning that operation X must complete before operation Y is done. Sequential consistency requires maintaining all four possible orderings: R→W, R→R, W→R, and W→W. The relaxed models are defined by which of these four sets of orderings they relax:

1. Relaxing the W→R ordering yields a model known as *total store ordering* or *processor consistency*. Because this ordering retains ordering among writes, many programs that operate under sequential consistency operate under this model, without additional synchronization.

2. Relaxing the W→W ordering yields a model known as *partial store order*.

3. Relaxing the R→W and R→R orderings yields a variety of models including *weak ordering*, the PowerPC consistency model, and *release consistency*, depending on the details of the ordering restrictions and how synchronization operations enforce ordering.

By relaxing these orderings, the processor can possibly obtain significant performance advantages. There are, however, many complexities in describing relaxed consistency models, including the advantages and complexities of relaxing different orders, defining precisely what it means for a write to complete, and deciding when processors can see values that the processor itself has written. For more information about the complexities, implementation issues, and performance potential from relaxed models, we highly recommend the excellent tutorial by Adve and Gharachorloo [1996].

Final Remarks on Consistency Models

At the present time, many multiprocessors being built support some sort of relaxed consistency model, varying from processor consistency to release consistency. Since synchronization is highly multiprocessor specific and error prone, the expectation is that most programmers will use standard synchronization libraries and will write synchronized programs, making the choice of a weak consistency model invisible to the programmer and yielding higher performance.

An alternative viewpoint, which we discuss more extensively in the next section, argues that with speculation much of the performance advantage of relaxed consistency models can be obtained with sequential or processor consistency.

A key part of this argument in favor of relaxed consistency revolves around the role of the compiler and its ability to optimize memory access to potentially shared variables; this topic is also discussed in Section 5.7.

5.7   Crosscutting Issues

Because multiprocessors redefine many system characteristics (e.g., performance assessment, memory latency, and the importance of scalability), they introduce interesting design problems that cut across the spectrum, affecting both hardware and software. In this section, we give several examples related to the issue of memory consistency. We then examine the performance gained when multithreading is added to multiprocessing.

Compiler Optimization and the Consistency Model

Another reason for defining a model for memory consistency is to specify the range of legal compiler optimizations that can be performed on shared data. In explicitly parallel programs, unless the synchronization points are clearly defined and the programs are synchronized, the compiler cannot interchange a read and a write of two different shared data items because such transformations might affect the semantics of the program. This prevents even relatively simple optimizations, such as register allocation of shared data, because such a process usually interchanges reads and writes. In implicitly parallelized programs—for example, those written in High Performance FORTRAN (HPF)—programs must be synchronized and the synchronization points are known, so this issue does not arise. Whether compilers can get significant advantage from more relaxed consistency models remains an open question, both from a research viewpoint and from a practical viewpoint, where the lack of uniform models is likely to retard progress on deploying compilers.

Using Speculation to Hide Latency in Strict Consistency Models

As we saw in Chapter 3, speculation can be used to hide memory latency. It can also be used to hide latency arising from a strict consistency model, giving much of the benefit of a relaxed memory model. The key idea is for the processor to use dynamic scheduling to reorder memory references, letting them possibly execute out of order. Executing the memory references out of order may generate violations of sequential consistency, which might affect the execution of the program. This possibility is avoided by using the delayed commit feature of a speculative processor. Assume the coherency protocol is based on invalidation. If the processor receives an invalidation for a memory reference before the memory reference is committed, the processor uses speculation recovery to back out of the computation and restart with the memory reference whose address was invalidated.

If the reordering of memory requests by the processor yields an execution order that could result in an outcome that differs from what would have been seen under sequential consistency, the processor will redo the execution. The key to using this approach is that the processor need only guarantee that the result would be the same as if all accesses were completed in order, and it can achieve this by detecting when the results might differ. The approach is attractive because the speculative restart will rarely be triggered. It will only be triggered when there are unsynchronized accesses that actually cause a race [Gharachorloo, Gupta, and Hennessy 1992].

Hill [1998] advocated the combination of sequential or processor consistency together with speculative execution as the consistency model of choice. His argument has three parts. First, an aggressive implementation of either sequential consistency or processor consistency will gain most of the advantage of a more relaxed model. Second, such an implementation adds very little to the implementation cost of a speculative processor. Third, such an approach allows the programmer to reason using the simpler programming models of either sequential or processor consistency. The MIPS R10000 design team had this insight in the mid-1990s and used the R10000's out-of-order capability to support this type of aggressive implementation of sequential consistency.

One open question is how successful compiler technology will be in optimizing memory references to shared variables. The state of optimization technology and the fact that shared data are often accessed via pointers or array indexing have limited the use of such optimizations. If this technology became available and led to significant performance advantages, compiler writers would want to be able to take advantage of a more relaxed programming model.

Inclusion and Its Implementation

All multiprocessors use multilevel cache hierarchies to reduce both the demand on the global interconnect and the latency of cache misses. If the cache also provides *multilevel inclusion*—every level of cache hierarchy is a subset of the level further away from the processor—then we can use the multilevel structure to reduce the contention between coherence traffic and processor traffic that occurs when snoops and processor cache accesses must contend for the cache. Many multiprocessors with multilevel caches enforce the inclusion property, although recent multiprocessors with smaller L1 caches and different block sizes have sometimes chosen not to enforce inclusion. This restriction is also called the *subset property* because each cache is a subset of the cache below it in the hierarchy.

At first glance, preserving the multilevel inclusion property seems trivial. Consider a two-level example: Any miss in L1 either hits in L2 or generates a miss in L2, causing it to be brought into both L1 and L2. Likewise, any invalidate that hits in L2 must be sent to L1, where it will cause the block to be invalidated if it exists.

The catch is what happens when the block sizes of L1 and L2 are different. Choosing different block sizes is quite reasonable, since L2 will be much larger and have a much longer latency component in its miss penalty, and thus will want to use a larger block size. What happens to our "automatic" enforcement of inclusion when the block sizes differ? A block in L2 represents multiple blocks in L1, and a miss in L2 causes the replacement of data that is equivalent to multiple L1 blocks. For example, if the block size of L2 is four times that of L1, then a miss in L2 will replace the equivalent of four L1 blocks. Let's consider a detailed example.

Example   Assume that L2 has a block size four times that of L1. Show how a miss for an address that causes a replacement in L1 and L2 can lead to violation of the inclusion property.

Answer   Assume that L1 and L2 are direct mapped and that the block size of L1 is b bytes and the block size of L2 is $4b$ bytes. Suppose L1 contains two blocks with starting addresses x and $x + b$ and that x mod $4b = 0$, meaning that x also is the starting address of a block in L2; then that single block in L2 contains the L1 blocks x, $x + b$, $x + 2b$, and $x + 3b$. Suppose the processor generates a reference to block y that maps to the block containing x in both caches and hence misses. Since L2 missed, it fetches $4b$ bytes and replaces the block containing x, $x + b$, $x + 2b$, and $x + 3b$, while L1 takes b bytes and replaces the block containing x. Since L1 still contains $x + b$, but L2 does not, the inclusion property no longer holds.

To maintain inclusion with multiple block sizes, we must probe the higher levels of the hierarchy when a replacement is done at the lower level to ensure that any words replaced in the lower level are invalidated in the higher-level caches; different levels of associativity create the same sort of problems. In 2011, designers still appear to be split on the enforcement of inclusion. Baer and Wang [1988] described the advantages and challenges of inclusion in detail. The Intel i7 uses inclusion for L3, meaning that L3 always includes the contents of all of L2 and L1. This allows them to implement a straightforward directory scheme at L3 and to minimize the interference from snooping on L1 and L2 to those circumstances where the directory indicates that L1 or L2 have a cached copy. The AMD Opteron, in contrast, makes L2 inclusive of L1 but has no such restriction for L3. They use a snooping protocol, but only needs to snoop at L2 unless there is a hit, in which case a snoop is sent to L1.

Performance Gains from Using Multiprocessing and Multithreading

In this section, we look at two different studies of the effectiveness of using multithreading on a multicore processor; we will return to this topic in the next section, when we examine the performance of the Intel i7. Our two studies are based on the Sun T1, which we introduced in Chapter 3, and the IBM Power5 processor.

We look at the performance of the T1 multicore using the same three server-oriented benchmarks—TPC-C, SPECJBB (the SPEC Java Business Benchmark), and SPECWeb99—that we examined in Chapter 3. The SPECWeb99 benchmark is only run on a four-core version of T1 because it cannot scale to use the full 32 threads of an eight-core processor; the other two benchmarks are run with eight cores and four threads each for a total of 32 threads. Figure 5.25 shows the per-thread and per-core CPIs and the effective CPI and instructions per clock (IPC) for the eight-core T1.

The IBM Power 5 is a dual-core that supports simultaneous multithreading (SMT). To examine the performance of multithreading in a multiprocessor, measurements were made on an IBM system with eight Power 5 processors, using only one core on each one. Figure 5.26 shows the speedup for an eight-processor Power5 multiprocessor, with and without SMT, for the SPECRate2000 benchmarks, as described in the caption. On average, the SPECintRate is 1.23 times faster, while the SPECfpRate is 1.16 times faster. Note that a few floating-point

Benchmark	Per-thread CPI	Per-core CPI	Effective CPI for eight cores	Effective IPC for eight cores
TPC-C	7.2	1.8	0.225	4.4
SPECJBB	5.6	1.40	0.175	5.7
SPECWeb99	6.6	1.65	0.206	4.8

Figure 5.25 The per-thread CPI, the per-core CPI, the effective eight-core CPI, and the effective IPC (inverse of CPI) for the eight-core Sun T1 processor.

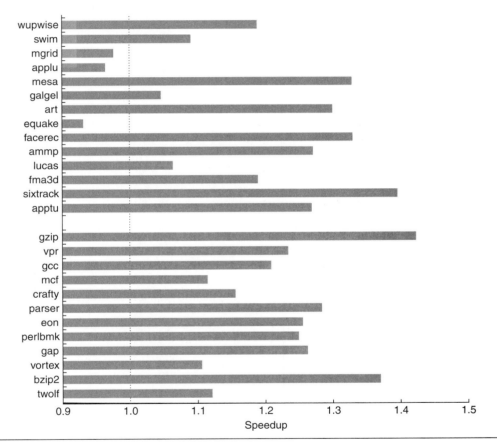

Figure 5.26 A comparison of SMT and single-thread (ST) performance on the eight-processor IBM eServer p5 575. Note that the *y*-axis starts at a speedup of 0.9, a performance loss. Only one processor in each Power5 core is active, which should slightly improve the results from SMT by decreasing destructive interference in the memory system. The SMT results are obtained by creating 16 user threads, while the ST results use only eight threads; with only one thread per processor, the Power5 is switched to single-threaded mode by the OS. These results were collected by John McCalpin of IBM. As we can see from the data, the standard deviation of the results for the SPECfpRate is higher than for SPECintRate (0.13 versus 0.07), indicating that the SMT improvement for FP programs is likely to vary widely.

Chapter Five Thread-Level Parallelism

benchmarks experience a slight decrease in performance in SMT mode, with the maximum reduction in speedup being 0.93. Although one might expect that SMT would do a better job of hiding the higher miss rates of the SPECFP benchmarks, it appears that limits in the memory system are encountered when running in SMT mode on such benchmarks.

5.8 Putting It All Together: Multicore Processors and Their Performance

In 2011, multicore is a theme of all new processors. The implementations vary widely, as does their support for larger multichip multiprocessors. In this section, we examine the design of four different multicore processors and some performance characteristics.

Figure 5.27 shows the key characteristics of four multicore processors designed for server applications. The Intel Xeon is based on the same design as the i7, but it has more cores, a slightly slower clock rate (power is the limitation), and a larger L3 cache. The AMD Opteron and desktop Phenom share the same basic core, while the SUN T2 is related to the SUN T1 we encountered in Chapter 3. The Power7 is an extension of the Power5 with more cores and bigger caches.

First, we compare the performance and performance scalability of three of these multicore processors (omitting the AMD Opteron where insufficient data are available) when configured as multichip multiprocessors.

In addition to how these three microprocessors differ in their emphasis on ILP versus TLP, there are significant differences in their target markets. Thus, our focus will be less on comparative absolute performance and more on scalability of performance as additional processors are added. After we examine this data, we will examine the multicore performance of the Intel Core i7 in more detail.

We show the performance for three benchmark sets: SPECintRate, SPECfpRate, and SPECjbb2005. The SPECRate benchmarks, which we clump together, illustrate the performance of these multiprocessors for request-level parallelism, since it is characterized by the parallel and overlapped execution of independent programs. In particular, nothing other than systems services is shared. SPECjbb2005 is a scalable Java business benchmark that models a three-tier client/server system, with the focus on the server, and is similar to the benchmark used in SPECPower, which we examined in Chapter 1. The benchmark exercises the implementations of the Java Virtual Machine, just in time compiler, garbage collection, threads, and some aspects of the operating system; it also tests scalability of multiprocessor systems.

Figure 5.28 shows the performance of the SPECRate CPU benchmarks as core counts are increased. Nearly linear speedup is achieved as the number of processor chips and hence the core count is increased.

Figure 5.29 shows similar data for the SPECjbb2005 benchmark. The trade-offs between exploiting more ILP and focusing on just TLP are complex and are highly workload dependent. SPECjbb2005 is a workload that scales up as additional processors are added, holding the time, rather than the problem size,

Feature	AMD Opteron 8439	IBM Power 7	Intel Xenon 7560	Sun T2
Transistors	904 M	1200 M	2300 M	500 M
Power (nominal)	137 W	140 W	130 W	95 W
Max. cores/chip	6	8	8	8
Multithreading	No	SMT	SMT	Fine-grained
Threads/core	1	4	2	8
Instruction issue/clock	3 from one thread	6 from one thread	4 from one thread	2 from 2 threads
Clock rate	2.8 GHz	4.1 GHz	2.7 GHz	1.6 GHz
Outermost cache	L3; 6 MB; shared	L3; 32 MB (using embedded DRAM); shared or private/core	L3; 24 MB; shared	L2; 4 MB; shared
Inclusion	No, although L2 is superset of L1	Yes, L3 superset	Yes, L3 superset	Yes
Multicore coherence protocol	MOESI	Extended MESI with behavioral and locality hints (13-state protocol)	MESIF	MOESI
Multicore coherence implementation	Snooping	Directory at L3	Directory at L3	Directory at L2
Extended coherence support	Up to 8 processor chips can be connected with HyperTransport in a ring, using directory or snooping. System is NUMA.	Up to 32 processor chips can be connected with the SMP links. Dynamic distributed directory structure. Memory access is symmetric outside of an 8-core chip.	Up to 8 processor cores can be implemented via Quickpath Interconnect. Support for directories with external logic.	Implemented via four coherence links per processor that can be used to snoop. Up to two chips directly connect, and up to four connect using external ASICs.

Figure 5.27 Summary of the characteristics of four recent high-end multicore processors (2010 releases) designed for servers. The table includes the highest core count versions of these processors; there are versions with lower core counts and higher clock rates for several of these processors. The L3 in the IBM Power7 can be all shared or partitioned into faster private regions dedicated to individual cores. We include only single-chip implementations of multicores.

constant. In this case, there appears to be ample parallelism to get linear speedup through 64 cores. We will return to this topic in the concluding remarks, but first let's take a more detailed look at the performance of the Intel Core i7 in a single-chip, four-core mode.

Performance and Energy Efficiency of the Intel Core i7 Multicore

In this section, we examine the performance of the i7 on the same two groups of benchmarks we considered in Chapter 3: the parallel Java benchmarks and the parallel PARSEC benchmarks (described in detail in Figure 3.34 on page 231).

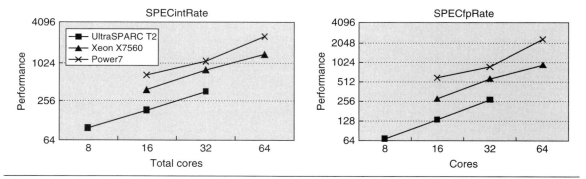

Figure 5.28 The performance on the SPECRate benchmarks for three multicore processors as the number of processor chips is increased. Notice for this highly parallel benchmark, nearly linear speedup is achieved. Both plots are on a log-log scale, so linear speedup is a straight line.

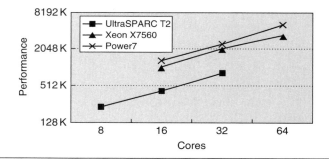

Figure 5.29 The performance on the SPECjbb2005 benchmark for three multicore processors as the number of processor chips is increased. Notice for this parallel benchmark, nearly linear speedup is achieved.

First, we look at the multicore performance and scaling versus a single-core without the use of SMT. Then, we combine both the multicore and SMT capability. All the data in this section, like that in the earlier i7 SMT evaluation (Chapter 3, Section 3.13) come from Esmaeilzadeh et al. [2011]. The dataset is the same as that used earlier (see Figure 3.34 on page 231), except that the Java benchmarks tradebeans and pjbb2005 are removed (leaving only the five scalable Java benchmarks); tradebeans and pjbb2005 never achieve speedup above 1.55 even with four cores and a total of eight threads, and thus are not appropriate for evaluating more cores.

Figure 5.30 plots both the speedup and energy efficiency of the Java and PARSEC benchmarks without the use of SMT. Showing energy efficiency means we are plotting the ratio of the energy consumed by the two- or four-core run by the energy consumed by the single-core run; thus, higher energy efficiency is better, with a value of 1.0 being the break-even point. The unused cores in all cases were in deep sleep mode, which minimized their power consumption by

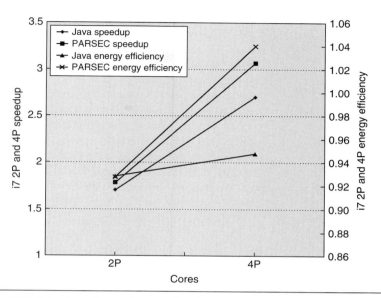

Figure 5.30 **This chart shows the speedup for two- and four-core executions of the parallel Java and PARSEC workloads without SMT.** These data were collected by Esmaeilzadeh et al. [2011] using the same setup as described in Chapter 3. Turbo Boost is turned off. The speedup and energy efficiency are summarized using harmonic mean, implying a workload where the total time spent running each 2p benchmark is equivalent.

essentially turning them off. In comparing the data for the single-core and multicore benchmarks, it is important to remember that the full energy cost of the L3 cache and memory interface is paid in the single-core (as well as the multicore) case. This fact increases the likelihood that energy consumption will improve for applications that scale reasonably well. Harmonic mean is used to summarize results with the implication described in the caption.

As the figure shows, the PARSEC benchmarks get better speedup than the Java benchmarks, achieving 76% speedup efficiency (i.e., actual speedup divided by processor count) on four cores, while the Java benchmarks achieve 67% speedup efficiency on four cores. Although this observation is clear from the data, analyzing why this difference exists is difficult. For example, it is quite possible that Amdahl's law effects have reduced the speedup for the Java workload. In addition, interaction between the processor architecture and the application, which affects issues such as the cost of synchronization or communication, may also play a role. In particular, well-parallelized applications, such as those in PARSEC, sometimes benefit from an advantageous ratio between computation and communication, which reduces the dependence on communications costs. (See Appendix I.)

These differences in speedup translate to differences in energy efficiency. For example, the PARSEC benchmarks actually slightly improve energy efficiency over the single-core version; this result may be significantly affected by the fact that the L3 cache is more effectively used in the multicore runs than in the single-core case and the energy cost is identical in both cases. Thus, for the PARSEC benchmarks, the multicore approach achieves what designers hoped for when they switched from an ILP-focused design to a multicore design; namely, it scales performance as fast or faster than scaling power, resulting in constant or even improved energy efficiency. In the Java case, we see that neither the two- or four-core runs break even in energy efficiency due to the lower speedup levels of the Java workload (although Java energy efficiency for the 2p run is the same as for PARSEC!). The energy efficiency in the four-core Java case is reasonably high (0.94). It is likely that an ILP-centric processor would need *even more* power to achieve a comparable speedup on either the PARSEC or Java workload. Thus, the TLP-centric approach is also certainly better than the ILP-centric approach for improving performance for these applications.

Putting Multicore and SMT Together

Finally, we consider the combination of multicore and multithreading by measuring the two benchmark sets for two to four processors and one to two threads (a total of four data points and up to eight threads). Figure 5.31 shows the

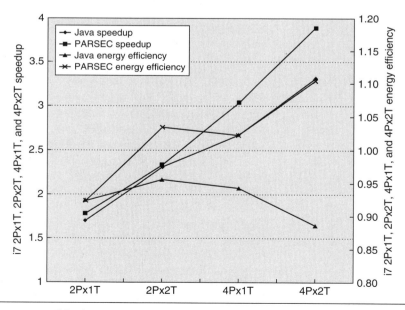

Figure 5.31 This chart shows the speedup for two- and four-core executions of the parallel Java and PARSEC workloads both with and without SMT. Remember that the results above vary in the number of threads from two to eight, and reflect both architectural effects and application characteristics. Harmonic mean is used to summarize results, as discussed in the caption of Figure 5.30.

speedup and energy efficiency obtained on the Intel i7 when the processor count is two or four and SMT is or is not employed, using harmonic mean to summarize the two benchmarks sets. Clearly, SMT can add to performance when there is sufficient thread-level parallelism available even in the multicore situation. For example, in the four-core, no-SMT case the speedup efficiencies were 67% and 76% for Java and PARSEC, respectively. With SMT on four cores, those ratios are an astonishing 83% and 97%!

Energy efficiency presents a slightly different picture. In the case of PARSEC, speedup is essentially linear for the four-core SMT case (eight threads), and power scales more slowly, resulting in an energy efficiency of 1.1 for that case. The Java situation is more complex; energy efficiency peaks for the two-core SMT (four-thread) run at 0.97 and drops to 0.89 in the four-core SMT (8-thread) run. It seems highly likely that the Java benchmarks are encountering Amdahl's law effects when more than four threads are deployed. As some architects have observed, multicore does shift more responsibility for performance (and hence energy efficiency) to the programmer, and the results for the Java workload certainly bear this out.

5.9 Fallacies and Pitfalls

Given the lack of maturity in our understanding of parallel computing, there are many hidden pitfalls that will be uncovered either by careful designers or by unfortunate ones. Given the large amount of hype that has surrounded multiprocessors over the years, common fallacies abound. We have included a selection of these.

Pitfall *Measuring performance of multiprocessors by linear speedup versus execution time.*

"Mortar shot" graphs—plotting performance versus number of processors, showing linear speedup, a plateau, and then a falling off—have long been used to judge the success of parallel processors. Although speedup is one facet of a parallel program, it is not a direct measure of performance. The first question is the power of the processors being scaled: A program that linearly improves performance to equal 100 Intel Atom processors (the low-end processor used for netbooks) may be slower than the version run on an eight-core Xeon. Be especially careful of floating-point-intensive programs; processing elements without hardware assist may scale wonderfully but have poor collective performance.

Comparing execution times is fair only if you are comparing the best algorithms on each computer. Comparing the identical code on two computers may seem fair, but it is not; the parallel program may be slower on a uniprocessor than a sequential version. Developing a parallel program will sometimes lead to algorithmic improvements, so comparing the previously best-known sequential program with the parallel code—which seems fair—will not compare equivalent algorithms. To reflect this issue, the terms *relative speedup* (same program) and *true speedup* (best program) are sometimes used.

Results that suggest *superlinear* performance, when a program on *n* processors is more than *n* times faster than the equivalent uniprocessor, may indicate that the comparison is unfair, although there are instances where "real" superlinear speedups have been encountered. For example, some scientific applications regularly achieve superlinear speedup for small increases in processor count (2 or 4 to 8 or 16). These results usually arise because critical data structures that do not fit into the aggregate caches of a multiprocessor with 2 or 4 processors fit into the aggregate cache of a multiprocessor with 8 or 16 processors.

In summary, comparing performance by comparing speedups is at best tricky and at worst misleading. Comparing the speedups for two different multiprocessors does not necessarily tell us anything about the relative performance of the multiprocessors. Even comparing two different algorithms on the same multiprocessor is tricky, since we must use true speedup, rather than relative speedup, to obtain a valid comparison.

Fallacy   *Amdahl's law doesn't apply to parallel computers.*

In 1987, the head of a research organization claimed that Amdahl's law (see Section 1.9) had been broken by an MIMD multiprocessor. This statement hardly meant, however, that the law has been overturned for parallel computers; the neglected portion of the program will still limit performance. To understand the basis of the media reports, let's see what Amdahl [1967] originally said:

> A fairly obvious conclusion which can be drawn at this point is that the effort expended on achieving high parallel processing rates is wasted unless it is accompanied by achievements in sequential processing rates of very nearly the same magnitude. [p. 483]

One interpretation of the law was that, since portions of every program must be sequential, there is a limit to the useful economic number of processors—say, 100. By showing linear speedup with 1000 processors, this interpretation of Amdahl's law was disproved.

The basis for the statement that Amdahl's law had been "overcome" was the use of *scaled speedup*, also called *weak scaling*. The researchers scaled the benchmark to have a dataset size that was 1000 times larger and compared the uniprocessor and parallel execution times of the scaled benchmark. For this particular algorithm, the sequential portion of the program was constant independent of the size of the input, and the rest was fully parallel—hence, linear speedup with 1000 processors. Because the running time grew faster than linear, the program actually ran longer after scaling, even with 1000 processors.

Speedup that assumes scaling of the input is not the same as true speedup and reporting it as if it were is misleading. Since parallel benchmarks are often run on different-sized multiprocessors, it is important to specify what type of application scaling is permissible and how that scaling should be done. Although simply scaling the data size with processor count is rarely appropriate, assuming a fixed problem size for a much larger processor count (called *strong scaling*) is often inappropriate, as well, since it is likely that users given a much larger multiprocessor would opt to run a larger or more detailed version of an application. See Appendix I for more discussion on this important topic.

Fallacy *Linear speedups are needed to make multiprocessors cost effective.*

It is widely recognized that one of the major benefits of parallel computing is to offer a "shorter time to solution" than the fastest uniprocessor. Many people, however, also hold the view that parallel processors cannot be as cost effective as uniprocessors unless they can achieve perfect linear speedup. This argument says that, because the cost of the multiprocessor is a linear function of the number of processors, anything less than linear speedup means that the performance/cost ratio decreases, making a parallel processor less cost effective than using a uniprocessor.

The problem with this argument is that cost is not only a function of processor count but also depends on memory, I/O, and the overhead of the system (box, power supply, interconnect, and so on). It also makes less sense in the multicore era, when there are multiple processors per chip.

The effect of including memory in the system cost was pointed out by Wood and Hill [1995]. We use an example based on more recent data using TPC-C and SPECRate benchmarks, but the argument could also be made with a parallel scientific application workload, which would likely make the case even stronger.

Figure 5.32 shows the speedup for TPC-C, SPECintRate, and SPECfpRate on an IBM eServer p5 multiprocessor configured with 4 to 64 processors. The figure shows that only TPC-C achieves better than linear speedup. For SPECintRate and SPECfpRate, speedup is less than linear, but so is the cost, since unlike TPC-C the amount of main memory and disk required both scale less than linearly.

As Figure 5.33 shows, larger processor counts can actually be more cost effective than the four-processor configuration. In comparing the cost-performance of two computers, we must be sure to include accurate assessments of both total system cost and what performance is achievable. For many applications with larger memory demands, such a comparison can dramatically increase the attractiveness of using a multiprocessor.

Pitfall *Not developing the software to take advantage of, or optimize for, a multiprocessor architecture.*

There is a long history of software lagging behind on multiprocessors, probably because the software problems are much harder. We give one example to show the subtlety of the issues, but there are many examples we could choose from!

One frequently encountered problem occurs when software designed for a uniprocessor is adapted to a multiprocessor environment. For example, the SGI operating system in 2000 originally protected the page table data structure with a single lock, assuming that page allocation is infrequent. In a uniprocessor,

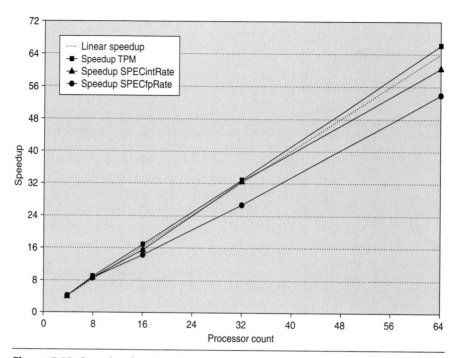

Figure 5.32 Speedup for three benchmarks on an IBM eServer p5 multiprocessor when configured with 4, 8, 16, 32, and 64 processors. The dashed line shows linear speedup.

this does not represent a performance problem. In a multiprocessor, it can become a major performance bottleneck for some programs. Consider a program that uses a large number of pages that are initialized at start-up, which UNIX does for statically allocated pages. Suppose the program is parallelized so that multiple processes allocate the pages. Because page allocation requires the use of the page table data structure, which is locked whenever it is in use, even an OS kernel that allows multiple threads in the OS will be serialized if the processes all try to allocate their pages at once (which is exactly what we might expect at initialization time!).

This page table serialization eliminates parallelism in initialization and has significant impact on overall parallel performance. This performance bottleneck persists even under multiprogramming. For example, suppose we split the parallel program apart into separate processes and run them, one process per processor, so that there is no sharing between the processes. (This is exactly what one user did, since he reasonably believed that the performance problem was due to unintended sharing or interference in his application.) Unfortunately, the lock still serializes all the processes, so even the multiprogramming performance is poor. This pitfall indicates the kind of subtle but significant performance bugs that can arise when software runs on multiprocessors. Like many other key software components, the OS

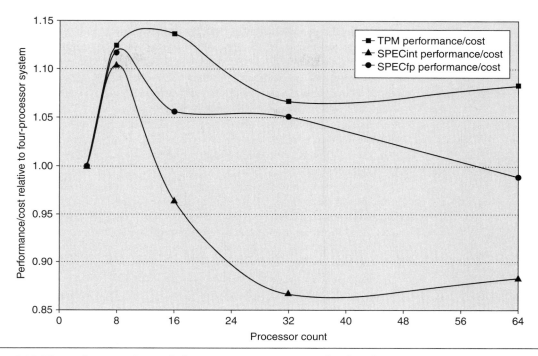

Figure 5.33 The performance/cost relative to a 4-processor system for three benchmarks run on an IBM eServer p5 multiprocessor containing from 4 to 64 processors shows that the larger processor counts can be as cost effective as the 4-processor configuration. For TPC-C the configurations are those used in the official runs, which means that disk and memory scale nearly linearly with processor count, and a 64-processor machine is approximately twice as expensive as a 32-processor version. In contrast, the disk and memory are scaled more slowly (although still faster than necessary to achieve the best SPECRate at 64 processors). In particular, the disk configurations go from one drive for the 4-processor version to four drives (140 GB) for the 64-processor version. Memory is scaled from 8 GB for the 4-processor system to 20 GB for the 64-processor system.

algorithms and data structures must be rethought in a multiprocessor context. Placing locks on smaller portions of the page table effectively eliminates the problem. Similar problems exist in memory structures, which increases the coherence traffic in cases where no sharing is actually occurring.

As multicore became the dominant theme in everything from desktops to servers, the lack of an adequate investment in parallel software became apparent. Given the lack of focus, it will likely be many years before the software systems we use adequately exploit this growing numbers of cores.

5.10   Concluding Remarks

For more than 30 years, researchers and designers have predicted the end of uniprocessors and their dominance by multiprocessors. Until the early years of this century, this prediction was constantly proven wrong. As we saw in Chapter 3, the costs of trying to find and exploit more ILP are prohibitive in efficiency (both in silicon area and in power). Of course, multicore does not solve the power problem, since it clearly increases both the transistor count and the active number of transistors switching, which are the two dominant contributions to power.

However, multicore does alter the game. By allowing idle cores to be placed in power-saving mode, some improvement in power efficiency can be achieved, as the results in this chapter have shown. More importantly, multicore shifts the burden for keeping the processor busy by relying more on TLP, which the application and programmer are responsible for identifying, rather than on ILP, for which the hardware is responsible. As we saw, these differences clearly played out in the multicore performance and energy efficiency of the Java versus the PARSEC benchmarks.

Although multicore provides some direct help with the energy efficiency challenge and shifts much of the burden to the software system, there remain difficult challenges and unresolved questions. For example, attempts to exploit thread-level versions of aggressive speculation have so far met the same fate as their ILP counterparts. That is, the performance gains have been modest and are likely less than the increase in energy consumption, so ideas such as speculative threads or hardware run-ahead have not been successfully incorporated in processors. As in speculation for ILP, unless the speculation is almost always right, the costs exceed the benefits.

In addition to the central problems of programming languages and compiler technology, multicore has reopened another long-standing question in computer architecture: Is it worthwhile to consider heterogeneous processors? Although no such multicore has yet been delivered and heterogeneous multiprocessors have had only limited success in special-purpose computers or embedded systems, the possibilities are much broader in a multicore environment. As with many issues in multiprocessing, the answer will likely depend on the software models and programming systems. If compilers and operating systems can effectively use heterogeneous processors, they will become more mainstream. At the present, dealing effectively with modest numbers of homogeneous core strains is beyond existing compiler capability for many applications, but multiprocessors that have heterogeneous cores with clear differences in functional capability and obvious methods to decompose an application are becoming more commonplace, including special processing units such as GPUs and media processors. Emphasis on energy efficiency could also lead to cores with different performance to power ratios being included.

In the 1995 edition of this text, we concluded the chapter with a discussion of two then-current controversial issues:

1. What architecture would very large-scale, microprocessor-based multiprocessors use?

2. What was the role for multiprocessing in the future of microprocessor architecture?

The intervening years have largely resolved these two questions.

Because very large-scale multiprocessors did not become a major and growing market, the only cost effective way to build such large-scale multiprocessors was to use clusters where the individual nodes are either single multicore microprocessors or small-scale, shared-memory multiprocessors (typically two to four multicores), and the interconnect technology is standard network technology. These clusters, which have been scaled to tens of thousands of processors and installed in specially designed "warehouses," are the subject of the next chapter.

The answer to the second question has become crystal clear in the last six or seven years: The future performance growth in microprocessors will come from the exploitation of thread-level parallelism through multicore processors rather than through exploiting more ILP.

As a consequence of this, cores have become the new building blocks of chips, and vendors offer a variety of chips based around one core design using varying numbers of cores and L3 caches. For example, Figure 5.34 shows the Intel processor family built using the just the Nehalem core (used in the Xeon 7560 and i7)!

In the 1980s and 1990s, with the birth and development of ILP, software in the form of optimizing compilers that could exploit ILP was key to its success. Similarly, the successful exploitation of thread-level parallelism will depend as much on the development of suitable software systems as it will on the contributions of computer architects. Given the slow progress on parallel software in the past 30-plus years, it is likely that exploiting thread-level parallelism broadly will remain challenging for years to come. Furthermore, your authors believe that there is significant opportunity for better multicore architectures. To design those architects will require a quantitative design discipline and the ability to accurately model tens to hundreds of cores running trillions of instructions, including large-scale applications and operating systems. Without such a methodology and capability, architects will be shooting in the dark. Sometimes you're lucky, but often you miss.

Processor	Series	Cores	L3 cache	Power (typical)	Clock rate (GHz)	Price
Xeon	7500	8	18–24 MB	130 W	2–2.3	$2837–3692
Xeon	5600	4–6 w/wo SMT	12 MB	40–130 W	1.86–3.33	$440–1663
Xeon	3400–3500	4 w/wo SMT	8 MB	45–130 W	1.86–3.3	$189–999
Xeon	5500	2–4	4–8 MB	80–130 W	1.86–3.3	$80–1600
i7	860–975	4	8 MB	82 W–130 W	2.53–3.33	$284–999
i7 mobile	720–970	4	6–8 MB	45–55 W	1.6–2.1	$364–378
i5	750–760	4 wo SMT	8 MB	80 W	2.4–2.8	$196–209
i3	330–350	2 w/wo SMT	3 MB	35 W	2.1–2.3	

Figure 5.34 The characteristics for a range of Intel parts based on the Nehalem microarchitecture. This chart still collapses a variety of entries in each row (from 2 to 8!). The price is for an order of 1000 units.

Historical Perspectives and References

Section L.7 (available online) looks at the history of multiprocessors and parallel processing. Divided by both time period and architecture, the section features discussions on early experimental multiprocessors and some of the great debates in parallel processing. Recent advances are also covered. References for further reading are included.

Case Studies and Exercises by Amr Zaky and David A. Wood

Case Study 1: Single-Chip Multicore Multiprocessor

Concepts illustrated by this case study

- Snooping Coherence Protocol Transitions
- Coherence Protocol Performance
- Coherence Protocol Optimizations
- Synchronization
- Memory Consistency Models Performance

The simple, multicore multiprocessor illustrated in Figure 5.35 represents a commonly implemented symmetric shared-memory architecture. Each processor has a single, private cache with coherence maintained using the snooping coherence protocol of Figure 5.7. Each cache is direct-mapped, with four blocks each holding two words. To simplify the illustration, the cache-address tag contains the full address, and each word shows only two hex characters, with the least significant word on the right. The coherence states are denoted M, S, and I (Modified, Shared, and Invalid).

5.1 [10/10/10/10/10/10/10] <5.2> For each part of this exercise, assume the initial cache and memory state as illustrated in Figure 5.35. Each part of this exercise specifies a sequence of one or more CPU operations of the form:

P#: <op> <address> [<value>]

where P# designates the CPU (e.g., P0), <op> is the CPU operation (e.g., read or write), <address> denotes the memory address, and <value> indicates the new word to be assigned on a write operation. Treat each action below as independently applied to the initial state as given in Figure 5.35. What is the resulting state (i.e., coherence state, tags, and data) of the caches and memory after the given action? Show only the blocks that change; for example, P0.B0: (I, 120, 00 01) indicates that CPU P0's block B0 has the final state of I, tag of 120, and data words 00 and 01. Also, what value is returned by each read operation?

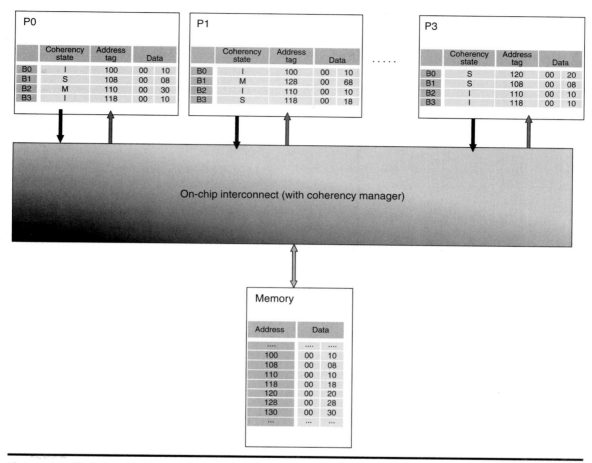

Figure 5.35 Multicore (point-to-point) multiprocessor.

a. [10] <5.2>   P0: read 120

b. [10] <5.2>   P0: write 120 <-- 80

c. [10] <5.2>   P3: write 120 <-- 80

d. [10] <5.2>   P1: read 110

e. [10] <5.2>   P0: write 108 <-- 48

f. [10] <5.2>   P0: write 130 <-- 78

g. [10] <5.2>   P3: write 130 <-- 78

5.2   [20/20/20/20] <5.3> The performance of a snooping cache-coherent multiprocessor depends on many detailed implementation issues that determine how quickly a cache responds with data in an exclusive or M state block. In some implementations, a CPU read miss to a cache block that is exclusive in another processor's cache is faster than a miss to a block in memory. This is because caches are smaller, and thus faster, than main memory. Conversely, in some implementations, misses satisfied by memory are faster than those satisfied by caches. This is because caches are generally optimized for "front side" or CPU references, rather than "back side" or snooping accesses. For the multiprocessor illustrated in Figure 5.35, consider the execution of a sequence of operations on a single CPU where

- CPU read and write hits generate no stall cycles.
- CPU read and write misses generate N_{memory} and N_{cache} stall cycles if satisfied by memory and cache, respectively.
- CPU write hits that generate an invalidate incur $N_{invalidate}$ stall cycles.
- A write-back of a block, due to either a conflict or another processor's request to an exclusive block, incurs an additional $N_{writeback}$ stall cycles.

Consider two implementations with different performance characteristics summarized in Figure 5.36. Consider the following sequence of operations assuming the initial cache state in Figure 5.35. For simplicity, assume that the second operation begins after the first completes (even though they are on different processors):

```
P1: read 110
P3: read 110
```

For Implementation 1, the first read generates 50 stall cycles because the read is satisfied by P0's cache. P1 stalls for 40 cycles while it waits for the block, and P0 stalls for 10 cycles while it writes the block back to memory in response to P1's request. Thus, the second read by P3 generates 100 stall cycles because its miss is satisfied by memory, and this sequence generates a total of 150 stall cycles. For the following sequences of operations, how many stall cycles are generated by each implementation?

Parameter	Implementation 1	Implementation 2
N_{memory}	100	100
N_{cache}	40	130
$N_{invalidate}$	15	15
$N_{writeback}$	10	10

Figure 5.36 Snooping coherence latencies.

a. [20] <5.3> P0: read 120
                P0: read 128
                P0: read 130

b. [20] <5.3> P0: read 100
                P0: write 108 <-- 48
                P0: write 130 <-- 78

c. [20] <5.3> P1: read 120
                P1: read 128
                P1: read 130

d. [20] <5.3> P1: read 100
                P1: write 108 <-- 48
                P1: write 130 <-- 78

5.3 [20] <5.2> Many snooping coherence protocols have additional states, state transitions, or bus transactions to reduce the overhead of maintaining cache coherency. In Implementation 1 of Exercise 5.2, misses are incurring fewer stall cycles when they are supplied by cache than when they are supplied by memory. Some coherence protocols try to improve performance by increasing the frequency of this case. A common protocol optimization is to introduce an Owned state (usually denoted O). The Owned state behaves like the Shared state in that nodes may only read Owned blocks, but it behaves like the Modified state in that nodes must supply data on other nodes' read and write misses to Owned blocks. A read miss to a block in either the Modified or Owned states supplies data to the requesting node and transitions to the Owned state. A write miss to a block in either state Modified or Owned supplies data to the requesting node and transitions to state Invalid. This optimized MOSI protocol only updates memory when a node replaces a block in state Modified or Owned. Draw new protocol diagrams with the additional state and transitions.

5.4 [20/20/20/20] <5.2> For the following code sequences and the timing parameters for the two implementations in Figure 5.36, compute the total stall cycles for the base MSI protocol and the optimized MOSI protocol in Exercise 5.3. Assume that state transitions that do not require bus transactions incur no additional stall cycles.

a. [20] <5.2> P0: read 110
                P3: read 110
                P0: read 110

b. [20] <5.2> P1: read 120
                P3: read 120
                P0: read 120

c. [20] <5.2> P0: write 120 <-- 80
                P3: read 120
                P0: read 120

d. [20] <5.2> P0: write 108 <-- 88
                P3: read 108
                P0: write 108 <-- 98

5.5 [20] <5.2> Some applications read a large dataset first, then modify most or all of it. The base MSI coherence protocol will first fetch all of the cache blocks in the Shared state and then be forced to perform an invalidate operation to upgrade them to the Modified state. The additional delay has a significant impact on some workloads. An additional protocol optimization eliminates the need to upgrade blocks that are read and later written by a single processor. This optimization adds the Exclusive (E) state to the protocol, indicating that no other node has a copy of the block, but it has not yet been modified. A cache block enters the Exclusive state when a read miss is satisfied by memory and no other node has a valid copy. CPU reads and writes to that block proceed with no further bus traffic, but CPU writes cause the coherence state to transition to Modified. Exclusive differs from Modified because the node may silently replace Exclusive blocks (while Modified blocks must be written back to memory). Also, a read miss to an Exclusive block results in a transition to Shared but does not require the node to respond with data (since memory has an up-to-date copy). Draw new protocol diagrams for a MESI protocol that adds the Exclusive state and transitions to the base MSI protocol's Modified, Shared, and Invalid states.

5.6 [20/20/20/20/20] <5.2> Assume the cache contents of Figure 5.35 and the timing of Implementation 1 in Figure 5.36. What are the total stall cycles for the following code sequences with both the base protocol and the new MESI protocol in Exercise 5.5? Assume that state transitions that do not require interconnect transactions incur no additional stall cycles.

a. [20] <5.2>
```
P0: read 100
P0: write 100 <-- 40
```

b. [20] <5.2>
```
P0: read 120
P0: write 120 <-- 60
```

c. [20] <5.2>
```
P0: read 100
P0: read 120
```

d. [20] <5.2>
```
P0: read 100
P1: write 100 <-- 60
```

e. [20] <5.2>
```
P0: read 100
P0: write 100 <-- 60
P1: write 100 <-- 40
```

5.7 [20/20/20/20] <5.5> The spin lock is the simplest synchronization mechanism possible on most commercial shared-memory machines. This spin lock relies on the exchange primitive to atomically load the old value and store a new value. The lock routine performs the exchange operation repeatedly until it finds the lock unlocked (i.e., the returned value is 0):

```
        DADDUI R2,R0,#1
lockit:     EXCH R2,0(R1)
            BNEZ R2, lockit
```

Unlocking a spin lock simply requires a store of the value 0:

```
unlock: SW R0,0(R1)
```

As discussed in Section 5.5, the more optimized spin lock employs cache coherence and uses a load to check the lock, allowing it to spin with a shared variable in the cache:

```
lockit:     LD      R2, 0(R1)
            BNEZ    R2, lockit
            DADDUI  R2,R0,#1
            EXCH    R2,0(R1)
            BNEZ    R2, lockit
```

Assume that processors P0, P1, and P3 are all trying to acquire a lock at address 0x100 (i.e., register R1 holds the value 0x100). Assume the cache contents from Figure 5.35 and the timing parameters from Implementation 1 in Figure 5.36. For simplicity, assume that the critical sections are 1000 cycles long.

a. [20] <5.5> Using the simple spin lock, determine *approximately* how many memory stall cycles each processor incurs before acquiring the lock.

b. [20] <5.5> Using the optimized spin lock, determine *approximately* how many memory stall cycles each processor incurs before acquiring the lock.

c. [20] <5.5> Using the simple spin lock, *approximately* how many interconnect transactions occur?

d. [20] <5.5> Using the test-and-test-and-set spin lock, *approximately* how many interconnect transactions occur?

5.8 [20/20/20/20] <5.6> Sequential consistency (SC) requires that all reads and writes appear to have executed in some total order. This may require the processor to stall in certain cases before committing a read or write instruction. Consider the following code sequence:

```
write A
read B
```

where the write A results in a cache miss and the read B results in a cache hit. Under SC, the processor must stall read B until after it can order (and thus perform) write A. Simple implementations of SC will stall the processor until the cache receives the data and can perform the write. Weaker consistency models relax the ordering constraints on reads and writes, reducing the cases that the processor must stall. The Total Store Order (TSO) consistency model requires that all writes appear to occur in a total order but allows a processor's reads to pass its own writes. This allows processors to implement write buffers that hold committed writes that have not yet been ordered with respect to other processors' writes. Reads are allowed to pass (and potentially bypass) the write buffer in TSO (which they could not do under SC). Assume that one memory operation can be performed per cycle and that operations that hit in the cache or that can be satisfied by the write buffer introduce no stall cycles. Operations that miss incur the latencies listed in Figure 5.36.

Assume the cache contents of Figure 5.35. How many stall cycles occur *prior* to each operation for both the SC and TSO consistency models?

a. [20] <5.6>   P0: write 110 <-- 80
                  P0: read 108

b. [20] <5.6>   P0: write 100 <-- 80
                  P0: read 108

c. [20] <5.6>   P0: write 110 <-- 80
                  P0: write 100 <-- 90

d. [20] <5.6>   P0: write 100 <-- 80
                  P0: write 110 <-- 90

Case Study 2: Simple Directory-Based Coherence

Concepts illustrated by this case study

■ Directory Coherence Protocol Transitions

■ Coherence Protocol Performance

■ Coherence Protocol Optimizations

Consider the distributed shared-memory system illustrated in Figure 5.37. It consists of two four-core chips. The processor in each chip share an L2 cache (L2$), and the two chips are connected via a point-to-point interconnect. The system memory is distributed across the two chips. Figure 5.38 zooms in on part of this system. Pi,j denotes processor *i* in chip *j*. Each processor has a single direct-mapped L1 cache that holds two blocks, each holding two words. Each chip has a single direct-mapped L2 cache that holds two blocks, each holding two words. To simplify the illustration, the cache address tags contain the full address and each word shows only two hex characters, with the least significant word on the right. The L1 cache states are denoted M, S, and I for Modified, Shared, and Invalid. Both the L2 caches and memories have directories. The directory states are denoted DM, DS, and DI for Directory Modified, Directory Shared, and Directory Invalid. The simple directory protocol is described in Figures 5.22 and 5.23. The L2 directory lists the local sharers/owners and additionally records if a line is shared externally in another chip; for example, P1,0;E denotes that a line is shared by local processor P1,0 and is externally shared in some other chip. The memory directory has a list of the chip sharers/owners of a line; for example, C0,C1 denotes that a line is shared in chips 0 and 1.

5.9   [10/10/10/10/15/15/15/15] <5.4> For each part of this exercise, assume the initial cache and memory state in Figure 5.38. Each part of this exercise specifies a sequence of one or more CPU operations of the form:

     P#: <op> <address> [<-- <value>]

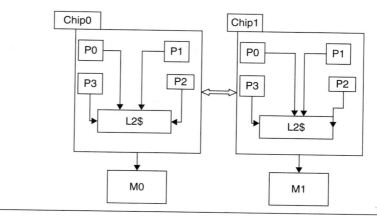

Figure 5.37 Multichip, multicore multiprocessor with DSM.

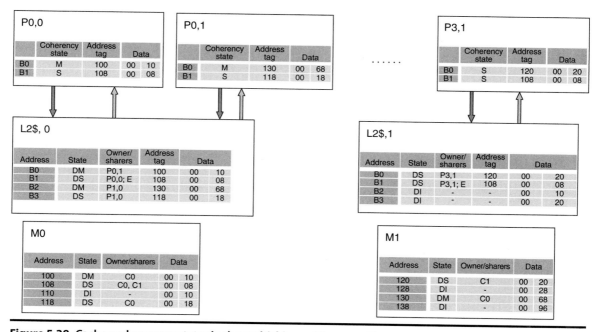

Figure 5.38 Cache and memory states in the multichip, multicore multiprocessor.

where P# designates the CPU (e.g., P0,0), <op> is the CPU operation (e.g., read or write), <address> denotes the memory address, and <value> indicates the new word to be assigned on a write operation. What is the final state (i.e., coherence state, sharers/owners, tags, and data) of the caches and memory after the given sequence of CPU operations has completed? Also, what value is returned by each read operation?

a. [10] <5.4>   P0,0: read 100

b. [10] <5.4>   P0,0: read 128

c. [10] <5.4>   P0,0: write 128 <-- 78

d. [10] <5.4>   P0,0: read 120

e. [15] <5.4>   P0,0: read 120
                 P1,0: read 120

f. [15] <5.4>   P0,0: read 120
                 P1,0: write 120 <-- 80

g. [15] <5.4>   P0,0: write 120 <-- 80
                 P1,0: read 120

h. [15] <5.4>   P0,0: write 120 <-- 80
                 P1,0: write 120 <-- 90

5.10   [10/10/10/10] <5.4> Directory protocols are more scalable than snooping proto-
        cols because they send explicit request and invalidate messages to those nodes
        that have copies of a block, while snooping protocols broadcast all requests and
        invalidates to all nodes. Consider the eight-processor system illustrated in
        Figure 5.37 and assume that all caches not shown have invalid blocks. For each
        of the sequences below, identify which nodes (chip/processor) receive each
        request and invalidate.

a. [10] <5.4>   P0,0: write 100 <-- 80

b. [10] <5.4>   P0,0: write 108 <-- 88

c. [10] <5.4>   P0,0: write 118 <-- 90

d. [10] <5.4>   P1,0: write 128 <-- 98

5.11   [25] <5.4> Exercise 5.3 asked you to add the Owned state to the simple MSI snoop-
        ing protocol. Repeat the question, but with the simple directory protocol above.

5.12   [25] <5.4> Discuss why adding an Exclusive state is much more difficult to do
        with the simple directory protocol than it is in a snooping protocol. Give an
        example of the kinds of issues that arise.

Case Study 3: Advanced Directory Protocol

Concepts illustrated by this case study

- Directory Coherence Protocol Implementation

- Coherence Protocol Performance

- Coherence Protocol Optimizations

The directory coherence protocol in Case Study 2 describes directory coherence at
an abstract level but assumes atomic transitions much like the simple snooping system. High-performance directory systems use pipelined, switched interconnects

that greatly improve bandwidth but also introduce transient states and nonatomic transactions. Directory cache coherence protocols are more scalable than snooping cache coherence protocols for two reasons. First, snooping cache coherence protocols broadcast requests to all nodes, limiting their scalability. Directory protocols use a level of indirection—a message to the directory—to ensure that requests are only sent to the nodes that have copies of a block. Second, the address network of a snooping system must deliver requests in a total order, while directory protocols can relax this constraint. Some directory protocols assume no network ordering, which is beneficial since it allows adaptive routing techniques to improve network bandwidth. Other protocols rely on point-to-point order (i.e., messages from node P0 to node P1 will arrive in order). Even with this ordering constraint, directory protocols usually have more transient states than snooping protocols. Figure 5.39

State	Read	Write	Replace-ment	Inv	Forwarded_GetS	Forwarded_GetM	PutM_Ack	Data	Last Ack
I	Send GetS/IS^D	Send GetM/IM^{AD}	error	Send Ack/I	error	error	error	error	error
S	Do read	Send GetM/IM^{AD}	I	Send Ack/I	error	error	error	error	error
M	Do read	Do write	Send PutM/MI^A	error	Send Data, send PutMS/MS^A	Send Data/I	error	error	error
IS^D	z	z	z	Send Ack/ISI^D	error	error	error	Save Data, do Read/S	error
ISI^D	z	z	z	Send Ack	error	error	error	Save Data, do Read/I	error
IM^{AD}	z	z	z	Send Ack	error	error	error	Save Data/IM^A	error
IM^A	z	z	z	error	IMS^A	IMI^A	error	error	Do Write/M
IMI^A	z	z	z	error	error	error	error	error	Do Write, send Data/I
IMS^A	z	z	z	Send Ack/IMI^A	z	z	error	error	Do write, send Data/S
MS^A	Do read	z	z	error	Send Data	Send Data MI^A	/S	error	error
MI^A	z	z	z	error	Send Data	Send Data/I	/I	error	error

Figure 5.39 Broadcast snooping cache controller transitions.

State	GetS	GetM	PutM (owner)	PutMS (nonowner)	PutM (owner)	PutMS (nonowner)
DI	Send Data, add to sharers/DS	Send Data, clear sharers, set owner/DM	error	Send PutM_Ack	error	Send PutM_Ack
DS	Send Data, add to sharers/DS	Send INVs to sharers, set owner, send Data/DM	error	Send PutM_Ack	error	Send PutM_Ack
DM	Forward GetS, add to sharers/DMS^D	Forward GetM, send INVs to sharers, clear sharers, set owner	Save Data, send PutM_Ack/DI	Send PutM_Ack	Save Data, add to sharers, send PutM_Ack/DS	Send PutM_Ack
DMS^D	Forward GetS, add to sharers	Forward GetM, send INVs to sharers, clear sharers, set owner/DM	Save Data, send PutM_Ack/DS	Send PutM_Ack	Save Data, add to sharers, send PutM_Ack/DS	Send PutM_Ack

Figure 5.40 Directory controller transitions.

presents the cache controller state transitions for a simplified directory protocol that relies on point-to-point network ordering. Figure 5.40 presents the directory controller's state transitions.

For each block, the directory maintains a state and a current owner field or a current sharers' list (if any). For the sake of the following discussion and ensuing problem, assume that the L2 caches are disabled. Assume that the memory directory lists sharers/owners at a processor granularity. For example, in Figure 5.38, the memory directory for line 108 would be "P0, 0; P3, 0" rather than "C0, C1". Also, assume that messages cross chip boundaries—if needed—in a transparent way.

The row is indexed by the current state, and the column by the event determines the <action/nextstate> tuple. If only a next state is listed, then no action is required. Impossible cases are marked "error" and represent error conditions; "z" means the requested event cannot currently be processed.

The following example illustrates the basic operation of this protocol. Suppose a processor attempts a write to a block in state I (Invalid). The corresponding tuple is "send GetM/IM^{AD}," indicating that the cache controller should send a GetM (GetModified) request to the directory and transition to state IM^{AD}. In the simplest case, the request message finds the directory in state DI (Directory Invalid), indicating that no other cache has a copy. The directory responds with a Data message that also contains the number of Acks to expect (in this case, zero). In this simplified protocol, the cache controller treats this single message as two messages: a Data message followed by a Last Ack event. The Data message is processed first, saving the data and transitioning to IM^A. The Last Ack event is then processed, transitioning to state M. Finally, the write can be performed in state M.

If the GetM finds the directory in state DS (Directory Shared), the directory will send Invalidate (INV) messages to all nodes on the sharers' list, send Data to the requester with the number of sharers, and transition to state M. When the INV messages arrive at the sharers, they will find the block in either state S or state I (if they have silently invalidated the block). In either case, the sharer will send an Ack directly to the requesting node. The requester will count the Acks it has received and compare that to the number sent back with the Data message. When all the Acks have arrived, the Last Ack event occurs, triggering the cache to transition to state M and allowing the write to proceed. Note that it is possible for all the Acks to arrive before the Data message, but not for the Last Ack event to occur. This is because the Data message contains the Ack count. Thus, the protocol assumes that the Data message is processed before the Last Ack event.

5.13 [10/10/10/10/10/10] <5.4> Consider the advanced directory protocol described above and the cache contents from Figure 5.38. What is the sequence of transient states that the affected cache blocks move through in each of the following cases?

   a. [10] <5.4>   P0,0: read 100

   b. [10] <5.4>   P0,0: read 120

   c. [10] <5.4>   P0,0: write 120 <-- 80

   d. [10] <5.4>   P3,1: write 120 <-- 80

   e. [10] <5.4>   P1,0: read 110

   f. [10] <5.4>   P0,0: write 108 <-- 48

5.14 [15/15/15/15/15/15/15] <5.4> Consider the advanced directory protocol described above and the cache contents from Figure 5.38. What is the sequence of transient states that the affected cache blocks move through in each of the following cases? In all cases, assume that the processors issue their requests in the same cycle, but the directory orders the requests in top-down order. Assume that the controllers' actions appear to be atomic (e.g., the directory controller will perform all the actions required for the DS --> DM transition before handling another request for the same block).

   a. [15] <5.4>   P0,0: read 120
                    P1,0: read 120

   b. [15] <5.4>   P0,0: read 120
                    P1,0: write 120 <-- 80

   c. [15] <5.4>   P0,0: write 120
                    P1,0: read 120

   d. [15] <5.4>   P0,0: write 120 <-- 80
                    P1,0: write 120 <-- 90

   e. [15] <5.4>   P0,0: replace 110
                    P1,0: read 110

   f. [15] <5.4>   P1,0: write 110 <-- 80
                    P0,0: replace 110

   g. [15] <5.4>   P1,0: read 110
                    P0,0: replace 110

5.15 [20/20/20/20/20] <5.4> For the multiprocessor illustrated in Figure 5.37 (with L2 caches disabled) implementing the protocol described in Figure 5.39 and Figure 5.40, assume the following latencies:

- CPU read and write hits generate no stall cycles.

- Completing a miss (e.g., do Read and do Write) takes L_{ack} cycles *only* if it is performed in response to the Last Ack event (otherwise, it gets done while the data are copied to cache).

- A CPU read or write that generates a replacement event issues the corresponding GetShared or GetModified message before the PutModified message (e.g., using a write-back buffer).

- A cache controller event that sends a request or acknowledgment message (e.g., GetShared) has latency L_{send_msg} cycles.

- A cache controller event that reads the cache and sends a data message has latency L_{send_data} cycles.

- A cache controller event that receives a data message and updates the cache has latency L_{rcv_data}.

- A memory controller incurs L_{send_msg} latency when it forwards a request message.

- A memory controller incurs an additional L_{inv} number of cycles for each invalidate that it must send.

- A cache controller incurs latency L_{send_msg} for each invalidate that it receives (latency is until it sends the Ack message).

- A memory controller has latency L_{read_memory} cycles to read memory and send a data message.

- A memory controller has latency L_{write_memory} to write a data message to memory (latency is until it sends the Ack message).

- A non-data message (e.g., request, invalidate, Ack) has network latency L_{req_msg} cycles.

- A data message has network latency L_{data_msg} cycles.

- Add a latency of 20 cycles to any message that crosses from chip 0 to chip 1 and *vice versa*.

Consider an implementation with the performance characteristics summarized in Figure 5.41.

For the sequences of operations below, the cache contents of Figure 5.38, and the directory protocol above, what is the latency observed by each processor node?

a. [20] <5.4> P0,0: read 100

b. [20] <5.4> P0,0: read 128

c. [20] <5.4> P0,0: write 128 <-- 68

d. [20] <5.4> P0,0: write 120 <-- 50

e. [20] <5.4> P0,0: write 108 <-- 80

Action	Latency
Send_msg	6
Send_data	20
Rcv_data	15
Read-memory	100
Write-memory	20
inv	1
ack	4
Req-msg	15
Data-msg	30

Figure 5.41 Directory coherence latencies.

5.16   [20] <5.4> In the case of a cache miss, both the switched snooping protocol described earlier and the directory protocol in this case study perform the read or write operation as soon as possible. In particular, they do the operation as part of the transition to the stable state, rather than transitioning to the stable state and simply retrying the operation. This is *not* an optimization. Rather, to ensure forward progress, protocol implementations must ensure that they perform at least one CPU operation before relinquishing a block. Suppose the coherence protocol implementation did not do this. Explain how this might lead to livelock. Give a simple code example that could stimulate this behavior.

5.17   [20/30] <5.4> Some directory protocols add an Owned (O) state to the protocol, similar to the optimization discussed for snooping protocols. The Owned state behaves like the Shared state in that nodes may only read Owned blocks, but it behaves like the Modified state in that nodes must supply data on other nodes' Get requests to Owned blocks. The Owned state eliminates the case where a GetShared request to a block in state Modified requires the node to send the data to both the requesting processor and the memory. In a MOSI directory protocol, a GetShared request to a block in either the Modified or Owned states supplies data to the requesting node and transitions to the Owned state. A GetModified request in state Owned is handled like a request in state Modified. This optimized MOSI protocol only updates memory when a node replaces a block in state Modified or Owned.

   a. [20] <5.4> Explain why the MSA state in the protocol is essentially a "transient" Owned state.

   b. [30] <5.4> Modify the cache and directory protocol tables to support a stable Owned state.

5.18   [25/25] <5.4> The advanced directory protocol described above relies on a point-to-point ordered interconnect to ensure correct operation. Assuming the initial cache contents of Figure 5.38 and the following sequences of operations, explain what problem could arise if the interconnect failed to maintain point-to-point ordering. Assume that the processors perform the requests at the same time, but they are processed by the directory in the order shown.

a. [25] <5.4>   P1,0: read 110
                  P3,1: write 110 <-- 90

b. [25] <5.4>   P1,0: read 110
                  P0,0: replace 110

Exercises

5.19 [15] <5.1> Assume that we have a function for an application of the form $F(i, p)$, which gives the fraction of time that exactly i processors are usable given that a total of p processors is available. That means that

$$\sum_{i=1}^{p} F(i, p) = 1$$

Assume that when i processors are in use, the applications run i times faster. Rewrite Amdahl's law so it gives the speedup as a function of p for some application.

5.20 [15/20/10] <5.1> In this exercise, we examine the effect of the interconnection network topology on the *clock cycles per instruction (CPI)* of programs running on a 64-processor distributed-memory multiprocessor. The processor clock rate is 3.3 GHz and the base CPI of an application with all references hitting in the cache is 0.5. Assume that 0.2% of the instructions involve a remote communication reference. The cost of a remote communication reference is $(100 + 10h)$ ns, where h is the number of communication network hops that a remote reference has to make to the remote processor memory and back. Assume that all communication links are bidirectional.

a. [15] <5.1> Calculate the worst-case remote communication cost when the 64 processors are arranged as a ring, as an 8×8 processor grid, or as a hypercube. (*Hint:* The longest communication path on a 2^n hypercube has n links.)

b. [20] <5.1> Compare the base CPI of the application with no remote communication to the CPI achieved with each of the three topologies in part (a).

c. [10] <5.1> How much faster is the application with no remote communication compared to its performance with remote communication on each of the three topologies in part (a).

5.21 [15] <5.2> Show how the basic snooping protocol of Figure 5.7 can be changed for a write-through cache. What is the major hardware functionality that is not needed with a write-through cache compared with a write-back cache?

5.22 [20] <5.2> Add a clean exclusive state to the basic snooping cache coherence protocol (Figure 5.7). Show the protocol in the format of Figure 5.7.

5.23 [15] <5.2> One proposed solution for the problem of false sharing is to add a valid bit per word. This would allow the protocol to invalidate a word without removing the entire block, letting a processor keep a portion of a block in its cache while another processor writes a different portion of the block. What extra complications are introduced into the basic snooping cache coherence protocol (Figure 5.7) if this capability is included? Remember to consider all possible protocol actions.

5.24 [15/20] <5.3> This exercise studies the impact of aggressive techniques to exploit instruction-level parallelism in the processor when used in the design of shared-memory multiprocessor systems. Consider two systems identical except for the processor. System A uses a processor with a simple single-issue in-order pipeline, while system B uses a processor with four-way issue, out-of-order execution, and a reorder buffer with 64 entries.

   a. [15] <5.3> Following the convention of Figure 5.11, let us divide the execution time into instruction execution, cache access, memory access, and other stalls. How would you expect each of these components to differ between system A and system B?

   b. [10] <5.3> Based on the discussion of the behavior of the On-Line Transaction Processing (OLTP) workload in Section 5.3, what is the important difference between the OLTP workload and other benchmarks that limits benefit from a more aggressive processor design?

5.25 [15] <5.3> How would you change the code of an application to avoid false sharing? What might be done by a compiler and what might require programmer directives?

5.26 [15] <5.4> Assume a directory-based cache coherence protocol. The directory currently has information that indicates that processor P1 has the data in "exclusive" mode. If the directory now gets a request for the same cache block from processor P1, what could this mean? What should the directory controller do? (Such cases are called *race conditions* and are the reason why coherence protocols are so difficult to design and verify.)

5.27 [20] <5.4> A directory controller can send invalidates for lines that have been replaced by the local cache controller. To avoid such messages and to keep the directory consistent, replacement hints are used. Such messages tell the controller that a block has been replaced. Modify the directory coherence protocol of Section 5.4 to use such replacement hints.

5.28 [20/30] <5.4> One downside of a straightforward implementation of directories using fully populated bit vectors is that the total size of the directory information scales as the product (i.e., processor count × memory blocks). If memory is grown linearly with processor count, the total size of the directory grows quadratically in the processor count. In practice, because the directory needs only 1 bit per memory block (which is typically 32 to 128 bytes), this problem is not serious for small to moderate processor counts. For example, assuming a 128-byte block, the amount of directory storage compared to main memory is the processor count/1024, or about 10% additional storage with 100 processors. This problem can be avoided by observing that we only need to keep an amount of information that is proportional to the cache size of each processor. We explore some solutions in these exercises.

a. [20] <5.4> One method to obtain a scalable directory protocol is to organize the multiprocessor as a logical hierarchy with the processors as leaves of the hierarchy and directories positioned at the root of each subtree. The directory at each subtree records which descendants cache which memory blocks, as well as which memory blocks with a home in that subtree are cached outside the subtree. Compute the amount of storage needed to record the processor information for the directories, assuming that each directory is fully associative. Your answer should also incorporate both the number of nodes at each level of the hierarchy as well as the total number of nodes.

b. [30] <5.4> An alternative approach to implementing directory schemes is to implement bit vectors that are not dense. There are two strategies; one reduces the number of bit vectors needed, and the other reduces the number of bits per vector. Using traces, you can compare these schemes. First, implement the directory as a four-way set associative cache storing full bit vectors, but only for the blocks that are cached outside the home node. If a directory cache miss occurs, choose a directory entry and invalidate the entry. Second, implement the directory so that every entry has 8 bits. If a block is cached in only one node outside its home, this field contains the node number. If the block is cached in more than one node outside its home, this field is a bit vector, with each bit indicating a group of eight processors, at least one of which caches the block. Using traces of 64-processor execution, simulate the behavior of these schemes. Assume a perfect cache for nonshared references so as to focus on coherency behavior. Determine the number of extraneous invalidations as the directory cache size in increased.

5.29   [10] <5.5> Implement the classical test-and-set instruction using the *load-linked/store-conditional* instruction pair.

5.30   [15] <5.5> One performance optimization commonly used is to pad synchronization variables to not have any other useful data in the same cache line as the synchronization variable. Construct a pathological example when not doing this can hurt performance. Assume a snooping write invalidate protocol.

5.31   [30] <5.5> One possible implementation of the *load-linked/store-conditional* pair for multicore processors is to constrain these instructions to using uncached memory operations. A monitor unit intercepts all reads and writes from any core to the memory. It keeps track of the source of the *load-linked* instructions and whether any intervening stores occur between the *load-linked* and its corresponding *store-conditional* instruction. The monitor can prevent any failing store conditional from writing any data and can use the interconnect signals to inform the processor that this store failed. Design such a monitor for a memory system supporting a four-core symmetric multiprocessor (SMP). Take into account that, generally, read and write requests can have different data sizes (4, 8, 16, 32 bytes). Any memory location can be the target of a *load-linked/store-conditional* pair, and the memory monitor should assume that *load-linked/store-conditional* references to any location can, possibly, be interleaved with regular accesses to the same location. The monitor complexity should be independent of the memory size.

5.32 [10/12/10/12] <5.6> As discussed in Section 5.6 the memory consistency model provides a specification of how the memory system will appear to the programmer. Consider the following code segment, where the initial values are

```
A=flag=C=0.
P1                          P2
A= 2000                     while (flag ==1){;}
flag=1                      C=A
```

a. [10] <5.6> At the end of the code segment, what is the value you would expect for C?

b. [12] <5.6> A system with a general-purpose interconnection network, a directory-based cache coherence protocol, and support for nonblocking loads generates a result where C is 0. Describe a scenario where this result is possible.

c. [10] <5.6> If you wanted to make the system sequentially consistent, what are the key constraints you would need to impose?

Assume that a processor supports a relaxed memory consistency model. A relaxed consistency model requires synchronization to be explicitly identified. Assume that the processor supports a "barrier" instruction, which ensures that all memory operations preceding the barrier instruction complete before any memory operations following the barrier are allowed to begin. Where would you include barrier instructions in the above code segment to ensure that you get the "intuitive results" of sequential consistency?

5.33 [25] <5.7> Prove that in a two-level cache hierarchy, where L1 is closer to the processor, inclusion is maintained with no extra action if L2 has at least as much associativity as L1, both caches use line replaceable unit (LRU) replacement, and both caches have the same block sizes.

5.34 [Discussion] <5.7> When trying to perform detailed performance evaluation of a multiprocessor system, system designers use one of three tools: analytical models, trace-driven simulation, and execution-driven simulation. Analytical models use mathematical expressions to model the behavior of programs. Trace-driven simulations run the applications on a real machine and generate a trace, typically of memory operations. These traces can be replayed through a cache simulator or a simulator with a simple processor model to predict the performance of the system when various parameters are changed. Execution-driven simulators simulate the entire execution maintaining an equivalent structure for the processor state and so on. What are the accuracy and speed trade-offs between these approaches?

5.35 [40] <5.7, 5.9> Multiprocessors and clusters usually show performance increases as you increase the number of the processors, with the ideal being $n\times$ speedup for n processors. The goal of this biased benchmark is to make a program that gets worse performance as you add processors. This means, for example, that one processor on the multiprocessor or cluster runs the program fastest, two are slower, four are slower than two, and so on. What are the key performance characteristics for each organization that give inverse linear speedup?

6

Warehouse-Scale Computers to Exploit Request-Level and Data-Level Parallelism

The datacenter is the computer.

Luiz André Barroso,
Google (2007)

A hundred years ago, companies stopped generating their own power with steam engines and dynamos and plugged into the newly built electric grid. The cheap power pumped out by electric utilities didn't just change how businesses operate. It set off a chain reaction of economic and social transformations that brought the modern world into existence. Today, a similar revolution is under way. Hooked up to the Internet's global computing grid, massive information-processing plants have begun pumping data and software code into our homes and businesses. This time, it's computing that's turning into a utility.

Nicholas Carr
The Big Switch: Rewiring the World, from
Edison to Google (2008)

6.1

Introduction

> Anyone can build a fast CPU. The trick is to build a fast system.
>
> **Seymour Cray**
> *Considered the father of the supercomputer*

The warehouse-scale computer (WSC)[1] is the foundation of Internet services many people use every day: search, social networking, online maps, video sharing, online shopping, email services, and so on. The tremendous popularity of such Internet services necessitated the creation of WSCs that could keep up with the rapid demands of the public. Although WSCs may appear to be just large datacenters, their architecture and operation are quite different, as we shall see. Today's WSCs act as one giant machine and cost on the order of $150M for the building, the electrical and cooling infrastructure, the servers, and the networking equipment that connects and houses 50,000 to 100,000 servers. Moreover, the rapid growth of cloud computing (see Section 6.5) makes WSCs available to anyone with a credit card.

Computer architecture extends naturally to designing WSCs. For example, Luiz Barroso of Google (quoted earlier) did his dissertation research in computer architecture. He believes an architect's skills of designing for scale, designing for dependability, and a knack for debugging hardware are very helpful in the creation and operation of WSCs.

At this extreme scale, which requires innovation in power distribution, cooling, monitoring, and operations, the WSC is the modern descendant of the supercomputer—making Seymour Cray the godfather of today's WSC architects. His extreme computers handled computations that could be done nowhere else, but were so expensive that only a few companies could afford them. This time the target is providing information technology for the world instead of high-performance computing (HPC) for scientists and engineers; hence, WSCs arguably play a more important role for society today than Cray's supercomputers did in the past.

Unquestionably, WSCs have many orders of magnitude more users than high-performance computing, and they represent a much larger share of the IT market. Whether measured by number of users or revenue, Google is at least 250 times larger than Cray Research ever was.

---

[1] This chapter is based on material from the book *The Datacenter as a Computer: An Introduction to the Design of Warehouse-Scale Machines*, by Luiz André Barroso and Urs Hölzle of Google [2009]; the blog Perspectives at mvdirona.com and the talks "Cloud-Computing Economies of Scale" and "Data Center Networks Are in My Way," by James Hamilton of Amazon Web Services [2009, 2010]; and the technical report *Above the Clouds: A Berkeley View of Cloud Computing*, by Michael Armbrust et al. [2009].

WSC architects share many goals and requirements with server architects:

- *Cost-performance*—Work done per dollar is critical in part because of the scale. Reducing the capital cost of a WSC by 10% could save $15M.

- *Energy efficiency*—Power distribution costs are functionally related to power consumption; you need sufficient power distribution before you can consume power. Mechanical system costs are functionally related to power: You need to get out the heat that you put in. Hence, peak power and consumed power drive both the cost of power distribution and the cost of cooling systems. Moreover, energy efficiency is an important part of environmental stewardship. Hence, work done per joule is critical for both WSCs and servers because of the high cost of building the power and mechanical infrastructure for a warehouse of computers and for the monthly utility bills to power servers.

- *Dependability via redundancy*—The long-running nature of Internet services means that the hardware and software in a WSC must collectively provide at least 99.99% of availability; that is, it must be down less than 1 hour per year. Redundancy is the key to dependability for both WSCs and servers. While server architects often utilize more hardware offered at higher costs to reach high availability, WSC architects rely instead on multiple cost-effective servers connected by a low-cost network and redundancy managed by software. Furthermore, if the goal is to go much beyond "four nines" of availability, you need multiple WSCs to mask events that can take out whole WSCs. Multiple WSCs also reduce latency for services that are widely deployed.

- *Network I/O*—Server architects must provide a good network interface to the external world, and WSC architects must also. Networking is needed to keep data consistent between multiple WSCs as well as to interface to the public.

- *Both interactive and batch processing workloads*—While you expect highly interactive workloads for services like search and social networking with millions of users, WSCs, like servers, also run massively parallel batch programs to calculate metadata useful to such services. For example, MapReduce jobs are run to convert the pages returned from crawling the Web into search indices (see Section 6.2).

Not surprisingly, there are also characteristics *not* shared with server architecture:

- *Ample parallelism*—A concern for a server architect is whether the applications in the targeted marketplace have enough parallelism to justify the amount of parallel hardware and whether the cost is too high for sufficient communication hardware to exploit this parallelism. A WSC architect has no such concern. First, batch applications benefit from the large number of independent datasets that require independent processing, such as billions of Web pages from a Web crawl. This processing is *data-level parallelism* applied to data in storage instead of data in memory, which we saw in Chapter 4. Second, interactive Internet service applications, also known as *software as a service* (*SaaS*), can benefit from millions of independent users of interactive Internet services. Reads and writes are rarely dependent in SaaS, so SaaS rarely needs to synchronize. For example, search uses a read-only index and email is normally reading- and writing-independent information. We call this type of easy parallelism *request-level parallelism*, as many independent efforts can proceed in parallel naturally with little need for communication or synchronization; for example, journal-based updating can reduce throughput demands. Given the success of SaaS and WSCs, more traditional applications such as relational databases have been weakened to rely on request-level parallelism. Even read-/write-dependent features are sometimes dropped to offer storage that can scale to the size of modern WSCs.

■ *Operational costs count*—Server architects usually design their systems for peak performance within a cost budget and worry about power only to make sure they don't exceed the cooling capacity of their enclosure. They usually ignore operational costs of a server, assuming that they pale in comparison to purchase costs. WSCs have longer lifetimes—the building and electrical and cooling infrastructure are often amortized over 10 or more years—so the operational costs add up: Energy, power distribution, and cooling represent more than 30% of the costs of a WSC in 10 years.

■ *Scale and the opportunities/problems associated with scale*—Often extreme computers are extremely expensive because they require custom hardware, and yet the cost of customization cannot be effectively amortized since few extreme computers are made. However, when you purchase 50,000 servers and the infrastructure that goes with it to construct a single WSC, you *do* get volume discounts. WSCs are so massive internally that you get economy of scale even if there are not many WSCs. As we shall see in Sections 6.5 and 6.10, these economies of scale led to cloud computing, as the lower per-unit costs of a WSC meant that companies could rent them at a profit below what it costs outsiders to do it themselves. The flip side of 50,000 servers is failures. Figure 6.1 shows outages and anomalies for 2400 servers. Even if a server had a mean time to failure (MTTF) of an amazing 25 years (200,000 hours), the WSC architect would need to design for 5 server failures a day. Figure 6.1 lists the annualized disk failure rate as 2% to 10%. If there were 4 disks per server and their annual failure rate was 4%, with 50,000 servers the WSC architect should expect to see one disk fail per *hour*.

Example   Calculate the availability of a service running on the 2400 servers in Figure 6.1. Unlike a service in a real WSC, in this example the service cannot tolerate hardware or software failures. Assume that the time to reboot software is 5 minutes and the time to repair hardware is 1 hour.

Answer   We can estimate service availability by calculating the time of outages due to failures of each component. We'll conservatively take the lowest number in each category in Figure 6.1 and split the 1000 outages evenly between four components. We ignore slow disks—the fifth component of the 1000 outages—since

Approx. number events in 1st year	Cause	Consequence
1 or 2	Power utility failures	Lose power to whole WSC; doesn't bring down WSC if UPS and generators work (generators work about 99% of time).
4	Cluster upgrades	Planned outage to upgrade infrastructure, many times for evolving networking needs such as recabling, to switch firmware upgrades, and so on. There are about 9 planned cluster outages for every unplanned outage.
1000s	Hard-drive failures	2% to 10% annual disk failure rate [Pinheiro 2007]
	Slow disks	Still operate, but run 10x to 20x more slowly
	Bad memories	One uncorrectable DRAM error per year [Schroeder et al. 2009]
	Misconfigured machines	Configuration led to ~30% of service disruptions [Barroso and Hölzle 2009]
	Flaky machines	1% of servers reboot more than once a week [Barroso and Hölzle 2009]
5000	Individual server crashes	Machine reboot, usually takes about 5 minutes

Figure 6.1 List of outages and anomalies with the approximate frequencies of occurrences in the first year of a new cluster of 2400 servers. We label what Google calls a cluster an *array*; see Figure 6.5. (Based on Barroso [2010].)

they hurt performance but not availability, and power utility failures, since the uninterruptible power supply (UPS) system hides 99% of them.

$$\text{Hours Outage}_{service} = (4 + 250 + 250 + 250) \times 1 \text{ hour } + (250 + 5000) \times 5 \text{ minutes}$$
$$= 754 + 438 = 1192 \text{ hours}$$

Since there are 365×24 or 8760 hours in a year, availability is:

$$\text{Availability}_{system} = \frac{(8760 - 1192)}{8760} = \frac{7568}{8760} = 86\%$$

That is, without software redundancy to mask the many outages, a service on those 2400 servers would be down on average one day a week, or *zero* nines of availability!

As Section 6.10 explains, the forerunners of WSCs are *computer clusters*. Clusters are collections of independent computers that are connected together using standard local area networks (LANs) and off-the-shelf switches. For workloads that did not require intensive communication, clusters offered much more cost-effective computing than shared memory multiprocessors. (Shared memory multiprocessors were the forerunners of the multicore computers discussed in Chapter 5.) Clusters became popular in the late 1990s for scientific computing and then later for Internet services. One view of WSCs is that they are just the logical evolution from clusters of hundreds of servers to tens of thousands of servers today.

A natural question is whether WSCs are similar to modern clusters for high-performance computing. Although some have similar scale and cost—there are HPC designs with a million processors that cost hundreds of millions of dollars—they generally have much faster processors and much faster networks between the nodes than are found in WSCs because the HPC applications are more interdependent and communicate more frequently (see Section 6.3). HPC designs also tend to use custom hardware—especially in the network—so they often don't get the cost benefits from using commodity chips. For example, the IBM Power 7 microprocessor alone can cost more and use more power than an entire server node in a Google WSC. The programming environment also emphasizes thread-level parallelism or data-level parallelism (see Chapters 4 and 5), typically emphasizing latency to complete a single task as opposed to bandwidth to complete many independent tasks via request-level parallelism. The HPC clusters also tend to have long-running jobs that keep the servers fully utilized, even for weeks at a time, while the utilization of servers in WSCs ranges between 10% and 50% (see Figure 6.3 on page 440) and varies every day.

How do WSCs compare to conventional datacenters? The operators of a conventional datacenter generally collect machines and third-party software from many parts of an organization and run them centrally for others. Their main focus tends to be consolidation of the many services onto fewer machines, which are isolated from each other to protect sensitive information. Hence, virtual machines are increasingly important in datacenters. Unlike WSCs, conventional datacenters tend to have a great deal of hardware and software heterogeneity to serve their varied customers inside an organization. WSC programmers customize third-party software or build their own, and WSCs have much more homogeneous hardware; the WSC goal is to make the hardware/software in the warehouse act like a single computer that typically runs a variety of applications. Often the largest cost in a conventional datacenter is the people to maintain it, whereas, as we shall see in Section 6.4, in a well-designed WSC the server hardware is the greatest cost, and people costs shift from the topmost to nearly irrelevant. Conventional datacenters also don't have the scale of a WSC, so they don't get the economic benefits of scale mentioned above. Hence, while you might consider a WSC as an extreme datacenter, in that computers are housed separately in a space with special electrical and cooling infrastructure, typical datacenters share little with the challenges and opportunities of a WSC, either architecturally or operationally.

Since few architects understand the software that runs in a WSC, we start with the workload and programming model of a WSC.

6.2 Programming Models and Workloads for Warehouse-Scale Computers

If a problem has no solution, it may not be a problem, but a fact—not to be solved, but to be coped with over time.

Shimon Peres

In addition to the public-facing Internet services such as search, video sharing, and social networking that make them famous, WSCs also run batch applications, such as converting videos into new formats or creating search indexes from Web crawls.

Today, the most popular framework for batch processing in a WSC is Map-Reduce [Dean and Ghemawat 2008] and its open-source twin Hadoop. Figure 6.2 shows the increasing popularity of MapReduce at Google over time. (Facebook runs Hadoop on 2000 batch-processing servers of the 60,000 servers it is estimated to have in 2011.) Inspired by the Lisp functions of the same name, Map first applies a programmer-supplied function to each logical input record. Map runs on thousands of computers to produce an intermediate result of key-value pairs. Reduce collects the output of those distributed tasks and collapses them using another programmer-defined function. With appropriate software support, both are highly parallel yet easy to understand and to use. Within 30 minutes, a novice programmer can run a MapReduce task on thousands of computers.

For example, one MapReduce program calculates the number of occurrences of every English word in a large collection of documents. Below is a simplified version of that program, which shows just the inner loop and assumes just one occurrence of all English words found in a document [Dean and Ghemawat 2008]:

```
map(String key, String value):
        // key: document name
        // value: document contents
        for each word w in value:
        EmitIntermediate(w, "1"); // Produce list of all words

reduce(String key, Iterator values):
        // key: a word
        // values: a list of counts
        int result = 0;
        for each v in values:

        result += ParseInt(v); // get integer from key-value pair
        Emit(AsString(result));
```

	Aug-04	Mar-06	Sep-07	Sep-09
Number of MapReduce jobs	29,000	171,000	2,217,000	3,467,000
Average completion time (seconds)	634	874	395	475
Server years used	217	2002	11,081	25,562
Input data read (terabytes)	3288	52,254	403,152	544,130
Intermediate data (terabytes)	758	6743	34,774	90,120
Output data written (terabytes)	193	2970	14,018	57,520
Average number of servers per job	157	268	394	488

Figure 6.2 Annual MapReduce usage at Google over time. Over five years the number of MapReduce jobs increased by a factor of 100 and the average number of servers per job increased by a factor of 3. In the last two years the increases were factors of 1.6 and 1.2, respectively [Dean 2009]. Figure 6.16 on page 459 estimates that running the 2009 workload on Amazon's cloud computing service EC2 would cost $133M.

The function EmitIntermediate used in the Map function emits each word in the document and the value one. Then the Reduce function sums all the values per word for each document using ParseInt() to get the number of occurrences per word in all documents. The MapReduce runtime environment schedules map tasks and reduce task to the nodes of a WSC. (The complete version of the program is found in Dean and Ghemawat [2004].)

MapReduce can be thought of as a generalization of the single-instruction, multiple-data (SIMD) operation (Chapter 4)—except that you pass a function to be applied to the data—that is followed by a function that is used in a reduction of the output from the Map task. Because reductions are commonplace even in SIMD programs, SIMD hardware often offers special operations for them. For example, Intel's recent AVX SIMD instructions include "horizontal" instructions that add pairs of operands that are adjacent in registers.

To accommodate variability in performance from thousands of computers, the MapReduce scheduler assigns new tasks based on how quickly nodes complete prior tasks. Obviously, a single slow task can hold up completion of a large MapReduce job. In a WSC, the solution to slow tasks is to provide software mechanisms to cope with such variability that is inherent at this scale. This approach is in sharp contrast to the solution for a server in a conventional datacenter, where traditionally slow tasks mean hardware is broken and needs to be replaced or that server software needs tuning and rewriting. Performance heterogeneity is the norm for 50,000 servers in a WSC. For example, toward the end of a MapReduce program, the system will start backup executions on other nodes of the tasks that haven't completed yet and take the result from whichever finishes first. In return for increasing resource usage a few percent, Dean and Ghemawat [2008] found that some large tasks complete 30% faster.

Another example of how WSCs differ is the use of data replication to overcome failures. Given the amount of equipment in a WSC, it's not surprising that failures are commonplace, as the prior example attests. To deliver on 99.99% availability, systems software must cope with this reality in a WSC. To reduce operational costs, all WSCs use automated monitoring software so that one operator can be responsible for more than 1000 servers.

Programming frameworks such as MapReduce for batch processing and externally facing SaaS such as search rely upon internal software services for their success. For example, MapReduce relies on the Google File System (GFS) (Ghemawat, Gobioff, and Leung [2003]) to supply files to any computer, so that MapReduce tasks can be scheduled anywhere.

In addition to GFS, examples of such scalable storage systems include Amazon's key value storage system Dynamo [DeCandia et al. 2007] and the Google record storage system Bigtable [Chang 2006]. Note that such systems often build upon each other. For example, Bigtable stores its logs and data on GFS, much as a relational database may use the file system provided by the kernel operating system.

These internal services often make different decisions than similar software running on single servers. As an example, rather than assuming storage is reliable, such as by using RAID storage servers, these systems often make complete replicas of the data. Replicas can help with read performance as well as with availability; with proper placement, replicas can overcome many other system failures, like those in Figure 6.1. Some systems use erasure encoding rather than full replicas, but the constant is cross-server redundancy rather than within-a-server or within-a-storage array redundancy. Hence, failure of the entire server or storage device doesn't negatively affect availability of the data.

Another example of the different approach is that WSC storage software often uses relaxed consistency rather than following all the ACID (atomicity, consistency, isolation, and durability) requirements of conventional database systems. The insight is that it's important for multiple replicas of data to agree *eventually*, but for most applications they need not be in agreement at all times. For example, eventual consistency is fine for video sharing. Eventual consistency makes storage systems much easier to scale, which is an absolute requirement for WSCs.

The workload demands of these public interactive services all vary considerably; even a popular global service such as Google search varies by a factor of two depending on the time of day. When you factor in weekends, holidays, and popular times of year for some applications—such as photograph sharing services after Halloween or online shopping before Christmas—you can see considerably greater variation in server utilization for Internet services. Figure 6.3 shows average utilization of 5000 Google servers over a 6-month period. Note that less than 0.5% of servers averaged 100% utilization, and most servers operated between 10% and 50% utilization. Stated alternatively, just 10% of all servers were utilized more than 50%. Hence, it's much more important for servers in a WSC to perform well while doing little than to just to perform efficiently at their peak, as they rarely operate at their peak.

In summary, WSC hardware and software must cope with variability in load based on user demand and in performance and dependability due to the vagaries of hardware at this scale.

Example   As a result of measurements like those in Figure 6.3, the SPECPower benchmark measures power and performance from 0% load to 100% in 10% increments (see Chapter 1). The overall single metric that summarizes this benchmark is the sum of all the performance measures (server-side Java operations per second) divided by the sum of all power measurements in watts. Thus, each level is equally likely. How would the numbers summary metric change if the levels were weighted by the utilization frequencies in Figure 6.3?

Answer   Figure 6.4 shows the original weightings and the new weighting that match Figure 6.3. These weightings reduce the performance summary by 30% from 3210 ssj_ops/watt to 2454.

Given the scale, software must handle failures, which means there is little reason to buy "gold-plated" hardware that reduces the frequency of failures. The primary impact would be to increase cost. Barroso and Hölzle [2009] found a factor of 20 difference in price-performance between a high-end

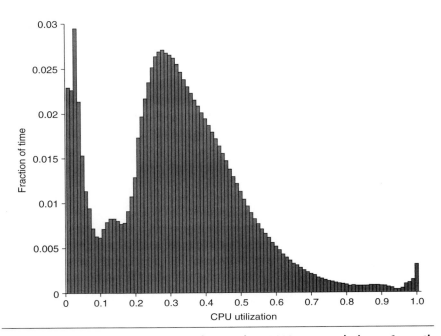

Figure 6.3 Average CPU utilization of more than 5000 servers during a 6-month period at Google. Servers are rarely completely idle or fully utilized, instead operating most of the time at between 10% and 50% of their maximum utilization. (From Figure 1 in Barroso and Hölzle [2007].) The column the third from the right in Figure 6.4 calculates percentages plus or minus 5% to come up with the weightings; thus, 1.2% for the 90% row means that 1.2% of servers were between 85% and 95% utilized.

Load	Performance	Watts	SPEC weightings	Weighted performance	Weighted watts	Figure 6.3 weightings	Weighted performance	Weighted watts
100%	2,889,020	662	9.09%	262,638	60	0.80%	22,206	5
90%	2,611,130	617	9.09%	237,375	56	1.20%	31,756	8
80%	2,319,900	576	9.09%	210,900	52	1.50%	35,889	9
70%	2,031,260	533	9.09%	184,660	48	2.10%	42,491	11
60%	1,740,980	490	9.09%	158,271	45	5.10%	88,082	25
50%	1,448,810	451	9.09%	131,710	41	11.50%	166,335	52
40%	1,159,760	416	9.09%	105,433	38	19.10%	221,165	79
30%	869,077	382	9.09%	79,007	35	24.60%	213,929	94
20%	581,126	351	9.09%	52,830	32	15.30%	88,769	54
10%	290,762	308	9.09%	26,433	28	8.00%	23,198	25
0%	0	181	9.09%	0	16	10.90%	0	20
Total	15,941,825	4967		1,449,257	452		933,820	380
				ssj_ops/Watt	3210		ssj_ops/Watt	2454

Figure 6.4 SPECPower result from Figure 6.17 using the weightings from Figure 6.3 instead of even weightings.

HP shared-memory multiprocessor and a commodity HP server when running the TPC-C database benchmark. Unsurprisingly, Google buys low-end commodity servers.

Such WSC services also tend to develop their own software rather than buy third-party commercial software, in part to cope with the huge scale and in part to save money. For example, even on the best price-performance platform for TPC-C in 2011, including the cost of the Oracle database and Windows operating system doubles the cost of the Dell Poweredge 710 server. In contrast, Google runs Bigtable and the Linux operating system on its servers, for which it pays no licensing fees.

Given this review of the applications and systems software of a WSC, we are ready to look at the computer architecture of a WSC.

6.3 Computer Architecture of Warehouse-Scale Computers

Networks are the connective tissue that binds 50,000 servers together. Analogous to the memory hierarchy of Chapter 2, WSCs use a hierarchy of networks. Figure 6.5 shows one example. Ideally, the combined network would provide nearly the performance of a custom high-end switch for 50,000 servers at nearly the cost per port of a commodity switch designed for 50 servers. As we shall see in Section 6.6, the current solutions are far from that ideal, and networks for WSCs are an area of active exploration.

The 19-inch (48.26-cm) rack is still the standard framework to hold servers, despite this standard going back to railroad hardware from the 1930s. Servers are measured in the number of rack units (U) that they occupy in a rack. One U is 1.75 inches (4.45 cm) high, and that is the minimum space a server can occupy.

A 7-foot (213.36-cm) rack offers 48 U, so it's not a coincidence that the most popular switch for a rack is a 48-port Ethernet switch. This product has become a commodity that costs as little as $30 per port for a 1 Gbit/sec Ethernet link in 2011 [Barroso and Hölzle 2009]. Note that the bandwidth within the rack is the same for each server, so it does not matter where the software places the sender and the receiver as long as they are within the same rack. This flexibility is ideal from a software perspective.

These switches typically offer two to eight uplinks, which leave the rack to go to the next higher switch in the network hierarchy. Thus, the bandwidth leaving the rack is 6 to 24 times smaller—48/8 to 48/2—than the bandwidth within the rack. This ratio is called *oversubscription*. Alas, large oversubscription means programmers must be aware of the performance consequences when placing senders and receivers in different racks. This increased software-scheduling burden is another argument for network switches designed specifically for the datacenter.

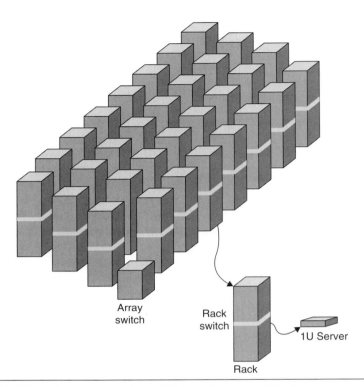

Figure 6.5 Hierarchy of switches in a WSC. (Based on Figure 1.2 of Barroso and Hölzle [2009].)

Storage

A natural design is to fill a rack with servers, minus whatever space you need for the commodity Ethernet rack switch. This design leaves open the question of where the storage is placed. From a hardware construction perspective, the simplest solution would be to include disks inside the server, and rely on Ethernet connectivity for access to information on the disks of remote servers. The alternative would be to use network attached storage (NAS), perhaps over a storage network like Infiniband. The NAS solution is generally more expensive per terabyte of storage, but it provides many features, including RAID techniques to improve dependability of the storage.

As you might expect from the philosophy expressed in the prior section, WSCs generally rely on local disks and provide storage software that handles connectivity and dependability. For example, GFS uses local disks and maintains at least three replicas to overcome dependability problems. This redundancy covers not just local disk failures, but also power failures to racks and to whole clusters. The eventual consistency flexibility of GFS lowers the cost of keeping replicas consistent, which also reduces the network bandwidth requirements of the storage system. Local access patterns also mean high bandwidth to local storage, as we'll see shortly.

Beware that there is confusion about the term *cluster* when talking about the architecture of a WSC. Using the definition in Section 6.1, a WSC is just an extremely large cluster. In contrast, Barroso and Hölzle [2009] used the term cluster to mean the next-sized grouping of computers, in this case about 30 racks. In this chapter, to avoid confusion we will use the term *array* to mean a collection of racks, preserving the original meaning of the word cluster to mean anything from a collection of networked computers within a rack to an entire warehouse full of networked computers.

Array Switch

The switch that connects an array of racks is considerably more expensive than the 48-port commodity Ethernet switch. This cost is due in part because of the higher connectivity and in part because the bandwidth through the switch must be much higher to reduce the oversubscription problem. Barroso and Hölzle [2009] reported that a switch that has 10 times the *bisection bandwidth*—basically, the worst-case internal bandwidth—of a rack switch costs about 100 times as much. One reason is that the cost of switch bandwidth for n ports can grow as n^2.

Another reason for the high costs is that these products offer high profit margins for the companies that produce them. They justify such prices in part by providing features such as packet inspection that are expensive because they must operate at very high rates. For example, network switches are major users of content-addressable memory chips and of field-programmable gate arrays (FPGAs), which help provide these features, but the chips themselves are expensive. While such features may be valuable for Internet settings, they are generally unused inside the datacenter.

WSC Memory Hierarchy

Figure 6.6 shows the latency, bandwidth, and capacity of memory hierarchy inside a WSC, and Figure 6.7 shows the same data visually. These figures are based on the following assumptions [Barroso and Hölzle 2009]:

	Local	Rack	Array
DRAM latency (microseconds)	0.1	100	300
Disk latency (microseconds)	10,000	11,000	12,000
DRAM bandwidth (MB/sec)	20,000	100	10
Disk bandwidth (MB/sec)	200	100	10
DRAM capacity (GB)	16	1040	31,200
Disk capacity (GB)	2000	160,000	4,800,000

Figure 6.6 **Latency, bandwidth, and capacity of the memory hierarchy of a WSC** [Barroso and Hölzle 2009]. Figure 6.7 plots this same information.

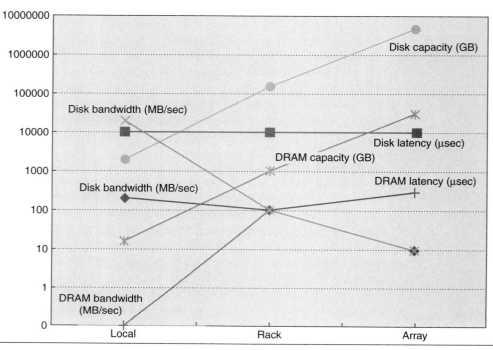

Figure 6.7 Graph of latency, bandwidth, and capacity of the memory hierarchy of a WSC for data in Figure 6.6 [Barroso and Hölzle 2009].

- Each server contains 16 GBytes of memory with a 100-nanosecond access time and transfers at 20 GBytes/sec and 2 terabytes of disk that offers a 10-millisecond access time and transfers at 200 MBytes/sec. There are two sockets per board, and they share one 1 Gbit/sec Ethernet port.

- Every pair of racks includes one rack switch and holds 80 2U servers (see Section 6.7). Networking software plus switch overhead increases the latency to DRAM to 100 microseconds and the disk access latency to 11 milliseconds. Thus, the total storage capacity of a rack is roughly 1 terabyte of DRAM and 160 terabytes of disk storage. The 1 Gbit/sec Ethernet limits the remote bandwidth to DRAM or disk within the rack to 100 MBytes/sec.

- The array switch can handle 30 racks, so storage capacity of an array goes up by a factor of 30: 30 terabytes of DRAM and 4.8 petabytes of disk. The array switch hardware and software increases latency to DRAM within an array to 500 microseconds and disk latency to 12 milliseconds. The bandwidth of the array switch limits the remote bandwidth to either array DRAM or array disk to 10 MBytes/sec.

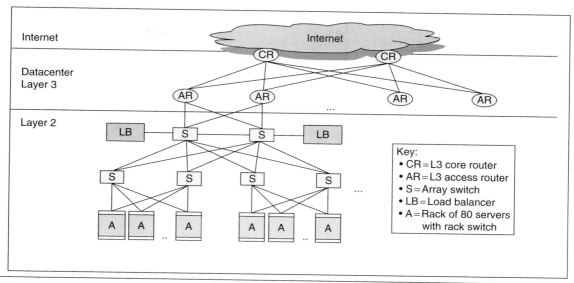

Figure 6.8 The Layer 3 network used to link arrays together and to the Internet [Greenberg et al. 2009]. Some WSCs use a separate *border router* to connect the Internet to the datacenter Layer 3 switches.

Figures 6.6 and 6.7 show that network overhead dramatically increases latency from local DRAM to rack DRAM and array DRAM, but both still have more than 10 times better latency than the local disk. The network collapses the difference in bandwidth between rack DRAM and rack disk and between array DRAM and array disk.

The WSC needs 20 arrays to reach 50,000 servers, so there is one more level of the networking hierarchy. Figure 6.8 shows the conventional Layer 3 routers to connect the arrays together and to the Internet.

Most applications fit on a single array within a WSC. Those that need more than one array use *sharding* or *partitioning*, meaning that the dataset is split into independent pieces and then distributed to different arrays. Operations on the whole dataset are sent to the servers hosting the pieces, and the results are coalesced by the client computer.

Example   What is the average memory latency assuming that 90% of accesses are local to the server, 9% are outside the server but within the rack, and 1% are outside the rack but within the array?

Answer   The average memory access time is

$$(90\% \times 0.1) + (9\% \times 100) + (1\% \times 300) = 0.09 + 9 + 3 = 12.09 \text{ microseconds}$$

or a factor of more than 120 slowdown versus 100% local accesses. Clearly, locality of access within a server is vital for WSC performance.

Example   How long does it take to transfer 1000 MB between disks within the server, between servers in the rack, and between servers in different racks in the array? How much faster is it to transfer 1000 MB between DRAM in the three cases?

Answer   A 1000 MB transfer between disks takes:

$$\text{Within server} = 1000/200 = 5 \text{ seconds}$$
$$\text{Within rack} = 1000/100 = 10 \text{ seconds}$$
$$\text{Within array} = 1000/10 = 100 \text{ seconds}$$

A memory-to-memory block transfer takes

$$\text{Within server} = 1000/20000 = 0.05 \text{ seconds}$$
$$\text{Within rack} = 1000/100 = 10 \text{ seconds}$$
$$\text{Within array} = 1000/10 = 100 \text{ seconds}$$

Thus, for block transfers outside a single server, it doesn't even matter whether the data are in memory or on disk since the rack switch and array switch are the bottlenecks. These performance limits affect the design of WSC software and inspire the need for higher performance switches (see Section 6.6).

Given the architecture of the IT equipment, we are now ready to see how to house, power, and cool it and to discuss the cost to build and operate the whole WSC, as compared to just the IT equipment within it.

6.4   Physical Infrastructure and Costs of Warehouse-Scale Computers

To build a WSC, you first need to build a warehouse. One of the first questions is where? Real estate agents emphasize location, but location for a WSC means proximity to Internet backbone optical fibers, low cost of electricity, and low risk from environmental disasters, such as earthquakes, floods, and hurricanes. For a company with many WSCs, another concern is finding a place geographically near a current or future population of Internet users, so as to reduce latency over the Internet. There are also many more mundane concerns, such as property tax rates.

Infrastructure costs for power distribution and cooling dwarf the construction costs of a WSC, so we concentrate on the former. Figures 6.9 and 6.10 show the power distribution and cooling infrastructure within a WSC.

Although there are many variations deployed, in North America electrical power typically goes through about five steps and four voltage changes on the way to the server, starting with the high-voltage lines at the utility tower of 115,000 volts:

1. The substation switches from 115,000 volts to medium-voltage lines of 13,200 volts, with an efficiency of 99.7%.

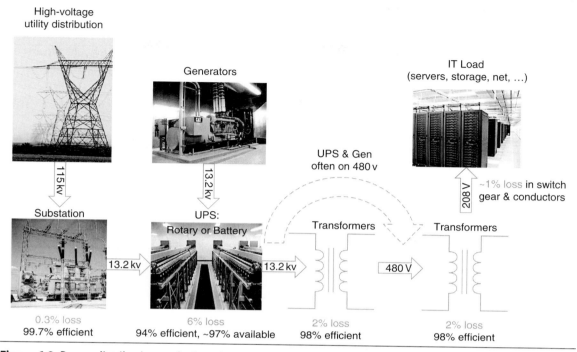

High-voltage
utility distribution

Generators

IT Load
(servers, storage, net, ...)

UPS & Gen
often on 480 v

~1% loss in switch
gear & conductors

115 kv

13.2 kv

208 V

Substation

UPS:
Rotary or Battery

Transformers

Transformers

13.2 kv

13.2 kv

480 V

0.3% loss
99.7% efficient

6% loss
94% efficient, ~97% available

2% loss
98% efficient

2% loss
98% efficient

Figure 6.9 Power distribution and where losses occur. Note that the best improvement is 11%. (From Hamilton [2010].)

2. To prevent the whole WSC from going offline if power is lost, a WSC has an uninterruptible power supply (UPS), just as some servers do. In this case, it involves large diesel engines that can take over from the utility company in an emergency and batteries or flywheels to maintain power after the service is lost but before the diesel engines are ready. The generators and batteries can take up so much space that they are typically located in a separate room from the IT equipment. The UPS plays three roles: power conditioning (maintain proper voltage levels and other characteristics), holding the electrical load while the generators start and come on line, and holding the electrical load when switching back from the generators to the electrical utility. The efficiency of this very large UPS is 94%, so the facility loses 6% of the power by having a UPS. The WSC UPS can account for 7% to 12% of the cost of all the IT equipment.

3. Next in the system is a power distribution unit (PDU) that converts to low-voltage, internal, three-phase power at 480 volts. The conversion efficiency is 98%. A typical PDU handles 75 to 225 kilowatts of load, or about 10 racks.

4. There is yet another down step to two-phase power at 208 volts that servers can use, once again at 98% efficiency. (Inside the server, there are more steps to bring the voltage down to what chips can use; see Section 6.7.)

5. The connectors, breakers, and electrical wiring to the server have a collective efficiency of 99%.

WSCs outside North America use different conversion values, but the overall design is similar.

Putting it all together, the efficiency of turning 115,000-volt power from the utility into 208-volt power that servers can use is 89%:

$$99.7\% \times 94\% \times 98\% \times 98\% \times 99\% = 89\%$$

This overall efficiency leaves only a little over 10% room for improvement, but as we shall see, engineers still try to make it better.

There is considerably more opportunity for improvement in the cooling infrastructure. The computer room air-conditioning (CRAC) unit cools the air in the server room using chilled water, similar to how a refrigerator removes heat by releasing it outside of the refrigerator. As a liquid absorbs heat, it evaporates. Conversely, when a liquid releases heat, it condenses. Air conditioners pump the liquid into coils under low pressure to evaporate and absorb heat, which is then sent to an external condenser where it is released. Thus, in a CRAC unit, fans push warm air past a set of coils filled with cold water and a pump moves the warmed water to the external chillers to be cooled down. The cool air for servers is typically between 64°F and 71°F (18°C and 22°C). Figure 6.10 shows the large collection of fans and water pumps that move air and water throughout the system.

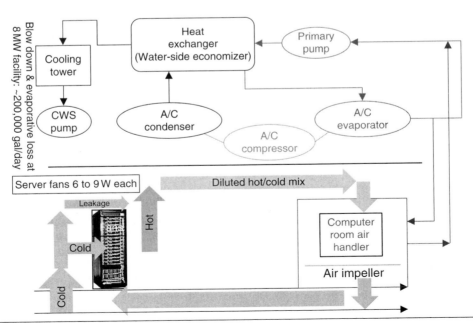

Figure 6.10 Mechanical design for cooling systems. CWS stands for circulating water system. (From Hamilton [2010].)

Clearly, one of the simplest ways to improve energy efficiency is simply to run the IT equipment at higher temperatures so that the air need not be cooled as much. Some WSCs run their equipment considerably above 71°F (22°C).

In addition to chillers, cooling towers are used in some datacenters to leverage the colder outside air to cool the water before it is sent to the chillers. The temperature that matters is called the *wet-bulb temperature*. The wet-bulb temperature is measured by blowing air on the bulb end of a thermometer that has water on it. It is the lowest temperature that can be achieved by evaporating water with air.

Warm water flows over a large surface in the tower, transferring heat to the outside air via evaporation and thereby cooling the water. This technique is called *airside economization*. An alternative is use cold water instead of cold air. Google's WSC in Belgium uses a water-to-water intercooler that takes cold water from an industrial canal to chill the warm water from inside the WSC.

Airflow is carefully planned for the IT equipment itself, with some designs even using airflow simulators. Efficient designs preserve the temperature of the cool air by reducing the chances of it mixing with hot air. For example, a WSC can have alternating aisles of hot air and cold air by orienting servers in opposite directions in alternating rows of racks so that hot exhaust blows in alternating directions.

In addition to energy losses, the cooling system also uses up a lot of water due to evaporation or to spills down sewer lines. For example, an 8 MW facility might use 70,000 to 200,000 gallons of water per day.

The relative power costs of cooling equipment to IT equipment in a typical datacenter [Barroso and Hölzle 2009] are as follows:

- Chillers account for 30% to 50% of the IT equipment power.
- CRAC accounts for 10% to 20% of the IT equipment power, due mostly to fans.

Surprisingly, it's not obvious to figure out how many servers a WSC can support after you subtract the overheads for power distribution and cooling. The so-called *nameplate power rating* from the server manufacturer is always conservative; it's the maximum power a server can draw. The first step then is to measure a single server under a variety of workloads to be deployed in the WSC. (Networking is typically about 5% of power consumption, so it can be ignored to start.)

To determine the number of servers for a WSC, the available power for IT could just be divided by the measured server power; however, this would again be too conservative according to Fan, Weber, and Barroso [2007]. They found that there is a significant gap between what thousands of servers could theoretically do in the worst case and what they will do in practice, since no real workloads will keep thousands of servers all simultaneously at their peaks. They found that they could safely oversubscribe the number of servers by as much as 40% based on the power of a single server. They recommended that WSC architects should do that to increase the average utilization of power within a WSC; however, they also suggested using extensive monitoring software along with a safety mechanism that deschedules lower priority tasks in case the workload shifts.

Breaking down power usage inside the IT equipment itself, Barroso and Hölzle [2009] reported the following for a Google WSC deployed in 2007:

- 33% of power for processors
- 30% for DRAM
- 10% for disks
- 5% for networking
- 22% for other reasons (inside the server)

Measuring Efficiency of a WSC

A widely used, simple metric to evaluate the efficiency of a datacenter or a WSC is called *power utilization effectiveness* (or *PUE*):

$$PUE = (Total\ facility\ power)/(IT\ equipment\ power)$$

Thus, PUE must be greater than or equal to 1, and the bigger the PUE the less efficient the WSC.

Greenberg et al. [2006] reported on the PUE of 19 datacenters and the portion of the overhead that went into the cooling infrastructure. Figure 6.11 shows what they found, sorted by PUE from most to least efficient. The median PUE is 1.69, with the cooling infrastructure using more than half as much power as the servers themselves—on average, 0.55 of the 1.69 is for cooling. Note that these are average PUEs, which can vary daily depending on workload and even external air temperature, as we shall see.

Since performance per dollar is the ultimate metric, we still need to measure performance. As Figure 6.7 above shows, bandwidth drops and latency increases depending on the distance to the data. In a WSC, the DRAM bandwidth within a server is 200 times larger than within a rack, which in turn is 10 times larger than within an array. Thus, there is another kind of locality to consider in the placement of data and programs within a WSC.

While designers of a WSC often focus on bandwidth, programmers developing applications on a WSC are also concerned with latency, since latency is visible to users. Users' satisfaction and productivity are tied to response time of a service. Several studies from the timesharing days report that user productivity is inversely proportional to time for an interaction, which was typically broken down into human entry time, system response time, and time for the person to think about the response before entering the next entry. The results of experiments showed that cutting system response time 30% shaved the time of an interaction by 70%. This implausible result is explained by human nature: People need less time to think when given a faster response, as they are less likely to get distracted and remain "on a roll."

Figure 6.12 shows the results of such an experiment for the Bing search engine, where delays of 50 ms to 2000 ms were inserted at the search server. As expected

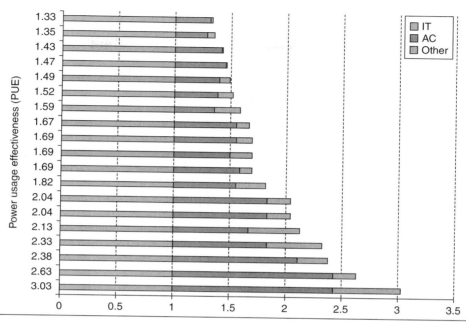

Figure 6.11 Power utilization efficiency of 19 datacenters in 2006 [Greenberg et al. 2006]. The power for air conditioning (AC) and other uses (such as power distribution) is normalized to the power for the IT equipment in calculating the PUE. Thus, power for IT equipment must be 1.0 and AC varies from about 0.30 to 1.40 times the power of the IT equipment. Power for "other" varies from about 0.05 to 0.60 of the IT equipment.

from previous studies, time to next click roughly doubled the delay; that is, a 200 ms delay at the server led to a 500 ms increase in time to next click. Revenue dropped linearly with increasing delay, as did user satisfaction. A separate study on the Google search engine found that these effects lingered long after the 4-week experiment ended. Five weeks later, there were 0.1% fewer searchers per day for users who experienced 200 ms delays, and there were 0.2% fewer searches from users who experienced 400 ms delays. Given the amount of money made in search, even such small changes are disconcerting. In fact, the results were so negative that they ended the experiment prematurely [Schurman and Brutlag 2009].

Server delay (ms)	Increased time to next click (ms)	Queries/ user	Any clicks/ user	User satisfaction	Revenue/ user
50	--	--	--	--	--
200	500	--	−0.3%	−0.4%	--
500	1200	--	−1.0%	−0.9%	−1.2%
1000	1900	−0.7%	−1.9%	−1.6%	−2.8%
2000	3100	−1.8%	−4.4%	−3.8%	−4.3%

Figure 6.12 Negative impact of delays at Bing search server on user behavior Schurman and Brutlag [2009].

Because of this extreme concern with satisfaction of all users of an Internet service, performance goals are typically specified that a high percentage of requests be below a latency threshold rather just offer a target for the average latency. Such threshold goals are called *service level objectives* (*SLOs*) or *service level agreements* (*SLAs*). An SLO might be that 99% of requests must be below 100 milliseconds. Thus, the designers of Amazon's Dynamo key-value storage system decided that, for services to offer good latency on top of Dynamo, their storage system had to deliver on its latency goal 99.9% of the time [DeCandia et al. 2007]. For example, one improvement of Dynamo helped the 99.9th percentile much more than the average case, which reflects their priorities.

Cost of a WSC

As mentioned in the introduction, unlike most architects, designers of WSCs worry about operational costs as well as the cost to build the WSC. Accounting labels the former costs as *operational expenditures* (*OPEX*) and the latter costs as *capital expenditures* (*CAPEX*).

To put the cost of energy into perspective, Hamilton [2010] did a case study to estimate the costs of a WSC. He determined that the CAPEX of this 8 MW facility was $88M, and that the roughly 46,000 servers and corresponding networking equipment added another $79M to the CAPEX for the WSC. Figure 6.13 shows the rest of the assumptions for the case study.

We can now price the total cost of energy, since U.S. accounting rules allow us to convert CAPEX into OPEX. We can just amortize CAPEX as a fixed amount each month for the effective life of the equipment. Figure 6.14 breaks down the monthly OPEX for this case study. Note that the amortization rates differ significantly, from 10 years for the facility to 4 years for the networking equipment and 3 years for the servers. Hence, the WSC facility lasts a decade, but you need to replace the servers every 3 years and the networking equipment every 4 years. By amortizing the CAPEX, Hamilton came up with a monthly OPEX, including accounting for the cost of borrowing money (5% annually) to pay for the WSC. At $3.8M, the monthly OPEX is about 2% of the CAPEX.

This figure allows us to calculate a handy guideline to keep in mind when making decisions about which components to use when being concerned about energy. The fully burdened cost of a watt per year in a WSC, including the cost of amortizing the power and cooling infrastructure, is

$$\frac{\text{Monthly cost of infrastructure + monthly cost of power}}{\text{Facility size in watts}} \times 12 = \frac{\$765K + \$475K}{8M} \times 12 = \$1.86$$

The cost is roughly $2 per watt-year. Thus, to reduce costs by saving energy you shouldn't spend more than $2 per watt-year (see Section 6.8).

Note that more than a third of OPEX is related to power, with that category trending up while server costs are trending down over time. The networking

Size of facility (critical load watts)	8,000,000
Average power usage (%)	80%
Power usage effectiveness	1.45
Cost of power ($/kwh)	$0.07
% Power and cooling infrastructure (% of total facility cost)	82%
CAPEX for facility (not including IT equipment)	**$88,000,000**
Number of servers	45,978
Cost/server	$1450
CAPEX for servers	**$66,700,000**
Number of rack switches	1150
Cost/rack switch	$4800
Number of array switches	22
Cost/array switch	$300,000
Number of layer 3 switches	2
Cost/layer 3 switch	$500,000
Number of border routers	2
Cost/border router	$144,800
CAPEX for networking gear	**$12,810,000**
Total CAPEX for WSC	**$167,510,000**
Server amortization time	3 years
Networking amortization time	4 years
Facilities amortization time	10 years
Annual cost of money	5%

Figure 6.13 Case study for a WSC, based on Hamilton [2010], rounded to nearest $5000. Internet bandwidth costs vary by application, so they are not included here. The remaining 18% of the CAPEX for the facility includes buying the property and the cost of construction of the building. We added people costs for security and facilities management in Figure 6.14, which were not part of the case study. Note that Hamilton's estimates were done before he joined Amazon, and they are not based on the WSC of a particular company.

equipment is significant at 8% of total OPEX and 19% of the server CAPEX, and networking equipment is not trending down as quickly as servers are. This difference is especially true for the switches in the networking hierarchy above the rack, which represent most of the networking costs (see Section 6.6). People costs for security and facilities management are just 2% of OPEX. Dividing the OPEX in Figure 6.14 by the number of servers and hours per month, the cost is about $0.11 per server per hour.

Expense (% total)	Category	Monthly cost	Percent monthly cost
Amortized CAPEX (85%)	Servers	$2,000,000	53%
	Networking equipment	$290,000	8%
	Power and cooling infrastructure	$765,000	20%
	Other infrastructure	$170,000	4%
OPEX (15%)	Monthly power use	$475,000	13%
	Monthly people salaries and benefits	$85,000	2%
	Total OPEX	$3,800,000	100%

Figure 6.14 Monthly OPEX for Figure 6.13, rounded to the nearest $5000. Note that the 3-year amortization for servers means you need to purchase new servers every 3 years, whereas the facility is amortized for 10 years. Hence, the amortized capital costs for servers are about 3 times more than for the facility. People costs include 3 security guard positions continuously for 24 hours a day, 365 days a year, at $20 per hour per person, and 1 facilities person for 24 hours a day, 365 days a year, at $30 per hour. Benefits are 30% of salaries. This calculation doesn't include the cost of network bandwidth to the Internet, as it varies by application, nor vendor maintenance fees, as that varies by equipment and by negotiations.

Example The cost of electricity varies by region in the United States from $0.03 to $0.15 per kilowatt-hour. What is the impact on hourly server costs of these two extreme rates?

Answer We multiply the critical load of 8 MW by the PUE and by the average power usage from Figure 6.13 to calculate the average power usage:

$$8 \times 1.45 \times 80\% = 9.28 \text{ Megawatts}$$

The monthly cost for power then goes from $475,000 in Figure 6.14 to $205,000 at $0.03 per kilowatt-hour and to $1,015,000 at $0.15 per kilowatt-hour. These changes in electricity cost change the hourly server costs from $0.11 to $0.10 and $0.13, respectively.

Example What would happen to monthly costs if the amortization times were all made to be the same—say, 5 years? How does that change the hourly cost per server?

Answer The spreadsheet is available online at *http://mvdirona.com/jrh/TalksAndPapers/ PerspectivesDataCenterCostAndPower.xls*. Changing the amortization time to 5 years changes the first four rows of Figure 6.14 to

Servers	$1,260,000	37%
Networking equipment	$242,000	7%
Power and cooling infrastructure	$1,115,000	33%
Other infrastructure	$245,000	7%

and the total monthly OPEX is $3,422,000. If we replaced everything every 5 years, the cost would be $0.103 per server hour, with more of the amortized costs now being for the facility rather than the servers, as in Figure 6.14.

The rate of $0.11 per server per hour can be much less than the cost for many companies that own and operate their own (smaller) conventional datacenters. The cost advantage of WSCs led large Internet companies to offer computing as a utility where, like electricity, you pay only for what you use. Today, utility computing is better known as cloud computing.

6.5   Cloud Computing: The Return of Utility Computing

If computers of the kind I have advocated become the computers of the future, then computing may someday be organized as a public utility just as the telephone system is a public utility. . . . The computer utility could become the basis of a new and important industry.

John McCarthy
MIT centennial celebration (1961)

Driven by the demand of an increasing number of users, Internet companies such as Amazon, Google, and Microsoft built increasingly larger warehouse-scale computers from commodity components. This demand led to innovations in systems software to support operating at this scale, including Bigtable, Dynamo, GFS, and MapReduce. It also demanded improvement in operational techniques to deliver a service available at least 99.99% of the time despite component failures and security attacks. Examples of these techniques include failover, firewalls, virtual machines, and protection against distributed denial-of-service attacks. With the software and expertise providing the ability to scale and increasing customer demand that justified the investment, WSCs with 50,000 to 100,000 servers have become commonplace in 2011.

With increasing scale came increasing economies of scale. Based on a study in 2006 that compared a WSC with a datacenter with only 1000 servers, Hamilton [2010] reported the following advantages:

- *5.7 times reduction in storage costs*—It cost the WSC $4.6 per GByte per year for disk storage versus $26 per GByte for the datacenter.

- *7.1 times reduction in administrative costs*—The ratio of servers per administrator was over 1000 for the WSC versus just 140 for the datacenter.

- *7.3 times reduction in networking costs*—Internet bandwidth cost the WSC $13 per Mbit/sec/month versus $95 for the datacenter. Unsurprisingly, you can negotiate a much better price per Mbit/sec if you order 1000 Mbit/sec than if you order 10 Mbit/sec.

Another economy of scale comes during purchasing. The high level of purchasing leads to volume discount prices on the servers and networking gear. It also allows optimization of the supply chain. Dell, IBM, and SGI will deliver on new orders in a week to a WSC instead of 4 to 6 months. Short delivery time makes it much easier to grow the utility to match the demand.

Economies of scale also apply to operational costs. From the prior section, we saw that many datacenters operate with a PUE of 2.0. Large firms can justify hiring mechanical and power engineers to develop WSCs with lower PUEs, in the range of 1.2 (see Section 6.7).

Internet services need to be distributed to multiple WSCs for both dependability and to reduce latency, especially for international markets. All large firms use multiple WSCs for that reason. It's much more expensive for individual firms to create multiple, small datacenters around the world than a single datacenter in the corporate headquarters.

Finally, for the reasons presented in Section 6.1, servers in datacenters tend to be utilized only 10% to 20% of the time. By making WSCs available to the public, uncorrelated peaks between different customers can raise average utilization above 50%.

Thus, economies of scale for a WSC offer factors of 5 to 7 for several components of a WSC plus a few factors of 1.5 to 2 for the entire WSC.

While there are many cloud computing providers, we feature Amazon Web Services (AWS) in part because of its popularity and in part because of the low level and hence more flexible abstraction of their service. Google App Engine and Microsoft Azure raise the level of abstraction to managed runtimes and to offer automatic scaling services, which are a better match to some customers, but not as good a match as AWS to the material in this book.

Amazon Web Services

Utility computing goes back to commercial timesharing systems and even batch processing systems of the 1960s and 1970s, where companies only paid for a terminal and a phone line and then were billed based on how much computing they used. Many efforts since the end of timesharing then have tried to offer such pay as you go services, but they were often met with failure.

When Amazon started offering utility computing via the Amazon Simple Storage Service (Amazon S3) and then Amazon Elastic Computer Cloud (Amazon EC2) in 2006, it made some novel technical and business decisions:

■ *Virtual Machines.* Building the WSC using x86-commodity computers running the Linux operating system and the Xen virtual machine solved several problems. First, it allowed Amazon to protect users from each other. Second, it simplified software distribution within a WSC, in that customers only need install an image and then AWS will automatically distribute it to all the instances being used. Third, the ability to kill a virtual machine reliably makes it easy for Amazon and customers to control resource usage. Fourth, since Virtual Machines can limit the rate at which they use the physical processors, disks, and the network as well as the amount of main memory, that gave AWS multiple price points: the lowest price option by packing multiple virtual cores on a single server, the highest price option of exclusive access to all the machine resources, as well as several intermediary points. Fifth, Virtual Machines hide the identity of older hardware, allowing AWS to continue to sell time on older machines that might otherwise be unattractive to customers if they knew their age. Finally, Virtual Machines allow AWS to introduce new and faster hardware by either packing even more virtual cores per server or simply by offering instances that have higher performance per virtual core; virtualization means that offered performance need not be an integer multiple of the performance of the hardware.

- *Very low cost.* When AWS announced a rate of $0.10 per hour per instance in 2006, it was a startlingly low amount. An instance is one Virtual Machine, and at $0.10 per hour AWS allocated two instances per core on a multicore server. Hence, one EC2 computer unit is equivalent to a 1.0 to 1.2 GHz AMD Opteron or Intel Xeon of that era.

- *(Initial) reliance on open source software.* The availability of good-quality software that had no licensing problems or costs associated with running on hundreds or thousands of servers made utility computing much more economical for both Amazon and its customers. More recently, AWS started offering instances including commercial third-party software at higher prices.

- *No (initial) guarantee of service.* Amazon originally promised only best effort. The low cost was so attractive that many could live without a service guarantee. Today, AWS provides availability SLAs of up to 99.95% on services such as Amazon EC2 and Amazon S3. Additionally, Amazon S3 was designed for 99.999999999% durability by saving multiple replicas of each object across multiple locations. That is, the chances of permanently losing an object are one in 100 billion. AWS also provides a Service Health Dashboard that shows the current operational status of each of the AWS services in real time, so that AWS uptime and performance are fully transparent.

- *No contract required.* In part because the costs are so low, all that is necessary to start using EC2 is a credit card.

Figure 6.15 shows the hourly price of the many types of EC2 instances in 2011. In addition to computation, EC2 charges for long-term storage and for Internet traffic. (There is no cost for network traffic inside AWS regions.) Elastic Block Storage costs $0.10 per GByte per month and $0.10 per million I/O requests. Internet traffic costs $0.10 per GByte going to EC2 and $0.08 to $0.15 per GByte leaving from EC2, depending on the volume. Putting this into historical perspective, for $100 per month you can use the equivalent capacity of the sum of the capacities of all magnetic disks produced in 1960!

Instance	Per hour	Ratio to small	Compute units	Virtual cores	Compute units/core	Memory (GB)	Disk (GB)	Address size
Micro	$0.020	0.5–2.0	0.5–2.0	1	0.5–2.0	0.6	EBS	32/64 bit
Standard Small	$0.085	1.0	1.0	1	1.00	1.7	160	32 bit
Standard Large	$0.340	4.0	4.0	2	2.00	7.5	850	64 bit
Standard Extra Large	$0.680	8.0	8.0	4	2.00	15.0	1690	64 bit
High-Memory Extra Large	$0.500	5.9	6.5	2	3.25	17.1	420	64 bit
High-Memory Double Extra Large	$1.000	11.8	13.0	4	3.25	34.2	850	64 bit
High-Memory Quadruple Extra Large	$2.000	23.5	26.0	8	3.25	68.4	1690	64 bit
High-CPU Medium	$0.170	2.0	5.0	2	2.50	1.7	350	32 bit
High-CPU Extra Large	$0.680	8.0	20.0	8	2.50	7.0	1690	64 bit
Cluster Quadruple Extra Large	$1.600	18.8	33.5	8	4.20	23.0	1690	64 bit

Figure 6.15 Price and characteristics of on-demand EC2 instances in the United States in the Virginia region in January 2011. Micro Instances are the newest and cheapest category, and they offer short bursts of up to 2.0 compute units for just $0.02 per hour. Customers report that Micro Instances average about 0.5 compute units. Cluster-Compute Instances in the last row, which AWS identifies as dedicated dual-socket Intel Xeon X5570 servers with four cores per socket running at 2.93 GHz, offer 10 Gigabit/sec networks. They are intended for HPC applications. AWS also offers Spot Instances at much less cost, where you set the price you are willing to pay and the number of instances you are willing to run, and then AWS will run them when the spot price drops below your level. They run until you stop them or the spot price exceeds your limit. One sample during the daytime in January 2011 found that the spot price was a factor of 2.3 to 3.1 lower, depending on the instance type. AWS also offers Reserved Instances for cases where customers know they will use most of the instance for a year. You pay a yearly fee per instance and then an hourly rate that is about 30% of column 1 to use it. If you used a Reserved Instance 100% for a whole year, the average cost per hour including amortization of the annual fee would be about 65% of the rate in the first column. The server equivalent to those in Figures 6.13 and 6.14 would be a Standard Extra Large or High-CPU Extra Large Instance, which we calculated to cost $0.11 per hour.

Example   Calculate the cost of running the average MapReduce jobs in Figure 6.2 on page 437 on EC2. Assume there are plenty of jobs, so there is no significant extra cost to round up so as to get an integer number of hours. Ignore the monthly storage costs, but include the cost of disk I/Os for AWS's Elastic Block Storage (EBS). Next calculate the cost per year to run all the MapReduce jobs.

Answer   The first question is what is the right size instance to match the typical server at Google? Figure 6.21 on page 467 in Section 6.7 shows that in 2007 a typical Google server had four cores running at 2.2 GHz with 8 GB of memory. Since a single instance is one virtual core that is equivalent to a 1 to 1.2 GHz AMD Opteron, the closest match in Figure 6.15 is a High-CPU Extra Large with eight virtual cores and 7.0 GB of memory. For simplicity, we'll assume the average EBS storage access is 64 KB in order to calculate the number of I/Os.

	Aug-04	Mar-06	Sep-07	Sep-09
Average completion time (hours)	0.15	0.21	0.10	0.11
Average number of servers per job	157	268	394	488
Cost per hour of EC2 High-CPU XL instance	$0.68	$0.68	$0.68	$0.68
Average EC2 cost per MapReduce job	$16.35	$38.47	$25.56	$38.07
Average number of EBS I/O requests (millions)	2.34	5.80	3.26	3.19
EBS cost per million I/O requests	$0.10	$0.10	$0.10	$0.10
Average EBS I/O cost per MapReduce job	$0.23	$0.58	$0.33	$0.32
Average total cost per MapReduce job	$16.58	$39.05	$25.89	$38.39
Annual number of MapReduce jobs	29,000	171,000	2,217,000	3,467,000
Total cost of MapReduce jobs on EC2/EBS	$480,910	$6,678,011	$57,394,985	$133,107,414

Figure 6.16 Estimated cost if you ran the Google MapReduce workload (Figure 6.2) using 2011 prices for AWS ECS and EBS (Figure 6.15). Since we are using 2011 prices, these estimates are less accurate for earlier years than for the more recent ones.

Figure 6.16 calculates the average and total cost per year of running the Google MapReduce workload on EC2. The average 2009 MapReduce job would cost a little under $40 on EC2, and the total workload for 2009 would cost $133M on AWS. Note that EBS accesses are about 1% of total costs for these jobs.

Example Given that the costs of MapReduce jobs are growing and already exceed $100M per year, imagine that your boss wants you to investigate ways to lower costs. Two potentially lower cost options are either AWS Reserved Instances or AWS Spot Instances. Which would you recommend?

Answer AWS Reserved Instances charge a fixed annual rate plus an hourly per-use rate. In 2011, the annual cost for the High-CPU Extra Large Instance is $1820 and the hourly rate is $0.24. Since we pay for the instances whether they are used or not, let's assume that the average utilization of Reserved Instances is 80%. Then the average price per hour becomes:

$$\frac{\frac{\text{Annual price}}{\text{Hours per year}} + \text{Hourly price}}{\text{Utilization}} = \frac{\frac{\$1820}{8760} + \$0.24}{80\%} = (0.21 + 0.24) \times 1.25 = \$0.56$$

Thus, the savings using Reserved Instances would be roughly 17% or $23M for the 2009 MapReduce workload.

Sampling a few days in January 2011, the hourly cost of a High-CPU Extra Large Spot Instance averages $0.235. Since that is the minimum price to bid to get one server, that cannot be the average cost since you usually want to run tasks to completion without being bumped. Let's assume you need to pay double the minimum price to run large MapReduce jobs to completion. The cost savings for Spot Instances for the 2009 workload would be roughly 31% or $41M.

Thus, you tentatively recommend Spot Instances to your boss since there is less of an up-front commitment and they may potentially save more money. However, you tell your boss you need to try to run MapReduce jobs on Spot Instances to see what you actually end up paying to ensure that jobs run to completion and that there really are hundreds of High-CPU Extra Large Instances available to run these jobs daily.

In addition to the low cost and a pay-for-use model of utility computing, another strong attractor for cloud computing users is that the cloud computing providers take on the risks of over-provisioning or under-provisioning. Risk avoidance is a godsend for startup companies, as either mistake could be fatal. If too much of the precious investment is spent on servers before the product is ready for heavy use, the company could run out of money. If the service suddenly became popular, but there weren't enough servers to match the demand, the company could make a very bad impression with the potential new customers it desperately needs to grow.

The poster child for this scenario is FarmVille from Zynga, a social networking game on Facebook. Before FarmVille was announced, the largest social game was about 5 million daily players. FarmVille had 1 million players 4 days after launch and 10 million players after 60 days. After 270 days, it had 28 million daily players and 75 million monthly players. Because they were deployed on AWS, they were able to grow seamlessly with the number of users. Moreover, it sheds load based on customer demand.

More established companies are taking advantage of the scalability of the cloud, as well. In 2011, Netflix migrated its Web site and streaming video service from a conventional datacenter to AWS. Netflix's goal was to let users watch a movie on, say, their cell phone while commuting home and then seamlessly switch to their television when they arrive home to continue watching their movie where they left off. This effort involves batch processing to convert new movies to the myriad formats they need to deliver movies on cell phones, tablets, laptops, game consoles, and digital video recorders. These batch AWS jobs can take thousands of machines several weeks to complete the conversions. The transactional backend for streaming is done in AWS and the delivery of encoded files is done via Content Delivery Networks such as Akamai and Level 3. The online service is much less expensive than mailing DVDs, and the resulting low cost has made the new service popular. One study put Netflix as 30% of Internet download traffic in the United States during peak evening periods. (In contrast, YouTube was just 10% in the same 8 p.m. to 10 p.m. period.) In fact, the overall average is 22% of Internet traffic, making Netflix alone responsible for the largest portion of Internet traffic in North America. Despite accelerating growth rates in Netflix subscriber accounts, the growth rate of Netflix's datacenter has been halted, and all capacity expansion going forward has been done via AWS.

Cloud computing has made the benefits of WSC available to everyone. Cloud computing offers cost associativity with the illusion of infinite scalability at no extra cost to the user: 1000 servers for 1 hour cost no more than 1 server for

1000 hours. It is up to the cloud computing provider to ensure that there are enough servers, storage, and Internet bandwidth available to meet the demand. The optimized supply chain mentioned above, which drops time-to-delivery to a week for new computers, is a considerable aid in providing that illusion without bankrupting the provider. This transfer of risks, cost associativity, and pay-as-you-go pricing is a powerful argument for companies of varying sizes to use cloud computing.

Two crosscutting issues that shape the cost-performance of WSCs and hence cloud computing are the WSC network and the efficiency of the server hardware and software.

6.6   Crosscutting Issues

Net gear is the SUV of the datacenter.

James Hamilton (2009)

WSC Network as a Bottleneck

Section 6.4 showed that the networking gear above the rack switch is a significant fraction of the cost of a WSC. Fully configured, the list price of a 128-port 1 Gbit datacenter switch from Juniper (EX8216) is $716,000 without optical interfaces and $908,000 with them. (These list prices are heavily discounted, but they still cost more than 50 times as much as a rack switch did.) These switches also tend be power hungry. For example, the EX8216 consumes about 19,200 watts, which is 500 to 1000 times more than a server in a WSC. Moreover, these large switches are manually configured and fragile at a large scale. Because of their price, it is difficult to afford more than dual redundancy in a WSC using these large switches, which limits the options for fault tolerance [Hamilton 2009].

However, the real impact on switches is how oversubscription affects the design of software and the placement of services and data within the WSC. The ideal WSC network would be a black box whose topology and bandwidth are uninteresting because there are no restrictions: You could run any workload in any place and optimize for server utilization rather than network traffic locality. The WSC network bottlenecks today constrain data placement, which in turn complicates WSC software. As this software is one of the most valuable assets of a WSC company, the cost of this added complexity can be significant.

For readers interested learning more about switch design, Appendix F describes the issues involved in the design of interconnection networks. In addition, Thacker [2007] proposed borrowing networking technology from supercomputing to overcome the price and performance problems. Vahdat et al. [2010] did as well, and proposed a networking infrastructure that can scale to 100,000 ports and 1 petabit/sec of bisection bandwidth. A major benefit of these novel datacenter switches is to simplify the software challenges due to oversubscription.

Using Energy Efficiently Inside the Server

While PUE measures the efficiency of a WSC, it has nothing to say about what goes on inside the IT equipment itself. Thus, another source of electrical inefficiency not covered in Figure 6.9 is the power supply *inside* the server, which converts input of 208 volts or 110 volts to the voltages that chips and disks use, typically 3.3, 5, and 12 volts. The 12 volts are further stepped down to 1.2 to 1.8 volts on the board, depending on what the microprocessor and memory require. In 2007, many power supplies were 60% to 80% efficient, which meant there were greater losses inside the server than there were going through the many steps and voltage changes from the high-voltage lines at the utility tower to supply the low-voltage lines at the server. One reason is that they have to supply a range of voltages to the chips and the disks, since they have no idea what is on the motherboard. A second reason is that the power supply is often oversized in watts for what is on the board. Moreover, such power supplies are often at their worst efficiency at 25% load or less, even though as Figure 6.3 on page 440 shows, many WSC servers operate in that range. Computer motherboards also have voltage regulator modules (VRMs), and they can have relatively low efficiency as well.

To improve the state of the art, Figure 6.17 shows the Climate Savers Computing Initiative standards [2007] for rating power supplies and their goals over time. Note that the standard specifies requirements at 20% and 50% loading in addition to 100% loading.

In addition to the power supply, Barroso and Hölzle [2007] said the goal for the whole server should be *energy proportionality*; that is, servers should consume energy in proportion to the amount of work performed. Figure 6.18 shows how far we are from achieving that ideal goal using SPECpower, a server benchmark that measures energy used at different performance levels (Chapter 1). The energy proportional line is added to the actual power usage of the most efficient server for SPECpower as of July 2010. Most servers will not be that efficient; it was up to 2.5 times better than other systems benchmarked that year, and late in a benchmark competition systems are often configured in ways to win the benchmark that are not typical of systems in the field. For example, the best-rated SPECpower servers use solid-state disks whose capacity is smaller than main memory! Even so, this very efficient system still uses almost 30% of the full

Loading conditioning	Base	Bronze (June 2008)	Silver (June 2009)	Gold (June 2010)
20%	80%	82%	85%	87%
50%	80%	85%	88%	90%
100%	80%	82%	85%	87%

Figure 6.17 Efficiency ratings and goals for power supplies over time of the Climate Savers Computing Initiative. These ratings are for Multi-Output Power Supply Units, which refer to desktop and server power supplies in nonredundant systems. There is a slightly higher standard for single-output PSUs, which are typically used in redundant configurations (1U/2U single-, dual-, and four-socket and blade servers).

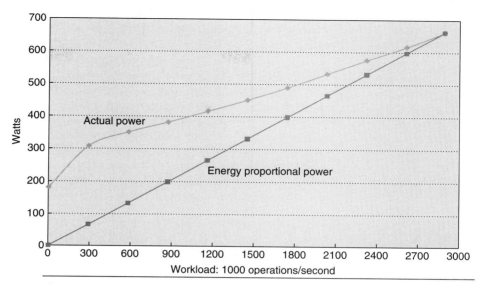

Figure 6.18 The best SPECpower results as of July 2010 versus the ideal energy proportional behavior. The system was the HP ProLiant SL2x170z G6, which uses a cluster of four dual-socket Intel Xeon L5640s with each socket having six cores running at 2.27 GHz. The system had 64 GB of DRAM and a tiny 60 GB SSD for secondary storage. (The fact that main memory is larger than disk capacity suggests that this system was tailored to this benchmark.) The software used was IBM Java Virtual Machine version 9 and Windows Server 2008, Enterprise Edition.

power when idle and almost 50% of full power at just 10% load. Thus, energy proportionality remains a lofty goal instead of a proud achievement.

Systems software is designed to use all of an available resource if it potentially improves performance, without concern for the energy implications. For example, operating systems use all of memory for program data or for file caches, despite the fact that much of the data will likely never be used. Software architects need to consider energy as well as performance in future designs [Carter and Rajamani 2010].

Example   Using the data of the kind in Figure 6.18, what is the saving in power going from five servers at 10% utilization versus one server at 50% utilization?

Answer   A single server at 10% load is 308 watts and at 50% load is 451 watts. The savings is then

$$5 \times 308 / 451 \ = \ (1540 / 451) \approx 3.4$$

or about a factor of 3.4. If we want to be good environmental stewards in our WSC, we must consolidate servers when utilizations drop, purchase servers that are more energy proportional, or find something else that is useful to run in periods of low activity.

Given the background from these six sections, we are now ready to appreciate the work of the Google WSC architects.

6.7 Putting It All Together: A Google Warehouse-Scale Computer

Since many companies with WSCs are competing vigorously in the marketplace, up until recently, they have been reluctant to share their latest innovations with the public (and each other). In 2009, Google described a state-of-the-art WSC as of 2005. Google graciously provided an update of the 2007 status of their WSC, making this section the most up-to-date description of a Google WSC [Clidaras, Johnson, and Felderman 2010]. Even more recently, Facebook decribed their latest datacenter as part of http://opencompute.org.

Containers

Both Google and Microsoft have built WSCs using shipping containers. The idea of building a WSC from containers is to make WSC design modular. Each container is independent, and the only external connections are networking, power, and water. The containers in turn supply networking, power, and cooling to the servers placed inside them, so the job of the WSC is to supply networking, power, and cold water to the containers and to pump the resulting warm water to external cooling towers and chillers.

The Google WSC that we are looking at contains 45 40-foot-long containers in a 300-foot by 250-foot space, or 75,000 square feet (about 7000 square meters). To fit in the warehouse, 30 of the containers are stacked two high, or 15 pairs of stacked containers. Although the location was not revealed, it was built at the time that Google developed WSCs in The Dalles, Oregon, which provides a moderate climate and is near cheap hydroelectric power and Internet backbone fiber. This WSC offers 10 megawatts with a PUE of 1.23 over the prior 12 months. Of that 0.230 of PUE overhead, 85% goes to cooling losses (0.195 PUE) and 15% (0.035) goes to power losses. The system went live in November 2005, and this section describes its state as of 2007.

A Google container can handle up to 250 kilowatts. That means the container can handle 780 watts per square foot (0.09 square meters), or 133 watts per square foot across the entire 75,000-square-foot space with 40 containers. However, the containers in this WSC average just 222 kilowatts

Figure 6.19 is a cutaway drawing of a Google container. A container holds up to 1160 servers, so 45 containers have space for 52,200 servers. (This WSC has about 40,000 servers.) The servers are stacked 20 high in racks that form two long rows of 29 racks (also called *bays*) each, with one row on each side of the container. The rack switches are 48-port, 1 Gbit/sec Ethernet switches, which are placed in every other rack.

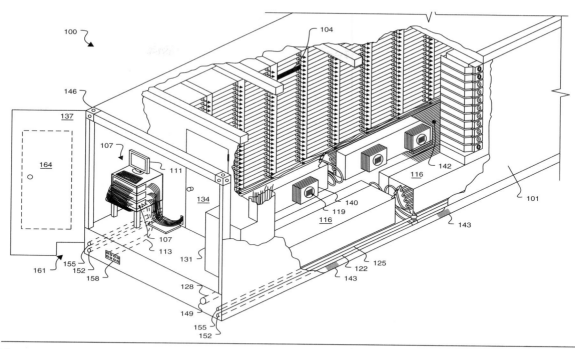

Figure 6.19   Google customizes a standard 1AAA container: 40 x 8 x 9.5 feet (12.2 x 2.4 x 2.9 meters). The servers are stacked up to 20 high in racks that form two long rows of 29 racks each, with one row on each side of the container. The cool aisle goes down the middle of the container, with the hot air return being on the outside. The hanging rack structure makes it easier to repair the cooling system without removing the servers. To allow people inside the container to repair components, it contains safety systems for fire detection and mist-based suppression, emergency egress and lighting, and emergency power shut-off. Containers also have many sensors: temperature, airflow pressure, air leak detection, and motion-sensing lighting. A video tour of the datacenter can be found at *http://www.google.com/corporate/green/datacenters/summit.html*. Microsoft, Yahoo!, and many others are now building modular datacenters based upon these ideas but they have stopped using ISO standard containers since the size is inconvenient.

Cooling and Power in the Google WSC

Figure 6.20 is a cross-section of the container that shows the airflow. The computer racks are attached to the ceiling of the container. The cooling is below a raised floor that blows into the aisle between the racks. Hot air is returned from behind the racks. The restricted space of the container prevents the mixing of hot and cold air, which improves cooling efficiency. Variable-speed fans are run at the lowest speed needed to cool the rack as opposed to a constant speed.

The "cold" air is kept 81°F (27°C), which is balmy compared to the temperatures in many conventional datacenters. One reason datacenters traditionally run so cold is not for the IT equipment, but so that hot spots within the datacenter don't cause isolated problems. By carefully controlling airflow to prevent hot spots, the container can run at a much higher temperature.

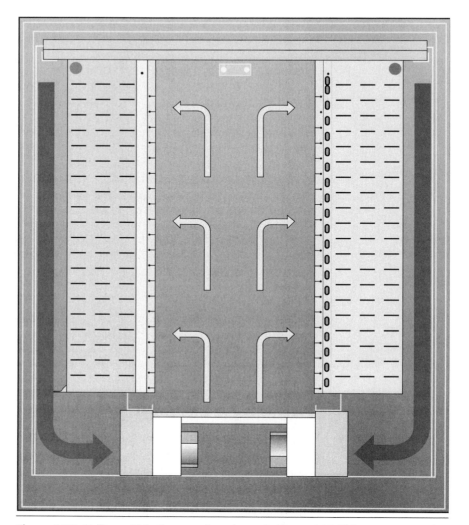

Figure 6.20 Airflow within the container shown in Figure 6.19. This cross-section diagram shows two racks on each side of the container. Cold air blows into the aisle in the middle of the container and is then sucked into the servers. Warm air returns at the edges of the container. This design isolates cold and warm airflows.

External chillers have cutouts so that, if the weather is right, only the outdoor cooling towers need cool the water. The chillers are skipped if the temperature of the water leaving the cooling tower is 70°F (21°C) or lower.

Note that if it's too cold outside, the cooling towers need heaters to prevent ice from forming. One of the advantages of placing a WSC in The Dalles is that the annual wet-bulb temperature ranges from 15°F to 66°F (–9°C to 19°C) with an average of 41°F (5°C), so the chillers can often be turned off. In contrast,

Figure 6.21 Server for Google WSC. The power supply is on the left and the two disks are on the top. The two fans below the left disk cover the two sockets of the AMD Barcelona microprocessor, each with two cores, running at 2.2 GHz. The eight DIMMs in the lower right each hold 1 GB, giving a total of 8 GB. There is no extra sheet metal, as the servers are plugged into the battery and a separate plenum is in the rack for each server to help control the airflow. In part because of the height of the batteries, 20 servers fit in a rack.

Las Vegas, Nevada, ranges from –42°F to 62°F (–41°C to 17°C) with an average of 29°F (–2°C). In addition, having to cool only to 81°F (27°C) inside the container makes it much more likely that Mother Nature will be able to cool the water.

Figure 6.21 shows the server designed by Google for this WSC. To improve efficiency of the power supply, it only supplies 12 volts to the motherboard and the motherboard supplies just enough for the number of disks it has on the board. (Laptops power their disks similarly.) The server norm is to supply the many voltage levels needed by the disks and chips directly. This simplification means the 2007 power supply can run at 92% efficiency, going far above the Gold rating for power supplies in 2010 (Figure 6.17).

Google engineers realized that 12 volts meant that the UPS could simply be a standard battery on each shelf. Hence, rather than have a separate battery room, which Figure 6.9 shows as 94% efficient, each server has its own lead acid battery that is 99.99% efficient. This "distributed UPS" is deployed incrementally with each machine, which means there is no money or power spent on overcapacity. They use standard off-the-shelf UPS units to protect network switches.

What about saving power by using dynamic voltage-frequency scaling (DVFS), which Chapter 1 describes? DVFS was not deployed in this family of machines since the impact on latency was such that it was only feasible in very low activity regions for online workloads, and even in those cases the system-wide savings were very small. The complex management control loop needed to deploy it therefore could not be justified.

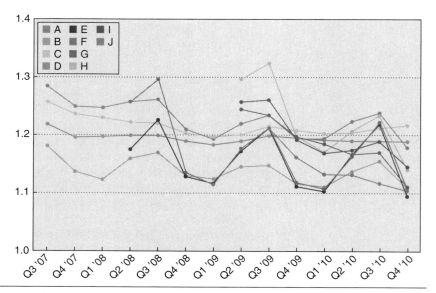

Figure 6.22 Power usage effectiveness (PUE) of 10 Google WSCs over time. Google A is the WSC described in this section. It is the highest line in Q3 '07 and Q2 '10. (From *www.google.com/corporate/green/datacenters/measuring.htm*.) Facebook recently announced a new datacenter that should deliver an impressive PUE of 1.07 (see *http://opencompute.org/*). The Prineville Oregon Facility has no air conditioning and no chilled water. It relies strictly on outside air, which is brought in one side of the building, filtered, cooled via misters, pumped across the IT equipment, and then sent out the building by exhaust fans. In addition, the servers use a custom power supply that allows the power distribution system to skip one of the voltage conversion steps in Figure 6.9.

One of the keys to achieving the PUE of 1.23 was to put measurement devices (called *current transformers*) in all circuits throughout the containers and elsewhere in the WSC to measure the actual power usage. These measurements allowed Google to tune the design of the WSC over time.

Google publishes the PUE of its WSCs each quarter. Figure 6.22 plots the PUE for 10 Google WSCs from the third quarter in 2007 to the second quarter in 2010; this section describes the WSC labeled Google A. Google E operates with a PUE of 1.16 with cooling being only 0.105, due to the higher operational temperatures and chiller cutouts. Power distribution is just 0.039, due to the distributed UPS and single voltage power supply. The best WSC result was 1.12, with Google A at 1.23. In April 2009, the trailing 12-month average weighted by usage across all datacenters was 1.19.

Servers in a Google WSC

The server in Figure 6.21 has two sockets, each containing a dual-core AMD Opteron processor running at 2.2 GHz. The photo shows eight DIMMS, and these servers are typically deployed with 8 GB of DDR2 DRAM. A novel feature is that the memory bus is downclocked to 533 MHz from the standard 666 MHz since the slower bus has little impact on performance but a significant impact on power.

The baseline design has a single network interface card (NIC) for a 1 Gbit/sec Ethernet link. Although the photo in Figure 6.21 shows two SATA disk drives, the baseline server has just one. The peak power of the baseline is about 160 watts, and idle power is 85 watts.

This baseline node is supplemented to offer a storage (or "diskfull") node. First, a second tray containing 10 SATA disks is connected to the server. To get one more disk, a second disk is placed into the empty spot on the motherboard, giving the storage node 12 SATA disks. Finally, since a storage node could saturate a single 1 Gbit/sec Ethernet link, a second Ethernet NIC was added. Peak power for a storage node is about 300 watts, and it idles at 198 watts.

Note that the storage node takes up two slots in the rack, which is one reason why Google deployed 40,000 instead of 52,200 servers in the 45 containers. In this facility, the ratio was about two compute nodes for every storage node, but that ratio varied widely across Google's WSCs. Hence, Google A had about 190,000 disks in 2007, or an average of almost 5 disks per server.

Networking in a Google WSC

The 40,000 servers are divided into three arrays of more than 10,000 servers each. (Arrays are called *clusters* in Google terminology.) The 48-port rack switch uses 40 ports to connect to servers, leaving 8 for uplinks to the array switches.

Array switches are configured to support up to 480 1 Gbit/sec Ethernet links and a few 10 Gbit/sec ports. The 1 Gigabit ports are used to connect to the rack switches, as each rack switch has a single link to each of the array switches. The 10 Gbit/sec ports connect to each of two datacenter routers, which aggregate all array routers and provide connectivity to the outside world. The WSC uses two datacenter routers for dependability, so a single datacenter router failure does not take out the whole WSC.

The number of uplink ports used per rack switch varies from a minimum of 2 to a maximum of 8. In the dual-port case, rack switches operate at an oversubscription rate of 20:1. That is, there is 20 times the network bandwidth inside the switch as there was exiting the switch. Applications with significant traffic demands beyond a rack tended to suffer from poor network performance. Hence, the 8-port uplink design, which provided a lower oversubscription rate of just 5:1, was used for arrays with more demanding traffic requirements.

Monitoring and Repair in a Google WSC

For a single operator to be responsible for more than 1000 servers, you need an extensive monitoring infrastructure and some automation to help with routine events.

Google deploys monitoring software to track the health of all servers and networking gear. Diagnostics are running all the time. When a system fails, many of the possible problems have simple automated solutions. In this case, the next step is to reboot the system and then to try to reinstall software components. Thus, the procedure handles the majority of the failures.

Machines that fail these first steps are added to a queue of machines to be repaired. The diagnosis of the problem is placed into the queue along with the ID of the failed machine.

To amortize the cost of repair, failed machines are addressed in batches by repair technicians. When the diagnosis software is confident in its assessment, the part is immediately replaced without going through the manual diagnosis process. For example, if the diagnostic says disk 3 of a storage node is bad, the disk is replaced immediately. Failed machines with no diagnostic or with low-confidence diagnostics are examined manually.

The goal is to have less than 1% of all nodes in the manual repair queue at any one time. The average time in the repair queue is a week, even though it takes much less time for repair technician to fix it. The longer latency suggests the importance of repair throughput, which affects cost of operations. Note that the automated repairs of the first step take minutes for a reboot/reinstall to hours for running directed stress tests to make sure the machine is indeed operational.

These latencies do not take into account the time to idle the broken servers. The reason is that a big variable is the amount of state in the node. A stateless node takes much less time than a storage node whose data may need to be evacuated before it can be replaced.

Summary

As of 2007, Google had already demonstrated several innovations to improve the energy efficiency of its WSCs to deliver a PUE of 1.23 in Google A:

- In addition to providing an inexpensive shell to enclose servers, the modified shipping containers separate hot and cold air plenums, which helps reduce the variation in intake air temperature for servers. With less severe worst-case hot spots, cold air can be delivered at warmer temperatures.

- These containers also shrink the distance of the air circulation loop, which reduces energy to move air.

- Operating servers at higher temperatures means that air only has to be chilled to 81°F (27°C) instead of the traditional 64°F to 71°F (18°C to 22°C).

- A higher target cold air temperature helps put the facility more often within the range that can be sustained by evaporative cooling solutions (cooling towers), which are more energy efficient than traditional chillers.

- Deploying WSCs in temperate climates to allow use of evaporative cooling exclusively for portions of the year.

- Deploying extensive monitoring hardware and software to measure actual PUE versus designed PUE improves operational efficiency.

- Operating more servers than the worst-case scenario for the power distribution system would suggest, since it's statistically unlikely that thousands of servers would all be highly busy simultaneously, yet rely on the monitoring system to off-load work in the unlikely case that they did [Fan, Weber, and Barroso 2007] [Ranganathan et al. 2006]. PUE improves because the facility is operating closer to its fully designed capacity, where it is at its most efficient because the servers and cooling systems are not energy proportional. Such increased utilization reduces demand for new servers and new WSCs.

- Designing motherboards that only need a single 12-volt supply so that the UPS function could be supplied by standard batteries associated with each server instead of a battery room, thereby lowering costs and reducing one source of inefficiency of power distribution within a WSC.

- Carefully designing the server board itself to improve its energy efficiency. For example, underclocking the front-side bus on these microprocessors reduces energy usage with negligible performance impact. (Note that such optimizations do not impact PUE but do reduce overall WSC energy consumption.)

WSC design must have improved in the intervening years, as Google's best WSC has dropped the PUE from 1.23 for Google A to 1.12. Facebook announced in 2011 that they had driven PUE down to 1.07 in their new datacenter (see *http://opencompute.org/*). It will be interesting to see what innovations remain to improve further the WSC efficiency so that we are good guardians of our environment. Perhaps in the future we will even consider the energy cost to *manufacture* the equipment within a WSC [Chang et al. 2010].

6.8 Fallacies and Pitfalls

Despite WSC being less than a decade old, WSC architects like those at Google have already uncovered many pitfalls and fallacies about WSCs, often learned the hard way. As we said in the introduction, WSC architects are today's Seymour Crays.

Fallacy *Cloud computing providers are losing money.*

A popular question about cloud computing is whether it's profitable at these low prices.

Based on AWS pricing from Figure 6.15, we could charge $0.68 per hour per server for computation. (The $0.085 per hour price is for a Virtual Machine equivalent to one EC2 compute unit, not a full server.) If we could sell 50% of the server hours, that would generate $0.34 of income per hour per server. (Note that customers pay no matter how little they use the servers they occupy, so selling 50% of the server hours doesn't necessarily mean that average server utilization is 50%.)

Another way to calculate income would be to use AWS *Reserved Instances*, where customers pay a yearly fee to reserve an instance and then a lower rate per hour to use it. Combining the charges together, AWS would receive $0.45 of income per hour per server for a full year.

If we could sell 750 GB per server for storage using AWS pricing, in addition to the computation income, that would generate another $75 per month per server, or another $0.10 per hour.

These numbers suggest an average income of $0.44 per hour per server (via On-Demand Instances) to $0.55 per hour (via Reserved Instances). From Figure 6.13, we calculated the cost per server as $0.11 per hour for the WSC in Section 6.4. Although the costs in Figure 6.13 are estimates that are *not* based on actual AWS costs and the 50% sales for server processing and 750 GB utilization of per server storage are just examples, these assumptions suggest a gross margin of 75% to 80%. Assuming these calculations are reasonable, they suggest that cloud computing is profitable, especially for a service business.

Fallacy   *Capital costs of the WSC facility are higher than for the servers that it houses.*

While a quick look at Figure 6.13 on page 453 might lead you to that conclusion, that glimpse ignores the length of amortization for each part of the full WSC. However, the facility lasts 10 to 15 years while the servers need to be repurchased every 3 or 4 years. Using the amortization times in Figure 6.13 of 10 years and 3 years, respectively, the capital expenditures over a decade are $72M for the facility and $3.3 \times$ $67M, or $221M, for servers. Thus, the capital costs for servers in a WSC over a decade are a factor of three higher than for the WSC facility.

Pitfall   *Trying to save power with inactive low power modes versus active low power modes.*

Figure 6.3 on page 440 shows that the average utilization of servers is between 10% and 50%. Given the concern on operational costs of a WSC from Section 6.4, you would think low power modes would be a huge help.

As Chapter 1 mentions, you cannot access DRAMs or disks in these *inactive low power modes*, so you must return to fully active mode to read or write, no matter how low the rate. The pitfall is that the time and energy required to return to fully active mode make inactive low power modes less attractive. Figure 6.3 shows that almost all servers average at least 10% utilization, so you might expect long periods of low activity but not long periods of inactivity.

In contrast, processors still run in lower power modes at a small multiple of the regular rate, so *active low power modes* are much easier to use. Note that the time to move to fully active mode for processors is also measured in microseconds, so active low power modes also address the latency concerns about low power modes.

Pitfall   *Using too wimpy a processor when trying to improve WSC cost-performance.*

Amdahl's law still applies to WSC, as there will be some serial work for each request, and that can increase request latency if it runs on a slow server [Hölzle 2010] [Lim et al. 2008]. If the serial work increases latency, then the cost of using a wimpy processor must include the software development costs to optimize the code to return it to the lower latency. The larger number of threads of many slow servers can also be more difficult to schedule and load balance, and thus the variability in thread performance can lead to longer latencies. A 1 in 1000 chance of bad scheduling is probably not an issue with 10 tasks, but it is with 1000 tasks when you have to wait for the longest task. Many smaller servers can also lead to lower utilization, as it's clearly easier to schedule when there are fewer things to schedule. Finally, even some parallel algorithms get less efficient when the problem is partitioned too finely. The Google rule of thumb is currently to use the low-end range of server class computers [Barroso and Hölzle 2009].

As a concrete example, Reddi et al. [2010] compared embedded microprocessors (Atom) and server microprocessors (Nehalem Xeon) running the Bing search engine. They found that the latency of a query was about three times longer on Atom than on Xeon. Moreover, the Xeon was more robust. As load increases on Xeon, quality of service degrades gradually and modestly. Atom quickly violates its quality-of-service target as it tries to absorb additional load.

This behavior translates directly into search quality. Given the importance of latency to the user, as Figure 6.12 suggests, the Bing search engine uses multiple strategies to refine search results if the query latency has not yet exceeded a cut-off latency. The lower latency of the larger Xeon nodes means they can spend more time refining search results. Hence, even when the Atom had almost no load, it gave worse answers in 1% of the queries than Xeon. At normal loads, 2% of the answers were worse.

Fallacy *Given improvements in DRAM dependability and the fault tolerance of WSC systems software, you don't need to spend extra for ECC memory in a WSC.*

Since ECC adds 8 bits to every 64 bits of DRAM, potentially you could save a ninth of the DRAM costs by eliminating error-correcting code (ECC), especially since measurements of DRAM had claimed failure rates of 1000 to 5000 FIT (failures per billion hours of operation) per megabit [Tezzaron Semiconductor 2004].

Schroeder, Pinheiro, and Weber [2009] studied measurements of the DRAMs with ECC protection at the majority of Google's WSCs, which was surely many hundreds of thousands of servers, over a 2.5-year period. They found 15 to 25 times higher FIT rates than had been published, or 25,000 to 70,000 failures per megabit. Failures affected more than 8% of DIMMs, and the average DIMM had 4000 correctable errors and 0.2 uncorrectable errors per year. Measured at the server, about a third experienced DRAM errors each year, with an average of 22,000 correctable errors and 1 uncorrectable error per year. That is, for one-third of the servers, one memory error is corrected every 2.5 hours. Note that these systems used the more powerful chipkill codes rather than the simpler SECDED codes. If the simpler scheme had been used, the uncorrectable error rates would have been 4 to 10 times higher.

In a WSC that only had parity error protection, the servers would have to reboot for each memory parity error. If the reboot time were 5 minutes, one-third of the machines would spend 20% of their time rebooting! Such behavior would lower the performance of the $150M facility by about 6%. Moreover, these systems would suffer many uncorrectable errors without operators being notified that they occurred.

In the early years, Google used DRAM that didn't even have parity protection. In 2000, during testing before shipping the next release of the search index, it started suggesting random documents in response to test queries [Barroso and Hölzle 2009]. The reason was a stuck-at-zero fault in some DRAMs, which corrupted the new index. Google added consistency checks to detect such errors in the future. As WSC grew in size and as ECC DIMMs became more affordable, ECC became the standard in Google WSCs. ECC has the added benefit of making it much easier to find broken DIMMs during repair.

Such data suggest why the Fermi GPU (Chapter 4) adds ECC to its memory where its predecessors didn't even have parity protection. Moreover, these FIT rates cast doubts on efforts to use the Intel Atom processor in a WSC—due to its improved power efficiency—since the 2011 chip set does not support ECC DRAM.

Fallacy   *Turning off hardware during periods of low activity improves cost-performance of a WSC.*

Figure 6.14 on page 454 shows that the cost of amortizing the power distribution and cooling infrastructure is 50% higher than the entire monthly power bill. Hence, while it certainly would save some money to compact workloads and turn off idle machines, even if you could save half the power it would only reduce the monthly operational bill by 7%. There would also be practical problems to overcome, since the extensive WSC monitoring infrastructure depends on being able to poke equipment and see it respond. Another advantage of energy proportionality and active low power modes is that they are compatible with the WSC monitoring infrastructure, which allows a single operator to be responsible for more than 1000 servers.

The conventional WSC wisdom is to run other valuable tasks during periods of low activity so as to recoup the investment in power distribution and cooling. A prime example is the batch MapReduce jobs that create indices for search. Another example of getting value from low utilization is spot pricing on AWS, which the caption in Figure 6.15 on page 458 describes. AWS users who are flexible about when their tasks are run can save a factor of 2.7 to 3 for computation by letting AWS schedule the tasks more flexibly using Spot Instances, such as when the WSC would otherwise have low utilization.

Fallacy   *Replacing all disks with Flash memory will improve cost-performance of a WSC.*

Flash memory is much faster than disk for some WSC workloads, such as those doing many random reads and writes. For example, Facebook deployed Flash memory packaged as solid-state disks (*SSDs*) as a write-back cache called Flashcache as part of its file system in its WSC, so that hot files stay in Flash and cold files stay on disk. However, since all performance improvements in a WSC must be judged on cost-performance, before replacing all the disks with SSD the question is really I/Os per second per dollar and storage capacity per dollar. As we saw in Chapter 2, Flash memory costs at least 20 times more per GByte than magnetic disks: $2.00/GByte versus $0.09/Gbyte.

Narayanan et al. [2009] looked at migrating workloads from disk to SSD by simulating workload traces from small and large datacenters. Their conclusion was that SSDs were not cost effective for any of their workloads due to the low storage capacity per dollar. To reach the break-even point, Flash memory storage devices need to improve capacity per dollar by a factor of 3 to 3000, depending on the workload.

Even when you factor power into the equation, it's hard to justify replacing disk with Flash for data that are infrequently accessed. A one-terabyte disk uses about 10 watts of power, so, using the $2 per watt-year rule of thumb from Section 6.4, the most you could save from reduced energy is $20 a year per disk. However, the CAPEX cost in 2011 for a terabyte of storage is $2000 for Flash and only $90 for disk.

6.9   Concluding Remarks

Inheriting the title of building the world's biggest computers, computer architects of WSCs are designing the large part of the future IT that completes the mobile client. Many of us use WSCs many times a day, and the number of times per day and the number of people using WSCs will surely increase in the next decade. Already more than half of the nearly seven billion people on the planet have cell phones. As these devices become Internet ready, many more people from around the world will be able to benefit from WSCs.

Moreover, the economies of scale uncovered by WSC have realized the long dreamed of goal of computing as a utility. Cloud computing means anyone anywhere with good ideas and business models can tap thousands of servers to deliver their vision almost instantly. Of course, there are important obstacles that could limit the growth of cloud computing around standards, privacy, and the rate of growth of Internet bandwidth, but we foresee them being addressed so that cloud computing can flourish.

Given the increasing number of cores per chip (see Chapter 5), clusters will increase to include thousands of cores. We believe the technologies developed to run WSC will prove useful and trickle down to clusters, so that clusters will run the same virtual machines and systems software developed for WSC. One advantage would be easy support of "hybrid" datacenters, where the workload could easily be shipped to the cloud in a crunch and then shrink back afterwards to relying only on local computing.

Among the many attractive features of cloud computing is that it offers economic incentives for conservation. Whereas it is hard to convince cloud computing *providers* to turn off unused equipment to save energy given the cost of the infrastructure investment, it is easy to convince cloud computing *users* to give up idle instances since they are paying for them whether or not they are doing anything useful. Similarly, charging by use encourages programmers to use computation, communication, and storage efficiently, which can be difficult to encourage without an understandable pricing scheme. The explicit pricing also makes it possible for researchers to evaluate innovations in cost-performance instead of just performance, since costs are now easily measured and believable. Finally, cloud computing means that researchers can evaluate their ideas at the scale of thousands of computers, which in the past only large companies could afford.

We believe that WSCs are changing the goals and principles of server design, just as the needs of mobile clients are changing the goals and principles of microprocessor design. Both are revolutionizing the software industry, as well. Performance per dollar and performance per joule drive both mobile client hardware and the WSC hardware, and parallelism is the key to delivering on those sets of goals.

Architects will play a vital role in both halves of this exciting future world. We look forward to seeing—and to using—what will come.

6.10 Historical Perspectives and References

Section L.8 (available online) covers the development of clusters that were the foundation of WSC and of utility computing. (Readers interested in learning more should start with Barroso and Hölzle [2009] and the blog postings and talks of James Hamilton at *http://perspectives.mvdirona.com.*)

Case Studies and Exercises by Parthasarathy Ranganathan

Case Study 1: Total Cost of Ownership Influencing Warehouse-Scale Computer Design Decisions

Concepts illustrated by this case study

■ Total Cost of Ownership (TCO)

■ Influence of Server Cost and Power on the Entire WSC

■ Benefits and Drawbacks of Low-Power Servers

Total cost of ownership is an important metric for measuring the effectiveness of a warehouse-scale computer (WSC). TCO includes both the CAPEX and OPEX described in Section 6.4 and reflects the ownership cost of the entire datacenter to achieve a certain level of performance. In considering different servers, networks, and storage architectures, TCO is often the important comparison metric used by datacenter owners to decide which options are best; however, TCO is a multidimensional computation that takes into account many different factors. The goal of this case study is to take a detailed look into WSCs, how different architectures influence TCO, and how TCO drives operator decisions. This case study will use the numbers from Figure 6.13 and Section 6.4, and assumes that the described WSC achieves the operator's target level of performance. TCO is often used to compare different server options that have multiple dimensions. The exercises in this case study examine how such comparisons are made in the context of WSCs and the complexity involved in making the decisions.

6.1 [5/5/10] <6.2, 6.4> In this chapter, data-level parallelism has been discussed as a way for WSCs to achieve high performance on large problems. Conceivably, even greater performance can be obtained by using high-end servers; however, higher performance servers often come with a nonlinear price increase.

    a. [5] <6.4> Assuming servers that are 10% faster at the same utilization, but 20% more expensive, what is the CAPEX for the WSC?

    b. [5] <6.4> If those servers also use 15% more power, what is the OPEX?

    c. [10] <6.2, 6.4> Given the speed improvement and power increase, what must the cost of the new servers be to be comparable to the original cluster? (*Hint:* Based on this TCO model, you may have to change the critical load of the facility.)

6.2 [5/10] <6.4, 6.8> To achieve a lower OPEX, one appealing alternative is to use low-power versions of servers to reduce the total electricity required to run the servers; however, similar to high-end servers, low-power versions of high-end components also have nonlinear trade-offs.

    a. [5] <6.4, 6.8> If low-power server options offered 15% lower power at the same performance but are 20% more expensive, are they a good trade-off?

    b. [10] <6.4, 6.8> At what cost do the servers become comparable to the original cluster? What if the price of electricity doubles?

6.3 [5/10/15] <6.4, 6.6> Servers that have different operating modes offer opportunities for dynamically running different configurations in the cluster to match workload usage. Use the data in Figure 6.23 for the power/performance modes for a given low-power server.

    a. [5] <6.4, 6.6> If a server operator decided to save power costs by running all servers at medium performance, how many servers would be needed to achieve the same level of performance?

Mode	Performance	Power
High	100%	100%
Medium	75%	60%
Low	59%	38%

Figure 6.23 Power–performance modes for low-power servers.

   b. [10] <6.4, 6.6> What are the CAPEX and OPEX of such a configuration?

   c. [15] <6.4, 6.6> If there was an alternative to purchase a server that is 20% cheaper but slower and uses less power, find the performance–power curve that provides a TCO comparable to the baseline server.

6.4 [Discussion] <6.4> Discuss the trade-offs and benefits of the two options in Exercise 6.3, assuming a constant workload being run on the servers.

6.5 [Discussion] <6.2, 6.4> Unlike high-performance computing (HPC) clusters, WSCs often experience significant workload fluctuation throughout the day. Discuss the trade-offs and benefits of the two options in Exercise 6.3, this time assuming a workload that varies.

6.6 [Discussion] <6.4, 6.7> The TCO model presented so far abstracts away a significant amount of lower level details. Discuss the impact of these abstractions to the overall accuracy of the TCO model. When are these abstractions safe to make? In what cases would greater detail provide significantly different answers?

Case Study 2: Resource Allocation in WSCs and TCO

Concepts illustrated by this case study

■ Server and Power Provisioning within a WSC

■ Time-Variance of Workloads

■ Effects of Variance on TCO

Some of the key challenges to deploying efficient WSCs are provisioning resources properly and utilizing them to their fullest. This problem is complex due to the size of WSCs as well as the potential variance of the workloads being run. The exercises in this case study show how different uses of resources can affect TCO.

6.7 [5/5/10] <6.4> One of the challenges in provisioning a WSC is determining the proper power load, given the facility size. As described in the chapter, nameplate power is often a peak value that is rarely encountered.

   a. [5] <6.4> Estimate how the per-server TCO changes if the nameplate server power is 200 watts and the cost is $3000.

   b. [5] <6.4> Also consider a higher power, but cheaper option whose power is 300 watts and costs $2000.

   c. [10] <6.4> How does the per-server TCO change if the actual average power usage of the servers is only 70% of the nameplate power?

6.8 [15/10] <6.2, 6.4> One assumption in the TCO model is that the critical load of the facility is fixed, and the amount of servers fits that critical load. In reality, due to the variations of server power based on load, the critical power used by a facility can vary at any given time. Operators must initially provision the datacenter based on its critical power resources and an estimate of how much power is used by the datacenter components.

    a. [15] <6.2, 6.4> Extend the TCO model to initially provision a WSC based on a server with a nameplate power of 300 watts, but also calculate the actual monthly critical power used and TCO assuming the server averages 40% utilization and 225 watts. How much capacity is left unused?

    b. [10] <6.2, 6.4> Repeat this exercise with a 500-watt server that averages 20% utilization and 300 watts.

6.9   [10] <6.4, 6.5> WSCs are often used in an interactive manner with end users, as mentioned in Section 6.5. This interactive usage often leads to time-of-day fluctuations, with peaks correlating to specific time periods. For example, for Netflix rentals, there is a peak during the evening periods of 8 to 10 p.m.; the entirety of these time-of-day effects is significant. Compare the per-server TCO of a datacenter with a capacity to match the utilization at 4 a.m. compared to 9 p.m.

6.10   [Discussion/15] <6.4, 6.5> Discuss some options to better utilize the excess servers during the off-peak hours or options to save costs. Given the interactive nature of WSCs, what are some of the challenges to aggressively reducing power usage?

6.11   [Discussion/25] <6.4, 6.6> Propose one possible way to improve TCO by focusing on reducing server power. What are the challenges to evaluating your proposal? Estimate the TCO improvements based on your proposal. What are advantages and drawbacks?

Exercises

6.12   [10/10/10] <6.1> One of the important enablers of WSC is ample request-level parallelism, in contrast to instruction or thread-level parallelism. This question explores the implication of different types of parallelism on computer architecture and system design.

    a. [10] <6.1> Discuss scenarios where improving the instruction- or thread-level parallelism would provide greater benefits than achievable through request-level parallelism.

    b. [10] <6.1> What are the software design implications of increasing request-level parallelism?

    c. [10] <6.1> What are potential drawbacks of increasing request-level parallelism?

6.13   [Discussion/15/15] <6.2> When a cloud computing service provider receives jobs consisting of multiple Virtual Machines (VMs) (e.g., a MapReduce job), many scheduling options exist. The VMs can be scheduled in a round-robin manner to spread across all available processors and servers or they can be consolidated to use as few processors as possible. Using these scheduling options, if a job with 24 VMs was submitted and 30 processors were available in the cloud (each able to run up to 3 VMs), round-robin would use 24 processors, while consolidated scheduling would use 8 processors. The scheduler can also find available processor cores at different scopes: socket, server, rack, and an array of racks.

a. [Discussion] <6.2> Assuming that the submitted jobs are all compute-heavy workloads, possibly with different memory bandwidth requirements, what are the pros and cons of round-robin versus consolidated scheduling in terms of power and cooling costs, performance, and reliability?

b. [15] <6.2> Assuming that the submitted jobs are all I/O-heavy workloads, what are the pros and cons of round-robin versus consolidated scheduling, at different scopes?

c. [15] <6.2> Assuming that the submitted jobs are network-heavy workloads, what are the pros and cons of round-robin versus consolidated scheduling, at different scopes?

6.14 [15/15/10/10] <6.2, 6.3> MapReduce enables large amounts of parallelism by having data-independent tasks run on multiple nodes, often using commodity hardware; however, there are limits to the level of parallelism. For example, for redundancy, MapReduce will write data blocks to multiple nodes, consuming disk and potentially network bandwidth. Assume a total dataset size of 300 GB, a network bandwidth of 1 Gb/sec, a 10 sec/GB map rate, and a 20 sec/GB reduce rate. Also assume that 30% of the data must be read from remote nodes, and each output file is written to two other nodes for redundancy. Use Figure 6.6 for all other parameters.

a. [15] <6.2, 6.3> Assume that all nodes are in the same rack. What is the expected runtime with 5 nodes? 10 nodes? 100 nodes? 1000 nodes? Discuss the bottlenecks at each node size.

b. [15] <6.2, 6.3> Assume that there are 40 nodes per rack and that any remote read/write has an equal chance of going to any node. What is the expected runtime at 100 nodes? 1000 nodes?

c. [10] <6.2, 6.3> An important consideration is minimizing data movement as much as possible. Given the significant slowdown of going from local to rack to array accesses, software must be strongly optimized to maximize locality. Assume that there are 40 nodes per rack, and 1000 nodes are used in the MapReduce job. What is the runtime if remote accesses are within the same rack 20% of the time? 50% of the time? 80% of the time?

d. [10] <6.2, 6.3> Given the simple MapReduce program in Section 6.2, discuss some possible optimizations to maximize the locality of the workload.

6.15 [20/20/10/20/20/20] <6.2> WSC programmers often use data replication to overcome failures in the software. Hadoop HDFS, for example, employs three-way replication (one local copy, one remote copy in the rack, and one remote copy in a separate rack), but it's worth examining when such replication is needed.

a. [20] <6.2> A Hadoop World 2010 attendee survey showed that over half of the Hadoop clusters had 10 nodes or less, with dataset sizes of 10 TB or less.

Using the failure frequency data in Figure 6.1, what kind of availability does a 10-node Hadoop cluster have with one-, two-, and three-way replications?

b. [20] <6.2> Assuming the failure data in Figure 6.1 and a 1000-node Hadoop cluster, what kind of availability does it have with one-, two-, and three-way replications?

c. [10] <6.2> The relative overhead of replication varies with the amount of data written per local compute hour. Calculate the amount of extra I/O traffic and network traffic (within and across rack) for a 1000-node Hadoop job that sorts 1 PB of data, where the intermediate results for data shuffling are written to the HDFS.

d. [20] <6.2> Using Figure 6.6, calculate the time overhead for two- and three-way replications. Using the failure rates shown in Figure 6.1, compare the expected execution times for no replication versus two- and three-way replications.

e. [20] <6.2> Now consider a database system applying replication on logs, assuming each transaction on average accesses the hard disk once and generates 1 KB of log data. Calculate the time overhead for two- and three-way replications. What if the transaction is executed in-memory and takes 10 μs?

f. [20] <6.2> Now consider a database system with ACID consistency that requires two network round-trips for two-phase commitment. What is the time overhead for maintaining consistency as well as replications?

6.16 [15/15/20/15/] <6.1, 6.2, 6.8> Although request-level parallelism allows many machines to work on a single problem in parallel, thereby achieving greater overall performance, one of the challenges is avoiding dividing the problem too finely. If we look at this problem in the context of service level agreements (SLAs), using smaller problem sizes through greater partitioning can require increased effort to achieve the target SLA. Assume an SLA of 95% of queries respond at 0.5 sec or faster, and a parallel architecture similar to MapReduce that can launch multiple redundant jobs to achieve the same result. For the following questions, assume the query–response time curve shown in Figure 6.24. The curve shows the latency of response, based on the number of queries per second, for a baseline server as well as a "small" server that uses a slower processor model.

a. [15] <6.1, 6.2, 6.8> How many servers are required to achieve that SLA, assuming that the WSC receives 30,000 queries per second, and the query–response time curve shown in Figure 6.24? How many "small" servers are required to achieve that SLA, given this response-time probability curve? Looking only at server costs, how much cheaper must the "wimpy" servers be than the normal servers to achieve a cost advantage for the target SLA?

b. [15] <6.1, 6.2, 6.8> Often "small" servers are also less reliable due to cheaper components. Using the numbers from Figure 6.1, assume that the number of events due to flaky machines and bad memories increases by 30%. How many "small" servers are required now? How much cheaper must those servers be than the standard servers?

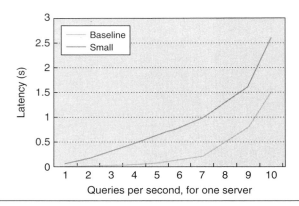

Figure 6.24 Query–response time curve.

c. [20] <6.1, 6.2, 6.8> Now assume a batch processing environment. The "small" servers provide 30% of the overall performance of the regular servers. Still assuming the reliability numbers from Exercise 6.15 part (b), how many "wimpy" nodes are required to provide the same expected throughput of a 2400-node array of standard servers, assuming perfect linear scaling of performance to node size and an average task length of 10 minutes per node? What if the scaling is 85%? 60%?

d. [15] <6.1, 6.2, 6.8> Often the scaling is not a linear function, but instead a logarithmic function. A natural response may be instead to purchase larger nodes that have more computational power per node to minimize the array size. Discuss some of the trade-offs with this architecture.

6.17 [10/10/15] <6.3, 6.8> One trend in high-end servers is toward the inclusion of nonvolatile Flash memory in the memory hierarchy, either through solid-state disks (SSDs) or PCI Express-attached cards. Typical SSDs have a bandwidth of 250 MB/sec and latency of 75 μs, whereas PCIe cards have a bandwidth of 600 MB/sec and latency of 35 μs.

a. [10] Take Figure 6.7 and include these points in the local server hierarchy. Assuming that identical performance scaling factors as DRAM are accessed at different hierarchy levels, how do these Flash memory devices compare when accessed across the rack? Across the array?

b. [10] Discuss some software-based optimizations that can utilize the new level of the memory hierarchy.

c. [25] Repeat part (a), instead assuming that each node has a 32 GB PCIe card that is able to cache 50% of all disk accesses.

d. [15] As discussed in "Fallacies and Pitfalls" (Section 6.8), replacing all disks with SSDs is not necessarily a cost-effective strategy. Consider a WSC operator that uses it to provide cloud services. Discuss some scenarios where using SSDs or other Flash memory would make sense.

6.18   [20/20/Discussion] <6.3> *Memory Hierarchy*: Caching is heavily used in some WSC designs to reduce latency, and there are multiple caching options to satisfy varying access patterns and requirements.

    a. [20] Let's consider the design options for streaming rich media from the Web (e.g., Netflix). First we need to estimate the number of movies, number of encode formats per movie, and concurrent viewing users. In 2010, Netflix had 12,000 titles for online streaming, each title having at least four encode formats (at 500, 1000, 1600, and 2200 kbps). Let's assume that there are 100,000 concurrent viewers for the entire site, and an average movie is one hour long. Estimate the total storage capacity, I/O and network bandwidths, and video-streaming-related computation requirements.

    b. [20] What are the access patterns and reference locality characteristics per user, per movie, and across all movies? (*Hint*: Random versus sequential, good versus poor temporal and spatial locality, relatively small versus large working set size.)

    c. [Discussion] What movie storage options exist by using DRAM, SSD, and hard drives? Compare them in performance and TCO.

6.19   [10/20/20/Discussion/Discussion] <6.3> Consider a social networking Web site with 100 million active users posting updates about themselves (in text and pictures) as well as browsing and interacting with updates in their social networks. To provide low latency, Facebook and many other Web sites use memcached as a caching layer before the backend storage/database tiers.

    a. [10] Estimate the data generation and request rates per user and across the entire site.

    b. [20] For the social networking Web site discussed here, how much DRAM is needed to host its working set? Using servers each having 96 GB DRAM, estimate how many local versus remote memory accesses are needed to generate a user's home page?

    c. [20] Now consider two candidate memcached server designs, one using conventional Xeon processors and the other using smaller cores, such as Atom processors. Given that memcached requires large physical memory but has low CPU utilization, what are the pros and cons of these two designs?

    d. [Discussion] Today's tight coupling between memory modules and processors often requires an increase in CPU socket count in order to provide large memory support. List other designs to provide large physical memory without proportionally increasing the number of sockets in a server. Compare them based on performance, power, costs, and reliability.

    e. [Discussion] The same user's information can be stored in both the memcached and storage servers, and such servers can be physically hosted in different ways. Discuss the pros and cons of the following server layout in the WSC: (1) memcached collocated on the same storage server, (2) memcached and storage server on separate nodes in the same rack, or (3) memcached servers on the same racks and storage servers collocated on separate racks.

6.20   [5/5/10/10/Discussion/Discussion] <6.3, 6.6> *Datacenter Networking*: Map-Reduce and WSC are a powerful combination to tackle large-scale data processing; for example, Google in 2008 sorted one petabyte (1 PB) of records in a little more than 6 hours using 4000 servers and 48,000 hard drives.

   a. [5] Derive disk bandwidth from Figure 6.1 and associated text. How many seconds does it take to read the data into main memory and write the sorted results back?

   b. [5] Assuming each server has two 1 Gb/sec Ethernet network interface cards (NICs) and the WSC switch infrastructure is oversubscribed by a factor of 4, how many seconds does it take to shuffle the entire dataset across 4000 servers?

   c. [10] Assuming network transfer is the performance bottleneck for petabyte sort, can you estimate what oversubscription ratio Google has in their datacenter?

   d. [10] Now let's examine the benefits of having 10 Gb/sec Ethernet without oversubscription—for example, using a 48-port 10 Gb/sec Ethernet (as used by the 2010 Indy sort benchmark winner TritonSort). How long does it take to shuffle the 1 PB of data?

   e. [Discussion] Compare the two approaches here: (1) the massively scale-out approach with high network oversubscription ratio, and (2) a relatively small-scale system with a high-bandwidth network. What are their potential bottlenecks? What are their advantages and disadvantages, in terms of scalability and TCO?

   f. [Discussion] Sort and many important scientific computing workloads are communication heavy, while many other workloads are not. List three example workloads that do not benefit from high-speed networking. What EC2 instances would you recommend to use for these two classes of workloads?

6.21   [10/25/Discussion] <6.4, 6.6> Because of the massive scale of WSCs, it is very important to properly allocate network resources based on the workloads that are expected to be run. Different allocations can have significant impacts on both the performance and total cost of ownership.

   a. [10] Using the numbers in the spreadsheet detailed in Figure 6.13, what is the oversubscription ratio at each access-layer switch? What is the impact on TCO if the oversubscription ratio is cut in half? What if it is doubled?

   b. [25] Reducing the oversubscription ratio can potentially improve the performance if a workload is network-limited. Assume a MapReduce job that uses 120 servers and reads 5 TB of data. Assume the same ratio of read/intermediate/output data as in Figure 6.2, Sep-09, and use Figure 6.6 to define the bandwidths of the memory hierarchy. For data reading, assume that 50% of data is read from remote disks; of that, 80% is read from within the rack and 20% is read from within the array. For intermediate data and output data, assume that 30% of the data uses remote disks; of that, 90% is within the rack and 10% is within the array. What is the overall performance improvement when reducing the oversubscription ratio by half? What is the performance if it is doubled? Calculate the TCO in each case.

c. [Discussion] We are seeing the trend to more cores per system. We are also seeing the increasing adoption of optical communication (with potentially higher bandwidth and improved energy efficiency). How do you think these and other emerging technology trends will affect the design of future WSCs?

6.22 [5/15/15/20/25] <6.5> *Realizing the Capability of Amazon Web Services*: Imagine you are the site operation and infrastructure manager of an Alexa.com top site and are considering using Amazon Web Services (AWS). What factors do you need to consider in determining whether to migrate to AWS, what services and instance types to use and how much cost could you save? You can use Alexa and site traffic information (e.g., Wikipedia provides page view stats) to estimate the amount of traffic received by a top site, or you can take concrete examples from the Web, such as the following example from DrupalCon San Francisco 2010: *http://2bits.com/sites/2bits.com/files/drupal-single-server-2.8-million-page-views-a-day.pdf*. The slides describe an Alexa #3400 site that receives 2.8 million page views per day, using a single server. The server has two quad-core Xeon 2.5 GHz processors with 8 GB DRAM and three 15 K RPM SAS hard drives in a RAID1 configuration, and it costs about $400 per month. The site uses caching heavily, and the CPU utilization ranges from 50% to 250% (roughly 0.5 to 2.5 cores busy).

a. [5] Looking at the available EC2 instances (*http://aws.amazon.com/ec2/instance-types/*), what instance types match or exceed the current server configuration?

b. [15] Looking at the EC2 pricing information (*http://aws.amazon.com/ec2/pricing/*), select the most cost-efficient EC2 instances (combinations allowed) to host the site on AWS. What's the monthly cost for EC2?

c. [15] Now add the costs for IP address and network traffic to the equation, and suppose the site transfers 100 GB/day in and out on the Internet. What's the monthly cost for the site now?

d. [20] AWS also offers the Micro Instance for free for 1 year to new customers and 15 GB bandwidth each for traffic going in and out across AWS. Based on your estimation of peak and average traffic from your department Web server, can you host it for free on AWS?

e. [25] A much larger site, Netflix.com, has also migrated their streaming and encoding infrastructure to AWS. Based on their service characteristics, what AWS services could be used by Netflix and for what purposes?

6.23 [Discussion/Discussion/20/20/Discussion] <6.4> Figure 6.12 shows the impact of user perceived response time on revenue, and motivates the need to achieve high-throughput while maintaining low latency.

a. [Discussion] Taking Web search as an example, what are the possible ways of reducing query latency?

b. [Discussion] What monitoring statistics can you collect to help understand where time is spent? How do you plan to implement such a monitoring tool?

c. [20] Assuming that the number of disk accesses per query follows a normal distribution, with an average of 2 and standard deviation of 3, what kind of disk access latency is needed to satisfy a latency SLA of 0.1 sec for 95% of the queries?

d. [20] In-memory caching can reduce the frequencies of long-latency events (e.g., accessing hard drives). Assuming a steady-state hit rate of 40%, hit latency of 0.05 sec, and miss latency of 0.2 sec, does caching help meet a latency SLA of 0.1 sec for 95% of the queries?

e. [Discussion] When can cached content become stale or even inconsistent? How often can this happen? How can you detect and invalidate such content?

6.24   [15/15/20] <6.4> The efficiency of typical power supply units (PSUs) varies as the load changes; for example, PSU efficiency can be about 80% at 40% load (e.g., output 40 watts from a 100-watt PSU), 75% when the load is between 20% and 40%, and 65% when the load is below 20%.

a. [15] Assume a power-proportional server whose actual power is proportional to CPU utilization, with a utilization curve as shown in Figure 6.3. What is the average PSU efficiency?

b. [15] Suppose the server employs 2*N* redundancy for PSUs (i.e., doubles the number of PSUs) to ensure stable power when one PSU fails. What is the average PSU efficiency?

c. [20] Blade server vendors use a shared pool of PSUs not only to provide redundancy but also to dynamically match the number of PSUs to the server's actual power consumption. The HP c7000 enclosure uses up to six PSUs for a total of 16 servers. In this case, what is the average PSU efficiency for the enclosure of server with the same utilization curve?

6.25   [5/Discussion/10/15/Discussion/Discussion/Discussion] <6.4> *Power stranding* is a term used to refer to power capacity that is provisioned but not used in a datacenter. Consider the data presented in Figure 6.25 [Fan, Weber, and Barroso 2007] for different groups of machines. (Note that what this paper calls a "cluster" is what we have referred to as an "array" in this chapter.)

a. [5] What is the stranded power at (1) the rack level, (2) the power distribution unit level, and (3) the array (cluster) level? What are the trends with oversubscription of power capacity at larger groups of machines?

b. [Discussion] What do you think causes the differences between power stranding at different groups of machines?

c. [10] Consider an array-level collection of machines where the total machines never use more than 72% of the aggregate power (this is sometimes also referred to as the ratio between the peak-of-sum and sum-of-peaks usage). Using the cost model in the case study, compute the cost savings from comparing a datacenter provisioned for peak capacity and one provisioned for actual use.

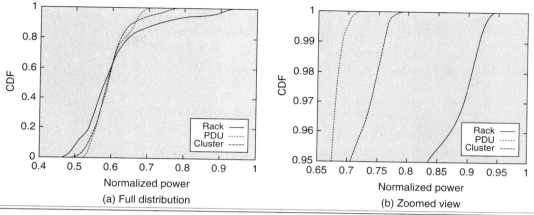

Figure 6.25 Cumulative distribution function (CDF) of a real datacenter.

d. [15] Assume that the datacenter designer chose to include additional servers at the array level to take advantage of the stranded power. Using the example configuration and assumptions in part (a), compute how many more servers can now be included in the warehouse-scale computer for the same total power provisioning.

e. [Discussion] What is needed to make the optimization of part (d) work in a real-world deployment? (*Hint*: Think about what needs to happen to cap power in the rare case when all the servers in the array are used at peak power.)

f. [Discussion] Two kinds of policies can be envisioned to manage power caps [Ranganathan et al. 2006]: (1) preemptive policies where power budgets are predetermined ("don't assume you can use more power; ask before you do!") or (2) reactive policies where power budgets are throttled in the event of a power budget violation ("use as much power as needed until told you can't!"). Discuss the trade-offs between these approaches and when you would use each type.

g. [Discussion] What happens to the total stranded power if systems become more energy proportional (assume workloads similar to that of Figure 6.4)?

6.26 [5/20/Discussion] <6.4, 6.7> Section 6.7 discussed the use of per-server battery sources in the Google design. Let us examine the consequences of this design.

a. [5] Assume that the use of a battery as a mini-server-level UPS is 99.99% efficient and eliminates the need for a facility-wide UPS that is only 92% efficient. Assume that substation switching is 99.7% efficient and that the efficiency for the PDU, step-down stages, and other electrical breakers are 98%, 98%, and 99%, respectively. Calculate the overall power infrastructure efficiency improvements from using a per-server battery backup.

    b. [20] Assume that the UPS is 10% of the cost of the IT equipment. Using the rest of the assumptions from the cost model in the case study, what is the break-even point for the costs of the battery (as a fraction of the cost of a single server) at which the total cost of ownership for a battery-based solution is better than that for a facility-wide UPS?

    c. [Discussion] What are the other trade-offs between these two approaches? In particular, how do you think the manageability and failure model will change across these two different designs?

6.27   [5/5/Discussion] <6.4> For this exercise, consider a simplified equation for the total operational power of a WSC as follows: Total operational power = (1 + Cooling inefficiency multiplier) * IT equipment power.

    a. [5] Assume an 8 MW datacenter at 80% power usage, electricity costs of $0.10 per kilowatt-hour, and a cooling-inefficiency multiplier of 0.8. Compare the cost savings from (1) an optimization that improves cooling efficiency by 20%, and (2) an optimization that improves the energy efficiency of the IT equipment by 20%.

    b. [5] What is the percentage improvement in IT equipment energy efficiency needed to match the cost savings from a 20% improvement in cooling efficiency?

    c. [Discussion/10] What conclusions can you draw about the relative importance of optimizations that focus on server energy efficiency and cooling energy efficiency?

6.28   [5/5/Discussion] <6.4> As discussed in this chapter, the cooling equipment in WSCs can themselves consume a lot of energy. Cooling costs can be lowered by proactively managing temperature. Temperature-aware workload placement is one optimization that has been proposed to manage temperature to reduce cooling costs. The idea is to identify the cooling profile of a given room and map the hotter systems to the cooler spots, so that at the WSC level the requirements for overall cooling are reduced.

    a. [5] The coefficient of performance (COP) of a CRAC unit is defined as the ratio of heat removed (Q) to the amount of work necessary (W) to remove that heat. The COP of a CRAC unit increases with the temperature of the air the CRAC unit pushes into the plenum. If air returns to the CRAC unit at 20 degrees Celsius and we remove 10KW of heat with a COP of 1.9, how much energy do we expend in the CRAC unit? If cooling the same volume of air, but now returning at 25 degrees Celsius, takes a COP of 3.1, how much energy do we expend in the CRAC unit now?

    b. [5] Assume a workload distribution algorithm is able to match the hot workloads well with the cool spots to allow the computer room air-conditioning (CRAC) unit to be run at higher temperature to improve cooling efficiencies like in the exercise above. What is the power savings between the two cases described above?

    c. [Discussion] Given the scale of WSC systems, power management can be a complex, multifaceted problem. Optimizations to improve energy efficiency can be implemented in hardware and in software, at the system level, and at the cluster level for the IT equipment or the cooling equipment, etc. It is important to consider these interactions when designing an overall energy-efficiency solution for the WSC. Consider a consolidation algorithm that looks at server utilization and consolidates different workload classes on the same server to increase server utilization (this can potentially have the server operating at higher energy efficiency if the system is not energy proportional). How would this optimization interact with a concurrent algorithm that tried to use different power states (see ACPI, Advanced Configuration Power Interface, for some examples)? What other examples can you think of where multiple optimizations can potentially conflict with one another in a WSC? How would you solve this problem?

6.29 [5/10/15/20] <6.2> Energy proportionality (sometimes also referred to as energy scale-down) is the attribute of the system to consume no power when idle, but more importantly gradually consume more power in proportion to the activity level and work done. In this exercise, we will examine the sensitivity of energy consumption to different energy proportionality models. In the exercises below, unless otherwise mentioned, use the data in Figure 6.4 as the default.

a. [5] A simple way to reason about energy proportionality is to assume linearity between activity and power usage. Using just the peak power and idle power data from Figure 6.4 and a linear interpolation, plot the energy-efficiency trends across varying activities. (Energy efficiency is expressed as performance per watt.) What happens if idle power (at 0% activity) is half of what is assumed in Figure 6.4? What happens if idle power is zero?

b. [10] Plot the energy-efficiency trends across varying activities, but use the data from column 3 of Figure 6.4 for power variation. Plot the energy efficiency assuming that the idle power (alone) is half of what is assumed in Figure 6.4. Compare these plots with the linear model in the previous exercise. What conclusions can you draw about the consequences of focusing purely on idle power alone?

c. [15] Assume the system utilization mix in column 7 of Figure 6.4. For simplicity, assume a discrete distribution across 1000 servers, with 109 servers at 0% utilization, 80 servers at 10% utilizations, etc. Compute the total performance and total energy for this workload mix using the assumptions in part (a) and part (b).

d. [20] One could potentially design a system that has a sublinear power versus load relationship in the region of load levels between 0% and 50%. This would have an energy-efficiency curve that peaks at lower utilizations (at the expense of higher utilizations). Create a new version of column 3 from Figure 6.4 that shows such an energy-efficiency curve. Assume the system utilization mix in column 7 of Figure 6.4. For simplicity, assume a discrete distribution across 1000 servers, with 109 servers at 0% utilization, 80 servers at 10% utilizations, etc. Compute the total performance and total energy for this workload mix.

Activity (%)	0	10	20	30	40	50	60	70	80	90	100
Power, case A (W)	181	308	351	382	416	451	490	533	576	617	662
Power, case B (W)	250	275	325	340	395	405	415	425	440	445	450

Figure 6.26 Power distribution for two servers.

Activity (%)	0	10	20	30	40	50	60	70	80	90	100
No. servers, case A and B	109	80	153	246	191	115	51	21	15	12	8
No. servers, case C	504	6	8	11	26	57	95	123	76	40	54

Figure 6.27 Utilization distributions across cluster, without and with consolidation.

6.30 [15/20/20] <6.2, 6.6> This exercise illustrates the interactions of energy proportionality models with optimizations such as server consolidation and energy-efficient server designs. Consider the scenarios shown in Figure 6.26 and Figure 6.27.

  a. [15] Consider two servers with the power distributions shown in Figure 6.26: case A (the server considered in Figure 6.4) and case B (a less energy-proportional but more energy-efficient server than case A). Assume the system utilization mix in column 7 of Figure 6.4. For simplicity, assume a discrete distribution across 1000 servers, with 109 servers at 0% utilization, 80 servers at 10% utilizations, etc., as shown in row 1 of Figure 6.27. Assume performance variation based on column 2 of Figure 6.4. Compare the total performance and total energy for this workload mix for the two server types.

  b. [20] Consider a cluster of 1000 servers with data similar to the data shown in Figure 6.4 (and summarized in the first rows of Figures 6.26 and 6.27). What are the total performance and total energy for the workload mix with these assumptions? Now assume that we were able to consolidate the workloads to model the distribution shown in case C (second row of Figure 6.27). What are the total performance and total energy now? How does the total energy compare with a system that has a linear energy-proportional model with idle power of zero watts and peak power of 662 watts?

  c. [20] Repeat part (b), but with the power model of server B, and compare with the results of part (a).

6.31 [10/Discussion] <6.2, 6.4, 6.6> *System-Level Energy Proportionality Trends*: Consider the following breakdowns of the power consumption of a server:

CPU, 50%; memory, 23%; disks, 11%; networking/other, 16%
CPU, 33%; memory, 30%; disks, 10%; networking/other, 27%

  a. [10] Assume a dynamic power range of 3.0× for the CPU (i.e., the power consumption of the CPU at idle is one-third that of its power consumption at

Tier 1	Single path for power and cooling distributions, without redundant components	99.0%
Tier 2	$(N + 1)$ redundancy = two power and cooling distribution paths	99.7%
Tier 3	$(N + 2)$ redundancy = three power and cooling distribution paths for uptime even during maintenance	99.98%
Tier 4	Two active power and cooling distribution paths, with redundant components in each path, to tolerate any single equipment failure without impacting the load	99.995%

Figure 6.28 Overview of data center tier classifications. (Adapted from Pitt Turner IV et al. [2008].)

peak). Assume that the dynamic range of the memory systems, disks, and the networking/other categories above are respectively 2.0×, 1.3×, and 1.2×. What is the overall dynamic range for the total system for the two cases?

b. [Discussion/10] What can you learn from the results of part (a)? How would we achieve better energy proportionality at the system level? (*Hint*: Energy proportionality at a system level cannot be achieved through CPU optimizations alone, but instead requires improvement across all components.)

6.32   [30] <6.4> Pitt Turner IV et al. [2008] presented a good overview of datacenter tier classifications. Tier classifications define site infrastructure performance. For simplicity, consider the key differences as shown in Figure 6.25 (adapted from Pitt Turner IV et al. [2008]). Using the TCO model in the case study, compare the cost implications of the different tiers shown.

6.33   [Discussion] <6.4> Based on the observations in Figure 6.13, what can you say qualitatively about the trade-offs between revenue loss from downtime and costs incurred for uptime?

6.34   [15/Discussion] <6.4> Some recent studies have defined a metric called TPUE, which stands for "true PUE" or "total PUE." TPUE is defined as PUE * SPUE. PUE, the power utilization effectiveness, is defined in Section 6.4 as the ratio of the total facility power over the total IT equipment power. SPUE, or server PUE, is a new metric analogous to PUE, but instead applied to computing equipment, and is defined as the ratio of total server input power to its useful power, where useful power is defined as the power consumed by the electronic components directly involved in the computation: motherboard, disks, CPUs, DRAM, I/O cards, and so on. In other words, the SPUE metric captures inefficiencies associated with the power supplies, voltage regulators, and fans housed on a server.

a. [15] <6.4> Consider a design that uses a higher supply temperature for the CRAC units. The efficiency of the CRAC unit is approximately a quadratic function of the temperature, and this design therefore improves the overall PUE, let's assume by 7%. (Assume baseline PUE of 1.7.) However, the higher temperature at the server level triggers the on-board fan controller to operate the fan at much higher speeds. The fan power is a cubic function of speed, and the increased fan speed leads to a degradation of SPUE. Assume a fan power model:

$$\text{Fan power} = 284 * ns * ns * ns - 75 * ns * ns,$$

where ns is the normalized fan speed = fan speed in rpm/18,000

and a baseline server power of 350 W. Compute the SPUE if the fan speed increases from (1) 10,000 rpm to 12,500 rpm and (2) 10,000 rpm to 18,000 rpm. Compare the PUE and TPUE in both these cases. (For simplicity, ignore the inefficiencies with power delivery in the SPUE model.)

b. [Discussion] Part (a) illustrates that, while PUE is an excellent metric to capture the overhead of the facility, it does not capture the inefficiencies within the IT equipment itself. Can you identify another design where TPUE is potentially lower than PUE? (*Hint*: See Exercise 6.26.)

6.35 [Discussion/30/Discussion] <6.2> Two recently released benchmarks provide a good starting point for energy-efficiency accounting in servers—the SPECpower_ssj2008 benchmark (available at *http://www.spec.org/power_ssj2008/*) and the JouleSort metric (available at *http://sortbenchmark.org/*).

a. [Discussion] <6.2> Look up the descriptions of the two benchmarks. How are they similar? How are they different? What would you do to improve these benchmarks to better address the goal of improving WSC energy efficiency?

b. [30] <6.2> JouleSort measures the total system energy to perform an out-of-core sort and attempts to derive a metric that enables the comparison of systems ranging from embedded devices to supercomputers. Look up the description of the JouleSort metric at *http://sortbenchmark.org*. Download a publicly available version of the sort algorithm and run it on different classes of machines—a laptop, a PC, a mobile phone, etc.—or with different configurations. What can you learn from the JouleSort ratings for different setups?

c. [Discussion] <6.2> Consider the system with the best JouleSort rating from your experiments above. How would you improve the energy efficiency? For example, try rewriting the sort code to improve the JouleSort rating.

6.36 [10/10/15] <6.1, 6.2> Figure 6.1 is a listing of outages in an array of servers. When dealing with the large scale of WSCs, it is important to balance cluster design and software architectures to achieve the required uptime without incurring significant costs. This question explores the implications of achieving availability through hardware only.

a. [10] <6.1, 6.2> Assuming that an operator wishes to achieve 95% availability through server hardware improvements alone, how many events of each type would have to be reduced? For now, assume that individual server crashes are completely handled through redundant machines.

b. [10] <6.1, 6.2> How does the answer to part (a) change if the individual server crashes are handled by redundancy 50% of the time? 20% of the time? None of the time?

c. [15] <6.1, 6.2> Discuss the importance of software redundancy to achieving a high level of availability. If a WSC operator considered buying machines that were cheaper, but 10% less reliable, what implications would that have on the software architecture? What are the challenges associated with software redundancy?

6.37 [15] <6.1, 6.8> Look up the current prices of standard DDR3 DRAM versus DDR3 DRAM that has error-correcting code (ECC). What is the increase in price per bit for achieving the higher reliability that ECC provides? Using the DRAM prices alone, and the data provided in Section 6.8, what is the uptime per dollar of a WSC with non-ECC versus ECC DRAM?

6.38 [5/Discussion] <6.1> *WSC Reliability and Manageability Concerns*:

a. [5] Consider a cluster of servers costing $2000 each. Assuming an annual failure rate of 5%, an average of an hour of service time per repair, and replacement parts requiring 10% of the system cost per failure, what is the annual maintenance cost per server? Assume an hourly rate of $100 per hour for a service technician.

b. [Discussion] Comment on the differences between this manageability model versus that in a traditional enterprise datacenter with a large number of small or medium-sized applications each running on its own dedicated hardware infrastructure.

A

Instruction Set Principles

A n   Add the number in storage location *n* into the accumulator.

E n   If the number in the accumulator is greater than or equal to zero execute next the order which stands in storage location *n;* otherwise proceed serially.

Z   Stop the machine and ring the warning bell.

Wilkes and Renwick
Selection from the List of 18 Machine
Instructions for the EDSAC (1949)

A.1   **Introduction**

In this appendix we concentrate on instruction set architecture—the portion of the computer visible to the programmer or compiler writer. Most of this material should be review for readers of this book; we include it here for background. This appendix introduces the wide variety of design alternatives available to the instruction set architect. In particular, we focus on four topics. First, we present a taxonomy of instruction set alternatives and give some qualitative assessment of the advantages and disadvantages of various approaches. Second, we present and analyze some instruction set measurements that are largely independent of a specific instruction set. Third, we address the issue of languages and compilers and their bearing on instruction set architecture. Finally, the "Putting It All Together" section shows how these ideas are reflected in the MIPS instruction set, which is typical of RISC architectures. We conclude with fallacies and pitfalls of instruction set design.

To illustrate the principles further, Appendix K also gives four examples of general-purpose RISC architectures (MIPS, PowerPC, Precision Architecture, SPARC), four embedded RISC processors (ARM, Hitachi SH, MIPS 16, Thumb), and three older architectures (80x86, IBM 360/370, and VAX). Before we discuss how to classify architectures, we need to say something about instruction set measurement.

Throughout this appendix, we examine a wide variety of architectural measurements. Clearly, these measurements depend on the programs measured and on the compilers used in making the measurements. The results should not be interpreted as absolute, and you might see different data if you did the measurement with a different compiler or a different set of programs. We believe that the measurements in this appendix are reasonably indicative of a class of typical applications. Many of the measurements are presented using a small set of benchmarks, so that the data can be reasonably displayed and the differences among programs can be seen. An architect for a new computer would want to analyze a much larger collection of programs before making architectural decisions. The measurements shown are usually *dynamic*—that is, the frequency of a measured event is weighed by the number of times that event occurs during execution of the measured program.

Before starting with the general principles, let's review the three application areas from Chapter 1. *Desktop computing* emphasizes the performance of programs with integer and floating-point data types, with little regard for program size. For example, code size has never been reported in the five generations of SPEC benchmarks. *Servers* today are used primarily for database, file server, and Web applications, plus some time-sharing applications for many users. Hence, floating-point performance is much less important for performance than integers and character strings, yet virtually every server processor still includes floating-point instructions. *Personal mobile devices* and *embedded applications* value cost and energy, so code size is important because less memory is both cheaper and lower energy, and some classes of instructions (such as floating point) may be optional to reduce chip costs.

Thus, instruction sets for all three applications are very similar. In fact, the MIPS architecture that drives this appendix has been used successfully in desktops, servers, and embedded applications.

One successful architecture very different from RISC is the 80x86 (see Appendix K). Surprisingly, its success does not necessarily belie the advantages of a RISC instruction set. The commercial importance of binary compatibility with PC software combined with the abundance of transistors provided by Moore's law led Intel to use a RISC instruction set internally while supporting an 80x86 instruction set externally. Recent 80x86 microprocessors, such as the Pentium 4, use hardware to translate from 80x86 instructions to RISC-like instructions and then execute the translated operations inside the chip. They maintain the illusion of 80x86 architecture to the programmer while allowing the computer designer to implement a RISC-style processor for performance.

Now that the background is set, we begin by exploring how instruction set architectures can be classified.

A.2   Classifying Instruction Set Architectures

The type of internal storage in a processor is the most basic differentiation, so in this section we will focus on the alternatives for this portion of the architecture. The major choices are a stack, an accumulator, or a set of registers. Operands may be named explicitly or implicitly: The operands in a *stack architecture* are implicitly on the top of the stack, and in an *accumulator architecture* one operand is implicitly the accumulator. The *general-purpose register architectures* have only explicit operands—either registers or memory locations. Figure A.1 shows a block diagram of such architectures, and Figure A.2 shows how the code sequence C = A + B would typically appear in these three classes of instruction sets. The explicit operands may be accessed directly from memory or may need to be first loaded into temporary storage, depending on the class of architecture and choice of specific instruction.

As the figures show, there are really two classes of register computers. One class can access memory as part of any instruction, called *register-memory* architecture, and the other can access memory only with load and store instructions, called *load-store* architecture. A third class, not found in computers shipping today, keeps all operands in memory and is called a *memory-memory* architecture. Some instruction set architectures have more registers than a single accumulator but place restrictions on uses of these special registers. Such an architecture is sometimes called an *extended accumulator* or *special-purpose register* computer.

Although most early computers used stack or accumulator-style architectures, virtually every new architecture designed after 1980 uses a load-store register architecture. The major reasons for the emergence of general-purpose register (GPR) computers are twofold. First, registers—like other forms of storage internal to the processor—are faster than memory. Second, registers are more efficient

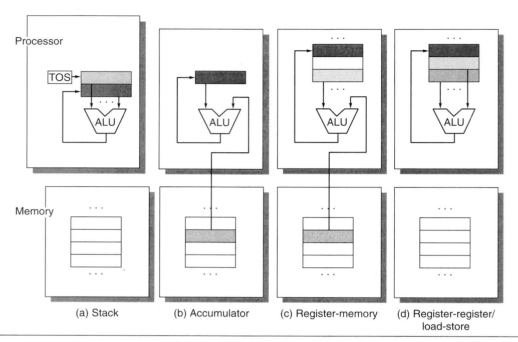

Figure A.1 **Operand locations for four instruction set architecture classes.** The arrows indicate whether the operand is an input or the result of the arithmetic-logical unit (ALU) operation, or both an input and result. Lighter shades indicate inputs, and the dark shade indicates the result. In (a), a Top Of Stack register (TOS) points to the top input operand, which is combined with the operand below. The first operand is removed from the stack, the result takes the place of the second operand, and TOS is updated to point to the result. All operands are implicit. In (b), the Accumulator is both an implicit input operand and a result. In (c), one input operand is a register, one is in memory, and the result goes to a register. All operands are registers in (d) and, like the stack architecture, can be transferred to memory only via separate instructions: push or pop for (a) and load or store for (d).

Stack	Accumulator	Register (register-memory)	Register (load-store)
Push A	Load A	Load R1,A	Load R1,A
Push B	Add B	Add R3,R1,B	Load R2,B
Add	Store C	Store R3,C	Add R3,R1,R2
Pop C			Store R3,C

Figure A.2 **The code sequence for C = A + B for four classes of instruction sets.** Note that the Add instruction has implicit operands for stack and accumulator architectures and explicit operands for register architectures. It is assumed that A, B, and C all belong in memory and that the values of A and B cannot be destroyed. Figure A.1 shows the Add operation for each class of architecture.

for a compiler to use than other forms of internal storage. For example, on a register computer the expression $(A * B) - (B * C) - (A * D)$ may be evaluated by doing the multiplications in any order, which may be more efficient because of the location of the operands or because of pipelining concerns (see Chapter 3). Nevertheless, on a stack computer the hardware must evaluate the expression in only one order, since operands are hidden on the stack, and it may have to load an operand multiple times.

More importantly, registers can be used to hold variables. When variables are allocated to registers, the memory traffic reduces, the program speeds up (since registers are faster than memory), and the code density improves (since a register can be named with fewer bits than can a memory location).

As explained in Section A.8, compiler writers would prefer that all registers be equivalent and unreserved. Older computers compromise this desire by dedicating registers to special uses, effectively decreasing the number of general-purpose registers. If the number of truly general-purpose registers is too small, trying to allocate variables to registers will not be profitable. Instead, the compiler will reserve all the uncommitted registers for use in expression evaluation.

How many registers are sufficient? The answer, of course, depends on the effectiveness of the compiler. Most compilers reserve some registers for expression evaluation, use some for parameter passing, and allow the remainder to be allocated to hold variables. Modern compiler technology and its ability to effectively use larger numbers of registers has led to an increase in register counts in more recent architectures.

Two major instruction set characteristics divide GPR architectures. Both characteristics concern the nature of operands for a typical arithmetic or logical instruction (ALU instruction). The first concerns whether an ALU instruction has two or three operands. In the three-operand format, the instruction contains one result operand and two source operands. In the two-operand format, one of the operands is both a source and a result for the operation. The second distinction among GPR architectures concerns how many of the operands may be memory addresses in ALU instructions. The number of memory operands supported by a typical ALU instruction may vary from none to three. Figure A.3 shows combinations of these two attributes with examples of computers. Although there are seven possible combinations, three serve to classify nearly all existing computers. As we mentioned earlier, these three are load-store (also called register-register), register-memory, and memory-memory.

Figure A.4 shows the advantages and disadvantages of each of these alternatives. Of course, these advantages and disadvantages are not absolutes: They are qualitative and their actual impact depends on the compiler and implementation strategy. A GPR computer with memory-memory operations could easily be ignored by the compiler and used as a load-store computer. One of the most pervasive architectural impacts is on instruction encoding and the number of instructions needed to perform a task. We see the impact of these architectural alternatives on implementation approaches in Appendix C and Chapter 3.

Number of memory addresses	Maximum number of operands allowed	Type of architecture	Examples
0	3	Load-store	Alpha, ARM, MIPS, PowerPC, SPARC, SuperH, TM32
1	2	Register-memory	IBM 360/370, Intel 80x86, Motorola 68000, TI TMS320C54x
2	2	Memory-memory	VAX (also has three-operand formats)
3	3	Memory-memory	VAX (also has two-operand formats)

Figure A.3 Typical combinations of memory operands and total operands per typical ALU instruction with examples of computers. Computers with no memory reference per ALU instruction are called load-store or register-register computers. Instructions with multiple memory operands per typical ALU instruction are called register-memory or memory-memory, according to whether they have one or more than one memory operand.

Type	Advantages	Disadvantages
Register-register (0, 3)	Simple, fixed-length instruction encoding. Simple code generation model. Instructions take similar numbers of clocks to execute (see Appendix C).	Higher instruction count than architectures with memory references in instructions. More instructions and lower instruction density lead to larger programs.
Register-memory (1, 2)	Data can be accessed without a separate load instruction first. Instruction format tends to be easy to encode and yields good density.	Operands are not equivalent since a source operand in a binary operation is destroyed. Encoding a register number and a memory address in each instruction may restrict the number of registers. Clocks per instruction vary by operand location.
Memory-memory (2, 2) or (3, 3)	Most compact. Doesn't waste registers for temporaries.	Large variation in instruction size, especially for three-operand instructions. In addition, large variation in work per instruction. Memory accesses create memory bottleneck. (Not used today.)

Figure A.4 Advantages and disadvantages of the three most common types of general-purpose register computers. The notation (*m, n*) means *m* memory operands and *n* total operands. In general, computers with fewer alternatives simplify the compiler's task since there are fewer decisions for the compiler to make (see Section A.8). Computers with a wide variety of flexible instruction formats reduce the number of bits required to encode the program. The number of registers also affects the instruction size since you need $\log_2$ (number of registers) for each register specifier in an instruction. Thus, doubling the number of registers takes 3 extra bits for a register-register architecture, or about 10% of a 32-bit instruction.

Summary: Classifying Instruction Set Architectures

Here and at the end of Sections A.3 through A.8 we summarize those characteristics we would expect to find in a new instruction set architecture, building the foundation for the MIPS architecture introduced in Section A.9. From this section we should clearly expect the use of general-purpose registers. Figure A.4, combined with Appendix C on pipelining, leads to the expectation of a load-store version of a general-purpose register architecture.

With the class of architecture covered, the next topic is addressing operands.

A.3   Memory Addressing

Independent of whether the architecture is load-store or allows any operand to be a memory reference, it must define how memory addresses are interpreted and how they are specified. The measurements presented here are largely, but not completely, computer independent. In some cases the measurements are significantly affected by the compiler technology. These measurements have been made using an optimizing compiler, since compiler technology plays a critical role.

Interpreting Memory Addresses

How is a memory address interpreted? That is, what object is accessed as a function of the address and the length? All the instruction sets discussed in this book are byte addressed and provide access for bytes (8 bits), half words (16 bits), and words (32 bits). Most of the computers also provide access for double words (64 bits).

There are two different conventions for ordering the bytes within a larger object. *Little Endian* byte order puts the byte whose address is "x . . . x000" at the least-significant position in the double word (the little end). The bytes are numbered:

7	6	5	4	3	2	1	0

Big Endian byte order puts the byte whose address is "x . . . x000" at the most-significant position in the double word (the big end). The bytes are numbered:

0	1	2	3	4	5	6	7

When operating within one computer, the byte order is often unnoticeable—only programs that access the same locations as both, say, words and bytes, can notice the difference. Byte order is a problem when exchanging data among computers with different orderings, however. Little Endian ordering also fails to match the normal ordering of words when strings are compared. Strings appear "SDRAWKCAB" (backwards) in the registers.

A second memory issue is that in many computers, accesses to objects larger than a byte must be *aligned*. An access to an object of size s bytes at byte address A is aligned if A mod $s = 0$. Figure A.5 shows the addresses at which an access is aligned or misaligned.

Why would someone design a computer with alignment restrictions? Misalignment causes hardware complications, since the memory is typically aligned on a multiple of a word or double-word boundary. A misaligned memory access

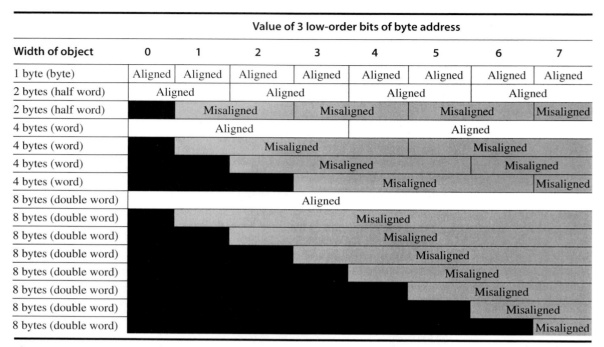

Width of object	Value of 3 low-order bits of byte address							
	0	1	2	3	4	5	6	7
1 byte (byte)	Aligned	Aligned	Aligned	Aligned	Aligned	Aligned	Aligned	Aligned
2 bytes (half word)	Aligned		Aligned		Aligned		Aligned	
2 bytes (half word)		Misaligned		Misaligned		Misaligned		Misaligned
4 bytes (word)	Aligned				Aligned			
4 bytes (word)		Misaligned				Misaligned		
4 bytes (word)			Misaligned				Misaligned	
4 bytes (word)				Misaligned				Misaligned
8 bytes (double word)	Aligned							
8 bytes (double word)		Misaligned						
8 bytes (double word)			Misaligned					
8 bytes (double word)				Misaligned				
8 bytes (double word)					Misaligned			
8 bytes (double word)						Misaligned		
8 bytes (double word)							Misaligned	
8 bytes (double word)								Misaligned

Figure A.5 Aligned and misaligned addresses of byte, half-word, word, and double-word objects for byte-addressed computers. For each misaligned example some objects require two memory accesses to complete. Every aligned object can always complete in one memory access, as long as the memory is as wide as the object. The figure shows the memory organized as 8 bytes wide. The byte offsets that label the columns specify the low-order 3 bits of the address.

may, therefore, take multiple aligned memory references. Thus, even in computers that allow misaligned access, programs with aligned accesses run faster.

Even if data are aligned, supporting byte, half-word, and word accesses requires an alignment network to align bytes, half words, and words in 64-bit registers. For example, in Figure A.5, suppose we read a byte from an address with its 3 low-order bits having the value 4. We will need to shift right 3 bytes to align the byte to the proper place in a 64-bit register. Depending on the instruction, the computer may also need to sign-extend the quantity. Stores are easy: Only the addressed bytes in memory may be altered. On some computers a byte, half-word, and word operation does not affect the upper portion of a register. Although all the computers discussed in this book permit byte, half-word, and word accesses to memory, only the IBM 360/370, Intel 80x86, and VAX support ALU operations on register operands narrower than the full width.

Now that we have discussed alternative interpretations of memory addresses, we can discuss the ways addresses are specified by instructions, called *addressing modes.*

Addressing Modes

Given an address, we now know what bytes to access in memory. In this subsection we will look at addressing modes—how architectures specify the address of an object they will access. Addressing modes specify constants and registers in addition to locations in memory. When a memory location is used, the actual memory address specified by the addressing mode is called the *effective address*.

Figure A.6 shows all the data addressing modes that have been used in recent computers. Immediates or literals are usually considered memory addressing

Addressing mode	Example instruction	Meaning	When used
Register	Add R4,R3	Regs[R4] ← Regs[R4] + Regs[R3]	When a value is in a register.
Immediate	Add R4,#3	Regs[R4] ← Regs[R4] + 3	For constants.
Displacement	Add R4,100(R1)	Regs[R4] ← Regs[R4] + Mem[100 + Regs[R1]]	Accessing local variables (+ simulates register indirect, direct addressing modes).
Register indirect	Add R4,(R1)	Regs[R4] ← Regs[R4] + Mem[Regs[R1]]	Accessing using a pointer or a computed address.
Indexed	Add R3,(R1 + R2)	Regs[R3] ← Regs[R3] + Mem[Regs[R1] + Regs[R2]]	Sometimes useful in array addressing: R1 = base of array; R2 = index amount.
Direct or absolute	Add R1,(1001)	Regs[R1] ← Regs[R1] + Mem[1001]	Sometimes useful for accessing static data; address constant may need to be large.
Memory indirect	Add R1,@(R3)	Regs[R1] ← Regs[R1] + Mem[Mem[Regs[R3]]]	If R3 is the address of a pointer p, then mode yields $*p$.
Autoincrement	Add R1,(R2)+	Regs[R1] ← Regs[R1] + Mem[Regs[R2]] Regs[R2] ← Regs[R2] + d	Useful for stepping through arrays within a loop. R2 points to start of array; each reference increments R2 by size of an element, d.
Autodecrement	Add R1, −(R2)	Regs[R2] ← Regs[R2] − d Regs[R1] ← Regs[R1] + Mem[Regs[R2]]	Same use as autoincrement. Autodecrement/-increment can also act as push/pop to implement a stack.
Scaled	Add R1,100(R2)[R3]	Regs[R1] ← Regs[R1] + Mem[100 + Regs[R2] + Regs[R3] * d]	Used to index arrays. May be applied to any indexed addressing mode in some computers.

Figure A.6 Selection of addressing modes with examples, meaning, and usage. In autoincrement/-decrement and scaled addressing modes, the variable d designates the size of the data item being accessed (i.e., whether the instruction is accessing 1, 2, 4, or 8 bytes). These addressing modes are only useful when the elements being accessed are adjacent in memory. RISC computers use displacement addressing to simulate register indirect with 0 for the address and to simulate direct addressing using 0 in the base register. In our measurements, we use the first name shown for each mode. The extensions to C used as hardware descriptions are defined on page A-36.

modes (even though the value they access is in the instruction stream), although registers are often separated since they don't normally have memory addresses. We have kept addressing modes that depend on the program counter, called *PC-relative addressing*, separate. PC-relative addressing is used primarily for specifying code addresses in control transfer instructions, discussed in Section A.6.

Figure A.6 shows the most common names for the addressing modes, though the names differ among architectures. In this figure and throughout the book, we will use an extension of the C programming language as a hardware description notation. In this figure, only one non-C feature is used: The left arrow (←) is used for assignment. We also use the array Mem as the name for main memory and the array Regs for registers. Thus, Mem[Regs[R1]] refers to the contents of the memory location whose address is given by the contents of register 1 (R1). Later, we will introduce extensions for accessing and transferring data smaller than a word.

Addressing modes have the ability to significantly reduce instruction counts; they also add to the complexity of building a computer and may increase the average clock cycles per instruction (CPI) of computers that implement those modes. Thus, the usage of various addressing modes is quite important in helping the architect choose what to include.

Figure A.7 shows the results of measuring addressing mode usage patterns in three programs on the VAX architecture. We use the old VAX architecture for a few measurements in this appendix because it has the richest set of addressing modes and the fewest restrictions on memory addressing. For example, Figure A.6 on page A-9 shows all the modes the VAX supports. Most measurements in this appendix, however, will use the more recent register-register architectures to show how programs use instruction sets of current computers.

As Figure A.7 shows, displacement and immediate addressing dominate addressing mode usage. Let's look at some properties of these two heavily used modes.

Displacement Addressing Mode

The major question that arises for a displacement-style addressing mode is that of the range of displacements used. Based on the use of various displacement sizes, a decision of what sizes to support can be made. Choosing the displacement field sizes is important because they directly affect the instruction length. Figure A.8 shows the measurements taken on the data access on a load-store architecture using our benchmark programs. We look at branch offsets in Section A.6—data accessing patterns and branches are different; little is gained by combining them, although in practice the immediate sizes are made the same for simplicity.

Immediate or Literal Addressing Mode

Immediates can be used in arithmetic operations, in comparisons (primarily for branches), and in moves where a constant is wanted in a register. The last case occurs for constants written in the code—which tend to be small—and for

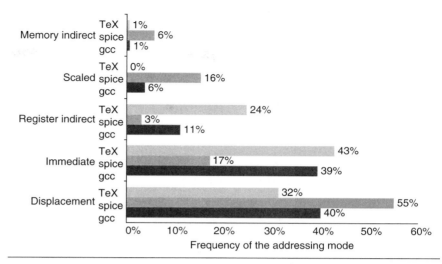

Figure A.7 Summary of use of memory addressing modes (including immediates). These major addressing modes account for all but a few percent (0% to 3%) of the memory accesses. Register modes, which are not counted, account for one-half of the operand references, while memory addressing modes (including immediate) account for the other half. Of course, the compiler affects what addressing modes are used; see Section A.8. The memory indirect mode on the VAX can use displacement, autoincrement, or autodecrement to form the initial memory address; in these programs, almost all the memory indirect references use displacement mode as the base. Displacement mode includes all displacement lengths (8, 16, and 32 bits). The PC-relative addressing modes, used almost exclusively for branches, are not included. Only the addressing modes with an average frequency of over 1% are shown.

address constants, which tend to be large. For the use of immediates it is important to know whether they need to be supported for all operations or for only a subset. Figure A.9 shows the frequency of immediates for the general classes of integer and floating-point operations in an instruction set.

Another important instruction set measurement is the range of values for immediates. Like displacement values, the size of immediate values affects instruction length. As Figure A.10 shows, small immediate values are most heavily used. Large immediates are sometimes used, however, most likely in addressing calculations.

Summary: Memory Addressing

First, because of their popularity, we would expect a new architecture to support at least the following addressing modes: displacement, immediate, and register indirect. Figure A.7 shows that they represent 75% to 99% of the addressing modes used in our measurements. Second, we would expect the size of the address for displacement mode to be at least 12 to 16 bits, since the caption in Figure A.8 suggests these sizes would capture 75% to 99% of the displacements.

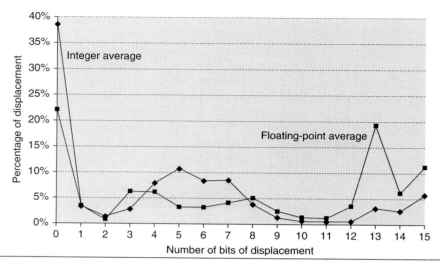

Figure A.8 Displacement values are widely distributed. There are both a large number of small values and a fair number of large values. The wide distribution of displacement values is due to multiple storage areas for variables and different displacements to access them (see Section A.8) as well as the overall addressing scheme the compiler uses. The *x*-axis is $\log_2$ of the displacement, that is, the size of a field needed to represent the magnitude of the displacement. Zero on the *x*-axis shows the percentage of displacements of value 0. The graph does not include the sign bit, which is heavily affected by the storage layout. Most displacements are positive, but a majority of the largest displacements (14+ bits) are negative. Since these data were collected on a computer with 16-bit displacements, they cannot tell us about longer displacements. These data were taken on the Alpha architecture with full optimization (see Section A.8) for SPEC CPU2000, showing the average of integer programs (CINT2000) and the average of floating-point programs (CFP2000).

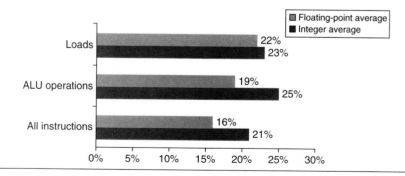

Figure A.9 About one-quarter of data transfers and ALU operations have an immediate operand. The bottom bars show that integer programs use immediates in about one-fifth of the instructions, while floating-point programs use immediates in about one-sixth of the instructions. For loads, the load immediate instruction loads 16 bits into either half of a 32-bit register. Load immediates are not loads in a strict sense because they do not access memory. Occasionally a pair of load immediates is used to load a 32-bit constant, but this is rare. (For ALU operations, shifts by a constant amount are included as operations with immediate operands.) The programs and computer used to collect these statistics are the same as in Figure A.8.

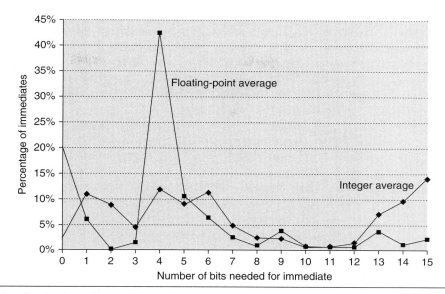

Figure A.10 **The distribution of immediate values.** The *x*-axis shows the number of bits needed to represent the magnitude of an immediate value—0 means the immediate field value was 0. The majority of the immediate values are positive. About 20% were negative for CINT2000, and about 30% were negative for CFP2000. These measurements were taken on an Alpha, where the maximum immediate is 16 bits, for the same programs as in Figure A.8. A similar measurement on the VAX, which supported 32-bit immediates, showed that about 20% to 25% of immediates were longer than 16 bits. Thus, 16 bits would capture about 80% and 8 bits about 50%.

Third, we would expect the size of the immediate field to be at least 8 to 16 bits. This claim is not substantiated by the caption of the figure to which it refers.

Having covered instruction set classes and decided on register-register architectures, plus the previous recommendations on data addressing modes, we next cover the sizes and meanings of data.

A.4   Type and Size of Operands

How is the type of an operand designated? Normally, encoding in the opcode designates the type of an operand—this is the method used most often. Alternatively, the data can be annotated with tags that are interpreted by the hardware. These tags specify the type of the operand, and the operation is chosen accordingly. Computers with tagged data, however, can only be found in computer museums.

Let's start with desktop and server architectures. Usually the type of an operand—integer, single-precision floating point, character, and so on—effectively gives its size. Common operand types include character (8 bits), half word (16 bits), word (32 bits), single-precision floating point (also 1 word), and double-precision floating point (2 words). Integers are almost universally represented as two's complement binary numbers. Characters are usually in ASCII, but the 16-bit Unicode (used in Java) is gaining popularity with the internationalization of computers. Until the early 1980s, most computer manufacturers chose their own floating-point representation. Almost all computers since that time follow the same standard for floating point, the IEEE standard 754. The IEEE floating-point standard is discussed in detail in Appendix J.

Some architectures provide operations on character strings, although such operations are usually quite limited and treat each byte in the string as a single character. Typical operations supported on character strings are comparisons and moves.

For business applications, some architectures support a decimal format, usually called *packed decimal* or *binary-coded decimal*—4 bits are used to encode the values 0 to 9, and 2 decimal digits are packed into each byte. Numeric character strings are sometimes called *unpacked decimal*, and operations—called *packing* and *unpacking*—are usually provided for converting back and forth between them.

One reason to use decimal operands is to get results that exactly match decimal numbers, as some decimal fractions do not have an exact representation in binary. For example, 0.10_{10} is a simple fraction in decimal, but in binary it requires an infinite set of repeating digits: $0.0001100110\overline{0011}\ldots_{2}$. Thus, calculations that are exact in decimal can be close but inexact in binary, which can be a problem for financial transactions. (See Appendix J to learn more about precise arithmetic.)

Our SPEC benchmarks use byte or character, half-word (short integer), word (integer), double-word (long integer), and floating-point data types. Figure A.11 shows the dynamic distribution of the sizes of objects referenced from memory for these programs. The frequency of access to different data types helps in deciding what types are most important to support efficiently. Should the computer have a 64-bit access path, or would taking two cycles to access a double word be satisfactory? As we saw earlier, byte accesses require an alignment network: How important is it to support bytes as primitives? Figure A.11 uses memory references to examine the types of data being accessed.

In some architectures, objects in registers may be accessed as bytes or half words. However, such access is very infrequent—on the VAX, it accounts for no more than 12% of register references, or roughly 6% of all operand accesses in these programs.

A.5 Operations in the Instruction Set

The operators supported by most instruction set architectures can be categorized as in Figure A.12. One rule of thumb across all architectures is that the most widely executed instructions are the simple operations of an instruction set. For example, Figure A.13 shows 10 simple instructions that account for 96% of

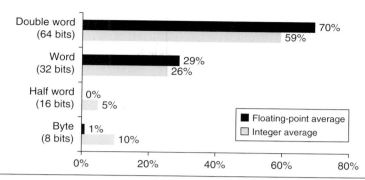

Figure A.11 Distribution of data accesses by size for the benchmark programs. The double-word data type is used for double-precision floating point in floating-point programs and for addresses, since the computer uses 64-bit addresses. On a 32-bit address computer the 64-bit addresses would be replaced by 32-bit addresses, and so almost all double-word accesses in integer programs would become single-word accesses.

Operator type	Examples
Arithmetic and logical	Integer arithmetic and logical operations: add, subtract, and, or, multiply, divide
Data transfer	Loads-stores (move instructions on computers with memory addressing)
Control	Branch, jump, procedure call and return, traps
System	Operating system call, virtual memory management instructions
Floating point	Floating-point operations: add, multiply, divide, compare
Decimal	Decimal add, decimal multiply, decimal-to-character conversions
String	String move, string compare, string search
Graphics	Pixel and vertex operations, compression/decompression operations

Figure A.12 Categories of instruction operators and examples of each. All computers generally provide a full set of operations for the first three categories. The support for system functions in the instruction set varies widely among architectures, but all computers must have some instruction support for basic system functions. The amount of support in the instruction set for the last four categories may vary from none to an extensive set of special instructions. Floating-point instructions will be provided in any computer that is intended for use in an application that makes much use of floating point. These instructions are sometimes part of an optional instruction set. Decimal and string instructions are sometimes primitives, as in the VAX or the IBM 360, or may be synthesized by the compiler from simpler instructions. Graphics instructions typically operate on many smaller data items in parallel—for example, performing eight 8-bit additions on two 64-bit operands.

Rank	80x86 instruction	Integer average (% total executed)
1	load	22%
2	conditional branch	20%
3	compare	16%
4	store	12%
5	add	8%
6	and	6%
7	sub	5%
8	move register-register	4%
9	call	1%
10	return	1%
Total		**96%**

Figure A.13 The top 10 instructions for the 80x86. Simple instructions dominate this list and are responsible for 96% of the instructions executed. These percentages are the average of the five SPECint92 programs.

instructions executed for a collection of integer programs running on the popular Intel 80x86. Hence, the implementor of these instructions should be sure to make these fast, as they are the common case.

As mentioned before, the instructions in Figure A.13 are found in every computer for every application—desktop, server, embedded—with the variations of operations in Figure A.12 largely depending on which data types that the instruction set includes.

A.6   Instructions for Control Flow

Because the measurements of branch and jump behavior are fairly independent of other measurements and applications, we now examine the use of control flow instructions, which have little in common with the operations of the previous sections.

There is no consistent terminology for instructions that change the flow of control. In the 1950s they were typically called *transfers*. Beginning in 1960 the name *branch* began to be used. Later, computers introduced additional names. Throughout this book we will use *jump* when the change in control is unconditional and *branch* when the change is conditional.

We can distinguish four different types of control flow change:

■ Conditional branches

■ Jumps

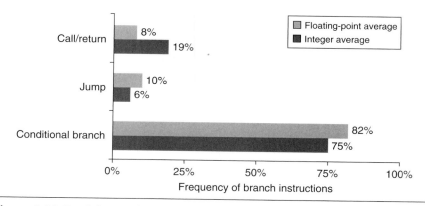

Figure A.14 Breakdown of control flow instructions into three classes: calls or returns, jumps, and conditional branches. Conditional branches clearly dominate. Each type is counted in one of three bars. The programs and computer used to collect these statistics are the same as those in Figure A.8.

- Procedure calls
- Procedure returns

We want to know the relative frequency of these events, as each event is different, may use different instructions, and may have different behavior. Figure A.14 shows the frequencies of these control flow instructions for a load-store computer running our benchmarks.

Addressing Modes for Control Flow Instructions

The destination address of a control flow instruction must always be specified. This destination is specified explicitly in the instruction in the vast majority of cases—procedure return being the major exception, since for return the target is not known at compile time. The most common way to specify the destination is to supply a displacement that is added to the *program counter* (PC). Control flow instructions of this sort are called *PC-relative*. PC-relative branches or jumps are advantageous because the target is often near the current instruction, and specifying the position relative to the current PC requires fewer bits. Using PC-relative addressing also permits the code to run independently of where it is loaded. This property, called *position independence*, can eliminate some work when the program is linked and is also useful in programs linked dynamically during execution.

To implement returns and indirect jumps when the target is not known at compile time, a method other than PC-relative addressing is required. Here, there must be a way to specify the target dynamically, so that it can change at runtime. This dynamic address may be as simple as naming a register that contains the target address; alternatively, the jump may permit any addressing mode to be used to supply the target address.

These register indirect jumps are also useful for four other important features:

- *Case* or *switch* statements, found in most programming languages (which select among one of several alternatives)

- *Virtual functions* or *methods* in object-oriented languages like C++ or Java (which allow different routines to be called depending on the type of the argument)

- *High-order functions* or *function pointers* in languages like C or C++ (which allow functions to be passed as arguments, giving some of the flavor of object-oriented programming)

- *Dynamically shared libraries* (which allow a library to be loaded and linked at runtime only when it is actually invoked by the program rather than loaded and linked statically before the program is run)

In all four cases the target address is not known at compile time, and hence is usually loaded from memory into a register before the register indirect jump.

As branches generally use PC-relative addressing to specify their targets, an important question concerns how far branch targets are from branches. Knowing the distribution of these displacements will help in choosing what branch offsets to support, and thus will affect the instruction length and encoding. Figure A.15 shows the distribution of displacements for PC-relative branches in instructions. About 75% of the branches are in the forward direction.

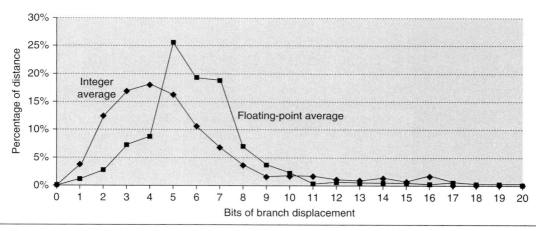

Figure A.15 Branch distances in terms of number of instructions between the target and the branch instruction. The most frequent branches in the integer programs are to targets that can be encoded in 4 to 8 bits. This result tells us that short displacement fields often suffice for branches and that the designer can gain some encoding density by having a shorter instruction with a smaller branch displacement. These measurements were taken on a load-store computer (Alpha architecture) with all instructions aligned on word boundaries. An architecture that requires fewer instructions for the same program, such as a VAX, would have shorter branch distances. However, the number of bits needed for the displacement may increase if the computer has variable-length instructions to be aligned on any byte boundary. The programs and computer used to collect these statistics are the same as those in Figure A.8.

Conditional Branch Options

Since most changes in control flow are branches, deciding how to specify the branch condition is important. Figure A.16 shows the three primary techniques in use today and their advantages and disadvantages.

One of the most noticeable properties of branches is that a large number of the comparisons are simple tests, and a large number are comparisons with zero. Thus, some architectures choose to treat these comparisons as special cases, especially if a *compare and branch* instruction is being used. Figure A.17 shows the frequency of different comparisons used for conditional branching.

Procedure Invocation Options

Procedure calls and returns include control transfer and possibly some state saving; at a minimum the return address must be saved somewhere, sometimes in a special link register or just a GPR. Some older architectures provide a mechanism to save many registers, while newer architectures require the compiler to generate stores and loads for each register saved and restored.

There are two basic conventions in use to save registers: either at the call site or inside the procedure being called. *Caller saving* means that the calling procedure must save the registers that it wants preserved for access after the call, and thus the called procedure need not worry about registers. *Callee saving* is the opposite: the called procedure must save the registers it wants to use, leaving the caller unrestrained. There are times when caller save must be used because of access patterns to globally visible variables in two different procedures. For

Name	Examples	How condition is tested	Advantages	Disadvantages
Condition code (CC)	80x86, ARM, PowerPC, SPARC, SuperH	Tests special bits set by ALU operations, possibly under program control.	Sometimes condition is set for free.	CC is extra state. Condition codes constrain the ordering of instructions since they pass information from one instruction to a branch.
Condition register	Alpha, MIPS	Tests arbitrary register with the result of a comparison.	Simple.	Uses up a register.
Compare and branch	PA-RISC, VAX	Compare is part of the branch. Often compare is limited to subset.	One instruction rather than two for a branch.	May be too much work per instruction for pipelined execution.

Figure A.16 The major methods for evaluating branch conditions, their advantages, and their disadvantages. Although condition codes can be set by ALU operations that are needed for other purposes, measurements on programs show that this rarely happens. The major implementation problems with condition codes arise when the condition code is set by a large or haphazardly chosen subset of the instructions, rather than being controlled by a bit in the instruction. Computers with compare and branch often limit the set of compares and use a condition register for more complex compares. Often, different techniques are used for branches based on floating-point comparison versus those based on integer comparison. This dichotomy is reasonable since the number of branches that depend on floating-point comparisons is much smaller than the number depending on integer comparisons.

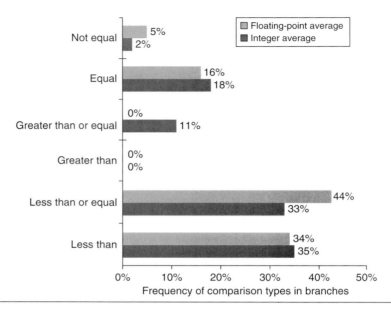

Figure A.17 Frequency of different types of compares in conditional branches. Less than (or equal) branches dominate this combination of compiler and architecture. These measurements include both the integer and floating-point compares in branches. The programs and computer used to collect these statistics are the same as those in Figure A.8.

example, suppose we have a procedure P1 that calls procedure P2, and both procedures manipulate the global variable *x*. If P1 had allocated *x* to a register, it must be sure to save *x* to a location known by P2 before the call to P2. A compiler's ability to discover when a called procedure may access register-allocated quantities is complicated by the possibility of separate compilation. Suppose P2 may not touch *x* but can call another procedure, P3, that may access *x,* yet P2 and P3 are compiled separately. Because of these complications, most compilers will conservatively caller save *any* variable that may be accessed during a call.

In the cases where either convention could be used, some programs will be more optimal with callee save and some will be more optimal with caller save. As a result, most real systems today use a combination of the two mechanisms. This convention is specified in an application binary interface (ABI) that sets down the basic rules as to which registers should be caller saved and which should be callee saved. Later in this appendix we will examine the mismatch between sophisticated instructions for automatically saving registers and the needs of the compiler.

Summary: Instructions for Control Flow

Control flow instructions are some of the most frequently executed instructions. Although there are many options for conditional branches, we would expect branch addressing in a new architecture to be able to jump to hundreds of instructions either above or below the branch. This requirement suggests a PC-relative branch displacement of at least 8 bits. We would also expect to see register indirect and PC-relative addressing for jump instructions to support returns as well as many other features of current systems.

We have now completed our instruction architecture tour at the level seen by an assembly language programmer or compiler writer. We are leaning toward a load-store architecture with displacement, immediate, and register indirect addressing modes. These data are 8-, 16-, 32-, and 64-bit integers and 32- and 64-bit floating-point data. The instructions include simple operations, PC-relative conditional branches, jump and link instructions for procedure call, and register indirect jumps for procedure return (plus a few other uses).

Now we need to select how to represent this architecture in a form that makes it easy for the hardware to execute.

A.7   Encoding an Instruction Set

Clearly, the choices mentioned above will affect how the instructions are encoded into a binary representation for execution by the processor. This representation affects not only the size of the compiled program but also the implementation of the processor, which must decode this representation to quickly find the operation and its operands. The operation is typically specified in one field, called the *opcode*. As we shall see, the important decision is how to encode the addressing modes with the operations.

This decision depends on the range of addressing modes and the degree of independence between opcodes and modes. Some older computers have one to five operands with 10 addressing modes for each operand (see Figure A.6). For such a large number of combinations, typically a separate *address specifier* is needed for each operand: The address specifier tells what addressing mode is used to access the operand. At the other extreme are load-store computers with only one memory operand and only one or two addressing modes; obviously, in this case, the addressing mode can be encoded as part of the opcode.

When encoding the instructions, the number of registers and the number of addressing modes both have a significant impact on the size of instructions, as the register field and addressing mode field may appear many times in a single instruction. In fact, for most instructions many more bits are consumed in encoding addressing modes and register fields than in specifying the opcode. The architect must balance several competing forces when encoding the instruction set:

1. The desire to have as many registers and addressing modes as possible.

2. The impact of the size of the register and addressing mode fields on the average instruction size and hence on the average program size.

3. A desire to have instructions encoded into lengths that will be easy to handle in a pipelined implementation. (The value of easily decoded instructions is discussed in Appendix C and Chapter 3.) As a minimum, the architect wants

instructions to be in multiples of bytes, rather than an arbitrary bit length. Many desktop and server architects have chosen to use a fixed-length instruction to gain implementation benefits while sacrificing average code size.

Figure A.18 shows three popular choices for encoding the instruction set. The first we call *variable,* since it allows virtually all addressing modes to be with all operations. This style is best when there are many addressing modes and operations. The second choice we call *fixed,* since it combines the operation and the addressing mode into the opcode. Often fixed encoding will have only a single size for all instructions; it works best when there are few addressing modes and operations. The trade-off between variable encoding and fixed encoding is size of programs versus ease of decoding in the processor. Variable tries to use as few bits as possible to represent the program, but individual instructions can vary widely in both size and the amount of work to be performed.

Let's look at an 80x86 instruction to see an example of the variable encoding:

add EAX,1000(EBX)

Operation and no. of operands	Address specifier 1	Address field 1		Address specifier *n*	Address field *n*

(a) Variable (e.g., Intel 80x86, VAX)

Operation	Address field 1	Address field 2	Address field 3

(b) Fixed (e.g., Alpha, ARM, MIPS, PowerPC, SPARC, SuperH)

Operation	Address specifier	Address field

Operation	Address specifier 1	Address specifier 2	Address field

Operation	Address specifier	Address field 1	Address field 2

(c) Hybrid (e.g., IBM 360/370, MIPS16, Thumb, TI TMS320C54x)

Figure A.18 Three basic variations in instruction encoding: variable length, fixed length, and hybrid. The variable format can support any number of operands, with each address specifier determining the addressing mode and the length of the specifier for that operand. It generally enables the smallest code representation, since unused fields need not be included. The fixed format always has the same number of operands, with the addressing modes (if options exist) specified as part of the opcode. It generally results in the largest code size. Although the fields tend not to vary in their location, they will be used for different purposes by different instructions. The hybrid approach has multiple formats specified by the opcode, adding one or two fields to specify the addressing mode and one or two fields to specify the operand address.

The name add means a 32-bit integer add instruction with two operands, and this opcode takes 1 byte. An 80x86 address specifier is 1 or 2 bytes, specifying the source/destination register (EAX) and the addressing mode (displacement in this case) and base register (EBX) for the second operand. This combination takes 1 byte to specify the operands. When in 32-bit mode (see Appendix K), the size of the address field is either 1 byte or 4 bytes. Since 1000 is bigger than 2^8, the total length of the instruction is

$$1 + 1 + 4 = 6 \text{ bytes}$$

The length of 80x86 instructions varies between 1 and 17 bytes. 80x86 programs are generally smaller than the RISC architectures, which use fixed formats (see Appendix K).

Given these two poles of instruction set design of variable and fixed, the third alternative immediately springs to mind: Reduce the variability in size and work of the variable architecture but provide multiple instruction lengths to reduce code size. This *hybrid* approach is the third encoding alternative, and we'll see examples shortly.

Reduced Code Size in RISCs

As RISC computers started being used in embedded applications, the 32-bit fixed format became a liability since cost and hence smaller code are important. In response, several manufacturers offered a new hybrid version of their RISC instruction sets, with both 16-bit and 32-bit instructions. The narrow instructions support fewer operations, smaller address and immediate fields, fewer registers, and the two-address format rather than the classic three-address format of RISC computers. Appendix K gives two examples, the ARM Thumb and MIPS MIPS16, which both claim a code size reduction of up to 40%.

In contrast to these instruction set extensions, IBM simply compresses its standard instruction set and then adds hardware to decompress instructions as they are fetched from memory on an instruction cache miss. Thus, the instruction cache contains full 32-bit instructions, but compressed code is kept in main memory, ROMs, and the disk. The advantage of MIPS16 and Thumb is that instruction caches act as if they are about 25% larger, while IBM's CodePack means that compilers need not be changed to handle different instruction sets and instruction decoding can remain simple.

CodePack starts with run-length encoding compression on any PowerPC program and then loads the resulting compression tables in a 2 KB table on chip. Hence, every program has its own unique encoding. To handle branches, which are no longer to an aligned word boundary, the PowerPC creates a hash table in memory that maps between compressed and uncompressed addresses. Like a TLB (see Chapter 2), it caches the most recently used address maps to reduce the number of memory accesses. IBM claims an overall performance cost of 10%, resulting in a code size reduction of 35% to 40%.

Hitachi simply invented a RISC instruction set with a fixed 16-bit format, called SuperH, for embedded applications (see Appendix K). It has 16 rather than

32 registers to make it fit the narrower format and fewer instructions but otherwise looks like a classic RISC architecture.

Summary: Encoding an Instruction Set

Decisions made in the components of instruction set design discussed in previous sections determine whether the architect has the choice between variable and fixed instruction encodings. Given the choice, the architect more interested in code size than performance will pick variable encoding, and the one more interested in performance than code size will pick fixed encoding. Appendix E gives 13 examples of the results of architects' choices. In Appendix C and Chapter 3, the impact of variability on performance of the processor will be discussed further.

We have almost finished laying the groundwork for the MIPS instruction set architecture that will be introduced in Section A.9. Before we do that, however, it will be helpful to take a brief look at compiler technology and its effect on program properties.

A.8   Crosscutting Issues: The Role of Compilers

Today almost all programming is done in high-level languages for desktop and server applications. This development means that since most instructions executed are the output of a compiler, an instruction set architecture is essentially a compiler target. In earlier times for these applications, architectural decisions were often made to ease assembly language programming or for a specific kernel. Because the compiler will significantly affect the performance of a computer, understanding compiler technology today is critical to designing and efficiently implementing an instruction set.

Once it was popular to try to isolate the compiler technology and its effect on hardware performance from the architecture and its performance, just as it was popular to try to separate architecture from its implementation. This separation is essentially impossible with today's desktop compilers and computers. Architectural choices affect the quality of the code that can be generated for a computer and the complexity of building a good compiler for it, for better or for worse.

In this section, we discuss the critical goals in the instruction set primarily from the compiler viewpoint. It starts with a review of the anatomy of current compilers. Next we discuss how compiler technology affects the decisions of the architect, and how the architect can make it hard or easy for the compiler to produce good code. We conclude with a review of compilers and multimedia operations, which unfortunately is a bad example of cooperation between compiler writers and architects.

The Structure of Recent Compilers

To begin, let's look at what optimizing compilers are like today. Figure A.19 shows the structure of recent compilers.

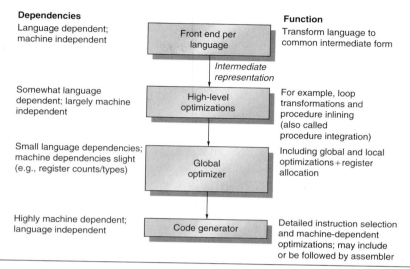

Figure A.19 Compilers typically consist of two to four passes, with more highly optimizing compilers having more passes. This structure maximizes the probability that a program compiled at various levels of optimization will produce the same output when given the same input. The optimizing passes are designed to be optional and may be skipped when faster compilation is the goal and lower-quality code is acceptable. A *pass* is simply one phase in which the compiler reads and transforms the entire program. (The term *phase* is often used interchangeably with *pass*.) Because the optimizing passes are separated, multiple languages can use the same optimizing and code generation passes. Only a new front end is required for a new language.

   A compiler writer's first goal is correctness—all valid programs must be compiled correctly. The second goal is usually speed of the compiled code. Typically, a whole set of other goals follows these two, including fast compilation, debugging support, and interoperability among languages. Normally, the passes in the compiler transform higher-level, more abstract representations into progressively lower-level representations. Eventually it reaches the instruction set. This structure helps manage the complexity of the transformations and makes writing a bug-free compiler easier.

   The complexity of writing a correct compiler is a major limitation on the amount of optimization that can be done. Although the multiple-pass structure helps reduce compiler complexity, it also means that the compiler must order and perform some transformations before others. In the diagram of the optimizing compiler in Figure A.19, we can see that certain high-level optimizations are performed long before it is known what the resulting code will look like. Once such a transformation is made, the compiler can't afford to go back and revisit all steps, possibly undoing transformations. Such iteration would be prohibitive, both in compilation time and in complexity. Thus, compilers make assumptions about the ability of later steps to deal with certain problems. For example, compilers usually have to choose which procedure calls to expand inline before they know the exact size of the procedure being called. Compiler writers call this problem the *phase-ordering problem*.

How does this ordering of transformations interact with the instruction set architecture? A good example occurs with the optimization called *global common subexpression elimination*. This optimization finds two instances of an expression that compute the same value and saves the value of the first computation in a temporary. It then uses the temporary value, eliminating the second computation of the common expression.

For this optimization to be significant, the temporary must be allocated to a register. Otherwise, the cost of storing the temporary in memory and later reloading it may negate the savings gained by not recomputing the expression. There are, in fact, cases where this optimization actually slows down code when the temporary is not register allocated. Phase ordering complicates this problem because register allocation is typically done near the end of the global optimization pass, just before code generation. Thus, an optimizer that performs this optimization must *assume* that the register allocator will allocate the temporary to a register.

Optimizations performed by modern compilers can be classified by the style of the transformation, as follows:

- *High-level optimizations* are often done on the source with output fed to later optimization passes.

- *Local optimizations* optimize code only within a straight-line code fragment (called a *basic block* by compiler people).

- *Global optimizations* extend the local optimizations across branches and introduce a set of transformations aimed at optimizing loops.

- *Register allocation* associates registers with operands.

- *Processor-dependent optimizations* attempt to take advantage of specific architectural knowledge.

Register Allocation

Because of the central role that register allocation plays, both in speeding up the code and in making other optimizations useful, it is one of the most important—if not the most important—of the optimizations. Register allocation algorithms today are based on a technique called *graph coloring*. The basic idea behind graph coloring is to construct a graph representing the possible candidates for allocation to a register and then to use the graph to allocate registers. Roughly speaking, the problem is how to use a limited set of colors so that no two adjacent nodes in a dependency graph have the same color. The emphasis in the approach is to achieve 100% register allocation of active variables. The problem of coloring a graph in general can take exponential time as a function of the size of the graph (NP-complete). There are heuristic algorithms, however, that work well in practice, yielding close allocations that run in near-linear time.

Graph coloring works best when there are at least 16 (and preferably more) general-purpose registers available for global allocation for integer variables and additional registers for floating point. Unfortunately, graph coloring does not work very well when the number of registers is small because the heuristic algorithms for coloring the graph are likely to fail.

Impact of Optimizations on Performance

It is sometimes difficult to separate some of the simpler optimizations—local and processor-dependent optimizations—from transformations done in the code generator. Examples of typical optimizations are given in Figure A.20. The last column of Figure A.20 indicates the frequency with which the listed optimizing transforms were applied to the source program.

Figure A.21 shows the effect of various optimizations on instructions executed for two programs. In this case, optimized programs executed roughly 25% to 90% fewer instructions than unoptimized programs. The figure illustrates the importance of looking at optimized code before suggesting new instruction set features, since a compiler might completely remove the instructions the architect was trying to improve.

The Impact of Compiler Technology on the Architect's Decisions

The interaction of compilers and high-level languages significantly affects how programs use an instruction set architecture. There are two important questions: How are variables allocated and addressed? How many registers are needed to allocate variables appropriately? To address these questions, we must look at the three separate areas in which current high-level languages allocate their data:

- The *stack* is used to allocate local variables. The stack is grown or shrunk on procedure call or return, respectively. Objects on the stack are addressed relative to the stack pointer and are primarily scalars (single variables) rather than arrays. The stack is used for activation records, *not* as a stack for evaluating expressions. Hence, values are almost never pushed or popped on the stack.

- The *global data area* is used to allocate statically declared objects, such as global variables and constants. A large percentage of these objects are arrays or other aggregate data structures.

- The *heap* is used to allocate dynamic objects that do not adhere to a stack discipline. Objects in the heap are accessed with pointers and are typically not scalars.

Register allocation is much more effective for stack-allocated objects than for global variables, and register allocation is essentially impossible for heap-allocated objects because they are accessed with pointers. Global variables and some stack variables are impossible to allocate because they are *aliased*—there

Optimization name	Explanation	Percentage of the total number of optimizing transforms
High-level	*At or near the source level; processor-independent*	
Procedure integration	Replace procedure call by procedure body	N.M.
Local	*Within straight-line code*	
Common subexpression elimination	Replace two instances of the same computation by single copy	18%
Constant propagation	Replace all instances of a variable that is assigned a constant with the constant	22%
Stack height reduction	Rearrange expression tree to minimize resources needed for expression evaluation	N.M.
Global	*Across a branch*	
Global common subexpression elimination	Same as local, but this version crosses branches	13%
Copy propagation	Replace all instances of a variable A that has been assigned X (i.e., $A = X$) with X	11%
Code motion	Remove code from a loop that computes same value each iteration of the loop	16%
Induction variable elimination	Simplify/eliminate array addressing calculations within loops	2%
Processor-dependent	*Depends on processor knowledge*	
Strength reduction	Many examples, such as replace multiply by a constant with adds and shifts	N.M.
Pipeline scheduling	Reorder instructions to improve pipeline performance	N.M.
Branch offset optimization	Choose the shortest branch displacement that reaches target	N.M.

Figure A.20 Major types of optimizations and examples in each class. These data tell us about the relative frequency of occurrence of various optimizations. The third column lists the static frequency with which some of the common optimizations are applied in a set of 12 small Fortran and Pascal programs. There are nine local and global optimizations done by the compiler included in the measurement. Six of these optimizations are covered in the figure, and the remaining three account for 18% of the total static occurrences. The abbreviation *N.M.* means that the number of occurrences of that optimization was not measured. Processor-dependent optimizations are usually done in a code generator, and none of those was measured in this experiment. The percentage is the portion of the static optimizations that are of the specified type. Data from Chow [1983] (collected using the Stanford UCODE compiler).

are multiple ways to refer to the address of a variable, making it illegal to put it into a register. (Most heap variables are effectively aliased for today's compiler technology.)

For example, consider the following code sequence, where & returns the address of a variable and * dereferences a pointer:

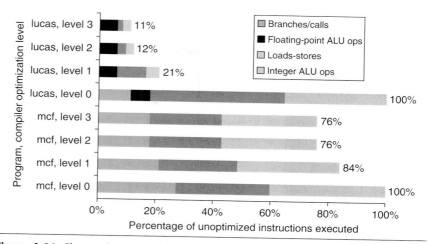

Figure A.21 Change in instruction count for the programs lucas and mcf from the SPEC2000 as compiler optimization levels vary. Level 0 is the same as unoptimized code. Level 1 includes local optimizations, code scheduling, and local register allocation. Level 2 includes global optimizations, loop transformations (software pipelining), and global register allocation. Level 3 adds procedure integration. These experiments were performed on Alpha compilers.

```
p = &a-- gets address of a in p
a = ...-- assigns to a directly
*p = ...-- uses p to assign to a
...a...-- accesses a
```

The variable a could not be register allocated across the assignment to *p without generating incorrect code. Aliasing causes a substantial problem because it is often difficult or impossible to decide what objects a pointer may refer to. A compiler must be conservative; some compilers will not allocate *any* local variables of a procedure in a register when there is a pointer that may refer to *one* of the local variables.

How the Architect Can Help the Compiler Writer

Today, the complexity of a compiler does not come from translating simple statements like A = B + C. Most programs are *locally simple*, and simple translations work fine. Rather, complexity arises because programs are large and globally complex in their interactions, and because the structure of compilers means decisions are made one step at a time about which code sequence is best.

Compiler writers often are working under their own corollary of a basic principle in architecture: *Make the frequent cases fast and the rare case correct.* That is, if we know which cases are frequent and which are rare, and if generating code for both is straightforward, then the quality of the code for the rare case may not be very important—but it must be correct!

Some instruction set properties help the compiler writer. These properties should not be thought of as hard-and-fast rules, but rather as guidelines that will make it easier to write a compiler that will generate efficient and correct code.

- *Provide regularity*—Whenever it makes sense, the three primary components of an instruction set—the operations, the data types, and the addressing modes—should be *orthogonal*. Two aspects of an architecture are said to be orthogonal if they are independent. For example, the operations and addressing modes are orthogonal if, for every operation to which one addressing mode can be applied, all addressing modes are applicable. This regularity helps simplify code generation and is particularly important when the decision about what code to generate is split into two passes in the compiler. A good counterexample of this property is restricting what registers can be used for a certain class of instructions. Compilers for special-purpose register architectures typically get stuck in this dilemma. This restriction can result in the compiler finding itself with lots of available registers, but none of the right kind!

- *Provide primitives, not solutions*—Special features that "match" a language construct or a kernel function are often unusable. Attempts to support high-level languages may work only with one language or do more or less than is required for a correct and efficient implementation of the language. An example of how such attempts have failed is given in Section A.10.

- *Simplify trade-offs among alternatives*—One of the toughest jobs a compiler writer has is figuring out what instruction sequence will be best for every segment of code that arises. In earlier days, instruction counts or total code size might have been good metrics, but—as we saw in Chapter 1—this is no longer true. With caches and pipelining, the trade-offs have become very complex. Anything the designer can do to help the compiler writer understand the costs of alternative code sequences would help improve the code. One of the most difficult instances of complex trade-offs occurs in a register-memory architecture in deciding how many times a variable should be referenced before it is cheaper to load it into a register. This threshold is hard to compute and, in fact, may vary among models of the same architecture.

- *Provide instructions that bind the quantities known at compile time as constants*—A compiler writer hates the thought of the processor interpreting at runtime a value that was known at compile time. Good counterexamples of this principle include instructions that interpret values that were fixed at compile time. For instance, the VAX procedure call instruction (calls) dynamically interprets a mask saying what registers to save on a call, but the mask is fixed at compile time (see Section A.10).

Compiler Support (or Lack Thereof) for Multimedia Instructions

Alas, the designers of the SIMD instructions (see Section 4.3 in Chapter 4) basically ignored the previous subsection. These instructions tend to be solutions, not primitives; they are short of registers; and the data types do not match existing programming languages. Architects hoped to find an inexpensive solution that would help some users, but often only a few low-level graphics library routines use them.

The SIMD instructions are really an abbreviated version of an elegant architecture style that has its own compiler technology. As explained in Section 4.2, *vector architectures* operate on vectors of data. Invented originally for scientific codes, multimedia kernels are often vectorizable as well, albeit often with shorter vectors. As Section 4.3 suggests, we can think of Intel's MMX and SSE or PowerPC's AltiVec as simply short vector computers: MMX with vectors of eight 8-bit elements, four 16-bit elements, or two 32-bit elements, and AltiVec with vectors twice that length. They are implemented as simply adjacent, narrow elements in wide registers.

These microprocessor architectures build the vector register size into the architecture: the sum of the sizes of the elements is limited to 64 bits for MMX and 128 bits for AltiVec. When Intel decided to expand to 128-bit vectors, it added a whole new set of instructions, called Streaming SIMD Extension (SSE).

A major advantage of vector computers is hiding latency of memory access by loading many elements at once and then overlapping execution with data transfer. The goal of vector addressing modes is to collect data scattered about memory, place them in a compact form so that they can be operated on efficiently, and then place the results back where they belong.

Vector computers include *strided addressing* and *gather/scatter addressing* (see Section 4.2) to increase the number of programs that can be vectorized. Strided addressing skips a fixed number of words between each access, so sequential addressing is often called *unit stride addressing*. Gather and scatter find their addresses in another vector register: Think of it as register indirect addressing for vector computers. From a vector perspective, in contrast, these short-vector SIMD computers support only unit strided accesses: Memory accesses load or store all elements at once from a single wide memory location. Since the data for multimedia applications are often streams that start and end in memory, strided and gather/scatter addressing modes are essential to successful vectorization (see Section 4.7).

Example   As an example, compare a vector computer to MMX for color representation conversion of pixels from RGB (red, green, blue) to YUV (luminosity chrominance), with each pixel represented by 3 bytes. The conversion is just three lines of C code placed in a loop:

```
Y = (9798*R + 19235*G + 3736*B) / 32768;
U = (-4784*R - 9437*G + 4221*B) / 32768 + 128;
V = (20218*R - 16941*G - 3277*B) / 32768 + 128;
```

A 64-bit-wide vector computer can calculate 8 pixels simultaneously. One vector computer for media with strided addresses takes

- 3 vector loads (to get RGB)
- 3 vector multiplies (to convert R)
- 6 vector multiply adds (to convert G and B)
- 3 vector shifts (to divide by 32,768)
- 2 vector adds (to add 128)
- 3 vector stores (to store YUV)

The total is 20 instructions to perform the 20 operations in the previous C code to convert 8 pixels [Kozyrakis 2000]. (Since a vector might have 32 64-bit elements, this code actually converts up to 32×8 or 256 pixels.)

In contrast, Intel's Web site shows that a library routine to perform the same calculation on 8 pixels takes 116 MMX instructions plus 6 80x86 instructions [Intel 2001]. This sixfold increase in instructions is due to the large number of instructions to load and unpack RGB pixels and to pack and store YUV pixels, since there are no strided memory accesses.

Having short, architecture-limited vectors with few registers and simple memory addressing modes makes it more difficult to use vectorizing compiler technology. Hence, these SIMD instructions are more likely to be found in hand-coded libraries than in compiled code.

Summary: The Role of Compilers

This section leads to several recommendations. First, we expect a new instruction set architecture to have at least 16 general-purpose registers—not counting separate registers for floating-point numbers—to simplify allocation of registers using graph coloring. The advice on orthogonality suggests that all supported addressing modes apply to all instructions that transfer data. Finally, the last three pieces of advice—provide primitives instead of solutions, simplify trade-offs between alternatives, don't bind constants at runtime—all suggest that it is better to err on the side of simplicity. In other words, understand that less is more in the design of an instruction set. Alas, SIMD extensions are more an example of good marketing than of outstanding achievement of hardware–software co-design.

A.9 Putting It All Together: The MIPS Architecture

In this section we describe a simple 64-bit load-store architecture called MIPS. The instruction set architecture of MIPS and RISC relatives was based on observations similar to those covered in the last sections. (In Section L.3 we discuss how and why these architectures became popular.) Reviewing our expectations from each section, for desktop applications:

- *Section A.2*—Use general-purpose registers with a load-store architecture.

- *Section A.3*—Support these addressing modes: displacement (with an address offset size of 12 to 16 bits), immediate (size 8 to 16 bits), and register indirect.

- *Section A.4*—Support these data sizes and types: 8-, 16-, 32-, and 64-bit integers and 64-bit IEEE 754 floating-point numbers.

- *Section A.5*—Support these simple instructions, since they will dominate the number of instructions executed: load, store, add, subtract, move register-register, and shift.

- *Section A.6*—Compare equal, compare not equal, compare less, branch (with a PC-relative address at least 8 bits long), jump, call, and return.

- *Section A.7*—Use fixed instruction encoding if interested in performance, and use variable instruction encoding if interested in code size.

- *Section A.8*—Provide at least 16 general-purpose registers, be sure all addressing modes apply to all data transfer instructions, and aim for a minimalist instruction set. This section didn't cover floating-point programs, but they often use separate floating-point registers. The justification is to increase the total number of registers without raising problems in the instruction format or in the speed of the general-purpose register file. This compromise, however, is not orthogonal.

We introduce MIPS by showing how it follows these recommendations. Like most recent computers, MIPS emphasizes

- A simple load-store instruction set

- Design for pipelining efficiency (discussed in Appendix C), including a fixed instruction set encoding

- Efficiency as a compiler target

MIPS provides a good architectural model for study, not only because of the popularity of this type of processor, but also because it is an easy architecture to understand. We will use this architecture again in Appendix C and in Chapter 3, and it forms the basis for a number of exercises and programming projects.

In the years since the first MIPS processor in 1985, there have been many versions of MIPS (see Appendix K). We will use a subset of what is now called MIPS64, which will often abbreviate to just MIPS, but the full instruction set is found in Appendix K.

Registers for MIPS

MIPS64 has 32 64-bit general-purpose registers (GPRs), named R0, R1, . . . , R31. GPRs are also sometimes known as *integer registers*. Additionally, there is a set of 32 floating-point registers (FPRs), named F0, F1, . . . , F31, which can hold 32 single-precision (32-bit) values or 32 double-precision (64-bit) values. (When holding one single-precision number, the other half of the FPR is unused.) Both single- and double-precision floating-point operations (32-bit and 64-bit) are provided. MIPS also includes instructions that operate on two single-precision operands in a single 64-bit floating-point register.

The value of R0 is always 0. We shall see later how we can use this register to synthesize a variety of useful operations from a simple instruction set.

A few special registers can be transferred to and from the general-purpose registers. An example is the floating-point status register, used to hold information about the results of floating-point operations. There are also instructions for moving between an FPR and a GPR.

Data Types for MIPS

The data types are 8-bit bytes, 16-bit half words, 32-bit words, and 64-bit double words for integer data and 32-bit single precision and 64-bit double precision for floating point. Half words were added because they are found in languages like C and are popular in some programs, such as the operating systems, concerned about size of data structures. They will also become more popular if Unicode becomes widely used. Single-precision floating-point operands were added for similar reasons. (Remember the early warning that you should measure many more programs before designing an instruction set.)

The MIPS64 operations work on 64-bit integers and 32- or 64-bit floating point. Bytes, half words, and words are loaded into the general-purpose registers with either zeros or the sign bit replicated to fill the 64 bits of the GPRs. Once loaded, they are operated on with the 64-bit integer operations.

Addressing Modes for MIPS Data Transfers

The only data addressing modes are immediate and displacement, both with 16-bit fields. Register indirect is accomplished simply by placing 0 in the 16-bit displacement field, and absolute addressing with a 16-bit field is accomplished by using register 0 as the base register. Embracing zero gives us four effective modes, although only two are supported in the architecture.

MIPS memory is byte addressable with a 64-bit address. It has a mode bit that allows software to select either Big Endian or Little Endian. As it is a load-store architecture, all references between memory and either GPRs or FPRs are through loads or stores. Supporting the data types mentioned above, memory accesses involving GPRs can be to a byte, half word, word, or double word. The FPRs may be loaded and stored with single-precision or double-precision numbers. All memory accesses must be aligned.

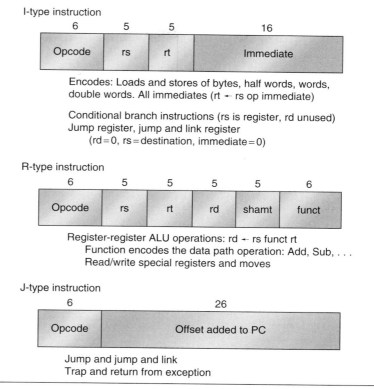

I-type instruction

6	5	5	16
Opcode	rs	rt	Immediate

Encodes: Loads and stores of bytes, half words, words, double words. All immediates (rt ← rs op immediate)

Conditional branch instructions (rs is register, rd unused)
Jump register, jump and link register
(rd = 0, rs = destination, immediate = 0)

R-type instruction

6	5	5	5	5	6
Opcode	rs	rt	rd	shamt	funct

Register-register ALU operations: rd ← rs funct rt
Function encodes the data path operation: Add, Sub, . . .
Read/write special registers and moves

J-type instruction

6	26
Opcode	Offset added to PC

Jump and jump and link
Trap and return from exception

Figure A.22 Instruction layout for MIPS. All instructions are encoded in one of three types, with common fields in the same location in each format.

MIPS Instruction Format

Since MIPS has just two addressing modes, these can be encoded into the opcode. Following the advice on making the processor easy to pipeline and decode, all instructions are 32 bits with a 6-bit primary opcode. Figure A.22 shows the instruction layout. These formats are simple while providing 16-bit fields for displacement addressing, immediate constants, or PC-relative branch addresses.

Appendix K shows a variant of MIPS—called MIPS16—which has 16-bit and 32-bit instructions to improve code density for embedded applications. We will stick to the traditional 32-bit format in this book.

MIPS Operations

MIPS supports the list of simple operations recommended above plus a few others. There are four broad classes of instructions: loads and stores, ALU operations, branches and jumps, and floating-point operations.

Any of the general-purpose or floating-point registers may be loaded or stored, except that loading R0 has no effect. Figure A.23 gives examples of the load and store instructions. Single-precision floating-point numbers occupy half a floating-point register. Conversions between single and double precision must be done explicitly. The floating-point format is IEEE 754 (see Appendix J). A list of all the MIPS instructions in our subset appears in Figure A.26 (page A-40).

To understand these figures we need to introduce a few additional extensions to our C description language used initially on page A-9:

■ A subscript is appended to the symbol ← whenever the length of the datum being transferred might not be clear. Thus, $\leftarrow_n$ means transfer an n-bit quantity. We use $x, y \leftarrow z$ to indicate that z should be transferred to x and y.

■ A subscript is used to indicate selection of a bit from a field. Bits are labeled from the most-significant bit starting at 0. The subscript may be a single digit (e.g., $\text{Regs}[\text{R4}]_0$ yields the sign bit of R4) or a subrange (e.g., $\text{Regs}[\text{R3}]_{56..63}$ yields the least-significant byte of R3).

■ The variable Mem, used as an array that stands for main memory, is indexed by a byte address and may transfer any number of bytes.

■ A superscript is used to replicate a field (e.g., 0^{48} yields a field of zeros of length 48 bits).

■ The symbol ## is used to concatenate two fields and may appear on either side of a data transfer.

Example instruction	Instruction name	Meaning
LD R1,30(R2)	Load double word	$\text{Regs}[\text{R1}] \leftarrow_{64} \text{Mem}[30+\text{Regs}[\text{R2}]]$
LD R1,1000(R0)	Load double word	$\text{Regs}[\text{R1}] \leftarrow_{64} \text{Mem}[1000+0]$
LW R1,60(R2)	Load word	$\text{Regs}[\text{R1}] \leftarrow_{64} (\text{Mem}[60+\text{Regs}[\text{R2}]]_0)^{32}\ \#\#\ \text{Mem}[60+\text{Regs}[\text{R2}]]$
LB R1,40(R3)	Load byte	$\text{Regs}[\text{R1}] \leftarrow_{64} (\text{Mem}[40+\text{Regs}[\text{R3}]]_0)^{56}\ \#\#$ $\text{Mem}[40+\text{Regs}[\text{R3}]]$
LBU R1,40(R3)	Load byte unsigned	$\text{Regs}[\text{R1}] \leftarrow_{64} 0^{56}\ \#\#\ \text{Mem}[40+\text{Regs}[\text{R3}]]$
LH R1,40(R3)	Load half word	$\text{Regs}[\text{R1}] \leftarrow_{64} (\text{Mem}[40+\text{Regs}[\text{R3}]]_0)^{48}\ \#\#$ $\text{Mem}[40+\text{Regs}[\text{R3}]]\ \#\#\ \text{Mem}[41+\text{Regs}[\text{R3}]]$
L.S F0,50(R3)	Load FP single	$\text{Regs}[\text{F0}] \leftarrow_{64} \text{Mem}[50+\text{Regs}[\text{R3}]]\ \#\#\ 0^{32}$
L.D F0,50(R2)	Load FP double	$\text{Regs}[\text{F0}] \leftarrow_{64} \text{Mem}[50+\text{Regs}[\text{R2}]]$
SD R3,500(R4)	Store double word	$\text{Mem}[500+\text{Regs}[\text{R4}]] \leftarrow_{64} \text{Regs}[\text{R3}]$
SW R3,500(R4)	Store word	$\text{Mem}[500+\text{Regs}[\text{R4}]] \leftarrow_{32} \text{Regs}[\text{R3}]_{32..63}$
S.S F0,40(R3)	Store FP single	$\text{Mem}[40+\text{Regs}[\text{R3}]] \leftarrow_{32} \text{Regs}[\text{F0}]_{0..31}$
S.D F0,40(R3)	Store FP double	$\text{Mem}[40+\text{Regs}[\text{R3}]] \leftarrow_{64} \text{Regs}[\text{F0}]$
SH R3,502(R2)	Store half	$\text{Mem}[502+\text{Regs}[\text{R2}]] \leftarrow_{16} \text{Regs}[\text{R3}]_{48..63}$
SB R2,41(R3)	Store byte	$\text{Mem}[41+\text{Regs}[\text{R3}]] \leftarrow_8 \text{Regs}[\text{R2}]_{56..63}$

Figure A.23 The load and store instructions in MIPS. All use a single addressing mode and require that the memory value be aligned. Of course, both loads and stores are available for all the data types shown.

Example instruction	Instruction name	Meaning
DADDU R1,R2,R3	Add unsigned	Regs[R1] ← Regs[R2]+Regs[R3]
DADDIU R1,R2,#3	Add immediate unsigned	Regs[R1] ← Regs[R2]+3
LUI R1,#42	Load upper immediate	Regs[R1] ← 0^{32}##42##0^{16}
DSLL R1,R2,#5	Shift left logical	Regs[R1] ← Regs[R2]<<5
SLT R1,R2,R3	Set less than	if (Regs[R2]<Regs[R3]) Regs[R1] ← 1 else Regs[R1]←0

Figure A.24 Examples of arithmetic/logical instructions on MIPS, both with and without immediates.

As an example, assuming that R8 and R10 are 64-bit registers:

$$Regs[R10]_{32..63} \leftarrow _{32}(Mem[Regs[R8]]_0)^{24} \; \#\# \; Mem[Regs[R8]]$$

means that the byte at the memory location addressed by the contents of register R8 is sign-extended to form a 32-bit quantity that is stored into the lower half of register R10. (The upper half of R10 is unchanged.)

All ALU instructions are register-register instructions. Figure A.24 gives some examples of the arithmetic/logical instructions. The operations include simple arithmetic and logical operations: add, subtract, AND, OR, XOR, and shifts. Immediate forms of all these instructions are provided using a 16-bit sign-extended immediate. The operation LUI (load upper immediate) loads bits 32 through 47 of a register, while setting the rest of the register to 0. LUI allows a 32-bit constant to be built in two instructions, or a data transfer using any constant 32-bit address in one extra instruction.

As mentioned above, R0 is used to synthesize popular operations. Loading a constant is simply an add immediate where the source operand is R0, and a register-register move is simply an add where one of the sources is R0. (We sometimes use the mnemonic LI, standing for load immediate, to represent the former, and the mnemonic MOV for the latter.)

MIPS Control Flow Instructions

MIPS provides compare instructions, which compare two registers to see if the first is less than the second. If the condition is true, these instructions place a 1 in the destination register (to represent true); otherwise, they place the value 0. Because these operations "set" a register, they are called set-equal, set-not-equal, set-less-than, and so on. There are also immediate forms of these compares.

Control is handled through a set of jumps and a set of branches. Figure A.25 gives some typical branch and jump instructions. The four jump instructions are differentiated by the two ways to specify the destination address and by whether or not a link is made. Two jumps use a 26-bit offset shifted 2 bits and then replace

Example instruction	Instruction name	Meaning
J name	Jump	$PC_{36..63} \leftarrow name$
JAL name	Jump and link	$Regs[R31] \leftarrow PC+8;\ PC_{36..63} \leftarrow name;$ $((PC+4)-2^{27}) \leq name < ((PC+4)+2^{27})$
JALR R2	Jump and link register	$Regs[R31] \leftarrow PC+8;\ PC \leftarrow Regs[R2]$
JR R3	Jump register	$PC \leftarrow Regs[R3]$
BEQZ R4,name	Branch equal zero	$if\ (Regs[R4]==0)\ PC \leftarrow name;$ $((PC+4)-2^{17}) \leq name < ((PC+4)+2^{17})$
BNE R3,R4,name	Branch not equal zero	$if\ (Regs[R3]\ !=\ Regs[R4])\ PC \leftarrow name;$ $((PC+4)-2^{17}) \leq name < ((PC+4)+2^{17})$
MOVZ R1,R2,R3	Conditional move if zero	$if\ (Regs[R3]==0)\ Regs[R1] \leftarrow Regs[R2]$

Figure A.25 Typical control flow instructions in MIPS. All control instructions, except jumps to an address in a register, are PC-relative. Note that the branch distances are longer than the address field would suggest; since MIPS instructions are all 32 bits long, the byte branch address is multiplied by 4 to get a longer distance.

the lower 28 bits of the program counter (of the instruction sequentially following the jump) to determine the destination address. The other two jump instructions specify a register that contains the destination address. There are two flavors of jumps: plain jump and jump and link (used for procedure calls). The latter places the return address—the address of the next sequential instruction—in R31.

All branches are conditional. The branch condition is specified by the instruction, which may test the register source for zero or nonzero; the register may contain a data value or the result of a compare. There are also conditional branch instructions to test for whether a register is negative and for equality between two registers. The branch-target address is specified with a 16-bit signed offset that is shifted left two places and then added to the program counter, which is pointing to the next sequential instruction. There is also a branch to test the floating-point status register for floating-point conditional branches, described later.

Appendix C and Chapter 3 show that conditional branches are a major challenge to pipelined execution; hence, many architectures have added instructions to convert a simple branch into a conditional arithmetic instruction. MIPS included conditional move on zero or not zero. The value of the destination register either is left unchanged or is replaced by a copy of one of the source registers depending on whether or not the value of the other source register is zero.

MIPS Floating-Point Operations

Floating-point instructions manipulate the floating-point registers and indicate whether the operation to be performed is single or double precision. The operations MOV.S and MOV.D copy a single-precision (MOV.S) or double-precision

(MOV.D) floating-point register to another register of the same type. The operations MFC1, MTC1, DMFC1, and DMTC1 move data between a single or double floating-point register and an integer register. Conversions from integer to floating point are also provided, and *vice versa*.

The floating-point operations are add, subtract, multiply, and divide; a suffix D is used for double precision, and a suffix S is used for single precision (e.g., ADD.D, ADD.S, SUB.D, SUB.S, MUL.D, MUL.S, DIV.D, DIV.S). Floating-point compares set a bit in the special floating-point status register that can be tested with a pair of branches: BC1T and BC1F, branch floating-point true and branch floating-point false.

To get greater performance for graphics routines, MIPS64 has instructions that perform two 32-bit floating-point operations on each half of the 64-bit floating-point register. These *paired single* operations include ADD.PS, SUB.PS, MUL.PS, and DIV.PS. (They are loaded and stored using double-precision loads and stores.)

Giving a nod toward the importance of multimedia applications, MIPS64 also includes both integer and floating-point multiply-add instructions: MADD, MADD.S, MADD.D, and MADD.PS. The registers are all the same width in these combined operations. Figure A.26 contains a list of a subset of MIPS64 operations and their meanings.

MIPS Instruction Set Usage

To give an idea of which instructions are popular, Figure A.27 shows the frequency of instructions and instruction classes for five SPECint2000 programs, and Figure A.28 shows the same data for five SPECfp2000 programs.

A.10	**Fallacies and Pitfalls**

Architects have repeatedly tripped on common, but erroneous, beliefs. In this section we look at a few of them.

Pitfall   *Designing a "high-level" instruction set feature specifically oriented to supporting a high-level language structure.*

Attempts to incorporate high-level language features in the instruction set have led architects to provide powerful instructions with a wide range of flexibility. However, often these instructions do more work than is required in the frequent case, or they don't exactly match the requirements of some languages. Many such efforts have been aimed at eliminating what in the 1970s was called the *semantic gap*. Although the idea is to supplement the instruction set with additions that bring the hardware up to the level of the language, the additions

Instruction type/opcode	Instruction meaning
Data transfers	*Move data between registers and memory, or between the integer and FP or special registers; only memory address mode is 16-bit displacement + contents of a GPR*
LB,LBU,SB	Load byte, load byte unsigned, store byte (to/from integer registers)
LH,LHU,SH	Load half word, load half word unsigned, store half word (to/from integer registers)
LW,LWU,SW	Load word, load word unsigned, store word (to/from integer registers)
LD,SD	Load double word, store double word (to/from integer registers)
L.S,L.D,S.S,S.D	Load SP float, load DP float, store SP float, store DP float
MFC0,MTC0	Copy from/to GPR to/from a special register
MOV.S,MOV.D	Copy one SP or DP FP register to another FP register
MFC1,MTC1	Copy 32 bits to/from FP registers from/to integer registers
Arithmetic/logical	*Operations on integer or logical data in GPRs; signed arithmetic trap on overflow*
DADD,DADDI,DADDU,DADDIU	Add, add immediate (all immediates are 16 bits); signed and unsigned
DSUB,DSUBU	Subtract; signed and unsigned
DMUL,DMULU,DDIV, DDIVU,MADD	Multiply and divide, signed and unsigned; multiply-add; all operations take and yield 64-bit values
AND,ANDI	And, and immediate
OR,ORI,XOR,XORI	Or, or immediate, exclusive or, exclusive or immediate
LUI	Load upper immediate; loads bits 32 to 47 of register with immediate, then sign-extends
DSLL,DSRL,DSRA,DSLLV, DSRLV,DSRAV	Shifts: both immediate (DS__) and variable form (DS__V); shifts are shift left logical, right logical, right arithmetic
SLT,SLTI,SLTU,SLTIU	Set less than, set less than immediate; signed and unsigned
Control	*Conditional branches and jumps; PC-relative or through register*
BEQZ,BNEZ	Branch GPRs equal/not equal to zero; 16-bit offset from PC + 4
BEQ,BNE	Branch GPR equal/not equal; 16-bit offset from PC + 4
BC1T,BC1F	Test comparison bit in the FP status register and branch; 16-bit offset from PC + 4
MOVN,MOVZ	Copy GPR to another GPR if third GPR is negative, zero
J,JR	Jumps: 26-bit offset from PC + 4 (J) or target in register (JR)
JAL,JALR	Jump and link: save PC + 4 in R31, target is PC-relative (JAL) or a register (JALR)
TRAP	Transfer to operating system at a vectored address
ERET	Return to user code from an exception; restore user mode
Floating point	*FP operations on DP and SP formats*
ADD.D,ADD.S,ADD.PS	Add DP, SP numbers, and pairs of SP numbers
SUB.D,SUB.S,SUB.PS	Subtract DP, SP numbers, and pairs of SP numbers
MUL.D,MUL.S,MUL.PS	Multiply DP, SP floating point, and pairs of SP numbers
MADD.D,MADD.S,MADD.PS	Multiply-add DP, SP numbers, and pairs of SP numbers
DIV.D,DIV.S,DIV.PS	Divide DP, SP floating point, and pairs of SP numbers
CVT._._	Convert instructions: CVT.x.y converts from type x to type y, where x and y are L (64-bit integer), W (32-bit integer), D (DP), or S (SP). Both operands are FPRs.
C.__.D,C.__.S	DP and SP compares: "__" = LT,GT,LE,GE,EQ,NE; sets bit in FP status register

Figure A.26 **Subset of the instructions in MIPS64.** Figure A.22 lists the formats of these instructions. SP = single precision; DP = double precision. This list can also be found on the back inside cover.

Instruction	gap	gcc	gzip	mcf	perlbmk	Integer average
load	26.5%	25.1%	20.1%	30.3%	28.7%	26%
store	10.3%	13.2%	5.1%	4.3%	16.2%	10%
add	21.1%	19.0%	26.9%	10.1%	16.7%	19%
sub	1.7%	2.2%	5.1%	3.7%	2.5%	3%
mul	1.4%	0.1%				0%
compare	2.8%	6.1%	6.6%	6.3%	3.8%	5%
load imm	4.8%	2.5%	1.5%	0.1%	1.7%	2%
cond branch	9.3%	12.1%	11.0%	17.5%	10.9%	12%
cond move	0.4%	0.6%	1.1%	0.1%	1.9%	1%
jump	0.8%	0.7%	0.8%	0.7%	1.7%	1%
call	1.6%	0.6%	0.4%	3.2%	1.1%	1%
return	1.6%	0.6%	0.4%	3.2%	1.1%	1%
shift	3.8%	1.1%	2.1%	1.1%	0.5%	2%
AND	4.3%	4.6%	9.4%	0.2%	1.2%	4%
OR	7.9%	8.5%	4.8%	17.6%	8.7%	9%
XOR	1.8%	2.1%	4.4%	1.5%	2.8%	3%
other logical	0.1%	0.4%	0.1%	0.1%	0.3%	0%
load FP						0%
store FP						0%
add FP						0%
sub FP						0%
mul FP						0%
div FP						0%
mov reg-reg FP						0%
compare FP						0%
cond mov FP						0%
other FP						0%

Figure A.27 MIPS dynamic instruction mix for five SPECint2000 programs. Note that integer register-register move instructions are included in the OR instruction. Blank entries have the value 0.0%.

can generate what Wulf, Levin, and Harbison [1981] have called a *semantic clash:*

> . . . by giving too much semantic content to the instruction, the computer designer made it possible to use the instruction only in limited contexts. [p. 43]

More often the instructions are simply overkill—they are too general for the most frequent case, resulting in unneeded work and a slower instruction. Again, the VAX CALLS is a good example. CALLS uses a callee save strategy (the registers

Instruction	applu	art	equake	lucas	swim	FP average
load	13.8%	18.1%	22.3%	10.6%	9.1%	15%
store	2.9%		0.8%	3.4%	1.3%	2%
add	30.4%	30.1%	17.4%	11.1%	24.4%	23%
sub	2.5%		0.1%	2.1%	3.8%	2%
mul	2.3%			1.2%		1%
compare		7.4%	2.1%			2%
load imm	13.7%		1.0%	1.8%	9.4%	5%
cond branch	2.5%	11.5%	2.9%	0.6%	1.3%	4%
cond mov		0.3%	0.1%			0%
jump			0.1%			0%
call			0.7%			0%
return			0.7%			0%
shift	0.7%		0.2%	1.9%		1%
AND			0.2%	1.8%		0%
OR	0.8%	1.1%	2.3%	1.0%	7.2%	2%
XOR		3.2%	0.1%			1%
other logical			0.1%			0%
load FP	11.4%	12.0%	19.7%	16.2%	16.8%	15%
store FP	4.2%	4.5%	2.7%	18.2%	5.0%	7%
add FP	2.3%	4.5%	9.8%	8.2%	9.0%	7%
sub FP	2.9%		1.3%	7.6%	4.7%	3%
mul FP	8.6%	4.1%	12.9%	9.4%	6.9%	8%
div FP	0.3%	0.6%	0.5%		0.3%	0%
mov reg-reg FP	0.7%	0.9%	1.2%	1.8%	0.9%	1%
compare FP		0.9%	0.6%	0.8%		0%
cond mov FP		0.6%		0.8%		0%
other FP				1.6%		0%

Figure A.28 MIPS dynamic instruction mix for five programs from SPECfp2000. Note that integer register-register move instructions are included in the OR instruction. Blank entries have the value 0.0%.

to be saved are specified by the callee), *but* the saving is done by the call instruction in the caller. The CALLS instruction begins with the arguments pushed on the stack, and then takes the following steps:

1. Align the stack if needed.

2. Push the argument count on the stack.

3. Save the registers indicated by the procedure call mask on the stack (as mentioned in Section A.8). The mask is kept in the called procedure's code—this

permits the callee to specify the registers to be saved by the caller even with separate compilation.

4. Push the return address on the stack, and then push the top and base of stack pointers (for the activation record).

5. Clear the condition codes, which sets the trap enable to a known state.

6. Push a word for status information and a zero word on the stack.

7. Update the two stack pointers.

8. Branch to the first instruction of the procedure.

The vast majority of calls in real programs do not require this amount of overhead. Most procedures know their argument counts, and a much faster linkage convention can be established using registers to pass arguments rather than the stack in memory. Furthermore, the CALLS instruction forces two registers to be used for linkage, while many languages require only one linkage register. Many attempts to support procedure call and activation stack management have failed to be useful, either because they do not match the language needs or because they are too general and hence too expensive to use.

The VAX designers provided a simpler instruction, JSB, that is much faster since it only pushes the return PC on the stack and jumps to the procedure. However, most VAX compilers use the more costly CALLS instructions. The call instructions were included in the architecture to standardize the procedure linkage convention. Other computers have standardized their calling convention by agreement among compiler writers and without requiring the overhead of a complex, very general procedure call instruction.

Fallacy   *There is such a thing as a typical program.*

Many people would like to believe that there is a single "typical" program that could be used to design an optimal instruction set. For example, see the synthetic benchmarks discussed in Chapter 1. The data in this appendix clearly show that programs can vary significantly in how they use an instruction set. For example, Figure A.29 shows the mix of data transfer sizes for four of the SPEC2000 programs: It would be hard to say what is typical from these four programs. The variations are even larger on an instruction set that supports a class of applications, such as decimal instructions, that are unused by other applications.

Pitfall   *Innovating at the instruction set architecture to reduce code size without accounting for the compiler.*

Figure A.30 shows the relative code sizes for four compilers for the MIPS instruction set. Whereas architects struggle to reduce code size by 30% to 40%, different compiler strategies can change code size by much larger factors. Similar to performance optimization techniques, the architect should start with the tightest code the compilers can produce before proposing hardware innovations to save space.

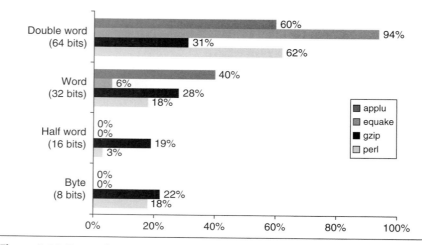

Figure A.29 **Data reference size of four programs from SPEC2000.** Although you can calculate an average size, it would be hard to claim the average is typical of programs.

Compiler	Apogee Software Version 4.1	Green Hills Multi2000 Version 2.0	Algorithmics SDE4.0B	IDT/c 7.2.1
Architecture	MIPS IV	MIPS IV	MIPS 32	MIPS 32
Processor	NEC VR5432	NEC VR5000	IDT 32334	IDT 79RC32364
Autocorrelation kernel	1.0	2.1	1.1	2.7
Convolutional encoder kernel	1.0	1.9	1.2	2.4
Fixed-point bit allocation kernel	1.0	2.0	1.2	2.3
Fixed-point complex FFT kernel	1.0	1.1	2.7	1.8
Viterbi GSM decoder kernel	1.0	1.7	0.8	1.1
Geometric mean of five kernels	1.0	1.7	1.4	2.0

Figure A.30 **Code size relative to Apogee Software Version 4.1 C compiler for Telecom application of EEMBC benchmarks.** The instruction set architectures are virtually identical, yet the code sizes vary by factors of 2. These results were reported February–June 2000.

Fallacy *An architecture with flaws cannot be successful.*

The 80x86 provides a dramatic example: The instruction set architecture is one only its creators could love (see Appendix K). Succeeding generations of Intel engineers have tried to correct unpopular architectural decisions made in designing the 80x86. For example, the 80x86 supports segmentation, whereas all others picked paging; it uses extended accumulators for integer data, but other processors use general-purpose registers; and it uses a stack for floating-point data, when everyone else abandoned execution stacks long before.

Despite these major difficulties, the 80x86 architecture has been enormously successful. The reasons are threefold: First, its selection as the microprocessor in the initial IBM PC makes 80x86 binary compatibility extremely valuable. Second, Moore's law provided sufficient resources for 80x86 microprocessors to translate to an internal RISC instruction set and then execute RISC-like instructions. This mix enables binary compatibility with the valuable PC software base and performance on par with RISC processors. Third, the very high volumes of PC microprocessors mean Intel can easily pay for the increased design cost of hardware translation. In addition, the high volumes allow the manufacturer to go up the learning curve, which lowers the cost of the product.

The larger die size and increased power for translation may be a liability for embedded applications, but it makes tremendous economic sense for the desktop. And its cost-performance in the desktop also makes it attractive for servers, with its main weakness for servers being 32-bit addresses, which was resolved with the 64-bit addresses of AMD64 (see Chapter 2).

Fallacy   *You can design a flawless architecture.*

All architecture design involves trade-offs made in the context of a set of hardware and software technologies. Over time those technologies are likely to change, and decisions that may have been correct at the time they were made look like mistakes. For example, in 1975 the VAX designers overemphasized the importance of code size efficiency, underestimating how important ease of decoding and pipelining would be five years later. An example in the RISC camp is delayed branch (see Appendix K). It was a simple matter to control pipeline hazards with five-stage pipelines, but a challenge for processors with longer pipelines that issue multiple instructions per clock cycle. In addition, almost all architectures eventually succumb to the lack of sufficient address space.

In general, avoiding such flaws in the long run would probably mean compromising the efficiency of the architecture in the short run, which is dangerous, since a new instruction set architecture must struggle to survive its first few years.

A.11   Concluding Remarks

The earliest architectures were limited in their instruction sets by the hardware technology of that time. As soon as the hardware technology permitted, computer architects began looking for ways to support high-level languages. This search led to three distinct periods of thought about how to support programs efficiently. In the 1960s, stack architectures became popular. They were viewed as being a good match for high-level languages—and they probably were, given the compiler technology of the day. In the 1970s, the main concern of architects was how to reduce software costs. This concern was met primarily by replacing software with hardware, or by providing high-level architectures that could simplify the task of software designers. The result was both the high-level language computer architecture movement and powerful architectures like the VAX, which has a large number of addressing modes, multiple data types, and a highly orthogonal architecture. In the 1980s, more sophisticated compiler technology and a renewed emphasis on processor performance saw a return to simpler architectures, based mainly on the load-store style of computer.

The following instruction set architecture changes occurred in the 1990s:

■ *Address size doubles*—The 32-bit address instruction sets for most desktop and server processors were extended to 64-bit addresses, expanding the width of the registers (among other things) to 64 bits. Appendix K gives three examples of architectures that have gone from 32 bits to 64 bits.

■ *Optimization of conditional branches via conditional execution*—In Chapter 3, we see that conditional branches can limit the performance of aggressive computer designs. Hence, there was interest in replacing conditional branches with conditional completion of operations, such as conditional move (see Appendix H), which was added to most instruction sets.

■ *Optimization of cache performance via prefetch*—Chapter 2 explains the increasing role of memory hierarchy in the performance of computers, with a cache miss on some computers taking as many instruction times as page faults took on earlier computers. Hence, prefetch instructions were added to try to hide the cost of cache misses by prefetching (see Chapter 2).

■ *Support for multimedia*—Most desktop and embedded instruction sets were extended with support for multimedia applications.

■ *Faster floating-point operations*—Appendix J describes operations added to enhance floating-point performance, such as operations that perform a multiply and an add and paired single execution. (We include them in MIPS.)

Between 1970 and 1985 many thought the primary job of the computer architect was the design of instruction sets. As a result, textbooks of that era emphasize instruction set design, much as computer architecture textbooks of the 1950s and 1960s emphasized computer arithmetic. The educated architect was expected to have strong opinions about the strengths and especially the weaknesses of the popular computers. The importance of binary compatibility in quashing innovations in instruction set design was unappreciated by many researchers and textbook writers, giving the impression that many architects would get a chance to design an instruction set.

The definition of computer architecture today has been expanded to include design and evaluation of the full computer system—not just the definition of the instruction set and not just the processor—and hence there are plenty of topics for the architect to study. In fact, the material in this appendix was a central point of the book in its first edition in 1990, but now is included in an appendix primarily as reference material!

Appendix K may satisfy readers interested in instruction set architecture; it describes a variety of instruction sets, which are either important in the marketplace today or historically important, and it compares nine popular load-store computers with MIPS.

A.12 Historical Perspective and References

Section L.4 (available online) features a discussion on the evolution of instruction sets and includes references for further reading and exploration of related topics.

Exercises by Gregory D. Peterson

A.1   [15] <A.9> Compute the effective CPI for MIPS using Figure A.27. Assume we have made the following measurements of average CPI for instruction types:

Instruction	Clock Cycles
All ALU instructions	1.0
Loads-stores	1.4
Conditional branches	
Taken	2.0
Not taken	1.5
Jumps	1.2

Assume that 60% of the conditional branches are taken and that all instructions in the "other" category of Figure A.27 are ALU instructions. Average the instruction frequencies of gap and gcc to obtain the instruction mix.

A.2   [15] <A.9> Compute the effective CPI for MIPS using Figure A.27 and the table above. Average the instruction frequencies of gzip and perlbmk to obtain the instruction mix.

A.3   [20] <A.9> Compute the effective CPI for MIPS using Figure A.28. Assume we have made the following measurements of average CPI for instruction types:

Instruction	Clock Cycles
All ALU instructions	1.0
Loads-stores	1.4
Conditional branches:	
Taken	2.0
Not taken	1.5
Jumps	1.2
FP multiply	6.0
FP add	4.0
FP divide	20.0
Load-store FP	1.5
Other FP	2.0

Assume that 60% of the conditional branches are taken and that all instructions in the "other" category of Figure A.28 are ALU instructions. Average the instruction frequencies of lucas and swim to obtain the instruction mix.

A.4 [20] <A.9> Compute the effective CPI for MIPS using Figure A.28 and the table above. Average the instruction frequencies of applu and art to obtain the instruction mix.

A.5 [10] <A.8> Consider this high-level code sequence of three statements:

```
A = B + C;
B = A + C;
D = A - B;
```

Use the technique of copy propagation (see Figure A.20) to transform the code sequence to the point where no operand is a computed value. Note the instances in which the transformation has reduced the computational work of a statement and those cases where the work has increased. What does this suggest about the technical challenge faced in trying to satisfy the desire for optimizing compilers?

A.6 [30] <A.8> Compiler optimizations may result in improvements to code size and/or performance. Consider one or more of the benchmark programs from the SPEC CPU2006 suite. Use a processor available to you and the GNU C compiler to optimize the program using no optimization, –O1, –O2, and –O3. Compare the performance and size of the resulting programs. Also compare your results to Figure A.21.

A.7 [20/20] <A.2, A.9> Consider the following fragment of C code:

```
for (i = 0; i <= 100; i++)
{ A[i] = B[i] + C; }
```

Assume that A and B are arrays of 64-bit integers, and C and i are 64-bit integers. Assume that all data values and their addresses are kept in memory (at addresses 1000, 3000, 5000, and 7000 for A, B, C, and i, respectively) except when they are operated on. Assume that values in registers are lost between iterations of the loop.

a. [20] <A.2, A.9> Write the code for MIPS. How many instructions are required dynamically? How many memory-data references will be executed? What is the code size in bytes?

b. [20] <A.2> Write the code for x86. How many instructions are required dynamically? How many memory-data references will be executed? What is the code size in bytes?

A.8 [10/10/10] <A.2, A.7> For the following we consider instruction encoding for instruction set architectures.

a. [10] <A.2, A.7> Consider the case of a processor with an instruction length of 12 bits and with 32 general-purpose registers so the size of the address fields is 5 bits. Is it possible to have instruction encodings for the following?

- 3 two-address instructions
- 30 one-address instructions
- 45 zero-address instructions

b. [10] <A.2, A.7> Assuming the same instruction length and address field sizes as above, determine if it is possible to have

- 3 two-address instructions
- 31 one-address instructions
- 35 zero-address instructions

Explain your answer.

c. [10] <A.2, A.7> Assume the same instruction length and address field sizes as above. Further assume there are already 3 two-address and 24 zero-address instructions. What is the maximum number of one-address instructions that can be encoded for this processor?

A.9 [10/15] <A.2> For the following assume that values A, B, C, D, E, and F reside in memory. Also assume that instruction operation codes are represented in 8 bits, memory addresses are 64 bits, and register addresses are 6 bits.

a. [10] <A.2> For each instruction set architecture shown in Figure A.2, how many addresses, or names, appear in each instruction for the code to compute C = A + B, and what is the total code size?

b. [15] <A.2> Some of the instruction set architectures in Figure A.2 destroy operands in the course of computation. This loss of data values from processor internal storage has performance consequences. For each architecture in Figure A.2, write the code sequence to compute:

```
C = A + B
D = A - E
F = C + D
```

In your code, mark each operand that is destroyed during execution and mark each "overhead" instruction that is included just to overcome this loss of data from processor internal storage. What is the total code size, the number of bytes of instructions and data moved to or from memory, the number of overhead instructions, and the number of overhead data bytes for each of your code sequences?

A.10 [20] <A.2, A.7, A.9> The design of MIPS provides for 32 general-purpose registers and 32 floating-point registers. If registers are good, are more registers better? List and discuss as many trade-offs as you can that should be considered by instruction set architecture designers examining whether to, and how much to, increase the number of MIPS registers.

A.11   [5] <A.3> Consider a C struct that includes the following members:

```
struct foo {
        char a;
        bool b;
        int c;
        double d;
        short e;
        float f;
        double g;
        char * cptr;
        float * fptr;
        int x;
};
```

For a 32-bit machine, what is the size of the foo struct? What is the minimum size required for this struct, assuming you may arrange the order of the struct members as you wish? What about for a 64-bit machine?

A.12   [30] <A.7> Many computer manufacturers now include tools or simulators that allow you to measure the instruction set usage of a user program. Among the methods in use are machine simulation, hardware-supported trapping, and a compiler technique that instruments the object code module by inserting counters. Find a processor available to you that includes such a tool. Use it to measure the instruction set mix for one of the SPEC CPU2006 benchmarks. Compare the results to those shown in this chapter.

A.13   [30] <A.8> Newer processors such as Intel's i7 Sandy Bridge include support for AVX vector/multimedia instructions. Write a dense matrix multiply function using single-precision values and compile it with different compilers and optimization flags. Linear algebra codes using Basic Linear Algebra Subroutine (BLAS) routines such as SGEMM include optimized versions of dense matrix multiply. Compare the code size and performance of your code to that of BLAS SGEMM. Explore what happens when using double-precision values and DGEMM.

A.14   [30] <A.8> For the SGEMM code developed above for the i7 processor, include the use of AVX intrinsics to improve the performance. In particular, try to vectorize your code to better utilize the AVX hardware. Compare the code size and performance to the original code.

A.15   [30] <A.7, A.9> SPIM is a popular simulator for simulating MIPS processors. Use SPIM to measure the instruction set mix for some SPEC CPU2006 benchmark programs.

A.16   [35/35/35/35] <A.2–A.8> gcc targets most modern instruction set architectures (see *www.gnu.org/software/gcc/*). Create a version of gcc for several architectures that you have access to, such as x86, MIPS, PowerPC, and ARM.

     a. [35] <A.2–A.8> Compile a subset of SPEC CPU2006 integer benchmarks and create a table of code sizes. Which architecture is best for each program?

b. [35] <A.2–A.8> Compile a subset of SPEC CPU2006 floating-point benchmarks and create a table of code sizes. Which architecture is best for each program?

c. [35] <A.2–A.8> Compile a subset of EEMBC AutoBench benchmarks (see *www.eembc.org/home.php*) and create a table of code sizes. Which architecture is best for each program?

d. [35] <A.2–A.8> Compile a subset of EEMBC FPBench floating-point benchmarks and create a table of code sizes. Which architecture is best for each program?

A.17 [40] <A.2–A.8> Power efficiency has become very important for modern processors, particularly for embedded systems. Create a version of gcc for two architectures that you have access to, such as x86, MIPS, PowerPC, and ARM. Compile a subset of EEMBC benchmarks while using EnergyBench to measure energy usage during execution. Compare code size, performance, and energy usage for the processors. Which is best for each program?

A.18 [20/15/15/20] Your task is to compare the memory efficiency of four different styles of instruction set architectures. The architecture styles are

- *Accumulator*—All operations occur between a single register and a memory location.

- *Memory-memory*—All instruction addresses reference only memory locations.

- *Stack*—All operations occur on top of the stack. Push and pop are the only instructions that access memory; all others remove their operands from the stack and replace them with the result. The implementation uses a hardwired stack for only the top two stack entries, which keeps the processor circuit very small and low cost. Additional stack positions are kept in memory locations, and accesses to these stack positions require memory references.

- *Load-store*—All operations occur in registers, and register-to-register instructions have three register names per instruction.

To measure memory efficiency, make the following assumptions about all four instruction sets:

- All instructions are an integral number of bytes in length.

- The opcode is always one byte (8 bits).

- Memory accesses use direct, or absolute, addressing.

- The variables A, B, C, and D are initially in memory.

a. [20] <A.2, A.3> Invent your own assembly language mnemonics (Figure A.2 provides a useful sample to generalize), and for each architecture write the best equivalent assembly language code for this high-level language code sequence:

```
A = B + C;
B = A + C;
D = A - B;
```

b. [15] <A.3> Label each instance in your assembly codes for part (a) where a value is loaded from memory after having been loaded once. Also label each instance in your code where the result of one instruction is passed to another instruction as an operand, and further classify these events as involving storage within the processor or storage in memory.

c. [15] <A.7> Assume that the given code sequence is from a small, embedded computer application, such as a microwave oven controller, that uses a 16-bit memory address and data operands. If a load-store architecture is used, assume it has 16 general-purpose registers. For each architecture answer the following questions: How many instruction bytes are fetched? How many bytes of data are transferred from/to memory? Which architecture is most efficient as measured by total memory traffic (code + data)?

d. [20] <A.7> Now assume a processor with 64-bit memory addresses and data operands. For each architecture answer the questions of part (c). How have the relative merits of the architectures changed for the chosen metrics?

A.19 [30] <A.2, A.3> Use the four different instruction set architecture styles from above, but assume that the memory operations supported include register indirect as well as direct addressing. Invent your own assembly language mnemonics (Figure A.2 provides a useful sample to generalize), and for each architecture write the best equivalent assembly language code for this fragment of C code:

```
for (i = 0; i <= 100; i++)
{ A[i] = B[i] + C; }
```

Assume that A and B are arrays of 64-bit integers, and C and i are 64-bit integers.

The second and third columns contain the cumulative percentage of the data references and branches, respectively, that can be accommodated with the corresponding number of bits of magnitude in the displacement. These are the average distances of all the integer and floating-point programs in Figures A.8 and A.15.

A.20 [20/20/20] <A.3> We are designing instruction set formats for a load-store architecture and are trying to decide whether it is worthwhile to have multiple offset lengths for branches and memory references. The length of an instruction would be equal to 16 bits + offset length in bits, so ALU instructions will be 16 bits. Figure A.31 contains data on offset size for the Alpha architecture with full optimization for SPEC CPU2000. For instruction set frequencies, use the data for MIPS from the average of the five benchmarks for the load-store machine in Figure A.27. Assume that the miscellaneous instructions are all ALU instructions that use only registers.

Number of offset magnitude bits	Cumulative data references	Cumulative branches
0	30.4%	0.1%
1	33.5%	2.8%
2	35.0%	10.5%
3	40.0%	22.9%
4	47.3%	36.5%
5	54.5%	57.4%
6	60.4%	72.4%
7	66.9%	85.2%
8	71.6%	90.5%
9	73.3%	93.1%
10	74.2%	95.1%
11	74.9%	96.0%
12	76.6%	96.8%
13	87.9%	97.4%
14	91.9%	98.1%
15	100%	98.5%
16	100%	99.5%
17	100%	99.8%
18	100%	99.9%
19	100%	100%
20	100%	100%
21	100%	100%

Figure A.31 Data on offset size for the Alpha architecture with full optimization for SPEC CPU2000.

a. [20] <A.3> Suppose offsets are permitted to be 0, 8, 16, or 24 bits in length, including the sign bit. What is the average length of an executed instruction?

b. [20] <A.3> Suppose we want a fixed-length instruction and we chose a 24-bit instruction length (for everything, including ALU instructions). For every offset of longer than 8 bits, additional instructions are required. Determine the number of instruction bytes fetched in this machine with fixed instruction size versus those fetched with a byte-variable-sized instruction as defined in part (a).

c. [20] <A.3> Now suppose we use a fixed offset length of 24 bits so that no additional instruction is ever required. How many instruction bytes would be required? Compare this result to your answer to part (b).

A.21 [20/20] <A.3, A.6, A.9> The size of displacement values needed for the displacement addressing mode or for PC-relative addressing can be extracted from compiled applications. Use a disassembler with one or more of the SPEC CPU2006 benchmarks compiled for the MIPS processor.

    a. [20] <A.3, A.9> For each instruction using displacement addressing, record the displacement value used. Create a histogram of displacement values. Compare the results to those shown in this chapter in Figure A.8.

    b. [20] <A.6, A.9> For each branch instruction using PC-relative addressing, record the displacement value used. Create a histogram of displacement values. Compare the results to those shown in this chapter in Figure A.15.

A.22 [15/15/10/10] <A.3> The value represented by the hexadecimal number 434F 4D50 5554 4552 is to be stored in an aligned 64-bit double word.

    a. [15] <A.3> Using the physical arrangement of the first row in Figure A.5, write the value to be stored using Big Endian byte order. Next, interpret each byte as an ASCII character and below each byte write the corresponding character, forming the character string as it would be stored in Big Endian order.

    b. [15] <A.3> Using the same physical arrangement as in part (a), write the value to be stored using Little Endian byte order, and below each byte write the corresponding ASCII character.

    c. [10] <A.3> What are the hexadecimal values of all misaligned 2-byte words that can be read from the given 64-bit double word when stored in Big Endian byte order?

    d. [10] <A.3> What are the hexadecimal values of all misaligned 4-byte words that can be read from the given 64-bit double word when stored in Little Endian byte order?

A.23 [Discussion] <A.2–A.12> Consider typical applications for desktop, server, cloud, and embedded computing. How would instruction set architecture be impacted for machines targeting each of these markets?

B

Review of Memory Hierarchy

Cache: a safe place for hiding or storing things.

**Webster's New World Dictionary of the
American Language**
Second College Edition (1976)

Introduction

This appendix is a quick refresher of the memory hierarchy, including the basics of cache and virtual memory, performance equations, and simple optimizations. This first section reviews the following 36 terms:

cache	*fully associative*	*write allocate*
virtual memory	*dirty bit*	*unified cache*
memory stall cycles	*block offset*	*misses per instruction*
direct mapped	*write-back*	*block*
valid bit	*data cache*	*locality*
block address	*hit time*	*address trace*
write-through	*cache miss*	*set*
instruction cache	*page fault*	*random replacement*
average memory access time	*miss rate*	*index field*
cache hit	*n-way set associative*	*no-write allocate*
page	*least recently used*	*write buffer*
miss penalty	*tag field*	*write stall*

If this review goes too quickly, you might want to look at Chapter 7 in *Computer Organization and Design*, which we wrote for readers with less experience.

Cache is the name given to the highest or first level of the memory hierarchy encountered once the address leaves the processor. Since the principle of locality applies at many levels, and taking advantage of locality to improve performance is popular, the term *cache* is now applied whenever buffering is employed to reuse commonly occurring items. Examples include *file caches, name caches,* and so on.

When the processor finds a requested data item in the cache, it is called a *cache hit*. When the processor does not find a data item it needs in the cache, a *cache miss* occurs. A fixed-size collection of data containing the requested word, called a *block* or line run, is retrieved from the main memory and placed into the cache. *Temporal locality* tells us that we are likely to need this word again in the near future, so it is useful to place it in the cache where it can be accessed quickly. Because of *spatial locality*, there is a high probability that the other data in the block will be needed soon.

The time required for the cache miss depends on both the latency and bandwidth of the memory. Latency determines the time to retrieve the first word of the block, and bandwidth determines the time to retrieve the rest of this block. A cache miss is handled by hardware and causes processors using in-order execution to pause, or stall, until the data are available. With out-of-order execution, an

Level	1	2	3	4
Name	Registers	Cache	Main memory	Disk storage
Typical size	<1 KB	32 KB–8 MB	<512 GB	>1 TB
Implementation technology	Custom memory with multiple ports, CMOS	On-chip CMOS SRAM	CMOS DRAM	Magnetic disk
Access time (ns)	0.15–0.30	0.5–15	30–200	5,000,000
Bandwidth (MB/sec)	100,000–1,000,000	10,000–40,000	5000–20,000	50–500
Managed by	Compiler	Hardware	Operating system	Operating system/operator
Backed by	Cache	Main memory	Disk	Other disks and DVD

Figure B.1 **The typical levels in the hierarchy slow down and get larger as we move away from the processor for a large workstation or small server.** Embedded computers might have no disk storage and much smaller memories and caches. The access times increase as we move to lower levels of the hierarchy, which makes it feasible to manage the transfer less responsively. The implementation technology shows the typical technology used for these functions. The access time is given in nanoseconds for typical values in 2006; these times will decrease over time. Bandwidth is given in megabytes per second between levels in the memory hierarchy. Bandwidth for disk storage includes both the media and the buffered interfaces.

instruction using the result must still wait, but other instructions may proceed during the miss.

Similarly, not all objects referenced by a program need to reside in main memory. *Virtual memory* means some objects may reside on disk. The address space is usually broken into fixed-size blocks, called *pages*. At any time, each page resides either in main memory or on disk. When the processor references an item within a page that is not present in the cache or main memory, a *palt* occurs, and the entire page is moved from the disk to main memory. Since page faults take so long, they are handled in software and the processor is not stalled. The processor usually switches to some other task while the disk access occurs. From a high-level perspective, the reliance on locality of references and the relative relationships in size and relative cost per bit of cache versus main memory are similar to those of main memory versus disk.

Figure B.1 shows the range of sizes and access times of each level in the memory hierarchy for computers ranging from high-end desktops to low-end servers.

Cache Performance Review

Because of locality and the higher speed of smaller memories, a memory hierarchy can substantially improve performance. One method to evaluate cache performance is to expand our processor execution time equation from Chapter 1.

We now account for the number of cycles during which the processor is stalled waiting for a memory access, which we call the *memory stall cycles*. The performance is then the product of the clock cycle time and the sum of the processor cycles and the memory stall cycles:

$$\text{CPU execution time} = (\text{CPU clock cycles} + \text{Memory stall cycles}) \times \text{Clock cycle time}$$

This equation assumes that the CPU clock cycles include the time to handle a cache hit and that the processor is stalled during a cache miss. Section B.2 reexamines this simplifying assumption.

The number of memory stall cycles depends on both the number of misses and the cost per miss, which is called the *miss penalty:*

$$
\begin{aligned}
\text{Memory stall cycles} &= \text{Number of misses} \times \text{Miss penalty} \\
&= \text{IC} \times \frac{\text{Misses}}{\text{Instruction}} \times \text{Miss penalty} \\
&= \text{IC} \times \frac{\text{Memory accesses}}{\text{Instruction}} \times \text{Miss rate} \times \text{Miss penalty}
\end{aligned}
$$

The advantage of the last form is that the components can be easily measured. We already know how to measure instruction count (IC). (For speculative processors, we only count instructions that commit.) Measuring the number of memory references per instruction can be done in the same fashion; every instruction requires an instruction access, and it is easy to decide if it also requires a data access.

Note that we calculated miss penalty as an average, but we will use it below as if it were a constant. The memory behind the cache may be busy at the time of the miss because of prior memory requests or memory refresh. The number of clock cycles also varies at interfaces between different clocks of the processor, bus, and memory. Thus, please remember that using a single number for miss penalty is a simplification.

The component *miss rate* is simply the fraction of cache accesses that result in a miss (i.e., number of accesses that miss divided by number of accesses). Miss rates can be measured with cache simulators that take an *address trace* of the instruction and data references, simulate the cache behavior to determine which references hit and which miss, and then report the hit and miss totals. Many microprocessors today provide hardware to count the number of misses and memory references, which is a much easier and faster way to measure miss rate.

The formula above is an approximation since the miss rates and miss penalties are often different for reads and writes. Memory stall clock cycles could then be defined in terms of the number of memory accesses per instruction, miss penalty (in clock cycles) for reads and writes, and miss rate for reads and writes:

$$
\begin{aligned}
\text{Memory stall clock cycles} = &\ \text{IC} \times \text{Reads per instruction} \times \text{Read miss rate} \times \text{Read miss penalty} \\
&+ \text{IC} \times \text{Writes per instruction} \times \text{Write miss rate} \times \text{Write miss penalty}
\end{aligned}
$$

We normally simplify the complete formula by combining the reads and writes and finding the average miss rates and miss penalty for reads *and* writes:

$$\text{Memory stall clock cycles} = \text{IC} \times \frac{\text{Memory accesses}}{\text{Instruction}} \times \text{Miss rate} \times \text{Miss penalty}$$

The miss rate is one of the most important measures of cache design, but, as we will see in later sections, not the only measure.

Example   Assume we have a computer where the cycles per instruction (CPI) is 1.0 when all memory accesses hit in the cache. The only data accesses are loads and stores, and these total 50% of the instructions. If the miss penalty is 25 clock cycles and the miss rate is 2%, how much faster would the computer be if all instructions were cache hits?

Answer   First compute the performance for the computer that always hits:

$$\begin{aligned} \text{CPU execution time} &= (\text{CPU clock cycles} + \text{Memory stall cycles}) \times \text{Clock cycle} \\ &= (\text{IC} \times \text{CPI} + 0) \times \text{Clock cycle} \\ &= \text{IC} \times 1.0 \times \text{Clock cycle} \end{aligned}$$

Now for the computer with the real cache, first we compute memory stall cycles:

$$\begin{aligned} \text{Memory stall cycles} &= \text{IC} \times \frac{\text{Memory accesses}}{\text{Instruction}} \times \text{Miss rate} \times \text{Miss penalty} \\ &= \text{IC} \times (1 + 0.5) \times 0.02 \times 25 \\ &= \text{IC} \times 0.75 \end{aligned}$$

where the middle term $(1 + 0.5)$ represents one instruction access and 0.5 data accesses per instruction. The total performance is thus

$$\begin{aligned} \text{CPU execution time}_{\text{cache}} &= (\text{IC} \times 1.0 + \text{IC} \times 0.75) \times \text{Clock cycle} \\ &= 1.75 \times \text{IC} \times \text{Clock cycle} \end{aligned}$$

The performance ratio is the inverse of the execution times:

$$\begin{aligned} \frac{\text{CPU execution time}_{\text{cache}}}{\text{CPU execution time}} &= \frac{1.75 \times \text{IC} \times \text{Clock cycle}}{1.0 \times \text{IC} \times \text{Clock cycle}} \\ &= 1.75 \end{aligned}$$

The computer with no cache misses is 1.75 times faster.

Some designers prefer measuring miss rate as *misses per instruction* rather than misses per memory reference. These two are related:

$$\frac{\text{Misses}}{\text{Instruction}} = \frac{\text{Miss rate} \times \text{Memory accesses}}{\text{Instruction count}} = \text{Miss rate} \times \frac{\text{Memory accesses}}{\text{Instruction}}$$

The latter formula is useful when you know the average number of memory accesses per instruction because it allows you to convert miss rate into misses per instruction, and vice versa. For example, we can turn the miss rate per memory reference in the previous example into misses per instruction:

$$\frac{\text{Misses}}{\text{Instruction}} = \text{Miss rate} \times \frac{\text{Memory accesses}}{\text{Instruction}} = 0.02 \times (1.5) = 0.030$$

By the way, misses per instruction are often reported as misses per 1000 instructions to show integers instead of fractions. Thus, the answer above could also be expressed as 30 misses per 1000 instructions.

The advantage of misses per instruction is that it is independent of the hardware implementation. For example, speculative processors fetch about twice as many instructions as are actually committed, which can artificially reduce the miss rate if measured as misses per memory reference rather than per instruction. The drawback is that misses per instruction is architecture dependent; for example, the average number of memory accesses per instruction may be very different for an 80x86 versus MIPS. Thus, misses per instruction are most popular with architects working with a single computer family, although the similarity of RISC architectures allows one to give insights into others.

Example To show equivalency between the two miss rate equations, let's redo the example above, this time assuming a miss rate per 1000 instructions of 30. What is memory stall time in terms of instruction count?

Answer Recomputing the memory stall cycles:

$$\text{Memory stall cycles} = \text{Number of misses} \times \text{Miss penalty}$$
$$= IC \times \frac{\text{Misses}}{\text{Instruction}} \times \text{Miss penalty}$$
$$= IC/1000 \times \frac{\text{Misses}}{\text{Instruction} \times 1000} \times \text{Miss penalty}$$
$$= IC/1000 \times 30 \times 25$$
$$= IC/1000 \times 750$$
$$= IC \times 0.75$$

We get the same answer as on page B-5, showing equivalence of the two equations.

Four Memory Hierarchy Questions

We continue our introduction to caches by answering the four common questions for the first level of the memory hierarchy:

Q1: Where can a block be placed in the upper level? (*block placement*)

Q2: How is a block found if it is in the upper level? (*block identification*)

Q3: Which block should be replaced on a miss? (*block replacement*)

Q4: What happens on a write? (*write strategy*)

The answers to these questions help us understand the different trade-offs of memories at different levels of a hierarchy; hence, we ask these four questions on every example.

Q1: Where Can a Block Be Placed in a Cache?

Figure B.2 shows that the restrictions on where a block is placed create three categories of cache organization:

■   If each block has only one place it can appear in the cache, the cache is said to be *direct mapped*. The mapping is usually

$$(\textit{Block address}) \text{ MOD } (\textit{Number of blocks in cache})$$

■   If a block can be placed anywhere in the cache, the cache is said to be *fully associative*.

■   If a block can be placed in a restricted set of places in the cache, the cache is *set associative*. A *set* is a group of blocks in the cache. A block is first mapped onto a set, and then the block can be placed anywhere within that set. The set is usually chosen by *bit selection*; that is,

$$(\textit{Block address}) \text{ MOD } (\textit{Number of sets in cache})$$

If there are n blocks in a set, the cache placement is called *n-way set associative*.

The range of caches from direct mapped to fully associative is really a continuum of levels of set associativity. Direct mapped is simply one-way set associative, and a fully associative cache with m blocks could be called "m-way set associative." Equivalently, direct mapped can be thought of as having m sets, and fully associative as having one set.

The vast majority of processor caches today are direct mapped, two-way set associative, or four-way set associative, for reasons we will see shortly.

Q2: How Is a Block Found If It Is in the Cache?

Caches have an address tag on each block frame that gives the block address. The tag of every cache block that might contain the desired information is checked to see if it matches the block address from the processor. As a rule, all possible tags are searched in parallel because speed is critical.

There must be a way to know that a cache block does not have valid information. The most common procedure is to add a *valid bit* to the tag to say whether or not this entry contains a valid address. If the bit is not set, there cannot be a match on this address.

Before proceeding to the next question, let's explore the relationship of a processor address to the cache. Figure B.3 shows how an address is divided. The first division is between the *block address* and the *block offset*. The block

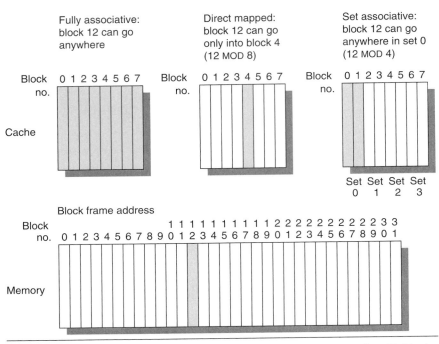

Figure B.2 This example cache has eight block frames and memory has 32 blocks. The three options for caches are shown left to right. In fully associative, block 12 from the lower level can go into any of the eight block frames of the cache. With direct mapped, block 12 can only be placed into block frame 4 (12 modulo 8). Set associative, which has some of both features, allows the block to be placed anywhere in set 0 (12 modulo 4). With two blocks per set, this means block 12 can be placed either in block 0 or in block 1 of the cache. Real caches contain thousands of block frames, and real memories contain millions of blocks. The set associative organization has four sets with two blocks per set, called *two-way set associative*. Assume that there is nothing in the cache and that the block address in question identifies lower-level block 12.

frame address can be further divided into the *tag field* and the *index field*. The block offset field selects the desired data from the block, the index field selects the set, and the tag field is compared against it for a hit. Although the comparison could be made on more of the address than the tag, there is no need because of the following:

■ The offset should not be used in the comparison, since the entire block is present or not, and hence all block offsets result in a match by definition.

■ Checking the index is redundant, since it was used to select the set to be checked. An address stored in set 0, for example, must have 0 in the index field or it couldn't be stored in set 0; set 1 must have an index value of 1; and so on. This optimization saves hardware and power by reducing the width of memory size for the cache tag.

Block address		Block
Tag	Index	offset

Figure B.3 The three portions of an address in a set associative or direct-mapped cache. The tag is used to check all the blocks in the set, and the index is used to select the set. The block offset is the address of the desired data within the block. Fully associative caches have no index field.

If the total cache size is kept the same, increasing associativity increases the number of blocks per set, thereby decreasing the size of the index and increasing the size of the tag. That is, the tag-index boundary in Figure B.3 moves to the right with increasing associativity, with the end point of fully associative caches having no index field.

Q3: Which Block Should Be Replaced on a Cache Miss?

When a miss occurs, the cache controller must select a block to be replaced with the desired data. A benefit of direct-mapped placement is that hardware decisions are simplified—in fact, so simple that there is no choice: Only one block frame is checked for a hit, and only that block can be replaced. With fully associative or set associative placement, there are many blocks to choose from on a miss. There are three primary strategies employed for selecting which block to replace:

- *Random*—To spread allocation uniformly, candidate blocks are randomly selected. Some systems generate pseudorandom block numbers to get reproducible behavior, which is particularly useful when debugging hardware.

- *Least recently used* (LRU)—To reduce the chance of throwing out information that will be needed soon, accesses to blocks are recorded. Relying on the past to predict the future, the block replaced is the one that has been unused for the longest time. LRU relies on a corollary of locality: If recently used blocks are likely to be used again, then a good candidate for disposal is the least recently used block.

- *First in, first out* (FIFO)—Because LRU can be complicated to calculate, this approximates LRU by determining the *oldest* block rather than the LRU.

A virtue of random replacement is that it is simple to build in hardware. As the number of blocks to keep track of increases, LRU becomes increasingly expensive and is usually only approximated. A common approximation (often called pseudo-LRU) has a set of bits for each set in the cache with each bit corresponding to a single way (a *way* is bank in a set associative cache; there are four ways in four-way set associative cache) in the cache. When a set is accessed, the bit corresponding to the way containing the desired block is turned on; if all the bits associated with a set are turned on, they are reset with the exception of the most recently turned on bit. When a block must be replaced, the

	Associativity								
	Two-way			Four-way			Eight-way		
Size	LRU	Random	FIFO	LRU	Random	FIFO	LRU	Random	FIFO
16 KB	114.1	117.3	115.5	111.7	115.1	113.3	109.0	111.8	110.4
64 KB	103.4	104.3	103.9	102.4	102.3	103.1	99.7	100.5	100.3
256 KB	92.2	92.1	92.5	92.1	92.1	92.5	92.1	92.1	92.5

Figure B.4 Data cache misses per 1000 instructions comparing least recently used, random, and first in, first out replacement for several sizes and associativities. There is little difference between LRU and random for the largest size cache, with LRU outperforming the others for smaller caches. FIFO generally outperforms random in the smaller cache sizes. These data were collected for a block size of 64 bytes for the Alpha architecture using 10 SPEC2000 benchmarks. Five are from SPECint2000 (gap, gcc, gzip, mcf, and perl) and five are from SPECfp2000 (applu, art, equake, lucas, and swim). We will use this computer and these benchmarks in most figures in this appendix.

processor chooses a block from the way whose bit is turned off, often randomly if more than one choice is available. This approximates LRU, since the block that is replaced will not have been accessed since the last time that all the blocks in the set were accessed. Figure B.4 shows the difference in miss rates between LRU, random, and FIFO replacement.

Q4: What Happens on a Write?

Reads dominate processor cache accesses. All instruction accesses are reads, and most instructions don't write to memory. Figures A.32 and A.33 in Appendix A suggest a mix of 10% stores and 26% loads for MIPS programs, making writes 10%/(100% + 26% + 10%) or about 7% of the overall memory traffic. Of the *data cache* traffic, writes are 10%/(26% + 10%) or about 28%. Making the common case fast means optimizing caches for reads, especially since processors traditionally wait for reads to complete but need not wait for writes. Amdahl's law (Section 1.9) reminds us, however, that high-performance designs cannot neglect the speed of writes.

Fortunately, the common case is also the easy case to make fast. The block can be read from the cache at the same time that the tag is read and compared, so the block read begins as soon as the block address is available. If the read is a hit, the requested part of the block is passed on to the processor immediately. If it is a miss, there is no benefit—but also no harm except more power in desktop and server computers; just ignore the value read.

Such optimism is not allowed for writes. Modifying a block cannot begin until the tag is checked to see if the address is a hit. Because tag checking cannot occur in parallel, writes normally take longer than reads. Another complexity is that the processor also specifies the size of the write, usually between 1 and 8 bytes; only that portion of a block can be changed. In contrast, reads can access more bytes than necessary without fear.

The write policies often distinguish cache designs. There are two basic options when writing to the cache:

- *Write-through*—The information is written to both the block in the cache *and* to the block in the lower-level memory.

- *Write-back*—The information is written only to the block in the cache. The modified cache block is written to main memory only when it is replaced.

To reduce the frequency of writing back blocks on replacement, a feature called the *dirty bit* is commonly used. This status bit indicates whether the block is *dirty* (modified while in the cache) or *clean* (not modified). If it is clean, the block is not written back on a miss, since identical information to the cache is found in lower levels.

Both write-back and write-through have their advantages. With write-back, writes occur at the speed of the cache memory, and multiple writes within a block require only one write to the lower-level memory. Since some writes don't go to memory, write-back uses less memory bandwidth, making write-back attractive in multiprocessors. Since write-back uses the rest of the memory hierarchy and memory interconnect less than write-through, it also saves power, making it attractive for embedded applications.

Write-through is easier to implement than write-back. The cache is always clean, so unlike write-back read misses never result in writes to the lower level. Write-through also has the advantage that the next lower level has the most current copy of the data, which simplifies data coherency. Data coherency is important for multiprocessors and for I/O, which we examine in Chapter 4 and Appendix D. Multilevel caches make write-through more viable for the upper-level caches, as the writes need only propagate to the next lower level rather than all the way to main memory.

As we will see, I/O and multiprocessors are fickle: They want write-back for processor caches to reduce the memory traffic and write-through to keep the cache consistent with lower levels of the memory hierarchy.

When the processor must wait for writes to complete during write-through, the processor is said to *write stall*. A common optimization to reduce write stalls is a *write buffer,* which allows the processor to continue as soon as the data are written to the buffer, thereby overlapping processor execution with memory updating. As we will see shortly, write stalls can occur even with write buffers.

Since the data are not needed on a write, there are two options on a write miss:

- *Write allocate*—The block is allocated on a write miss, followed by the write hit actions above. In this natural option, write misses act like read misses.

- *No-write allocate*—This apparently unusual alternative is write misses do *not* affect the cache. Instead, the block is modified only in the lower-level memory.

Thus, blocks stay out of the cache in no-write allocate until the program tries to read the blocks, but even blocks that are only written will still be in the cache with write allocate. Let's look at an example.

Example Assume a fully associative write-back cache with many cache entries that starts empty. Below is a sequence of five memory operations (the address is in square brackets):

```
Write Mem[100];
Write Mem[100];
Read  Mem[200];
Write Mem[200];
Write Mem[100].
```

What are the number of hits and misses when using no-write allocate versus write allocate?

Answer For no-write allocate, the address 100 is not in the cache, and there is no allocation on write, so the first two writes will result in misses. Address 200 is also not in the cache, so the read is also a miss. The subsequent write to address 200 is a hit. The last write to 100 is still a miss. The result for no-write allocate is four misses and one hit.

For write allocate, the first accesses to 100 and 200 are misses, and the rest are hits since 100 and 200 are both found in the cache. Thus, the result for write allocate is two misses and three hits.

Either write miss policy could be used with write-through or write-back. Normally, write-back caches use write allocate, hoping that subsequent writes to that block will be captured by the cache. Write-through caches often use no-write allocate. The reasoning is that even if there are subsequent writes to that block, the writes must still go to the lower-level memory, so what's to be gained?

An Example: The Opteron Data Cache

To give substance to these ideas, Figure B.5 shows the organization of the data cache in the AMD Opteron microprocessor. The cache contains 65,536 (64K) bytes of data in 64-byte blocks with two-way set associative placement, least-recently used replacement, write-back, and write allocate on a write miss.

Let's trace a cache hit through the steps of a hit as labeled in Figure B.5. (The four steps are shown as circled numbers.) As described in Section B.5, the Opteron presents a 48-bit virtual address to the cache for tag comparison, which is simultaneously translated into a 40-bit physical address.

The reason Opteron doesn't use all 64 bits of virtual address is that its designers don't think anyone needs that big of a virtual address space yet, and the

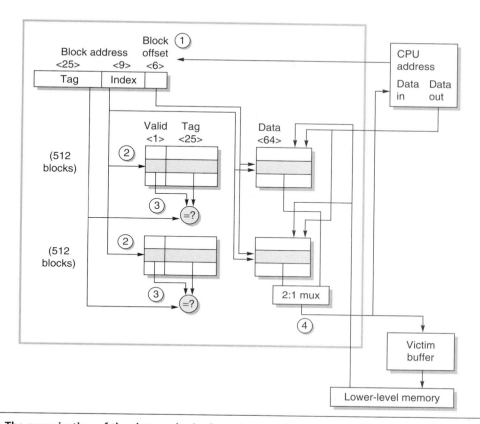

Figure B.5 The organization of the data cache in the Opteron microprocessor. The 64 KB cache is two-way set associative with 64-byte blocks. The 9-bit index selects among 512 sets. The four steps of a read hit, shown as circled numbers in order of occurrence, label this organization. Three bits of the block offset join the index to supply the RAM address to select the proper 8 bytes. Thus, the cache holds two groups of 4096 64-bit words, with each group containing half of the 512 sets. Although not exercised in this example, the line from lower-level memory to the cache is used on a miss to load the cache. The size of address leaving the processor is 40 bits because it is a physical address and not a virtual address. Figure B.24 on page B-47 explains how the Opteron maps from virtual to physical for a cache access.

smaller size simplifies the Opteron virtual address mapping. The designers plan to grow the virtual address in future microprocessors.

The physical address coming into the cache is divided into two fields: the 34-bit block address and the 6-bit block offset ($64 = 2^6$ and $34 + 6 = 40$). The block address is further divided into an address tag and cache index. Step 1 shows this division.

The cache index selects the tag to be tested to see if the desired block is in the cache. The size of the index depends on cache size, block size, and set associativity. For the Opteron cache the set associativity is set to two, and we calculate the index as follows:

$$2^{\text{Index}} = \frac{\text{Cache size}}{\text{Block size} \times \text{Set associativity}} = \frac{65{,}536}{64 \times 2} = 512 = 2^9$$

Hence, the index is 9 bits wide, and the tag is 34 – 9 or 25 bits wide. Although that is the index needed to select the proper block, 64 bytes is much more than the processor wants to consume at once. Hence, it makes more sense to organize the data portion of the cache memory 8 bytes wide, which is the natural data word of the 64-bit Opteron processor. Thus, in addition to 9 bits to index the proper cache block, 3 more bits from the block offset are used to index the proper 8 bytes. Index selection is step 2 in Figure B.5.

After reading the two tags from the cache, they are compared to the tag portion of the block address from the processor. This comparison is step 3 in the figure. To be sure the tag contains valid information, the valid bit must be set or else the results of the comparison are ignored.

Assuming one tag does match, the final step is to signal the processor to load the proper data from the cache by using the winning input from a 2:1 multiplexor. The Opteron allows 2 clock cycles for these four steps, so the instructions in the following 2 clock cycles would wait if they tried to use the result of the load.

Handling writes is more complicated than handling reads in the Opteron, as it is in any cache. If the word to be written is in the cache, the first three steps are the same. Since the Opteron executes out of order, only after it signals that the instruction has committed and the cache tag comparison indicates a hit are the data written to the cache.

So far we have assumed the common case of a cache hit. What happens on a miss? On a read miss, the cache sends a signal to the processor telling it the data are not yet available, and 64 bytes are read from the next level of the hierarchy. The latency is 7 clock cycles to the first 8 bytes of the block, and then 2 clock cycles per 8 bytes for the rest of the block. Since the data cache is set associative, there is a choice on which block to replace. Opteron uses LRU, which selects the block that was referenced longest ago, so every access must update the LRU bit. Replacing a block means updating the data, the address tag, the valid bit, and the LRU bit.

Since the Opteron uses write-back, the old data block could have been modified, and hence it cannot simply be discarded. The Opteron keeps 1 dirty bit per block to record if the block was written. If the "victim" was modified, its data and address are sent to the victim buffer. (This structure is similar to a *write buffer* in other computers.) The Opteron has space for eight victim blocks. In parallel with other cache actions, it writes victim blocks to the next level of the hierarchy. If the victim buffer is full, the cache must wait.

A write miss is very similar to a read miss, since the Opteron allocates a block on a read or a write miss.

We have seen how it works, but the *data* cache cannot supply all the memory needs of the processor: The processor also needs instructions. Although a single cache could try to supply both, it can be a bottleneck. For example, when a load or store instruction is executed, the pipelined processor will simultaneously request both a data word *and* an instruction word. Hence, a single cache would present a structural hazard for loads and stores, leading to stalls. One simple way to conquer this problem is to divide it: One cache is dedicated to instructions and another to data. Separate caches are found in most recent processors, including the Opteron. Hence, it has a 64 KB instruction cache as well as the 64 KB data cache.

The processor knows whether it is issuing an instruction address or a data address, so there can be separate ports for both, thereby doubling the bandwidth between the memory hierarchy and the processor. Separate caches also offer the opportunity of optimizing each cache separately: Different capacities, block sizes, and associativities may lead to better performance. (In contrast to the instruction caches and data caches of the Opteron, the terms *unified* or *mixed* are applied to caches that can contain either instructions or data.)

Figure B.6 shows that instruction caches have lower miss rates than data caches. Separating instructions and data removes misses due to conflicts between instruction blocks and data blocks, but the split also fixes the cache space devoted to each type. Which is more important to miss rates? A fair comparison of separate instruction and data caches to unified caches requires the total cache size to be the same. For example, a separate 16 KB instruction cache and 16 KB data cache should be compared to a 32 KB unified cache. Calculating the average miss rate with separate instruction and data caches necessitates knowing the percentage of memory references to each cache. From the data in Appendix A we find the split is 100%/(100% + 26% + 10%) or about 74% instruction references to (26% + 10%)/(100% + 26% + 10%) or about 26% data references. Splitting affects performance beyond what is indicated by the change in miss rates, as we will see shortly.

Size (KB)	Instruction cache	Data cache	Unified cache
8	8.16	44.0	63.0
16	3.82	40.9	51.0
32	1.36	38.4	43.3
64	0.61	36.9	39.4
128	0.30	35.3	36.2
256	0.02	32.6	32.9

Figure B.6 Miss per 1000 instructions for instruction, data, and unified caches of different sizes. The percentage of instruction references is about 74%. The data are for two-way associative caches with 64-byte blocks for the same computer and benchmarks as Figure B.4.

B.2   Cache Performance

Because instruction count is independent of the hardware, it is tempting to evaluate processor performance using that number. Such indirect performance measures have waylaid many a computer designer. The corresponding temptation for evaluating memory hierarchy performance is to concentrate on miss rate because it, too, is independent of the speed of the hardware. As we will see, miss rate can be just as misleading as instruction count. A better measure of memory hierarchy performance is the *average memory access time*:

$$\text{Average memory access time} = \text{Hit time} + \text{Miss rate} \times \text{Miss penalty}$$

where *hit time* is the time to hit in the cache; we have seen the other two terms before. The components of average access time can be measured either in absolute time—say, 0.25 to 1.0 nanoseconds on a hit—or in the number of clock cycles that the processor waits for the memory—such as a miss penalty of 150 to 200 clock cycles. Remember that average memory access time is still an indirect measure of performance; although it is a better measure than miss rate, it is not a substitute for execution time.

This formula can help us decide between split caches and a unified cache.

Example   Which has the lower miss rate: a 16 KB instruction cache with a 16 KB data cache or a 32 KB unified cache? Use the miss rates in Figure B.6 to help calculate the correct answer, assuming 36% of the instructions are data transfer instructions. Assume a hit takes 1 clock cycle and the miss penalty is 100 clock cycles. A load or store hit takes 1 extra clock cycle on a unified cache if there is only one cache port to satisfy two simultaneous requests. Using the pipelining terminology of Chapter 3, the unified cache leads to a structural hazard. What is the average memory access time in each case? Assume write-through caches with a write buffer and ignore stalls due to the write buffer.

Answer   First let's convert misses per 1000 instructions into miss rates. Solving the general formula from above, the miss rate is

$$\text{Miss rate} = \dfrac{\dfrac{\text{Misses}}{1000 \text{ Instructions}}/1000}{\dfrac{\text{Memory accesses}}{\text{Instruction}}}$$

Since every instruction access has exactly one memory access to fetch the instruction, the instruction miss rate is

$$\text{Miss rate}_{16 \text{ KB instruction}} = \frac{3.82/1000}{1.00} = 0.004$$

Since 36% of the instructions are data transfers, the data miss rate is

$$\text{Miss rate}_{16 \text{ KB data}} = \frac{40.9/1000}{0.36} = 0.114$$

The unified miss rate needs to account for instruction and data accesses:

$$\text{Miss rate}_{32\text{ KB unified}} = \frac{43.3/1000}{1.00 + 0.36} = 0.0318$$

As stated above, about 74% of the memory accesses are instruction references. Thus, the overall miss rate for the split caches is

$$(74\% \times 0.004) + (26\% \times 0.114) = 0.0326$$

Thus, a 32 KB unified cache has a slightly lower effective miss rate than two 16 KB caches.

The average memory access time formula can be divided into instruction and data accesses:

Average memory access time
$$= \% \text{ instructions} \times (\text{Hit time} + \text{Instruction miss rate} \times \text{Miss penalty})$$
$$+ \% \text{ data} \times (\text{Hit time} + \text{Data miss rate} \times \text{Miss penalty})$$

Therefore, the time for each organization is

Average memory access time$_{\text{split}}$
$$= 74\% \times (1 + 0.004 \times 200) + 26\% \times (1 + 0.114 \times 200)$$
$$= (74\% \times 1.80) + (26\% \times 23.80) = 1.332 + 6.188 = 7.52$$

Average memory access time$_{\text{unified}}$
$$= 74\% \times (1 + 0.0318 \times 200) + 26\% \times (1 + 1 + 0.0318 \times 200)$$
$$= (74\% \times 7.36) + (26\% \times 8.36) = 5.446 + 2.174 = 7.62$$

Hence, the split caches in this example—which offer two memory ports per clock cycle, thereby avoiding the structural hazard—have a better average memory access time than the single-ported unified cache despite having a worse effective miss rate.

Average Memory Access Time and Processor Performance

An obvious question is whether average memory access time due to cache misses predicts processor performance.

First, there are other reasons for stalls, such as contention due to I/O devices using memory. Designers often assume that all memory stalls are due to cache misses, since the memory hierarchy typically dominates other reasons for stalls. We use this simplifying assumption here, but be sure to account for *all* memory stalls when calculating final performance.

Second, the answer also depends on the processor. If we have an in-order execution processor (see Chapter 3), then the answer is basically yes. The processor stalls during misses, and the memory stall time is strongly correlated to average memory access time. Let's make that assumption for now, but we'll return to out-of-order processors in the next subsection.

As stated in the previous section, we can model CPU time as:

CPU time = (CPU execution clock cycles + Memory stall clock cycles) × Clock cycle time

This formula raises the question of whether the clock cycles for a cache hit should be considered part of CPU execution clock cycles or part of memory stall clock cycles. Although either convention is defensible, the most widely accepted is to include hit clock cycles in CPU execution clock cycles.

We can now explore the impact of caches on performance.

Example   Let's use an in-order execution computer for the first example. Assume that the cache miss penalty is 200 clock cycles, and all instructions normally take 1.0 clock cycles (ignoring memory stalls). Assume that the average miss rate is 2%, there is an average of 1.5 memory references per instruction, and the average number of cache misses per 1000 instructions is 30. What is the impact on performance when behavior of the cache is included? Calculate the impact using both misses per instruction and miss rate.

Answer $$\text{CPU time} = \text{IC} \times \left(\text{CPI}_{\text{execution}} + \frac{\text{Memory stall clock cycles}}{\text{Instruction}} \right) \times \text{Clock cycle time}$$

The performance, including cache misses, is

$$\begin{aligned} \text{CPU time}_{\text{with cache}} \quad &= \text{IC} \times [1.0 + (30/1000 \times 200)] \times \text{Clock cycle time} \\ &= \text{IC} \times 7.00 \times \text{Clock cycle time} \end{aligned}$$

Now calculating performance using miss rate:

$$\text{CPU time} = \text{IC} \times \left(\text{CPI}_{\text{execution}} + \text{Miss rate} \times \frac{\text{Memory accesses}}{\text{Instruction}} \times \text{Miss penalty} \right) \times \text{Clock cycle time}$$

$$\begin{aligned} \text{CPU time}_{\text{with cache}} \quad &= \text{IC} \times [1.0 + (1.5 \times 2\% \times 200)] \times \text{Clock cycle time} \\ &= \text{IC} \times 7.00 \times \text{Clock cycle time} \end{aligned}$$

The clock cycle time and instruction count are the same, with or without a cache. Thus, CPU time increases sevenfold, with CPI from 1.00 for a "perfect cache" to 7.00 with a cache that can miss. Without any memory hierarchy at all the CPI would increase again to 1.0 + 200 × 1.5 or 301—a factor of more than 40 times longer than a system with a cache!

As this example illustrates, cache behavior can have enormous impact on performance. Furthermore, cache misses have a double-barreled impact on a processor with a low CPI and a fast clock:

1. The lower the $\text{CPI}_{\text{execution}}$, the higher the *relative* impact of a fixed number of cache miss clock cycles.

2. When calculating CPI, the cache miss penalty is measured in processor clock cycles for a miss. Therefore, even if memory hierarchies for two computers

are identical, the processor with the higher clock rate has a larger number of clock cycles per miss and hence a higher memory portion of CPI.

The importance of the cache for processors with low CPI and high clock rates is thus greater, and, consequently, greater is the danger of neglecting cache behavior in assessing performance of such computers. Amdahl's law strikes again!

Although minimizing average memory access time is a reasonable goal—and we will use it in much of this appendix—keep in mind that the final goal is to reduce processor execution time. The next example shows how these two can differ.

Example   What is the impact of two different cache organizations on the performance of a processor? Assume that the CPI with a perfect cache is 1.6, the clock cycle time is 0.35 ns, there are 1.4 memory references per instruction, the size of both caches is 128 KB, and both have a block size of 64 bytes. One cache is direct mapped and the other is two-way set associative. Figure B.5 shows that for set associative caches we must add a multiplexor to select between the blocks in the set depending on the tag match. Since the speed of the processor can be tied directly to the speed of a cache hit, assume the processor clock cycle time must be stretched 1.35 times to accommodate the selection multiplexor of the set associative cache. To the first approximation, the cache miss penalty is 65 ns for either cache organization. (In practice, it is normally rounded up or down to an integer number of clock cycles.) First, calculate the average memory access time and then processor performance. Assume the hit time is 1 clock cycle, the miss rate of a direct-mapped 128 KB cache is 2.1%, and the miss rate for a two-way set associative cache of the same size is 1.9%.

Answer   Average memory access time is

$$\text{Average memory access time} = \text{Hit time} + \text{Miss rate} \times \text{Miss penalty}$$

Thus, the time for each organization is

$$\text{Average memory access time}_{1\text{-way}} = 0.35 + (.021 \times 65) = 1.72 \text{ ns}$$
$$\text{Average memory access time}_{2\text{-way}} = 0.35 \times 1.35 + (.019 \times 65) = 1.71 \text{ ns}$$

The average memory access time is better for the two-way set-associative cache. The processor performance is

$$\text{CPU time} = \text{IC} \times \left(\text{CPI}_{\text{execution}} + \frac{\text{Misses}}{\text{Instruction}} \times \text{Miss penalty} \right) \times \text{Clock cycle time}$$

$$= \text{IC} \times \left[\left(\text{CPI}_{\text{execution}} \times \text{Clock cycle time} \right) \right.$$

$$\left. + \left(\text{Miss rate} \times \frac{\text{Memory accesses}}{\text{Instruction}} \times \text{Miss penalty} \times \text{Clock cycle time} \right) \right]$$

Substituting 65 ns for (Miss penalty × Clock cycle time), the performance of each cache organization is

$$\text{CPU time}_{1\text{-way}} = IC \times [1.6 \times 0.35 + (0.021 \times 1.4 \times 65)] = 2.47 \times IC$$

$$\text{CPU time}_{2\text{-way}} = IC \times [1.6 \times 0.35 \times 1.35 + (0.019 \times 1.4 \times 65)] = 2.49 \times IC$$

and relative performance is

$$\frac{\text{CPU time}_{2\text{-way}}}{\text{CPU time}_{1\text{-way}}} = \frac{2.49 \times \text{Instruction count}}{2.47 \times \text{Instruction count}} = \frac{2.49}{2.47} = 1.01$$

In contrast to the results of average memory access time comparison, the direct-mapped cache leads to slightly better average performance because the clock cycle is stretched for *all* instructions for the two-way set associative case, even if there are fewer misses. Since CPU time is our bottom-line evaluation and since direct mapped is simpler to build, the preferred cache is direct mapped in this example.

Miss Penalty and Out-of-Order Execution Processors

For an out-of-order execution processor, how do you define "miss penalty"? Is it the full latency of the miss to memory, or is it just the "exposed" or nonoverlapped latency when the processor must stall? This question does not arise in processors that stall until the data miss completes.

Let's redefine memory stalls to lead to a new definition of miss penalty as nonoverlapped latency:

$$\frac{\text{Memory stall cycles}}{\text{Instruction}} = \frac{\text{Misses}}{\text{Instruction}} \times (\text{Total miss latency} - \text{Overlapped miss latency})$$

Similarly, as some out-of-order processors stretch the hit time, that portion of the performance equation could be divided by total hit latency less overlapped hit latency. This equation could be further expanded to account for contention for memory resources in an out-of-order processor by dividing total miss latency into latency without contention and latency due to contention. Let's just concentrate on miss latency.

We now have to decide the following:

■ *Length of memory latency*—What to consider as the start and the end of a memory operation in an out-of-order processor

■ *Length of latency overlap*—What is the start of overlap with the processor (or, equivalently, when do we say a memory operation is stalling the processor)

Given the complexity of out-of-order execution processors, there is no single correct definition.

Since only committed operations are seen at the retirement pipeline stage, we say a processor is stalled in a clock cycle if it does not retire the maximum possible number of instructions in that cycle. We attribute that stall to the first instruction that could not be retired. This definition is by no means foolproof. For example, applying an optimization to improve a certain stall time may not always improve execution time because another type of stall—hidden behind the targeted stall—may now be exposed.

For latency, we could start measuring from the time the memory instruction is queued in the instruction window, or when the address is generated, or when the instruction is actually sent to the memory system. Any option works as long as it is used in a consistent fashion.

Example   Let's redo the example above, but this time we assume the processor with the longer clock cycle time supports out-of-order execution yet still has a direct-mapped cache. Assume 30% of the 65 ns miss penalty can be overlapped; that is, the average CPU memory stall time is now 45.5 ns.

Answer   Average memory access time for the out-of-order (OOO) computer is

$$\text{Average memory access time}_{1\text{-way,OOO}} = 0.35 \times 1.35 + (0.021 \times 45.5) = 1.43 \text{ ns}$$

The performance of the OOO cache is

$$\text{CPU time}_{1\text{-way,OOO}} = IC \times [1.6 \times 0.35 \times 1.35 + (0.021 \times 1.4 \times 45.5)] = 2.09 \times IC$$

Hence, despite a much slower clock cycle time and the higher miss rate of a direct-mapped cache, the out-of-order computer can be slightly faster if it can hide 30% of the miss penalty.

In summary, although the state of the art in defining and measuring memory stalls for out-of-order processors is complex, be aware of the issues because they significantly affect performance. The complexity arises because out-of-order processors tolerate some latency due to cache misses without hurting performance. Consequently, designers normally use simulators of the out-of-order processor and memory when evaluating trade-offs in the memory hierarchy to be sure that an improvement that helps the average memory latency actually helps program performance.

To help summarize this section and to act as a handy reference, Figure B.7 lists the cache equations in this appendix.

$$2^{\text{index}} = \frac{\text{Cache size}}{\text{Block size} \times \text{Set associativity}}$$

$$\text{CPU execution time} = (\text{CPU clock cycles} + \text{Memory stall cycles}) \times \text{Clock cycle time}$$

$$\text{Memory stall cycles} = \text{Number of misses} \times \text{Miss penalty}$$

$$\text{Memory stall cycles} = \text{IC} \times \frac{\text{Misses}}{\text{Instruction}} \times \text{Miss penalty}$$

$$\frac{\text{Misses}}{\text{Instruction}} = \text{Miss rate} \times \frac{\text{Memory accesses}}{\text{Instruction}}$$

$$\text{Average memory access time} = \text{Hit time} + \text{Miss rate} \times \text{Miss penalty}$$

$$\text{CPU execution time} = \text{IC} \times \left(\text{CPI}_{\text{execution}} + \frac{\text{Memory stall clock cycles}}{\text{Instruction}} \right) \times \text{Clock cycle time}$$

$$\text{CPU execution time} = \text{IC} \times \left(\text{CPI}_{\text{execution}} + \frac{\text{Misses}}{\text{Instruction}} \times \text{Miss penalty} \right) \times \text{Clock cycle time}$$

$$\text{CPU execution time} = \text{IC} \times \left(\text{CPI}_{\text{execution}} + \text{Miss rate} \times \frac{\text{Memory accesses}}{\text{Instruction}} \times \text{Miss penalty} \right) \times \text{Clock cycle time}$$

$$\frac{\text{Memory stall cycles}}{\text{Instruction}} = \frac{\text{Misses}}{\text{Instruction}} \times (\text{Total miss latency} - \text{Overlapped miss latency})$$

$$\text{Average memory access time} = \text{Hit time}_{L1} + \text{Miss rate}_{L1} \times (\text{Hit time}_{L2} + \text{Miss rate}_{L2} \times \text{Miss penalty}_{L2})$$

$$\frac{\text{Memory stall cycles}}{\text{Instruction}} = \frac{\text{Misses}_{L1}}{\text{Instruction}} \times \text{Hit time}_{L2} + \frac{\text{Misses}_{L2}}{\text{Instruction}} \times \text{Miss penalty}_{L2}$$

Figure B.7 Summary of performance equations in this appendix. The first equation calculates the cache index size, and the rest help evaluate performance. The final two equations deal with multilevel caches, which are explained early in the next section. They are included here to help make the figure a useful reference.

B.3 Six Basic Cache Optimizations

The average memory access time formula gave us a framework to present cache optimizations for improving cache performance:

$$\text{Average memory access time} = \text{Hit time} + \text{Miss rate} \times \text{Miss penalty}$$

Hence, we organize six cache optimizations into three categories:

- *Reducing the miss rate*—larger block size, larger cache size, and higher associativity

- *Reducing the miss penalty*—multilevel caches and giving reads priority over writes

- *Reducing the time to hit in the cache*—avoiding address translation when indexing the cache

Figure B.18 on page B-40 concludes this section with a summary of the implementation complexity and the performance benefits of these six techniques.

The classical approach to improving cache behavior is to reduce miss rates, and we present three techniques to do so. To gain better insights into the causes of misses, we first start with a model that sorts all misses into three simple categories:

- *Compulsory*—The very first access to a block *cannot* be in the cache, so the block must be brought into the cache. These are also called *cold-start misses* or *first-reference misses.*

- *Capacity*—If the cache cannot contain all the blocks needed during execution of a program, capacity misses (in addition to compulsory misses) will occur because of blocks being discarded and later retrieved.

- *Conflict*—If the block placement strategy is set associative or direct mapped, conflict misses (in addition to compulsory and capacity misses) will occur because a block may be discarded and later retrieved if too many blocks map to its set. These misses are also called *collision misses*. The idea is that hits in a fully associative cache that become misses in an n-way set-associative cache are due to more than n requests on some popular sets.

(Chapter 5 adds a fourth C, for *coherency* misses due to cache flushes to keep multiple caches coherent in a multiprocessor; we won't consider those here.)

Figure B.8 shows the relative frequency of cache misses, broken down by the three C's. Compulsory misses are those that occur in an infinite cache. Capacity misses are those that occur in a fully associative cache. Conflict misses are those that occur going from fully associative to eight-way associative, four-way associative, and so on. Figure B.9 presents the same data graphically. The top graph shows absolute miss rates; the bottom graph plots the percentage of all the misses by type of miss as a function of cache size.

To show the benefit of associativity, conflict misses are divided into misses caused by each decrease in associativity. Here are the four divisions of conflict misses and how they are calculated:

- *Eight-way*—Conflict misses due to going from fully associative (no conflicts) to eight-way associative

- *Four-way*—Conflict misses due to going from eight-way associative to four-way associative

- *Two-way*—Conflict misses due to going from four-way associative to two-way associative

- *One-way*—Conflict misses due to going from two-way associative to one-way associative (direct mapped)

As we can see from the figures, the compulsory miss rate of the SPEC2000 programs is very small, as it is for many long-running programs.

Having identified the three C's, what can a computer designer do about them? Conceptually, conflicts are the easiest: Fully associative placement avoids all conflict misses. Full associativity is expensive in hardware, however, and may slow the processor clock rate (see the example on page B-29), leading to lower overall performance.

Cache size (KB)	Degree associative	Total miss rate	Miss rate components (relative percent) (sum = 100% of total miss rate)					
			Compulsory		Capacity		Conflict	
4	1-way	0.098	0.0001	0.1%	0.070	72%	0.027	28%
4	2-way	0.076	0.0001	0.1%	0.070	93%	0.005	7%
4	4-way	0.071	0.0001	0.1%	0.070	99%	0.001	1%
4	8-way	0.071	0.0001	0.1%	0.070	100%	0.000	0%
8	1-way	0.068	0.0001	0.1%	0.044	65%	0.024	35%
8	2-way	0.049	0.0001	0.1%	0.044	90%	0.005	10%
8	4-way	0.044	0.0001	0.1%	0.044	99%	0.000	1%
8	8-way	0.044	0.0001	0.1%	0.044	100%	0.000	0%
16	1-way	0.049	0.0001	0.1%	0.040	82%	0.009	17%
16	2-way	0.041	0.0001	0.2%	0.040	98%	0.001	2%
16	4-way	0.041	0.0001	0.2%	0.040	99%	0.000	0%
16	8-way	0.041	0.0001	0.2%	0.040	100%	0.000	0%
32	1-way	0.042	0.0001	0.2%	0.037	89%	0.005	11%
32	2-way	0.038	0.0001	0.2%	0.037	99%	0.000	0%
32	4-way	0.037	0.0001	0.2%	0.037	100%	0.000	0%
32	8-way	0.037	0.0001	0.2%	0.037	100%	0.000	0%
64	1-way	0.037	0.0001	0.2%	0.028	77%	0.008	23%
64	2-way	0.031	0.0001	0.2%	0.028	91%	0.003	9%
64	4-way	0.030	0.0001	0.2%	0.028	95%	0.001	4%
64	8-way	0.029	0.0001	0.2%	0.028	97%	0.001	2%
128	1-way	0.021	0.0001	0.3%	0.019	91%	0.002	8%
128	2-way	0.019	0.0001	0.3%	0.019	100%	0.000	0%
128	4-way	0.019	0.0001	0.3%	0.019	100%	0.000	0%
128	8-way	0.019	0.0001	0.3%	0.019	100%	0.000	0%
256	1-way	0.013	0.0001	0.5%	0.012	94%	0.001	6%
256	2-way	0.012	0.0001	0.5%	0.012	99%	0.000	0%
256	4-way	0.012	0.0001	0.5%	0.012	99%	0.000	0%
256	8-way	0.012	0.0001	0.5%	0.012	99%	0.000	0%
512	1-way	0.008	0.0001	0.8%	0.005	66%	0.003	33%
512	2-way	0.007	0.0001	0.9%	0.005	71%	0.002	28%
512	4-way	0.006	0.0001	1.1%	0.005	91%	0.000	8%
512	8-way	0.006	0.0001	1.1%	0.005	95%	0.000	4%

Figure B.8 Total miss rate for each size cache and percentage of each according to the three C's. Compulsory misses are independent of cache size, while capacity misses decrease as capacity increases, and conflict misses decrease as associativity increases. Figure B.9 shows the same information graphically. Note that a direct-mapped cache of size *N* has about the same miss rate as a two-way set-associative cache of size *N*/2 up through 128 K. Caches larger than 128 KB do not prove that rule. Note that the Capacity column is also the fully associative miss rate. Data were collected as in Figure B.4 using LRU replacement.

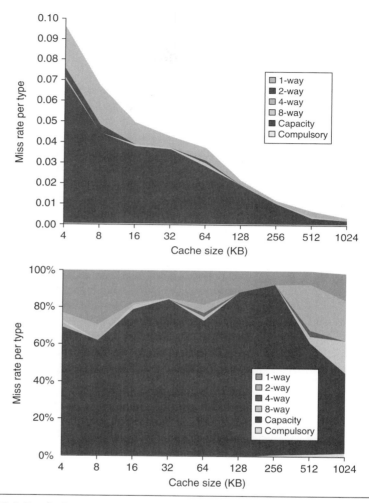

Figure B.9 Total miss rate (top) and distribution of miss rate (bottom) for each size cache according to the three C's for the data in Figure B.8. The top diagram shows the actual data cache miss rates, while the bottom diagram shows the percentage in each category. (Space allows the graphs to show one extra cache size than can fit in Figure B.8.)

There is little to be done about capacity except to enlarge the cache. If the upper-level memory is much smaller than what is needed for a program, and a significant percentage of the time is spent moving data between two levels in the hierarchy, the memory hierarchy is said to *thrash*. Because so many replacements are required, thrashing means the computer runs close to the speed of the lower-level memory, or maybe even slower because of the miss overhead.

Another approach to improving the three C's is to make blocks larger to reduce the number of compulsory misses, but, as we will see shortly, large blocks can increase other kinds of misses.

The three C's give insight into the cause of misses, but this simple model has its limits; it gives you insight into average behavior but may not explain an individual miss. For example, changing cache size changes conflict misses as well as capacity misses, since a larger cache spreads out references to more blocks. Thus, a miss might move from a capacity miss to a conflict miss as cache size changes. Note that the three C's also ignore replacement policy, since it is difficult to model and since, in general, it is less significant. In specific circumstances the replacement policy can actually lead to anomalous behavior, such as poorer miss rates for larger associativity, which contradicts the three C's model. (Some have proposed using an address trace to determine optimal placement in memory to avoid placement misses from the three C's model; we've not followed that advice here.)

Alas, many of the techniques that reduce miss rates also increase hit time or miss penalty. The desirability of reducing miss rates using the three optimizations must be balanced against the goal of making the whole system fast. This first example shows the importance of a balanced perspective.

First Optimization: Larger Block Size to Reduce Miss Rate

The simplest way to reduce miss rate is to increase the block size. Figure B.10 shows the trade-off of block size versus miss rate for a set of programs and cache sizes. Larger block sizes will reduce also compulsory misses. This reduction occurs because the principle of locality has two components: temporal locality and spatial locality. Larger blocks take advantage of spatial locality.

At the same time, larger blocks increase the miss penalty. Since they reduce the number of blocks in the cache, larger blocks may increase conflict misses and even capacity misses if the cache is small. Clearly, there is little reason to increase the block size to such a size that it *increases* the miss rate. There is also no benefit to reducing miss rate if it increases the average memory access time. The increase in miss penalty may outweigh the decrease in miss rate.

Example   Figure B.11 shows the actual miss rates plotted in Figure B.10. Assume the memory system takes 80 clock cycles of overhead and then delivers 16 bytes every 2 clock cycles. Thus, it can supply 16 bytes in 82 clock cycles, 32 bytes in 84 clock cycles, and so on. Which block size has the smallest average memory access time for each cache size in Figure B.11?

Answer   Average memory access time is

$$\text{Average memory access time} = \text{Hit time} + \text{Miss rate} \times \text{Miss penalty}$$

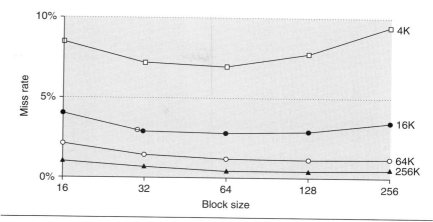

Figure B.10 Miss rate versus block size for five different-sized caches. Note that miss rate actually goes up if the block size is too large relative to the cache size. Each line represents a cache of different size. Figure B.11 shows the data used to plot these lines. Unfortunately, SPEC2000 traces would take too long if block size were included, so these data are based on SPEC92 on a DECstation 5000 [Gee et al. 1993].

If we assume the hit time is 1 clock cycle independent of block size, then the access time for a 16-byte block in a 4 KB cache is

$$\text{Average memory access time} = 1 + (8.57\% \times 82) = 8.027 \text{ clock cycles}$$

and for a 256-byte block in a 256 KB cache the average memory access time is

$$\text{Average memory access time} = 1 + (0.49\% \times 112) = 1.549 \text{ clock cycles}$$

	Cache size			
Block size	**4K**	**16K**	**64K**	**256K**
16	8.57%	3.94%	2.04%	1.09%
32	7.24%	2.87%	1.35%	0.70%
64	7.00%	2.64%	1.06%	0.51%
128	7.78%	2.77%	1.02%	0.49%
256	9.51%	3.29%	1.15%	0.49%

Figure B.11 Actual miss rate versus block size for the five different-sized caches in Figure B.10. Note that for a 4 KB cache, 256-byte blocks have a higher miss rate than 32-byte blocks. In this example, the cache would have to be 256 KB in order for a 256-byte block to decrease misses.

Block size	Miss penalty	Cache size			
		4K	16K	64K	256K
16	82	8.027	4.231	2.673	1.894
32	84	**7.082**	3.411	2.134	1.588
64	88	7.160	**3.323**	**1.933**	**1.449**
128	96	8.469	3.659	1.979	1.470
256	112	11.651	4.685	2.288	1.549

Figure B.12 Average memory access time versus block size for five different-sized caches in Figure B.10. Block sizes of 32 and 64 bytes dominate. The smallest average time per cache size is boldfaced.

Figure B.12 shows the average memory access time for all block and cache sizes between those two extremes. The boldfaced entries show the fastest block size for a given cache size: 32 bytes for 4 KB and 64 bytes for the larger caches. These sizes are, in fact, popular block sizes for processor caches today.

As in all of these techniques, the cache designer is trying to minimize both the miss rate and the miss penalty. The selection of block size depends on both the latency and bandwidth of the lower-level memory. High latency and high bandwidth encourage large block size since the cache gets many more bytes per miss for a small increase in miss penalty. Conversely, low latency and low bandwidth encourage smaller block sizes since there is little time saved from a larger block. For example, twice the miss penalty of a small block may be close to the penalty of a block twice the size. The larger number of small blocks may also reduce conflict misses. Note that Figures B.10 and B.12 show the difference between selecting a block size based on minimizing miss rate versus minimizing average memory access time.

After seeing the positive and negative impact of larger block size on compulsory and capacity misses, the next two subsections look at the potential of higher capacity and higher associativity.

Second Optimization: Larger Caches to Reduce Miss Rate

The obvious way to reduce capacity misses in Figures B.8 and B.9 is to increase capacity of the cache. The obvious drawback is potentially longer hit time and higher cost and power. This technique has been especially popular in off-chip caches.

Third Optimization: Higher Associativity to Reduce Miss Rate

Figures B.8 and B.9 show how miss rates improve with higher associativity. There are two general rules of thumb that can be gleaned from these figures. The first is that eight-way set associative is for practical purposes as effective in reducing misses for these sized caches as fully associative. You can see the difference by comparing the eight-way entries to the capacity miss column in Figure B.8, since capacity misses are calculated using fully associative caches.

The second observation, called the *2:1 cache rule of thumb*, is that a direct-mapped cache of size N has about the same miss rate as a two-way set associative cache of size $N/2$. This held in three C's figures for cache sizes less than 128 KB.

Like many of these examples, improving one aspect of the average memory access time comes at the expense of another. Increasing block size reduces miss rate while increasing miss penalty, and greater associativity can come at the cost of increased hit time. Hence, the pressure of a fast processor clock cycle encourages simple cache designs, but the increasing miss penalty rewards associativity, as the following example suggests.

Example   Assume that higher associativity would increase the clock cycle time as listed below:

$$\text{Clock cycle time}_{2\text{-way}} = 1.36 \times \text{Clock cycle time}_{1\text{-way}}$$
$$\text{Clock cycle time}_{4\text{-way}} = 1.44 \times \text{Clock cycle time}_{1\text{-way}}$$
$$\text{Clock cycle time}_{8\text{-way}} = 1.52 \times \text{Clock cycle time}_{1\text{-way}}$$

Assume that the hit time is 1 clock cycle, that the miss penalty for the direct-mapped case is 25 clock cycles to a level 2 cache (see next subsection) that never misses, and that the miss penalty need not be rounded to an integral number of clock cycles. Using Figure B.8 for miss rates, for which cache sizes are each of these three statements true?

$$\text{Average memory access time}_{8\text{-way}} < \text{Average memory access time}_{4\text{-way}}$$
$$\text{Average memory access time}_{4\text{-way}} < \text{Average memory access time}_{2\text{-way}}$$
$$\text{Average memory access time}_{2\text{-way}} < \text{Average memory access time}_{1\text{-way}}$$

Cache size (KB)	Associativity			
	1-way	2-way	4-way	8-way
4	3.44	3.25	3.22	**3.28**
8	2.69	2.58	2.55	**2.62**
16	2.23	**2.40**	**2.46**	**2.53**
32	2.06	**2.30**	**2.37**	**2.45**
64	1.92	**2.14**	**2.18**	**2.25**
128	1.52	**1.84**	**1.92**	**2.00**
256	1.32	**1.66**	**1.74**	**1.82**
512	1.20	**1.55**	**1.59**	**1.66**

Figure B.13 Average memory access time using miss rates in Figure B.8 for parameters in the example. Boldface type means that this time is higher than the number to the left, that is, higher associativity *increases* average memory access time.

Answer Average memory access time for each associativity is

$$\text{Average memory access time}_{8\text{-way}} = \text{Hit time}_{8\text{-way}} + \text{Miss rate}_{8\text{-way}} \times \text{Miss penalty}_{8\text{-way}}$$
$$= 1.52 + \text{Miss rate}_{8\text{-way}} \times 25$$
$$\text{Average memory access time}_{4\text{-way}} = 1.44 + \text{Miss rate}_{4\text{-way}} \times 25$$
$$\text{Average memory access time}_{2\text{-way}} = 1.36 + \text{Miss rate}_{2\text{-way}} \times 25$$
$$\text{Average memory access time}_{1\text{-way}} = 1.00 + \text{Miss rate}_{1\text{-way}} \times 25$$

The miss penalty is the same time in each case, so we leave it as 25 clock cycles. For example, the average memory access time for a 4 KB direct-mapped cache is

$$\text{Average memory access time}_{1\text{-way}} = 1.00 + (0.098 \times 25) = 3.44$$

and the time for a 512 KB, eight-way set associative cache is

$$\text{Average memory access time}_{8\text{-way}} = 1.52 + (0.006 \times 25) = 1.66$$

Using these formulas and the miss rates from Figure B.8, Figure B.13 shows the average memory access time for each cache and associativity. The figure shows that the formulas in this example hold for caches less than or equal to 8 KB for up to four-way associativity. Starting with 16 KB, the greater hit time of larger associativity outweighs the time saved due to the reduction in misses.

Note that we did not account for the slower clock rate on the rest of the program in this example, thereby understating the advantage of direct-mapped cache.

Fourth Optimization: Multilevel Caches to Reduce Miss Penalty

Reducing cache misses had been the traditional focus of cache research, but the cache performance formula assures us that improvements in miss penalty can be just as beneficial as improvements in miss rate. Moreover, Figure 2.2 on page 74 shows that technology trends have improved the speed of processors faster than DRAMs, making the relative cost of miss penalties increase over time.

This performance gap between processors and memory leads the architect to this question: Should I make the cache faster to keep pace with the speed of processors, or make the cache larger to overcome the widening gap between the processor and main memory?

One answer is, do both. Adding another level of cache between the original cache and memory simplifies the decision. The first-level cache can be small enough to match the clock cycle time of the fast processor. Yet, the second-level cache can be large enough to capture many accesses that would go to main memory, thereby lessening the effective miss penalty.

Although the concept of adding another level in the hierarchy is straightforward, it complicates performance analysis. Definitions for a second level of cache are not always straightforward. Let's start with the definition of *average memory access time* for a two-level cache. Using the subscripts L1 and L2 to refer, respectively, to a first-level and a second-level cache, the original formula is

$$\text{Average memory access time} = \text{Hit time}_{L1} + \text{Miss rate}_{L1} \times \text{Miss penalty}_{L1}$$

and

$$\text{Miss penalty}_{L1} = \text{Hit time}_{L2} + \text{Miss rate}_{L2} \times \text{Miss penalty}_{L2}$$

so

$$\text{Average memory access time} = \text{Hit time}_{L1} + \text{Miss rate}_{L1}$$
$$\times (\text{Hit time}_{L2} + \text{Miss rate}_{L2} \times \text{Miss penalty}_{L2})$$

In this formula, the second-level miss rate is measured on the leftovers from the first-level cache. To avoid ambiguity, these terms are adopted here for a two-level cache system:

■ *Local miss rate*—This rate is simply the number of misses in a cache divided by the total number of memory accesses to this cache. As you would expect, for the first-level cache it is equal to Miss rate$_{L1}$, and for the second-level cache it is Miss rate$_{L2}$.

■ *Global miss rate*—The number of misses in the cache divided by the total number of memory accesses generated by the processor. Using the terms above, the global miss rate for the first-level cache is still just Miss rate$_{L1}$, but for the second-level cache it is Miss rate$_{L1}$ × Miss rate$_{L2}$.

This local miss rate is large for second-level caches because the first-level cache skims the cream of the memory accesses. This is why the global miss rate is the more useful measure: It indicates what fraction of the memory accesses that leave the processor go all the way to memory.

Here is a place where the misses per instruction metric shines. Instead of confusion about local or global miss rates, we just expand memory stalls per instruction to add the impact of a second-level cache.

$$\text{Average memory stalls per instruction} = \text{Misses per instruction}_{L1} \times \text{Hit time}_{L2}$$
$$+ \text{Misses per instruction}_{L2} \times \text{Miss penalty}_{L2}$$

Example   Suppose that in 1000 memory references there are 40 misses in the first-level cache and 20 misses in the second-level cache. What are the various miss rates? Assume the miss penalty from the L2 cache to memory is 200 clock cycles, the hit time of the L2 cache is 10 clock cycles, the hit time of L1 is 1 clock cycle, and there are 1.5 memory references per instruction. What is the average memory access time and average stall cycles per instruction? Ignore the impact of writes.

Answer   The miss rate (either local or global) for the first-level cache is 40/1000 or 4%. The local miss rate for the second-level cache is 20/40 or 50%. The global miss rate of the second-level cache is 20/1000 or 2%. Then

$$\text{Average memory access time} = \text{Hit time}_{L1} + \text{Miss rate}_{L1} \times (\text{Hit time}_{L2} + \text{Miss rate}_{L2} \times \text{Miss penalty}_{L2})$$
$$= 1 + 4\% \times (10 + 50\% \times 200) = 1 + 4\% \times 110 = 5.4 \text{ clock cycles}$$

To see how many misses we get per instruction, we divide 1000 memory references by 1.5 memory references per instruction, which yields 667 instructions. Thus, we need to multiply the misses by 1.5 to get the number of misses per 1000 instructions. We have 40×1.5 or 60 L1 misses, and 20×1.5 or 30 L2 misses, per 1000 instructions. For average memory stalls per instruction, assuming the misses are distributed uniformly between instructions and data:

$$\text{Average memory stalls per instruction} = \text{Misses per instruction}_{L1} \times \text{Hit time}_{L2} + \text{Misses per instruction}_{L2}$$
$$\times \text{Miss penalty}_{L2}$$
$$= (60/1000) \times 10 + (30/1000) \times 200$$
$$= 0.060 \times 10 + 0.030 \times 200 = 6.6 \text{ clock cycles}$$

If we subtract the L1 hit time from the average memory access time (AMAT) and then multiply by the average number of memory references per instruction, we get the same average memory stalls per instruction:

$$(5.4 - 1.0) \times 1.5 = 4.4 \times 1.5 = 6.6 \text{ clock cycles}$$

As this example shows, there may be less confusion with multilevel caches when calculating using misses per instruction versus miss rates.

Note that these formulas are for combined reads and writes, assuming a write-back first-level cache. Obviously, a write-through first-level cache will send *all* writes to the second level, not just the misses, and a write buffer might be used.

Figures B.14 and B.15 show how miss rates and relative execution time change with the size of a second-level cache for one design. From these figures we can gain two insights. The first is that the global cache miss rate is very similar to the single cache miss rate of the second-level cache, provided that the second-level cache is much larger than the first-level cache. Hence, our intuition and knowledge about the first-level caches apply. The second insight is that the local cache miss rate is *not* a good measure of secondary caches; it is a function of the miss rate of the first-level cache, and hence can vary by changing the first-level cache. Thus, the global cache miss rate should be used when evaluating second-level caches.

With these definitions in place, we can consider the parameters of second-level caches. The foremost difference between the two levels is that the speed of the first-level cache affects the clock rate of the processor, while the speed of the second-level cache only affects the miss penalty of the first-level cache. Thus, we can consider many alternatives in the second-level cache that would be ill chosen for the first-level cache. There are two major questions for the design of the second-level cache: Will it lower the average memory access time portion of the CPI, and how much does it cost?

The initial decision is the size of a second-level cache. Since everything in the first-level cache is likely to be in the second-level cache, the second-level cache should be much bigger than the first. If second-level caches are just a little bigger, the local miss rate will be high. This observation inspires the design of huge second-level caches—the size of main memory in older computers!

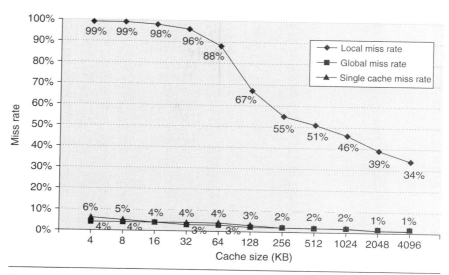

Figure B.14 Miss rates versus cache size for multilevel caches. Second-level caches *smaller* than the sum of the two 64 KB first-level caches make little sense, as reflected in the high miss rates. After 256 KB the single cache is within 10% of the global miss rates. The miss rate of a single-level cache versus size is plotted against the local miss rate and global miss rate of a second-level cache using a 32 KB first-level cache. The L2 caches (unified) were two-way set associative with replacement. Each had split L1 instruction and data caches that were 64 KB two-way set associative with LRU replacement. The block size for both L1 and L2 caches was 64 bytes. Data were collected as in Figure B.4.

One question is whether set associativity makes more sense for second-level caches.

Example   Given the data below, what is the impact of second-level cache associativity on its miss penalty?

- Hit time$_{L2}$ for direct mapped = 10 clock cycles.
- Two-way set associativity increases hit time by 0.1 clock cycle to 10.1 clock cycles.
- Local miss rate$_{L2}$ for direct mapped = 25%.
- Local miss rate$_{L2}$ for two-way set associative = 20%.
- Miss penalty$_{L2}$ = 200 clock cycles.

Answer   For a direct-mapped second-level cache, the first-level cache miss penalty is

$$\text{Miss penalty}_{\text{1-way L2}} = 10 + 25\% \times 200 = 60.0 \text{ clock cycles}$$

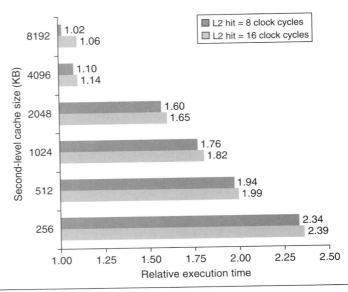

Figure B.15 Relative execution time by second-level cache size. The two bars are for different clock cycles for an L2 cache hit. The reference execution time of 1.00 is for an 8192 KB second-level cache with a 1-clock-cycle latency on a second-level hit. These data were collected the same way as in Figure B.14, using a simulator to imitate the Alpha 21264.

Adding the cost of associativity increases the hit cost only 0.1 clock cycle, making the new first-level cache miss penalty:

$$\text{Miss penalty}_{\text{2-way L2}} = 10.1 + 20\% \times 200 = 50.1 \text{ clock cycles}$$

In reality, second-level caches are almost always synchronized with the first-level cache and processor. Accordingly, the second-level hit time must be an integral number of clock cycles. If we are lucky, we shave the second-level hit time to 10 cycles; if not, we round up to 11 cycles. Either choice is an improvement over the direct-mapped second-level cache:

$$\text{Miss penalty}_{\text{2-way L2}} = 10 + 20\% \times 200 = 50.0 \text{ clock cycles}$$
$$\text{Miss penalty}_{\text{2-way L2}} = 11 + 20\% \times 200 = 51.0 \text{ clock cycles}$$

Now we can reduce the miss penalty by reducing the *miss rate* of the second-level caches.

Another consideration concerns whether data in the first-level cache are in the second-level cache. *Multilevel inclusion* is the natural policy for memory hierarchies: L1 data are always present in L2. Inclusion is desirable because consistency between I/O and caches (or among caches in a multiprocessor) can be determined just by checking the second-level cache.

One drawback to inclusion is that measurements can suggest smaller blocks for the smaller first-level cache and larger blocks for the larger second-level cache. For example, the Pentium 4 has 64-byte blocks in its L1 caches and 128-byte blocks in its L2 cache. Inclusion can still be maintained with more work on a second-level miss. The second-level cache must invalidate all first-level blocks that map onto the second-level block to be replaced, causing a slightly higher first-level miss rate. To avoid such problems, many cache designers keep the block size the same in all levels of caches.

However, what if the designer can only afford an L2 cache that is slightly bigger than the L1 cache? Should a significant portion of its space be used as a redundant copy of the L1 cache? In such cases a sensible opposite policy is *multilevel exclusion*: L1 data are *never* found in an L2 cache. Typically, with exclusion a cache miss in L1 results in a swap of blocks between L1 and L2 instead of a replacement of an L1 block with an L2 block. This policy prevents wasting space in the L2 cache. For example, the AMD Opteron chip obeys the exclusion property using two 64 KB L1 caches and 1 MB L2 cache.

As these issues illustrate, although a novice might design the first- and second-level caches independently, the designer of the first-level cache has a simpler job given a compatible second-level cache. It is less of a gamble to use a write-through, for example, if there is a write-back cache at the next level to act as a backstop for repeated writes and it uses multilevel inclusion.

The essence of all cache designs is balancing fast hits and few misses. For second-level caches, there are many fewer hits than in the first-level cache, so the emphasis shifts to fewer misses. This insight leads to much larger caches and techniques to lower the miss rate, such as higher associativity and larger blocks.

Fifth Optimization: Giving Priority to Read Misses over Writes to Reduce Miss Penalty

This optimization serves reads before writes have been completed. We start with looking at the complexities of a write buffer.

With a write-through cache the most important improvement is a write buffer of the proper size. Write buffers, however, do complicate memory accesses because they might hold the updated value of a location needed on a read miss.

Example   Look at this code sequence:

```
SW R3, 512(R0)      ;M[512] ← R3      (cache index 0)
LW R1, 1024(R0)     ;R1 ← M[1024]     (cache index 0)
LW R2, 512(R0)      ;R2 ← M[512]      (cache index 0)
```

Assume a direct-mapped, write-through cache that maps 512 and 1024 to the same block, and a four-word write buffer that is not checked on a read miss. Will the value in R2 always be equal to the value in R3?

Answer   Using the terminology from Chapter 2, this is a read-after-write data hazard in memory. Let's follow a cache access to see the danger. The data in R3 are placed into the write buffer after the store. The following load uses the same cache index and is therefore a miss. The second load instruction tries to put the value in location 512 into register R2; this also results in a miss. If the write buffer hasn't completed writing to location 512 in memory, the read of location 512 will put the old, wrong value into the cache block, and then into R2. Without proper precautions, R3 would not be equal to R2!

The simplest way out of this dilemma is for the read miss to wait until the write buffer is empty. The alternative is to check the contents of the write buffer on a read miss, and if there are no conflicts and the memory system is available, let the read miss continue. Virtually all desktop and server processors use the latter approach, giving reads priority over writes.

The cost of writes by the processor in a write-back cache can also be reduced. Suppose a read miss will replace a dirty memory block. Instead of writing the dirty block to memory, and then reading memory, we could copy the dirty block to a buffer, then read memory, and *then* write memory. This way the processor read, for which the processor is probably waiting, will finish sooner. Similar to the previous situation, if a read miss occurs, the processor can either stall until the buffer is empty or check the addresses of the words in the buffer for conflicts.

Now that we have five optimizations that reduce cache miss penalties or miss rates, it is time to look at reducing the final component of average memory access time. Hit time is critical because it can affect the clock rate of the processor; in many processors today the cache access time limits the clock cycle rate, even for processors that take multiple clock cycles to access the cache. Hence, a fast hit time is multiplied in importance beyond the average memory access time formula because it helps everything.

Sixth Optimization: Avoiding Address Translation during Indexing of the Cache to Reduce Hit Time

Even a small and simple cache must cope with the translation of a virtual address from the processor to a physical address to access memory. As described in Section B.4, processors treat main memory as just another level of the memory hierarchy, and thus the address of the virtual memory that exists on disk must be mapped onto the main memory.

The guideline of making the common case fast suggests that we use virtual addresses for the cache, since hits are much more common than misses. Such caches are termed *virtual caches*, with *physical cache* used to identify the traditional cache that uses physical addresses. As we will shortly see, it is important to distinguish two tasks: indexing the cache and comparing addresses. Thus, the issues are whether a virtual or physical address is used to index the cache and whether a virtual or physical address is used in the tag comparison. Full virtual addressing for both indices and tags eliminates address translation time from a cache hit. Then why doesn't everyone build virtually addressed caches?

One reason is protection. Page-level protection is checked as part of the virtual to physical address translation, and it must be enforced no matter what. One solution is to copy the protection information from the TLB on a miss, add a field to hold it, and check it on every access to the virtually addressed cache.

Another reason is that every time a process is switched, the virtual addresses refer to different physical addresses, requiring the cache to be flushed. Figure B.16 shows the impact on miss rates of this flushing. One solution is to increase the width of the cache address tag with a *process-identifier tag* (PID). If the operating system assigns these tags to processes, it only need flush the cache when a PID is recycled; that is, the PID distinguishes whether or not the data in the cache are for

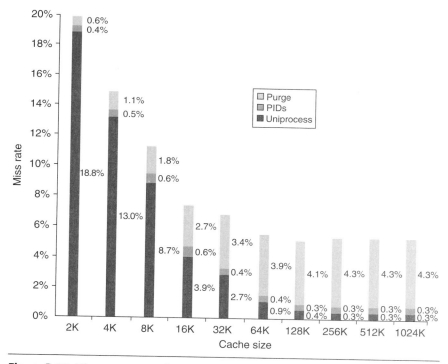

Figure B.16 Miss rate versus virtually addressed cache size of a program measured three ways: without process switches (uniprocess), with process switches using a process-identifier tag (PID), and with process switches but without PIDs (purge). PIDs increase the uniprocess absolute miss rate by 0.3% to 0.6% and save 0.6% to 4.3% over purging. Agarwal [1987] collected these statistics for the Ultrix operating system running on a VAX, assuming direct-mapped caches with a block size of 16 bytes. Note that the miss rate goes up from 128K to 256K. Such nonintuitive behavior can occur in caches because changing size changes the mapping of memory blocks onto cache blocks, which can change the conflict miss rate.

this program. Figure B.16 shows the improvement in miss rates by using PIDs to avoid cache flushes.

A third reason why virtual caches are not more popular is that operating systems and user programs may use two different virtual addresses for the same physical address. These duplicate addresses, called *synonyms* or *aliases*, could result in two copies of the same data in a virtual cache; if one is modified, the other will have the wrong value. With a physical cache this wouldn't happen, since the accesses would first be translated to the same physical cache block.

Hardware solutions to the synonym problem, called *antialiasing*, guarantee every cache block a unique physical address. For example, the AMD Opteron uses a 64 KB instruction cache with a 4 KB page and two-way set associativity; hence, the hardware must handle aliases involved with the three virtual address bits in the set index. It avoids aliases by simply checking all eight possible locations on a miss—two blocks in each of four sets—to be sure that none matches the physical address of the data being fetched. If one is found, it is invalidated, so when the new data are loaded into the cache their physical address is guaranteed to be unique.

Software can make this problem much easier by forcing aliases to share some address bits. An older version of UNIX from Sun Microsystems, for example, required all aliases to be identical in the last 18 bits of their addresses; this restriction is called *page coloring*. Note that page coloring is simply set associative mapping applied to virtual memory: The 4 KB (2^{12}) pages are mapped using 64 (2^6) sets to ensure that the physical and virtual addresses match in the last 18 bits. This restriction means a direct-mapped cache that is 2^{18} (256K) bytes or smaller can never have duplicate physical addresses for blocks. From the perspective of the cache, page coloring effectively increases the page offset, as software guarantees that the last few bits of the virtual and physical page address are identical.

The final area of concern with virtual addresses is I/O. I/O typically uses physical addresses and thus would require mapping to virtual addresses to interact with a virtual cache. (The impact of I/O on caches is further discussed in Appendix D.)

One alternative to get the best of both virtual and physical caches is to use part of the page offset—the part that is identical in both virtual and physical addresses—to index the cache. At the same time as the cache is being read using that index, the virtual part of the address is translated, and the tag match uses physical addresses.

This alternative allows the cache read to begin immediately, and yet the tag comparison is still with physical addresses. The limitation of this *virtually indexed, physically tagged* alternative is that a direct-mapped cache can be no bigger than the page size. For example, in the data cache in Figure B.5 on page B-13, the index is 9 bits and the cache block offset is 6 bits. To use this trick, the virtual page size would have to be at least $2^{(9+6)}$ bytes or 32 KB. If not, a portion of the index must be translated from virtual to physical address. Figure B.17 shows the organization of the caches, translation lookaside buffers (TLBs), and virtual memory when this technique is used.

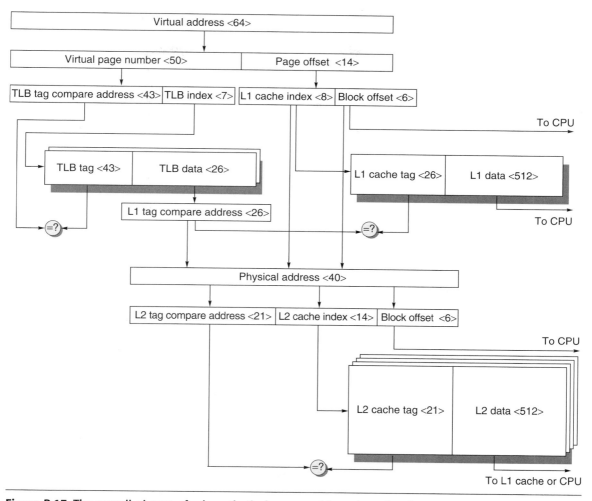

Figure B.17 The overall picture of a hypothetical memory hierarchy going from virtual address to L2 cache access. The page size is 16 KB. The TLB is two-way set associative with 256 entries. The L1 cache is a direct-mapped 16 KB, and the L2 cache is a four-way set associative with a total of 4 MB. Both use 64-byte blocks. The virtual address is 64 bits and the physical address is 40 bits.

Associativity can keep the index in the physical part of the address and yet still support a large cache. Recall that the size of the index is controlled by this formula:

$$2^{\text{Index}} = \frac{\text{Cache size}}{\text{Block size} \times \text{Set associativity}}$$

For example, doubling associativity and doubling the cache size does not change the size of the index. The IBM 3033 cache, as an extreme example, is 16-way set associative, even though studies show there is little benefit to miss

Technique	Hit time	Miss penalty	Miss rate	Hardware complexity	Comment
Larger block size		−	+	0	Trivial; Pentium 4 L2 uses 128 bytes
Larger cache size	−		+	1	Widely used, especially for L2 caches
Higher associativity	−		+	1	Widely used
Multilevel caches		+		2	Costly hardware; harder if L1 block size ≠ L2 block size; widely used
Read priority over writes		+		1	Widely used
Avoiding address translation during cache indexing	+			1	Widely used

Figure B.18 Summary of basic cache optimizations showing impact on cache performance and complexity for the techniques in this appendix. Generally a technique helps only one factor. + means that the technique improves the factor, − means it hurts that factor, and blank means it has no impact. The complexity measure is subjective, with 0 being the easiest and 3 being a challenge.

rates above 8-way set associativity. This high associativity allows a 64 KB cache to be addressed with a physical index, despite the handicap of 4 KB pages in the IBM architecture.

Summary of Basic Cache Optimization

The techniques in this section to improve miss rate, miss penalty, and hit time generally impact the other components of the average memory access equation as well as the complexity of the memory hierarchy. Figure B.18 summarizes these techniques and estimates the impact on complexity, with + meaning that the technique improves the factor, − meaning it hurts that factor, and blank meaning it has no impact. No optimization in this figure helps more than one category.

B.4 Virtual Memory

. . . a system has been devised to make the core drum combination appear to the programmer as a single level store, the requisite transfers taking place automatically.

Kilburn et al. [1962]

At any instant in time computers are running multiple processes, each with its own address space. (Processes are described in the next section.) It would be too expensive to dedicate a full address space worth of memory for each process, especially since many processes use only a small part of their address space. Hence, there must be a means of sharing a smaller amount of physical memory among many processes.

One way to do this, *virtual memory*, divides physical memory into blocks and allocates them to different processes. Inherent in such an approach must be a *protection* scheme that restricts a process to the blocks belonging only to that process. Most forms of virtual memory also reduce the time to start a program, since not all code and data need be in physical memory before a program can begin.

Although protection provided by virtual memory is essential for current computers, sharing is not the reason that virtual memory was invented. If a program became too large for physical memory, it was the programmer's job to make it fit. Programmers divided programs into pieces, then identified the pieces that were mutually exclusive, and loaded or unloaded these *overlays* under user program control during execution. The programmer ensured that the program never tried to access more physical main memory than was in the computer, and that the proper overlay was loaded at the proper time. As you can well imagine, this responsibility eroded programmer productivity.

Virtual memory was invented to relieve programmers of this burden; it automatically manages the two levels of the memory hierarchy represented by main memory and secondary storage. Figure B.19 shows the mapping of virtual memory to physical memory for a program with four pages.

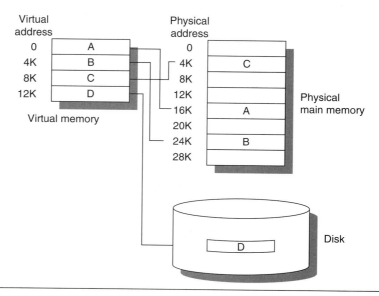

Figure B.19 **The logical program in its contiguous virtual address space is shown on the left.** It consists of four pages, A, B, C, and D. The actual location of three of the blocks is in physical main memory and the other is located on the disk.

In addition to sharing protected memory space and automatically managing the memory hierarchy, virtual memory also simplifies loading the program for execution. Called *relocation*, this mechanism allows the same program to run in any location in physical memory. The program in Figure B.19 can be placed anywhere in physical memory or disk just by changing the mapping between them. (Prior to the popularity of virtual memory, processors would include a relocation register just for that purpose.) An alternative to a hardware solution would be software that changed all addresses in a program each time it was run.

Several general memory hierarchy ideas from Chapter 1 about caches are analogous to virtual memory, although many of the terms are different. *Page* or *segment* is used for block, and *page fault* or *address fault* is used for miss. With virtual memory, the processor produces *virtual addresses* that are translated by a combination of hardware and software to *physical addresses*, which access main memory. This process is called *memory mapping* or *address translation*. Today, the two memory hierarchy levels controlled by virtual memory are DRAMs and magnetic disks. Figure B.20 shows a typical range of memory hierarchy parameters for virtual memory.

There are further differences between caches and virtual memory beyond those quantitative ones mentioned in Figure B.20:

■ Replacement on cache misses is primarily controlled by hardware, while virtual memory replacement is primarily controlled by the operating system. The longer miss penalty means it's more important to make a good decision, so the operating system can be involved and take time deciding what to replace.

■ The size of the processor address determines the size of virtual memory, but the cache size is independent of the processor address size.

Parameter	First-level cache	Virtual memory
Block (page) size	16–128 bytes	4096–65,536 bytes
Hit time	1–3 clock cycles	100–200 clock cycles
Miss penalty	8–200 clock cycles	1,000,000–10,000,000 clock cycles
(access time)	(6–160 clock cycles)	(800,000–8,000,000 clock cycles)
(transfer time)	(2–40 clock cycles)	(200,000–2,000,000 clock cycles)
Miss rate	0.1–10%	0.00001–0.001%
Address mapping	25–45-bit physical address to 14–20-bit cache address	32–64-bit virtual address to 25–45-bit physical address

Figure B.20 Typical ranges of parameters for caches and virtual memory. Virtual memory parameters represent increases of 10 to 1,000,000 times over cache parameters. Normally, first-level caches contain at most 1 MB of data, whereas physical memory contains 256 MB to 1 TB.

■ In addition to acting as the lower-level backing store for main memory in the hierarchy, secondary storage is also used for the file system. In fact, the file system occupies most of secondary storage. It is not normally in the address space.

Virtual memory also encompasses several related techniques. Virtual memory systems can be categorized into two classes: those with fixed-size blocks, called *pages*, and those with variable-size blocks, called *segments*. Pages are typically fixed at 4096 to 8192 bytes, while segment size varies. The largest segment supported on any processor ranges from 2^{16} bytes up to 2^{32} bytes; the smallest segment is 1 byte. Figure B.21 shows how the two approaches might divide code and data.

The decision to use paged virtual memory versus segmented virtual memory affects the processor. Paged addressing has a single fixed-size address divided into page number and offset within a page, analogous to cache addressing. A single

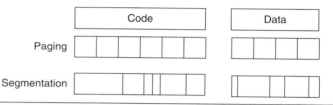

Figure B.21 Example of how paging and segmentation divide a program.

	Page	Segment
Words per address	One	Two (segment and offset)
Programmer visible?	Invisible to application programmer	May be visible to application programmer
Replacing a block	Trivial (all blocks are the same size)	Difficult (must find contiguous, variable-size, unused portion of main memory)
Memory use inefficiency	Internal fragmentation (unused portion of page)	External fragmentation (unused pieces of main memory)
Efficient disk traffic	Yes (adjust page size to balance access time and transfer time)	Not always (small segments may transfer just a few bytes)

Figure B.22 Paging versus segmentation. Both can waste memory, depending on the block size and how well the segments fit together in main memory. Programming languages with unrestricted pointers require both the segment and the address to be passed. A hybrid approach, called *paged segments*, shoots for the best of both worlds: Segments are composed of pages, so replacing a block is easy, yet a segment may be treated as a logical unit.

address does not work for segmented addresses; the variable size of segments requires 1 word for a segment number and 1 word for an offset within a segment, for a total of 2 words. An unsegmented address space is simpler for the compiler.

The pros and cons of these two approaches have been well documented in operating systems textbooks; Figure B.22 summarizes the arguments. Because of the replacement problem (the third line of the figure), few computers today use pure segmentation. Some computers use a hybrid approach, called *paged segments*, in which a segment is an integral number of pages. This simplifies replacement because memory need not be contiguous, and the full segments need not be in main memory. A more recent hybrid is for a computer to offer multiple page sizes, with the larger sizes being powers of 2 times the smallest page size. The IBM 405CR embedded processor, for example, allows 1 KB, 4 KB ($2^2 \times$ 1 KB), 16 KB ($2^4 \times$ 1 KB), 64 KB ($2^6 \times$ 1 KB), 256 KB ($2^8 \times$ 1 KB), 1024 KB ($2^{10} \times$ 1 KB), and 4096 KB ($2^{12} \times$ 1 KB) to act as a single page.

Four Memory Hierarchy Questions Revisited

We are now ready to answer the four memory hierarchy questions for virtual memory.

Q1: Where Can a Block Be Placed in Main Memory?

The miss penalty for virtual memory involves access to a rotating magnetic storage device and is therefore quite high. Given the choice of lower miss rates or a simpler placement algorithm, operating systems designers normally pick lower miss rates because of the exorbitant miss penalty. Thus, operating systems allow blocks to be placed anywhere in main memory. According to the terminology in Figure B.2 on page B-8, this strategy would be labeled fully associative.

Q2: How Is a Block Found If It Is in Main Memory?

Both paging and segmentation rely on a data structure that is indexed by the page or segment number. This data structure contains the physical address of the block. For segmentation, the offset is added to the segment's physical address to obtain the final physical address. For paging, the offset is simply concatenated to this physical page address (see Figure B.23).

This data structure, containing the physical page addresses, usually takes the form of a *page table*. Indexed by the virtual page number, the size of the table is the number of pages in the virtual address space. Given a 32-bit virtual address, 4 KB pages, and 4 bytes per page table entry (PTE), the size of the page table would be $(2^{32}/2^{12}) \times 2^2 = 2^{22}$ or 4 MB.

To reduce the size of this data structure, some computers apply a hashing function to the virtual address. The hash allows the data structure to be the length of the number of *physical* pages in main memory. This number could be much smaller than the number of virtual pages. Such a structure is called an *inverted page table*. Using the previous example, a 512 MB physical memory would only need 1 MB (8×512 MB/4 KB) for an inverted page table; the extra 4 bytes per

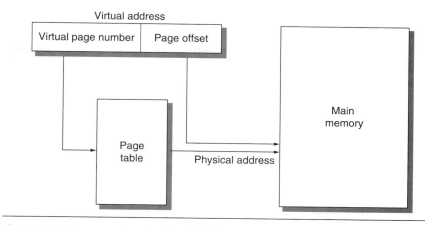

Figure B.23 **The mapping of a virtual address to a physical address via a page table.**

page table entry are for the virtual address. The HP/Intel IA-64 covers both bases by offering both traditional pages tables *and* inverted page tables, leaving the choice of mechanism to the operating system programmer.

To reduce address translation time, computers use a cache dedicated to these address translations, called a *translation lookaside buffer*, or simply *translation buffer*, described in more detail shortly.

Q3: Which Block Should Be Replaced on a Virtual Memory Miss?

As mentioned earlier, the overriding operating system guideline is minimizing page faults. Consistent with this guideline, almost all operating systems try to replace the least recently used (LRU) block because if the past predicts the future, that is the one less likely to be needed.

To help the operating system estimate LRU, many processors provide a *use bit* or *reference bit*, which is logically set whenever a page is accessed. (To reduce work, it is actually set only on a translation buffer miss, which is described shortly.) The operating system periodically clears the use bits and later records them so it can determine which pages were touched during a particular time period. By keeping track in this way, the operating system can select a page that is among the least recently referenced.

Q4: What Happens on a Write?

The level below main memory contains rotating magnetic disks that take millions of clock cycles to access. Because of the great discrepancy in access time, no one has yet built a virtual memory operating system that writes through main memory to disk on every store by the processor. (This remark should not be interpreted as an opportunity to become famous by being the first to build one!) Thus, the write strategy is always write-back.

Since the cost of an unnecessary access to the next-lower level is so high, virtual memory systems usually include a dirty bit. It allows blocks to be written to disk only if they have been altered since being read from the disk.

Techniques for Fast Address Translation

Page tables are usually so large that they are stored in main memory and are sometimes paged themselves. Paging means that every memory access logically takes at least twice as long, with one memory access to obtain the physical address and a second access to get the data. As mentioned in Chapter 2, we use locality to avoid the extra memory access. By keeping address translations in a special cache, a memory access rarely requires a second access to translate the data. This special address translation cache is referred to as a *translation look aside buffer* (TLB), also called a *translation buffer* (TB).

A TLB entry is like a cache entry where the tag holds portions of the virtual address and the data portion holds a physical page frame number, protection field, valid bit, and usually a use bit and dirty bit. To change the physical page frame number or protection of an entry in the page table, the operating system must make sure the old entry is not in the TLB; otherwise, the system won't behave properly. Note that this dirty bit means the corresponding *page* is dirty, not that the address translation in the TLB is dirty nor that a particular block in the data cache is dirty. The operating system resets these bits by changing the value in the page table and then invalidates the corresponding TLB entry. When the entry is reloaded from the page table, the TLB gets an accurate copy of the bits.

Figure B.24 shows the Opteron data TLB organization, with each step of the translation labeled. This TLB uses fully associative placement; thus, the translation begins (steps 1 and 2) by sending the virtual address to all tags. Of course, the tag must be marked valid to allow a match. At the same time, the type of memory access is checked for a violation (also in step 2) against protection information in the TLB.

For reasons similar to those in the cache case, there is no need to include the 12 bits of the page offset in the TLB. The matching tag sends the corresponding physical address through effectively a 40:1 multiplexor (step 3). The page offset is then combined with the physical page frame to form a full physical address (step 4). The address size is 40 bits.

Address translation can easily be on the critical path determining the clock cycle of the processor, so the Opteron uses virtually addressed, physically tagged L1 caches.

Selecting a Page Size

The most obvious architectural parameter is the page size. Choosing the page is a question of balancing forces that favor a larger page size versus those favoring a smaller size. The following favor a larger size:

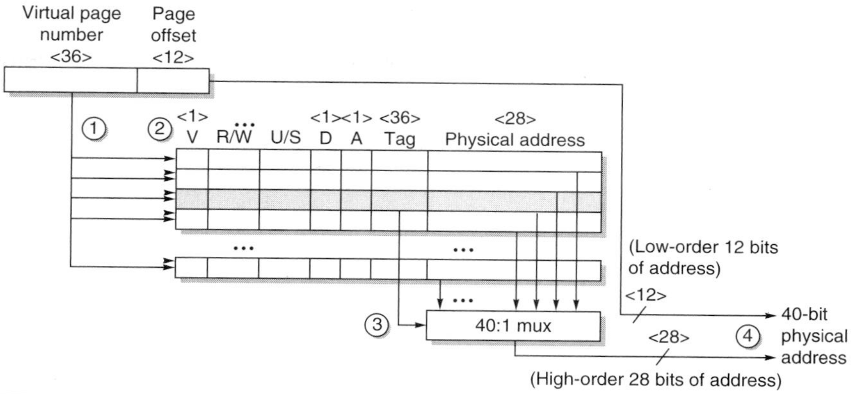

Figure B.24 Operation of the Opteron data TLB during address translation. The four steps of a TLB hit are shown as circled numbers. This TLB has 40 entries. Section B.5 describes the various protection and access fields of an Opteron page table entry.

- The size of the page table is inversely proportional to the page size; memory (or other resources used for the memory map) can therefore be saved by making the pages bigger.

- As mentioned in Section B.3, a larger page size can allow larger caches with fast cache hit times.

- Transferring larger pages to or from secondary storage, possibly over a network, is more efficient than transferring smaller pages.

- The number of TLB entries is restricted, so a larger page size means that more memory can be mapped efficiently, thereby reducing the number of TLB misses.

It is for this final reason that recent microprocessors have decided to support multiple page sizes; for some programs, TLB misses can be as significant on CPI as the cache misses.

The main motivation for a smaller page size is conserving storage. A small page size will result in less wasted storage when a contiguous region of virtual memory is not equal in size to a multiple of the page size. The term for this unused memory in a page is *internal fragmentation*. Assuming that each process has three primary segments (text, heap, and stack), the average wasted storage per process will be 1.5 times the page size. This amount is negligible for computers with hundreds of megabytes of memory and page sizes of 4 KB to 8 KB. Of course, when the page sizes become very large (more than 32 KB), storage (both main and secondary) could be wasted, as well as I/O bandwidth. A final concern is process start-up time; many processes are small, so a large page size would lengthen the time to invoke a process.

Summary of Virtual Memory and Caches

With virtual memory, TLBs, first-level caches, and second-level caches all mapping portions of the virtual and physical address space, it can get confusing what bits go where. Figure B.25 gives a hypothetical example going from a 64-bit virtual address to a 41-bit physical address with two levels of cache. This L1 cache is virtually indexed, physically tagged since both the cache size and the page size are 8 KB. The L2 cache is 4 MB. The block size for both is 64 bytes.

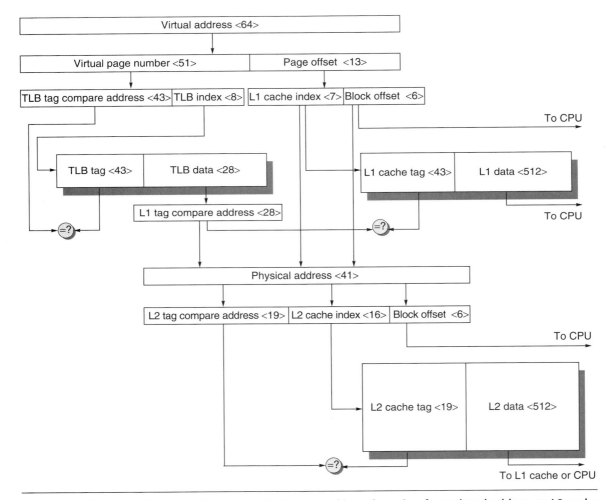

Figure B.25 The overall picture of a hypothetical memory hierarchy going from virtual address to L2 cache access. The page size is 8 KB. The TLB is direct mapped with 256 entries. The L1 cache is a direct-mapped 8 KB, and the L2 cache is a direct-mapped 4 MB. Both use 64-byte blocks. The virtual address is 64 bits and the physical address is 41 bits. The primary difference between this simple figure and a real cache is replication of pieces of this figure.

First, the 64-bit virtual address is logically divided into a virtual page number and page offset. The former is sent to the TLB to be translated into a physical address, and the high bit of the latter is sent to the L1 cache to act as an index. If the TLB match is a hit, then the physical page number is sent to the L1 cache tag to check for a match. If it matches, it's an L1 cache hit. The block offset then selects the word for the processor.

If the L1 cache check results in a miss, the physical address is then used to try the L2 cache. The middle portion of the physical address is used as an index to the 4 MB L2 cache. The resulting L2 cache tag is compared to the upper part of the physical address to check for a match. If it matches, we have an L2 cache hit, and the data are sent to the processor, which uses the block offset to select the desired word. On an L2 miss, the physical address is then used to get the block from memory.

Although this is a simple example, the major difference between this drawing and a real cache is replication. First, there is only one L1 cache. When there are two L1 caches, the top half of the diagram is duplicated. Note that this would lead to two TLBs, which is typical. Hence, one cache and TLB is for instructions, driven from the PC, and one cache and TLB is for data, driven from the effective address.

The second simplification is that all the caches and TLBs are direct mapped. If any were n-way set associative, then we would replicate each set of tag memory, comparators, and data memory n times and connect data memories with an $n{:}1$ multiplexor to select a hit. Of course, if the total cache size remained the same, the cache index would also shrink by $\log 2n$ bits according to the formula in Figure B.7 on page B-22.

B.5   Protection and Examples of Virtual Memory

The invention of multiprogramming, where a computer would be shared by several programs running concurrently, led to new demands for protection and sharing among programs. These demands are closely tied to virtual memory in computers today, and so we cover the topic here along with two examples of virtual memory.

Multiprogramming leads to the concept of a *process*. Metaphorically, a process is a program's breathing air and living space—that is, a running program plus any state needed to continue running it. Time-sharing is a variation of multiprogramming that shares the processor and memory with several interactive users at the same time, giving the illusion that all users have their own computers. Thus, at any instant it must be possible to switch from one process to another. This exchange is called a *process switch* or *context switch*.

A process must operate correctly whether it executes continuously from start to finish, or it is interrupted repeatedly and switched with other processes. The responsibility for maintaining correct process behavior is shared by designers of the computer and the operating system. The computer designer must ensure that the processor portion of the process state can be saved and restored. The operating system designer must guarantee that processes do not interfere with each others' computations.

The safest way to protect the state of one process from another would be to copy the current information to disk. However, a process switch would then take seconds—far too long for a time-sharing environment.

This problem is solved by operating systems partitioning main memory so that several different processes have their state in memory at the same time. This division means that the operating system designer needs help from the computer designer to provide protection so that one process cannot modify another. Besides protection, the computers also provide for sharing of code and data between processes, to allow communication between processes or to save memory by reducing the number of copies of identical information.

Protecting Processes

Processes can be protected from one another by having their own page tables, each pointing to distinct pages of memory. Obviously, user programs must be prevented from modifying their page tables or protection would be circumvented.

Protection can be escalated, depending on the apprehension of the computer designer or the purchaser. *Rings* added to the processor protection structure expand memory access protection from two levels (user and kernel) to many more. Like a military classification system of top secret, secret, confidential, and unclassified, concentric rings of security levels allow the most trusted to access anything, the second most trusted to access everything except the innermost level, and so on. The "civilian" programs are the least trusted and, hence, have the most limited range of accesses. There may also be restrictions on what pieces of memory can contain code—execute protection—and even on the entrance point between the levels. The Intel 80x86 protection structure, which uses rings, is described later in this section. It is not clear whether rings are an improvement in practice over the simple system of user and kernel modes.

As the designer's apprehension escalates to trepidation, these simple rings may not suffice. Restricting the freedom given a program in the inner sanctum requires a new classification system. Instead of a military model, the analogy of this system is to keys and locks: A program can't unlock access to the data unless it has the key. For these keys, or *capabilities*, to be useful, the hardware and operating system must be able to explicitly pass them from one program to another without allowing a program itself to forge them. Such checking requires a great deal of hardware support if time for checking keys is to be kept low.

The 80x86 architecture has tried several of these alternatives over the years. Since backwards compatibility is one of the guidelines of this architecture, the most recent versions of the architecture include all of its experiments in virtual memory. We'll go over two of the options here: first the older segmented address space and then the newer flat, 64-bit address space.

A Segmented Virtual Memory Example: Protection in the Intel Pentium

The second system is the most dangerous system a man ever designs. . . . The general tendency is to over-design the second system, using all the ideas and frills that were cautiously sidetracked on the first one.

F. P. Brooks, Jr.
The Mythical Man-Month (1975)

The original 8086 used segments for addressing, yet it provided nothing for virtual memory or for protection. Segments had base registers but no bound registers and no access checks, and before a segment register could be loaded the corresponding segment had to be in physical memory. Intel's dedication to virtual memory and protection is evident in the successors to the 8086, with a few fields extended to support larger addresses. This protection scheme is elaborate, with many details carefully designed to try to avoid security loopholes. We'll refer to it as IA-32. The next few pages highlight a few of the Intel safeguards; if you find the reading difficult, imagine the difficulty of implementing them!

The first enhancement is to double the traditional two-level protection model: The IA-32 has four levels of protection. The innermost level (0) corresponds to the traditional kernel mode, and the outermost level (3) is the least privileged mode. The IA-32 has separate stacks for each level to avoid security breaches between the levels. There are also data structures analogous to traditional page tables that contain the physical addresses for segments, as well as a list of checks to be made on translated addresses.

The Intel designers did not stop there. The IA-32 divides the address space, allowing both the operating system and the user access to the full space. The IA-32 user can call an operating system routine in this space and even pass parameters to it while retaining full protection. This safe call is not a trivial action, since the stack for the operating system is different from the user's stack. Moreover, the IA-32 allows the operating system to maintain the protection level of the *called* routine for the parameters that are passed to it. This potential loophole in protection is prevented by not allowing the user process to ask the operating system to access something indirectly that it would not have been able to access itself. (Such security loopholes are called *Trojan horses*.)

The Intel designers were guided by the principle of trusting the operating system as little as possible, while supporting sharing and protection. As an example of the use of such protected sharing, suppose a payroll program writes checks and also updates the year-to-date information on total salary and benefits payments. Thus, we want to give the program the ability to read the salary and year-to-date information and modify the year-to-date information but not the salary. We will see the mechanism to support such features shortly. In the rest of this subsection, we will look at the big picture of the IA-32 protection and examine its motivation.

Adding Bounds Checking and Memory Mapping

The first step in enhancing the Intel processor was getting the segmented addressing to check bounds as well as supply a base. Rather than a base address, the segment registers in the IA-32 contain an index to a virtual memory data structure called a *descriptor table*. Descriptor tables play the role of traditional page tables. On the IA-32 the equivalent of a page table entry is a *segment descriptor*. It contains fields found in PTEs:

■ *Present bit*—Equivalent to the PTE valid bit, used to indicate this is a valid translation

■ *Base field*—Equivalent to a page frame address, containing the physical address of the first byte of the segment

■ *Access bit*—Like the reference bit or use bit in some architectures that is helpful for replacement algorithms

■ *Attributes field*—Specifies the valid operations and protection levels for operations that use this segment

There is also a *limit field,* not found in paged systems, which establishes the upper bound of valid offsets for this segment. Figure B.26 shows examples of IA-32 segment descriptors.

IA-32 provides an optional paging system in addition to this segmented addressing. The upper portion of the 32-bit address selects the segment descriptor, and the middle portion is an index into the page table selected by the descriptor. We describe below the protection system that does not rely on paging.

Adding Sharing and Protection

To provide for protected sharing, half of the address space is shared by all processes and half is unique to each process, called *global address space* and *local address space*, respectively. Each half is given a descriptor table with the appropriate name. A descriptor pointing to a shared segment is placed in the global descriptor table, while a descriptor for a private segment is placed in the local descriptor table.

A program loads an IA-32 segment register with an index to the table *and* a bit saying which table it desires. The operation is checked according to the attributes in the descriptor, the physical address being formed by adding the offset in the processor to the base in the descriptor, provided the offset is less than the limit field. Every segment descriptor has a separate 2-bit field to give the legal access level of this segment. A violation occurs only if the program tries to use a segment with a lower protection level in the segment descriptor.

We can now show how to invoke the payroll program mentioned above to update the year-to-date information without allowing it to update salaries. The program could be given a descriptor to the information that has the writable field clear, meaning it can read but not write the data. A trusted program can then be supplied that will only write the year-to-date information. It is given a descriptor

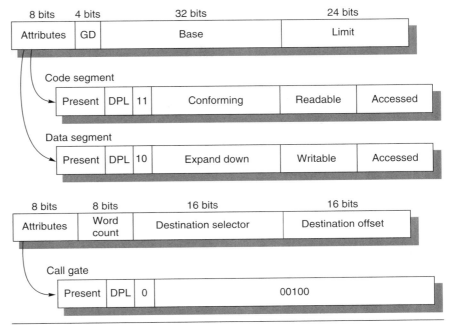

Figure B.26 The IA-32 segment descriptors are distinguished by bits in the attributes field. *Base, limit, present, readable,* and *writable* are all self-explanatory. D gives the default addressing size of the instructions: 16 bits or 32 bits. G gives the granularity of the segment limit: 0 means in bytes and 1 means in 4 KB pages. G is set to 1 when paging is turned on to set the size of the page tables. DPL means *descriptor privilege level*—this is checked against the code privilege level to see if the access will be allowed. *Conforming* says the code takes on the privilege level of the code being called rather than the privilege level of the caller; it is used for library routines. The *expand-down field* flips the check to let the base field be the high-water mark and the limit field be the low-water mark. As you might expect, this is used for stack segments that grow down. *Word count* controls the number of words copied from the current stack to the new stack on a call gate. The other two fields of the call gate descriptor, *destination selector* and *destination offset,* select the descriptor of the destination of the call and the offset into it, respectively. There are many more than these three segment descriptors in the IA-32 protection model.

with the writable field set (Figure B.26). The payroll program invokes the trusted code using a code segment descriptor with the conforming field set. This setting means the called program takes on the privilege level of the code being called rather than the privilege level of the caller. Hence, the payroll program can read the salaries and call a trusted program to update the year-to-date totals, yet the payroll program cannot modify the salaries. If a Trojan horse exists in this system, to be effective it must be located in the trusted code whose only job is to update the year-to-date information. The argument for this style of protection is that limiting the scope of the vulnerability enhances security.

Adding Safe Calls from User to OS Gates and Inheriting Protection Level for Parameters

Allowing the user to jump into the operating system is a bold step. How, then, can a hardware designer increase the chances of a safe system without trusting the operating system or any other piece of code? The IA-32 approach is to restrict where the user can enter a piece of code, to safely place parameters on the proper stack, and to make sure the user parameters don't get the protection level of the called code.

To restrict entry into others' code, the IA-32 provides a special segment descriptor, or *call gate*, identified by a bit in the attributes field. Unlike other descriptors, call gates are full physical addresses of an object in memory; the offset supplied by the processor is ignored. As stated above, their purpose is to prevent the user from randomly jumping anywhere into a protected or more privileged code segment. In our programming example, this means the only place the payroll program can invoke the trusted code is at the proper boundary. This restriction is needed to make conforming segments work as intended.

What happens if caller and callee are "mutually suspicious," so that neither trusts the other? The solution is found in the word count field in the bottom descriptor in Figure B.26. When a call instruction invokes a call gate descriptor, the descriptor copies the number of words specified in the descriptor from the local stack onto the stack corresponding to the level of this segment. This copying allows the user to pass parameters by first pushing them onto the local stack. The hardware then safely transfers them onto the correct stack. A return from a call gate will pop the parameters off both stacks and copy any return values to the proper stack. Note that this model is incompatible with the current practice of passing parameters in registers.

This scheme still leaves open the potential loophole of having the operating system use the user's address, passed as parameters, with the operating system's security level, instead of with the user's level. The IA-32 solves this problem by dedicating 2 bits in every processor segment register to the *requested protection level*. When an operating system routine is invoked, it can execute an instruction that sets this 2-bit field in all address parameters with the protection level of the user that called the routine. Thus, when these address parameters are loaded into the segment registers, they will set the requested protection level to the proper value. The IA-32 hardware then uses the requested protection level to prevent any foolishness: No segment can be accessed from the system routine using those parameters if it has a more privileged protection level than requested.

A Paged Virtual Memory Example: The 64-Bit Opteron Memory Management

AMD engineers found few uses of the elaborate protection model described above. The popular model is a flat, 32-bit address space, introduced by the 80386, which sets all the base values of the segment registers to zero. Hence,

AMD dispensed with the multiple segments in the 64-bit mode. It assumes that the segment base is zero and ignores the limit field. The page sizes are 4 KB, 2 MB, and 4 MB.

The 64-bit virtual address of the AMD64 architecture is mapped onto 52-bit physical addresses, although implementations can implement fewer bits to simplify hardware. The Opteron, for example, uses 48-bit virtual addresses and 40-bit physical addresses. AMD64 requires that the upper 16 bits of the virtual address be just the sign extension of the lower 48 bits, which it calls *canonical form*.

The size of page tables for the 64-bit address space is alarming. Hence, AMD64 uses a multilevel hierarchical page table to map the address space to keep the size reasonable. The number of levels depends on the size of the virtual address space. Figure B.27 shows the four-level translation of the 48-bit virtual addresses of the Opteron.

The offsets for each of these page tables come from four 9-bit fields. Address translation starts with adding the first offset to the page-map level 4 base register and then reading memory from this location to get the base of the next-level page

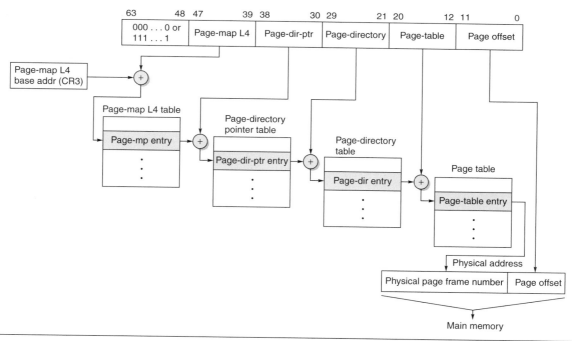

Figure B.27   The mapping of an Opteron virtual address. The Opteron virtual memory implementation with four page table levels supports an effective physical address size of 40 bits. Each page table has 512 entries, so each level field is 9 bits wide. The AMD64 architecture document allows the virtual address size to grow from the current 48 bits to 64 bits, and the physical address size to grow from the current 40 bits to 52 bits.

table. The next address offset is in turn added to this newly fetched address, and memory is accessed again to determine the base of the third page table. It happens again in the same fashion. The last address field is added to this final base address, and memory is read using this sum to (finally) get the physical address of the page being referenced. This address is concatenated with the 12-bit page offset to get the full physical address. Note that the page table in the Opteron architecture fits within a single 4 KB page.

The Opteron uses a 64-bit entry in each of these page tables. The first 12 bits are reserved for future use, the next 52 bits contain the physical page frame number, and the last 12 bits give the protection and use information. Although the fields vary some between the page table levels, here are the basic ones:

■ *Presence*—Says that page is present in memory.

■ *Read/write*—Says whether page is read-only or read-write.

■ *User/supervisor*—Says whether a user can access the page or if it is limited to the upper three privilege levels.

■ *Dirty*—Says if page has been modified.

■ *Accessed*—Says if page has been read or written since the bit was last cleared.

■ *Page size*—Says whether the last level is for 4 KB pages or 4 MB pages; if it's the latter, then the Opteron only uses three instead of four levels of pages.

■ *No execute*—Not found in the 80386 protection scheme, this bit was added to prevent code from executing in some pages.

■ *Page level cache disable*—Says whether the page can be cached or not.

■ *Page level write-through*—Says whether the page allows write-back or write-through for data caches.

Since the Opteron normally goes through four levels of tables on a TLB miss, there are three potential places to check protection restrictions. The Opteron obeys only the bottom-level PTE, checking the others only to be sure the valid bit is set.

As the entry is 8 bytes long, each page table has 512 entries, and the Opteron has 4 KB pages, the page tables are exactly one page long. Each of the four level fields are 9 bits long, and the page offset is 12 bits. This derivation leaves $64 - (4 \times 9 + 12)$ or 16 bits to be sign extended to ensure canonical addresses.

Although we have explained translation of legal addresses, what prevents the user from creating illegal address translations and getting into mischief? The page tables themselves are protected from being written by user programs. Thus, the user can try any virtual address, but by controlling the page table entries the operating system controls what physical memory is accessed. Sharing of memory between processes is accomplished by having a page table entry in each address space point to the same physical memory page.

The Opteron employs four TLBs to reduce address translation time, two for instruction accesses and two for data accesses. Like multilevel caches, the

Parameter	Description
Block size	1 PTE (8 bytes)
L1 hit time	1 clock cycle
L2 hit time	7 clock cycles
L1 TLB size	Same for instruction and data TLBs: 40 PTEs per TLBs, with 32 4 KB pages and 8 for 2 MB or 4 MB pages
L2 TLB size	Same for instruction and data TLBs: 512 PTEs of 4 KB pages
Block selection	LRU
Write strategy	(Not applicable)
L1 block placement	Fully associative
L2 block placement	4-way set associative

Figure B.28 Memory hierarchy parameters of the Opteron L1 and L2 instruction and data TLBs.

Opteron reduces TLB misses by having two larger L2 TLBs: one for instructions and one for data. Figure B.28 describes the data TLB.

Summary: Protection on the 32-Bit Intel Pentium vs. the 64-Bit AMD Opteron

Memory management in the Opteron is typical of most desktop or server computers today, relying on page-level address translation and correct operation of the operating system to provide safety to multiple processes sharing the computer. Although presented as alternatives, Intel has followed AMD's lead and embraced the AMD64 architecture. Hence, both AMD and Intel support the 64-bit extension of 80x86; yet, for compatibility reasons, both support the elaborate segmented protection scheme.

If the segmented protection model looks harder to build than the AMD64 model, that's because it is. This effort must be especially frustrating for the engineers, since few customers use the elaborate protection mechanism. In addition, the fact that the protection model is a mismatch to the simple paging protection of UNIX-like systems means it will be used only by someone writing an operating system especially for this computer, which hasn't happened yet.

B.6   Fallacies and Pitfalls

Even a review of memory hierarchy has fallacies and pitfalls!

Pitfall   *Too small an address space.*

Just five years after DEC and Carnegie Mellon University collaborated to design the new PDP-11 computer family, it was apparent that their creation had a fatal flaw. An architecture announced by IBM six years *before* the PDP-11 was still thriving, with minor modifications, 25 years later. And the DEC VAX, criticized for including unnecessary functions, sold millions of units after the PDP-11 went out of production. Why?

The fatal flaw of the PDP-11 was the size of its addresses (16 bits) as compared to the address sizes of the IBM 360 (24 to 31 bits) and the VAX (32 bits). Address size limits the program length, since the size of a program and the amount of data needed by the program must be less than $2^{\text{Address size}}$. The reason the address size is so hard to change is that it determines the minimum width of anything that can contain an address: PC, register, memory word, and effective-address arithmetic. If there is no plan to expand the address from the start, then the chances of successfully changing address size are so slim that it normally means the end of that computer family. Bell and Strecker [1976] put it like this:

> There is only one mistake that can be made in computer design that is difficult to recover from—not having enough address bits for memory addressing and memory management. The PDP-11 followed the unbroken tradition of nearly every known computer. [p. 2]

A partial list of successful computers that eventually starved to death for lack of address bits includes the PDP-8, PDP-10, PDP-11, Intel 8080, Intel 8086, Intel 80186, Intel 80286, Motorola 6800, AMI 6502, Zilog Z80, CRAY-1, and CRAY X-MP.

The venerable 80x86 line bears the distinction of having been extended twice, first to 32 bits with the Intel 80386 in 1985 and recently to 64 bits with the AMD Opteron.

Pitfall   *Ignoring the impact of the operating system on the performance of the memory hierarchy.*

Figure B.29 shows the memory stall time due to the operating system spent on three large workloads. About 25% of the stall time is either spent in misses in the operating system or results from misses in the application programs because of interference with the operating system.

Pitfall   *Relying on the operating systems to change the page size over time.*

The Alpha architects had an elaborate plan to grow the architecture over time by growing its page size, even building it into the size of its virtual address. When it came time to grow page sizes with later Alphas, the operating system designers balked and the virtual memory system was revised to grow the address space while maintaining the 8 KB page.

Architects of other computers noticed very high TLB miss rates, and so added multiple, larger page sizes to the TLB. The hope was that operating systems programmers would allocate an object to the largest page that made sense, thereby preserving TLB entries. After a decade of trying, most operating systems use these "superpages" only for handpicked functions: mapping the display memory or other I/O devices, or using very large pages for the database code.

Workload	Misses		Time						
			% Time due to application misses		% Time due directly to OS misses				% Time OS misses and application conflicts
	% in applications	% in OS	Inherent application misses	OS conflicts with applications	OS instruction misses	Data misses for migration	Data misses in block operations	Rest of OS misses	
Pmake	47%	53%	14.1%	4.8%	10.9%	1.0%	6.2%	2.9%	25.8%
Multipgm	53%	47%	21.6%	3.4%	9.2%	4.2%	4.7%	3.4%	24.9%
Oracle	73%	27%	25.7%	10.2%	10.6%	2.6%	0.6%	2.8%	26.8%

Figure B.29 Misses and time spent in misses for applications and operating system. The operating system adds about 25% to the execution time of the application. Each processor has a 64 KB instruction cache and a two-level data cache with 64 KB in the first level and 256 KB in the second level; all caches are direct mapped with 16-byte blocks. Collected on Silicon Graphics POWER station 4D/340, a multiprocessor with four 33 MHz R3000 processors running three application workloads under a UNIX System V—Pmake, a parallel compile of 56 files; Multipgm, the parallel numeric program MP3D running concurrently with Pmake and a five-screen edit session; and Oracle, running a restricted version of the TP-1 benchmark using the Oracle database. (Data from Torrellas, Gupta, and Hennessy [1992].)

B.7   Concluding Remarks

The difficulty of building a memory system to keep pace with faster processors is underscored by the fact that the raw material for main memory is the same as that found in the cheapest computer. It is the principle of locality that helps us here—its soundness is demonstrated at all levels of the memory hierarchy in current computers, from disks to TLBs.

However, the increasing relative latency to memory, taking hundreds of clock cycles in 2011, means that programmers and compiler writers must be aware of the parameters of the caches and TLBs if they want their programs to perform well.

B.8   Historical Perspective and References

In Section L.3 (available online) we examine the history of caches, virtual memory, and virtual machines. (The historical section covers both this appendix and Chapter 3.) IBM plays a prominent role in the history of all three. References for further reading are included.

Exercises by Amr Zaky

B.1 [10/10/10/15] <B.1> You are trying to appreciate how important the principle of locality is in justifying the use of a cache memory, so you experiment with a computer having an L1 data cache and a main memory (you exclusively focus on data accesses). The latencies (in CPU cycles) of the different kinds of accesses are as follows: cache hit, 1 cycle; cache miss, 105 cycles; main memory access with cache disabled, 100 cycles.

a. [10] <B.1> When you run a program with an overall miss rate of 5%, what will the average memory access time (in CPU cycles) be?

b. [10] <B.1> Next, you run a program specifically designed to produce completely random data addresses with no locality. Toward that end, you use an array of size 256 MB (all of it fits in the main memory). Accesses to random elements of this array are continuously made (using a uniform random number generator to generate the elements indices). If your data cache size is 64 KB, what will the average memory access time be?

c. [10] <B.1> If you compare the result obtained in part (b) with the main memory access time when the cache is disabled, what can you conclude about the role of the principle of locality in justifying the use of cache memory?

d. [15] <B.1> You observed that a cache hit produces a gain of 99 cycles (1 cycle vs. 100), but it produces a loss of 5 cycles in the case of a miss (105 cycles vs. 100). In the general case, we can express these two quantities as G (gain) and L (loss). Using these two quantities (G and L), identify the highest miss rate after which the cache use would be disadvantageous.

B.2 [15/15] <B.1> For the purpose of this exercise, we assume that we have 512-byte cache with 64-byte blocks. We will also assume that the main memory is 2 KB large. We can regard the memory as an array of 64-byte blocks: M0, M1, ..., M31. Figure B.30 sketches the memory blocks that can reside in different cache blocks if the cache was fully associative.

a. [15] <B.1> Show the contents of the table if cache is organized as a direct-mapped cache.

b. [15] <B.1> Repeat part (a) with the cache organized as a four-way set associative cache.

B.3 [10/10/10/10/15/10/15/20] <B.1> Cache organization is often influenced by the desire to reduce the cache's power consumption. For that purpose we assume that the cache is physically distributed into a data array (holding the data), tag array (holding the tags), and replacement array (holding information needed by replacement policy). Furthermore, every one of these arrays is physically distributed into multiple sub-arrays (one per way) that can be individually accessed; for example, a four-way set associative least recently used (LRU) cache would have

Cache block	Set	Way	Memory blocks that can reside in cache block
0	0	0	M0, M1, M2, ..., M31
1	0	1	M0, M1, M2, ..., M31
2	0	2	M0, M1, M2, ..., M31
3	0	3	M0, M1, M2, ..., M31
4	0	4	M0, M1, M2, ..., M31
5	0	5	M0, M1, M2, ..., M31
6	0	6	M0, M1, M2, ..., M31
7	0	7	M0, M1, M2, ..., M31

Figure B.30 Memory blocks that can reside in cache block.

four data sub-arrays, four tag sub-arrays, and four replacement sub-arrays. We assume that the replacement sub-arrays are accessed once per access when the LRU replacement policy is used, and once per miss if the first-in, first-out (FIFO) replacement policy is used. It is not needed when a random replacement policy is used. For a specific cache, it was determined that the accesses to the different arrays have the following power consumption weights:

Array	Power consumption weight (per way accessed)
Data array	20 units
Tag	Array 5 units
Miscellaneous array	1 unit

Estimate the cache power usage (in power units) for the following configurations. We assume the cache is four-way set associative. Main memory access power—albeit important—is not considered here. Provide answers for the LRU, FIFO, and random replacement policies.

a. [10]<B.1> A cache read hit. All arrays are read simultaneously.

b. [10] <B.1> Repeat part (a) for a cache read miss.

c. [10] <B.1> Repeat part (a) assuming that the cache access is split across two cycles. In the first cycle, all the tag sub-arrays are accessed. In the second cycle, only the sub-array whose tag matched will be accessed.

d. [10] <B.1> Repeat part (c) for a cache read miss (no data array accesses in the second cycle).

e. [15] <B.1> Repeat part (c) assuming that logic is added to predict the cache way to be accessed. Only the tag sub-array for the predicted way is accessed in cycle one. A way hit (address match in predicted way) implies a cache hit. A way miss dictates examining all the tag sub-arrays in the second cycle. In case of a way hit, only one data sub-array (the one whose tag matched) is accessed in cycle two. Assume there is way hit.

f. [10] <B.1> Repeat part (e) assuming that the way predictor missed (the way it chose is wrong). When it fails, the way predictor adds an extra cycle in which it accesses all the tag sub-arrays. Assume a cache read hit.

g. [15] <B.1> Repeat part (f) assuming a cache read miss.

h. [20] <B.1> Use parts (e), (f), and (g) for the general case where the workload has the following statistics: way-predictor miss rate = 5% and cache miss rate = 3%. (Consider different replacement policies.)

B.4 [10/10/15/15/15/20] <B.1> We compare the write bandwidth requirements of write-through versus write-back caches using a concrete example. Let us assume that we have a 64 KB cache with a line size of 32 bytes. The cache will allocate a line on a write miss. If configured as a write-back cache, it will write back the whole dirty line if it needs to be replaced. We will also assume that the cache is connected to the lower level in the hierarchy through a 64-bit-wide (8-byte-wide) bus. The number of CPU cycles for a B-bytes write access on this bus is

$$10 + 5\left(\left\lceil \frac{B}{8} \right\rceil - 1\right)$$

For example, an 8-byte write would take $10 + 5\left(\left\lceil \frac{B}{8} \right\rceil - 1\right)$ cycles, whereas using the same formula a 12-byte write would take 15 cycles. Answer the following questions while referring to the C code snippet below:

...

```
#define PORTION 1 … Base = 8*i; for (unsigned int j=base;
j < base+PORTION; j++) //assume j is stored in a register
data[j] = j;
```

a. [10] <B.1> For a write-through cache, how many CPU cycles are spent on write transfers to the memory for the all the combined iterations of the j loop?

b. [10] <B.1> If the cache is configured as a write-back cache, how many CPU cycles are spent on writing back a cache line?

c. [15] <B.1> Change PORTION to 8 and repeat part (a).

d. [15] <B.1> What is the minimum number of array updates to the same cache line (before replacing it) that would render the write-back cache superior?

e. [15] <B.1> Think of a scenario where all the words of the cache line will be written (not necessarily using the above code) and a write-through cache will require fewer total CPU cycles than the write-back cache.

B.5 [10/10/10/10/] <B.2> You are building a system around a processor with in-order execution that runs at 1.1 GHz and has a CPI of 0.7 excluding memory accesses. The only instructions that read or write data from memory are loads

(20% of all instructions) and stores (5% of all instructions). The memory system for this computer is composed of a split L1 cache that imposes no penalty on hits. Both the I-cache and D-cache are direct mapped and hold 32 KB each. The I-cache has a 2% miss rate and 32-byte blocks, and the D-cache is write-through with a 5% miss rate and 16-byte blocks. There is a write buffer on the D-cache that eliminates stalls for 95% of all writes. The 512 KB write-back, unified L2 cache has 64-byte blocks and an access time of 15 ns. It is connected to the L1 cache by a 128-bit data bus that runs at 266 MHz and can transfer one 128-bit word per bus cycle. Of all memory references sent to the L2 cache in this system, 80% are satisfied without going to main memory. Also, 50% of all blocks replaced are dirty. The 128-bit-wide main memory has an access latency of 60 ns, after which any number of bus words may be transferred at the rate of one per cycle on the 128-bit-wide 133 MHz main memory bus.

   a. [10] <B.2> What is the average memory access time for instruction accesses?

   b. [10] <B.2> What is the average memory access time for data reads?

   c. [10] <B.2> What is the average memory access time for data writes?

   d. [10] <B.2> What is the overall CPI, including memory accesses?

B.6 [10/15/15] <B.2> Converting miss rate (misses per reference) into misses per instruction relies upon two factors: references per instruction fetched and the fraction of fetched instructions that actually commits.

   a. [10] <B.2> The formula for misses per instruction on page B-5 is written first in terms of three factors: miss rate, memory accesses, and instruction count. Each of these factors represents actual events. What is different about writing misses per instruction as miss rate times the factor *memory accesses per instruction?*

   b. [15] <B.2> Speculative processors will fetch instructions that do not commit. The formula for misses per instruction on page B-5 refers to misses per instruction on the execution path, that is, only the instructions that must actually be executed to carry out the program. Convert the formula for misses per instruction on page B-5 into one that uses only miss rate, references per instruction fetched, and fraction of fetched instructions that commit. Why rely upon these factors rather than those in the formula on page B-5?

   c. [15] <B.2> The conversion in part (b) could yield an incorrect value to the extent that the value of the factor references per instruction fetched is not equal to the number of references for any particular instruction. Rewrite the formula of part (b) to correct this deficiency.

B.7 [20] <B.1, B.3> In systems with a write-through L1 cache backed by a write-back L2 cache instead of main memory, a merging write buffer can be simplified. Explain how this can be done. Are there situations where having a full write buffer (instead of the simple version you've just proposed) could be helpful?

B.8 [20/20/15/25] <B.3> The LRU replacement policy is based on the assumption that if address A1 is accessed less recently than address A2 in the past, then A2 will be accessed again before A1 in the future. Hence, A2 is given priority over A1. Discuss how this assumption fails to hold when the a loop larger than the instruction cache is being continuously executed. For example, consider a fully associative 128-byte instruction cache with a 4-byte block (every block can exactly hold one instruction). The cache uses an LRU replacement policy.

a. [20] <B.3> What is the asymptotic instruction miss rate for a 64-byte loop with a large number of iterations?

b. [20] <B.3> Repeat part (a) for loop sizes 192 bytes and 320 bytes.

c. [15] <B.3> If the cache replacement policy is changed to most recently used (MRU) (replace the most recently accessed cache line), which of the three above cases (64-, 192-, or 320-byte loops) would benefit from this policy?

d. [25] <B.3> Suggest additional replacement policies that might outperform LRU.

B.9 [20] < B.3> Increasing a cache's associativity (with all other parameters kept constant), *statistically* reduces the miss rate. However, there can be pathological cases where increasing a cache's associativity would increase the miss rate for a particular workload. Consider the case of direct mapped compared to a two-way set associative cache of equal size. Assume that the set associative cache uses the LRU replacement policy. To simplify, assume that the block size is one word. Now construct a trace of word accesses that would produce more misses in the two-way associative cache. (*Hint*: Focus on constructing a trace of accesses that are exclusively directed to a single set of the two-way set associative cache, such that the same trace would exclusively access two blocks in the direct-mapped cache.)

B.10 [10/10/15] <B.3> Consider a two-level memory hierarchy made of L1 and L2 data caches. Assume that both caches use write-back policy on write hit and both have the same block size. List the actions taken in response to the following events:

a. [10] <B.3> An L1 cache miss when the caches are organized in an inclusive hierarchy.

b. [10] <B.3> An L1 cache miss when the caches are organized in an exclusive hierarchy.

c. [15] <B.3> In both parts (a) and (b), consider the possibility that the evicted line might be clean or dirty.

B.11 [15/20] <B.2, B.3> Excluding some instructions from entering the cache can reduce conflict misses.

a. [15] <B.3> Sketch a program hierarchy where parts of the program would be better excluded from entering the instruction cache. (*Hint*: Consider a program with code blocks that are placed in deeper loop nests than other blocks.)

b. [20] <B.2, B.3> Suggest software or hardware techniques to enforce exclusion of certain blocks from the instruction cache.

B.12 [15] <B.4> A program is running on a computer with a four-entry fully associative (micro) translation lookaside buffer (TLB):

VP#	PP#	Entry valid
5	30	1
7	1	0
10	10	1
15	25	1

The following is a trace of virtual page numbers accessed by a program. For each access indicate whether it produces a TLB hit/miss and, if it accesses the page table, whether it produces a page hit or fault. Put an X under the page table column if it is not accessed.

Virtual page index	Physical page #	Present
0	3	Y
1	7	N
2	6	N
3	5	Y
4	14	Y
5	30	Y
6	26	Y
7	11	Y
8	13	N
9	18	N
10	10	Y
11	56	Y
12	110	Y
13	33	Y
14	12	N
15	25	Y

Virtual page accessed	TLB (hit or miss)	Page table (hit or fault)
1		
5		
9		
14		
10		
6		
15		
12		
7		
2		

B.13 [15/15/15/15/] <B.4> Some memory systems handle TLB misses in software (as an exception), while others use hardware for TLB misses.

a. [15] <B.4> What are the trade-offs between these two methods for handling TLB misses?

b. [15] <B.4> Will TLB miss handling in software always be slower than TLB miss handling in hardware? Explain.

c. [15] <B.4> Are there page table structures that would be difficult to handle in hardware but possible in software? Are there any such structures that would be difficult for software to handle but easy for hardware to manage?

d. [15] <B.4> Why are TLB miss rates for floating-point programs generally higher than those for integer programs?

B.14 [25/25/25/25/20] <B.4> How big should a TLB be? TLB misses are usually very fast (fewer than 10 instructions plus the cost of an exception), so it may not be worth having a huge TLB just to lower the TLB miss rate a bit. Using the SimpleScalar simulator (*www.cs.wisc.edu/~mscalar/simplescalar.html*) and one or more SPEC95 benchmarks, calculate the TLB miss rate and the TLB overhead (in percentage of time wasted handling TLB misses) for the following TLB configurations. Assume that each TLB miss requires 20 instructions.

a. [25] <B.4> 128 entries, two-way set associative, 4 KB to 64 KB pages (going by powers of 2).

b. [25] <B.4> 256 entries, two-way set associative, 4 KB to 64 KB pages (going by powers of 2).

c. [25] <B.4> 512 entries, two-way set associative, 4 KB to 64 KB pages (going by powers of 2).

d. [25] <B.4> 1024 entries, two-way set associative, 4 KB to 64 KB pages (going by powers of 2).

e. [20] <B.4> What would be the effect on TLB miss rate and overhead for a multitasking environment? How would the context switch frequency affect the overhead?

B.15 [15/20/20] <B.5> It is possible to provide more flexible protection than that in the Intel Pentium architecture by using a protection scheme similar to that used in the Hewlett-Packard Precision Architecture (HP/PA). In such a scheme, each page table entry contains a "protection ID" (key) along with access rights for the page. On each reference, the CPU compares the protection ID in the page table entry with those stored in each of four protection ID registers (access to these registers requires that the CPU be in supervisor mode). If there is no match for the protection ID in the page table entry or if the access is not a permitted access (writing to a read-only page, for example), an exception is generated.

a. [15] <B.5> How could a process have more than four valid protection IDs at any given time? In other words, suppose a process wished to have 10 protection IDs simultaneously. Propose a mechanism by which this could be done (perhaps with help from software).

b. [20] <B.5> Explain how this model could be used to facilitate the construction of operating systems from relatively small pieces of code that can't overwrite each other (microkernels). What advantages might such an operating system have over a monolithic operating system in which any code in the OS can write to any memory location?

c. [20] <B.5> A simple design change to this system would allow two protection IDs for each page table entry, one for read access and the other for either write or execute access (the field is unused if neither the writable nor executable bit is set). What advantages might there be from having different protection IDs for read and write capabilities? (*Hint:* Could this make it easier to share data and code between processes?)

C

Pipelining: Basic and Intermediate Concepts

It is quite a three-pipe problem.

Sir Arthur Conan Doyle
The Adventures of Sherlock Holmes

C.1 Introduction

Many readers of this text will have covered the basics of pipelining in another text (such as our more basic text *Computer Organization and Design*) or in another course. Because Chapter 3 builds heavily on this material, readers should ensure that they are familiar with the concepts discussed in this appendix before proceeding. As you read Chapter 2, you may find it helpful to turn to this material for a quick review.

We begin the appendix with the basics of pipelining, including discussing the data path implications, introducing hazards, and examining the performance of pipelines. This section describes the basic five-stage RISC pipeline that is the basis for the rest of the appendix. Section C.2 describes the issue of hazards, why they cause performance problems, and how they can be dealt with. Section C.3 discusses how the simple five-stage pipeline is actually implemented, focusing on control and how hazards are dealt with.

Section C.4 discusses the interaction between pipelining and various aspects of instruction set design, including discussing the important topic of exceptions and their interaction with pipelining. Readers unfamiliar with the concepts of precise and imprecise interrupts and resumption after exceptions will find this material useful, since they are key to understanding the more advanced approaches in Chapter 3.

Section C.5 discusses how the five-stage pipeline can be extended to handle longer-running floating-point instructions. Section C.6 puts these concepts together in a case study of a deeply pipelined processor, the MIPS R4000/4400, including both the eight-stage integer pipeline and the floating-point pipeline.

Section C.7 introduces the concept of dynamic scheduling and the use of scoreboards to implement dynamic scheduling. It is introduced as a crosscutting issue, since it can be used to serve as an introduction to the core concepts in Chapter 3, which focused on dynamically scheduled approaches. Section C.7 is also a gentle introduction to the more complex Tomasulo's algorithm covered in Chapter 3. Although Tomasulo's algorithm can be covered and understood without introducing scoreboarding, the scoreboarding approach is simpler and easier to comprehend.

What Is Pipelining?

Pipelining is an implementation technique whereby multiple instructions are overlapped in execution; it takes advantage of parallelism that exists among the actions needed to execute an instruction. Today, pipelining is the key implementation technique used to make fast CPUs.

A pipeline is like an assembly line. In an automobile assembly line, there are many steps, each contributing something to the construction of the car. Each step operates in parallel with the other steps, although on a different car. In a computer pipeline, each step in the pipeline completes a part of an instruction. Like the assembly line, different steps are completing different parts of different instructions in parallel. Each of these steps is called a *pipe stage* or a *pipe segment*. The stages are connected one to the next to form a pipe—instructions enter at one end, progress through the stages, and exit at the other end, just as cars would in an assembly line.

In an automobile assembly line, *throughput* is defined as the number of cars per hour and is determined by how often a completed car exits the assembly line. Likewise, the throughput of an instruction pipeline is determined by how often an instruction exits the pipeline. Because the pipe stages are hooked together, all the stages must be ready to proceed at the same time, just as we would require in an assembly line. The time required between moving an instruction one step down the pipeline is a *processor cycle*. Because all stages proceed at the same time, the length of a processor cycle is determined by the time required for the slowest pipe stage, just as in an auto assembly line the longest step would determine the time between advancing the line. In a computer, this processor cycle is usually 1 clock cycle (sometimes it is 2, rarely more).

The pipeline designer's goal is to balance the length of each pipeline stage, just as the designer of the assembly line tries to balance the time for each step in the process. If the stages are perfectly balanced, then the time per instruction on the pipelined processor—assuming ideal conditions—is equal to

$$\frac{\text{Time per instruction on unpipelined machine}}{\text{Number of pipe stages}}$$

Under these conditions, the speedup from pipelining equals the number of pipe stages, just as an assembly line with *n* stages can ideally produce cars *n* times as fast. Usually, however, the stages will not be perfectly balanced; furthermore, pipelining does involve some overhead. Thus, the time per instruction on the pipelined processor will not have its minimum possible value, yet it can be close.

Pipelining yields a reduction in the average execution time per instruction. Depending on what you consider as the baseline, the reduction can be viewed as decreasing the number of clock cycles per instruction (CPI), as decreasing the clock cycle time, or as a combination. If the starting point is a processor that takes multiple clock cycles per instruction, then pipelining is usually viewed as reducing the CPI. This is the primary view we will take. If the starting point is a processor that takes 1 (long) clock cycle per instruction, then pipelining decreases the clock cycle time.

Pipelining is an implementation technique that exploits parallelism among the instructions in a sequential instruction stream. It has the substantial advantage that, unlike some speedup techniques (see Chapter 4), it is not visible to the programmer. In this appendix we will first cover the concept of pipelining using a classic five-stage pipeline; other chapters investigate the more sophisticated pipelining techniques in use in modern processors. Before we say more about pipelining and its use in a processor, we need a simple instruction set, which we introduce next.

The Basics of a RISC Instruction Set

Throughout this book we use a RISC (reduced instruction set computer) architecture or load-store architecture to illustrate the basic concepts, although nearly all the ideas we introduce in this book are applicable to other processors. In this section we introduce the core of a typical RISC architecture. In this appendix, and throughout the book, our default RISC architecture is MIPS. In many places, the concepts are significantly similar that they will apply to any RISC. RISC architectures are characterized by a few key properties, which dramatically simplify their implementation:

■ All operations on data apply to data in registers and typically change the entire register (32 or 64 bits per register).

■ The only operations that affect memory are load and store operations that move data from memory to a register or to memory from a register, respectively. Load and store operations that load or store less than a full register (e.g., a byte, 16 bits, or 32 bits) are often available.

■ The instruction formats are few in number, with all instructions typically being one size.

These simple properties lead to dramatic simplifications in the implementation of pipelining, which is why these instruction sets were designed this way.

For consistency with the rest of the text, we use MIPS64, the 64-bit version of the MIPS instruction set. The extended 64-bit instructions are generally designated by having a D on the start or end of the mnemonic. For example DADD is the 64-bit version of an add instruction, while LD is the 64-bit version of a load instruction.

Like other RISC architectures, the MIPS instruction set provides 32 registers, although register 0 always has the value 0. Most RISC architectures, like MIPS, have three classes of instructions (see Appendix A for more detail):

1. *ALU instructions*—These instructions take either two registers or a register and a sign-extended immediate (called *ALU immediate instructions*, they have a 16-bit offset in MIPS), operate on them, and store the result into a third register. Typical operations include add (DADD), subtract (DSUB), and logical operations (such as AND or OR), which do not differentiate between 32-bit and 64-bit versions. Immediate versions of these instructions use the same mnemonics with a suffix of I. In MIPS, there are both signed and unsigned forms of the arithmetic instructions; the unsigned forms, which do not generate overflow exceptions—and thus are the same in 32-bit and 64-bit mode—have a U at the end (e.g., DADDU, DSUBU, DADDIU).

2. *Load and store instructions*—These instructions take a register source, called the *base register,* and an immediate field (16-bit in MIPS), called the *offset,* as operands. The sum—called the *effective address*—of the contents of the base register and the sign-extended offset is used as a memory address. In the case of a load instruction, a second register operand acts as the destination for the

data loaded from memory. In the case of a store, the second register operand is the source of the data that is stored into memory. The instructions load word (LD) and store word (SD) load or store the entire 64-bit register contents.

3. *Branches and jumps*—Branches are conditional transfers of control. There are usually two ways of specifying the branch condition in RISC architectures: with a set of condition bits (sometimes called a *condition code*) or by a limited set of comparisons between a pair of registers or between a register and zero. MIPS uses the latter. For this appendix, we consider only comparisons for equality between two registers. In all RISC architectures, the branch destination is obtained by adding a sign-extended offset (16 bits in MIPS) to the current PC. Unconditional jumps are provided in many RISC architectures, but we will not cover jumps in this appendix.

A Simple Implementation of a RISC Instruction Set

To understand how a RISC instruction set can be implemented in a pipelined fashion, we need to understand how it is implemented *without* pipelining. This section shows a simple implementation where every instruction takes at most 5 clock cycles. We will extend this basic implementation to a pipelined version, resulting in a much lower CPI. Our unpipelined implementation is not the most economical or the highest-performance implementation without pipelining. Instead, it is designed to lead naturally to a pipelined implementation. Implementing the instruction set requires the introduction of several temporary registers that are not part of the architecture; these are introduced in this section to simplify pipelining. Our implementation will focus only on a pipeline for an integer subset of a RISC architecture that consists of load-store word, branch, and integer ALU operations.

Every instruction in this RISC subset can be implemented in at most 5 clock cycles. The 5 clock cycles are as follows.

1. *Instruction fetch cycle* (IF):

   Send the program counter (PC) to memory and fetch the current instruction from memory. Update the PC to the next sequential PC by adding 4 (since each instruction is 4 bytes) to the PC.

2. *Instruction decode/register fetch cycle* (ID):

   Decode the instruction and read the registers corresponding to register source specifiers from the register file. Do the equality test on the registers as they are read, for a possible branch. Sign-extend the offset field of the instruction in case it is needed. Compute the possible branch target address by adding the sign-extended offset to the incremented PC. In an aggressive implementation, which we explore later, the branch can be completed at the end of this stage by storing the branch-target address into the PC, if the condition test yielded true.

   Decoding is done in parallel with reading registers, which is possible because the register specifiers are at a fixed location in a RISC architecture.

This technique is known as *fixed-field decoding*. Note that we may read a register we don't use, which doesn't help but also doesn't hurt performance. (It does waste energy to read an unneeded register, and power-sensitive designs might avoid this.) Because the immediate portion of an instruction is also located in an identical place, the sign-extended immediate is also calculated during this cycle in case it is needed.

3. *Execution/effective address cycle* (EX):

   The ALU operates on the operands prepared in the prior cycle, performing one of three functions depending on the instruction type.

   ■ Memory reference—The ALU adds the base register and the offset to form the effective address.

   ■ Register-Register ALU instruction—The ALU performs the operation specified by the ALU opcode on the values read from the register file.

   ■ Register-Immediate ALU instruction—The ALU performs the operation specified by the ALU opcode on the first value read from the register file and the sign-extended immediate.

   In a load-store architecture the effective address and execution cycles can be combined into a single clock cycle, since no instruction needs to simultaneously calculate a data address and perform an operation on the data.

4. *Memory access* (MEM):

   If the instruction is a load, the memory does a read using the effective address computed in the previous cycle. If it is a store, then the memory writes the data from the second register read from the register file using the effective address.

5. *Write-back cycle* (WB):

   ■ Register-Register ALU instruction or load instruction:

   Write the result into the register file, whether it comes from the memory system (for a load) or from the ALU (for an ALU instruction).

   In this implementation, branch instructions require 2 cycles, store instructions require 4 cycles, and all other instructions require 5 cycles. Assuming a branch frequency of 12% and a store frequency of 10%, a typical instruction distribution leads to an overall CPI of 4.54. This implementation, however, is not optimal either in achieving the best performance or in using the minimal amount of hardware given the performance level; we leave the improvement of this design as an exercise for you and instead focus on pipelining this version.

The Classic Five-Stage Pipeline for a RISC Processor

We can pipeline the execution described above with almost no changes by simply starting a new instruction on each clock cycle. (See why we chose this design?)

	Clock number								
Instruction number	**1**	**2**	**3**	**4**	**5**	**6**	**7**	**8**	**9**
Instruction i	IF	ID	EX	MEM	WB				
Instruction $i + 1$		IF	ID	EX	MEM	WB			
Instruction $i + 2$			IF	ID	EX	MEM	WB		
Instruction $i + 3$				IF	ID	EX	MEM	WB	
Instruction $i + 4$					IF	ID	EX	MEM	WB

Figure C.1 Simple RISC pipeline. On each clock cycle, another instruction is fetched and begins its five-cycle execution. If an instruction is started every clock cycle, the performance will be up to five times that of a processor that is not pipelined. The names for the stages in the pipeline are the same as those used for the cycles in the unpipelined implementation: IF = instruction fetch, ID = instruction decode, EX = execution, MEM = memory access, and WB = write-back.

Each of the clock cycles from the previous section becomes a *pipe stage*—a cycle in the pipeline. This results in the execution pattern shown in Figure C.1, which is the typical way a pipeline structure is drawn. Although each instruction takes 5 clock cycles to complete, during each clock cycle the hardware will initiate a new instruction and will be executing some part of the five different instructions.

You may find it hard to believe that pipelining is as simple as this; it's not. In this and the following sections, we will make our RISC pipeline "real" by dealing with problems that pipelining introduces.

To start with, we have to determine what happens on every clock cycle of the processor and make sure we don't try to perform two different operations with the same data path resource on the same clock cycle. For example, a single ALU cannot be asked to compute an effective address and perform a subtract operation at the same time. Thus, we must ensure that the overlap of instructions in the pipeline cannot cause such a conflict. Fortunately, the simplicity of a RISC instruction set makes resource evaluation relatively easy. Figure C.2 shows a simplified version of a RISC data path drawn in pipeline fashion. As you can see, the major functional units are used in different cycles, and hence overlapping the execution of multiple instructions introduces relatively few conflicts. There are three observations on which this fact rests.

First, we use separate instruction and data memories, which we would typically implement with separate instruction and data caches (discussed in Chapter 2). The use of separate caches eliminates a conflict for a single memory that would arise between instruction fetch and data memory access. Notice that if our pipelined processor has a clock cycle that is equal to that of the unpipelined version, the memory system must deliver five times the bandwidth. This increased demand is one cost of higher performance.

Second, the register file is used in the two stages: one for reading in ID and one for writing in WB. These uses are distinct, so we simply show the register file in two places. Hence, we need to perform two reads and one write every clock cycle. To handle reads and a write to the same register (and for another reason, which will become obvious shortly), we perform the register write in the first half of the clock cycle and the read in the second half.

Third, Figure C.2 does not deal with the PC. To start a new instruction every clock, we must increment and store the PC every clock, and this must be done during the IF stage in preparation for the next instruction. Furthermore, we must also have an adder to compute the potential branch target during ID. One further problem is that a branch does not change the PC until the ID stage. This causes a problem, which we ignore for now, but will handle shortly.

Although it is critical to ensure that instructions in the pipeline do not attempt to use the hardware resources at the same time, we must also ensure that instructions in different stages of the pipeline do not interfere with one another. This separation is done by introducing *pipeline registers* between successive stages of the pipeline, so that at the end of a clock cycle all the results from a given stage are stored into a register that is used as the input to the next stage on the next clock cycle. Figure C.3 shows the pipeline drawn with these pipeline registers.

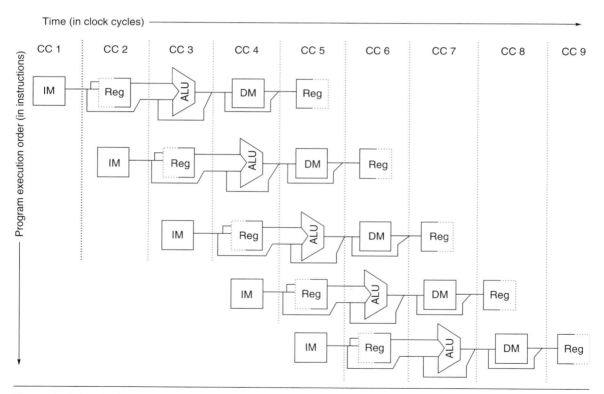

Figure C.2 The pipeline can be thought of as a series of data paths shifted in time. This shows the overlap among the parts of the data path, with clock cycle 5 (CC 5) showing the steady-state situation. Because the register file is used as a source in the ID stage and as a destination in the WB stage, it appears twice. We show that it is read in one part of the stage and written in another by using a solid line, on the right or left, respectively, and a dashed line on the other side. The abbreviation IM is used for instruction memory, DM for data memory, and CC for clock cycle.

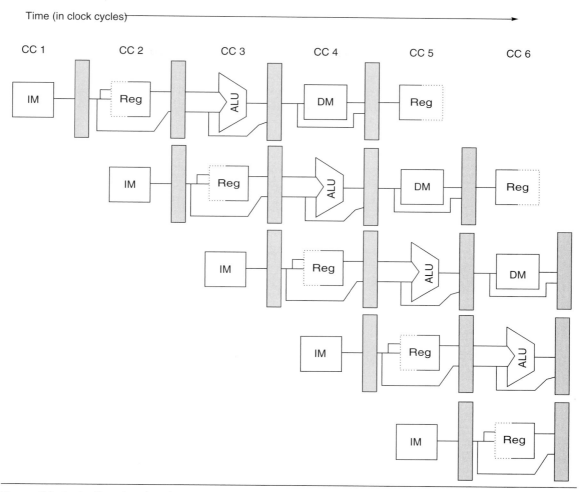

Figure C.3 A pipeline showing the pipeline registers between successive pipeline stages. Notice that the registers prevent interference between two different instructions in adjacent stages in the pipeline. The registers also play the critical role of carrying data for a given instruction from one stage to the other. The edge-triggered property of registers—that is, that the values change instantaneously on a clock edge—is critical. Otherwise, the data from one instruction could interfere with the execution of another!

Although many figures will omit such registers for simplicity, they are required to make the pipeline operate properly and must be present. Of course, similar registers would be needed even in a multicycle data path that had no pipelining (since only values in registers are preserved across clock boundaries). In the case of a pipelined processor, the pipeline registers also play the key role of carrying intermediate results from one stage to another where the source and destination may not be directly adjacent. For example, the register value to be stored during a store instruction is read during ID, but not actually used until MEM; it is passed through two pipeline registers to reach the data memory during the MEM stage. Likewise, the result of an ALU instruction is computed during EX, but not actually stored until WB; it arrives there by passing through two pipeline registers. It is sometimes useful to name the pipeline registers, and we follow the convention of naming them by the pipeline stages they connect, so that the registers are called IF/ID, ID/EX, EX/MEM, and MEM/WB.

Basic Performance Issues in Pipelining

Pipelining increases the CPU instruction throughput—the number of instructions completed per unit of time—but it does not reduce the execution time of an individual instruction. In fact, it usually slightly increases the execution time of each instruction due to overhead in the control of the pipeline. The increase in instruction throughput means that a program runs faster and has lower total execution time, even though no single instruction runs faster!

The fact that the execution time of each instruction does not decrease puts limits on the practical depth of a pipeline, as we will see in the next section. In addition to limitations arising from pipeline latency, limits arise from imbalance among the pipe stages and from pipelining overhead. Imbalance among the pipe stages reduces performance since the clock can run no faster than the time needed for the slowest pipeline stage. Pipeline overhead arises from the combination of pipeline register delay and clock skew. The pipeline registers add setup time, which is the time that a register input must be stable before the clock signal that triggers a write occurs, plus propagation delay to the clock cycle. Clock skew, which is maximum delay between when the clock arrives at any two registers, also contributes to the lower limit on the clock cycle. Once the clock cycle is as small as the sum of the clock skew and latch overhead, no further pipelining is useful, since there is no time left in the cycle for useful work. The interested reader should see Kunkel and Smith [1986]. As we saw in Chapter 3, this overhead affected the performance gains achieved by the Pentium 4 versus the Pentium III.

Example　Consider the unpipelined processor in the previous section. Assume that it has a 1 ns clock cycle and that it uses 4 cycles for ALU operations and branches and 5 cycles for memory operations. Assume that the relative frequencies of these operations are 40%, 20%, and 40%, respectively. Suppose that due to clock skew and setup, pipelining the processor adds 0.2 ns of overhead to the clock. Ignoring any latency impact, how much speedup in the instruction execution rate will we gain from a pipeline?

Answer　The average instruction execution time on the unpipelined processor is

$$
\begin{aligned}
\text{Average instruction execution time} &= \text{Clock cycle} \times \text{Average CPI} \\
&= 1 \text{ ns} \times [(40\% + 20\%) \times 4 + 40\% \times 5] \\
&= 1 \text{ ns} \times 4.4 \\
&= 4.4 \text{ ns}
\end{aligned}
$$

In the pipelined implementation, the clock must run at the speed of the slowest stage plus overhead, which will be $1 + 0.2$ or 1.2 ns; this is the average instruction execution time. Thus, the speedup from pipelining is

$$\text{Speedup from pipelining} = \frac{\text{Average instruction time unpipelined}}{\text{Average instruction time pipelined}}$$

$$= \frac{4.4 \text{ ns}}{1.2 \text{ ns}} = 3.7 \text{ times}$$

The 0.2 ns overhead essentially establishes a limit on the effectiveness of pipelining. If the overhead is not affected by changes in the clock cycle, Amdahl's law tells us that the overhead limits the speedup.

This simple RISC pipeline would function just fine for integer instructions if every instruction were independent of every other instruction in the pipeline. In reality, instructions in the pipeline can depend on one another; this is the topic of the next section.

C.2   The Major Hurdle of Pipelining—Pipeline Hazards

There are situations, called *hazards*, that prevent the next instruction in the instruction stream from executing during its designated clock cycle. Hazards reduce the performance from the ideal speedup gained by pipelining. There are three classes of hazards:

1. *Structural hazards* arise from resource conflicts when the hardware cannot support all possible combinations of instructions simultaneously in overlapped execution.

2. *Data hazards* arise when an instruction depends on the results of a previous instruction in a way that is exposed by the overlapping of instructions in the pipeline.

3. *Control hazards* arise from the pipelining of branches and other instructions that change the PC.

Hazards in pipelines can make it necessary to *stall* the pipeline. Avoiding a hazard often requires that some instructions in the pipeline be allowed to proceed while others are delayed. For the pipelines we discuss in this appendix, when an instruction is stalled, all instructions issued *later* than the stalled instruction—and hence not as far along in the pipeline—are also stalled. Instructions issued *earlier* than the stalled instruction—and hence farther along in the pipeline—must continue, since otherwise the hazard will never clear. As a result, no new instructions are fetched during the stall. We will see several examples of how pipeline stalls operate in this section—don't worry, they aren't as complex as they might sound!

Performance of Pipelines with Stalls

A stall causes the pipeline performance to degrade from the ideal performance. Let's look at a simple equation for finding the actual speedup from pipelining, starting with the formula from the previous section:

$$\text{Speedup from pipelining} = \frac{\text{Average instruction time unpipelined}}{\text{Average instruction time pipelined}}$$

$$= \frac{\text{CPI unpipelined} \times \text{Clock cycle unpipelined}}{\text{CPI pipelined} \times \text{Clock cycle pipelined}}$$

$$= \frac{\text{CPI unpipelined}}{\text{CPI pipelined}} \times \frac{\text{Clock cycle unpipelined}}{\text{Clock cycle pipelined}}$$

Pipelining can be thought of as decreasing the CPI or the clock cycle time. Since it is traditional to use the CPI to compare pipelines, let's start with that assumption. The ideal CPI on a pipelined processor is almost always 1. Hence, we can compute the pipelined CPI:

$$\text{CPI pipelined} = \text{Ideal CPI} + \text{Pipeline stall clock cycles per instruction}$$

$$= 1 + \text{Pipeline stall clock cycles per instruction}$$

If we ignore the cycle time overhead of pipelining and assume that the stages are perfectly balanced, then the cycle time of the two processors can be equal, leading to

$$\text{Speedup} = \frac{\text{CPI unpipelined}}{1 + \text{Pipeline stall cycles per instruction}}$$

One important simple case is where all instructions take the same number of cycles, which must also equal the number of pipeline stages (also called the *depth of the pipeline*). In this case, the unpipelined CPI is equal to the depth of the pipeline, leading to

$$\text{Speedup} = \frac{\text{Pipeline depth}}{1 + \text{Pipeline stall cycles per instruction}}$$

If there are no pipeline stalls, this leads to the intuitive result that pipelining can improve performance by the depth of the pipeline.

Alternatively, if we think of pipelining as improving the clock cycle time, then we can assume that the CPI of the unpipelined processor, as well as that of the pipelined processor, is 1. This leads to

$$\text{Speedup from pipelining} = \frac{\text{CPI unpipelined}}{\text{CPI pipelined}} \times \frac{\text{Clock cycle unpipelined}}{\text{Clock cycle pipelined}}$$

$$= \frac{1}{1 + \text{Pipeline stall cycles per instruction}} \times \frac{\text{Clock cycle unpipelined}}{\text{Clock cycle pipelined}}$$

In cases where the pipe stages are perfectly balanced and there is no overhead, the clock cycle on the pipelined processor is smaller than the clock cycle of the unpipelined processor by a factor equal to the pipelined depth:

$$\text{Clock cycle pipelined} = \frac{\text{Clock cycle unpipelined}}{\text{Pipeline depth}}$$

$$\text{Pipeline depth} = \frac{\text{Clock cycle unpipelined}}{\text{Clock cycle pipelined}}$$

This leads to the following:

$$\text{Speedup from pipelining} = \frac{1}{1 + \text{Pipeline stall cycles per instruction}} \times \frac{\text{Clock cycle unpipelined}}{\text{Clock cycle pipelined}}$$

$$= \frac{1}{1 + \text{Pipeline stall cycles per instruction}} \times \text{Pipeline depth}$$

Thus, if there are no stalls, the speedup is equal to the number of pipeline stages, matching our intuition for the ideal case.

Structural Hazards

When a processor is pipelined, the overlapped execution of instructions requires pipelining of functional units and duplication of resources to allow all possible combinations of instructions in the pipeline. If some combination of instructions cannot be accommodated because of resource conflicts, the processor is said to have a *structural hazard.*

The most common instances of structural hazards arise when some functional unit is not fully pipelined. Then a sequence of instructions using that unpipelined unit cannot proceed at the rate of one per clock cycle. Another common way that structural hazards appear is when some resource has not been duplicated enough to allow all combinations of instructions in the pipeline to execute. For example, a processor may have only one register-file write port, but under certain circumstances, the pipeline might want to perform two writes in a clock cycle. This will generate a structural hazard.

When a sequence of instructions encounters this hazard, the pipeline will stall one of the instructions until the required unit is available. Such stalls will increase the CPI from its usual ideal value of 1.

Some pipelined processors have shared a single-memory pipeline for data and instructions. As a result, when an instruction contains a data memory reference, it will conflict with the instruction reference for a later instruction, as shown in Figure C.4. To resolve this hazard, we stall the pipeline for 1 clock cycle when the data memory access occurs. A stall is commonly called a *pipeline bubble* or just *bubble*, since it floats through the pipeline taking space but carrying no useful work. We will see another type of stall when we talk about data hazards.

Designers often indicate stall behavior using a simple diagram with only the pipe stage names, as in Figure C.5. The form of Figure C.5 shows the stall by indicating the cycle when no action occurs and simply shifting instruction 3 to

Time (in clock cycles)

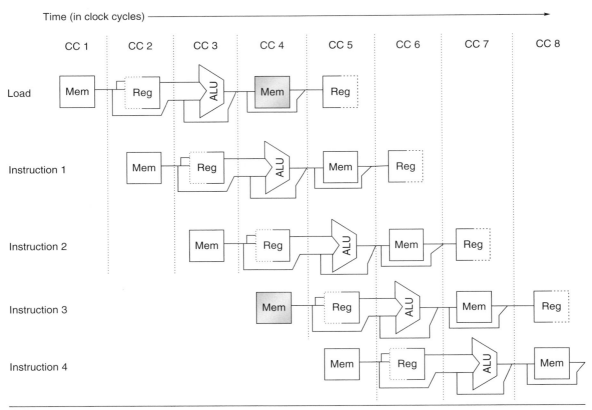

Figure C.4 A processor with only one memory port will generate a conflict whenever a memory reference occurs. In this example the load instruction uses the memory for a data access at the same time instruction 3 wants to fetch an instruction from memory.

the right (which delays its execution start and finish by 1 cycle). The effect of the pipeline bubble is actually to occupy the resources for that instruction slot as it travels through the pipeline.

Example   Let's see how much the load structural hazard might cost. Suppose that data references constitute 40% of the mix, and that the ideal CPI of the pipelined processor, ignoring the structural hazard, is 1. Assume that the processor with the structural hazard has a clock rate that is 1.05 times higher than the clock rate of the processor without the hazard. Disregarding any other performance losses, is the pipeline with or without the structural hazard faster, and by how much?

Answer   There are several ways we could solve this problem. Perhaps the simplest is to compute the average instruction time on the two processors:

$$\text{Average instruction time} = \text{CPI} \times \text{Clock cycle time}$$

	Clock cycle number									
Instruction	1	2	3	4	5	6	7	8	9	10
Load instruction	IF	ID	EX	MEM	WB					
Instruction $i + 1$		IF	ID	EX	MEM	WB				
Instruction $i + 2$			IF	ID	EX	MEM	WB			
Instruction $i + 3$				Stall	IF	ID	EX	MEM	WB	
Instruction $i + 4$						IF	ID	EX	MEM	WB
Instruction $i + 5$							IF	ID	EX	MEM
Instruction $i + 6$								IF	ID	EX

Figure C.5   A pipeline stalled for a structural hazard—a load with one memory port. As shown here, the load instruction effectively steals an instruction-fetch cycle, causing the pipeline to stall—no instruction is initiated on clock cycle 4 (which normally would initiate instruction $i + 3$). Because the instruction being fetched is stalled, all other instructions in the pipeline before the stalled instruction can proceed normally. The stall cycle will continue to pass through the pipeline, so that no instruction completes on clock cycle 8. Sometimes these pipeline diagrams are drawn with the stall occupying an entire horizontal row and instruction 3 being moved to the next row; in either case, the effect is the same, since instruction $i + 3$ does not begin execution until cycle 5. We use the form above, since it takes less space in the figure. Note that this figure assumes that instructions $i + 1$ and $i + 2$ are not memory references.

Since it has no stalls, the average instruction time for the ideal processor is simply the Clock cycle time$_{ideal}$. The average instruction time for the processor with the structural hazard is

$$\text{Average instruction time} = \text{CPI} \times \text{Clock cycle time}$$
$$= (1 + 0.4 \times 1) \times \frac{\text{Clock cycle time}_{ideal}}{1.05}$$
$$= 1.3 \times \text{Clock cycle time}_{ideal}$$

Clearly, the processor without the structural hazard is faster; we can use the ratio of the average instruction times to conclude that the processor without the hazard is 1.3 times faster.

As an alternative to this structural hazard, the designer could provide a separate memory access for instructions, either by splitting the cache into separate instruction and data caches or by using a set of buffers, usually called *instruction buffers*, to hold instructions. Chapter 5 discusses both the split cache and instruction buffer ideas.

If all other factors are equal, a processor without structural hazards will always have a lower CPI. Why, then, would a designer allow structural hazards? The primary reason is to reduce cost of the unit, since pipelining all the functional units, or duplicating them, may be too costly. For example, processors that support both an instruction and a data cache access every cycle (to prevent the structural hazard of the above example) require twice as much total memory bandwidth and often have higher bandwidth at the pins. Likewise, fully pipelining a floating-point (FP) multiplier consumes lots of gates. If the structural hazard is rare, it may not be worth the cost to avoid it.

Data Hazards

A major effect of pipelining is to change the relative timing of instructions by overlapping their execution. This overlap introduces data and control hazards. Data hazards occur when the pipeline changes the order of read/write accesses to operands so that the order differs from the order seen by sequentially executing instructions on an unpipelined processor. Consider the pipelined execution of these instructions:

```
DADD      R1,R2,R3
DSUB      R4,R1,R5
AND       R6,R1,R7
OR        R8,R1,R9
XOR       R10,R1,R11
```

All the instructions after the DADD use the result of the DADD instruction. As shown in Figure C.6, the DADD instruction writes the value of R1 in the WB pipe stage, but the DSUB instruction reads the value during its ID stage. This problem is called a *data hazard*. Unless precautions are taken to prevent it, the DSUB instruction will read the wrong value and try to use it. In fact, the value used by the DSUB instruction is not even deterministic: Though we might think it logical to assume that DSUB would always use the value of R1 that was assigned by an instruction prior to DADD, this is not always the case. If an interrupt should occur between the DADD and DSUB instructions, the WB stage of the DADD will complete, and the value of R1 at that point will be the result of the DADD. This unpredictable behavior is obviously unacceptable.

The AND instruction is also affected by this hazard. As we can see from Figure C.6, the write of R1 does not complete until the end of clock cycle 5. Thus, the AND instruction that reads the registers during clock cycle 4 will receive the wrong results.

The XOR instruction operates properly because its register read occurs in clock cycle 6, after the register write. The OR instruction also operates without incurring a hazard because we perform the register file reads in the second half of the cycle and the writes in the first half.

The next subsection discusses a technique to eliminate the stalls for the hazard involving the DSUB and AND instructions.

Minimizing Data Hazard Stalls by Forwarding

The problem posed in Figure C.6 can be solved with a simple hardware technique called *forwarding* (also called *bypassing* and sometimes *short-circuiting*). The key insight in forwarding is that the result is not really needed by the DSUB until

Time (in clock cycles)

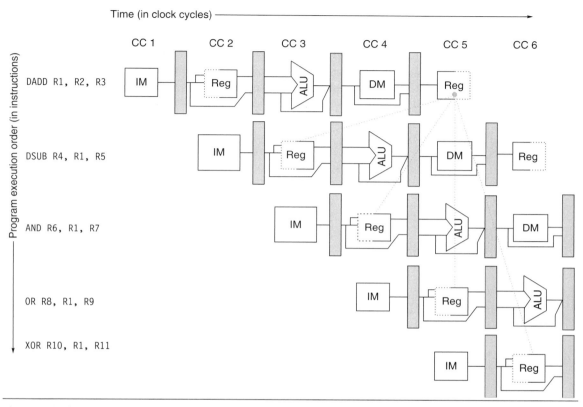

Figure C.6 The use of the result of the DADD instruction in the next three instructions causes a hazard, since the register is not written until after those instructions read it.

after the DADD actually produces it. If the result can be moved from the pipeline register where the DADD stores it to where the DSUB needs it, then the need for a stall can be avoided. Using this observation, forwarding works as follows:

1. The ALU result from both the EX/MEM and MEM/WB pipeline registers is always fed back to the ALU inputs.

2. If the forwarding hardware detects that the previous ALU operation has written the register corresponding to a source for the current ALU operation, control logic selects the forwarded result as the ALU input rather than the value read from the register file.

Notice that with forwarding, if the DSUB is stalled, the DADD will be completed and the bypass will not be activated. This relationship is also true for the case of an interrupt between the two instructions.

As the example in Figure C.6 shows, we need to forward results not only from the immediately previous instruction but also possibly from an instruction that started 2 cycles earlier. Figure C.7 shows our example with the bypass paths in place and highlighting the timing of the register read and writes. This code sequence can be executed without stalls.

Forwarding can be generalized to include passing a result directly to the functional unit that requires it: A result is forwarded from the pipeline register corresponding to the output of one unit to the input of another, rather than just from the result of a unit to the input of the same unit. Take, for example, the following sequence:

```
DADD    R1,R2,R3
LD      R4,0(R1)
SD      R4,12(R1)
```

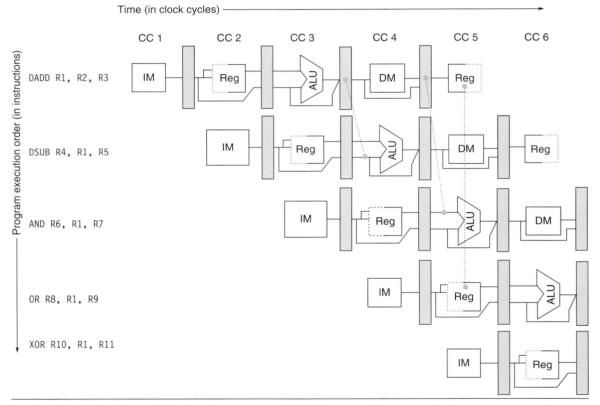

Figure C.7 A set of instructions that depends on the DADD result uses forwarding paths to avoid the data hazard. The inputs for the DSUB and AND instructions forward from the pipeline registers to the first ALU input. The OR receives its result by forwarding through the register file, which is easily accomplished by reading the registers in the second half of the cycle and writing in the first half, as the dashed lines on the registers indicate. Notice that the forwarded result can go to either ALU input; in fact, both ALU inputs could use forwarded inputs from either the same pipeline register or from different pipeline registers. This would occur, for example, if the AND instruction was AND R6,R1,R4.

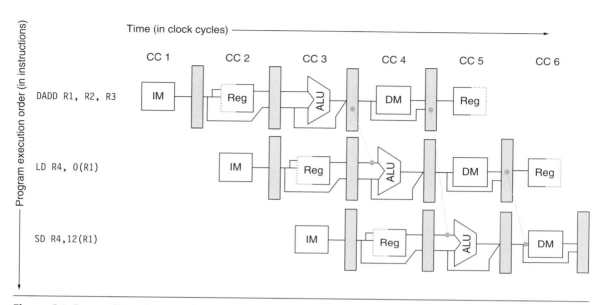

Figure C.8 Forwarding of operand required by stores during MEM. The result of the load is forwarded from the memory output to the memory input to be stored. In addition, the ALU output is forwarded to the ALU input for the address calculation of both the load and the store (this is no different than forwarding to another ALU operation). If the store depended on an immediately preceding ALU operation (not shown above), the result would need to be forwarded to prevent a stall.

To prevent a stall in this sequence, we would need to forward the values of the ALU output and memory unit output from the pipeline registers to the ALU and data memory inputs. Figure C.8 shows all the forwarding paths for this example.

Data Hazards Requiring Stalls

Unfortunately, not all potential data hazards can be handled by bypassing. Consider the following sequence of instructions:

```
LD      R1,0(R2)
DSUB    R4,R1,R5
AND     R6,R1,R7
OR      R8,R1,R9
```

The pipelined data path with the bypass paths for this example is shown in Figure C.9. This case is different from the situation with back-to-back ALU operations. The LD instruction does not have the data until the end of clock cycle 4 (its MEM cycle), while the DSUB instruction needs to have the data by the beginning of that clock cycle. Thus, the data hazard from using the result of a load instruction cannot be completely eliminated with simple hardware. As Figure C.9 shows, such a forwarding path would have to operate backward

Time (in clock cycles) ⟶

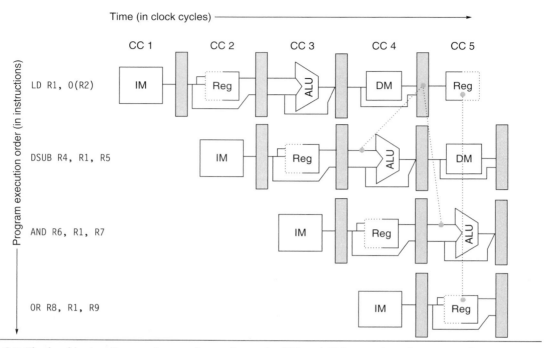

Figure C.9 The load instruction can bypass its results to the AND and OR instructions, but not to the DSUB, since that would mean forwarding the result in "negative time."

in time—a capability not yet available to computer designers! We *can* forward the result immediately to the ALU from the pipeline registers for use in the AND operation, which begins 2 clock cycles after the load. Likewise, the OR instruction has no problem, since it receives the value through the register file. For the DSUB instruction, the forwarded result arrives too late—at the end of a clock cycle, when it is needed at the beginning.

The load instruction has a delay or latency that cannot be eliminated by forwarding alone. Instead, we need to add hardware, called a *pipeline interlock*, to preserve the correct execution pattern. In general, a pipeline interlock detects a hazard and stalls the pipeline until the hazard is cleared. In this case, the interlock stalls the pipeline, beginning with the instruction that wants to use the data until the source instruction produces it. This pipeline interlock introduces a stall or bubble, just as it did for the structural hazard. The CPI for the stalled instruction increases by the length of the stall (1 clock cycle in this case).

Figure C.10 shows the pipeline before and after the stall using the names of the pipeline stages. Because the stall causes the instructions starting with the DSUB to move 1 cycle later in time, the forwarding to the AND instruction now goes through the register file, and no forwarding at all is needed for the OR instruction. The insertion of the bubble causes the number of cycles to complete this sequence to grow by one. No instruction is started during clock cycle 4 (and none finishes during cycle 6).

LD R1,0(R2)	IF	ID	EX	MEM	WB				
DSUB R4,R1,R5		IF	ID	EX	MEM	WB			
AND R6,R1,R7			IF	ID	EX	MEM	WB		
OR R8,R1,R9				IF	ID	EX	MEM	WB	

LD R1,0(R2)	IF	ID	EX	MEM	WB				
DSUB R4,R1,R5		IF	ID	stall	EX	MEM	WB		
AND R6,R1,R7			IF	stall	ID	EX	MEM	WB	
OR R8,R1,R9				stall	IF	ID	EX	MEM	WB

Figure C.10 In the top half, we can see why a stall is needed: The MEM cycle of the load produces a value that is needed in the EX cycle of the DSUB, which occurs at the same time. This problem is solved by inserting a stall, as shown in the bottom half.

Branch Hazards

Control hazards can cause a greater performance loss for our MIPS pipeline than do data hazards. When a branch is executed, it may or may not change the PC to something other than its current value plus 4. Recall that if a branch changes the PC to its target address, it is a *taken* branch; if it falls through, it is *not taken*, or *untaken*. If instruction *i* is a taken branch, then the PC is normally not changed until the end of ID, after the completion of the address calculation and comparison.

Figure C.11 shows that the simplest method of dealing with branches is to redo the fetch of the instruction following a branch, once we detect the branch during ID (when instructions are decoded). The first IF cycle is essentially a stall, because it never performs useful work. You may have noticed that if the branch is untaken, then the repetition of the IF stage is unnecessary since the correct instruction was indeed fetched. We will develop several schemes to take advantage of this fact shortly.

One stall cycle for every branch will yield a performance loss of 10% to 30% depending on the branch frequency, so we will examine some techniques to deal with this loss.

Branch instruction	IF	ID	EX	MEM	WB			
Branch successor		IF	IF	ID	EX	MEM	WB	
Branch successor + 1				IF	ID	EX	MEM	
Branch successor + 2					IF	ID	EX	

Figure C.11 A branch causes a one-cycle stall in the five-stage pipeline. The instruction after the branch is fetched, but the instruction is ignored, and the fetch is restarted once the branch target is known. It is probably obvious that if the branch is not taken, the second IF for branch successor is redundant. This will be addressed shortly.

Reducing Pipeline Branch Penalties

There are many methods for dealing with the pipeline stalls caused by branch delay; we discuss four simple compile time schemes in this subsection. In these four schemes the actions for a branch are static—they are fixed for each branch during the entire execution. The software can try to minimize the branch penalty using knowledge of the hardware scheme and of branch behavior. Chapter 3 looks at more powerful hardware and software techniques for both static and dynamic branch prediction.

The simplest scheme to handle branches is to *freeze* or *flush* the pipeline, holding or deleting any instructions after the branch until the branch destination is known. The attractiveness of this solution lies primarily in its simplicity both for hardware and software. It is the solution used earlier in the pipeline shown in Figure C.11. In this case, the branch penalty is fixed and cannot be reduced by software.

A higher-performance, and only slightly more complex, scheme is to treat every branch as not taken, simply allowing the hardware to continue as if the branch were not executed. Here, care must be taken not to change the processor state until the branch outcome is definitely known. The complexity of this scheme arises from having to know when the state might be changed by an instruction and how to "back out" such a change.

In the simple five-stage pipeline, this *predicted-not-taken* or *predicted-untaken* scheme is implemented by continuing to fetch instructions as if the branch were a normal instruction. The pipeline looks as if nothing out of the ordinary is happening. If the branch is taken, however, we need to turn the fetched instruction into a no-op and restart the fetch at the target address. Figure C.12 shows both situations.

Untaken branch instruction	IF	ID	EX	MEM	WB				
Instruction $i + 1$		IF	ID	EX	MEM	WB			
Instruction $i + 2$			IF	ID	EX	MEM	WB		
Instruction $i + 3$				IF	ID	EX	MEM	WB	
Instruction $i + 4$					IF	ID	EX	MEM	WB
Taken branch instruction	IF	ID	EX	MEM	WB				
Instruction $i + 1$		IF	idle	idle	idle	idle			
Branch target			IF	ID	EX	MEM	WB		
Branch target + 1				IF	ID	EX	MEM	WB	
Branch target + 2					IF	ID	EX	MEM	WB

Figure C.12 The predicted-not-taken scheme and the pipeline sequence when the branch is untaken (top) and taken (bottom). When the branch is untaken, determined during ID, we fetch the fall-through and just continue. If the branch is taken during ID, we restart the fetch at the branch target. This causes all instructions following the branch to stall 1 clock cycle.

An alternative scheme is to treat every branch as taken. As soon as the branch is decoded and the target address is computed, we assume the branch to be taken and begin fetching and executing at the target. Because in our five-stage pipeline we don't know the target address any earlier than we know the branch outcome, there is no advantage in this approach for this pipeline. In some processors—especially those with implicitly set condition codes or more powerful (and hence slower) branch conditions—the branch target is known before the branch outcome, and a predicted-taken scheme might make sense. In either a predicted-taken or predicted-not-taken scheme, the compiler can improve performance by organizing the code so that the most frequent path matches the hardware's choice. Our fourth scheme provides more opportunities for the compiler to improve performance.

A fourth scheme in use in some processors is called *delayed branch*. This technique was heavily used in early RISC processors and works reasonably well in the five-stage pipeline. In a delayed branch, the execution cycle with a branch delay of one is

```
branch instruction
sequential successor₁
branch target if taken
```

The sequential successor is in the *branch delay slot*. This instruction is executed whether or not the branch is taken. The pipeline behavior of the five-stage pipeline with a branch delay is shown in Figure C.13. Although it is possible to have a branch delay longer than one, in practice almost all processors with delayed branch have a single instruction delay; other techniques are used if the pipeline has a longer potential branch penalty.

Untaken branch instruction	IF	ID	EX	MEM	WB			
Branch delay instruction ($i + 1$)		IF	ID	EX	MEM	WB		
Instruction $i + 2$			IF	ID	EX	MEM	WB	
Instruction $i + 3$				IF	ID	EX	MEM	WB
Instruction $i + 4$					IF	ID	EX	MEM	WB
Taken branch instruction	IF	ID	EX	MEM	WB			
Branch delay instruction ($i + 1$)		IF	ID	EX	MEM	WB		
Branch target			IF	ID	EX	MEM	WB	
Branch target + 1				IF	ID	EX	MEM	WB
Branch target + 2					IF	ID	EX	MEM	WB

Figure C.13 The behavior of a delayed branch is the same whether or not the branch is taken. The instructions in the delay slot (there is only one delay slot for MIPS) are executed. If the branch is untaken, execution continues with the instruction after the branch delay instruction; if the branch is taken, execution continues at the branch target. When the instruction in the branch delay slot is also a branch, the meaning is unclear: If the branch is not taken, what should happen to the branch in the branch delay slot? Because of this confusion, architectures with delay branches often disallow putting a branch in the delay slot.

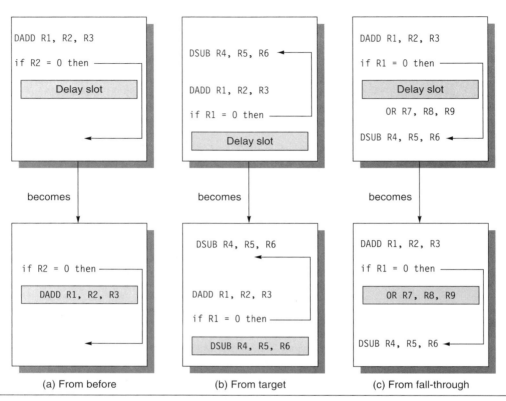

Figure C.14 Scheduling the branch delay slot. The top box in each pair shows the code before scheduling; the bottom box shows the scheduled code. In (a), the delay slot is scheduled with an independent instruction from before the branch. This is the best choice. Strategies (b) and (c) are used when (a) is not possible. In the code sequences for (b) and (c), the use of R1 in the branch condition prevents the DADD instruction (whose destination is R1) from being moved after the branch. In (b), the branch delay slot is scheduled from the target of the branch; usually the target instruction will need to be copied because it can be reached by another path. Strategy (b) is preferred when the branch is taken with high probability, such as a loop branch. Finally, the branch may be scheduled from the not-taken fall-through as in (c). To make this optimization legal for (b) or (c), it must be OK to execute the moved instruction when the branch goes in the unexpected direction. By OK we mean that the work is wasted, but the program will still execute correctly. This is the case, for example, in (c) if R7 were an unused temporary register when the branch goes in the unexpected direction.

The job of the compiler is to make the successor instructions valid and useful. A number of optimizations are used. Figure C.14 shows the three ways in which the branch delay can be scheduled.

The limitations on delayed-branch scheduling arise from: (1) the restrictions on the instructions that are scheduled into the delay slots, and (2) our ability to predict at compile time whether a branch is likely to be taken or not. To improve the ability of the compiler to fill branch delay slots, most processors with conditional branches have introduced a *canceling* or *nullifying* branch. In a canceling branch, the instruction includes the direction that the branch was predicted. When the branch behaves as predicted, the instruction in the branch delay slot is simply executed as it would normally be with a delayed branch. When the branch is incorrectly predicted, the instruction in the branch delay slot is simply turned into a no-op.

Performance of Branch Schemes

What is the effective performance of each of these schemes? The effective pipeline speedup with branch penalties, assuming an ideal CPI of 1, is

$$\text{Pipeline speedup} = \frac{\text{Pipeline depth}}{1 + \text{Pipeline stall cycles from branches}}$$

Because of the following:

$$\text{Pipeline stall cycles from branches} = \text{Branch frequency} \times \text{Branch penalty}$$

we obtain:

$$\text{Pipeline speedup} = \frac{\text{Pipeline depth}}{1 + \text{Branch frequency} \times \text{Branch penalty}}$$

The branch frequency and branch penalty can have a component from both unconditional and conditional branches. However, the latter dominate since they are more frequent.

Example   For a deeper pipeline, such as that in a MIPS R4000, it takes at least three pipeline stages before the branch-target address is known and an additional cycle before the branch condition is evaluated, assuming no stalls on the registers in the conditional comparison. A three-stage delay leads to the branch penalties for the three simplest prediction schemes listed in Figure C.15.

Find the effective addition to the CPI arising from branches for this pipeline, assuming the following frequencies:

Unconditional branch	4%
Conditional branch, untaken	6%
Conditional branch, taken	10%

Branch scheme	Penalty unconditional	Penalty untaken	Penalty taken
Flush pipeline	2	3	3
Predicted taken	2	3	2
Predicted untaken	2	0	3

Figure C.15 Branch penalties for the three simplest prediction schemes for a deeper pipeline.

Branch scheme	Additions to the CPI from branch costs			
	Unconditional branches	Untaken conditional branches	Taken conditional branches	All branches
Frequency of event	4%	6%	10%	20%
Stall pipeline	0.08	0.18	0.30	0.56
Predicted taken	0.08	0.18	0.20	0.46
Predicted untaken	0.08	0.00	0.30	0.38

Figure C.16 CPI penalties for three branch-prediction schemes and a deeper pipeline.

Answer   We find the CPIs by multiplying the relative frequency of unconditional, conditional untaken, and conditional taken branches by the respective penalties. The results are shown in Figure C.16.

The differences among the schemes are substantially increased with this longer delay. If the base CPI were 1 and branches were the only source of stalls, the ideal pipeline would be 1.56 times faster than a pipeline that used the stall-pipeline scheme. The predicted-untaken scheme would be 1.13 times better than the stall-pipeline scheme under the same assumptions.

Reducing the Cost of Branches through Prediction

As pipelines get deeper and the potential penalty of branches increases, using delayed branches and similar schemes becomes insufficient. Instead, we need to turn to more aggressive means for predicting branches. Such schemes fall into two classes: low-cost static schemes that rely on information available at compile time and strategies that predict branches dynamically based on program behavior. We discuss both approaches here.

Static Branch Prediction

A key way to improve compile-time branch prediction is to use profile information collected from earlier runs. The key observation that makes this worthwhile is that the behavior of branches is often bimodally distributed; that is, an individual branch is often highly biased toward taken or untaken. Figure C.17 shows the success of branch prediction using this strategy. The same input data were used for runs and for collecting the profile; other studies have shown that changing the input so that the profile is for a different run leads to only a small change in the accuracy of profile-based prediction.

The effectiveness of any branch prediction scheme depends both on the accuracy of the scheme and the frequency of conditional branches, which vary in SPEC from 3% to 24%. The fact that the misprediction rate for the integer programs is higher and such programs typically have a higher branch frequency is a major limitation for static branch prediction. In the next section, we consider dynamic branch predictors, which most recent processors have employed.

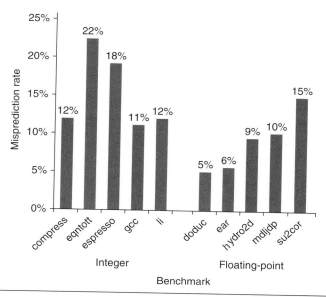

Figure C.17 Misprediction rate on SPEC92 for a profile-based predictor varies widely but is generally better for the floating-point programs, which have an average misprediction rate of 9% with a standard deviation of 4%, than for the integer programs, which have an average misprediction rate of 15% with a standard deviation of 5%. The actual performance depends on both the prediction accuracy and the branch frequency, which vary from 3% to 24%.

Dynamic Branch Prediction and Branch-Prediction Buffers

The simplest dynamic branch-prediction scheme is a *branch-prediction buffer* or *branch history table*. A branch-prediction buffer is a small memory indexed by the lower portion of the address of the branch instruction. The memory contains a bit that says whether the branch was recently taken or not. This scheme is the simplest sort of buffer; it has no tags and is useful only to reduce the branch delay when it is longer than the time to compute the possible target PCs.

With such a buffer, we don't know, in fact, if the prediction is correct—it may have been put there by another branch that has the same low-order address bits. But this doesn't matter. The prediction is a hint that is assumed to be correct, and fetching begins in the predicted direction. If the hint turns out to be wrong, the prediction bit is inverted and stored back.

This buffer is effectively a cache where every access is a hit, and, as we will see, the performance of the buffer depends on both how often the prediction is for the branch of interest and how accurate the prediction is when it matches. Before we analyze the performance, it is useful to make a small, but important, improvement in the accuracy of the branch-prediction scheme.

This simple 1-bit prediction scheme has a performance shortcoming: Even if a branch is almost always taken, we will likely predict incorrectly twice, rather than once, when it is not taken, since the misprediction causes the prediction bit to be flipped.

To remedy this weakness, 2-bit prediction schemes are often used. In a 2-bit scheme, a prediction must miss twice before it is changed. Figure C.18 shows the finite-state processor for a 2-bit prediction scheme.

A branch-prediction buffer can be implemented as a small, special "cache" accessed with the instruction address during the IF pipe stage, or as a pair of bits attached to each block in the instruction cache and fetched with the instruction. If the instruction is decoded as a branch and if the branch is predicted as taken, fetching begins from the target as soon as the PC is known. Otherwise, sequential fetching and executing continue. As Figure C.18 shows, if the prediction turns out to be wrong, the prediction bits are changed.

What kind of accuracy can be expected from a branch-prediction buffer using 2 bits per entry on real applications? Figure C.19 shows that for the SPEC89

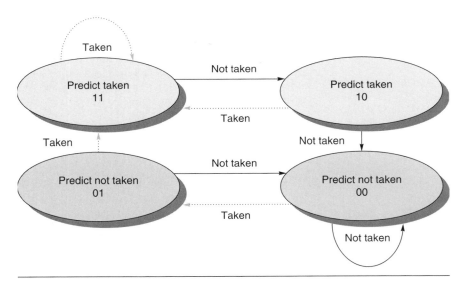

Figure C.18 The states in a 2-bit prediction scheme. By using 2 bits rather than 1, a branch that strongly favors taken or not taken—as many branches do—will be mispredicted less often than with a 1-bit predictor. The 2 bits are used to encode the four states in the system. The 2-bit scheme is actually a specialization of a more general scheme that has an n-bit saturating counter for each entry in the prediction buffer. With an n-bit counter, the counter can take on values between 0 and $2^n - 1$: When the counter is greater than or equal to one-half of its maximum value ($2^n - 1$), the branch is predicted as taken; otherwise, it is predicted as untaken. Studies of n-bit predictors have shown that the 2-bit predictors do almost as well, thus most systems rely on 2-bit branch predictors rather than the more general n-bit predictors.

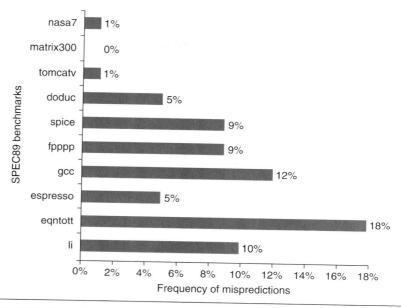

Figure C.19 **Prediction accuracy of a 4096-entry 2-bit prediction buffer for the SPEC89 benchmarks.** The misprediction rate for the integer benchmarks (gcc, espresso, eqntott, and li) is substantially higher (average of 11%) than that for the floating-point programs (average of 4%). Omitting the floating-point kernels (nasa7, matrix300, and tomcatv) still yields a higher accuracy for the FP benchmarks than for the integer benchmarks. These data, as well as the rest of the data in this section, are taken from a branch-prediction study done using the IBM Power architecture and optimized code for that system. See Pan, So, and Rameh [1992]. Although these data are for an older version of a subset of the SPEC benchmarks, the newer benchmarks are larger and would show slightly worse behavior, especially for the integer benchmarks.

benchmarks a branch-prediction buffer with 4096 entries results in a prediction accuracy ranging from over 99% to 82%, or a *misprediction rate* of 1% to 18%. A 4K entry buffer, like that used for these results, is considered small by 2005 standards, and a larger buffer could produce somewhat better results.

As we try to exploit more ILP, the accuracy of our branch prediction becomes critical. As we can see in Figure C.19, the accuracy of the predictors for integer programs, which typically also have higher branch frequencies, is lower than for the loop-intensive scientific programs. We can attack this problem in two ways: by increasing the size of the buffer and by increasing the accuracy of the scheme we use for each prediction. A buffer with 4K entries, however, as Figure C.20 shows, performs quite comparably to an infinite buffer, at least for benchmarks like those in SPEC. The data in Figure C.20 make it clear that the hit rate of the buffer is not the major limiting factor. As we mentioned above, simply increasing

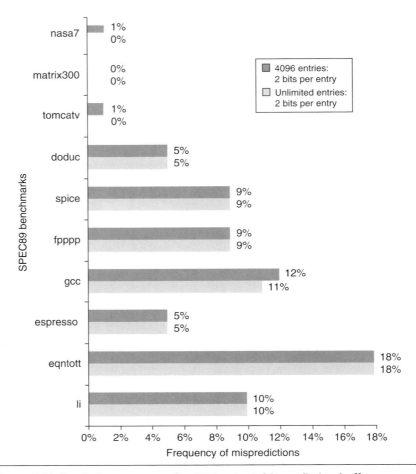

Figure C.20 Prediction accuracy of a 4096-entry 2-bit prediction buffer versus an infinite buffer for the SPEC89 benchmarks. Although these data are for an older version of a subset of the SPEC benchmarks, the results would be comparable for newer versions with perhaps as many as 8K entries needed to match an infinite 2-bit predictor.

the number of bits per predictor without changing the predictor structure also has little impact. Instead, we need to look at how we might increase the accuracy of each predictor.

C.3   How Is Pipelining Implemented?

Before we proceed to basic pipelining, we need to review a simple implementation of an unpipelined version of MIPS.

A Simple Implementation of MIPS

In this section we follow the style of Section C.1, showing first a simple unpipe-lined implementation and then the pipelined implementation. This time, however, our example is specific to the MIPS architecture.

In this subsection, we focus on a pipeline for an integer subset of MIPS that consists of load-store word, branch equal to zero, and integer ALU operations. Later in this appendix we will incorporate the basic floating-point operations. Although we discuss only a subset of MIPS, the basic principles can be extended to handle all the instructions. We initially used a less aggressive implementation of a branch instruction. We show how to implement the more aggressive version at the end of this section.

Every MIPS instruction can be implemented in at most 5 clock cycles. The 5 clock cycles are as follows:

1. *Instruction fetch cycle* (IF):

   ```
   IR ← Mem[PC];
   NPC ← PC + 4;
   ```

   Operation—Send out the PC and fetch the instruction from memory into the instruction register (IR); increment the PC by 4 to address the next sequential instruction. The IR is used to hold the instruction that will be needed on sub-sequent clock cycles; likewise, the register NPC is used to hold the next sequential PC.

2. *Instruction decode/register fetch cycle* (ID):

   ```
   A ← Regs[rs];
   B ← Regs[rt];
   Imm ← sign-extended immediate field of IR;
   ```

   Operation—Decode the instruction and access the register file to read the registers (rs and rt are the register specifiers). The outputs of the general-purpose registers are read into two temporary registers (A and B) for use in later clock cycles. The lower 16 bits of the IR are also sign extended and stored into the temporary register Imm, for use in the next cycle.

   Decoding is done in parallel with reading registers, which is possible because these fields are at a fixed location in the MIPS instruction format. Because the immediate portion of an instruction is located in an identical place in every MIPS format, the sign-extended immediate is also calculated during this cycle in case it is needed in the next cycle.

3. *Execution/effective address cycle* (EX):

   The ALU operates on the operands prepared in the prior cycle, performing one of four functions depending on the MIPS instruction type:

   - Memory reference:

     ```
     ALUOutput ← A + Imm;
     ```

Operation—The ALU adds the operands to form the effective address and places the result into the register ALUOutput.

- Register-register ALU instruction:

```
ALUOutput ← A func B;
```

Operation—The ALU performs the operation specified by the function code on the value in register A and on the value in register B. The result is placed in the temporary register ALUOutput.

- Register-Immediate ALU instruction:

```
ALUOutput ← A op Imm;
```

Operation—The ALU performs the operation specified by the opcode on the value in register A and on the value in register Imm. The result is placed in the temporary register ALUOutput.

- Branch:

```
ALUOutput ← NPC + (Imm << 2);
Cond ← (A == 0)
```

Operation—The ALU adds the NPC to the sign-extended immediate value in Imm, which is shifted left by 2 bits to create a word offset, to compute the address of the branch target. Register A, which has been read in the prior cycle, is checked to determine whether the branch is taken. Since we are considering only one form of branch (BEQZ), the comparison is against 0. Note that BEQZ is actually a pseudoinstruction that translates to a BEQ with R0 as an operand. For simplicity, this is the only form of branch we consider.

The load-store architecture of MIPS means that effective address and execution cycles can be combined into a single clock cycle, since no instruction needs to simultaneously calculate a data address, calculate an instruction target address, and perform an operation on the data. The other integer instructions not included above are jumps of various forms, which are similar to branches.

4. *Memory access/branch completion cycle* (MEM):

The PC is updated for all instructions: PC ← NPC;

- Memory reference:

```
LMD ← Mem[ALUOutput] or
Mem[ALUOutput] ← B;
```

Operation—Access memory if needed. If instruction is a load, data return from memory and are placed in the LMD (load memory data) register; if it is a store, then the data from the B register are written into memory. In either case, the address used is the one computed during the prior cycle and stored in the register ALUOutput.

- Branch:

```
if (cond) PC ← ALUOutput
```

Operation—If the instruction branches, the PC is replaced with the branch destination address in the register ALUOutput.

5. *Write-back cycle* (WB):

   ■ Register-register ALU instruction:

   Regs[rd] ← ALUOutput;

   ■ Register-immediate ALU instruction:

   Regs[rt] ← ALUOutput;

   ■ Load instruction:

   Regs[rt] ← LMD;

   Operation—Write the result into the register file, whether it comes from the memory system (which is in LMD) or from the ALU (which is in ALUOutput); the register destination field is also in one of two positions (rd or rt) depending on the effective opcode.

Figure C.21 shows how an instruction flows through the data path. At the end of each clock cycle, every value computed during that clock cycle and required on a later clock cycle (whether for this instruction or the next) is written into a storage device, which may be memory, a general-purpose register, the PC, or a temporary register (i.e., LMD, Imm, A, B, IR, NPC, ALUOutput, or Cond). The temporary registers hold values between clock cycles for one instruction, while the other storage elements are visible parts of the state and hold values between successive instructions.

Although all processors today are pipelined, this multicycle implementation is a reasonable approximation of how most processors would have been implemented in earlier times. A simple finite-state machine could be used to implement the control following the 5-cycle structure shown above. For a much more complex processor, microcode control could be used. In either event, an instruction sequence like that above would determine the structure of the control.

There are some hardware redundancies that could be eliminated in this multicycle implementation. For example, there are two ALUs: one to increment the PC and one used for effective address and ALU computation. Since they are not needed on the same clock cycle, we could merge them by adding additional multiplexers and sharing the same ALU. Likewise, instructions and data could be stored in the same memory, since the data and instruction accesses happen on different clock cycles.

Rather than optimize this simple implementation, we will leave the design as it is in Figure C.21, since this provides us with a better base for the pipelined implementation.

As an alternative to the multicycle design discussed in this section, we could also have implemented the CPU so that every instruction takes 1 long clock cycle. In such cases, the temporary registers would be deleted, since there would not be any communication across clock cycles within an instruction. Every instruction would execute in 1 long clock cycle, writing the result into the data memory, registers, or PC at the end of the clock cycle. The CPI would be one for such a processor.

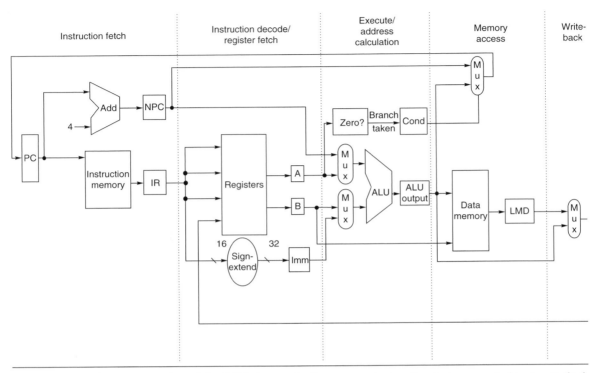

Figure C.21 The implementation of the MIPS data path allows every instruction to be executed in 4 or 5 clock cycles. Although the PC is shown in the portion of the data path that is used in instruction fetch and the registers are shown in the portion of the data path that is used in instruction decode/register fetch, both of these functional units are read as well as written by an instruction. Although we show these functional units in the cycle corresponding to where they are read, the PC is written during the memory access clock cycle and the registers are written during the write-back clock cycle. In both cases, the writes in later pipe stages are indicated by the multiplexer output (in memory access or write-back), which carries a value back to the PC or registers. These backward-flowing signals introduce much of the complexity of pipelining, since they indicate the possibility of hazards.

The clock cycle, however, would be roughly equal to five times the clock cycle of the multicycle processor, since every instruction would need to traverse all the functional units. Designers would never use this single-cycle implementation for two reasons. First, a single-cycle implementation would be very inefficient for most CPUs that have a reasonable variation among the amount of work, and hence in the clock cycle time, needed for different instructions. Second, a single-cycle implementation requires the duplication of functional units that could be shared in a multicycle implementation. Nonetheless, this single-cycle data path allows us to illustrate how pipelining can improve the clock cycle time, as opposed to the CPI, of a processor.

A Basic Pipeline for MIPS

As before, we can pipeline the data path of Figure C.21 with almost no changes by starting a new instruction on each clock cycle. Because every pipe stage is active on every clock cycle, all operations in a pipe stage must complete in 1 clock cycle and any combination of operations must be able to occur at once. Furthermore, pipelining the data path requires that values passed from one pipe stage to the next must be placed in registers. Figure C.22 shows the MIPS pipeline with the appropriate registers, called *pipeline registers* or *pipeline latches*, between each pipeline stage. The registers are labeled with the names of the stages they connect. Figure C.22 is drawn so that connections through the pipeline registers from one stage to another are clear.

All of the registers needed to hold values temporarily between clock cycles within one instruction are subsumed into these pipeline registers. The fields of the instruction register (IR), which is part of the IF/ID register, are labeled when they are used to supply register names. The pipeline registers carry both data and control from one pipeline stage to the next. Any value needed on a later pipeline stage must be placed in such a register and copied from one pipeline register to the next, until it is no longer needed. If we tried to just use the temporary registers we had in our earlier unpipelined data path, values could be overwritten before all uses were completed. For example, the field of a register operand used

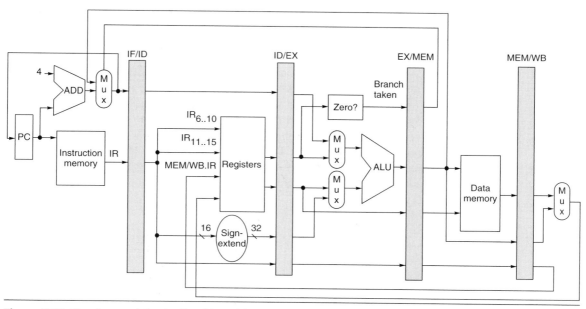

Figure C.22   The data path is pipelined by adding a set of registers, one between each pair of pipe stages. The registers serve to convey values and control information from one stage to the next. We can also think of the PC as a pipeline register, which sits before the IF stage of the pipeline, leading to one pipeline register for each pipe stage. Recall that the PC is an edge-triggered register written at the end of the clock cycle; hence, there is no race condition in writing the PC. The selection multiplexer for the PC has been moved so that the PC is written in exactly one stage (IF). If we didn't move it, there would be a conflict when a branch occurred, since two instructions would try to write different values into the PC. Most of the data paths flow from left to right, which is from earlier in time to later. The paths flowing from right to left (which carry the register write-back information and PC information on a branch) introduce complications into our pipeline.

for a write on a load or ALU operation is supplied from the MEM/WB pipeline register rather than from the IF/ID register. This is because we want a load or ALU operation to write the register designated by that operation, not the register field of the instruction currently transitioning from IF to ID! This destination register field is simply copied from one pipeline register to the next, until it is needed during the WB stage.

Any instruction is active in exactly one stage of the pipeline at a time; therefore, any actions taken on behalf of an instruction occur between a pair of pipeline registers. Thus, we can also look at the activities of the pipeline by examining what has to happen on any pipeline stage depending on the instruction type. Figure C.23 shows this view. Fields of the pipeline registers are named so as to show the flow of data from one stage to the next. Notice that the actions in the first two stages are independent of the current instruction type; they must be independent because the instruction is not decoded until the end of the ID stage. The IF activity depends on whether the instruction in EX/MEM is a taken branch. If so, then the branch-target address of the branch instruction in EX/MEM is written into the PC at the end of IF; otherwise, the incremented PC will be written back. (As we said earlier, this effect of branches leads to complications in the pipeline that we deal with in the next few sections.) The fixed-position encoding of the register source operands is critical to allowing the registers to be fetched during ID.

To control this simple pipeline we need only determine how to set the control for the four multiplexers in the data path of Figure C.22. The two multiplexers in the ALU stage are set depending on the instruction type, which is dictated by the IR field of the ID/EX register. The top ALU input multiplexer is set by whether the instruction is a branch or not, and the bottom multiplexer is set by whether the instruction is a register-register ALU operation or any other type of operation. The multiplexer in the IF stage chooses whether to use the value of the incremented PC or the value of the EX/MEM.ALUOutput (the branch target) to write into the PC. This multiplexer is controlled by the field EX/MEM.cond. The fourth multiplexer is controlled by whether the instruction in the WB stage is a load or an ALU operation. In addition to these four multiplexers, there is one additional multiplexer needed that is not drawn in Figure C.22, but whose existence is clear from looking at the WB stage of an ALU operation. The destination register field is in one of two different places depending on the instruction type (register-register ALU versus either ALU immediate or load). Thus, we will need a multiplexer to choose the correct portion of the IR in the MEM/WB register to specify the register destination field, assuming the instruction writes a register.

Implementing the Control for the MIPS Pipeline

The process of letting an instruction move from the instruction decode stage (ID) into the execution stage (EX) of this pipeline is usually called *instruction issue*; an instruction that has made this step is said to have *issued*. For the MIPS integer pipeline, all the data hazards can be checked during the ID phase of the pipeline. If a data hazard exists, the instruction is stalled before it is issued. Likewise, we can determine what forwarding will be needed during ID and set the appropriate

Stage	Any instruction		
IF	IF/ID.IR ← Mem[PC]; IF/ID.NPC,PC ← (if ((EX/MEM.opcode == branch) & EX/MEM.cond){EX/MEM.ALUOutput} else {PC+4});		
ID	ID/EX.A ← Regs[IF/ID.IR[rs]]; ID/EX.B ← Regs[IF/ID.IR[rt]]; ID/EX.NPC ← IF/ID.NPC; ID/EX.IR ← IF/ID.IR; ID/EX.Imm ← sign-extend(IF/ID.IR[immediate field]);		
	ALU instruction	**Load or store instruction**	**Branch instruction**
EX	EX/MEM.IR ← ID/EX.IR; EX/MEM.ALUOutput ← ID/EX.A func ID/EX.B; or EX/MEM.ALUOutput ← ID/EX.A op ID/EX.Imm;	EX/MEM.IR to ID/EX.IR EX/MEM.ALUOutput ← ID/EX.A + ID/EX.Imm; EX/MEM.B ← ID/EX.B;	EX/MEM.ALUOutput ← ID/EX.NPC + (ID/EX.Imm << 2); EX/MEM.cond ← (ID/EX.A == 0);
MEM	MEM/WB.IR ← EX/MEM.IR; MEM/WB.ALUOutput ← EX/MEM.ALUOutput;	MEM/WB.IR ← EX/MEM.IR; MEM/WB.LMD ← Mem[EX/MEM.ALUOutput]; or Mem[EX/MEM.ALUOutput] ← EX/MEM.B;	
WB	Regs[MEM/WB.IR[rd]] ← MEM/WB.ALUOutput; or Regs[MEM/WB.IR[rt]] ← MEM/WB.ALUOutput;	For load only: Regs[MEM/WB.IR[rt]] ← MEM/WB.LMD;	

Figure C.23 Events on every pipe stage of the MIPS pipeline. Let's review the actions in the stages that are specific to the pipeline organization. In IF, in addition to fetching the instruction and computing the new PC, we store the incremented PC both into the PC and into a pipeline register (NPC) for later use in computing the branch-target address. This structure is the same as the organization in Figure C.22, where the PC is updated in IF from one of two sources. In ID, we fetch the registers, extend the sign of the lower 16 bits of the IR (the immediate field), and pass along the IR and NPC. During EX, we perform an ALU operation or an address calculation; we pass along the IR and the B register (if the instruction is a store). We also set the value of cond to 1 if the instruction is a taken branch. During the MEM phase, we cycle the memory, write the PC if needed, and pass along values needed in the final pipe stage. Finally, during WB, we update the register field from either the ALU output or the loaded value. For simplicity we always pass the entire IR from one stage to the next, although as an instruction proceeds down the pipeline, less and less of the IR is needed.

controls then. Detecting interlocks early in the pipeline reduces the hardware complexity because the hardware never has to suspend an instruction that has updated the state of the processor, unless the entire processor is stalled. Alternatively, we can detect the hazard or forwarding at the beginning of a clock cycle that uses an operand (EX and MEM for this pipeline). To show the differences in these two approaches, we will show how the interlock for a read after write (RAW) hazard with the source coming from a load instruction (called a *load interlock*) can be implemented by a check in ID, while the implementation of forwarding paths

Situation	Example code sequence	Action
No dependence	LD **R1**,45(R2) DADD R5,R6,R7 DSUB R8,R6,R7 OR R9,R6,R7	No hazard possible because no dependence exists on R1 in the immediately following three instructions.
Dependence requiring stall	LD **R1**,45(R2) DADD R5,**R1**,R7 DSUB R8,R6,R7 OR R9,R6,R7	Comparators detect the use of R1 in the DADD and stall the DADD (and DSUB and OR) before the DADD begins EX.
Dependence overcome by forwarding	LD **R1**,45(R2) DADD R5,R6,R7 DSUB R8,**R1**,R7 OR R9,R6,R7	Comparators detect use of R1 in DSUB and forward result of load to ALU in time for DSUB to begin EX.
Dependence with accesses in order	LD **R1**,45(R2) DADD R5,R6,R7 DSUB R8,R6,R7 OR R9,**R1**,R7	No action required because the read of R1 by OR occurs in the second half of the ID phase, while the write of the loaded data occurred in the first half.

Figure C.24 Situations that the pipeline hazard detection hardware can see by comparing the destination and sources of adjacent instructions. This table indicates that the only comparison needed is between the destination and the sources on the two instructions following the instruction that wrote the destination. In the case of a stall, the pipeline dependences will look like the third case once execution continues. Of course, hazards that involve R0 can be ignored since the register always contains 0, and the test above could be extended to do this.

to the ALU inputs can be done during EX. Figure C.24 lists the variety of circumstances that we must handle.

Let's start with implementing the load interlock. If there is a RAW hazard with the source instruction being a load, the load instruction will be in the EX stage when an instruction that needs the load data will be in the ID stage. Thus, we can describe all the possible hazard situations with a small table, which can be directly translated to an implementation. Figure C.25 shows a table that detects all load interlocks when the instruction using the load result is in the ID stage.

Once a hazard has been detected, the control unit must insert the pipeline stall and prevent the instructions in the IF and ID stages from advancing. As we said earlier, all the control information is carried in the pipeline registers. (Carrying the instruction along is enough, since all control is derived from it.) Thus, when we detect a hazard we need only change the control portion of the ID/EX pipeline register to all 0s, which happens to be a no-op (an instruction that does nothing, such as DADD R0,R0,R0). In addition, we simply recirculate the contents of the IF/ID registers to hold the stalled instruction. In a pipeline with more complex hazards, the same ideas would apply: We can detect the hazard by comparing some set of pipeline registers and shift in no-ops to prevent erroneous execution.

Implementing the forwarding logic is similar, although there are more cases to consider. The key observation needed to implement the forwarding logic is

Opcode field of ID/EX (ID/EX.IR$_{0..5}$)	Opcode field of IF/ID (IF/ID.IR$_{0..5}$)	Matching operand fields
Load	Register-register ALU	ID/EX.IR[rt] == IF/ID.IR[rs]
Load	Register-register ALU	ID/EX.IR[rt] == IF/ID.IR[rt]
Load	Load, store, ALU immediate, or branch	ID/EX.IR[rt] == IF/ID.IR[rs]

Figure C.25 The logic to detect the need for load interlocks during the ID stage of an instruction requires three comparisons. Lines 1 and 2 of the table test whether the load destination register is one of the source registers for a register-register operation in ID. Line 3 of the table determines if the load destination register is a source for a load or store effective address, an ALU immediate, or a branch test. Remember that the IF/ID register holds the state of the instruction in ID, which potentially uses the load result, while ID/EX holds the state of the instruction in EX, which is the load instruction.

that the pipeline registers contain both the data to be forwarded as well as the source and destination register fields. All forwarding logically happens from the ALU or data memory output to the ALU input, the data memory input, or the zero detection unit. Thus, we can implement the forwarding by a comparison of the destination registers of the IR contained in the EX/MEM and MEM/WB stages against the source registers of the IR contained in the ID/EX and EX/MEM registers. Figure C.26 shows the comparisons and possible forwarding operations where the destination of the forwarded result is an ALU input for the instruction currently in EX.

In addition to the comparators and combinational logic that we must determine when a forwarding path needs to be enabled, we also must enlarge the multiplexers at the ALU inputs and add the connections from the pipeline registers that are used to forward the results. Figure C.27 shows the relevant segments of the pipelined data path with the additional multiplexers and connections in place.

For MIPS, the hazard detection and forwarding hardware is reasonably simple; we will see that things become somewhat more complicated when we extend this pipeline to deal with floating point. Before we do that, we need to handle branches.

Dealing with Branches in the Pipeline

In MIPS, the branches (BEQ and BNE) require testing a register for equality to another register, which may be R0. If we consider only the cases of BEQZ and BNEZ, which require a zero test, it is possible to complete this decision by the end of the ID cycle by moving the zero test into that cycle. To take advantage of an early decision on whether the branch is taken, both PCs (taken and untaken) must be computed early. Computing the branch-target address during ID requires an additional adder because the main ALU, which has been used for this function so

Pipeline register containing source instruction	Opcode of source instruction	Pipeline register containing destination instruction	Opcode of destination instruction	Destination of the forwarded result	Comparison (if equal then forward)
EX/MEM	Register-register ALU	ID/EX	Register-register ALU, ALU immediate, load, store, branch	Top ALU input	`EX/MEM.IR[rd] == ID/EX.IR[rs]`
EX/MEM	Register-register ALU	ID/EX	Register-register ALU	Bottom ALU input	`EX/MEM.IR[rd] == ID/EX.IR[rt]`
MEM/WB	Register-register ALU	ID/EX	Register-register ALU, ALU immediate, load, store, branch	Top ALU input	`MEM/WB.IR[rd] == ID/EX.IR[rs]`
MEM/WB	Register-register ALU	ID/EX	Register-register ALU	Bottom ALU input	`MEM/WB.IR[rd] == ID/EX.IR[rt]`
EX/MEM	ALU immediate	ID/EX	Register-register ALU, ALU immediate, load, store, branch	Top ALU input	`EX/MEM.IR[rt] == ID/EX.IR[rs]`
EX/MEM	ALU immediate	ID/EX	Register-register ALU	Bottom ALU input	`EX/MEM.IR[rt] == ID/EX.IR[rt]`
MEM/WB	ALU immediate	ID/EX	Register-register ALU, ALU immediate, load, store, branch	Top ALU input	`MEM/WB.IR[rt] == ID/EX.IR[rs]`
MEM/WB	ALU immediate	ID/EX	Register-register ALU	Bottom ALU input	`MEM/WB.IR[rt] == ID/EX.IR[rt]`
MEM/WB	Load	ID/EX	Register-register ALU, ALU immediate, load, store, branch	Top ALU input	`MEM/WB.IR[rt] == ID/EX.IR[rs]`
MEM/WB	Load	ID/EX	Register-register ALU	Bottom ALU input	`MEM/WB.IR[rt] == ID/EX.IR[rt]`

Figure C.26 Forwarding of data to the two ALU inputs (for the instruction in EX) can occur from the ALU result (in EX/MEM or in MEM/WB) or from the load result in MEM/WB. There are 10 separate comparisons needed to tell whether a forwarding operation should occur. The top and bottom ALU inputs refer to the inputs corresponding to the first and second ALU source operands, respectively, and are shown explicitly in Figure C.21 on page C-34 and in Figure C.27 on page C-41. Remember that the pipeline latch for destination instruction in EX is ID/EX, while the source values come from the ALUOutput portion of EX/MEM or MEM/WB or the LMD portion of MEM/WB. There is one complication not addressed by this logic: dealing with multiple instructions that write the same register. For example, during the code sequence DADD R1, R2, R3; DADDI R1, R1, #2; DSUB R4, R3, R1, the logic must ensure that the DSUB instruction uses the result of the DADDI instruction rather than the result of the DADD instruction. The logic shown above can be extended to handle this case by simply testing that forwarding from MEM/WB is enabled only when forwarding from EX/MEM is not enabled for the same input. Because the DADDI result will be in EX/MEM, it will be forwarded, rather than the DADD result in MEM/WB.

far, is not usable until EX. Figure C.28 shows the revised pipelined data path. With the separate adder and a branch decision made during ID, there is only a 1-clock-cycle stall on branches. Although this reduces the branch delay to 1 cycle,

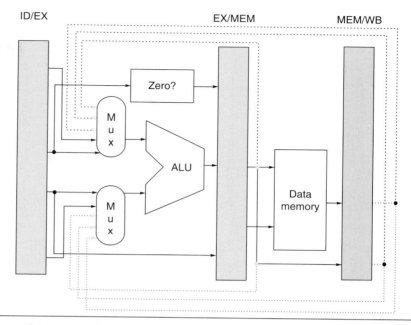

Figure C.27 **Forwarding of results to the ALU requires the addition of three extra inputs on each ALU multiplexer and the addition of three paths to the new inputs.** The paths correspond to a bypass of: (1) the ALU output at the end of the EX, (2) the ALU output at the end of the MEM stage, and (3) the memory output at the end of the MEM stage.

it means that an ALU instruction followed by a branch on the result of the instruction will incur a data hazard stall. Figure C.29 shows the branch portion of the revised pipeline table from Figure C.23.

In some processors, branch hazards are even more expensive in clock cycles than in our example, since the time to evaluate the branch condition and compute the destination can be even longer. For example, a processor with separate decode and register fetch stages will probably have a *branch delay*—the length of the control hazard—that is at least 1 clock cycle longer. The branch delay, unless it is dealt with, turns into a branch penalty. Many older CPUs that implement more complex instruction sets have branch delays of 4 clock cycles or more, and large, deeply pipelined processors often have branch penalties of 6 or 7. In general, the deeper the pipeline, the worse the branch penalty in clock cycles. Of course, the relative performance effect of a longer branch penalty depends on the overall CPI of the processor. A low-CPI processor can afford to have more expensive branches because the percentage of the processor's performance that will be lost from branches is less.

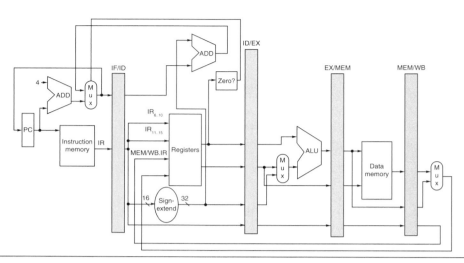

Figure C.28 **The stall from branch hazards can be reduced by moving the zero test and branch-target calcula-tion into the ID phase of the pipeline.** Notice that we have made two important changes, each of which removes 1 cycle from the 3-cycle stall for branches. The first change is to move both the branch-target address calculation and the branch condition decision to the ID cycle. The second change is to write the PC of the instruction in the IF phase, using either the branch-target address computed during ID or the incremented PC computed during IF. In compari-son, Figure C.22 obtained the branch-target address from the EX/MEM register and wrote the result during the MEM clock cycle. As mentioned in Figure C.22, the PC can be thought of as a pipeline register (e.g., as part of ID/IF), which is written with the address of the next instruction at the end of each IF cycle.

Pipe stage	Branch instruction
IF	IF/ID.IR ← Mem[PC]; IF/ID.NPC,PC ← (if ((IF/ID.opcode == branch) & (Regs[IF/ID.IR$_{6..10}$] op 0)) {IF/ID.NPC + sign-extended (IF/ID.IR[immediate field] << 2) else {PC + 4});
ID	ID/EX.A ← Regs[IF/ID.IR$_{6..10}$]; ID/EX.B ← Regs[IF/ID.IR$_{11..15}$]; ID/EX.IR ← IF/ID.IR; ID/EX.Imm ← (IF/ID.IR$_{16}$)^{16}##IF/ID.IR$_{16..31}$
EX	
MEM	
WB	

Figure C.29 **This revised pipeline structure is based on the original in Figure C.23.** It uses a separate adder, as in Figure C.28, to compute the branch-target address during ID. The operations that are new or have changed are in bold. Because the branch-target address addition happens during ID, it will happen for all instructions; the branch condition (Regs[IF/ID.IR$_{6..10}$] op 0) will also be done for all instructions. The selection of the sequential PC or the branch-target PC still occurs during IF, but it now uses values from the ID stage that correspond to the values set by the previous instruction. This change reduces the branch penalty by 2 cycles: one from evaluating the branch target and condition earlier and one from controlling the PC selection on the same clock rather than on the next clock. Since the value of cond is set to 0, unless the instruction in ID is a taken branch, the processor must decode the instruction before the end of ID. Because the branch is done by the end of ID, the EX, MEM, and WB stages are unused for branches. An additional complication arises for jumps that have a longer offset than branches. We can resolve this by using an additional adder that sums the PC and lower 26 bits of the IR after shifting left by 2 bits.

What Makes Pipelining Hard to Implement?

Now that we understand how to detect and resolve hazards, we can deal with some complications that we have avoided so far. The first part of this section considers the challenges of exceptional situations where the instruction execution order is changed in unexpected ways. In the second part of this section, we discuss some of the challenges raised by different instruction sets.

Dealing with Exceptions

Exceptional situations are harder to handle in a pipelined CPU because the overlapping of instructions makes it more difficult to know whether an instruction can safely change the state of the CPU. In a pipelined CPU, an instruction is executed piece by piece and is not completed for several clock cycles. Unfortunately, other instructions in the pipeline can raise exceptions that may force the CPU to abort the instructions in the pipeline before they complete. Before we discuss these problems and their solutions in detail, we need to understand what types of situations can arise and what architectural requirements exist for supporting them.

Types of Exceptions and Requirements

The terminology used to describe exceptional situations where the normal execution order of instruction is changed varies among CPUs. The terms *interrupt*, *fault*, and *exception* are used, although not in a consistent fashion. We use the term *exception* to cover all these mechanisms, including the following:

- I/O device request
- Invoking an operating system service from a user program
- Tracing instruction execution
- Breakpoint (programmer-requested interrupt)
- Integer arithmetic overflow
- FP arithmetic anomaly
- Page fault (not in main memory)
- Misaligned memory accesses (if alignment is required)
- Memory protection violation
- Using an undefined or unimplemented instruction
- Hardware malfunctions
- Power failure

When we wish to refer to some particular class of such exceptions, we will use a longer name, such as I/O interrupt, floating-point exception, or page fault. Figure C.30 shows the variety of different names for the common exception events above.

Exception event	IBM 360	VAX	Motorola 680x0	Intel 80x86
I/O device request	Input/output interruption	Device interrupt	Exception (L0 to L7 autovector)	Vectored interrupt
Invoking the operating system service from a user program	Supervisor call interruption	Exception (change mode supervisor trap)	Exception (unimplemented instruction)— on Macintosh	Interrupt (INT instruction)
Tracing instruction execution	Not applicable	Exception (trace fault)	Exception (trace)	Interrupt (single-step trap)
Breakpoint	Not applicable	Exception (breakpoint fault)	Exception (illegal instruction or breakpoint)	Interrupt (breakpoint trap)
Integer arithmetic overflow or underflow; FP trap	Program interruption (overflow or underflow exception)	Exception (integer overflow trap or floating underflow fault)	Exception (floating-point coprocessor errors)	Interrupt (overflow trap or math unit exception)
Page fault (not in main memory)	Not applicable (only in 370)	Exception (translation not valid fault)	Exception (memory-management unit errors)	Interrupt (page fault)
Misaligned memory accesses	Program interruption (specification exception)	Not applicable	Exception (address error)	Not applicable
Memory protection violations	Program interruption (protection exception)	Exception (access control violation fault)	Exception (bus error)	Interrupt (protection exception)
Using undefined instructions	Program interruption (operation exception)	Exception (opcode privileged/reserved fault)	Exception (illegal instruction or break-point/unimplemented instruction)	Interrupt (invalid opcode)
Hardware malfunctions	Machine-check interruption	Exception (machine-check abort)	Exception (bus error)	Not applicable
Power failure	Machine-check interruption	Urgent interrupt	Not applicable	Nonmaskable interrupt

Figure C.30 The names of common exceptions vary across four different architectures. Every event on the IBM 360 and 80x86 is called an *interrupt*, while every event on the 680x0 is called an *exception*. VAX divides events into *interrupts* or *exceptions*. The adjectives *device*, *software*, and *urgent* are used with VAX interrupts, whereas VAX exceptions are subdivided into *faults*, *traps*, and *aborts*.

Although we use the term *exception* to cover all of these events, individual events have important characteristics that determine what action is needed in the hardware. The requirements on exceptions can be characterized on five semi-independent axes:

1. *Synchronous versus asynchronous*—If the event occurs at the same place every time the program is executed with the same data and memory allocation,

the event is *synchronous*. With the exception of hardware malfunctions, *asynchronous* events are caused by devices external to the CPU and memory. Asynchronous events usually can be handled after the completion of the current instruction, which makes them easier to handle.

2. *User requested versus coerced*—If the user task directly asks for it, it is a *user-requested* event. In some sense, user-requested exceptions are not really exceptions, since they are predictable. They are treated as exceptions, however, because the same mechanisms that are used to save and restore the state are used for these user-requested events. Because the only function of an instruction that triggers this exception is to cause the exception, user-requested exceptions can always be handled after the instruction has completed. *Coerced* exceptions are caused by some hardware event that is not under the control of the user program. Coerced exceptions are harder to implement because they are not predictable.

3. *User maskable versus user nonmaskable*—If an event can be masked or disabled by a user task, it is *user maskable*. This mask simply controls whether the hardware responds to the exception or not.

4. *Within versus between instructions*—This classification depends on whether the event prevents instruction completion by occurring in the middle of execution—no matter how short—or whether it is recognized *between* instructions. Exceptions that occur *within* instructions are usually synchronous, since the instruction triggers the exception. It's harder to implement exceptions that occur within instructions than those between instructions, since the instruction must be stopped and restarted. Asynchronous exceptions that occur within instructions arise from catastrophic situations (e.g., hardware malfunction) and always cause program termination.

5. *Resume versus terminate*—If the program's execution always stops after the interrupt, it is a *terminating* event. If the program's execution continues after the interrupt, it is a *resuming* event. It is easier to implement exceptions that terminate execution, since the CPU need not be able to restart execution of the same program after handling the exception.

Figure C.31 classifies the examples from Figure C.30 according to these five categories. The difficult task is implementing interrupts occurring within instructions where the instruction must be resumed. Implementing such exceptions requires that another program must be invoked to save the state of the executing program, correct the cause of the exception, and then restore the state of the program before the instruction that caused the exception can be tried again. This process must be effectively invisible to the executing program. If a pipeline provides the ability for the processor to handle the exception, save the state, and restart without affecting the execution of the program, the pipeline or processor is said to be *restartable*. While early supercomputers and microprocessors often lacked this property, almost all processors today support it, at least for the integer pipeline, because it is needed to implement virtual memory (see Chapter 2).

Exception type	Synchronous vs. asynchronous	User request vs. coerced	User maskable vs. nonmaskable	Within vs. between instructions	Resume vs. terminate
I/O device request	Asynchronous	Coerced	Nonmaskable	Between	Resume
Invoke operating system	Synchronous	User request	Nonmaskable	Between	Resume
Tracing instruction execution	Synchronous	User request	User maskable	Between	Resume
Breakpoint	Synchronous	User request	User maskable	Between	Resume
Integer arithmetic overflow	Synchronous	Coerced	User maskable	Within	Resume
Floating-point arithmetic overflow or underflow	Synchronous	Coerced	User maskable	Within	Resume
Page fault	Synchronous	Coerced	Nonmaskable	Within	Resume
Misaligned memory accesses	Synchronous	Coerced	User maskable	Within	Resume
Memory protection violations	Synchronous	Coerced	Nonmaskable	Within	Resume
Using undefined instructions	Synchronous	Coerced	Nonmaskable	Within	Terminate
Hardware malfunctions	Asynchronous	Coerced	Nonmaskable	Within	Terminate
Power failure	Asynchronous	Coerced	Nonmaskable	Within	Terminate

Figure C.31 Five categories are used to define what actions are needed for the different exception types shown in Figure C.30. Exceptions that must allow resumption are marked as resume, although the software may often choose to terminate the program. Synchronous, coerced exceptions occurring within instructions that can be resumed are the most difficult to implement. We might expect that memory protection access violations would always result in termination; however, modern operating systems use memory protection to detect events such as the first attempt to use a page or the first write to a page. Thus, CPUs should be able to resume after such exceptions.

Stopping and Restarting Execution

As in unpipelined implementations, the most difficult exceptions have two properties: (1) they occur within instructions (that is, in the middle of the instruction execution corresponding to EX or MEM pipe stages), and (2) they must be restartable. In our MIPS pipeline, for example, a virtual memory page fault resulting from a data fetch cannot occur until sometime in the MEM stage of the instruction. By the time that fault is seen, several other instructions will be in execution. A page fault must be restartable and requires the intervention of another process, such as the operating system. Thus, the pipeline must be safely shut down and the state saved so that the instruction can be restarted in the correct state. Restarting is usually implemented by saving the PC of the instruction at which to restart. If the restarted instruction is not a branch, then we will continue to fetch the sequential successors and begin their execution in the normal fashion. If the restarted instruction is a branch, then we will reevaluate the branch condition and begin fetching from either the target or the fall-through. When an exception occurs, the pipeline control can take the following steps to save the pipeline state safely:

1. Force a trap instruction into the pipeline on the next IF.

2. Until the trap is taken, turn off all writes for the faulting instruction and for all instructions that follow in the pipeline; this can be done by placing zeros into

the pipeline latches of all instructions in the pipeline, starting with the instruction that generates the exception, but not those that precede that instruction. This prevents any state changes for instructions that will not be completed before the exception is handled.

3. After the exception-handling routine in the operating system receives control, it immediately saves the PC of the faulting instruction. This value will be used to return from the exception later.

When we use delayed branches, as mentioned in the last section, it is no longer possible to re-create the state of the processor with a single PC because the instructions in the pipeline may not be sequentially related. So we need to save and restore as many PCs as the length of the branch delay plus one. This is done in the third step above.

After the exception has been handled, special instructions return the processor from the exception by reloading the PCs and restarting the instruction stream (using the instruction RFE in MIPS). If the pipeline can be stopped so that the instructions just before the faulting instruction are completed and those after it can be restarted from scratch, the pipeline is said to have *precise exceptions*. Ideally, the faulting instruction would not have changed the state, and correctly handling some exceptions requires that the faulting instruction have no effects. For other exceptions, such as floating-point exceptions, the faulting instruction on some processors writes its result before the exception can be handled. In such cases, the hardware must be prepared to retrieve the source operands, even if the destination is identical to one of the source operands. Because floating-point operations may run for many cycles, it is highly likely that some other instruction may have written the source operands (as we will see in the next section, floating-point operations often complete out of order). To overcome this, many recent high-performance CPUs have introduced two modes of operation. One mode has precise exceptions and the other (fast or performance mode) does not. Of course, the precise exception mode is slower, since it allows less overlap among floating-point instructions. In some high-performance CPUs, including the Alpha 21064, Power2, and MIPS R8000, the precise mode is often much slower (>10 times) and thus useful only for debugging of codes.

Supporting precise exceptions is a requirement in many systems, while in others it is "just" valuable because it simplifies the operating system interface. At a minimum, any processor with demand paging or IEEE arithmetic trap handlers must make its exceptions precise, either in the hardware or with some software support. For integer pipelines, the task of creating precise exceptions is easier, and accommodating virtual memory strongly motivates the support of precise exceptions for memory references. In practice, these reasons have led designers and architects to always provide precise exceptions for the integer pipeline. In this section we describe how to implement precise exceptions for the MIPS integer pipeline. We will describe techniques for handling the more complex challenges arising in the floating-point pipeline in Section C.5.

Exceptions in MIPS

Figure C.32 shows the MIPS pipeline stages and which problem exceptions might occur in each stage. With pipelining, multiple exceptions may occur in the same clock cycle because there are multiple instructions in execution. For example, consider this instruction sequence:

LD	IF	ID	EX	MEM	WB	
DADD		IF	ID	EX	MEM	WB

This pair of instructions can cause a data page fault and an arithmetic exception at the same time, since the LD is in the MEM stage while the DADD is in the EX stage. This case can be handled by dealing with only the data page fault and then restarting the execution. The second exception will reoccur (but not the first, if the software is correct), and when the second exception occurs it can be handled independently.

In reality, the situation is not as straightforward as this simple example. Exceptions may occur out of order; that is, an instruction may cause an exception before an earlier instruction causes one. Consider again the above sequence of instructions, LD followed by DADD. The LD can get a data page fault, seen when the instruction is in MEM, and the DADD can get an instruction page fault, seen when the DADD instruction is in IF. The instruction page fault will actually occur first, even though it is caused by a later instruction!

Since we are implementing precise exceptions, the pipeline is required to handle the exception caused by the LD instruction first. To explain how this works, let's call the instruction in the position of the LD instruction i, and the instruction in the position of the DADD instruction $i + 1$. The pipeline cannot simply handle an exception when it occurs in time, since that will lead to exceptions occurring out of the unpipelined order. Instead, the hardware posts all exceptions caused by a given instruction in a status vector associated with that instruction. The exception status vector is carried along as the instruction goes down the pipeline. Once an exception indication is set in the exception status vector, any control signal that may cause a data value to be written is turned off (this includes

Pipeline stage	Problem exceptions occurring
IF	Page fault on instruction fetch; misaligned memory access; memory protection violation
ID	Undefined or illegal opcode
EX	Arithmetic exception
MEM	Page fault on data fetch; misaligned memory access; memory protection violation
WB	None

Figure C.32 Exceptions that may occur in the MIPS pipeline. Exceptions raised from instruction or data memory access account for six out of eight cases.

both register writes and memory writes). Because a store can cause an exception during MEM, the hardware must be prepared to prevent the store from completing if it raises an exception.

When an instruction enters WB (or is about to leave MEM), the exception status vector is checked. If any exceptions are posted, they are handled in the order in which they would occur in time on an unpipelined processor—the exception corresponding to the earliest instruction (and usually the earliest pipe stage for that instruction) is handled first. This guarantees that all exceptions will be seen on instruction i before any are seen on $i + 1$. Of course, any action taken in earlier pipe stages on behalf of instruction i may be invalid, but since writes to the register file and memory were disabled, no state could have been changed. As we will see in Section C.5, maintaining this precise model for FP operations is much harder.

In the next subsection we describe problems that arise in implementing exceptions in the pipelines of processors with more powerful, longer-running instructions.

Instruction Set Complications

No MIPS instruction has more than one result, and our MIPS pipeline writes that result only at the end of an instruction's execution. When an instruction is guaranteed to complete, it is called *committed*. In the MIPS integer pipeline, all instructions are committed when they reach the end of the MEM stage (or beginning of WB) and no instruction updates the state before that stage. Thus, precise exceptions are straightforward. Some processors have instructions that change the state in the middle of the instruction execution, before the instruction and its predecessors are guaranteed to complete. For example, autoincrement addressing modes in the IA-32 architecture cause the update of registers in the middle of an instruction execution. In such a case, if the instruction is aborted because of an exception, it will leave the processor state altered. Although we know which instruction caused the exception, without additional hardware support the exception will be imprecise because the instruction will be half finished. Restarting the instruction stream after such an imprecise exception is difficult. Alternatively, we could avoid updating the state before the instruction commits, but this may be difficult or costly, since there may be dependences on the updated state: Consider a VAX instruction that autoincrements the same register multiple times. Thus, to maintain a precise exception model, most processors with such instructions have the ability to back out any state changes made before the instruction is committed. If an exception occurs, the processor uses this ability to reset the state of the processor to its value before the interrupted instruction started. In the next section, we will see that a more powerful MIPS floating-point pipeline can introduce similar problems, and Section C.7 introduces techniques that substantially complicate exception handling.

A related source of difficulties arises from instructions that update memory state during execution, such as the string copy operations on the VAX or IBM 360 (see Appendix K). To make it possible to interrupt and restart these instructions, the instructions are defined to use the general-purpose registers as working registers. Thus, the state of the partially completed instruction is always in the registers, which are saved on an exception and restored after the exception, allowing the instruction to continue. In the VAX an additional bit of state records when an instruction has started updating the memory state, so that when the pipeline is restarted the CPU knows whether to restart the instruction from the beginning or from the middle of the instruction. The IA-32 string instructions also use the registers as working storage, so that saving and restoring the registers saves and restores the state of such instructions.

A different set of difficulties arises from odd bits of state that may create additional pipeline hazards or may require extra hardware to save and restore. Condition codes are a good example of this. Many processors set the condition codes implicitly as part of the instruction. This approach has advantages, since condition codes decouple the evaluation of the condition from the actual branch. However, implicitly set condition codes can cause difficulties in scheduling any pipeline delays between setting the condition code and the branch, since most instructions set the condition code and cannot be used in the delay slots between the condition evaluation and the branch.

Additionally, in processors with condition codes, the processor must decide when the branch condition is fixed. This involves finding out when the condition code has been set for the last time before the branch. In most processors with implicitly set condition codes, this is done by delaying the branch condition evaluation until all previous instructions have had a chance to set the condition code.

Of course, architectures with explicitly set condition codes allow the delay between condition test and the branch to be scheduled; however, pipeline control must still track the last instruction that sets the condition code to know when the branch condition is decided. In effect, the condition code must be treated as an operand that requires hazard detection for RAW hazards with branches, just as MIPS must do on the registers.

A final thorny area in pipelining is multicycle operations. Imagine trying to pipeline a sequence of VAX instructions such as this:

```
MOVL    R1,R2                      ;moves between registers
ADDL3   42(R1),56(R1)+,@(R1)       ;adds memory locations
SUBL2   R2,R3                      ;subtracts registers
MOVC3   @(R1)[R2],74(R2),R3        ;moves a character string
```

These instructions differ radically in the number of clock cycles they will require, from as low as one up to hundreds of clock cycles. They also require different numbers of data memory accesses, from zero to possibly hundreds. The data hazards are very complex and occur both between and within instructions. The simple solution of making all instructions execute for the same number of clock cycles is unacceptable because it introduces an enormous number of hazards and bypass conditions and makes an immensely long pipeline. Pipelining the VAX at the instruction level is difficult, but a clever solution was found by the VAX 8800 designers. They pipeline the *microinstruction* execution; a microinstruction is a simple instruction used in sequences to implement a more complex instruction set. Because the microinstructions are simple (they look a lot like MIPS), the pipeline control is much easier. Since 1995, all Intel IA-32 microprocessors have used this strategy of converting the IA-32 instructions into microoperations, and then pipelining the microoperations.

In comparison, load-store processors have simple operations with similar amounts of work and pipeline more easily. If architects realize the relationship between instruction set design and pipelining, they can design architectures for more efficient pipelining. In the next section, we will see how the MIPS pipeline deals with long-running instructions, specifically floating-point operations.

For many years, the interaction between instruction sets and implementations was believed to be small, and implementation issues were not a major focus in designing instruction sets. In the 1980s, it became clear that the difficulty and inefficiency of pipelining could both be increased by instruction set complications. In the 1990s, all companies moved to simpler instructions sets with the goal of reducing the complexity of aggressive implementations.

C.5   Extending the MIPS Pipeline to Handle Multicycle Operations

We now want to explore how our MIPS pipeline can be extended to handle floating-point operations. This section concentrates on the basic approach and the design alternatives, closing with some performance measurements of a MIPS floating-point pipeline.

It is impractical to require that all MIPS FP operations complete in 1 clock cycle, or even in 2. Doing so would mean accepting a slow clock or using enormous amounts of logic in the FP units, or both. Instead, the FP pipeline will allow for a longer latency for operations. This is easier to grasp if we imagine the FP instructions as having the same pipeline as the integer instructions, with two important changes. First, the EX cycle may be repeated as many times as needed to complete the operation—the number of repetitions can vary for different operations. Second, there may be multiple FP functional units. A stall will occur if the instruction to be issued will cause either a structural hazard for the functional unit it uses or a data hazard.

For this section, let's assume that there are four separate functional units in our MIPS implementation:

1. The main integer unit that handles loads and stores, integer ALU operations, and branches

2. FP and integer multiplier

3. FP adder that handles FP add, subtract, and conversion

4. FP and integer divider

If we also assume that the execution stages of these functional units are not pipelined, then Figure C.33 shows the resulting pipeline structure. Because EX is not pipelined, no other instruction using that functional unit may issue until

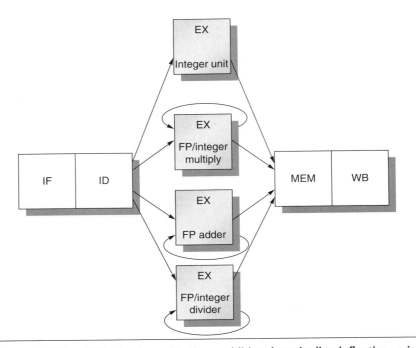

Figure C.33 The MIPS pipeline with three additional unpipelined, floating-point, functional units. Because only one instruction issues on every clock cycle, all instructions go through the standard pipeline for integer operations. The FP operations simply loop when they reach the EX stage. After they have finished the EX stage, they proceed to MEM and WB to complete execution.

the previous instruction leaves EX. Moreover, if an instruction cannot proceed to the EX stage, the entire pipeline behind that instruction will be stalled.

In reality, the intermediate results are probably not cycled around the EX unit as Figure C.33 suggests; instead, the EX pipeline stage has some number of clock delays larger than 1. We can generalize the structure of the FP pipeline shown in Figure C.33 to allow pipelining of some stages and multiple ongoing operations. To describe such a pipeline, we must define both the latency of the functional units and also the *initiation interval* or *repeat interval*. We define latency the same way we defined it earlier: the number of intervening cycles between an instruction that produces a result and an instruction that uses the result. The initiation or repeat interval is the number of cycles that must elapse between issuing two operations of a given type. For example, we will use the latencies and initiation intervals shown in Figure C.34.

With this definition of latency, integer ALU operations have a latency of 0, since the results can be used on the next clock cycle, and loads have a latency of 1, since their results can be used after one intervening cycle. Since most operations consume their operands at the beginning of EX, the latency is usually the number of stages after EX that an instruction produces a result—for example,

Functional unit	Latency	Initiation interval
Integer ALU	0	1
Data memory (integer and FP loads)	1	1
FP add	3	1
FP multiply (also integer multiply)	6	1
FP divide (also integer divide)	24	25

Figure C.34 Latencies and initiation intervals for functional units.

zero stages for ALU operations and one stage for loads. The primary exception is stores, which consume the value being stored 1 cycle later. Hence, the latency to a store for the value being stored, but not for the base address register, will be 1 cycle less. Pipeline latency is essentially equal to 1 cycle less than the depth of the execution pipeline, which is the number of stages from the EX stage to the stage that produces the result. Thus, for the example pipeline just above, the number of stages in an FP add is four, while the number of stages in an FP multiply is seven. To achieve a higher clock rate, designers need to put fewer logic levels in each pipe stage, which makes the number of pipe stages required for more complex operations larger. The penalty for the faster clock rate is thus longer latency for operations.

The example pipeline structure in Figure C.34 allows up to four outstanding FP adds, seven outstanding FP/integer multiplies, and one FP divide. Figure C.35 shows how this pipeline can be drawn by extending Figure C.33. The repeat interval is implemented in Figure C.35 by adding additional pipeline stages, which will be separated by additional pipeline registers. Because the units are independent, we name the stages differently. The pipeline stages that take multiple clock cycles, such as the divide unit, are further subdivided to show the latency of those stages. Because they are not complete stages, only one operation may be active. The pipeline structure can also be shown using the familiar diagrams from earlier in the appendix, as Figure C.36 shows for a set of independent FP operations and FP loads and stores. Naturally, the longer latency of the FP operations increases the frequency of RAW hazards and resultant stalls, as we will see later in this section.

The structure of the pipeline in Figure C.35 requires the introduction of the additional pipeline registers (e.g., A1/A2, A2/A3, A3/A4) and the modification of the connections to those registers. The ID/EX register must be expanded to connect ID to EX, DIV, M1, and A1; we can refer to the portion of the register associated with one of the next stages with the notation ID/EX, ID/DIV, ID/M1, or ID/A1. The pipeline register between ID and all the other stages may be thought of as logically separate registers and may, in fact, be implemented as separate registers. Because only one operation can be in a pipe stage at a time, the control information can be associated with the register at the head of the stage.

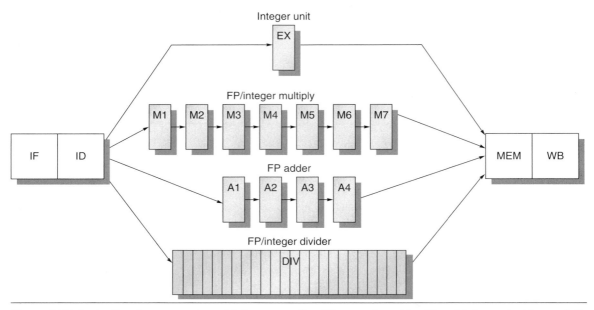

Figure C.35 A pipeline that supports multiple outstanding FP operations. The FP multiplier and adder are fully pipelined and have a depth of seven and four stages, respectively. The FP divider is not pipelined, but requires 24 clock cycles to complete. The latency in instructions between the issue of an FP operation and the use of the result of that operation without incurring a RAW stall is determined by the number of cycles spent in the execution stages. For example, the fourth instruction after an FP add can use the result of the FP add. For integer ALU operations, the depth of the execution pipeline is always one and the next instruction can use the results.

MUL.D	IF	ID	*M1*	M2	M3	M4	M5	M6	**M7**	MEM	WB
ADD.D		IF	ID	*A1*	A2	A3	**A4**	**MEM**	WB		
L.D			IF	ID	*EX*	**MEM**	WB				
S.D				IF	ID	*EX*	*MEM*	WB			

Figure C.36 The pipeline timing of a set of independent FP operations. The stages in italics show where data are needed, while the stages in bold show where a result is available. The ".D" extension on the instruction mnemonic indicates double-precision (64-bit) floating-point operations. FP loads and stores use a 64-bit path to memory so that the pipelining timing is just like an integer load or store.

Hazards and Forwarding in Longer Latency Pipelines

There are a number of different aspects to the hazard detection and forwarding for a pipeline like that shown in Figure C.35.

1. Because the divide unit is not fully pipelined, structural hazards can occur. These will need to be detected and issuing instructions will need to be stalled.

2. Because the instructions have varying running times, the number of register writes required in a cycle can be larger than 1.

3. Write after write (WAW) hazards are possible, since instructions no longer reach WB in order. Note that write after read (WAR) hazards are not possible, since the register reads always occur in ID.

4. Instructions can complete in a different order than they were issued, causing problems with exceptions; we deal with this in the next subsection.

5. Because of longer latency of operations, stalls for RAW hazards will be more frequent.

The increase in stalls arising from longer operation latencies is fundamentally the same as that for the integer pipeline. Before describing the new problems that arise in this FP pipeline and looking at solutions, let's examine the potential impact of RAW hazards. Figure C.37 shows a typical FP code sequence and the resultant stalls. At the end of this section, we'll examine the performance of this FP pipeline for our SPEC subset.

Now look at the problems arising from writes, described as (2) and (3) in the earlier list. If we assume that the FP register file has one write port, sequences of FP operations, as well as an FP load together with FP operations, can cause conflicts for the register write port. Consider the pipeline sequence shown in Figure C.38. In clock cycle 11, all three instructions will reach WB and want to write the register file. With only a single register file write port, the processor must serialize the instruction completion. This single register port represents a structural hazard. We could increase the number of write ports to solve this, but that solution may be unattractive since the additional write ports would be used only rarely. This is because the maximum steady-state number of write ports needed is 1. Instead, we choose to detect and enforce access to the write port as a structural hazard.

There are two different ways to implement this interlock. The first is to track the use of the write port in the ID stage and to stall an instruction before it issues,

									Clock cycle number								
Instruction	1	2	3	4	5	6	7	8	9	10	11	12	13	14	15	16	17
L.D F4,0(R2)	IF	ID	EX	MEM	WB												
MUL.D F0,F4,F6		IF	ID	Stall	M1	M2	M3	M4	M5	M6	M7	MEM	WB				
ADD.D F2,F0,F8			IF	Stall	ID	Stall	Stall	Stall	Stall	Stall	Stall	A1	A2	A3	A4	MEM	WB
S.D F2,0(R2)					IF	Stall	Stall	Stall	Stall	Stall	Stall	ID	EX	Stall	Stall	Stall	MEM

Figure C.37 A typical FP code sequence showing the stalls arising from RAW hazards. The longer pipeline substantially raises the frequency of stalls versus the shallower integer pipeline. Each instruction in this sequence is dependent on the previous and proceeds as soon as data are available, which assumes the pipeline has full bypassing and forwarding. The S.D must be stalled an extra cycle so that its MEM does not conflict with the ADD.D. Extra hardware could easily handle this case.

Instruction	Clock cycle number										
	1	2	3	4	5	6	7	8	9	10	11
MUL.D F0,F4,F6	IF	ID	M1	M2	M3	M4	M5	M6	M7	MEM	WB
...		IF	ID	EX	MEM	WB					
...			IF	ID	EX	MEM	WB				
ADD.D F2,F4,F6				IF	ID	A1	A2	A3	A4	MEM	WB
...					IF	ID	EX	MEM	WB		
...						IF	ID	EX	MEM	WB	
L.D F2,0(R2)							IF	ID	EX	MEM	WB

Figure C.38 Three instructions want to perform a write-back to the FP register file simultaneously, as shown in clock cycle 11. This is *not* the worst case, since an earlier divide in the FP unit could also finish on the same clock. Note that although the MUL.D, ADD.D, and L.D all are in the MEM stage in clock cycle 10, only the L.D actually uses the memory, so no structural hazard exists for MEM.

just as we would for any other structural hazard. Tracking the use of the write port can be done with a shift register that indicates when already-issued instructions will use the register file. If the instruction in ID needs to use the register file at the same time as an instruction already issued, the instruction in ID is stalled for a cycle. On each clock the reservation register is shifted 1 bit. This implementation has an advantage: It maintains the property that all interlock detection and stall insertion occurs in the ID stage. The cost is the addition of the shift register and write conflict logic. We will assume this scheme throughout this section.

An alternative scheme is to stall a conflicting instruction when it tries to enter either the MEM or WB stage. If we wait to stall the conflicting instructions until they want to enter the MEM or WB stage, we can choose to stall either instruction. A simple, though sometimes suboptimal, heuristic is to give priority to the unit with the longest latency, since that is the one most likely to have caused another instruction to be stalled for a RAW hazard. The advantage of this scheme is that it does not require us to detect the conflict until the entrance of the MEM or WB stage, where it is easy to see. The disadvantage is that it complicates pipeline control, as stalls can now arise from two places. Notice that stalling before entering MEM will cause the EX, A4, or M7 stage to be occupied, possibly forcing the stall to trickle back in the pipeline. Likewise, stalling before WB would cause MEM to back up.

Our other problem is the possibility of WAW hazards. To see that these exist, consider the example in Figure C.38. If the L.D instruction were issued one cycle earlier and had a destination of F2, then it would create a WAW hazard, because it would write F2 one cycle earlier than the ADD.D. Note that this hazard only occurs when the result of the ADD.D is overwritten *without* any instruction ever using it! If there were a use of F2 between the ADD.D and the L.D, the pipeline would need to be stalled for a RAW hazard, and the L.D would not issue until the

ADD.D was completed. We could argue that, for our pipeline, WAW hazards only occur when a useless instruction is executed, but we must still detect them and make sure that the result of the L.D appears in F2 when we are done. (As we will see in Section C.8, such sequences sometimes *do* occur in reasonable code.)

There are two possible ways to handle this WAW hazard. The first approach is to delay the issue of the load instruction until the ADD.D enters MEM. The second approach is to stamp out the result of the ADD.D by detecting the hazard and changing the control so that the ADD.D does not write its result. Then the L.D can issue right away. Because this hazard is rare, either scheme will work fine—you can pick whatever is simpler to implement. In either case, the hazard can be detected during ID when the L.D is issuing, and stalling the L.D or making the ADD.D a no-op is easy. The difficult situation is to detect that the L.D might finish before the ADD.D, because that requires knowing the length of the pipeline and the current position of the ADD.D. Luckily, this code sequence (two writes with no intervening read) will be very rare, so we can use a simple solution: If an instruction in ID wants to write the same register as an instruction already issued, do not issue the instruction to EX. In Section C.7, we will see how additional hardware can eliminate stalls for such hazards. First, let's put together the pieces for implementing the hazard and issue logic in our FP pipeline.

In detecting the possible hazards, we must consider hazards among FP instructions, as well as hazards between an FP instruction and an integer instruction. Except for FP loads-stores and FP-integer register moves, the FP and integer registers are distinct. All integer instructions operate on the integer registers, while the FP operations operate only on their own registers. Thus, we need only consider FP loads-stores and FP register moves in detecting hazards between FP and integer instructions. This simplification of pipeline control is an additional advantage of having separate register files for integer and floating-point data. (The main advantages are a doubling of the number of registers, without making either set larger, and an increase in bandwidth without adding more ports to either set. The main disadvantage, beyond the need for an extra register file, is the small cost of occasional moves needed between the two register sets.) Assuming that the pipeline does all hazard detection in ID, there are three checks that must be performed before an instruction can issue:

1. *Check for structural hazards*—Wait until the required functional unit is not busy (this is only needed for divides in this pipeline) and make sure the register write port is available when it will be needed.

2. *Check for a RAW data hazard*—Wait until the source registers are not listed as pending destinations in a pipeline register that will not be available when this instruction needs the result. A number of checks must be made here, depending on both the source instruction, which determines when the result will be available, and the destination instruction, which determines when the value is needed. For example, if the instruction in ID is an FP operation with source register F2, then F2 cannot be listed as a destination in ID/A1, A1/A2, or A2/A3, which correspond to FP add instructions that will not be finished when the instruction in ID needs a result. (ID/A1 is the portion of the output register of

ID that is sent to A1.) Divide is somewhat more tricky, if we want to allow the last few cycles of a divide to be overlapped, since we need to handle the case when a divide is close to finishing as special. In practice, designers might ignore this optimization in favor of a simpler issue test.

3. *Check for a WAW data hazard*—Determine if any instruction in A1, . . . , A4, D, M1, . . . , M7 has the same register destination as this instruction. If so, stall the issue of the instruction in ID.

Although the hazard detection is more complex with the multicycle FP operations, the concepts are the same as for the MIPS integer pipeline. The same is true for the forwarding logic. The forwarding can be implemented by checking if the destination register in any of the EX/MEM, A4/MEM, M7/MEM, D/MEM, or MEM/WB registers is one of the source registers of a floating-point instruction. If so, the appropriate input multiplexer will have to be enabled so as to choose the forwarded data. In the exercises, you will have the opportunity to specify the logic for the RAW and WAW hazard detection as well as for forwarding.

Multicycle FP operations also introduce problems for our exception mechanisms, which we deal with next.

Maintaining Precise Exceptions

Another problem caused by these long-running instructions can be illustrated with the following sequence of code:

```
DIV.D    F0,F2,F4
ADD.D    F10,F10,F8
SUB.D    F12,F12,F14
```

This code sequence looks straightforward; there are no dependences. A problem arises, however, because an instruction issued early may complete after an instruction issued later. In this example, we can expect ADD.D and SUB.D to complete *before* the DIV.D completes. This is called *out-of-order completion* and is common in pipelines with long-running operations (see Section C.7). Because hazard detection will prevent any dependence among instructions from being violated, why is out-of-order completion a problem? Suppose that the SUB.D causes a floating-point arithmetic exception at a point where the ADD.D has completed but the DIV.D has not. The result will be an imprecise exception, something we are trying to avoid. It may appear that this could be handled by letting the floating-point pipeline drain, as we do for the integer pipeline. But the exception may be in a position where this is not possible. For example, if the DIV.D decided to take a floating-point-arithmetic exception after the add completed, we could not have a precise exception at the hardware level. In fact, because the ADD.D destroys one of its operands, we could not restore the state to what it was before the DIV.D, even with software help.

This problem arises because instructions are completing in a different order than they were issued. There are four possible approaches to dealing with out-of-order completion. The first is to ignore the problem and settle for imprecise exceptions. This approach was used in the 1960s and early 1970s. It is still used in some supercomputers, where certain classes of exceptions are not allowed or are handled by the hardware without stopping the pipeline. It is difficult to use this approach in most processors built today because of features such as virtual memory and the IEEE floating-point standard that essentially require precise exceptions through a combination of hardware and software. As mentioned earlier, some recent processors have solved this problem by introducing two modes of execution: a fast, but possibly imprecise mode and a slower, precise mode. The slower precise mode is implemented either with a mode switch or by insertion of explicit instructions that test for FP exceptions. In either case, the amount of overlap and reordering permitted in the FP pipeline is significantly restricted so that effectively only one FP instruction is active at a time. This solution is used in the DEC Alpha 21064 and 21164, in the IBM Power1 and Power2, and in the MIPS R8000.

A second approach is to buffer the results of an operation until all the operations that were issued earlier are complete. Some CPUs actually use this solution, but it becomes expensive when the difference in running times among operations is large, since the number of results to buffer can become large. Furthermore, results from the queue must be bypassed to continue issuing instructions while waiting for the longer instruction. This requires a large number of comparators and a very large multiplexer.

There are two viable variations on this basic approach. The first is a *history file*, used in the CYBER 180/990. The history file keeps track of the original values of registers. When an exception occurs and the state must be rolled back earlier than some instruction that completed out of order, the original value of the register can be restored from the history file. A similar technique is used for autoincrement and autodecrement addressing on processors such as VAXes. Another approach, the *future file*, proposed by Smith and Pleszkun [1988], keeps the newer value of a register; when all earlier instructions have completed, the main register file is updated from the future file. On an exception, the main register file has the precise values for the interrupted state. In Chapter 3, we saw extensions of this idea which are used in processors such as the PowerPC 620 and the MIPS R10000 to allow overlap and reordering while preserving precise exceptions.

A third technique in use is to allow the exceptions to become somewhat imprecise, but to keep enough information so that the trap-handling routines can create a precise sequence for the exception. This means knowing what operations were in the pipeline and their PCs. Then, after handling the exception, the software finishes any instructions that precede the latest instruction completed, and the sequence can restart. Consider the following worst-case code sequence:

Instruction$_1$—A long-running instruction that eventually interrupts execution.

Instruction$_2$, . . . , Instruction$_{n-1}$—A series of instructions that are not completed.

Instruction$_n$—An instruction that is finished.

Given the PCs of all the instructions in the pipeline and the exception return PC, the software can find the state of instruction$_1$ and instruction$_n$. Because instruction$_n$ has completed, we will want to restart execution at instruction$_{n+1}$. After handling the exception, the software must simulate the execution of instruction$_1$, . . . , instruction$_{n-1}$. Then we can return from the exception and restart at instruction$_{n+1}$. The complexity of executing these instructions properly by the handler is the major difficulty of this scheme.

There is an important simplification for simple MIPS-like pipelines: If instruction$_2$, . . . , instruction$_n$ are all integer instructions, we know that if instruction$_n$ has completed then all of instruction$_2$, . . . , instruction$_{n-1}$ have also completed. Thus, only FP operations need to be handled. To make this scheme tractable, the number of floating-point instructions that can be overlapped in execution can be limited. For example, if we only overlap two instructions, then only the interrupting instruction need be completed by software. This restriction may reduce the potential throughput if the FP pipelines are deep or if there are a significant number of FP functional units. This approach is used in the SPARC architecture to allow overlap of floating-point and integer operations.

The final technique is a hybrid scheme that allows the instruction issue to continue only if it is certain that all the instructions before the issuing instruction will complete without causing an exception. This guarantees that when an exception occurs, no instructions after the interrupting one will be completed and all of the instructions before the interrupting one can be completed. This sometimes means stalling the CPU to maintain precise exceptions. To make this scheme work, the floating-point functional units must determine if an exception is possible early in the EX stage (in the first 3 clock cycles in the MIPS pipeline), so as to prevent further instructions from completing. This scheme is used in the MIPS R2000/3000, the R4000, and the Intel Pentium. It is discussed further in Appendix J.

Performance of a MIPS FP Pipeline

The MIPS FP pipeline of Figure C.35 on page C-54 can generate both structural stalls for the divide unit and stalls for RAW hazards (it also can have WAW hazards, but this rarely occurs in practice). Figure C.39 shows the number of stall cycles for each type of floating-point operation on a per-instance basis (i.e., the first bar for each FP benchmark shows the number of FP result stalls for each FP add, subtract, or convert). As we might expect, the stall cycles per operation track the latency of the FP operations, varying from 46% to 59% of the latency of the functional unit.

Figure C.40 gives the complete breakdown of integer and FP stalls for five SPECfp benchmarks. There are four classes of stalls shown: FP result stalls, FP compare stalls, load and branch delays, and FP structural delays. The compiler tries to schedule both load and FP delays before it schedules branch delays. The total number of stalls per instruction varies from 0.65 to 1.21.

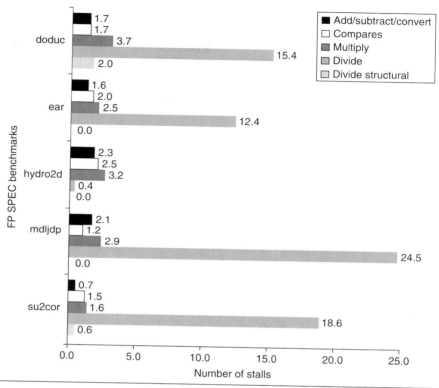

Figure C.39 Stalls per FP operation for each major type of FP operation for the SPEC89 FP benchmarks. Except for the divide structural hazards, these data do not depend on the frequency of an operation, only on its latency and the number of cycles before the result is used. The number of stalls from RAW hazards roughly tracks the latency of the FP unit. For example, the average number of stalls per FP add, subtract, or convert is 1.7 cycles, or 56% of the latency (3 cycles). Likewise, the average number of stalls for multiplies and divides are 2.8 and 14.2, respectively, or 46% and 59% of the corresponding latency. Structural hazards for divides are rare, since the divide frequency is low.

C.6   Putting It All Together: The MIPS R4000 Pipeline

In this section, we look at the pipeline structure and performance of the MIPS R4000 processor family, which includes the 4400. The R4000 implements MIPS64 but uses a deeper pipeline than that of our five-stage design both for integer and FP programs. This deeper pipeline allows it to achieve higher clock rates by decomposing the five-stage integer pipeline into eight stages. Because cache access is particularly time critical, the extra pipeline stages come from decomposing the memory access. This type of deeper pipelining is sometimes called *superpipelining*.

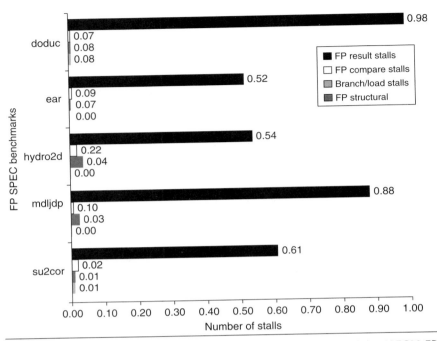

Figure C.40 The stalls occurring for the MIPS FP pipeline for five of the SPEC89 FP benchmarks. The total number of stalls per instruction ranges from 0.65 for su2cor to 1.21 for doduc, with an average of 0.87. FP result stalls dominate in all cases, with an average of 0.71 stalls per instruction, or 82% of the stalled cycles. Compares generate an average of 0.1 stalls per instruction and are the second largest source. The divide structural hazard is only significant for doduc.

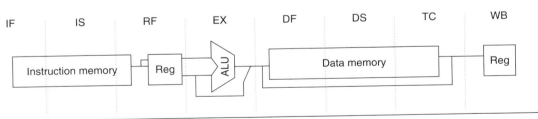

Figure C.41 The eight-stage pipeline structure of the R4000 uses pipelined instruction and data caches. The pipe stages are labeled and their detailed function is described in the text. The vertical dashed lines represent the stage boundaries as well as the location of pipeline latches. The instruction is actually available at the end of IS, but the tag check is done in RF, while the registers are fetched. Thus, we show the instruction memory as operating through RF. The TC stage is needed for data memory access, since we cannot write the data into the register until we know whether the cache access was a hit or not.

Figure C.41 shows the eight-stage pipeline structure using an abstracted version of the data path. Figure C.42 shows the overlap of successive instructions in the pipeline. Notice that, although the instruction and data memory

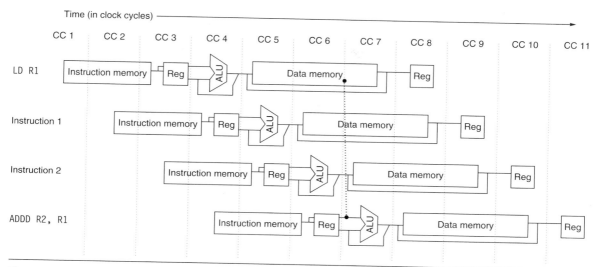

Figure C.42 The structure of the R4000 integer pipeline leads to a 2-cycle load delay. A 2-cycle delay is possible because the data value is available at the end of DS and can be bypassed. If the tag check in TC indicates a miss, the pipeline is backed up a cycle, when the correct data are available.

occupy multiple cycles, they are fully pipelined, so that a new instruction can start on every clock. In fact, the pipeline uses the data before the cache hit detection is complete; Chapter 2 discusses how this can be done in more detail.

The function of each stage is as follows:

- IF—First half of instruction fetch; PC selection actually happens here, together with initiation of instruction cache access.

- IS—Second half of instruction fetch, complete instruction cache access.

- RF—Instruction decode and register fetch, hazard checking, and instruction cache hit detection.

- EX—Execution, which includes effective address calculation, ALU operation, and branch-target computation and condition evaluation.

- DF—Data fetch, first half of data cache access.

- DS—Second half of data fetch, completion of data cache access.

- TC—Tag check, to determine whether the data cache access hit.

- WB—Write-back for loads and register-register operations.

In addition to substantially increasing the amount of forwarding required, this longer-latency pipeline increases both the load and branch delays. Figure C.42 shows that load delays are 2 cycles, since the data value is available at the end of

	Clock number								
Instruction number	1	2	3	4	5	6	7	8	9
LD R1,...	IF	IS	RF	EX	DF	DS	TC	WB	
DADD R2,R1,...		IF	IS	RF	Stall	Stall	EX	DF	DS
DSUB R3,R1,...			IF	IS	Stall	Stall	RF	EX	DF
OR R4,R1,...				IF	Stall	Stall	IS	RF	EX

Figure C.43 **A load instruction followed by an immediate use results in a 2-cycle stall.** Normal forwarding paths can be used after 2 cycles, so the DADD and DSUB get the value by forwarding after the stall. The OR instruction gets the value from the register file. Since the two instructions after the load could be independent and hence not stall, the bypass can be to instructions that are 3 or 4 cycles after the load.

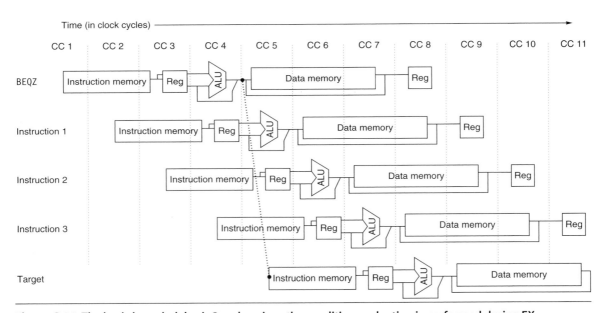

Figure C.44 **The basic branch delay is 3 cycles, since the condition evaluation is performed during EX.**

DS. Figure C.43 shows the shorthand pipeline schedule when a use immediately follows a load. It shows that forwarding is required for the result of a load instruction to a destination that is 3 or 4 cycles later.

Figure C.44 shows that the basic branch delay is 3 cycles, since the branch condition is computed during EX. The MIPS architecture has a single-cycle delayed branch. The R4000 uses a predicted-not-taken strategy for the remaining 2 cycles of the branch delay. As Figure C.45 shows, untaken branches are simply 1-cycle delayed branches, while taken branches have a 1-cycle delay slot followed by 2 idle cycles. The instruction set provides a branch-likely instruction, which we described earlier and which helps in filling the branch

Instruction number	Clock number								
	1	2	3	4	5	6	7	8	9
Branch instruction	IF	IS	RF	EX	DF	DS	TC	WB	
Delay slot		IF	IS	RF	EX	DF	DS	TC	WB
Stall			Stall	Stall	Stall	Stall	Stall	Stall	Stall
Stall				Stall	Stall	Stall	Stall	Stall	Stall
Branch target					IF	IS	RF	EX	DF

Instruction number	Clock number								
	1	2	3	4	5	6	7	8	9
Branch instruction	IF	IS	RF	EX	DF	DS	TC	WB	
Delay slot		IF	IS	RF	EX	DF	DS	TC	WB
Branch instruction + 2			IF	IS	RF	EX	DF	DS	TC
Branch instruction + 3				IF	IS	RF	EX	DF	DS

Figure C.45 A taken branch, shown in the top portion of the figure, has a 1-cycle delay slot followed by a 2-cycle stall, while an untaken branch, shown in the bottom portion, has simply a 1-cycle delay slot. The branch instruction can be an ordinary delayed branch or a branch-likely, which cancels the effect of the instruction in the delay slot if the branch is untaken.

delay slot. Pipeline interlocks enforce both the 2-cycle branch stall penalty on a taken branch and any data hazard stall that arises from use of a load result.

In addition to the increase in stalls for loads and branches, the deeper pipeline increases the number of levels of forwarding for ALU operations. In our MIPS five-stage pipeline, forwarding between two register-register ALU instructions could happen from the ALU/MEM or the MEM/WB registers. In the R4000 pipeline, there are four possible sources for an ALU bypass: EX/DF, DF/DS, DS/TC, and TC/WB.

The Floating-Point Pipeline

The R4000 floating-point unit consists of three functional units: a floating-point divider, a floating-point multiplier, and a floating-point adder. The adder logic is used on the final step of a multiply or divide. Double-precision FP operations can take from 2 cycles (for a negate) up to 112 cycles (for a square root). In addition, the various units have different initiation rates. The FP functional unit can be thought of as having eight different stages, listed in Figure C.46; these stages are combined in different orders to execute various FP operations.

There is a single copy of each of these stages, and various instructions may use a stage zero or more times and in different orders. Figure C.47 shows the

Stage	Functional unit	Description
A	FP adder	Mantissa ADD stage
D	FP divider	Divide pipeline stage
E	FP multiplier	Exception test stage
M	FP multiplier	First stage of multiplier
N	FP multiplier	Second stage of multiplier
R	FP adder	Rounding stage
S	FP adder	Operand shift stage
U		Unpack FP numbers

Figure C.46 The eight stages used in the R4000 floating-point pipelines.

FP instruction	Latency	Initiation interval	Pipe stages
Add, subtract	4	3	U, S + A, A + R, R + S
Multiply	8	4	U, E + M, M, M, M, N, N + A, R
Divide	36	35	U, A, R, D^{28}, D + A, D + R, D + A, D + R, A, R
Square root	112	111	U, E, $(A+R)^{108}$, A, R
Negate	2	1	U, S
Absolute value	2	1	U, S
FP compare	3	2	U, A, R

Figure C.47 The latencies and initiation intervals for the FP operations both depend on the FP unit stages that a given operation must use. The latency values assume that the destination instruction is an FP operation; the latencies are 1 cycle less when the destination is a store. The pipe stages are shown in the order in which they are used for any operation. The notation S + A indicates a clock cycle in which both the S and A stages are used. The notation D^{28} indicates that the D stage is used 28 times in a row.

latency, initiation rate, and pipeline stages used by the most common double-precision FP operations.

From the information in Figure C.47, we can determine whether a sequence of different, independent FP operations can issue without stalling. If the timing of the sequence is such that a conflict occurs for a shared pipeline stage, then a stall will be needed. Figures C.48, C.49, C.50, and C.51 show four common possible two-instruction sequences: a multiply followed by an add, an add followed by a multiply, a divide followed by an add, and an add followed by a divide. The figures show all the interesting starting positions for the second instruction and whether that second instruction will issue or stall for each position. Of course, there could be three instructions active, in which case the possibilities for stalls are much higher and the figures more complex.

Operation	Issue/stall	Clock cycle												
		0	1	2	3	4	5	6	7	8	9	10	11	12
Multiply	Issue	U	E + M	M	M	M	N	N + A	R					
Add	Issue		U	S + A	A + R	R + S								
	Issue			U	S + A	A + R	R + S							
	Issue				U	S + A	A + R	R + S						
	Stall					U	S + A	**A + R**	**R + S**					
	Stall						U	**S + A**	**A + R**	R + S				
	Issue							U	S + A	A + R	R + S			
	Issue								U	S + A	A + R	R + S		

Figure C.48 An FP multiply issued at clock 0 is followed by a single FP add issued between clocks 1 and 7. The second column indicates whether an instruction of the specified type stalls when it is issued *n* cycles later, where *n* is the clock cycle number in which the U stage of the second instruction occurs. The stage or stages that cause a stall are in bold. Note that this table deals with only the interaction between the multiply and *one* add issued between clocks 1 and 7. In this case, the add will stall if it is issued 4 or 5 cycles after the multiply; otherwise, it issues without stalling. Notice that the add will be stalled for 2 cycles if it issues in cycle 4 since on the next clock cycle it will still conflict with the multiply; if, however, the add issues in cycle 5, it will stall for only 1 clock cycle, since that will eliminate the conflicts.

Operation	Issue/stall	Clock cycle												
		0	1	2	3	4	5	6	7	8	9	10	11	12
Add	Issue	U	S + A	A + R	R + S									
Multiply	Issue		U	E + M	M	M	M	N	N + A	R				
	Issue			U	M	M	M	M	N	N + A	R			

Figure C.49 A multiply issuing after an add can always proceed without stalling, since the shorter instruction clears the shared pipeline stages before the longer instruction reaches them.

Performance of the R4000 Pipeline

In this section, we examine the stalls that occur for the SPEC92 benchmarks when running on the R4000 pipeline structure. There are four major causes of pipeline stalls or losses:

1. *Load stalls*—Delays arising from the use of a load result 1 or 2 cycles after the load

2. *Branch stalls*—Two-cycle stalls on every taken branch plus unfilled or canceled branch delay slots

3. *FP result stalls*—Stalls because of RAW hazards for an FP operand

Operation	Issue/stall	Clock cycle											
		25	26	27	28	29	30	31	32	33	34	35	36
Divide	Issued in cycle 0. . .	D	D	D	D	D	D + A	D + R	D + A	D + R	A	R	
Add	Issue		U	S + A	A + R	R + S							
	Issue			U	S + A	A + R	R + S						
	Stall				U	S + A	A + R	R + S					
	Stall					U	S + A	A + R	R + S				
	Stall						U	S + A	A + R	R + S			
	Stall							U	S + A	A + R	R + S		
	Stall								U	S + A	A + R	R + S	
	Stall									U	S + A	A + R	R + S
	Issue										U	S + A	A + R
	Issue											U	S + A
	Issue												U

Figure C.50 An FP divide can cause a stall for an add that starts near the end of the divide. The divide starts at cycle 0 and completes at cycle 35; the last 10 cycles of the divide are shown. Since the divide makes heavy use of the rounding hardware needed by the add, it stalls an add that starts in any of cycles 28 to 33. Notice that the add starting in cycle 28 will be stalled until cycle 36. If the add started right after the divide, it would not conflict, since the add could complete before the divide needed the shared stages, just as we saw in Figure C.49 for a multiply and add. As in the earlier figure, this example assumes *exactly* one add that reaches the U stage between clock cycles 26 and 35.

Operation	Issue/stall	Clock cycle												
		0	1	2	3	4	5	6	7	8	9	10	11	12
Add	Issue	U	S + A	A + R	R + S									
Divide	Stall		U	A	R	D	D	D	D	D	D	D	D	D
	Issue			U	A	R	D	D	D	D	D	D	D	D
	Issue				U	A	R	D	D	D	D	D	D	D

Figure C.51 A double-precision add is followed by a double-precision divide. If the divide starts 1 cycle after the add, the divide stalls, but after that there is no conflict.

4. *FP structural stalls*—Delays because of issue restrictions arising from conflicts for functional units in the FP pipeline

Figure C.52 shows the pipeline CPI breakdown for the R4000 pipeline for the 10 SPEC92 benchmarks. Figure C.53 shows the same data but in tabular form.

From the data in Figures C.52 and C.53, we can see the penalty of the deeper pipelining. The R4000's pipeline has much longer branch delays than the classic

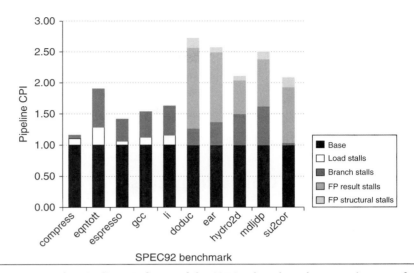

Figure C.52 The pipeline CPI for 10 of the SPEC92 benchmarks, assuming a perfect cache. The pipeline CPI varies from 1.2 to 2.8. The leftmost five programs are integer programs, and branch delays are the major CPI contributor for these. The rightmost five programs are FP, and FP result stalls are the major contributor for these. Figure C.53 shows the numbers used to construct this plot.

Benchmark	Pipeline CPI	Load stalls	Branch stalls	FP result stalls	FP structural stalls
Compress	1.20	0.14	0.06	0.00	0.00
Eqntott	1.88	0.27	0.61	0.00	0.00
Espresso	1.42	0.07	0.35	0.00	0.00
Gcc	1.56	0.13	0.43	0.00	0.00
Li	1.64	0.18	0.46	0.00	0.00
Integer average	1.54	0.16	0.38	0.00	0.00
Doduc	2.84	0.01	0.22	1.39	0.22
Mdljdp2	2.66	0.01	0.31	1.20	0.15
Ear	2.17	0.00	0.46	0.59	0.12
Hydro2d	2.53	0.00	0.62	0.75	0.17
Su2cor	2.18	0.02	0.07	0.84	0.26
FP average	2.48	0.01	0.33	0.95	0.18
Overall average	2.00	0.10	0.36	0.46	0.09

Figure C.53 The total pipeline CPI and the contributions of the four major sources of stalls are shown. The major contributors are FP result stalls (both for branches and for FP inputs) and branch stalls, with loads and FP structural stalls adding less.

five-stage pipeline. The longer branch delay substantially increases the cycles spent on branches, especially for the integer programs with a higher branch frequency. An interesting effect for the FP programs is that the latency of the FP functional units leads to more result stalls than the structural hazards, which arise both from the initiation interval limitations and from conflicts for functional units from different FP instructions. Thus, reducing the latency of FP operations should be the first target, rather than more pipelining or replication of the functional units. Of course, reducing the latency would probably increase the structural stalls, since many potential structural stalls are hidden behind data hazards.

C.7 Crosscutting Issues

RISC Instruction Sets and Efficiency of Pipelining

We have already discussed the advantages of instruction set simplicity in building pipelines. Simple instruction sets offer another advantage: They make it easier to schedule code to achieve efficiency of execution in a pipeline. To see this, consider a simple example: Suppose we need to add two values in memory and store the result back to memory. In some sophisticated instruction sets this will take only a single instruction; in others, it will take two or three. A typical RISC architecture would require four instructions (two loads, an add, and a store). These instructions cannot be scheduled sequentially in most pipelines without intervening stalls.

With a RISC instruction set, the individual operations are separate instructions and may be individually scheduled either by the compiler (using the techniques we discussed earlier and more powerful techniques discussed in Chapter 3) or using dynamic hardware scheduling techniques (which we discuss next and in further detail in Chapter 3). These efficiency advantages, coupled with the greater ease of implementation, appear to be so significant that almost all recent pipelined implementations of complex instruction sets actually translate their complex instructions into simple RISC-like operations, and then schedule and pipeline those operations. Chapter 3 shows that both the Pentium III and Pentium 4 use this approach.

Dynamically Scheduled Pipelines

Simple pipelines fetch an instruction and issue it, unless there is a data dependence between an instruction already in the pipeline and the fetched instruction that cannot be hidden with bypassing or forwarding. Forwarding logic reduces the effective pipeline latency so that certain dependences do not result in hazards. If there is an unavoidable hazard, then the hazard detection hardware stalls the pipeline (starting with the instruction that uses the result). No new instructions are fetched or issued until the dependence is cleared. To overcome these performance losses, the compiler can attempt to schedule instructions to avoid the hazard; this approach is called *compiler* or *static scheduling*.

Several early processors used another approach, called *dynamic scheduling*, whereby the hardware rearranges the instruction execution to reduce the stalls. This section offers a simpler introduction to dynamic scheduling by explaining the scoreboarding technique of the CDC 6600. Some readers will find it easier to read this material before plunging into the more complicated Tomasulo scheme, which is covered in Chapter 3.

All the techniques discussed in this appendix so far use in-order instruction issue, which means that if an instruction is stalled in the pipeline, no later instructions can proceed. With in-order issue, if two instructions have a hazard between them, the pipeline will stall, even if there are later instructions that are independent and would not stall.

In the MIPS pipeline developed earlier, both structural and data hazards were checked during instruction decode (ID): When an instruction could execute properly, it was issued from ID. To allow an instruction to begin execution as soon as its operands are available, even if a predecessor is stalled, we must separate the issue process into two parts: checking the structural hazards and waiting for the absence of a data hazard. We decode and issue instructions in order; however, we want the instructions to begin execution as soon as their data operands are available. Thus, the pipeline will do *out-of-order execution*, which implies *out-of-order completion*. To implement out-of-order execution, we must split the ID pipe stage into two stages:

1. *Issue*—Decode instructions, check for structural hazards.

2. *Read operands*—Wait until no data hazards, then read operands.

The IF stage proceeds the issue stage, and the EX stage follows the read operands stage, just as in the MIPS pipeline. As in the MIPS floating-point pipeline, execution may take multiple cycles, depending on the operation. Thus, we may need to distinguish when an instruction *begins execution* and when it *completes execution*; between the two times, the instruction is *in execution*. This allows multiple instructions to be in execution at the same time. In addition to these changes to the pipeline structure, we will also change the functional unit design by varying the number of units, the latency of operations, and the functional unit pipelining so as to better explore these more advanced pipelining techniques.

Dynamic Scheduling with a Scoreboard

In a dynamically scheduled pipeline, all instructions pass through the issue stage in order (in-order issue); however, they can be stalled or bypass each other in the second stage (read operands) and thus enter execution out of order. *Scoreboarding* is a technique for allowing instructions to execute out of order when there are sufficient resources and no data dependences; it is named after the CDC 6600 scoreboard, which developed this capability.

Before we see how scoreboarding could be used in the MIPS pipeline, it is important to observe that WAR hazards, which did not exist in the MIPS floating-point or integer pipelines, may arise when instructions execute out of order. For example, consider the following code sequence:

```
DIV.D    F0,F2,F4
ADD.D    F10,F0,F8
SUB.D    F8,F8,F14
```

There is an antidependence between the ADD.D and the SUB.D: If the pipeline executes the SUB.D before the ADD.D, it will violate the antidependence, yielding incorrect execution. Likewise, to avoid violating output dependences, WAW hazards (e.g., as would occur if the destination of the SUB.D were F10) must also be detected. As we will see, both these hazards are avoided in a scoreboard by stalling the later instruction involved in the antidependence.

The goal of a scoreboard is to maintain an execution rate of one instruction per clock cycle (when there are no structural hazards) by executing an instruction as early as possible. Thus, when the next instruction to execute is stalled, other instructions can be issued and executed if they do not depend on any active or stalled instruction. The scoreboard takes full responsibility for instruction issue and execution, including all hazard detection. Taking advantage of out-of-order execution requires multiple instructions to be in their EX stage simultaneously. This can be achieved with multiple functional units, with pipelined functional units, or with both. Since these two capabilities—pipelined functional units and multiple functional units—are essentially equivalent for the purposes of pipeline control, we will assume the processor has multiple functional units.

The CDC 6600 had 16 separate functional units, including 4 floating-point units, 5 units for memory references, and 7 units for integer operations. On a processor for the MIPS architecture, scoreboards make sense primarily on the floating-point unit since the latency of the other functional units is very small. Let's assume that there are two multipliers, one adder, one divide unit, and a single integer unit for all memory references, branches, and integer operations. Although this example is simpler than the CDC 6600, it is sufficiently powerful to demonstrate the principles without having a mass of detail or needing very long examples. Because both MIPS and the CDC 6600 are load-store architectures, the techniques are nearly identical for the two processors. Figure C.54 shows what the processor looks like.

Every instruction goes through the scoreboard, where a record of the data dependences is constructed; this step corresponds to instruction issue and replaces part of the ID step in the MIPS pipeline. The scoreboard then determines when the instruction can read its operands and begin execution. If the scoreboard decides the instruction cannot execute immediately, it monitors every change in the hardware and decides when the instruction *can* execute. The scoreboard also controls when an instruction can write its result into the destination register. Thus, all hazard detection and resolution are centralized in the scoreboard. We will see a picture of the scoreboard later (Figure C.55 on page C-76), but

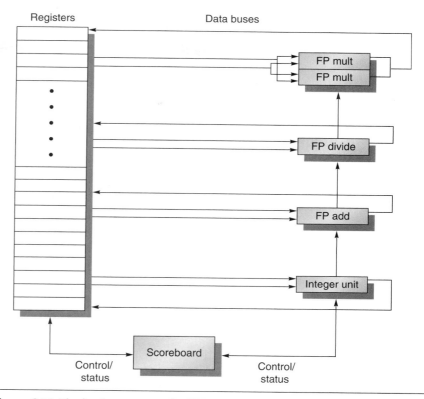

Figure C.54 The basic structure of a MIPS processor with a scoreboard. The scoreboard's function is to control instruction execution (vertical control lines). All of the data flow between the register file and the functional units over the buses (the horizontal lines, called *trunks* in the CDC 6600). There are two FP multipliers, an FP divider, an FP adder, and an integer unit. One set of buses (two inputs and one output) serves a group of functional units. The details of the scoreboard are shown in Figures C.55 to C.58.

first we need to understand the steps in the issue and execution segment of the pipeline.

Each instruction undergoes four steps in executing. (Since we are concentrating on the FP operations, we will not consider a step for memory access.) Let's first examine the steps informally and then look in detail at how the scoreboard keeps the necessary information that determines when to progress from one step to the next. The four steps, which replace the ID, EX, and WB steps in the standard MIPS pipeline, are as follows:

1. *Issue*—If a functional unit for the instruction is free and no other active instruction has the same destination register, the scoreboard issues the instruction to the functional unit and updates its internal data structure. This step replaces a portion of the ID step in the MIPS pipeline. By ensuring that

no other active functional unit wants to write its result into the destination register, we guarantee that WAW hazards cannot be present. If a structural or WAW hazard exists, then the instruction issue stalls, and no further instructions will issue until these hazards are cleared. When the issue stage stalls, it causes the buffer between instruction fetch and issue to fill; if the buffer is a single entry, instruction fetch stalls immediately. If the buffer is a queue with multiple instructions, it stalls when the queue fills.

2. *Read operands*—The scoreboard monitors the availability of the source operands. A source operand is available if no earlier issued active instruction is going to write it. When the source operands are available, the scoreboard tells the functional unit to proceed to read the operands from the registers and begin execution. The scoreboard resolves RAW hazards dynamically in this step, and instructions may be sent into execution out of order. This step, together with issue, completes the function of the ID step in the simple MIPS pipeline.

3. *Execution*—The functional unit begins execution upon receiving operands. When the result is ready, it notifies the scoreboard that it has completed execution. This step replaces the EX step in the MIPS pipeline and takes multiple cycles in the MIPS FP pipeline.

4. *Write result*—Once the scoreboard is aware that the functional unit has completed execution, the scoreboard checks for WAR hazards and stalls the completing instruction, if necessary.

A WAR hazard exists if there is a code sequence like our earlier example with ADD.D and SUB.D that both use F8. In that example, we had the code

```
DIV.D    F0,F2,F4
ADD.D    F10,F0,F8
SUB.D    F8,F8,F14
```

ADD.D has a source operand F8, which is the same register as the destination of SUB.D. But ADD.D actually depends on an earlier instruction. The scoreboard will still stall the SUB.D in its write result stage until ADD.D reads its operands. In general, then, a completing instruction cannot be allowed to write its results when:

■ There is an instruction that has not read its operands that precedes (i.e., in order of issue) the completing instruction, and

■ One of the operands is the same register as the result of the completing instruction.

If this WAR hazard does not exist, or when it clears, the scoreboard tells the functional unit to store its result to the destination register. This step replaces the WB step in the simple MIPS pipeline.

At first glance, it might appear that the scoreboard will have difficulty separating RAW and WAR hazards.

Because the operands for an instruction are read only when both operands are available in the register file, this scoreboard does not take advantage of forwarding. Instead, registers are only read when they are both available. This is not as large a penalty as you might initially think. Unlike our simple pipeline of earlier, instructions will write their result into the register file as soon as they complete execution (assuming no WAR hazards), rather than wait for a statically assigned write slot that may be several cycles away. The effect is reduced pipeline latency and benefits of forwarding. There is still one additional cycle of latency that arises since the write result and read operand stages cannot overlap. We would need additional buffering to eliminate this overhead.

Based on its own data structure, the scoreboard controls the instruction progression from one step to the next by communicating with the functional units. There is a small complication, however. There are only a limited number of source operand buses and result buses to the register file, which represents a structural hazard. The scoreboard must guarantee that the number of functional units allowed to proceed into steps 2 and 4 does not exceed the number of buses available. We will not go into further detail on this, other than to mention that the CDC 6600 solved this problem by grouping the 16 functional units together into four groups and supplying a set of buses, called *data trunks*, for each group. Only one unit in a group could read its operands or write its result during a clock.

Now let's look at the detailed data structure maintained by a MIPS scoreboard with five functional units. Figure C.55 shows what the scoreboard's information looks like partway through the execution of this simple sequence of instructions:

```
L.D      F6,34(R2)
L.D      F2,45(R3)
MUL.D    F0,F2,F4
SUB.D    F8,F6,F2
DIV.D    F10,F0,F6
ADD.D    F6,F8,F2
```

There are three parts to the scoreboard:

1. *Instruction status*—Indicates which of the four steps the instruction is in.

2. *Functional unit status*—Indicates the state of the functional unit (FU). There are nine fields for each functional unit:

    ■ Busy—Indicates whether the unit is busy or not.

    ■ Op—Operation to perform in the unit (e.g., add or subtract).

    ■ Fi—Destination register.

    ■ Fj, Fk—Source-register numbers.

    ■ Qj, Qk—Functional units producing source registers Fj, Fk.

    ■ Rj, Rk—Flags indicating when Fj, Fk are ready and not yet read. Set to No after operands are read.

Instruction status					
Instruction		**Issue**	**Read operands**	**Execution complete**	**Write result**
L.D	F6,34(R2)	√	√	√	√
L.D	F2,45(R3)	√	√	√	
MUL.D	F0,F2,F4	√			
SUB.D	F8,F6,F2	√			
DIV.D	F10,F0,F6	√			
ADD.D	F6,F8,F2				

Functional unit status									
Name	**Busy**	**Op**	**Fi**	**Fj**	**Fk**	**Qj**	**Qk**	**Rj**	**Rk**
Integer	Yes	Load	F2	R3				No	
Mult1	Yes	Mult	F0	F2	F4	Integer		No	Yes
Mult2	No								
Add	Yes	Sub	F8	F6	F2		Integer	Yes	No
Divide	Yes	Div	F10	F0	F6	Mult1		No	Yes

Register result status								
	F0	**F2**	**F4**	**F6**	**F8**	**F10**	**F12**	**...**	**F30**
FU	Mult1	Integer			Add	Divide			

Figure C.55 Components of the scoreboard. Each instruction that has issued or is pending issue has an entry in the instruction status table. There is one entry in the functional unit status table for each functional unit. Once an instruction issues, the record of its operands is kept in the functional unit status table. Finally, the register result table indicates which unit will produce each pending result; the number of entries is equal to the number of registers. The instruction status table says that: (1) the first L.D has completed and written its result, and (2) the second L.D has completed execution but has not yet written its result. The MUL.D, SUB.D, and DIV.D have all issued but are stalled, waiting for their operands. The functional unit status says that the first multiply unit is waiting for the integer unit, the add unit is waiting for the integer unit, and the divide unit is waiting for the first multiply unit. The ADD.D instruction is stalled because of a structural hazard; it will clear when the SUB.D completes. If an entry in one of these scoreboard tables is not being used, it is left blank. For example, the Rk field is not used on a load and the Mult2 unit is unused, hence their fields have no meaning. Also, once an operand has been read, the Rj and Rk fields are set to No. Figure C.58 shows why this last step is crucial.

3. *Register result status*—Indicates which functional unit will write each register, if an active instruction has the register as its destination. This field is set to blank whenever there are no pending instructions that will write that register.

Now let's look at how the code sequence begun in Figure C.55 continues execution. After that, we will be able to examine in detail the conditions that the scoreboard uses to control execution.

Example   Assume the following EX cycle latencies (chosen to illustrate the behavior and not representative) for the floating-point functional units: Add is 2 clock cycles, multiply is 10 clock cycles, and divide is 40 clock cycles. Using the code segment in Figure C.55 and beginning with the point indicated by the instruction status in Figure C.55, show what the status tables look like when MUL.D and DIV.D are each ready to go to the write result state.

Answer   There are RAW data hazards from the second L.D to MUL.D, ADD.D, and SUB.D, from MUL.D to DIV.D, and from SUB.D to ADD.D. There is a WAR data hazard between DIV.D and ADD.D and SUB.D. Finally, there is a structural hazard on the add functional unit for ADD.D and SUB.D. What the tables look like when MUL.D and DIV.D are ready to write their results is shown in Figures C.56 and C.57, respectively.

Now we can see how the scoreboard works in detail by looking at what has to happen for the scoreboard to allow each instruction to proceed. Figure C.58 shows what the scoreboard requires for each instruction to advance and the bookkeeping action necessary when the instruction does advance. The scoreboard records operand specifier information, such as register numbers. For example, we must record the source registers when an instruction is issued. Because we refer to the contents of a register as Regs[D], where D is a register name, there is no ambiguity. For example, Fj[FU] ← S1 causes the register *name* S1 to be placed in Fj[FU], rather than the *contents* of register S1.

The costs and benefits of scoreboarding are interesting considerations. The CDC 6600 designers measured a performance improvement of 1.7 for FORTRAN programs and 2.5 for hand-coded assembly language. However, this was measured in the days before software pipeline scheduling, semiconductor main memory, and caches (which lower memory access time). The scoreboard on the CDC 6600 had about as much logic as one of the functional units, which is surprisingly low. The main cost was in the large number of buses—about four times as many as would be required if the CPU only executed instructions in order (or if it only initiated one instruction per execute cycle). The recently increasing interest in dynamic scheduling is motivated by attempts to issue more instructions per clock (so the cost of more buses must be paid anyway) and by ideas like speculation (explored in Section 4.7) that naturally build on dynamic scheduling.

A scoreboard uses the available ILP to minimize the number of stalls arising from the program's true data dependences. In eliminating stalls, a scoreboard is limited by several factors:

1. *The amount of parallelism available among the instructions*—This determines whether independent instructions can be found to execute. If each instruction depends on its predecessor, no dynamic scheduling scheme can reduce stalls. If the instructions in the pipeline simultaneously must be chosen from the same basic block (as was true in the 6600), this limit is likely to be quite severe.

Instruction		Instruction status			
		Issue	Read operands	Execution complete	Write result
L.D	F6,34(R2)	√	√	√	√
L.D	F2,45(R3)	√	√	√	√
MUL.D	F0,F2,F4	√	√	√	
SUB.D	F8,F6,F2	√	√	√	√
DIV.D	F10,F0,F6	√			
ADD.D	F6,F8,F2	√	√	√	

				Functional unit status					
Name	Busy	Op	Fi	Fj	Fk	Qj	Qk	Rj	Rk
Integer	No								
Mult1	Yes	Mult	F0	F2	F4			No	No
Mult2	No								
Add	Yes	Add	F6	F8	F2			No	No
Divide	Yes	Div	F10	F0	F6	Mult1		No	Yes

				Register result status					
	F0	F2	F4	F6	F8	F10	F12	...	F30
FU	Mult 1			Add		Divide			

Figure C.56 Scoreboard tables just before the MUL.D goes to write result. The DIV.D has not yet read either of its operands, since it has a dependence on the result of the multiply. The ADD.D has read its operands and is in execution, although it was forced to wait until the SUB.D finished to get the functional unit. ADD.D cannot proceed to write result because of the WAR hazard on F6, which is used by the DIV.D. The Q fields are only relevant when a functional unit is waiting for another unit.

2. *The number of scoreboard entries*—This determines how far ahead the pipeline can look for independent instructions. The set of instructions examined as candidates for potential execution is called the *window*. The size of the scoreboard determines the size of the window. In this section, we assume a window does not extend beyond a branch, so the window (and the scoreboard) always contains straight-line code from a single basic block. Chapter 3 shows how the window can be extended beyond a branch.

3. *The number and types of functional units*—This determines the importance of structural hazards, which can increase when dynamic scheduling is used.

Instruction		Instruction status			
		Issue	Read operands	Execution complete	Write result
L.D	F6,34(R2)d	√	√	√	√
L.D	F2,45(R3)	√	√	√	√
MUL.D	F0,F2,F4	√	√	√	√
SUB.D	F8,F6,F2	√	√	√	√
DIV.D	F10,F0,F6	√	√	√	
ADD.D	F6,F8,F2	√	√	√	√

		Functional unit status							
Name	Busy	Op	Fi	Fj	Fk	Qj	Qk	Rj	Rk
Integer	No								
Mult1	Yes	Mult	F0	F2	F4			No	No
Mult2	No								
Add	Yes	Add	F6	F8	F2			No	No
Divide	Yes	Div	F10	F0	F6			No	Yes

	Register result status								
	F0	F2	F4	F6	F8	F10	F12	...	F30
FU	Mult 1			Add		Divide			

Figure C.57 Scoreboard tables just before the DIV.D goes to write result. ADD.D was able to complete as soon as DIV.D passed through read operands and got a copy of F6. Only the DIV.D remains to finish.

4. *The presence of antidependences and output dependences*—These lead to WAR and WAW stalls.

Chapter 3 focuses on techniques that attack the problem of exposing and better utilizing available instruction-level parallelism (ILP). The second and third factors can be attacked by increasing the size of the scoreboard and the number of functional units; however, these changes have cost implications and may also affect cycle time. WAW and WAR hazards become more important in dynamically scheduled processors because the pipeline exposes more name dependences. WAW hazards also become more important if we use dynamic scheduling with a branch-prediction scheme that allows multiple iterations of a loop to overlap.

Instruction status	Wait until	Bookkeeping

Issue	Not busy [FU] and not result [D]	`Busy[FU]←yes; Op[FU]←op; Fi[FU]←D;`
		`Fj[FU]←S1; Fk[FU]←S2;`
		`Qj←Result[S1]; Qk← Result[S2];`
		`Rj← not Qj; Rk← not Qk; Result[D]←FU;`

Read operands	Rj and Rk	`Rj← No; Rk← No; Qj←0; Qk←0`
Execution complete	Functional unit done	

Write result	$\forall f((\text{Fj}[f] \mid \text{Fi}[\text{FU}] \text{ or } \text{Rj}[f] = \text{No})$ &
	$(\text{Fk}[f] \mid \text{Fi}[\text{FU}] \text{ or } \text{Rk}[f] = \text{No}))$
		`∀f(if Qj[f]=FU then Rj[f]←Yes);`
		`∀f(if Qk[f]=FU then Rk[f]←Yes);`
		`Result[Fi[FU]]← 0; Busy[FU]← No`

Figure C.58 Required checks and bookkeeping actions for each step in instruction execution. FU stands for the functional unit used by the instruction, D is the destination register name, S1 and S2 are the source register names, and op is the operation to be done. To access the scoreboard entry named Fj for functional unit FU we use the notation Fj[FU]. Result[D] is the name of the functional unit that will write register D. The test on the write result case prevents the write when there is a WAR hazard, which exists if another instruction has this instruction's destination (Fi[FU]) as a source (Fj[f] or Fk[f]) and if some other instruction has written the register (Rj = Yes or Rk = Yes). The variable f is used for any functional unit.

C.8 Fallacies and Pitfalls

Pitfall *Unexpected execution sequences may cause unexpected hazards.*

At first glance, WAW hazards look like they should never occur in a code sequence because no compiler would ever generate two writes to the same register without an intervening read, but they can occur when the sequence is unexpected. For example, the first write might be in the delay slot of a taken branch when the scheduler thought the branch would not be taken. Here is the code sequence that could cause this:

```
        BNEZ    R1,foo
        DIV.D   F0,F2,F4; moved into delay slot
                ;from fall through
        .....
        .....
foo:    L.D     F0,qrs
```

If the branch is taken, then before the DIV.D can complete, the L.D will reach WB, causing a WAW hazard. The hardware must detect this and may stall the issue of the L.D. Another way this can happen is if the second write is in a trap routine. This occurs when an instruction that traps and is writing results continues and completes after an instruction that writes the same register in the trap handler. The hardware must detect and prevent this as well.

Pitfall *Extensive pipelining can impact other aspects of a design, leading to overall worse cost-performance.*

The best example of this phenomenon comes from two implementations of the VAX, the 8600 and the 8700. When the 8600 was initially delivered, it had a cycle time of 80 ns. Subsequently, a redesigned version, called the 8650, with a 55 ns clock was introduced. The 8700 has a much simpler pipeline that operates at the microinstruction level, yielding a smaller CPU with a faster clock cycle of 45 ns. The overall outcome is that the 8650 has a CPI advantage of about 20%, but the 8700 has a clock rate that is about 20% faster. Thus, the 8700 achieves the same performance with much less hardware.

Pitfall *Evaluating dynamic or static scheduling on the basis of unoptimized code.*

Unoptimized code—containing redundant loads, stores, and other operations that might be eliminated by an optimizer—is much easier to schedule than "tight" optimized code. This holds for scheduling both control delays (with delayed branches) and delays arising from RAW hazards. In gcc running on an R3000, which has a pipeline almost identical to that of Section C.1, the frequency of idle clock cycles increases by 18% from the unoptimized and scheduled code to the optimized and scheduled code. Of course, the optimized program is much faster, since it has fewer instructions. To fairly evaluate a compile-time scheduler or runtime dynamic scheduling, you must use optimized code, since in the real system you will derive good performance from other optimizations in addition to scheduling.

C.9   Concluding Remarks

At the beginning of the 1980s, pipelining was a technique reserved primarily for supercomputers and large multimillion dollar mainframes. By the mid-1980s, the first pipelined microprocessors appeared and helped transform the world of computing, allowing microprocessors to bypass minicomputers in performance and eventually to take on and outperform mainframes. By the early 1990s, high-end embedded microprocessors embraced pipelining, and desktops were headed toward the use of the sophisticated dynamically scheduled, multiple-issue approaches discussed in Chapter 3. The material in this appendix, which was considered reasonably advanced for graduate students when this text first appeared in 1990, is now considered basic undergraduate material and can be found in processors costing less than $2!

C.10   Historical Perspective and References

Section L.5 (available online) features a discussion on the development of pipelining and instruction-level parallelism covering both this appendix and the material in Chapter 3. We provide numerous references for further reading and exploration of these topics.

Updated Exercises by Diana Franklin

C.1   [15/15/15/15/25/10/15] <A.2> Use the following code fragment:

```
Loop:    LD      R1,0(R2)      ;load R1 from address 0+R2
         DADDI   R1,R1,#1      ;R1=R1+1
         SD      R1,0,(R2)     ;store R1 at address 0+R2
         DADDI   R2,R2,#4      ;R2=R2+4
         DSUB    R4,R3,R2      ;R4=R3-R2
         BNEZ    R4,Loop       ;branch to Loop if R4!=0
```

Assume that the initial value of R3 is R2 + 396.

a.   [15] <C.2> Data hazards are caused by data dependences in the code. Whether a dependency causes a hazard depends on the machine implementation (i.e., number of pipeline stages). List all of the data dependences in the code above. Record the register, source instruction, and destination instruction; for example, there is a data dependency for register R1 from the LD to the DADDI.

b.   [15] <C.2> Show the timing of this instruction sequence for the 5-stage RISC pipeline without any forwarding or bypassing hardware but assuming that a register read and a write in the same clock cycle "forwards" through the register file, as shown in Figure C.6. Use a pipeline timing chart like that in Figure C.5. Assume that the branch is handled by flushing the pipeline. If all memory references take 1 cycle, how many cycles does this loop take to execute?

c.   [15] <C.2> Show the timing of this instruction sequence for the 5-stage RISC pipeline with full forwarding and bypassing hardware. Use a pipeline timing chart like that shown in Figure C.5. Assume that the branch is handled by predicting it as not taken. If all memory references take 1 cycle, how many cycles does this loop take to execute?

d.   [15] <C.2> Show the timing of this instruction sequence for the 5-stage RISC pipeline with full forwarding and bypassing hardware. Use a pipeline timing chart like that shown in Figure C.5. Assume that the branch is handled by predicting it as taken. If all memory references take 1 cycle, how many cycles does this loop take to execute?

e.   [25] <C.2> High-performance processors have very deep pipelines—more than 15 stages. Imagine that you have a 10-stage pipeline in which every stage of the 5-stage pipeline has been split in two. The only catch is that, for data forwarding, data are forwarded from the end of a pair of stages to the beginning of the two stages where they are needed. For example, data are forwarded from the output of the second execute stage to the input of the first execute stage, still causing a 1-cycle delay. Show the timing of this instruction sequence for the 10-stage RISC pipeline with full forwarding and bypassing hardware. Use a pipeline timing chart like that shown in Figure C.5. Assume that the branch is handled by predicting it as taken. If all memory references take 1 cycle, how many cycles does this loop take to execute?

f. [10] <C.2> Assume that in the 5-stage pipeline the longest stage requires 0.8 ns, and the pipeline register delay is 0.1 ns. What is the clock cycle time of the 5-stage pipeline? If the 10-stage pipeline splits all stages in half, what is the cycle time of the 10-stage machine?

g. [15] <C.2> Using your answers from parts (d) and (e), determine the cycles per instruction (CPI) for the loop on a 5-stage pipeline and a 10-stage pipeline. Make sure you count only from when the first instruction reaches the write-back stage to the end. Do not count the start-up of the first instruction. Using the clock cycle time calculated in part (f), calculate the average instruction execute time for each machine.

C.2 [15/15] <C.2> Suppose the branch frequencies (as percentages of all instructions) are as follows:

Conditional branches	15%
Jumps and calls	1%
Taken conditional branches	60% are taken

a. [15] <C.2> We are examining a four-deep pipeline where the branch is resolved at the end of the second cycle for unconditional branches and at the end of the third cycle for conditional branches. Assuming that only the first pipe stage can always be done independent of whether the branch goes and ignoring other pipeline stalls, how much faster would the machine be without any branch hazards?

b. [15] <C.2> Now assume a high-performance processor in which we have a 15-deep pipeline where the branch is resolved at the end of the fifth cycle for unconditional branches and at the end of the tenth cycle for conditional branches. Assuming that only the first pipe stage can always be done independent of whether the branch goes and ignoring other pipeline stalls, how much faster would the machine be without any branch hazards?

C.3 [5/15/10/10] <C.2> We begin with a computer implemented in single-cycle implementation. When the stages are split by functionality, the stages do not require exactly the same amount of time. The original machine had a clock cycle time of 7 ns. After the stages were split, the measured times were IF, 1 ns; ID, 1.5 ns; EX, 1 ns; MEM, 2 ns; and WB, 1.5 ns. The pipeline register delay is 0.1 ns.

a. [5] <C.2> What is the clock cycle time of the 5-stage pipelined machine?

b. [15] <C.2> If there is a stall every 4 instructions, what is the CPI of the new machine?

c. [10] <C.2> What is the speedup of the pipelined machine over the single-cycle machine?

d. [10] <C.2> If the pipelined machine had an infinite number of stages, what would its speedup be over the single-cycle machine?

C.4 [15] <C.1, C.2> A reduced hardware implementation of the classic five-stage RISC pipeline might use the EX stage hardware to perform a branch instruction comparison and then not actually deliver the branch target PC to the IF stage until the clock cycle in which the branch instruction reaches the MEM stage. Control hazard stalls can be reduced by resolving branch instructions in ID, but improving performance in one respect may reduce performance in other circumstances. Write a small snippet of code in which calculating the branch in the ID stage causes a data hazard, even with data forwarding.

C.5 [12/13/20/20/15/15] <C.2, C.3> For these problems, we will explore a pipeline for a register-memory architecture. The architecture has two instruction formats: a register-register format and a register-memory format. There is a single-memory addressing mode (offset + base register). There is a set of ALU operations with the format:

        ALUop Rdest, Rsrc1, Rsrc2

or

        ALUop Rdest, Rsrc1, MEM

where the ALUop is one of the following: add, subtract, AND, OR, load (Rsrc1 ignored), or store. Rsrc or Rdest are registers. MEM is a base register and offset pair. Branches use a full compare of two registers and are PC relative. Assume that this machine is pipelined so that a new instruction is started every clock cycle. The pipeline structure, similar to that used in the VAX 8700 micropipeline [Clark 1987], is

IF	RF	ALU1	MEM	WB			
	IF	RF	ALU1	MEM	ALU2	WB	
		IF	RF	ALU1	MEM	ALU2	WB
			IF	RF	ALU1	MEM	ALU2	WB
				IF	RF	ALU1	MEM	ALU2	WB
					IF	RF	ALU1	MEM	ALU2	WB

The first ALU stage is used for effective address calculation for memory references and branches. The second ALU cycle is used for operations and branch comparison. RF is both a decode and register-fetch cycle. Assume that when a register read and a register write of the same register occur in the same clock the write data are forwarded.

a. [12] <C.2> Find the number of adders needed, counting any adder or incrementer; show a combination of instructions and pipe stages that justify this answer. You need only give one combination that maximizes the adder count.

b. [13] <C.2> Find the number of register read and write ports and memory read and write ports required. Show that your answer is correct by showing a combination of instructions and pipeline stage indicating the instruction and the number of read ports and write ports required for that instruction.

c. [20] <C.3> Determine any data forwarding for any ALUs that will be needed. Assume that there are separate ALUs for the ALU1 and ALU2 pipe stages. Put in all forwarding among ALUs necessary to avoid or reduce stalls. Show the relationship between the two instructions involved in forwarding using the format of the table in Figure C.26 but ignoring the last two columns. Be careful to consider forwarding across an intervening instruction—for example,

```
ADD            R1, ...
any instruction
ADD            ..., R1, ...
```

d. [20] <C.3> Show all of the data forwarding requirements necessary to avoid or reduce stalls when either the source or destination unit is not an ALU. Use the same format as in Figure C.26, again ignoring the last two columns. Remember to forward to and from memory references.

e. [15] <C.3> Show all the remaining hazards that involve at least one unit other than an ALU as the source or destination unit. Use a table like that shown in Figure C.25, but replace the last column with the lengths of the hazards.

f. [15] <C.2> Show all control hazards by example and state the length of the stall. Use a format like that shown in Figure C.11, labeling each example.

C.6 [12/13/13/15/15] <C.1, C.2, C.3> We will now add support for register-memory ALU operations to the classic five-stage RISC pipeline. To offset this increase in complexity, *all* memory addressing will be restricted to register indirect (i.e., all addresses are simply a value held in a register; no offset or displacement may be added to the register value). For example, the register-memory instruction ADD R4, R5, (R1) means add the contents of register R5 to the contents of the memory location with address equal to the value in register R1 and put the sum in register R4. Register-register ALU operations are unchanged. The following items apply to the integer RISC pipeline:

a. [12] <C.1> List a rearranged order of the five traditional stages of the RISC pipeline that will support register-memory operations implemented exclusively by register indirect addressing.

b. [13] <C.2, C.3> Describe what new forwarding paths are needed for the rearranged pipeline by stating the source, destination, and information transferred on each needed new path.

c. [13] <C.2, C.3> For the reordered stages of the RISC pipeline, what new data hazards are created by this addressing mode? Give an instruction sequence illustrating each new hazard.

d. [15] <C.3> List all of the ways that the RISC pipeline with register-memory ALU operations can have a different instruction count for a given program than the original RISC pipeline. Give a pair of specific instruction sequences, one for the original pipeline and one for the rearranged pipeline, to illustrate each way.

e. [15] <C.3> Assume that all instructions take 1 clock cycle per stage. List all of the ways that the register-memory RISC can have a different CPI for a given program as compared to the original RISC pipeline.

C.7 [10/10] <C.3> In this problem, we will explore how deepening the pipeline affects performance in two ways: faster clock cycle and increased stalls due to data and control hazards. Assume that the original machine is a 5-stage pipeline with a 1 ns clock cycle. The second machine is a 12-stage pipeline with a 0.6 ns clock cycle. The 5-stage pipeline experiences a stall due to a data hazard every 5 instructions, whereas the 12-stage pipeline experiences 3 stalls every 8 instructions. In addition, branches constitute 20% of the instructions, and the misprediction rate for both machines is 5%.

a. [10] <C.3> What is the speedup of the 12-stage pipeline over the 5-stage pipeline, taking into account only data hazards?

b. [10] <C.3> If the branch mispredict penalty for the first machine is 2 cycles but the second machine is 5 cycles, what are the CPIs of each, taking into account the stalls due to branch mispredictions?

C.8 [15] <C.5> Create a table showing the forwarding logic for the R4000 integer pipeline using the same format as that shown in Figure C.26. Include only the MIPS instructions we considered in Figure C.26.

C.9 [15] <C.5> Create a table showing the R4000 integer hazard detection using the same format as that shown in Figure C.25. Include only the MIPS instructions we considered in Figure C.26.

C.10 [25] <C.5> Suppose MIPS had only one register set. Construct the forwarding table for the FP and integer instructions using the format of Figure C.26. Ignore FP and integer divides.

C.11 [15] <C.5> Construct a table like that shown in Figure C.25 to check for WAW stalls in the MIPS FP pipeline of Figure C.35. Do not consider FP divides.

C.12 [20/22/22] <C.4, C.6> In this exercise, we will look at how a common vector loop runs on statically and dynamically scheduled versions of the MIPS pipeline. The loop is the so-called DAXPY loop (discussed extensively in Appendix G) and the central operation in Gaussian elimination. The loop implements the vector operation $Y = a * X + Y$ for a vector of length 100. Here is the MIPS code for the loop:

```
foo:    L.D      F2, 0(R1)      ; load X(i)
        MUL.D    F4, F2, F0     ; multiply a*X(i)
        L.D      F6, 0($2)      ; load Y(i)
        ADD.D    F6, F4, F6     ; add a*X(i) + Y(i)
        S.D      0(R2), F6      ; store Y(i)
        DADDIU   R1, R1, #8     ; increment X index
        DADDIU   R2, R2, #8     ; increment Y index
        SGTIU    R3, R1, done   ; test if done
        BEQZ     R3, foo        ; loop if not done
```

For parts (a) to (c), assume that integer operations issue and complete in 1 clock cycle (including loads) and that their results are fully bypassed. Ignore the branch delay. You will use the FP latencies (only) shown in Figure C.34, but assume that the FP unit is fully pipelined. For scoreboards below, assume that an instruction waiting for a result from another function unit can pass through read operands at the same time the result is written. Also assume that an instruction in WR completing will allow a currently active instruction that is waiting on the same functional unit to issue in the same clock cycle in which the first instruction completes WR.

a. [20] <C.5> For this problem, use the MIPS pipeline of Section C.5 with the pipeline latencies from Figure C.34, but a fully pipelined FP unit, so the initiation interval is 1. Draw a timing diagram, similar to Figure C.37, showing the timing of each instruction's execution. How many clock cycles does each loop iteration take, counting from when the first instruction enters the WB stage to when the last instruction enters the WB stage?

b. [22] <C.6> Using the MIPS code for DAXPY above, show the state of the scoreboard tables (as in Figure C.56) when the SGTIU instruction reaches write result. Assume that issue and read operands each take a cycle. Assume that there is one integer functional unit that takes only a single execution cycle (the latency to use is 0 cycles, including loads and stores). Assume the FP unit configuration of Figure C.54 with the FP latencies of Figure C.34. The branch should not be included in the scoreboard.

c. [22] <C.6> Using the MIPS code for DAXPY above, assume a scoreboard with the FP functional units described in Figure C.54, plus one integer functional unit (also used for load-store). Assume the latencies shown in Figure C.59. Show the state of the scoreboard (as in Figure C.56) when the branch issues for the second time. Assume that the branch was correctly predicted taken and took 1 cycle. How many clock cycles does each loop iteration take? You may ignore any register port/bus conflicts.

C.13 [25] <C.8> It is critical that the scoreboard be able to distinguish RAW and WAR hazards, because a WAR hazard requires stalling the instruction doing the writing until the instruction reading an operand initiates execution, but a RAW hazard

Instruction producing result	Instruction using result	Latency in clock cycles
FP multiply	FP ALU op	6
FP add	FP ALU op	4
FP multiply	FP store	5
FP add	FP store	3
Integer operation (including load)	Any	0

Figure C.59 Pipeline latencies where latency is number.

requires delaying the reading instruction until the writing instruction finishes—just the opposite. For example, consider the sequence:

```
MUL.D      F0,F6,F4
DSUB.D     F8,F0,F2
ADD.D      F2,F10,F2
```

The DSUB.D depends on the MUL.D (a RAW hazard), thus the MUL.D must be allowed to complete before the DSUB.D. If the MUL.D were stalled for the DSUB.D due to the inability to distinguish between RAW and WAR hazards, the processor will deadlock. This sequence contains a WAR hazard between the ADD.D and the DSUB.D, and the ADD.D cannot be allowed to complete until the DSUB.D begins execution. The difficulty lies in distinguishing the RAW hazard between MUL.D and DSUB.D, and the WAR hazard between the DSUB.D and ADD.D. To see just why the three-instruction scenario is important, trace the handling of each instruction stage by stage through issue, read operands, execute, and write result. Assume that each scoreboard stage other than execute takes 1 clock cycle. Assume that the MUL.D instruction requires 3 clock cycles to execute and that the DSUB.D and ADD.D instructions each take 1 cycle to execute. Finally, assume that the processor has two multiply function units and two add function units. Present the trace as follows.

1. Make a table with the column headings Instruction, Issue, Read Operands, Execute, Write Result, and Comment. In the first column, list the instructions in program order (be generous with space between instructions; larger table cells will better hold the results of your analysis). Start the table by writing a 1 in the Issue column of the MUL.D instruction row to show that MUL.D completes the issue stage in clock cycle 1. Now, fill in the stage columns of the table through the cycle at which the scoreboard first stalls an instruction.

2. For a stalled instruction write the words "waiting at clock cycle X," where X is the number of the current clock cycle, in the appropriate table column to show that the scoreboard is resolving an RAW or WAR hazard by stalling that stage. In the Comment column, state what type of hazard and what dependent instruction is causing the wait.

3. Adding the words "completes with clock cycle Y" to a "waiting" table entry, fill in the rest of the table through the time when all instructions are complete. For an instruction that stalled, add a description in the Comments column telling why the wait ended when it did and how deadlock was avoided. (*Hint*: Think about how WAW hazards are prevented and what this implies about active instruction sequences.) Note the completion order of the three instructions as compared to their program order.

C.14 [10/10/10] <C.5> For this problem, you will create a series of small snippets that illustrate the issues that arise when using functional units with different latencies. For each one, draw a timing diagram similar to Figure C.38 that illustrates each concept, and clearly indicate the problem.

   a. [10] <C.5> Demonstrate, using code different from that used in Figure C.38, the structural hazard of having the hardware for only one MEM and WB stage.

   b. [10] <C.5> Demonstrate a WAW hazard requiring a stall.

References

Adve, S. V., and K. Gharachorloo [1996]. "Shared memory consistency models: A tutorial," *IEEE Computer* 29:12 (December), 66–76.

Adve, S. V., and M. D. Hill [1990]. "Weak ordering—a new definition," *Proc. 17th Annual Int'l. Symposium on Computer Architecture (ISCA)*, May 28–31, 1990, Seattle, Wash., 2–14.

Agarwal, A. [1987]. "Analysis of Cache Performance for Operating Systems and Multi-programming," Ph.D. thesis, Tech. Rep. No. CSL-TR-87-332, Stanford University, Palo Alto, Calif.

Agarwal, A. [1991]. "Limits on interconnection network performance," *IEEE Trans. on Parallel and Distributed Systems* 2:4 (April), 398–412.

Agarwal, A., and S. D. Pudar [1993]. "Column-associative caches: A technique for reducing the miss rate of direct-mapped caches," *20th Annual Int'l. Symposium on Computer Architecture (ISCA)*, May 16–19, 1993, San Diego, Calif. Also appears in *Computer Architecture News* 21:2 (May), 179–190, 1993.

Agarwal, A., R. Bianchini, D. Chaiken, K. Johnson, and D. Kranz [1995]. "The MIT Alewife machine: Architecture and performance," *Int'l. Symposium on Computer Architecture* (Denver, Colo.), June, 2–13.

Agarwal, A., J. L. Hennessy, R. Simoni, and M. A. Horowitz [1988]. "An evaluation of directory schemes for cache coherence," *Proc. 15th Int'l. Symposium on Computer Architecture* (June), 280–289.

Agarwal, A., J. Kubiatowicz, D. Kranz, B.-H. Lim, D. Yeung, G. D'Souza, and M. Parkin [1993]. "Sparcle: An evolutionary processor design for large-scale multiprocessors," *IEEE Micro* 13 (June), 48–61.

Agerwala, T., and J. Cocke [1987]. *High Performance Reduced Instruction Set Processors*, IBM Tech. Rep. RC12434, IBM, Armonk, N.Y.

Akeley, K. and T. Jermoluk [1988]. "High-Performance Polygon Rendering," *Proc. 15th Annual Conf. on Computer Graphics and Interactive Techniques (SIGGRAPH 1988)*, August 1–5, 1988, Atlanta, Ga., 239–246.

Alexander, W. G., and D. B. Wortman [1975]. "Static and dynamic characteristics of XPL programs," *IEEE Computer* 8:11 (November), 41–46.

Alles, A. [1995]. "ATM Internetworking," White Paper (May), Cisco Systems, Inc., San Jose, Calif. (*www.cisco.com/warp/public/614/12.html*).

Alliant. [1987]. *Alliant FX/Series: Product Summary*, Alliant Computer Systems Corp., Acton, Mass.

Almasi, G. S., and A. Gottlieb [1989]. *Highly Parallel Computing*, Benjamin/Cummings, Redwood City, Calif.

Alverson, G., R. Alverson, D. Callahan, B. Koblenz, A. Porterfield, and B. Smith [1992]. "Exploiting heterogeneous parallelism on a multithreaded multiprocessor," *Proc. ACM/IEEE Conf. on Supercomputing*, November 16–20, 1992, Minneapolis, Minn., 188–197.

Amdahl, G. M. [1967]. "Validity of the single processor approach to achieving large scale computing capabilities," *Proc. AFIPS Spring Joint Computer Conf.*, April 18–20, 1967, Atlantic City, N.J., 483–485.

Amdahl, G. M., G. A. Blaauw, and F. P. Brooks, Jr. [1964]. "Architecture of the IBM System 360," *IBM J. Research and Development* 8:2 (April), 87–101.

Amza, C., A. L. Cox, S. Dwarkadas, P. Keleher, H. Lu, R. Rajamony, W. Yu, and W. Zwaenepoel [1996]. "Treadmarks: Shared memory computing on networks of workstations," *IEEE Computer* 29:2 (February), 18–28.

Anderson, D. [2003]. "You don't know jack about disks," *Queue*, 1:4 (June), 20–30.

Anderson, D., J. Dykes, and E. Riedel [2003]. "SCSI vs. ATA—More than an interface," *Proc. 2nd USENIX Conf. on File and Storage Technology (FAST '03)*, March 31–April 2, 2003, San Francisco.

Anderson, D. W., F. J. Sparacio, and R. M. Tomasulo [1967]. "The IBM 360 Model 91: Processor philosophy and instruction handling," *IBM J. Research and Development* 11:1 (January), 8–24.

Anderson, M. H. [1990]. "Strength (and safety) in numbers (RAID, disk storage technology)," *Byte* 15:13 (December), 337–339.

Anderson, T. E., D. E. Culler, and D. Patterson [1995]. "A case for NOW (networks of workstations)," *IEEE Micro* 15:1 (February), 54–64.

Ang, B., D. Chiou, D. Rosenband, M. Ehrlich, L. Rudolph, and Arvind [1998]. "StarT-Voyager: A flexible platform for exploring scalable SMP issues," *Proc. ACM/IEEE Conf. on Supercomputing*, November 7–13, 1998, Orlando, FL.

Anjan, K. V., and T. M. Pinkston [1995]. "An efficient, fully-adaptive deadlock recovery scheme: Disha," *Proc. 22nd Annual Int'l. Symposium on Computer Architecture (ISCA)*, June 22–24, 1995, Santa Margherita, Italy.

Anon. et al. [1985]. *A Measure of Transaction Processing Power*, Tandem Tech. Rep. TR85.2. Also appears in *Datamation* 31:7 (April), 112–118, 1985.

Apache Hadoop. [2011]. *http://hadoop.apache.org*.

Archibald, J., and J.-L. Baer [1986]. "Cache coherence protocols: Evaluation using a multiprocessor simulation model," *ACM Trans. on Computer Systems* 4:4 (November), 273–298.

Armbrust, M., A. Fox, R. Griffith, A. D. Joseph, R. Katz, A. Konwinski, G. Lee, D. Patterson, A. Rabkin, I. Stoica, and M. Zaharia [2009]. *Above the Clouds: A Berkeley View of Cloud Computing*, Tech. Rep. UCB/EECS-2009-28, University of California, Berkeley (*http://www.eecs.berkeley.edu/Pubs/TechRpts/2009/EECS-2009-28.html*).

Arpaci, R. H., D. E. Culler, A. Krishnamurthy, S. G. Steinberg, and K. Yelick [1995]. "Empirical evaluation of the CRAY-T3D: A compiler perspective," *22nd Annual Int'l. Symposium on Computer Architecture (ISCA)*, June 22–24, 1995, Santa Margherita, Italy.

Asanovic, K. [1998]. "Vector Microprocessors," Ph.D. thesis, Computer Science Division, University of California, Berkeley.

Associated Press. [2005]. "Gap Inc. shuts down two Internet stores for major overhaul," *USATODAY.com*, August 8, 2005.

Atanasoff, J. V. [1940]. *Computing Machine for the Solution of Large Systems of Linear Equations*, Internal Report, Iowa State University, Ames.

Atkins, M. [1991]. Performance and the i860 Microprocessor, *IEEE Micro*, 11:5 (September), 24–27, 72–78.

Austin, T. M., and G. Sohi [1992]. "Dynamic dependency analysis of ordinary programs," *Proc. 19th Annual Int'l. Symposium on Computer Architecture (ISCA)*, May 19–21, 1992, Gold Coast, Australia, 342–351.

Babbay, F., and A. Mendelson [1998]. "Using value prediction to increase the power of speculative execution hardware," *ACM Trans. on Computer Systems* 16:3 (August), 234–270.

Baer, J.-L., and W.-H. Wang [1988]. "On the inclusion property for multi-level cache hierarchies," *Proc. 15th Annual Int'l. Symposium on Computer Architecture*, May 30–June 2, 1988, Honolulu, Hawaii, 73–80.

Bailey, D. H., E. Barszcz, J. T. Barton, D. S. Browning, R. L. Carter, L. Dagum, R. A. Fatoohi, P. O. Frederickson, T. A. Lasinski, R. S. Schreiber, H. D. Simon, V. Venkatakrishnan, and S. K. Weeratunga [1991]. "The NAS parallel benchmarks," *Int'l. J. Supercomputing Applications* 5, 63–73.

Bakoglu, H. B., G. F. Grohoski, L. E. Thatcher, J. A. Kaeli, C. R. Moore, D. P. Tattle, W. E. Male, W. R. Hardell, D. A. Hicks, M. Nguyen Phu, R. K. Montoye, W. T. Glover, and S. Dhawan [1989]. "IBM second-generation RISC processor organization," *Proc. IEEE Int'l. Conf. on Computer Design*, September 30–October 4, 1989, Rye, N.Y., 138–142.

Balakrishnan, H., V. N. Padmanabhan, S. Seshan, and R. H. Katz [1997]. "A comparison of mechanisms for improving TCP performance over wireless links," *IEEE/ACM Trans. on Networking* 5:6 (December), 756–769.

Ball, T., and J. Larus [1993]. "Branch prediction for free," *Proc. ACM SIGPLAN'93 Conference on Programming Language Design and Implementation (PLDI)*, June 23–25, 1993, Albuquerque, N.M., 300–313.

Banerjee, U. [1979]. "Speedup of Ordinary Programs," Ph.D. thesis, Dept. of Computer Science, University of Illinois at Urbana-Champaign.

Barham, P., B. Dragovic, K. Fraser, S. Hand, T. Harris, A. Ho, and R. Neugebauer [2003]. "Xen and the art of virtualization," *Proc. of the 19th ACM Symposium on Operating Systems Principles*, October 19–22, 2003, Bolton Landing, N.Y.

Barroso, L. A. [2010]. "Warehouse Scale Computing [keynote address]," *Proc. ACM SIGMOD*, June 8–10, 2010, Indianapolis, Ind.

Barroso, L. A., and U. Hölzle [2007], "The case for energy-proportional computing," *IEEE Computer*, 40:12 (December), 33–37.

Barroso, L. A., and U. Hölzle [2009]. *The Datacenter as a Computer: An Introduction to the Design of Warehouse-Scale Machines*, Morgan & Claypool, San Rafael, Calif.

Barroso, L. A., K. Gharachorloo, and E. Bugnion [1998]. "Memory system characterization of commercial workloads," *Proc. 25th Annual Int'l. Symposium on Computer Architecture (ISCA)*, July 3–14, 1998, Barcelona, Spain, 3–14.

Barton, R. S. [1961]. "A new approach to the functional design of a computer," *Proc. Western Joint Computer Conf.*, May 9–11, 1961, Los Angeles, Calif., 393–396.

Bashe, C. J., W. Buchholz, G. V. Hawkins, J. L. Ingram, and N. Rochester [1981]. "The architecture of IBM's early computers," *IBM J. Research and Development* 25:5 (September), 363–375.

Bashe, C. J., L. R. Johnson, J. H. Palmer, and E. W. Pugh [1986]. *IBM's Early Computers*, MIT Press, Cambridge, Mass.

Baskett, F., and T. W. Keller [1977]. "An evaluation of the Cray-1 processor," in *High Speed Computer and Algorithm Organization*, D. J. Kuck, D. H. Lawrie, and A. H. Sameh, eds., Academic Press, San Diego, 71–84.

Baskett, F., T. Jermoluk, and D. Solomon [1988]. "The 4D-MP graphics superworkstation: Computing + graphics = 40 MIPS + 40 MFLOPS and 10,000 lighted polygons per second," *Proc. IEEE COMPCON*, February 29–March 4, 1988, San Francisco, 468–471.

BBN Laboratories. [1986]. *Butterfly Parallel Processor Overview*, Tech. Rep. 6148, BBN Laboratories, Cambridge, Mass.

Bell, C. G. [1984]. "The mini and micro industries," *IEEE Computer* 17:10 (October), 14–30.

Bell, C. G. [1985]. "Multis: A new class of multiprocessor computers," *Science* 228 (April 26), 462–467.

Bell, C. G. [1989]. "The future of high performance computers in science and engineering," *Communications of the ACM* 32:9 (September), 1091–1101.

Bell, G., and J. Gray [2001]. *Crays, Clusters and Centers*, Tech. Rep. MSR-TR-2001-76, Microsoft Research, Redmond, Wash.

Bell, C. G., and J. Gray [2002]. "What's next in high performance computing?" *CACM* 45:2 (February), 91–95.

Bell, C. G., and A. Newell [1971]. *Computer Structures: Readings and Examples*, McGraw-Hill, New York.

Bell, C. G., and W. D. Strecker [1976]. "Computer structures: What have we learned from the PDP-11?," *Third Annual Int'l. Symposium on Computer Architecture (ISCA)*, January 19–21, 1976, Tampa, Fla., 1–14.

Bell, C. G., and W. D. Strecker [1998]. "Computer structures: What have we learned from the PDP-11?" *25 Years of the International Symposia on Computer Architecture (Selected Papers)*, ACM, New York, 138–151.

Bell, C. G., J. C. Mudge, and J. E. McNamara [1978]. *A DEC View of Computer Engineering*, Digital Press, Bedford, Mass.

Bell, C. G., R. Cady, H. McFarland, B. DeLagi, J. O'Laughlin, R. Noonan, and W. Wulf [1970]. "A new architecture for mini-computers: The DEC PDP-11," *Proc. AFIPS Spring Joint Computer Conf.*, May 5–May 7, 1970, Atlantic City, N.J., 657–675.

Benes, V. E. [1962]. "Rearrangeable three stage connecting networks," *Bell System Technical Journal* 41, 1481–1492.

Bertozzi, D., A. Jalabert, S. Murali, R. Tamhankar, S. Stergiou, L. Benini, and G. De Micheli [2005]. "NoC synthesis flow for customized domain specific multiprocessor systems-on-chip," *IEEE Trans. on Parallel and Distributed Systems* 16:2 (February), 113–130.

Bhandarkar, D. P. [1995]. *Alpha Architecture and Implementations*, Digital Press, Newton, Mass.

Bhandarkar, D. P., and D. W. Clark [1991]. "Performance from architecture: Comparing a RISC and a CISC with similar hardware organizations," *Proc. Fourth Int'l. Conf. on Architectural Support for Programming Languages and Operating Systems (ASPLOS)*, April 8–11, 1991, Palo Alto, Calif., 310–319.

Bhandarkar, D. P., and J. Ding [1997]. "Performance characterization of the Pentium Pro processor," *Proc. Third Int'l. Symposium on High-Performance Computer Architecture*, February 1–February 5, 1997, San Antonio, Tex., 288–297.

Bhuyan, L. N., and D. P. Agrawal [1984]. "Generalized hypercube and hyperbus structures for a computer network," *IEEE Trans. on Computers* 32:4 (April), 322–333.

Bienia, C., S. Kumar, P. S. Jaswinder, and K. Li [2008]. *The Parsec Benchmark Suite: Characterization and Architectural Implications*, Tech. Rep. TR-811-08, Princeton University, Princeton, N.J.

Bier, J. [1997]. "The Evolution of DSP Processors," presentation at Univesity of California, Berkeley, November 14.

Bird, S., A. Phansalkar, L. K. John, A. Mericas, and R. Indukuru [2007]. "Characterization of performance of SPEC CPU benchmarks on Intel's Core Microarchitecture based processor," *Proc. 2007 SPEC Benchmark Workshop*, January 21, 2007, Austin, Tex.

Birman, M., A. Samuels, G. Chu, T. Chuk, L. Hu, J. McLeod, and J. Barnes [1990]. "Developing the WRL3170/3171 SPARC floating-point coprocessors," *IEEE Micro* 10:1, 55–64.

Blackburn, M., R. Garner, C. Hoffman, A. M. Khan, K. S. McKinley, R. Bentzur, A. Diwan, D. Feinberg, D. Frampton, S. Z. Guyer, M. Hirzel, A. Hosking, M. Jump, H. Lee, J. E. B. Moss, A. Phansalkar, D. Stefanovic, T. VanDrunen, D. von Dincklage, and B. Wiedermann [2006]. "The DaCapo benchmarks: Java benchmarking development and analysis," *ACM SIGPLAN Conference on Object-Oriented Programming, Systems, Languages, and Applications (OOPSLA)*, October 22–26, 2006, 169–190.

Blaum, M., J. Bruck, and A. Vardy [1996]. "MDS array codes with independent parity symbols," *IEEE Trans. on Information Theory*, IT-42 (March), 529–42.

Blaum, M., J. Brady, J. Bruck, and J. Menon [1994]. "EVENODD: An optimal scheme for tolerating double disk failures in RAID architectures," *Proc. 21st Annual Int'l. Symposium on Computer Architecture (ISCA)*, April 18–21, 1994, Chicago, 245–254.

Blaum, M., J. Brady, J. Bruck, and J. Menon [1995]. "EVENODD: An optimal scheme for tolerating double disk failures in RAID architectures," *IEEE Trans. on Computers* 44:2 (February), 192–202.

Blaum, M., J. Brady, J., Bruck, J. Menon, and A. Vardy [2001]. "The EVENODD code and its generalization," in H. Jin, T. Cortes, and R. Buyya, eds., *High Performance Mass Storage and Parallel I/O: Technologies and Applications*, Wiley–IEEE, New York, 187–208.

Bloch, E. [1959]. "The engineering design of the Stretch computer," *1959 Proceedings of the Eastern Joint Computer Conf.*, December 1–3, 1959, Boston, Mass., 48–59.

Boddie, J. R. [2000]. "History of DSPs," *www.lucent.com/micro/dsp/dsphist.html.*

Bolt, K. M. [2005]. "Amazon sees sales rise, profit fall," *Seattle Post-Intelligencer*, October 25 (http://seattlepi.nwsource.com/business/245943_techearns26.html).

Bordawekar, R., U. Bondhugula, R. Rao [2010]. "Believe It or Not!: Multi-core CPUs can Match GPU Performance for a FLOP-Intensive Application!" *19th International Conference on Parallel Architecture and Compilation Techniques (PACT 2010)*. Vienna, Austria, September 11–15, 2010, 537–538.

Borg, A., R. E. Kessler, and D. W. Wall [1990]. "Generation and analysis of very long address traces," *19th Annual Int'l. Symposium on Computer Architecture (ISCA)*, May 19–21, 1992, Gold Coast, Australia, 270–279.

Bouknight, W. J., S. A. Deneberg, D. E. McIntyre, J. M. Randall, A. H. Sameh, and D. L. Slotnick [1972]. "The Illiac IV system," *Proc. IEEE* 60:4, 369–379. Also appears in D. P. Siewiorek, C. G. Bell, and A. Newell, *Computer Structures: Principles and Examples*, McGraw-Hill, New York, 1982, 306–316.

Brady, J. T. [1986]. "A theory of productivity in the creative process," *IEEE CG&A* (May), 25–34.

Brain, M. [2000]. "Inside a Digital Cell Phone," *www.howstuffworks.com/inside-cellphone.htm.*

Brandt, M., J. Brooks, M. Cahir, T. Hewitt, E. Lopez-Pineda, and D. Sandness [2000]. *The Benchmarker's Guide for Cray SV1 Systems*. Cray Inc., Seattle, Wash.

Brent, R. P., and H. T. Kung [1982]. "A regular layout for parallel adders," *IEEE Trans. on Computers* C-31, 260–264.

Brewer, E. A., and B. C. Kuszmaul [1994]. "How to get good performance from the CM-5 data network," *Proc. Eighth Int'l. Parallel Processing Symposium*, April 26–27, 1994, Cancun, Mexico.

Brin, S., and L. Page [1998]. "The anatomy of a large-scale hypertextual Web search engine," *Proc. 7th Int'l. World Wide Web Conf.*, April 14–18, 1998, Brisbane, Queensland, Australia, 107–117.

Brown, A., and D. A. Patterson [2000]. "Towards maintainability, availability, and growth benchmarks: A case study of software RAID systems." *Proc. 2000 USENIX Annual Technical Conf.*, June 18–23, 2000, San Diego, Calif.

Bucher, I. V., and A. H. Hayes [1980]. "I/O performance measurement on Cray-1 and CDC 7000 computers," *Proc. Computer Performance Evaluation Users Group, 16th Meeting*, NBS 500-65, 245–254.

Bucher, I. Y. [1983]. "The computational speed of supercomputers," *Proc. Int'l. Conf. on Measuring and Modeling of Computer Systems (SIGMETRICS 1983)*, August 29–31, 1983, Minneapolis, Minn., 151–165.

Bucholtz, W. [1962]. *Planning a Computer System: Project Stretch*, McGraw-Hill, New York.

Burgess, N., and T. Williams [1995]. "Choices of operand truncation in the SRT division algorithm," *IEEE Trans. on Computers* 44:7, 933–938.

Burkhardt III, H., S. Frank, B. Knobe, and J. Rothnie [1992]. *Overview of the KSR1 Computer System*, Tech. Rep. KSR-TR-9202001, Kendall Square Research, Boston, Mass.

Burks, A. W., H. H. Goldstine, and J. von Neumann [1946]. "Preliminary discussion of the logical design of an electronic computing instrument," Report to the U.S. Army Ordnance Department, p. 1; also appears in *Papers of John von Neumann*, W. Aspray and A. Burks, eds., MIT Press, Cambridge, Mass., and Tomash Publishers, Los Angeles, Calif., 1987, 97–146.

Calder, B., G. Reinman, and D. M. Tullsen [1999]. "Selective value prediction," *Proc. 26th Annual Int'l. Symposium on Computer Architecture (ISCA)*, May 2–4, 1999, Atlanta, Ga.

Calder, B., D. Grunwald, M. Jones, D. Lindsay, J. Martin, M. Mozer, and B. Zorn [1997]. "Evidence-based static branch prediction using machine learning," *ACM Trans. Program. Lang. Syst.* 19:1, 188–222.

Callahan, D., J. Dongarra, and D. Levine [1988]. "Vectorizing compilers: A test suite and results," *Proc. ACM/IEEE Conf. on Supercomputing*, November 12–17, 1988, Orland, Fla., 98–105.

Cantin, J. F., and M. D. Hill [2001]. "Cache Performance for Selected SPEC CPU2000 Benchmarks," *www.jfred.org/cache-data.html* (June).

Cantin, J. F., and M. D. Hill [2003]. "Cache Performance for SPEC CPU2000 Benchmarks, Version 3.0," *www.cs.wisc.edu/multifacet/misc/spec2000cache-data/index.html*.

Carles, S. [2005]. "Amazon reports record Xmas season, top game picks," *Gamasutra*, December 27 (*http://www.gamasutra.com/php-bin/news_index.php?story=7630.*)

Carter, J., and K. Rajamani [2010]. "Designing energy-efficient servers and data centers," *IEEE Computer* 43:7 (July), 76–78.

Case, R. P., and A. Padegs [1978]. "The architecture of the IBM System/370," *Communications of the ACM* 21:1, 73–96. Also appears in D. P. Siewiorek, C. G. Bell, and A. Newell, *Computer Structures: Principles and Examples*, McGraw-Hill, New York, 1982, 830–855.

Censier, L., and P. Feautrier [1978]. "A new solution to coherence problems in multicache systems," *IEEE Trans. on Computers* C-27:12 (December), 1112–1118.

Chandra, R., S. Devine, B. Verghese, A. Gupta, and M. Rosenblum [1994]. "Scheduling and page migration for multiprocessor compute servers," *Sixth Int'l. Conf. on Architectural Support for Programming Languages and Operating Systems (ASPLOS)*, October 4–7, 1994, San Jose, Calif., 12–24.

Chang, F., J. Dean, S. Ghemawat, W. C. Hsieh, D. A. Wallach, M. Burrows, T. Chandra, A. Fikes, and R. E. Gruber [2006]. "Bigtable: A distributed storage system for structured data," *Proc. 7th USENIX Symposium on Operating Systems Design and Implementation (OSDI '06)*, November 6–8, 2006, Seattle, Wash.

Chang, J., J. Meza, P. Ranganathan, C. Bash, and A. Shah [2010]. "Green server design: Beyond operational energy to sustainability," *Proc. Workshop on Power Aware Computing and Systems (HotPower '10)*, October 3, 2010, Vancouver, British Columbia.

Chang, P. P., S. A. Mahlke, W. Y. Chen, N. J. Warter, and W. W. Hwu [1991]. "IMPACT: An architectural framework for multiple-instruction-issue processors," *18th Annual Int'l. Symposium on Computer Architecture (ISCA)*, May 27–30, 1991, Toronto, Canada, 266–275.

Charlesworth, A. E. [1981]. "An approach to scientific array processing: The architecture design of the AP-120B/FPS-164 family," *Computer* 14:9 (September), 18–27.

Charlesworth, A. [1998]. "Starfire: Extending the SMP envelope," *IEEE Micro* 18:1 (January/February), 39–49.

Chen, P. M., and E. K. Lee [1995]. "Striping in a RAID level 5 disk array," *Proc. ACM SIGMETRICS Conf. on Measurement and Modeling of Computer Systems*, May 15–19, 1995, Ottawa, Canada, 136–145.

Chen, P. M., G. A. Gibson, R. H. Katz, and D. A. Patterson [1990]. "An evaluation of redundant arrays of inexpensive disks using an Amdahl 5890," *Proc. ACM SIGMETRICS Conf. on Measurement and Modeling of Computer Systems*, May 22–25, 1990, Boulder, Colo.

Chen, P. M., E. K. Lee, G. A. Gibson, R. H. Katz, and D. A. Patterson [1994]. "RAID: High-performance, reliable secondary storage," *ACM Computing Surveys* 26:2 (June), 145–188.

Chen, S. [1983]. "Large-scale and high-speed multiprocessor system for scientific applications," *Proc. NATO Advanced Research Workshop on High-Speed Computing*, June 20–22, 1983, Jülich, West Germany. Also appears in K. Hwang, ed., "Superprocessors: Design and applications," *IEEE* (August), 602–609, 1984.

Chen, T. C. [1980]. "Overlap and parallel processing," in H. Stone, ed., *Introduction to Computer Architecture*, Science Research Associates, Chicago, 427–486.

Chow, F. C. [1983]. "A Portable Machine-Independent Global Optimizer—Design and Measurements," Ph.D. thesis, Stanford University, Palo Alto, Calif.

Chrysos, G. Z., and J. S. Emer [1998]. "Memory dependence prediction using store sets," *Proc. 25th Annual Int'l. Symposium on Computer Architecture (ISCA)*, July 3–14, 1998, Barcelona, Spain, 142–153.

Clark, B., T. Deshane, E. Dow, S. Evanchik, M. Finlayson, J. Herne, and J. Neefe Matthews [2004]. "Xen and the art of repeated research," *Proc. USENIX Annual Technical Conf.*, June 27–July 2, 2004, 135–144.

Clark, D. W. [1983]. "Cache performance of the VAX-11/780," *ACM Trans. on Computer Systems* 1:1, 24–37.

Clark, D. W. [1987]. "Pipelining and performance in the VAX 8800 processor," *Proc. Second Int'l. Conf. on Architectural Support for Programming Languages and Operating Systems (ASPLOS)*, October 5–8, 1987, Palo Alto, Calif., 173–177.

Clark, D. W., and J. S. Emer [1985]. "Performance of the VAX-11/780 translation buffer: Simulation and measurement," *ACM Trans. on Computer Systems* 3:1 (February), 31–62.

Clark, D., and H. Levy [1982]. "Measurement and analysis of instruction set use in the VAX-11/780," *Proc. Ninth Annual Int'l. Symposium on Computer Architecture (ISCA)*, April 26–29, 1982, Austin, Tex., 9–17.

Clark, D., and W. D. Strecker [1980]. "Comments on 'the case for the reduced instruction set computer,'" *Computer Architecture News* 8:6 (October), 34–38.

Clark, W. A. [1957]. "The Lincoln TX-2 computer development," *Proc. Western Joint Computer Conference*, February 26–28, 1957, Los Angeles, 143–145.

Clidaras, J., C. Johnson, and B. Felderman [2010]. Private communication.

Climate Savers Computing Initiative. [2007]. "Efficiency Specs," *http://www.climatesaverscomputing.org/*.

Clos, C. [1953]. "A study of non-blocking switching networks," *Bell Systems Technical Journal* 32 (March), 406–424.

Cody, W. J., J. T. Coonen, D. M. Gay, K. Hanson, D. Hough, W. Kahan, R. Karpinski, J. Palmer, F. N. Ris, and D. Stevenson [1984]. "A proposed radix- and word-lengthindependent standard for floating-point arithmetic," *IEEE Micro* 4:4, 86–100.

Colwell, R. P., and R. Steck [1995]. "A 0.6 μm BiCMOS processor with dynamic execution." *Proc. of IEEE Int'l. Symposium on Solid State Circuits (ISSCC)*, February 15–17, 1995, San Francisco, 176–177.

Colwell, R. P., R. P. Nix, J. J. O'Donnell, D. B. Papworth, and P. K. Rodman [1987]. "A VLIW architecture for a trace scheduling compiler," *Proc. Second Int'l. Conf. on Architectural Support for Programming Languages and Operating Systems (ASPLOS)*, October 5–8, 1987, Palo Alto, Calif., 180–192.

Comer, D. [1993]. *Internetworking with TCP/IP*, 2nd ed., Prentice Hall, Englewood Cliffs, N.J.

Compaq Computer Corporation. [1999]. *Compiler Writer's Guide for the Alpha 21264*, Order Number EC-RJ66A-TE, June, *www1.support.compaq.com/alpha-tools/documentation/current/21264_EV67/ec-rj66a-te_comp_writ_gde_for_alpha21264.pdf.*

Conti, C., D. H. Gibson, and S. H. Pitkowsky [1968]. "Structural aspects of the System/360 Model 85. Part I. General organization," *IBM Systems J.* 7:1, 2–14.

Coonen, J. [1984]. "Contributions to a Proposed Standard for Binary Floating-Point Arithmetic," Ph.D. thesis, University of California, Berkeley.

Corbett, P., B. English, A. Goel, T. Grcanac, S. Kleiman, J. Leong, and S. Sankar [2004]. "Row-diagonal parity for double disk failure correction," *Proc. 3rd USENIX Conf. on File and Storage Technology (FAST '04)*, March 31–April 2, 2004, San Francisco.

Crawford, J., and P. Gelsinger [1988]. *Programming the 80386*, Sybex Books, Alameda, Calif.

Culler, D. E., J. P. Singh, and A. Gupta [1999]. *Parallel Computer Architecture: A Hardware/Software Approach*, Morgan Kaufmann, San Francisco.

Curnow, H. J., and B. A. Wichmann [1976]. "A synthetic benchmark," *The Computer J.* 19:1, 43–49.

Cvetanovic, Z., and R. E. Kessler [2000]. "Performance analysis of the Alpha 21264-based Compaq ES40 system," *Proc. 27th Annual Int'l. Symposium on Computer Architecture (ISCA)*, June 10–14, 2000, Vancouver, Canada, 192–202.

Dally, W. J. [1990]. "Performance analysis of k-ary n-cube interconnection networks," *IEEE Trans. on Computers* 39:6 (June), 775–785.

Dally, W. J. [1992]. "Virtual channel flow control," *IEEE Trans. on Parallel and Distributed Systems* 3:2 (March), 194–205.

Dally, W. J. [1999]. "Interconnect limited VLSI architecture," *Proc. of the International Interconnect Technology Conference*, May 24–26, 1999, San Francisco.

Dally, W. J., and C. I. Seitz [1986]. "The torus routing chip," *Distributed Computing* 1:4, 187–196.

Dally, W. J., and B. Towles [2001]. "Route packets, not wires: On-chip interconnection networks," *Proc. 38th Design Automation Conference*, June 18–22, 2001, Las Vegas.

Dally, W. J., and B. Towles [2003]. *Principles and Practices of Interconnection Networks*, Morgan Kaufmann, San Francisco.

Darcy, J. D., and D. Gay [1996]. "FLECKmarks: Measuring floating point performance using a full IEEE compliant arithmetic benchmark," CS 252 class project, University of California, Berkeley (see *HTTP.CS.Berkeley.EDU/~darcy/Projects/cs252/*).

Darley, H. M. et al. [1989]. "Floating Point/Integer Processor with Divide and Square Root Functions," U.S. Patent 4,878,190, October 31.

Davidson, E. S. [1971]. "The design and control of pipelined function generators," *Proc. IEEE Conf. on Systems, Networks, and Computers*, January 19–21, 1971, Oaxtepec, Mexico, 19–21.

Davidson, E. S., A. T. Thomas, L. E. Shar, and J. H. Patel [1975]. "Effective control for pipelined processors," *Proc. IEEE COMPCON*, February 25–27, 1975, San Francisco, 181–184.

Davie, B. S., L. L. Peterson, and D. Clark [1999]. *Computer Networks: A Systems Approach*, 2nd ed., Morgan Kaufmann, San Francisco.

Dean, J. [2009]. "Designs, lessons and advice from building large distributed systems [keynote address]," *Proc. 3rd ACM SIGOPS Int'l. Workshop on Large-Scale Distributed Systems and Middleware, Co-located with the 22nd ACM Symposium on Operating Systems Principles*, October 11–14, 2009, Big Sky, Mont.

Dean, J., and S. Ghemawat [2004]. "MapReduce: Simplified data processing on large clusters." In *Proc. Operating Systems Design and Implementation (OSDI)*, December 6–8, 2004, San Francisco, Calif., 137–150.

Dean, J., and S. Ghemawat [2008]. "MapReduce: Simplified data processing on large clusters," *Communications of the ACM*, 51:1, 107–113.

DeCandia, G., D. Hastorun, M. Jampani, G. Kakulapati, A. Lakshman, A. Pilchin, S. Sivasubramanian, P. Vosshall, and W. Vogels [2007]. "Dynamo: Amazon's highly available key-value store," *Proc. 21st ACM Symposium on Operating Systems Principles*, October 14–17, 2007, Stevenson, Wash.

Dehnert, J. C., P. Y.-T. Hsu, and J. P. Bratt [1989]. "Overlapped loop support on the Cydra 5," *Proc. Third Int'l. Conf. on Architectural Support for Programming Languages and Operating Systems (ASPLOS)*, April 3–6, 1989, Boston, Mass., 26–39.

Demmel, J. W., and X. Li [1994]. "Faster numerical algorithms via exception handling," *IEEE Trans. on Computers* 43:8, 983–992.

Denehy, T. E., J. Bent, F. I. Popovici, A. C. Arpaci-Dusseau, and R. H. Arpaci-Dusseau [2004]. "Deconstructing storage arrays," *Proc. 11th Int'l. Conf. on Architectural Support for Programming Languages and Operating Systems (ASPLOS)*, October 7–13, 2004, Boston, Mass., 59–71.

Desurvire, E. [1992]. "Lightwave communications: The fifth generation," *Scientific American* (International Edition) 266:1 (January), 96–103.

Diep, T. A., C. Nelson, and J. P. Shen [1995]. "Performance evaluation of the PowerPC 620 microarchitecture," *Proc. 22nd Annual Int'l. Symposium on Computer Architecture (ISCA)*, June 22–24, 1995, Santa Margherita, Italy.

Digital Semiconductor. [1996]. *Alpha Architecture Handbook, Version 3*, Digital Press, Maynard, Mass.

Ditzel, D. R., and H. R. McLellan [1987]. "Branch folding in the CRISP microprocessor: Reducing the branch delay to zero," *Proc. 14th Annual Int'l. Symposium on Computer Architecture (ISCA)*, June 2–5, 1987, Pittsburgh, Penn., 2–7.

Ditzel, D. R., and D. A. Patterson [1980]. "Retrospective on high-level language computer architecture," *Proc. Seventh Annual Int'l. Symposium on Computer Architecture (ISCA)*, May 6–8, 1980, La Baule, France, 97–104.

Doherty, W. J., and R. P. Kelisky [1979]. "Managing VM/CMS systems for user effectiveness," *IBM Systems J.* 18:1, 143–166.

Dongarra, J. J. [1986]. "A survey of high performance processors," *Proc. IEEE COMPCON*, March 3–6, 1986, San Francisco, 8–11.

Dongarra, J., T. Sterling, H. Simon, and E. Strohmaier [2005]. "High-performance computing: Clusters, constellations, MPPs, and future directions," *Computing in Science & Engineering*, 7:2 (March/April), 51–59.

Douceur, J. R., and W. J. Bolosky [1999]. "A large scale study of file-system contents," *Proc. ACM SIGMETRICS Conf. on Measurement and Modeling of Computer Systems*, May 1–9, 1999, Atlanta, Ga., 59–69.

Douglas, J. [2005]. "Intel 8xx series and Paxville Xeon-MP microprocessors," paper presented at Hot Chips 17, August 14–16, 2005, Stanford University, Palo Alto, Calif.

Duato, J. [1993]. "A new theory of deadlock-free adaptive routing in wormhole networks," *IEEE Trans. on Parallel and Distributed Systems* 4:12 (December) 1320–1331.

Duato, J., and T. M. Pinkston [2001]. "A general theory for deadlock-free adaptive routing using a mixed set of resources," *IEEE Trans. on Parallel and Distributed Systems* 12:12 (December), 1219–1235.

Duato, J., S. Yalamanchili, and L. Ni [2003]. *Interconnection Networks: An Engineering Approach*, 2nd printing, Morgan Kaufmann, San Francisco.

Duato, J., I. Johnson, J. Flich, F. Naven, P. Garcia, and T. Nachiondo [2005a]. "A new scalable and cost-effective congestion management strategy for lossless multistage interconnection networks," *Proc. 11th Int'l. Symposium on High-Performance Computer Architecture*, February 12–16, 2005, San Francisco.

Duato, J., O. Lysne, R. Pang, and T. M. Pinkston [2005b]. "Part I: A theory for deadlock-free dynamic reconfiguration of interconnection networks," *IEEE Trans. on Parallel and Distributed Systems* 16:5 (May), 412–427.

Dubois, M., C. Scheurich, and F. Briggs [1988]. "Synchronization, coherence, and event ordering," *IEEE Computer* 21:2 (February), 9–21.

Dunigan, W., K. Vetter, K. White, and P. Worley [2005]. "Performance evaluation of the Cray X1 distributed shared memory architecture," *IEEE Micro* January/February, 30–40.

Eden, A., and T. Mudge [1998]. "The YAGS branch prediction scheme," *Proc. of the 31st Annual ACM/IEEE Int'l. Symposium on Microarchitecture*, November 30–December 2, 1998, Dallas, Tex., 69–80.

Edmondson, J. H., P. I. Rubinfield, R. Preston, and V. Rajagopalan [1995]. "Superscalar instruction execution in the 21164 Alpha microprocessor," *IEEE Micro* 15:2, 33–43.

Eggers, S. [1989]. "Simulation Analysis of Data Sharing in Shared Memory Multiprocessors," Ph.D. thesis, University of California, Berkeley.

Elder, J., A. Gottlieb, C. K. Kruskal, K. P. McAuliffe, L. Randolph, M. Snir, P. Teller, and J. Wilson [1985]. "Issues related to MIMD shared-memory computers: The NYU Ultracomputer approach," *Proc. 12th Annual Int'l. Symposium on Computer Architecture (ISCA)*, June 17–19, 1985, Boston, Mass., 126–135.

Ellis, J. R. [1986]. *Bulldog: A Compiler for VLIW Architectures*, MIT Press, Cambridge, Mass.

Emer, J. S., and D. W. Clark [1984]. "A characterization of processor performance in the VAX-11/780," *Proc. 11th Annual Int'l. Symposium on Computer Architecture (ISCA)*, June 5–7, 1984, Ann Arbor, Mich., 301–310.

Enriquez, P. [2001]. "What happened to my dial tone? A study of FCC service disruption reports," poster, *Richard Tapia Symposium on the Celebration of Diversity in Computing*, October 18–20, Houston, Tex.

Erlichson, A., N. Nuckolls, G. Chesson, and J. L. Hennessy [1996]. "SoftFLASH: Analyzing the performance of clustered distributed virtual shared memory," *Proc. Seventh Int'l. Conf. on Architectural Support for Programming Languages and Operating Systems (ASPLOS)*, October 1–5, 1996, Cambridge, Mass., 210–220.

Esmaeilzadeh, H., T. Cao, Y. Xi, S. M. Blackburn, and K. S. McKinley [2011]. "Looking Back on the Language and Hardware Revolution: Measured Power, Performance, and Scaling," *Proc. 16th Int'l. Conf. on Architectural Support for Programming Languages and Operating Systems (ASPLOS)*, March 5–11, 2011, Newport Beach, Calif.

Evers, M., S. J. Patel, R. S. Chappell, and Y. N. Patt [1998]. "An analysis of correlation and predictability: What makes two-level branch predictors work," *Proc. 25th Annual Int'l. Symposium on Computer Architecture (ISCA)*, July 3–14, 1998, Barcelona, Spain, 52–61.

Fabry, R. S. [1974]. "Capability based addressing," *Communications of the ACM* 17:7 (July), 403–412.

Falsafi, B., and D. A. Wood [1997]. "Reactive NUMA: A design for unifying S-COMA and CC-NUMA," *Proc. 24th Annual Int'l. Symposium on Computer Architecture (ISCA)*, June 2–4, 1997, Denver, Colo., 229–240.

Fan, X., W. Weber, and L. A. Barroso [2007]. "Power provisioning for a warehouse-sized computer," *Proc. 34th Annual Int'l. Symposium on Computer Architecture (ISCA)*, June 9–13, 2007, San Diego, Calif.

Farkas, K. I., and N. P. Jouppi [1994]. "Complexity/performance trade-offs with non-blocking loads," *Proc. 21st Annual Int'l. Symposium on Computer Architecture (ISCA)*, April 18–21, 1994, Chicago.

Farkas, K. I., N. P. Jouppi, and P. Chow [1995]. "How useful are non-blocking loads, stream buffers and speculative execution in multiple issue processors?," *Proc. First IEEE Symposium on High-Performance Computer Architecture*, January 22–25, 1995, Raleigh, N.C., 78–89.

Farkas, K. I., P. Chow, N. P. Jouppi, and Z. Vranesic [1997]. "Memory-system design considerations for dynamically-scheduled processors," *Proc. 24th Annual Int'l. Symposium on Computer Architecture (ISCA)*, June 2–4, 1997, Denver, Colo., 133–143.

Fazio, D. [1987]. "It's really much more fun building a supercomputer than it is simply inventing one," *Proc. IEEE COMPCON*, February 23–27, 1987, San Francisco, 102–105.

Fisher, J. A. [1981]. "Trace scheduling: A technique for global microcode compaction," *IEEE Trans. on Computers* 30:7 (July), 478–490.

Fisher, J. A. [1983]. "Very long instruction word architectures and ELI-512," *10th Annual Int'l. Symposium on Computer Architecture (ISCA)*, June 5–7, 1982, Stockholm, Sweden, 140–150.

Fisher, J. A., and S. M. Freudenberger [1992]. "Predicting conditional branches from previous runs of a program," *Proc. Fifth Int'l. Conf. on Architectural Support for Programming Languages and Operating Systems (ASPLOS)*, October 12–15, 1992, Boston, Mass., 85–95.

Fisher, J. A., and B. R. Rau [1993]. *Journal of Supercomputing*, January (special issue).

Fisher, J. A., J. R. Ellis, J. C. Ruttenberg, and A. Nicolau [1984]. "Parallel processing: A smart compiler and a dumb processor," *Proc. SIGPLAN Conf. on Compiler Construction*, June 17–22, 1984, Montreal, Canada, 11–16.

Flemming, P. J., and J. J. Wallace [1986]. "How not to lie with statistics: The correct way to summarize benchmarks results," *Communications of the ACM* 29:3 (March), 218–221.

Flynn, M. J. [1966]. "Very high-speed computing systems," *Proc. IEEE* 54:12 (December), 1901–1909.

Forgie, J. W. [1957]. "The Lincoln TX-2 input-output system," *Proc. Western Joint Computer Conference* (February), Institute of Radio Engineers, Los Angeles, 156–160.

Foster, C. C., and E. M. Riseman [1972]. "Percolation of code to enhance parallel dispatching and execution," *IEEE Trans. on Computers* C-21:12 (December), 1411–1415.

Frank, S. J. [1984]. "Tightly coupled multiprocessor systems speed memory access time," *Electronics* 57:1 (January), 164–169.

Freiman, C. V. [1961]. "Statistical analysis of certain binary division algorithms," *Proc. IRE* 49:1, 91–103.

Friesenborg, S. E., and R. J. Wicks [1985]. *DASD Expectations: The 3380, 3380-23, and MVS/XA*, Tech. Bulletin GG22-9363-02, IBM Washington Systems Center, Gaithersburg, Md.

Fuller, S. H., and W. E. Burr [1977]. "Measurement and evaluation of alternative computer architectures," *Computer* 10:10 (October), 24–35.

Furber, S. B. [1996]. *ARM System Architecture*, Addison-Wesley, Harlow, England (see *www.cs.man.ac.uk/amulet/publications/books/ARMsysArch*).

Gagliardi, U. O. [1973]. "Report of workshop 4—software-related advances in computer hardware," *Proc. Symposium on the High Cost of Software*, September 17–19, 1973, Monterey, Calif., 99–120.

Gajski, D., D. Kuck, D. Lawrie, and A. Sameh [1983]. "CEDAR—a large scale multiprocessor," *Proc. Int'l. Conf. on Parallel Processing (ICPP)*, August, Columbus, Ohio, 524–529.

Gallagher, D. M., W. Y. Chen, S. A. Mahlke, J. C. Gyllenhaal, and W. W. Hwu [1994]. "Dynamic memory disambiguation using the memory conflict buffer," *Proc. Sixth Int'l. Conf. on Architectural Support for Programming Languages and Operating Systems (ASPLOS)*, October 4–7, Santa Jose, Calif., 183–193.

Galles, M. [1996]. "Scalable pipelined interconnect for distributed endpoint routing: The SGI SPIDER chip," *Proc. IEEE HOT Interconnects '96*, August 15–17, 1996, Stanford University, Palo Alto, Calif.

Game, M., and A. Booker [1999]. "CodePack code compression for PowerPC processors," *MicroNews*, 5:1, *www.chips.ibm.com/micronews/vol5_no1/codepack.html*.

Gao, Q. S. [1993]. "The Chinese remainder theorem and the prime memory system," *20th Annual Int'l. Symposium on Computer Architecture (ISCA)*, May 16–19, 1993, San Diego, Calif. (*Computer Architecture News* 21:2 (May), 337–340).

Gap. [2005]. "Gap Inc. Reports Third Quarter Earnings," *http://gapinc.com/public/documents/PR_Q405EarningsFeb2306.pdf*.

Gap. [2006]. "Gap Inc. Reports Fourth Quarter and Full Year Earnings," *http://gapinc.com/public/documents/Q32005PressRelease_Final22.pdff*.

Garner, R., A. Agarwal, F. Briggs, E. Brown, D. Hough, B. Joy, S. Kleiman, S. Muchnick, M. Namjoo, D. Patterson, J. Pendleton, and R. Tuck [1988]. "Scalable processor architecture (SPARC)," *Proc. IEEE COMPCON*, February 29–March 4, 1988, San Francisco, 278–283.

Gebis, J., and D. Patterson [2007]. "Embracing and extending 20th-century instruction set architectures," *IEEE Computer* 40:4 (April), 68–75.

Gee, J. D., M. D. Hill, D. N. Pnevmatikatos, and A. J. Smith [1993]. "Cache performance of the SPEC92 benchmark suite," *IEEE Micro* 13:4 (August), 17–27.

Gehringer, E. F., D. P. Siewiorek, and Z. Segall [1987]. *Parallel Processing: The Cm* Experience*, Digital Press, Bedford, Mass.

Gharachorloo, K., A. Gupta, and J. L. Hennessy [1992]. "Hiding memory latency using dynamic scheduling in shared-memory multiprocessors," *Proc. 19th Annual Int'l. Symposium on Computer Architecture (ISCA)*, May 19–21, 1992, Gold Coast, Australia.

Gharachorloo, K., D. Lenoski, J. Laudon, P. Gibbons, A. Gupta, and J. L. Hennessy [1990]. "Memory consistency and event ordering in scalable shared-memory multiprocessors," *Proc. 17th Annual Int'l. Symposium on Computer Architecture (ISCA)*, May 28–31, 1990, Seattle, Wash., 15–26.

Ghemawat, S., H. Gobioff, and S.-T. Leung [2003]. "The Google file system," *Proc. 19th ACM Symposium on Operating Systems Principles*, October 19–22, 2003, Bolton Landing, N.Y.

Gibson, D. H. [1967]. "Considerations in block-oriented systems design," *AFIPS Conf. Proc.* 30, 75–80.

Gibson, G. A. [1992]. *Redundant Disk Arrays: Reliable, Parallel Secondary Storage*, ACM Distinguished Dissertation Series, MIT Press, Cambridge, Mass.

Gibson, J. C. [1970]. "The Gibson mix," Rep. TR. 00.2043, IBM Systems Development Division, Poughkeepsie, N.Y. (research done in 1959).

Gibson, J., R. Kunz, D. Ofelt, M. Horowitz, J. Hennessy, and M. Heinrich [2000]. "FLASH vs. (simulated) FLASH: Closing the simulation loop," *Proc. Ninth Int'l. Conf. on Architectural Support for Programming Languages and Operating Systems (ASPLOS)*, November 12–15, Cambridge, Mass., 49–58.

Glass, C. J., and L. M. Ni [1992]. "The Turn Model for adaptive routing," *19th Annual Int'l. Symposium on Computer Architecture (ISCA)*, May 19–21, 1992, Gold Coast, Australia.

Goldberg, D. [1991]. "What every computer scientist should know about floating-point arithmetic," *Computing Surveys* 23:1, 5–48.

Goldberg, I. B. [1967]. "27 bits are not enough for 8-digit accuracy," *Communications of the ACM* 10:2, 105–106.

Goldstein, S. [1987]. *Storage Performance—An Eight Year Outlook*, Tech. Rep. TR 03.308-1, Santa Teresa Laboratory, IBM Santa Teresa Laboratory, San Jose, Calif.

Goldstine, H. H. [1972]. *The Computer: From Pascal to von Neumann*, Princeton University Press, Princeton, N.J.

González, J., and A. González [1998]. "Limits of instruction level parallelism with data speculation," *Proc. Vector and Parallel Processing (VECPAR) Conf.*, June 21–23, 1998, Porto, Portugal, 585–598.

Goodman, J. R. [1983]. "Using cache memory to reduce processor memory traffic," *Proc. 10th Annual Int'l. Symposium on Computer Architecture (ISCA)*, June 5–7, 1982, Stockholm, Sweden, 124–131.

Goralski, W. [1997]. *SONET: A Guide to Synchronous Optical Network*, McGraw-Hill, New York.

Gosling, J. B. [1980]. *Design of Arithmetic Units for Digital Computers*, Springer-Verlag, New York.

Gray, J. [1990]. "A census of Tandem system availability between 1985 and 1990," *IEEE Trans. on Reliability*, 39:4 (October), 409–418.

Gray, J. (ed.) [1993]. *The Benchmark Handbook for Database and Transaction Processing Systems*, 2nd ed., Morgan Kaufmann, San Francisco.

Gray, J. [2006]. Sort benchmark home page, *http://sortbenchmark.org/*.

Gray, J., and A. Reuter [1993]. *Transaction Processing: Concepts and Techniques*, Morgan Kaufmann, San Francisco.

Gray, J., and D. P. Siewiorek [1991]. "High-availability computer systems," *Computer* 24:9 (September), 39–48.

Gray, J., and C. van Ingen [2005]. *Empirical Measurements of Disk Failure Rates and Error Rates*, MSR-TR-2005-166, Microsoft Research, Redmond, Wash.

Greenberg, A., N. Jain, S. Kandula, C. Kim, P. Lahiri, D. Maltz, P. Patel, and S. Sengupta [2009]. "VL2: A Scalable and Flexible Data Center Network," in *Proc. ACM SIGCOMM*, August 17–21, 2009, Barcelona, Spain.

Grice, C., and M. Kanellos [2000]. "Cell phone industry at crossroads: Go high or low?," *CNET News*, August 31, *technews.netscape.com/news/0-1004-201-2518386-0.html?tag=st.ne.1002.tgif.sf.*

Groe, J. B., and L. E. Larson [2000]. *CDMA Mobile Radio Design*, Artech House, Boston.

Gunther, K. D. [1981]. "Prevention of deadlocks in packet-switched data transport systems," *IEEE Trans. on Communications* COM–29:4 (April), 512–524.

Hagersten, E., and M. Koster [1998]. "WildFire: A scalable path for SMPs," *Proc. Fifth Int'l. Symposium on High-Performance Computer Architecture*, January 9–12, 1999, Orlando, Fla.

Hagersten, E., A. Landin, and S. Haridi [1992]. "DDM—a cache-only memory architecture," *IEEE Computer* 25:9 (September), 44–54.

Hamacher, V. C., Z. G. Vranesic, and S. G. Zaky [1984]. *Computer Organization*, 2nd ed., McGraw-Hill, New York.

Hamilton, J. [2009]. "Data center networks are in my way," paper presented at the Stanford Clean Slate CTO Summit, October 23, 2009 (*http://mvdirona.com/jrh/TalksAndPapers/JamesHamilton_CleanSlateCTO2009.pdf*).

Hamilton, J. [2010]. "Cloud computing economies of scale," paper presented at the *AWS Workshop on Genomics and Cloud Computing*, June 8, 2010, Seattle, Wash. (*http://mvdirona.com/jrh/TalksAndPapers/JamesHamilton_GenomicsCloud20100608.pdf*).

Handy, J. [1993]. *The Cache Memory Book*, Academic Press, Boston.

Hauck, E. A., and B. A. Dent [1968]. "Burroughs' B6500/B7500 stack mechanism," *Proc. AFIPS Spring Joint Computer Conf.*, April 30–May 2, 1968, Atlantic City, N.J., 245–251.

Heald, R., K. Aingaran, C. Amir, M. Ang, M. Boland, A. Das, P. Dixit, G. Gouldsberry, J. Hart, T. Horel, W.-J. Hsu, J. Kaku, C. Kim, S. Kim, F. Klass, H. Kwan, R. Lo, H. McIntyre, A. Mehta, D. Murata, S. Nguyen, Y.-P. Pai, S. Patel, K. Shin, K. Tam, S. Vishwanthaiah, J. Wu, G. Yee, and H. You [2000]. "Implementation of third-generation SPARC V9 64-b microprocessor," *ISSCC Digest of Technical Papers*, 412–413 and slide supplement.

Heinrich, J. [1993]. *MIPS R4000 User's Manual*, Prentice Hall, Englewood Cliffs, N.J.

Henly, M., and B. McNutt [1989]. *DASD I/O Characteristics: A Comparison of MVS to VM*," Tech. Rep. TR 02.1550 (May), IBM General Products Division, San Jose, Calif.

Hennessy, J. [1984]. "VLSI processor architecture," *IEEE Trans. on Computers* C-33:11 (December), 1221–1246.

Hennessy, J. [1985]. "VLSI RISC processors," *VLSI Systems Design* 6:10 (October), 22–32.

Hennessy, J., N. Jouppi, F. Baskett, and J. Gill [1981]. "MIPS: A VLSI processor architecture," in *CMU Conference on VLSI Systems and Computations*, Computer Science Press, Rockville, Md.

Hewlett-Packard. [1994]. *PA-RISC 2.0 Architecture Reference Manual*, 3rd ed., Hewlett-Packard, Palo Alto, Calif.

Hewlett-Packard. [1998]. "HP's '5NINES:5MINUTES' Vision Extends Leadership and Redefines High Availability in Mission-Critical Environments," February 10, *www.future.enterprisecomputing.hp.com/ia64/news/5nines_vision_pr.html*.

Hill, M. D. [1987]. "Aspects of Cache Memory and Instruction Buffer Performance," Ph.D. thesis, Tech. Rep. UCB/CSD 87/381, Computer Science Division, University of California, Berkeley.

Hill, M. D. [1988]. "A case for direct mapped caches," *Computer* 21:12 (December), 25–40.

Hill, M. D. [1998]. "Multiprocessors should support simple memory consistency models," *IEEE Computer* 31:8 (August), 28–34.

Hillis, W. D. [1985]. *The Connection Multiprocessor*, MIT Press, Cambridge, Mass.

Hillis, W. D. and G. L. Steele [1986]. "Data parallel algorithms," *Communications of the ACM* 29:12 (December), 1170–1183. (*http://doi.acm.org/10.1145/7902.7903*).

Hinton, G., D. Sager, M. Upton, D. Boggs, D. Carmean, A. Kyker, and P. Roussel [2001]. "The microarchitecture of the Pentium 4 processor," *Intel Technology Journal*, February.

Hintz, R. G., and D. P. Tate [1972]. "Control data STAR-100 processor design," *Proc. IEEE COMPCON*, September 12–14, 1972, San Francisco, 1–4.

Hirata, H., K. Kimura, S. Nagamine, Y. Mochizuki, A. Nishimura, Y. Nakase, and T. Nishizawa [1992]. "An elementary processor architecture with simultaneous instruction issuing from multiple threads," *Proc. 19th Annual Int'l. Symposium on Computer Architecture (ISCA)*, May 19–21, 1992, Gold Coast, Australia, 136–145.

Hitachi. [1997]. *SuperH RISC Engine SH7700 Series Programming Manual*, Hitachi, Santa Clara, Calif. (see *www.halsp.hitachi.com/tech_prod/* and search for title).

Ho, R., K. W. Mai, and M. A. Horowitz [2001]. "The future of wires," *Proc. of the IEEE* 89:4 (April), 490–504.

Hoagland, A. S. [1963]. *Digital Magnetic Recording*, Wiley, New York.

Hockney, R. W., and C. R. Jesshope [1988]. *Parallel Computers 2: Architectures, Programming and Algorithms*, Adam Hilger, Ltd., Bristol, England.

Holland, J. H. [1959]. "A universal computer capable of executing an arbitrary number of subprograms simultaneously," *Proc. East Joint Computer Conf.* 16, 108–113.

Holt, R. C. [1972]. "Some deadlock properties of computer systems," *ACM Computer Surveys* 4:3 (September), 179–196.

Hopkins, M. [2000]. "A critical look at IA-64: Massive resources, massive ILP, but can it deliver?" *Microprocessor Report*, February.

Hord, R. M. [1982]. *The Illiac-IV, The First Supercomputer*, Computer Science Press, Rockville, Md.

Horel, T., and G. Lauterbach [1999]. "UltraSPARC-III: Designing third-generation 64-bit performance," *IEEE Micro* 19:3 (May–June), 73–85.

Hospodor, A. D., and A. S. Hoagland [1993]. "The changing nature of disk controllers." *Proc. IEEE* 81:4 (April), 586–594.

Hölzle, U. [2010]. "Brawny cores still beat wimpy cores, most of the time," *IEEE Micro* 30:4 (July/August).

Hristea, C., D. Lenoski, and J. Keen [1997]. "Measuring memory hierarchy performance of cache-coherent multiprocessors using micro benchmarks," *Proc. ACM/IEEE Conf. on Supercomputing*, November 16–21, 1997, San Jose, Calif.

Hsu, P. [1994]. "Designing the TFP microprocessor," *IEEE Micro* 18:2 (April), 2333.

Huck, J. et al. [2000]. "Introducing the IA-64 Architecture" *IEEE Micro*, 20:5 (September–October), 12–23.

Hughes, C. J., P. Kaul, S. V. Adve, R. Jain, C. Park, and J. Srinivasan [2001]. "Variability in the execution of multimedia applications and implications for architecture," *Proc. 28th Annual Int'l. Symposium on Computer Architecture (ISCA)*, June 30–July 4, 2001, Goteborg, Sweden, 254–265.

Hwang, K. [1979]. *Computer Arithmetic: Principles, Architecture, and Design*, Wiley, New York.

Hwang, K. [1993]. *Advanced Computer Architecture and Parallel Programming*, McGraw-Hill, New York.

Hwu, W.-M., and Y. Patt [1986]. "HPSm, a high performance restricted data flow architecture having minimum functionality," *Proc. 13th Annual Int'l. Symposium on Computer Architecture (ISCA)*, June 2–5, 1986, Tokyo, 297–307.

Hwu, W. W., S. A. Mahlke, W. Y. Chen, P. P. Chang, N. J. Warter, R. A. Bringmann, R. O. Ouellette, R. E. Hank, T. Kiyohara, G. E. Haab, J. G. Holm, and D. M. Lavery [1993]. "The superblock: An effective technique for VLIW and superscalar compilation," *J. Supercomputing* 7:1, 2 (March), 229–248.

IBM. [1982]. *The Economic Value of Rapid Response Time*, GE20-0752-0, IBM, White Plains, N.Y., 11–82.

IBM. [1990]. "The IBM RISC System/6000 processor" (collection of papers), *IBM J. Research and Development* 34:1 (January).

IBM. [1994]. *The PowerPC Architecture*, Morgan Kaufmann, San Francisco.

IBM. [2005]. "Blue Gene," *IBM J. Research and Development*, 49:2/3 (special issue).

IEEE. [1985]. "IEEE standard for binary floating-point arithmetic," *SIGPLAN Notices* 22:2, 9–25.

IEEE. [2005]. "Intel virtualization technology, computer," *IEEE Computer Society* 38:5 (May), 48–56.

IEEE. 754-2008 Working Group. [2006]. "DRAFT Standard for Floating-Point Arithmetic 754-2008," *http://dx.doi.org/10.1109/IEEESTD.2008.4610935*.

Imprimis Product Specification, 97209 Sabre Disk Drive IPI-2 Interface 1.2 GB, Document No. 64402302, Imprimis, Dallas, Tex.

InfiniBand Trade Association. [2001]. *InfiniBand Architecture Specifications Release 1.0.a, www.infinibandta.org.*

Intel. [2001]. "Using MMX Instructions to Convert RGB to YUV Color Conversion," *cedar.intel.com/cgi-bin/ids.dll/content/content.jsp?cntKey=Legacy::irtm_AP548_9996& cntType=IDS_ EDITORIAL.*

Internet Retailer. [2005]. "The Gap launches a new site—after two weeks of downtime," *Internet® Retailer,* September 28, *http://www.internetretailer.com/2005/09/28/the-gap-launches-a-new-site-after-two-weeks-of-downtime.*

Jain, R. [1991]. *The Art of Computer Systems Performance Analysis: Techniques for Experimental Design, Measurement, Simulation, and Modeling,* Wiley, New York.

Jantsch, A., and H. Tenhunen (eds.) [2003]. *Networks on Chips,* Kluwer Academic Publishers, The Netherlands.

Jimenez, D. A., and C. Lin [2002]. "Neural methods for dynamic branch prediction," *ACM Trans. on Computer Systems* 20:4 (November), 369–397.

Johnson, M. [1990]. *Superscalar Microprocessor Design,* Prentice Hall, Englewood Cliffs, N.J.

Jordan, H. F. [1983]. "Performance measurements on HEP—a pipelined MIMD computer," *Proc. 10th Annual Int'l. Symposium on Computer Architecture (ISCA),* June 5–7, 1982, Stockholm, Sweden, 207–212.

Jordan, K. E. [1987]. "Performance comparison of large-scale scientific processors: Scalar mainframes, mainframes with vector facilities, and supercomputers," *Computer* 20:3 (March), 10–23.

Jouppi, N. P. [1990]. "Improving direct-mapped cache performance by the addition of a small fully-associative cache and prefetch buffers," *Proc. 17th Annual Int'l. Symposium on Computer Architecture (ISCA),* May 28–31, 1990, Seattle, Wash., 364–373.

Jouppi, N. P. [1998]. "Retrospective: Improving direct-mapped cache performance by the addition of a small fully-associative cache and prefetch buffers," *25 Years of the International Symposia on Computer Architecture (Selected Papers),* ACM, New York, 71–73.

Jouppi, N. P., and D. W. Wall [1989]. "Available instruction-level parallelism for superscalar and superpipelined processors," *Proc. Third Int'l. Conf. on Architectural Support for Programming Languages and Operating Systems (ASPLOS),* April 3–6, 1989, Boston, 272–282.

Jouppi, N. P., and S. J. E. Wilton [1994]. "Trade-offs in two-level on-chip caching," *Proc. 21st Annual Int'l. Symposium on Computer Architecture (ISCA),* April 18–21, 1994, Chicago, 34–45.

Kaeli, D. R., and P. G. Emma [1991]. "Branch history table prediction of moving target branches due to subroutine returns," *Proc. 18th Annual Int'l. Symposium on Computer Architecture (ISCA),* May 27–30, 1991, Toronto, Canada, 34–42.

Kahan, J. [1990]. "On the advantage of the 8087's stack," unpublished course notes, Computer Science Division, University of California, Berkeley.

Kahan, W. [1968]. "7094-II system support for numerical analysis," *SHARE Secretarial Distribution* SSD-159, Department of Computer Science, University of Toronto.

Kahaner, D. K. [1988]. "Benchmarks for 'real' programs," *SIAM News,* November.

Kahn, R. E. [1972]. "Resource-sharing computer communication networks," *Proc. IEEE* 60:11 (November), 1397–1407.

Kane, G. [1986]. *MIPS R2000 RISC Architecture,* Prentice Hall, Englewood Cliffs, N.J.

Kane, G. [1996]. *PA-RISC 2.0 Architecture,* Prentice Hall, Upper Saddle River, N.J.

Kane, G., and J. Heinrich [1992]. *MIPS RISC Architecture,* Prentice Hall, Englewood Cliffs, N.J.

Katz, R. H., D. A. Patterson, and G. A. Gibson [1989]. "Disk system architectures for high performance computing," *Proc. IEEE* 77:12 (December), 1842–1858.

Keckler, S. W., and W. J. Dally [1992]. "Processor coupling: Integrating compile time and runtime scheduling for parallelism," *Proc. 19th Annual Int'l. Symposium on Computer Architecture (ISCA)*, May 19–21, 1992, Gold Coast, Australia, 202–213.

Keller, R. M. [1975]. "Look-ahead processors," *ACM Computing Surveys* 7:4 (December), 177–195.

Keltcher, C. N., K. J. McGrath, A. Ahmed, and P. Conway [2003]. "The AMD Opteron processor for multiprocessor servers," *IEEE Micro* 23:2 (March–April), 66–76 (dx.doi.org/10.1109.MM.2003.119116).

Kembel, R. [2000]. "Fibre Channel: A comprehensive introduction," *Internet Week*, April.

Kermani, P., and L. Kleinrock [1979]. "Virtual Cut-Through: A New Computer Communication Switching Technique," *Computer Networks* 3 (January), 267–286.

Kessler, R. [1999]. "The Alpha 21264 microprocessor," *IEEE Micro* 19:2 (March/April) 24–36.

Kilburn, T., D. B. G. Edwards, M. J. Lanigan, and F. H. Sumner [1962]. "One-level storage system," *IRE Trans. on Electronic Computers* EC-11 (April) 223–235. Also appears in D. P. Siewiorek, C. G. Bell, and A. Newell, *Computer Structures: Principles and Examples*, McGraw-Hill, New York, 1982, 135–148.

Killian, E. [1991]. "MIPS R4000 technical overview–64 bits/100 MHz or bust," *Hot Chips III Symposium Record*, August 26–27, 1991, Stanford University, Palo Alto, Calif., 1.6–1.19.

Kim, M. Y. [1986]. "Synchronized disk interleaving," *IEEE Trans. on Computers* C-35:11 (November), 978–988.

Kissell, K. D. [1997]. "MIPS16: High-density for the embedded market," *Proc. Real Time Systems '97*, June 15, 1997, Las Vegas, Nev. (see *www.sgi.com/MIPS/arch/MIPS16/ MIPS16.whitepaper.pdf*).

Kitagawa, K., S. Tagaya, Y. Hagihara, and Y. Kanoh [2003]. "A hardware overview of SX-6 and SX-7 supercomputer," *NEC Research & Development J.* 44:1 (January), 2–7.

Knuth, D. [1981]. *The Art of Computer Programming*, Vol. II, 2nd ed., Addison-Wesley, Reading, Mass.

Kogge, P. M. [1981]. *The Architecture of Pipelined Computers*, McGraw-Hill, New York.

Kohn, L., and S.-W. Fu [1989]. "A 1,000,000 transistor microprocessor," *Proc. of IEEE Int'l. Symposium on Solid State Circuits (ISSCC)*, February 15–17, 1989, New York, 54–55.

Kohn, L., and N. Margulis [1989]. "Introducing the Intel i860 64-Bit Microprocessor," *IEEE Micro*, 9:4 (July), 15–30.

Kontothanassis, L., G. Hunt, R. Stets, N. Hardavellas, M. Cierniak, S. Parthasarathy, W. Meira, S. Dwarkadas, and M. Scott [1997]. "VM-based shared memory on low-latency, remote-memory-access networks," *Proc. 24th Annual Int'l. Symposium on Computer Architecture (ISCA)*, June 2–4, 1997, Denver, Colo.

Koren, I. [1989]. *Computer Arithmetic Algorithms*, Prentice Hall, Englewood Cliffs, N.J.

Kozyrakis, C. [2000]. "Vector IRAM: A media-oriented vector processor with embedded DRAM," paper presented at Hot Chips 12, August 13–15, 2000, Palo Alto, Calif, 13–15.

Kozyrakis, C., and D. Patterson, [2002]. "Vector vs. superscalar and VLIW architectures for embedded multimedia benchmarks," *Proc. 35th Annual Int'l. Symposium on Microarchitecture (MICRO-35)*, November 18–22, 2002, Istanbul, Turkey.

Kroft, D. [1981]. "Lockup-free instruction fetch/prefetch cache organization," *Proc. Eighth Annual Int'l. Symposium on Computer Architecture (ISCA)*, May 12–14, 1981, Minneapolis, Minn., 81–87.

Kroft, D. [1998]. "Retrospective: Lockup-free instruction fetch/prefetch cache organization," *25 Years of the International Symposia on Computer Architecture (Selected Papers)*, ACM, New York, 20–21.

Kuck, D., P. P. Budnik, S.-C. Chen, D. H. Lawrie, R. A. Towle, R. E. Strebendt, E. W. Davis, Jr., J. Han, P. W. Kraska, and Y. Muraoka [1974]. "Measurements of parallelism in ordinary FORTRAN programs," *Computer* 7:1 (January), 37–46.

Kuhn, D. R. [1997]. "Sources of failure in the public switched telephone network," *IEEE Computer* 30:4 (April), 31–36.

Kumar, A. [1997]. "The HP PA-8000 RISC CPU," *IEEE Micro* 17:2 (March/April), 27–32.

Kunimatsu, A., N. Ide, T. Sato, Y. Endo, H. Murakami, T. Kamei, M. Hirano, F. Ishihara, H. Tago, M. Oka, A. Ohba, T. Yutaka, T. Okada, and M. Suzuoki [2000]. "Vector unit architecture for emotion synthesis," *IEEE Micro* 20:2 (March–April), 40–47.

Kunkel, S. R., and J. E. Smith [1986]. "Optimal pipelining in supercomputers," *Proc. 13th Annual Int'l. Symposium on Computer Architecture (ISCA)*, June 2–5, 1986, Tokyo, 404–414.

Kurose, J. F., and K. W. Ross [2001]. *Computer Networking: A Top-Down Approach Featuring the Internet*, Addison-Wesley, Boston.

Kuskin, J., D. Ofelt, M. Heinrich, J. Heinlein, R. Simoni, K. Gharachorloo, J. Chapin, D. Nakahira, J. Baxter, M. Horowitz, A. Gupta, M. Rosenblum, and J. L. Hennessy [1994]. "The Stanford FLASH multiprocessor," *Proc. 21st Annual Int'l. Symposium on Computer Architecture (ISCA)*, April 18–21, 1994, Chicago.

Lam, M. [1988]. "Software pipelining: An effective scheduling technique for VLIW processors," *SIGPLAN Conf. on Programming Language Design and Implementation*, June 22–24, 1988, Atlanta, Ga., 318–328.

Lam, M. S., and R. P. Wilson [1992]. "Limits of control flow on parallelism," *Proc. 19th Annual Int'l. Symposium on Computer Architecture (ISCA)*, May 19–21, 1992, Gold Coast, Australia, 46–57.

Lam, M. S., E. E. Rothberg, and M. E. Wolf [1991]. "The cache performance and optimizations of blocked algorithms," *Proc. Fourth Int'l. Conf. on Architectural Support for Programming Languages and Operating Systems (ASPLOS)*, April 8–11, 1991, Santa Clara, Calif. (*SIGPLAN Notices* 26:4 (April), 63–74).

Lambright, D. [2000]. "Experiences in measuring the reliability of a cache-based storage system," *Proc. of First Workshop on Industrial Experiences with Systems Software (WIESS 2000), Co-Located with the 4th Symposium on Operating Systems Design and Implementation (OSDI)*, October 22, 2000, San Diego, Calif.

Lamport, L. [1979]. "How to make a multiprocessor computer that correctly executes multiprocess programs," *IEEE Trans. on Computers* C-28:9 (September), 241–248.

Lang, W., J. M. Patel, and S. Shankar [2010]. "Wimpy node clusters: What about non-wimpy workloads?" *Proc. Sixth International Workshop on Data Management on New Hardware (DaMoN)*, June 7, Indianapolis, Ind.

Laprie, J.-C. [1985]. "Dependable computing and fault tolerance: Concepts and terminology," *Proc. 15th Annual Int'l. Symposium on Fault-Tolerant Computing*, June 19–21, 1985, Ann Arbor, Mich., 2–11.

Larson, E. R. [1973]. "Findings of fact, conclusions of law, and order for judgment," File No. 4-67, Civ. 138, *Honeywell v. Sperry-Rand and Illinois Scientific Development*, U.S. District Court for the State of Minnesota, Fourth Division (October 19).

Laudon, J., and D. Lenoski [1997]. "The SGI Origin: A ccNUMA highly scalable server," *Proc. 24th Annual Int'l. Symposium on Computer Architecture (ISCA)*, June 2–4, 1997, Denver, Colo., 241–251.

Laudon, J., A. Gupta, and M. Horowitz [1994]. "Interleaving: A multithreading technique targeting multiprocessors and workstations," *Proc. Sixth Int'l. Conf. on Architectural Support for Programming Languages and Operating Systems (ASPLOS)*, October 4–7, San Jose, Calif., 308–318.

Lauterbach, G., and T. Horel [1999]. "UltraSPARC-III: Designing third generation 64-bit performance," *IEEE Micro* 19:3 (May/June).

Lazowska, E. D., J. Zahorjan, G. S. Graham, and K. C. Sevcik [1984]. *Quantitative System Performance: Computer System Analysis Using Queueing Network Models*, Prentice Hall, Englewood Cliffs, N.J. (Although out of print, it is available online at *www.cs.washington.edu/homes/lazowska/qsp/.*)

Lebeck, A. R., and D. A. Wood [1994]. "Cache profiling and the SPEC benchmarks: A case study," *Computer* 27:10 (October), 15–26.

Lee, R. [1989]. "Precision architecture," *Computer* 22:1 (January), 78–91.

Lee, W. V. et al. [2010]. "Debunking the 100X GPU vs. CPU myth: An evaluation of throughput computing on CPU and GPU," *Proc. 37th Annual Int'l. Symposium on Computer Architecture (ISCA)*, June 19–23, 2010, Saint-Malo, France.

Leighton, F. T. [1992]. *Introduction to Parallel Algorithms and Architectures: Arrays, Trees, Hypercubes*, Morgan Kaufmann, San Francisco.

Leiner, A. L. [1954]. "System specifications for the DYSEAC," *J. ACM* 1:2 (April), 57–81.

Leiner, A. L., and S. N. Alexander [1954]. "System organization of the DYSEAC," *IRE Trans. of Electronic Computers* EC-3:1 (March), 1–10.

Leiserson, C. E. [1985]. "Fat trees: Universal networks for hardware-efficient supercomputing," *IEEE Trans. on Computers* C-34:10 (October), 892–901.

Lenoski, D., J. Laudon, K. Gharachorloo, A. Gupta, and J. L. Hennessy [1990]. "The Stanford DASH multiprocessor," *Proc. 17th Annual Int'l. Symposium on Computer Architecture (ISCA)*, May 28–31, 1990, Seattle, Wash., 148–159.

Lenoski, D., J. Laudon, K. Gharachorloo, W.-D. Weber, A. Gupta, J. L. Hennessy, M. A. Horowitz, and M. Lam [1992]. "The Stanford DASH multiprocessor," *IEEE Computer* 25:3 (March), 63–79.

Levy, H., and R. Eckhouse [1989]. *Computer Programming and Architecture: The VAX*, Digital Press, Boston.

Li, K. [1988]. "IVY: A shared virtual memory system for parallel computing," *Proc. 1988 Int'l. Conf. on Parallel Processing*, Pennsylvania State University Press, University Park, Penn.

Li, S., K. Chen, J. B. Brockman, and N. Jouppi [2011]. "Performance Impacts of Nonblocking Caches in Out-of-order Processors," HP Labs Tech Report HPL-2011-65 (full text available at http://Library.hp.com/techpubs/2011/Hpl-2011-65.html).

Lim, K., P. Ranganathan, J. Chang, C. Patel, T. Mudge, and S. Reinhardt [2008]. "Understanding and designing new system architectures for emerging warehouse-computing environments," *Proc. 35th Annual Int'l. Symposium on Computer Architecture (ISCA)*, June 21–25, 2008, Beijing, China.

Lincoln, N. R. [1982]. "Technology and design trade offs in the creation of a modern supercomputer," *IEEE Trans. on Computers* C-31:5 (May), 363–376.

Lindholm, T., and F. Yellin [1999]. *The Java Virtual Machine Specification*, 2nd ed., Addison-Wesley, Reading, Mass. (also available online at *java.sun.com/docs/ books/ vmspec/*).

Lipasti, M. H., and J. P. Shen [1996]. "Exceeding the dataflow limit via value prediction," *Proc. 29th Int'l. Symposium on Microarchitecture*, December 2–4, 1996, Paris, France.

Lipasti, M. H., C. B. Wilkerson, and J. P. Shen [1996]. "Value locality and load value prediction," *Proc. Seventh Conf. on Architectural Support for Programming Languages and Operating Systems (ASPLOS)*, October 1–5, 1996, Cambridge, Mass., 138–147.

Liptay, J. S. [1968]. "Structural aspects of the System/360 Model 85, Part II: The cache," *IBM Systems J.* 7:1, 15–21.

Lo, J., L. Barroso, S. Eggers, K. Gharachorloo, H. Levy, and S. Parekh [1998]. "An analysis of database workload performance on simultaneous multithreaded processors," *Proc. 25th Annual Int'l. Symposium on Computer Architecture (ISCA)*, July 3–14, 1998, Barcelona, Spain, 39–50.

Lo, J., S. Eggers, J. Emer, H. Levy, R. Stamm, and D. Tullsen [1997]. "Converting thread-level parallelism into instruction-level parallelism via simultaneous multithreading," *ACM Trans. on Computer Systems* 15:2 (August), 322–354.

Lovett, T., and S. Thakkar [1988]. "The Symmetry multiprocessor system," *Proc. 1988 Int'l. Conf. of Parallel Processing*, University Park, Penn., 303–310.

Lubeck, O., J. Moore, and R. Mendez [1985]. "A benchmark comparison of three super-computers: Fujitsu VP-200, Hitachi S810/20, and Cray X-MP/2," *Computer* 18:12 (December), 10–24.

Luk, C.-K., and T. C Mowry [1999]. "Automatic compiler-inserted prefetching for pointer-based applications," *IEEE Trans. on Computers* 48:2 (February), 134–141.

Lunde, A. [1977]. "Empirical evaluation of some features of instruction set processor architecture," *Communications of the ACM* 20:3 (March), 143–152.

Luszczek, P., J. J. Dongarra, D. Koester, R. Rabenseifner, B. Lucas, J. Kepner, J. McCalpin, D. Bailey, and D. Takahashi [2005]. "Introduction to the HPC challenge benchmark suite," Lawrence Berkeley National Laboratory, Paper LBNL-57493 (April 25), *repositories.cdlib.org/lbnl/LBNL-57493*.

Maberly, N. C. [1966]. *Mastering Speed Reading*, New American Library, New York.

Magenheimer, D. J., L. Peters, K. W. Pettis, and D. Zuras [1988]. "Integer multiplication and division on the HP precision architecture," *IEEE Trans. on Computers* 37:8, 980–990.

Mahlke, S. A., W. Y. Chen, W.-M. Hwu, B. R. Rau, and M. S. Schlansker [1992]. "Sentinel scheduling for VLIW and superscalar processors," *Proc. Fifth Int'l. Conf. on Architectural Support for Programming Languages and Operating Systems (ASPLOS)*, October 12–15, 1992, Boston, 238–247.

Mahlke, S. A., R. E. Hank, J. E. McCormick, D. I. August, and W. W. Hwu [1995]. "A comparison of full and partial predicated execution support for ILP processors," *Proc. 22nd Annual Int'l. Symposium on Computer Architecture (ISCA)*, June 22–24, 1995, Santa Margherita, Italy, 138–149.

Major, J. B. [1989]. "Are queuing models within the grasp of the unwashed?," *Proc. Int'l. Conf. on Management and Performance Evaluation of Computer Systems*, December 11–15, 1989, Reno, Nev., 831–839.

Markstein, P. W. [1990]. "Computation of elementary functions on the IBM RISC System/6000 processor," *IBM J. Research and Development* 34:1, 111–119.

Mathis, H. M., A. E. Mercias, J. D. McCalpin, R. J. Eickemeyer, and S. R. Kunkel [2005]. "Characterization of the multithreading (SMT) efficiency in Power5," *IBM J. Research and Development*, 49:4/5 (July/September), 555–564.

McCalpin, J. [2005]. "STREAM: Sustainable Memory Bandwidth in High Performance Computers," *www.cs.virginia.edu/stream/*.

McCalpin, J., D. Bailey, and D. Takahashi [2005]. *Introduction to the HPC Challenge Benchmark Suite*, Paper LBNL-57493 Lawrence Berkeley National Laboratory, University of California, Berkeley, *repositories.cdlib.org/lbnl/LBNL-57493*.

McCormick, J., and A. Knies [2002]. "A brief analysis of the SPEC CPU2000 benchmarks on the Intel Itanium 2 processor," paper presented at Hot Chips 14, August 18–20, 2002, Stanford University, Palo Alto, Calif.

McFarling, S. [1989]. "Program optimization for instruction caches," *Proc. Third Int'l. Conf. on Architectural Support for Programming Languages and Operating Systems (ASPLOS)*, April 3–6, 1989, Boston, 183–191.

McFarling, S. [1993]. *Combining Branch Predictors*, WRL Technical Note TN-36, Digital Western Research Laboratory, Palo Alto, Calif.

McFarling, S., and J. Hennessy [1986]. "Reducing the cost of branches," *Proc. 13th Annual Int'l. Symposium on Computer Architecture (ISCA)*, June 2–5, 1986, Tokyo, 396–403.

McGhan, H., and M. O'Connor [1998]. "PicoJava: A direct execution engine for Java bytecode," *Computer* 31:10 (October), 22–30.

McKeeman, W. M. [1967]. "Language directed computer design," *Proc. AFIPS Fall Joint Computer Conf.*, November 14–16, 1967, Washington, D.C., 413–417.

McMahon, F. M. [1986]. *"The Livermore FORTRAN Kernels: A Computer Test of Numerical Performance Range,"* Tech. Rep. UCRL-55745, Lawrence Livermore National Laboratory, University of California, Livermore.

McNairy, C., and D. Soltis [2003]. "Itanium 2 processor microarchitecture," *IEEE Micro* 23:2 (March–April), 44–55.

Mead, C., and L. Conway [1980]. *Introduction to VLSI Systems*, Addison-Wesley, Reading, Mass.

Mellor-Crummey, J. M., and M. L. Scott [1991]. "Algorithms for scalable synchronization on shared-memory multiprocessors," *ACM Trans. on Computer Systems* 9:1 (February), 21–65.

Menabrea, L. F. [1842]. "Sketch of the analytical engine invented by Charles Babbage," *Bibliothèque Universelle de Genève*, 82 (October).

Menon, A., J. Renato Santos, Y. Turner, G. Janakiraman, and W. Zwaenepoel [2005]. "Diagnosing performance overheads in the xen virtual machine environment," *Proc. First ACM/USENIX Int'l. Conf. on Virtual Execution Environments*, June 11–12, 2005, Chicago, 13–23.

Merlin, P. M., and P. J. Schweitzer [1980]. "Deadlock avoidance in store-and-forward networks. Part I. Store-and-forward deadlock," *IEEE Trans. on Communications* COM-28:3 (March), 345–354.

Metcalfe, R. M. [1993]. "Computer/network interface design: Lessons from Arpanet and Ethernet," *IEEE J. on Selected Areas in Communications* 11:2 (February), 173–180.

Metcalfe, R. M., and D. R. Boggs [1976]. "Ethernet: Distributed packet switching for local computer networks," *Communications of the ACM* 19:7 (July), 395–404.

Metropolis, N., J. Howlett, and G. C. Rota (eds.) [1980]. *A History of Computing in the Twentieth Century*, Academic Press, New York.

Meyer, R. A., and L. H. Seawright [1970]. A virtual machine time sharing system, *IBM Systems J.* 9:3, 199–218.

Meyers, G. J. [1978]. "The evaluation of expressions in a storage-to-storage architecture," *Computer Architecture News* 7:3 (October), 20–23.

Meyers, G. J. [1982]. *Advances in Computer Architecture*, 2nd ed., Wiley, New York.

Micron. [2004]. "Calculating Memory System Power for DDR2," *http://download.micron.com/pdf/pubs/designline/dl1Q04.pdf*.

Micron. [2006]. "The Micron® System-Power Calculator," *http://www.micron.com/systemcalc*.

MIPS. [1997]. "MIPS16 Application Specific Extension Product Description," *www.sgi.com/MIPS/arch/MIPS16/mips16.pdf*.

Miranker, G. S., J. Rubenstein, and J. Sanguinetti [1988]. "Squeezing a Cray-class supercomputer into a single-user package," *Proc. IEEE COMPCON*, February 29–March 4, 1988, San Francisco, 452–456.

Mitchell, D. [1989]. "The Transputer: The time is now," *Computer Design* (RISC suppl.), 40–41.

Mitsubishi. [1996]. *Mitsubishi 32-Bit Single Chip Microcomputer M32R Family Software Manual*, Mitsubishi, Cypress, Calif.

Miura, K., and K. Uchida [1983]. "FACOM vector processing system: VP100/200," *Proc. NATO Advanced Research Workshop on High-Speed Computing*, June 20–22, 1983, Jülich, West Germany. Also appears in K. Hwang, ed., "Superprocessors: Design and applications," *IEEE* (August 1984), 59–73.

Miya, E. N. [1985]. "Multiprocessor/distributed processing bibliography," *Computer Architecture News* 13:1, 27–29.

Montoye, R. K., E. Hokenek, and S. L. Runyon [1990]. "Design of the IBM RISC System/6000 floating-point execution," *IBM J. Research and Development* 34:1, 59–70.

Moore, B., A. Padegs, R. Smith, and W. Bucholz [1987]. "Concepts of the System/370 vector architecture," *14th Annual Int'l. Symposium on Computer Architecture (ISCA)*, June 2–5, 1987, Pittsburgh, Penn., 282–292.

Moore, G. E. [1965]. "Cramming more components onto integrated circuits," *Electronics*, 38:8 (April 19), 114–117.

Morse, S., B. Ravenal, S. Mazor, and W. Pohlman [1980]. "Intel microprocessors—8080 to 8086," *Computer* 13:10 (October).

Moshovos, A., and G. S. Sohi [1997]. "Streamlining inter-operation memory communication via data dependence prediction," *Proc. 30th Annual Int'l. Symposium on Microarchitecture*, December 1–3, Research Triangle Park, N.C., 235–245.

Moshovos, A., S. Breach, T. N. Vijaykumar, and G. S. Sohi [1997]. "Dynamic speculation and synchronization of data dependences," *24th Annual Int'l. Symposium on Computer Architecture (ISCA)*, June 2–4, 1997, Denver, Colo.

Moussouris, J., L. Crudele, D. Freitas, C. Hansen, E. Hudson, S. Przybylski, T. Riordan, and C. Rowen [1986]. "A CMOS RISC processor with integrated system functions," *Proc. IEEE COMPCON*, March 3–6, 1986, San Francisco, 191.

Mowry, T. C., S. Lam, and A. Gupta [1992]. "Design and evaluation of a compiler algorithm for prefetching," *Proc. Fifth Int'l. Conf. on Architectural Support for Programming Languages and Operating Systems (ASPLOS)*, October 12–15, 1992, Boston (*SIGPLAN Notices* 27:9 (September), 62–73).

MSN Money. [2005]. "Amazon Shares Tumble after Rally Fizzles," *http://moneycentral.msn.com/content/CNBCTV/Articles/Dispatches/P133695.asp.*

Muchnick, S. S. [1988]. "Optimizing compilers for SPARC," *Sun Technology* 1:3 (Summer), 64–77.

Mueller, M., L. C. Alves, W. Fischer, M. L. Fair, and I. Modi [1999]. "RAS strategy for IBM S/390 G5 and G6," *IBM J. Research and Development* 43:5–6 (September–November), 875–888.

Mukherjee, S. S., C. Weaver, J. S. Emer, S. K. Reinhardt, and T. M. Austin [2003]. "Measuring architectural vulnerability factors," *IEEE Micro* 23:6, 70–75.

Murphy, B., and T. Gent [1995]. "Measuring system and software reliability using an automated data collection process," *Quality and Reliability Engineering International* 11:5 (September–October), 341–353.

Myer, T. H., and I. E. Sutherland [1968]. "On the design of display processors," *Communications of the ACM* 11:6 (June), 410–414.

Narayanan, D., E. Thereska, A. Donnelly, S. Elnikety, and A. Rowstron [2009]. "Migrating server storage to SSDs: Analysis of trade-offs," *Proc. 4th ACM European Conf. on Computer Systems*, April 1–3, 2009, Nuremberg, Germany.

National Research Council. [1997]. *The Evolution of Untethered Communications*, Computer Science and Telecommunications Board, National Academy Press, Washington, D.C.

National Storage Industry Consortium. [1998]. "Tape Roadmap," *www.nsic.org.*

Nelson, V. P. [1990]. "Fault-tolerant computing: Fundamental concepts," *Computer* 23:7 (July), 19–25.

Ngai, T.-F., and M. J. Irwin [1985]. "Regular, area-time efficient carry-lookahead adders," *Proc. Seventh IEEE Symposium on Computer Arithmetic*, June 4–6, 1985, University of Illinois, Urbana, 9–15.

Nicolau, A., and J. A. Fisher [1984]. "Measuring the parallelism available for very long instruction word architectures," *IEEE Trans. on Computers* C-33:11 (November), 968–976.

Nikhil, R. S., G. M. Papadopoulos, and Arvind [1992]. "*T: A multithreaded massively parallel architecture," *Proc. 19th Annual Int'l. Symposium on Computer Architecture (ISCA)*, May 19–21, 1992, Gold Coast, Australia, 156–167.

Noordergraaf, L., and R. van der Pas [1999]. "Performance experiences on Sun's WildFire prototype," *Proc. ACM/IEEE Conf. on Supercomputing*, November 13–19, 1999, Portland, Ore.

Nyberg, C. R., T. Barclay, Z. Cvetanovic, J. Gray, and D. Lomet [1994]. "AlphaSort: A RISC machine sort," *Proc. ACM SIGMOD*, May 24–27, 1994, Minneapolis, Minn.

Oka, M., and M. Suzuoki [1999]. "Designing and programming the emotion engine," *IEEE Micro* 19:6 (November–December), 20–28.

Okada, S., S. Okada, Y. Matsuda, T. Yamada, and A. Kobayashi [1999]. "System on a chip for digital still camera," *IEEE Trans. on Consumer Electronics* 45:3 (August), 584–590.

Oliker, L., A. Canning, J. Carter, J. Shalf, and S. Ethier [2004]. "Scientific computations on modern parallel vector systems," *Proc. ACM/IEEE Conf. on Supercomputing*, November 6–12, 2004, Pittsburgh, Penn., 10.

Pabst, T. [2000]. "Performance Showdown at 133 MHz FSB—The Best Platform for Coppermine," *www6.tomshardware.com/mainboard/00q1/000302/*.

Padua, D., and M. Wolfe [1986]. "Advanced compiler optimizations for supercomputers," *Communications of the ACM* 29:12 (December), 1184–1201.

Palacharla, S., and R. E. Kessler [1994]. "Evaluating stream buffers as a secondary cache replacement," *Proc. 21st Annual Int'l. Symposium on Computer Architecture (ISCA)*, April 18–21, 1994, Chicago, 24–33.

Palmer, J., and S. Morse [1984]. *The 8087 Primer*, John Wiley & Sons, New York, 93.

Pan, S.-T., K. So, and J. T. Rameh [1992]. "Improving the accuracy of dynamic branch prediction using branch correlation," *Proc. Fifth Int'l. Conf. on Architectural Support for Programming Languages and Operating Systems (ASPLOS)*, October 12–15, 1992, Boston, 76–84.

Partridge, C. [1994]. *Gigabit Networking*, Addison-Wesley, Reading, Mass.

Patterson, D. [1985]. "Reduced instruction set computers," *Communications of the ACM* 28:1 (January), 8–21.

Patterson, D. [2004]. "Latency lags bandwidth," *Communications of the ACM* 47:10 (October), 71–75.

Patterson, D. A., and D. R. Ditzel [1980]. "The case for the reduced instruction set computer," *Computer Architecture News* 8:6 (October), 25–33.

Patterson, D. A., and J. L. Hennessy [2004]. *Computer Organization and Design: The Hardware/Software Interface*, 3rd ed., Morgan Kaufmann, San Francisco.

Patterson, D. A., G. A. Gibson, and R. H. Katz [1987]. *A Case for Redundant Arrays of Inexpensive Disks (RAID)*, Tech. Rep. UCB/CSD 87/391, University of California, Berkeley. Also appeared in *Proc. ACM SIGMOD*, June 1–3, 1988, Chicago, 109–116.

Patterson, D. A., P. Garrison, M. Hill, D. Lioupis, C. Nyberg, T. Sippel, and K. Van Dyke [1983]. "Architecture of a VLSI instruction cache for a RISC," *10th Annual Int'l. Conf. on Computer Architecture Conf. Proc.*, June 13–16, 1983, Stockholm, Sweden, 108–116.

Pavan, P., R. Bez, P. Olivo, and E. Zanoni [1997]. "Flash memory cells—an overview." *Proc. IEEE* 85:8 (August), 1248–1271.

Peh, L. S., and W. J. Dally [2001]. "A delay model and speculative architecture for pipelined routers," *Proc. 7th Int'l. Symposium on High-Performance Computer Architecture*, January 22–24, 2001, Monterrey, Mexico.

Peng, V., S. Samudrala, and M. Gavrielov [1987]. "On the implementation of shifters, multipliers, and dividers in VLSI floating point units," *Proc. 8th IEEE Symposium on Computer Arithmetic*, May 19–21, 1987, Como, Italy, 95–102.

Pfister, G. F. [1998]. *In Search of Clusters*, 2nd ed., Prentice Hall, Upper Saddle River, N.J.

Pfister, G. F., W. C. Brantley, D. A. George, S. L. Harvey, W. J. Kleinfekder, K. P. McAuliffe, E. A. Melton, V. A. Norton, and J. Weiss [1985]. "The IBM research parallel processor prototype (RP3): Introduction and architecture," *Proc. 12th Annual Int'l. Symposium on Computer Architecture (ISCA)*, June 17–19, 1985, Boston, Mass., 764–771.

Pinheiro, E., W. D. Weber, and L. A. Barroso [2007]. "Failure trends in a large disk drive population," *Proc. 5th USENIX Conference on File and Storage Technologies (FAST '07)*, February 13–16, 2007, San Jose, Calif.

Pinkston, T. M. [2004]. "Deadlock characterization and resolution in interconnection networks," in M. C. Zhu and M. P. Fanti, eds., *Deadlock Resolution in Computer-Integrated Systems*, CRC Press, Boca Raton, FL, 445–492.

Pinkston, T. M., and J. Shin [2005]. "Trends toward on-chip networked microsystems," *Int'l. J. of High Performance Computing and Networking* 3:1, 3–18.

Pinkston, T. M., and S. Warnakulasuriya [1997]. "On deadlocks in interconnection networks," *24th Annual Int'l. Symposium on Computer Architecture (ISCA)*, June 2–4, 1997, Denver, Colo.

Pinkston, T. M., A. Benner, M. Krause, I. Robinson, and T. Sterling [2003]. "InfiniBand: The 'de facto' future standard for system and local area networks or just a scalable replacement for PCI buses?" *Cluster Computing* (special issue on communication architecture for clusters) 6:2 (April), 95–104.

Postiff, M. A., D. A. Greene, G. S. Tyson, and T. N. Mudge [1999]. "The limits of instruction level parallelism in SPEC95 applications," *Computer Architecture News* 27:1 (March), 31–40.

Przybylski, S. A. [1990]. *Cache Design: A Performance-Directed Approach*, Morgan Kaufmann, San Francisco.

Przybylski, S. A., M. Horowitz, and J. L. Hennessy [1988]. "Performance trade-offs in cache design," *15th Annual Int'l. Symposium on Computer Architecture*, May 30–June 2, 1988, Honolulu, Hawaii, 290–298.

Puente, V., R. Beivide, J. A. Gregorio, J. M. Prellezo, J. Duato, and C. Izu [1999]. "Adaptive bubble router: A design to improve performance in torus networks," *Proc. 28th Int'l. Conference on Parallel Processing*, September 21–24, 1999, Aizu-Wakamatsu, Fukushima, Japan.

Radin, G. [1982]. "The 801 minicomputer," *Proc. Symposium Architectural Support for Programming Languages and Operating Systems (ASPLOS)*, March 1–3, 1982, Palo Alto, Calif., 39–47.

Rajesh Bordawekar, Uday Bondhugula, Ravi Rao: Believe it or not!: mult-core CPUs can match GPU performance for a FLOP-intensive application! 19th International Conference on Parallel Architecture and Compilation Techniques (PACT 2010), Vienna, Austria, September 11-15, 2010: 537-538.

Ramamoorthy, C. V., and H. F. Li [1977]. "Pipeline architecture," *ACM Computing Surveys* 9:1 (March), 61–102.

Ranganathan, P., P. Leech, D. Irwin, and J. Chase [2006]. "Ensemble-Level Power Management for Dense Blade Servers," *Proc. 33rd Annual Int'l. Symposium on Computer Architecture (ISCA)*, June 17–21, 2006, Boston, Mass., 66–77.

Rau, B. R. [1994]. "Iterative modulo scheduling: An algorithm for software pipelining loops," *Proc. 27th Annual Int'l. Symposium on Microarchitecture*, November 30–December 2, 1994, San Jose, Calif., 63–74.

Rau, B. R., C. D. Glaeser, and R. L. Picard [1982]. "Efficient code generation for horizontal architectures: Compiler techniques and architectural support," *Proc. Ninth Annual Int'l. Symposium on Computer Architecture (ISCA)*, April 26–29, 1982, Austin, Tex., 131–139.

Rau, B. R., D. W. L. Yen, W. Yen, and R. A. Towle [1989]. "The Cydra 5 departmental supercomputer: Design philosophies, decisions, and trade-offs," *IEEE Computers* 22:1 (January), 12–34.

Reddi, V. J. , B. C. Lee, T. Chilimbi, and K. Vaid [2010]. "Web search using mobile cores: Quantifying and mitigating the price of efficiency," *Proc. 37th Annual Int'l. Symposium on Computer Architecture (ISCA)*, June 19–23, 2010, Saint-Malo, France.

Redmond, K. C., and T. M. Smith [1980]. *Project Whirlwind—The History of a Pioneer Computer*, Digital Press, Boston.

Reinhardt, S. K., J. R. Larus, and D. A. Wood [1994]. "Tempest and Typhoon: User-level shared memory," *21st Annual Int'l. Symposium on Computer Architecture (ISCA)*, April 18–21, 1994, Chicago, 325–336.

Reinman, G., and N. P. Jouppi. [1999]. "Extensions to CACTI," *research.compaq.com/ wrl/people/jouppi/CACTI.html*.

Rettberg, R. D., W. R. Crowther, P. P. Carvey, and R. S. Towlinson [1990]. "The Monarch parallel processor hardware design," *IEEE Computer* 23:4 (April), 18–30.

Riemens, A., K. A. Vissers, R. J. Schutten, F. W. Sijstermans, G. J. Hekstra, and G. D. La Hei [1999]."Trimedia CPU64 application domain and benchmark suite," *Proc. IEEE Int'l. Conf. on Computer Design: VLSI in Computers and Processors (ICCD'99)*, October 10–13, 1999, Austin, Tex., 580–585.

Riseman, E. M., and C. C. Foster [1972]. "Percolation of code to enhance paralled dispatching and execution," *IEEE Trans. on Computers* C-21:12 (December), 1411–1415.

Robin, J., and C. Irvine [2000]. "Analysis of the Intel Pentium's ability to support a secure virtual machine monitor." *Proc. USENIX Security Symposium*, August 14–17, 2000, Denver, Colo.

Robinson, B., and L. Blount [1986]. *The VM/HPO 3880-23 Performance Results*, IBM Tech. Bulletin GG66-0247-00, IBM Washington Systems Center, Gaithersburg, Md.

Ropers, A., H. W. Lollman, and J. Wellhausen [1999]. *DSPstone: Texas Instruments TMS320C54x*, Tech. Rep. IB 315 1999/9-ISS-Version 0.9, Aachen University of Technology, Aaachen, Germany (*www.ert.rwth-aachen.de/Projekte/Tools/coal/ dspstone_c54x/index.html*).

Rosenblum, M., S. A. Herrod, E. Witchel, and A. Gupta [1995]. "Complete computer simulation: The SimOS approach," in *IEEE Parallel and Distributed Technology* (now called *Concurrency*) 4:3, 34–43.

Rowen, C., M. Johnson, and P. Ries [1988]. "The MIPS R3010 floating-point coprocessor," *IEEE Micro* 8:3 (June), 53–62.

Russell, R. M. [1978]. "The Cray-1 processor system," *Communications of the ACM* 21:1 (January), 63–72.

Rymarczyk, J. [1982]. "Coding guidelines for pipelined processors," *Proc. Symposium Architectural Support for Programming Languages and Operating Systems (ASPLOS)*, March 1–3, 1982, Palo Alto, Calif., 12–19.

Saavedra-Barrera, R. H. [1992]. "CPU Performance Evaluation and Execution Time Prediction Using Narrow Spectrum Benchmarking," Ph.D. dissertation, University of California, Berkeley.

Salem, K., and H. Garcia-Molina [1986]. "Disk striping," *Proc. 2nd Int'l. IEEE Conf. on Data Engineering*, February 5–7, 1986, Washington, D.C., 249–259.

Saltzer, J. H., D. P. Reed, and D. D. Clark [1984]. "End-to-end arguments in system design," *ACM Trans. on Computer Systems* 2:4 (November), 277–288.

Samples, A. D., and P. N. Hilfinger [1988]. *Code Reorganization for Instruction Caches,* Tech. Rep. UCB/CSD 88/447, University of California, Berkeley.

Santoro, M. R., G. Bewick, and M. A. Horowitz [1989]. "Rounding algorithms for IEEE multipliers," *Proc. Ninth IEEE Symposium on Computer Arithmetic,* September 6–8, Santa Monica, Calif., 176–183.

Satran, J., D. Smith, K. Meth, C. Sapuntzakis, M. Wakeley, P. Von Stamwitz, R. Haagens, E. Zeidner, L. Dalle Ore, and Y. Klein [2001]. "iSCSI," IPS Working Group of IETF, Internet draft *www.ietf.org/internet-drafts/draft-ietf-ips-iscsi-07.txt.*

Saulsbury, A., T. Wilkinson, J. Carter, and A. Landin [1995]. "An argument for Simple COMA," *Proc. First IEEE Symposium on High-Performance Computer Architectures,* January 22–25, 1995, Raleigh, N.C., 276–285.

Schneck, P. B. [1987]. *Superprocessor Architecture,* Kluwer Academic Publishers, Norwell, Mass.

Schroeder, B., and G. A. Gibson [2007]. "Understanding failures in petascale computers," *J. of Physics Conf. Series* 78(1), 188–198.

Schroeder, B., E. Pinheiro, and W.-D. Weber [2009]. "DRAM errors in the wild: a large-scale field study," *Proc. Eleventh Int'l. Joint Conf. on Measurement and Modeling of Computer Systems (SIGMETRICS),* June 15–19, 2009, Seattle, Wash.

Schurman, E., and J. Brutlag [2009]. "The user and business impact of server delays," *Proc. Velocity: Web Performance and Operations Conf.,* June 22–24, 2009, San Jose, Calif.

Schwartz, J. T. [1980]. "Ultracomputers," *ACM Trans. on Programming Languages and Systems* 4:2, 484–521.

Scott, N. R. [1985]. *Computer Number Systems and Arithmetic,* Prentice Hall, Englewood Cliffs, N.J.

Scott, S. L. [1996]. "Synchronization and communication in the T3E multiprocessor," *Seventh Int'l. Conf. on Architectural Support for Programming Languages and Operating Systems (ASPLOS),* October 1–5, 1996, Cambridge, Mass.

Scott, S. L., and J. Goodman [1994]. "The impact of pipelined channels on *k*-ary *n*-cube networks," *IEEE Trans. on Parallel and Distributed Systems* 5:1 (January), 1–16.

Scott, S. L., and G. M. Thorson [1996]. "The Cray T3E network: Adaptive routing in a high performance 3D torus," *Proc. IEEE HOT Interconnects '96,* August 15–17, 1996, Stanford University, Palo Alto, Calif., 14–156.

Scranton, R. A., D. A. Thompson, and D. W. Hunter [1983]. *The Access Time Myth,"* Tech. Rep. RC 10197 (45223), IBM, Yorktown Heights, N.Y.

Seagate. [2000]. *Seagate Cheetah 73 Family: ST173404LW/LWV/LC/LCV Product Manual,* Vol. 1, Seagate, Scotts Valley, Calif. (*www.seagate.com/support/disc/manuals/scsi/29478b.pdf*).

Seitz, C. L. [1985]. "The Cosmic Cube (concurrent computing)," *Communications of the ACM* 28:1 (January), 22–33.

Senior, J. M. [1993]. *Optical Fiber Commmunications: Principles and Practice,* 2nd ed., Prentice Hall, Hertfordshire, U.K.

Sharangpani, H., and K. Arora [2000]. "Itanium Processor Microarchitecture," *IEEE Micro* 20:5 (September–October), 24–43.

Shurkin, J. [1984]. *Engines of the Mind: A History of the Computer,* W. W. Norton, New York.

Shustek, L. J. [1978]. "Analysis and Performance of Computer Instruction Sets," Ph.D. dissertation, Stanford University, Palo Alto, Calif.

Silicon Graphics. [1996]. *MIPS V Instruction Set* (see http://www.sgi.com/MIPS/arch/ISA5/#MIPSV_indx).

Singh, J. P., J. L. Hennessy, and A. Gupta [1993]. "Scaling parallel programs for multiprocessors: Methodology and examples," *Computer* 26:7 (July), 22–33.

Sinharoy, B., R. N. Koala, J. M. Tendler, R. J. Eickemeyer, and J. B. Joyner [2005]. "POWER5 system microarchitecture," *IBM J. Research and Development*, 49:4–5, 505–521.

Sites, R. [1979]. *Instruction Ordering for the CRAY-1 Computer*, Tech. Rep. 78-CS-023, Dept. of Computer Science, University of California, San Diego.

Sites, R. L. (ed.) [1992]. *Alpha Architecture Reference Manual*, Digital Press, Burlington, Mass.

Sites, R. L., and R. Witek, (eds.) [1995]. *Alpha Architecture Reference Manual*, 2nd ed., Digital Press, Newton, Mass.

Skadron, K., and D. W. Clark [1997]. "Design issues and tradeoffs for write buffers," *Proc. Third Int'l. Symposium on High-Performance Computer Architecture*, February 1–5, 1997, San Antonio, Tex., 144–155.

Skadron, K., P. S. Ahuja, M. Martonosi, and D. W. Clark [1999]. "Branch prediction, instruction-window size, and cache size: Performance tradeoffs and simulation techniques," *IEEE Trans. on Computers* 48:11 (November).

Slater, R. [1987]. *Portraits in Silicon*, MIT Press, Cambridge, Mass.

Slotnick, D. L., W. C. Borck, and R. C. McReynolds [1962]. "The Solomon computer," *Proc. AFIPS Fall Joint Computer Conf.*, December 4–6, 1962, Philadelphia, Penn., 97–107.

Smith, A. J. [1982]. "Cache memories," *Computing Surveys* 14:3 (September), 473–530.

Smith, A., and J. Lee [1984]. "Branch prediction strategies and branch-target buffer design," *Computer* 17:1 (January), 6–22.

Smith, B. J. [1978]. "A pipelined, shared resource MIMD computer," *Proc. Int'l. Conf. on Parallel Processing (ICPP)*, August, Bellaire, Mich., 6–8.

Smith, B. J. [1981]. "Architecture and applications of the HEP multiprocessor system," *Real-Time Signal Processing IV* 298 (August), 241–248.

Smith, J. E. [1981]. "A study of branch prediction strategies," *Proc. Eighth Annual Int'l. Symposium on Computer Architecture (ISCA)*, May 12–14, 1981, Minneapolis, Minn., 135–148.

Smith, J. E. [1984]. "Decoupled access/execute computer architectures," *ACM Trans. on Computer Systems* 2:4 (November), 289–308.

Smith, J. E. [1988]. "Characterizing computer performance with a single number," *Communications of the ACM* 31:10 (October), 1202–1206.

Smith, J. E. [1989]. "Dynamic instruction scheduling and the Astronautics ZS-1," *Computer* 22:7 (July), 21–35.

Smith, J. E., and J. R. Goodman [1983]. "A study of instruction cache organizations and replacement policies," *Proc. 10th Annual Int'l. Symposium on Computer Architecture (ISCA)*, June 5–7, 1982, Stockholm, Sweden, 132–137.

Smith, J. E., and A. R. Pleszkun [1988]. "Implementing precise interrupts in pipelined processors," *IEEE Trans. on Computers* 37:5 (May), 562–573. (This paper is based on an earlier paper that appeared in *Proc. 12th Annual Int'l. Symposium on Computer Architecture (ISCA)*, June 17–19, 1985, Boston, Mass.)

Smith, J. E., G. E. Dermer, B. D. Vanderwarn, S. D. Klinger, C. M. Rozewski, D. L. Fowler, K. R. Scidmore, and J. P. Laudon [1987]. "The ZS-1 central processor," *Proc. Second Int'l. Conf. on Architectural Support for Programming Languages and Operating Systems (ASPLOS)*, October 5–8, 1987, Palo Alto, Calif., 199–204.

Smith, M. D., M. Horowitz, and M. S. Lam [1992]. "Efficient superscalar performance through boosting," *Proc. Fifth Int'l. Conf. on Architectural Support for Programming Languages and Operating Systems (ASPLOS)*, October 12–15, 1992, Boston, 248–259.

Smith, M. D., M. Johnson, and M. A. Horowitz [1989]. "Limits on multiple instruction issue," *Proc. Third Int'l. Conf. on Architectural Support for Programming Languages and Operating Systems (ASPLOS)*, April 3–6, 1989, Boston, 290–302.

Smotherman, M. [1989]. "A sequencing-based taxonomy of I/O systems and review of historical machines," *Computer Architecture News* 17:5 (September), 5–15. Reprinted in *Computer Architecture Readings*, M. D. Hill, N. P. Jouppi, and G. S. Sohi, eds., Morgan Kaufmann, San Francisco, 1999, 451–461.

Sodani, A., and G. Sohi [1997]. "Dynamic instruction reuse," *Proc. 24th Annual Int'l. Symposium on Computer Architecture (ISCA)*, June 2–4, 1997, Denver, Colo.

Sohi, G. S. [1990]. "Instruction issue logic for high-performance, interruptible, multiple functional unit, pipelined computers," *IEEE Trans. on Computers* 39:3 (March), 349–359.

Sohi, G. S., and S. Vajapeyam [1989]. "Tradeoffs in instruction format design for horizontal architectures," *Proc. Third Int'l. Conf. on Architectural Support for Programming Languages and Operating Systems (ASPLOS)*, April 3–6, 1989, Boston, 15–25.

Soundararajan, V., M. Heinrich, B. Verghese, K. Gharachorloo, A. Gupta, and J. L. Hennessy [1998]. "Flexible use of memory for replication/migration in cache-coherent DSM multiprocessors," *Proc. 25th Annual Int'l. Symposium on Computer Architecture (ISCA)*, July 3–14, 1998, Barcelona, Spain, 342–355.

SPEC. [1989]. *SPEC Benchmark Suite Release 1.0* (October 2).

SPEC. [1994]. *SPEC Newsletter* (June).

Sporer, M., F. H. Moss, and C. J. Mathais [1988]. "An introduction to the architecture of the Stellar Graphics supercomputer," *Proc. IEEE COMPCON*, February 29–March 4, 1988, San Francisco, 464.

Spurgeon, C. [2001]. "Charles Spurgeon's Ethernet Web Site," *wwwhost.ots.utexas.edu/ethernet/ethernet-home.html*.

Spurgeon, C. [2006]. "Charles Spurgeon's Ethernet Web SITE," *www.ethermanage.com/ethernet/ethernet.html*.

Stenström, P., T. Joe, and A. Gupta [1992]. "Comparative performance evaluation of cache-coherent NUMA and COMA architectures," *Proc. 19th Annual Int'l. Symposium on Computer Architecture (ISCA)*, May 19–21, 1992, Gold Coast, Australia, 80–91.

Sterling, T. [2001]. *Beowulf PC Cluster Computing with Windows and Beowulf PC Cluster Computing with Linux*, MIT Press, Cambridge, Mass.

Stern, N. [1980]. "Who invented the first electronic digital computer?" *Annals of the History of Computing* 2:4 (October), 375–376.

Stevens, W. R. [1994–1996]. *TCP/IP Illustrated* (three volumes), Addison-Wesley, Reading, Mass.

Stokes, J. [2000]. "Sound and Vision: A Technical Overview of the Emotion Engine," arstechnica.com/reviews/1q00/playstation2/ee-1.html.

Stone, H. [1991]. *High Performance Computers*, Addison-Wesley, New York.

Strauss, W. [1998]. "DSP Strategies 2002," www.usadata.com/ market_research/spr_05/spr_r127-005.htm.

Strecker, W. D. [1976]. "Cache memories for the PDP-11?," *Proc. Third Annual Int'l. Symposium on Computer Architecture (ISCA)*, January 19–21, 1976, Tampa, Fla., 155–158.

Strecker, W. D. [1978]. "VAX-11/780: A virtual address extension of the PDP-11 family," *Proc. AFIPS National Computer Conf.*, June 5–8, 1978, Anaheim, Calif., 47, 967–980.

Sugumar, R. A., and S. G. Abraham [1993]. "Efficient simulation of caches under optimal replacement with applications to miss characterization," *Proc. ACM SIGMETRICS Conf. on Measurement and Modeling of Computer Systems*, May 17–21, 1993, Santa Clara, Calif., 24–35.

Sun Microsystems. [1989]. *The SPARC Architectural Manual*, Version 8, Part No. 8001399-09, Sun Microsystems, Santa Clara, Calif.

Sussenguth, E. [1999]. "IBM's ACS-1 Machine," *IEEE Computer* 22:11 (November).

Swan, R. J., S. H. Fuller, and D. P. Siewiorek [1977]. "Cm*—a modular, multi-microprocessor," *Proc. AFIPS National Computing Conf.*, June 13–16, 1977, Dallas, Tex., 637–644.

Swan, R. J., A. Bechtolsheim, K. W. Lai, and J. K. Ousterhout [1977]. "The implementation of the Cm* multi-microprocessor," *Proc. AFIPS National Computing Conf.*, June 13–16, 1977, Dallas, Tex., 645–654.

Swartzlander, E. (ed.) [1990]. *Computer Arithmetic*, IEEE Computer Society Press, Los Alamitos, Calif.

Takagi, N., H. Yasuura, and S. Yajima [1985]. "High-speed VLSI multiplication algorithm with a redundant binary addition tree," *IEEE Trans. on Computers* C-34:9, 789–796.

Talagala, N. [2000]. "Characterizing Large Storage Systems: Error Behavior and Performance Benchmarks," Ph.D. dissertation, Computer Science Division, University of California, Berkeley.

Talagala, N., and D. Patterson [1999]. *An Analysis of Error Behavior in a Large Storage System*, Tech. Report UCB//CSD-99-1042, Computer Science Division, University of California, Berkeley.

Talagala, N., R. Arpaci-Dusseau, and D. Patterson [2000]. *Micro-Benchmark Based Extraction of Local and Global Disk Characteristics*, CSD-99-1063, Computer Science Division, University of California, Berkeley.

Talagala, N., S. Asami, D. Patterson, R. Futernick, and D. Hart [2000]. "The art of massive storage: A case study of a Web image archive," *Computer* (November).

Tamir, Y., and G. Frazier [1992]. "Dynamically-allocated multi-queue buffers for VLSI communication switches," *IEEE Trans. on Computers* 41:6 (June), 725–734.

Tanenbaum, A. S. [1978]. "Implications of structured programming for machine architecture," *Communications of the ACM* 21:3 (March), 237–246.

Tanenbaum, A. S. [1988]. *Computer Networks*, 2nd ed., Prentice Hall, Englewood Cliffs, N.J.

Tang, C. K. [1976]. "Cache design in the tightly coupled multiprocessor system," *Proc. AFIPS National Computer Conf.*, June 7–10, 1976, New York, 749–753.

Tanqueray, D. [2002]. "The Cray X1 and supercomputer road map," *Proc. 13th Daresbury Machine Evaluation Workshop*, December 11–12, 2002, Daresbury Laboratories, Daresbury, Cheshire, U.K.

Tarjan, D., S. Thoziyoor, and N. Jouppi [2005]. "HPL Technical Report on CACTI 4.0," www.hpl.hp.com/techeports/2006/HPL=2006+86.html.

Taylor, G. S. [1981]. "Compatible hardware for division and square root," *Proc. 5th IEEE Symposium on Computer Arithmetic*, May 18–19, 1981, University of Michigan, Ann Arbor, Mich., 127–134.

Taylor, G. S. [1985]. "Radix 16 SRT dividers with overlapped quotient selection stages," *Proc. Seventh IEEE Symposium on Computer Arithmetic*, June 4–6, 1985, University of Illinois, Urbana, Ill., 64–71.

Taylor, G., P. Hilfinger, J. Larus, D. Patterson, and B. Zorn [1986]. "Evaluation of the SPUR LISP architecture," *Proc. 13th Annual Int'l. Symposium on Computer Architecture (ISCA)*, June 2–5, 1986, Tokyo.

Taylor, M. B., W. Lee, S. P. Amarasinghe, and A. Agarwal [2005]. "Scalar operand networks," *IEEE Trans. on Parallel and Distributed Systems* 16:2 (February), 145–162.

Tendler, J. M., J. S. Dodson, J. S. Fields, Jr., H. Le, and B. Sinharoy [2002]. "Power4 system microarchitecture," *IBM J. Research and Development* 46:1, 5–26.

Texas Instruments. [2000]. "History of Innovation: 1980s," www.ti.com/corp/docs/company/ history/1980s.shtml.

Tezzaron Semiconductor. [2004]. *Soft Errors in Electronic Memory*, White Paper, Tezzaron Semiconductor, Naperville, Ill. (*http://www.tezzaron.com/about/papers/soft_errors_1_1_secure.pdf*).

Thacker, C. P., E. M. McCreight, B. W. Lampson, R. F. Sproull, and D. R. Boggs [1982]. "Alto: A personal computer," in D. P. Siewiorek, C. G. Bell, and A. Newell, eds., *Computer Structures: Principles and Examples*, McGraw-Hill, New York, 549–572.

Thadhani, A. J. [1981]. "Interactive user productivity," *IBM Systems J.* 20:4, 407–423.

Thekkath, R., A. P. Singh, J. P. Singh, S. John, and J. L. Hennessy [1997]. "An evaluation of a commercial CC-NUMA architecture—the CONVEX Exemplar SPP1200," *Proc. 11th Int'l. Parallel Processing Symposium (IPPS)*, April 1–7, 1997, Geneva, Switzerland.

Thorlin, J. F. [1967]. "Code generation for PIE (parallel instruction execution) computers," *Proc. Spring Joint Computer Conf.*, April 18–20, 1967, Atlantic City, N.J., 27.

Thornton, J. E. [1964]. "Parallel operation in the Control Data 6600," *Proc. AFIPS Fall Joint Computer Conf., Part II*, October 27–29, 1964, San Francisco, 26, 33–40.

Thornton, J. E. [1970]. *Design of a Computer, the Control Data 6600*, Scott, Foresman, Glenview, Ill.

Tjaden, G. S., and M. J. Flynn [1970]. "Detection and parallel execution of independent instructions," *IEEE Trans. on Computers* C-19:10 (October), 889–895.

Tomasulo, R. M. [1967]. "An efficient algorithm for exploiting multiple arithmetic units," *IBM J. Research and Development* 11:1 (January), 25–33.

Torrellas, J., A. Gupta, and J. Hennessy [1992]. "Characterizing the caching and synchronization performance of a multiprocessor operating system," *Proc. Fifth Int'l. Conf. on Architectural Support for Programming Languages and Operating Systems (ASPLOS)*, October 12–15, 1992, Boston (*SIGPLAN Notices* 27:9 (September), 162–174).

Touma, W. R. [1993]. *The Dynamics of the Computer Industry: Modeling the Supply of Workstations and Their Components*, Kluwer Academic, Boston.

Tuck, N., and D. Tullsen [2003]. "Initial observations of the simultaneous multithreading Pentium 4 processor," *Proc. 12th Int. Conf. on Parallel Architectures and Compilation Techniques (PACT'03)*, September 27–October 1, 2003, New Orleans, La., 26–34.

Tullsen, D. M., S. J. Eggers, and H. M. Levy [1995]. "Simultaneous multithreading: Maximizing on-chip parallelism," *Proc. 22nd Annual Int'l. Symposium on Computer Architecture (ISCA)*, June 22–24, 1995, Santa Margherita, Italy, 392–403.

Tullsen, D. M., S. J. Eggers, J. S. Emer, H. M. Levy, J. L. Lo, and R. L. Stamm [1996]. "Exploiting choice: Instruction fetch and issue on an implementable simultaneous multithreading processor," *Proc. 23rd Annual Int'l. Symposium on Computer Architecture (ISCA)*, May 22–24, 1996, Philadelphia, Penn., 191–202.

Ungar, D., R. Blau, P. Foley, D. Samples, and D. Patterson [1984]. "Architecture of SOAR: Smalltalk on a RISC," *Proc. 11th Annual Int'l. Symposium on Computer Architecture (ISCA)*, June 5–7, 1984, Ann Arbor, Mich., 188–197.

Unger, S. H. [1958]. "A computer oriented towards spatial problems," *Proc. Institute of Radio Engineers* 46:10 (October), 1744–1750.

Vahdat, A., M. Al-Fares, N. Farrington, R. Niranjan Mysore, G. Porter, and S. Radhakrishnan [2010]. "Scale-Out Networking in the Data Center," *IEEE Micro* 30:4 (July/August), 29–41.

Vaidya, A. S., A Sivasubramaniam, and C. R. Das [1997]. "Performance benefits of virtual channels and adaptive routing: An application-driven study," *Proc. ACM/IEEE Conf. on Supercomputing*, November 16–21, 1997, San Jose, Calif.

Vajapeyam, S. [1991]. "Instruction-Level Characterization of the Cray Y-MP Processor," Ph.D. thesis, Computer Sciences Department, University of Wisconsin-Madison.

van Eijndhoven, J. T. J., F. W. Sijstermans, K. A. Vissers, E. J. D. Pol, M. I. A. Tromp, P. Struik, R. H. J. Bloks, P. van der Wolf, A. D. Pimentel, and H. P. E. Vranken [1999]. "Trimedia CPU64 architecture," *Proc. IEEE Int'l. Conf. on Computer Design: VLSI in Computers and Processors (ICCD'99)*, October 10–13, 1999, Austin, Tex., 586–592.

Van Vleck, T. [2005]. "The IBM 360/67 and CP/CMS," http://www.multicians.org/thvv/360-67.html.

von Eicken, T., D. E. Culler, S. C. Goldstein, and K. E. Schauser [1992]. "Active Messages: A mechanism for integrated communication and computation," *Proc. 19th Annual Int'l. Symposium on Computer Architecture (ISCA)*, May 19–21, 1992, Gold Coast, Australia.

Waingold, E., M. Taylor, D. Srikrishna, V. Sarkar, W. Lee, V. Lee, J. Kim, M. Frank, P. Finch, R. Barua, J. Babb, S. Amarasinghe, and A. Agarwal [1997]. "Baring it all to software: Raw Machines," *IEEE Computer* 30 (September), 86–93.

Wakerly, J. [1989]. *Microcomputer Architecture and Programming*, Wiley, New York.

Wall, D. W. [1991]. "Limits of instruction-level parallelism," *Proc. Fourth Int'l. Conf. on Architectural Support for Programming Languages and Operating Systems (ASPLOS)*, April 8–11, 1991, Palo Alto, Calif., 248–259.

Wall, D. W. [1993]. *Limits of Instruction-Level Parallelism*, Research Rep. 93/6, Western Research Laboratory, Digital Equipment Corp., Palo Alto, Calif.

Walrand, J. [1991]. *Communication Networks: A First Course*, Aksen Associates/Irwin, Homewood, Ill.

Wang, W.-H., J.-L. Baer, and H. M. Levy [1989]. "Organization and performance of a two-level virtual-real cache hierarchy," *Proc. 16th Annual Int'l. Symposium on Computer Architecture (ISCA)*, May 28–June 1, 1989, Jerusalem, 140–148.

Watanabe, T. [1987]. "Architecture and performance of the NEC supercomputer SX system," *Parallel Computing* 5, 247–255.

Waters, F. (ed.) [1986]. *IBM RT Personal Computer Technology*, SA 23-1057, IBM, Austin, Tex.

Watson, W. J. [1972]. "The TI ASC—a highly modular and flexible super processor architecture," *Proc. AFIPS Fall Joint Computer Conf.*, December 5–7, 1972, Anaheim, Calif., 221–228.

Weaver, D. L., and T. Germond [1994]. *The SPARC Architectural Manual*, Version 9, Prentice Hall, Englewood Cliffs, N.J.

Weicker, R. P. [1984]. "Dhrystone: A synthetic systems programming benchmark," *Communications of the ACM* 27:10 (October), 1013–1030.

Weiss, S., and J. E. Smith [1984]. "Instruction issue logic for pipelined supercomputers," *Proc. 11th Annual Int'l. Symposium on Computer Architecture (ISCA)*, June 5–7, 1984, Ann Arbor, Mich., 110–118.

Weiss, S., and J. E. Smith [1987]. "A study of scalar compilation techniques for pipelined supercomputers," *Proc. Second Int'l. Conf. on Architectural Support for Programming Languages and Operating Systems (ASPLOS)*, October 5–8, 1987, Palo Alto, Calif., 105–109.

Weiss, S., and J. E. Smith [1994]. *Power and PowerPC*, Morgan Kaufmann, San Francisco.

Wendel, D., R. Kalla, J. Friedrich, J. Kahle, J. Leenstra, C. Lichtenau, B. Sinharoy, W. Starke, and V. Zyuban [2010]. "The Power7 processor SoC," *Proc. Int'l. Conf. on IC Design and Technology*, June 2–4, 2010, Grenoble, France, 71–73.

Weste, N., and K. Eshraghian [1993]. *Principles of CMOS VLSI Design: A Systems Perspective*, 2nd ed., Addison-Wesley, Reading, Mass.

Wiecek, C. [1982]. "A case study of the VAX 11 instruction set usage for compiler execution," *Proc. Symposium on Architectural Support for Programming Languages and Operating Systems (ASPLOS)*, March 1–3, 1982, Palo Alto, Calif., 177–184.

Wilkes, M. [1965]. "Slave memories and dynamic storage allocation," *IEEE Trans. Electronic Computers* EC-14:2 (April), 270–271.

Wilkes, M. V. [1982]. "Hardware support for memory protection: Capability implementations," *Proc. Symposium on Architectural Support for Programming Languages and Operating Systems (ASPLOS)*, March 1–3, 1982, Palo Alto, Calif., 107–116.

Wilkes, M. V. [1985]. *Memoirs of a Computer Pioneer*, MIT Press, Cambridge, Mass.

Wilkes, M. V. [1995]. *Computing Perspectives*, Morgan Kaufmann, San Francisco.

Wilkes, M. V., D. J. Wheeler, and S. Gill [1951]. *The Preparation of Programs for an Electronic Digital Computer*, Addison-Wesley, Cambridge, Mass.

Williams, S., A. Waterman, and D. Patterson [2009]. "Roofline: An insightful visual performance model for multicore architectures," *Communications of the ACM*, 52:4 (April), 65–76.

Williams, T. E., M. Horowitz, R. L. Alverson, and T. S. Yang [1987]. "A self-timed chip for division," in P. Losleben, ed., *1987 Stanford Conference on Advanced Research in VLSI*, MIT Press, Cambridge, Mass.

Wilson, A. W., Jr. [1987]. "Hierarchical cache/bus architecture for shared-memory multiprocessors," *Proc. 14th Annual Int'l. Symposium on Computer Architecture (ISCA)*, June 2–5, 1987, Pittsburgh, Penn., 244–252.

Wilson, R. P., and M. S. Lam [1995]. "Efficient context-sensitive pointer analysis for C programs," *Proc. ACM SIGPLAN'95 Conf. on Programming Language Design and Implementation*, June 18–21, 1995, La Jolla, Calif., 1–12.

Wolfe, A., and J. P. Shen [1991]. "A variable instruction stream extension to the VLIW architecture," *Proc. Fourth Int'l. Conf. on Architectural Support for Programming Languages and Operating Systems (ASPLOS)*, April 8–11, 1991, Palo Alto, Calif., 2–14.

Wood, D. A., and M. D. Hill [1995]. "Cost-effective parallel computing," *IEEE Computer* 28:2 (February), 69–72.

Wulf, W. [1981]. "Compilers and computer architecture," *Computer* 14:7 (July), 41–47.

Wulf, W., and C. G. Bell [1972]. "C.mmp—A multi-mini-processor," *Proc. AFIPS Fall Joint Computer Conf.*, December 5–7, 1972, Anaheim, Calif., 765–777.

Wulf, W., and S. P. Harbison [1978]. "Reflections in a pool of processors—an experience report on C.mmp/Hydra," *Proc. AFIPS National Computing Conf.* June 5–8, 1978, Anaheim, Calif., 939–951.

Wulf, W. A., and S. A. McKee [1995]. "Hitting the memory wall: Implications of the obvious," *ACM SIGARCH Computer Architecture News*, 23:1 (March), 20–24.

Wulf, W. A., R. Levin, and S. P. Harbison [1981]. *Hydra/C.mmp: An Experimental Computer System*, McGraw-Hill, New York.

Yamamoto, W., M. J. Serrano, A. R. Talcott, R. C. Wood, and M. Nemirosky [1994]. "Performance estimation of multistreamed, superscalar processors," *Proc. 27th Annual Hawaii Int'l. Conf. on System Sciences*, January 4–7, 1994, Maui, 195–204.

Yang, Y., and G. Mason [1991]. "Nonblocking broadcast switching networks," *IEEE Trans. on Computers* 40:9 (September), 1005–1015.

Yeager, K. [1996]. "The MIPS R10000 superscalar microprocessor," *IEEE Micro* 16:2 (April), 28–40.

Yeh, T., and Y. N. Patt [1993a]. "Alternative implementations of two-level adaptive branch prediction," *Proc. 19th Annual Int'l. Symposium on Computer Architecture (ISCA)*, May 19–21, 1992, Gold Coast, Australia, 124–134.

Yeh, T., and Y. N. Patt [1993b]. "A comparison of dynamic branch predictors that use two levels of branch history," *Proc. 20th Annual Int'l. Symposium on Computer Architecture (ISCA)*, May 16–19, 1993, San Diego, Calif., 257–266.

Index

Page references in bold represent figures and tables.

Numbers

2:1 cache rule of thumb, definition, B-29

80x86, *see* Intel 80x86 processors

A

ABC (Atanasoff Berry Computer), L-5

ABI, *see* Application binary interface (ABI)

Absolute addressing mode, Intel 80x86, K-47

Accelerated Strategic Computing Initiative (ASCI)
ASCI Red, F-100
ASCI White, F-67, F-100
system area network history, F-101

Access 1/Access 2 stages, TI 320C55 DSP, E-7

Access bit,
IA-32 descriptor table, B-52

Access time, *see also* Average Memory Access Time (AMAT)
vs. block size, **B-28**
distributed-memory multiprocessor, **348**
DRAM/magnetic disk, **D-3**
memory hierarchy basics, **77**
miss penalties, 218, B-42
NUMA, 348
paging, B-43
shared-memory multiprocessor, 347, 363
slowdown causes, B-3
TLP workloads, 369–370

during write, B-45
WSC memory hierarchy, 444

Access time gap, disk storage, D-3

ACID, *see* Atomicity-consistency-isolation-durability (ACID)

Acknowledgment, packets, F-16

ACM, *see* Association of Computing Machinery (ACM)

ACS project, L-28 to L-29

Active low power modes, WSCs, 472

Ada language, integer division/remainder, **J-12**

Adaptive routing
definition, F-47
vs. deterministic routing, F-52 to F-55, **F-54**
network fault tolerance, F-94
and overhead, F-93 to F-94

Adders
carry-lookahead, J-37 to J-41
chip comparison, J-60
full, J-2, **J-3**
half, J-2
integer division speedup, J-54 to J-58
integer multiplication speedup
even/odd array, **J-52**
many adders, **J-50**, J-50 to J-54
multipass array multiplier, **J-51**
signed-digit addition table, **J-54**
single adder, J-47 to J-49, **J-48 to J-49**
Wallace tree, **J-53**
radix-2 division, **J-55**
radix-4 division, **J-56**
radix-4 SRT division, **J-57**
ripple-carry, J-3, **J-3**

time/space requirements, **J-44**

Addition operations
chip comparison, J-61
floating point
denormals, J-26 to J-27
overview, J-21 to J-25
rules, **J-24**
speedup, J-25 to J-26
integer, speedup
carry-lookahead, J-37 to J-41
carry-lookahead circuit, **J-38**
carry-lookahead tree, **J-40**
carry-lookahead tree adder, **J-41**
carry-select adder, **J-43**, J-43 to J-44, **J-44**
carry-skip adder, J-41 to J43, **J-42**
overview, J-37
ripply-carry addition, **J-3**

Address aliasing prediction
definition, 213
ideal processor, 214
ILP for realizable processors, 216

Address Coalescing Unit
function, 310
gather-scatter, 329
GPUs, 300
Multithreaded SIMD Processor block diagram, **294**
vector processor, **310**

Address fault, virtual memory definition, B-42

Addressing modes
comparison, **A-11**
compiler writing-architecture relationship, A-30
control flow instructions, A-17 to A-18
desktop architectures, **K-5**

IBM 360 (*continued*)
  instruction operator categories,
    A-15
  instruction set, K-85 to K-88
  instruction set complications, C-49
    to C-50
  integer/FP R-R operations, K-85
  I/O bus history, L-81
  memory hierarchy development,
    L-9 to L-10
  parallel processing debates, L-57
  protection and ISA, 112
  R-R instructions, K-86
  RS and SI format instructions,
    K-87
  RX format instructions, K-86 to
    K-87
  SS format instructions, K-85 to
    K-88
IBM 360/85, L-10 to L-11, L-27
IBM 360/91
  dynamic scheduling with
    Tomasulo's algorithm,
    170–171
  early computer arithmetic, J-63
  history, L-27
  speculation concept origins, L-29
IBM 370
  architecture, K-83 to K-84
  characteristics, **K-42**
  early computer arithmetic, J-63
  integer overflow, **J-11**
  protection and ISA, 112
  vector processor history, G-27
  Virtual Machines, 110
IBM 370/158, L-7
IBM 650, L-6
IBM 701, L-5 to L-6
IBM 702, L-5 to L-6
IBM 704, L-6, L-26
IBM 705, L-6
IBM 801, L-19
IBM 3081, L-61
IBM 3090 Vector Facility, vector
    processor history, G-27
IBM 3840 cartridge, L-77
IBM 7030, L-26
IBM 9840 cartridge, L-77
IBM AS/400, L-79
IBM Blue Gene/L, F-4
  adaptive routing, F-93
  cluster history, L-63

commercial interconnection
    networks, F-63
  computing node, I-42 to I-44, **I-43**
  as custom cluster, I-41 to I-42
  deterministic *vs.* adaptive routing,
    F-52 to F-55
  fault tolerance, F-66 to F-67
  link bandwidth, F-89
  low-dimensional topologies, F-100
  parallel processing debates, L-58
  software overhead, F-91
  switch microarchitecture, F-62
  system, **I-44**
  system area network history, F-101
    to F-102
  3D torus network, F-72 to F-74
  topology, F-30, F-39
IBM CodePack, RISC code size, A-23
IBM CoreConnect
  cross-company interoperability,
    F-64
  OCNs, F-3
IBM eServer p5 processor
  performance/cost benchmarks, **409**
  SMT and ST performance, **399**
  speedup benchmarks, **408**,
    408–409
IBM Federation network interfaces,
    F-17 to F-18
IBM J9 JVM
  real-world server considerations,
    52–55
  WSC performance, **463**
IBM PCs, architecture flaws *vs.*
    success, A-45
IBM Power processors
  branch-prediction buffers, **C-29**
  characteristics, **247**
  exception stopping/restarting, C-47
  MIPS precise exceptions, C-59
  shared-memory multiprogramming
    workload, 378
IBM Power 1, L-29
IBM Power 2, L-29
IBM Power 4
  multithreading history, L-35
  peak performance, **58**
  recent advances, L-33 to L-34
IBM Power 5
  characteristics, **F-73**
  Itanium 2 comparison, **H-43**
  manufacturing cost, **62**

multiprocessing/
    multithreading-based
    performance, 398–400
  multithreading history, L-35
IBM Power 7
  vs. Google WSC, 436
  ideal processors, 214–215
  multicore processor performance,
    400–401
  multithreading, **225**
IBM Pulsar processor, L-34
IBM RP3, L-60
IBM RS/6000, L-57
IBM RT-PC, L-20
IBM SAGE, L-81
IBM servers, economies of scale, 456
IBM Stretch, L-6
IBM zSeries, vector processor history,
    G-27
IC, *see* Instruction count (IC)
I-caches
  case study examples, B-63
  way prediction, 81–82
ICR, *see* Idle Control Register (ICR)
ID, *see* Instruction decode (ID)
Ideal pipeline cycles per instruction,
    ILP concepts, 149
Ideal processors, ILP hardware model,
    214–215, 219–220
IDE disks, Berkeley's Tertiary Disk
    project, D-12
Idle Control Register (ICR), TI
    TMS320C55 DSP, E-8
Idle domains, TI TMS320C55 DSP,
    E-8
IEEE 754 floating-point standard, **J-16**
IEEE 1394, Sony PlayStation 2
    Emotion Engine case
    study, E-15
IEEE arithmetic
  floating point, J-13 to J-14
    addition, J-21 to J-25
    exceptions, J-34 to J-35
    remainder, J-31 to J-32
    underflow, J-36
  historical background, J-63 to J-64
  iterative division, J-30
  $-x$ *vs.* $0 -x$, J-62
  NaN, J-14
  rounding modes, **J-20**
  single-precision numbers, J-15 to
    J-16

Translation between GPU terms in book and official NVIDIA and OpenCL terms.

Type	More Descriptive Name used in this Book	Official CUDA/ NVIDIA Term	Book Definition and OpenCL Terms	Official CUDA/NVIDIA Definition
Program Abstractions	Vectorizable Loop	Grid	A vectorizable loop, executed on the GPU, made up of 1 or more "Thread Blocks" (or bodies of vectorized loop) that can execute in parallel. OpenCL name is "index range."	A Grid is an array of Thread Blocks that can execute concurrently, sequentially, or a mixture.
	Body of Vectorized Loop	Thread Block	A vectorized loop executed on a "Streaming Multiprocessor" (multithreaded SIMD processor), made up of 1 or more "Warps" (or threads of SIMD instructions). These "Warps" (SIMD Threads) can communicate via "Shared Memory" (Local Memory). OpenCL calls a thread block a "work group."	A Thread Block is an array of CUDA threads that execute concurrently together and can cooperate and communicate via Shared Memory and barrier synchronization. A Thread Block has a Thread Block ID within its Grid.
	Sequence of SIMD Lane Operations	CUDA Thread	A vertical cut of a "Warp" (or thread of SIMD instructions) corresponding to one element executed by one "Thread Processor" (or SIMD lane). Result is stored depending on mask. OpenCL calls a CUDA thread a "work item."	A CUDA Thread is a lightweight thread that executes a sequential program and can cooperate with other CUDA threads executing in the same Thread Block. A CUDA thread has a thread ID within its Thread Block.
Machine Object	A Thread of SIMD Instructions	Warp	A traditional thread, but it contains just SIMD instructions that are executed on a "Streaming Multiprocessor" (multithreaded SIMD processor). Results stored depending on a per element mask.	A Warp is a set of parallel CUDA Threads (e.g., 32) that execute the same instruction together in a multithreaded SIMT/SIMD processor.
	SIMD Instruction	PTX Instruction	A single SIMD instruction executed across the "Thread Processors" (SIMD lanes).	A PTX instruction specifies an instruction executed by a CUDA Thread.
Processing Hardware	Multithreaded SIMD Processor	Streaming Multiprocessor	Multithreaded SIMD processor that executes "Warps" (thread of SIMD instructions), independent of other SIMD processors. OpenCL calls it a "Compute Unit." However, CUDA programmer writes program for one lane rather than for a "vector" of multiple SIMD lanes.	A Streaming Multiprocessor (SM) is a multithreaded SIMT/SIMD processor that executes Warps of CUDA Threads. A SIMT program specifies the execution of one CUDA thread, rather than a vector of multiple SIMD lanes.
	Thread Block Scheduler	Giga Thread Engine	Assigns multiple "Thread Blocks" (or body of vectorized loop) to "Streaming Multiprocessors" (multithreaded SIMD processors).	Distributes and schedules Thread Blocks of a Grid to Streaming Multiprocessors as resources become available.
	SIMD Thread Scheduler	Warp Scheduler	Hardware unit that schedules and issues "Warps" (threads of SIMD instructions) when they are ready to execute; includes a scoreboard to track "Warp" (SIMD thread) execution.	A Warp Scheduler in a Streaming Multiprocessor schedules Warps for execution when their next instruction is ready to execute.
	SIMD Lane	Thread Processor	Hardware SIMD Lane that executes the operations in a "Warp" (thread of SIMD instructions) on a single element. Results stored depending on mask. OpenCL calls it a "Processing Element."	A Thread Processor is a datapath and register file portion of a Streaming Multiprocessor that executes operations for one or more lanes of a Warp.
Memory Hardware	GPU Memory	Global Memory	DRAM memory accessible by all "Streaming Multiprocessors" (or multithreaded SIMD processors) in a GPU. OpenCL calls it "Global Memory."	Global Memory is accessible by all CUDA Threads in any Thread Block in any Grid. Implemented as a region of DRAM, and may be cached.
	Private Memory	Local Memory	Portion of DRAM memory private to each "Thread Processor" (SIMD lane). OpenCL calls it "Private Memory."	Private "thread-local" memory for a CUDA Thread. Implemented as a cached region of DRAM.
	Local Memory	Shared Memory	Fast local SRAM for one "Streaming Multiprocessor" (multithreaded SIMD processor), unavailable to other Streaming Multiprocessors. OpenCL calls it "Local Memory."	Fast SRAM memory shared by the CUDA Threads composing a Thread Block, and private to that Thread Block. Used for communication among CUDA Threads in a Thread Block at barrier synchronization points.
	SIMD Lane Registers	Registers	Registers in a single "Thread Processor" (SIMD lane) allocated across full "Thread Block" (or body of vectorized loop).	Private registers for a CUDA Thread. Implemented as multithreaded register file for certain lanes of several warps for each thread processor.